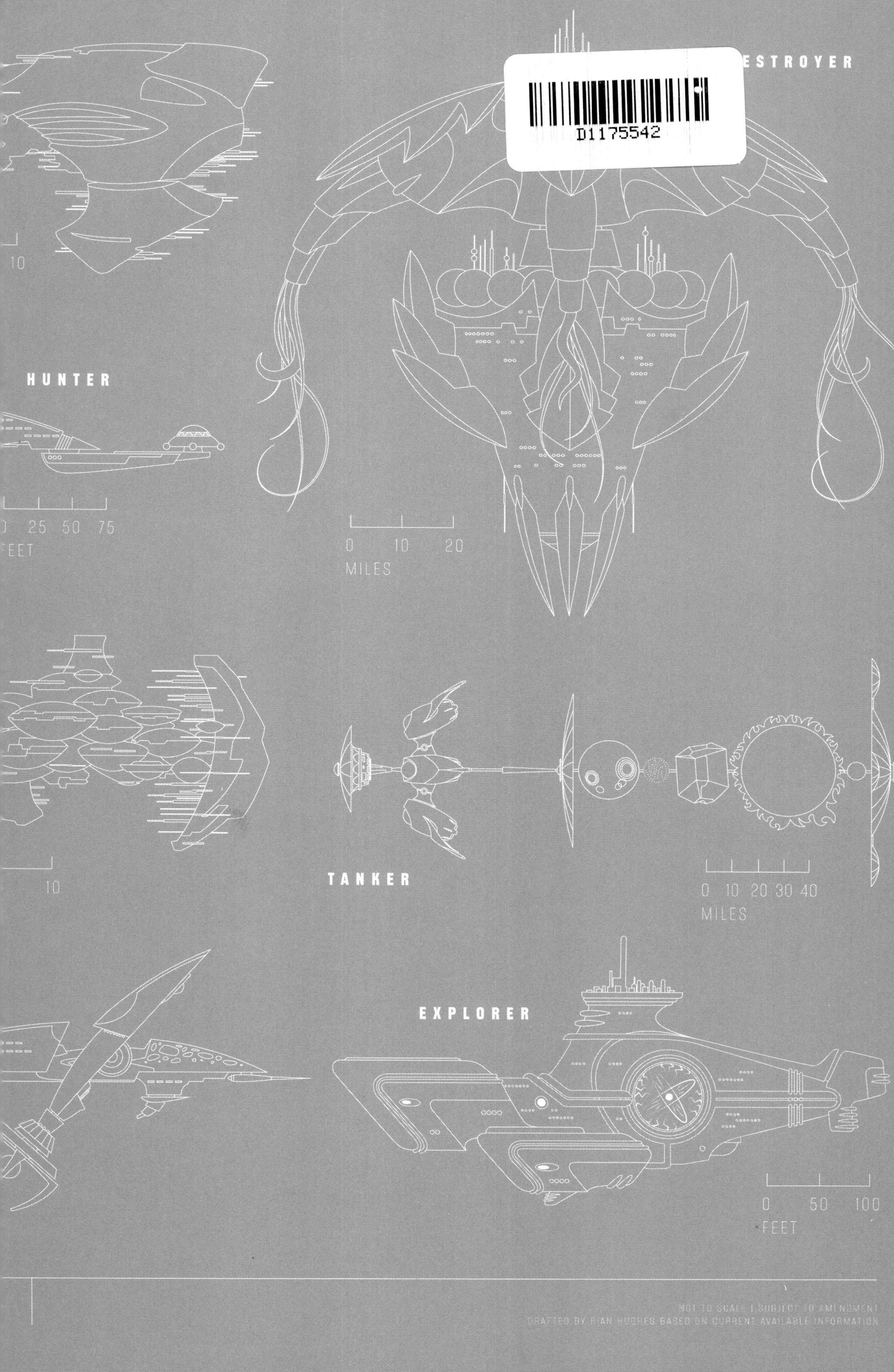
ESTROYER
0 10 20
MILES
HUNTER
25 50 75
FEET
10
10
TANKER
0 10 20 30 40
MILES
EXPLORER
0 50 100
FEET
NOT TO SCALE | SUBJECT TO AMENDMENT
DRAFTED BY RIAN HUGHES BASED ON CURRENT AVAILABLE INFORMATION

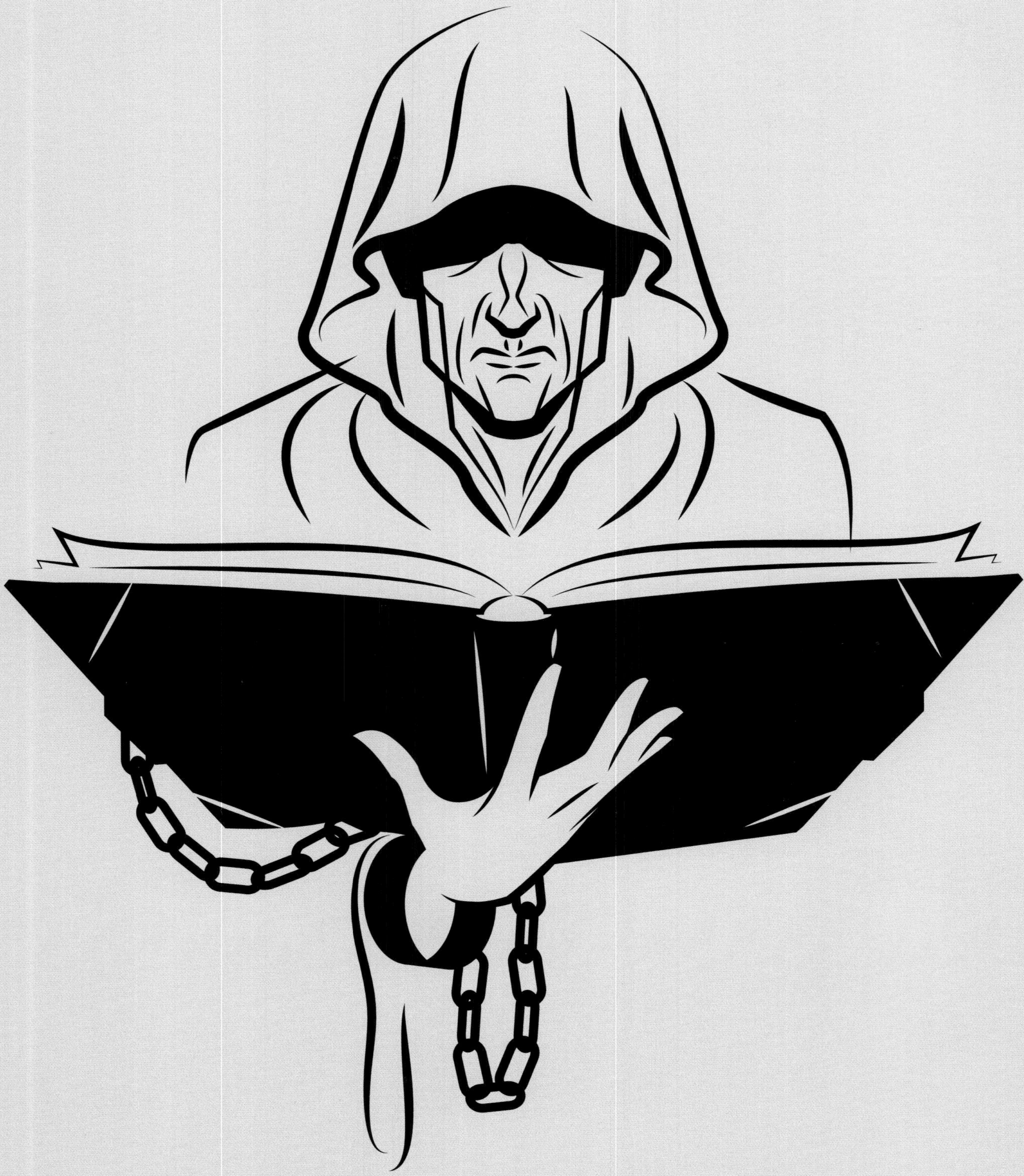

THE ABSOLUTE MULTIVERSITY

Written by
GRANT MORRISON

Art by
IVAN REIS
JOE PRADO
CHRIS SPROUSE
KARL STORY
WALDEN WONG
BEN OLIVER
FRANK QUITELY
CAMERON STEWART
MARCUS TO
PAULO SIQUEIRA
JIM LEE
SCOTT WILLIAMS
SANDRA HOPE
MARK IRWIN
JONATHAN GLAPION
DOUG MAHNKE
CHRISTIAN ALAMY
KEITH CHAMPAGNE
JAIME MENDOZA
EBER FERREIRA

Colors by
NEI RUFFINO
DAVE McCAIG
BEN OLIVER
DAN BROWN
NATHAN FAIRBAIRN
HI-FI
ALEX SINCLAIR
JEROMY COX
GABE ELTAEB
DAVID BARON
JASON WRIGHT
BLOND

Letters by
TODD KLEIN
CARLOS M. MANGUAL
CLEM ROBINS
ROB LEIGH
STEVE WANDS

Cover, slipcase, logos, Multiverse map, and original series cover designs by
RIAN HUGHES

SUPERMAN created by
JERRY SIEGEL and
JOE SHUSTER
SUPERBOY created by
JERRY SIEGEL
By special arrangement with the Jerry Siegel family

THE ABSOLUTE MULTIVERSITY

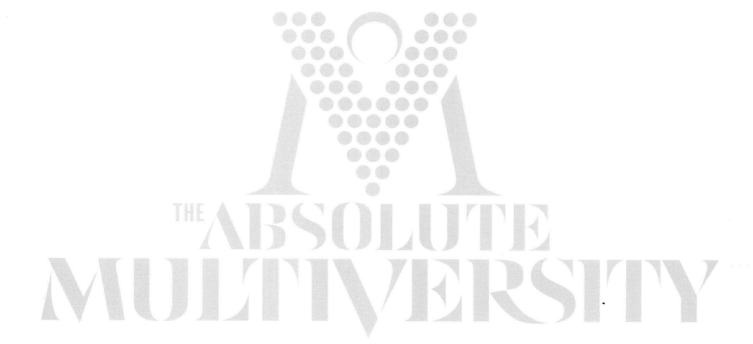

COLOPHON

RICKEY PURDIN
EDDIE BERGANZA   Editors – Original Series
ANDREW MARINO   Assistant Editor – Original Series
REZA LOKMAN   Editor – Collected Edition
STEVE COOK   Design Director – Books
RIAN HUGHES   Publication Design
CURTIS KING JR.
CHRISTY SAWYER   Publication Production

MARIE JAVINS   Editor-in-Chief, DC Comics

ANNE DePIES   Senior VP – General Manager
JIM LEE   Publisher & Chief Creative Officer
DON FALLETTI   VP – Manufacturing Operations & Workflow Management
LAWRENCE GANEM   VP – Talent Services
ALISON GILL   Senior VP – Manufacturing and Operations
JEFFREY KAUFMAN   VP – Editorial Strategy & Programming
NICK J. NAPOLITANO   VP – Manufacturing Administration & Design
NANCY SPEARS   VP – Revenue

THE ABSOLUTE MULTIVERSITY
Published by DC Comics.
Compilation, cover, and all new material
Copyright © 2022 DC Comics.
All Rights Reserved.
Originally published in single magazine form in
The Multiversity 1-2
The Multiversity: Society of Super-Heroes 1
The Multiversity: The Just 1
The Multiversity: Pax Americana 1
The Multiversity: Thunderworld Adventures 1
The Multiversity Guidebook 1
The Multiversity: Mastermen 1
The Multiversity: Ultra Comics 1
The Multiversity 1 & 2 Director's Cut
The Multiversity: Pax Americana Director's Cut
Copyright 2014, 2015 DC Comics.
All Rights Reserved.
All characters, their distinctive likenesses, and related elements
featured in this publication are trademarks of DC Comics.
The stories, characters, and incidents featured in this
publication are entirely fictional.
DC Comics does not read or accept unsolicited submissions
of ideas, stories, or artwork.

DC Comics, 100 S. California Street, Burbank, CA 91505
Printed by Friesens, Altona, MB, Canada. 9/2/22.
First Printing.
ISBN: 978-1-77951-561-2

Library of Congress Cataloging-in-Publication Data is available.

MIX
Paper from
responsible sources
FSC www.fsc.org   FSC® C016245

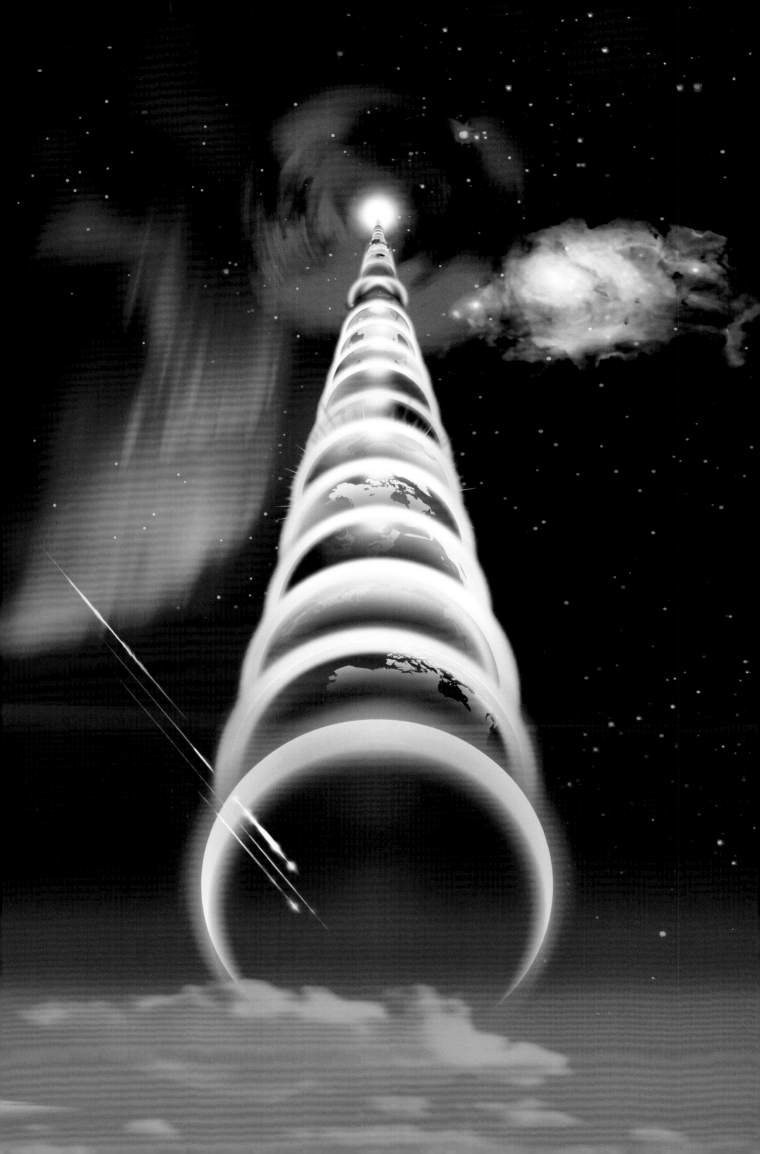

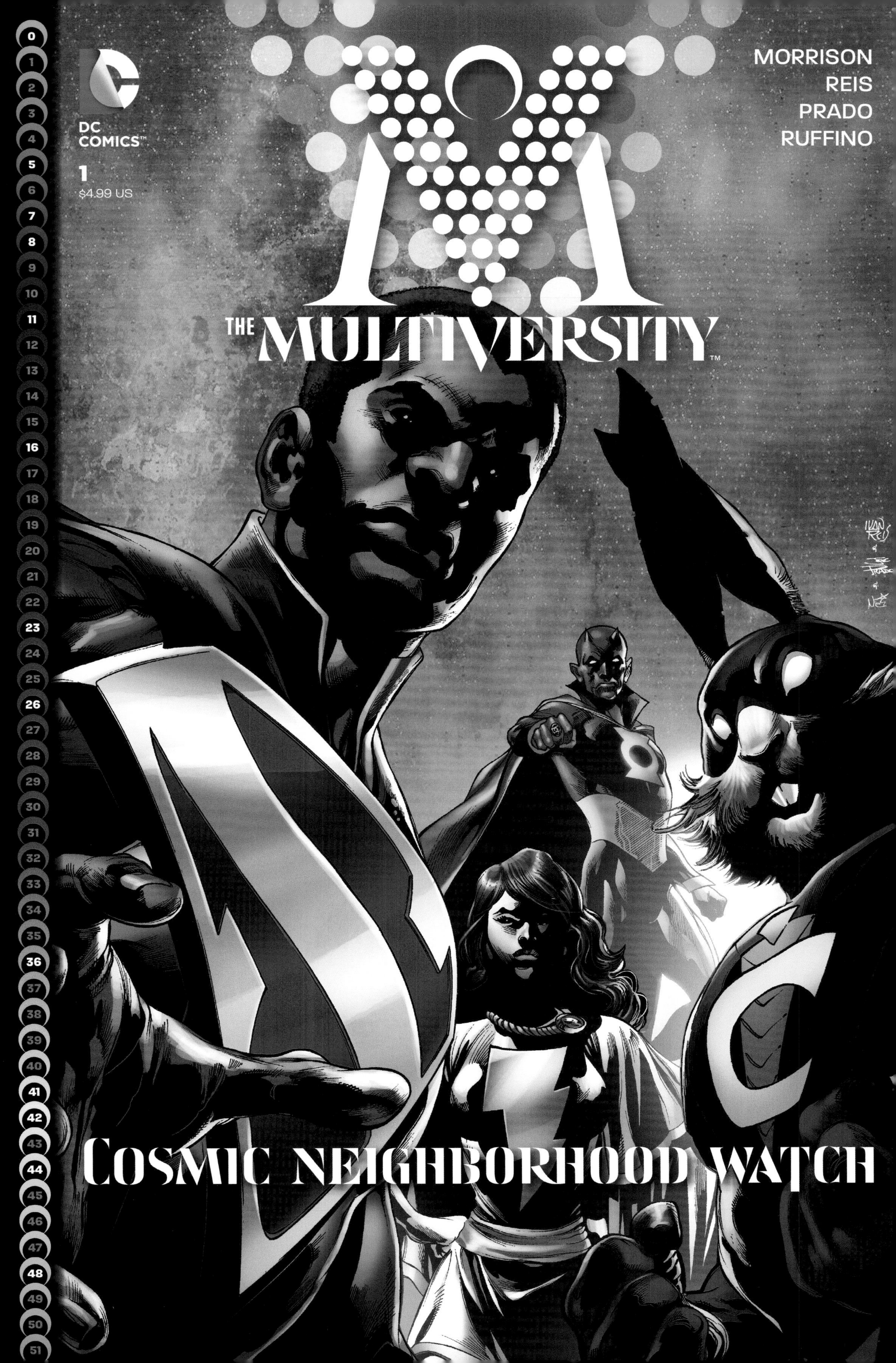
DC COMICS
1
$4.99 US
MORRISON
REIS
PRADO
RUFFINO
THE MULTIVERSITY
COSMIC NEIGHBORHOOD WATCH

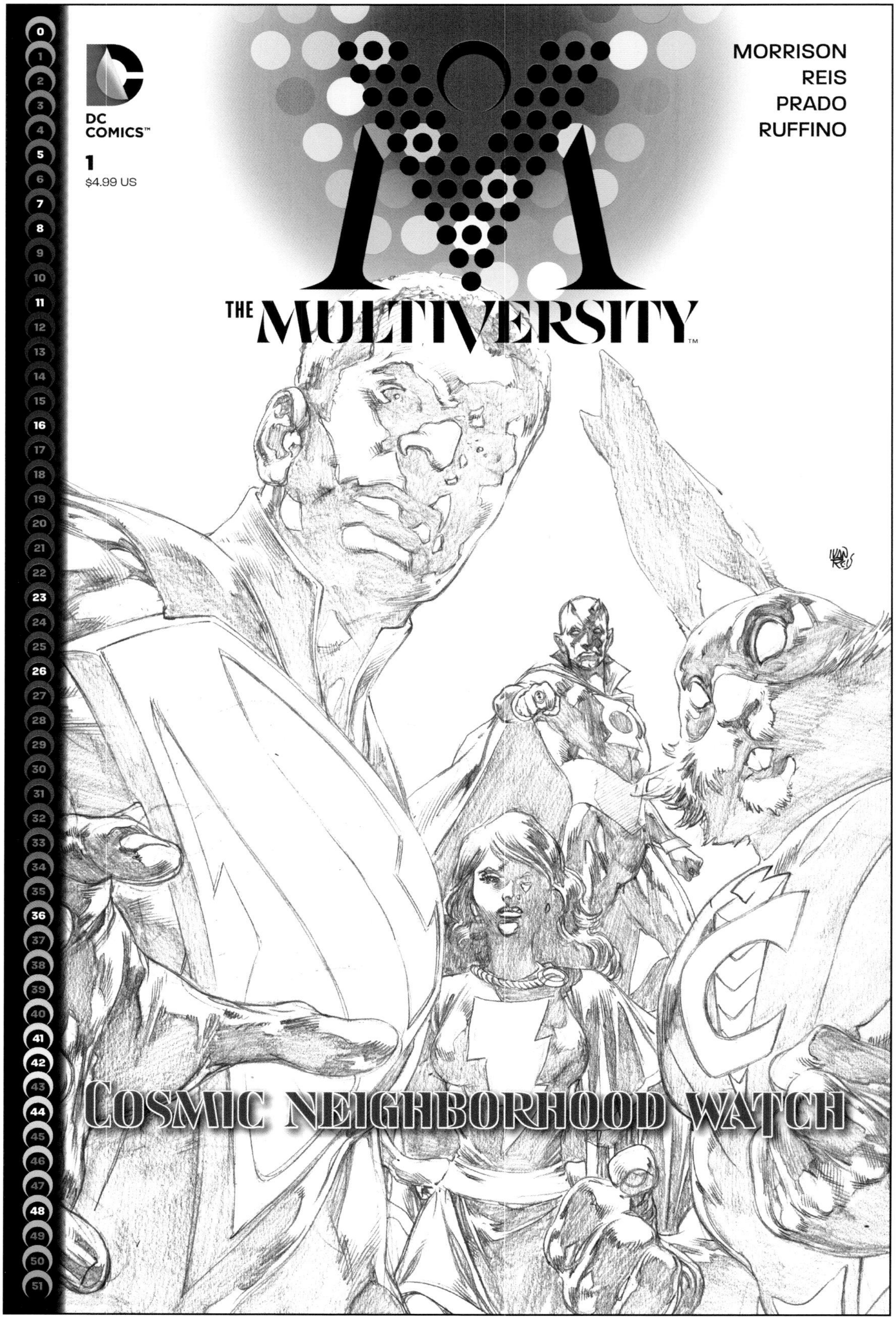
DC COMICS™
1
$4.99 US
MORRISON
REIS
PRADO
RUFFINO
THE MULTIVERSITY™
COSMIC NEIGHBORHOOD WATCH

THE MULTIVERSITY #1

Written by
GRANT MORRISON

Penciller
IVAN REIS

Inker
JOE PRADO

Colorist
NEI RUFFINO

Letterer
TODD KLEIN

Cover artists
IVAN REIS and **JOE PRADO** with **NEI RUFFINO**

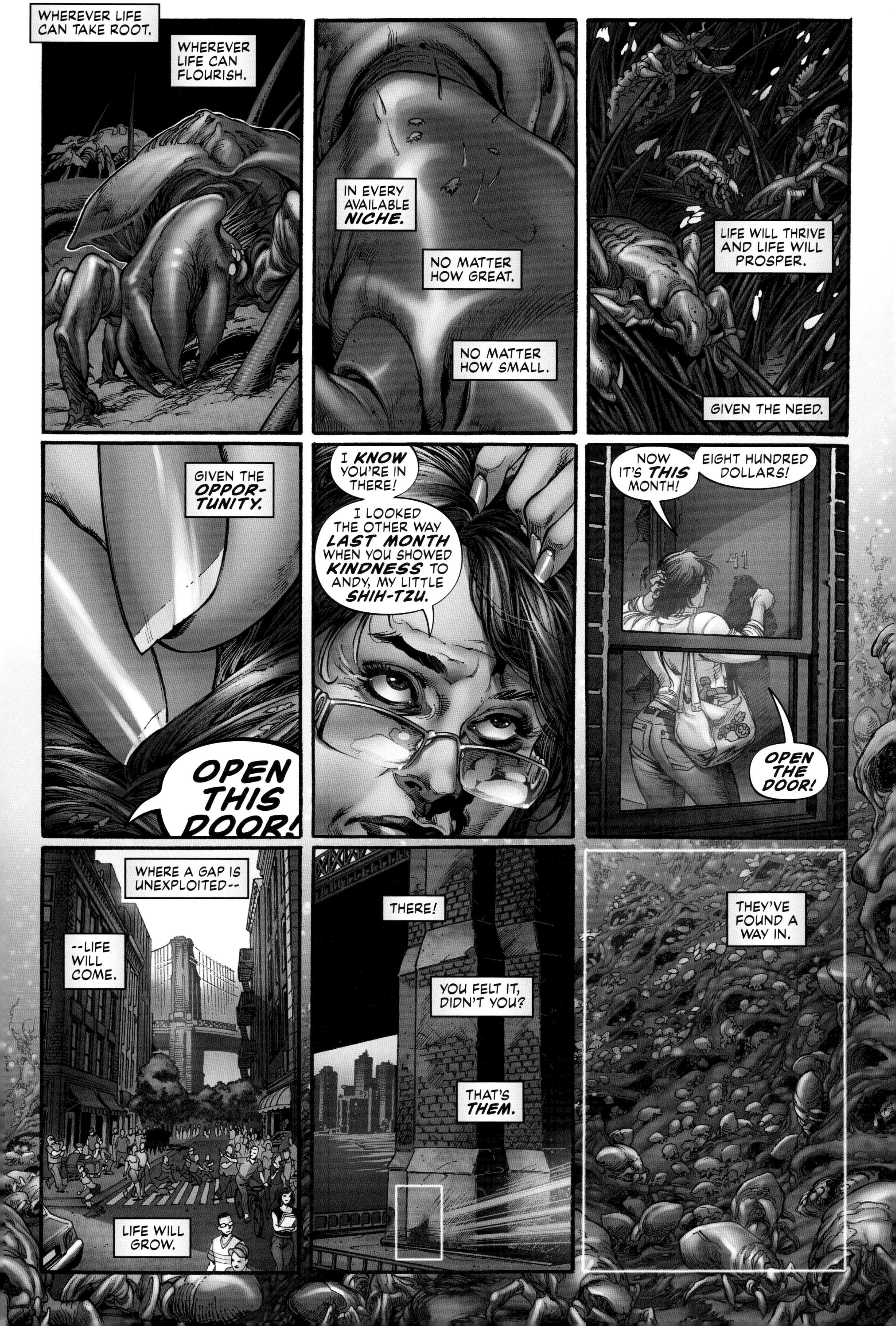
WHEREVER LIFE CAN TAKE ROOT.
WHEREVER LIFE CAN FLOURISH.
IN EVERY AVAILABLE NICHE.
NO MATTER HOW GREAT.
NO MATTER HOW SMALL.
LIFE WILL THRIVE AND LIFE WILL PROSPER.
GIVEN THE NEED.
GIVEN THE OPPOR-TUNITY.
OPEN THIS DOOR!
I KNOW YOU'RE IN THERE!
I LOOKED THE OTHER WAY LAST MONTH WHEN YOU SHOWED KINDNESS TO ANDY, MY LITTLE SHIH-TZU.
NOW IT'S THIS MONTH!
EIGHT HUNDRED DOLLARS!
OPEN THE DOOR!
WHERE A GAP IS UNEXPLOITED--
--LIFE WILL COME.
LIFE WILL GROW.
THERE!
YOU FELT IT, DIDN'T YOU?
THAT'S THEM.
THEY'VE FOUND A WAY IN.

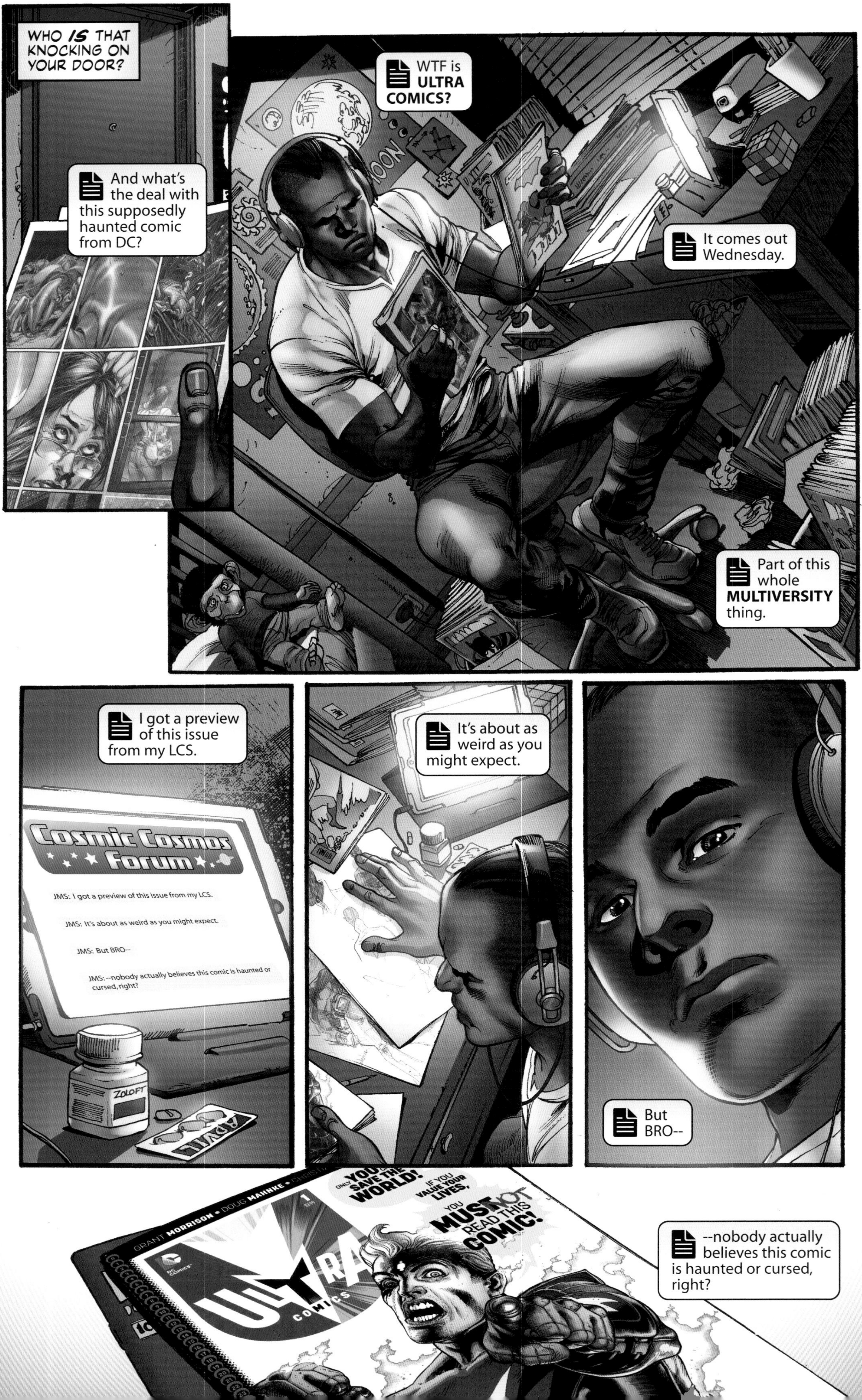

WHO *IS* THAT KNOCKING ON YOUR DOOR?
And what's the deal with this supposedly haunted comic from DC?
WTF is **ULTRA COMICS?**
It comes out Wednesday.
Part of this whole **MULTIVERSITY** thing.
I got a preview of this issue from my LCS.
Cosmic Cosmos Forum
JMS: I got a preview of this issue from my LCS.
JMS: It's about as weird as you might expect.
JMS: But BRO--
JMS: --nobody actually believes this comic is haunted or cursed, right?
ZOLOFT
ADVIL
It's about as weird as you might expect.
But BRO--
IF YOU VALUE YOUR LIVES,
YOU MUST NOT READ THIS COMIC!
ULTRA COMICS
--nobody actually believes this comic is haunted or cursed, right?

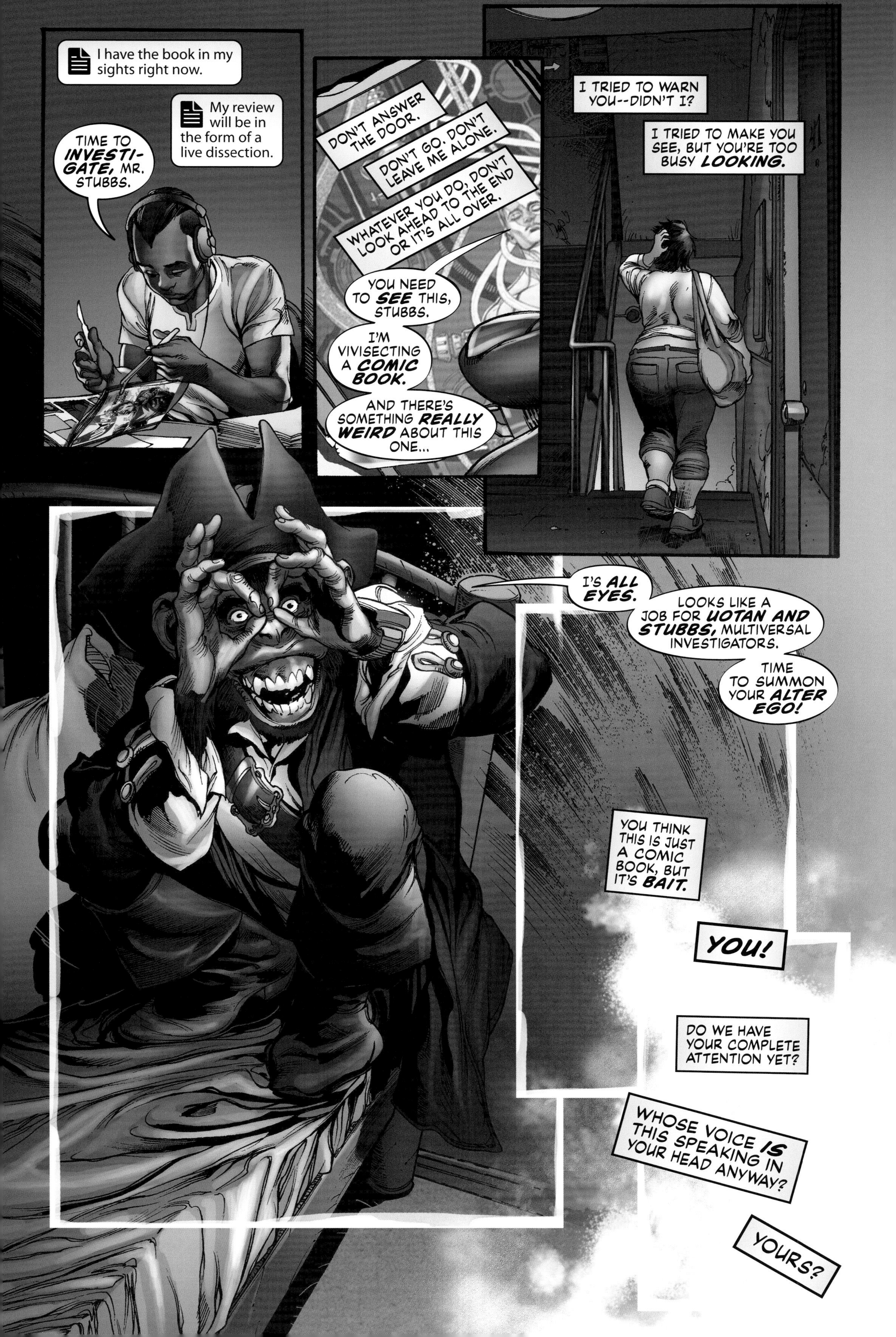
I have the book in my sights right now.
My review will be in the form of a live dissection.
TIME TO INVESTIGATE, MR. STUBBS.
DON'T ANSWER THE DOOR.
DON'T GO. DON'T LEAVE ME ALONE.
WHATEVER YOU DO, DON'T LOOK AHEAD TO THE END OR IT'S ALL OVER.
YOU NEED TO SEE THIS, STUBBS.
I'M VIVISECTING A COMIC BOOK.
AND THERE'S SOMETHING REALLY WEIRD ABOUT THIS ONE...
I TRIED TO WARN YOU--DIDN'T I?
I TRIED TO MAKE YOU SEE, BUT YOU'RE TOO BUSY LOOKING.
I'S ALL EYES.
LOOKS LIKE A JOB FOR UOTAN AND STUBBS, MULTIVERSAL INVESTIGATORS.
TIME TO SUMMON YOUR ALTER EGO!
YOU THINK THIS IS JUST A COMIC BOOK, BUT IT'S BAIT.
YOU!
DO WE HAVE YOUR COMPLETE ATTENTION YET?
WHOSE VOICE IS THIS SPEAKING IN YOUR HEAD ANYWAY?
YOURS?

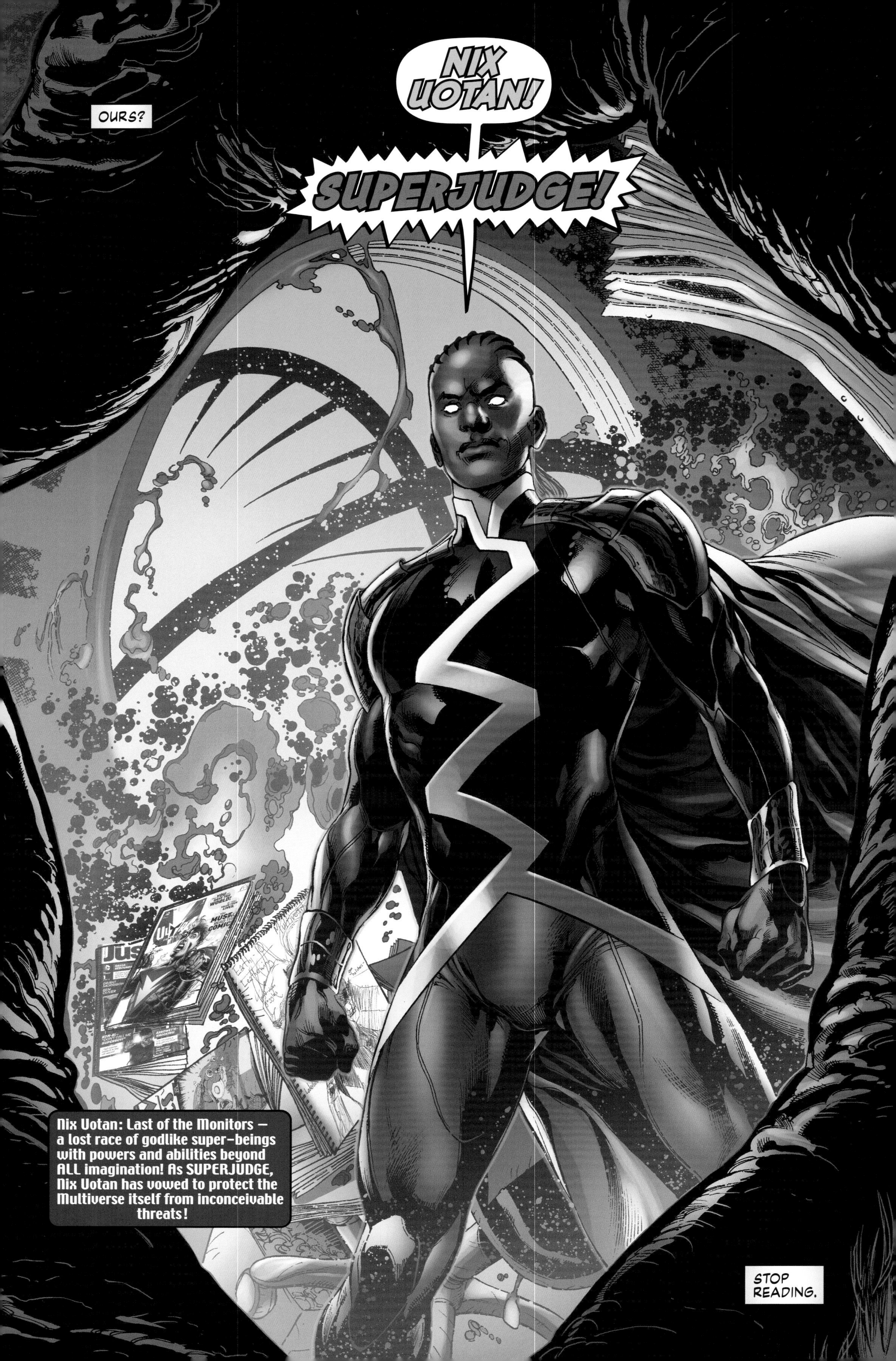

OURS?
NIX UOTAN!
SUPERJUDGE!
Nix Uotan: Last of the Monitors — a lost race of godlike super-beings with powers and abilities beyond ALL imagination! As SUPERJUDGE, Nix Uotan has vowed to protect the Multiverse itself from inconceivable threats!
STOP READING.

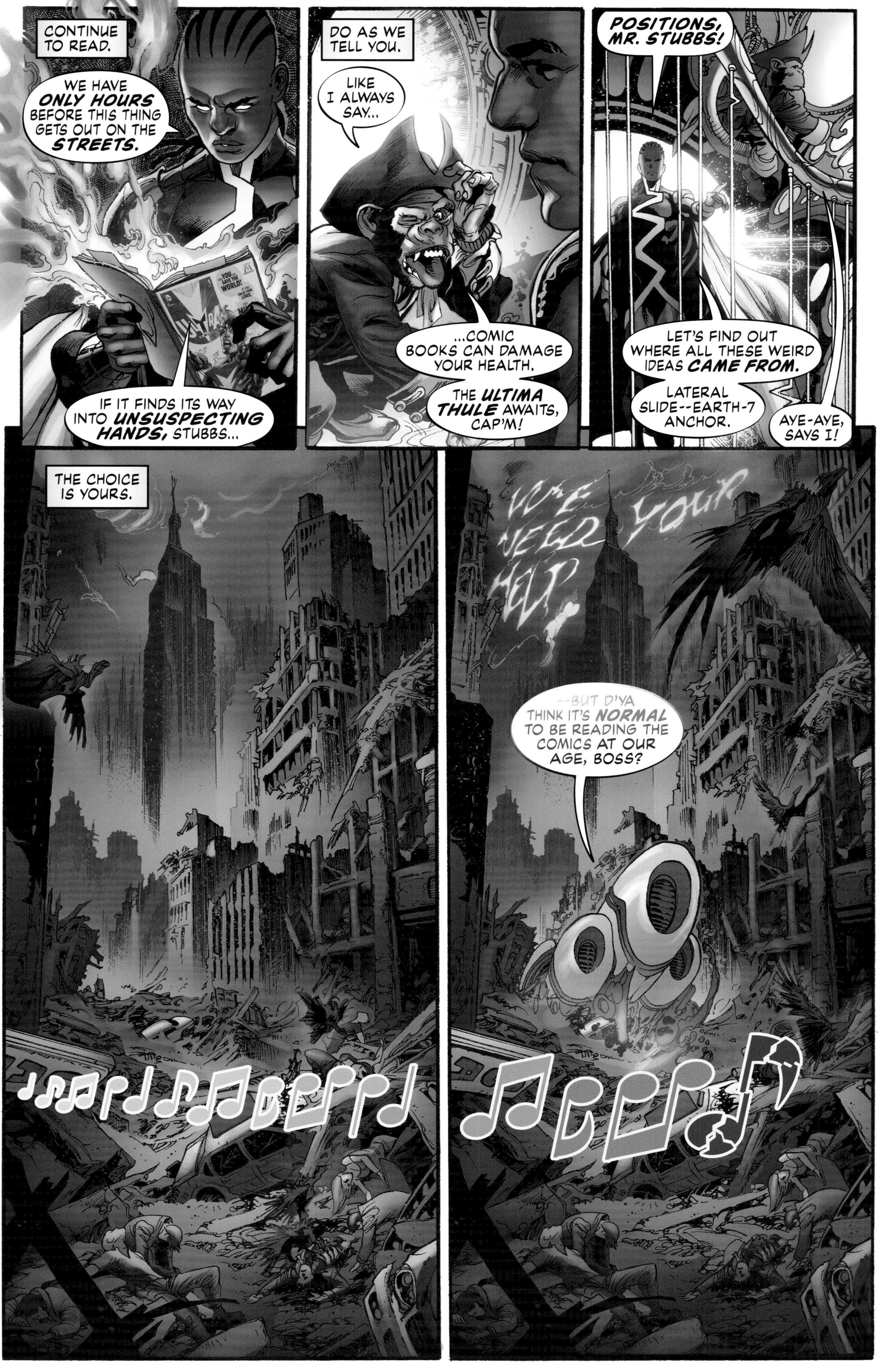
CONTINUE TO READ.
WE HAVE ONLY HOURS BEFORE THIS THING GETS OUT ON THE STREETS.
IF IT FINDS ITS WAY INTO UNSUSPECTING HANDS, STUBBS...
DO AS WE TELL YOU.
LIKE I ALWAYS SAY...
...COMIC BOOKS CAN DAMAGE YOUR HEALTH.
THE ULTIMA THULE AWAITS, CAP'M!
POSITIONS, MR. STUBBS!
LET'S FIND OUT WHERE ALL THESE WEIRD IDEAS CAME FROM.
LATERAL SLIDE--EARTH-7 ANCHOR.
AYE-AYE, SAYS I!
THE CHOICE IS YOURS.
WE NEED YOUR HELP
--BUT D'YA THINK IT'S NORMAL TO BE READING THE COMICS AT OUR AGE, BOSS?

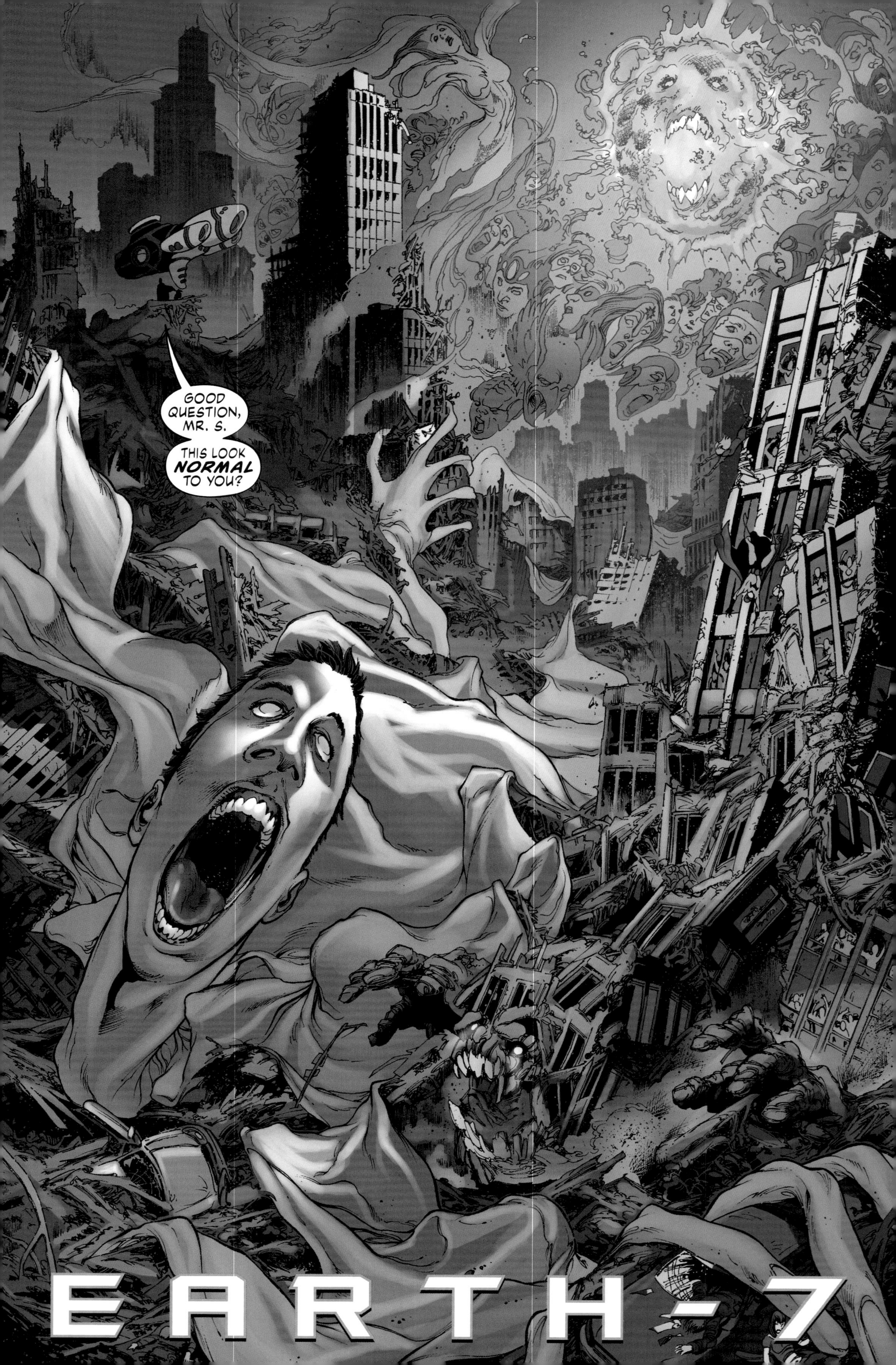
GOOD QUESTION, MR. S.
THIS LOOK NORMAL TO YOU?
EARTH-7

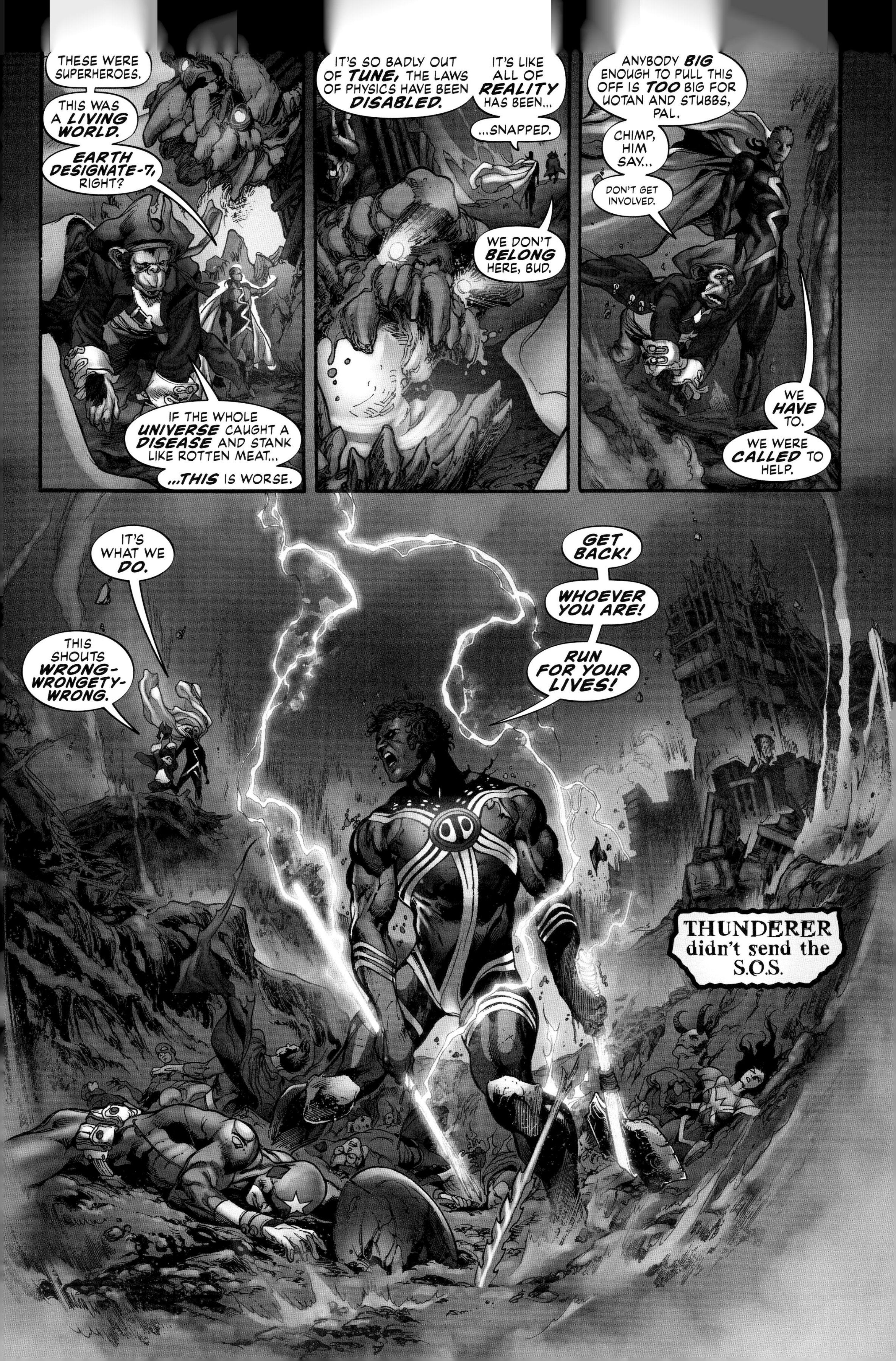

THESE WERE SUPERHEROES.
THIS WAS A LIVING WORLD.
EARTH DESIGNATE-7, RIGHT?
IF THE WHOLE UNIVERSE CAUGHT A DISEASE AND STANK LIKE ROTTEN MEAT...
...THIS IS WORSE.
IT'S SO BADLY OUT OF TUNE, THE LAWS OF PHYSICS HAVE BEEN DISABLED.
IT'S LIKE ALL OF REALITY HAS BEEN...
...SNAPPED.
WE DON'T BELONG HERE, BUD.
ANYBODY BIG ENOUGH TO PULL THIS OFF IS TOO BIG FOR UOTAN AND STUBBS, PAL.
CHIMP, HIM SAY...
DON'T GET INVOLVED.
WE HAVE TO.
WE WERE CALLED TO HELP.
IT'S WHAT WE DO.
THIS SHOUTS WRONG-WRONGETY-WRONG.
GET BACK!
WHOEVER YOU ARE!
RUN FOR YOUR LIVES!
THUNDERER didn't send the S.O.S.

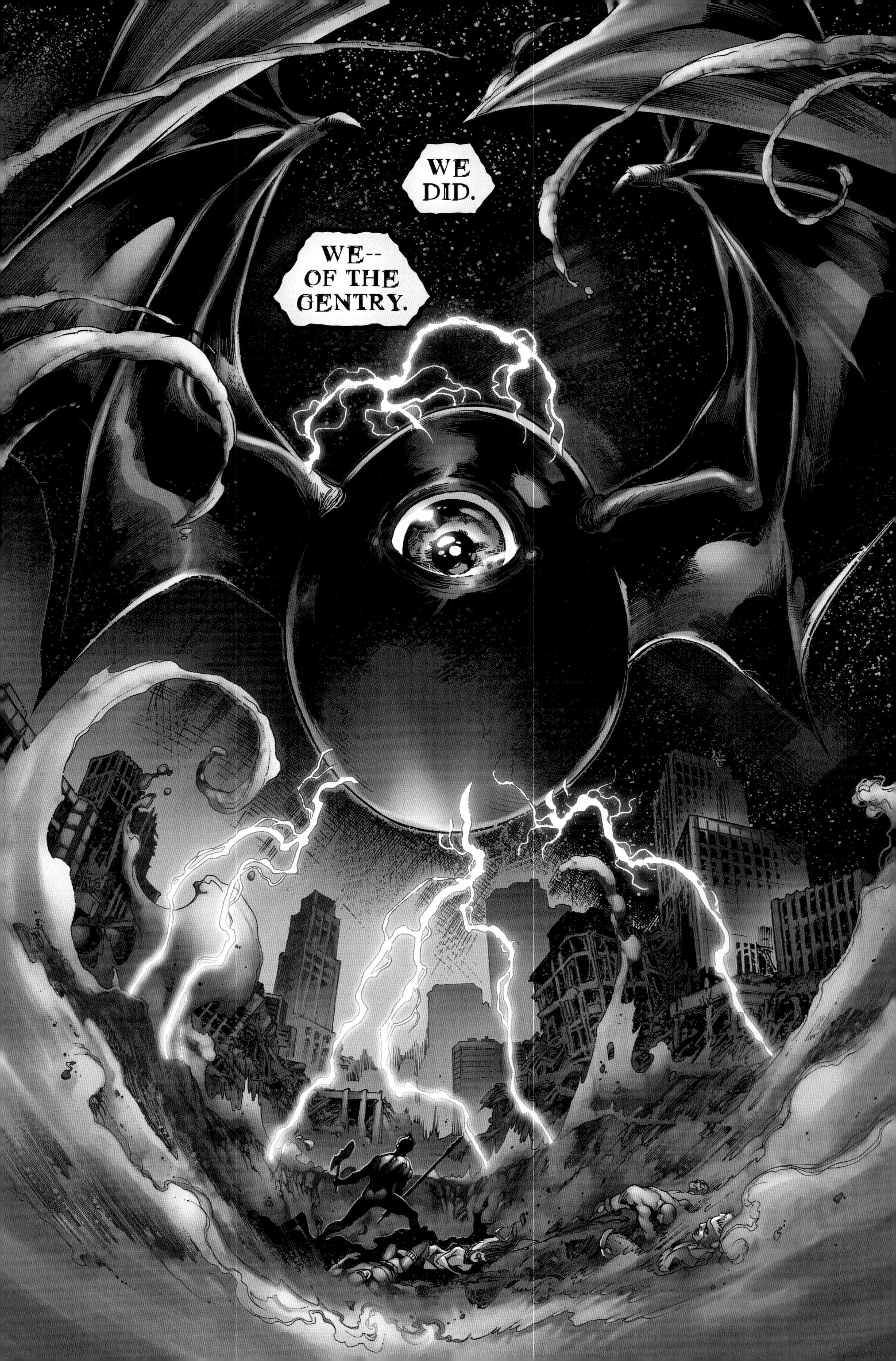
WE DID.
WE-- OF THE GENTRY.

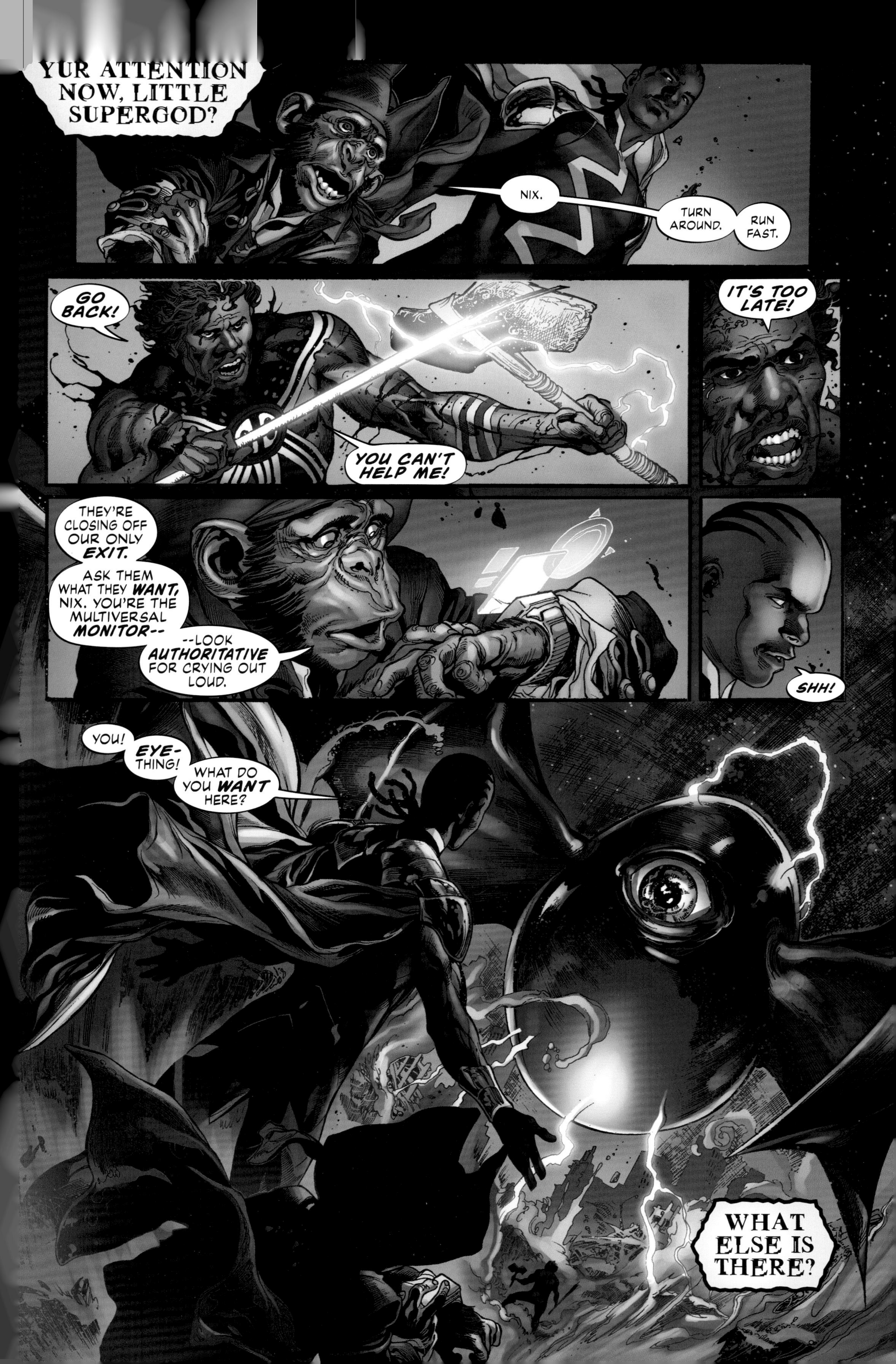
YUR ATTENTION NOW, LITTLE SUPERGOD?
NIX.
TURN AROUND.
RUN FAST.
GO BACK!
YOU CAN'T HELP ME!
IT'S TOO LATE!
THEY'RE CLOSING OFF OUR ONLY EXIT.
ASK THEM WHAT THEY WANT, NIX. YOU'RE THE MULTIVERSAL MONITOR--
--LOOK AUTHORITATIVE FOR CRYING OUT LOUD.
SHH!
YOU!
EYE-THING!
WHAT DO YOU WANT HERE?
WHAT ELSE IS THERE?

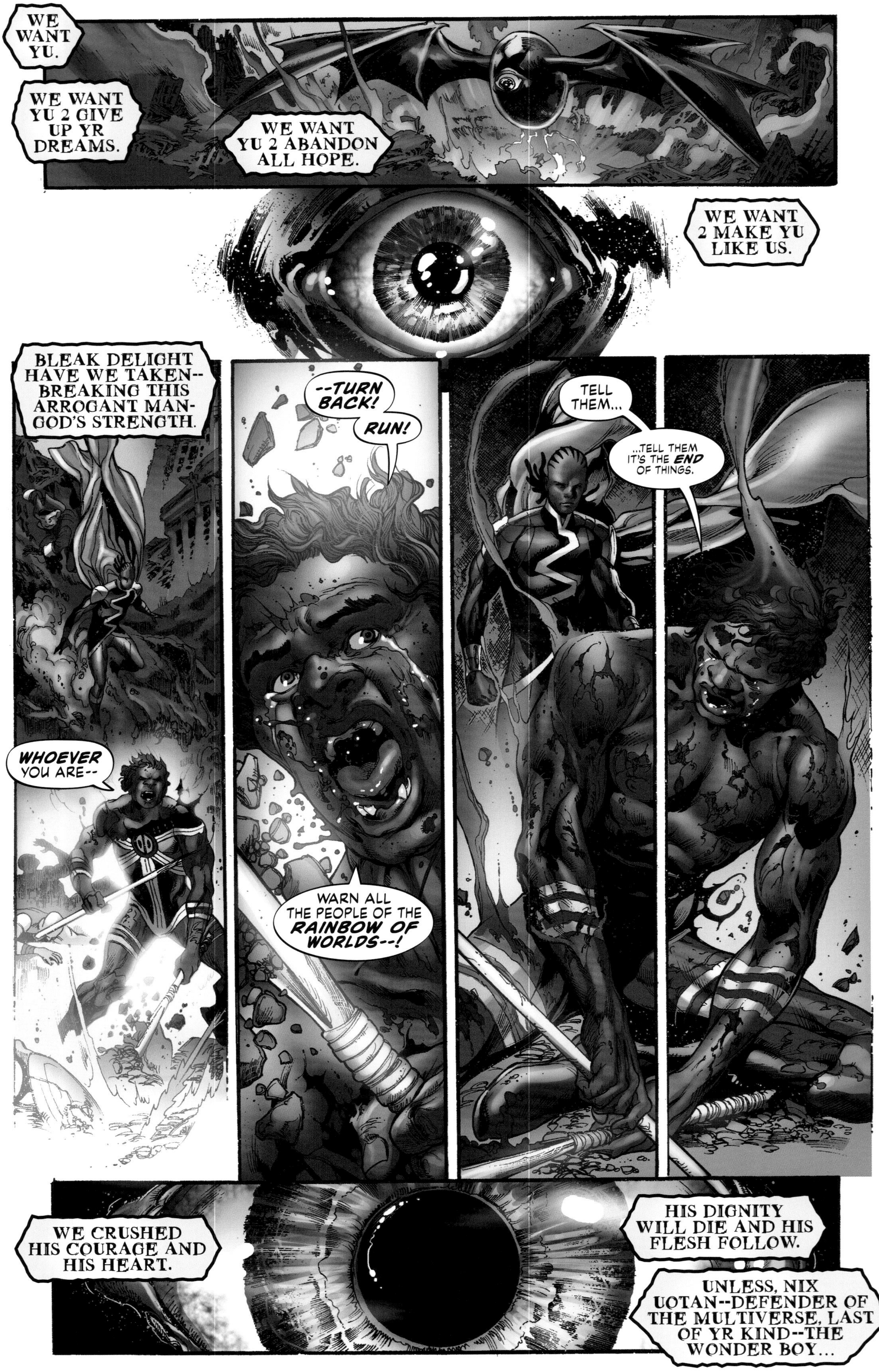
WE WANT YU.
WE WANT YU 2 GIVE UP YR DREAMS.
WE WANT YU 2 ABANDON ALL HOPE.
WE WANT 2 MAKE YU LIKE US.
BLEAK DELIGHT HAVE WE TAKEN--BREAKING THIS ARROGANT MAN-GOD'S STRENGTH.
WHOEVER YOU ARE--
--TURN BACK!
RUN!
WARN ALL THE PEOPLE OF THE RAINBOW OF WORLDS--!
TELL THEM...
...TELL THEM IT'S THE END OF THINGS.
WE CRUSHED HIS COURAGE AND HIS HEART.
HIS DIGNITY WILL DIE AND HIS FLESH FOLLOW.
UNLESS, NIX UOTAN--DEFENDER OF THE MULTIVERSE, LAST OF YR KIND--THE WONDER BOY...

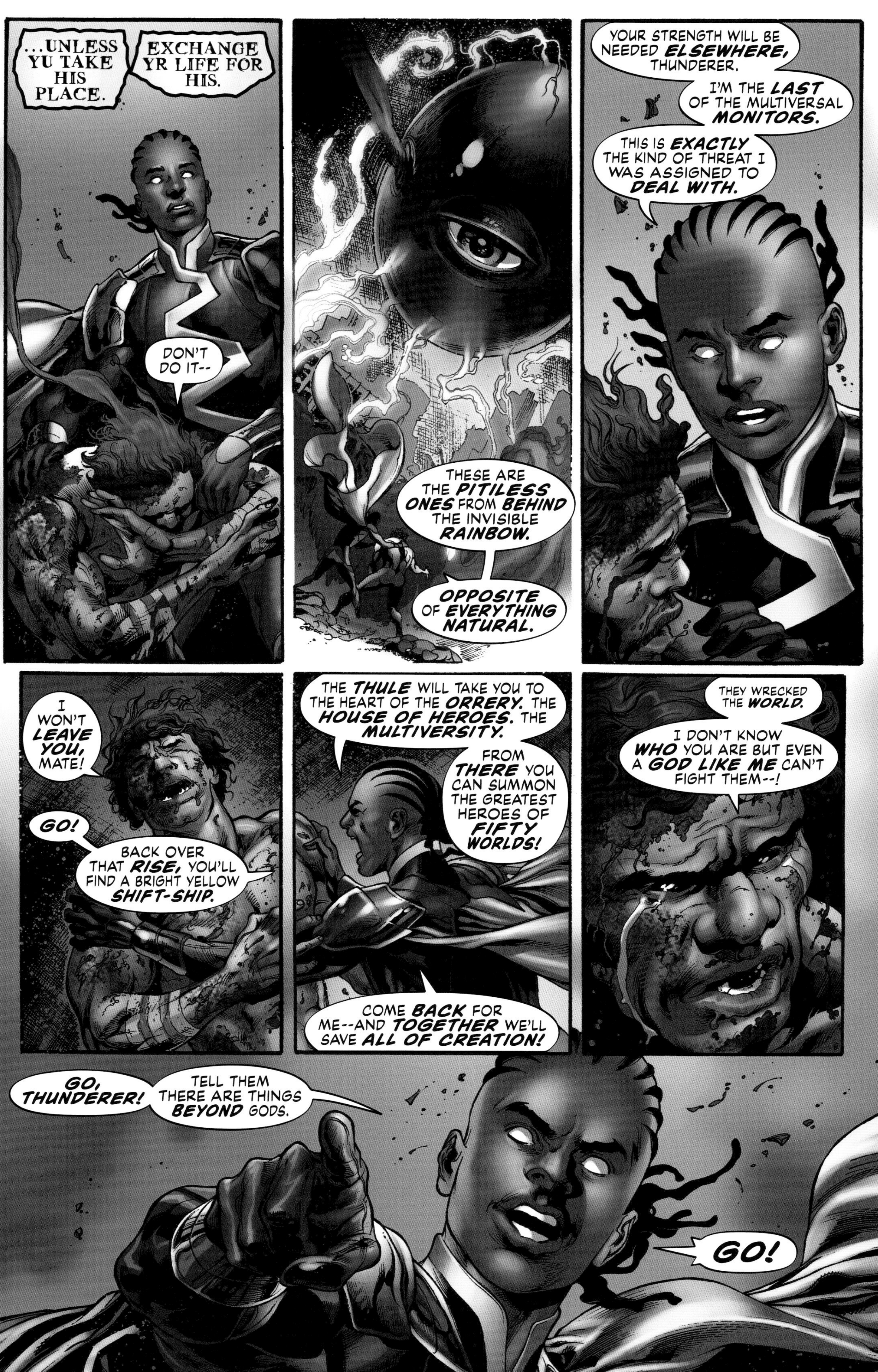
...UNLESS YU TAKE HIS PLACE.
EXCHANGE YR LIFE FOR HIS.
DON'T DO IT--
THESE ARE THE PITILESS ONES FROM BEHIND THE INVISIBLE RAINBOW.
OPPOSITE OF EVERYTHING NATURAL.
YOUR STRENGTH WILL BE NEEDED ELSEWHERE, THUNDERER.
I'M THE LAST OF THE MULTIVERSAL MONITORS.
THIS IS EXACTLY THE KIND OF THREAT I WAS ASSIGNED TO DEAL WITH.
I WON'T LEAVE YOU, MATE!
GO!
BACK OVER THAT RISE, YOU'LL FIND A BRIGHT YELLOW SHIFT-SHIP.
THE THULE WILL TAKE YOU TO THE HEART OF THE ORRERY. THE HOUSE OF HEROES. THE MULTIVERSITY.
FROM THERE YOU CAN SUMMON THE GREATEST HEROES OF FIFTY WORLDS!
COME BACK FOR ME--AND TOGETHER WE'LL SAVE ALL OF CREATION!
THEY WRECKED THE WORLD.
I DON'T KNOW WHO YOU ARE BUT EVEN A GOD LIKE ME CAN'T FIGHT THEM--!
GO, THUNDERER!
TELL THEM THERE ARE THINGS BEYOND GODS.
GO!

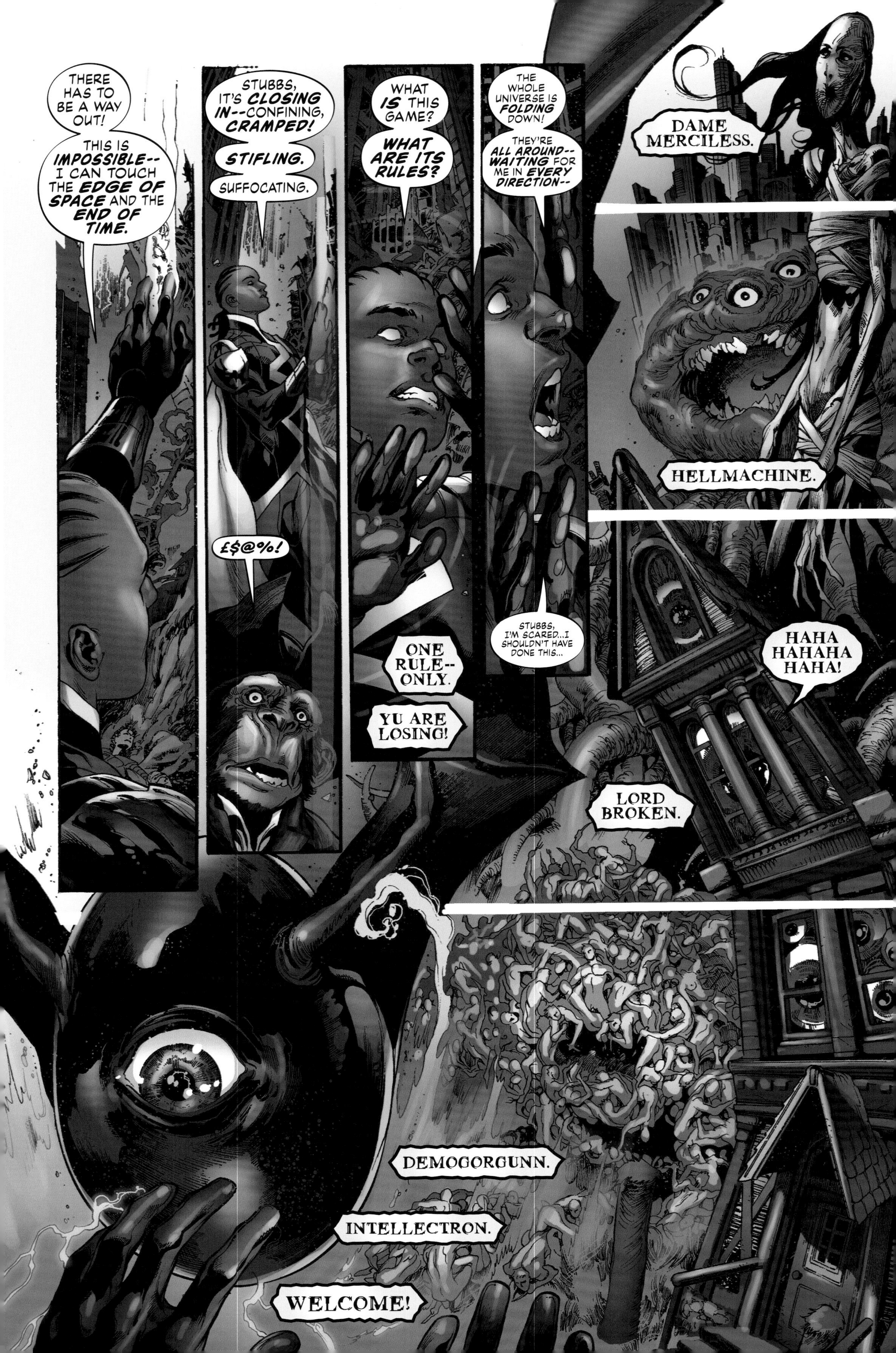

THERE HAS TO BE A WAY OUT!
THIS IS IMPOSSIBLE-- I CAN TOUCH THE EDGE OF SPACE AND THE END OF TIME.
STUBBS, IT'S CLOSING IN--CONFINING, CRAMPED!
STIFLING.
SUFFOCATING.
£$@%!
WHAT IS THIS GAME?
WHAT ARE ITS RULES?
ONE RULE-- ONLY.
YU ARE LOSING!
THE WHOLE UNIVERSE IS FOLDING DOWN!
THEY'RE ALL AROUND-- WAITING FOR ME IN EVERY DIRECTION--
STUBBS, I'M SCARED...I SHOULDN'T HAVE DONE THIS...
DAME MERCILESS.
HELLMACHINE.
HAHA HAHAHA HAHA!
LORD BROKEN.
DEMOGORGUNN.
INTELLECTRON.
WELCOME!

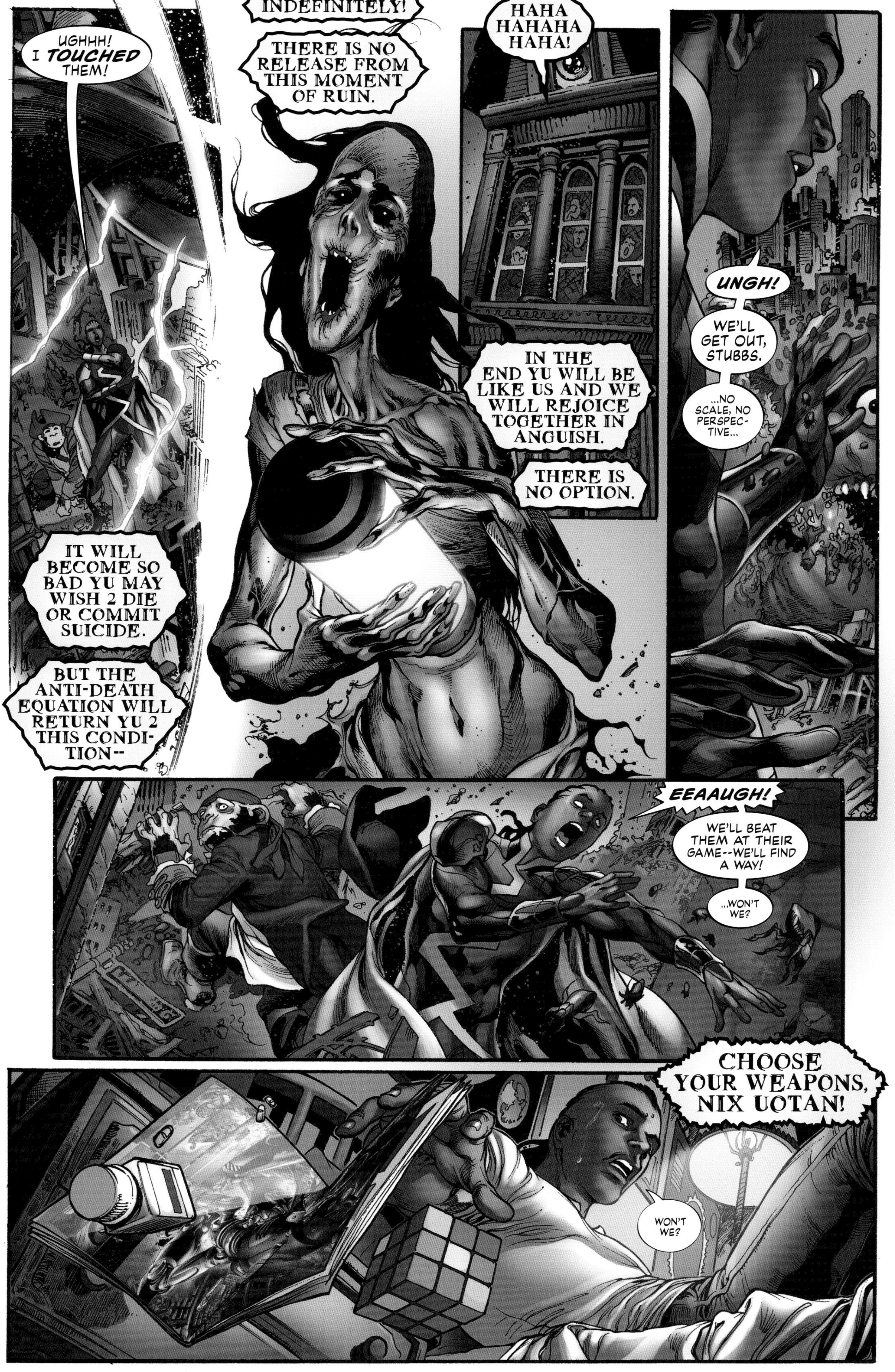

UGHHH! I TOUCHED THEM!
INDEFINITELY!
THERE IS NO RELEASE FROM THIS MOMENT OF RUIN.
IT WILL BECOME SO BAD YU MAY WISH 2 DIE OR COMMIT SUICIDE.
BUT THE ANTI-DEATH EQUATION WILL RETURN YU 2 THIS CONDITION--
HAHA HAHAHA HAHA!
IN THE END YU WILL BE LIKE US AND WE WILL REJOICE TOGETHER IN ANGUISH.
THERE IS NO OPTION.
UNGH!
WE'LL GET OUT, STUBBS.
...NO SCALE, NO PERSPECTIVE...
EEAAUGH!
WE'LL BEAT THEM AT THEIR GAME--WE'LL FIND A WAY!
...WON'T WE?
CHOOSE YOUR WEAPONS, NIX UOTAN!
WON'T WE?

EARTH-23

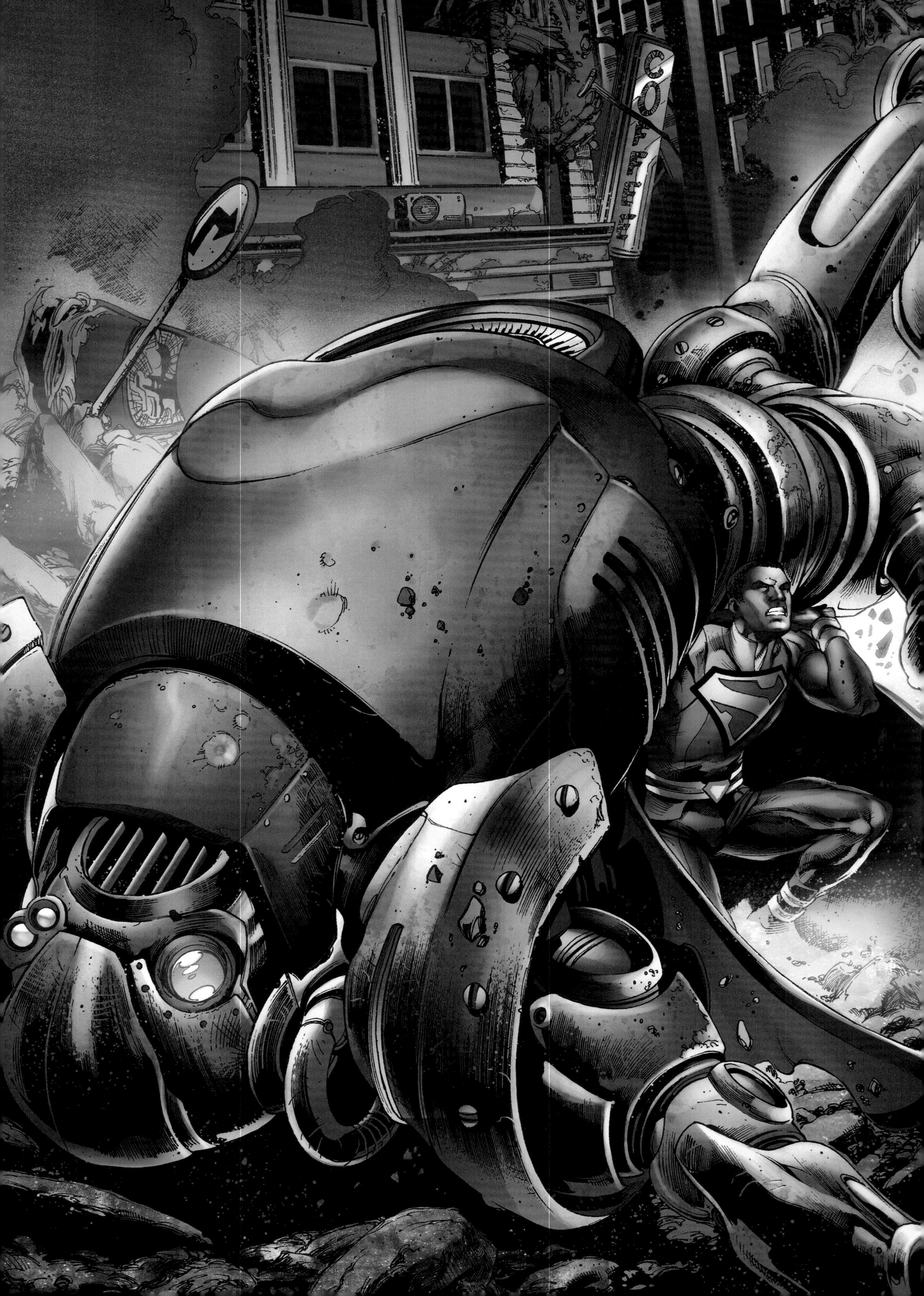

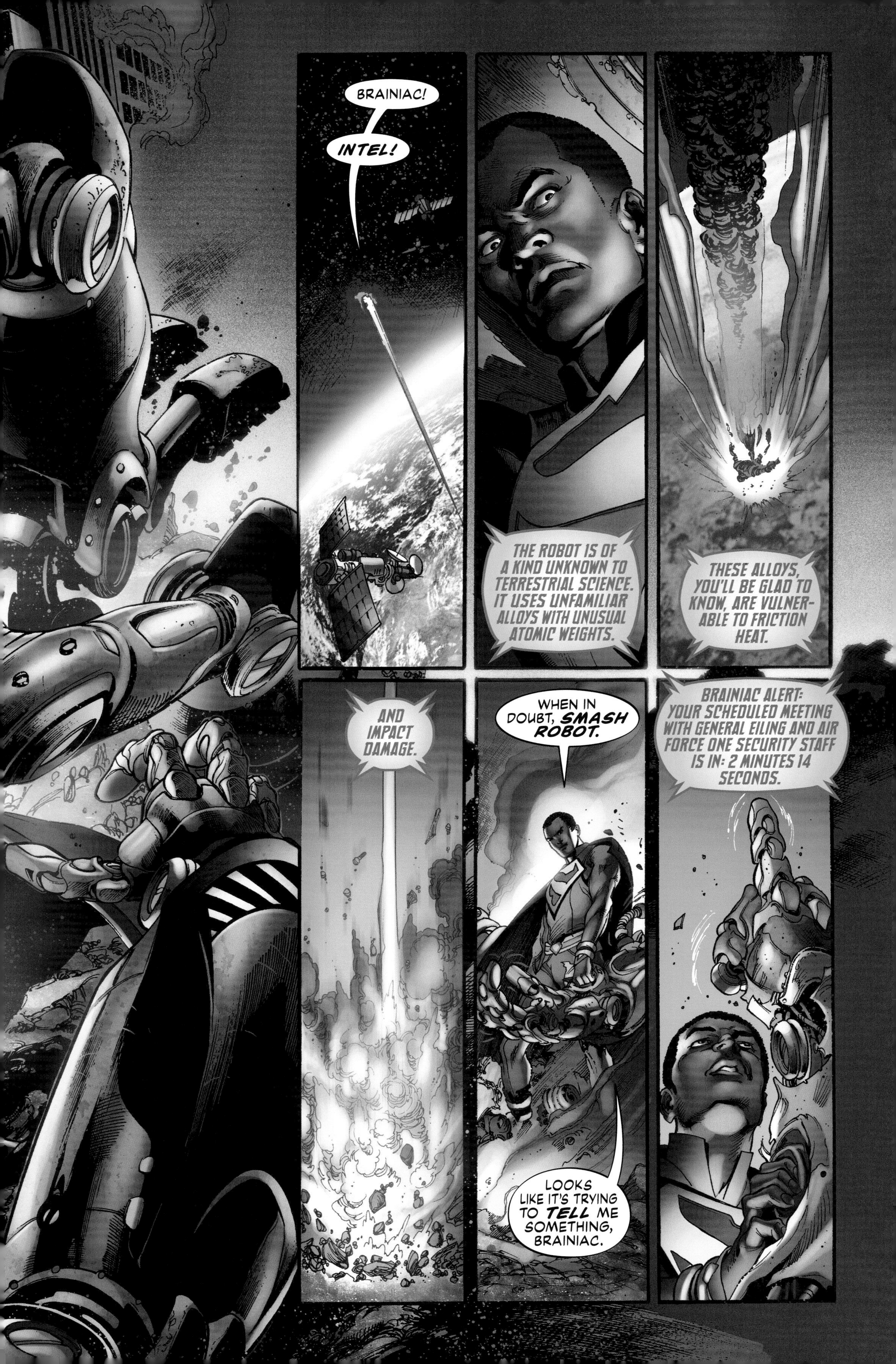
BRAINIAC!
INTEL!
THE ROBOT IS OF A KIND UNKNOWN TO TERRESTRIAL SCIENCE. IT USES UNFAMILIAR ALLOYS WITH UNUSUAL ATOMIC WEIGHTS.
THESE ALLOYS, YOU'LL BE GLAD TO KNOW, ARE VULNERABLE TO FRICTION HEAT.
AND IMPACT DAMAGE.
WHEN IN DOUBT, SMASH ROBOT.
LOOKS LIKE IT'S TRYING TO TELL ME SOMETHING, BRAINIAC.
BRAINIAC ALERT: YOUR SCHEDULED MEETING WITH GENERAL EILING AND AIR FORCE ONE SECURITY STAFF IS IN: 2 MINUTES 14 SECONDS.

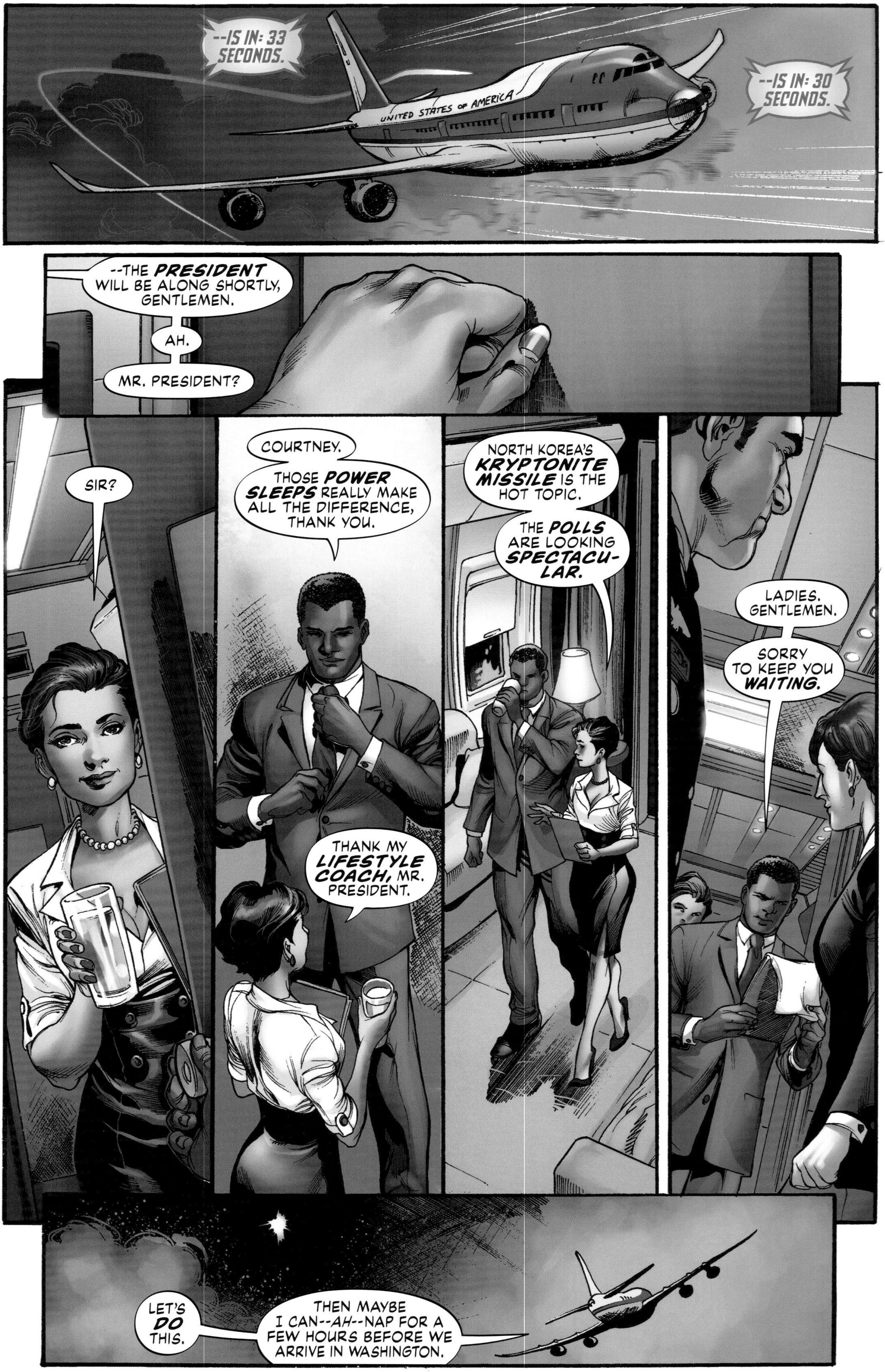
--IS IN: 33 SECONDS.
--IS IN: 30 SECONDS.
--THE PRESIDENT WILL BE ALONG SHORTLY, GENTLEMEN.
AH.
MR. PRESIDENT?
SIR?
COURTNEY.
THOSE POWER SLEEPS REALLY MAKE ALL THE DIFFERENCE, THANK YOU.
THANK MY LIFESTYLE COACH, MR. PRESIDENT.
NORTH KOREA'S KRYPTONITE MISSILE IS THE HOT TOPIC.
THE POLLS ARE LOOKING SPECTACU-LAR.
LADIES. GENTLEMEN.
SORRY TO KEEP YOU WAITING.
LET'S DO THIS.
THEN MAYBE I CAN--AH--NAP FOR A FEW HOURS BEFORE WE ARRIVE IN WASHINGTON.
UNITED STATES OF AMERICA

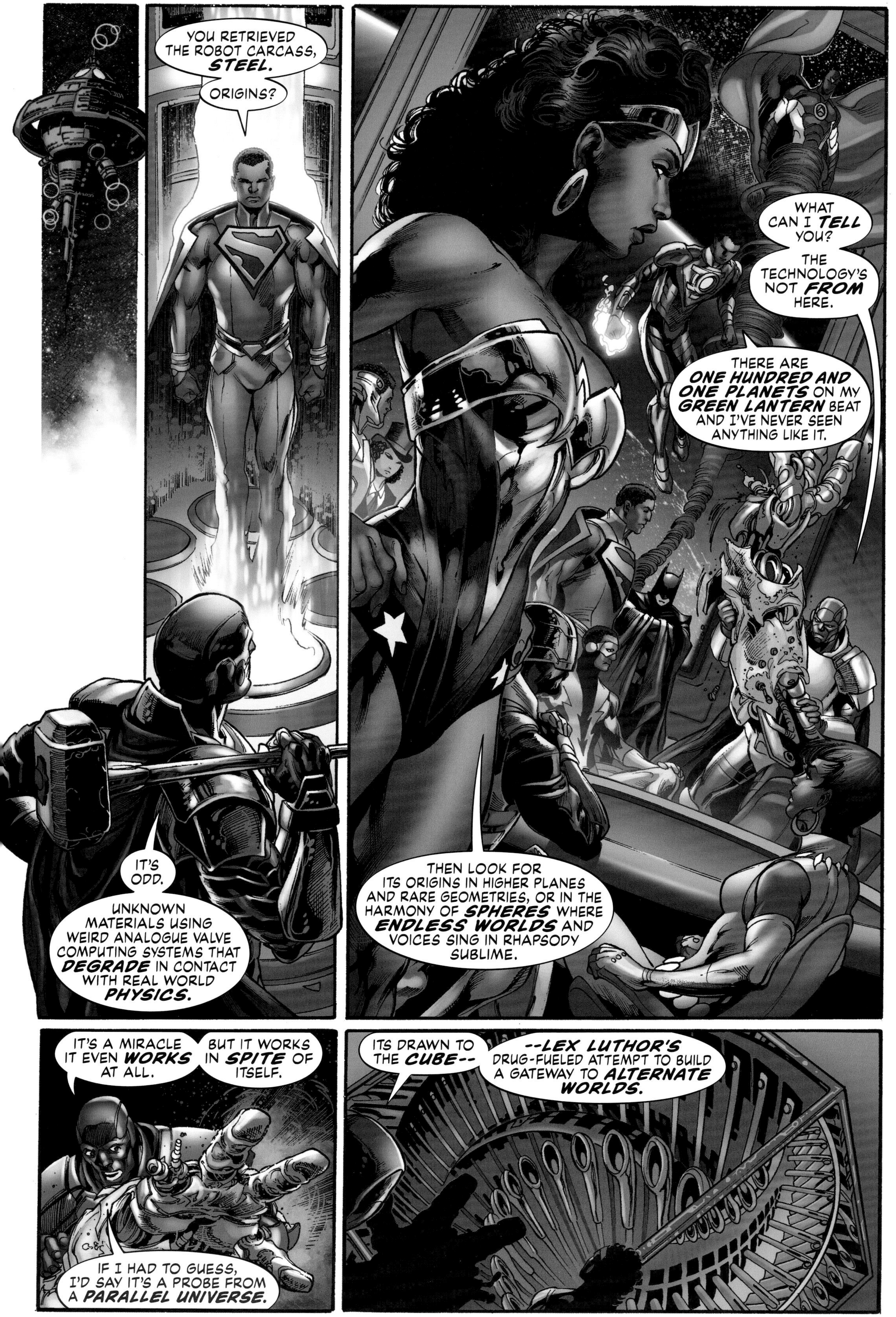
YOU RETRIEVED THE ROBOT CARCASS, STEEL.
ORIGINS?
IT'S ODD.
UNKNOWN MATERIALS USING WEIRD ANALOGUE VALVE COMPUTING SYSTEMS THAT DEGRADE IN CONTACT WITH REAL WORLD PHYSICS.
WHAT CAN I TELL YOU?
THE TECHNOLOGY'S NOT FROM HERE.
THERE ARE ONE HUNDRED AND ONE PLANETS ON MY GREEN LANTERN BEAT AND I'VE NEVER SEEN ANYTHING LIKE IT.
THEN LOOK FOR ITS ORIGINS IN HIGHER PLANES AND RARE GEOMETRIES, OR IN THE HARMONY OF SPHERES WHERE ENDLESS WORLDS AND VOICES SING IN RHAPSODY SUBLIME.
IT'S A MIRACLE IT EVEN WORKS AT ALL.
BUT IT WORKS IN SPITE OF ITSELF.
IF I HAD TO GUESS, I'D SAY IT'S A PROBE FROM A PARALLEL UNIVERSE.
ITS DRAWN TO THE CUBE--
--LEX LUTHOR'S DRUG-FUELED ATTEMPT TO BUILD A GATEWAY TO ALTERNATE WORLDS.

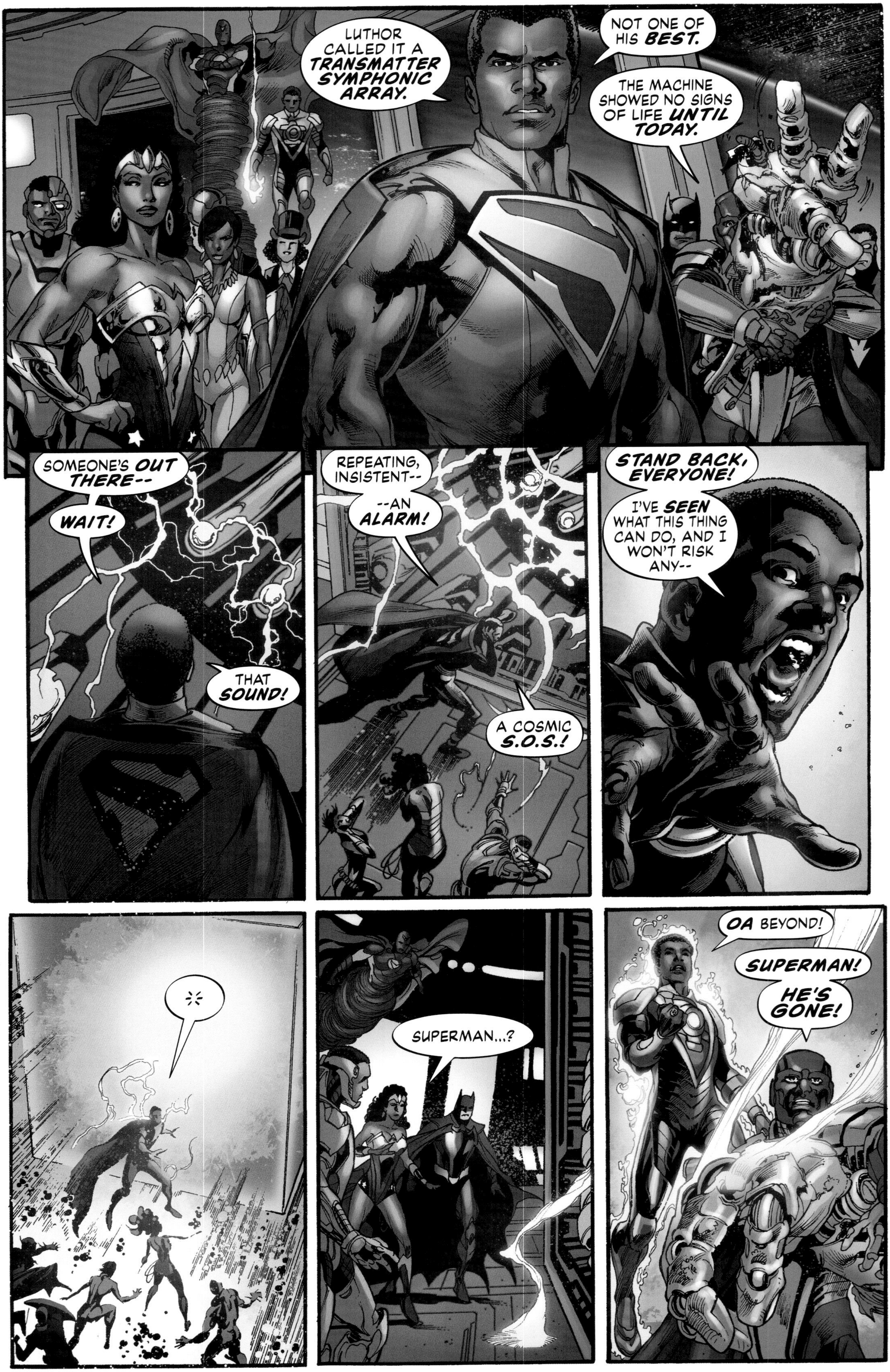
LUTHOR CALLED IT A TRANSMATTER SYMPHONIC ARRAY.
NOT ONE OF HIS BEST.
THE MACHINE SHOWED NO SIGNS OF LIFE UNTIL TODAY.
SOMEONE'S OUT THERE--
WAIT!
THAT SOUND!
REPEATING, INSISTENT--
--AN ALARM!
A COSMIC S.O.S.!
STAND BACK, EVERYONE!
I'VE SEEN WHAT THIS THING CAN DO, AND I WON'T RISK ANY--
SUPERMAN...?
OA BEYOND!
SUPERMAN!
HE'S GONE!

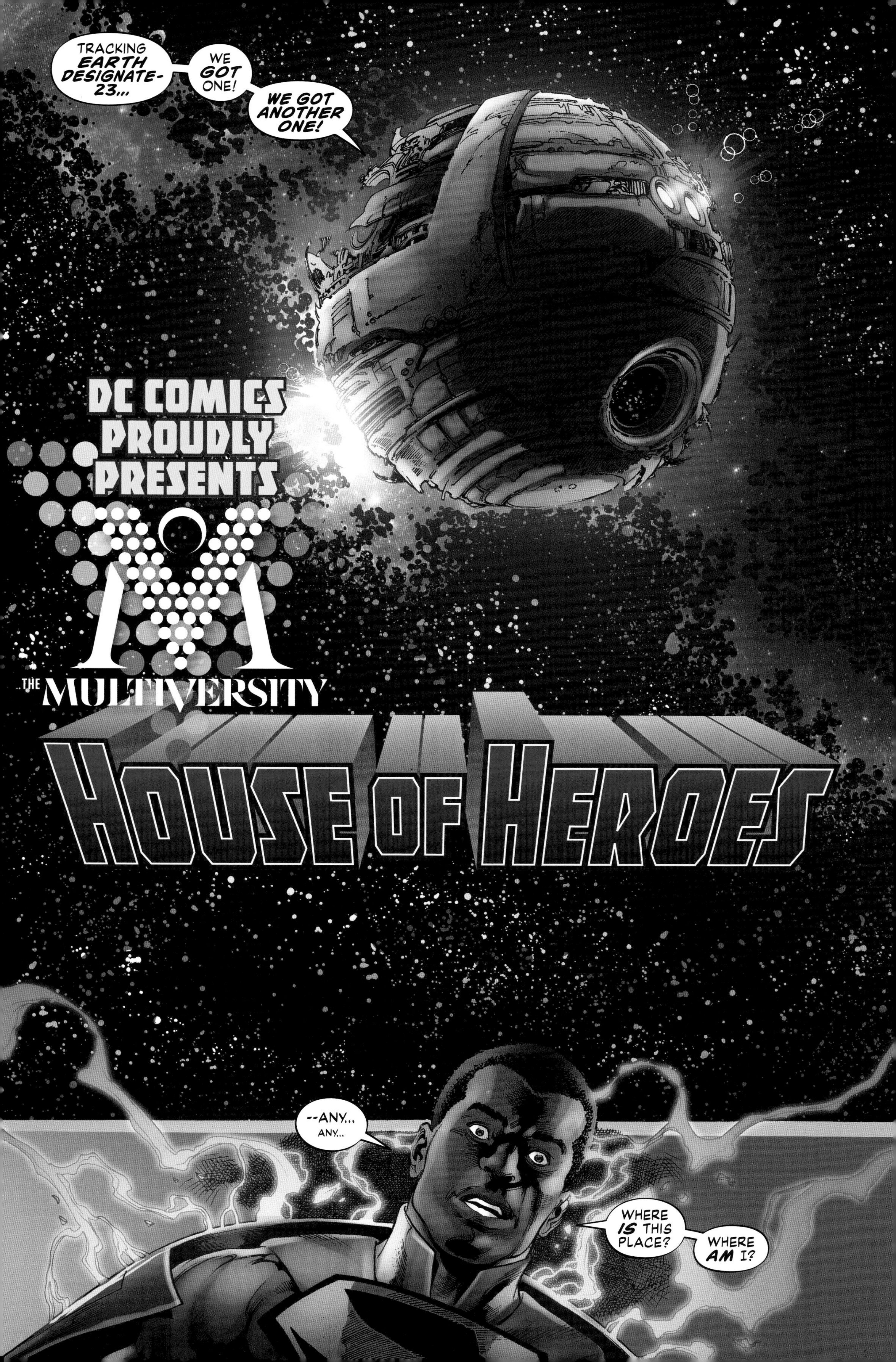
TRACKING EARTH DESIGNATE-23...
WE GOT ONE!
WE GOT ANOTHER ONE!
DC COMICS PROUDLY PRESENTS
THE MULTIVERSITY
HOUSE OF HEROES
--ANY... ANY...
WHERE IS THIS PLACE?
WHERE AM I?

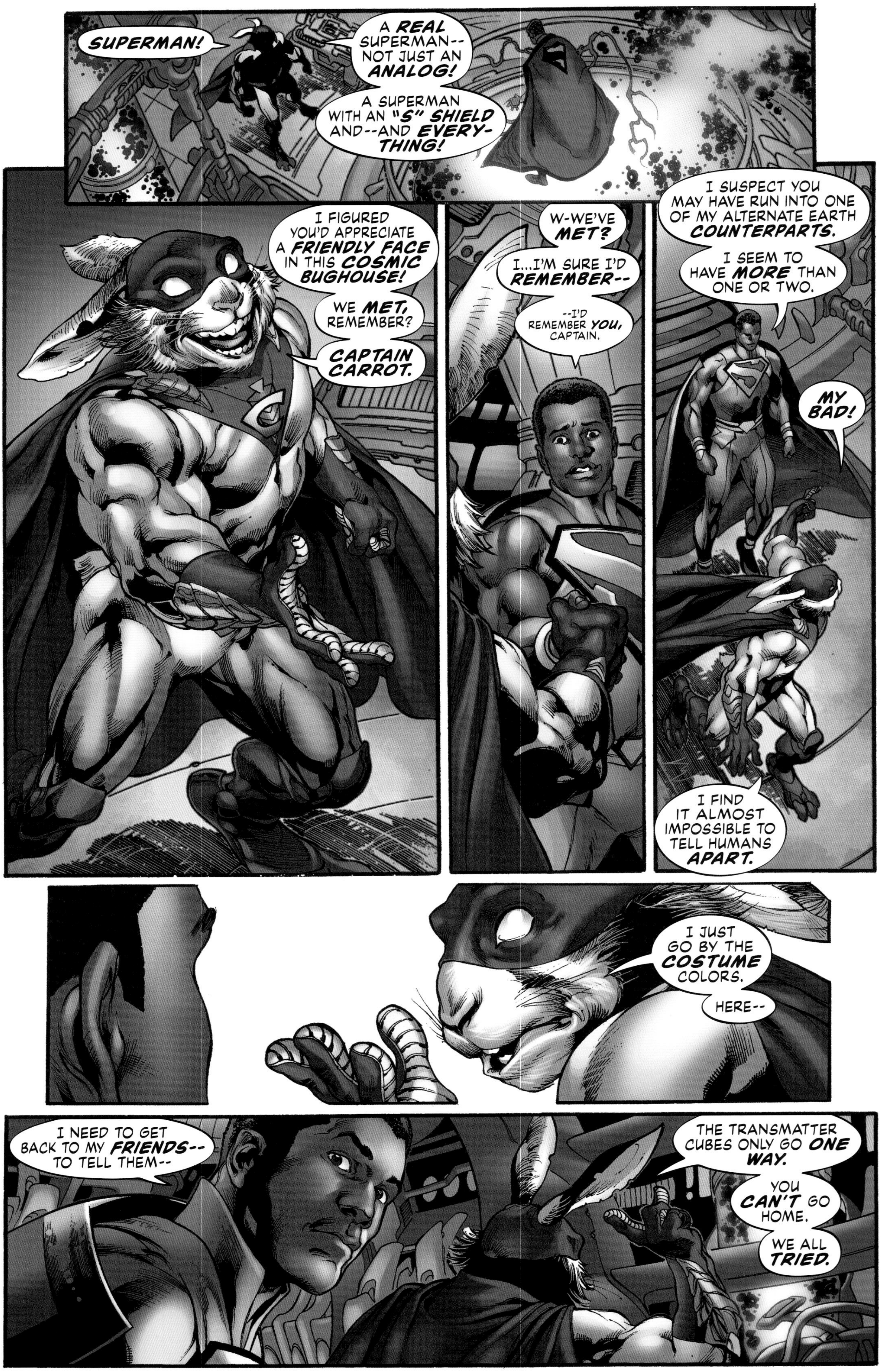
SUPERMAN!
A REAL SUPERMAN-- NOT JUST AN ANALOG!
A SUPERMAN WITH AN "S" SHIELD AND--AND EVERY-THING!
I FIGURED YOU'D APPRECIATE A FRIENDLY FACE IN THIS COSMIC BUGHOUSE!
WE MET, REMEMBER?
CAPTAIN CARROT.
W-WE'VE MET?
I...I'M SURE I'D REMEMBER--
--I'D REMEMBER YOU, CAPTAIN.
I SUSPECT YOU MAY HAVE RUN INTO ONE OF MY ALTERNATE EARTH COUNTERPARTS.
I SEEM TO HAVE MORE THAN ONE OR TWO.
MY BAD!
I FIND IT ALMOST IMPOSSIBLE TO TELL HUMANS APART.
I JUST GO BY THE COSTUME COLORS.
HERE--
I NEED TO GET BACK TO MY FRIENDS-- TO TELL THEM--
THE TRANSMATTER CUBES ONLY GO ONE WAY.
YOU CAN'T GO HOME.
WE ALL TRIED.

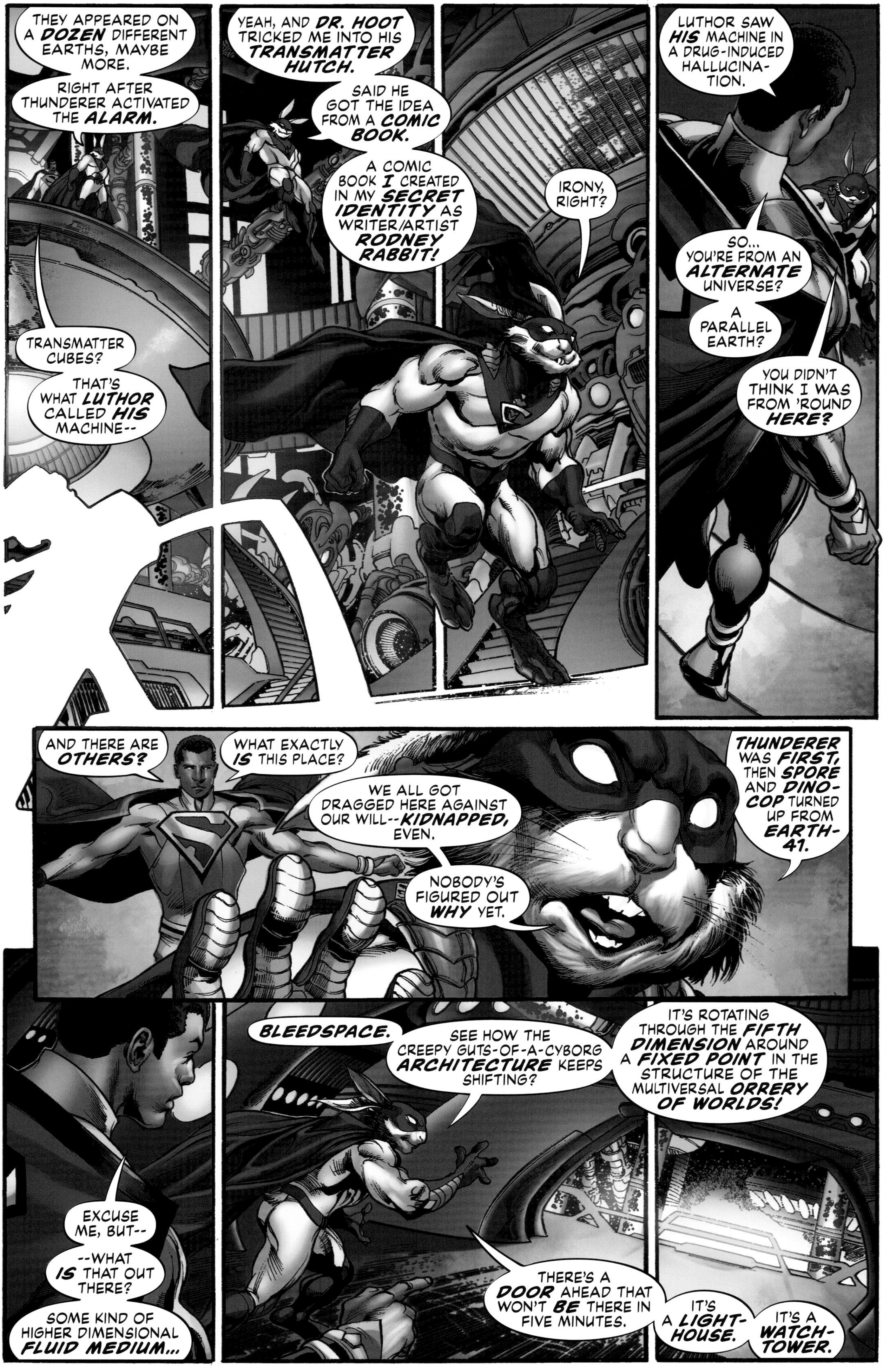
THEY APPEARED ON A DOZEN DIFFERENT EARTHS, MAYBE MORE.
RIGHT AFTER THUNDERER ACTIVATED THE ALARM.
TRANSMATTER CUBES?
THAT'S WHAT LUTHOR CALLED HIS MACHINE--
YEAH, AND DR. HOOT TRICKED ME INTO HIS TRANSMATTER HUTCH.
SAID HE GOT THE IDEA FROM A COMIC BOOK.
A COMIC BOOK I CREATED IN MY SECRET IDENTITY AS WRITER/ARTIST RODNEY RABBIT!
IRONY, RIGHT?
LUTHOR SAW HIS MACHINE IN A DRUG-INDUCED HALLUCINA-TION.
SO... YOU'RE FROM AN ALTERNATE UNIVERSE?
A PARALLEL EARTH?
YOU DIDN'T THINK I WAS FROM 'ROUND HERE?
AND THERE ARE OTHERS?
WHAT EXACTLY IS THIS PLACE?
WE ALL GOT DRAGGED HERE AGAINST OUR WILL--KIDNAPPED, EVEN.
NOBODY'S FIGURED OUT WHY YET.
THUNDERER WAS FIRST, THEN SPORE AND DINO-COP TURNED UP FROM EARTH-41.
EXCUSE ME, BUT--
--WHAT IS THAT OUT THERE?
SOME KIND OF HIGHER DIMENSIONAL FLUID MEDIUM...
BLEEDSPACE.
SEE HOW THE CREEPY GUTS-OF-A-CYBORG ARCHITECTURE KEEPS SHIFTING?
IT'S ROTATING THROUGH THE FIFTH DIMENSION AROUND A FIXED POINT IN THE STRUCTURE OF THE MULTIVERSAL ORRERY OF WORLDS!
THERE'S A DOOR AHEAD THAT WON'T BE THERE IN FIVE MINUTES.
IT'S A LIGHT-HOUSE.
IT'S A WATCH-TOWER.

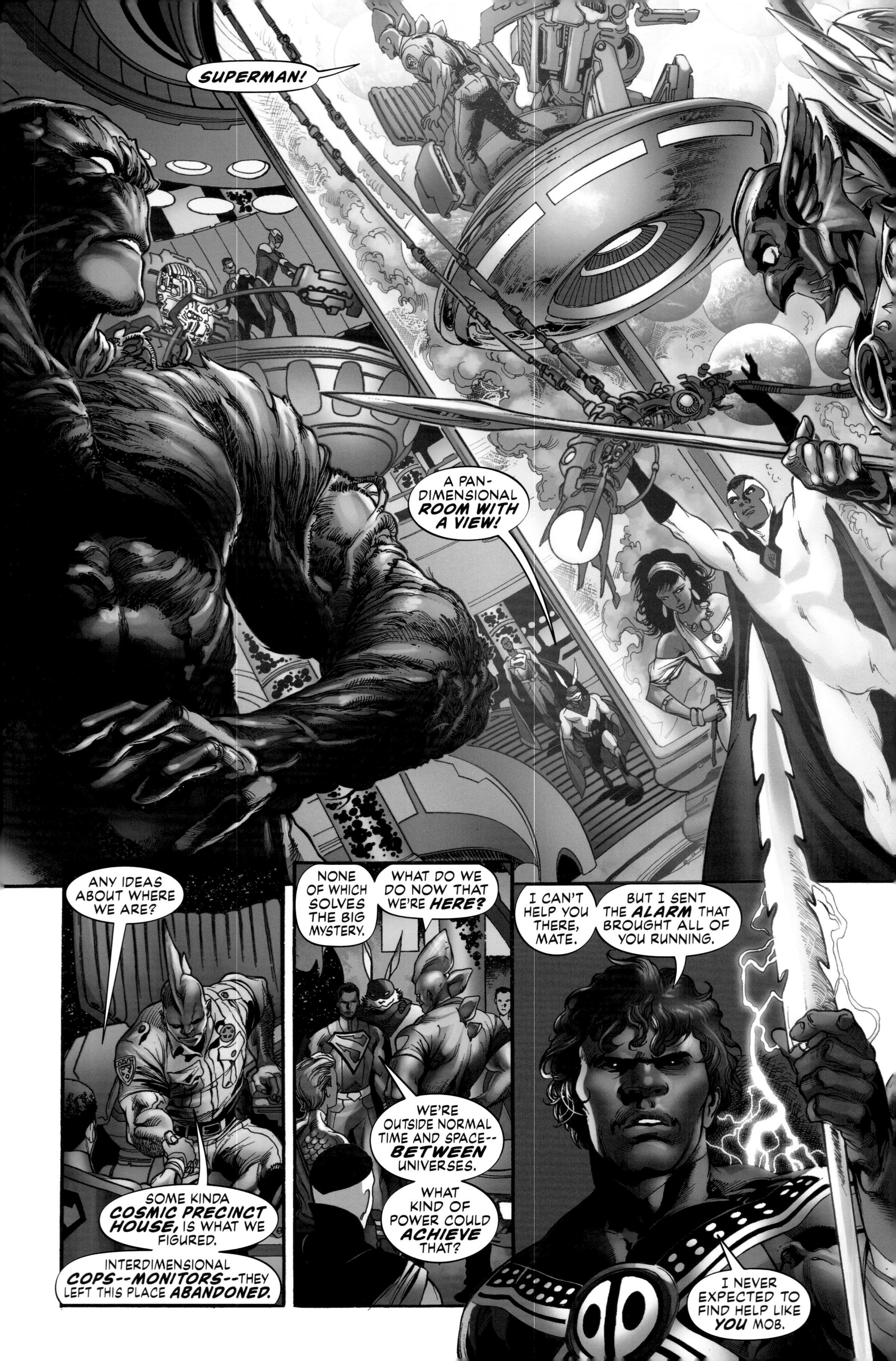
SUPERMAN!
A PAN-DIMENSIONAL ROOM WITH A VIEW!
ANY IDEAS ABOUT WHERE WE ARE?
SOME KINDA COSMIC PRECINCT HOUSE, IS WHAT WE FIGURED.
INTERDIMENSIONAL COPS--MONITORS--THEY LEFT THIS PLACE ABANDONED.
NONE OF WHICH SOLVES THE BIG MYSTERY.
WHAT DO WE DO NOW THAT WE'RE HERE?
WE'RE OUTSIDE NORMAL TIME AND SPACE--BETWEEN UNIVERSES.
WHAT KIND OF POWER COULD ACHIEVE THAT?
I CAN'T HELP YOU THERE, MATE.
BUT I SENT THE ALARM THAT BROUGHT ALL OF YOU RUNNING.
I NEVER EXPECTED TO FIND HELP LIKE YOU MOB.

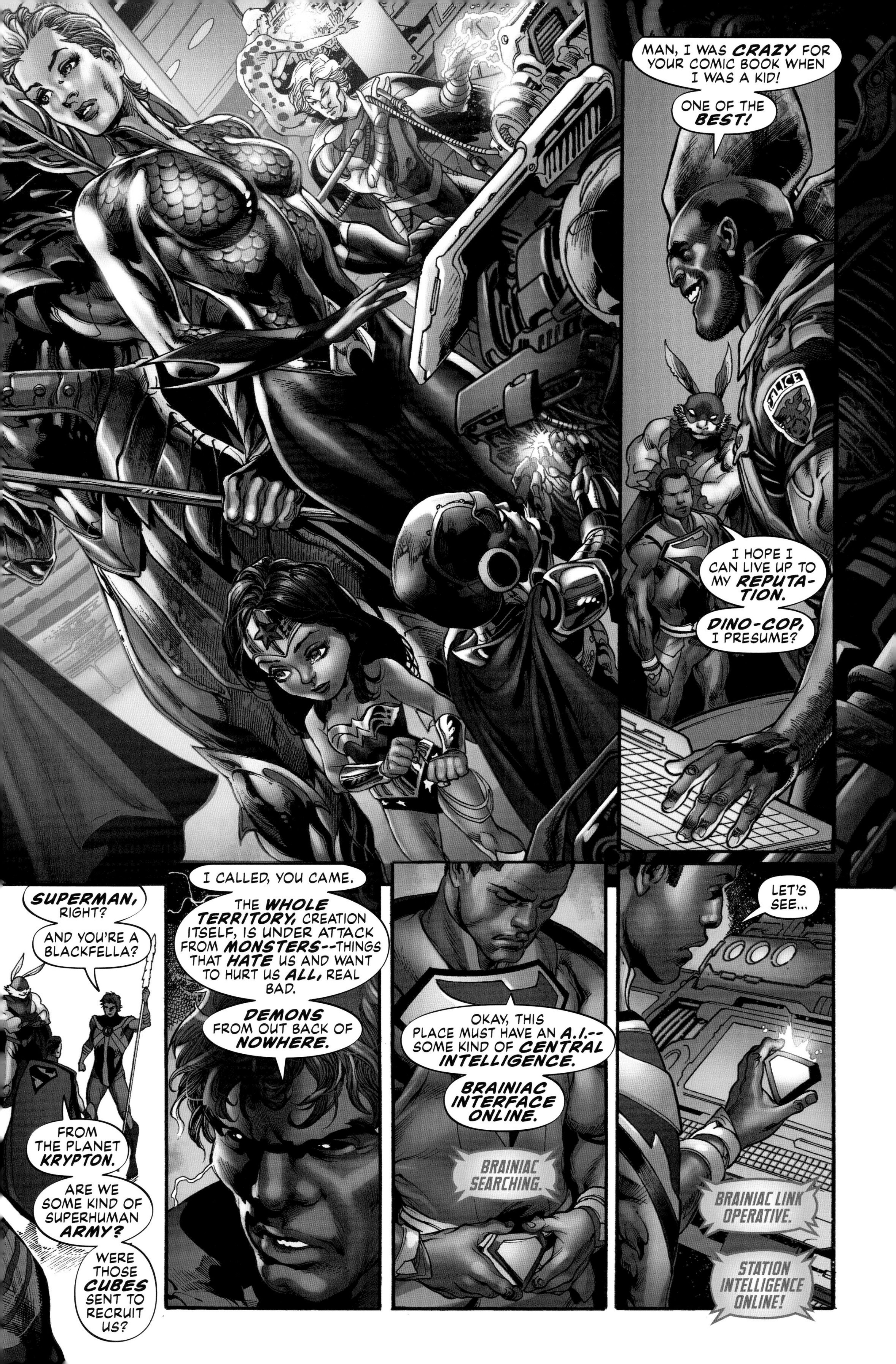
MAN, I WAS CRAZY FOR YOUR COMIC BOOK WHEN I WAS A KID!
ONE OF THE BEST!
I HOPE I CAN LIVE UP TO MY REPUTA-TION.
DINO-COP, I PRESUME?
SUPERMAN, RIGHT?
AND YOU'RE A BLACKFELLA?
FROM THE PLANET KRYPTON.
ARE WE SOME KIND OF SUPERHUMAN ARMY?
WERE THOSE CUBES SENT TO RECRUIT US?
I CALLED, YOU CAME.
THE WHOLE TERRITORY, CREATION ITSELF, IS UNDER ATTACK FROM MONSTERS--THINGS THAT HATE US AND WANT TO HURT US ALL, REAL BAD.
DEMONS FROM OUT BACK OF NOWHERE.
OKAY, THIS PLACE MUST HAVE AN A.I.--SOME KIND OF CENTRAL INTELLIGENCE.
BRAINIAC INTERFACE ONLINE.
BRAINIAC SEARCHING.
LET'S SEE...
BRAINIAC LINK OPERATIVE.
STATION INTELLIGENCE ONLINE!

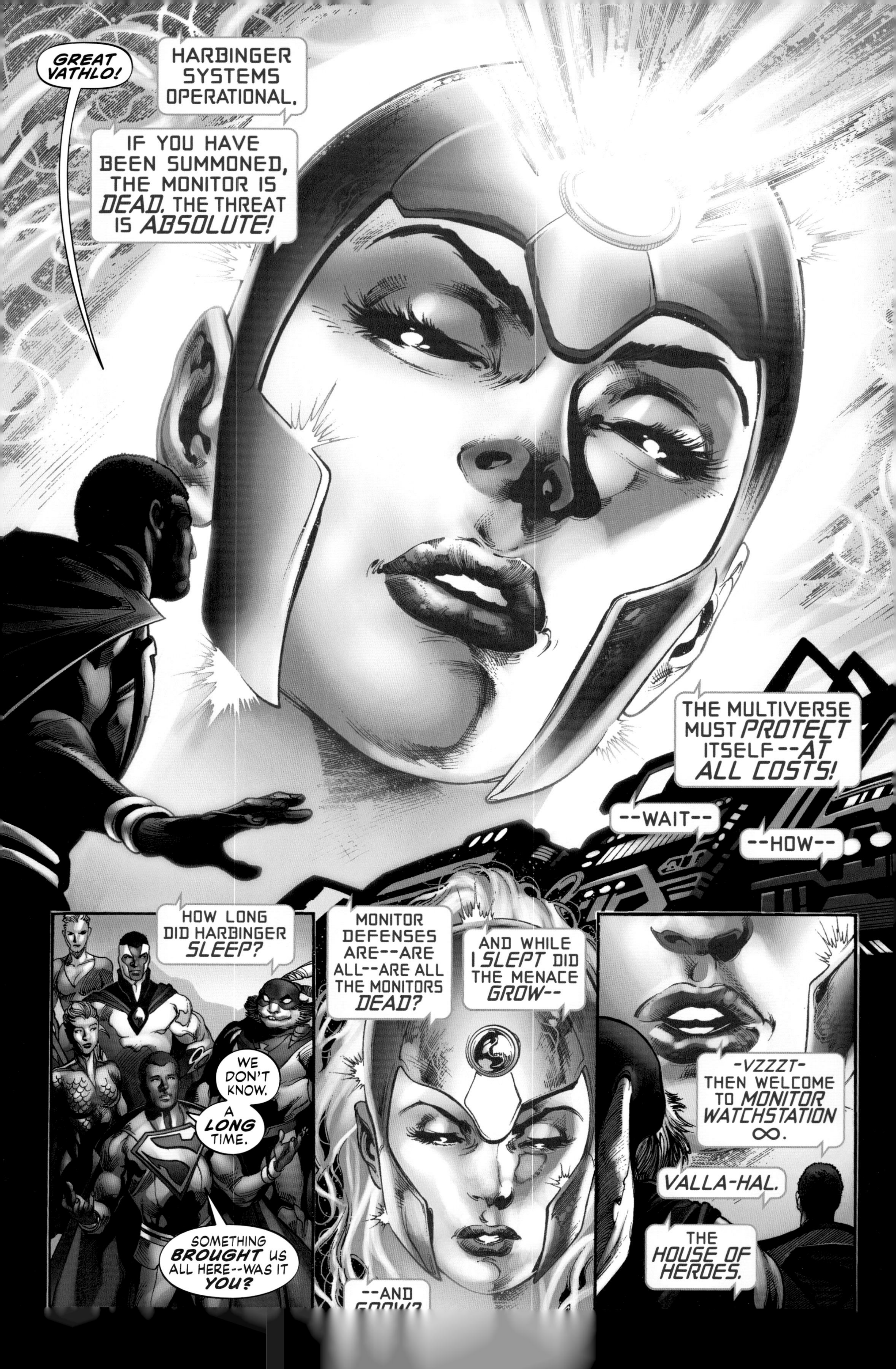
GREAT VATHLO!
HARBINGER SYSTEMS OPERATIONAL.
IF YOU HAVE BEEN SUMMONED, THE MONITOR IS DEAD, THE THREAT IS ABSOLUTE!
THE MULTIVERSE MUST PROTECT ITSELF--AT ALL COSTS!
--WAIT--
--HOW--
HOW LONG DID HARBINGER SLEEP?
WE DON'T KNOW.
A LONG TIME.
SOMETHING BROUGHT US ALL HERE--WAS IT YOU?
MONITOR DEFENSES ARE--ARE ALL--ARE ALL THE MONITORS DEAD?
AND WHILE I SLEPT DID THE MENACE GROW--
--AND
-VZZZT- THEN WELCOME TO MONITOR WATCHSTATION ∞.
VALLA-HAL.
THE HOUSE OF HEROES.

WELCOME TO THE **MULTIVERSITY.**

HOW MAY **HARBINGER** ASSIST?

WE WERE HOPING YOU COULD TELL US **WHY** WE'RE **HERE.**

YEAH. WHAT **THIS** GUY SAYS!

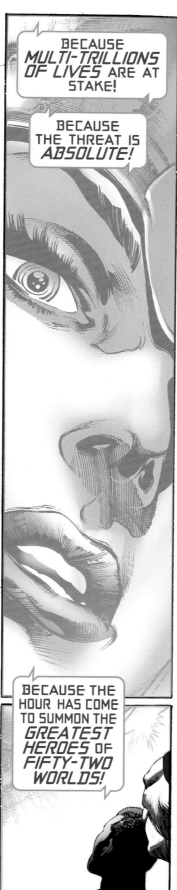

BECAUSE **MULTI-TRILLIONS OF LIVES** ARE AT STAKE!

BECAUSE THE THREAT IS **ABSOLUTE!**

BECAUSE THE HOUR HAS COME TO SUMMON THE **GREATEST HEROES** OF **FIFTY-TWO WORLDS!**

OKAY. **I'M** GAME.

THEN WE HAVE TO GO TO **HELL** TO SAVE **NIX UOTAN.**

HE GAVE **HIMSELF** TO SAVE US **ALL.**

THE **CORRUPTION** OF THE **ORRERY** IS UNDERWAY.

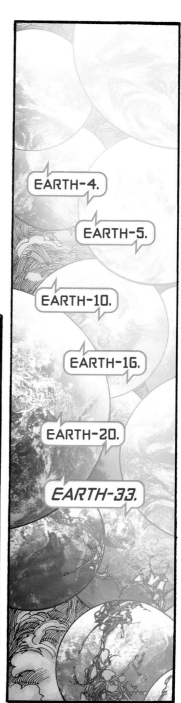

EARTH-4.

EARTH-5.

EARTH-10.

EARTH-16.

EARTH-20.

EARTH-33.

THE **MULTIVERSE** NEEDS YOU!

FINALLY, I GET THE *HANG* OF THIS FANCY *CYBER-CHAIR*, JUST IN TIME TO FACE DOWN A BUNCH OF BAD-ASS *COSMIC DESTROYERS.*

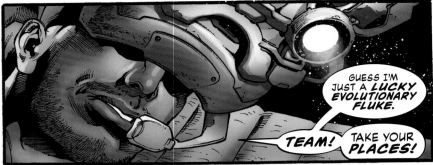

GUESS I'M JUST A *LUCKY EVOLUTIONARY FLUKE.*

TEAM! TAKE YOUR *PLACES!*

I'M THE RESIDENT *COMIC-BOOK NERD* HERE, SUPERMAN.

I'M A *HUGE* FAN AND I'D GIVE *ANYTHING* TO BE PART OF THIS.

I'M, UH, FROM *EARTH-36--RED RACER.*

?

MY *OTHER IDENTITY* IS AN *OPEN SECRET* HERE.

MY *REAL LIFE* IS *PUBLISHED* AS A MONTHLY *COMIC.*

THIS IS *INCREDI-BLE.*

NEXT: SUPERMAN JOURNEYS BEYOND THE *VOID!* MEET THE *THUNDERER* OF EARTH-7 AND THE STRANGEST GUEST STARS OF ALL-- IN "*HOUSE OF HEROES!*"

I ALWAYS SUSPECTED THAT ONE WORLD'S *REALITY* IS ANOTHER'S *FICTION.*

THAT'S WHY I *LIKE HAPPY ENDINGS!*

THESE COMIC BOOKS ARE SHOWING US WHAT'S *REALLY* HAPPENING ON ALL OUR DIFFERENT EARTHS.

MESSAGES IN BOTTLES FROM *NEIGHBORING UNIVERSES.* IT'S-- IT'S *AMAZING!*

I'M FROM *EARTH-11,* APPARENTLY.

AQUA-WOMAN, QUEEN OF ATLANTIS--

I'M *VOLUNTEERING* TO JOIN THE *WAR PARTY.*

YOU'RE *WELCOME.*

BUT I'D PREFER TO THINK OF THIS AS A *FACT-FINDING MISSION.*

≤TFF≥

WE'LL SEE.

THE NEW 52! ACTION COMICS

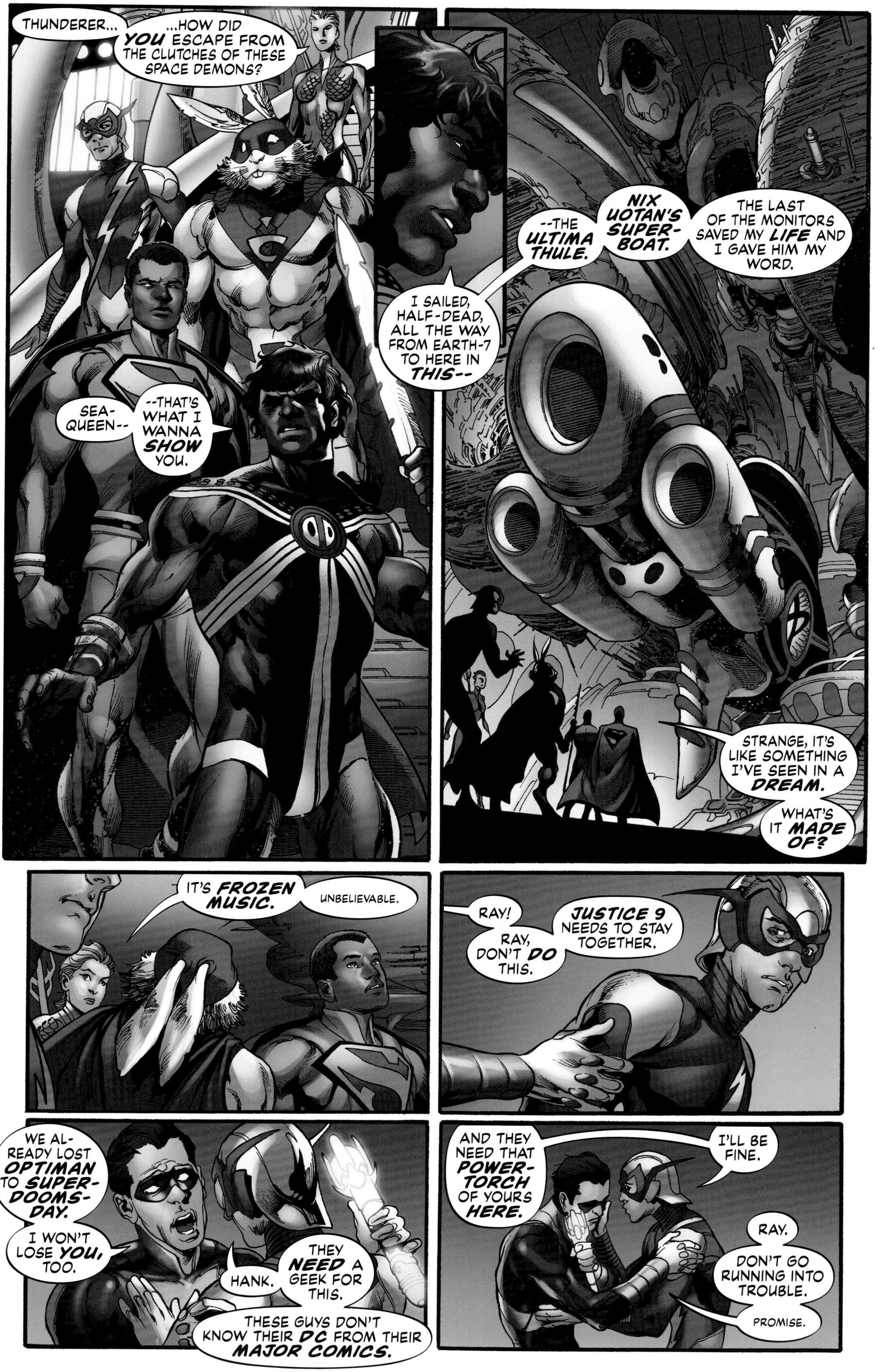
THUNDERER...
...HOW DID YOU ESCAPE FROM THE CLUTCHES OF THESE SPACE DEMONS?
SEA-QUEEN--
--THAT'S WHAT I WANNA SHOW YOU.
I SAILED, HALF-DEAD, ALL THE WAY FROM EARTH-7 TO HERE IN THIS--
--THE ULTIMA THULE.
NIX UOTAN'S SUPER-BOAT.
THE LAST OF THE MONITORS SAVED MY LIFE AND I GAVE HIM MY WORD.
STRANGE, IT'S LIKE SOMETHING I'VE SEEN IN A DREAM.
WHAT'S IT MADE OF?
IT'S FROZEN MUSIC.
UNBELIEVABLE.
RAY!
RAY, DON'T DO THIS.
JUSTICE 9 NEEDS TO STAY TOGETHER.
WE AL-READY LOST OPTIMAN TO SUPER-DOOMS-DAY.
I WON'T LOSE YOU, TOO.
HANK.
THEY NEED A GEEK FOR THIS.
THESE GUYS DON'T KNOW THEIR DC FROM THEIR MAJOR COMICS.
AND THEY NEED THAT POWER-TORCH OF YOURS HERE.
I'LL BE FINE.
RAY.
DON'T GO RUNNING INTO TROUBLE.
PROMISE.

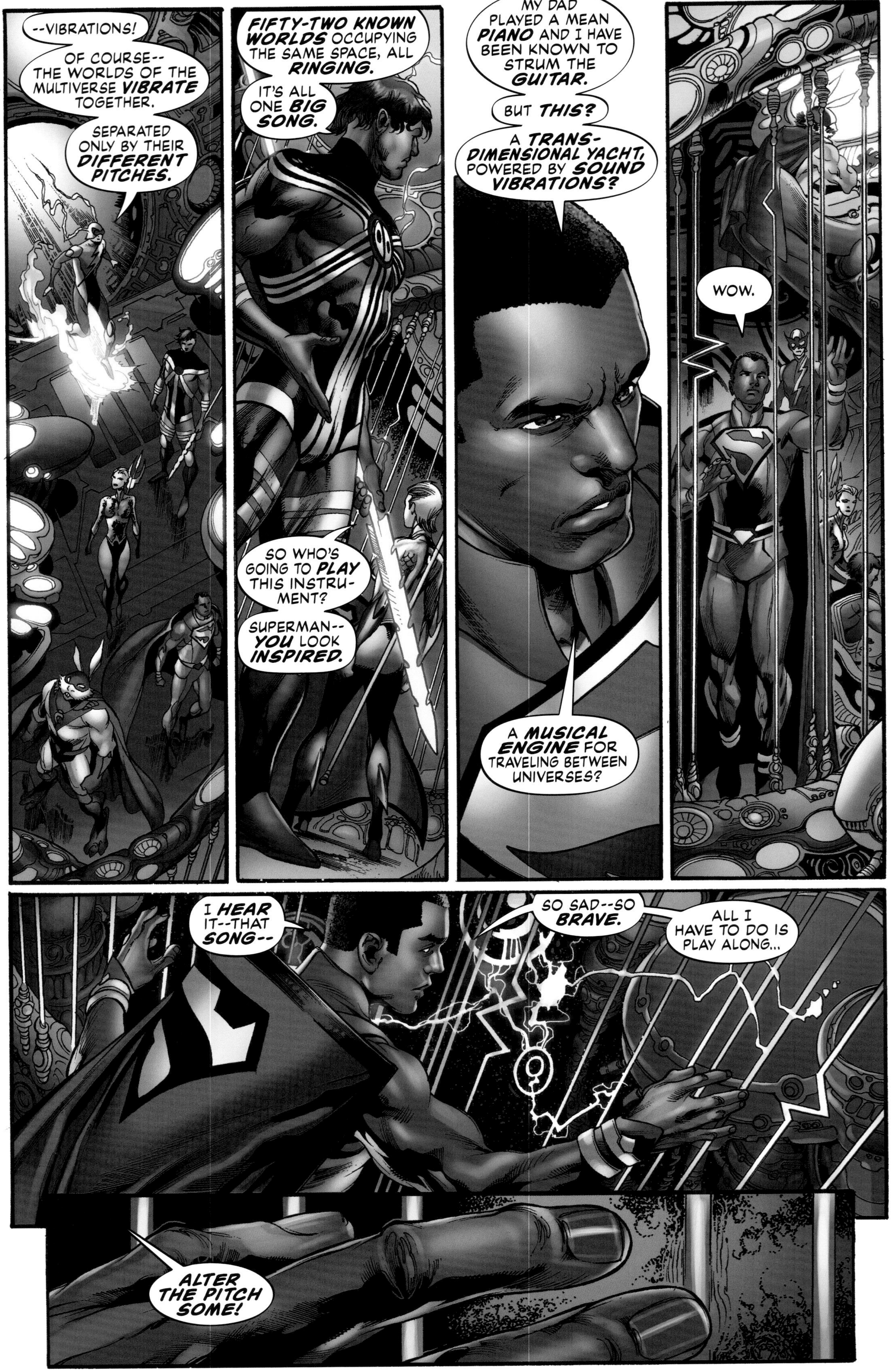
--VIBRATIONS!
OF COURSE-- THE WORLDS OF THE MULTIVERSE VIBRATE TOGETHER.
SEPARATED ONLY BY THEIR DIFFERENT PITCHES.
FIFTY-TWO KNOWN WORLDS OCCUPYING THE SAME SPACE, ALL RINGING.
IT'S ALL ONE BIG SONG.
SO WHO'S GOING TO PLAY THIS INSTRU-MENT?
SUPERMAN-- YOU LOOK INSPIRED.
MY DAD PLAYED A MEAN PIANO AND I HAVE BEEN KNOWN TO STRUM THE GUITAR.
BUT THIS?
A TRANS-DIMENSIONAL YACHT, POWERED BY SOUND VIBRATIONS?
A MUSICAL ENGINE FOR TRAVELING BETWEEN UNIVERSES?
WOW.
I HEAR IT--THAT SONG--
SO SAD--SO BRAVE.
ALL I HAVE TO DO IS PLAY ALONG...
ALTER THE PITCH SOME!

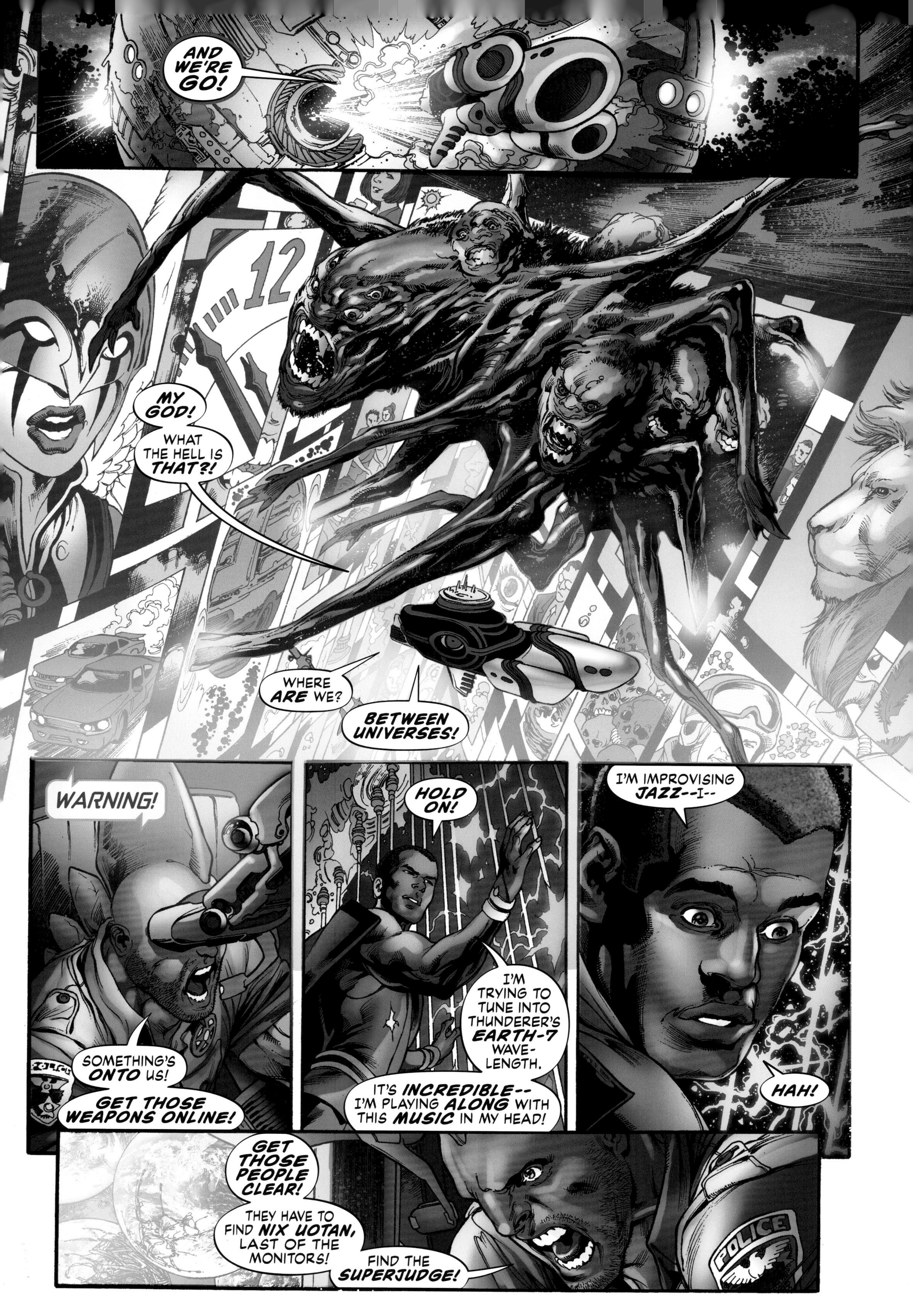
AND WE'RE GO!
MY GOD! WHAT THE HELL IS THAT?!
WHERE ARE WE?
BETWEEN UNIVERSES!
WARNING!
SOMETHING'S ONTO US!
GET THOSE WEAPONS ONLINE!
HOLD ON!
I'M TRYING TO TUNE INTO THUNDERER'S EARTH-7 WAVE-LENGTH.
IT'S INCREDIBLE-- I'M PLAYING ALONG WITH THIS MUSIC IN MY HEAD!
I'M IMPROVISING JAZZ--I--
HAH!
GET THOSE PEOPLE CLEAR!
THEY HAVE TO FIND NIX UOTAN, LAST OF THE MONITORS!
FIND THE SUPERJUDGE!

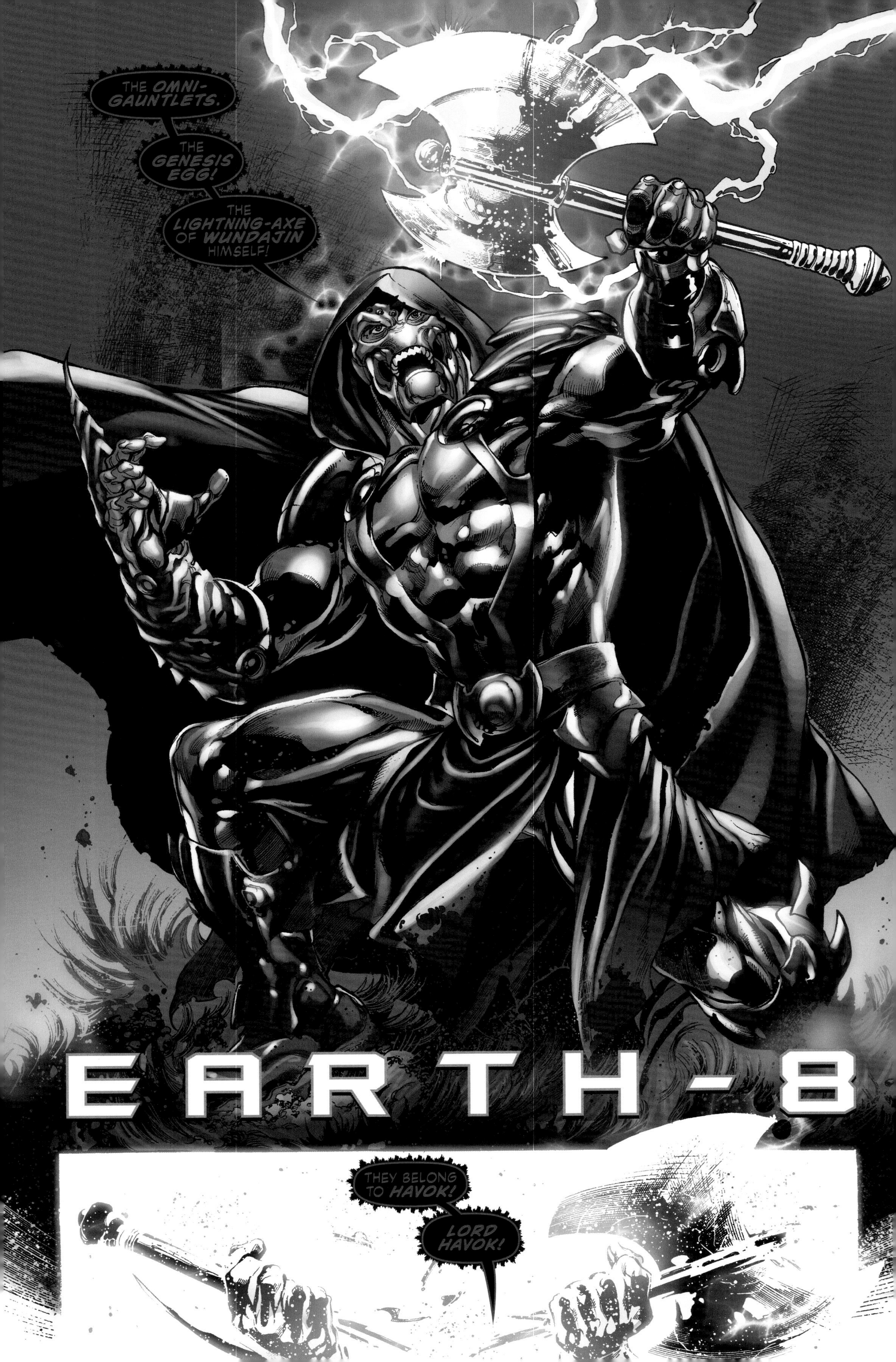
THE OMNI-GAUNTLETS.
THE GENESIS EGG!
THE LIGHTNING-AXE OF WUNDAJIN HIMSELF!
EARTH-8
THEY BELONG TO HAVOK!
LORD HAVOK!

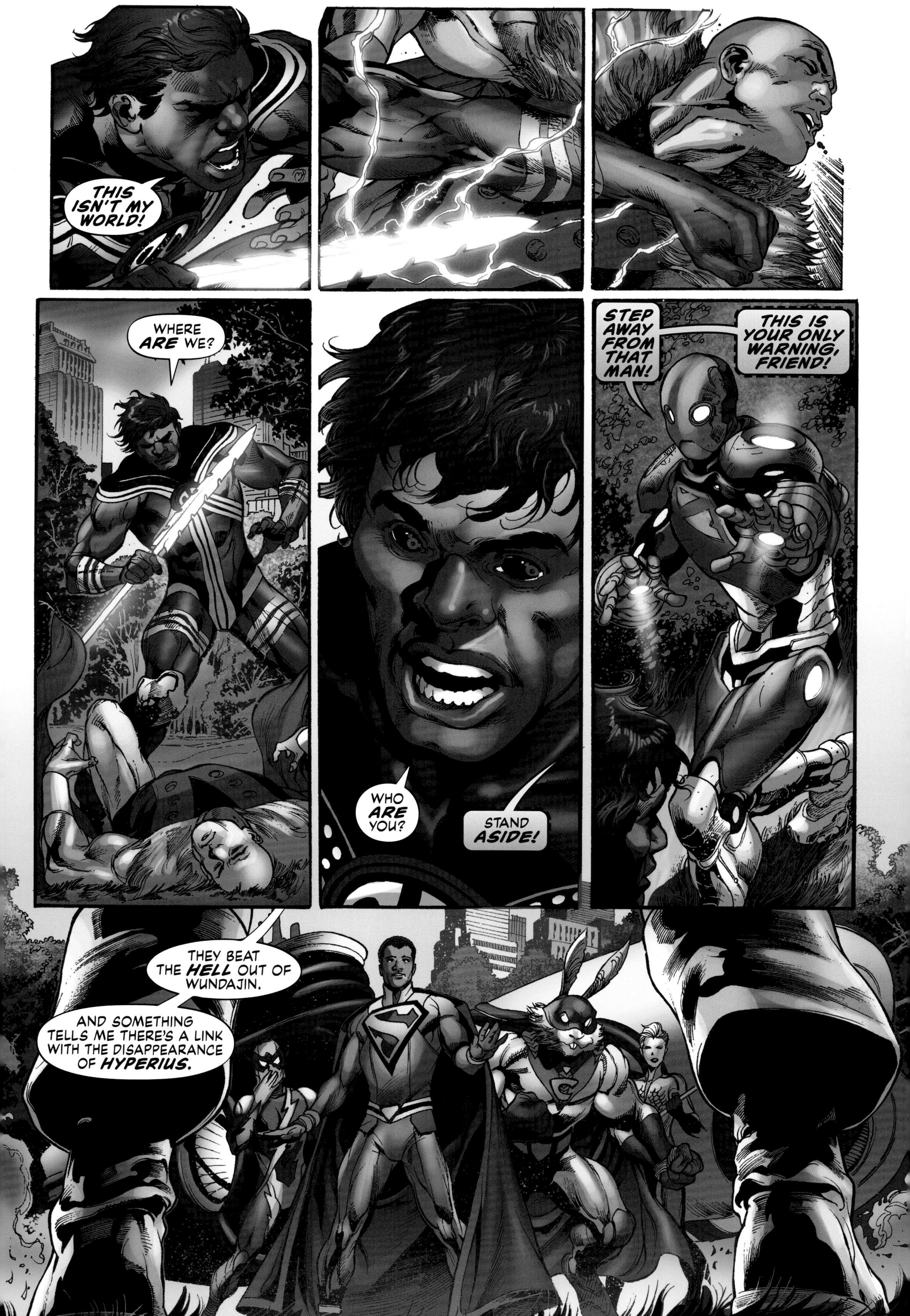

THIS ISN'T MY WORLD!
WHERE ARE WE?
WHO ARE YOU?
STAND ASIDE!
STEP AWAY FROM THAT MAN!
THIS IS YOUR ONLY WARNING, FRIEND!
THEY BEAT THE HELL OUT OF WUNDAJIN.
AND SOMETHING TELLS ME THERE'S A LINK WITH THE DISAPPEARANCE OF HYPERIUS.

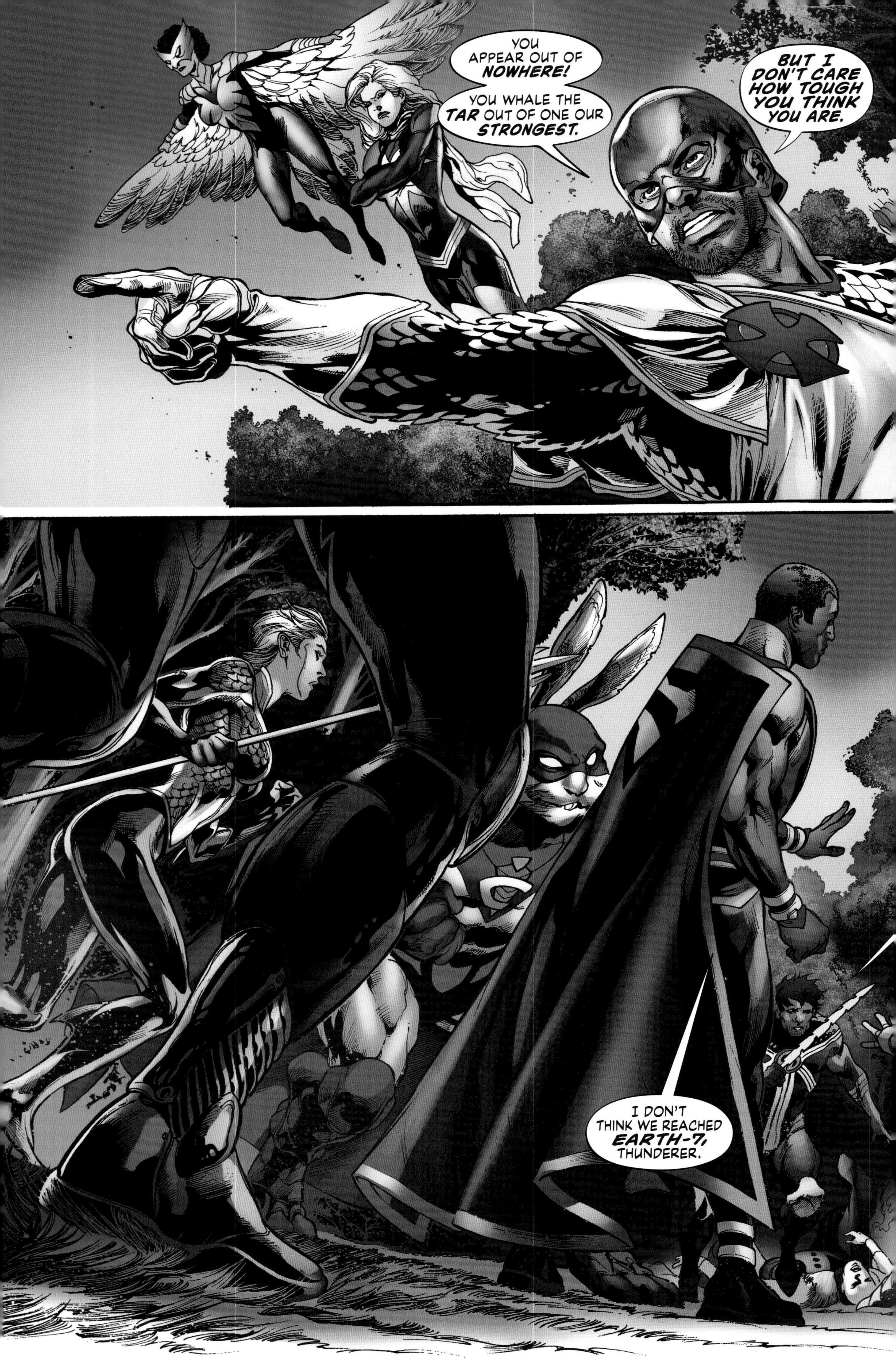
YOU APPEAR OUT OF NOWHERE!
YOU WHALE THE TAR OUT OF ONE OUR STRONGEST.
BUT I DON'T CARE HOW TOUGH YOU THINK YOU ARE.
I DON'T THINK WE REACHED EARTH-7, THUNDERER.

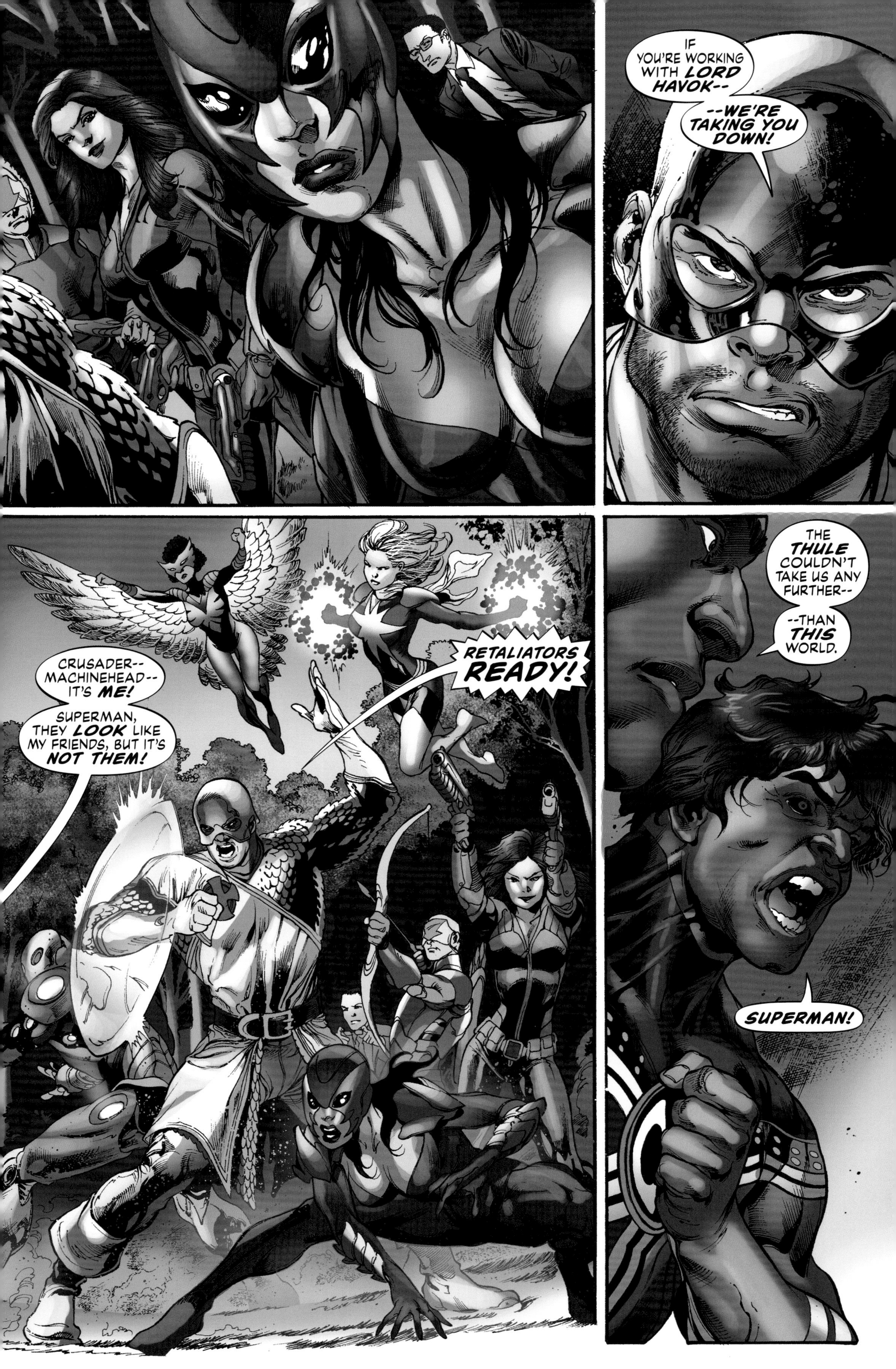
IF YOU'RE WORKING WITH LORD HAVOK--
--WE'RE TAKING YOU DOWN!
CRUSADER-- MACHINEHEAD-- IT'S ME!
SUPERMAN, THEY LOOK LIKE MY FRIENDS, BUT IT'S NOT THEM!
RETALIATORS READY!
THE THULE COULDN'T TAKE US ANY FURTHER--
--THAN THIS WORLD.
SUPERMAN!

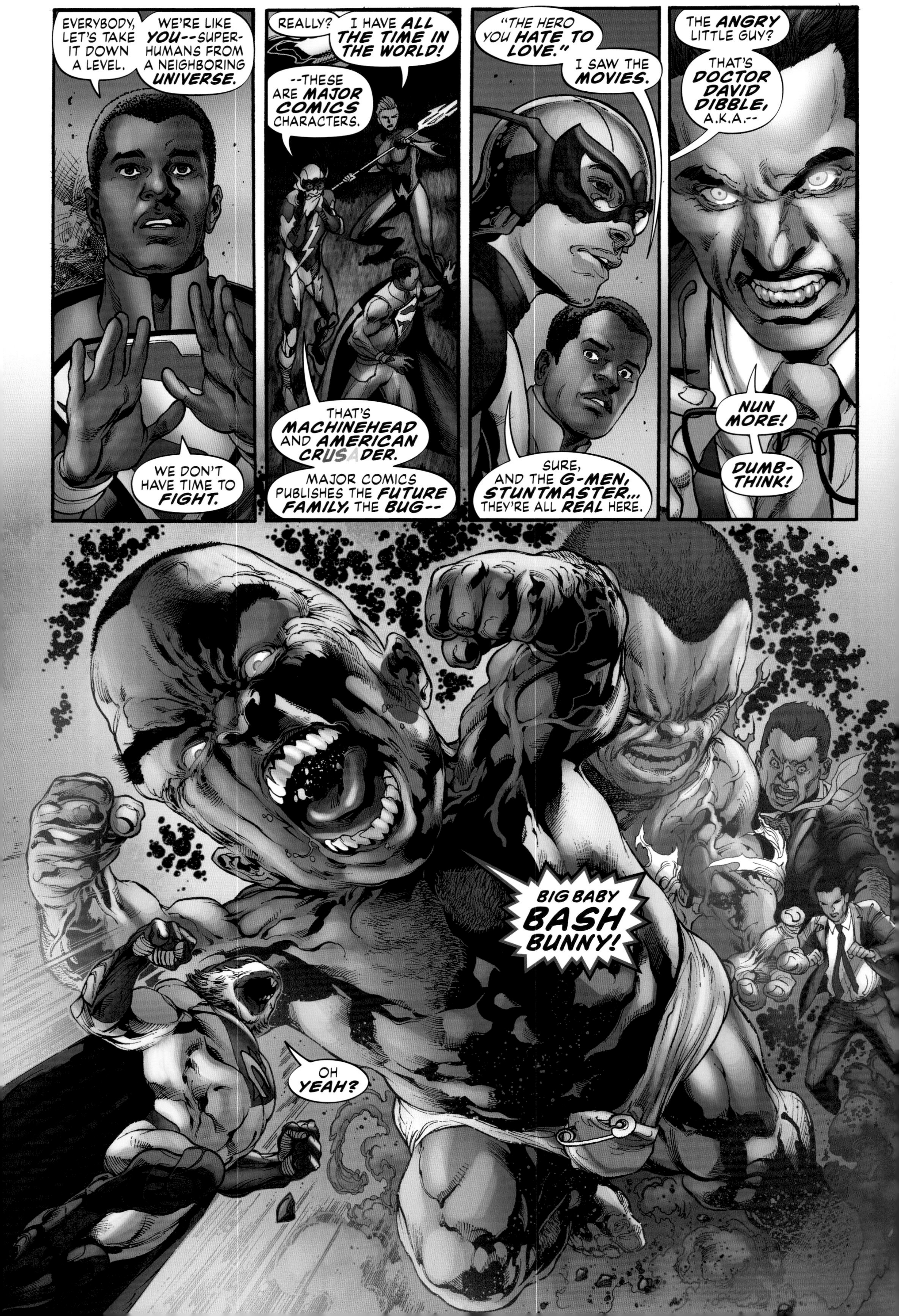
EVERYBODY, LET'S TAKE IT DOWN A LEVEL.
WE'RE LIKE YOU--SUPER-HUMANS FROM A NEIGHBORING UNIVERSE.
WE DON'T HAVE TIME TO FIGHT.
REALLY?
I HAVE ALL THE TIME IN THE WORLD!
--THESE ARE MAJOR COMICS CHARACTERS.
THAT'S MACHINEHEAD AND AMERICAN CRUSADER.
MAJOR COMICS PUBLISHES THE FUTURE FAMILY, THE BUG--
"THE HERO YOU HATE TO LOVE."
I SAW THE MOVIES.
SURE, AND THE G-MEN, STUNTMASTER... THEY'RE ALL REAL HERE.
THE ANGRY LITTLE GUY?
THAT'S DOCTOR DAVID DIBBLE, A.K.A.--
NUN MORE!
DUMB-THINK!
BIG BABY BASH BUNNY!
OH YEAH?

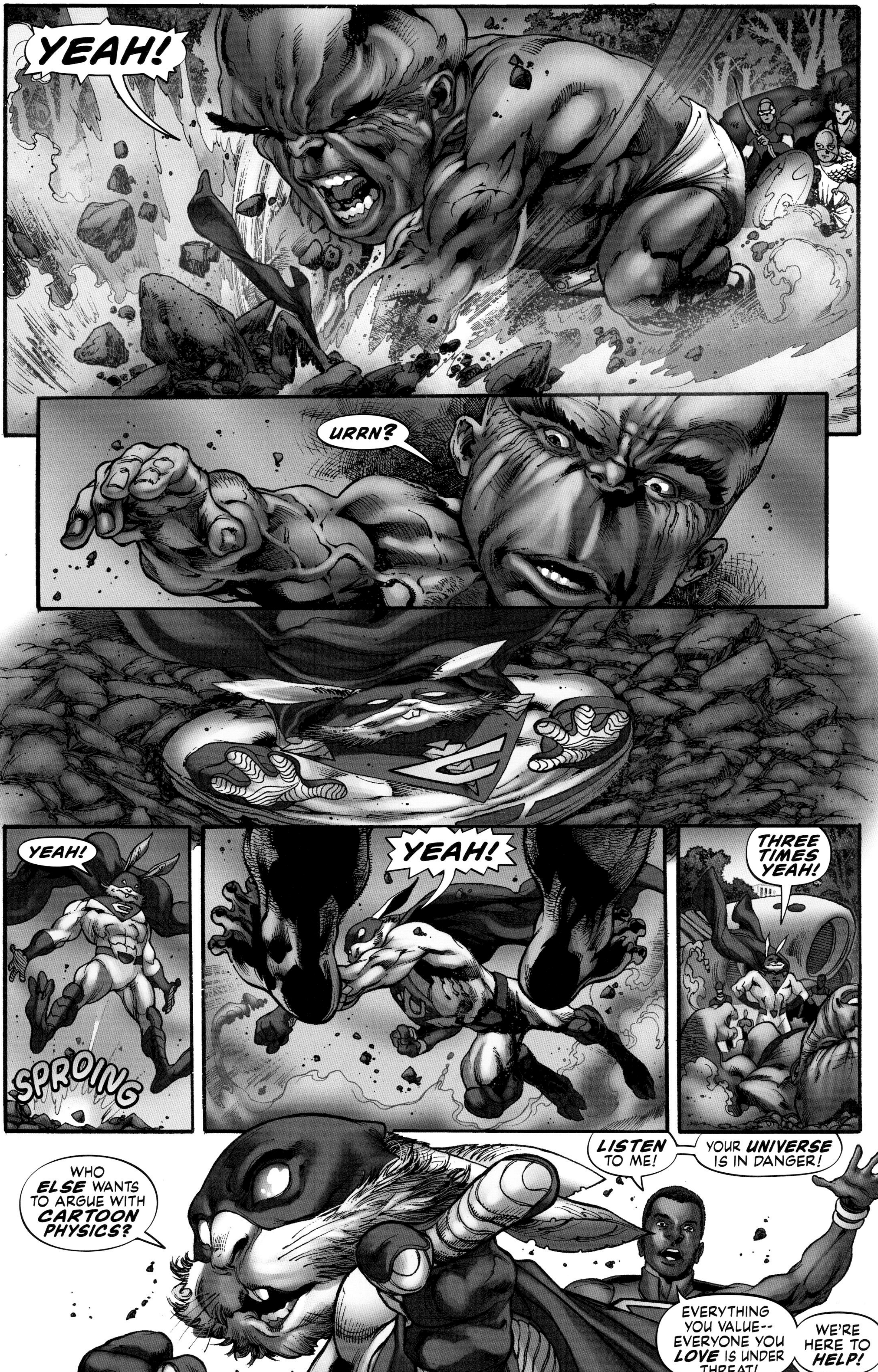
YEAH!
URRN?
YEAH!
SPROING
YEAH!
THREE TIMES YEAH!
WHO ELSE WANTS TO ARGUE WITH CARTOON PHYSICS?
LISTEN TO ME!
YOUR UNIVERSE IS IN DANGER!
EVERYTHING YOU VALUE-- EVERYONE YOU LOVE IS UNDER THREAT!
WE'RE HERE TO HELP!

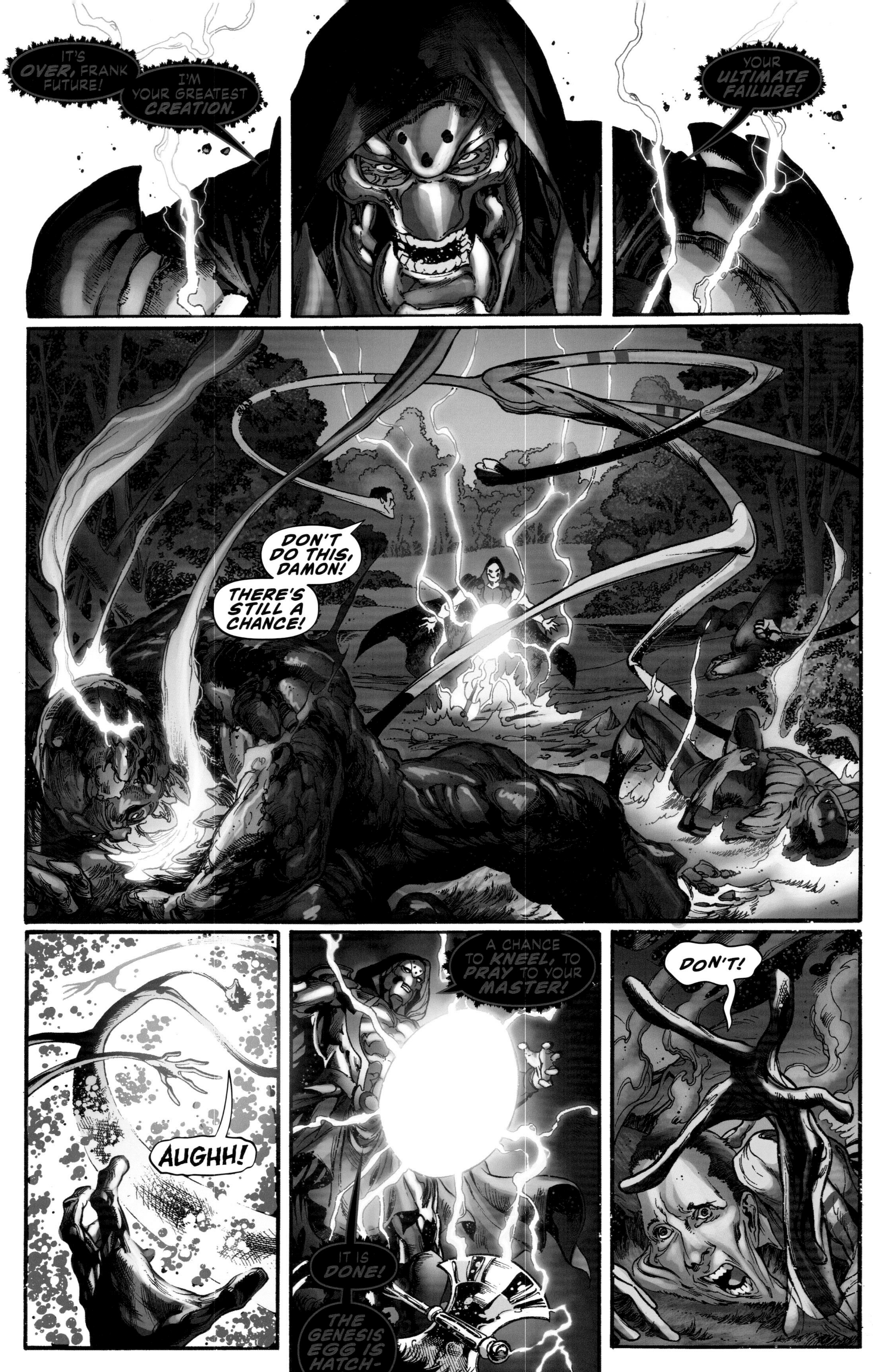
IT'S OVER, FRANK FUTURE!
I'M YOUR GREATEST CREATION.
YOUR ULTIMATE FAILURE!
DON'T DO THIS, DAMON!
THERE'S STILL A CHANCE!
AUGHH!
A CHANCE TO KNEEL, TO PRAY TO YOUR MASTER!
IT IS DONE!
THE GENESIS EGG IS HATCH-ING!
DON'T!

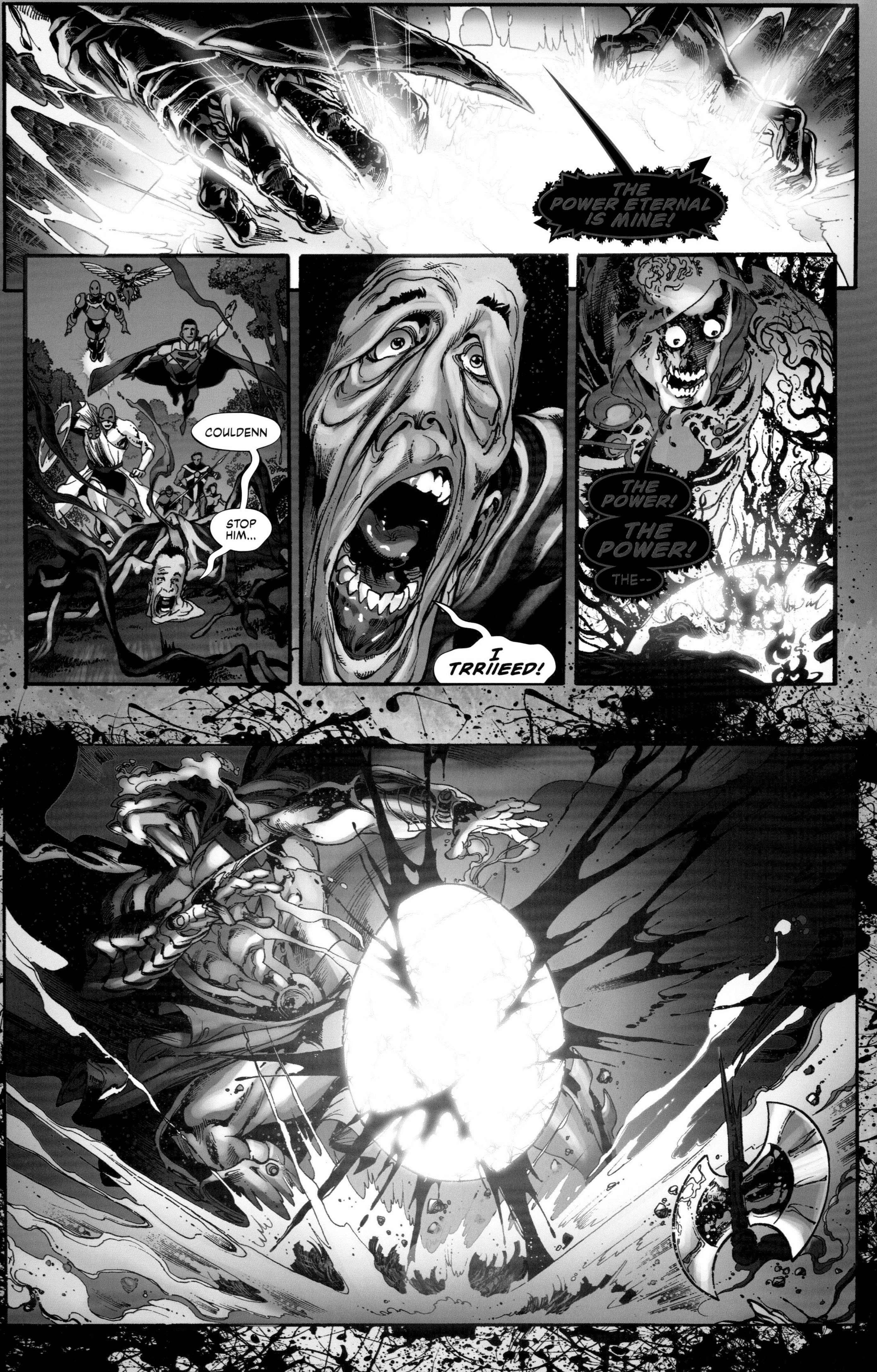

THE POWER ETERNAL IS MINE!
COULDENN
STOP HIM...
I TRRIIEED!
THE POWER!
THE POWER!
THE--

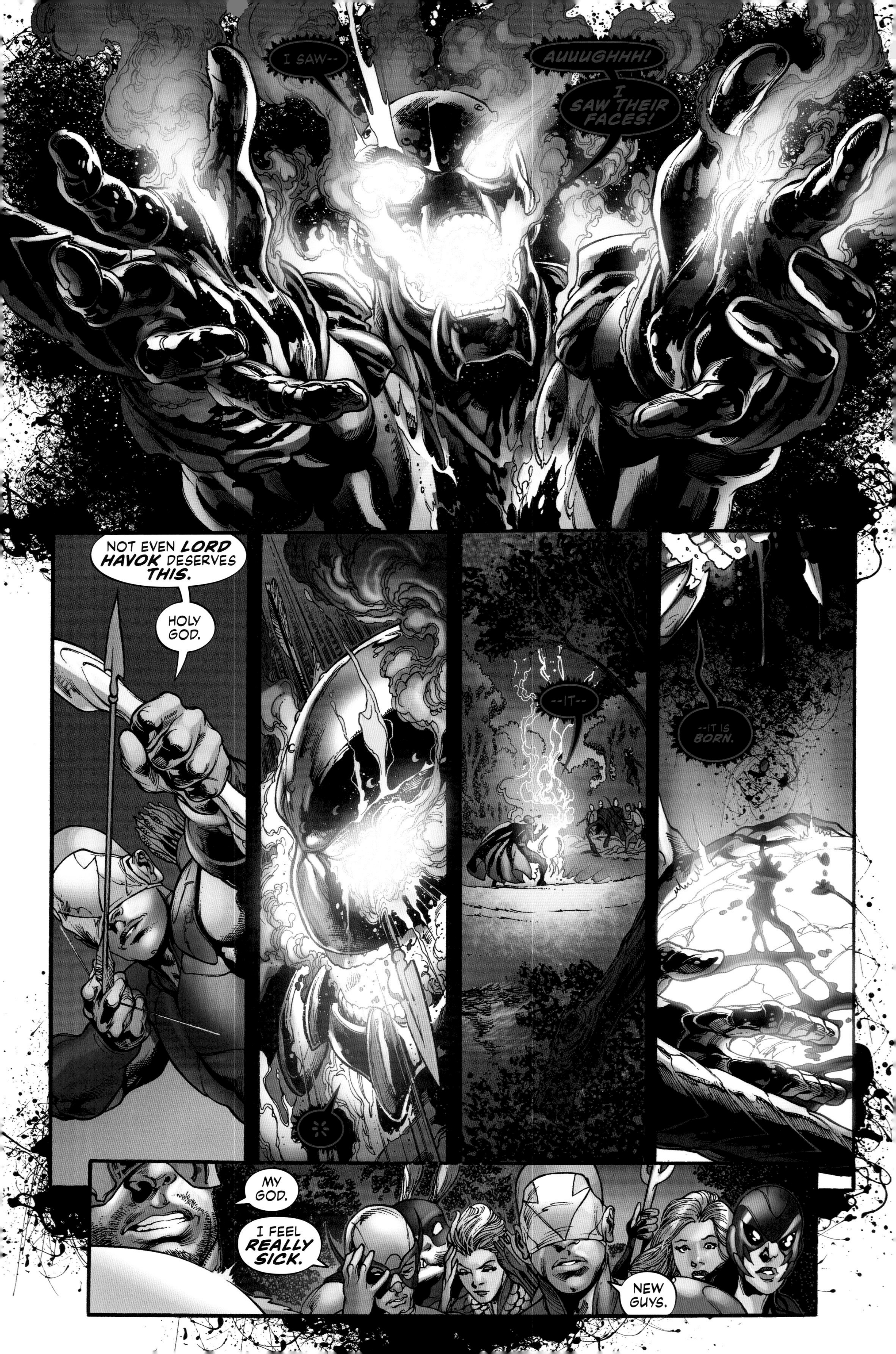
I SAW--
AUUUGHHH!
I SAW THEIR FACES!
NOT EVEN LORD HAVOK DESERVES THIS.
HOLY GOD.
--IT--
--IT IS BORN.
MY GOD.
I FEEL REALLY SICK.
NEW GUYS.

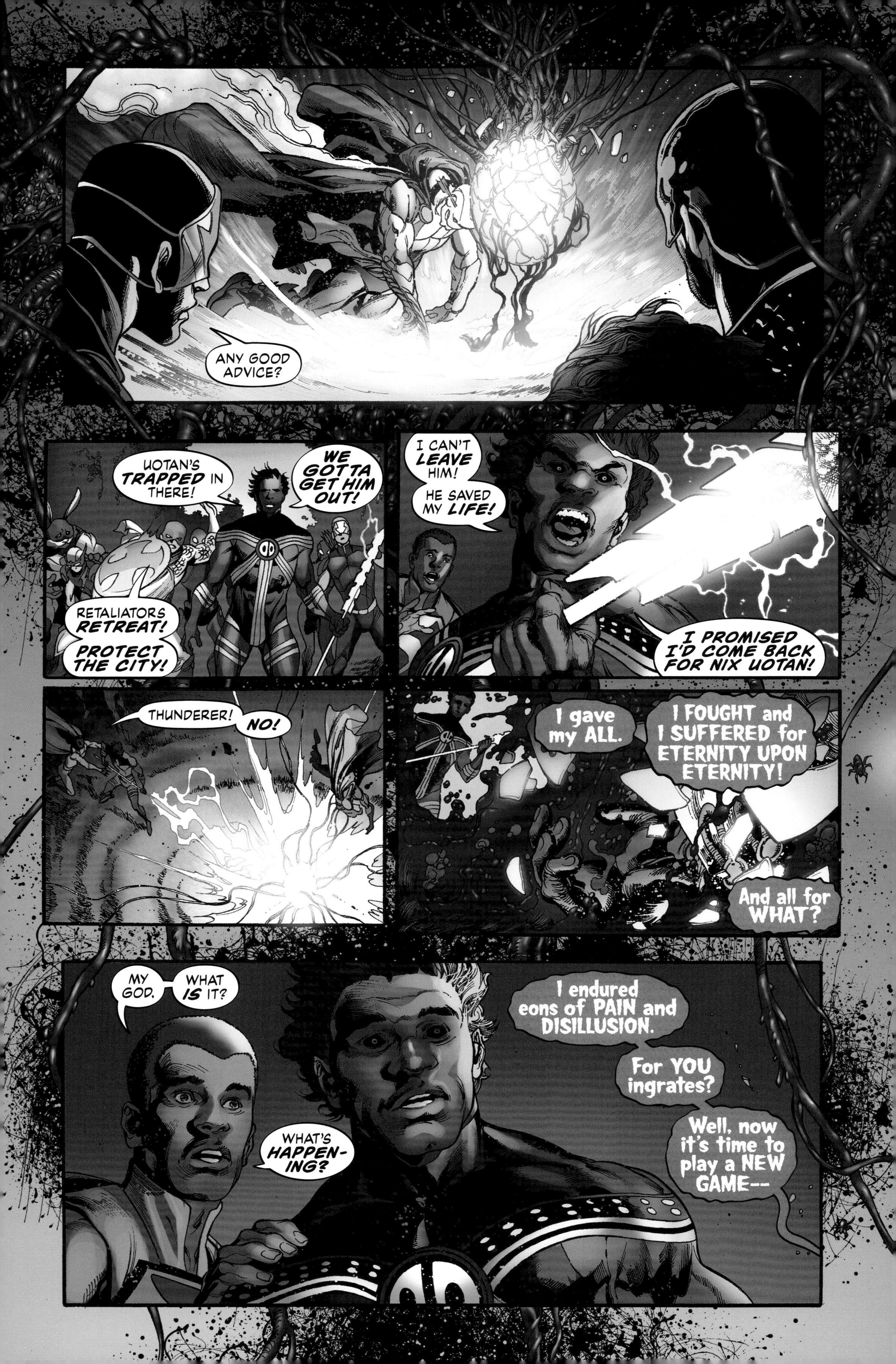
ANY GOOD ADVICE?
UOTAN'S TRAPPED IN THERE!
WE GOTTA GET HIM OUT!
RETALIATORS RETREAT!
PROTECT THE CITY!
I CAN'T LEAVE HIM!
HE SAVED MY LIFE!
I PROMISED I'D COME BACK FOR NIX UOTAN!
THUNDERER!
NO!
I gave my ALL.
I FOUGHT and I SUFFERED for ETERNITY UPON ETERNITY!
And all for WHAT?
MY GOD.
WHAT IS IT?
WHAT'S HAPPEN-ING?
I endured eons of PAIN and DISILLUSION.
For YOU ingrates?
Well, now it's time to play a NEW GAME--

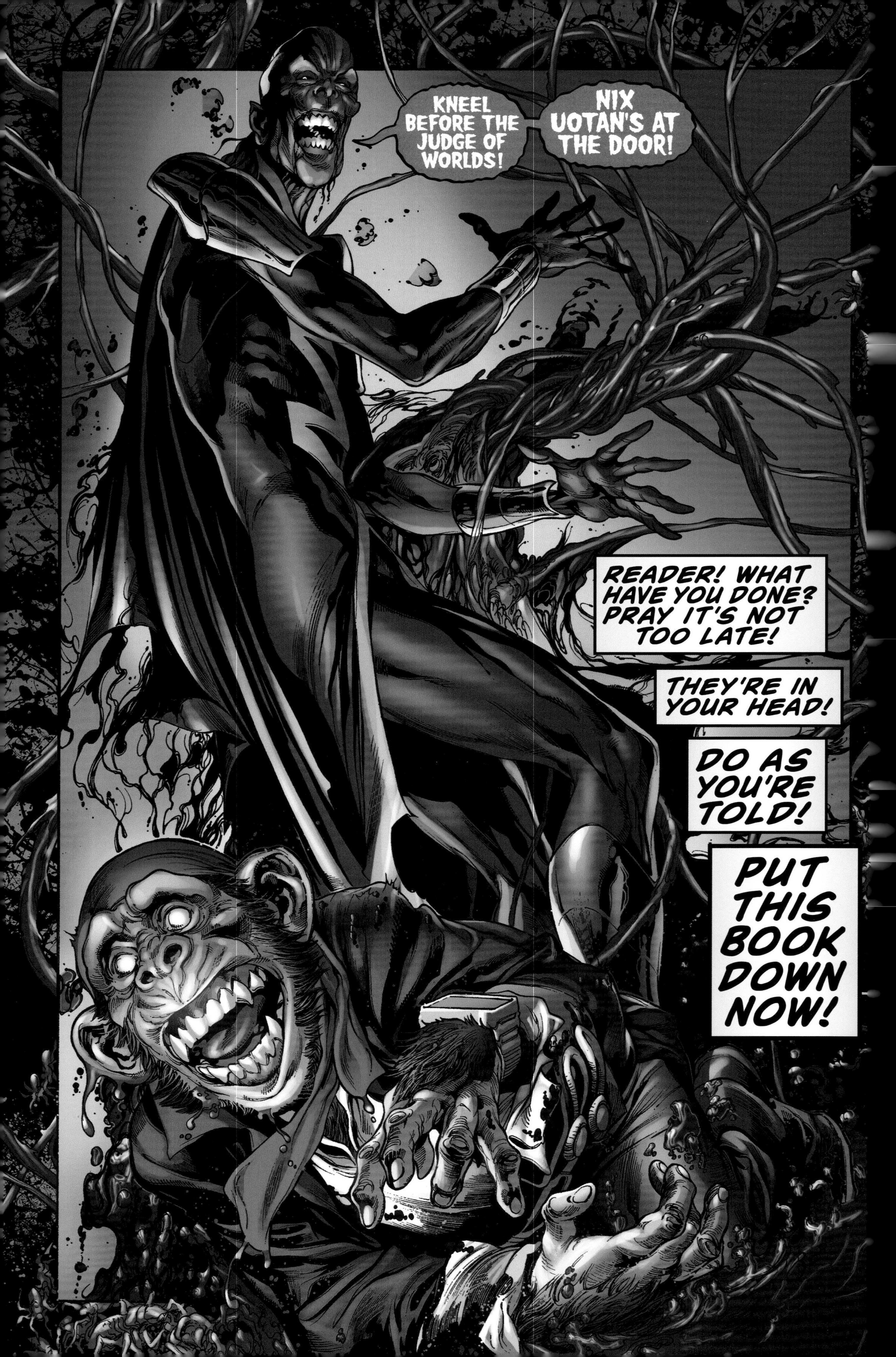
KNEEL BEFORE THE JUDGE OF WORLDS!
NIX UOTAN'S AT THE DOOR!
READER! WHAT HAVE YOU DONE? PRAY IT'S NOT TOO LATE!
THEY'RE IN YOUR HEAD!
DO AS YOU'RE TOLD!
PUT THIS BOOK DOWN NOW!

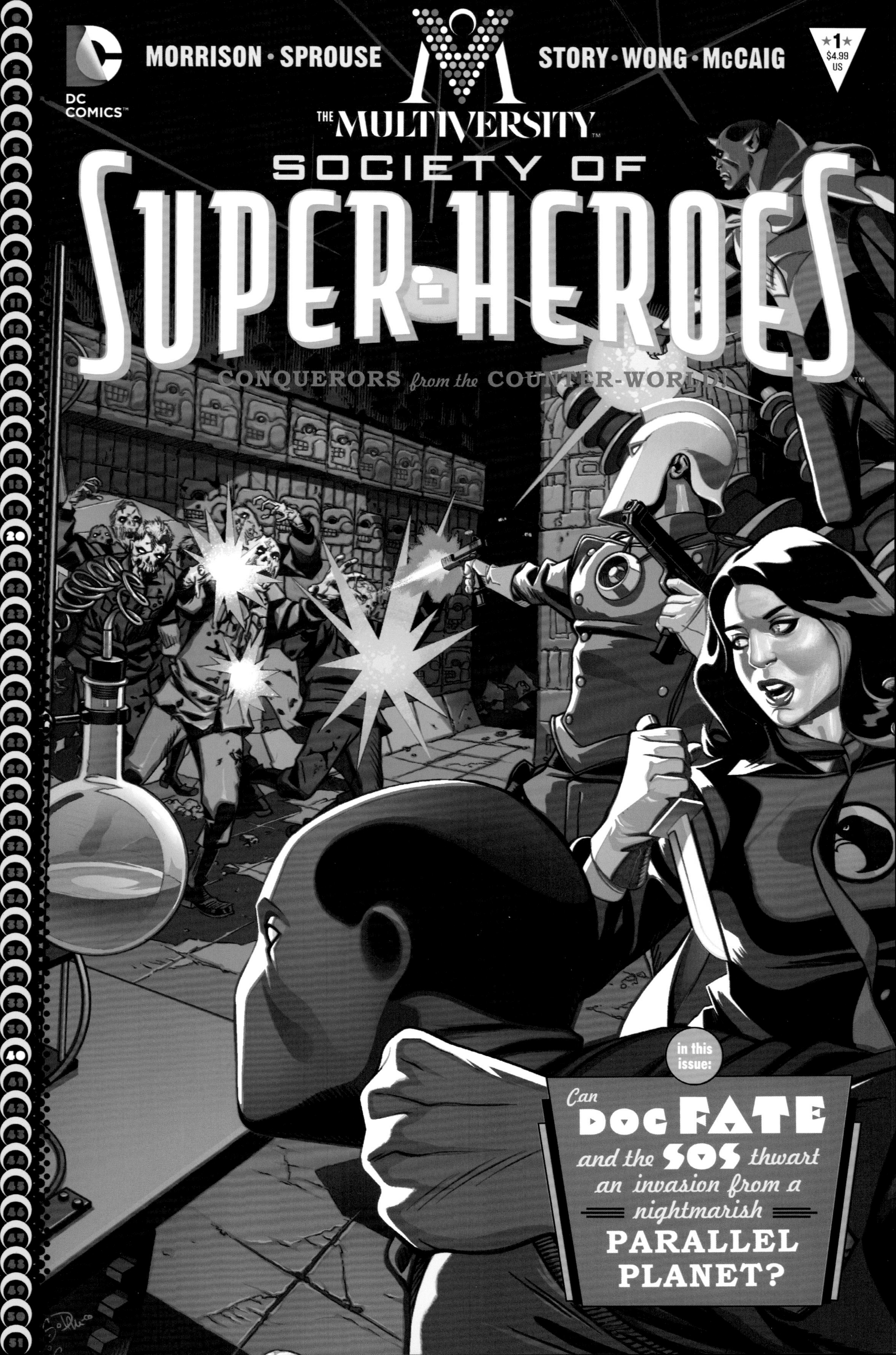
DC COMICS
MORRISON · SPROUSE
STORY · WONG · McCAIG
1
$4.99 US
THE MULTIVERSITY
SOCIETY OF SUPER-HEROES
CONQUERORS from the COUNTER-WORLD!
in this issue:
Can DOC FATE and the SOS thwart an invasion from a nightmarish PARALLEL PLANET?

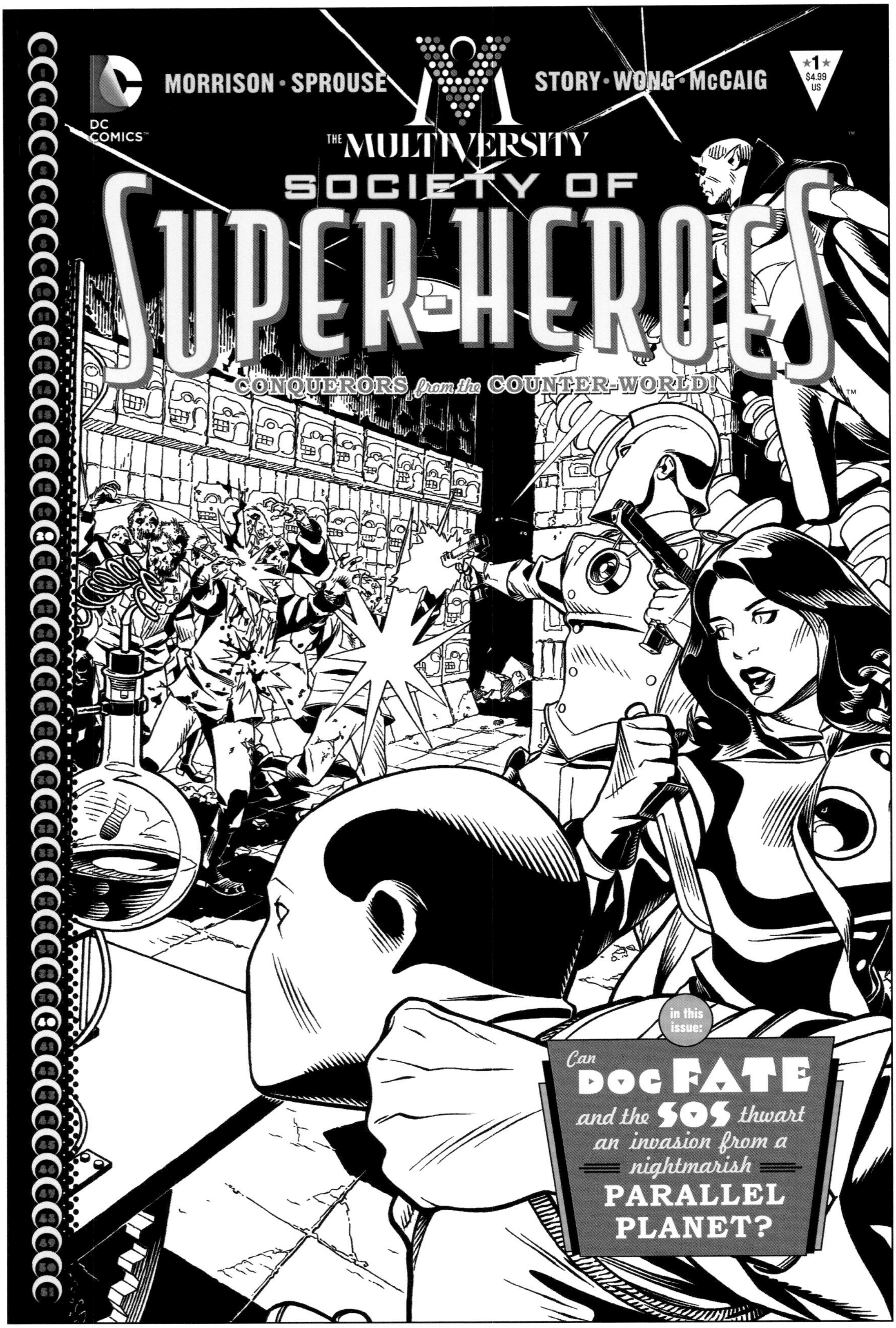
MORRISON · SPROUSE
STORY · WONG · McCAIG
DC COMICS
★1★ $4.99 US
THE MULTIVERSITY
SOCIETY OF
SUPER-HEROES
CONQUERORS from the COUNTER-WORLD!
in this issue:
Can DOC FATE and the SOS thwart an invasion from a nightmarish PARALLEL PLANET?

THE MULTIVERSITY: SOCIETY OF SUPER-HEROES #1

Written by
GRANT MORRISON

Penciller
CHRIS SPROUSE

Inkers
KARL STORY
WALDEN WONG

Colorist
DAVE McCAIG

Letterer
CARLOS M. MANGUAL

Cover artists
CHRIS SPROUSE with
DAVE McCAIG

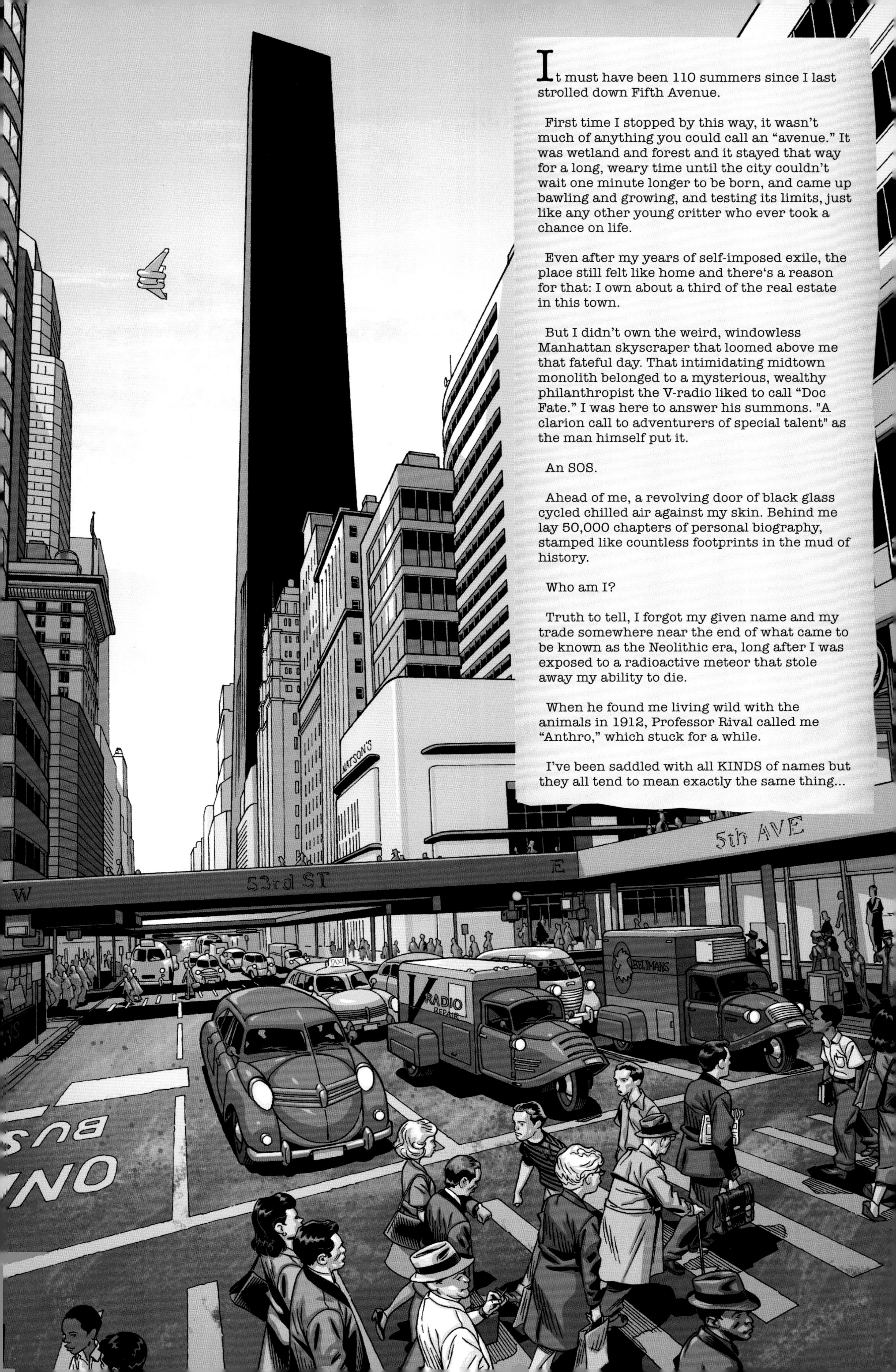
It must have been 110 summers since I last strolled down Fifth Avenue.
First time I stopped by this way, it wasn't much of anything you could call an "avenue." It was wetland and forest and it stayed that way for a long, weary time until the city couldn't wait one minute longer to be born, and came up bawling and growing, and testing its limits, just like any other young critter who ever took a chance on life.
Even after my years of self-imposed exile, the place still felt like home and there's a reason for that: I own about a third of the real estate in this town.
But I didn't own the weird, windowless Manhattan skyscraper that loomed above me that fateful day. That intimidating midtown monolith belonged to a mysterious, wealthy philanthropist the V-radio liked to call "Doc Fate." I was here to answer his summons. "A clarion call to adventurers of special talent" as the man himself put it.
An SOS.
Ahead of me, a revolving door of black glass cycled chilled air against my skin. Behind me lay 50,000 chapters of personal biography, stamped like countless footprints in the mud of history.
Who am I?
Truth to tell, I forgot my given name and my trade somewhere near the end of what came to be known as the Neolithic era, long after I was exposed to a radioactive meteor that stole away my ability to die.
When he found me living wild with the animals in 1912, Professor Rival called me "Anthro," which stuck for a while.
I've been saddled with all KINDS of names but they all tend to mean exactly the same thing...
5th AVE
W
53rd ST
E
TAXI
RADIO
REPAIR

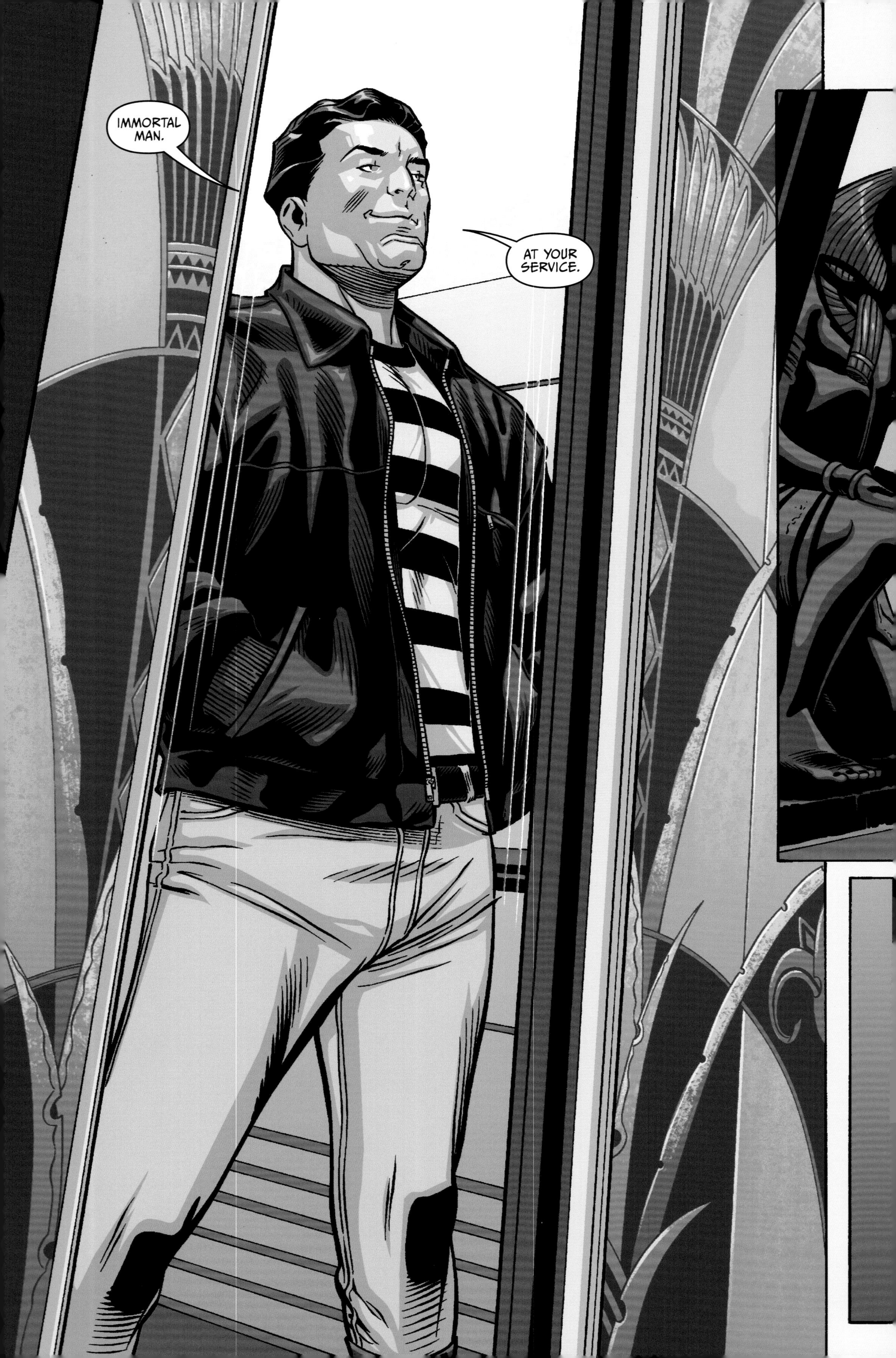
IMMORTAL MAN.
AT YOUR SERVICE.

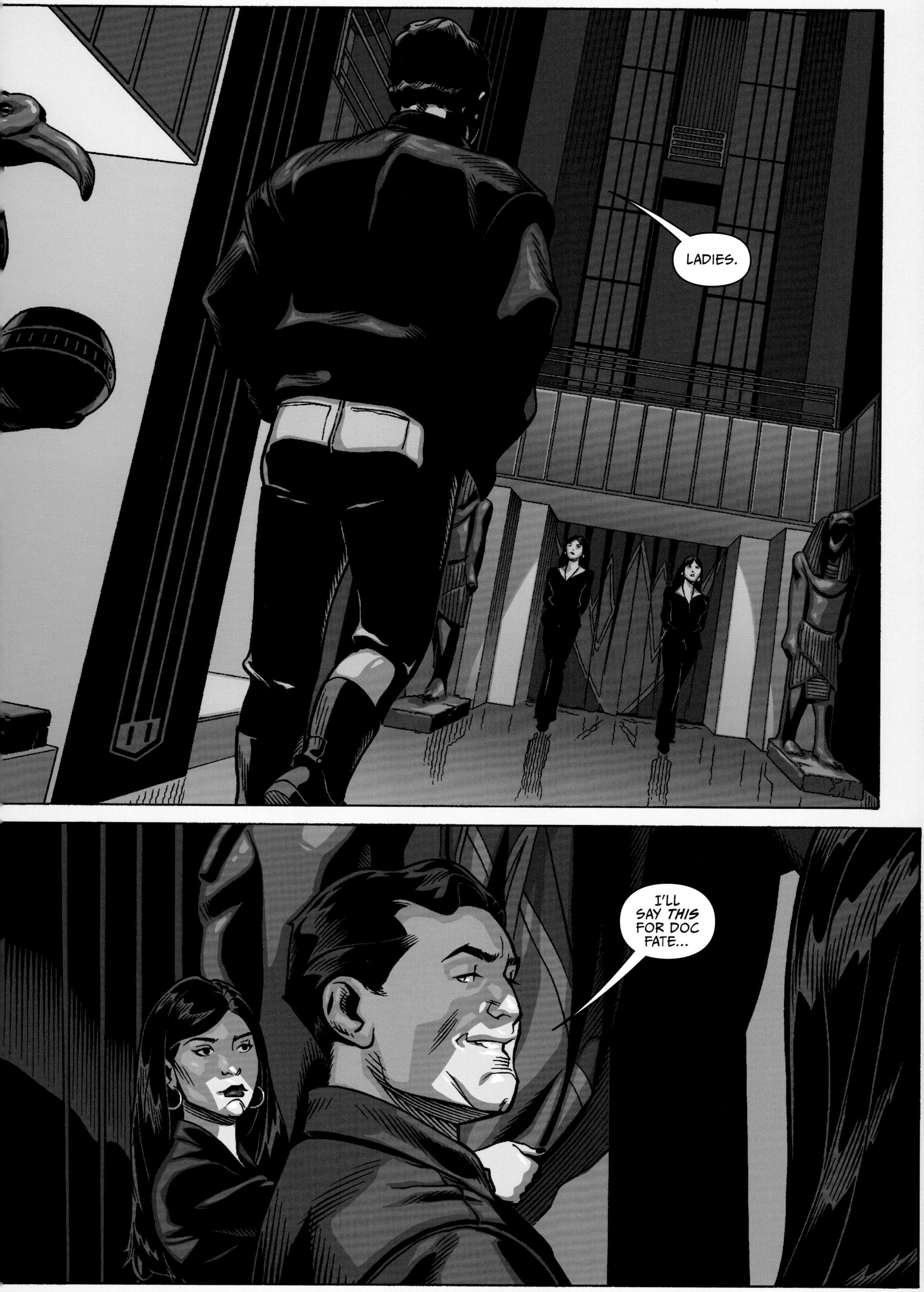
LADIES.
I'LL SAY *THIS* FOR DOC FATE...

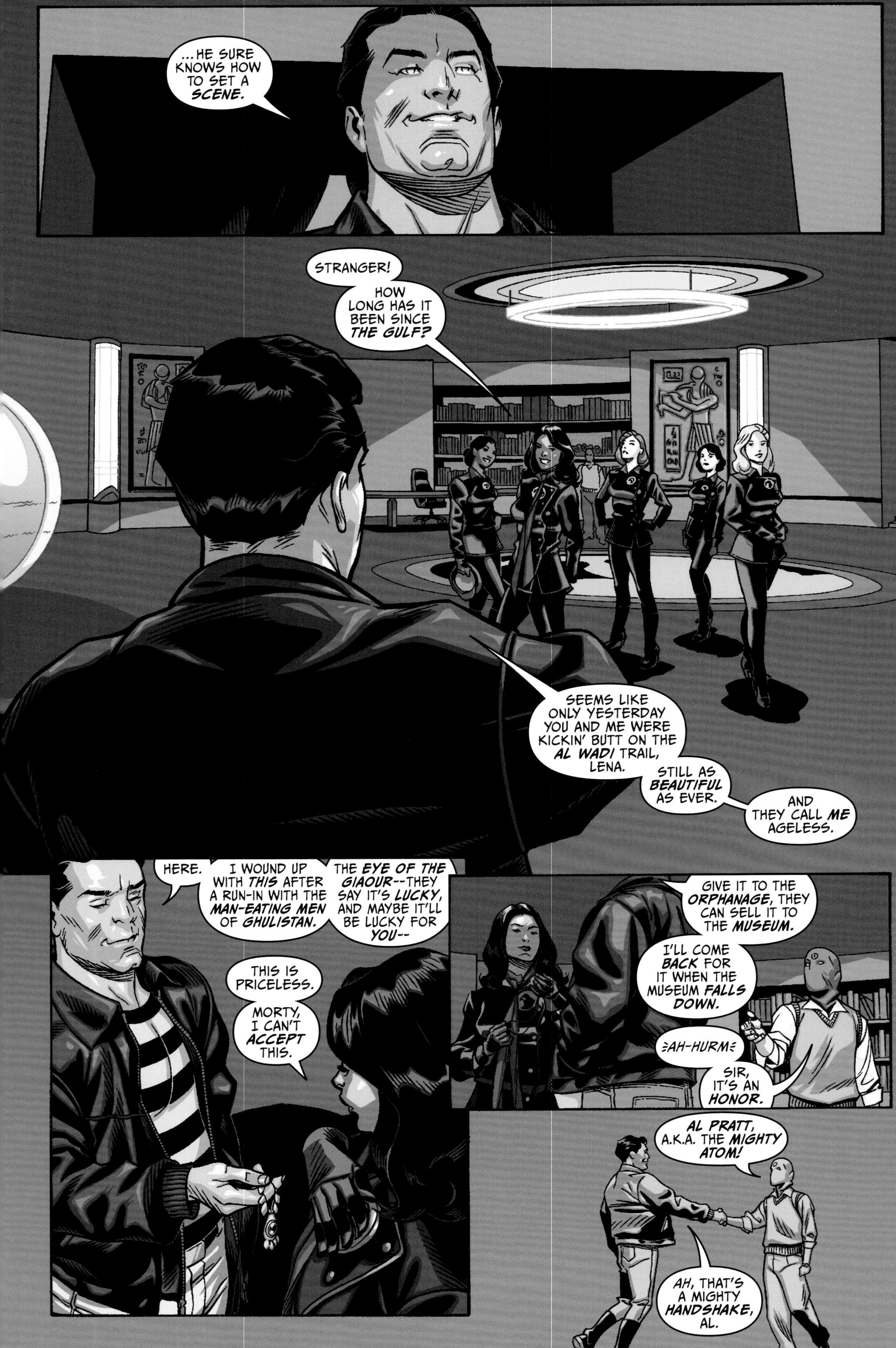
...HE SURE KNOWS HOW TO SET A *SCENE.*
STRANGER!
HOW LONG HAS IT BEEN SINCE *THE GULF?*
SEEMS LIKE ONLY YESTERDAY YOU AND ME WERE KICKIN' BUTT ON THE *AL WADI* TRAIL, LENA.
STILL AS *BEAUTIFUL* AS EVER.
AND THEY CALL *ME* AGELESS.
HERE.
I WOUND UP WITH *THIS* AFTER A RUN-IN WITH THE *MAN-EATING MEN* OF *GHULISTAN.*
THE *EYE OF THE GIAOUR*--THEY SAY IT'S *LUCKY,* AND MAYBE IT'LL BE LUCKY FOR *YOU*--
THIS IS PRICELESS.
MORTY, I CAN'T *ACCEPT* THIS.
GIVE IT TO THE *ORPHANAGE,* THEY CAN SELL IT TO THE *MUSEUM.*
I'LL COME *BACK* FOR IT WHEN THE MUSEUM *FALLS DOWN.*
AH-HURM
SIR, IT'S AN *HONOR.*
AL PRATT, A.K.A. THE *MIGHTY ATOM!*
AH, THAT'S A MIGHTY *HANDSHAKE,* AL.

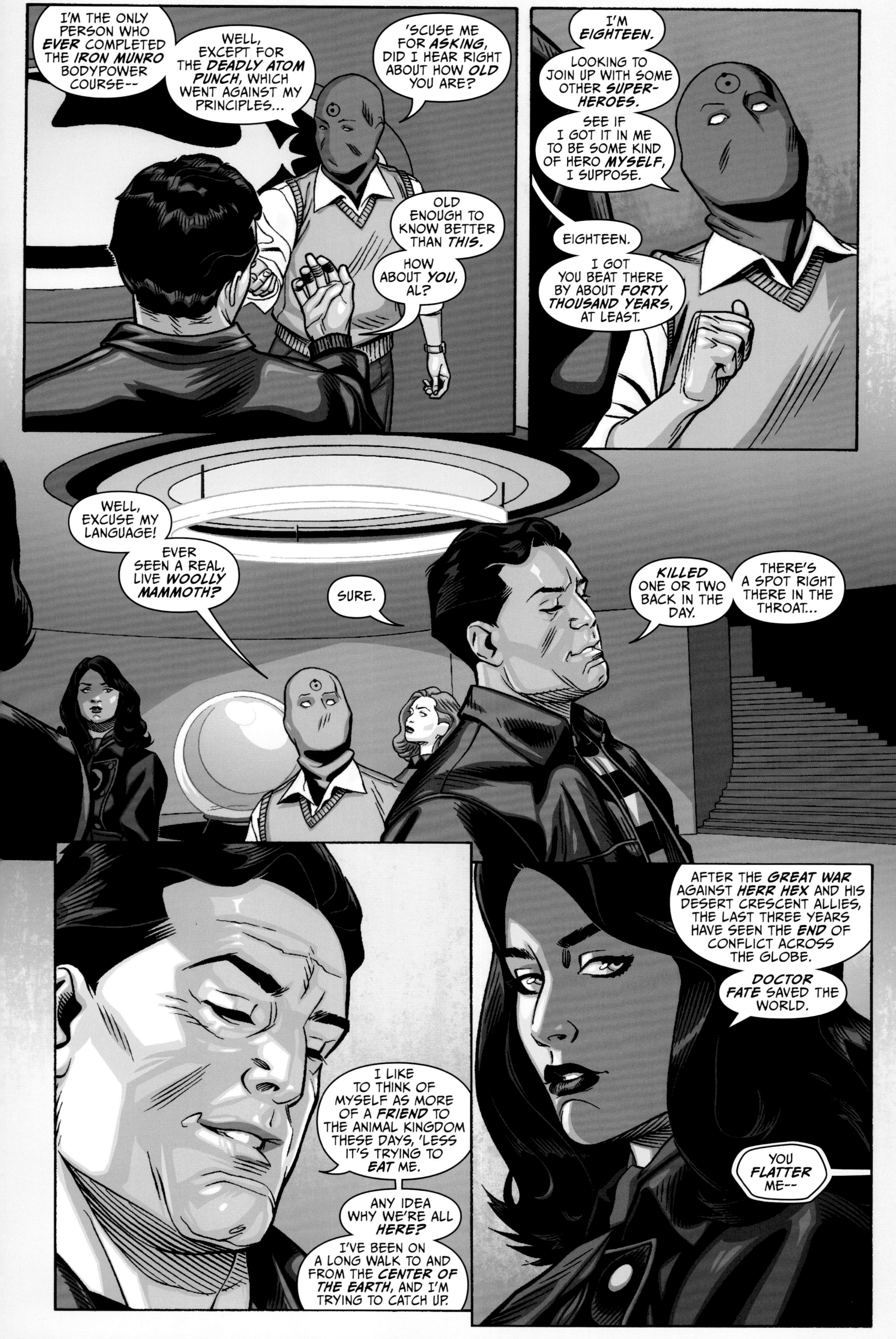
I'M THE ONLY PERSON WHO EVER COMPLETED THE IRON MUNRO BODYPOWER COURSE--
WELL, EXCEPT FOR THE DEADLY ATOM PUNCH, WHICH WENT AGAINST MY PRINCIPLES...
'SCUSE ME FOR ASKING, DID I HEAR RIGHT ABOUT HOW OLD YOU ARE?
OLD ENOUGH TO KNOW BETTER THAN THIS.
HOW ABOUT YOU, AL?
I'M EIGHTEEN.
LOOKING TO JOIN UP WITH SOME OTHER SUPER-HEROES.
SEE IF I GOT IT IN ME TO BE SOME KIND OF HERO MYSELF, I SUPPOSE.
EIGHTEEN.
I GOT YOU BEAT THERE BY ABOUT FORTY THOUSAND YEARS, AT LEAST.
WELL, EXCUSE MY LANGUAGE!
EVER SEEN A REAL, LIVE WOOLLY MAMMOTH?
SURE.
KILLED ONE OR TWO BACK IN THE DAY.
THERE'S A SPOT RIGHT THERE IN THE THROAT...
I LIKE TO THINK OF MYSELF AS MORE OF A FRIEND TO THE ANIMAL KINGDOM THESE DAYS, 'LESS IT'S TRYING TO EAT ME.
ANY IDEA WHY WE'RE ALL HERE?
I'VE BEEN ON A LONG WALK TO AND FROM THE CENTER OF THE EARTH, AND I'M TRYING TO CATCH UP.
AFTER THE GREAT WAR AGAINST HERR HEX AND HIS DESERT CRESCENT ALLIES, THE LAST THREE YEARS HAVE SEEN THE END OF CONFLICT ACROSS THE GLOBE.
DOCTOR FATE SAVED THE WORLD.
YOU FLATTER ME--

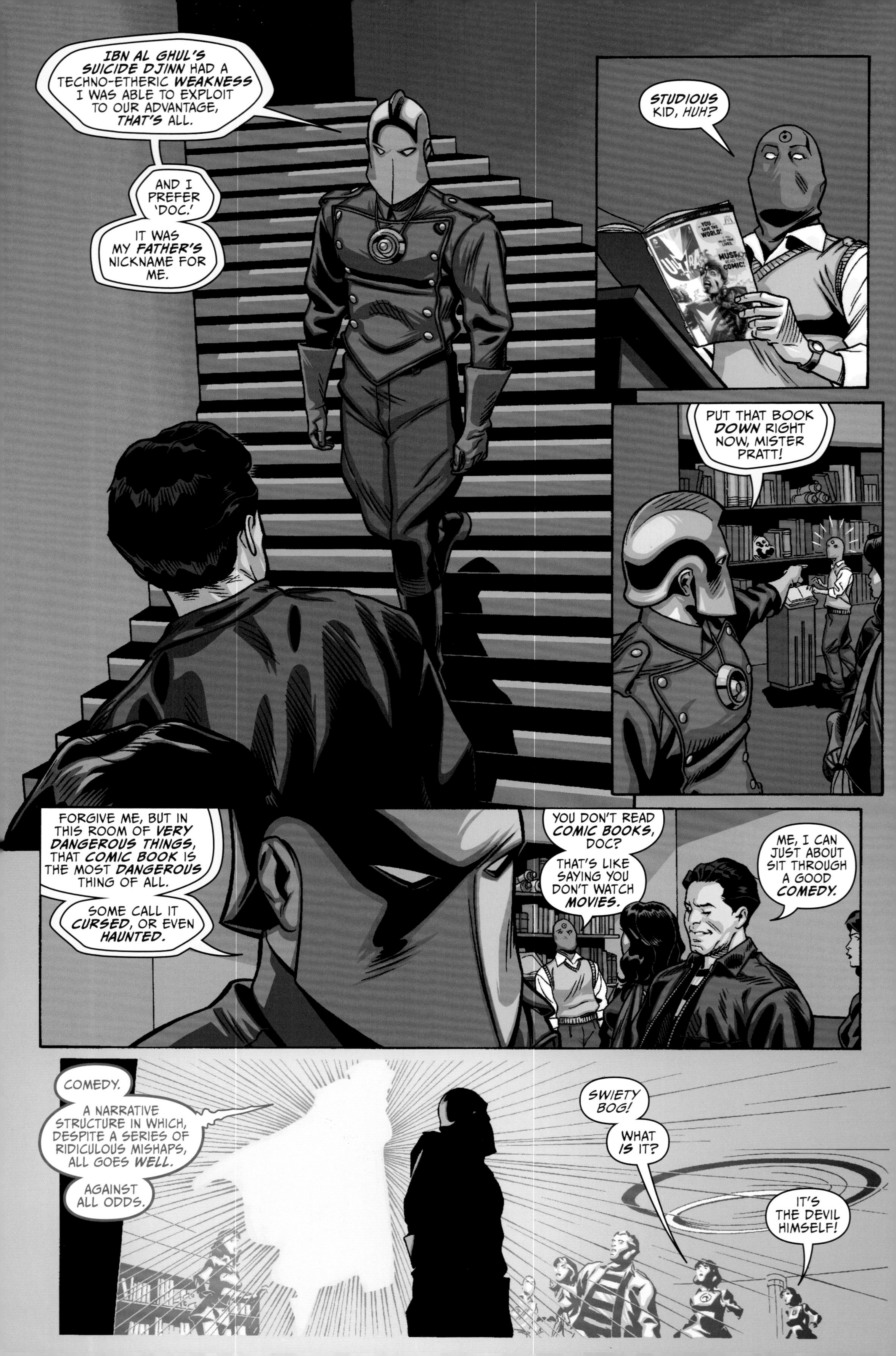
IBN AL GHUL'S SUICIDE DJINN HAD A TECHNO-ETHERIC WEAKNESS I WAS ABLE TO EXPLOIT TO OUR ADVANTAGE, THAT'S ALL.
AND I PREFER 'DOC.'
IT WAS MY FATHER'S NICKNAME FOR ME.
STUDIOUS KID, HUH?
PUT THAT BOOK DOWN RIGHT NOW, MISTER PRATT!
FORGIVE ME, BUT IN THIS ROOM OF VERY DANGEROUS THINGS, THAT COMIC BOOK IS THE MOST DANGEROUS THING OF ALL.
SOME CALL IT CURSED, OR EVEN HAUNTED.
YOU DON'T READ COMIC BOOKS, DOC?
THAT'S LIKE SAYING YOU DON'T WATCH MOVIES.
ME, I CAN JUST ABOUT SIT THROUGH A GOOD COMEDY.
COMEDY.
A NARRATIVE STRUCTURE IN WHICH, DESPITE A SERIES OF RIDICULOUS MISHAPS, ALL GOES WELL.
AGAINST ALL ODDS.
SWIETY BOG!
WHAT IS IT?
IT'S THE DEVIL HIMSELF!

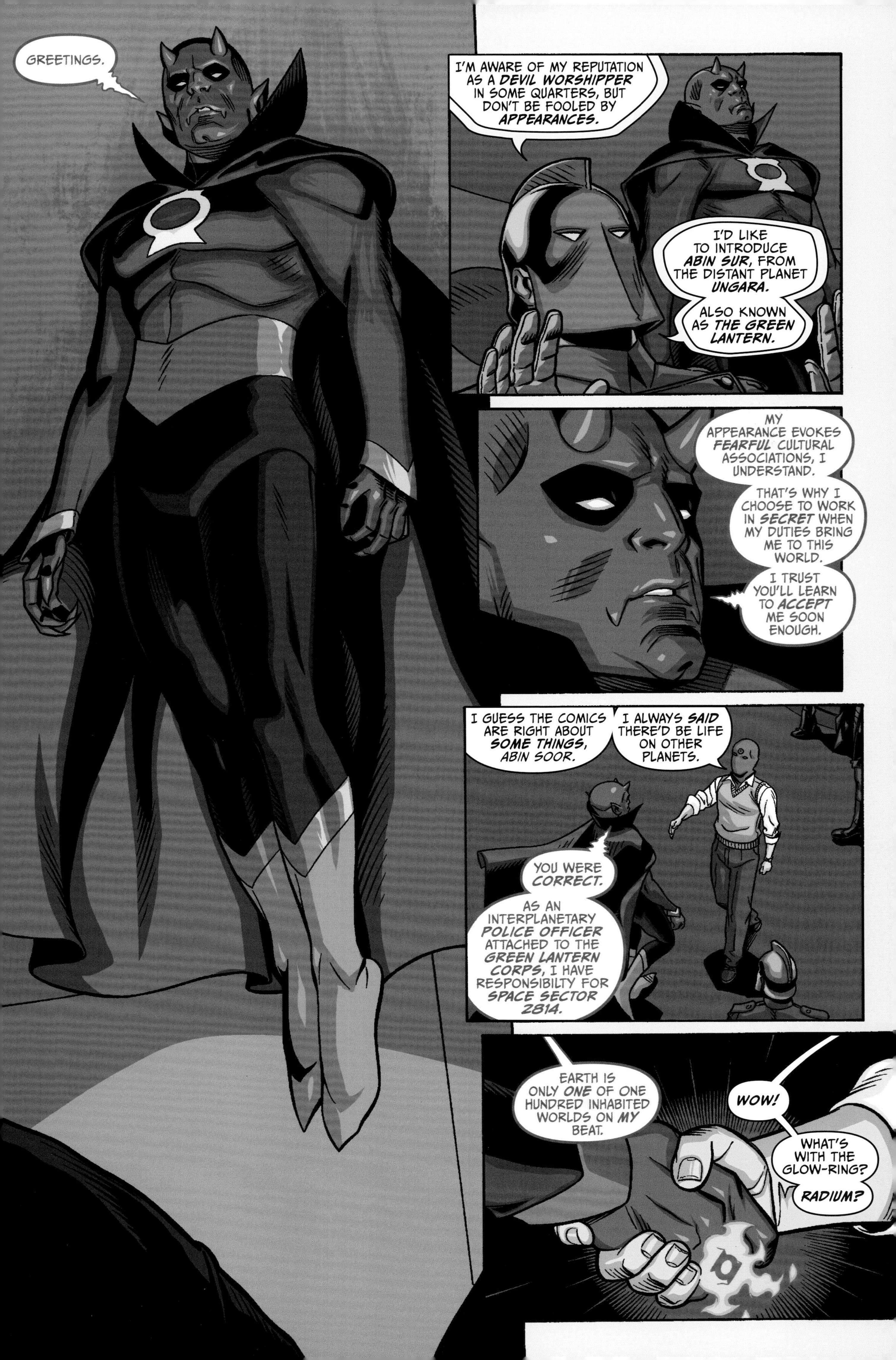
GREETINGS.
I'M AWARE OF MY REPUTATION AS A DEVIL WORSHIPPER IN SOME QUARTERS, BUT DON'T BE FOOLED BY APPEARANCES.
I'D LIKE TO INTRODUCE ABIN SUR, FROM THE DISTANT PLANET UNGARA.
ALSO KNOWN AS THE GREEN LANTERN.
MY APPEARANCE EVOKES FEARFUL CULTURAL ASSOCIATIONS, I UNDERSTAND.
THAT'S WHY I CHOOSE TO WORK IN SECRET WHEN MY DUTIES BRING ME TO THIS WORLD.
I TRUST YOU'LL LEARN TO ACCEPT ME SOON ENOUGH.
I GUESS THE COMICS ARE RIGHT ABOUT SOME THINGS, ABIN SOOR.
I ALWAYS SAID THERE'D BE LIFE ON OTHER PLANETS.
YOU WERE CORRECT.
AS AN INTERPLANETARY POLICE OFFICER ATTACHED TO THE GREEN LANTERN CORPS, I HAVE RESPONSIBILTY FOR SPACE SECTOR 2814.
EARTH IS ONLY ONE OF ONE HUNDRED INHABITED WORLDS ON MY BEAT.
WOW!
WHAT'S WITH THE GLOW-RING?
RADIUM?

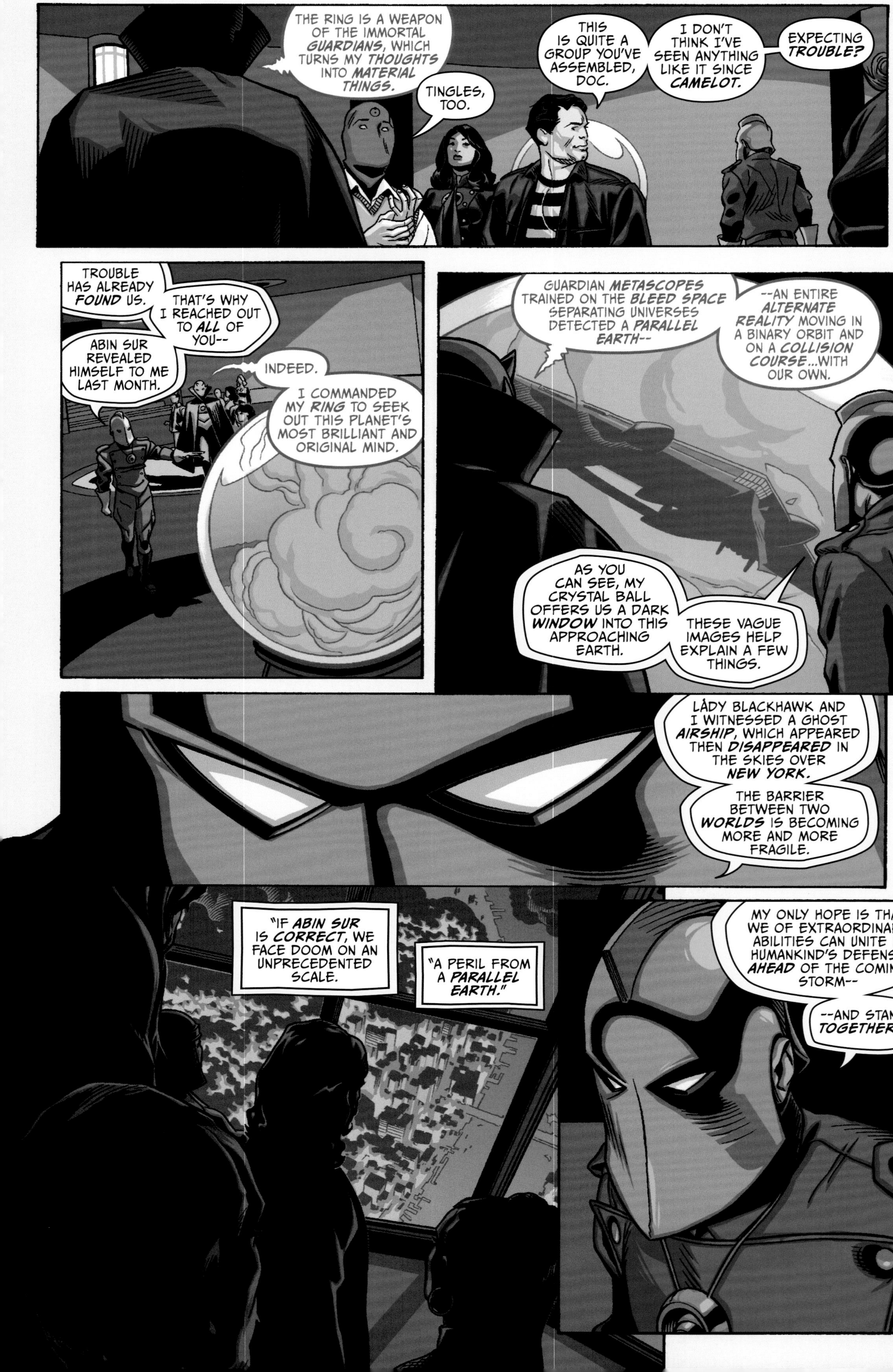
THE RING IS A WEAPON OF THE IMMORTAL GUARDIANS, WHICH TURNS MY THOUGHTS INTO MATERIAL THINGS.
TINGLES, TOO.
THIS IS QUITE A GROUP YOU'VE ASSEMBLED, DOC.
I DON'T THINK I'VE SEEN ANYTHING LIKE IT SINCE CAMELOT.
EXPECTING TROUBLE?
TROUBLE HAS ALREADY FOUND US.
THAT'S WHY I REACHED OUT TO ALL OF YOU--
ABIN SUR REVEALED HIMSELF TO ME LAST MONTH.
INDEED.
I COMMANDED MY RING TO SEEK OUT THIS PLANET'S MOST BRILLIANT AND ORIGINAL MIND.
GUARDIAN METASCOPES TRAINED ON THE BLEED SPACE SEPARATING UNIVERSES DETECTED A PARALLEL EARTH--
--AN ENTIRE ALTERNATE REALITY MOVING IN A BINARY ORBIT AND ON A COLLISION COURSE...WITH OUR OWN.
AS YOU CAN SEE, MY CRYSTAL BALL OFFERS US A DARK WINDOW INTO THIS APPROACHING EARTH.
THESE VAGUE IMAGES HELP EXPLAIN A FEW THINGS.
LÅDY BLACKHAWK AND I WITNESSED A GHOST AIRSHIP, WHICH APPEARED THEN DISAPPEARED IN THE SKIES OVER NEW YORK.
THE BARRIER BETWEEN TWO WORLDS IS BECOMING MORE AND MORE FRAGILE.
"IF ABIN SUR IS CORRECT, WE FACE DOOM ON AN UNPRECEDENTED SCALE.
"A PERIL FROM A PARALLEL EARTH."
MY ONLY HOPE IS THAT WE OF EXTRAORDINARY ABILITIES CAN UNITE IN HUMANKIND'S DEFENSE AHEAD OF THE COMING STORM--
--AND STAND TOGETHER--

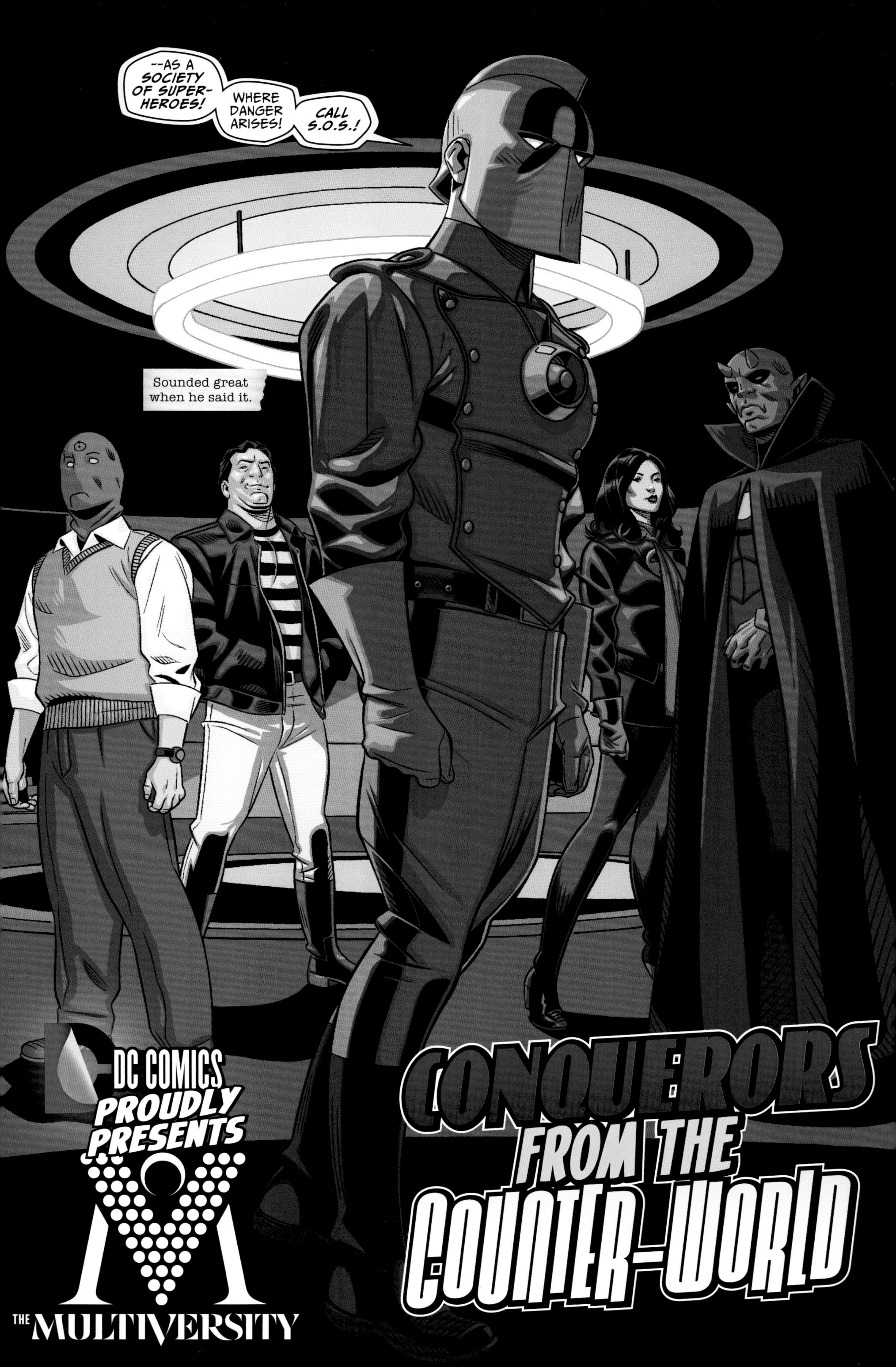
--AS A SOCIETY OF SUPER-HEROES!
WHERE DANGER ARISES!
CALL S.O.S.!
Sounded great when he said it.
DC COMICS PROUDLY PRESENTS
THE MULTIVERSITY
CONQUERORS FROM THE COUNTER-WORLD

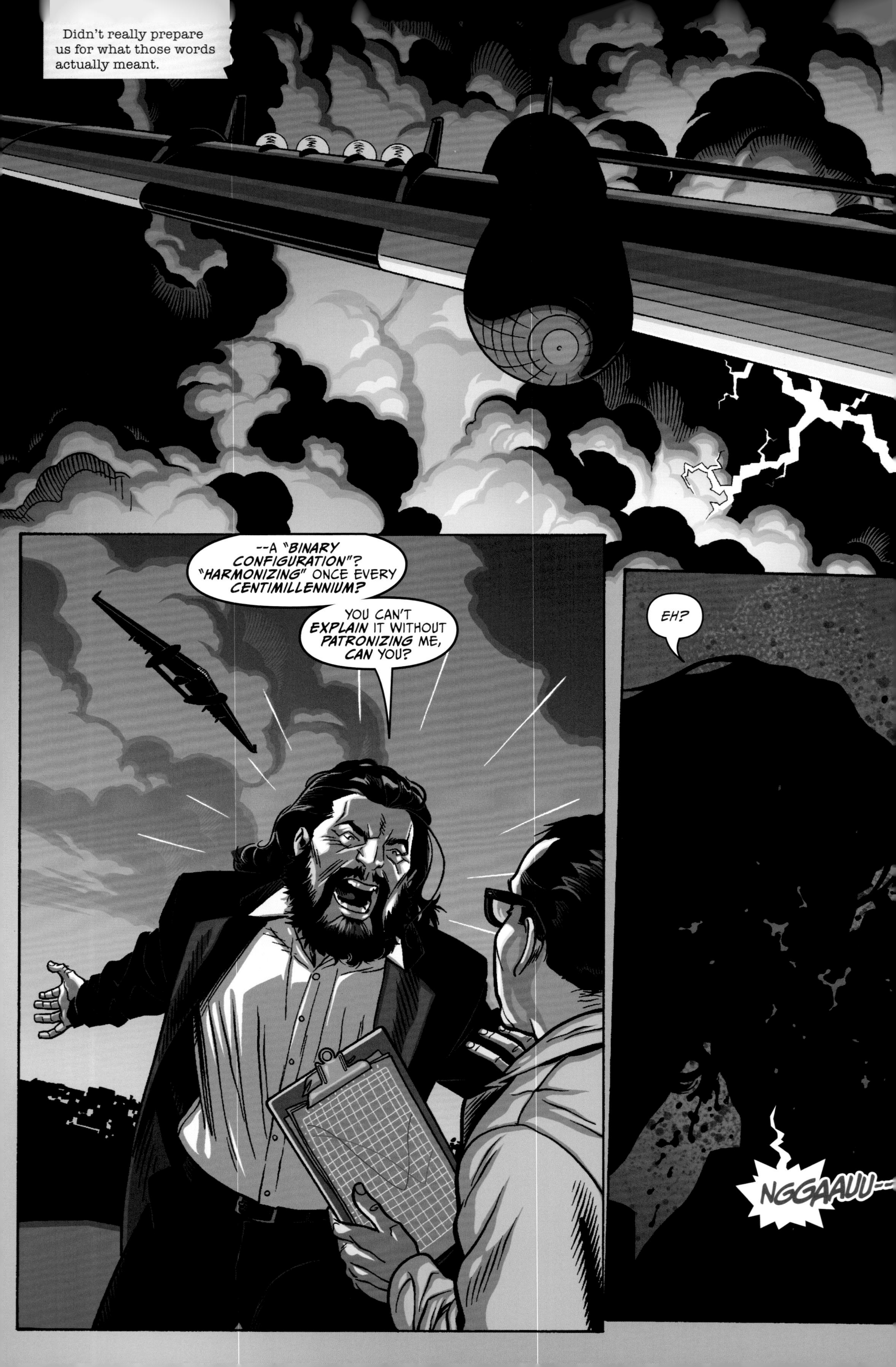
Didn't really prepare us for what those words actually meant.
--A "BINARY CONFIGURATION"? "HARMONIZING" ONCE EVERY CENTIMILLENNIUM?
YOU CAN'T EXPLAIN IT WITHOUT PATRONIZING ME, CAN YOU?
EH?
NGGAAUU--

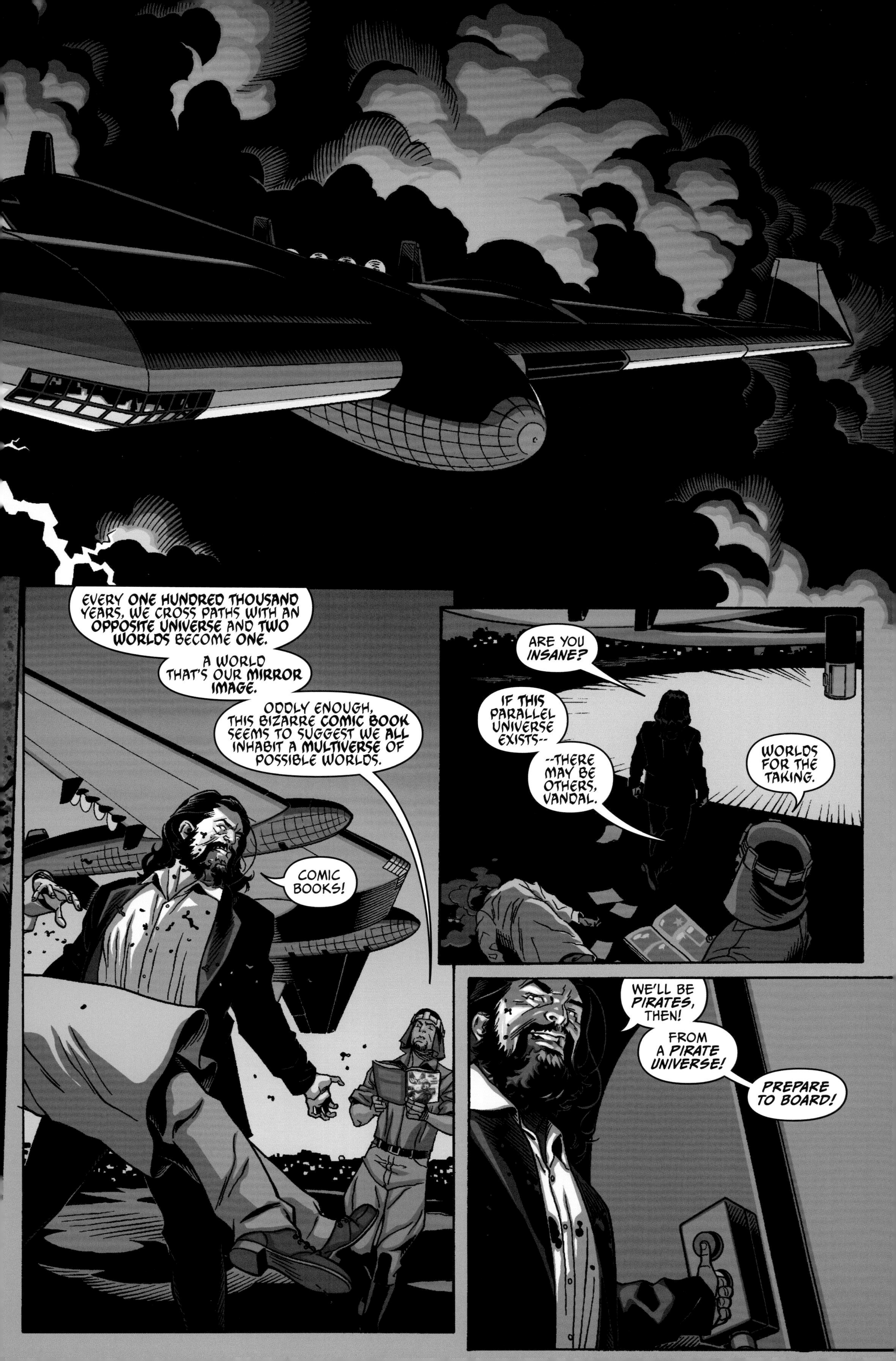
EVERY ONE HUNDRED THOUSAND YEARS, WE CROSS PATHS WITH AN OPPOSITE UNIVERSE AND TWO WORLDS BECOME ONE.
A WORLD THAT'S OUR MIRROR IMAGE.
ODDLY ENOUGH, THIS BIZARRE COMIC BOOK SEEMS TO SUGGEST WE ALL INHABIT A MULTIVERSE OF POSSIBLE WORLDS.
COMIC BOOKS!
ARE YOU INSANE?
IF THIS PARALLEL UNIVERSE EXISTS--
--THERE MAY BE OTHERS, VANDAL.
WORLDS FOR THE TAKING.
WE'LL BE PIRATES, THEN!
FROM A PIRATE UNIVERSE!
PREPARE TO BOARD!

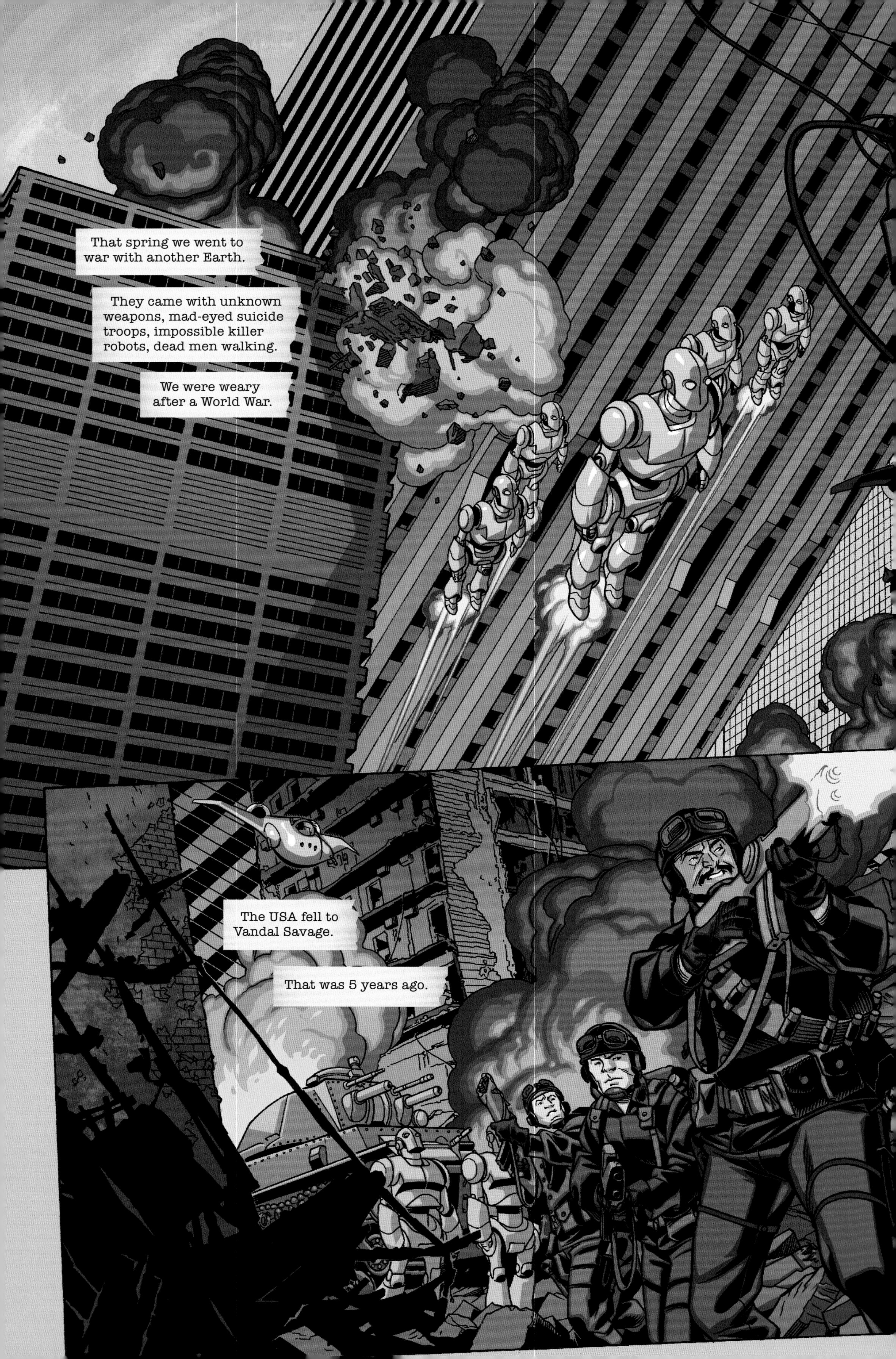
That spring we went to war with another Earth.
They came with unknown weapons, mad-eyed suicide troops, impossible killer robots, dead men walking.
We were weary after a World War.
The USA fell to Vandal Savage.
That was 5 years ago.

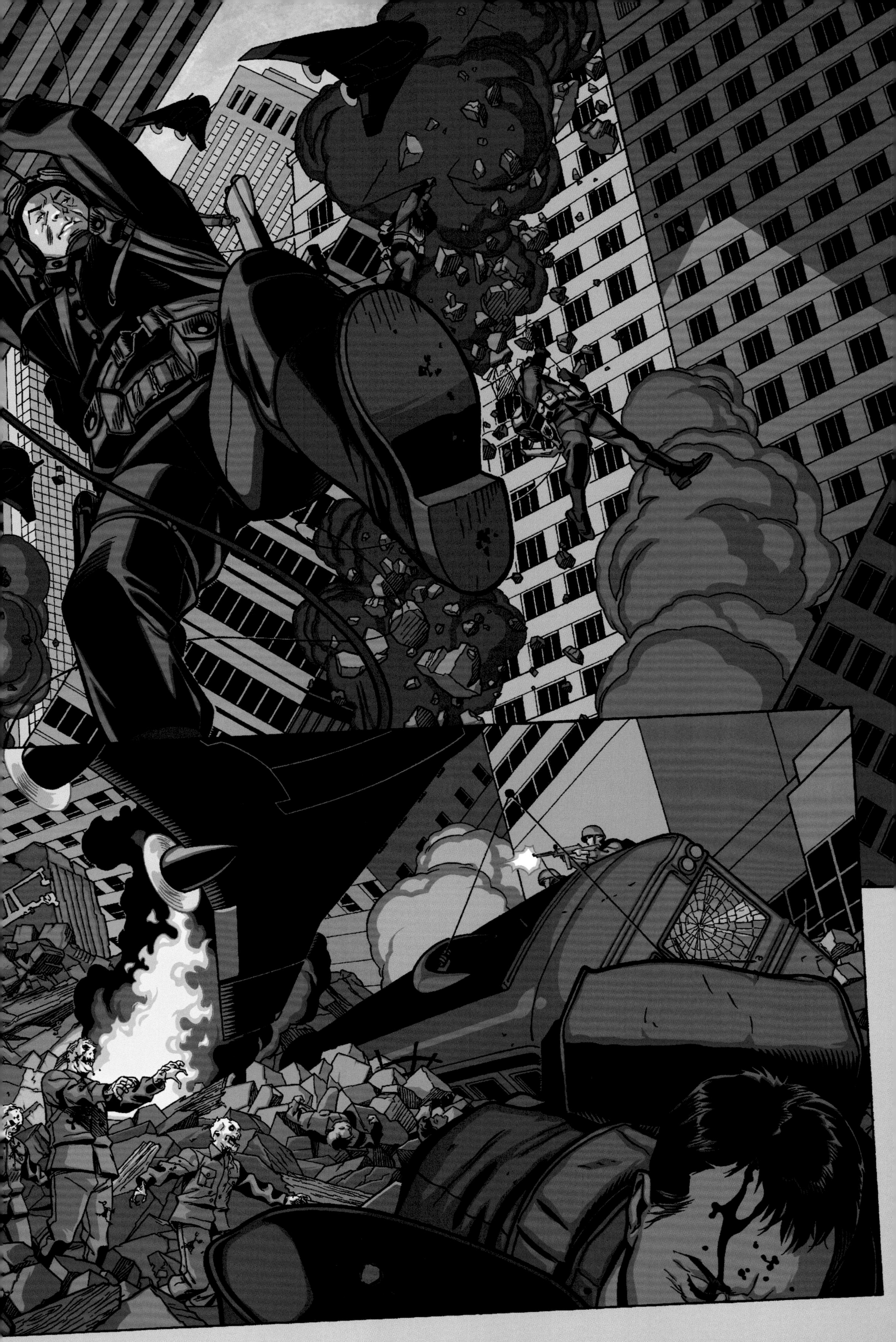

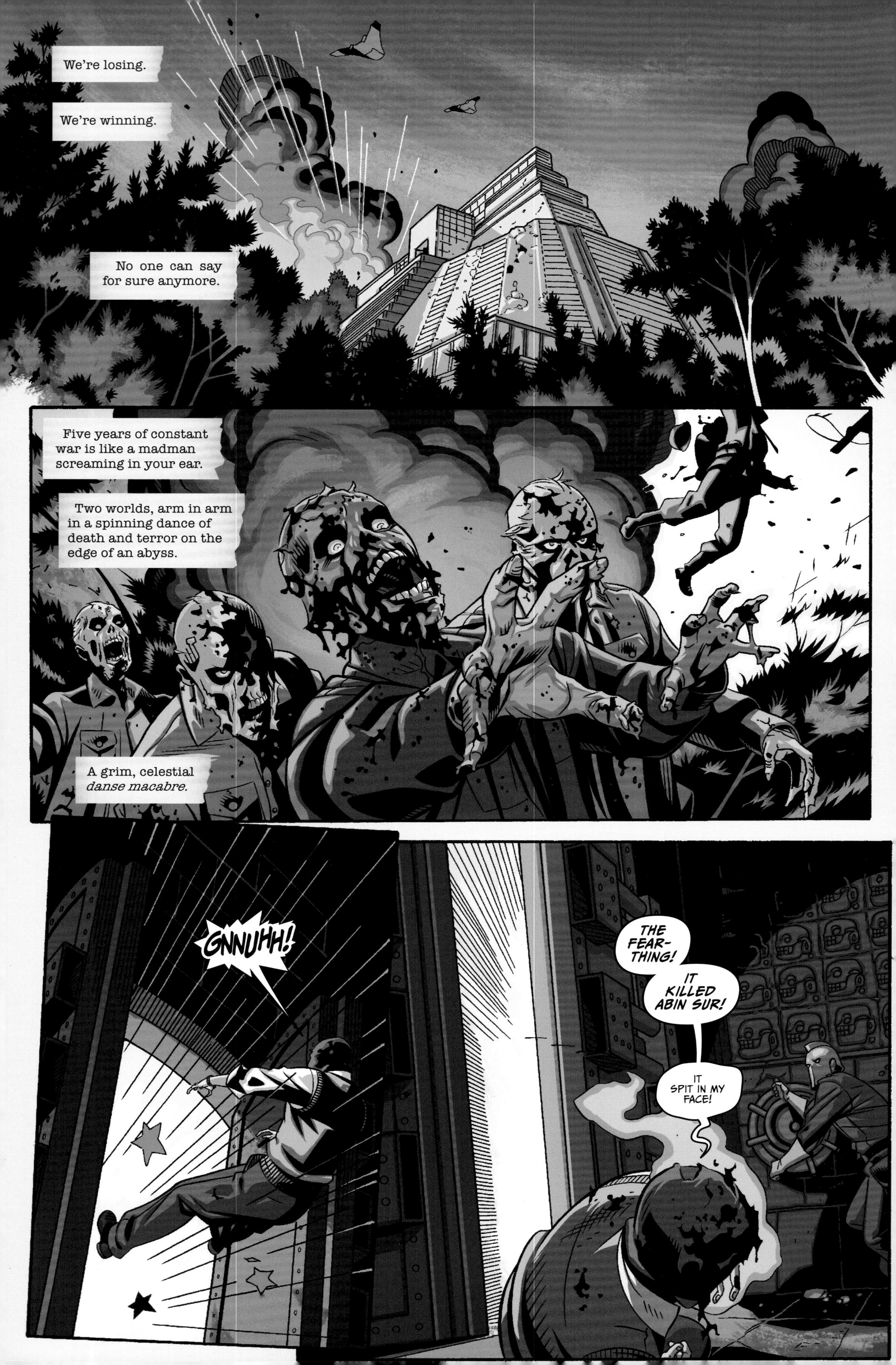
We're losing.
We're winning.
No one can say for sure anymore.
Five years of constant war is like a madman screaming in your ear.
Two worlds, arm in arm in a spinning dance of death and terror on the edge of an abyss.
A grim, celestial *danse macabre.*
GNNUHH!
THE FEAR-THING!
IT KILLED ABIN SUR!
IT SPIT IN MY FACE!

MY FACE!

I SAW IT, DOC!

MY FACE IS ON *FIRE!*

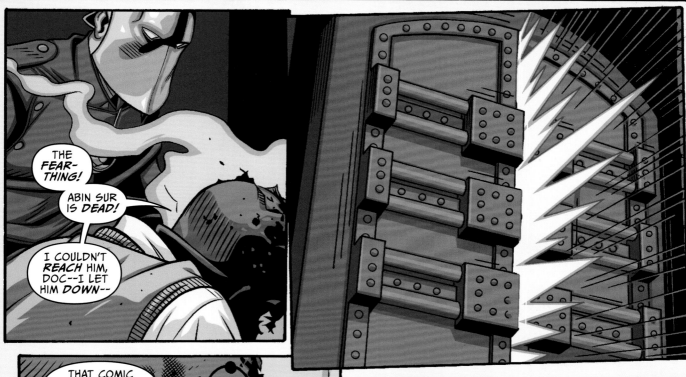

THE *FEAR-THING!*

ABIN SUR IS *DEAD!*

I COULDN'T *REACH* HIM, DOC--I LET HIM *DOWN*--

THAT COMIC BOOK--YOU SAID IT WAS *CURSED*-- YOU SAID--

YOU WERE *RIGHT,* I SHOULDN'T HAVE *LOOKED.*

SEE WHAT IT'S *DONE* TO ME!

AL!

LOOK AT ME.

YOU'RE GOING INTO *SHOCK.*

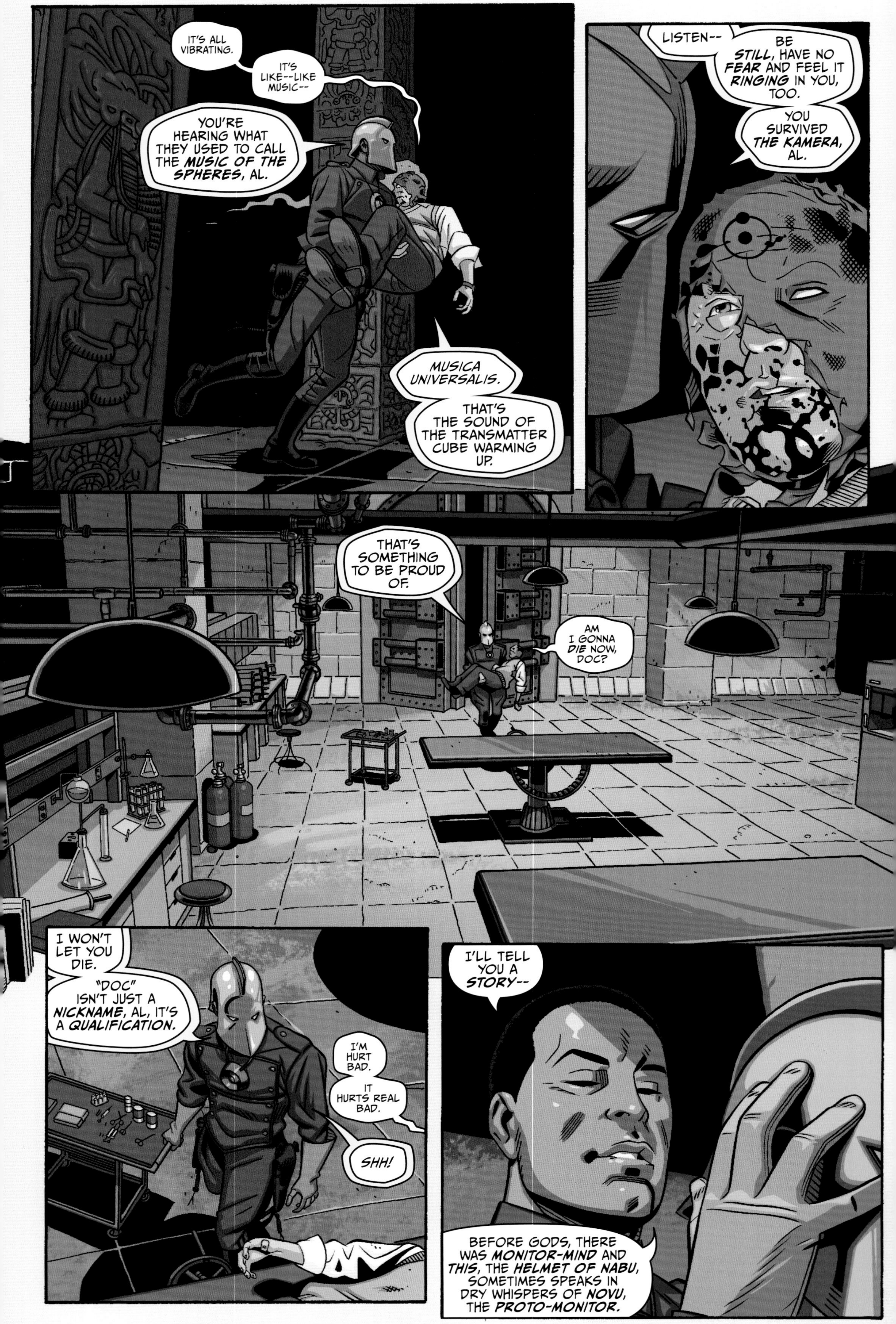
IT'S ALL VIBRATING.
IT'S LIKE--LIKE MUSIC--
YOU'RE HEARING WHAT THEY USED TO CALL THE MUSIC OF THE SPHERES, AL.
MUSICA UNIVERSALIS.
THAT'S THE SOUND OF THE TRANSMATTER CUBE WARMING UP.
LISTEN--
BE STILL, HAVE NO FEAR AND FEEL IT RINGING IN YOU, TOO.
YOU SURVIVED THE KAMERA, AL.
THAT'S SOMETHING TO BE PROUD OF.
AM I GONNA DIE NOW, DOC?
I WON'T LET YOU DIE.
"DOC" ISN'T JUST A NICKNAME, AL, IT'S A QUALIFICATION.
I'M HURT BAD.
IT HURTS REAL BAD.
SHH!
I'LL TELL YOU A STORY--
BEFORE GODS, THERE WAS MONITOR-MIND AND THIS, THE HELMET OF NABU, SOMETIMES SPEAKS IN DRY WHISPERS OF NOVU, THE PROTO-MONITOR.

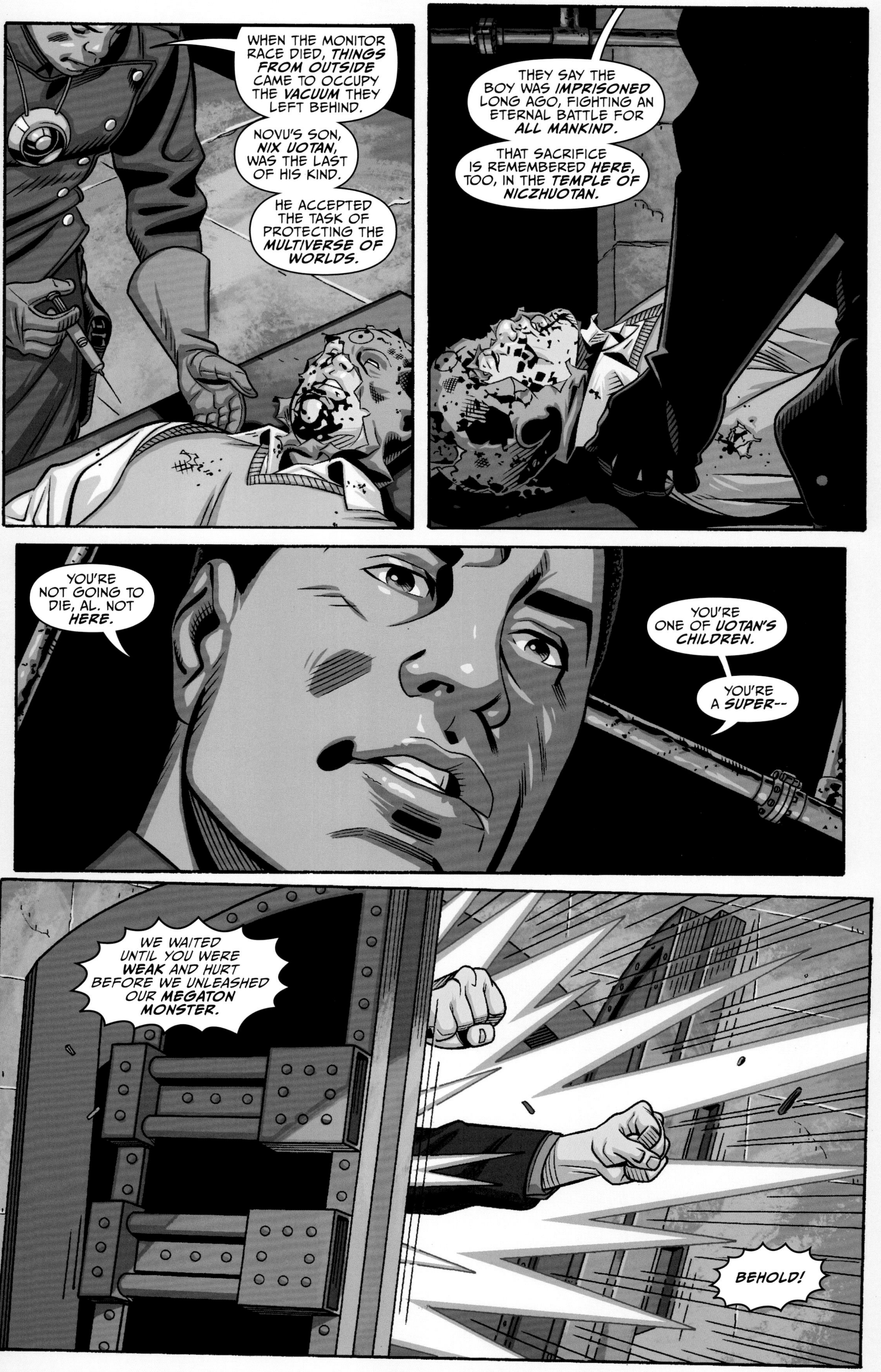
WHEN THE MONITOR RACE DIED, THINGS FROM OUTSIDE CAME TO OCCUPY THE VACUUM THEY LEFT BEHIND.
NOVU'S SON, NIX UOTAN, WAS THE LAST OF HIS KIND.
HE ACCEPTED THE TASK OF PROTECTING THE MULTIVERSE OF WORLDS.
THEY SAY THE BOY WAS IMPRISONED LONG AGO, FIGHTING AN ETERNAL BATTLE FOR ALL MANKIND.
THAT SACRIFICE IS REMEMBERED HERE, TOO, IN THE TEMPLE OF NICZHUOTAN.
YOU'RE NOT GOING TO DIE, AL. NOT HERE.
YOU'RE ONE OF UOTAN'S CHILDREN.
YOU'RE A SUPER--
WE WAITED UNTIL YOU WERE WEAK AND HURT BEFORE WE UNLEASHED OUR MEGATON MONSTER.
BEHOLD!

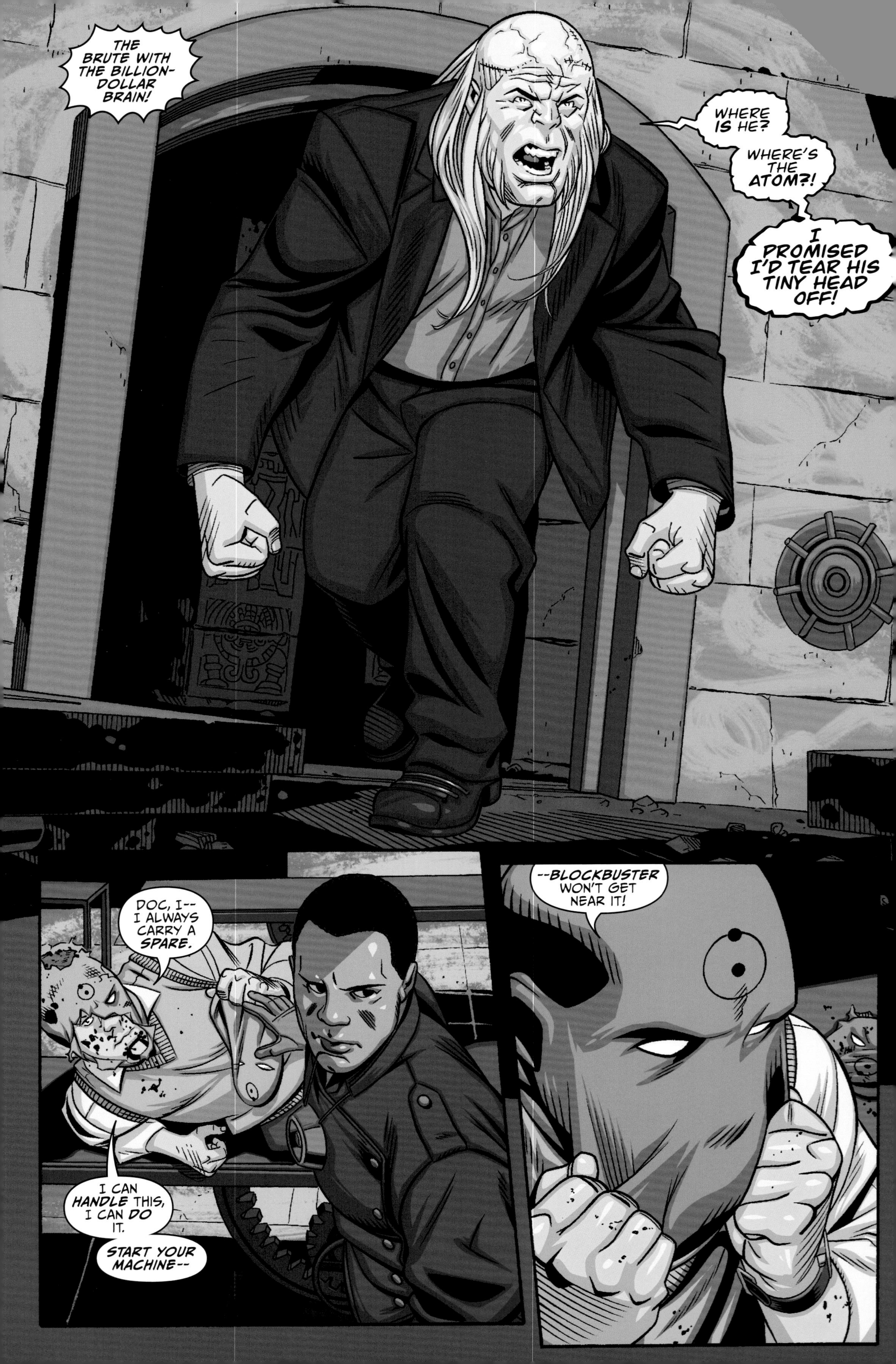
THE BRUTE WITH THE BILLION-DOLLAR BRAIN!
WHERE IS HE?
WHERE'S THE ATOM?!
I PROMISED I'D TEAR HIS TINY HEAD OFF!
DOC, I-- I ALWAYS CARRY A SPARE.
I CAN HANDLE THIS, I CAN DO IT.
START YOUR MACHINE--
--BLOCKBUSTER WON'T GET NEAR IT!

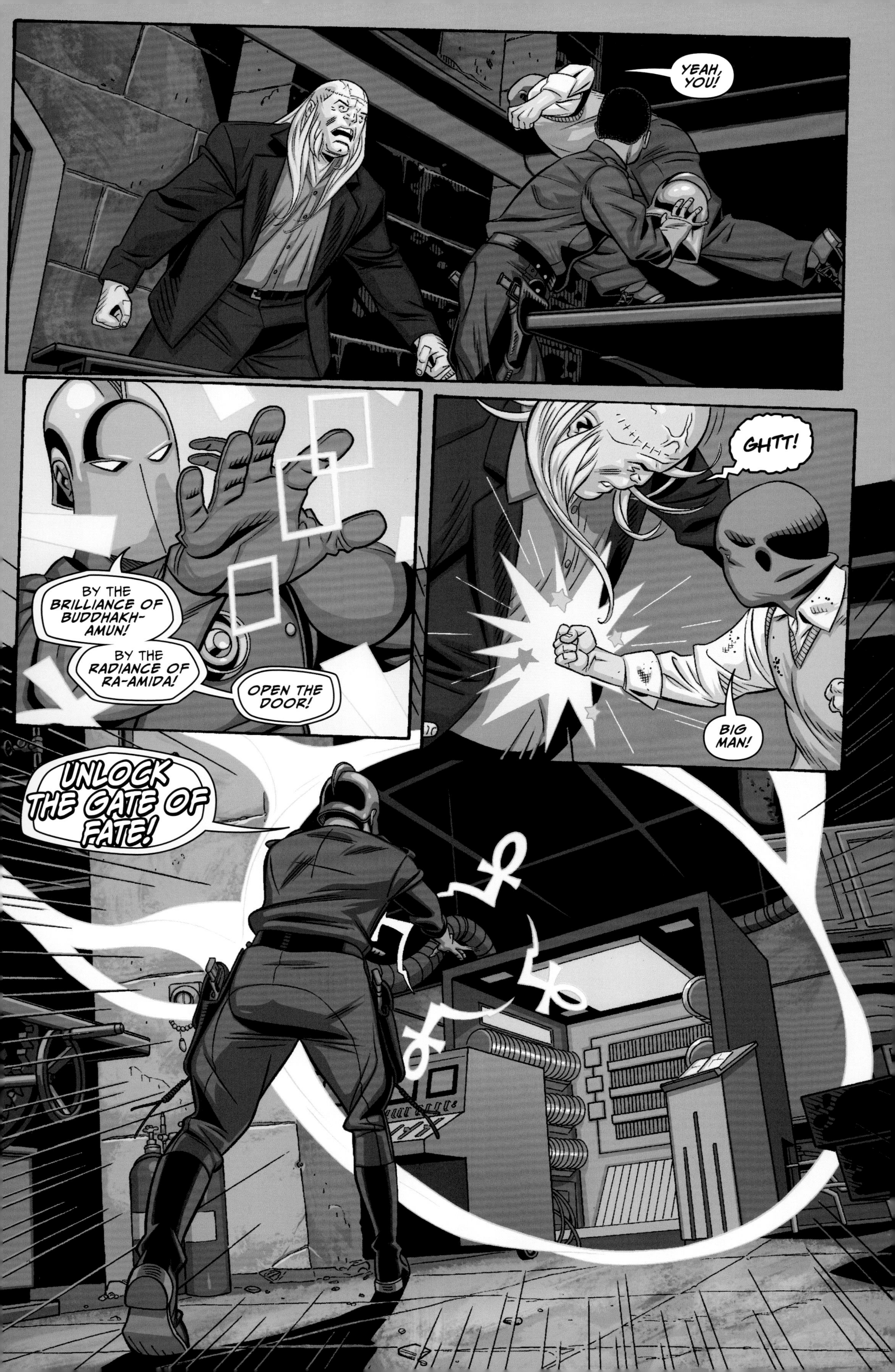

YEAH, YOU!
BY THE BRILLIANCE OF BUDDHAKH-AMUN!
BY THE RADIANCE OF RA-AMIDA!
OPEN THE DOOR!
GHTT!
BIG MAN!
UNLOCK THE GATE OF FATE!

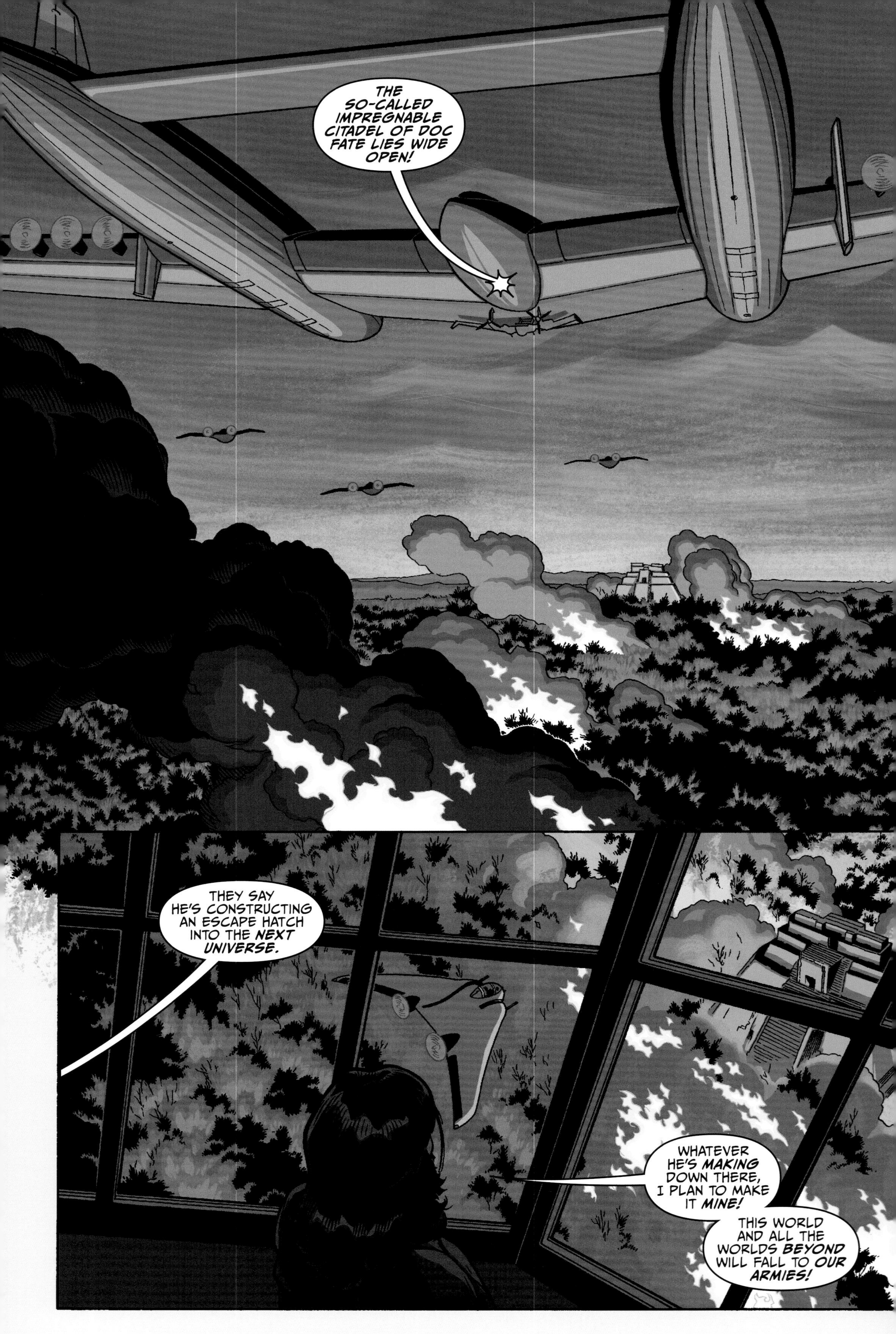
THE SO-CALLED IMPREGNABLE CITADEL OF DOC FATE LIES WIDE OPEN!
THEY SAY HE'S CONSTRUCTING AN ESCAPE HATCH INTO THE NEXT UNIVERSE.
WHATEVER HE'S MAKING DOWN THERE, I PLAN TO MAKE IT MINE!
THIS WORLD AND ALL THE WORLDS BEYOND WILL FALL TO OUR ARMIES!

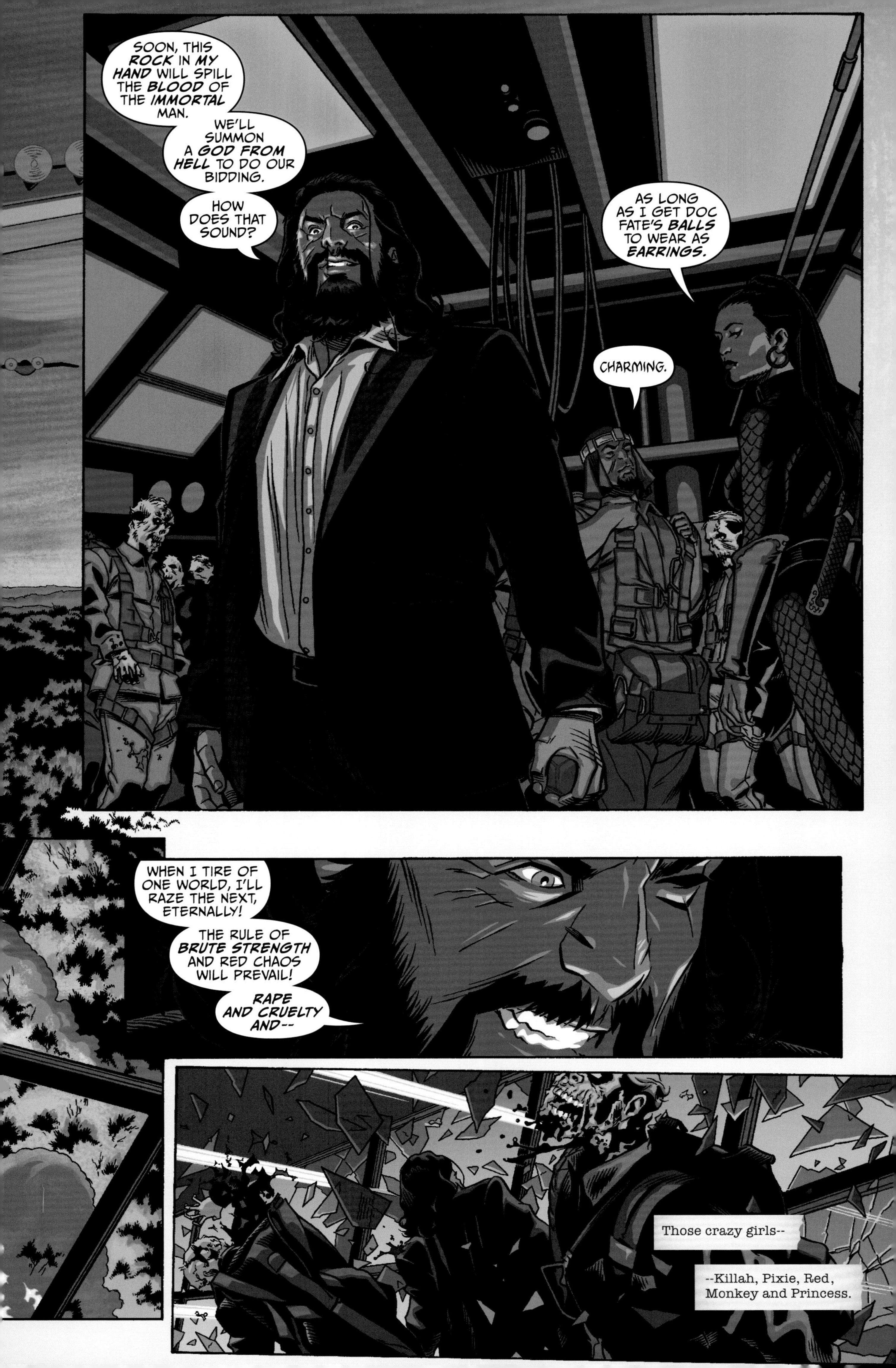
SOON, THIS ROCK IN MY HAND WILL SPILL THE BLOOD OF THE IMMORTAL MAN.
WE'LL SUMMON A GOD FROM HELL TO DO OUR BIDDING.
HOW DOES THAT SOUND?
AS LONG AS I GET DOC FATE'S BALLS TO WEAR AS EARRINGS.
CHARMING.
WHEN I TIRE OF ONE WORLD, I'LL RAZE THE NEXT, ETERNALLY!
THE RULE OF BRUTE STRENGTH AND RED CHAOS WILL PREVAIL!
RAPE AND CRUELTY AND--
Those crazy girls--
--Killah, Pixie, Red, Monkey and Princess.

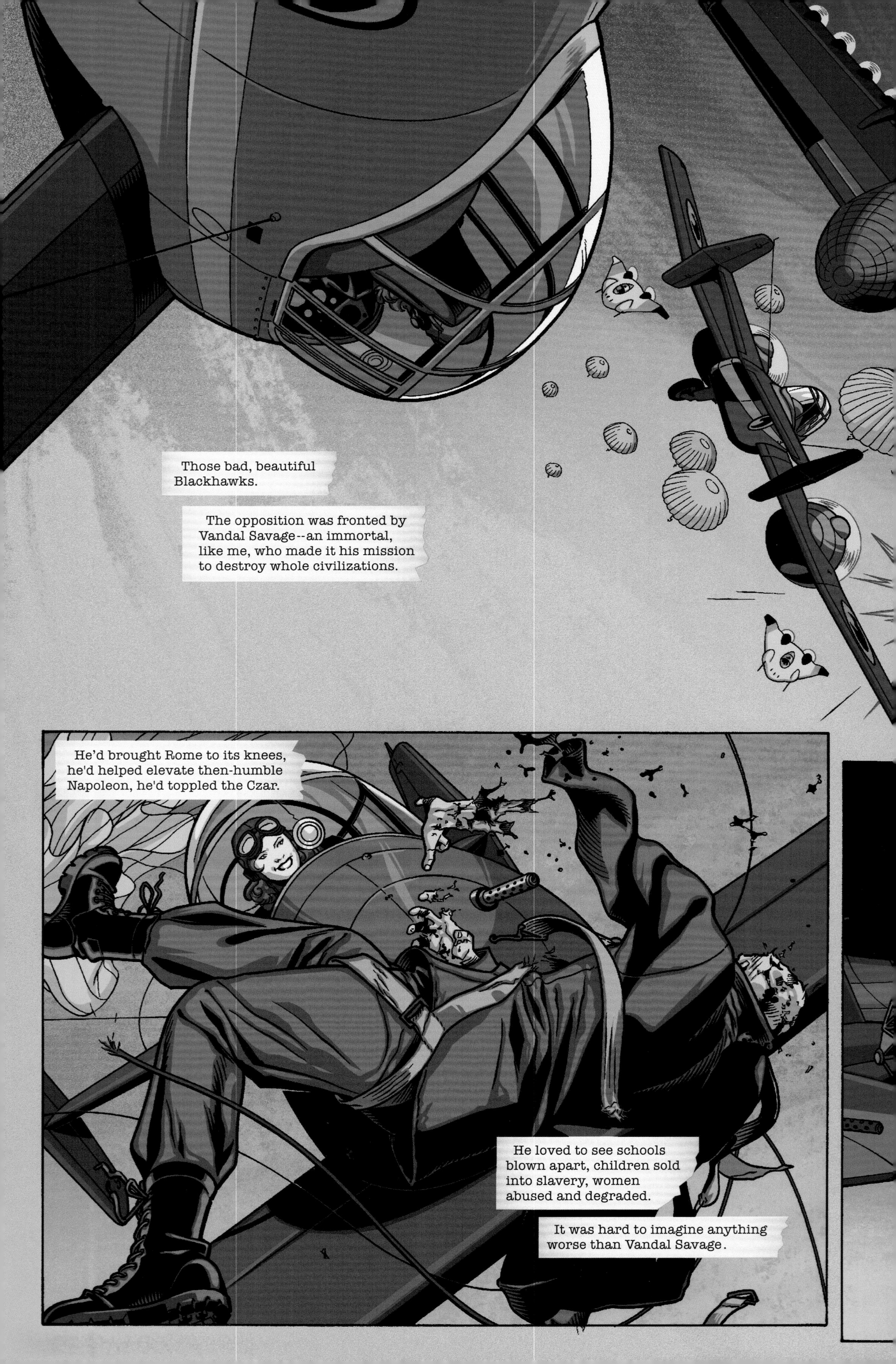
Those bad, beautiful Blackhawks.
The opposition was fronted by Vandal Savage--an immortal, like me, who made it his mission to destroy whole civilizations.
He'd brought Rome to its knees, he'd helped elevate then-humble Napoleon, he'd toppled the Czar.
He loved to see schools blown apart, children sold into slavery, women abused and degraded.
It was hard to imagine anything worse than Vandal Savage.

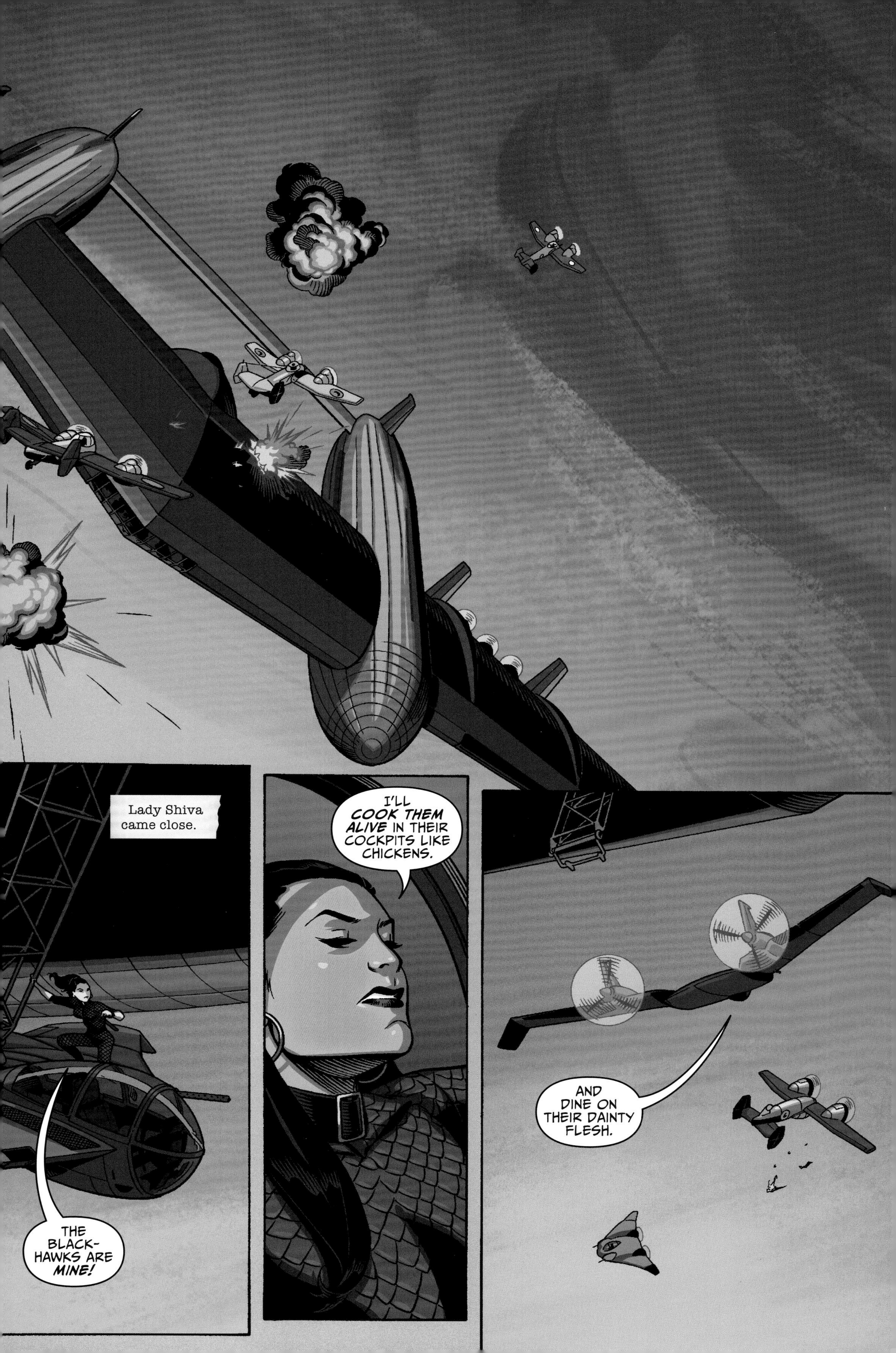

Lady Shiva came close.
THE BLACK-HAWKS ARE MINE!
I'LL COOK THEM ALIVE IN THEIR COCKPITS LIKE CHICKENS.
AND DINE ON THEIR DAINTY FLESH.

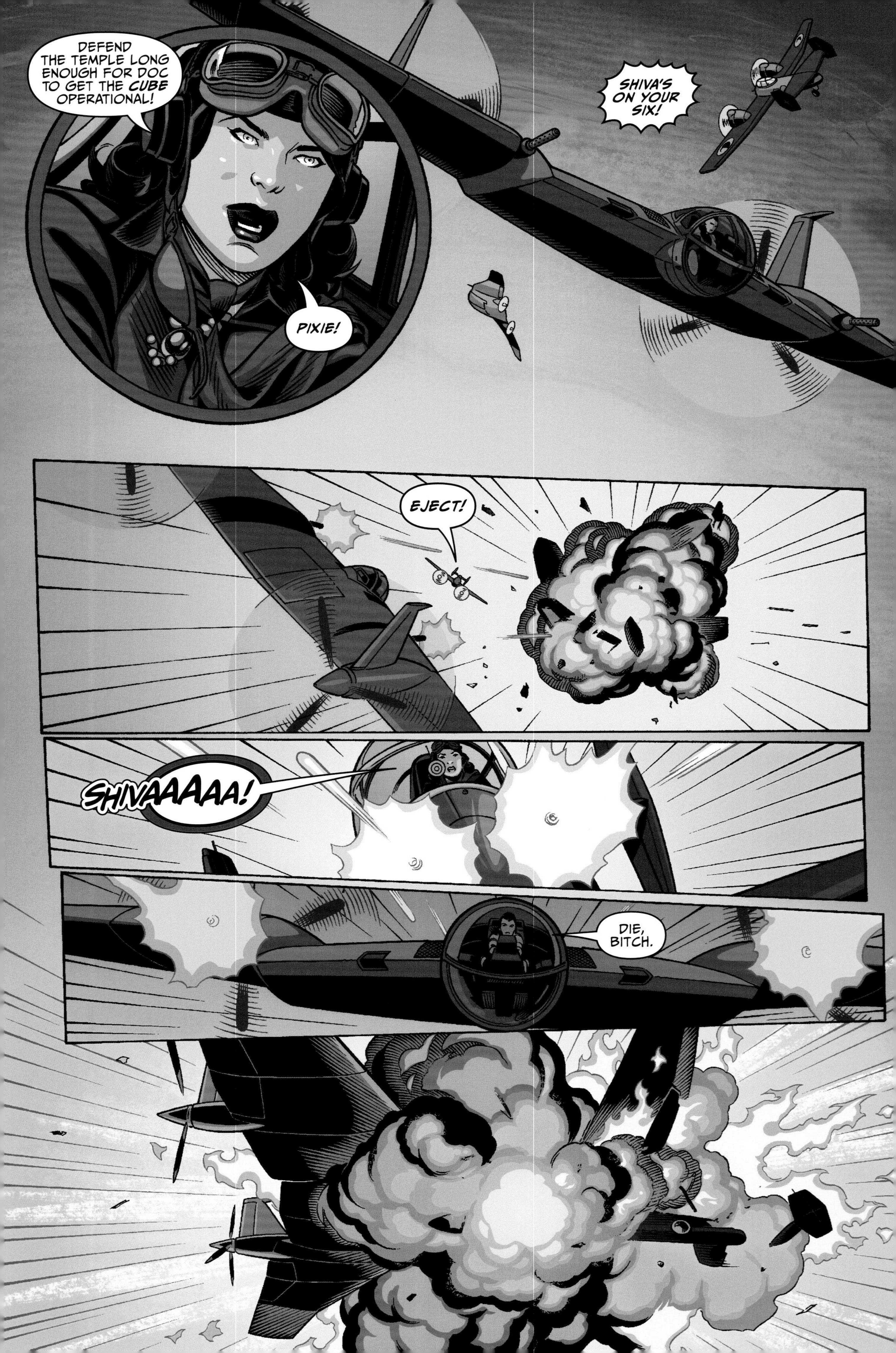
DEFEND THE TEMPLE LONG ENOUGH FOR DOC TO GET THE CUBE OPERATIONAL!
PIXIE!
SHIVA'S ON YOUR SIX!
EJECT!
SHIVAAAAA!
DIE, BITCH.

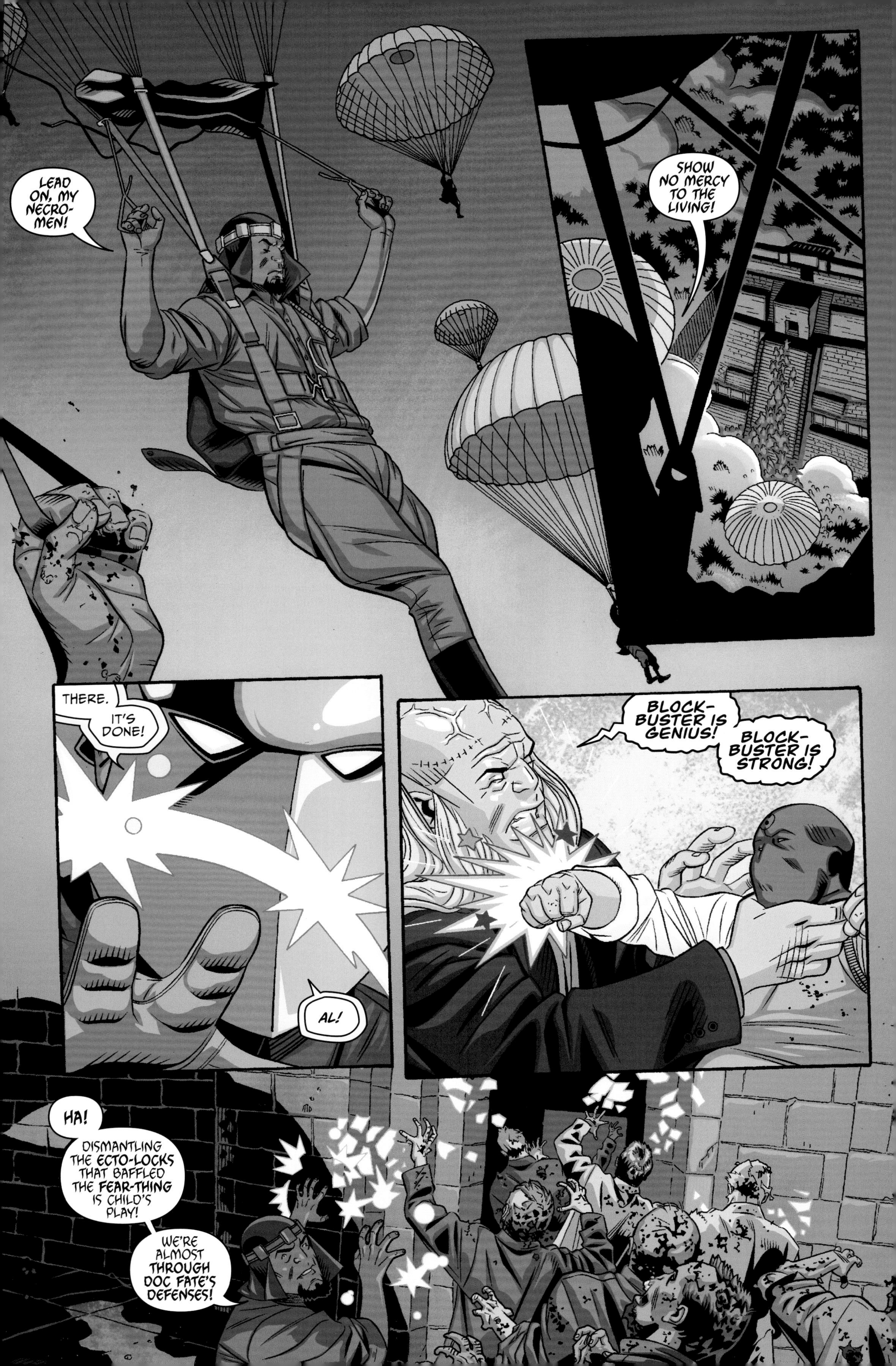
LEAD ON, MY NECRO-MEN!
SHOW NO MERCY TO THE LIVING!
THERE.
IT'S DONE!
AL!
BLOCK-BUSTER IS GENIUS!
BLOCK-BUSTER IS STRONG!
HA!
DISMANTLING THE ECTO-LOCKS THAT BAFFLED THE FEAR-THING IS CHILD'S PLAY!
WE'RE ALMOST THROUGH DOC FATE'S DEFENSES!

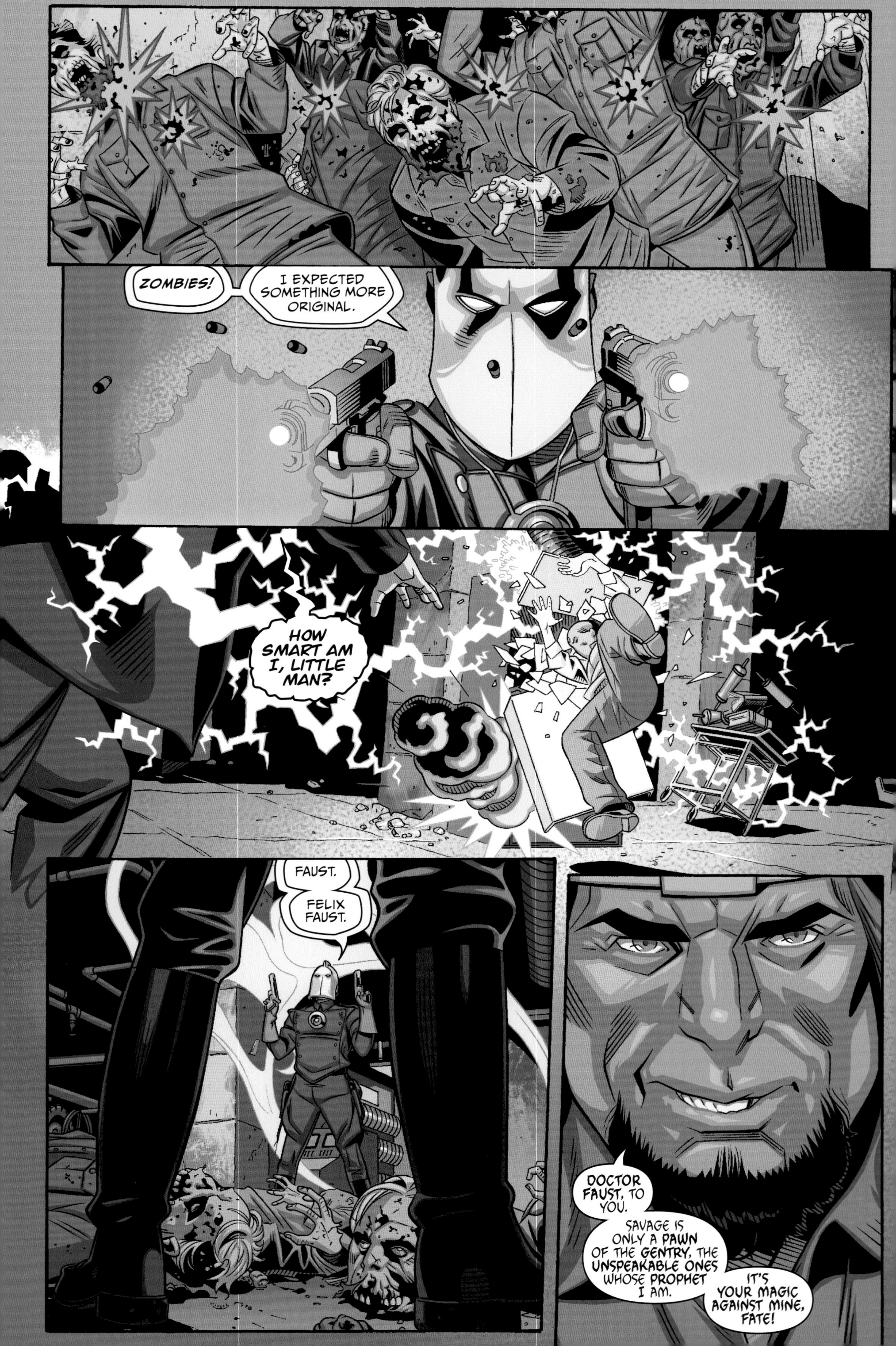
ZOMBIES!
I EXPECTED SOMETHING MORE ORIGINAL.
HOW SMART AM I, LITTLE MAN?
FAUST.
FELIX FAUST.
DOCTOR FAUST, TO YOU.
SAVAGE IS ONLY A PAWN OF THE GENTRY, THE UNSPEAKABLE ONES WHOSE PROPHET I AM.
IT'S YOUR MAGIC AGAINST MINE, FATE!

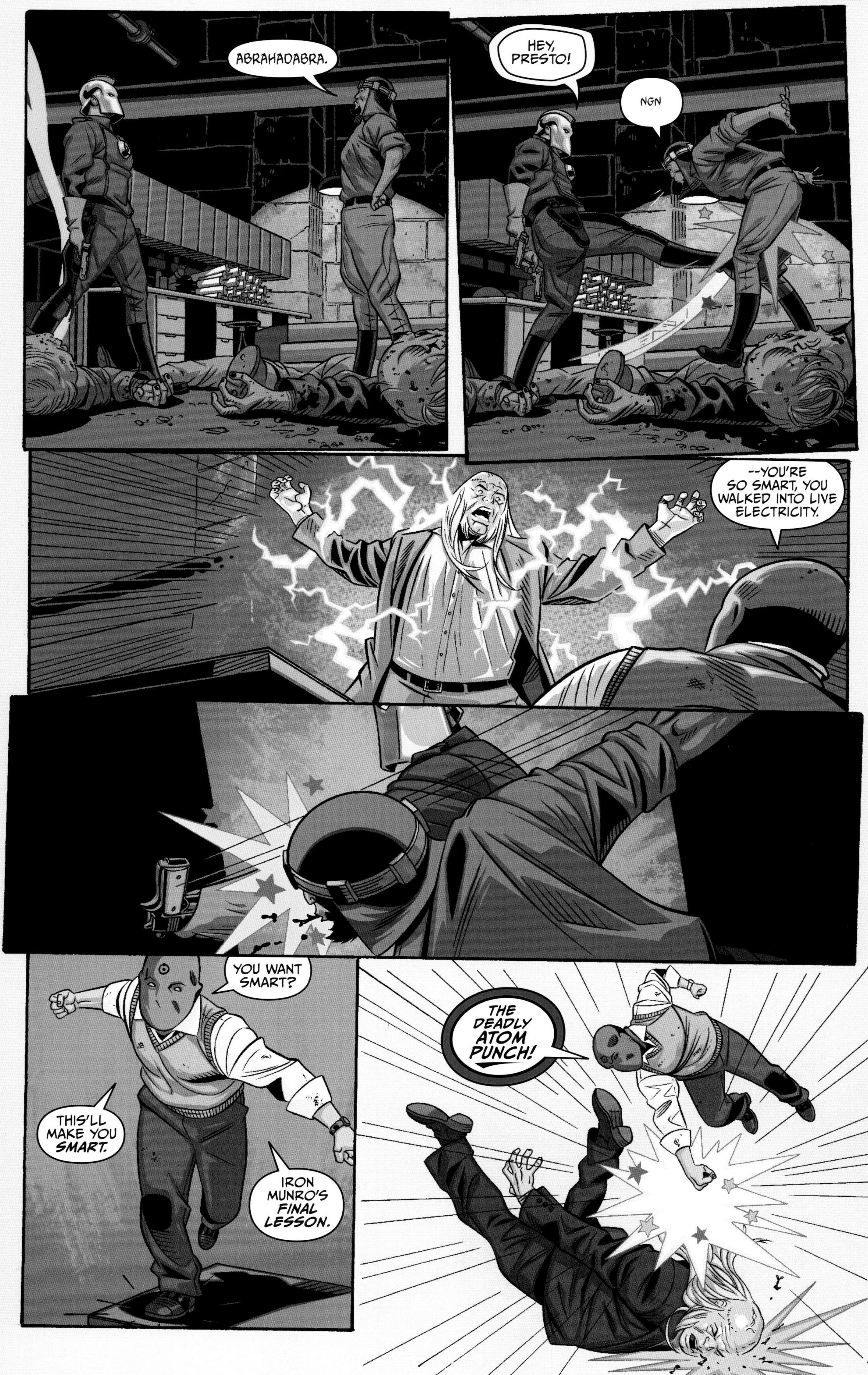
ABRAHADABRA.
HEY, PRESTO!
NGN
--YOU'RE SO SMART, YOU WALKED INTO LIVE ELECTRICITY.
YOU WANT SMART?
THIS'LL MAKE YOU SMART.
IRON MUNRO'S FINAL LESSON.
THE DEADLY ATOM PUNCH!

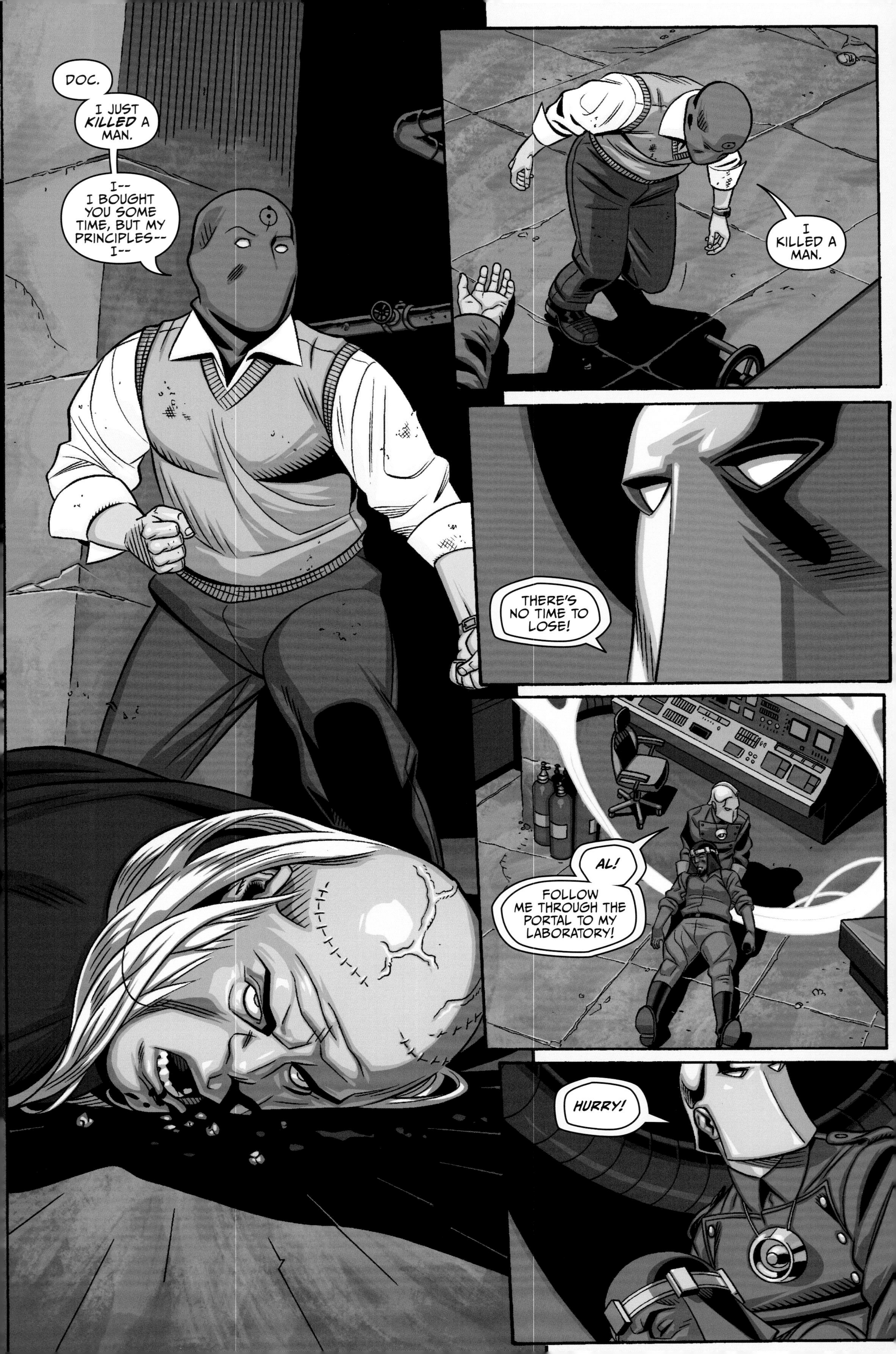
DOC.
I JUST *KILLED* A MAN.
I-- I BOUGHT YOU SOME TIME, BUT MY PRINCIPLES-- I--
I KILLED A MAN.
THERE'S NO TIME TO LOSE!
AL!
FOLLOW ME THROUGH THE PORTAL TO MY LABORATORY!
HURRY!

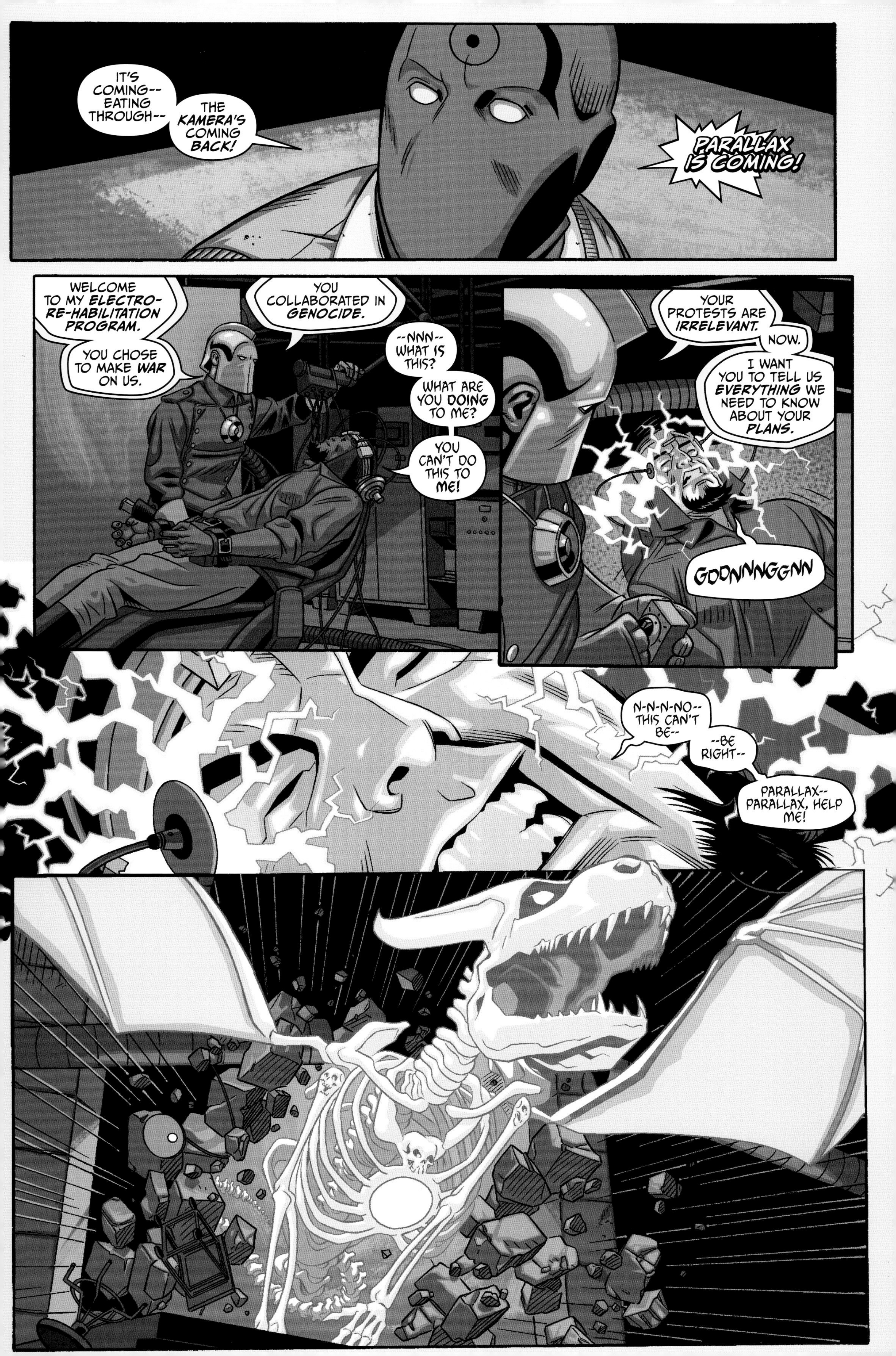
IT'S COMING-- EATING THROUGH--
THE KAMERA'S COMING BACK!
PARALLAX IS COMING!
WELCOME TO MY ELECTRO-RE-HABILITATION PROGRAM.
YOU CHOSE TO MAKE WAR ON US.
YOU COLLABORATED IN GENOCIDE.
--NNN-- WHAT IS THIS?
WHAT ARE YOU DOING TO ME?
YOU CAN'T DO THIS TO ME!
YOUR PROTESTS ARE IRRELEVANT.
NOW.
I WANT YOU TO TELL US EVERYTHING WE NEED TO KNOW ABOUT YOUR PLANS.
GOONNNGGNN
N-N-N-NO-- THIS CAN'T BE--
--BE RIGHT--
PARALLAX-- PARALLAX, HELP ME!

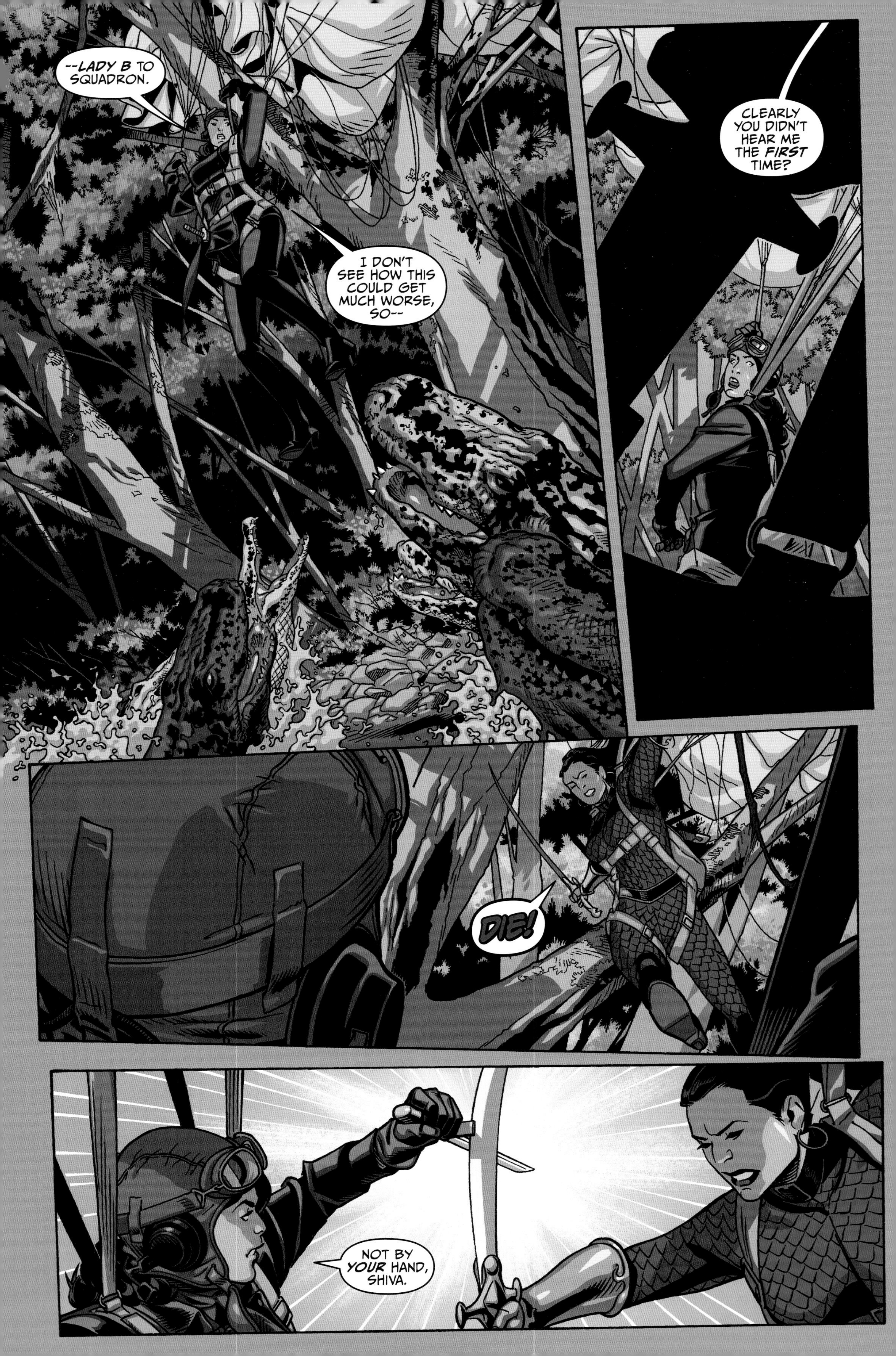
--LADY B TO SQUADRON.
I DON'T SEE HOW THIS COULD GET MUCH WORSE, SO--
CLEARLY YOU DIDN'T HEAR ME THE FIRST TIME?
DIE!
NOT BY YOUR HAND, SHIVA.

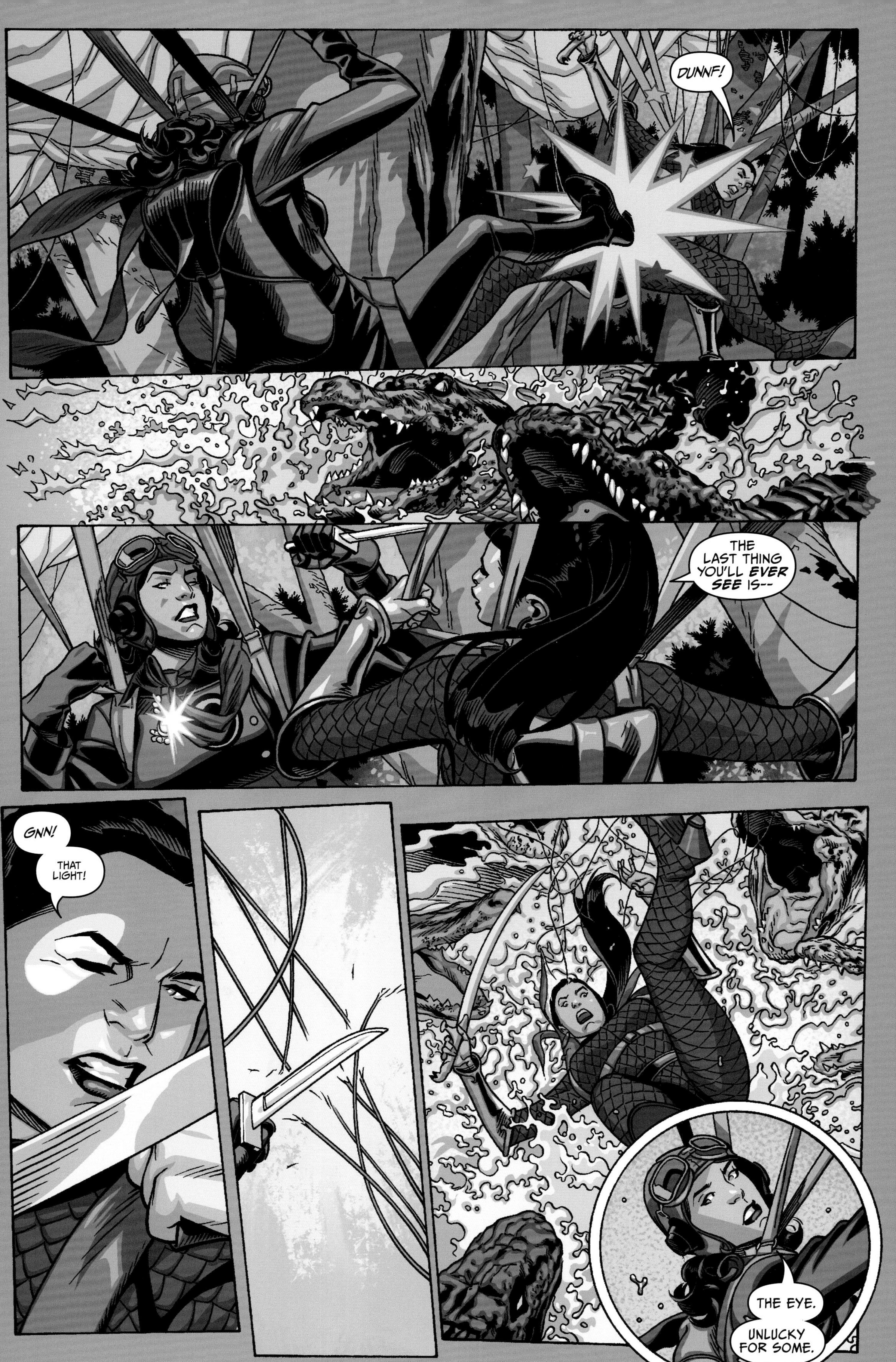
DUNNF!
THE LAST THING YOU'LL EVER SEE IS--
GNN!
THAT LIGHT!
THE EYE.
UNLUCKY FOR SOME.

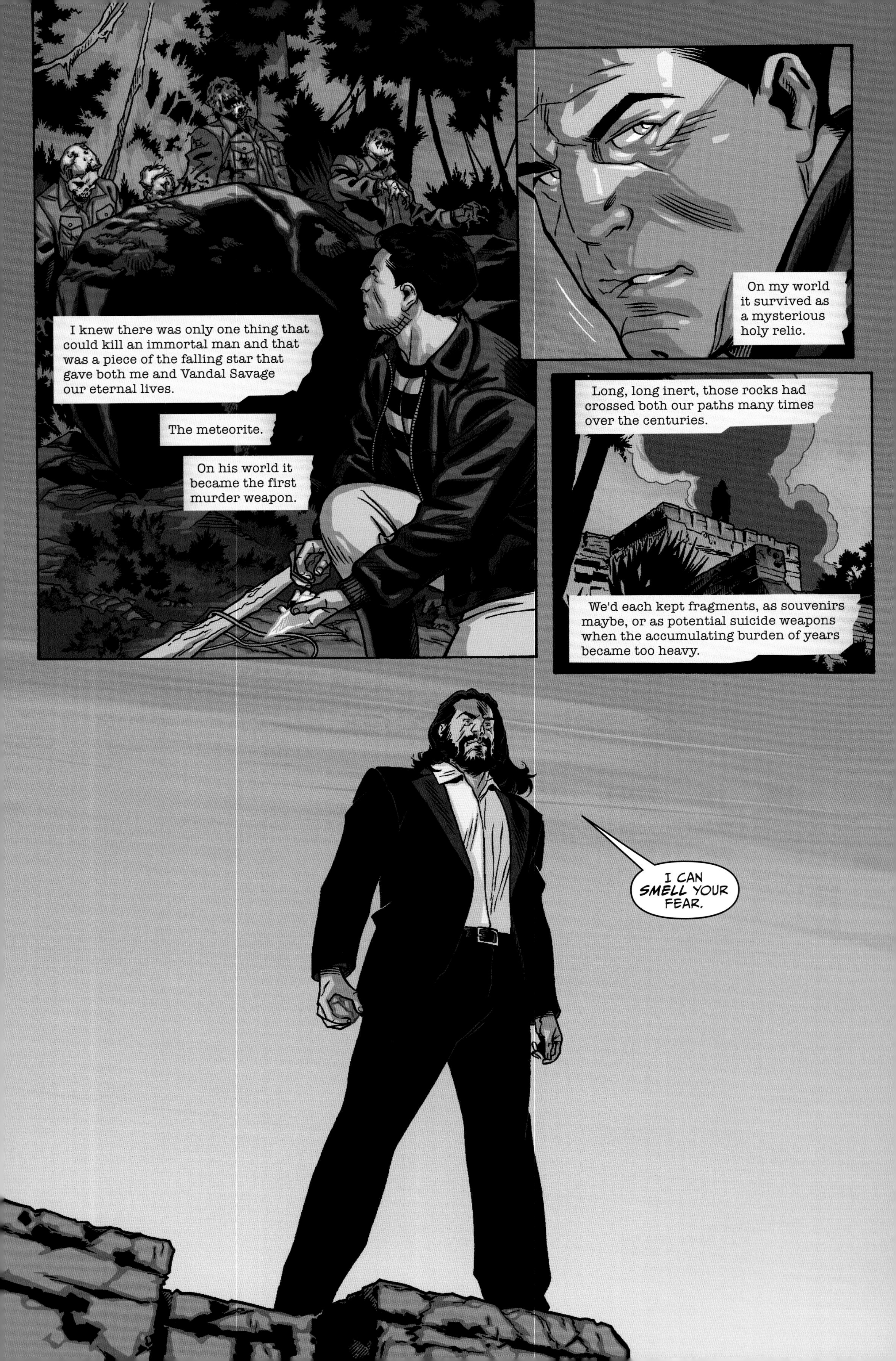
I knew there was only one thing that could kill an immortal man and that was a piece of the falling star that gave both me and Vandal Savage our eternal lives.
The meteorite.
On his world it became the first murder weapon.
On my world it survived as a mysterious holy relic.
Long, long inert, those rocks had crossed both our paths many times over the centuries.
We'd each kept fragments, as souvenirs maybe, or as potential suicide weapons when the accumulating burden of years became too heavy.
I CAN SMELL YOUR FEAR.

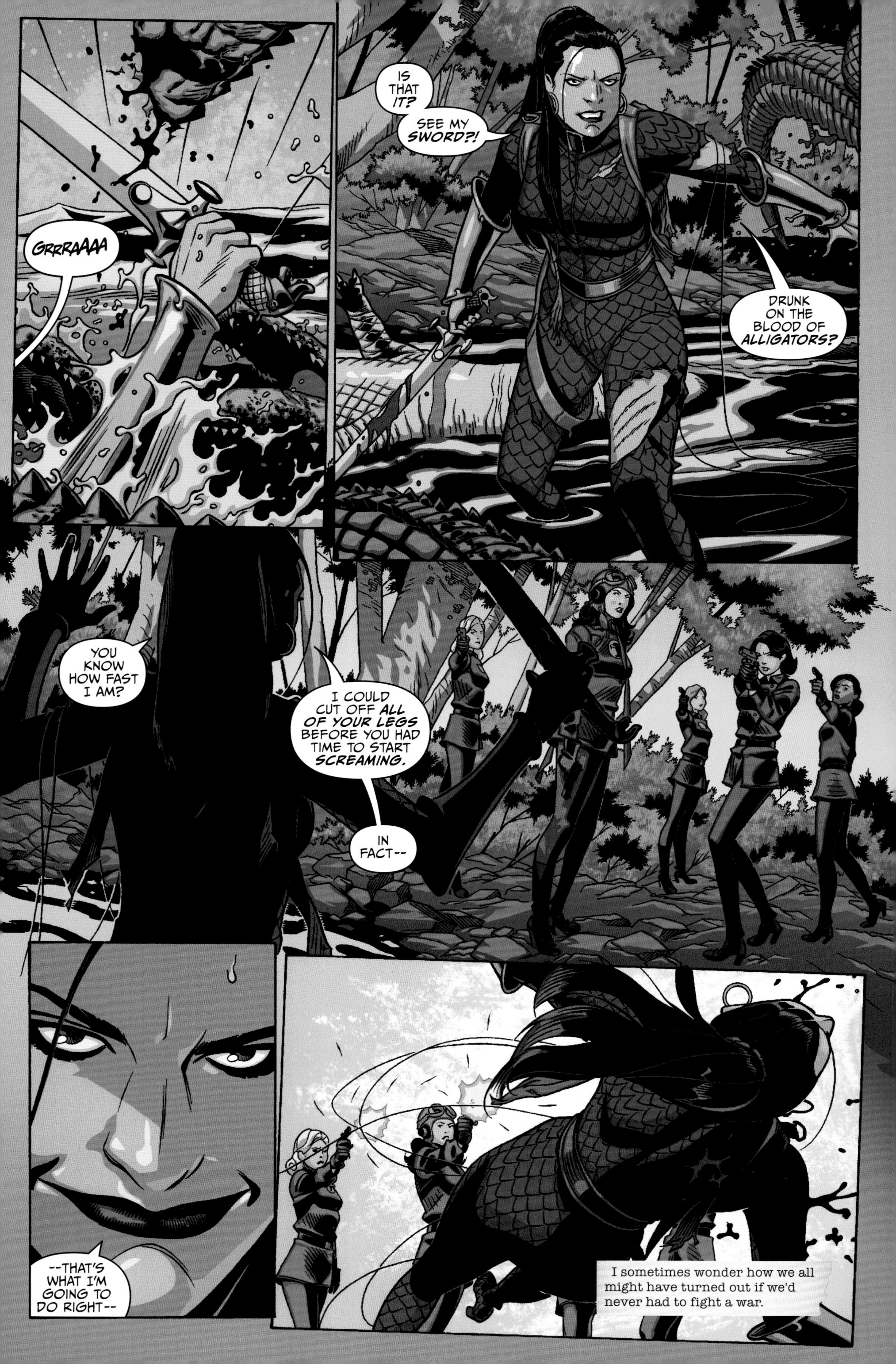
GRRRAAAA
IS THAT IT?
SEE MY SWORD?!
DRUNK ON THE BLOOD OF ALLIGATORS?
YOU KNOW HOW FAST I AM?
I COULD CUT OFF ALL OF YOUR LEGS BEFORE YOU HAD TIME TO START SCREAMING.
IN FACT--
--THAT'S WHAT I'M GOING TO DO RIGHT--
I sometimes wonder how we all might have turned out if we'd never had to fight a war.

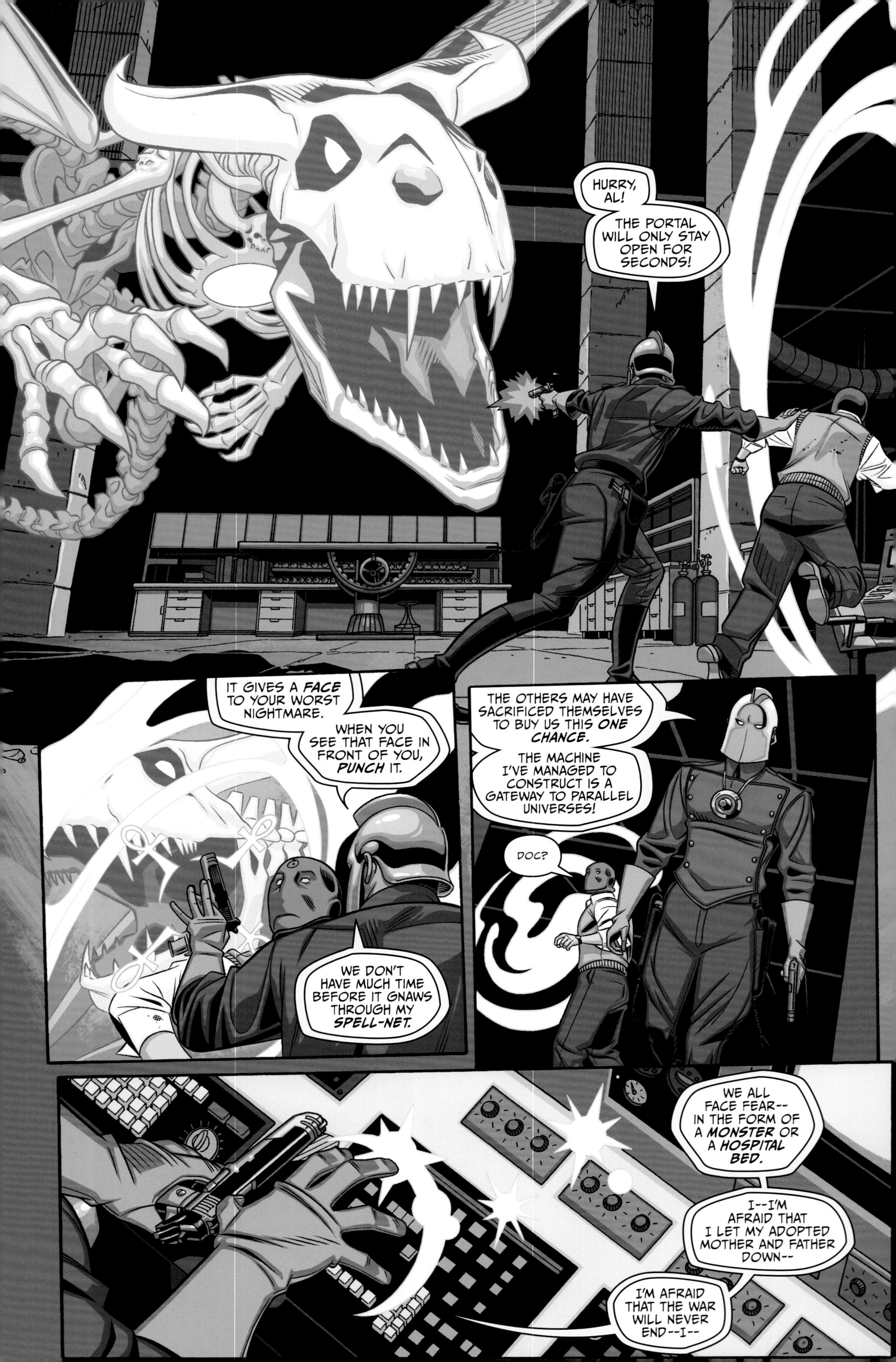
HURRY, AL!
THE PORTAL WILL ONLY STAY OPEN FOR SECONDS!
IT GIVES A FACE TO YOUR WORST NIGHTMARE.
WHEN YOU SEE THAT FACE IN FRONT OF YOU, PUNCH IT.
WE DON'T HAVE MUCH TIME BEFORE IT GNAWS THROUGH MY SPELL-NET.
THE OTHERS MAY HAVE SACRIFICED THEMSELVES TO BUY US THIS ONE CHANCE.
THE MACHINE I'VE MANAGED TO CONSTRUCT IS A GATEWAY TO PARALLEL UNIVERSES!
DOC?
WE ALL FACE FEAR-- IN THE FORM OF A MONSTER OR A HOSPITAL BED.
I--I'M AFRAID THAT I LET MY ADOPTED MOTHER AND FATHER DOWN--
I'M AFRAID THAT THE WAR WILL NEVER END--I--

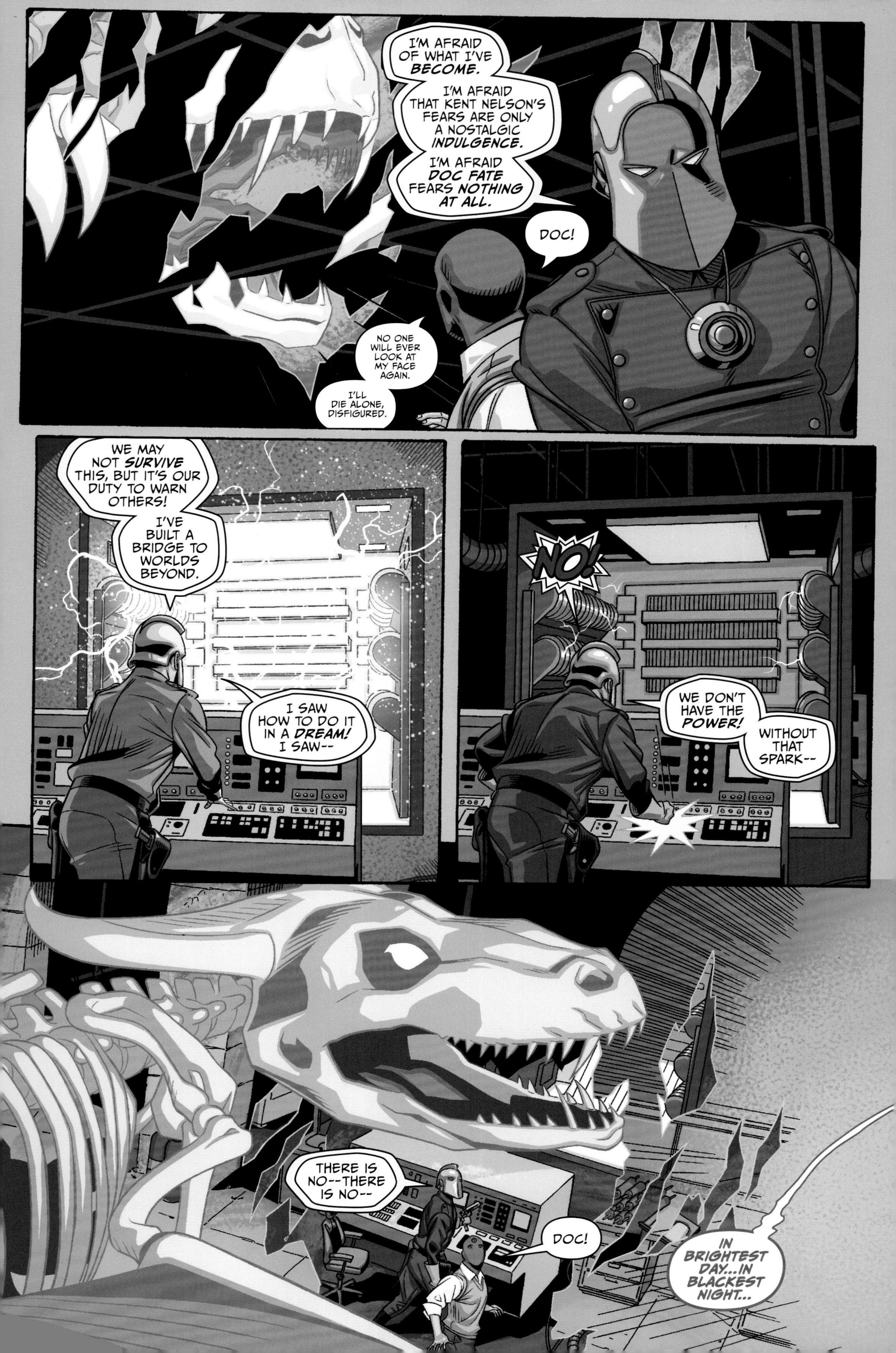
I'M AFRAID OF WHAT I'VE BECOME.
I'M AFRAID THAT KENT NELSON'S FEARS ARE ONLY A NOSTALGIC INDULGENCE.
I'M AFRAID DOC FATE FEARS NOTHING AT ALL.
DOC!
NO ONE WILL EVER LOOK AT MY FACE AGAIN.
I'LL DIE ALONE, DISFIGURED.
WE MAY NOT SURVIVE THIS, BUT IT'S OUR DUTY TO WARN OTHERS!
I'VE BUILT A BRIDGE TO WORLDS BEYOND.
I SAW HOW TO DO IT IN A DREAM! I SAW--
NO!
WE DON'T HAVE THE POWER!
WITHOUT THAT SPARK--
THERE IS NO--THERE IS NO--
DOC!
IN BRIGHTEST DAY...IN BLACKEST NIGHT...

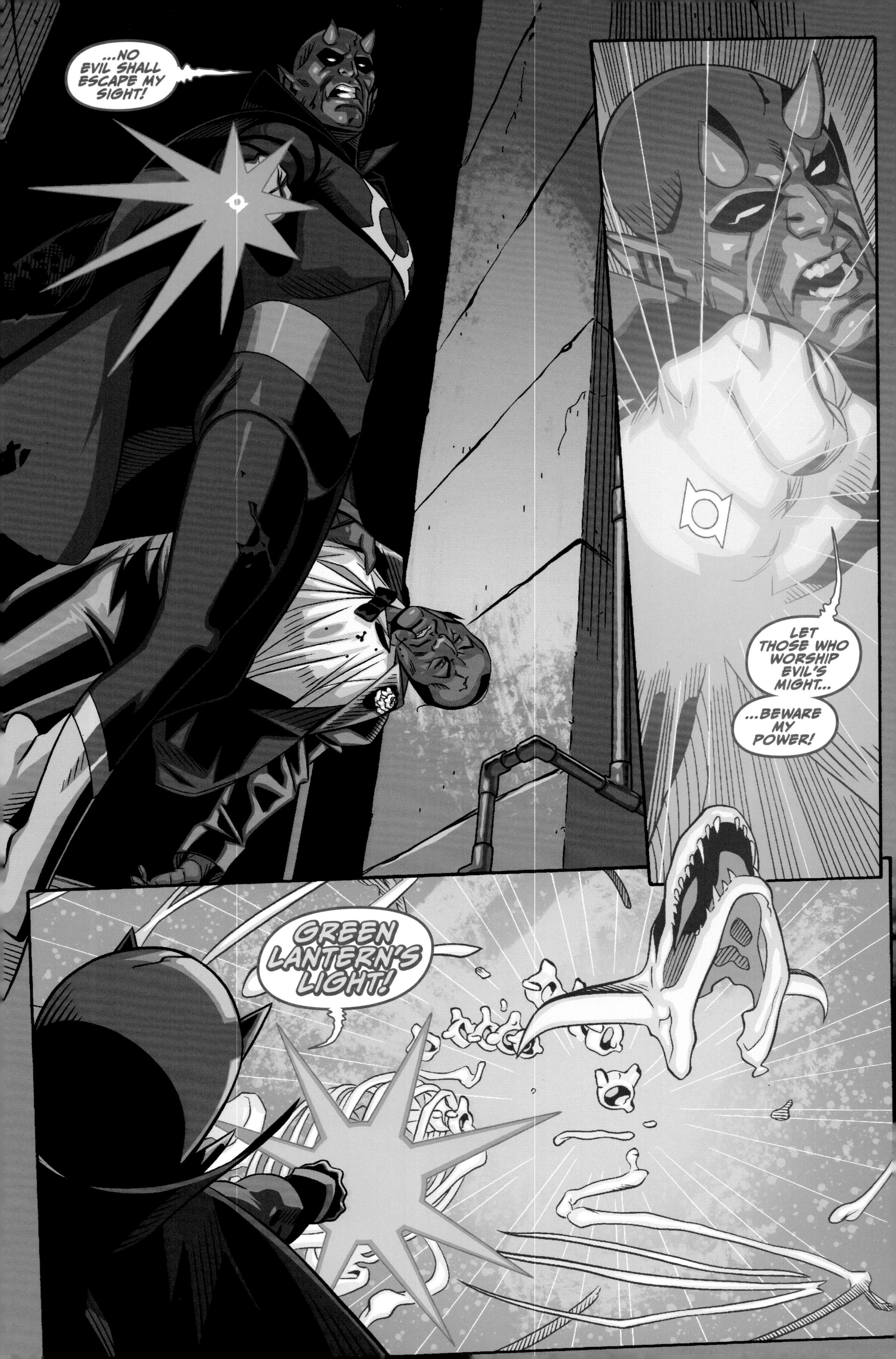
...NO EVIL SHALL ESCAPE MY SIGHT!
LET THOSE WHO WORSHIP EVIL'S MIGHT...
...BEWARE MY POWER!
GREEN LANTERN'S LIGHT!

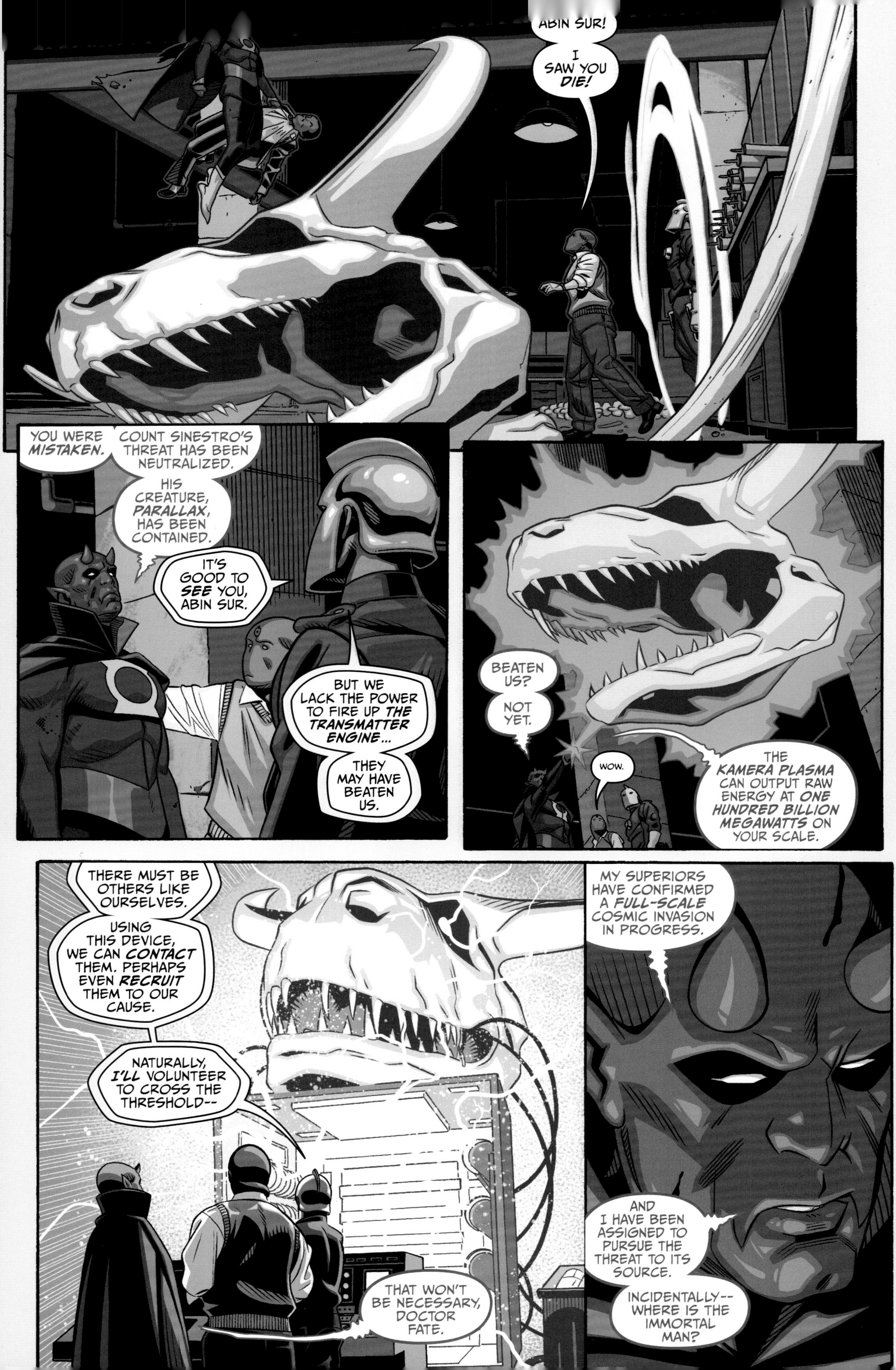
ABIN SUR!
I SAW YOU DIE!
YOU WERE MISTAKEN.
COUNT SINESTRO'S THREAT HAS BEEN NEUTRALIZED.
HIS CREATURE, PARALLAX, HAS BEEN CONTAINED.
IT'S GOOD TO SEE YOU, ABIN SUR.
BUT WE LACK THE POWER TO FIRE UP THE TRANSMATTER ENGINE...
THEY MAY HAVE BEATEN US.
BEATEN US?
NOT YET.
WOW.
THE KAMERA PLASMA CAN OUTPUT RAW ENERGY AT ONE HUNDRED BILLION MEGAWATTS ON YOUR SCALE.
THERE MUST BE OTHERS LIKE OURSELVES.
USING THIS DEVICE, WE CAN CONTACT THEM. PERHAPS EVEN RECRUIT THEM TO OUR CAUSE.
NATURALLY, I'LL VOLUNTEER TO CROSS THE THRESHOLD--
THAT WON'T BE NECESSARY, DOCTOR FATE.
MY SUPERIORS HAVE CONFIRMED A FULL-SCALE COSMIC INVASION IN PROGRESS.
AND I HAVE BEEN ASSIGNED TO PURSUE THE THREAT TO ITS SOURCE.
INCIDENTALLY-- WHERE IS THE IMMORTAL MAN?

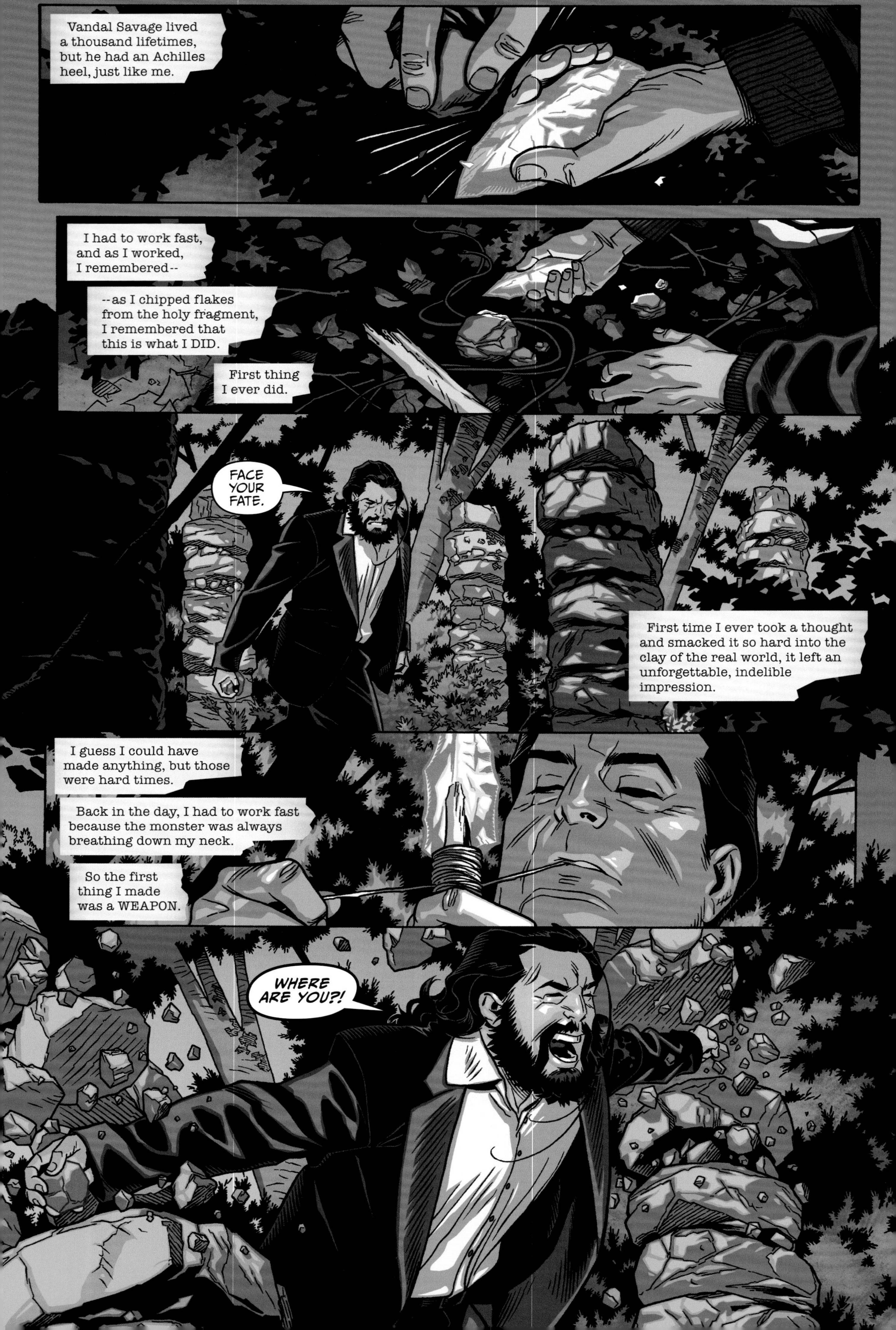
Vandal Savage lived a thousand lifetimes, but he had an Achilles heel, just like me.
I had to work fast, and as I worked, I remembered--
--as I chipped flakes from the holy fragment, I remembered that this is what I DID.
First thing I ever did.
FACE YOUR FATE.
First time I ever took a thought and smacked it so hard into the clay of the real world, it left an unforgettable, indelible impression.
I guess I could have made anything, but those were hard times.
Back in the day, I had to work fast because the monster was always breathing down my neck.
So the first thing I made was a WEAPON.
WHERE ARE YOU?!

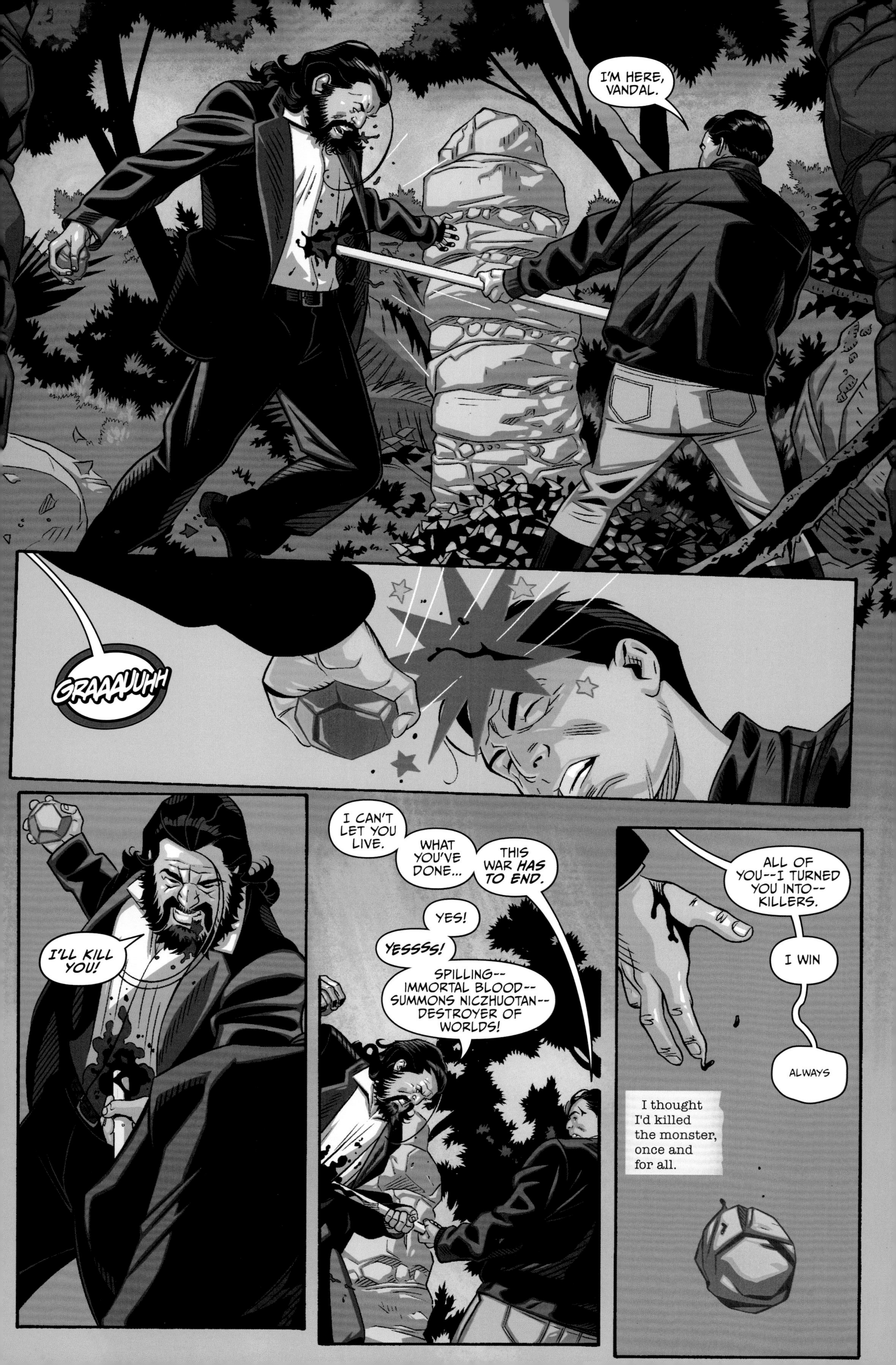
I'M HERE, VANDAL.
GRAAAUUHH
I'LL KILL YOU!
I CAN'T LET YOU LIVE.
WHAT YOU'VE DONE...
THIS WAR HAS TO END.
YES!
YESSSS!
SPILLING-- IMMORTAL BLOOD-- SUMMONS NICZHUOTAN-- DESTROYER OF WORLDS!
ALL OF YOU--I TURNED YOU INTO-- KILLERS.
I WIN
ALWAYS
I thought I'd killed the monster, once and for all.

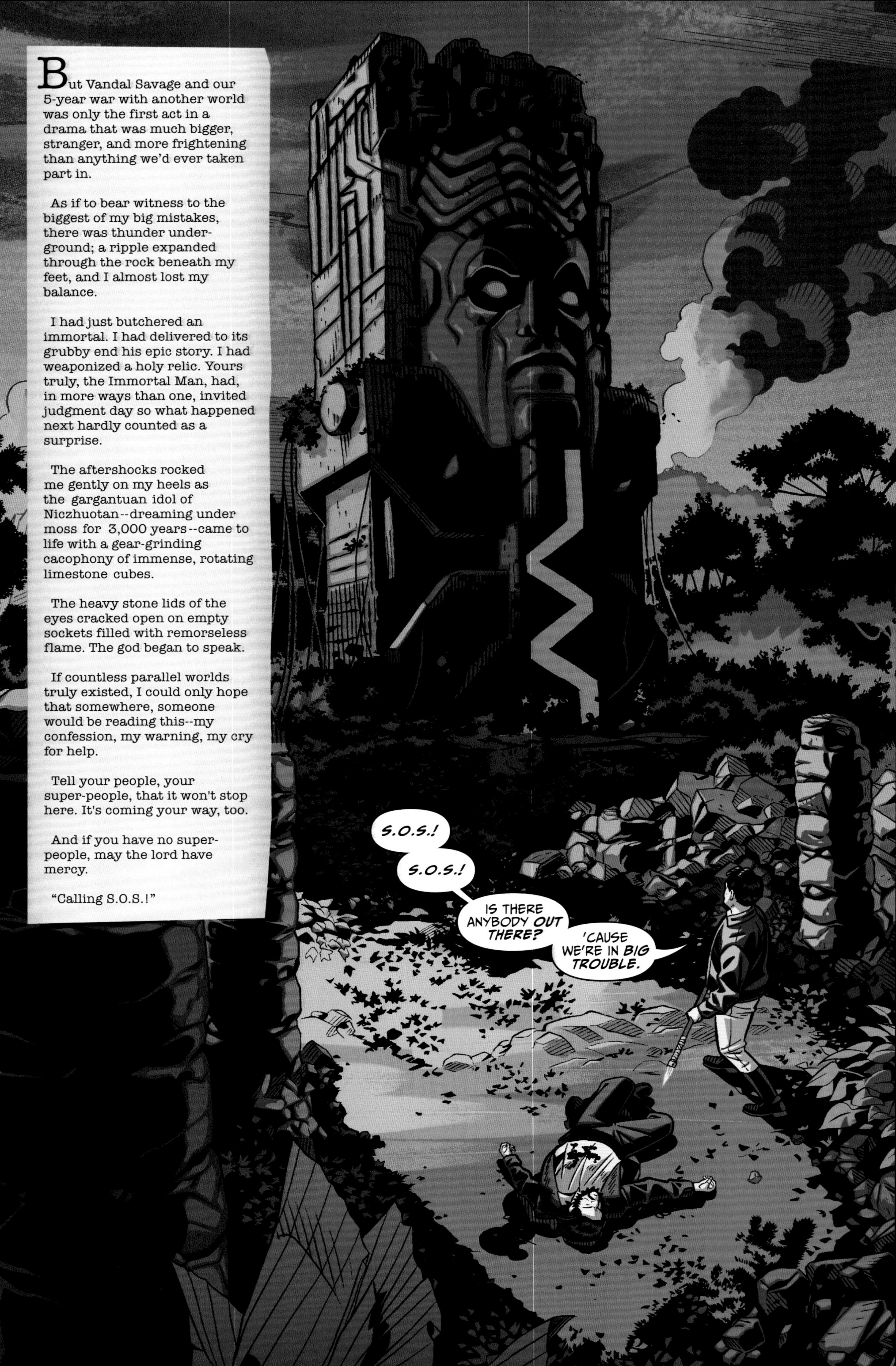
But Vandal Savage and our 5-year war with another world was only the first act in a drama that was much bigger, stranger, and more frightening than anything we'd ever taken part in.
As if to bear witness to the biggest of my big mistakes, there was thunder underground; a ripple expanded through the rock beneath my feet, and I almost lost my balance.
I had just butchered an immortal. I had delivered to its grubby end his epic story. I had weaponized a holy relic. Yours truly, the Immortal Man, had, in more ways than one, invited judgment day so what happened next hardly counted as a surprise.
The aftershocks rocked me gently on my heels as the gargantuan idol of Niczhuotan--dreaming under moss for 3,000 years--came to life with a gear-grinding cacophony of immense, rotating limestone cubes.
The heavy stone lids of the eyes cracked open on empty sockets filled with remorseless flame. The god began to speak.
If countless parallel worlds truly existed, I could only hope that somewhere, someone would be reading this--my confession, my warning, my cry for help.
Tell your people, your super-people, that it won't stop here. It's coming your way, too.
And if you have no super-people, may the lord have mercy.
"Calling S.O.S.!"
S.O.S.!
S.O.S.!
IS THERE ANYBODY OUT THERE?
'CAUSE WE'RE IN BIG TROUBLE.

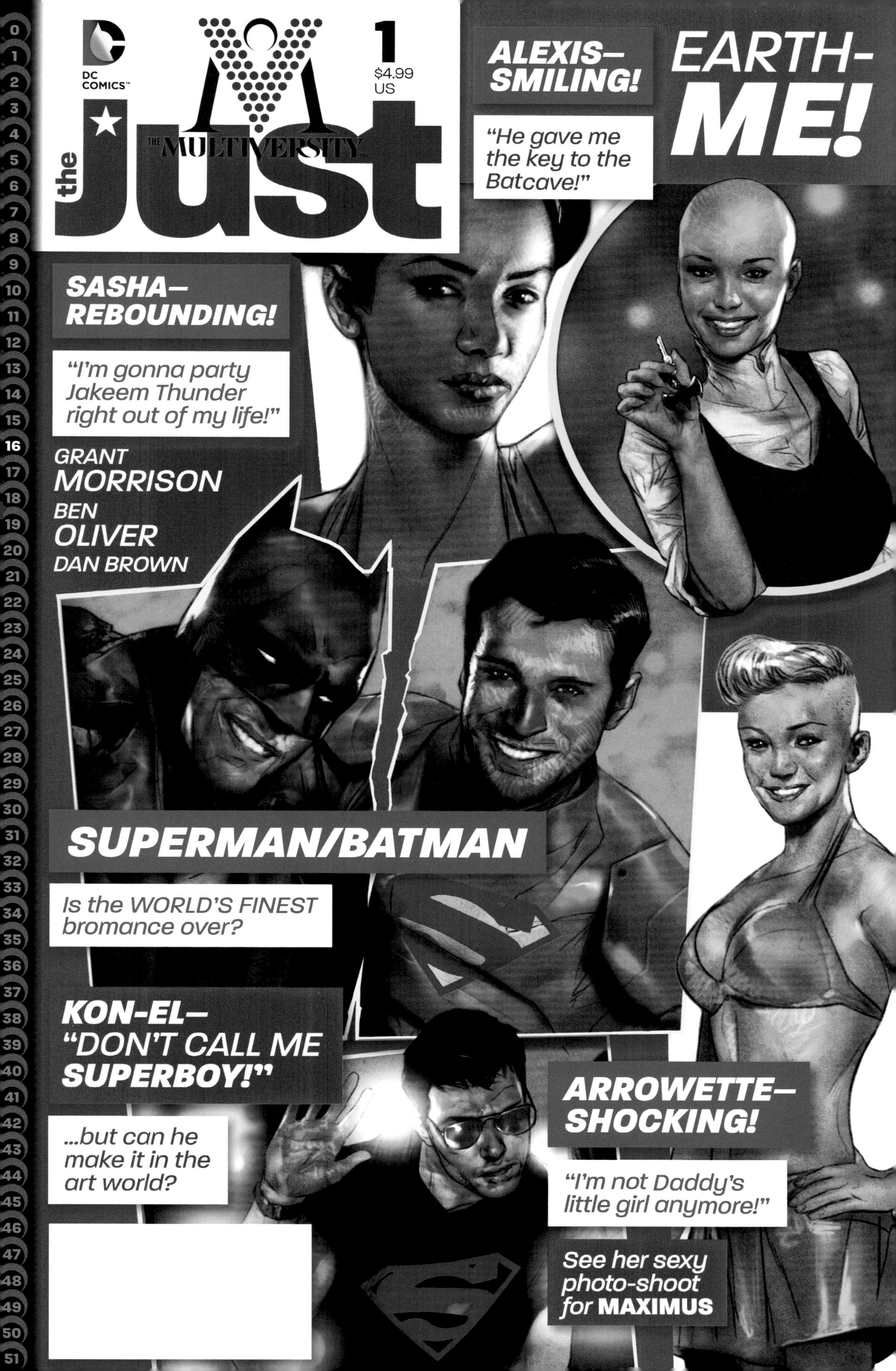
DC COMICS
1
$4.99
US
THE MULTIVERSITY
the Just
ALEXIS–
SMILING!
"He gave me
the key to the
Batcave!"
EARTH-
ME!
SASHA–
REBOUNDING!
"I'm gonna party
Jakeem Thunder
right out of my life!"
GRANT
MORRISON
BEN
OLIVER
DAN BROWN
SUPERMAN/BATMAN
Is the WORLD'S FINEST
bromance over?
KON-EL–
"DON'T CALL ME
SUPERBOY!"
...but can he
make it in the
art world?
ARROWETTE–
SHOCKING!
"I'm not Daddy's
little girl anymore!"
See her sexy
photo-shoot
for MAXIMUS

THE MULTIVERSITY: THE JUST
#1

Written by
GRANT MORRISON

Artist
BEN OLIVER

Colorists
BEN OLIVER
DAN BROWN

Letterer
CLEM ROBINS

Cover artist
BEN OLIVER

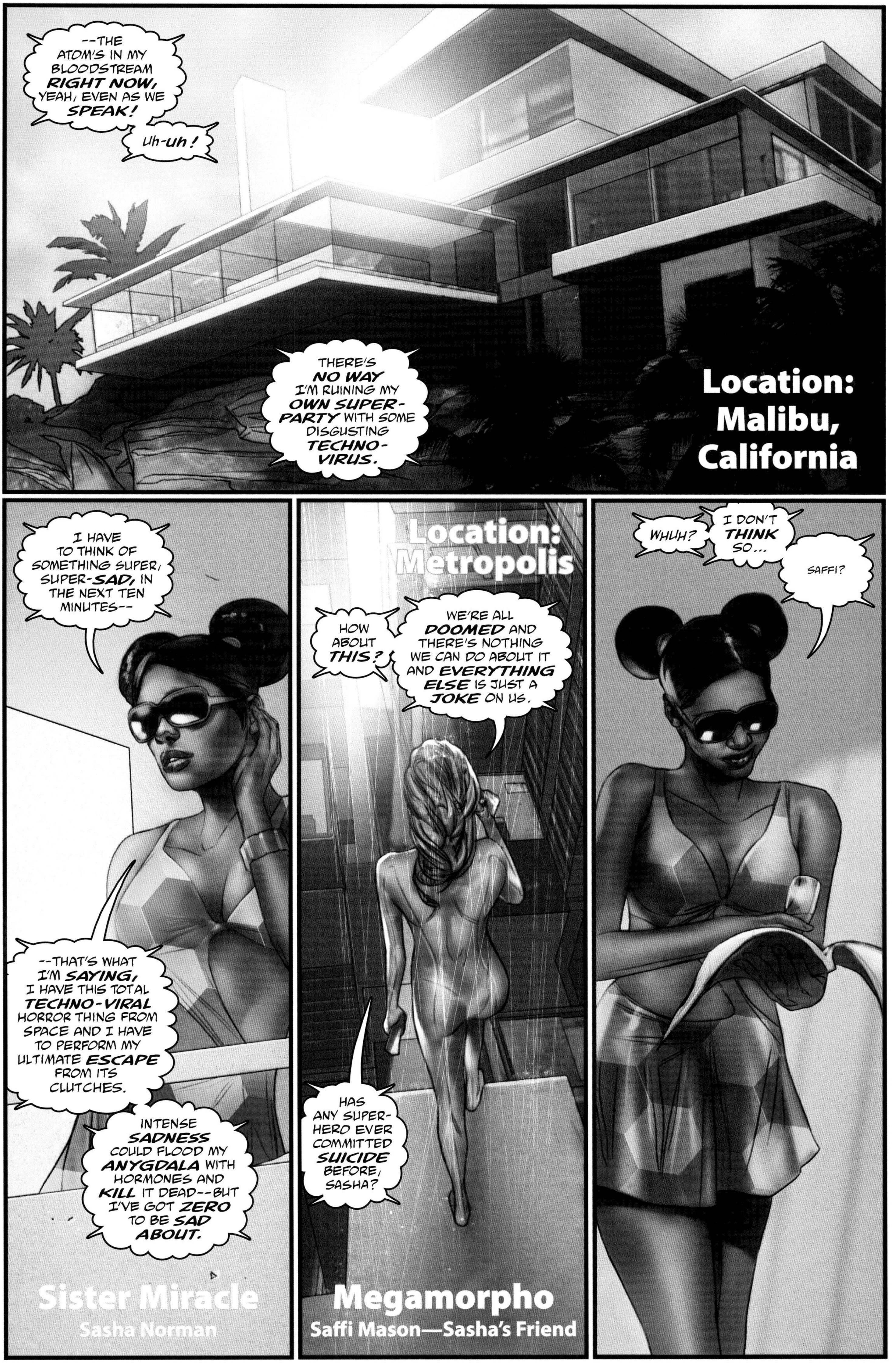
--THE ATOM'S IN MY BLOODSTREAM RIGHT NOW, YEAH, EVEN AS WE SPEAK!
Uh-uh!
THERE'S NO WAY I'M RUINING MY OWN SUPER-PARTY WITH SOME DISGUSTING TECHNO-VIRUS.
Location: Malibu, California
I HAVE TO THINK OF SOMETHING SUPER, SUPER-SAD, IN THE NEXT TEN MINUTES--
--THAT'S WHAT I'M SAYING, I HAVE THIS TOTAL TECHNO-VIRAL HORROR THING FROM SPACE AND I HAVE TO PERFORM MY ULTIMATE ESCAPE FROM ITS CLUTCHES.
INTENSE SADNESS COULD FLOOD MY ANYGDALA WITH HORMONES AND KILL IT DEAD--BUT I'VE GOT ZERO TO BE SAD ABOUT.
Sister Miracle
Sasha Norman
Location: Metropolis
HOW ABOUT THIS?
WE'RE ALL DOOMED AND THERE'S NOTHING WE CAN DO ABOUT IT AND EVERYTHING ELSE IS JUST A JOKE ON US.
HAS ANY SUPER-HERO EVER COMMITTED SUICIDE BEFORE, SASHA?
Megamorpho
Saffi Mason—Sasha's Friend
WHUH?
I DON'T THINK SO...
SAFFI?

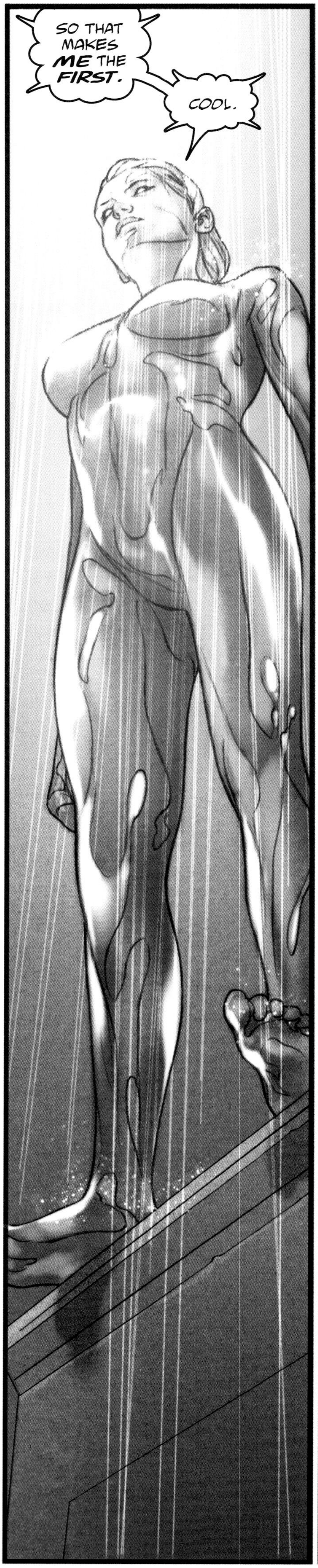
SO THAT MAKES **ME** THE **FIRST.**
COOL.

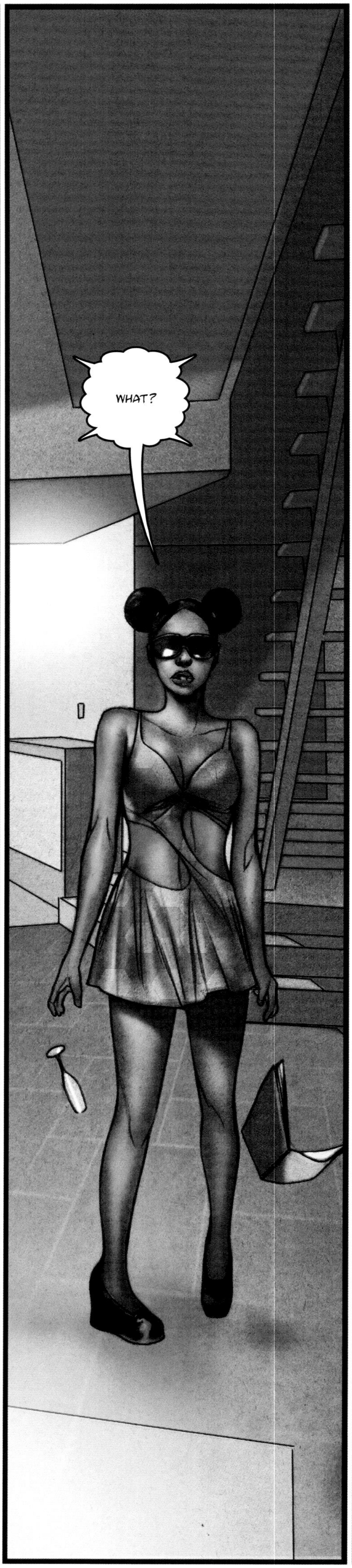
WHAT?

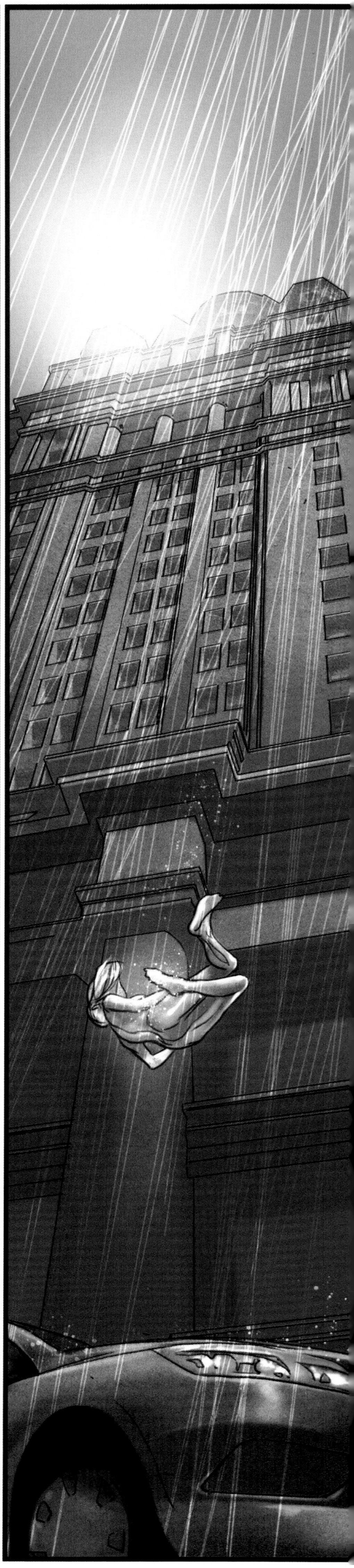

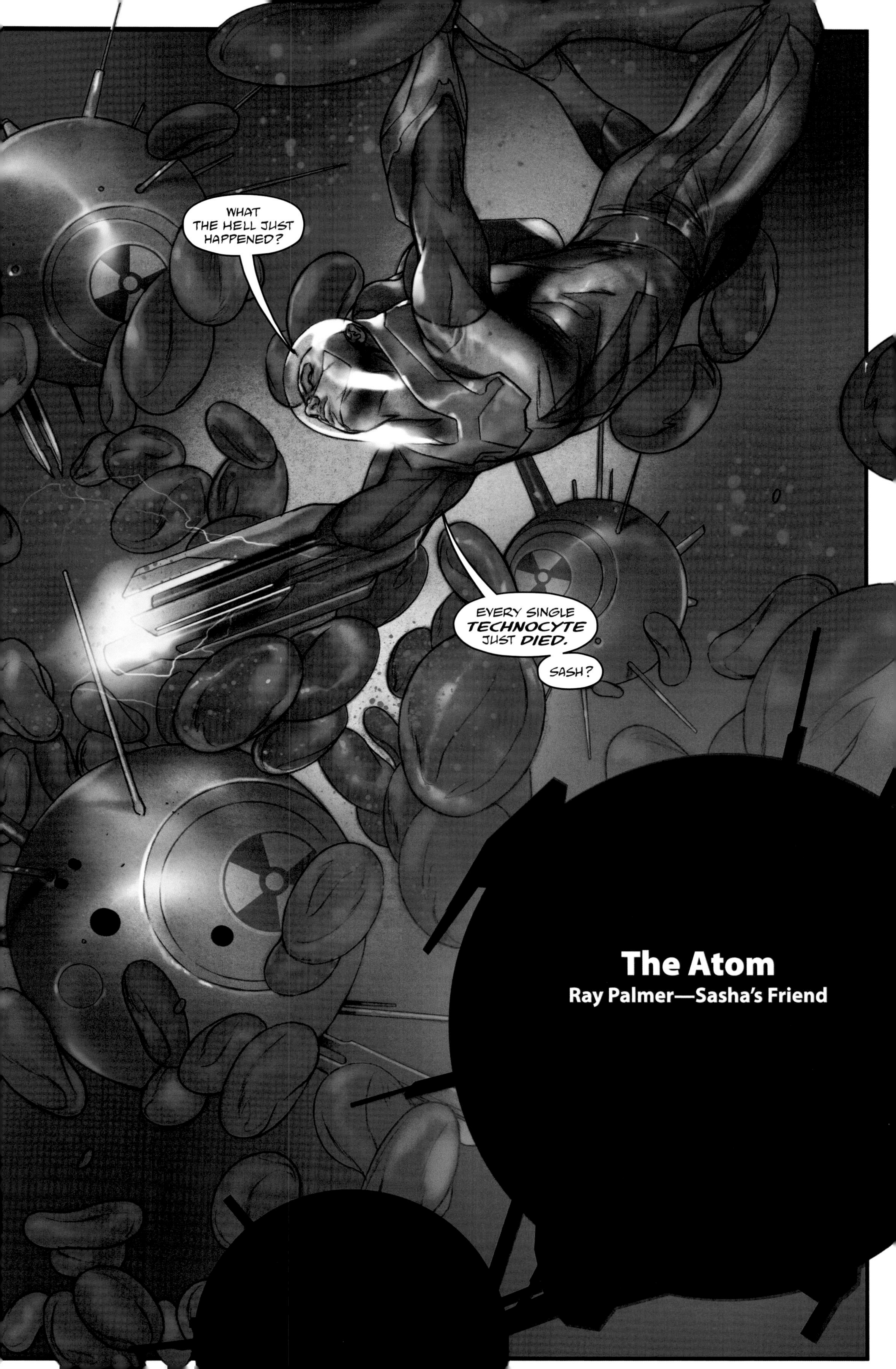
WHAT THE HELL JUST HAPPENED?
EVERY SINGLE TECHNOCYTE JUST DIED.
SASH?

The Atom
Ray Palmer—Sasha's Friend

WHAT'S *YOUR* TAKE ON THE WHOLE *COMIC BOOKS MMM-MIGHT BE ART* THING, DAMIAN?

Location: Gotham City

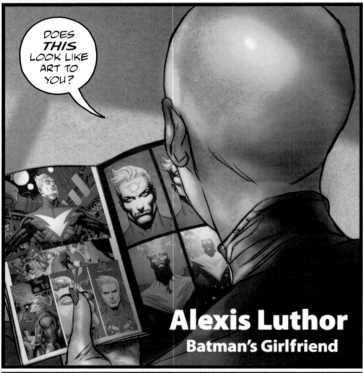

DOES *THIS* LOOK LIKE ART TO YOU?

Alexis Luthor
Batman's Girlfriend

WHAT ARE YOU *TALKING* ABOUT?

WHAT TAKE?

I DON'T *HAVE* A TAKE.

Batman
Damian Wayne

I'M *THE BATMAN.*

YOU SHOULD *SEE* THIS.

I SAW IT ONLINE.

THEY'RE FROM *ANOTHER* BORING *UNIVERSE* AND THEY'VE DECIDED TO--> YAWN <--

--TO INVADE REALITY ET CETERA ET CETERA ET CETERA...

MEANWHILE, I'M RIGHT HERE AND YOU'RE DELIBERATELY IGNORING MY OBVIOUS PHYSICAL AND INTELLECTUAL CHARMS.

IS BATMAN *GAY*?

TWO THOUSAND WORDS BY WEDNESDAY, STUDENTS.

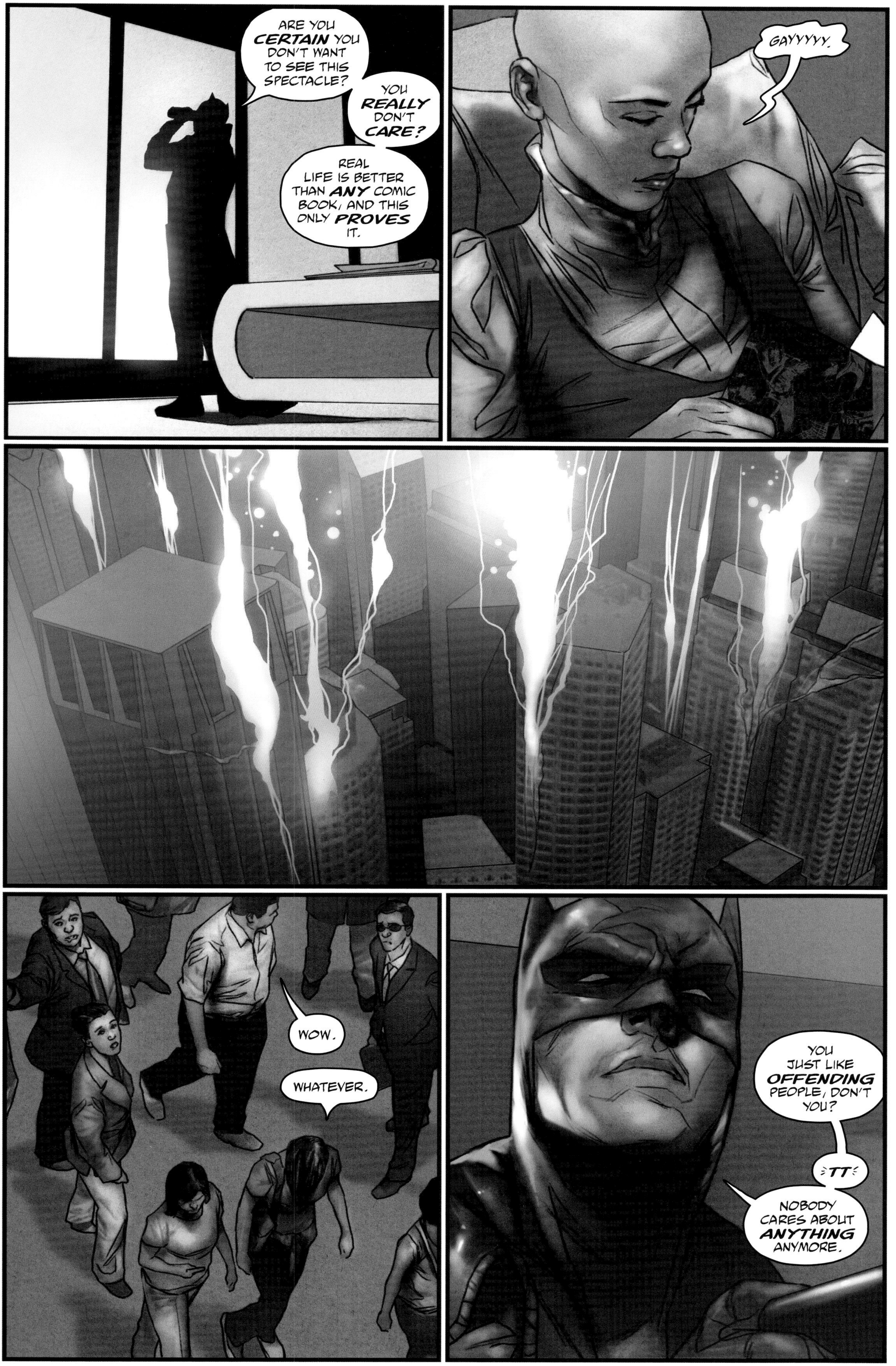
ARE YOU CERTAIN YOU DON'T WANT TO SEE THIS SPECTACLE?
YOU REALLY DON'T CARE?
REAL LIFE IS BETTER THAN ANY COMIC BOOK, AND THIS ONLY PROVES IT.
GAYYYYY.
WOW.
WHATEVER.
YOU JUST LIKE OFFENDING PEOPLE, DON'T YOU?
TT
NOBODY CARES ABOUT ANYTHING ANYMORE.

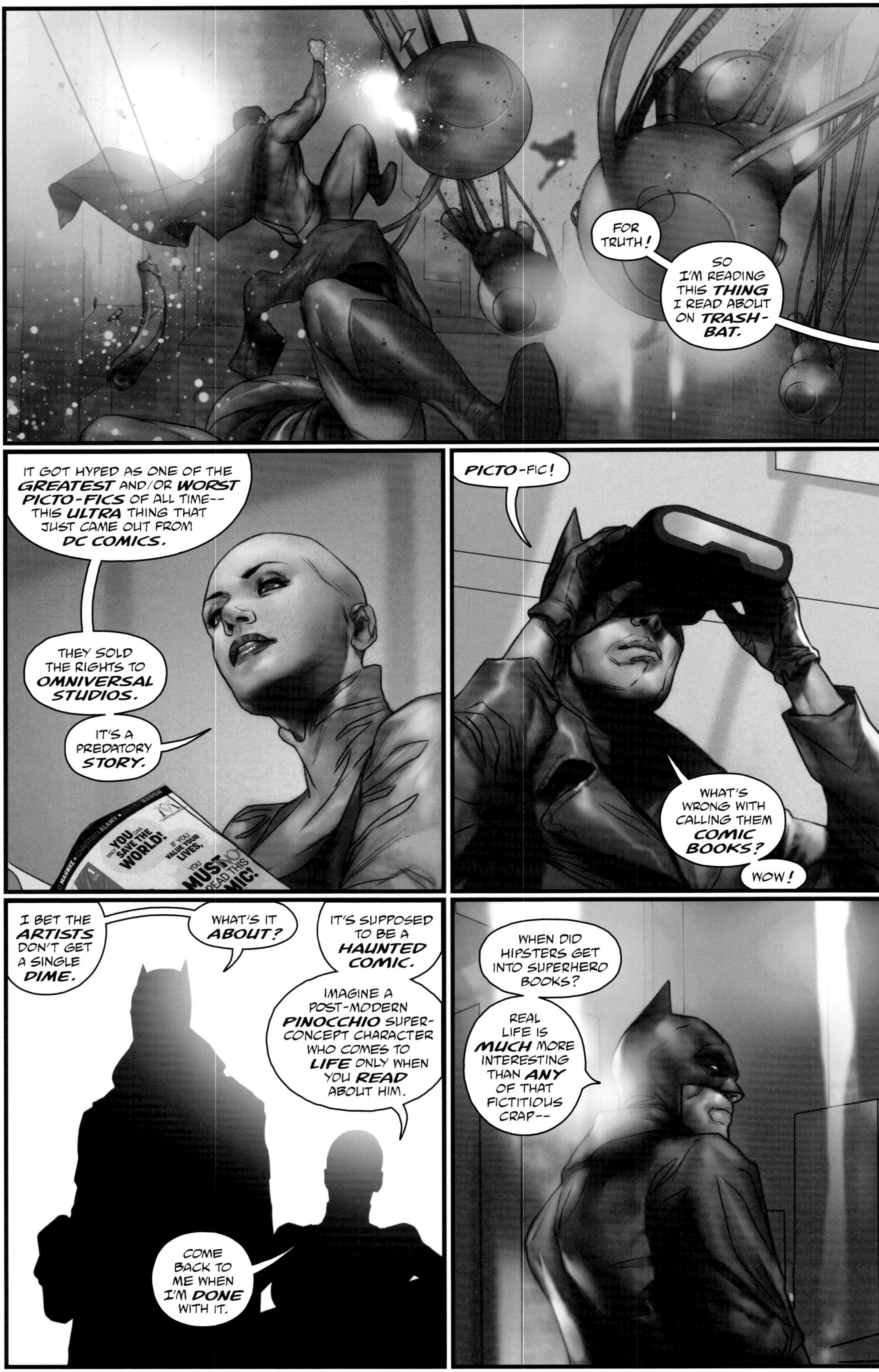
FOR TRUTH!
SO I'M READING THIS THING I READ ABOUT ON TRASH-BAT.
IT GOT HYPED AS ONE OF THE GREATEST AND/OR WORST PICTO-FICS OF ALL TIME-- THIS ULTRA THING THAT JUST CAME OUT FROM DC COMICS.
THEY SOLD THE RIGHTS TO OMNIVERSAL STUDIOS.
IT'S A PREDATORY STORY.
PICTO-FIC!
WHAT'S WRONG WITH CALLING THEM COMIC BOOKS?
WOW!
I BET THE ARTISTS DON'T GET A SINGLE DIME.
WHAT'S IT ABOUT?
IT'S SUPPOSED TO BE A HAUNTED COMIC.
IMAGINE A POST-MODERN PINOCCHIO SUPER-CONCEPT CHARACTER WHO COMES TO LIFE ONLY WHEN YOU READ ABOUT HIM.
COME BACK TO ME WHEN I'M DONE WITH IT.
WHEN DID HIPSTERS GET INTO SUPERHERO BOOKS?
REAL LIFE IS MUCH MORE INTERESTING THAN ANY OF THAT FICTITIOUS CRAP--

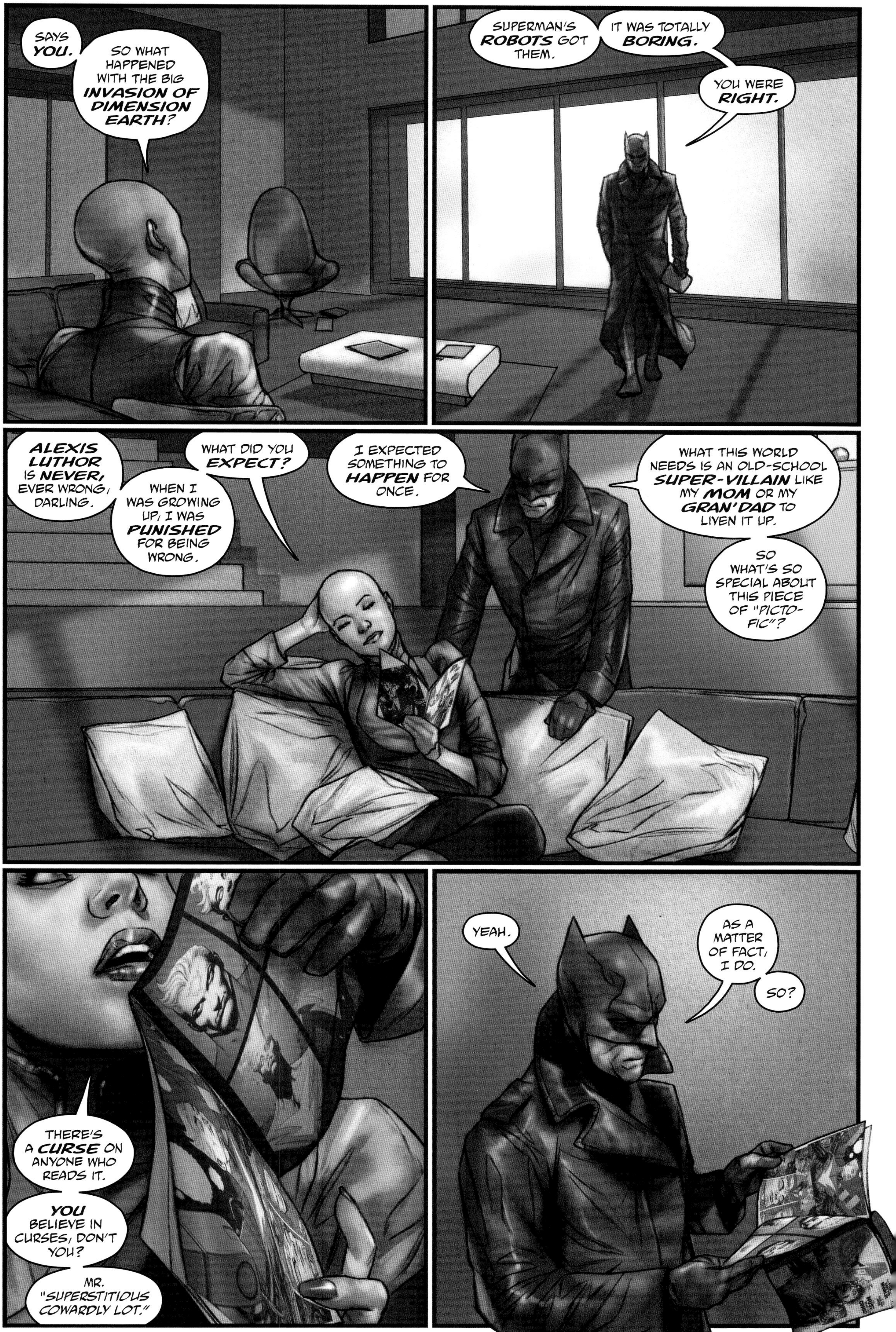
SAYS YOU.
SO WHAT HAPPENED WITH THE BIG INVASION OF DIMENSION EARTH?
SUPERMAN'S ROBOTS GOT THEM.
IT WAS TOTALLY BORING.
YOU WERE RIGHT.
ALEXIS LUTHOR IS NEVER, EVER WRONG, DARLING.
WHAT DID YOU EXPECT?
WHEN I WAS GROWING UP, I WAS PUNISHED FOR BEING WRONG.
I EXPECTED SOMETHING TO HAPPEN FOR ONCE.
WHAT THIS WORLD NEEDS IS AN OLD-SCHOOL SUPER-VILLAIN LIKE MY MOM OR MY GRAN'DAD TO LIVEN IT UP.
SO WHAT'S SO SPECIAL ABOUT THIS PIECE OF "PICTO-FIC"?
THERE'S A CURSE ON ANYONE WHO READS IT.
YOU BELIEVE IN CURSES, DON'T YOU?
MR. "SUPERSTITIOUS COWARDLY LOT."
YEAH.
AS A MATTER OF FACT, I DO.
SO?

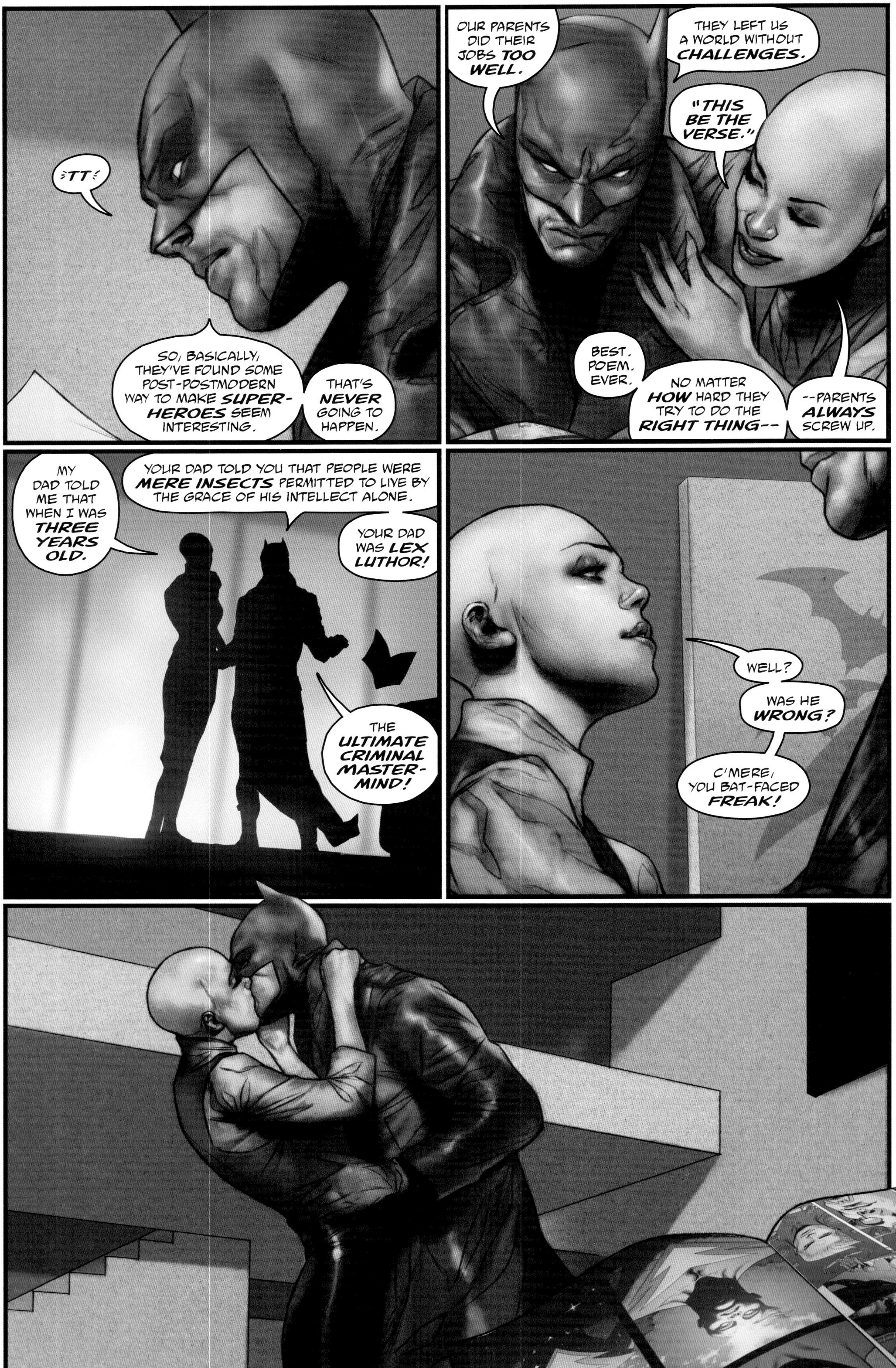

TT
SO, BASICALLY, THEY'VE FOUND SOME POST-POSTMODERN WAY TO MAKE SUPER-HEROES SEEM INTERESTING.
THAT'S NEVER GOING TO HAPPEN.
OUR PARENTS DID THEIR JOBS TOO WELL.
THEY LEFT US A WORLD WITHOUT CHALLENGES.
"THIS BE THE VERSE."
BEST. POEM. EVER.
NO MATTER HOW HARD THEY TRY TO DO THE RIGHT THING--
--PARENTS ALWAYS SCREW UP.
MY DAD TOLD ME THAT WHEN I WAS THREE YEARS OLD.
YOUR DAD TOLD YOU THAT PEOPLE WERE MERE INSECTS PERMITTED TO LIVE BY THE GRACE OF HIS INTELLECT ALONE.
YOUR DAD WAS LEX LUTHOR!
THE ULTIMATE CRIMINAL MASTER-MIND!
WELL?
WAS HE WRONG?
C'MERE, YOU BAT-FACED FREAK!

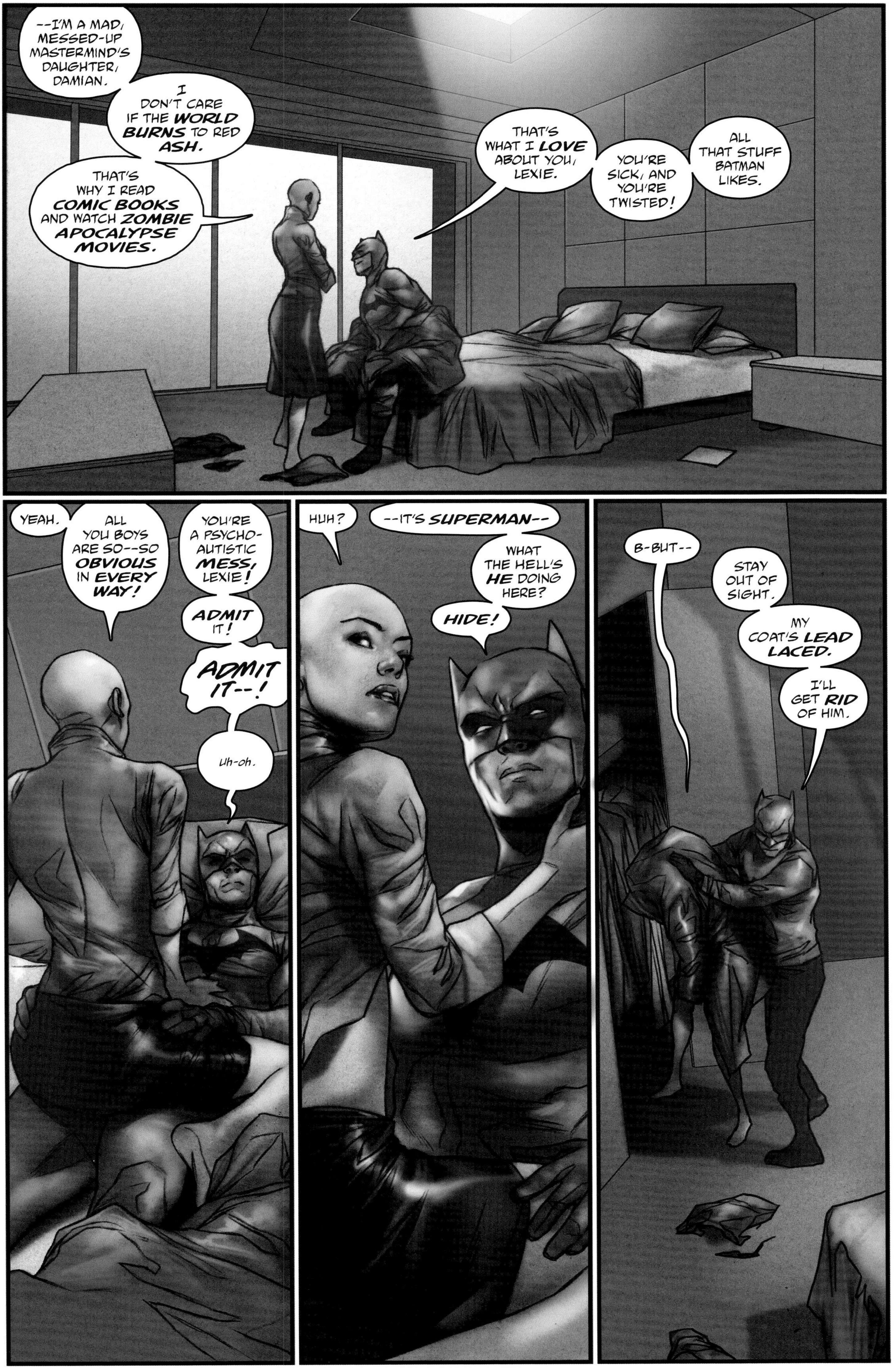
--I'M A MAD, MESSED-UP MASTERMIND'S DAUGHTER, DAMIAN.
I DON'T CARE IF THE WORLD BURNS TO RED ASH.
THAT'S WHY I READ COMIC BOOKS AND WATCH ZOMBIE APOCALYPSE MOVIES.
THAT'S WHAT I LOVE ABOUT YOU, LEXIE.
YOU'RE SICK, AND YOU'RE TWISTED!
ALL THAT STUFF BATMAN LIKES.
YEAH.
ALL YOU BOYS ARE SO--SO OBVIOUS IN EVERY WAY!
YOU'RE A PSYCHO-AUTISTIC MESS, LEXIE!
ADMIT IT!
ADMIT IT--!
uh-oh.
HUH?
--IT'S SUPERMAN--
WHAT THE HELL'S HE DOING HERE?
HIDE!
B-BUT--
STAY OUT OF SIGHT.
MY COAT'S LEAD LACED.
I'LL GET RID OF HIM.

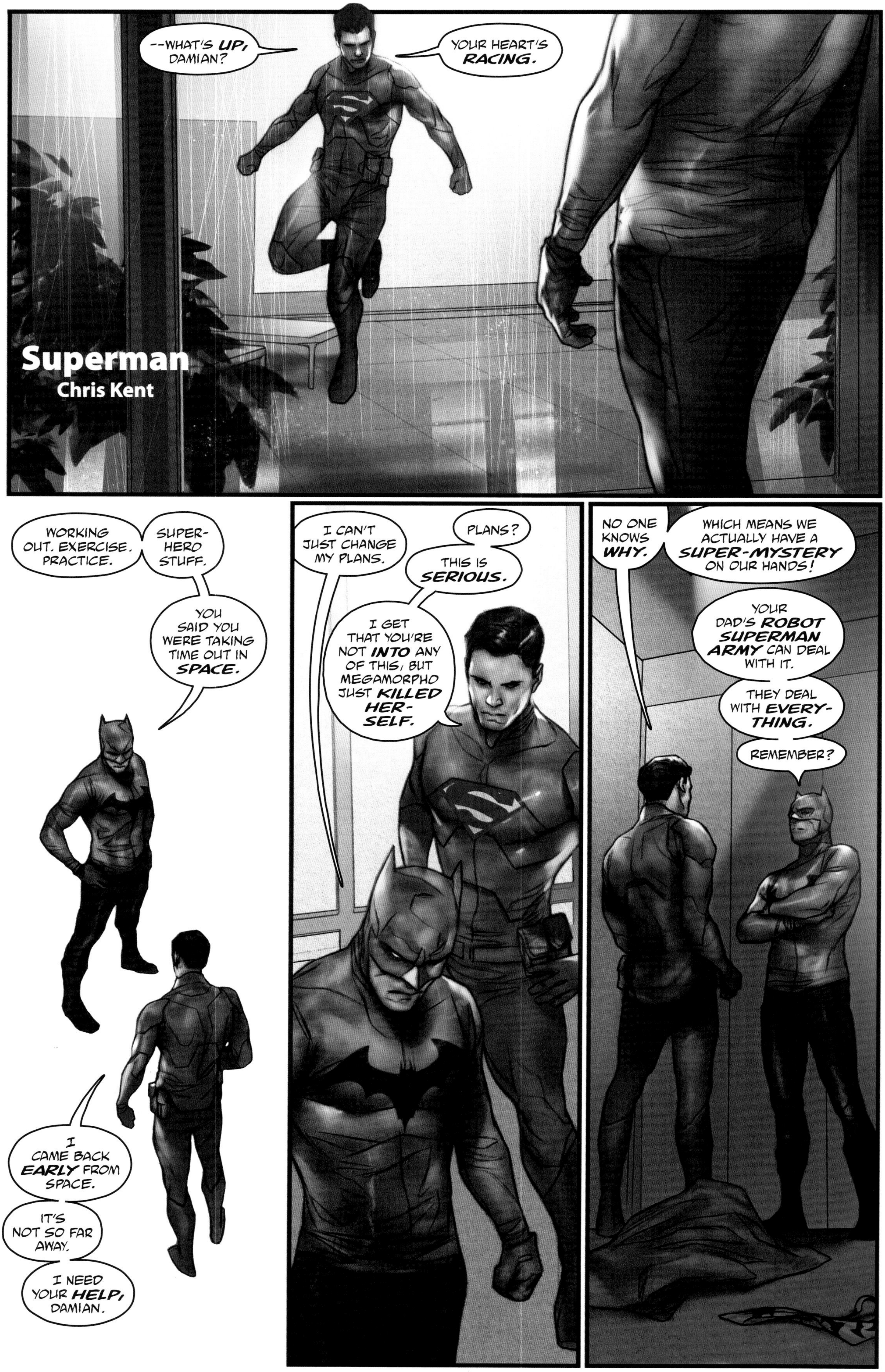
--WHAT'S UP, DAMIAN?
YOUR HEART'S RACING.
Superman
Chris Kent
WORKING OUT. EXERCISE. PRACTICE.
SUPER-HERO STUFF.
YOU SAID YOU WERE TAKING TIME OUT IN SPACE.
I CAME BACK EARLY FROM SPACE.
IT'S NOT SO FAR AWAY.
I NEED YOUR HELP, DAMIAN.
I CAN'T JUST CHANGE MY PLANS.
PLANS?
THIS IS SERIOUS.
I GET THAT YOU'RE NOT INTO ANY OF THIS, BUT MEGAMORPHO JUST KILLED HER-SELF.
NO ONE KNOWS WHY.
WHICH MEANS WE ACTUALLY HAVE A SUPER-MYSTERY ON OUR HANDS!
YOUR DAD'S ROBOT SUPERMAN ARMY CAN DEAL WITH IT.
THEY DEAL WITH EVERY-THING.
REMEMBER?

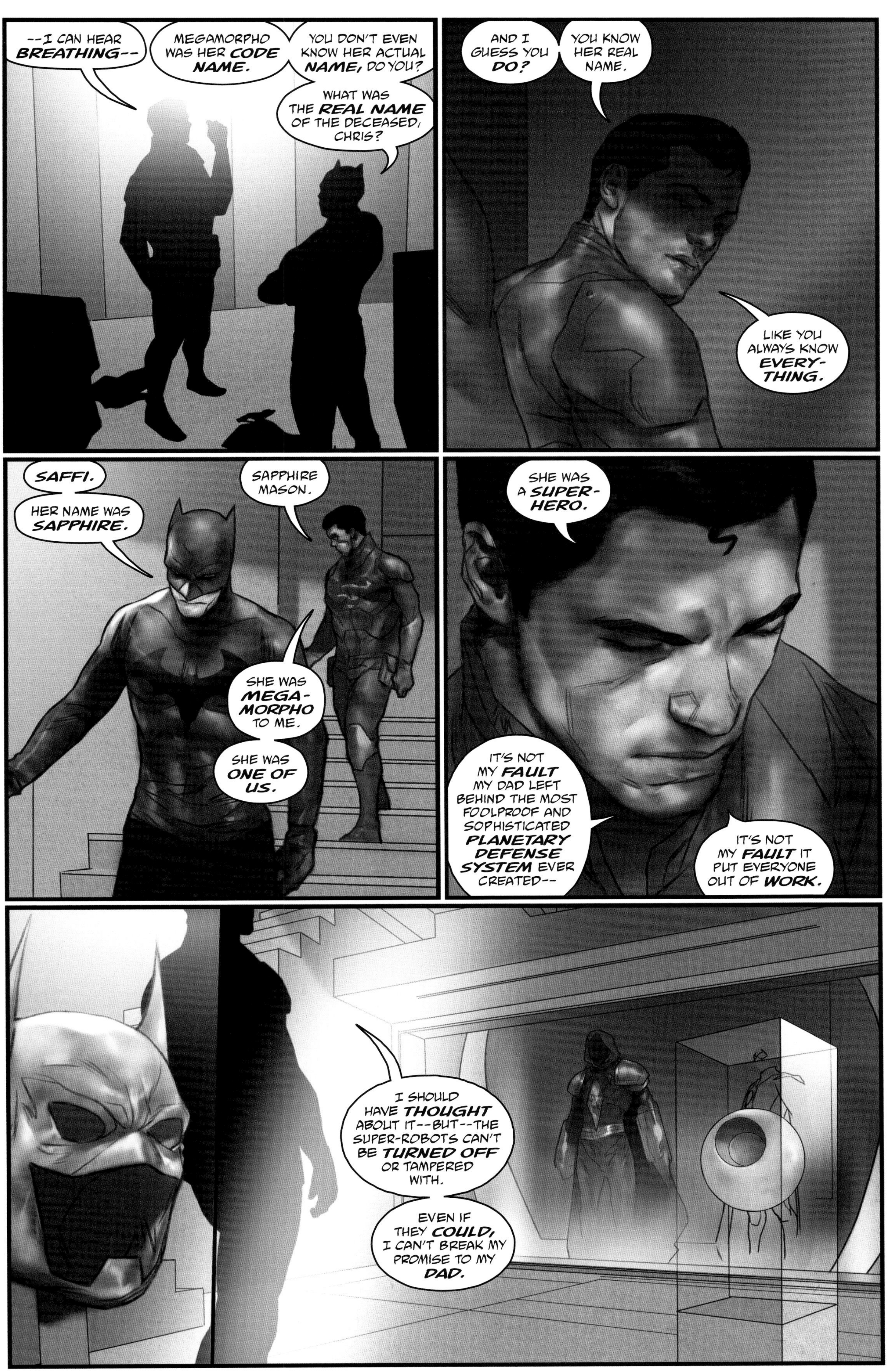
--I CAN HEAR BREATHING--
MEGAMORPHO WAS HER CODE NAME.
YOU DON'T EVEN KNOW HER ACTUAL NAME, DO YOU?
WHAT WAS THE REAL NAME OF THE DECEASED, CHRIS?
AND I GUESS YOU DO?
YOU KNOW HER REAL NAME.
LIKE YOU ALWAYS KNOW EVERY-THING.
SAFFI.
HER NAME WAS SAPPHIRE.
SAPPHIRE MASON.
SHE WAS MEGA-MORPHO TO ME.
SHE WAS ONE OF US.
SHE WAS A SUPER-HERO.
IT'S NOT MY FAULT MY DAD LEFT BEHIND THE MOST FOOLPROOF AND SOPHISTICATED PLANETARY DEFENSE SYSTEM EVER CREATED--
IT'S NOT MY FAULT IT PUT EVERYONE OUT OF WORK.
I SHOULD HAVE THOUGHT ABOUT IT--BUT--THE SUPER-ROBOTS CAN'T BE TURNED OFF OR TAMPERED WITH.
EVEN IF THEY COULD, I CAN'T BREAK MY PROMISE TO MY DAD.

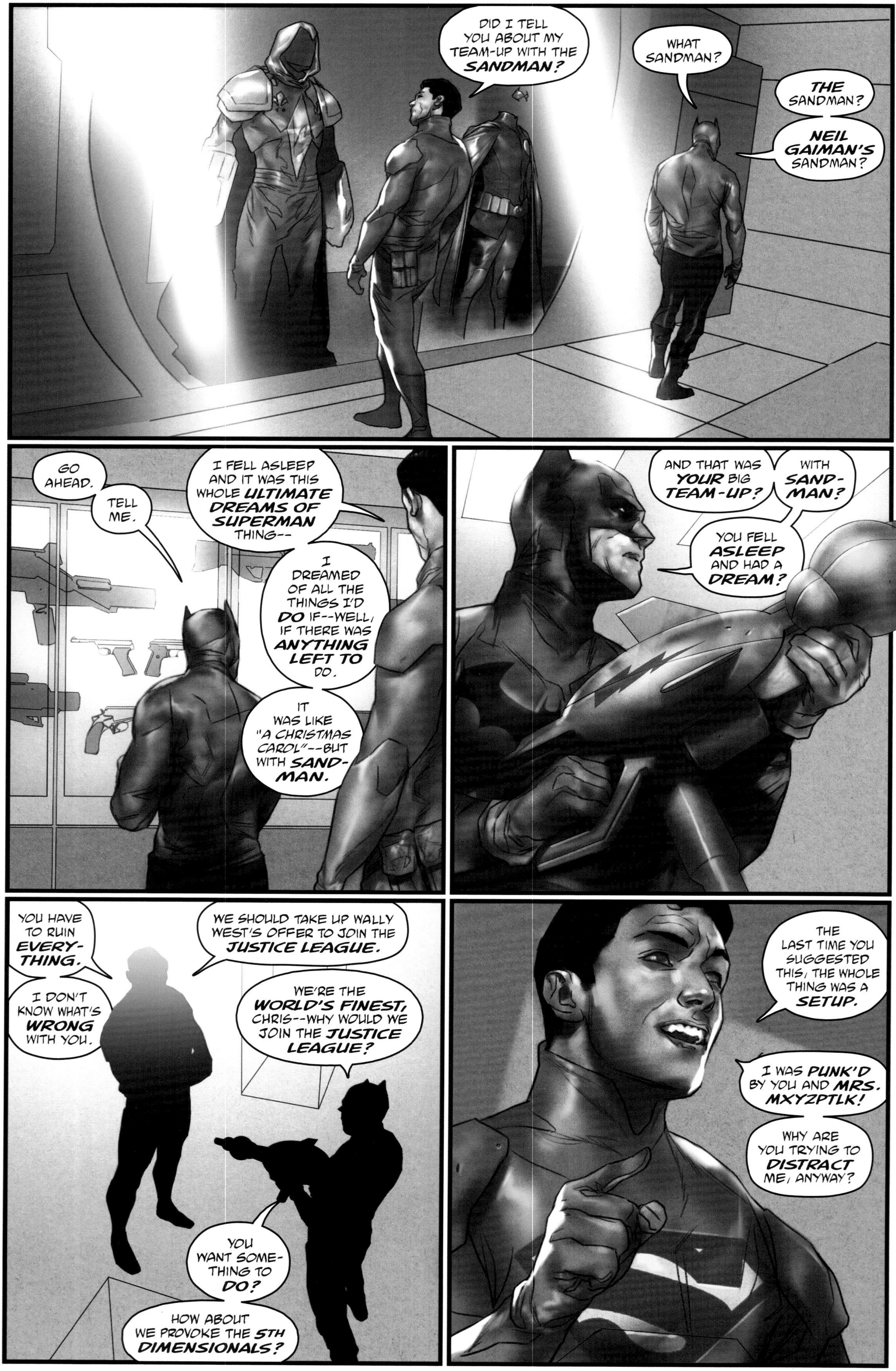
DID I TELL YOU ABOUT MY TEAM-UP WITH THE SANDMAN?
WHAT SANDMAN?
THE SANDMAN?
NEIL GAIMAN'S SANDMAN?
GO AHEAD.
TELL ME.
I FELL ASLEEP AND IT WAS THIS WHOLE ULTIMATE DREAMS OF SUPERMAN THING--
I DREAMED OF ALL THE THINGS I'D DO IF--WELL, IF THERE WAS ANYTHING LEFT TO DO.
IT WAS LIKE "A CHRISTMAS CAROL"--BUT WITH SAND-MAN.
AND THAT WAS YOUR BIG TEAM-UP?
WITH SAND-MAN?
YOU FELL ASLEEP AND HAD A DREAM?
YOU HAVE TO RUIN EVERY-THING.
I DON'T KNOW WHAT'S WRONG WITH YOU.
WE SHOULD TAKE UP WALLY WEST'S OFFER TO JOIN THE JUSTICE LEAGUE.
WE'RE THE WORLD'S FINEST, CHRIS--WHY WOULD WE JOIN THE JUSTICE LEAGUE?
YOU WANT SOME-THING TO DO?
HOW ABOUT WE PROVOKE THE 5TH DIMENSIONALS?
THE LAST TIME YOU SUGGESTED THIS, THE WHOLE THING WAS A SETUP.
I WAS PUNK'D BY YOU AND MRS. MXYZPTLK!
WHY ARE YOU TRYING TO DISTRACT ME, ANYWAY?

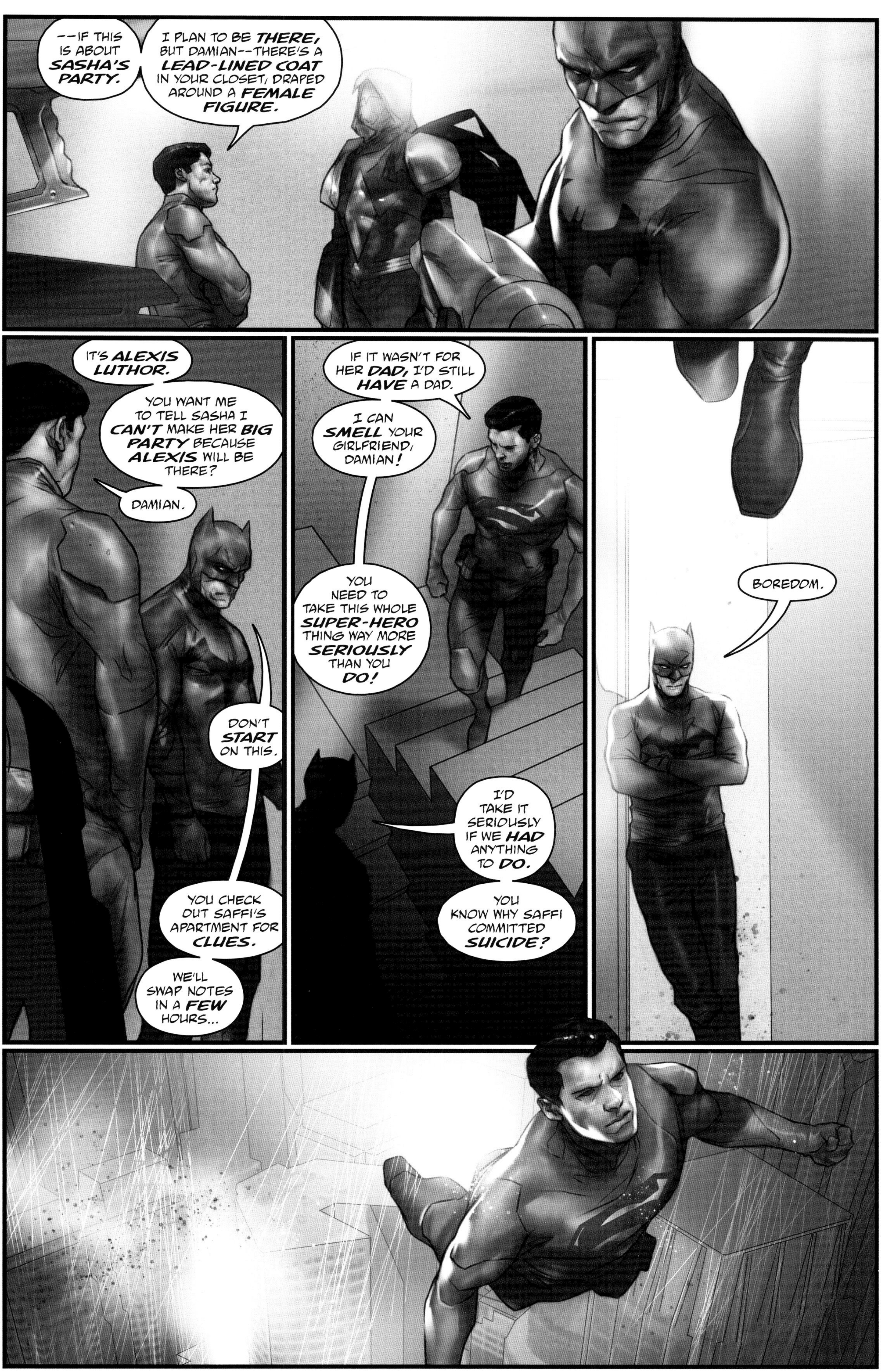
--IF THIS IS ABOUT SASHA'S PARTY.
I PLAN TO BE THERE, BUT DAMIAN--THERE'S A LEAD-LINED COAT IN YOUR CLOSET, DRAPED AROUND A FEMALE FIGURE.
IT'S ALEXIS LUTHOR.
YOU WANT ME TO TELL SASHA I CAN'T MAKE HER BIG PARTY BECAUSE ALEXIS WILL BE THERE?
DAMIAN.
DON'T START ON THIS.
YOU CHECK OUT SAFFI'S APARTMENT FOR CLUES.
WE'LL SWAP NOTES IN A FEW HOURS...
IF IT WASN'T FOR HER DAD, I'D STILL HAVE A DAD.
I CAN SMELL YOUR GIRLFRIEND, DAMIAN!
YOU NEED TO TAKE THIS WHOLE SUPER-HERO THING WAY MORE SERIOUSLY THAN YOU DO!
I'D TAKE IT SERIOUSLY IF WE HAD ANYTHING TO DO.
YOU KNOW WHY SAFFI COMMITTED SUICIDE?
BOREDOM.

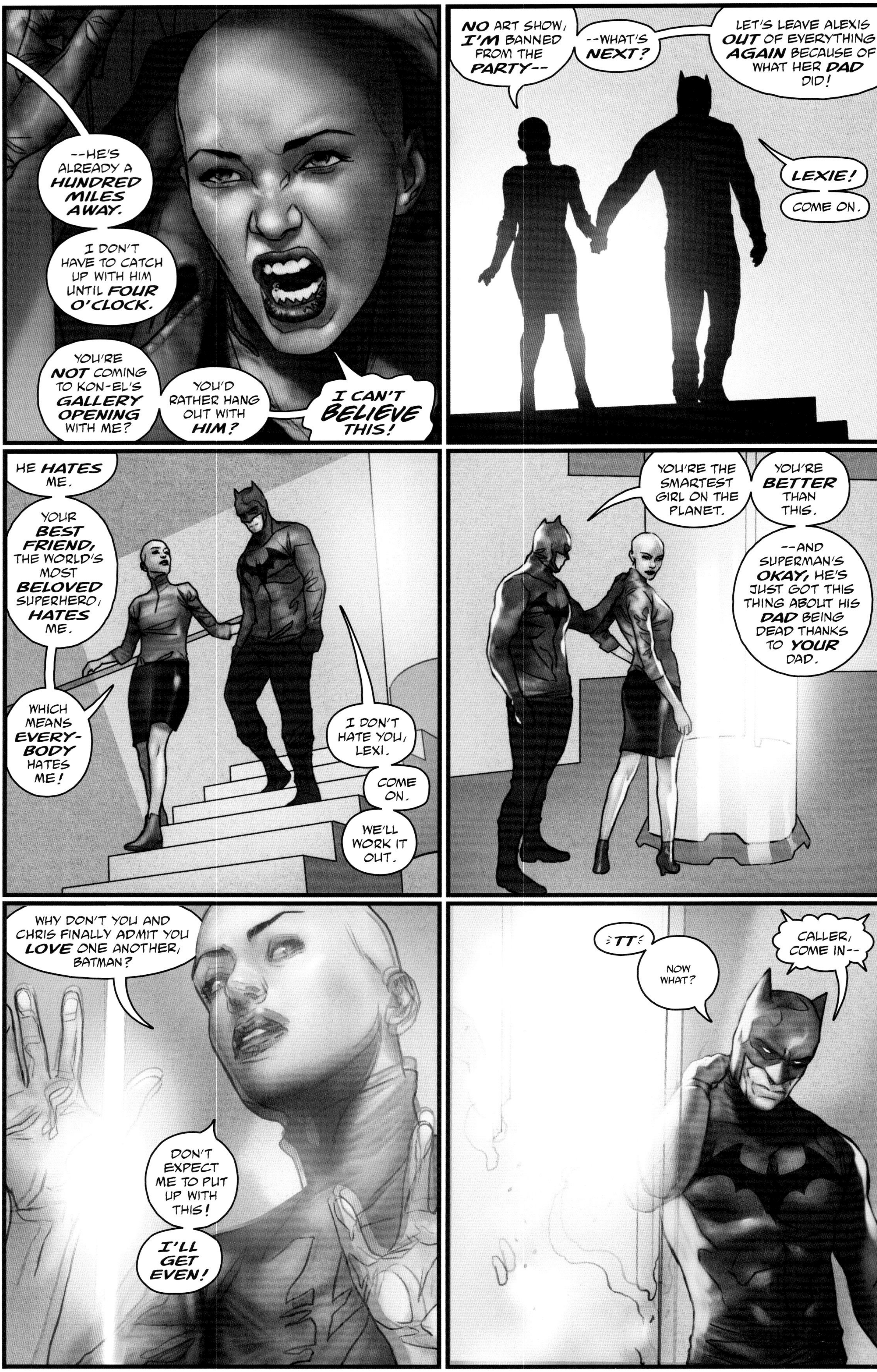
--HE'S ALREADY A HUNDRED MILES AWAY.
I DON'T HAVE TO CATCH UP WITH HIM UNTIL FOUR O'CLOCK.
YOU'RE NOT COMING TO KON-EL'S GALLERY OPENING WITH ME?
YOU'D RATHER HANG OUT WITH HIM?
I CAN'T BELIEVE THIS!
NO ART SHOW, I'M BANNED FROM THE PARTY--
--WHAT'S NEXT?
LET'S LEAVE ALEXIS OUT OF EVERYTHING AGAIN BECAUSE OF WHAT HER DAD DID!
LEXIE!
COME ON.
HE HATES ME.
YOUR BEST FRIEND, THE WORLD'S MOST BELOVED SUPERHERO, HATES ME.
WHICH MEANS EVERY-BODY HATES ME!
I DON'T HATE YOU, LEXI.
COME ON.
WE'LL WORK IT OUT.
YOU'RE THE SMARTEST GIRL ON THE PLANET.
YOU'RE BETTER THAN THIS.
--AND SUPERMAN'S OKAY, HE'S JUST GOT THIS THING ABOUT HIS DAD BEING DEAD THANKS TO YOUR DAD.
WHY DON'T YOU AND CHRIS FINALLY ADMIT YOU LOVE ONE ANOTHER, BATMAN?
DON'T EXPECT ME TO PUT UP WITH THIS!
I'LL GET EVEN!
TT
NOW WHAT?
CALLER, COME IN--

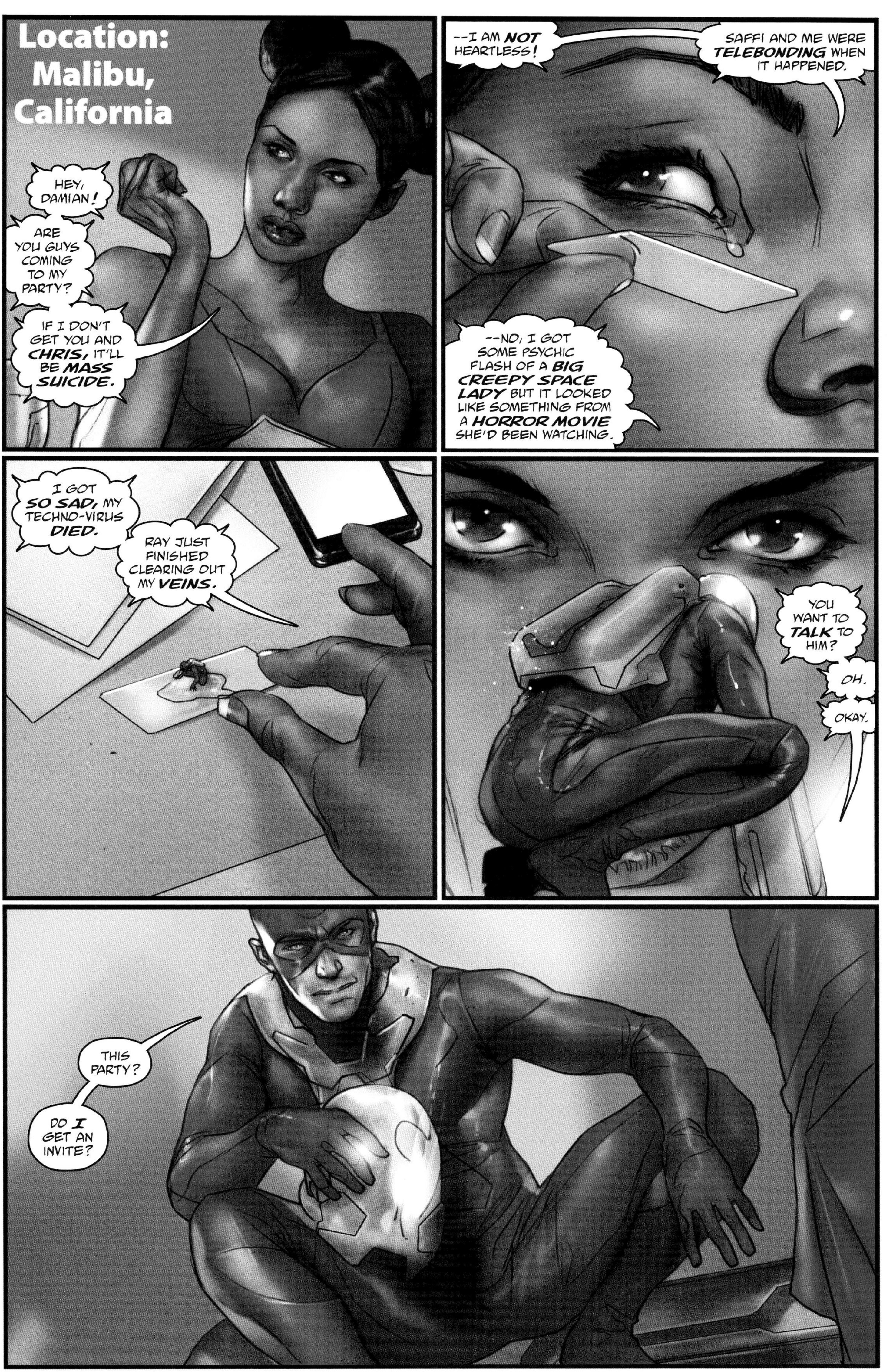

Location: Malibu, California
HEY, DAMIAN!
ARE YOU GUYS COMING TO MY PARTY?
IF I DON'T GET YOU AND CHRIS, IT'LL BE MASS SUICIDE.
--I AM NOT HEARTLESS!
SAFFI AND ME WERE TELEBONDING WHEN IT HAPPENED.
--NO, I GOT SOME PSYCHIC FLASH OF A BIG CREEPY SPACE LADY BUT IT LOOKED LIKE SOMETHING FROM A HORROR MOVIE SHE'D BEEN WATCHING.
I GOT SO SAD, MY TECHNO-VIRUS DIED.
RAY JUST FINISHED CLEARING OUT MY VEINS.
YOU WANT TO TALK TO HIM?
OH.
OKAY.
THIS PARTY?
DO I GET AN INVITE?

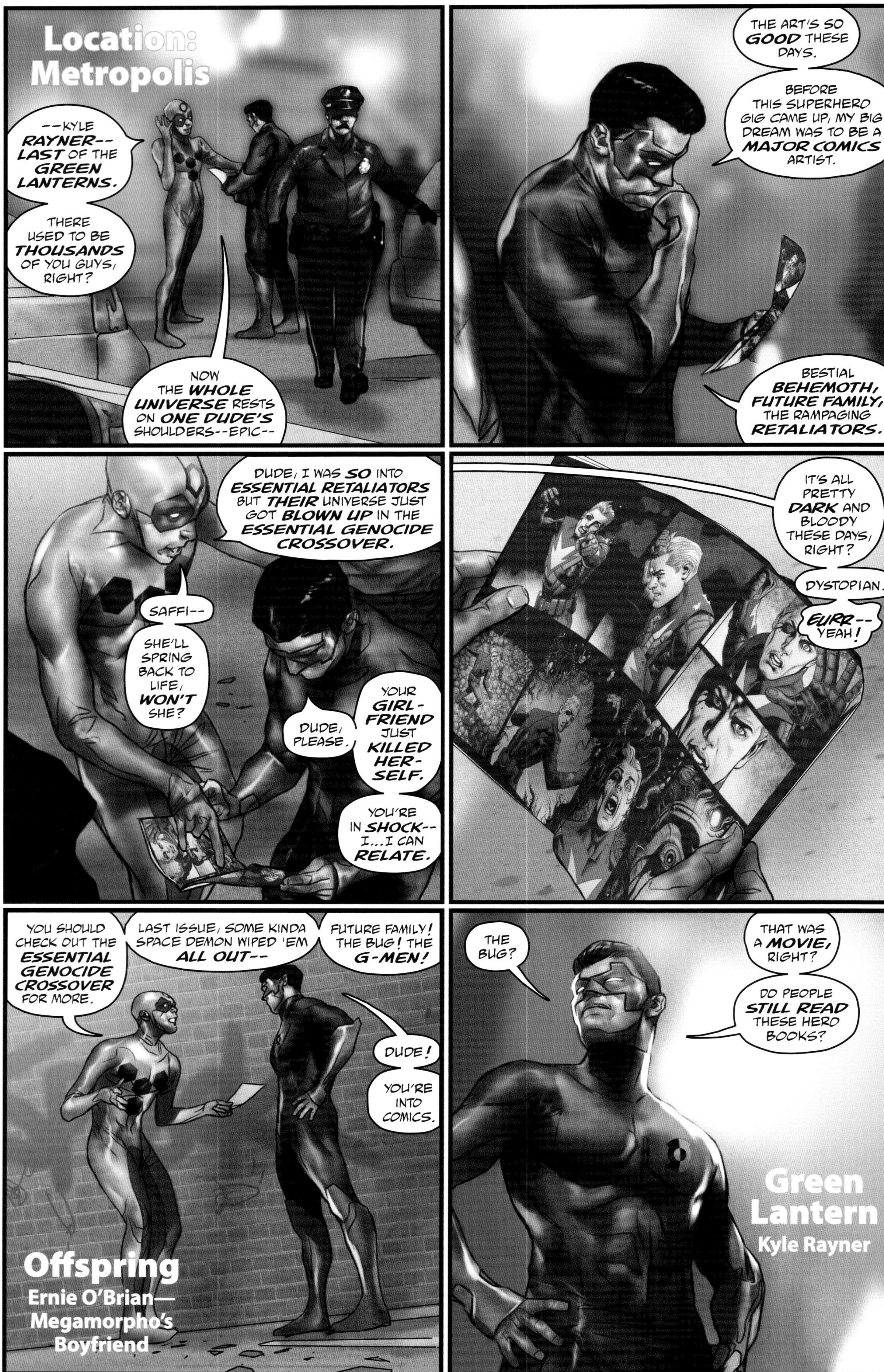
Location: Metropolis
--KYLE RAYNER--LAST OF THE GREEN LANTERNS.
THERE USED TO BE THOUSANDS OF YOU GUYS, RIGHT?
NOW THE WHOLE UNIVERSE RESTS ON ONE DUDE'S SHOULDERS--EPIC--
THE ART'S SO GOOD THESE DAYS.
BEFORE THIS SUPERHERO GIG CAME UP, MY BIG DREAM WAS TO BE A MAJOR COMICS ARTIST.
BESTIAL BEHEMOTH, FUTURE FAMILY, THE RAMPAGING RETALIATORS.
DUDE, I WAS SO INTO ESSENTIAL RETALIATORS BUT THEIR UNIVERSE JUST GOT BLOWN UP IN THE ESSENTIAL GENOCIDE CROSSOVER.
SAFFI--
SHE'LL SPRING BACK TO LIFE, WON'T SHE?
DUDE, PLEASE.
YOUR GIRL-FRIEND JUST KILLED HER-SELF.
YOU'RE IN SHOCK--I...I CAN RELATE.
IT'S ALL PRETTY DARK AND BLOODY THESE DAYS, RIGHT?
DYSTOPIAN.
EURR--YEAH!
YOU SHOULD CHECK OUT THE ESSENTIAL GENOCIDE CROSSOVER FOR MORE.
LAST ISSUE, SOME KINDA SPACE DEMON WIPED 'EM ALL OUT--
FUTURE FAMILY! THE BUG! THE G-MEN!
DUDE!
YOU'RE INTO COMICS.
Offspring
Ernie O'Brian—Megamorpho's Boyfriend
THE BUG?
THAT WAS A MOVIE, RIGHT?
DO PEOPLE STILL READ THESE HERO BOOKS?
Green Lantern
Kyle Rayner

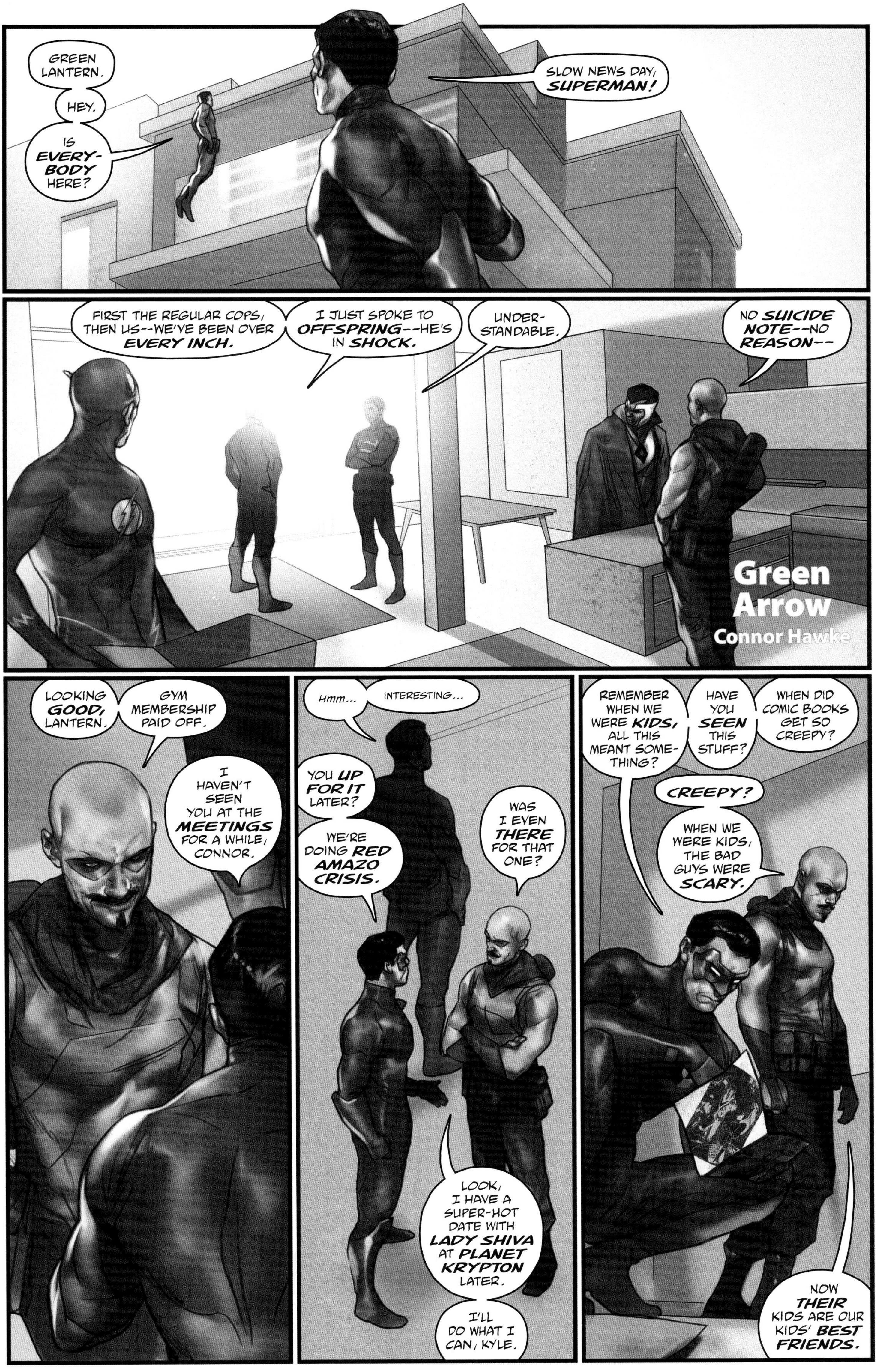

GREEN LANTERN.
HEY.
IS EVERY-BODY HERE?
SLOW NEWS DAY, SUPERMAN!
FIRST THE REGULAR COPS, THEN US--WE'VE BEEN OVER EVERY INCH.
I JUST SPOKE TO OFFSPRING--HE'S IN SHOCK.
UNDER-STANDABLE.
NO SUICIDE NOTE--NO REASON--
Green Arrow
Connor Hawke
LOOKING GOOD, LANTERN.
GYM MEMBERSHIP PAID OFF.
I HAVEN'T SEEN YOU AT THE MEETINGS FOR A WHILE, CONNOR.
Hmm...
INTERESTING...
YOU UP FOR IT LATER?
WE'RE DOING RED AMAZO CRISIS.
WAS I EVEN THERE FOR THAT ONE?
LOOK, I HAVE A SUPER-HOT DATE WITH LADY SHIVA AT PLANET KRYPTON LATER.
I'LL DO WHAT I CAN, KYLE.
REMEMBER WHEN WE WERE KIDS, ALL THIS MEANT SOME-THING?
HAVE YOU SEEN THIS STUFF?
WHEN DID COMIC BOOKS GET SO CREEPY?
CREEPY?
WHEN WE WERE KIDS, THE BAD GUYS WERE SCARY.
NOW THEIR KIDS ARE OUR KIDS' BEST FRIENDS.

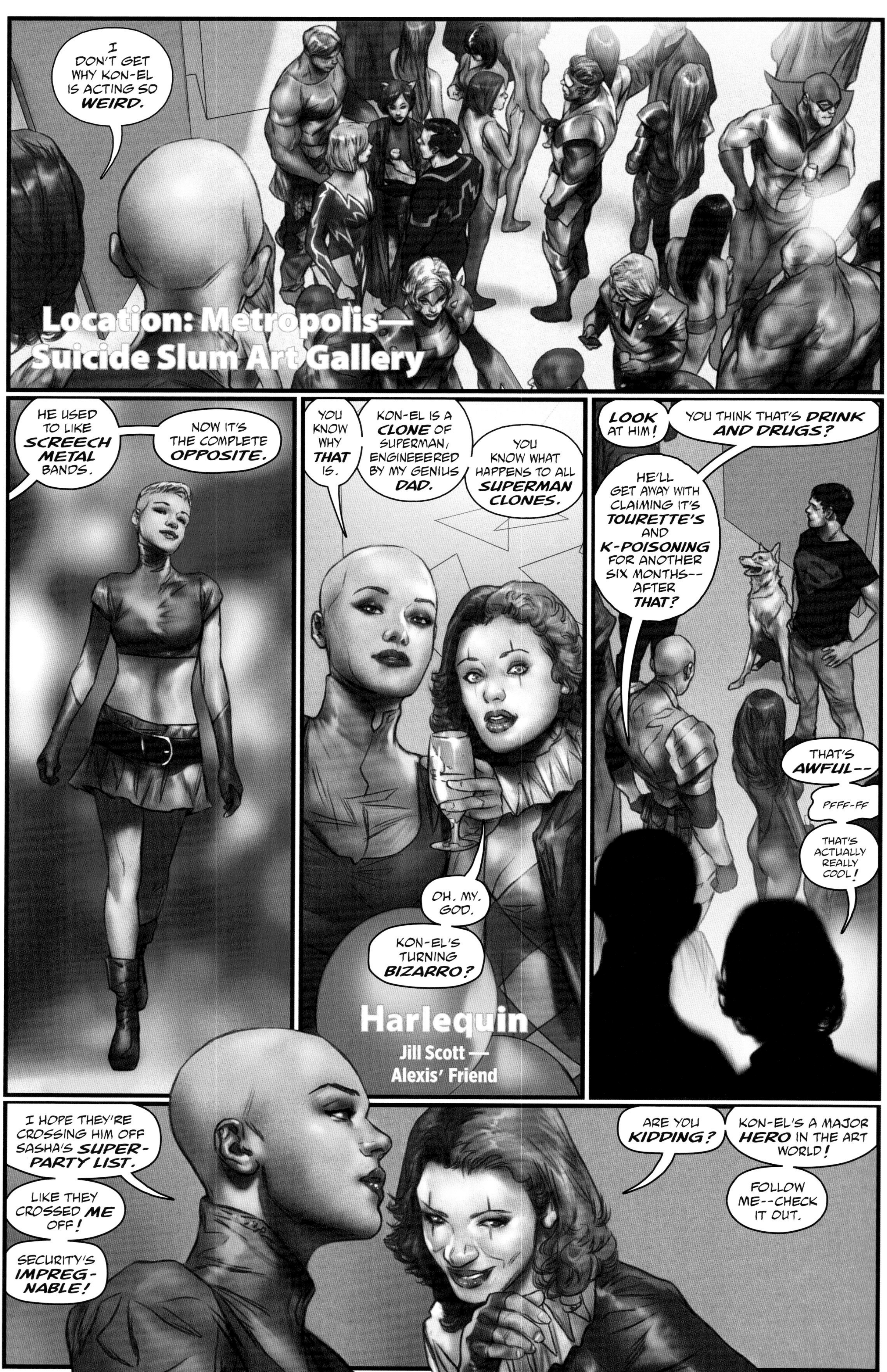
I DON'T GET WHY KON-EL IS ACTING SO WEIRD.
Location: Metropolis—
Suicide Slum Art Gallery
HE USED TO LIKE SCREECH METAL BANDS.
NOW IT'S THE COMPLETE OPPOSITE.
YOU KNOW WHY THAT IS.
KON-EL IS A CLONE OF SUPERMAN, ENGINEEERED BY MY GENIUS DAD.
YOU KNOW WHAT HAPPENS TO ALL SUPERMAN CLONES.
OH. MY. GOD.
KON-EL'S TURNING BIZARRO?
Harlequin
Jill Scott —
Alexis' Friend
LOOK AT HIM!
YOU THINK THAT'S DRINK AND DRUGS?
HE'LL GET AWAY WITH CLAIMING IT'S TOURETTE'S AND K-POISONING FOR ANOTHER SIX MONTHS-- AFTER THAT?
THAT'S AWFUL--
PFFF-FF
THAT'S ACTUALLY REALLY COOL!
I HOPE THEY'RE CROSSING HIM OFF SASHA'S SUPER-PARTY LIST.
LIKE THEY CROSSED ME OFF!
SECURITY'S IMPREG-NABLE!
ARE YOU KIDDING?
KON-EL'S A MAJOR HERO IN THE ART WORLD!
FOLLOW ME--CHECK IT OUT.

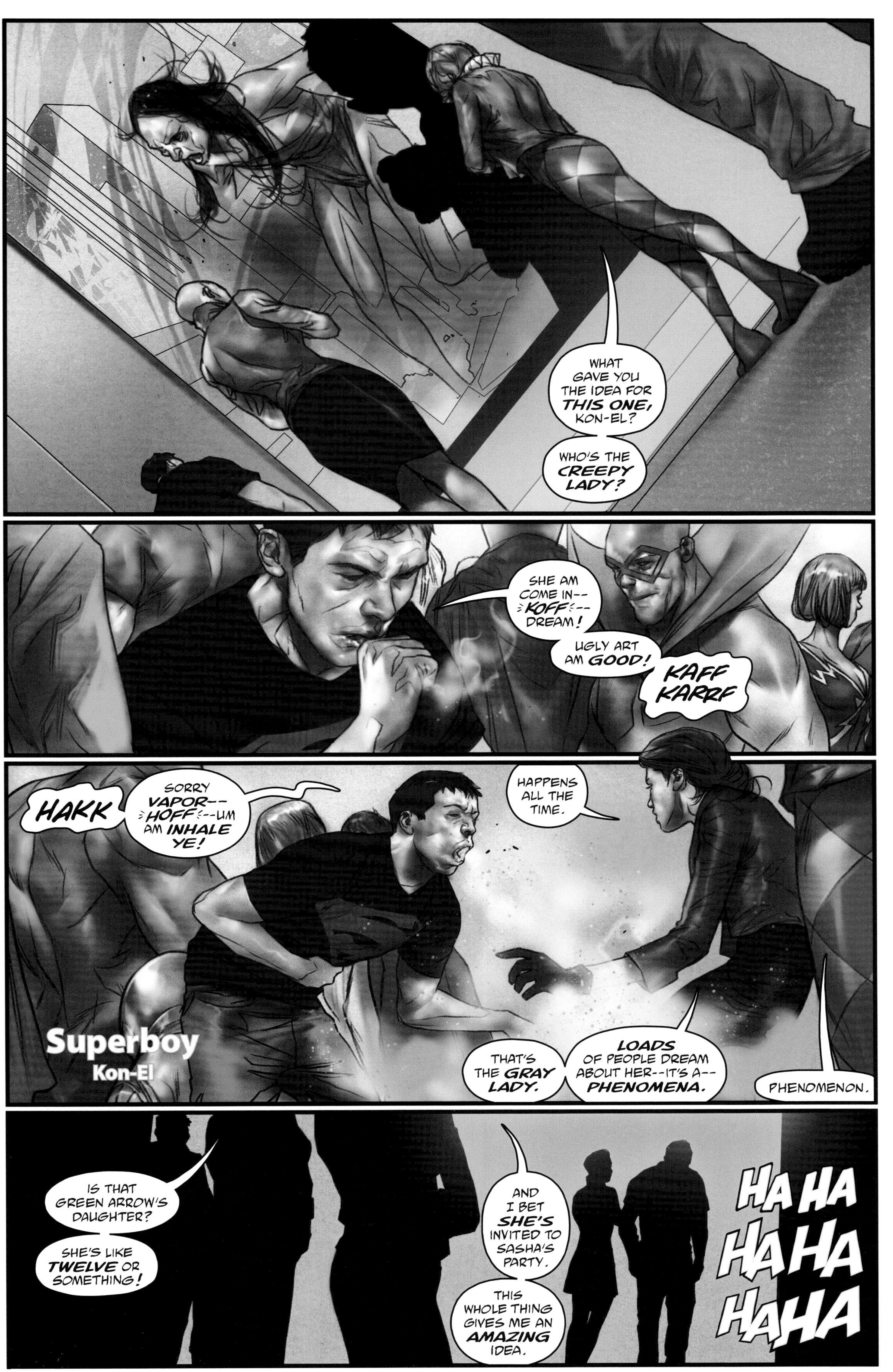

WHAT GAVE YOU THE IDEA FOR THIS ONE, KON-EL?
WHO'S THE CREEPY LADY?
SHE AM COME IN-- KOFF --DREAM!
UGLY ART AM GOOD!
KAFF KARRF
HAKK
SORRY VAPOR-- HOFF --UM AM INHALE YE!
HAPPENS ALL THE TIME.
Superboy
Kon-El
THAT'S THE GRAY LADY.
LOADS OF PEOPLE DREAM ABOUT HER--IT'S A-- PHENOMENA.
PHENOMENON.
IS THAT GREEN ARROW'S DAUGHTER?
SHE'S LIKE TWELVE OR SOMETHING!
AND I BET SHE'S INVITED TO SASHA'S PARTY.
THIS WHOLE THING GIVES ME AN AMAZING IDEA.
HA HA HA HA HA HA

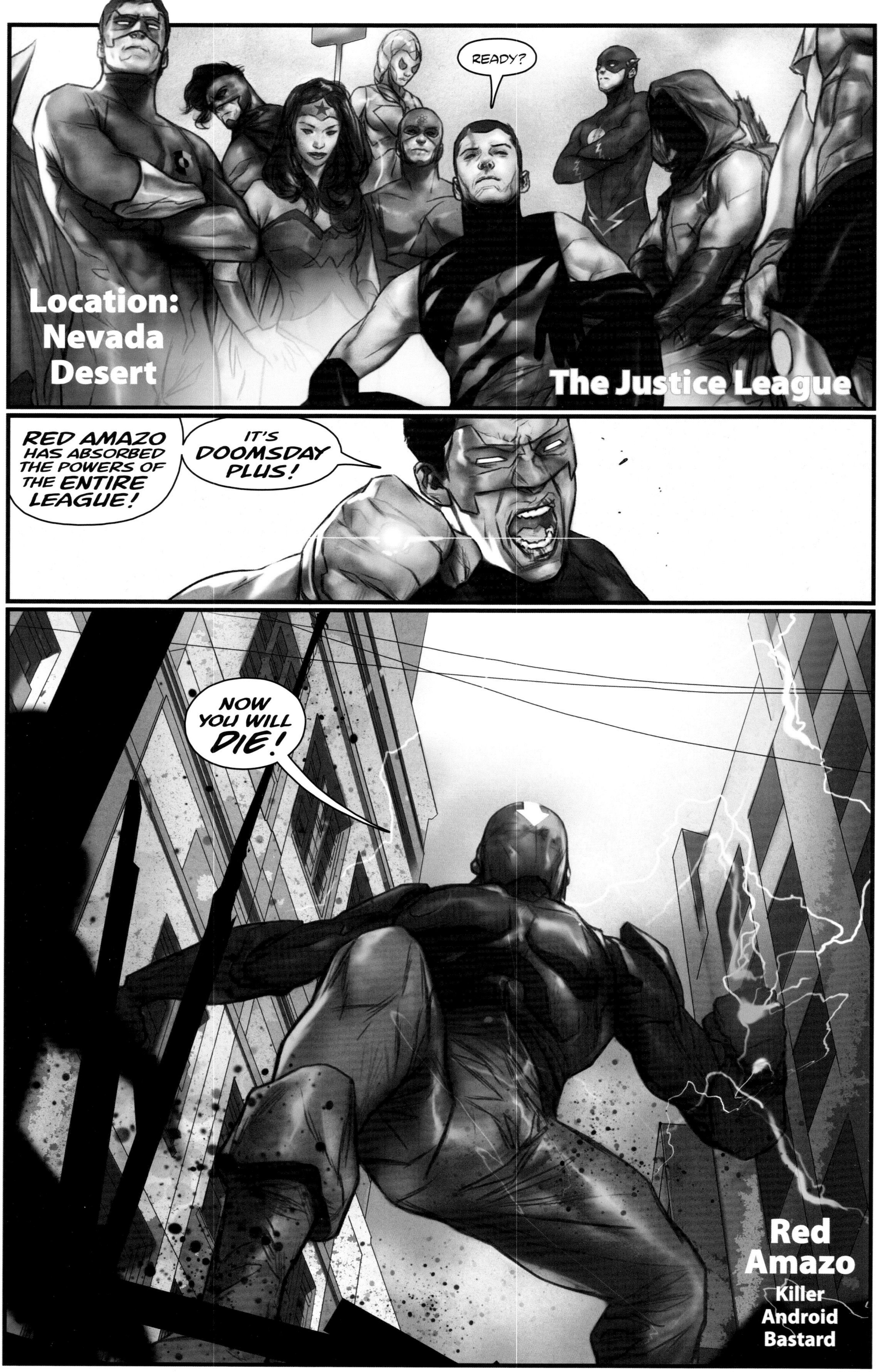

READY?
Location: Nevada Desert
The Justice League
RED AMAZO HAS ABSORBED THE POWERS OF THE ENTIRE LEAGUE!
IT'S DOOMSDAY PLUS!
NOW YOU WILL DIE!
Red Amazo
Killer Android Bastard

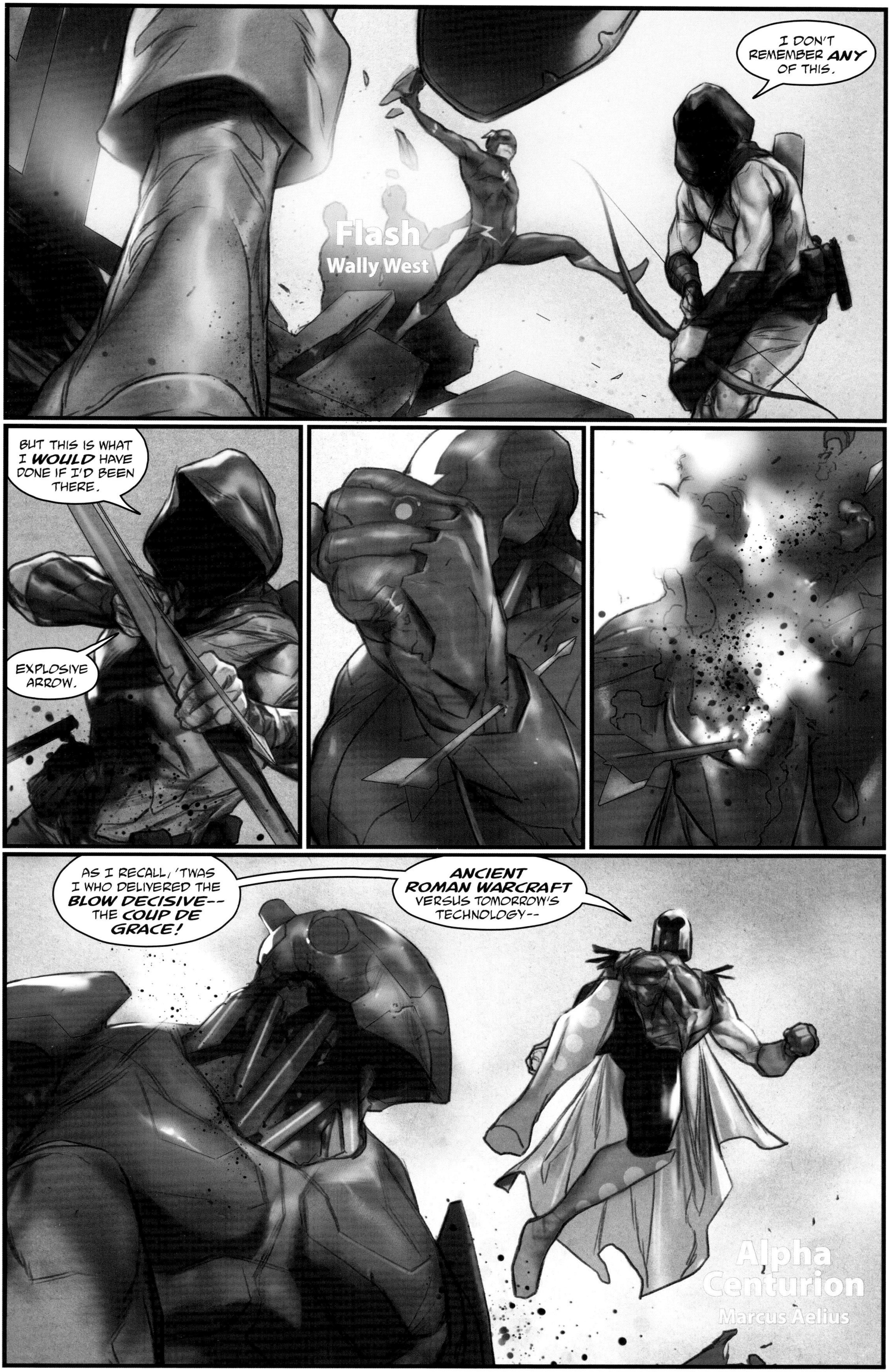
I DON'T REMEMBER ANY OF THIS.
Flash
Wally West
BUT THIS IS WHAT I WOULD HAVE DONE IF I'D BEEN THERE.
EXPLOSIVE ARROW.
AS I RECALL, 'TWAS I WHO DELIVERED THE BLOW DECISIVE-- THE COUP DE GRACE!
ANCIENT ROMAN WARCRAFT VERSUS TOMORROW'S TECHNOLOGY--
Alpha Centurion
Marcus Aelius

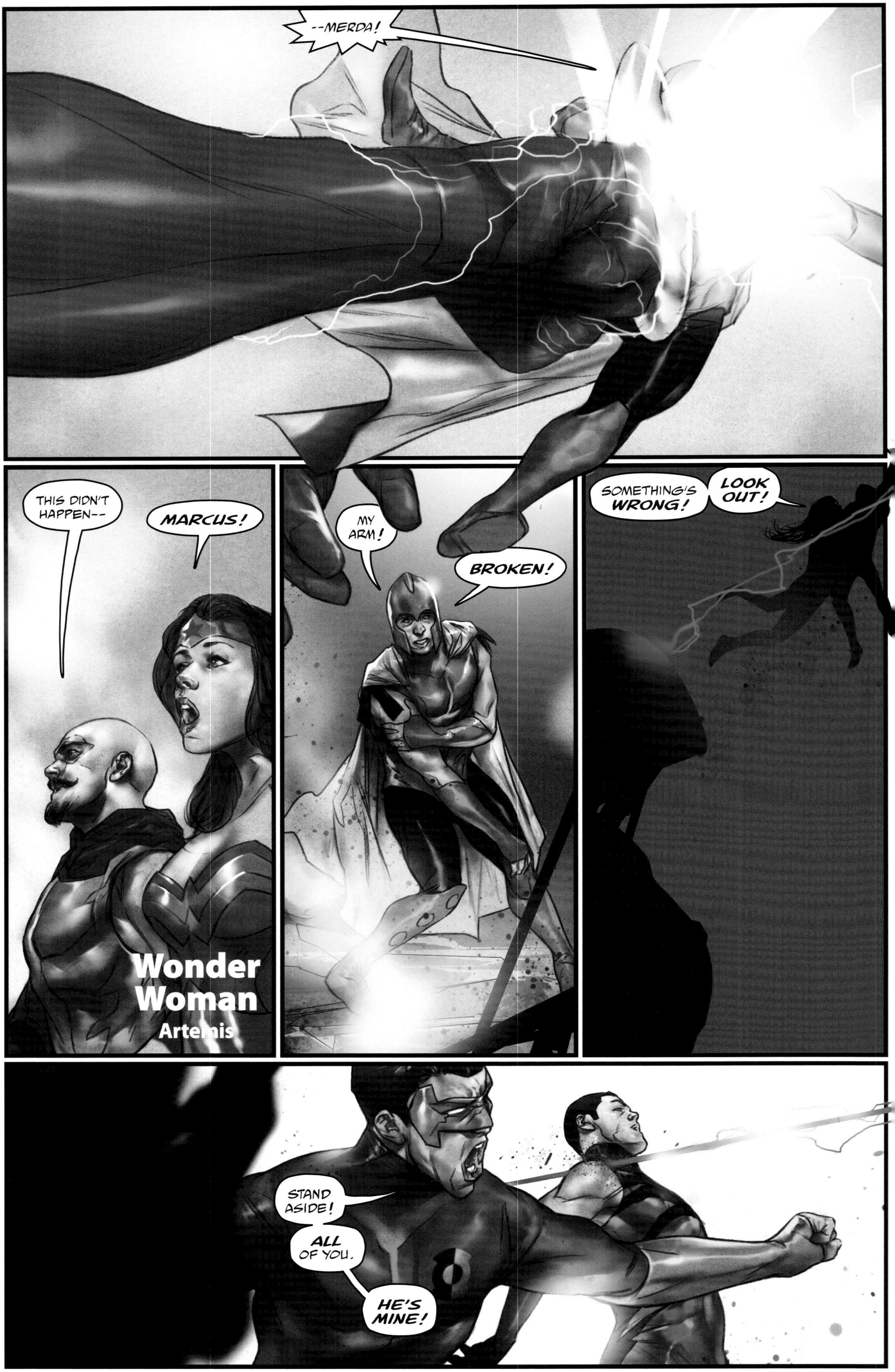
--MERDA!
THIS DIDN'T HAPPEN--
MARCUS!
Wonder Woman
Artemis
MY ARM!
BROKEN!
SOMETHING'S WRONG!
LOOK OUT!
STAND ASIDE!
ALL OF YOU.
HE'S MINE!

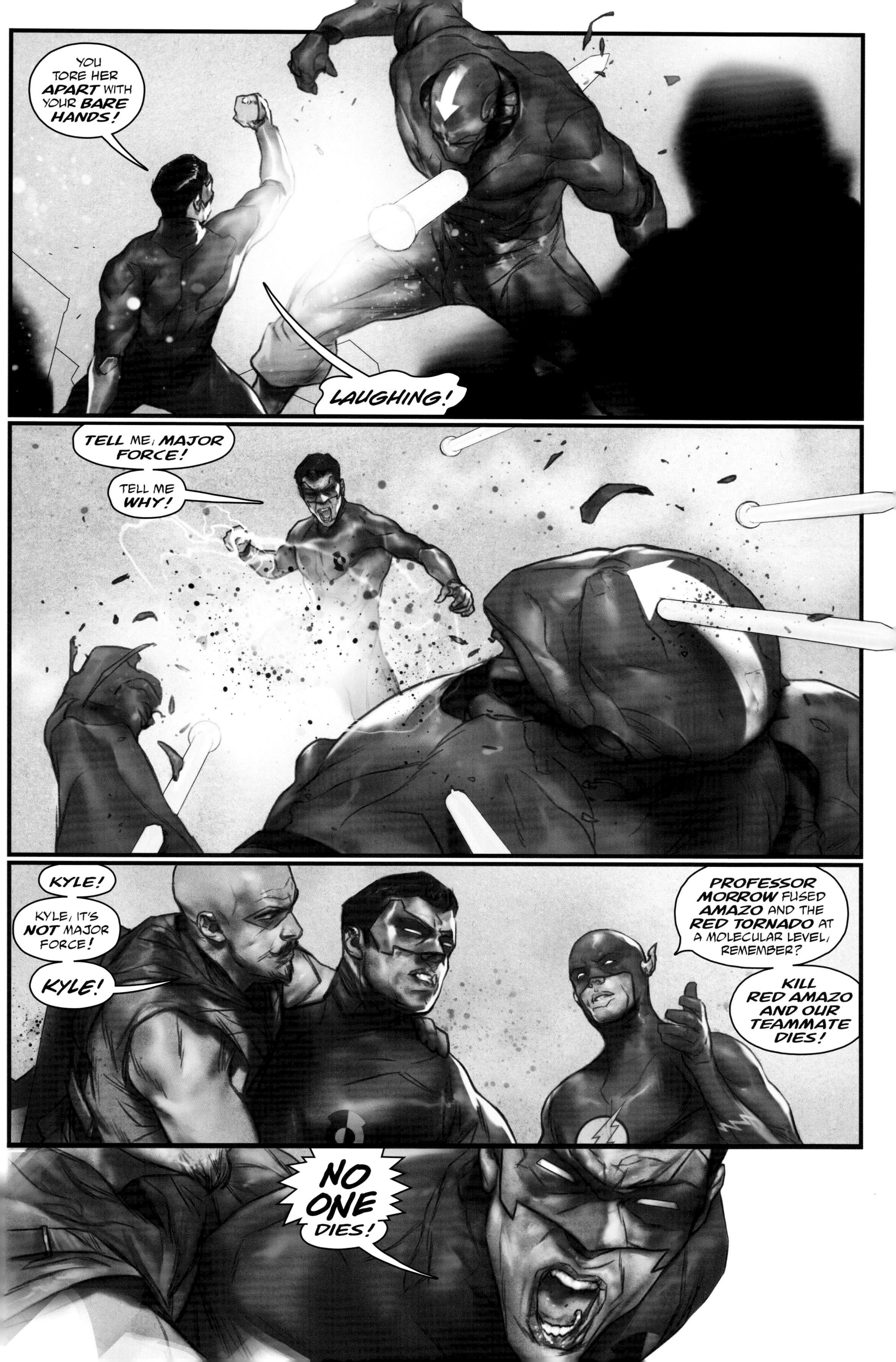
YOU TORE HER APART WITH YOUR BARE HANDS!
LAUGHING!
TELL ME, MAJOR FORCE!
TELL ME WHY!
KYLE!
KYLE, IT'S NOT MAJOR FORCE!
KYLE!
PROFESSOR MORROW FUSED AMAZO AND THE RED TORNADO AT A MOLECULAR LEVEL, REMEMBER?
KILL RED AMAZO AND OUR TEAMMATE DIES!
NO ONE DIES!

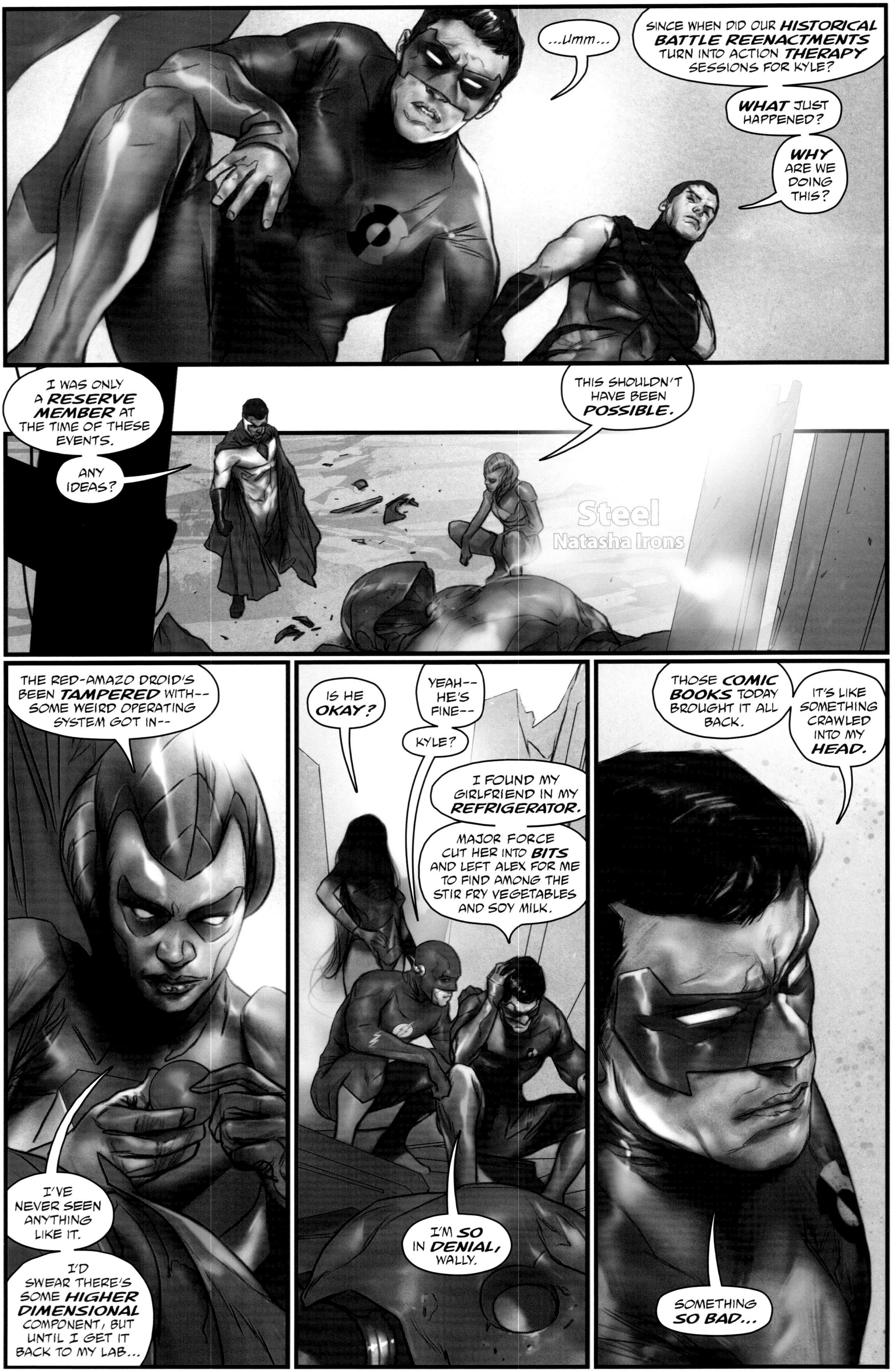
...UMM...
SINCE WHEN DID OUR HISTORICAL BATTLE REENACTMENTS TURN INTO ACTION THERAPY SESSIONS FOR KYLE?
WHAT JUST HAPPENED?
WHY ARE WE DOING THIS?
I WAS ONLY A RESERVE MEMBER AT THE TIME OF THESE EVENTS.
ANY IDEAS?
THIS SHOULDN'T HAVE BEEN POSSIBLE.
Steel
Natasha Irons
THE RED-AMAZO DROID'S BEEN TAMPERED WITH-- SOME WEIRD OPERATING SYSTEM GOT IN--
I'VE NEVER SEEN ANYTHING LIKE IT.
I'D SWEAR THERE'S SOME HIGHER DIMENSIONAL COMPONENT, BUT UNTIL I GET IT BACK TO MY LAB...
IS HE OKAY?
YEAH-- HE'S FINE--
KYLE?
I FOUND MY GIRLFRIEND IN MY REFRIGERATOR.
MAJOR FORCE CUT HER INTO BITS AND LEFT ALEX FOR ME TO FIND AMONG THE STIR FRY VEGETABLES AND SOY MILK.
I'M SO IN DENIAL, WALLY.
THOSE COMIC BOOKS TODAY BROUGHT IT ALL BACK.
IT'S LIKE SOMETHING CRAWLED INTO MY HEAD.
SOMETHING SO BAD...

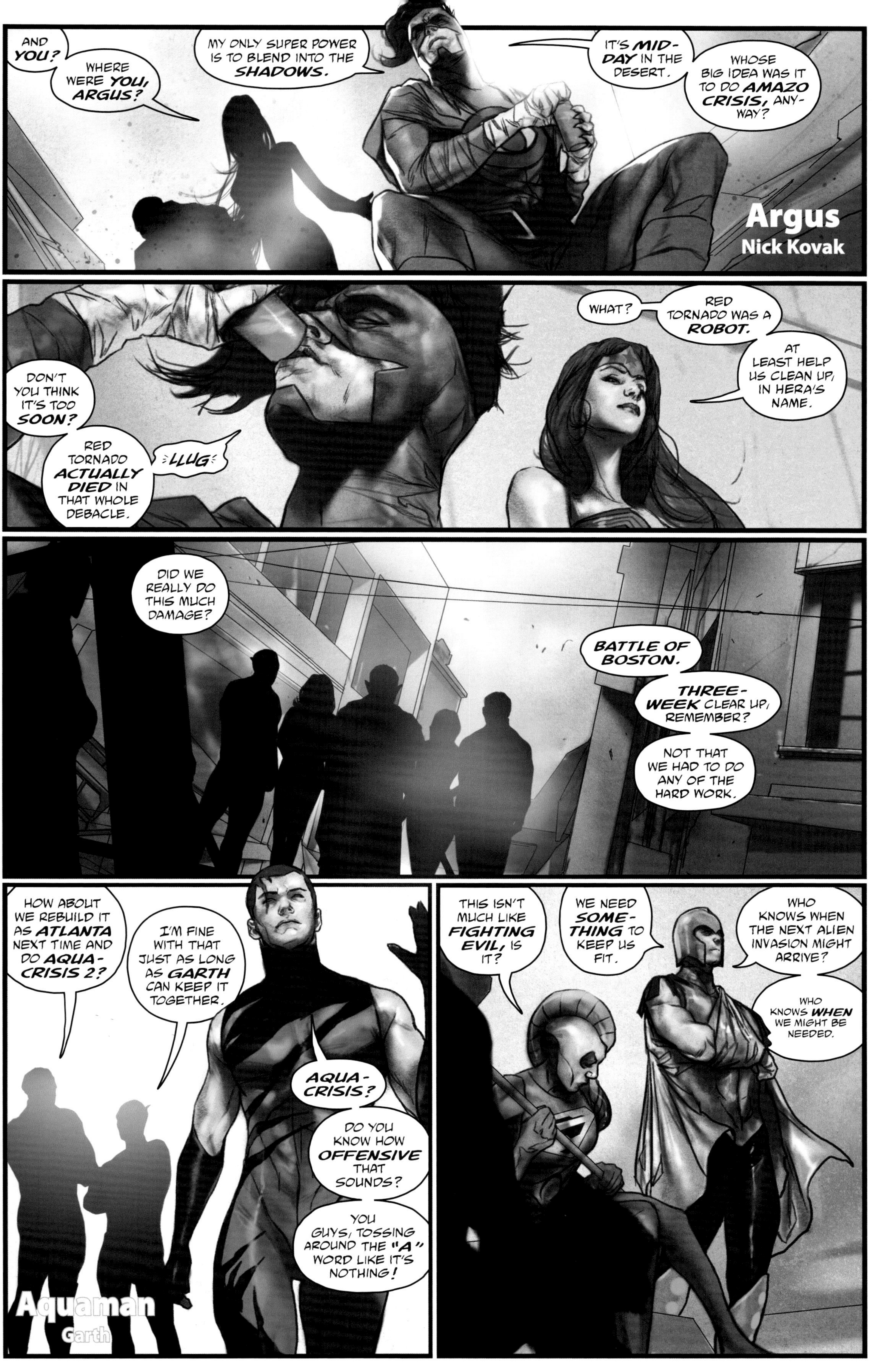
AND YOU?
WHERE WERE YOU, ARGUS?
MY ONLY SUPER POWER IS TO BLEND INTO THE SHADOWS.
IT'S MID-DAY IN THE DESERT.
WHOSE BIG IDEA WAS IT TO DO AMAZO CRISIS, ANY-WAY?
Argus
Nick Kovak
DON'T YOU THINK IT'S TOO SOON?
RED TORNADO ACTUALLY DIED IN THAT WHOLE DEBACLE.
LLUG
WHAT?
RED TORNADO WAS A ROBOT.
AT LEAST HELP US CLEAN UP, IN HERA'S NAME.
DID WE REALLY DO THIS MUCH DAMAGE?
BATTLE OF BOSTON.
THREE-WEEK CLEAR UP, REMEMBER?
NOT THAT WE HAD TO DO ANY OF THE HARD WORK.
HOW ABOUT WE REBUILD IT AS ATLANTA NEXT TIME AND DO AQUA-CRISIS 2?
I'M FINE WITH THAT JUST AS LONG AS GARTH CAN KEEP IT TOGETHER.
AQUA-CRISIS?
DO YOU KNOW HOW OFFENSIVE THAT SOUNDS?
YOU GUYS, TOSSING AROUND THE "A" WORD LIKE IT'S NOTHING!
Aquaman
Garth
THIS ISN'T MUCH LIKE FIGHTING EVIL, IS IT?
WE NEED SOME-THING TO KEEP US FIT.
WHO KNOWS WHEN THE NEXT ALIEN INVASION MIGHT ARRIVE?
WHO KNOWS WHEN WE MIGHT BE NEEDED.

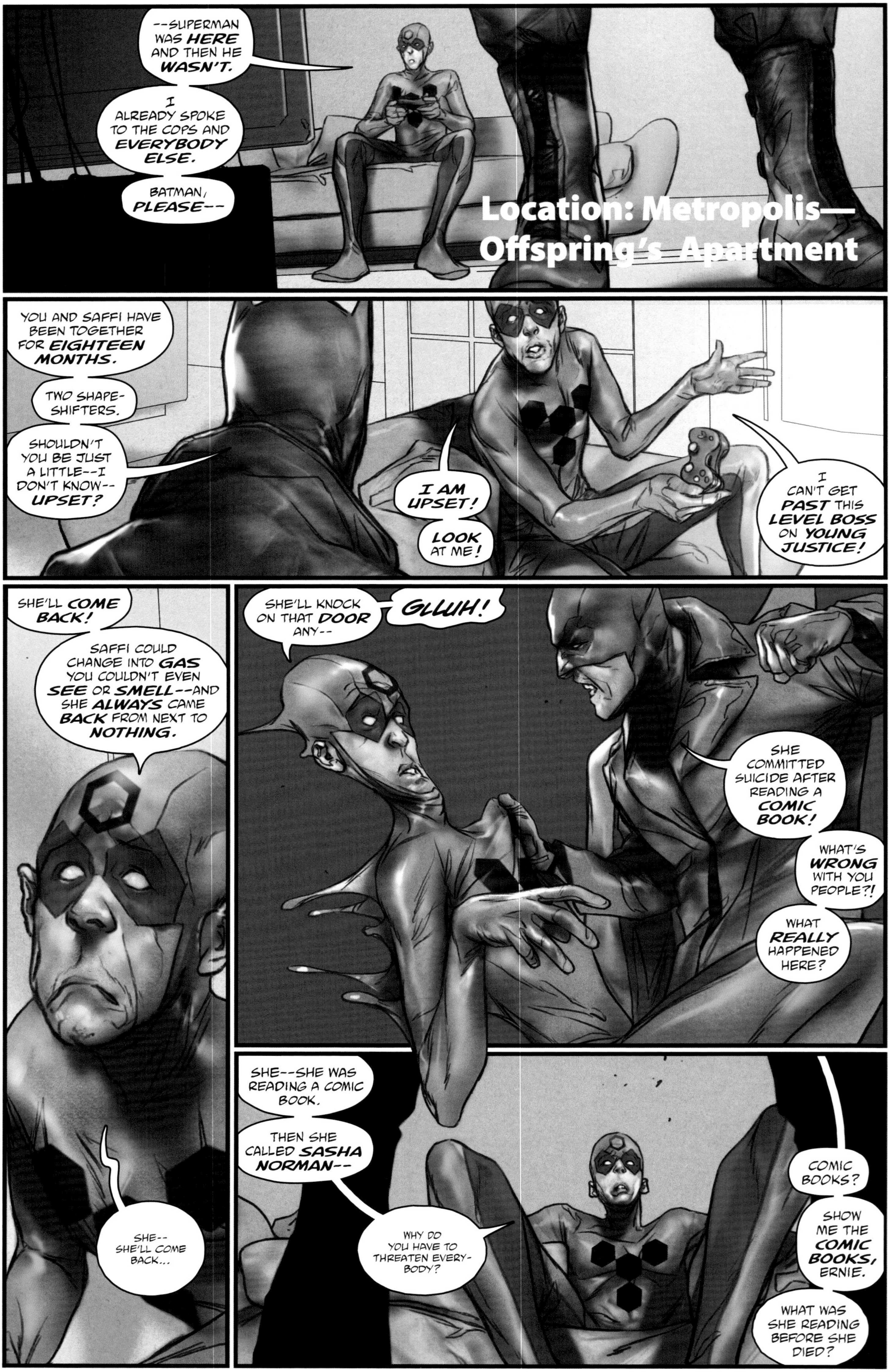

--SUPERMAN WAS HERE AND THEN HE WASN'T.
I ALREADY SPOKE TO THE COPS AND EVERYBODY ELSE.
BATMAN, PLEASE--
Location: Metropolis—Offspring's Apartment
YOU AND SAFFI HAVE BEEN TOGETHER FOR EIGHTEEN MONTHS.
TWO SHAPE-SHIFTERS.
SHOULDN'T YOU BE JUST A LITTLE--I DON'T KNOW--UPSET?
I AM UPSET!
LOOK AT ME!
I CAN'T GET PAST THIS LEVEL BOSS ON YOUNG JUSTICE!
SHE'LL COME BACK!
SAFFI COULD CHANGE INTO GAS YOU COULDN'T EVEN SEE OR SMELL--AND SHE ALWAYS CAME BACK FROM NEXT TO NOTHING.
SHE'LL KNOCK ON THAT DOOR ANY--
GLLUH!
SHE COMMITTED SUICIDE AFTER READING A COMIC BOOK!
WHAT'S WRONG WITH YOU PEOPLE?!
WHAT REALLY HAPPENED HERE?
SHE-- SHE'LL COME BACK...
SHE--SHE WAS READING A COMIC BOOK.
THEN SHE CALLED SASHA NORMAN--
WHY DO YOU HAVE TO THREATEN EVERY-BODY?
COMIC BOOKS?
SHOW ME THE COMIC BOOKS, ERNIE.
WHAT WAS SHE READING BEFORE SHE DIED?

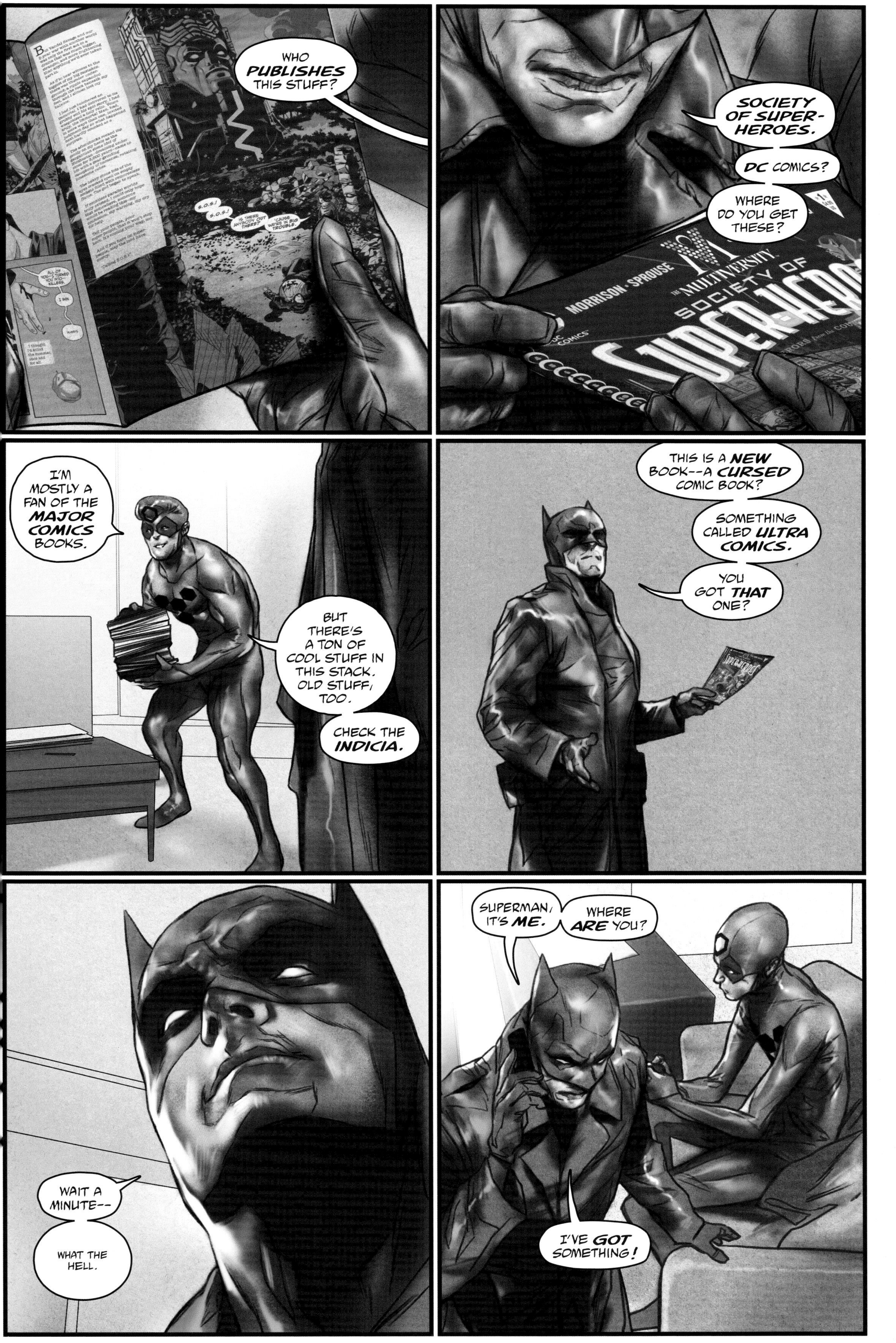
WHO PUBLISHES THIS STUFF?
SOCIETY OF SUPER-HEROES.
DC COMICS?
WHERE DO YOU GET THESE?
THE MULTIVERSITY
MORRISON · SPROUSE
SOCIETY OF SUPER-HEROES
DC COMICS
I'M MOSTLY A FAN OF THE MAJOR COMICS BOOKS.
BUT THERE'S A TON OF COOL STUFF IN THIS STACK. OLD STUFF, TOO.
CHECK THE INDICIA.
THIS IS A NEW BOOK--A CURSED COMIC BOOK?
SOMETHING CALLED ULTRA COMICS.
YOU GOT THAT ONE?
WAIT A MINUTE--
WHAT THE HELL.
SUPERMAN, IT'S ME.
WHERE ARE YOU?
I'VE GOT SOMETHING!

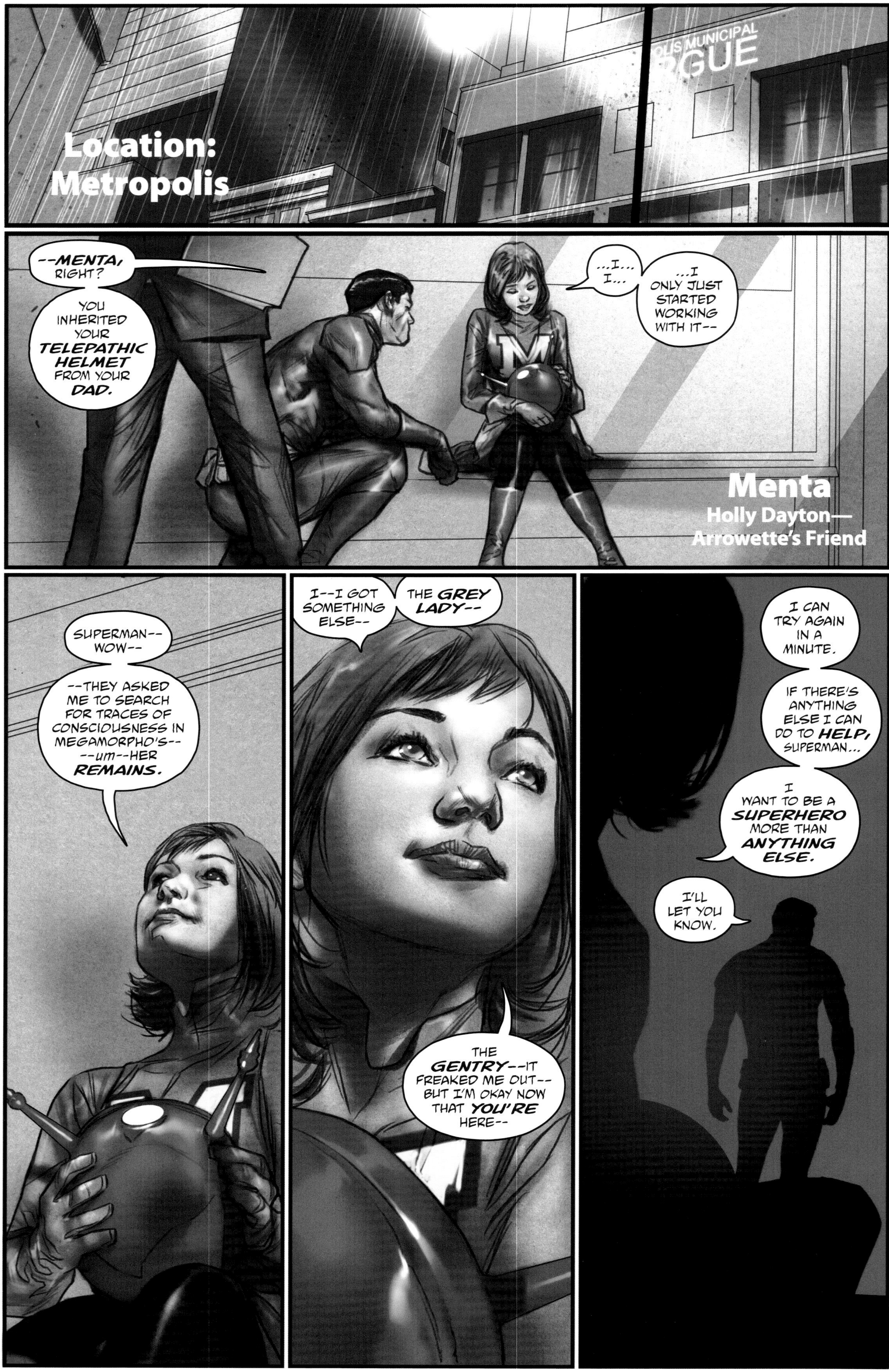
OLIS MUNICIPAL
RGUE
Location: Metropolis
--MENTA, RIGHT?
YOU INHERITED YOUR TELEPATHIC HELMET FROM YOUR DAD.
...I... I...
...I ONLY JUST STARTED WORKING WITH IT--
Menta
Holly Dayton—Arrowette's Friend
SUPERMAN--WOW--
--THEY ASKED ME TO SEARCH FOR TRACES OF CONSCIOUSNESS IN MEGAMORPHO'S-- --um--HER REMAINS.
I--I GOT SOMETHING ELSE--
THE GREY LADY--
THE GENTRY--IT FREAKED ME OUT--BUT I'M OKAY NOW THAT YOU'RE HERE--
I CAN TRY AGAIN IN A MINUTE.
IF THERE'S ANYTHING ELSE I CAN DO TO HELP, SUPERMAN...
I WANT TO BE A SUPERHERO MORE THAN ANYTHING ELSE.
I'LL LET YOU KNOW.

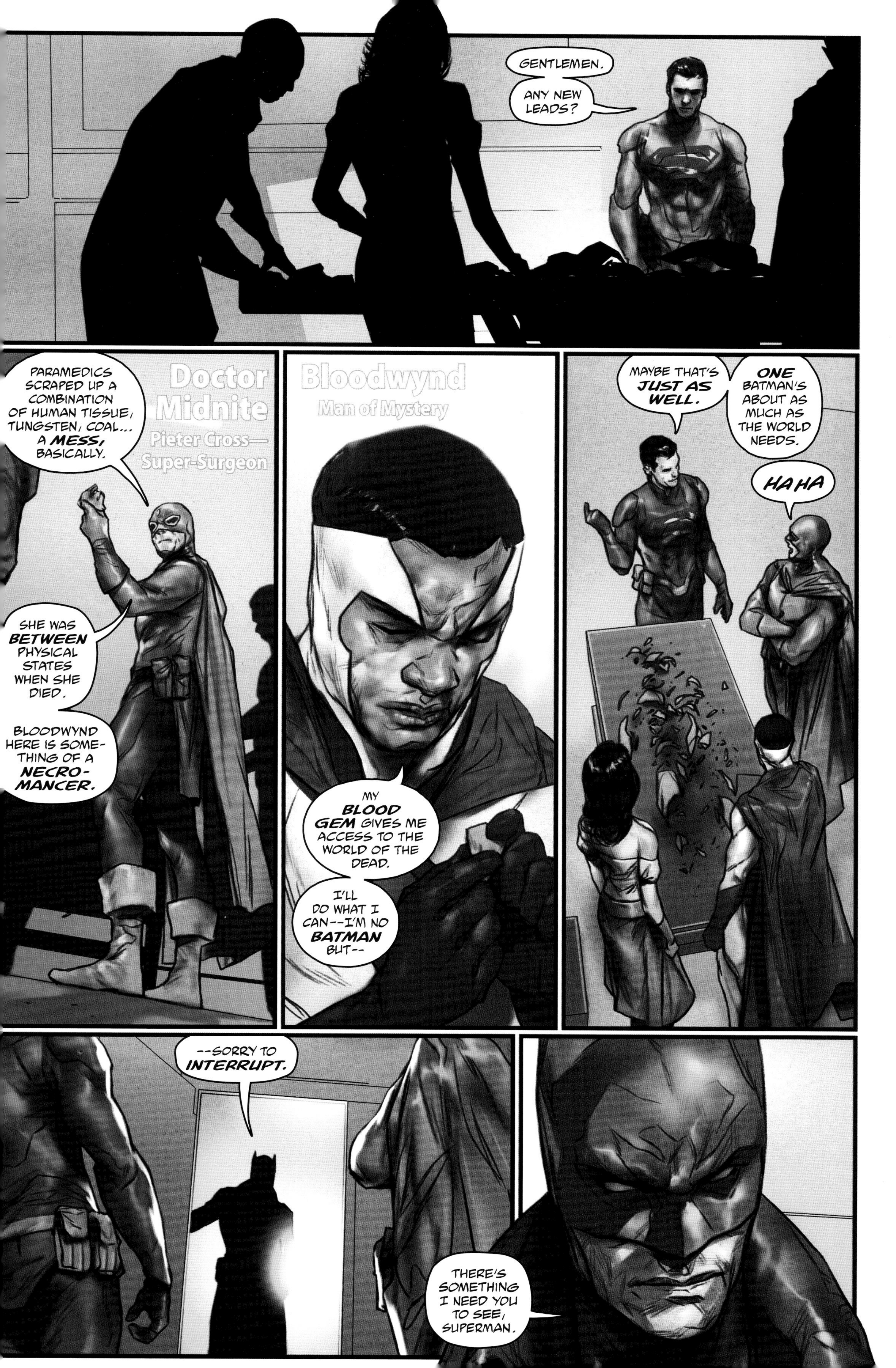

GENTLEMEN.
ANY NEW LEADS?
PARAMEDICS SCRAPED UP A COMBINATION OF HUMAN TISSUE, TUNGSTEN, COAL... A MESS, BASICALLY.
Doctor Midnite
Pieter Cross—Super-Surgeon
SHE WAS BETWEEN PHYSICAL STATES WHEN SHE DIED.
BLOODWYND HERE IS SOMETHING OF A NECROMANCER.
Bloodwynd
Man of Mystery
MY BLOOD GEM GIVES ME ACCESS TO THE WORLD OF THE DEAD.
I'LL DO WHAT I CAN--I'M NO BATMAN BUT--
MAYBE THAT'S JUST AS WELL.
ONE BATMAN'S ABOUT AS MUCH AS THE WORLD NEEDS.
HA HA
--SORRY TO INTERRUPT.
THERE'S SOMETHING I NEED YOU TO SEE, SUPERMAN.

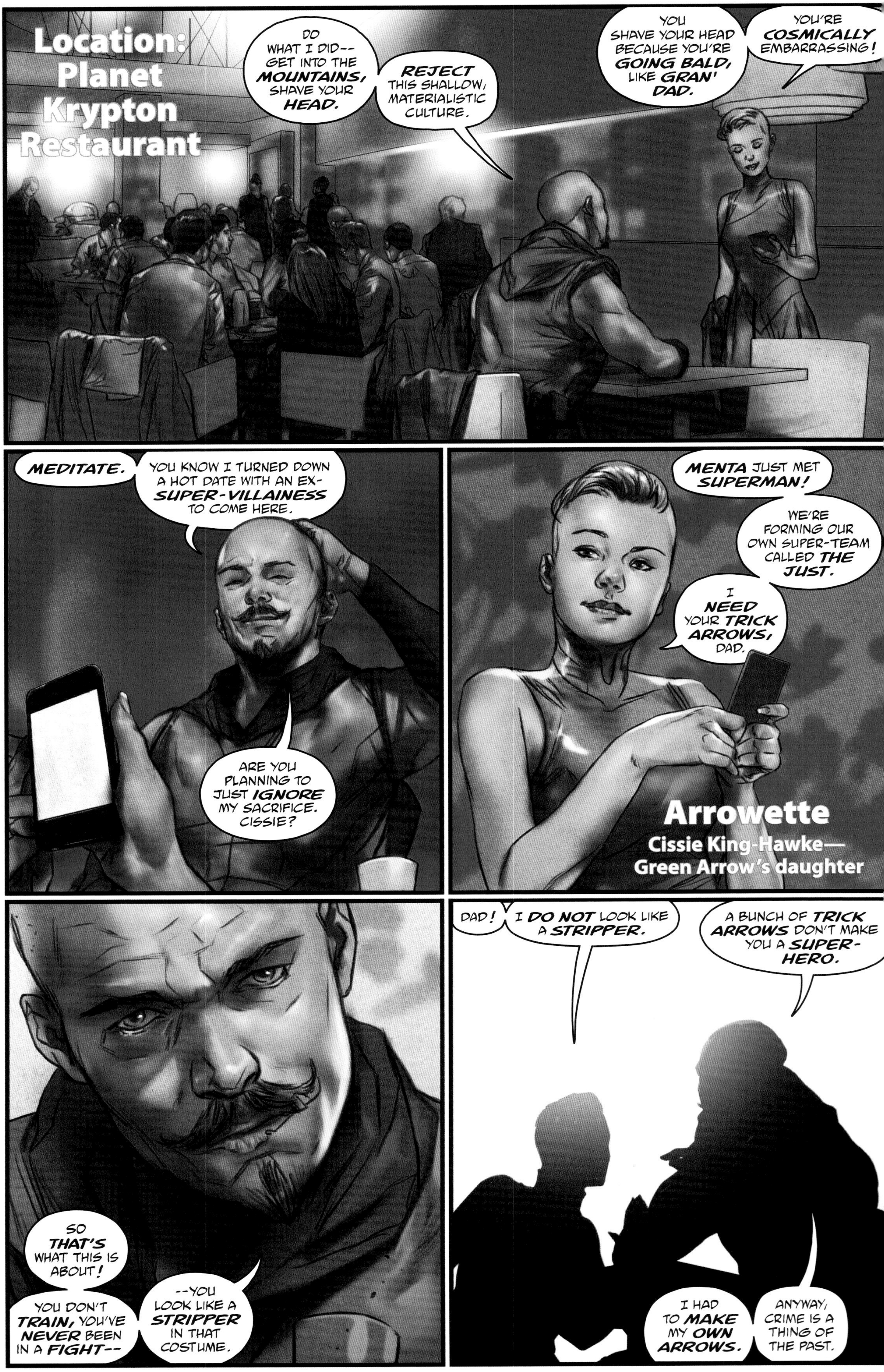
Location: Planet Krypton Restaurant
DO WHAT I DID-- GET INTO THE MOUNTAINS, SHAVE YOUR HEAD.
REJECT THIS SHALLOW, MATERIALISTIC CULTURE.
YOU SHAVE YOUR HEAD BECAUSE YOU'RE GOING BALD, LIKE GRAN' DAD.
YOU'RE COSMICALLY EMBARRASSING!
MEDITATE.
YOU KNOW I TURNED DOWN A HOT DATE WITH AN EX-SUPER-VILLAINESS TO COME HERE.
ARE YOU PLANNING TO JUST IGNORE MY SACRIFICE. CISSIE?
MENTA JUST MET SUPERMAN!
WE'RE FORMING OUR OWN SUPER-TEAM CALLED THE JUST.
I NEED YOUR TRICK ARROWS, DAD.
Arrowette
Cissie King-Hawke—Green Arrow's daughter
SO THAT'S WHAT THIS IS ABOUT!
YOU DON'T TRAIN, YOU'VE NEVER BEEN IN A FIGHT--
--YOU LOOK LIKE A STRIPPER IN THAT COSTUME.
DAD!
I DO NOT LOOK LIKE A STRIPPER.
A BUNCH OF TRICK ARROWS DON'T MAKE YOU A SUPER-HERO.
I HAD TO MAKE MY OWN ARROWS.
ANYWAY, CRIME IS A THING OF THE PAST.

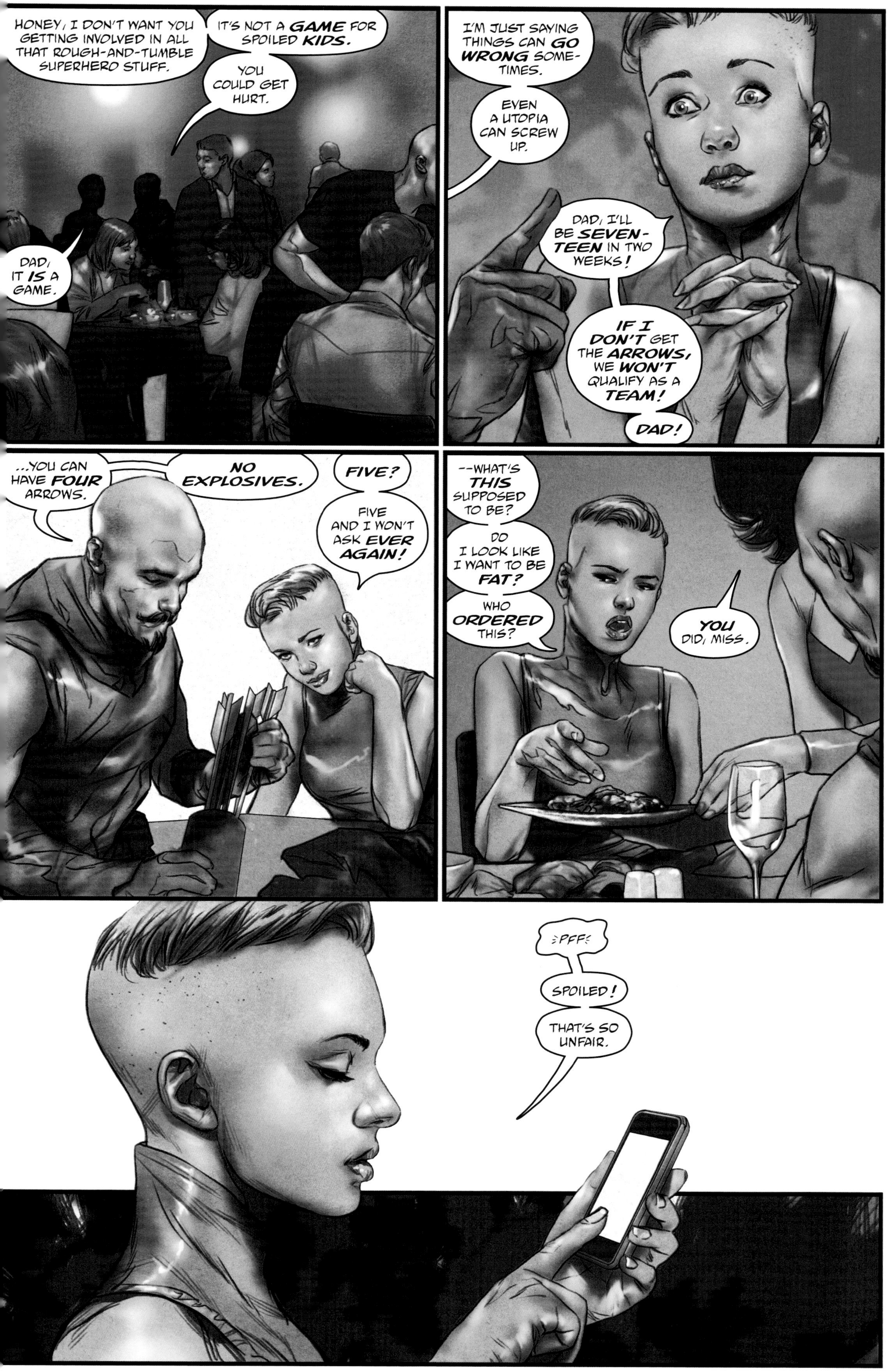
HONEY, I DON'T WANT YOU GETTING INVOLVED IN ALL THAT ROUGH-AND-TUMBLE SUPERHERO STUFF.
IT'S NOT A **GAME** FOR SPOILED **KIDS.**
YOU COULD GET HURT.
DAD, IT **IS** A GAME.
I'M JUST SAYING THINGS CAN **GO WRONG** SOME-TIMES.
EVEN A UTOPIA CAN SCREW UP.
DAD, I'LL BE **SEVENTEEN** IN TWO WEEKS!
IF I DON'T GET THE **ARROWS,** WE **WON'T** QUALIFY AS A **TEAM!**
DAD!
...YOU CAN HAVE **FOUR** ARROWS.
NO EXPLOSIVES.
FIVE?
FIVE AND I WON'T ASK **EVER AGAIN!**
--WHAT'S **THIS** SUPPOSED TO BE?
DO I LOOK LIKE I WANT TO BE **FAT?**
WHO **ORDERED** THIS?
YOU DID, MISS.
PFF
SPOILED!
THAT'S SO UNFAIR.

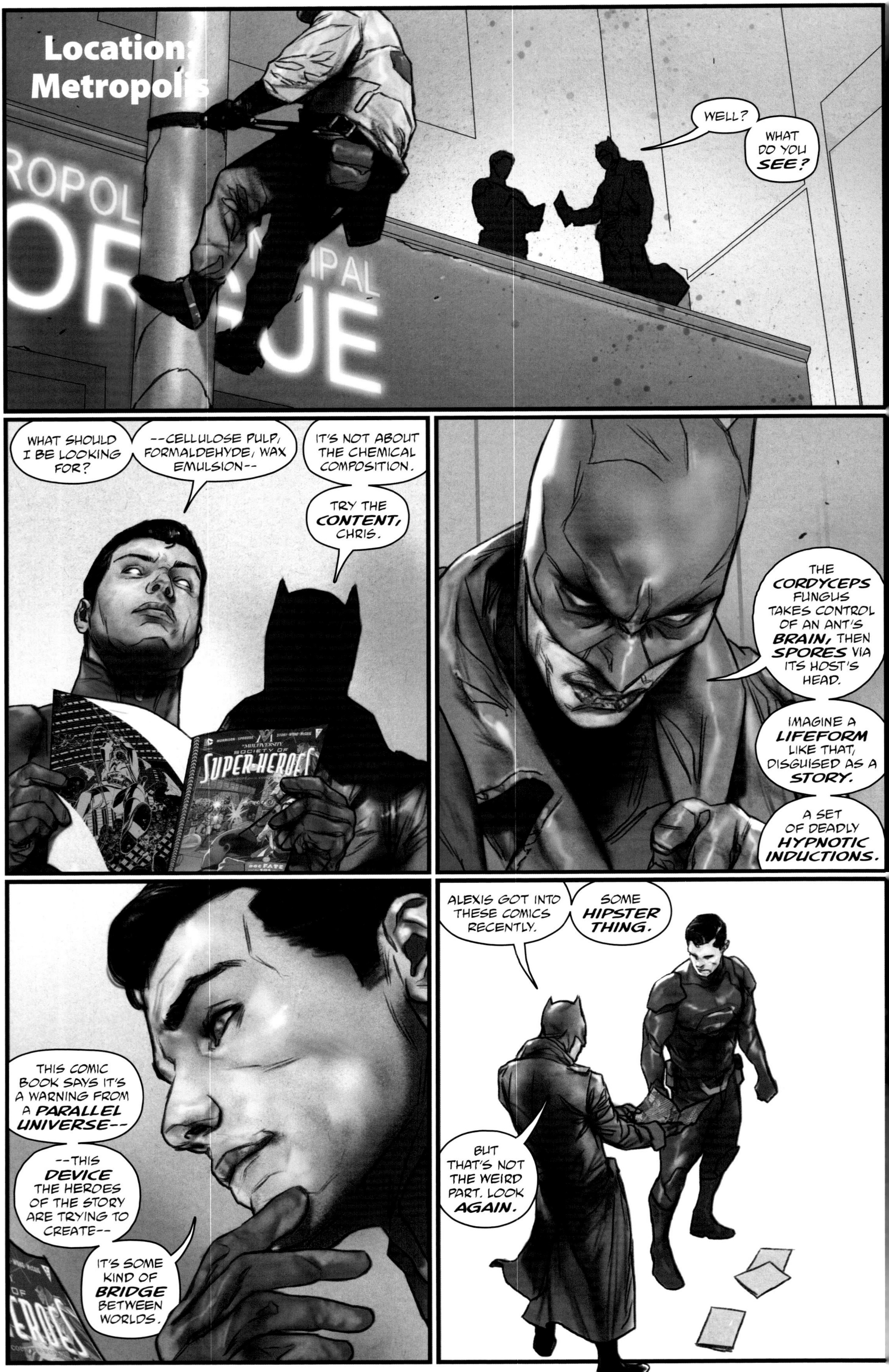
Location: Metropolis
ROPOL
MUNICIPAL
MORGUE
WELL?
WHAT DO YOU SEE?
WHAT SHOULD I BE LOOKING FOR?
--CELLULOSE PULP, FORMALDEHYDE, WAX EMULSION--
IT'S NOT ABOUT THE CHEMICAL COMPOSITION.
TRY THE CONTENT, CHRIS.
THE MULTIVERSITY SOCIETY OF SUPER-HEROES
THE CORDYCEPS FUNGUS TAKES CONTROL OF AN ANT'S BRAIN, THEN SPORES VIA ITS HOST'S HEAD.
IMAGINE A LIFEFORM LIKE THAT, DISGUISED AS A STORY.
A SET OF DEADLY HYPNOTIC INDUCTIONS.
THIS COMIC BOOK SAYS IT'S A WARNING FROM A PARALLEL UNIVERSE--
--THIS DEVICE THE HEROES OF THE STORY ARE TRYING TO CREATE--
IT'S SOME KIND OF BRIDGE BETWEEN WORLDS.
ALEXIS GOT INTO THESE COMICS RECENTLY.
SOME HIPSTER THING.
BUT THAT'S NOT THE WEIRD PART. LOOK AGAIN.

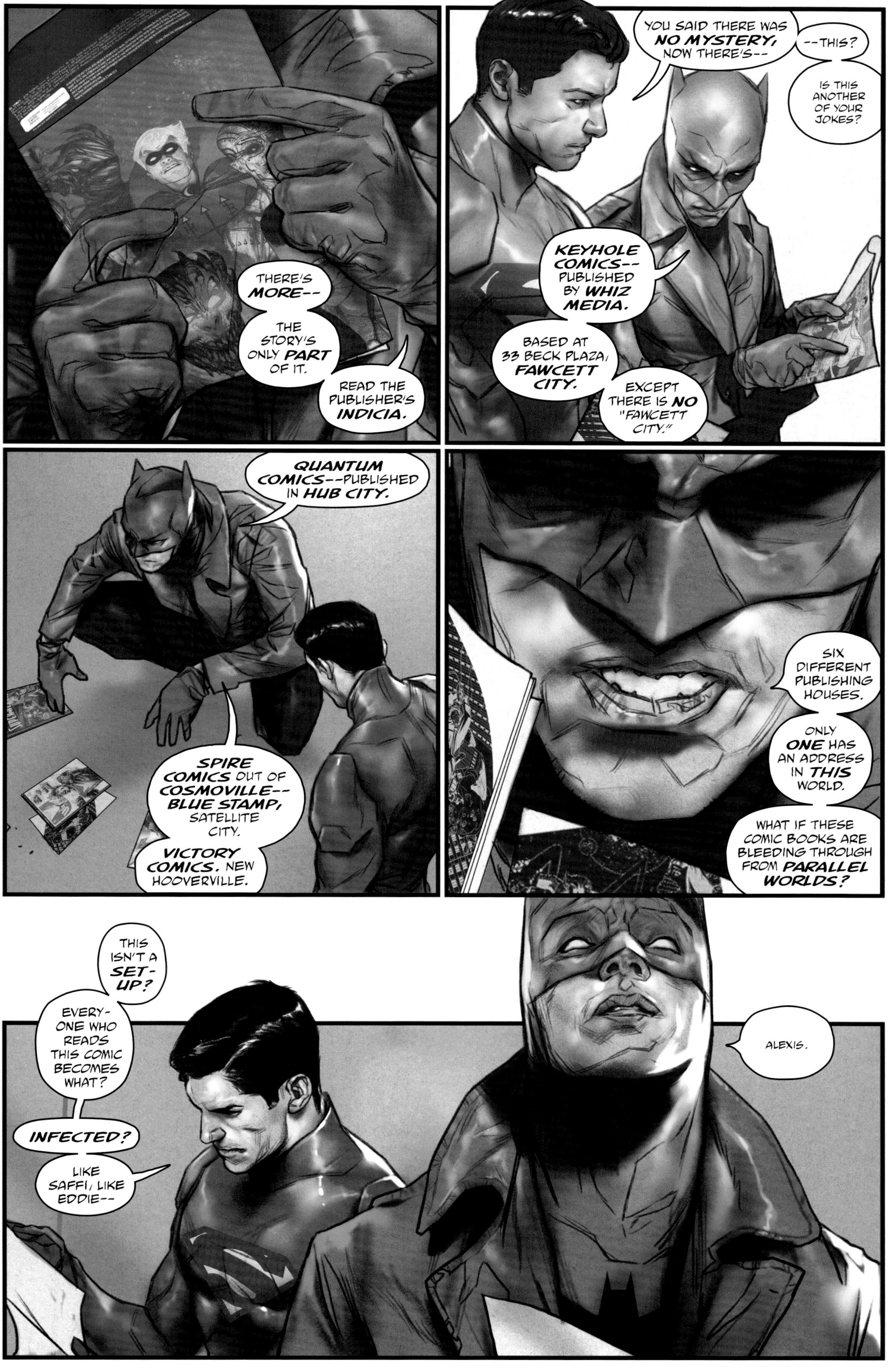
THERE'S MORE--
THE STORY'S ONLY PART OF IT.
READ THE PUBLISHER'S INDICIA.
YOU SAID THERE WAS NO MYSTERY, NOW THERE'S--
--THIS?
IS THIS ANOTHER OF YOUR JOKES?
KEYHOLE COMICS--PUBLISHED BY WHIZ MEDIA.
BASED AT 33 BECK PLAZA, FAWCETT CITY.
EXCEPT THERE IS NO "FAWCETT CITY."
QUANTUM COMICS--PUBLISHED IN HUB CITY.
SPIRE COMICS OUT OF COSMOVILLE--BLUE STAMP, SATELLITE CITY.
VICTORY COMICS. NEW HOOVERVILLE.
SIX DIFFERENT PUBLISHING HOUSES.
ONLY ONE HAS AN ADDRESS IN THIS WORLD.
WHAT IF THESE COMIC BOOKS ARE BLEEDING THROUGH FROM PARALLEL WORLDS?
THIS ISN'T A SET-UP?
EVERY-ONE WHO READS THIS COMIC BECOMES WHAT?
INFECTED?
LIKE SAFFI, LIKE EDDIE--
ALEXIS.

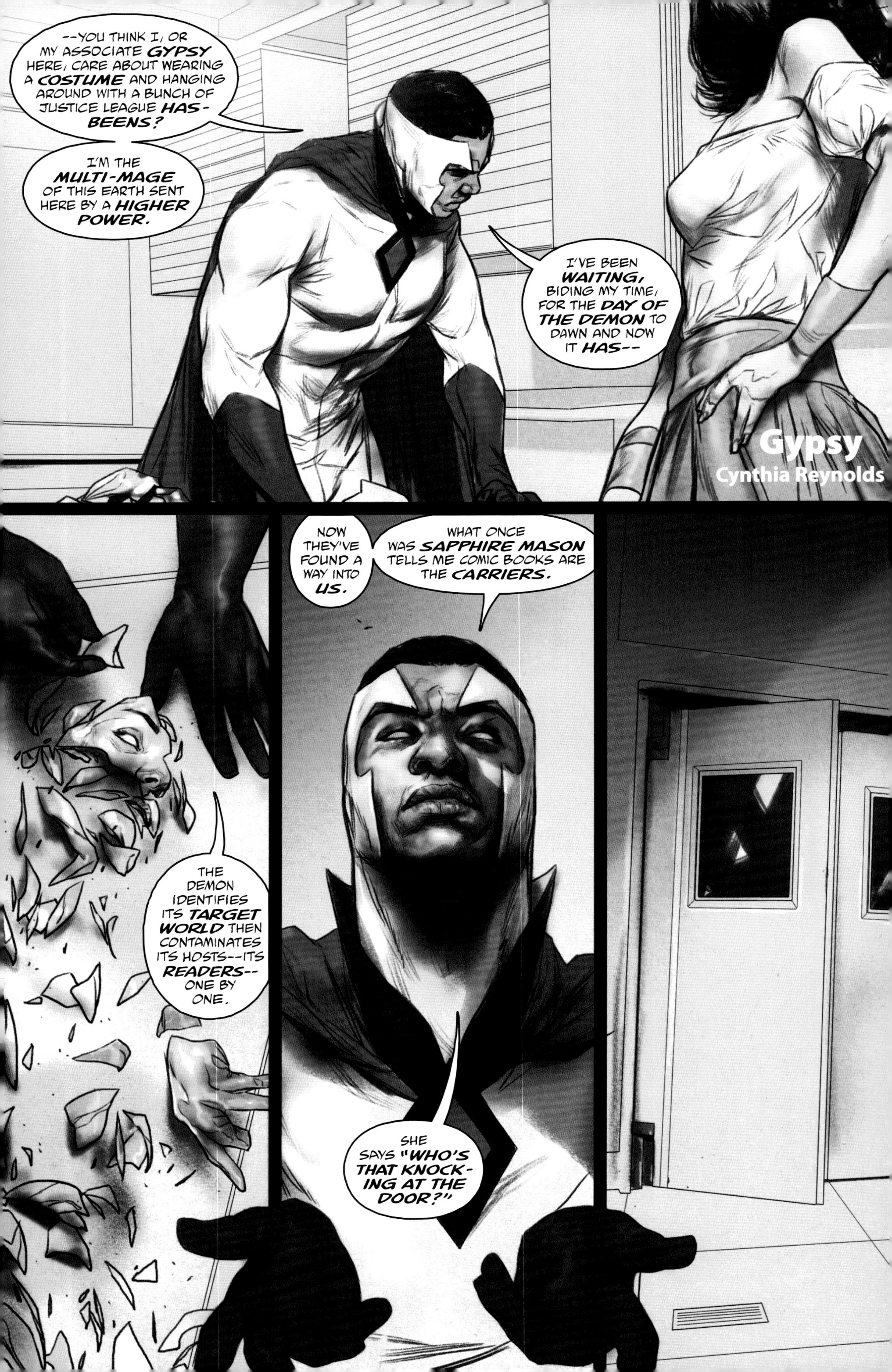
--YOU THINK I, OR MY ASSOCIATE GYPSY HERE, CARE ABOUT WEARING A COSTUME AND HANGING AROUND WITH A BUNCH OF JUSTICE LEAGUE HAS-BEENS?
I'M THE MULTI-MAGE OF THIS EARTH SENT HERE BY A HIGHER POWER.
I'VE BEEN WAITING, BIDING MY TIME, FOR THE DAY OF THE DEMON TO DAWN AND NOW IT HAS--
Gypsy
Cynthia Reynolds
THE DEMON IDENTIFIES ITS TARGET WORLD THEN CONTAMINATES ITS HOSTS--ITS READERS--ONE BY ONE.
NOW THEY'VE FOUND A WAY INTO US.
WHAT ONCE WAS SAPPHIRE MASON TELLS ME COMIC BOOKS ARE THE CARRIERS.
SHE SAYS "WHO'S THAT KNOCKING AT THE DOOR?"

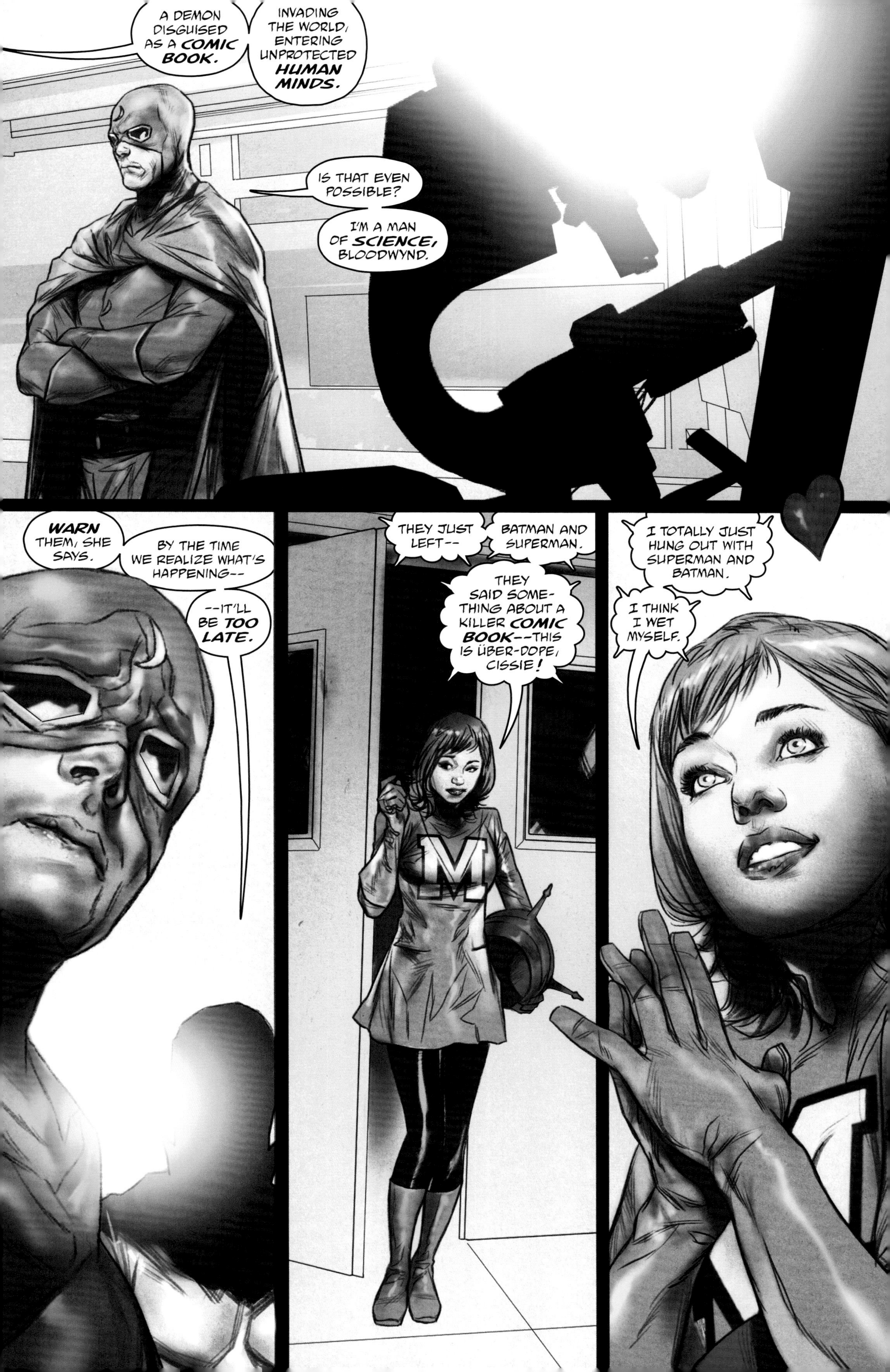
A DEMON DISGUISED AS A COMIC BOOK.
INVADING THE WORLD, ENTERING UNPROTECTED HUMAN MINDS.
IS THAT EVEN POSSIBLE?
I'M A MAN OF SCIENCE, BLOODWYND.
WARN THEM, SHE SAYS.
BY THE TIME WE REALIZE WHAT'S HAPPENING--
--IT'LL BE TOO LATE.
THEY JUST LEFT--
BATMAN AND SUPERMAN.
THEY SAID SOME-THING ABOUT A KILLER COMIC BOOK--THIS IS ÜBER-DOPE, CISSIE!
I TOTALLY JUST HUNG OUT WITH SUPERMAN AND BATMAN.
I THINK I WET MYSELF.

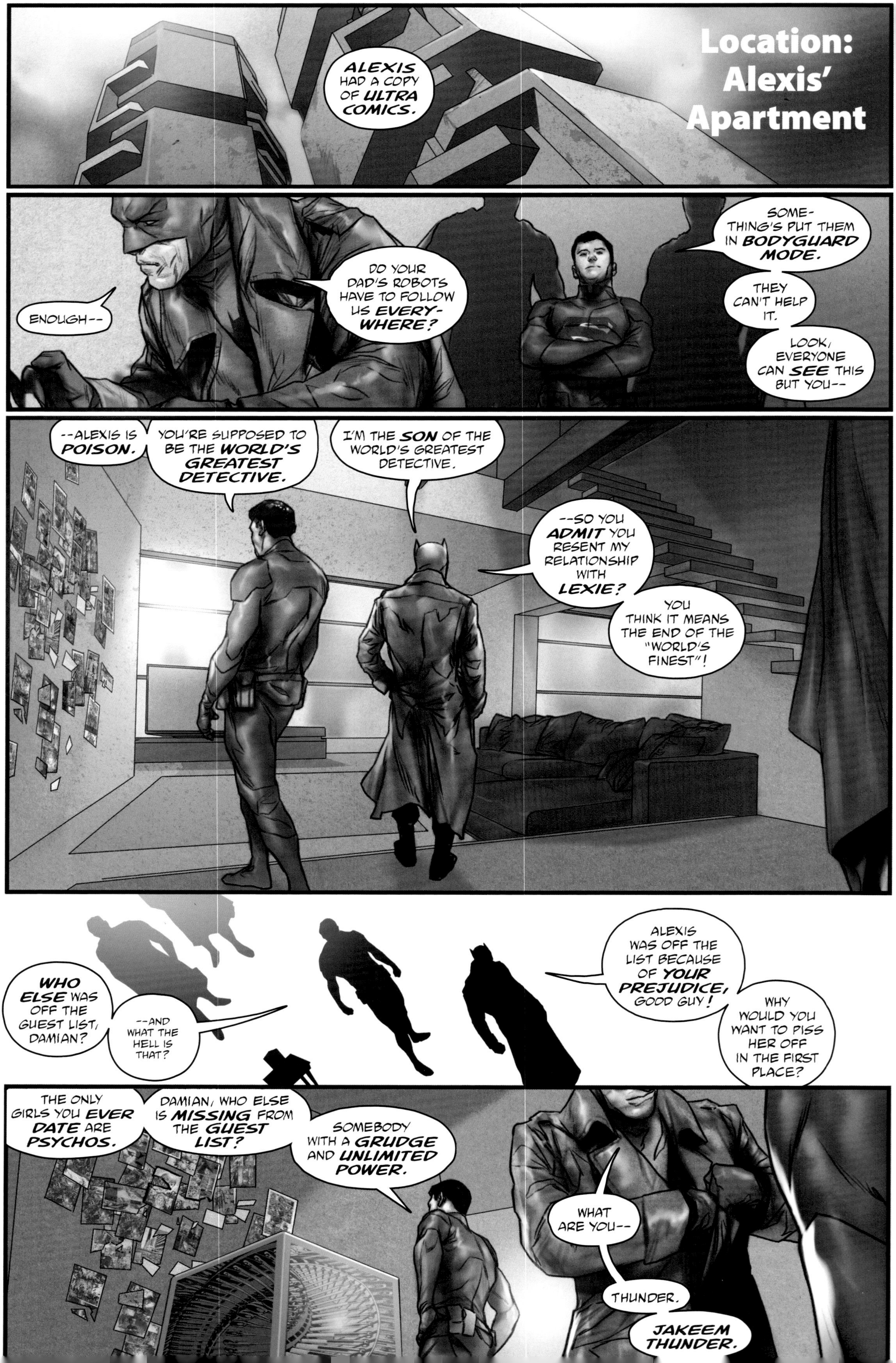
Location: Alexis' Apartment
ALEXIS HAD A COPY OF ULTRA COMICS.
ENOUGH--
DO YOUR DAD'S ROBOTS HAVE TO FOLLOW US EVERY-WHERE?
SOME-THING'S PUT THEM IN BODYGUARD MODE.
THEY CAN'T HELP IT.
LOOK, EVERYONE CAN SEE THIS BUT YOU--
--ALEXIS IS POISON.
YOU'RE SUPPOSED TO BE THE WORLD'S GREATEST DETECTIVE.
I'M THE SON OF THE WORLD'S GREATEST DETECTIVE.
--SO YOU ADMIT YOU RESENT MY RELATIONSHIP WITH LEXIE?
YOU THINK IT MEANS THE END OF THE "WORLD'S FINEST"!
WHO ELSE WAS OFF THE GUEST LIST, DAMIAN?
--AND WHAT THE HELL IS THAT?
ALEXIS WAS OFF THE LIST BECAUSE OF YOUR PREJUDICE, GOOD GUY!
WHY WOULD YOU WANT TO PISS HER OFF IN THE FIRST PLACE?
THE ONLY GIRLS YOU EVER DATE ARE PSYCHOS.
DAMIAN, WHO ELSE IS MISSING FROM THE GUEST LIST?
SOMEBODY WITH A GRUDGE AND UNLIMITED POWER.
WHAT ARE YOU--
THUNDER.
JAKEEM THUNDER.

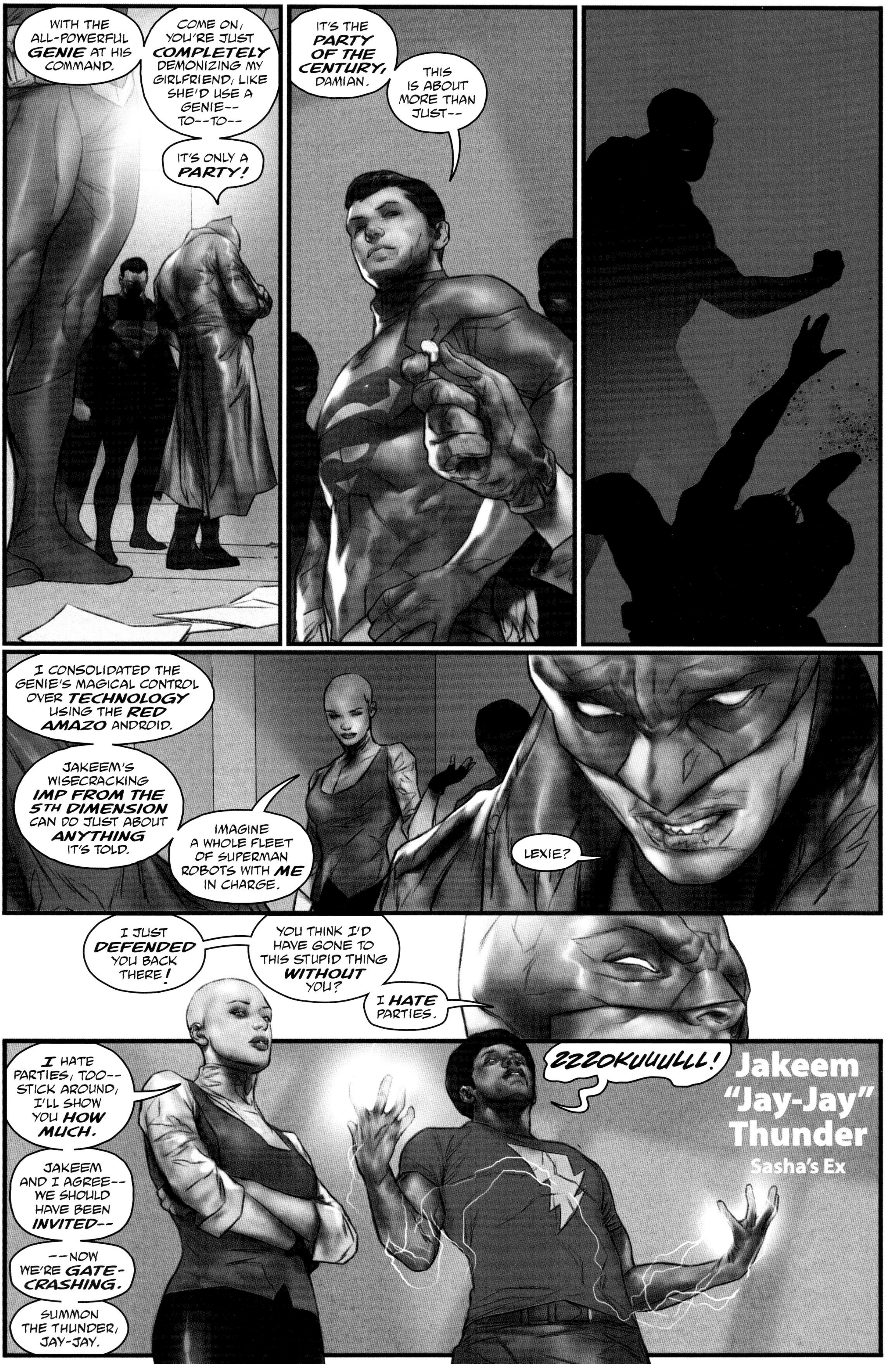
WITH THE ALL-POWERFUL GENIE AT HIS COMMAND.
COME ON, YOU'RE JUST COMPLETELY DEMONIZING MY GIRLFRIEND, LIKE SHE'D USE A GENIE-- TO--TO--
IT'S ONLY A PARTY!
IT'S THE PARTY OF THE CENTURY, DAMIAN.
THIS IS ABOUT MORE THAN JUST--
I CONSOLIDATED THE GENIE'S MAGICAL CONTROL OVER TECHNOLOGY USING THE RED AMAZO ANDROID.
JAKEEM'S WISECRACKING IMP FROM THE 5TH DIMENSION CAN DO JUST ABOUT ANYTHING IT'S TOLD.
IMAGINE A WHOLE FLEET OF SUPERMAN ROBOTS WITH ME IN CHARGE.
LEXIE?
I JUST DEFENDED YOU BACK THERE!
YOU THINK I'D HAVE GONE TO THIS STUPID THING WITHOUT YOU?
I HATE PARTIES.
I HATE PARTIES, TOO-- STICK AROUND, I'LL SHOW YOU HOW MUCH.
JAKEEM AND I AGREE-- WE SHOULD HAVE BEEN INVITED--
--NOW WE'RE GATE-CRASHING.
SUMMON THE THUNDER, JAY-JAY.
ZZZOKUUULLL!
Jakeem "Jay-Jay" Thunder
Sasha's Ex

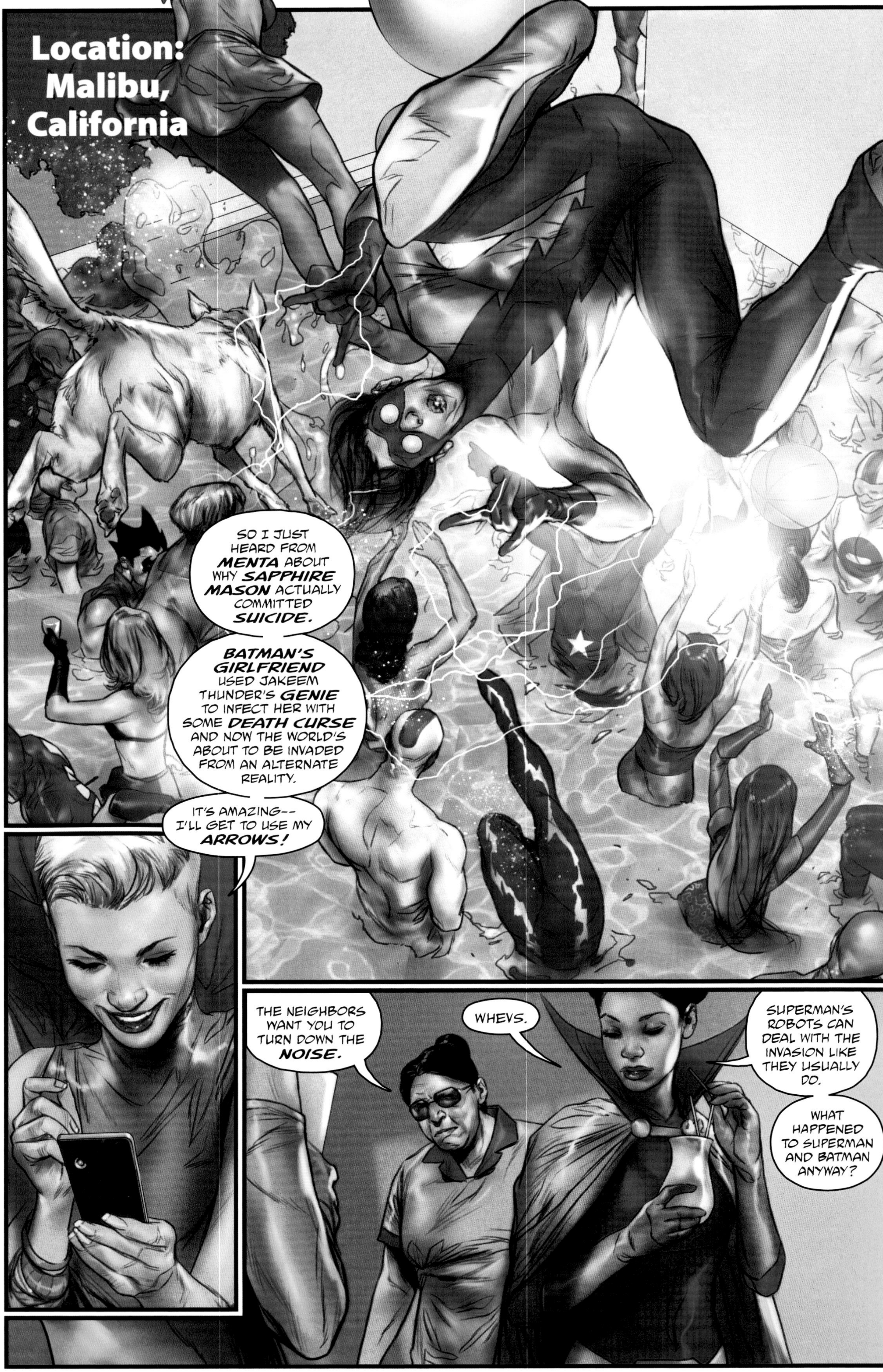
Location: Malibu, California
SO I JUST HEARD FROM MENTA ABOUT WHY SAPPHIRE MASON ACTUALLY COMMITTED SUICIDE.
BATMAN'S GIRLFRIEND USED JAKEEM THUNDER'S GENIE TO INFECT HER WITH SOME DEATH CURSE AND NOW THE WORLD'S ABOUT TO BE INVADED FROM AN ALTERNATE REALITY.
IT'S AMAZING-- I'LL GET TO USE MY ARROWS!
THE NEIGHBORS WANT YOU TO TURN DOWN THE NOISE.
WHEVS.
SUPERMAN'S ROBOTS CAN DEAL WITH THE INVASION LIKE THEY USUALLY DO.
WHAT HAPPENED TO SUPERMAN AND BATMAN ANYWAY?

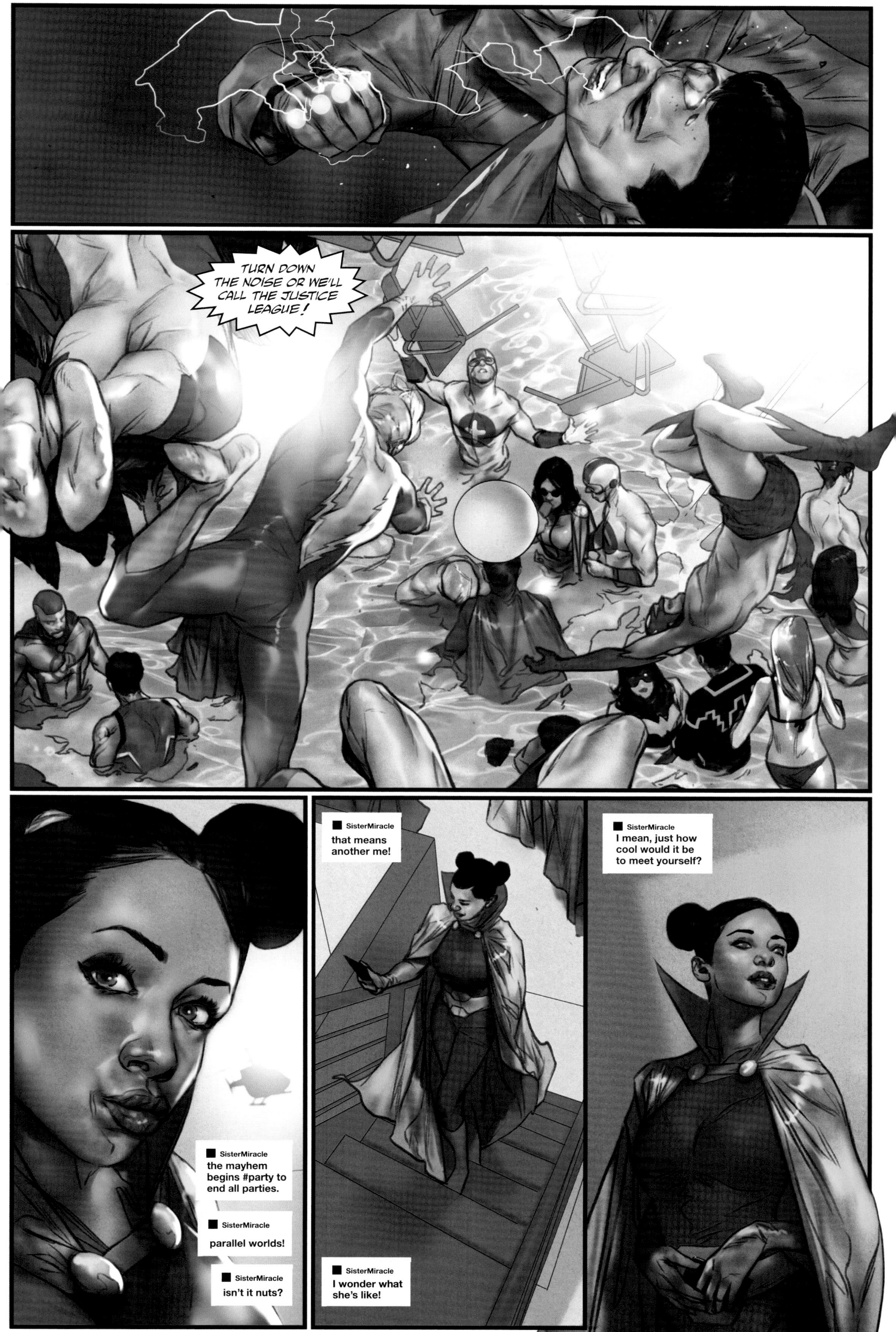
TURN DOWN THE NOISE OR WE'LL CALL THE JUSTICE LEAGUE!
SisterMiracle
the mayhem begins #party to end all parties.
SisterMiracle
parallel worlds!
SisterMiracle
isn't it nuts?
SisterMiracle
that means another me!
SisterMiracle
I wonder what she's like!
SisterMiracle
I mean, just how cool would it be to meet yourself?

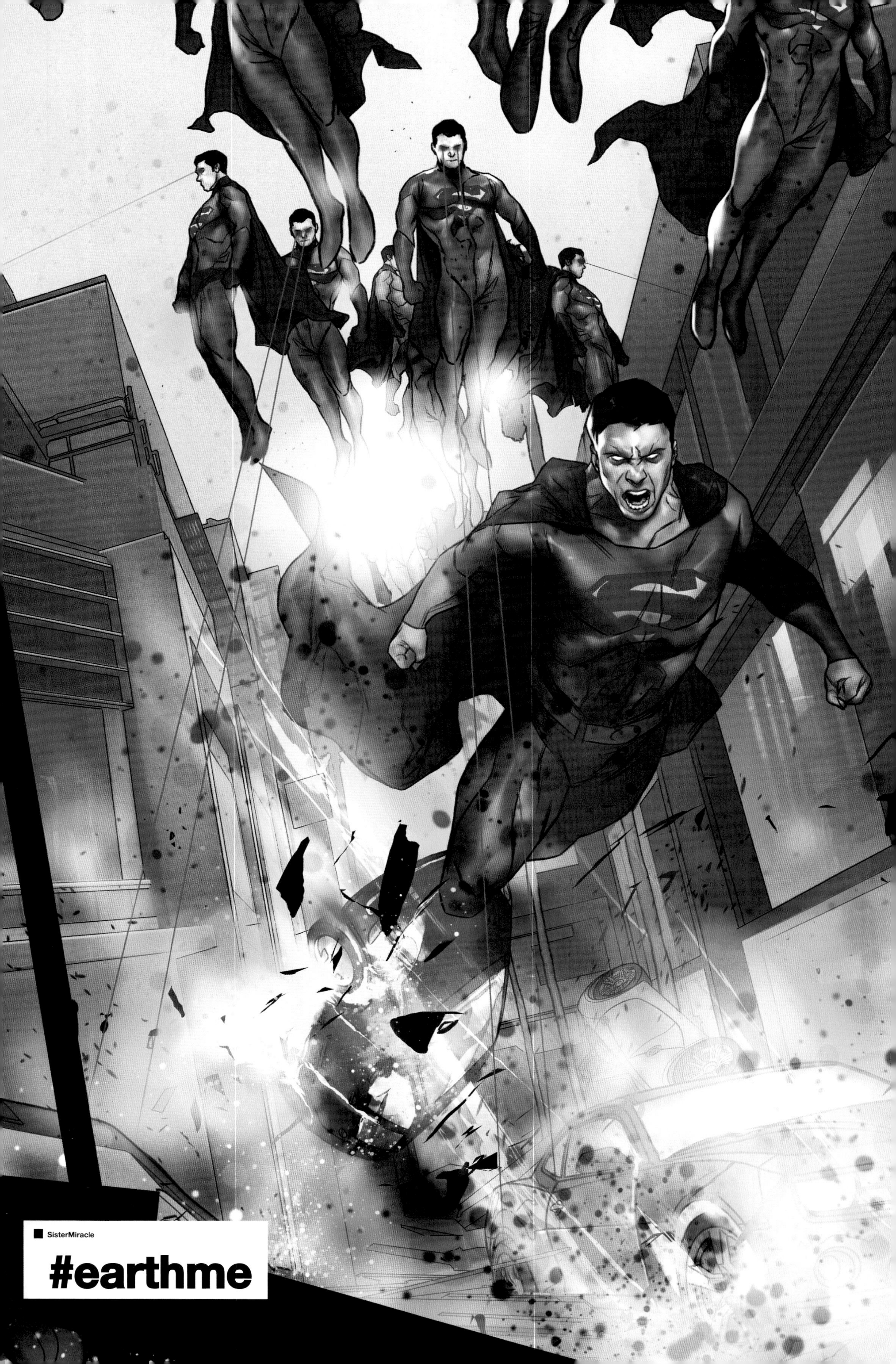
SisterMiracle
#earthme

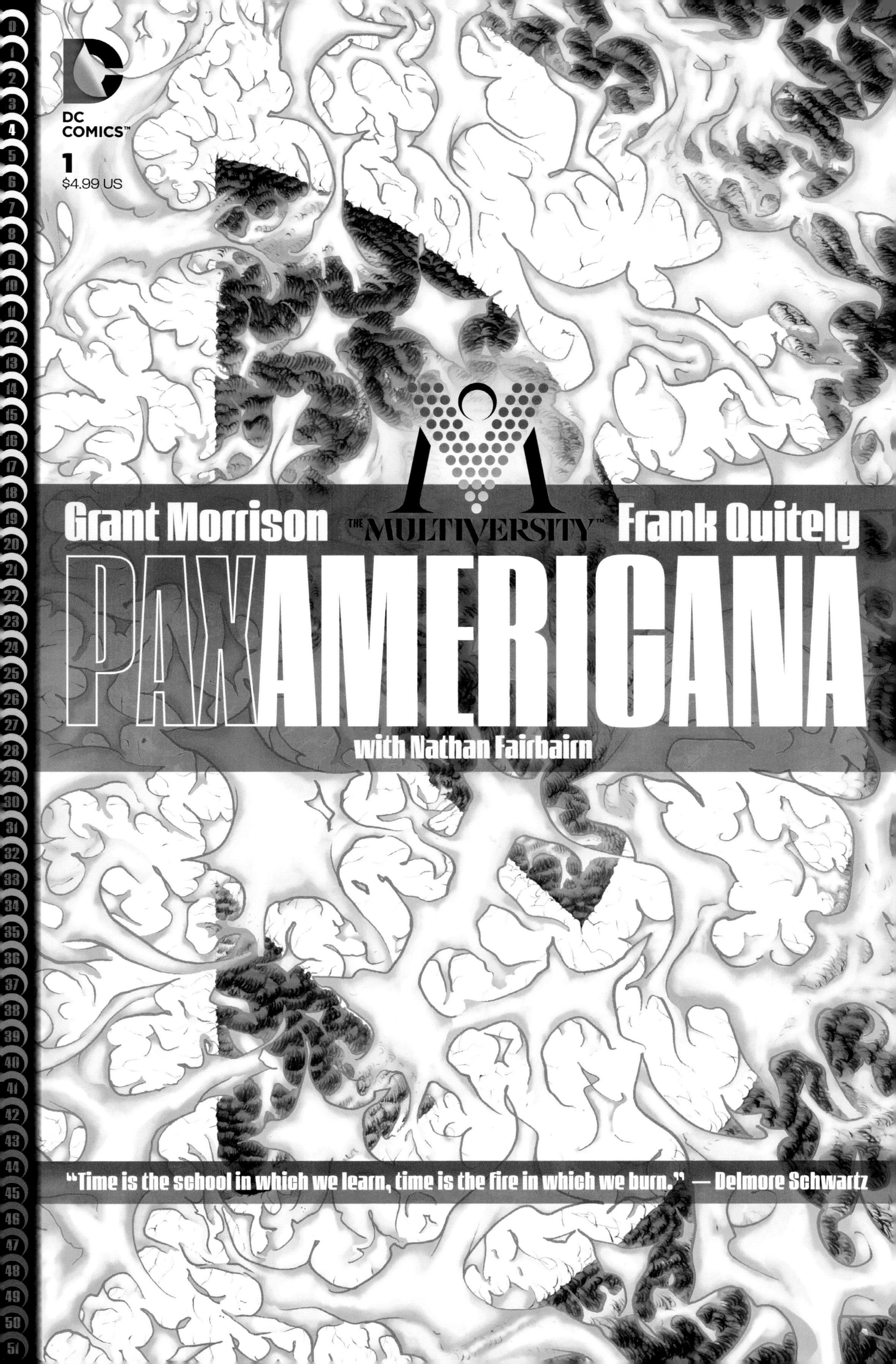
DC COMICS™
1
$4.99 US
Grant Morrison
THE MULTIVERSITY™
Frank Quitely
PAX AMERICANA
with Nathan Fairbairn
“Time is the school in which we learn, time is the fire in which we burn.” — Delmore Schwartz

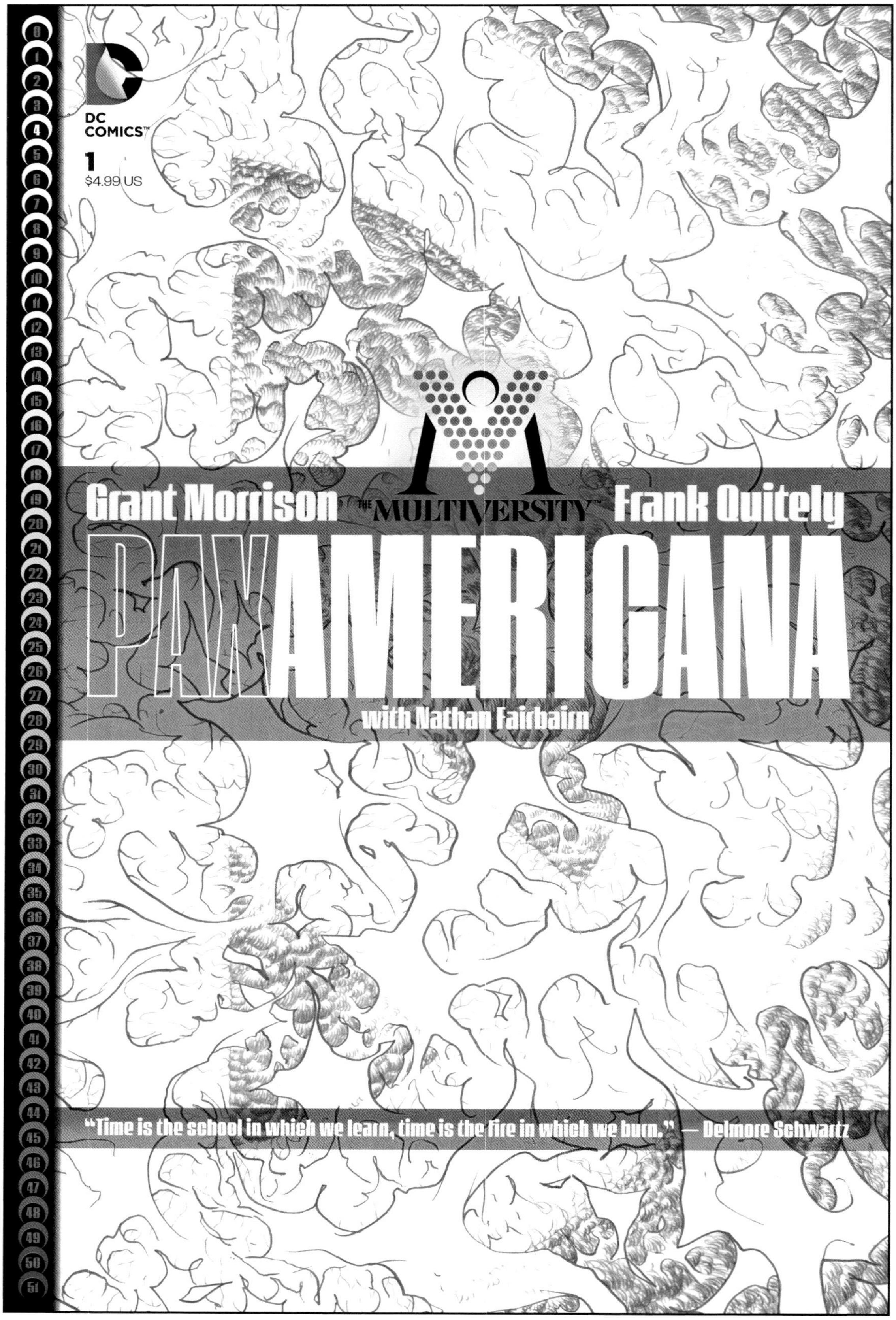
DC COMICS
1
$4.99 US
Grant Morrison
THE MULTIVERSITY
Frank Quitely
PAX AMERICANA
with Nathan Fairbairn
"Time is the school in which we learn, time is the fire in which we burn." — Delmore Schwartz

THE MULTIVERSITY: PAX AMERICANA
#1

Written by
GRANT MORRISON

Artist
FRANK QUITELY

Colorist
NATHAN FAIRBAIRN

Letterer
ROB LEIGH

Cover artists
FRANK QUITELY with
NATHAN FAIRBAIRN

PAX
STATES

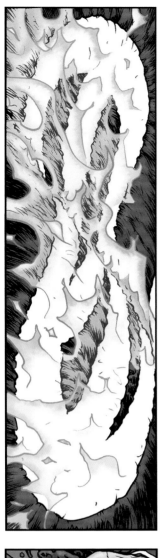

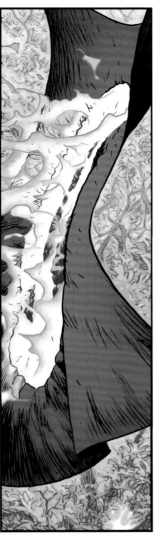

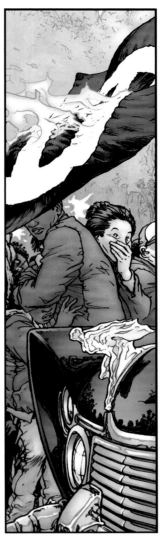

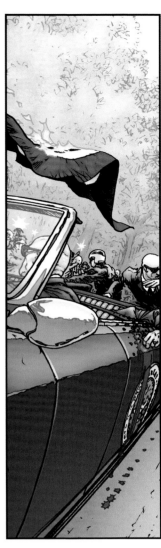

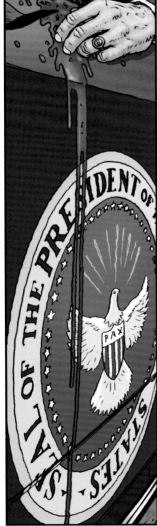

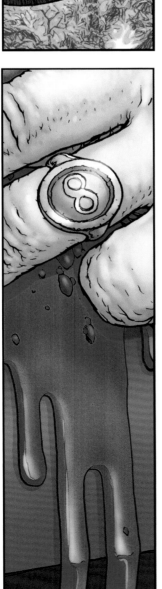

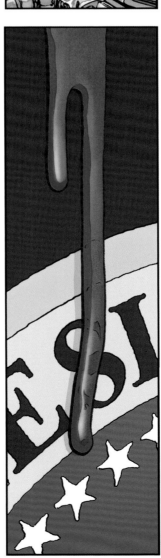

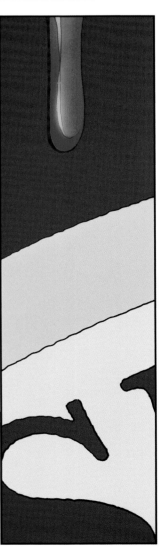

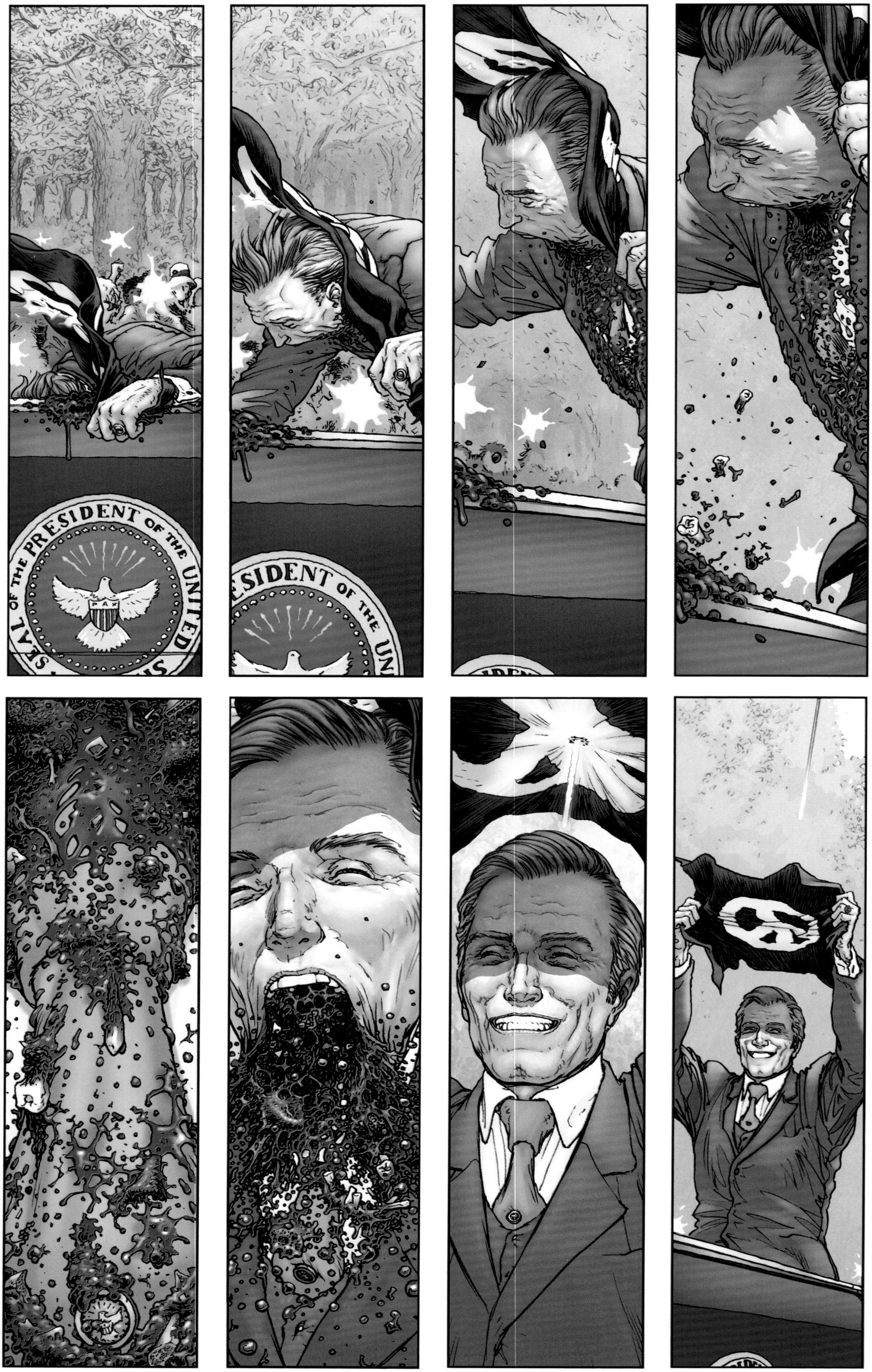
SEAL OF THE PRESIDENT OF THE UNITED

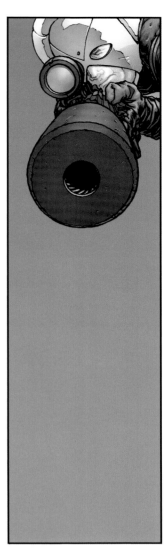

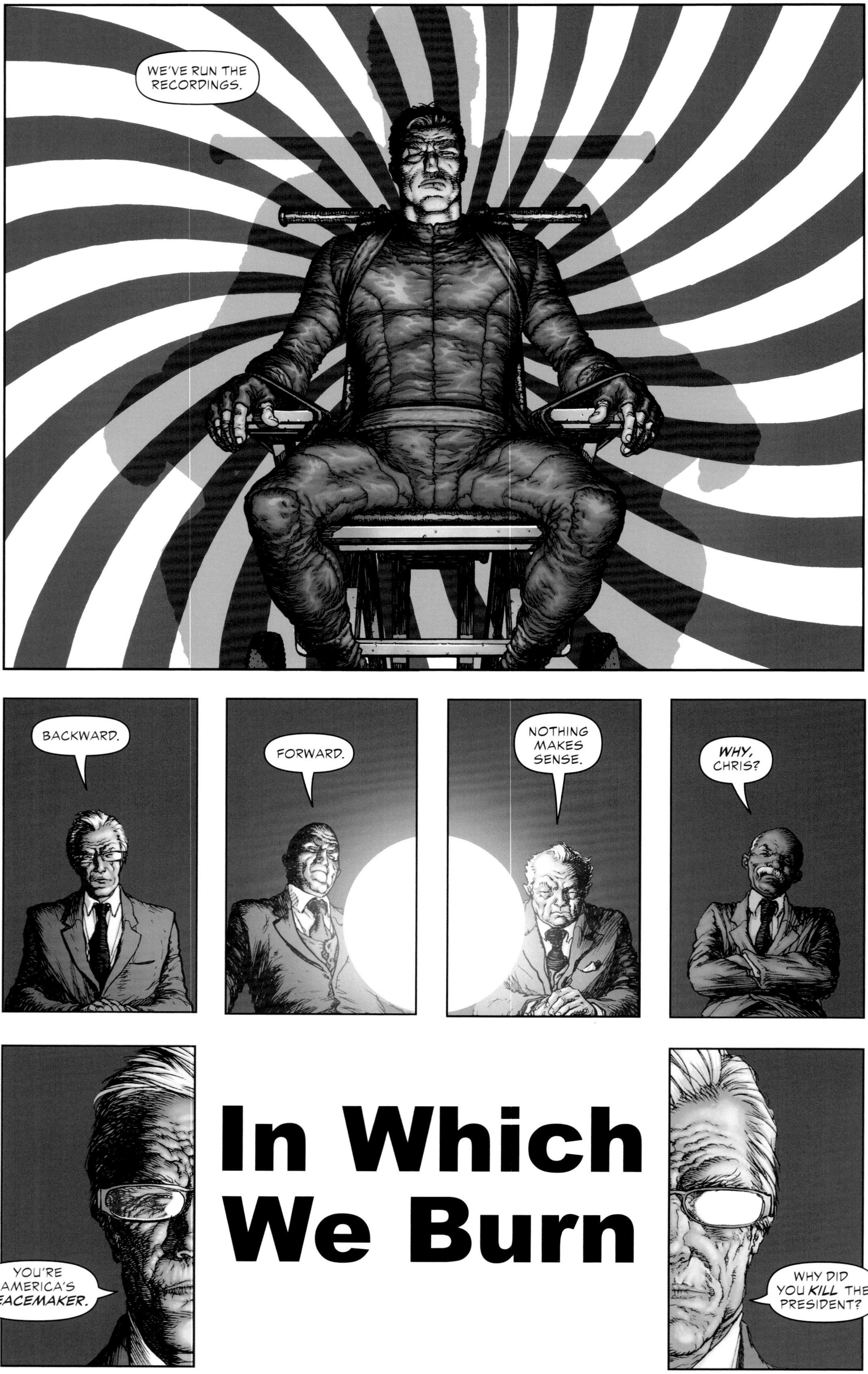
WE'VE RUN THE RECORDINGS.
BACKWARD.
FORWARD.
NOTHING MAKES SENSE.
WHY, CHRIS?
YOU'RE AMERICA'S *PEACEMAKER.*
In Which We Burn
WHY DID YOU *KILL* THE PRESIDENT?

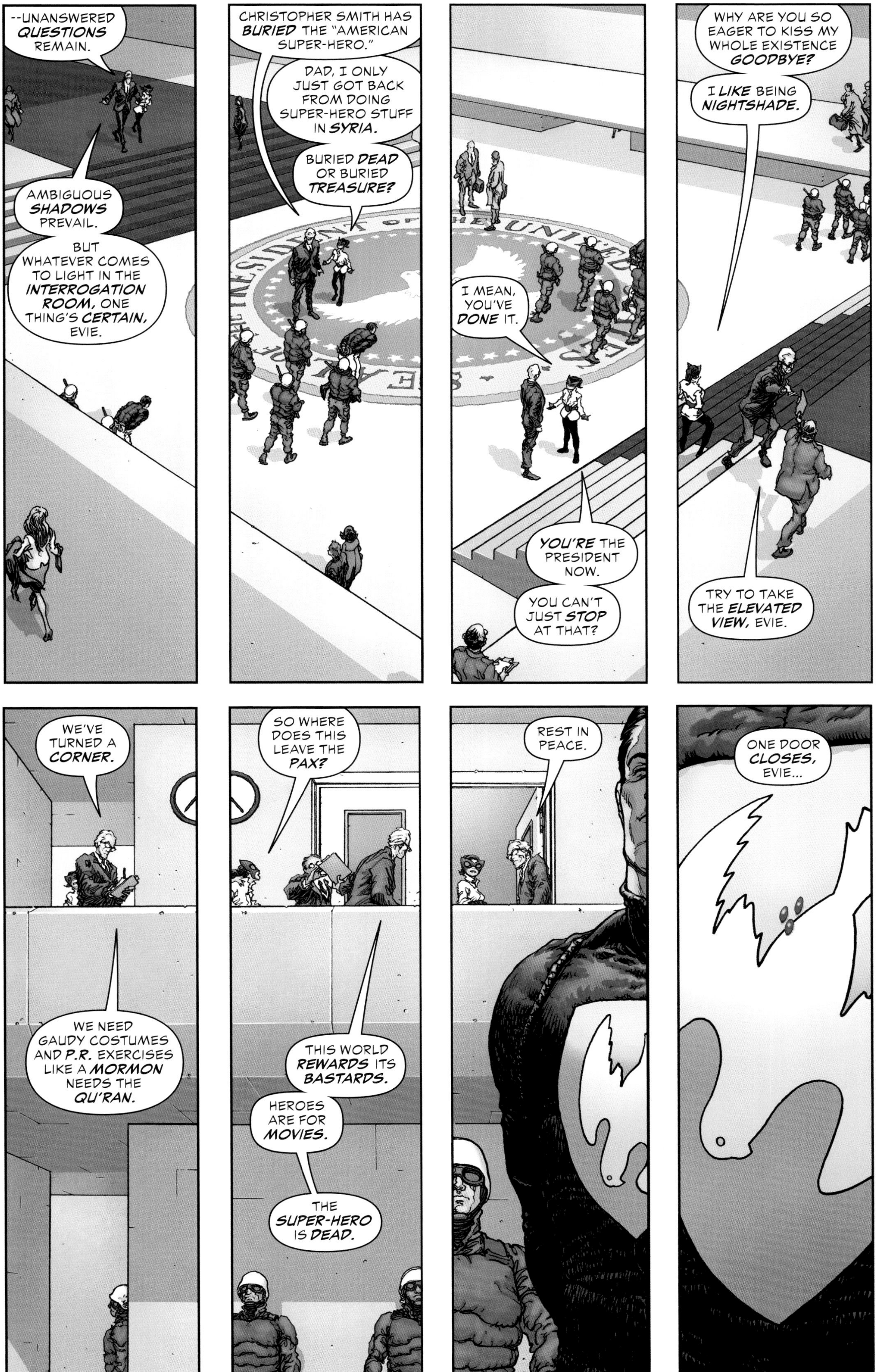
--UNANSWERED QUESTIONS REMAIN.
AMBIGUOUS SHADOWS PREVAIL.
BUT WHATEVER COMES TO LIGHT IN THE INTERROGATION ROOM, ONE THING'S CERTAIN, EVIE.
CHRISTOPHER SMITH HAS BURIED THE "AMERICAN SUPER-HERO."
DAD, I ONLY JUST GOT BACK FROM DOING SUPER-HERO STUFF IN SYRIA.
BURIED DEAD OR BURIED TREASURE?
I MEAN, YOU'VE DONE IT.
YOU'RE THE PRESIDENT NOW.
YOU CAN'T JUST STOP AT THAT?
WHY ARE YOU SO EAGER TO KISS MY WHOLE EXISTENCE GOODBYE?
I LIKE BEING NIGHTSHADE.
TRY TO TAKE THE ELEVATED VIEW, EVIE.
WE'VE TURNED A CORNER.
WE NEED GAUDY COSTUMES AND P.R. EXERCISES LIKE A MORMON NEEDS THE QU'RAN.
SO WHERE DOES THIS LEAVE THE PAX?
THIS WORLD REWARDS ITS BASTARDS.
HEROES ARE FOR MOVIES.
THE SUPER-HERO IS DEAD.
REST IN PEACE.
ONE DOOR CLOSES, EVIE...

...ANOTHER *OPENS.*

"SUPER-HERO" JUST BECAME A *DIRTY WORD.*

BUT THAT DOESN'T MEAN IT'S *ALL OVER.*

MOM WAS *RIGHT* ABOUT YOU...

YOUR MOTHER CLAIMED SHE WAS BORN IN THE *"SHADOW DIMENSION."*

AS FOR THE *OTHER* ACCUSATIONS...

MOM'S NOT *WELL.*

EVIE, THE *AMERICAN EMPIRE* FACES A DESCENT INTO *CHAOS.*

UNLESS *WE* TAKE STEPS TO PREVENT THE DECLINE--

VALUES *CHANGE* WITH AGE, YOU'LL *SEE.*

YOU TWIST *EVERYTHING.*

ENEMIES BECOME *FRIENDS.*

REFLECTION IS THE MOTHER OF *COMPROMISE.*

--EVERYTHING GOES INTO *REVERSE.*

THAT SHOULD SUIT *YOU.*

YOU GO BACK ON *EVERYTHING* YOU SAY, DAD!

HEROES AND VILLAINS?

MASKS?

OLD-FASHIONED *POLITICS* WILL TURN THIS COUNTRY AROUND.

WHAT ABOUT *MY LIFE?*

THE COUNTRY'S HIT ROCK BOTTOM.

THE MOST POPULAR PRESIDENT IN *DECADES,* SHOT DEAD BY HIS *BODYGUARD.*

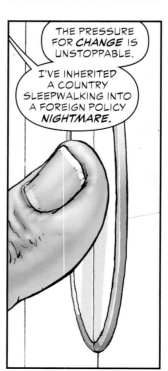

THE PRESSURE FOR *CHANGE* IS UNSTOPPABLE.

I'VE INHERITED A COUNTRY SLEEPWALKING INTO A FOREIGN POLICY *NIGHTMARE.*

WHAT WE NEED NOW IS A CONVINCING *EXIT STRATEGY.*

YOU MEAN A RETREAT INTO THE *PAST?*

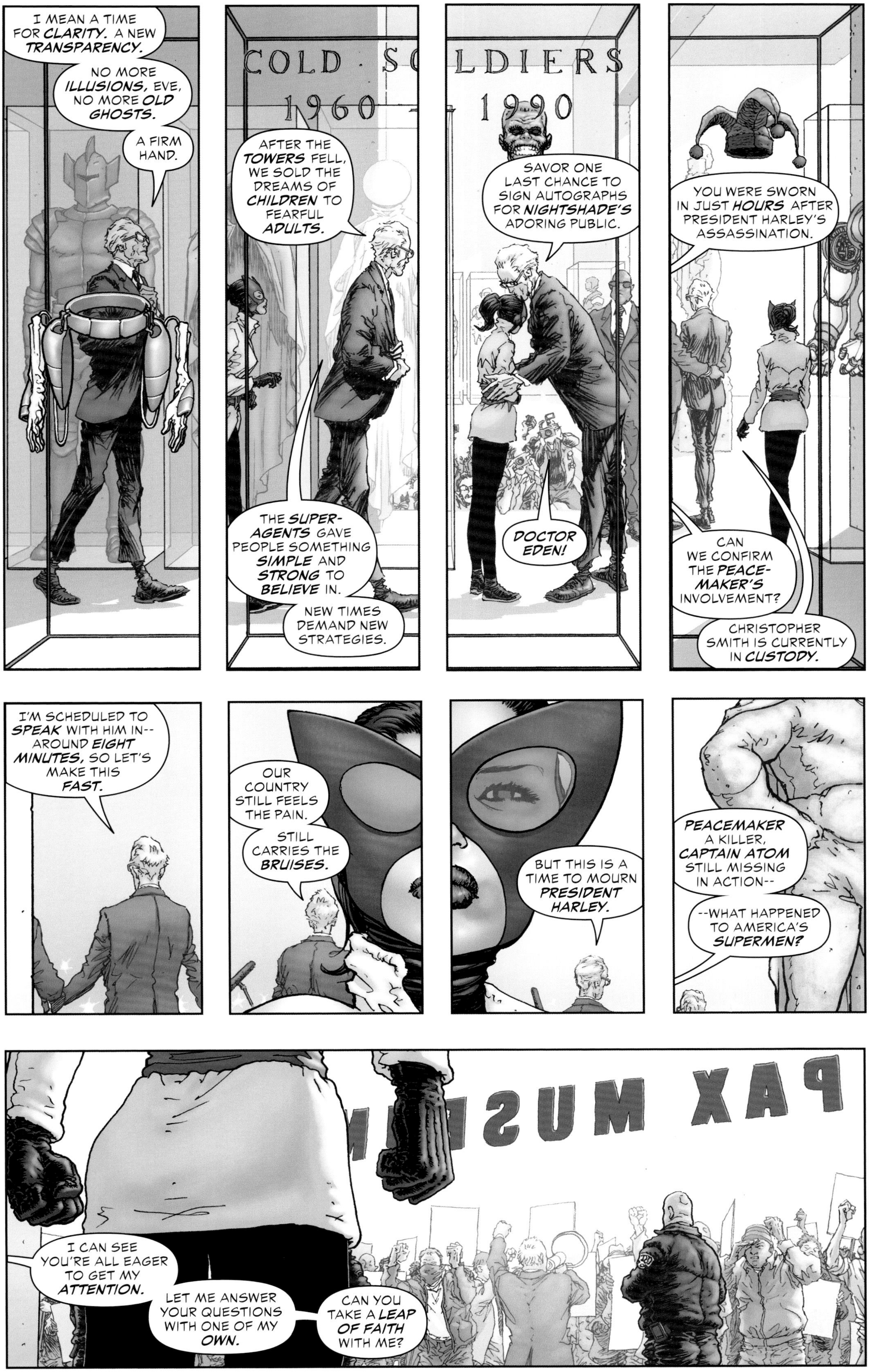
I MEAN A TIME FOR CLARITY. A NEW TRANSPARENCY.
NO MORE ILLUSIONS, EVE, NO MORE OLD GHOSTS.
A FIRM HAND.
COLD · SOLDIERS 1960 – 1990
AFTER THE TOWERS FELL, WE SOLD THE DREAMS OF CHILDREN TO FEARFUL ADULTS.
THE SUPER-AGENTS GAVE PEOPLE SOMETHING SIMPLE AND STRONG TO BELIEVE IN.
NEW TIMES DEMAND NEW STRATEGIES.
SAVOR ONE LAST CHANCE TO SIGN AUTOGRAPHS FOR NIGHTSHADE'S ADORING PUBLIC.
DOCTOR EDEN!
YOU WERE SWORN IN JUST HOURS AFTER PRESIDENT HARLEY'S ASSASSINATION.
CAN WE CONFIRM THE PEACE-MAKER'S INVOLVEMENT?
CHRISTOPHER SMITH IS CURRENTLY IN CUSTODY.
I'M SCHEDULED TO SPEAK WITH HIM IN-- AROUND EIGHT MINUTES, SO LET'S MAKE THIS FAST.
OUR COUNTRY STILL FEELS THE PAIN.
STILL CARRIES THE BRUISES.
BUT THIS IS A TIME TO MOURN PRESIDENT HARLEY.
PEACEMAKER A KILLER, CAPTAIN ATOM STILL MISSING IN ACTION--
--WHAT HAPPENED TO AMERICA'S SUPERMEN?
I CAN SEE YOU'RE ALL EAGER TO GET MY ATTENTION.
LET ME ANSWER YOUR QUESTIONS WITH ONE OF MY OWN.
CAN YOU TAKE A LEAP OF FAITH WITH ME?

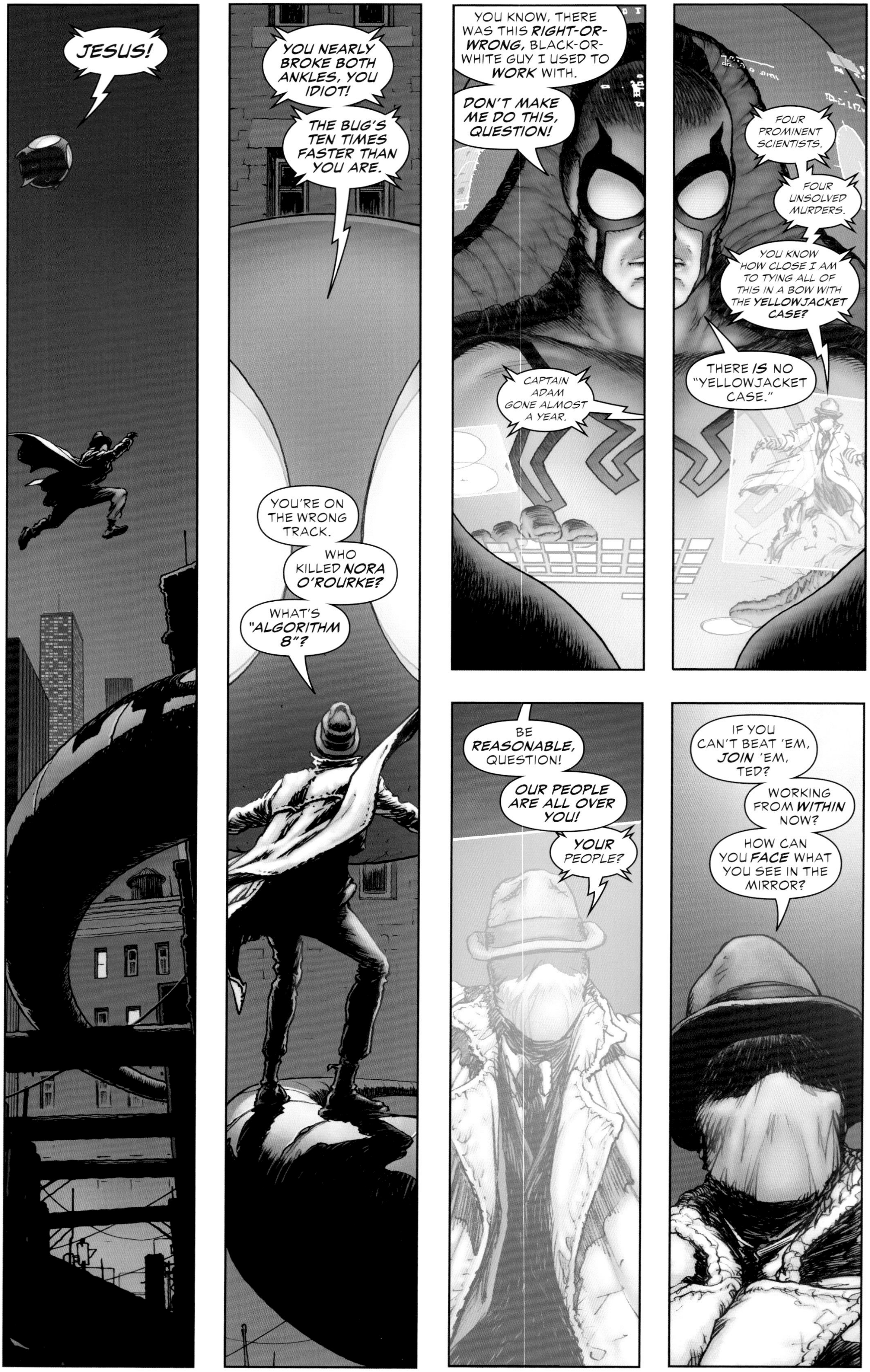

JESUS!
YOU NEARLY BROKE BOTH ANKLES, YOU IDIOT!
THE BUG'S TEN TIMES FASTER THAN YOU ARE.
YOU'RE ON THE WRONG TRACK.
WHO KILLED NORA O'ROURKE?
WHAT'S "ALGORITHM 8"?
YOU KNOW, THERE WAS THIS RIGHT-OR-WRONG, BLACK-OR-WHITE GUY I USED TO WORK WITH.
DON'T MAKE ME DO THIS, QUESTION!
CAPTAIN ADAM GONE ALMOST A YEAR.
FOUR PROMINENT SCIENTISTS.
FOUR UNSOLVED MURDERS.
YOU KNOW HOW CLOSE I AM TO TYING ALL OF THIS IN A BOW WITH THE YELLOWJACKET CASE?
THERE IS NO "YELLOWJACKET CASE."
BE REASONABLE, QUESTION!
OUR PEOPLE ARE ALL OVER YOU!
YOUR PEOPLE?
IF YOU CAN'T BEAT 'EM, JOIN 'EM, TED?
WORKING FROM WITHIN NOW?
HOW CAN YOU FACE WHAT YOU SEE IN THE MIRROR?

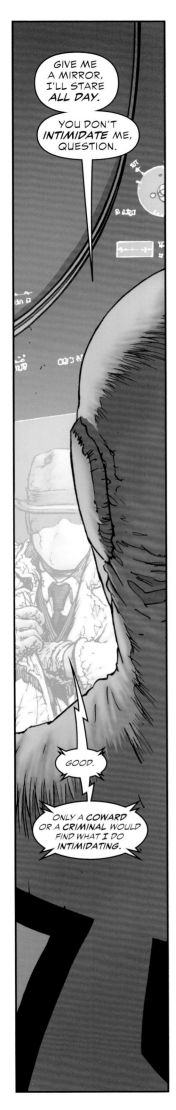

GIVE ME A MIRROR, I'LL STARE *ALL DAY*.

YOU DON'T *INTIMIDATE* ME, QUESTION.

GOOD.

ONLY A *COWARD* OR A *CRIMINAL* WOULD FIND WHAT I DO INTIMIDATING.

I MADE MY PEACE WITH *OSI* AND THE *PAX*.

WHAT HAPPENED TO *YOU*?

YOU MADE COMPROMISES YOU CAN BARELY *LIVE* WITH.

ANXIETY ATTACKS, AN *ULCER*, ERECTILE DYSFUNCTION--

AND YOU'RE SO DEEP IN THE CLOSET, YOU PAY RENT IN NARNIA.

WHAT'S THAT?

WHAT'S IN YOUR HAND?!

FAIRY TALES?

IF I TOLD YOU WE COULD *END* CRIME.

END IT ALL WITH A *SINGLE MAGIC FORMULA*.

WHAT WOULD *YOU* SACRIFICE?

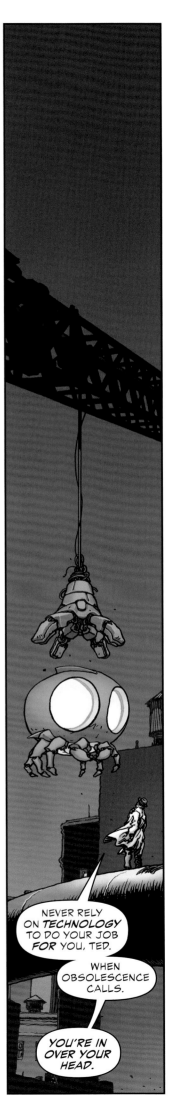

NEVER RELY ON *TECHNOLOGY* TO DO YOUR JOB *FOR* YOU, TED.

WHEN OBSOLESCENCE CALLS.

YOU'RE IN OVER YOUR HEAD.

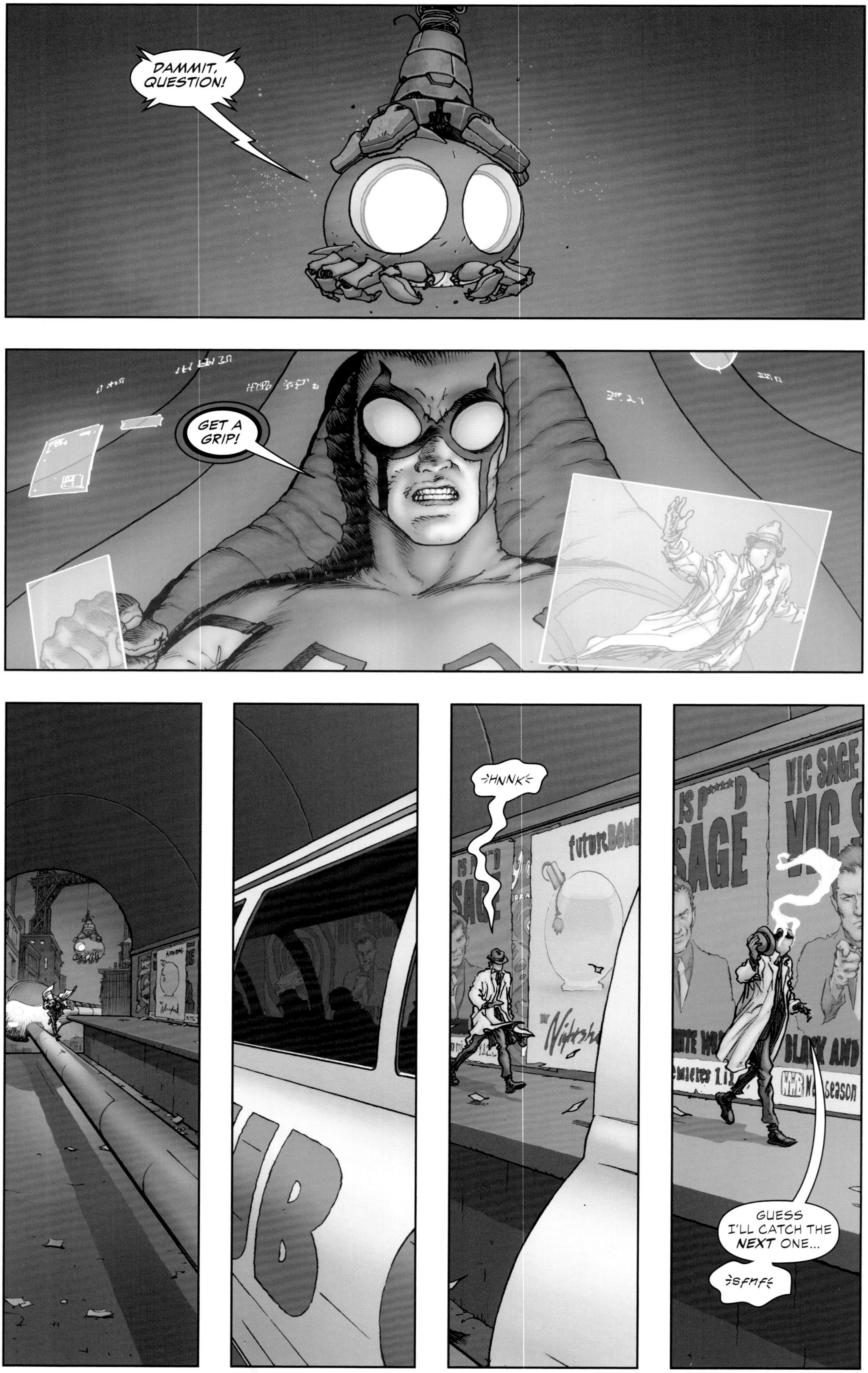
DAMMIT, QUESTION!
GET A GRIP!
HNNK
VIC SAGE
SAGE
BLACK AND
GUESS I'LL CATCH THE NEXT ONE...
SFNF

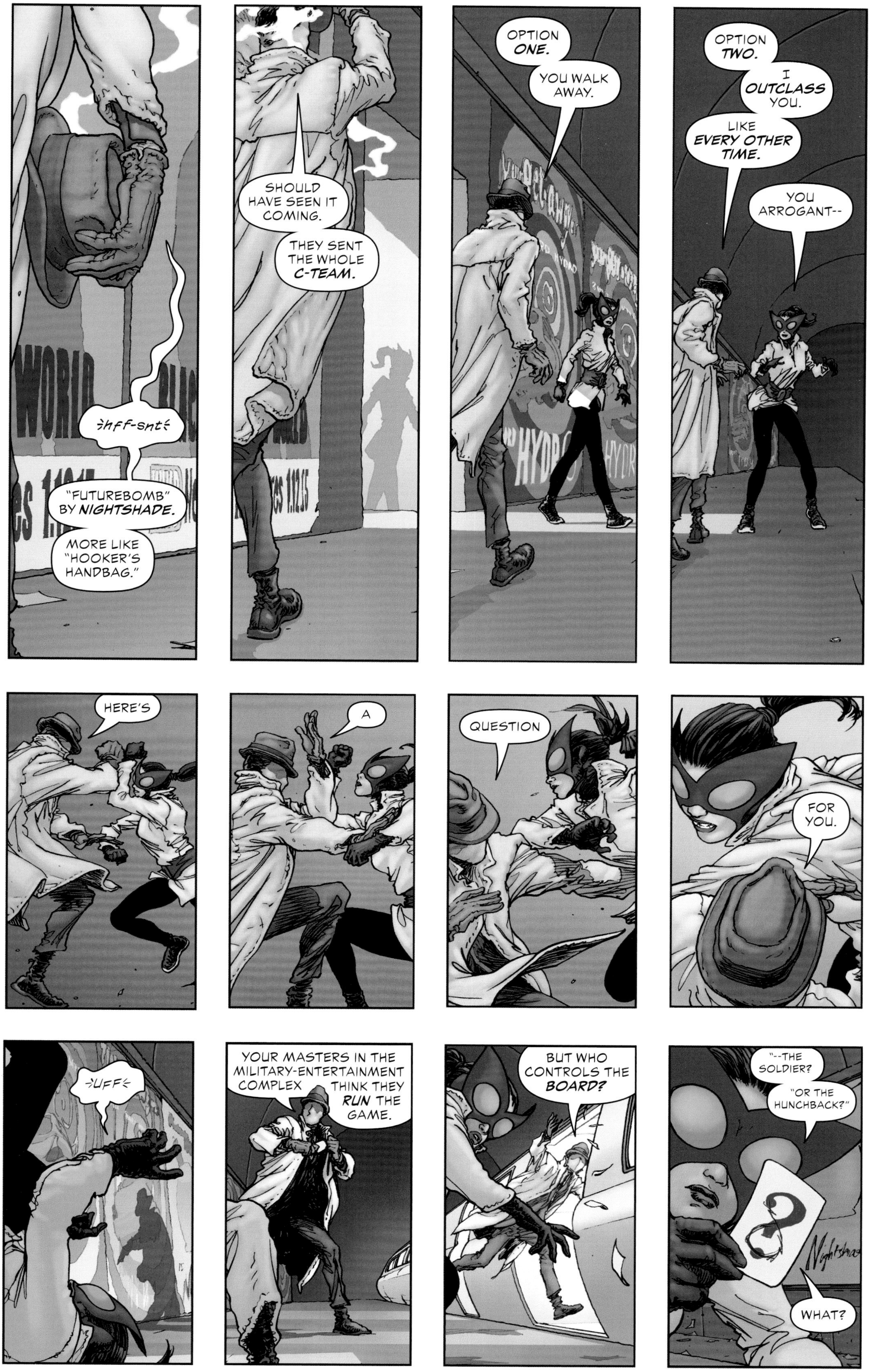

WORLD
>hff-snt<
"FUTUREBOMB" BY NIGHTSHADE.
MORE LIKE "HOOKER'S HANDBAG."
SHOULD HAVE SEEN IT COMING.
THEY SENT THE WHOLE C-TEAM.
OPTION ONE.
YOU WALK AWAY.
HYDRO
OPTION TWO.
I OUTCLASS YOU.
LIKE EVERY OTHER TIME.
YOU ARROGANT--
HERE'S
A
QUESTION
FOR YOU.
>UFF<
YOUR MASTERS IN THE MILITARY-ENTERTAINMENT COMPLEX THINK THEY RUN THE GAME.
BUT WHO CONTROLS THE BOARD?
"--THE SOLDIER?
"OR THE HUNCHBACK?"
WHAT?

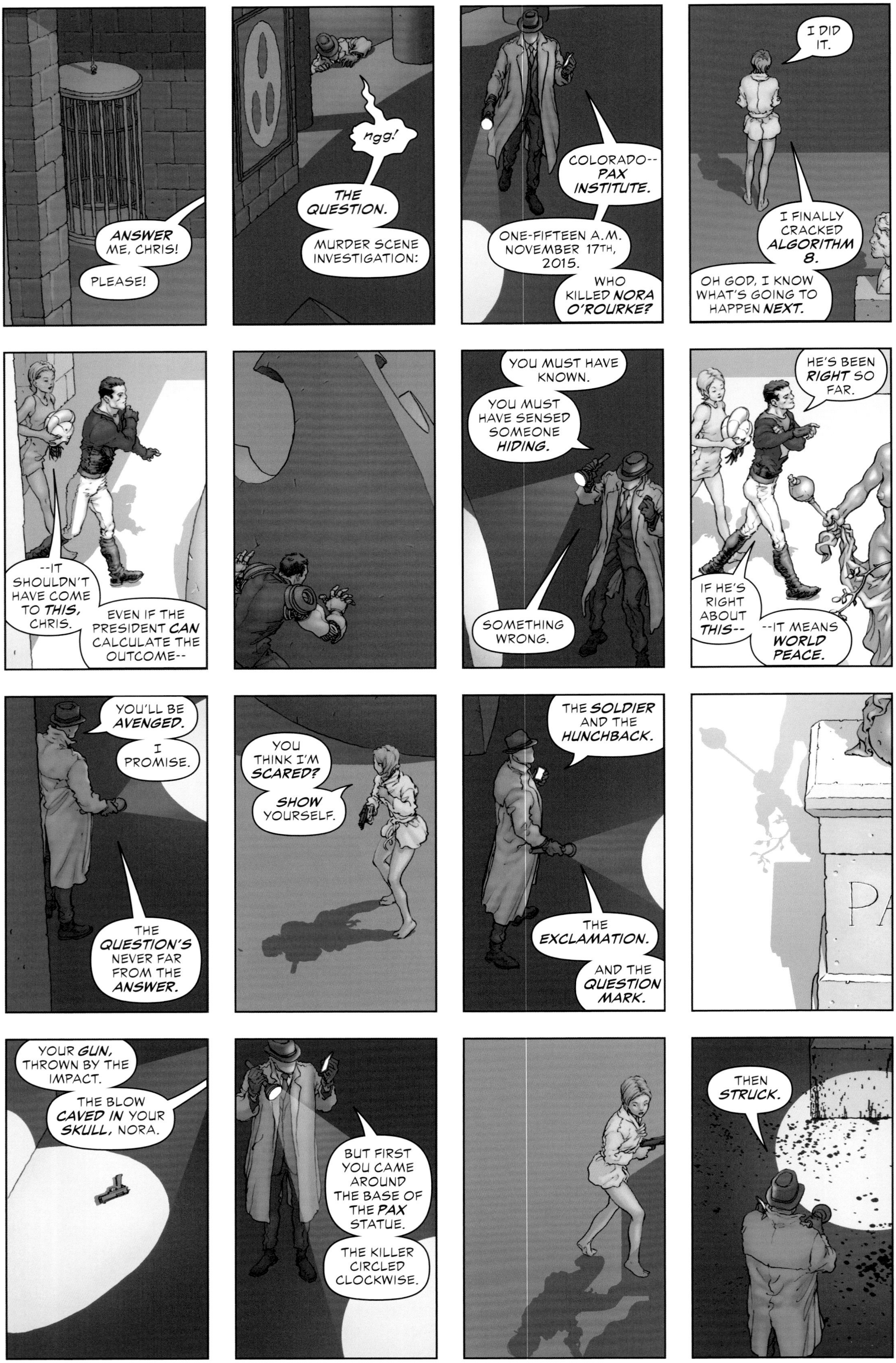
ANSWER ME, CHRIS!
PLEASE!
ngg!
THE QUESTION.
MURDER SCENE INVESTIGATION:
COLORADO-- PAX INSTITUTE.
ONE-FIFTEEN A.M. NOVEMBER 17TH, 2015.
WHO KILLED NORA O'ROURKE?
I DID IT.
I FINALLY CRACKED ALGORITHM 8.
OH GOD, I KNOW WHAT'S GOING TO HAPPEN NEXT.
--IT SHOULDN'T HAVE COME TO THIS, CHRIS.
EVEN IF THE PRESIDENT CAN CALCULATE THE OUTCOME--
YOU MUST HAVE KNOWN.
YOU MUST HAVE SENSED SOMEONE HIDING.
SOMETHING WRONG.
HE'S BEEN RIGHT SO FAR.
IF HE'S RIGHT ABOUT THIS--
--IT MEANS WORLD PEACE.
YOU'LL BE AVENGED.
I PROMISE.
THE QUESTION'S NEVER FAR FROM THE ANSWER.
YOU THINK I'M SCARED?
SHOW YOURSELF.
THE SOLDIER AND THE HUNCHBACK.
THE EXCLAMATION.
AND THE QUESTION MARK.
PA
YOUR GUN, THROWN BY THE IMPACT.
THE BLOW CAVED IN YOUR SKULL, NORA.
BUT FIRST YOU CAME AROUND THE BASE OF THE PAX STATUE.
THE KILLER CIRCLED CLOCKWISE.
THEN STRUCK.

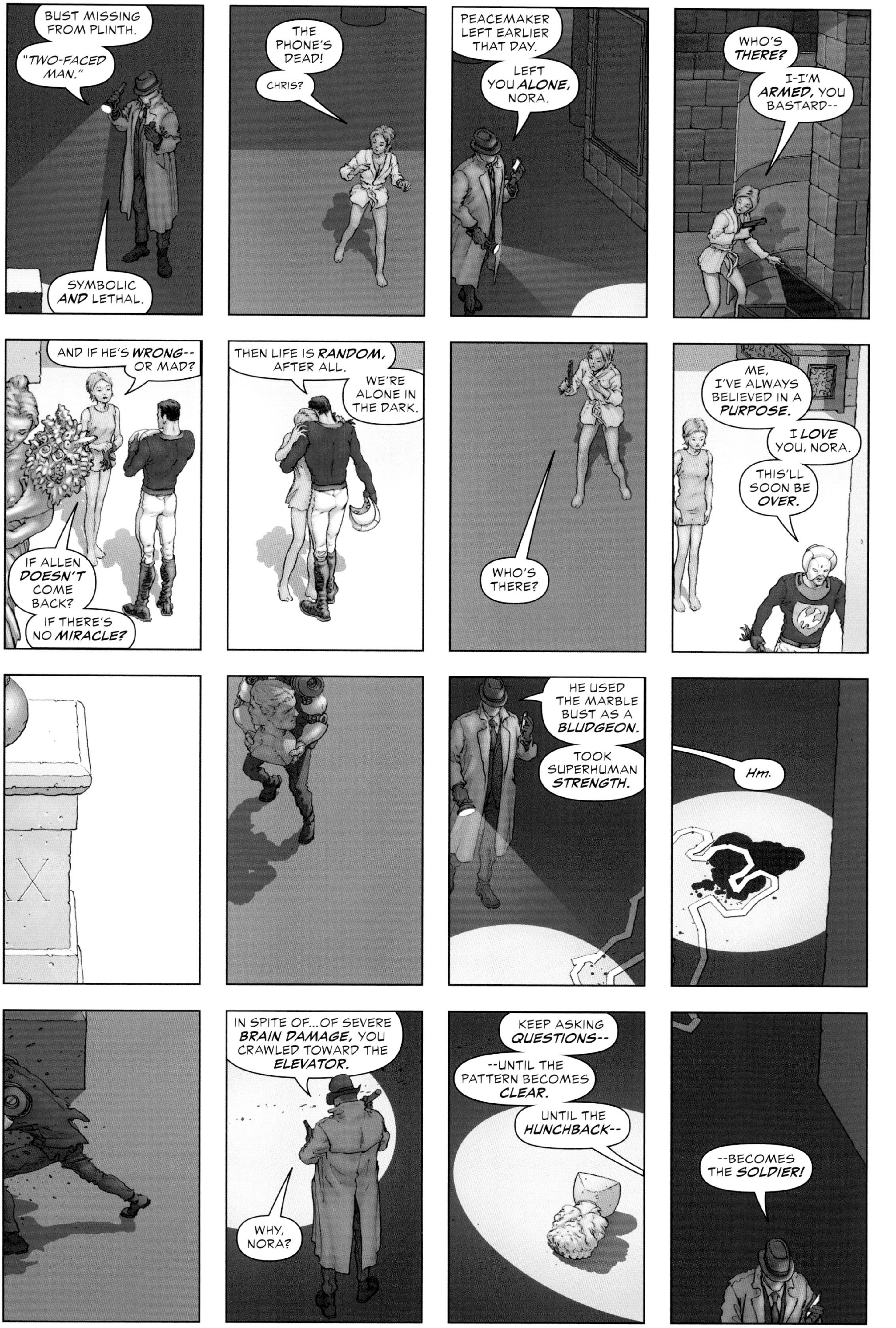

BUST MISSING FROM PLINTH.
"TWO-FACED MAN."
SYMBOLIC AND LETHAL.
THE PHONE'S DEAD!
CHRIS?
PEACEMAKER LEFT EARLIER THAT DAY.
LEFT YOU ALONE, NORA.
WHO'S THERE?
I-I'M ARMED, YOU BASTARD--
AND IF HE'S WRONG-- OR MAD?
IF ALLEN DOESN'T COME BACK?
IF THERE'S NO MIRACLE?
THEN LIFE IS RANDOM, AFTER ALL.
WE'RE ALONE IN THE DARK.
WHO'S THERE?
ME, I'VE ALWAYS BELIEVED IN A PURPOSE.
I LOVE YOU, NORA.
THIS'LL SOON BE OVER.
HE USED THE MARBLE BUST AS A BLUDGEON.
TOOK SUPERHUMAN STRENGTH.
Hm.
IN SPITE OF...OF SEVERE BRAIN DAMAGE, YOU CRAWLED TOWARD THE ELEVATOR.
WHY, NORA?
KEEP ASKING QUESTIONS--
--UNTIL THE PATTERN BECOMES CLEAR.
UNTIL THE HUNCHBACK--
--BECOMES THE SOLDIER!

--ON PAGES *12 AND 13*, I CAUGHT SIGHT OF A MASSLESS TIME-SYMMETRICAL *BOSON*.

A *MÖBIUS LOOP* CURVING THROUGH *EIGHT* DIMENSIONS.

I HEARD SOMETHING KNOCKING ON THE *DOOR* TO *GET IN*--

Um, *ah*, CAPTAIN, THIS IS *DOCTOR McDOUGALL* IN THE *CONTROL ROOM*.

CAN WE PUT AWAY THE COMIC BOOK, PLEASE?

I'M THINKING HOW *OUR* UNIVERSE APPEARS FROM A *HIGHER DIMENSIONAL* PERSPECTIVE.

FLAT.

CAPTAIN--PLEASE *CONCENTRATE*.

THIS IS *PROFESSOR LYONS*.

COMMENCING *PARTICLE ACCELERATION*, ARE YOU READY?

COMPLETE YET ALWAYS BEGINNING AND ENDING.

ALWAYS *DIFFERENT*.

THE STORY'S *LINEAR*, BUT I CAN FLIP THROUGH THE PAGES IN *ANY* ORDER, ANY DIRECTION.

FORWARD IN TIME TO THE *CONCLUSION*.

BACK TO THE *OPENING SCENE*.

THE CHARACTERS REMAIN *UNAWARE* OF MY SCRUTINY, BUT *THEIR* THOUGHTS ARE *TRANSPARENT*, WEIGHTLESS IN LITTLE CLOUDS.

THIS IS HOW A *2-DIMENSIONAL CONTINUUM* LOOKS TO *YOU*.

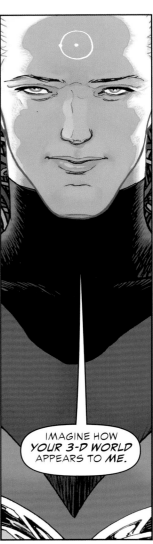

IMAGINE HOW *YOUR 3-D WORLD* APPEARS TO *ME*.

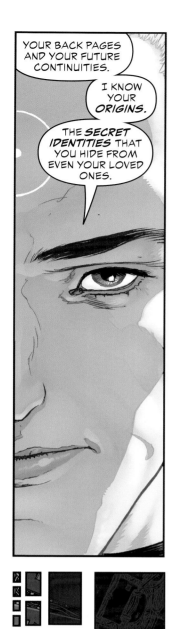

YOUR BACK PAGES AND YOUR FUTURE CONTINUITIES.

I KNOW YOUR ORIGINS.

THE SECRET IDENTITIES THAT YOU HIDE FROM EVEN YOUR LOVED ONES.

I CAN READ YOUR THOUGHT BALLOONS.

I KNOW WHAT YOU'RE PLANNING.

NOW!

EXECUTE PORTI BELLI!

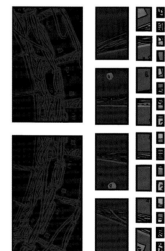

MY GOD.

HE'S GONE.

7:20 PM, JANUARY 31ST, 2015-- CAPTAIN ATOM HAS LEFT THE UNIVERSE.

MEN--

THE LORD *SPAKE,* SAYING--

"LET THERE BE LIGHT."

AND *LO.*

WE MADE THE WORLD'S *FIRST* ARTIFICIAL *BLACK HOLE.*

IN ALLEN ADAM'S *SKULL.*

WE DID EVERYTHING THEY ASKED, SERGEANT--

AND THE TIME HAS COME FOR YOUR *JUST REWARD.*

FREELY AND *WITHOUT CONSCIENCE,* YOU OPENED THE *GATES OF HELL,* MY FRIENDS.

I'M WHAT *CRAWLED OUT* TO *PUNISH* YOU.

SCIENTISTS.

CAN'T GET IT STRAIGHT, *CAN* YOU?

MY MOTHER--

PLEASE!

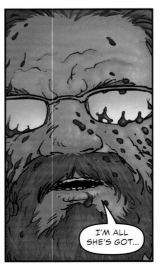

I'M ALL SHE'S GOT...

THE *BIG BANG'S* WHAT COMES AT THE *END.*

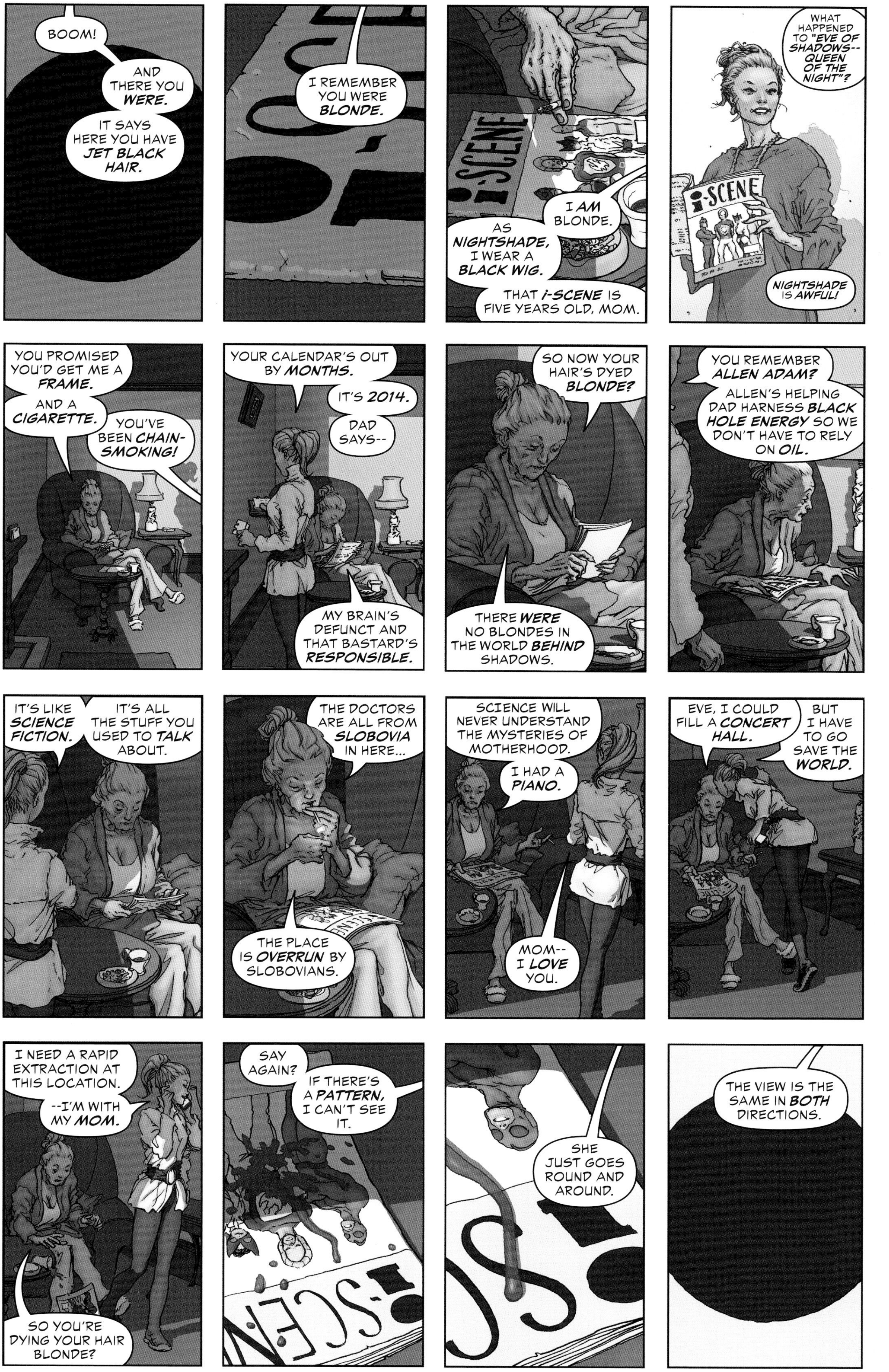
BOOM!
AND THERE YOU WERE.
IT SAYS HERE YOU HAVE JET BLACK HAIR.
I REMEMBER YOU WERE BLONDE.
i-SCENE
I AM BLONDE.
AS NIGHTSHADE, I WEAR A BLACK WIG.
THAT i-SCENE IS FIVE YEARS OLD, MOM.
WHAT HAPPENED TO "EVE OF SHADOWS--QUEEN OF THE NIGHT"?
i-SCENE
NIGHTSHADE IS AWFUL!
YOU PROMISED YOU'D GET ME A FRAME.
AND A CIGARETTE.
YOU'VE BEEN CHAIN-SMOKING!
YOUR CALENDAR'S OUT BY MONTHS.
IT'S 2014.
DAD SAYS--
MY BRAIN'S DEFUNCT AND THAT BASTARD'S RESPONSIBLE.
SO NOW YOUR HAIR'S DYED BLONDE?
THERE WERE NO BLONDES IN THE WORLD BEHIND SHADOWS.
YOU REMEMBER ALLEN ADAM?
ALLEN'S HELPING DAD HARNESS BLACK HOLE ENERGY SO WE DON'T HAVE TO RELY ON OIL.
IT'S LIKE SCIENCE FICTION.
IT'S ALL THE STUFF YOU USED TO TALK ABOUT.
THE DOCTORS ARE ALL FROM SLOBOVIA IN HERE...
THE PLACE IS OVERRUN BY SLOBOVIANS.
SCIENCE WILL NEVER UNDERSTAND THE MYSTERIES OF MOTHERHOOD.
I HAD A PIANO.
MOM--I LOVE YOU.
EVE, I COULD FILL A CONCERT HALL.
BUT I HAVE TO GO SAVE THE WORLD.
I NEED A RAPID EXTRACTION AT THIS LOCATION.
--I'M WITH MY MOM.
SO YOU'RE DYING YOUR HAIR BLONDE?
SAY AGAIN?
IF THERE'S A PATTERN, I CAN'T SEE IT.
SHE JUST GOES ROUND AND AROUND.
THE VIEW IS THE SAME IN BOTH DIRECTIONS.

JANUS WAS THE GUARDIAN OF **DOORS AND GATES** IN ANCIENT ROME.

THEN THERE'S THE LAST COMIC BOOK STORY HARLEY'S **DAD** WROTE.

"JANUS THE EVERYWAY MAN."

ALL THIS BLUE SKY THINKING, I'VE COME UP **EMPTY-HANDED.**

I WONDERED ABOUT YOUR LATEST **ART PROJECT.**

TWO HEADS ARE BETTER THAN ONE?

SO FORGET THE PAST.

YOUR PAST RECORD IS SPOTLESS.

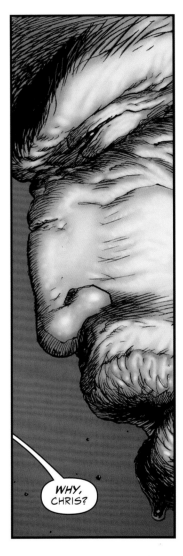

WHY, CHRIS?

TWO YEARS TO **VERIFY** THE EXISTENCE OF **ALGORITHM 8.**

THE **PAX INSTITUTE** WILL HAVE TRAINED THE **NEXT GENERATION** OF **PEACEMAKER** AGENTS BY THEN.

AFTER HE **WINS** THE 2015 ELECTION.

WHEN I'VE **DONE** WHAT HAS TO BE DONE, WE'LL GO WHERE THEY'LL NEVER FIND US.

JUST **YOU AND ME,** NORA.

SURE, IF I HAD YOUR *ULTIMATE ALGORITHM*, I'D BE SEARCHING THE *FUTURE* FOR INSPIRATION.

LET THAT *SUPER-BRAIN* OF YOURS LOOSE ON THE MATH.

IF HARLEY WON'T LET US INTO HIS SECRET, IT'S DOWN TO *YOU*.

AN *INTRUDER* KILLED HIS FATHER.

OPEN AND SHUT CASE, APPARENTLY.

HOW LONG DO I GET?

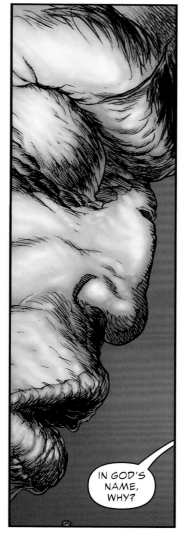

IN GOD'S NAME, WHY?

YOUR FUTURE SAFETY CANNOT BE GUARANTEED.

KMFF

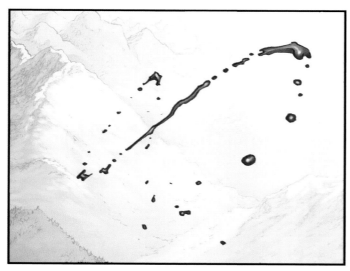

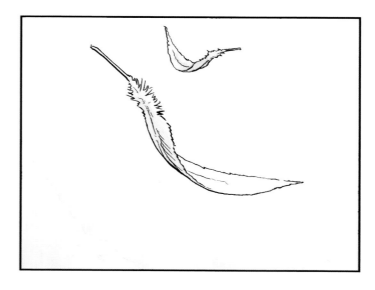

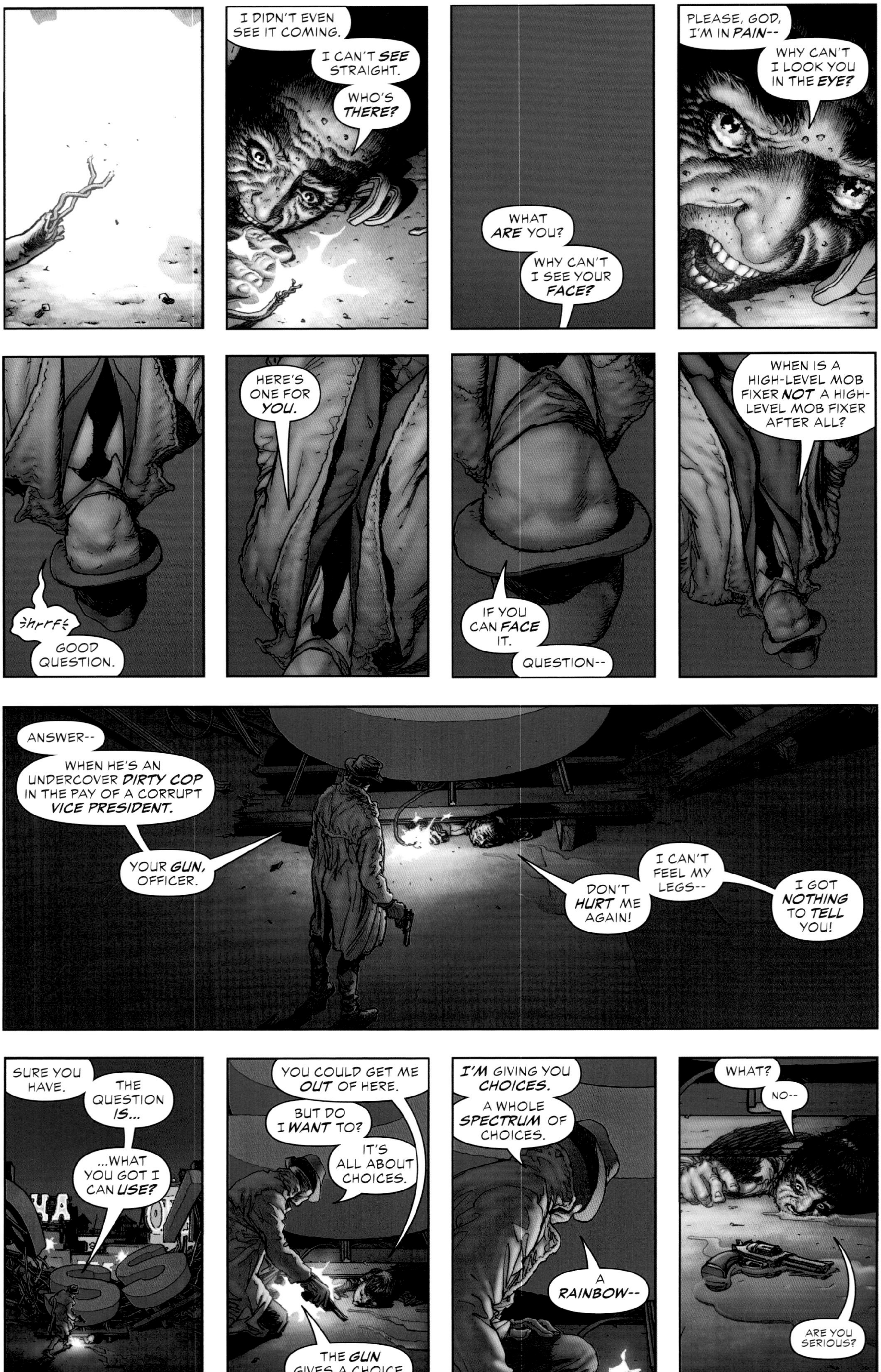
I DIDN'T EVEN SEE IT COMING.
I CAN'T SEE STRAIGHT.
WHO'S THERE?
WHAT ARE YOU?
WHY CAN'T I SEE YOUR FACE?
PLEASE, GOD, I'M IN PAIN--
WHY CAN'T I LOOK YOU IN THE EYE?
hrrf
GOOD QUESTION.
HERE'S ONE FOR YOU.
IF YOU CAN FACE IT.
QUESTION--
WHEN IS A HIGH-LEVEL MOB FIXER NOT A HIGH-LEVEL MOB FIXER AFTER ALL?
ANSWER--
WHEN HE'S AN UNDERCOVER DIRTY COP IN THE PAY OF A CORRUPT VICE PRESIDENT.
YOUR GUN, OFFICER.
DON'T HURT ME AGAIN!
I CAN'T FEEL MY LEGS--
I GOT NOTHING TO TELL YOU!
SURE YOU HAVE.
THE QUESTION IS...
...WHAT YOU GOT I CAN USE?
YOU COULD GET ME OUT OF HERE.
BUT DO I WANT TO?
IT'S ALL ABOUT CHOICES.
THE GUN GIVES A CHOICE.
I'M GIVING YOU CHOICES.
A WHOLE SPECTRUM OF CHOICES.
A RAINBOW--
WHAT?
NO--
ARE YOU SERIOUS?

AS THEY *GROW*, SOCIETIES, LIKE INDIVIDUALS, PASS THROUGH IDENTICAL STAGES OF *DEVELOPMENT*. IT BREAKS DOWN INTO AN *EIGHT-STAGE COLOR-CODED* SYSTEM, WHERE THE FIRST LEVEL IS *BEIGE*, CORRESPONDING TO INFANCY.

TH... ...OF PRI... ...WHERE... ...SU... ...ICAL ...ARE PA... ...UNT.

THIS IS WHY THEY KICKED YOU OUTTA THE PAX!

NEXT COMES *PURPLE*, EQUIVALENT TO *MAGICAL THINKING* AND THE STAGE AT WHICH HUNTER/GATHERER SUBSISTENCE SOCIETIES EX...

RED IS ...POWER POLIT... ...ET GANGS, WAR... ...IETIES-- THE ...TWOS.

BLUE... ...ENTALIST RE... ...NGE IS THE S... ...TIONAL ...ET THE ...EA.

WESTERN SOCIETY'S AT PLURALISTIC *GREEN* RIGHT NOW, BUT *YELLOW* COMES NEXT.

IF WE *MAKE* IT THAT FAR.

YELLOW INTEGRA... PLURAL...

A *TURQUOISE* SOCIETY WOULD RUN ON HOLISTIC, SYNERGISTIC... ...PLES.

ME?

I TAKE A *FULL SPECTRUM* APPROACH TO PROBLEMS.

WITH *YOUR* KIND I EMPHASIZE THEMES OF PAIN, FEAR, *BASIC SURVIVAL*.

--PLEASE CALL AN *AMBULANCE*--

MY ORDERS COME FROM THE *SARGE*...

I CAN'T REACH--

THOSE ARE THE GUYS YOU *WANT*!

I'M *DEAD* WHEN THE SPARKS HIT THE WATER!

THAT'S A *DIRTY, ROTTEN* WAY TO GO!

I--I GOT *RUMORS* IS ALL--

--ABOUT KILLING *CAPTAIN ATOM*.

A SECRET *FORMULA*...

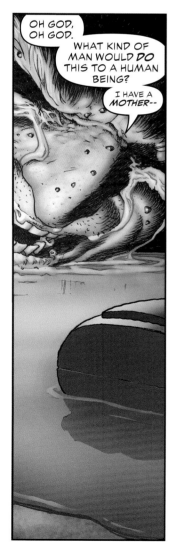

OH GOD, OH GOD.

WHAT KIND OF MAN WOULD *DO* THIS TO A HUMAN BEING?

I HAVE A *MOTHER*--

I'LL LET HER KNOW HER SON DIED *YELLOW*.

AS FOR *ME*--

--I'M A REGISTERED, CARD-CARRYING *SUPER-HERO*.

I DON'T SAVE *BAD GUYS*.

--*COMIC BOOKS*, PEOPLE.

AS AMERICAN AS *HOLLYWOOD* AND *POP ART.*

STARTING TODAY, WE ARE *HOMELAND SECURITY* MEETS *SHOWBIZ.*

THESE UNIFORMS ARE *RIDICULOUS* AND *DEMEANING,* SERGEANT LANE.

AND THE NAMES-- *"TIGER"!*

OSI WAS A *COVERT* OPERATION!

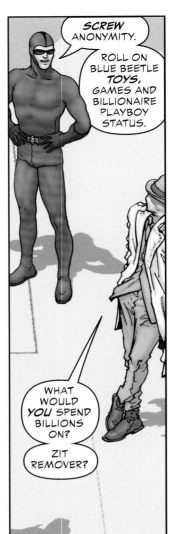

SCREW ANONYMITY.

ROLL ON BLUE BEETLE *TOYS,* GAMES AND BILLIONAIRE PLAYBOY STATUS.

WHAT WOULD *YOU* SPEND BILLIONS ON?

ZIT REMOVER?

SOMEBODY HAS TO SAY IT, MIGHT AS WELL BE *ME.*

WELCOME TO THE *JUSTICE LEAGUE OF AMERICA.*

HOW ABOUT *THE SENTINELS?*

EFF YOU.

WE ARE--

WE ARE *THE LAW.*

MR. PRESIDENT!

I JUST WANT YOU TO KNOW I VOTED FOR YOU.

AT EASE.

YOUR DESIGNERS DID YOU PROUD.

I HOPE YOU'LL *AGREE.*

AS OF TODAY, YOUR *CODE NAMES* AND *TRADEMARKS* BELONG TO *UNCLE SAM.*

YOU'LL REPRESENT A NEW, FUTURISTIC, *UPBEAT* AMERICA--

Hrrm

I'D LIKE TO RETAIN THE QUESTION "TRADEMARK." SUCH AS IT IS.

"THE QUESTION"?

I HAVE A QUESTION FOR *YOU,* MY FRIEND.

ARE YOU IN THE BOX OR OUT OF THE BOX-- MR. SAGE?

--AT THE PEAK OF THE ROMAN EMPIRE, THE PEACE THAT REIGNED FOR TWO CENTURIES WAS KNOWN AS THE PAX ROMANA.
I PROMISED TO CHANGE THE WORLD IF YOU VOTED FOR ME.
HERE'S WHERE I DELIVER.
HARLEY
MY FATHER, VINCE HARLEY, FOUGHT IN VIETNAM BEFORE HE BECAME A COMIC BOOK ARTIST.
MY DAD WAS A DREAMER.
TODAY IS FOR HIM.
FOR ALL THE DREAMERS.
THIS IS NOT A HOAX.
THIS IS NOT AN IMAGINARY STORY OR AN ALTERNATE REALITY.
MEET THE PAX AMERICANA!
WARRIORS OF PEACE.
AND THEIR COMMANDER--
CAPTAIN!
ATOM!
HARLEY
LOOK!
UP IN THE SKY!
WHERE TWO TOWERS FELL!
2008 HARLEY 2008

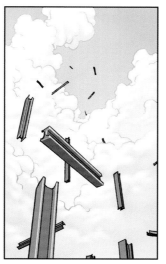

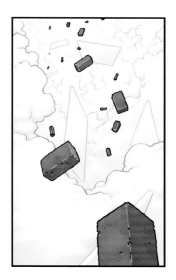

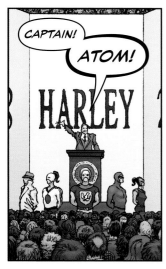

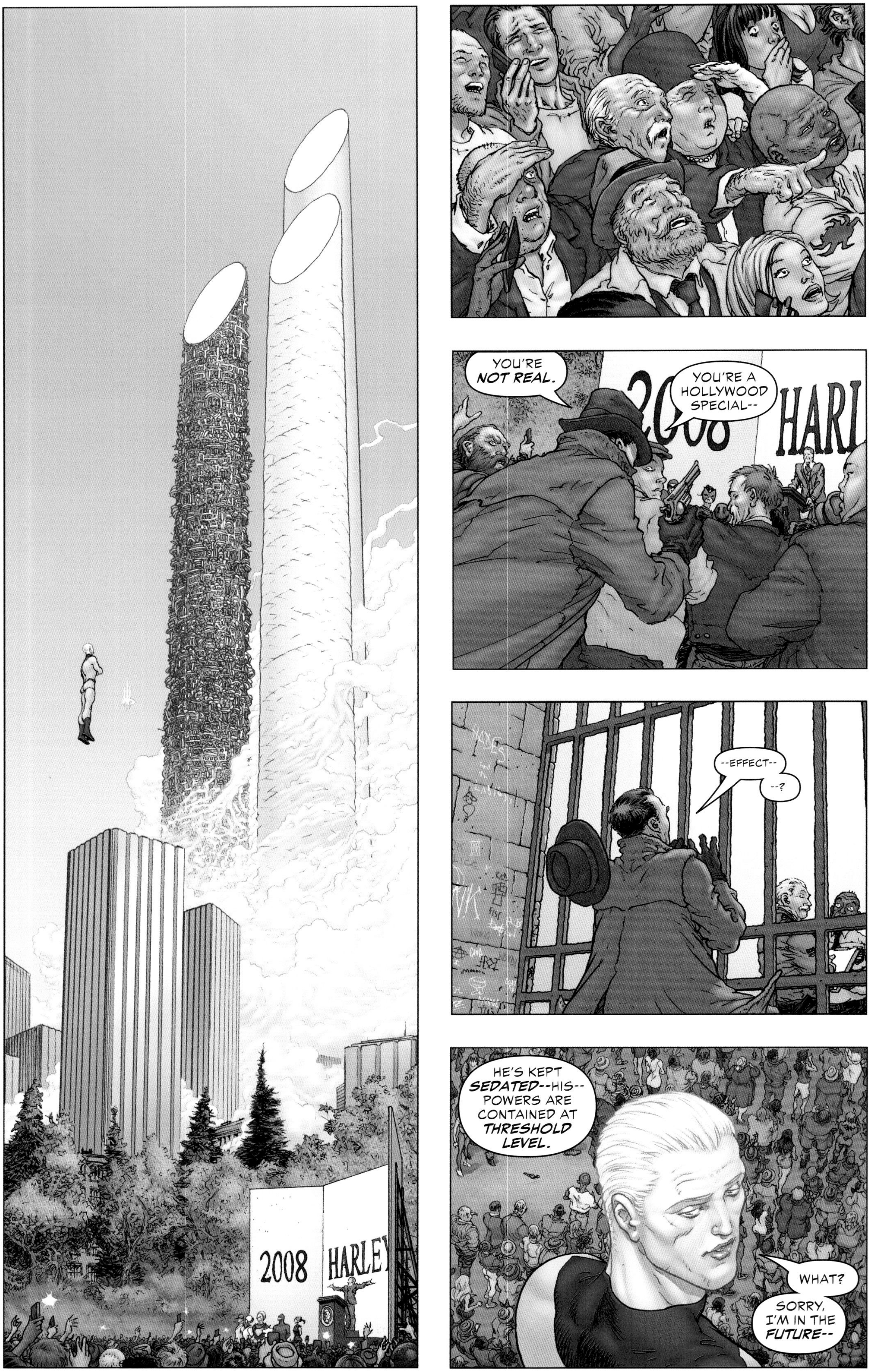
2008
HARLEY
YOU'RE NOT REAL.
YOU'RE A HOLLYWOOD SPECIAL--
2008
HARL
--EFFECT--
--?
HE'S KEPT SEDATED--HIS-- POWERS ARE CONTAINED AT THRESHOLD LEVEL.
WHAT?
SORRY, I'M IN THE FUTURE--

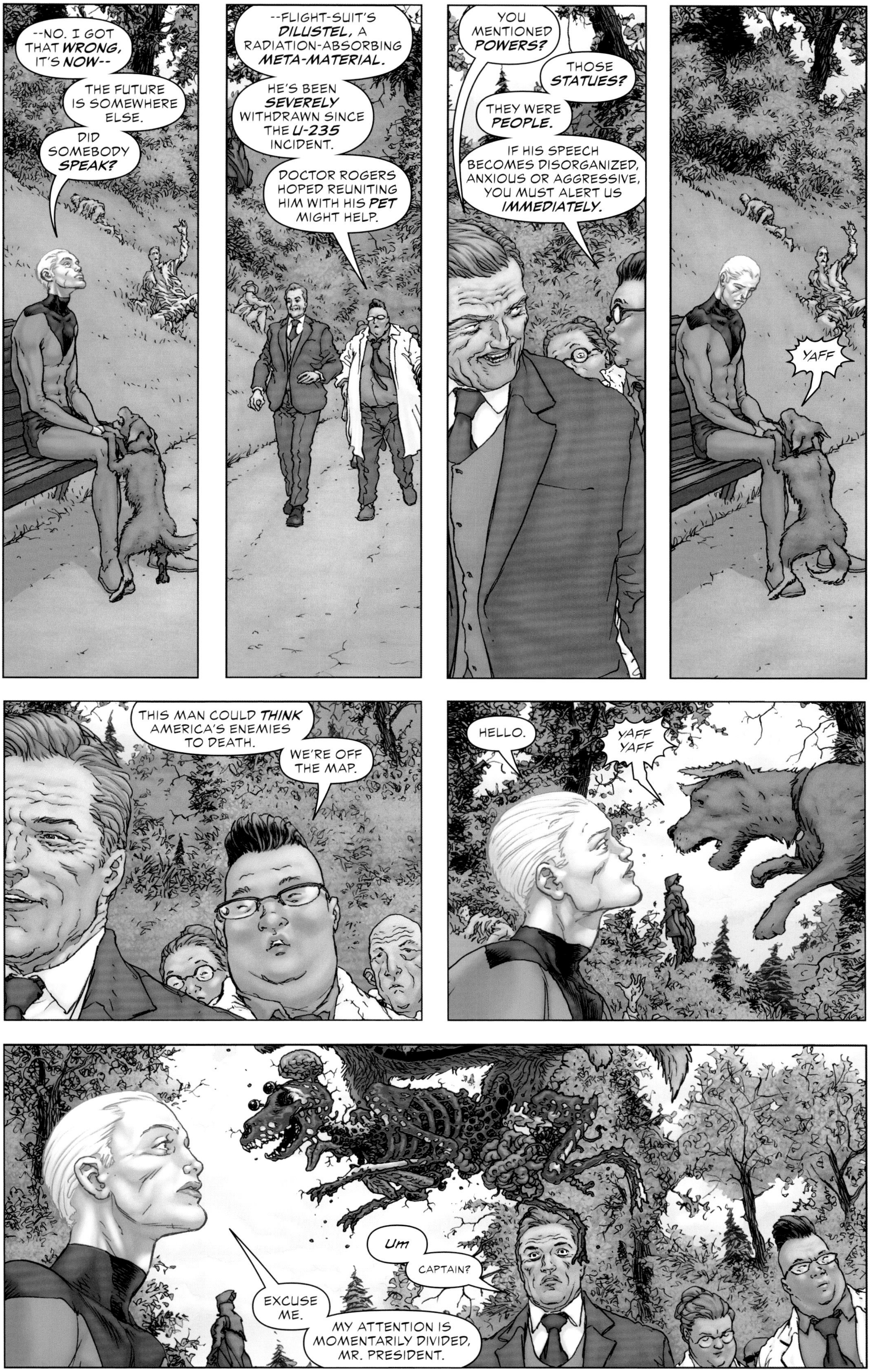
--NO. I GOT THAT WRONG, IT'S NOW--
THE FUTURE IS SOMEWHERE ELSE.
DID SOMEBODY SPEAK?
--FLIGHT-SUIT'S DILUSTEL, A RADIATION-ABSORBING META-MATERIAL.
HE'S BEEN SEVERELY WITHDRAWN SINCE THE U-235 INCIDENT.
DOCTOR ROGERS HOPED REUNITING HIM WITH HIS PET MIGHT HELP.
YOU MENTIONED POWERS?
THOSE STATUES?
THEY WERE PEOPLE.
IF HIS SPEECH BECOMES DISORGANIZED, ANXIOUS OR AGGRESSIVE, YOU MUST ALERT US IMMEDIATELY.
YAFF
THIS MAN COULD THINK AMERICA'S ENEMIES TO DEATH.
WE'RE OFF THE MAP.
HELLO.
YAFF YAFF
Um
CAPTAIN?
EXCUSE ME.
MY ATTENTION IS MOMENTARILY DIVIDED, MR. PRESIDENT.

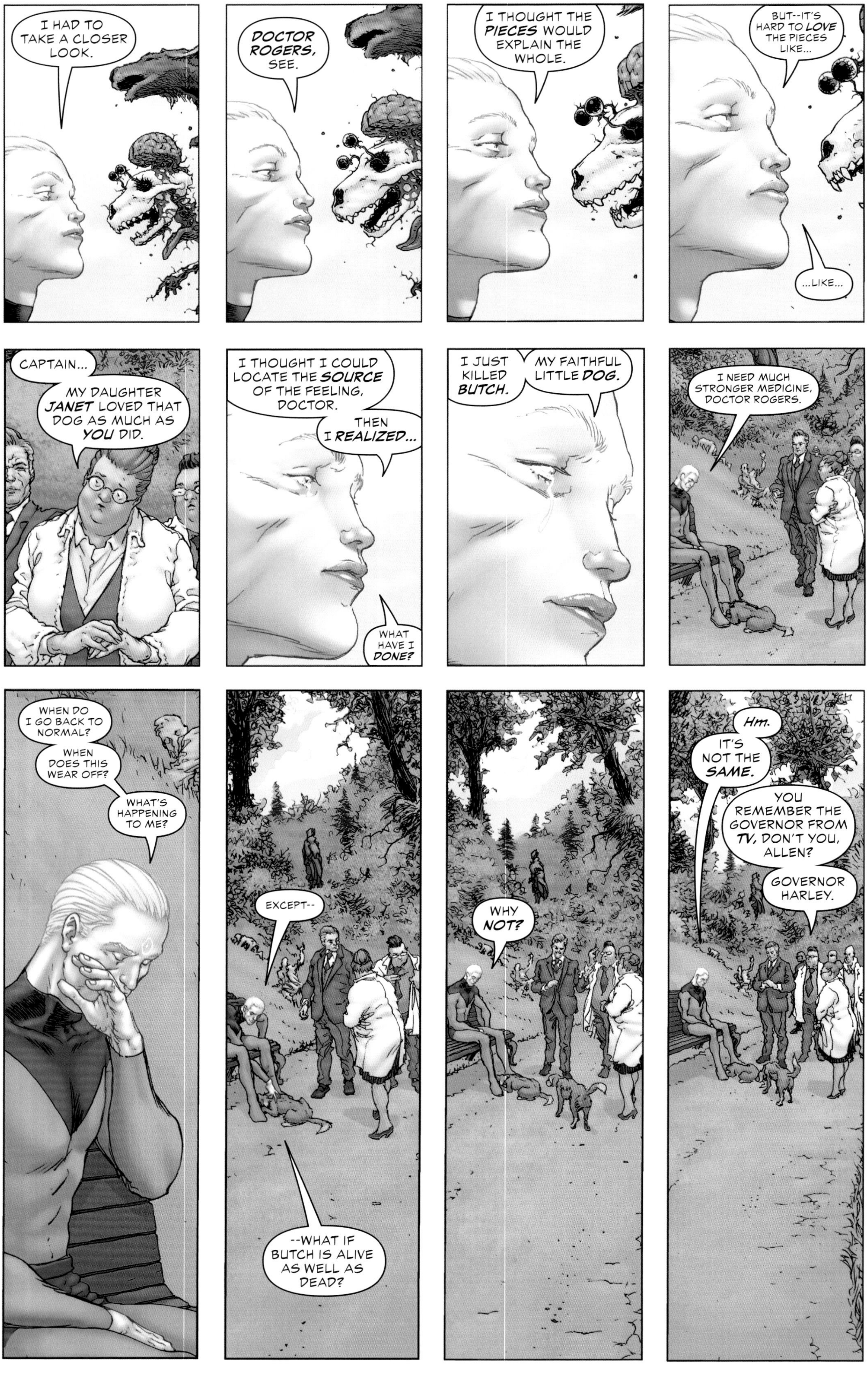
I HAD TO TAKE A CLOSER LOOK.
DOCTOR ROGERS, SEE.
I THOUGHT THE PIECES WOULD EXPLAIN THE WHOLE.
BUT--IT'S HARD TO LOVE THE PIECES LIKE...
...LIKE...
CAPTAIN...
MY DAUGHTER JANET LOVED THAT DOG AS MUCH AS YOU DID.
I THOUGHT I COULD LOCATE THE SOURCE OF THE FEELING, DOCTOR.
THEN I REALIZED...
WHAT HAVE I DONE?
I JUST KILLED BUTCH.
MY FAITHFUL LITTLE DOG.
I NEED MUCH STRONGER MEDICINE, DOCTOR ROGERS.
WHEN DO I GO BACK TO NORMAL?
WHEN DOES THIS WEAR OFF?
WHAT'S HAPPENING TO ME?
EXCEPT--
--WHAT IF BUTCH IS ALIVE AS WELL AS DEAD?
WHY NOT?
Hm.
IT'S NOT THE SAME.
YOU REMEMBER THE GOVERNOR FROM TV, DON'T YOU, ALLEN?
GOVERNOR HARLEY.

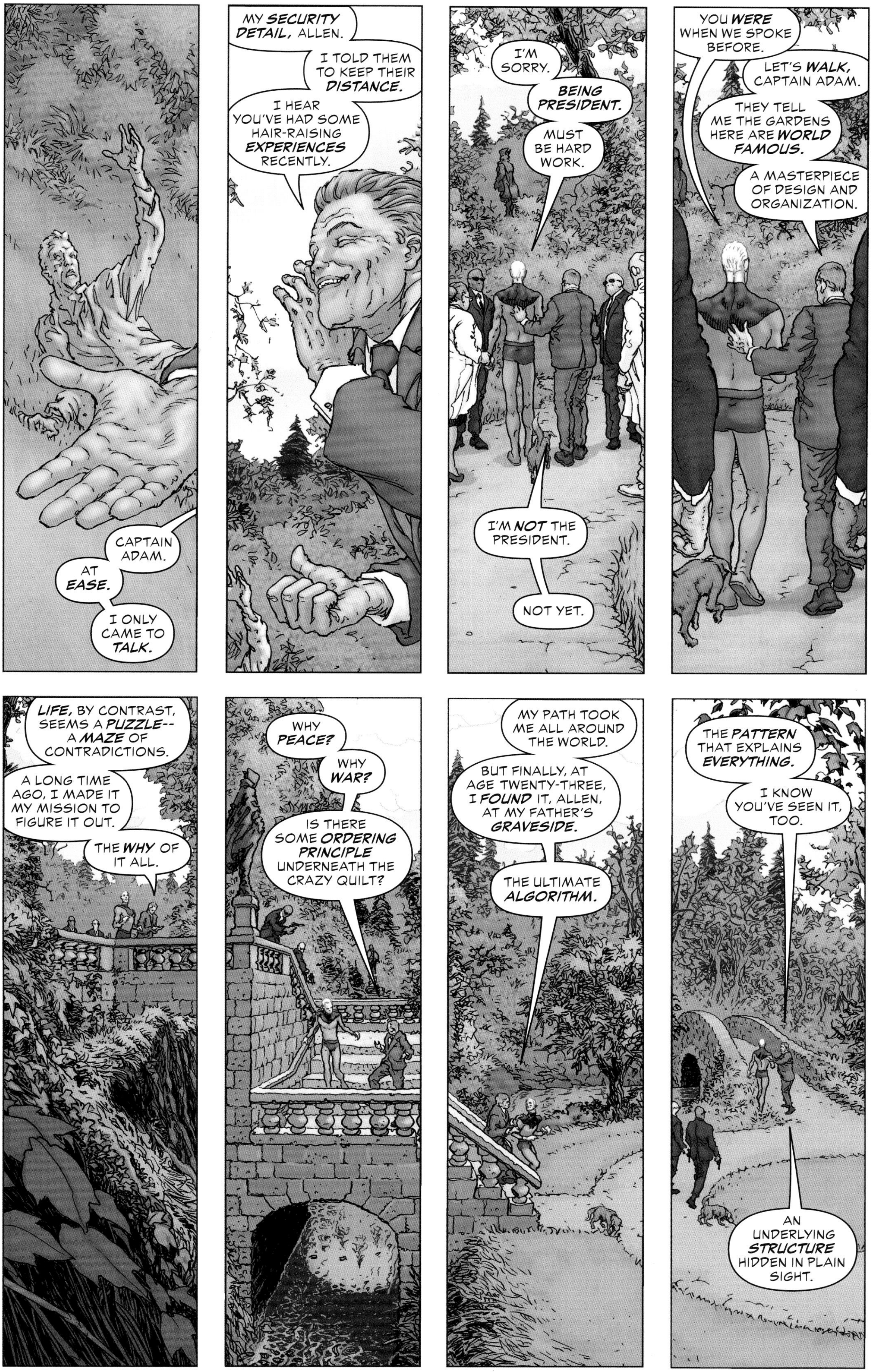
CAPTAIN ADAM.
AT EASE.
I ONLY CAME TO TALK.
MY SECURITY DETAIL, ALLEN.
I TOLD THEM TO KEEP THEIR DISTANCE.
I HEAR YOU'VE HAD SOME HAIR-RAISING EXPERIENCES RECENTLY.
I'M SORRY.
BEING PRESIDENT.
MUST BE HARD WORK.
I'M NOT THE PRESIDENT.
NOT YET.
YOU WERE WHEN WE SPOKE BEFORE.
LET'S WALK, CAPTAIN ADAM.
THEY TELL ME THE GARDENS HERE ARE WORLD FAMOUS.
A MASTERPIECE OF DESIGN AND ORGANIZATION.
LIFE, BY CONTRAST, SEEMS A PUZZLE-- A MAZE OF CONTRADICTIONS.
A LONG TIME AGO, I MADE IT MY MISSION TO FIGURE IT OUT.
THE WHY OF IT ALL.
WHY PEACE?
WHY WAR?
IS THERE SOME ORDERING PRINCIPLE UNDERNEATH THE CRAZY QUILT?
MY PATH TOOK ME ALL AROUND THE WORLD.
BUT FINALLY, AT AGE TWENTY-THREE, I FOUND IT, ALLEN, AT MY FATHER'S GRAVESIDE.
THE ULTIMATE ALGORITHM.
THE PATTERN THAT EXPLAINS EVERYTHING.
I KNOW YOU'VE SEEN IT, TOO.
AN UNDERLYING STRUCTURE HIDDEN IN PLAIN SIGHT.

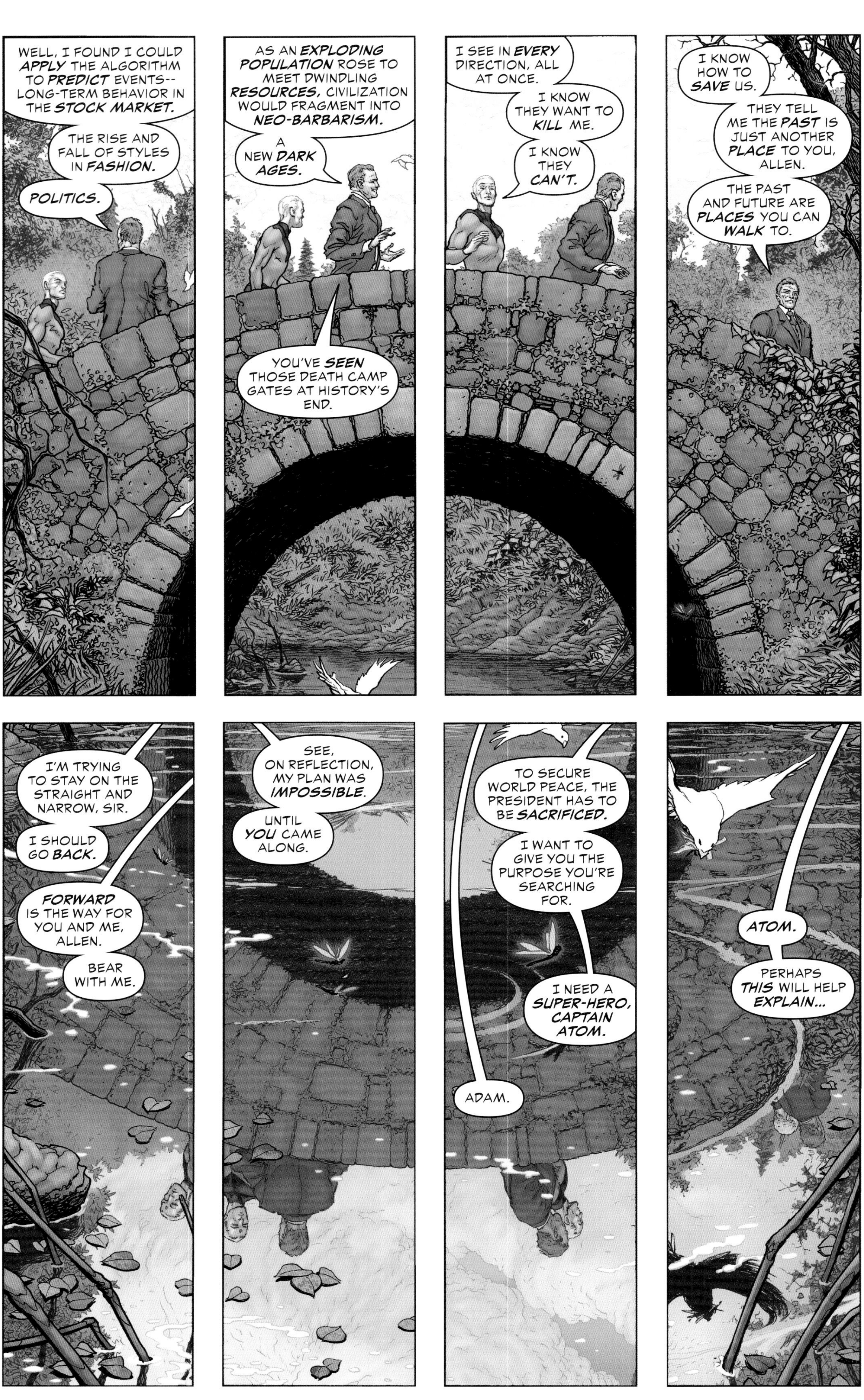
WELL, I FOUND I COULD APPLY THE ALGORITHM TO PREDICT EVENTS-- LONG-TERM BEHAVIOR IN THE STOCK MARKET.
THE RISE AND FALL OF STYLES IN FASHION.
POLITICS.
AS AN EXPLODING POPULATION ROSE TO MEET DWINDLING RESOURCES, CIVILIZATION WOULD FRAGMENT INTO NEO-BARBARISM.
A NEW DARK AGES.
YOU'VE SEEN THOSE DEATH CAMP GATES AT HISTORY'S END.
I SEE IN EVERY DIRECTION, ALL AT ONCE.
I KNOW THEY WANT TO KILL ME.
I KNOW THEY CAN'T.
I KNOW HOW TO SAVE US.
THEY TELL ME THE PAST IS JUST ANOTHER PLACE TO YOU, ALLEN.
THE PAST AND FUTURE ARE PLACES YOU CAN WALK TO.
I'M TRYING TO STAY ON THE STRAIGHT AND NARROW, SIR.
I SHOULD GO BACK.
FORWARD IS THE WAY FOR YOU AND ME, ALLEN.
BEAR WITH ME.
SEE, ON REFLECTION, MY PLAN WAS IMPOSSIBLE.
UNTIL YOU CAME ALONG.
TO SECURE WORLD PEACE, THE PRESIDENT HAS TO BE SACRIFICED.
I WANT TO GIVE YOU THE PURPOSE YOU'RE SEARCHING FOR.
I NEED A SUPER-HERO, CAPTAIN ATOM.
ADAM.
ATOM.
PERHAPS THIS WILL HELP EXPLAIN...

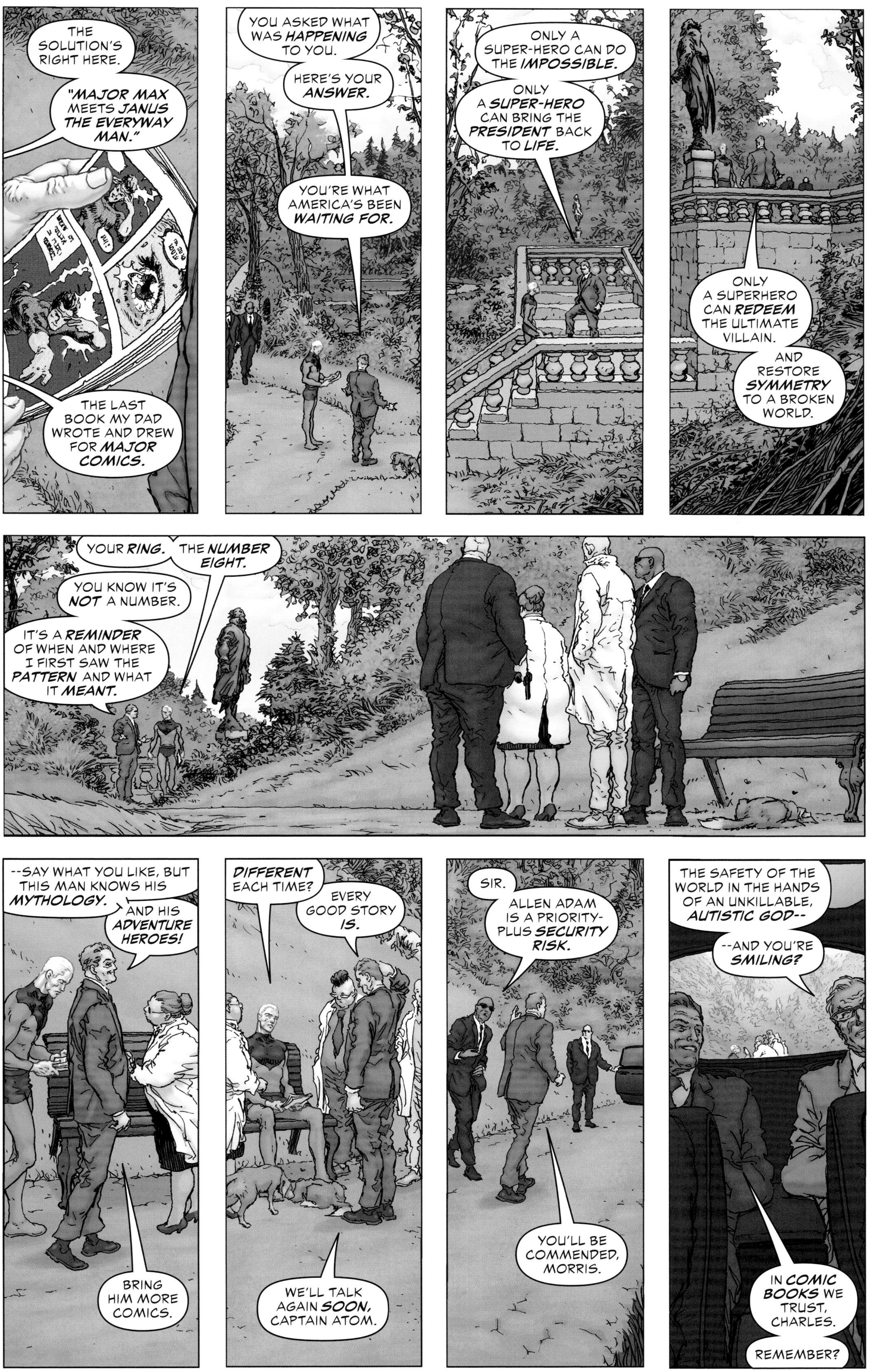

THE SOLUTION'S RIGHT HERE.
"MAJOR MAX MEETS JANUS THE EVERYWAY MAN."
THE LAST BOOK MY DAD WROTE AND DREW FOR MAJOR COMICS.
YOU ASKED WHAT WAS HAPPENING TO YOU.
HERE'S YOUR ANSWER.
YOU'RE WHAT AMERICA'S BEEN WAITING FOR.
ONLY A SUPER-HERO CAN DO THE IMPOSSIBLE.
ONLY A SUPER-HERO CAN BRING THE PRESIDENT BACK TO LIFE.
ONLY A SUPERHERO CAN REDEEM THE ULTIMATE VILLAIN.
AND RESTORE SYMMETRY TO A BROKEN WORLD.
YOUR RING.
THE NUMBER EIGHT.
YOU KNOW IT'S NOT A NUMBER.
IT'S A REMINDER OF WHEN AND WHERE I FIRST SAW THE PATTERN AND WHAT IT MEANT.
--SAY WHAT YOU LIKE, BUT THIS MAN KNOWS HIS MYTHOLOGY.
AND HIS ADVENTURE HEROES!
BRING HIM MORE COMICS.
DIFFERENT EACH TIME?
EVERY GOOD STORY IS.
WE'LL TALK AGAIN SOON, CAPTAIN ATOM.
SIR.
ALLEN ADAM IS A PRIORITY-PLUS SECURITY RISK.
YOU'LL BE COMMENDED, MORRIS.
THE SAFETY OF THE WORLD IN THE HANDS OF AN UNKILLABLE, AUTISTIC GOD--
--AND YOU'RE SMILING?
IN COMIC BOOKS WE TRUST, CHARLES.
REMEMBER?

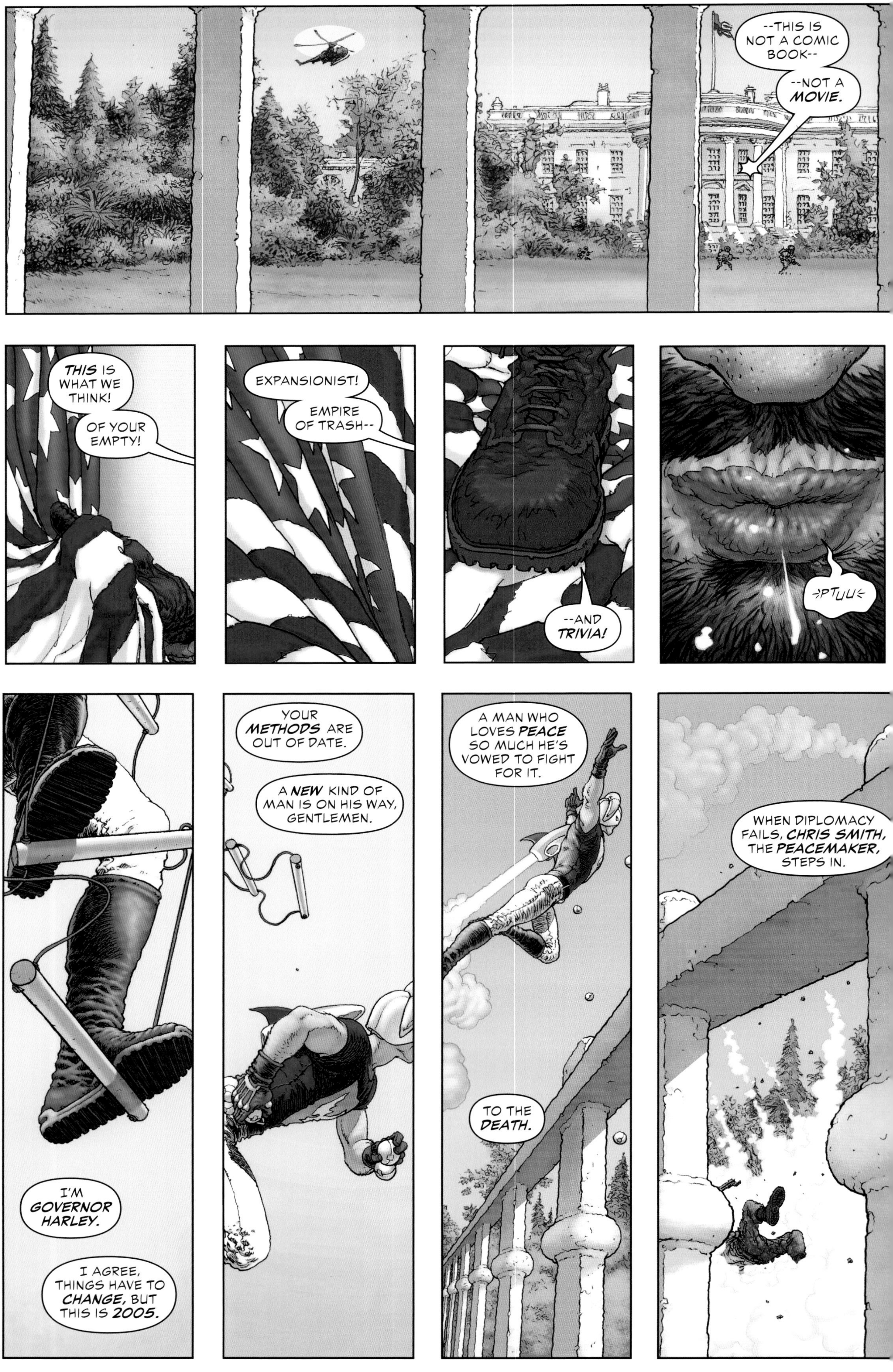

--THIS IS NOT A COMIC BOOK--
--NOT A MOVIE.
THIS IS WHAT WE THINK!
OF YOUR EMPTY!
EXPANSIONIST!
EMPIRE OF TRASH--
--AND TRIVIA!
PTUU
I'M GOVERNOR HARLEY.
I AGREE, THINGS HAVE TO CHANGE, BUT THIS IS 2005.
YOUR METHODS ARE OUT OF DATE.
A NEW KIND OF MAN IS ON HIS WAY, GENTLEMEN.
A MAN WHO LOVES PEACE SO MUCH HE'S VOWED TO FIGHT FOR IT.
TO THE DEATH.
WHEN DIPLOMACY FAILS, CHRIS SMITH, THE PEACEMAKER, STEPS IN.

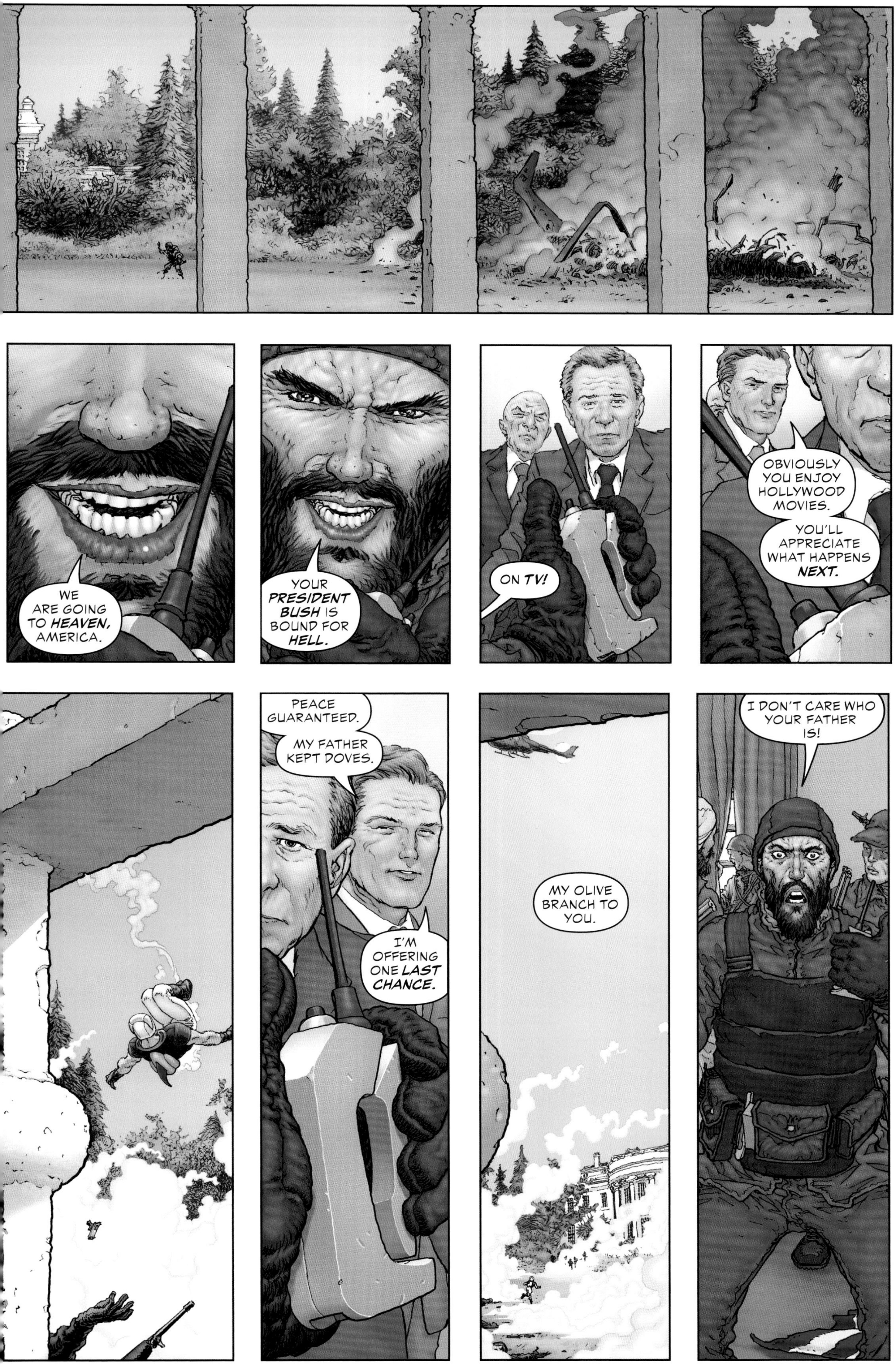
WE ARE GOING TO HEAVEN, AMERICA.
YOUR PRESIDENT BUSH IS BOUND FOR HELL.
ON TV!
OBVIOUSLY YOU ENJOY HOLLYWOOD MOVIES.
YOU'LL APPRECIATE WHAT HAPPENS NEXT.
PEACE GUARANTEED.
MY FATHER KEPT DOVES.
I'M OFFERING ONE LAST CHANCE.
MY OLIVE BRANCH TO YOU.
I DON'T CARE WHO YOUR FATHER IS!

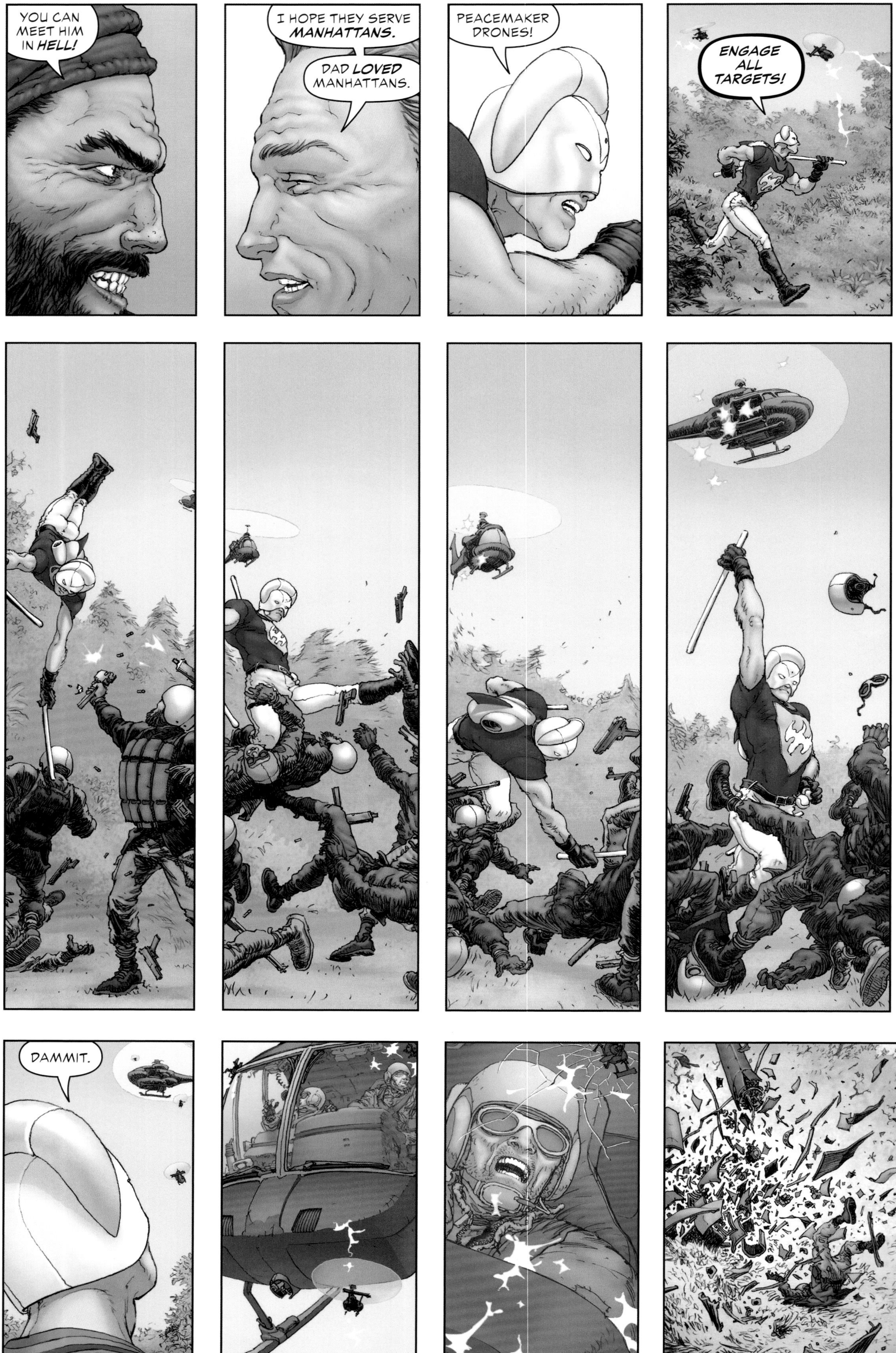
YOU CAN MEET HIM IN HELL!
I HOPE THEY SERVE MANHATTANS.
DAD LOVED MANHATTANS.
PEACEMAKER DRONES!
ENGAGE ALL TARGETS!
DAMMIT.

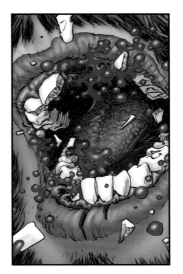

CASUALTIES?

MUST TRY HARDER NEXT TIME.

PEACEMAKER?

SOON THERE WILL BE MORE JUST LIKE HIM.

YOUR WORLD HAS COME TO AN END TODAY.

YOU AND YOUR KIND ARE *FINISHED.*

DONE WITH.

THANKS TO *YOU.*

YOU'RE A STRONG MAN, CHRIS.

THE DRUG IS *MUCH STRONGER.*

IT *DESTROYS* YOUR RESISTANCE.

IT CREEPS UP ON YOU.

I'LL ASK THE QUESTION *AGAIN.*

WHY?

SUVV

SUVVA WORLL

FROM WHOM?

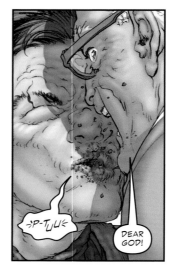

→P-T,U,U‹

DEAR GOD!

HE'S *LOOSE!*

HE--

BANG!

GT

--I ASKED HIM THE *REAL* REASON HE'D CHOSEN TO *BECOME* THE SACRIFICIAL VICTIM.

"I DESERVE IT," HE SAID.

"LET THE PUNISHMENT FIT THE CRIME."

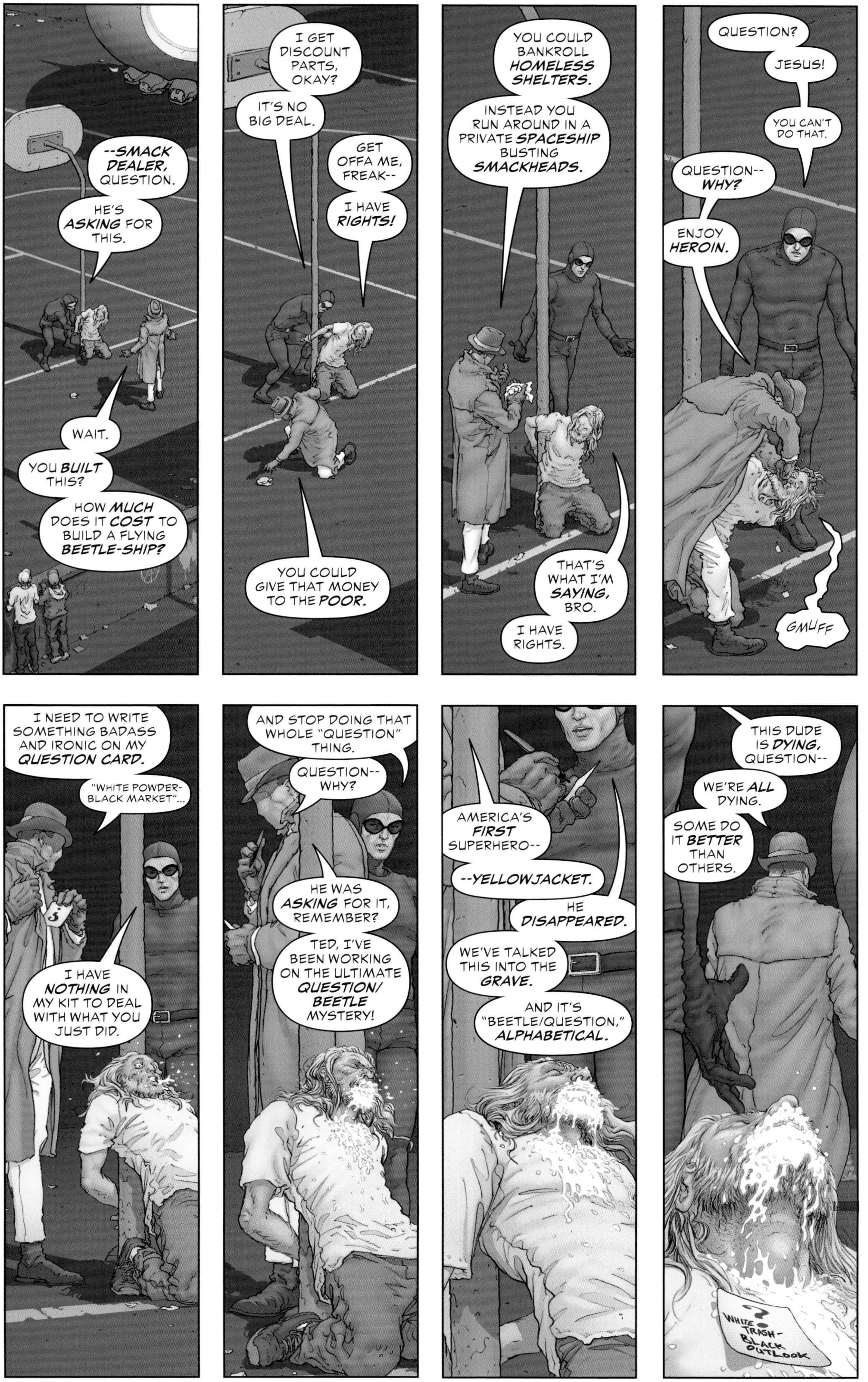
--SMACK DEALER, QUESTION.
HE'S ASKING FOR THIS.
WAIT.
YOU BUILT THIS?
HOW MUCH DOES IT COST TO BUILD A FLYING BEETLE-SHIP?
I GET DISCOUNT PARTS, OKAY?
IT'S NO BIG DEAL.
GET OFFA ME, FREAK--
I HAVE RIGHTS!
YOU COULD GIVE THAT MONEY TO THE POOR.
YOU COULD BANKROLL HOMELESS SHELTERS.
INSTEAD YOU RUN AROUND IN A PRIVATE SPACESHIP BUSTING SMACKHEADS.
THAT'S WHAT I'M SAYING, BRO.
I HAVE RIGHTS.
QUESTION?
JESUS!
YOU CAN'T DO THAT.
QUESTION-- WHY?
ENJOY HEROIN.
GMUFF
I NEED TO WRITE SOMETHING BADASS AND IRONIC ON MY QUESTION CARD.
"WHITE POWDER-BLACK MARKET"...
I HAVE NOTHING IN MY KIT TO DEAL WITH WHAT YOU JUST DID.
AND STOP DOING THAT WHOLE "QUESTION" THING.
QUESTION-- WHY?
HE WAS ASKING FOR IT, REMEMBER?
TED, I'VE BEEN WORKING ON THE ULTIMATE QUESTION/BEETLE MYSTERY!
AMERICA'S FIRST SUPERHERO--
--YELLOWJACKET.
HE DISAPPEARED.
WE'VE TALKED THIS INTO THE GRAVE.
AND IT'S "BEETLE/QUESTION," ALPHABETICAL.
THIS DUDE IS DYING, QUESTION--
WE'RE ALL DYING.
SOME DO IT BETTER THAN OTHERS.
WHITE TRASH-BLACK OUTLOOK

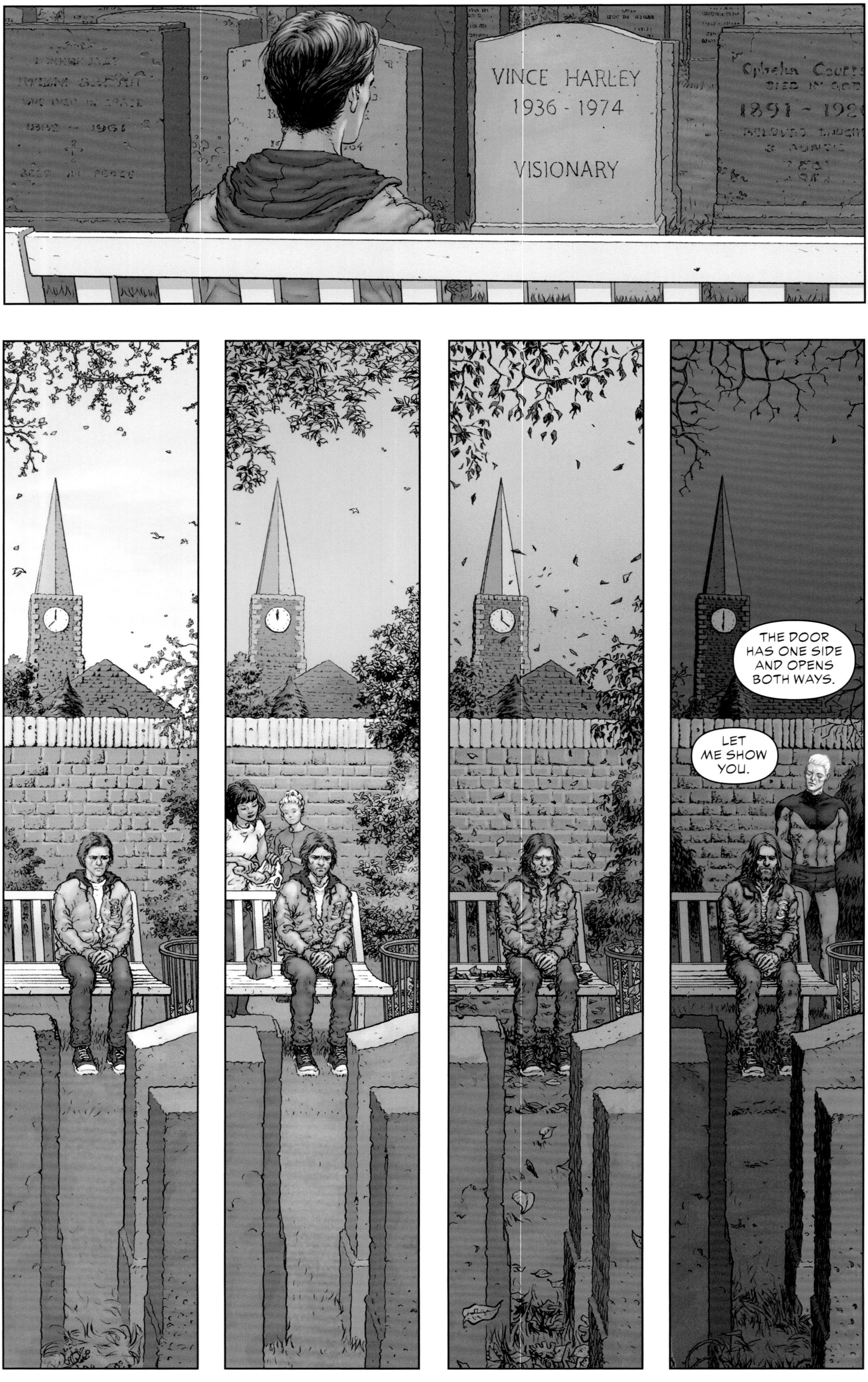
VINCE HARLEY
1936 - 1974
VISIONARY
THE DOOR HAS ONE SIDE AND OPENS BOTH WAYS.
LET ME SHOW YOU.

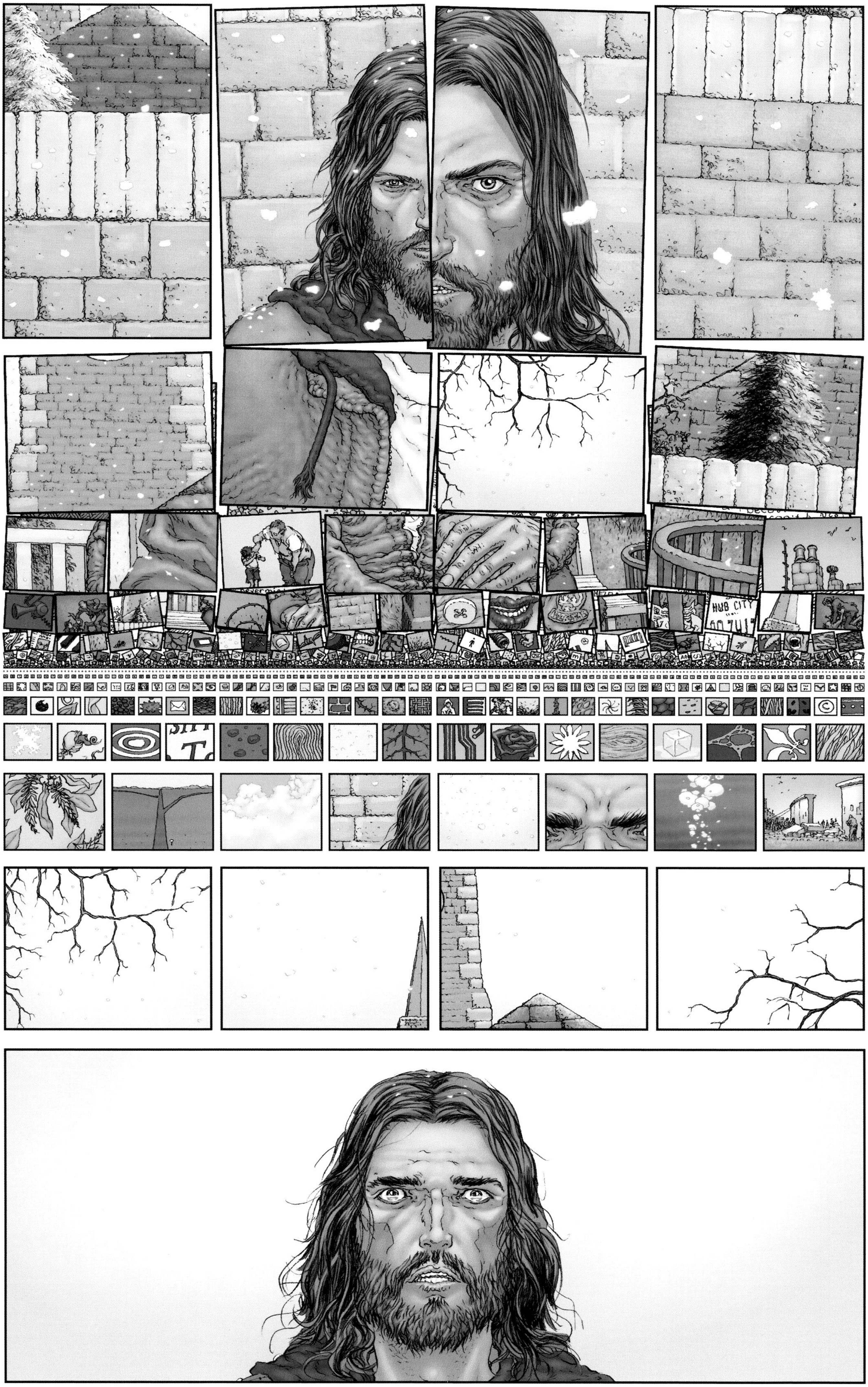
HUB CITY

IT'S SO OBVIOUS.

THE ANSWER IS STARING US IN THE FACE.

YELLOWJACKET IS NO OSI-SPONSORED COLD WAR SUPER-AGENT LIKE DAN GARRETT--

--HE'S ONE OF US!

AN ORDINARY CITIZEN, SICKENED BY TOP-DOWN HYPOCRISY FROM NIXON TO CITY HALL!

THEY CALL HIM DANGEROUS AND DERANGED!

I CALL HIM MR. 1970s AMERICA.

A NEW BREED IS ON ITS WAY, AND THEY'RE MAD AS HELL.

THEY SEE THINGS DIFFERENTLY.

THEY'VE HAD ENOUGH OF ANARCHY ON OUR STREETS.

THEY'RE PREPARED TO TAKE RESPONSIBILITY FOR THEIR COMMUNITIES.

AND GOD HELP US ALL.

MYSTERY MAN SMASHES DRUG RING

WHO IS YELLOWJACKET

MASKED HERO

THEY DON'T MIND TAKING THE LAW INTO THEIR OWN HANDS, EITHER.

I'M WALTER WYLIE, WWB.

I LEAVE YOU WITH THE DREAM OF A COUNTRY THAT MIGHT HAVE BEEN, IN THE WORDS OF JOHN F. KENNEDY.

HE SAID, "WHAT KIND OF PEACE DO I MEAN AND WHAT KIND OF PEACE DO WE SEEK?"

"NOT A PAX AMERICANA ENFORCED ON THE WORLD BY AMERICAN WEAPONS OF WAR.

"NOT THE PEACE OF THE GRAVE OR THE SECURITY OF THE SLAVE."

"I AM TALKING ABOUT GENUINE PEACE."

FORGOT MY KEY, KID.

AAAAAAAAA

"THE KIND OF PEACE THAT MAKES LIFE ON EARTH WORTH LIVING--

"AND THE KIND THAT ENABLES NATIONS TO GROW AND TO HOPE--

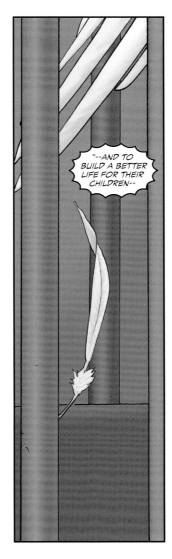

"--AND TO BUILD A BETTER LIFE FOR THEIR CHILDREN--

"--NOT MERELY PEACE FOR AMERICANS, BUT PEACE FOR ALL MEN AND WOMEN."

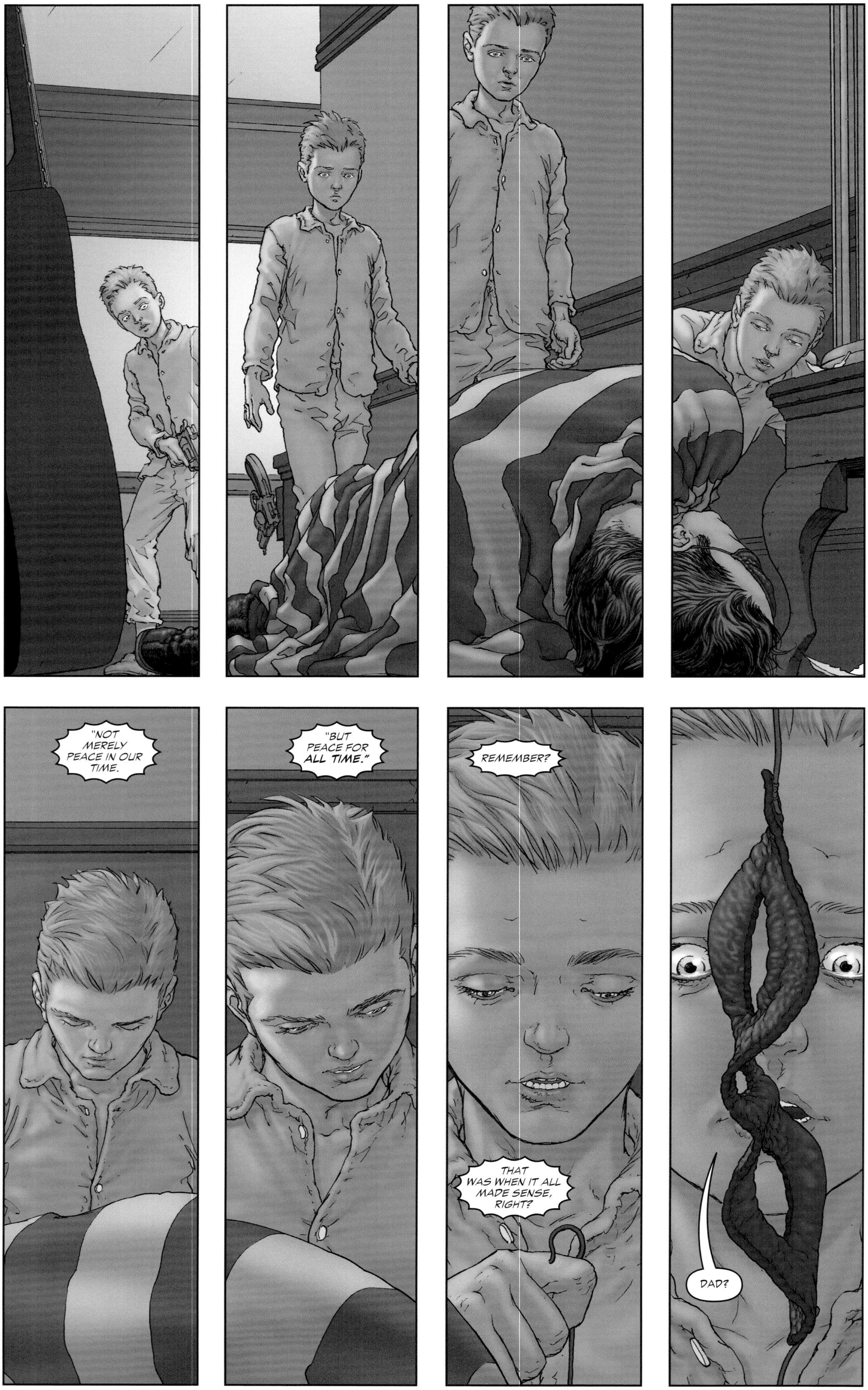
"NOT MERELY PEACE IN OUR TIME.
"BUT PEACE FOR ALL TIME."
REMEMBER?
THAT WAS WHEN IT ALL MADE SENSE, RIGHT?
DAD?

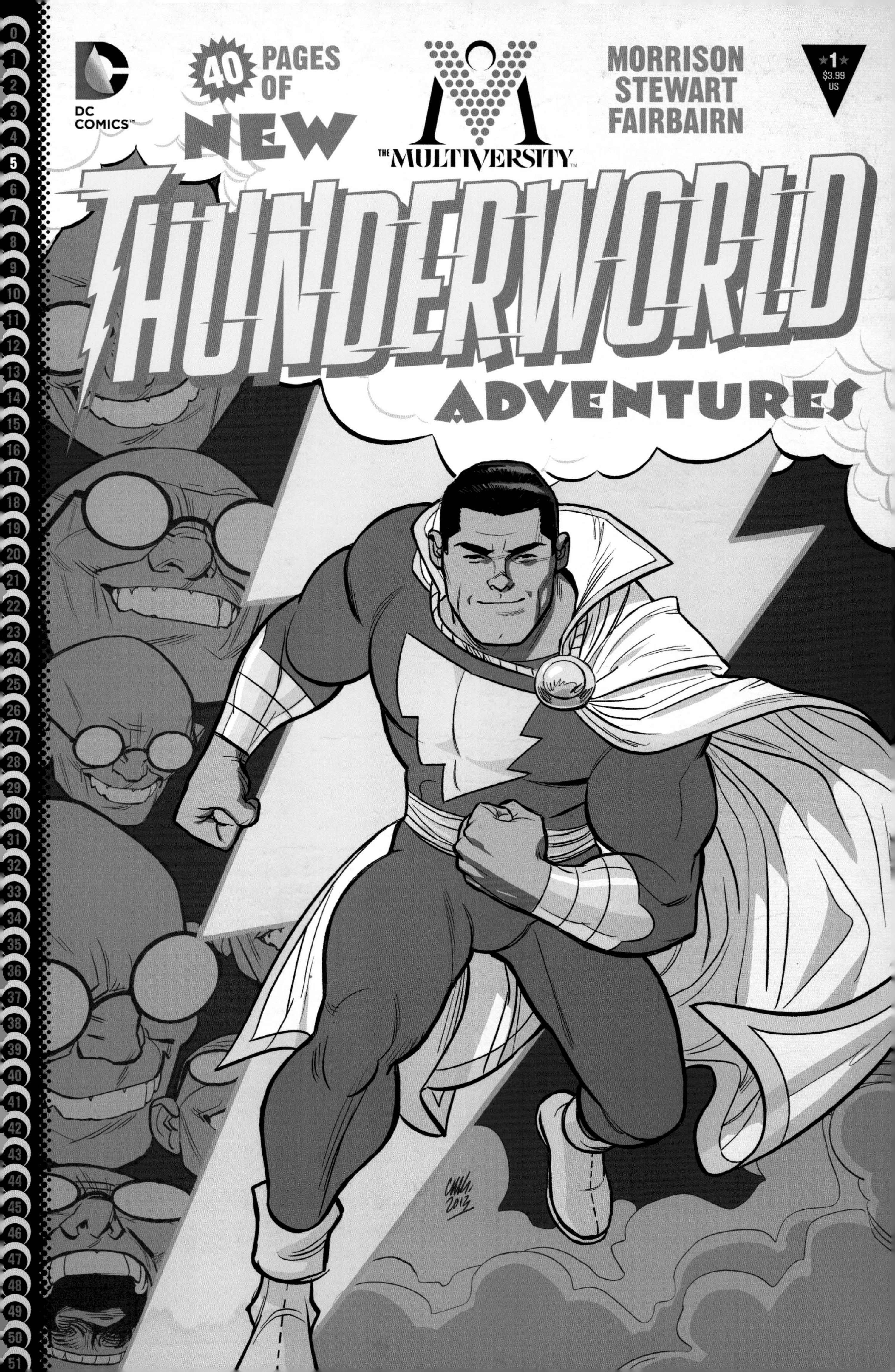
DC COMICS
40 PAGES OF
NEW
THE MULTIVERSITY
MORRISON
STEWART
FAIRBAIRN
1
$3.99
US
THUNDERWORLD
ADVENTURES

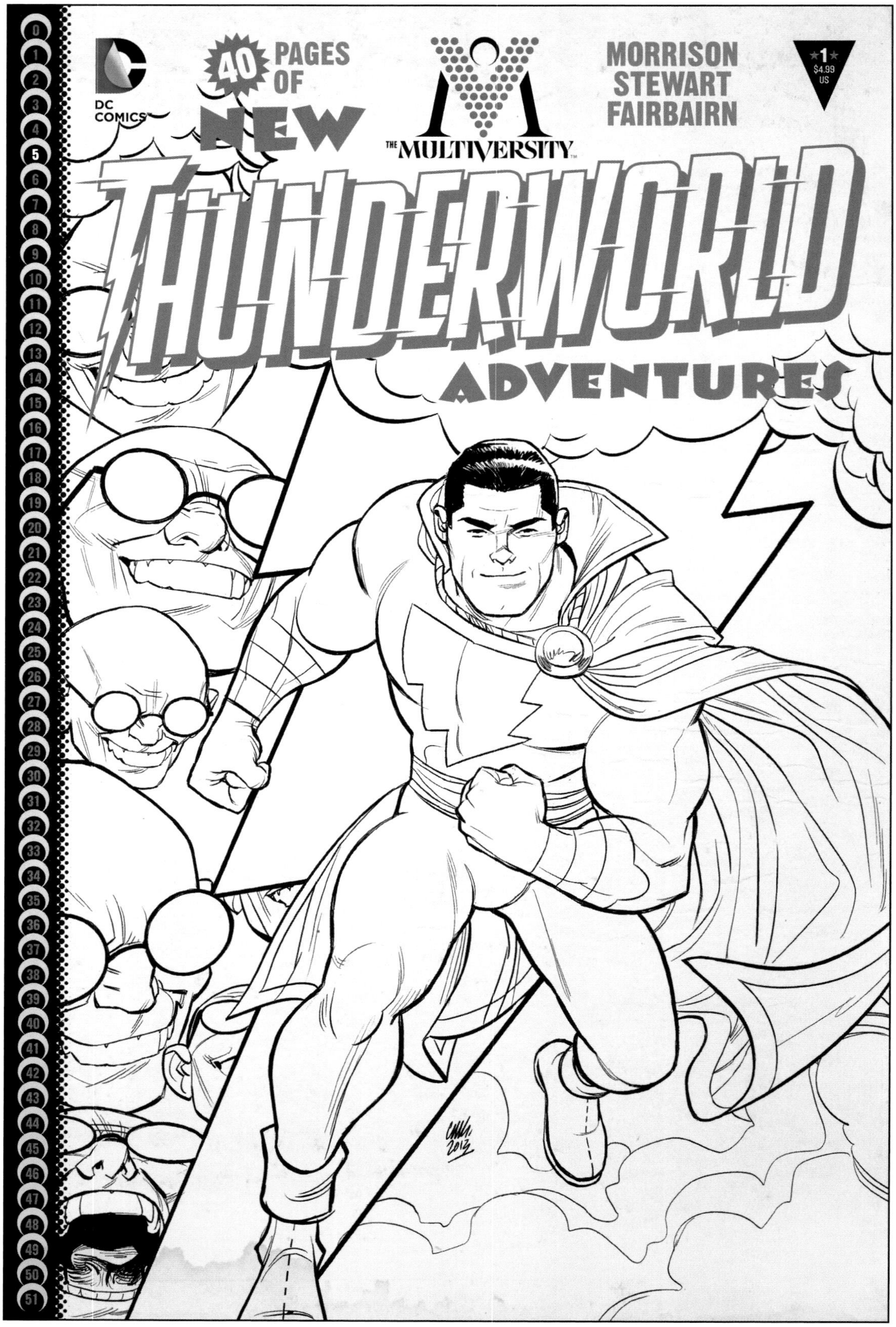
40 PAGES OF
NEW
THE MULTIVERSITY
MORRISON
STEWART
FAIRBAIRN
DC COMICS
1
$4.99
US
THUNDERWORLD
ADVENTURES

THE MULTIVERSITY: THUNDERWORLD ADVENTURES
#1

Written by
GRANT MORRISON

Artist
CAMERON STEWART

Letterer
STEVE WANDS

Colorist
NATHAN FAIRBAIRN

Cover artist
CAMERON STEWART

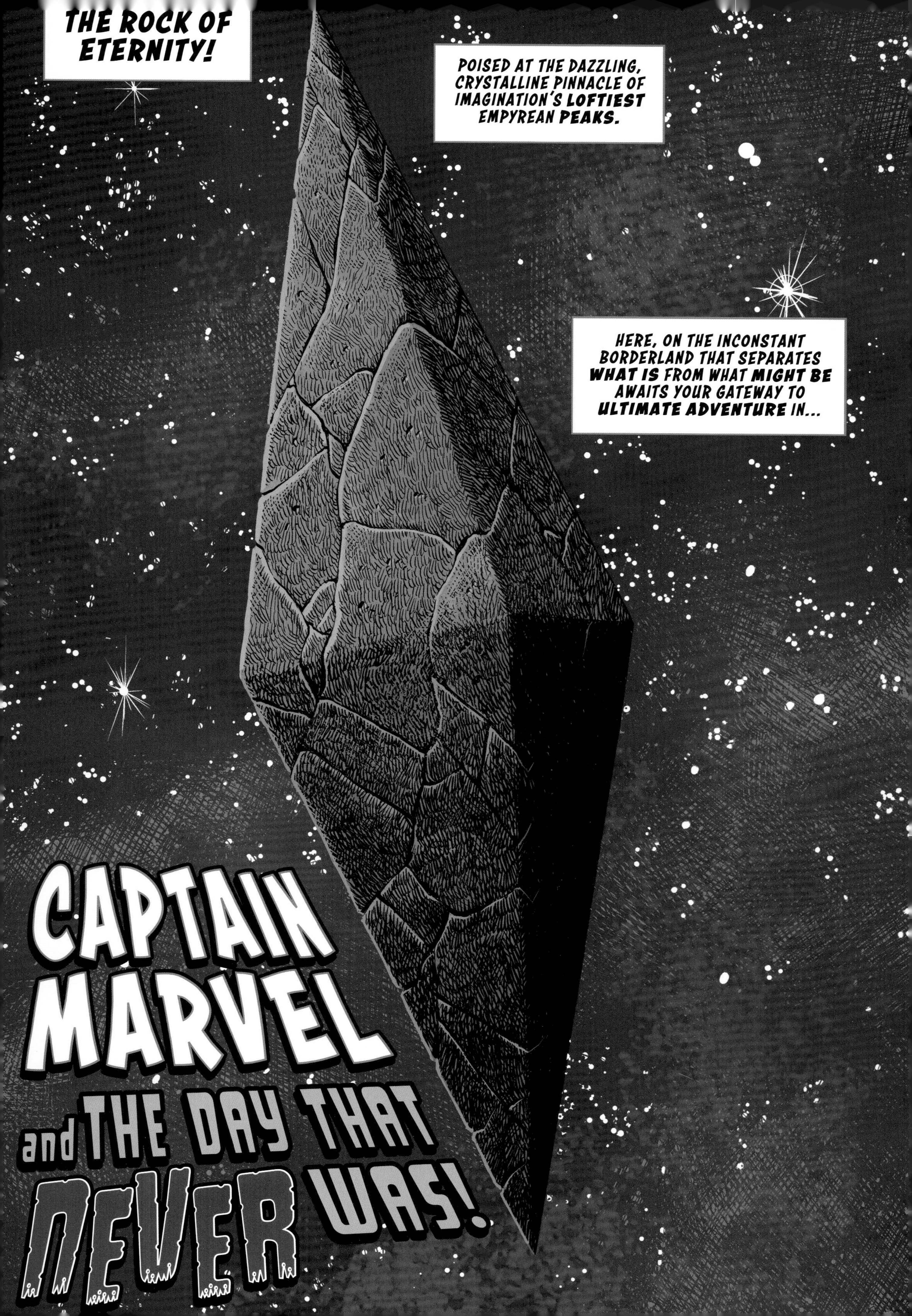
THE ROCK OF ETERNITY!
POISED AT THE DAZZLING, CRYSTALLINE PINNACLE OF IMAGINATION'S LOFTIEST EMPYREAN PEAKS.
HERE, ON THE INCONSTANT BORDERLAND THAT SEPARATES WHAT IS FROM WHAT MIGHT BE AWAITS YOUR GATEWAY TO ULTIMATE ADVENTURE IN...
CAPTAIN MARVEL and THE DAY THAT NEVER WAS!

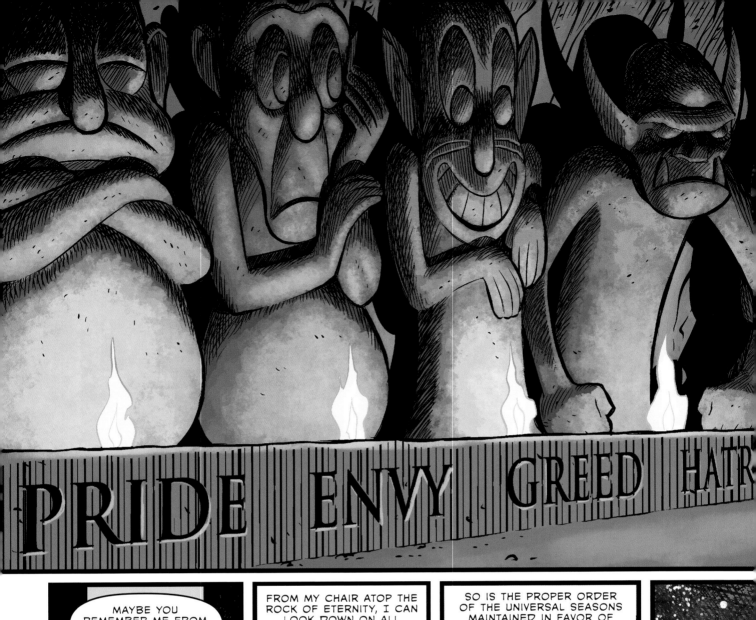

PRIDE ENVY GREED HATR

MAYBE YOU REMEMBER ME FROM *BEFORE.* MAYBE NOT, BUT *DON'T WORRY,* WE'LL GET THERE IN THE END.

I ∋HRMPPH∈ AM THE GUARDIAN OF TIME'S STARRY *OVERLOOK.*

KNOWN TO ALL AS THE WIZARD *SHAZAM.*

FROM MY CHAIR ATOP THE ROCK OF ETERNITY, I CAN LOOK DOWN ON ALL CREATION WITH AN EAGLE EYE PEELED FOR TROUBLE.

AND WHERE TROUBLE ARISES, I CAN INSTANTLY SEND MY SUPER-CHAMPION...

...CAPTAIN MARVEL.

SO IS THE PROPER ORDER OF THE UNIVERSAL SEASONS MAINTAINED IN FAVOR OF THE FORCES OF--

ODD...

THERE'S AN UNFAMILIAR *DAY* ON THE *COSMIC CALENDAR*--ONE I'VE NEVER *SEEN* BEFORE.

MONDAY TUESDAY WEDNESDAY THURSDAY...

HERE, WHERE THE CLOCKS TICK *ONCE AND FOREVER,* WAITS THE *WIZARD* OF ETERNITY--

--HMM, IT'S *YOU* AGAIN. I WAS JUST PRACTICING MY *OMNISCIENT NARRATOR* VOICE.

COME *CLOSER,* PLEASE.

SELFISHNESS | LAZINESS | INJUSTICE

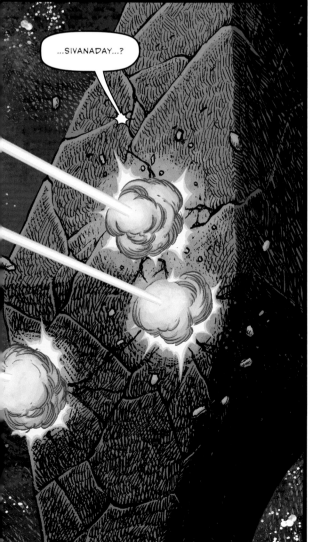

...SIVANADAY...?

IMPOSSIBLE!

THE ROCK OF ETERNITY IS UNDER ATTACK FOR THE FIRST TIME IN-- IN--ETERNITY!

I MUST ALERT MY *CHAMPION!*

HOW CAN THIS BE?

A *SECOND* ETERNITY?

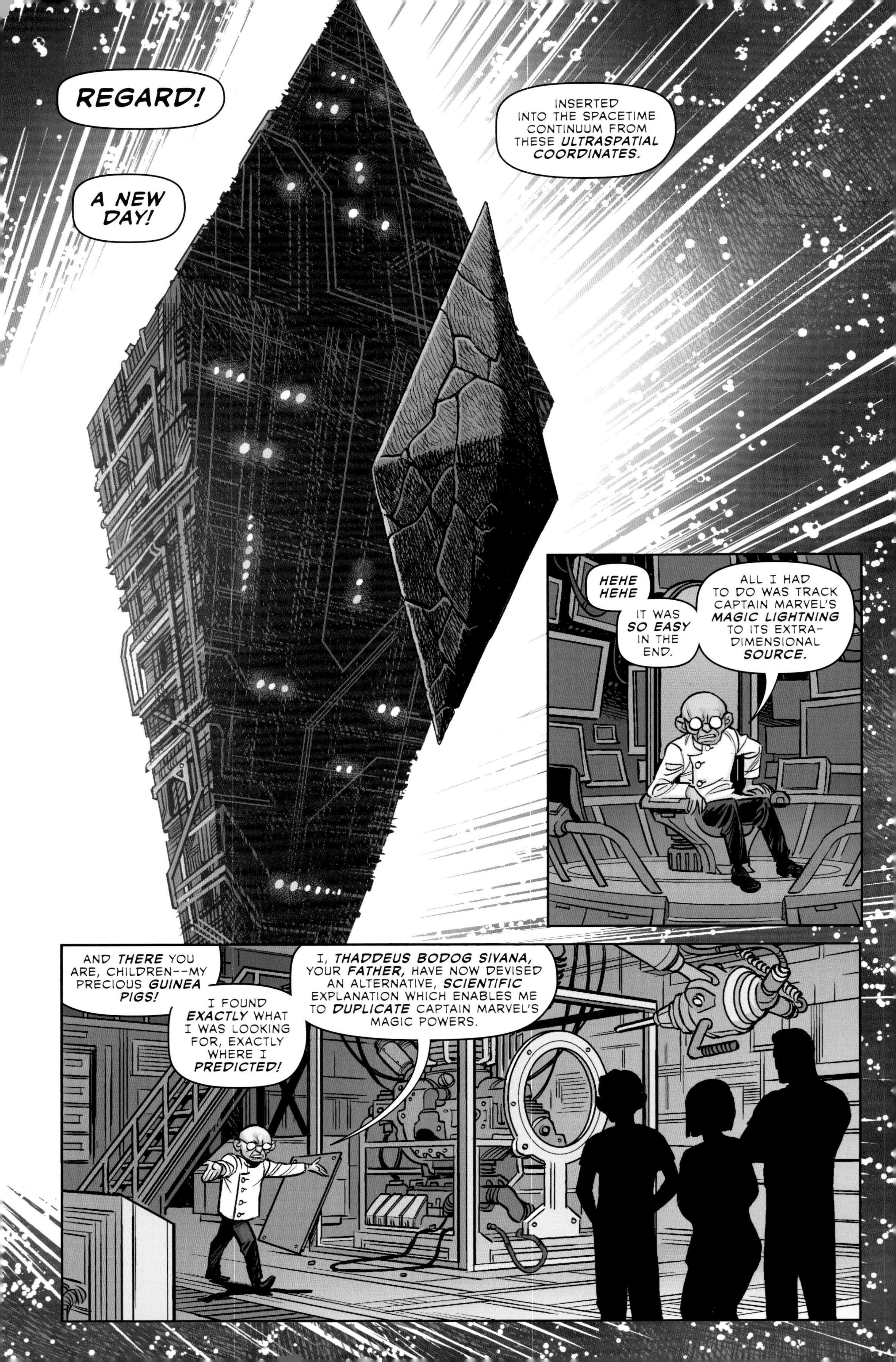
REGARD!
A NEW DAY!
INSERTED INTO THE SPACETIME CONTINUUM FROM THESE ULTRASPATIAL COORDINATES.
HEHE HEHE
IT WAS SO EASY IN THE END.
ALL I HAD TO DO WAS TRACK CAPTAIN MARVEL'S MAGIC LIGHTNING TO ITS EXTRA-DIMENSIONAL SOURCE.
AND THERE YOU ARE, CHILDREN--MY PRECIOUS GUINEA PIGS!
I FOUND EXACTLY WHAT I WAS LOOKING FOR, EXACTLY WHERE I PREDICTED!
I, THADDEUS BODOG SIVANA, YOUR FATHER, HAVE NOW DEVISED AN ALTERNATIVE, SCIENTIFIC EXPLANATION WHICH ENABLES ME TO DUPLICATE CAPTAIN MARVEL'S MAGIC POWERS.

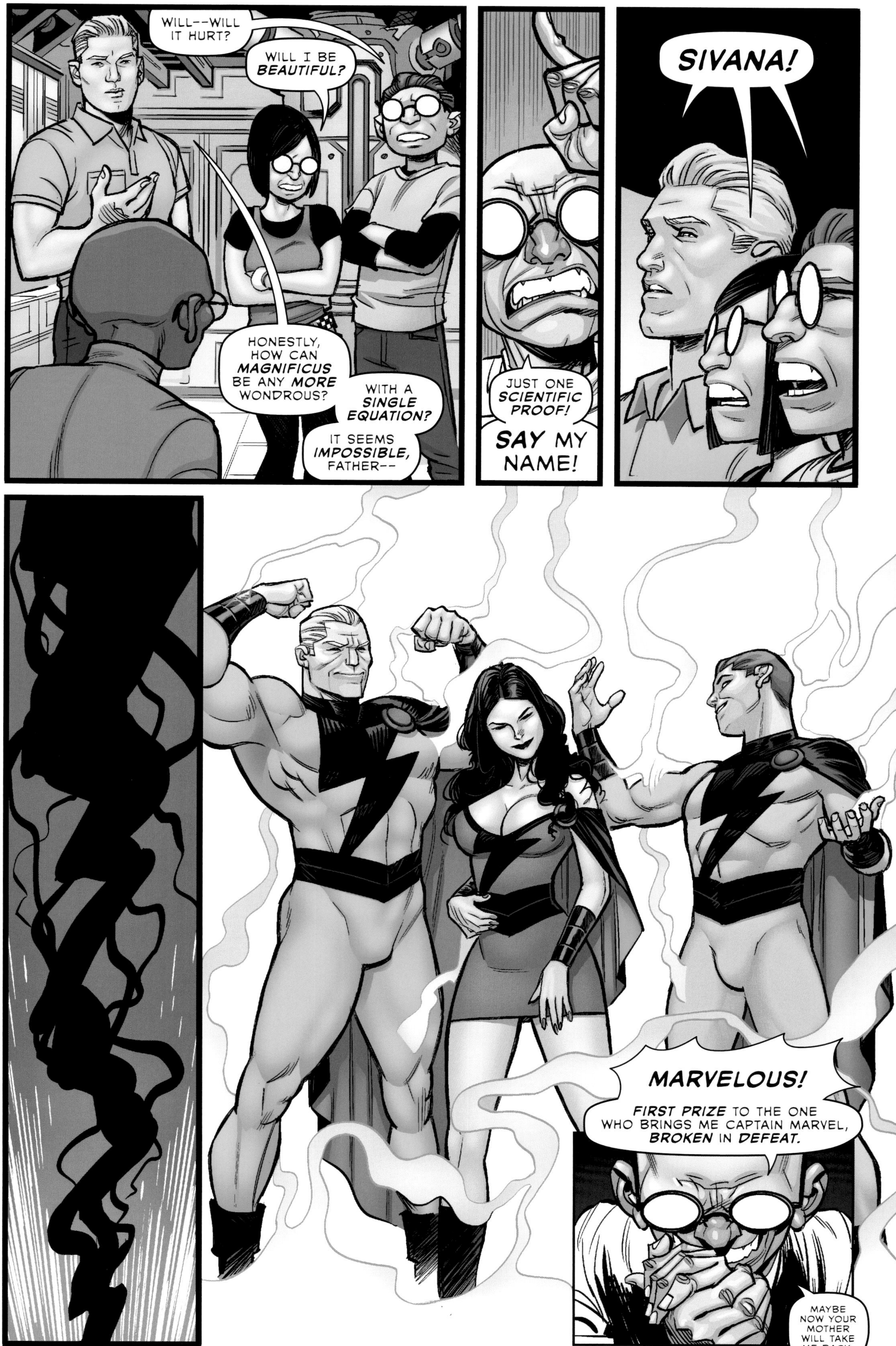
WILL--WILL IT HURT?
WILL I BE *BEAUTIFUL?*
HONESTLY, HOW CAN *MAGNIFICUS* BE ANY *MORE* WONDROUS?
WITH A *SINGLE EQUATION?*
IT SEEMS *IMPOSSIBLE,* FATHER--
JUST ONE *SCIENTIFIC PROOF!*
SAY MY NAME!
SIVANA!
MARVELOUS!
FIRST PRIZE TO THE ONE WHO BRINGS ME CAPTAIN MARVEL, *BROKEN* IN *DEFEAT.*
MAYBE NOW YOUR MOTHER WILL TAKE ME BACK.

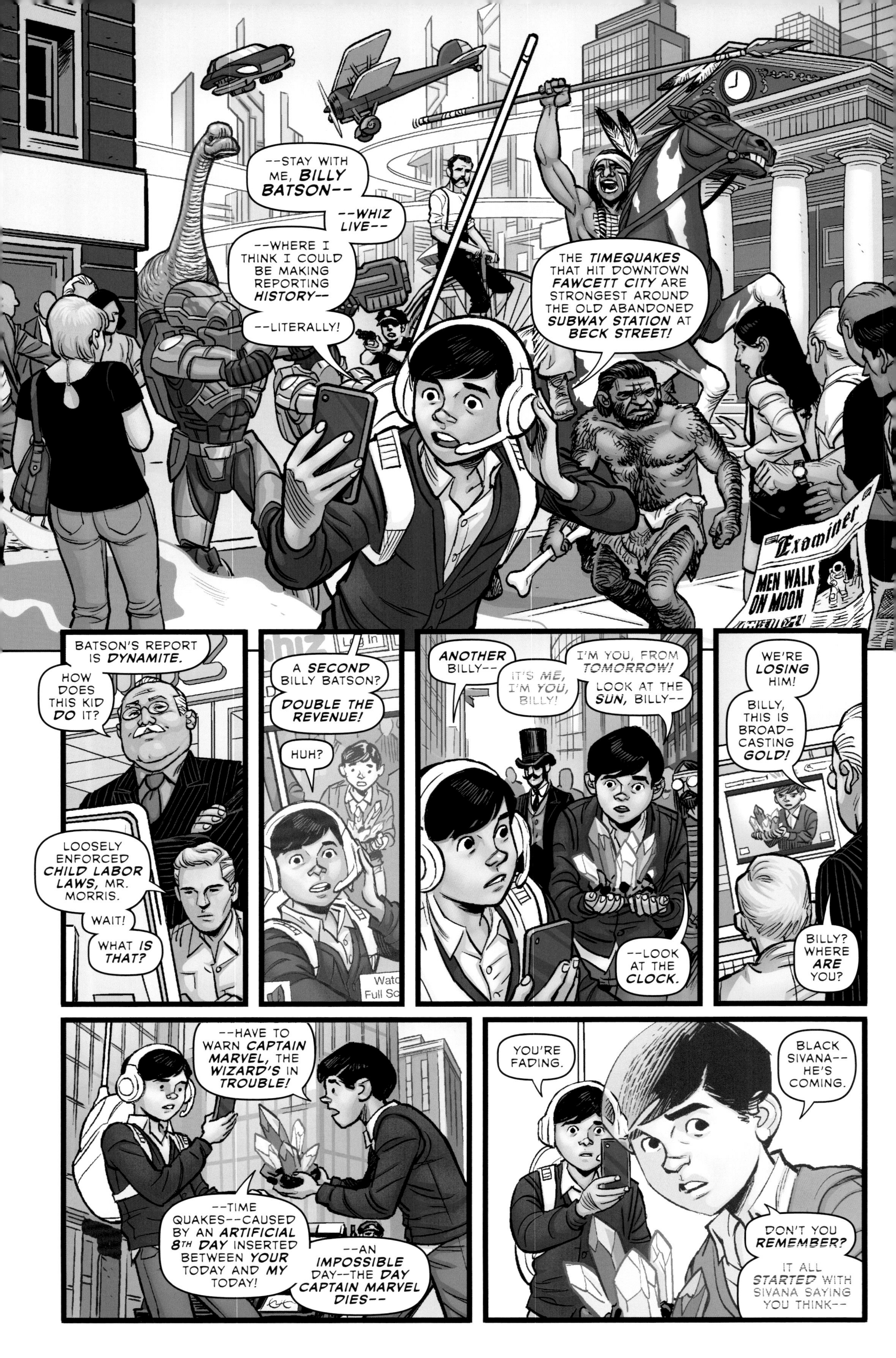
--STAY WITH ME, BILLY BATSON--
--WHIZ LIVE--
--WHERE I THINK I COULD BE MAKING REPORTING HISTORY--
--LITERALLY!
THE TIMEQUAKES THAT HIT DOWNTOWN FAWCETT CITY ARE STRONGEST AROUND THE OLD ABANDONED SUBWAY STATION AT BECK STREET!
Examiner
MEN WALK ON MOON
BATSON'S REPORT IS DYNAMITE.
HOW DOES THIS KID DO IT?
LOOSELY ENFORCED CHILD LABOR LAWS, MR. MORRIS.
WAIT!
WHAT IS THAT?
A SECOND BILLY BATSON?
DOUBLE THE REVENUE!
HUH?
ANOTHER BILLY--
IT'S ME, I'M YOU, BILLY!
I'M YOU, FROM TOMORROW!
LOOK AT THE SUN, BILLY--
--LOOK AT THE CLOCK.
WE'RE LOSING HIM!
BILLY, THIS IS BROAD-CASTING GOLD!
BILLY? WHERE ARE YOU?
--HAVE TO WARN CAPTAIN MARVEL, THE WIZARD'S IN TROUBLE!
--TIME QUAKES--CAUSED BY AN ARTIFICIAL 8TH DAY INSERTED BETWEEN YOUR TODAY AND MY TODAY!
--AN IMPOSSIBLE DAY--THE DAY CAPTAIN MARVEL DIES--
YOU'RE FADING.
BLACK SIVANA--HE'S COMING.
DON'T YOU REMEMBER?
IT ALL STARTED WITH SIVANA SAYING YOU THINK--

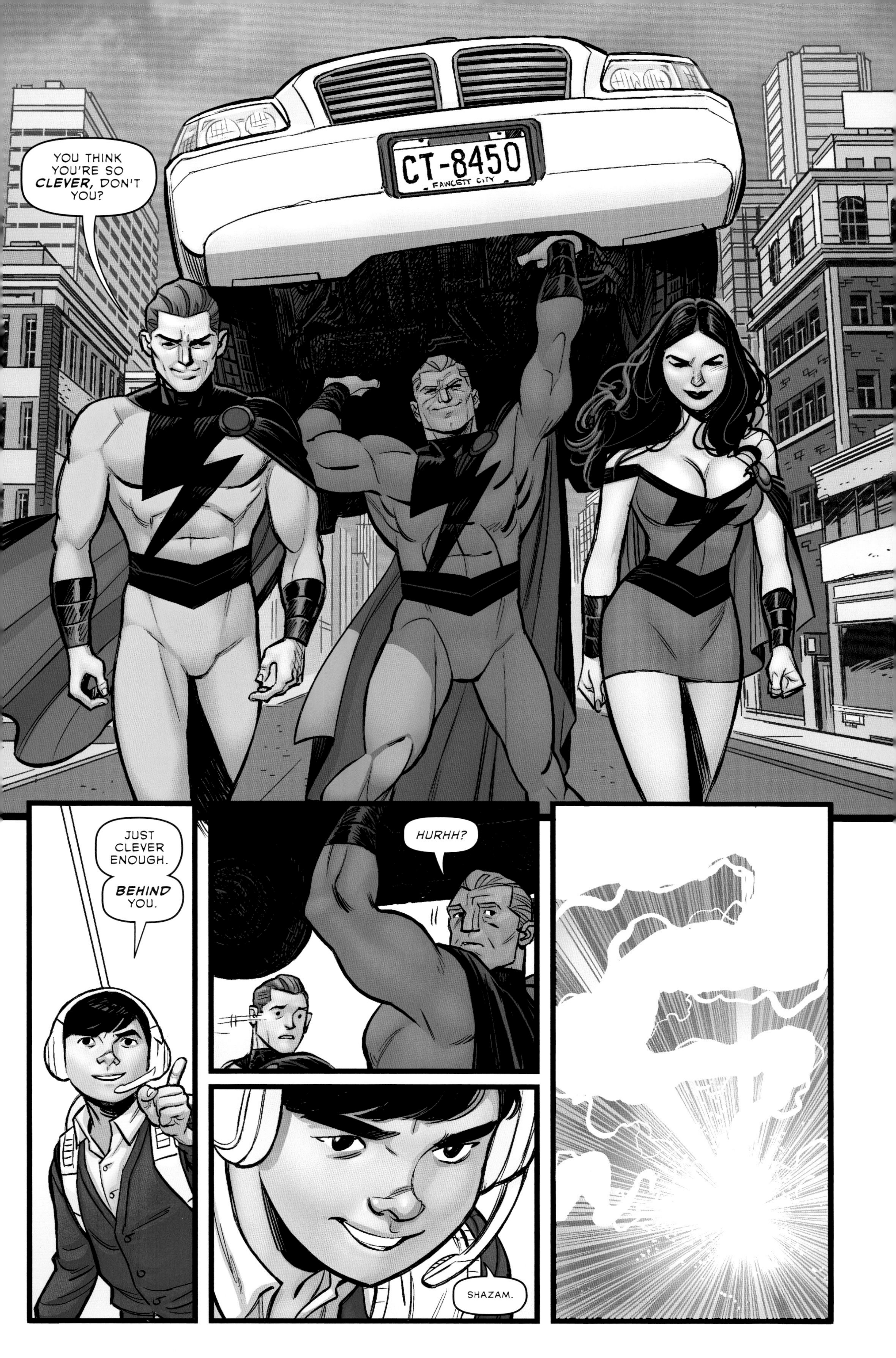
CT-8450
FAWCETT CITY
YOU THINK YOU'RE SO CLEVER, DON'T YOU?
JUST CLEVER ENOUGH.
BEHIND YOU.
HURHH?
SHAZAM.

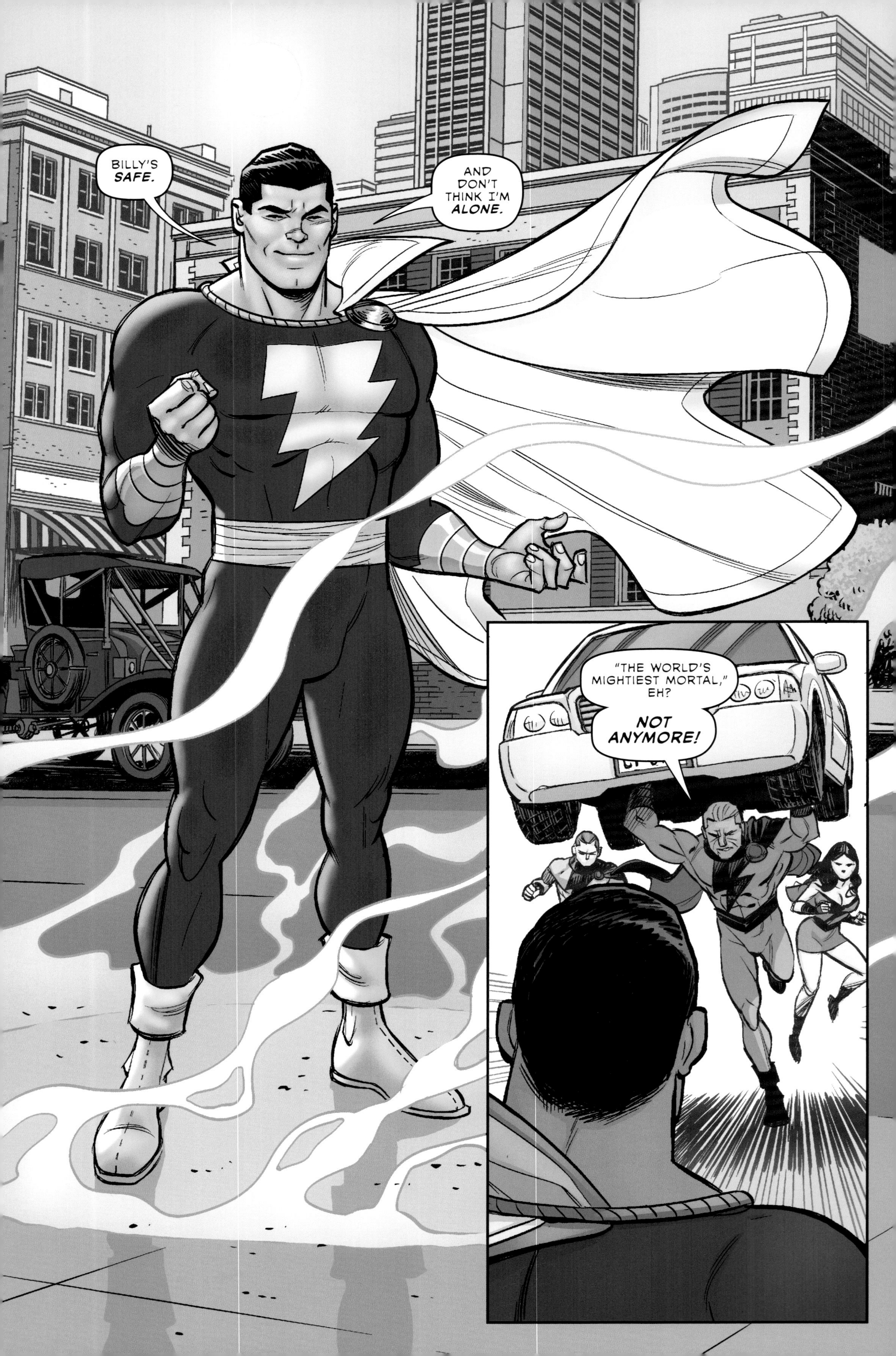
BILLY'S SAFE.
AND DON'T THINK I'M ALONE.
"THE WORLD'S MIGHTIEST MORTAL," EH?
NOT ANYMORE!

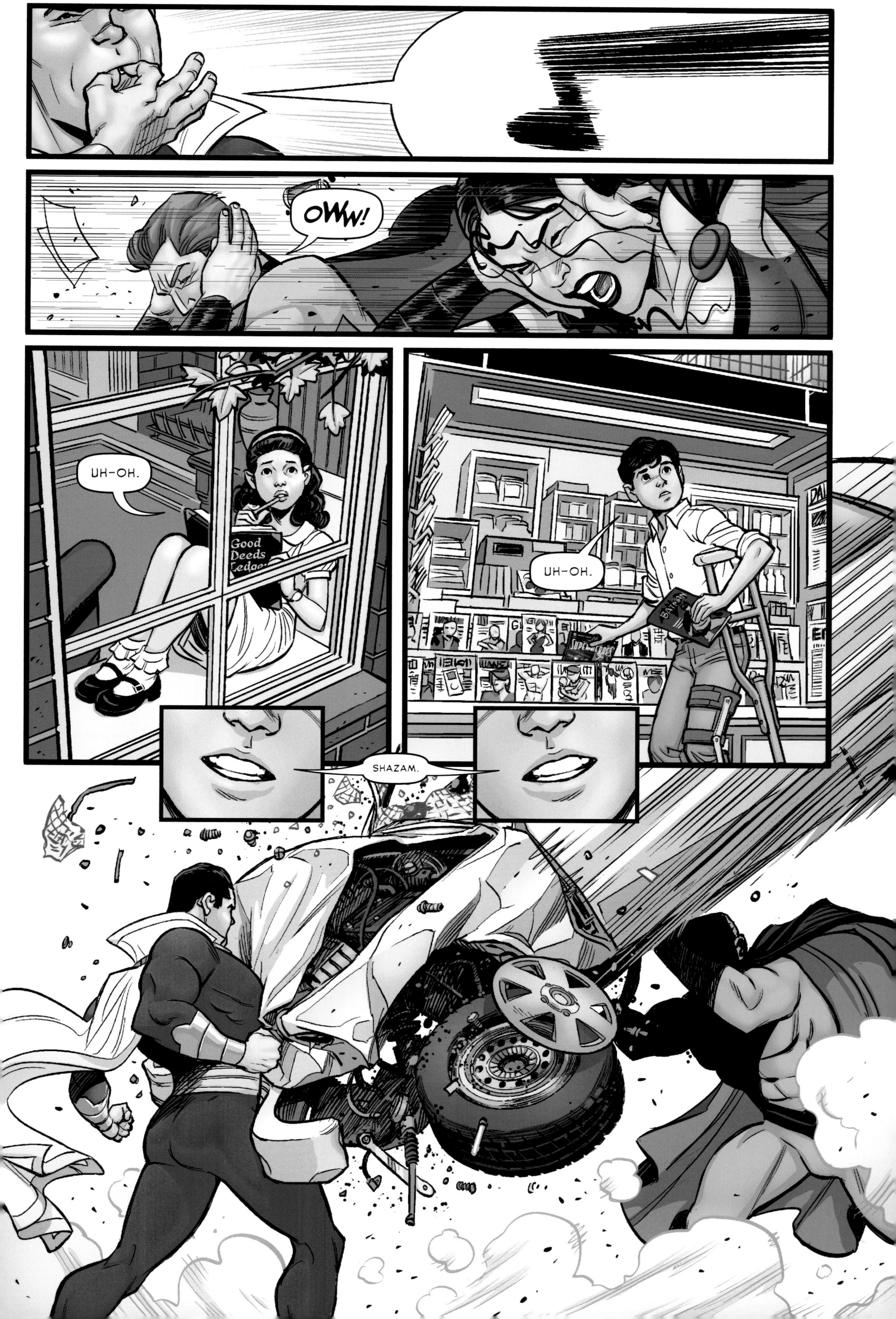
OWW!
UH-OH.
UH-OH.
SHAZAM.

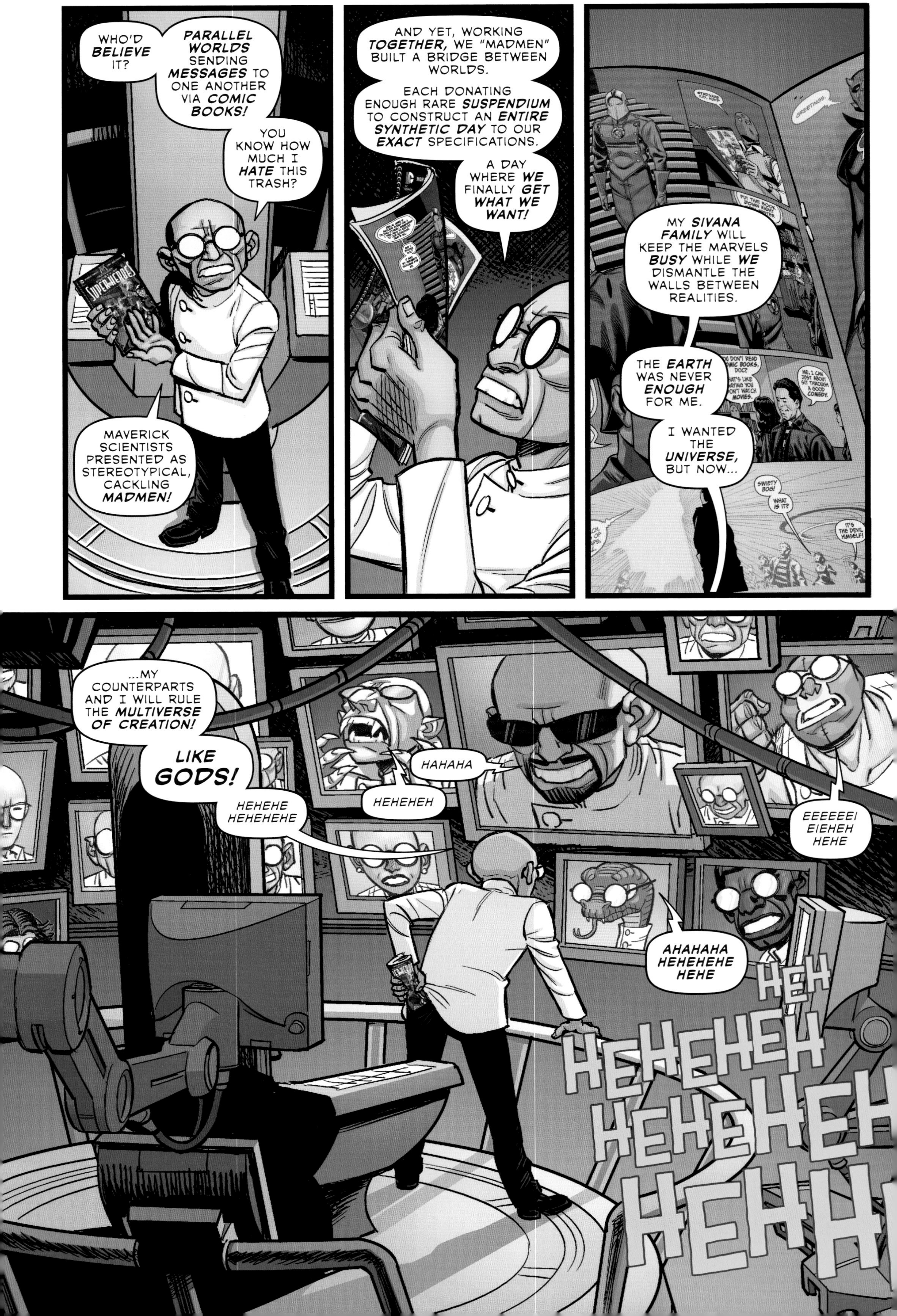

WHO'D BELIEVE IT?
PARALLEL WORLDS SENDING MESSAGES TO ONE ANOTHER VIA COMIC BOOKS!
YOU KNOW HOW MUCH I HATE THIS TRASH?
MAVERICK SCIENTISTS PRESENTED AS STEREOTYPICAL, CACKLING MADMEN!
AND YET, WORKING TOGETHER, WE "MADMEN" BUILT A BRIDGE BETWEEN WORLDS.
EACH DONATING ENOUGH RARE SUSPENDIUM TO CONSTRUCT AN ENTIRE SYNTHETIC DAY TO OUR EXACT SPECIFICATIONS.
A DAY WHERE WE FINALLY GET WHAT WE WANT!
GREETINGS.
MY SIVANA FAMILY WILL KEEP THE MARVELS BUSY WHILE WE DISMANTLE THE WALLS BETWEEN REALITIES.
ME, I CAN JUST ABOUT SIT THROUGH A GOOD COMEDY.
THE EARTH WAS NEVER ENOUGH FOR ME.
I WANTED THE UNIVERSE, BUT NOW...
SWIETY BOG!
WHAT IS IT?
IT'S THE DEVIL HIMSELF!
...MY COUNTERPARTS AND I WILL RULE THE MULTIVERSE OF CREATION!
LIKE GODS!
HAHAHA
HEHEHEH
HEHEHE HEHEHEHE
EEEEEEI EIEHEH HEHE
AHAHAHA HEHEHEHE HEHE
HEH
HEHEHEH
HEHEHEH
HEHH

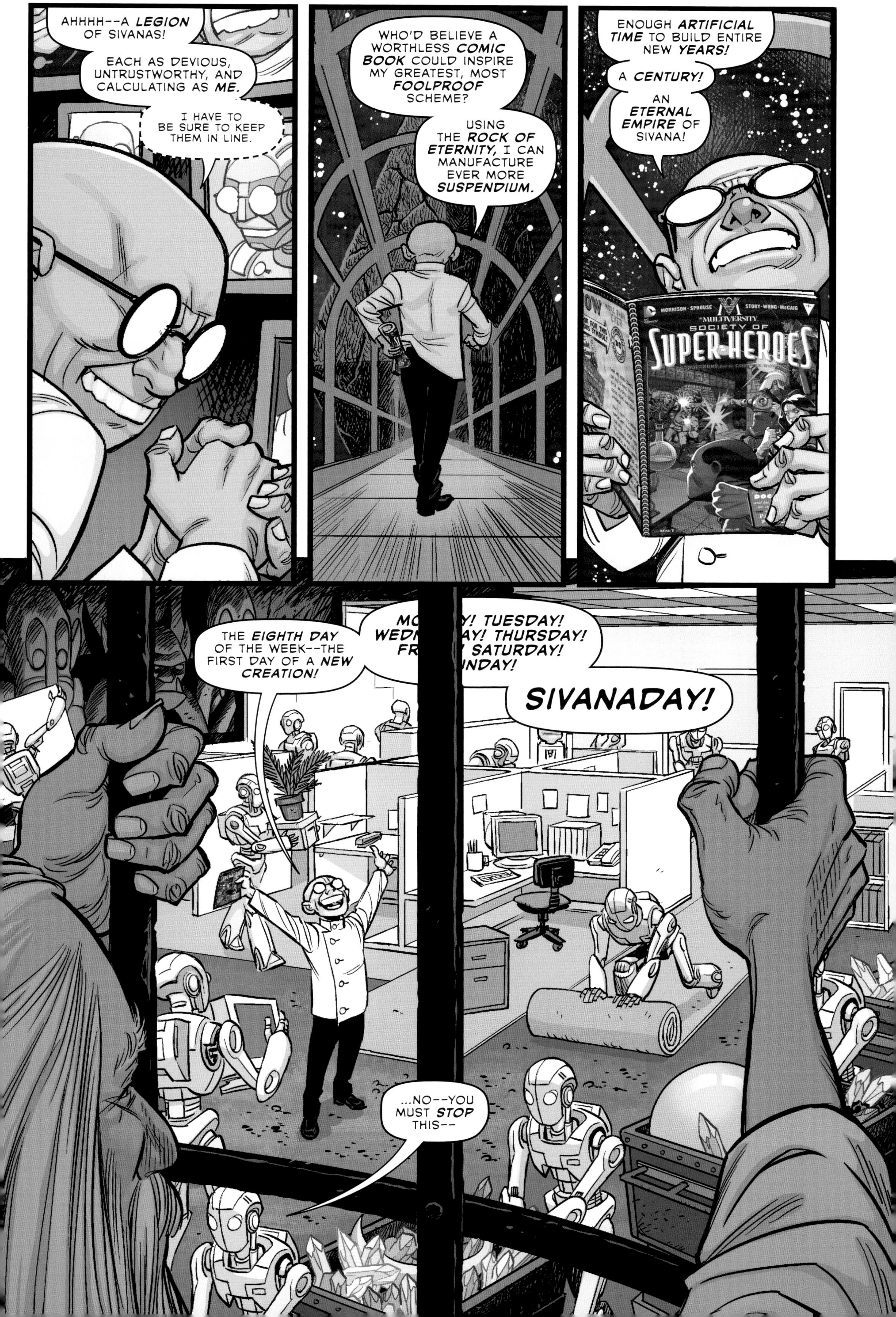

AHHHH--A LEGION OF SIVANAS!
EACH AS DEVIOUS, UNTRUSTWORTHY, AND CALCULATING AS ME.
I HAVE TO BE SURE TO KEEP THEM IN LINE.
WHO'D BELIEVE A WORTHLESS COMIC BOOK COULD INSPIRE MY GREATEST, MOST FOOLPROOF SCHEME?
USING THE ROCK OF ETERNITY, I CAN MANUFACTURE EVER MORE SUSPENDIUM.
ENOUGH ARTIFICIAL TIME TO BUILD ENTIRE NEW YEARS!
A CENTURY!
AN ETERNAL EMPIRE OF SIVANA!
MORRISON · SPROUSE
STORY · WONG · McCAIG
THE MULTIVERSITY
SOCIETY OF SUPER-HEROES
THE EIGHTH DAY OF THE WEEK--THE FIRST DAY OF A NEW CREATION!
MO AY! TUESDAY! WEDN AY! THURSDAY! FR SATURDAY! NDAY!
SIVANADAY!
...NO--YOU MUST STOP THIS--

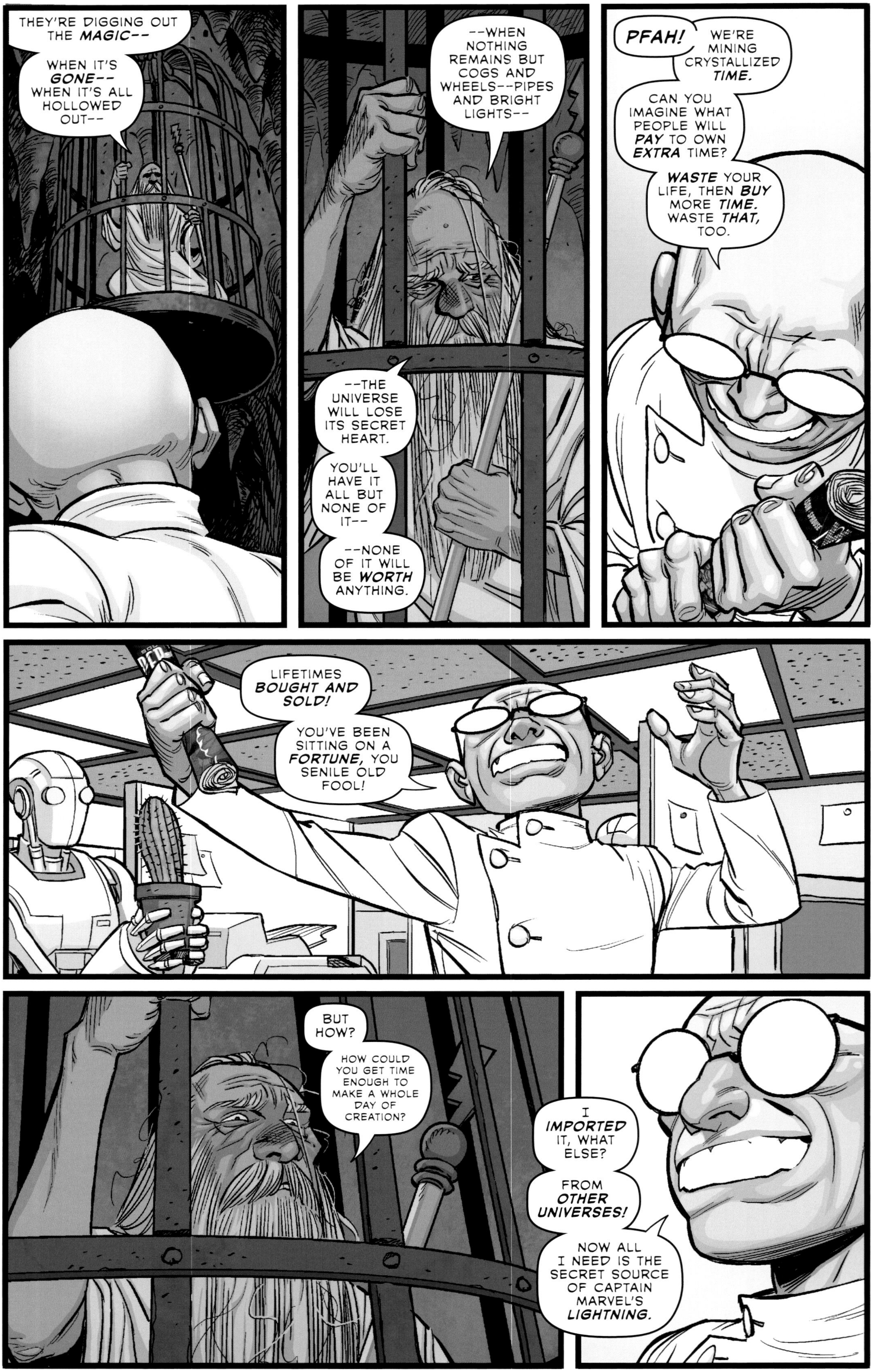
THEY'RE DIGGING OUT THE MAGIC--
WHEN IT'S GONE-- WHEN IT'S ALL HOLLOWED OUT--
--WHEN NOTHING REMAINS BUT COGS AND WHEELS--PIPES AND BRIGHT LIGHTS--
--THE UNIVERSE WILL LOSE ITS SECRET HEART.
YOU'LL HAVE IT ALL BUT NONE OF IT--
--NONE OF IT WILL BE WORTH ANYTHING.
PFAH!
WE'RE MINING CRYSTALLIZED TIME.
CAN YOU IMAGINE WHAT PEOPLE WILL PAY TO OWN EXTRA TIME?
WASTE YOUR LIFE, THEN BUY MORE TIME. WASTE THAT, TOO.
LIFETIMES BOUGHT AND SOLD!
YOU'VE BEEN SITTING ON A FORTUNE, YOU SENILE OLD FOOL!
BUT HOW?
HOW COULD YOU GET TIME ENOUGH TO MAKE A WHOLE DAY OF CREATION?
I IMPORTED IT, WHAT ELSE?
FROM OTHER UNIVERSES!
NOW ALL I NEED IS THE SECRET SOURCE OF CAPTAIN MARVEL'S LIGHTNING.

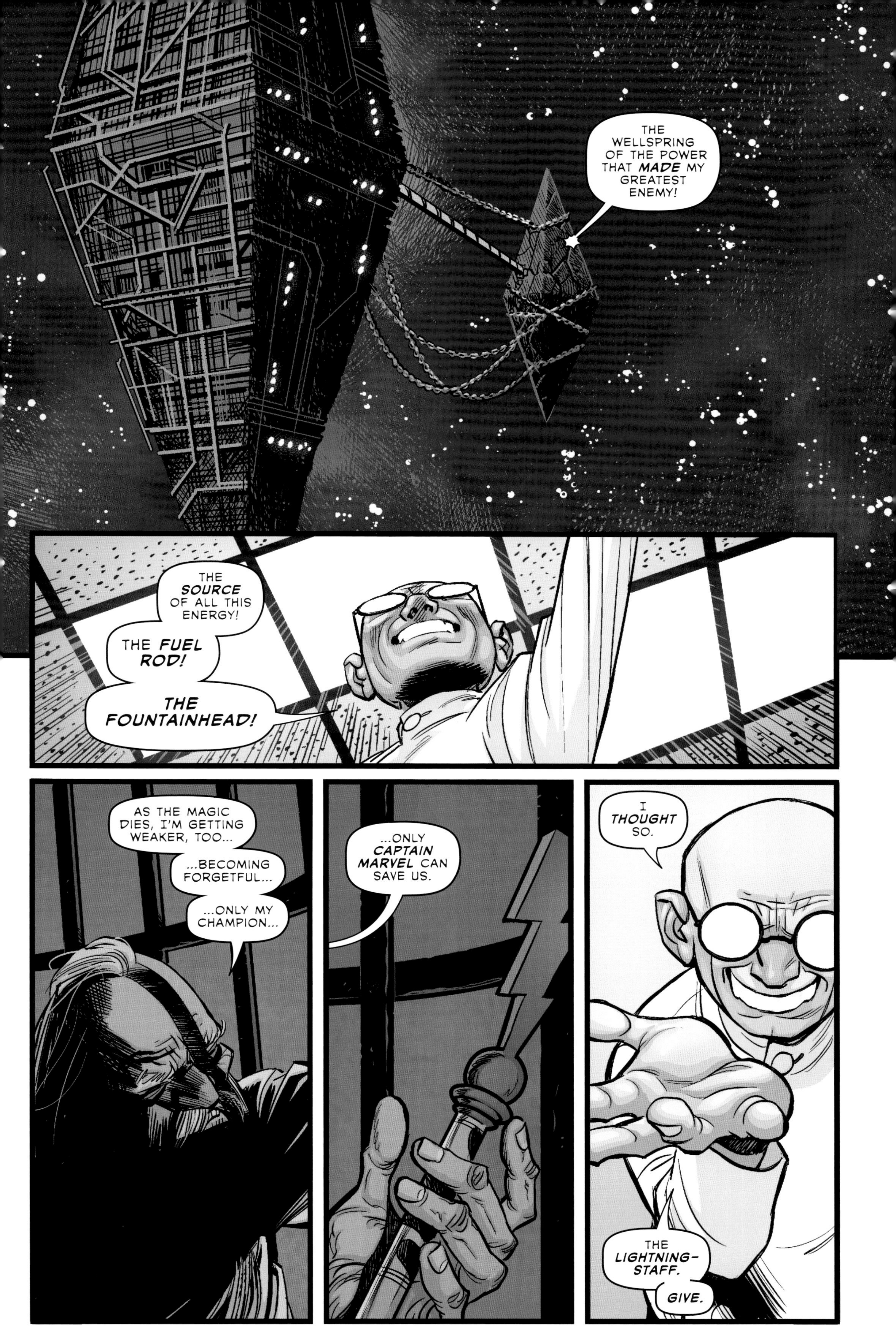
THE WELLSPRING OF THE POWER THAT MADE MY GREATEST ENEMY!
THE SOURCE OF ALL THIS ENERGY!
THE FUEL ROD!
THE FOUNTAINHEAD!
AS THE MAGIC DIES, I'M GETTING WEAKER, TOO...
...BECOMING FORGETFUL...
...ONLY MY CHAMPION...
...ONLY CAPTAIN MARVEL CAN SAVE US.
I THOUGHT SO.
THE LIGHTNING-STAFF.
GIVE.

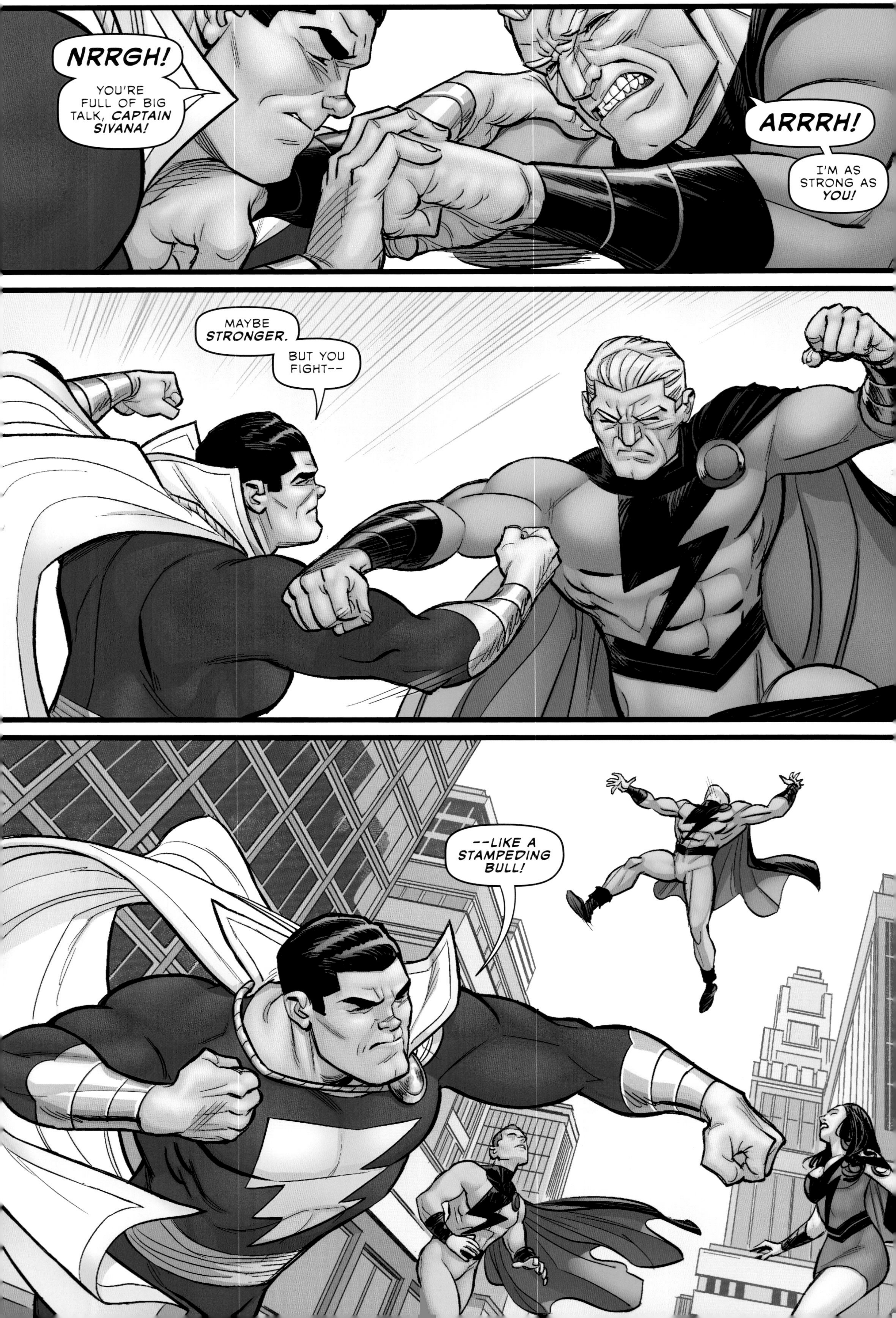
NRRGH!
YOU'RE FULL OF BIG TALK, CAPTAIN SIVANA!
ARRRH!
I'M AS STRONG AS YOU!
MAYBE STRONGER.
BUT YOU FIGHT--
--LIKE A STAMPEDING BULL!

I GOT HIM!

NO!

HE'S MINE!

I HAVE TO *STOP* HIM YOU, IDIOTS.

HE'S HEADING FOR THE *RAIL TRACK*--

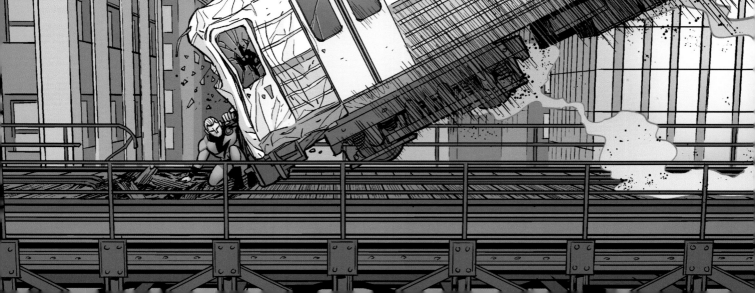

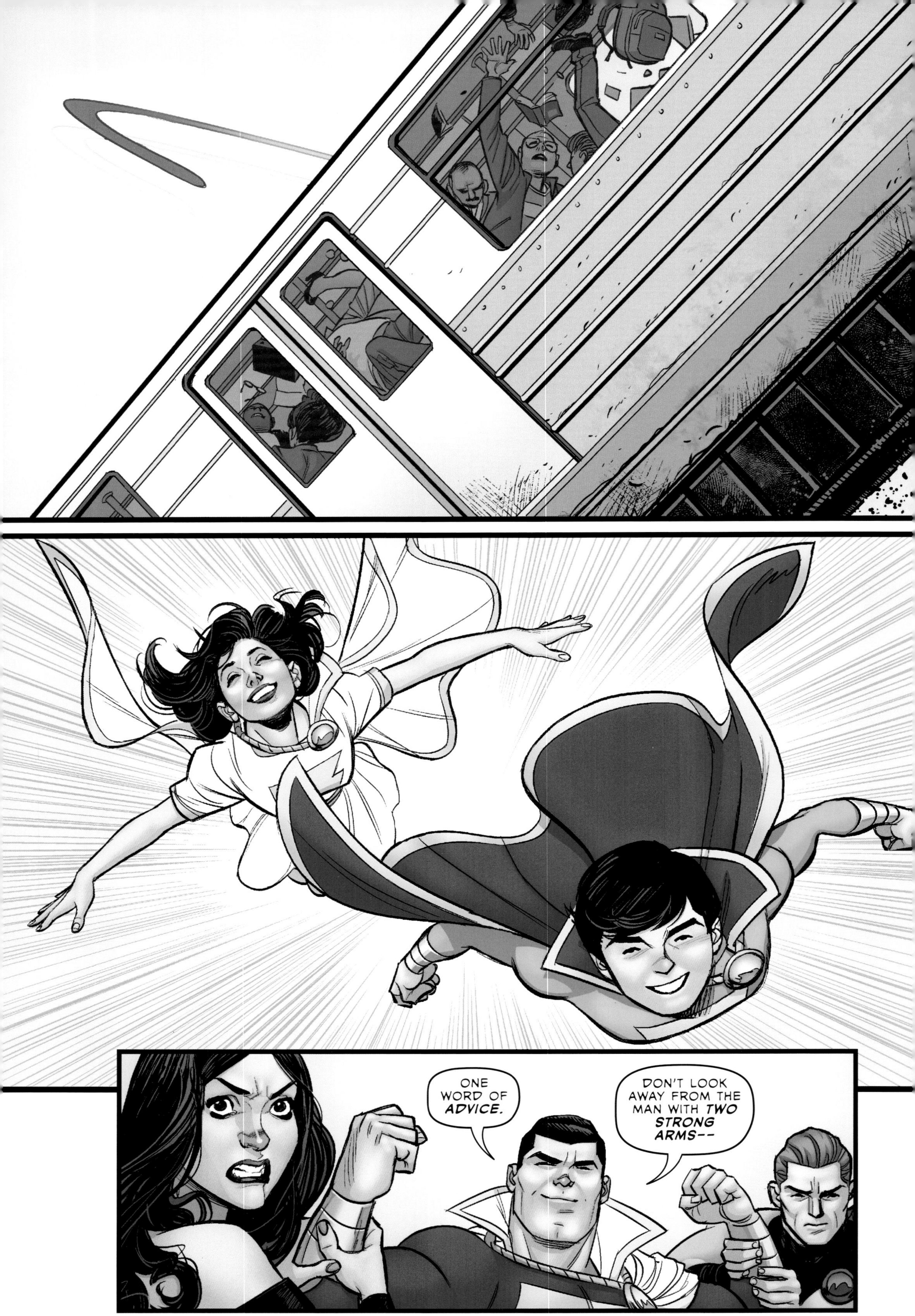
ONE WORD OF ADVICE.
DON'T LOOK AWAY FROM THE MAN WITH TWO STRONG ARMS--

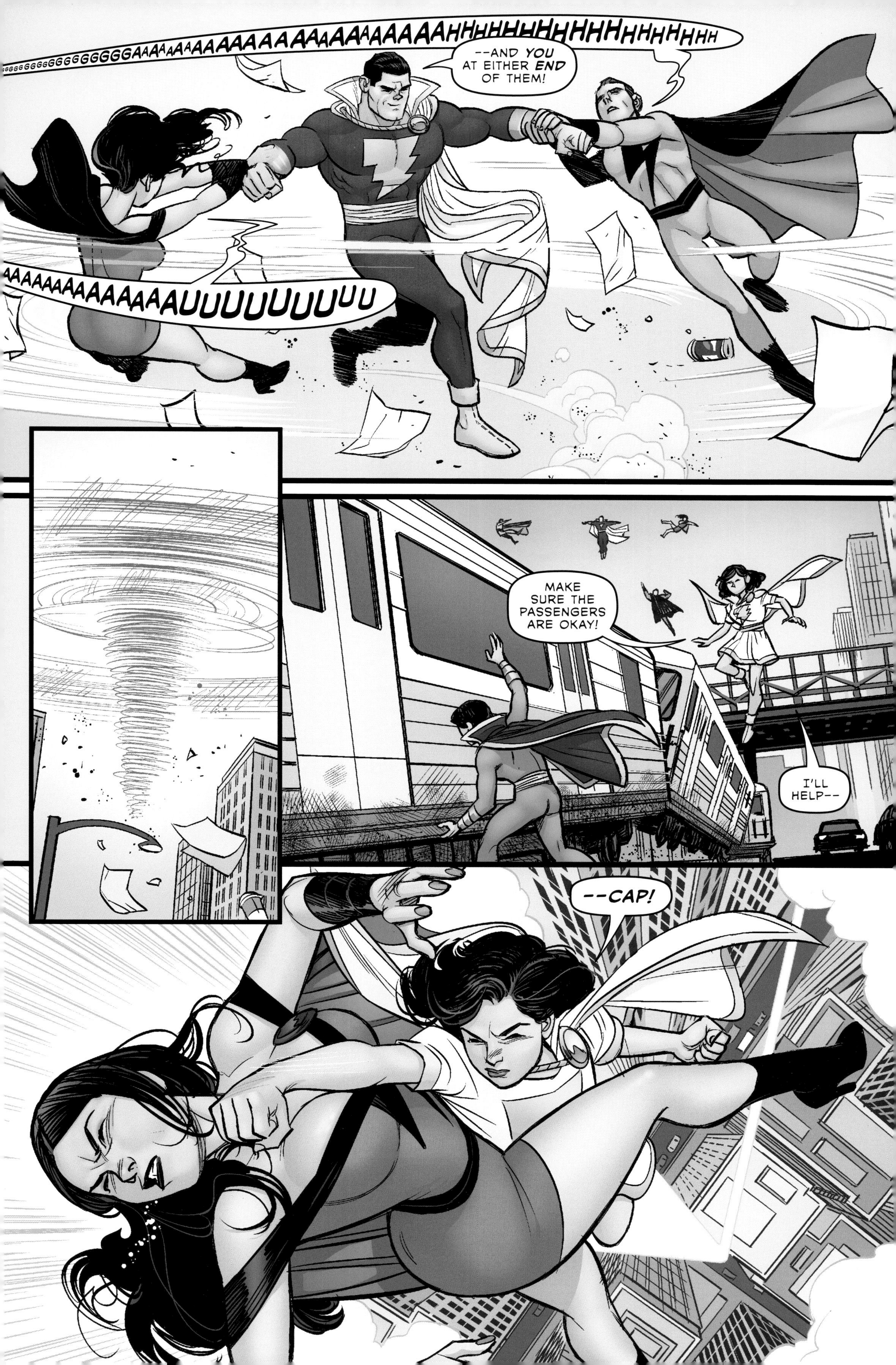
GGGGGGGGGGGGGGGGGGGAAAAAAAAAAAAAAAAAAAAAAAAAAAHHHHHHHHHHHHHHHHH
--AND YOU AT EITHER END OF THEM!
AAAAAAAAAAAAAAAAUUUUUUUUUU
MAKE SURE THE PASSENGERS ARE OKAY!
I'LL HELP--
--CAP!

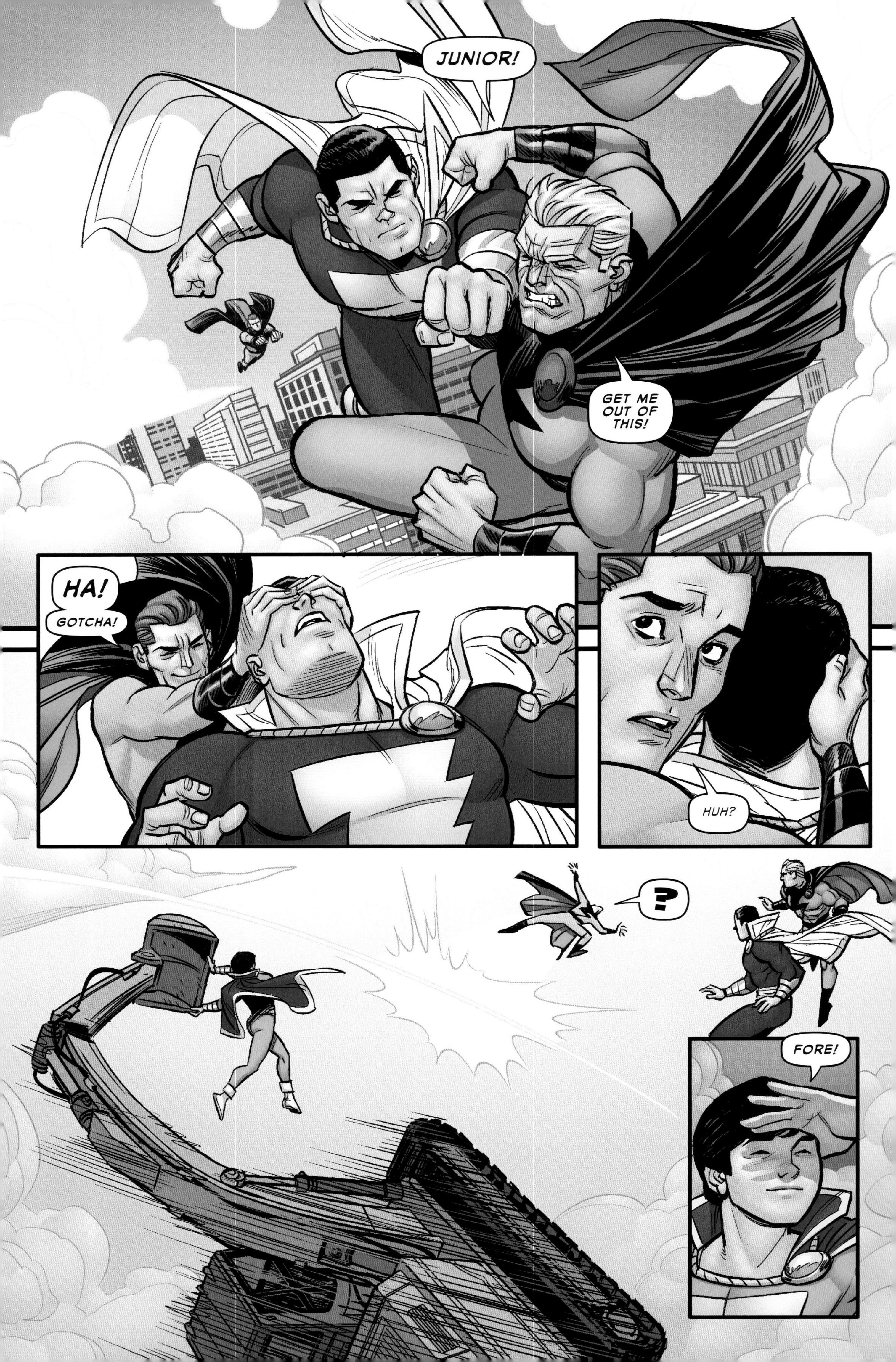
JUNIOR!
GET ME OUT OF THIS!
HA!
GOTCHA!
HUH?
?
FORE!

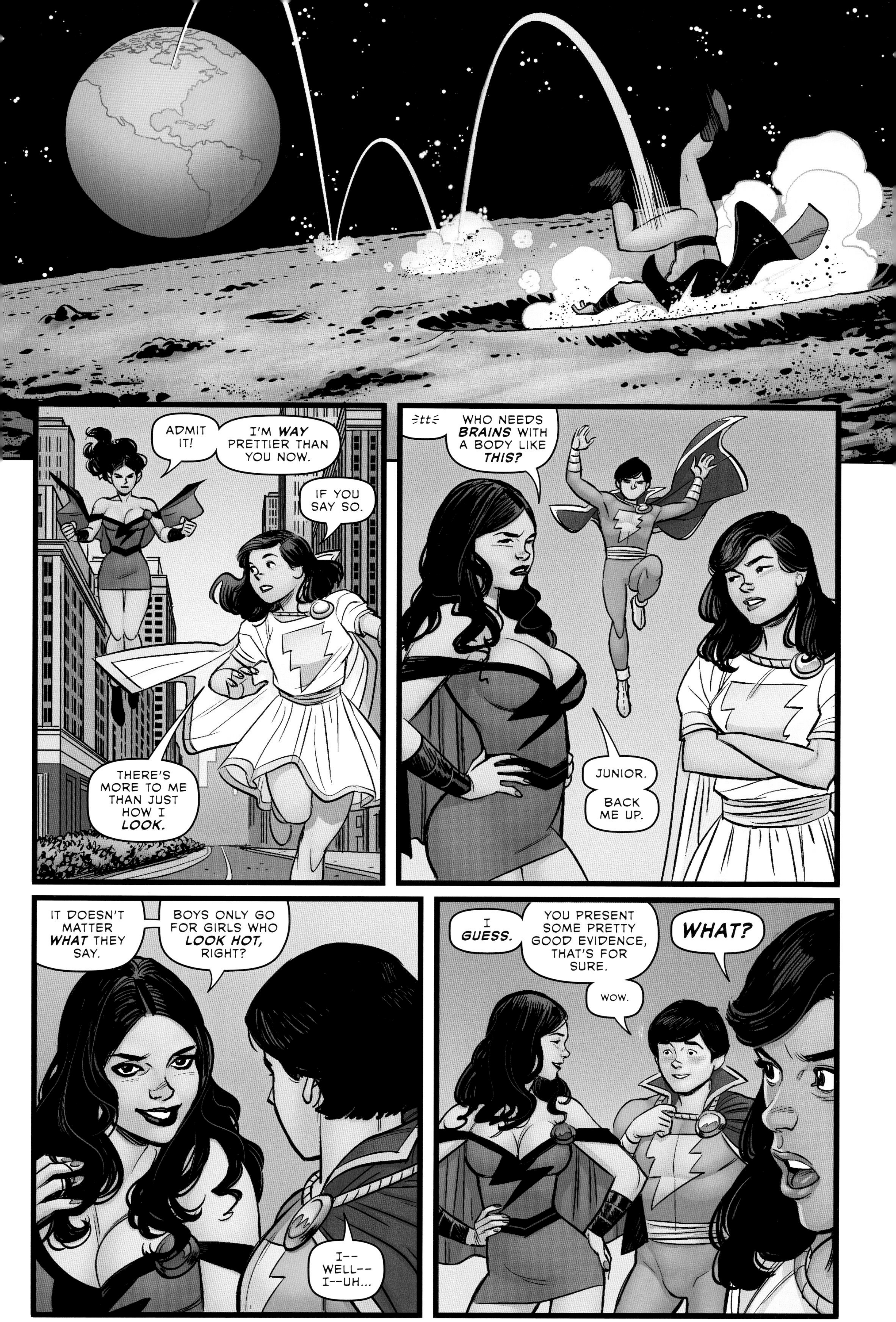
ADMIT IT!
I'M *WAY* PRETTIER THAN YOU NOW.
IF YOU SAY SO.
THERE'S MORE TO ME THAN JUST HOW I *LOOK.*
tt
WHO NEEDS *BRAINS* WITH A BODY LIKE *THIS?*
JUNIOR.
BACK ME UP.
IT DOESN'T MATTER *WHAT* THEY SAY.
BOYS ONLY GO FOR GIRLS WHO *LOOK HOT,* RIGHT?
I-- WELL-- I--UH...
I *GUESS.*
YOU PRESENT SOME PRETTY GOOD EVIDENCE, THAT'S FOR SURE.
WOW.
WHAT?

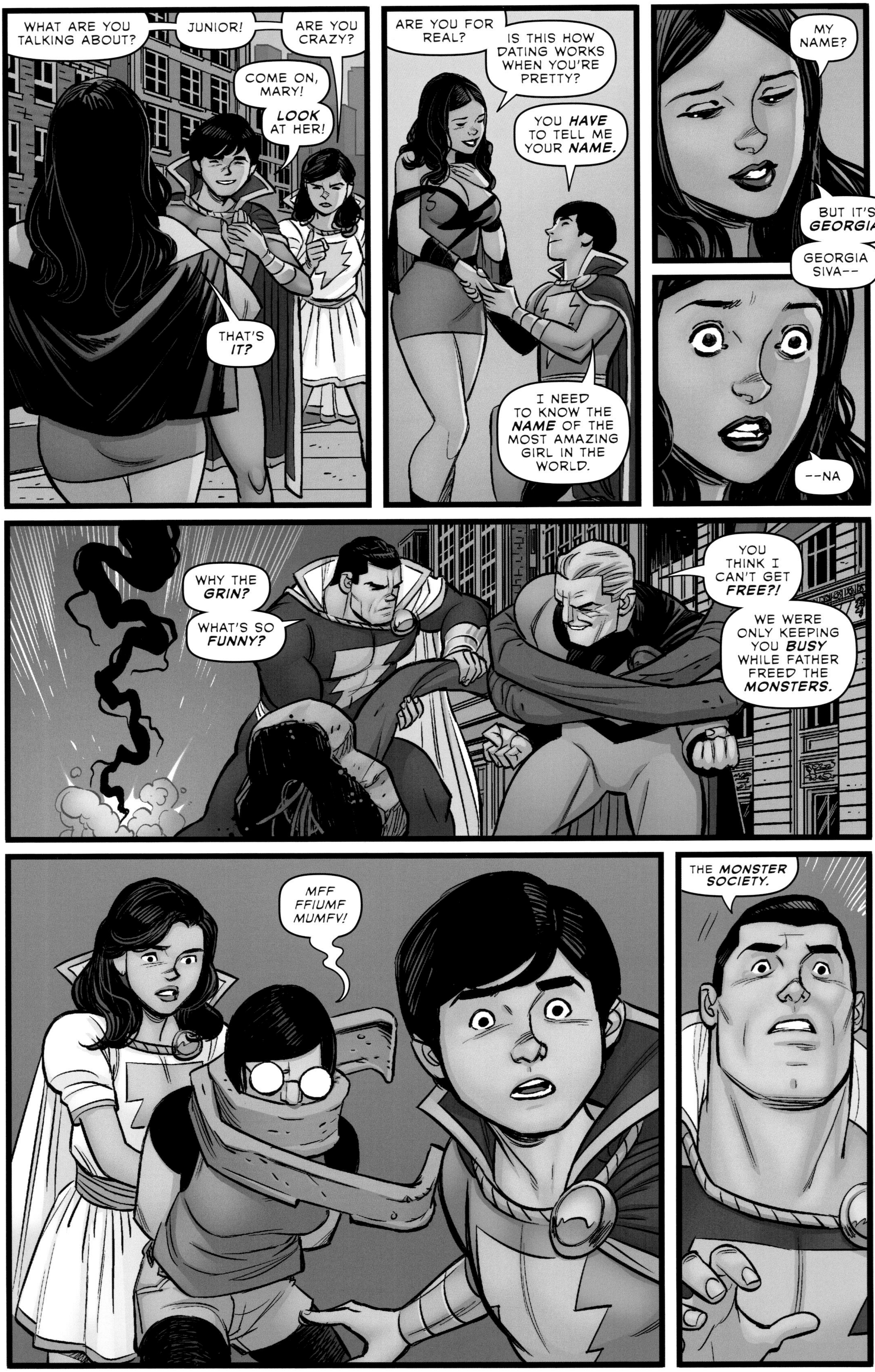
WHAT ARE YOU TALKING ABOUT?
JUNIOR!
ARE YOU CRAZY?
COME ON, MARY!
LOOK AT HER!
THAT'S IT?
ARE YOU FOR REAL?
IS THIS HOW DATING WORKS WHEN YOU'RE PRETTY?
YOU HAVE TO TELL ME YOUR NAME.
I NEED TO KNOW THE NAME OF THE MOST AMAZING GIRL IN THE WORLD.
MY NAME?
BUT IT'S GEORGIA.
GEORGIA SIVA--
--NA
WHY THE GRIN?
WHAT'S SO FUNNY?
YOU THINK I CAN'T GET FREE?!
WE WERE ONLY KEEPING YOU BUSY WHILE FATHER FREED THE MONSTERS.
MFF FFIUMF MUMFV!
THE MONSTER SOCIETY.

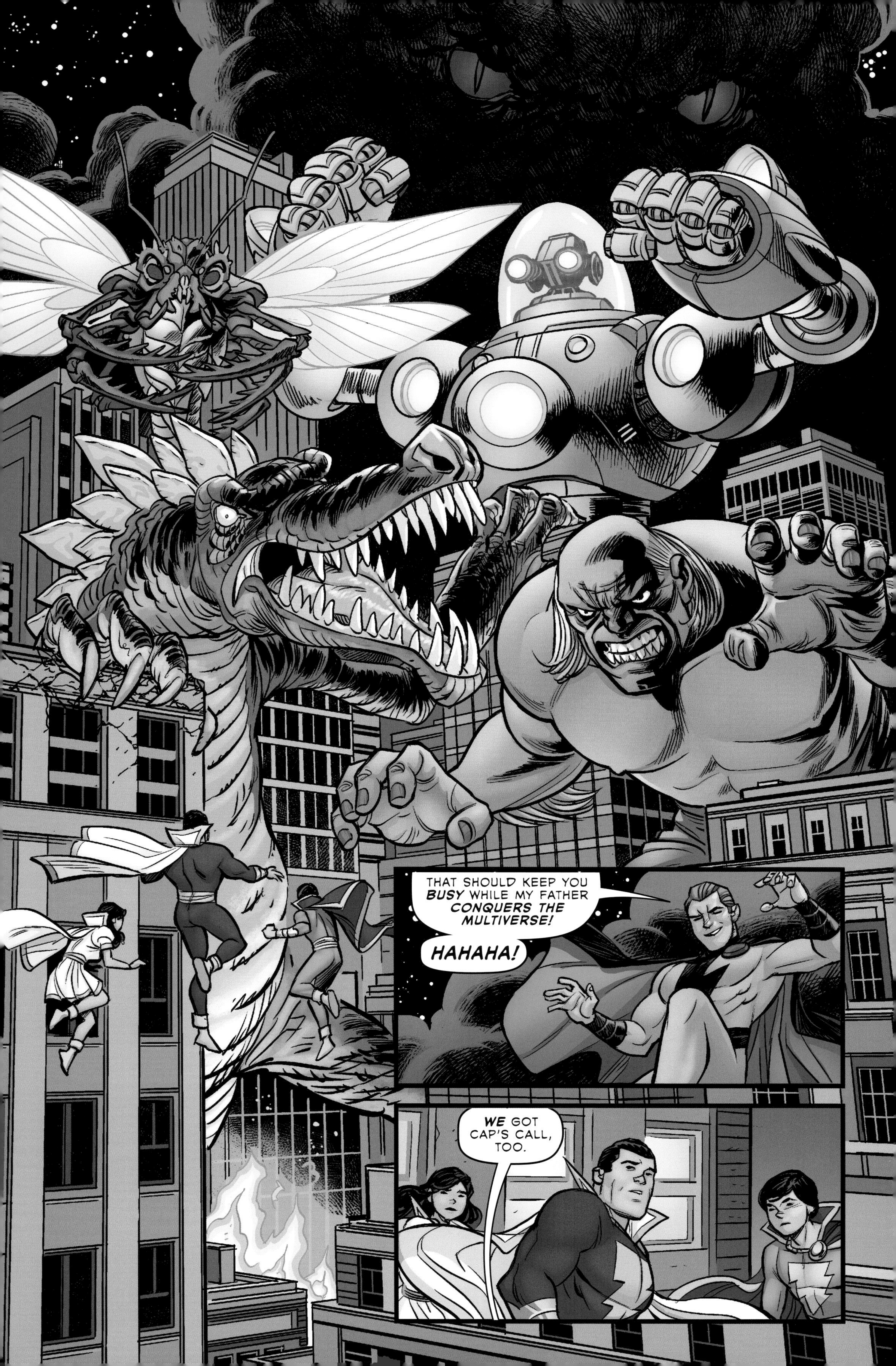
THAT SHOULD KEEP YOU BUSY WHILE MY FATHER CONQUERS THE MULTIVERSE!
HAHAHA!
WE GOT CAP'S CALL, TOO.

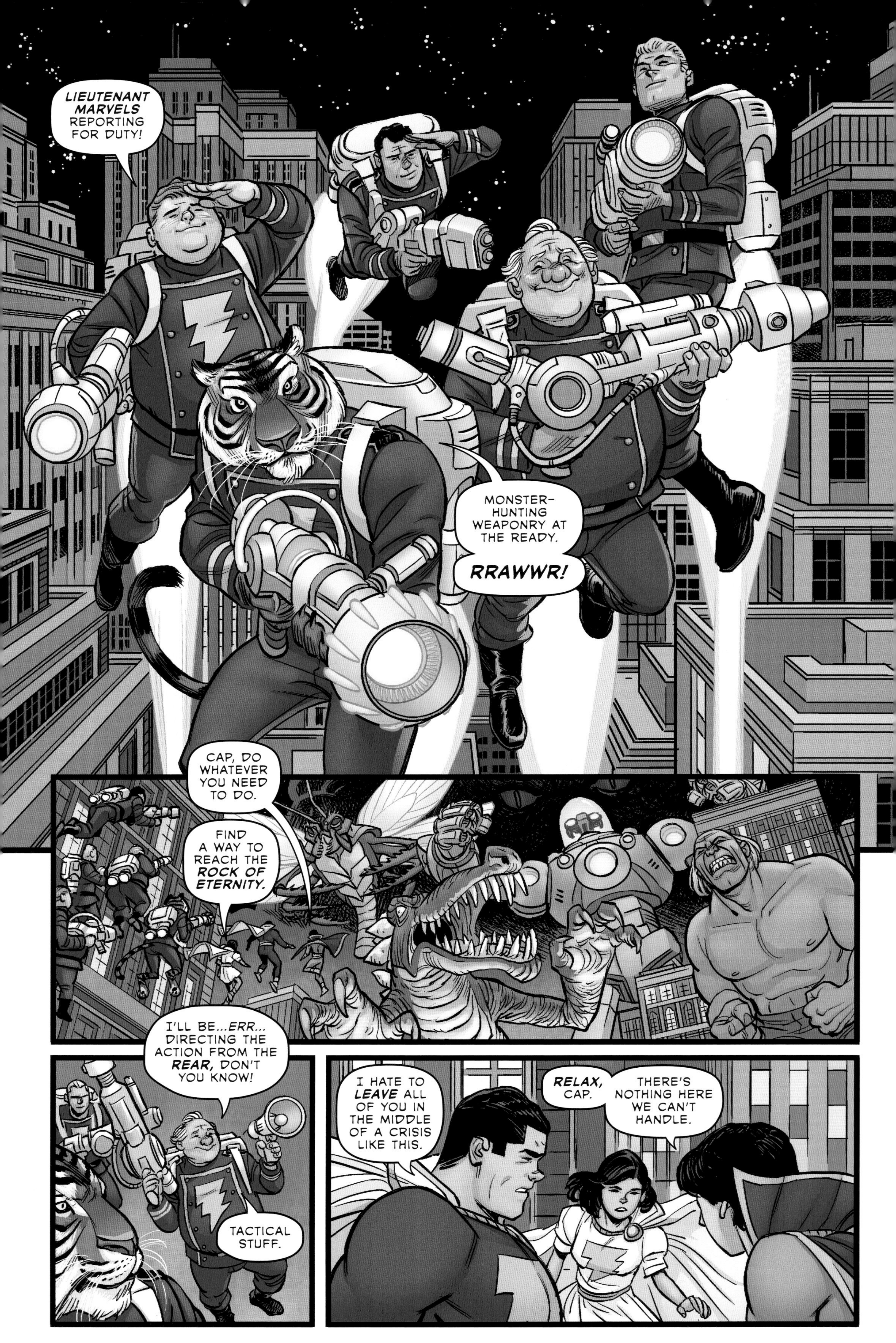
LIEUTENANT MARVELS REPORTING FOR DUTY!
MONSTER-HUNTING WEAPONRY AT THE READY.
RRAWWR!
CAP, DO WHATEVER YOU NEED TO DO.
FIND A WAY TO REACH THE ROCK OF ETERNITY.
I'LL BE...ERR... DIRECTING THE ACTION FROM THE REAR, DON'T YOU KNOW!
TACTICAL STUFF.
I HATE TO LEAVE ALL OF YOU IN THE MIDDLE OF A CRISIS LIKE THIS.
RELAX, CAP.
THERE'S NOTHING HERE WE CAN'T HANDLE.

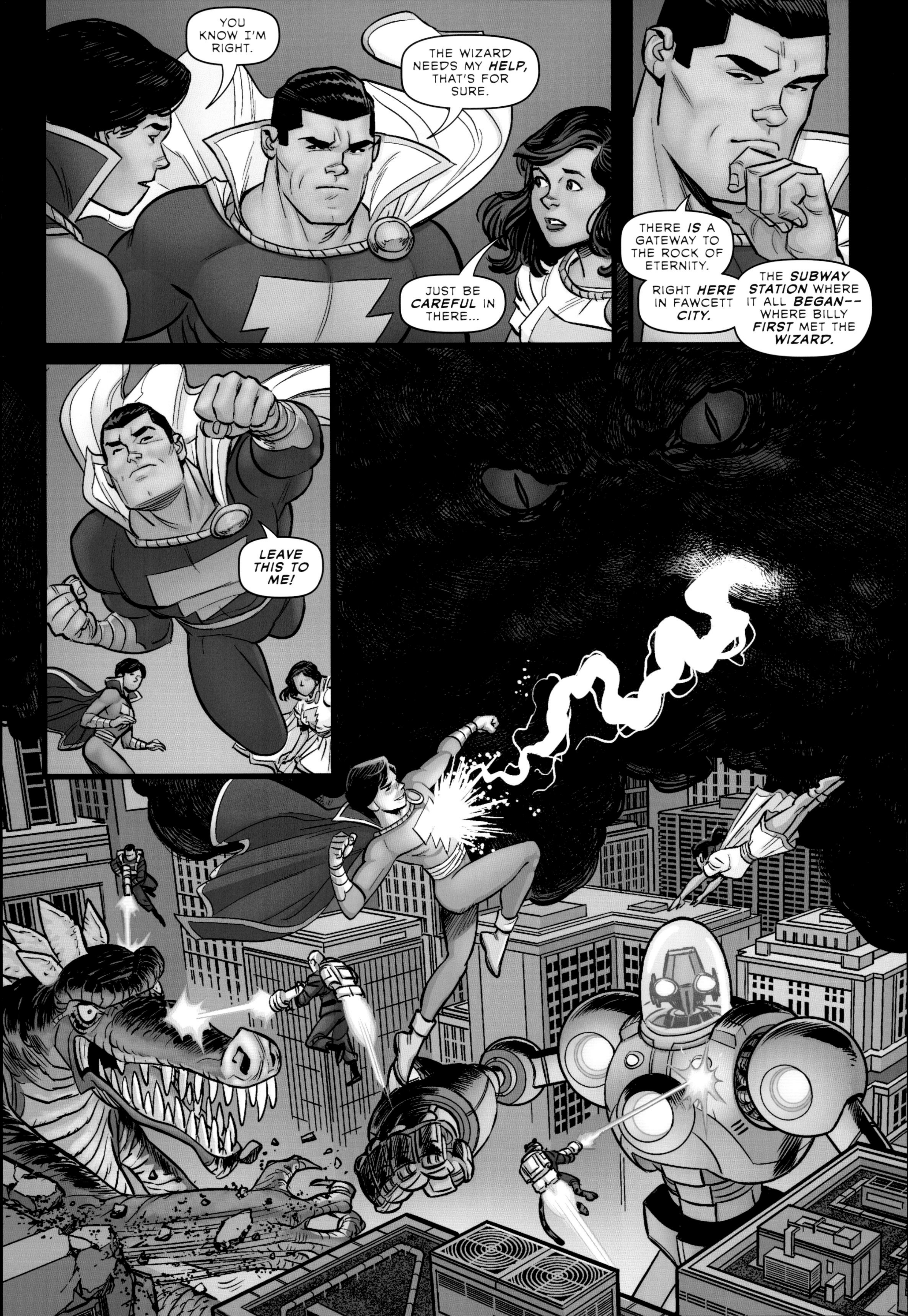

YOU KNOW I'M RIGHT.
THE WIZARD NEEDS MY *HELP,* THAT'S FOR SURE.
JUST BE *CAREFUL* IN THERE...
THERE *IS* A GATEWAY TO THE ROCK OF ETERNITY.
RIGHT *HERE* IN FAWCETT *CITY.*
THE *SUBWAY STATION* WHERE IT ALL *BEGAN*-- WHERE BILLY *FIRST* MET THE *WIZARD.*
LEAVE THIS TO ME!

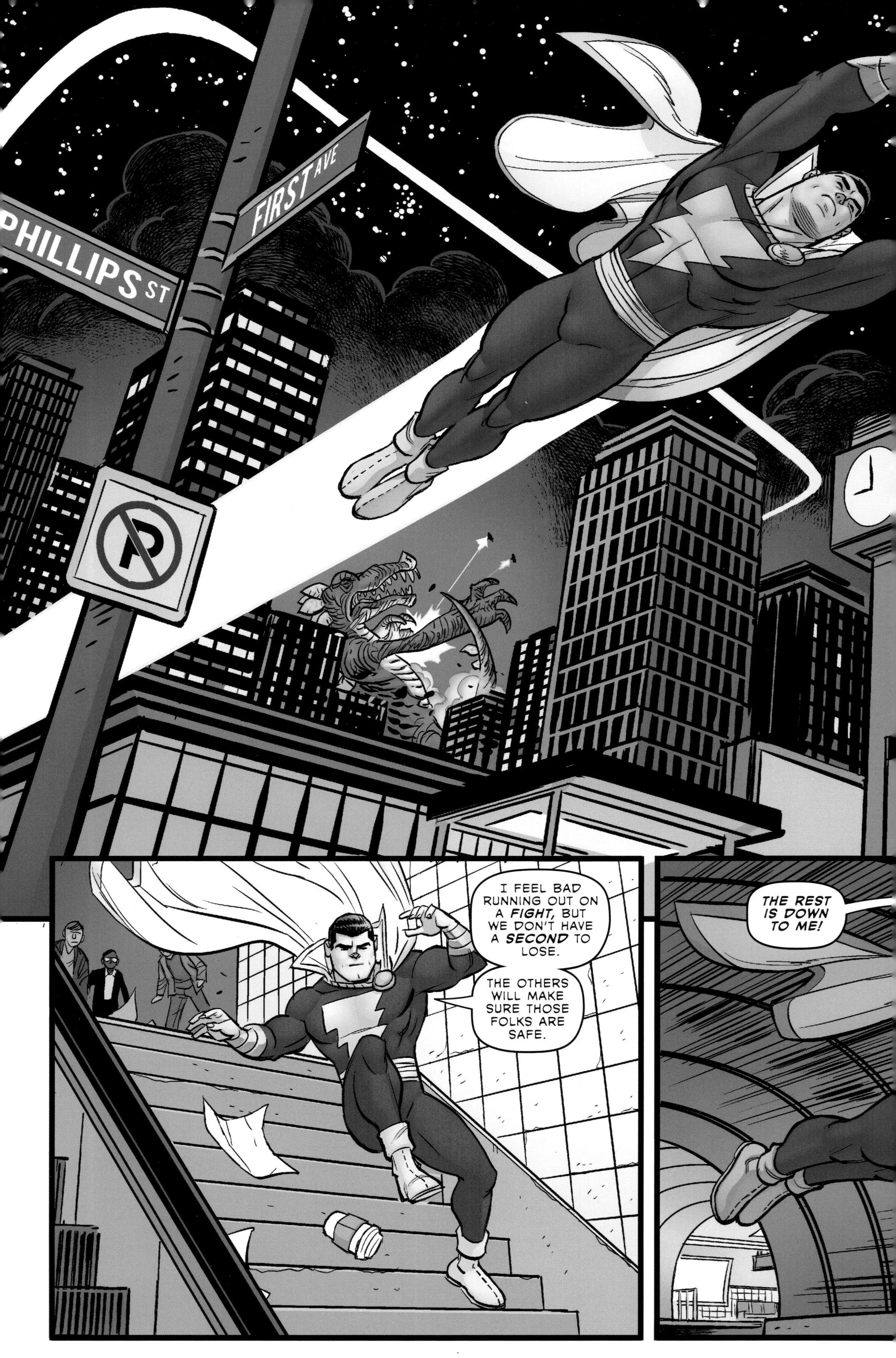
PHILLIPS ST
FIRST AVE
I FEEL BAD RUNNING OUT ON A FIGHT, BUT WE DON'T HAVE A SECOND TO LOSE.
THE OTHERS WILL MAKE SURE THOSE FOLKS ARE SAFE.
THE REST IS DOWN TO ME!

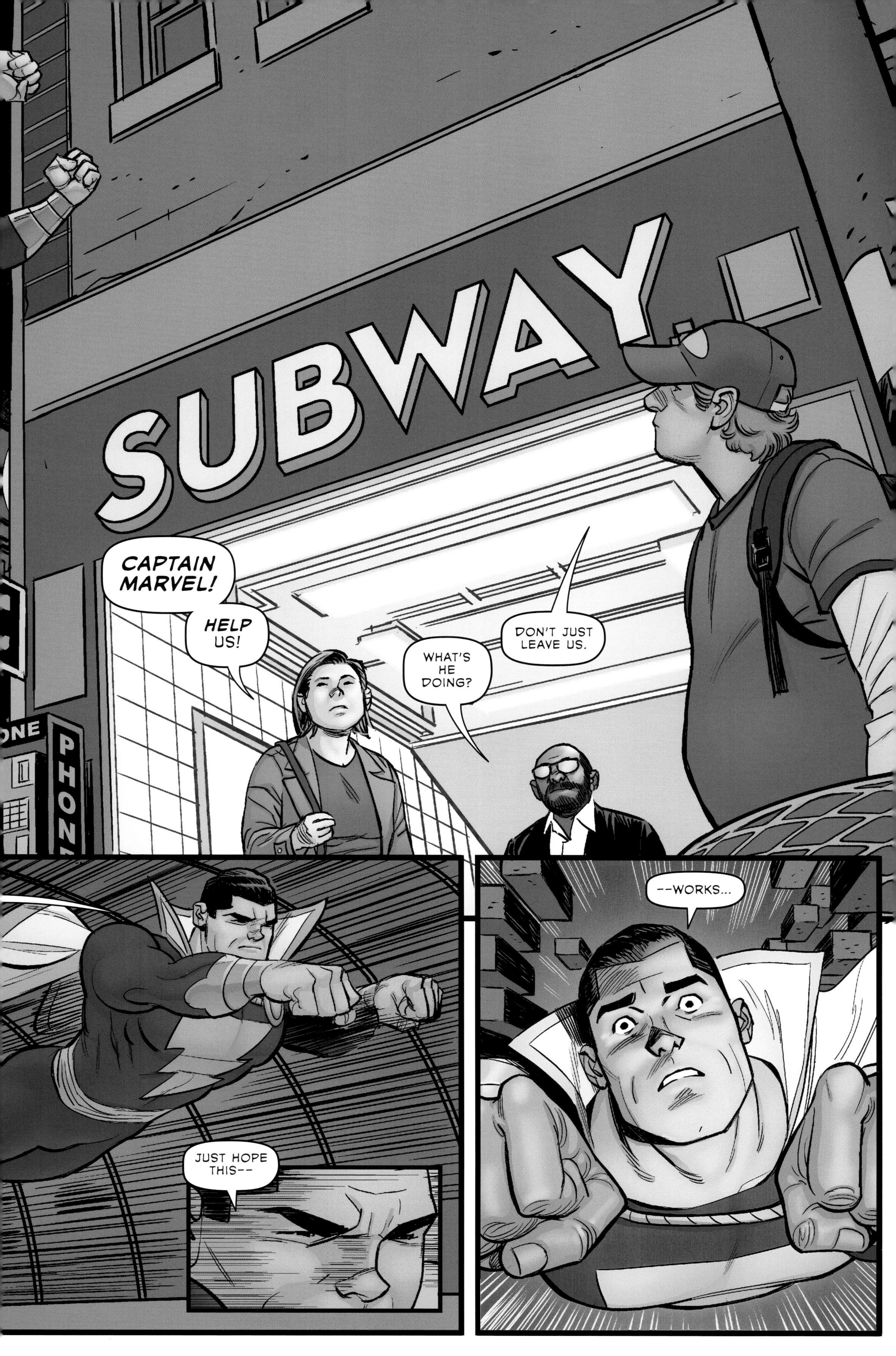
SUBWAY
CAPTAIN MARVEL!
HELP US!
WHAT'S HE DOING?
DON'T JUST LEAVE US.
ONE
PHON
JUST HOPE THIS--
--WORKS...

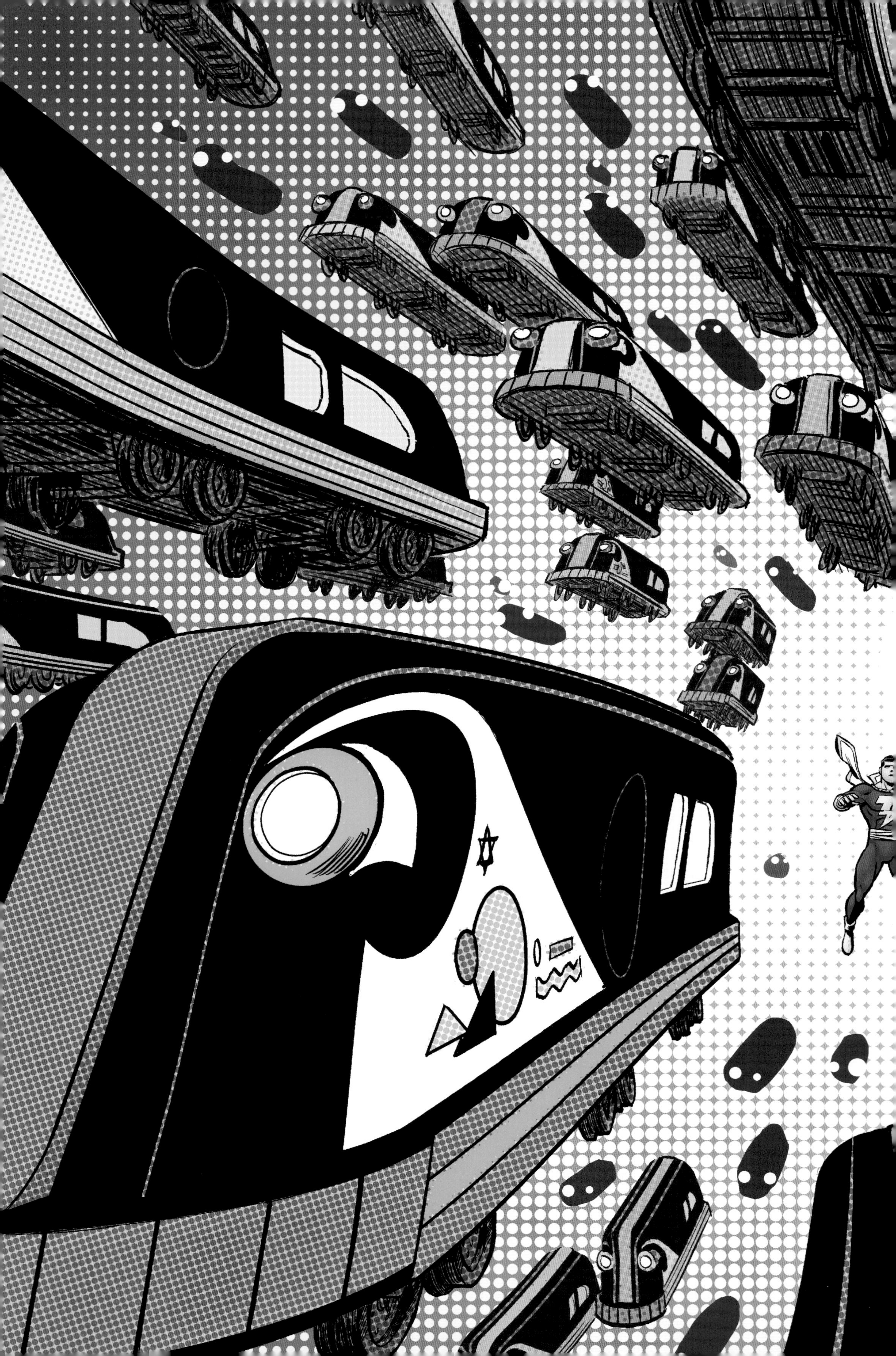

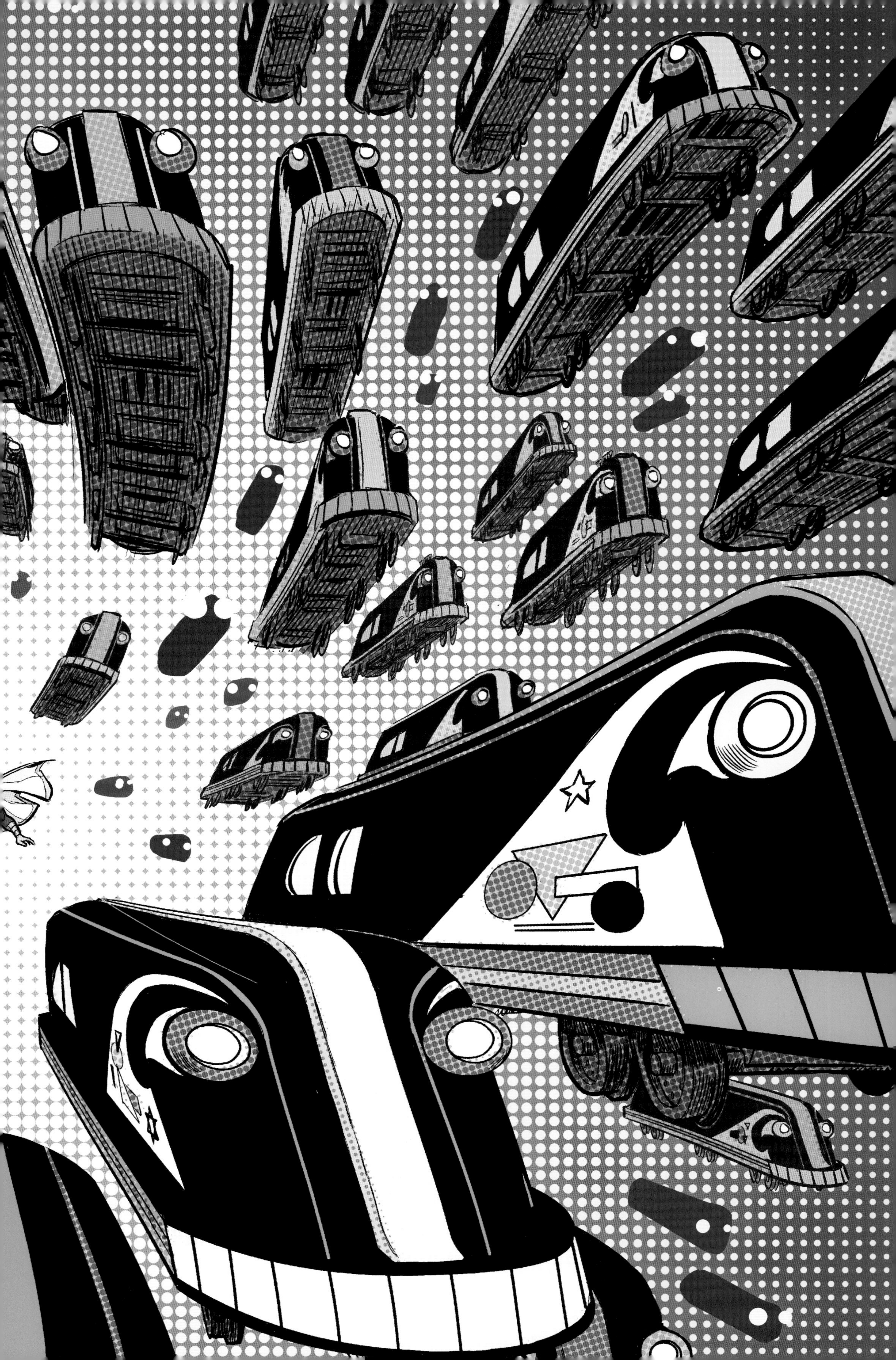

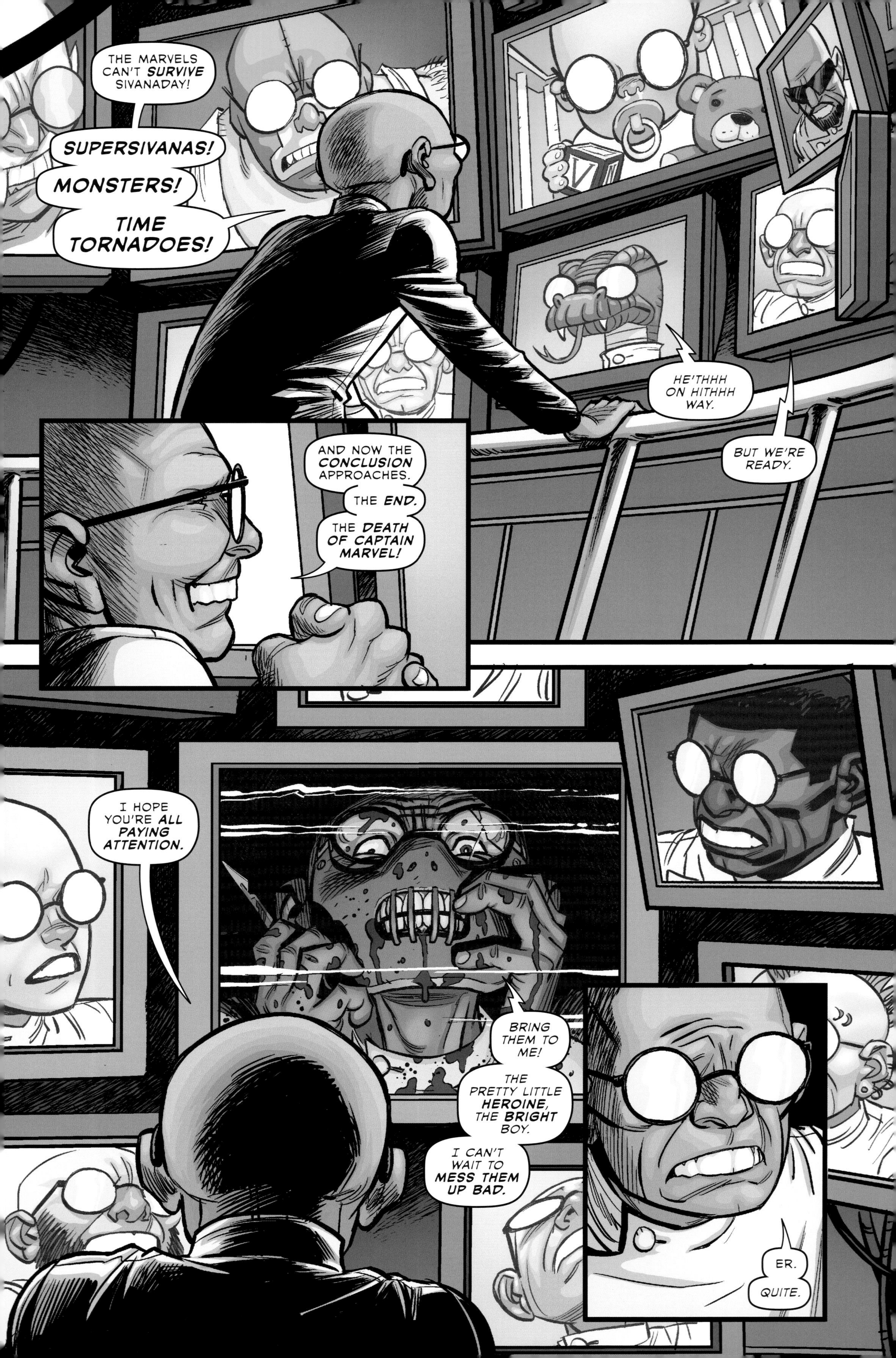
THE MARVELS CAN'T SURVIVE SIVANADAY!
SUPERSIVANAS!
MONSTERS!
TIME TORNADOES!
HE'THHH ON HITHHH WAY.
BUT WE'RE READY.
AND NOW THE CONCLUSION APPROACHES.
THE END.
THE DEATH OF CAPTAIN MARVEL!
I HOPE YOU'RE ALL PAYING ATTENTION.
BRING THEM TO ME!
THE PRETTY LITTLE HEROINE, THE BRIGHT BOY.
I CAN'T WAIT TO MESS THEM UP BAD.
ER.
QUITE.

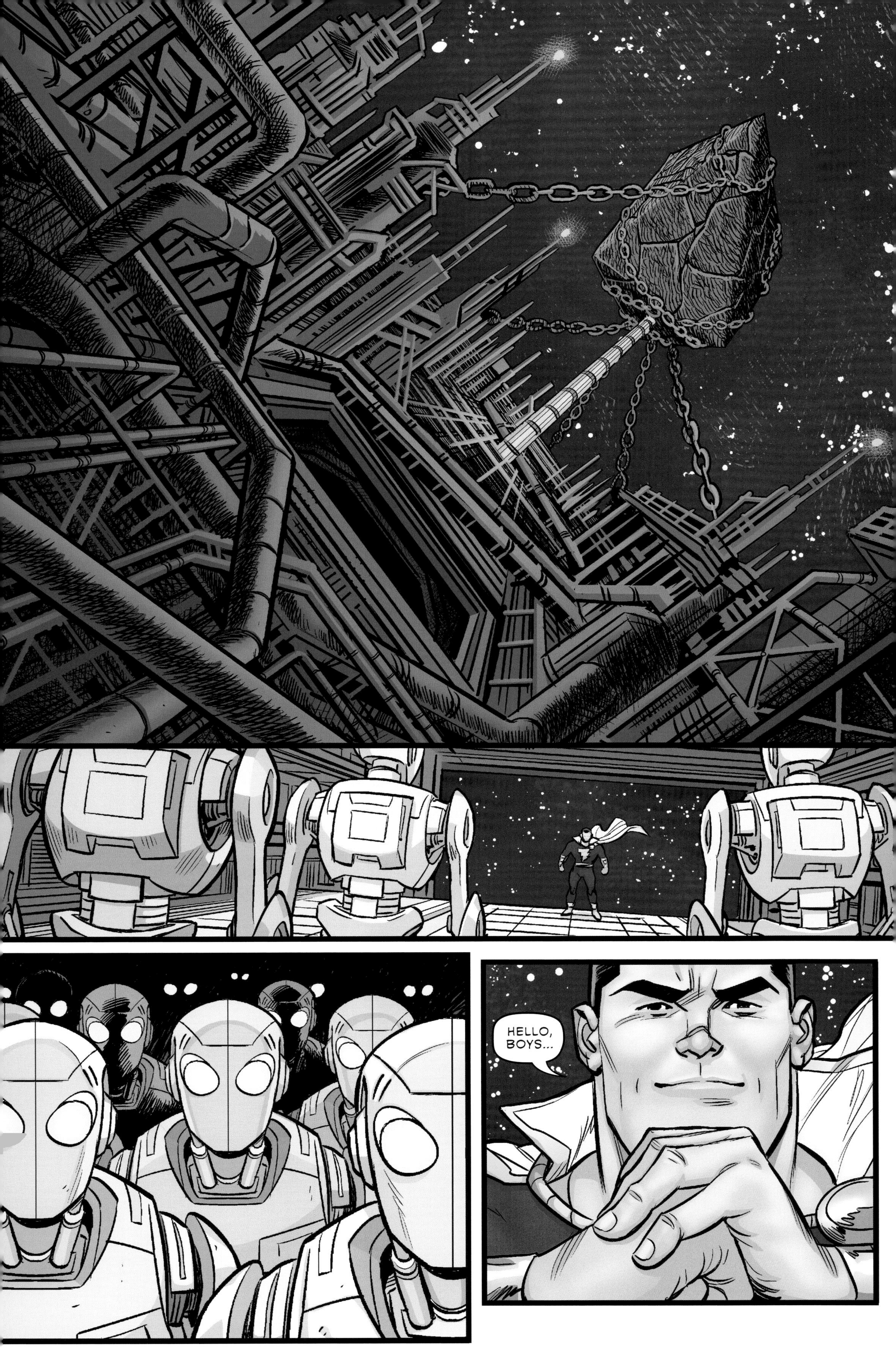
HELLO, BOYS...

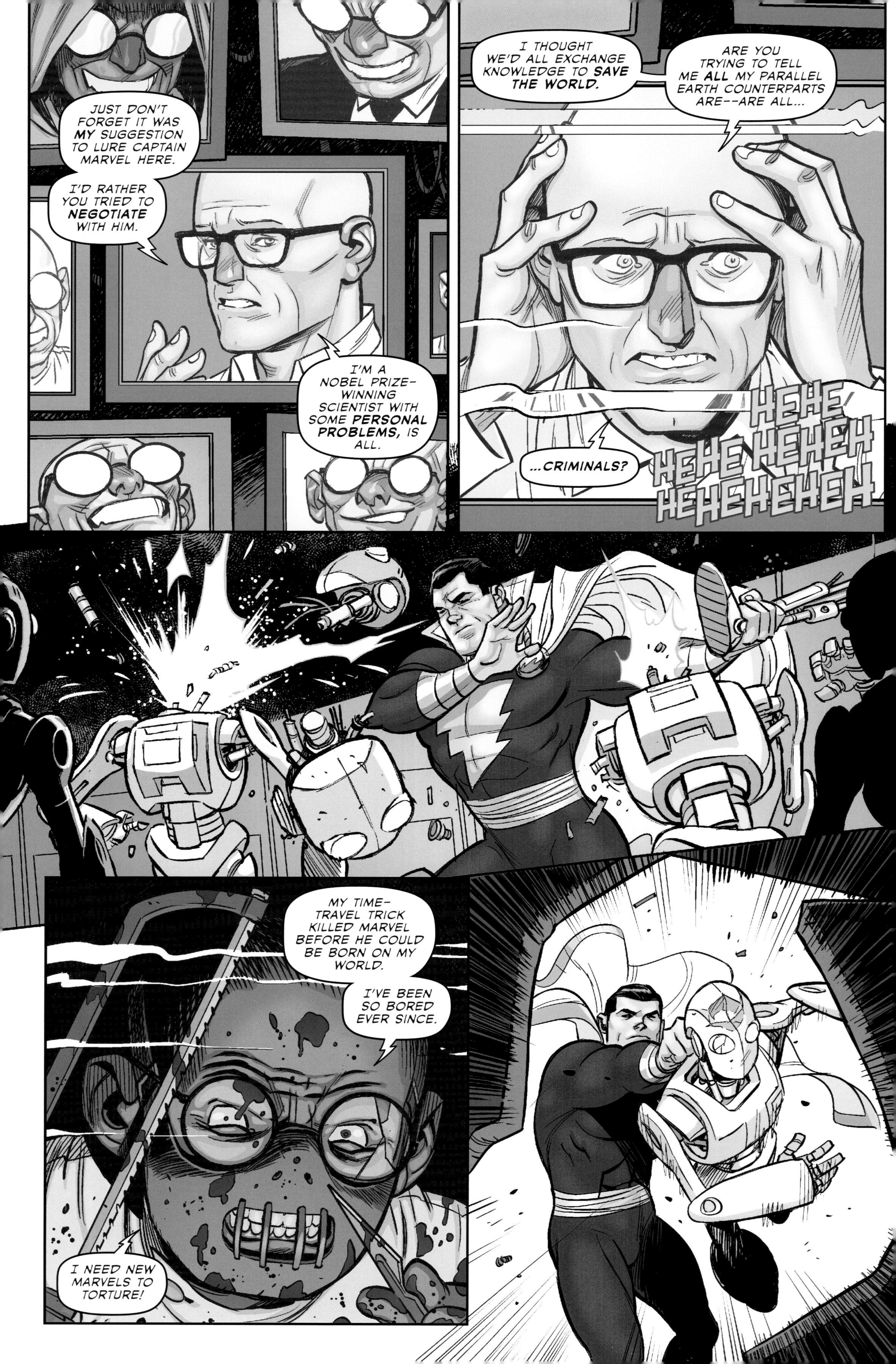
JUST DON'T FORGET IT WAS MY SUGGESTION TO LURE CAPTAIN MARVEL HERE.
I'D RATHER YOU TRIED TO NEGOTIATE WITH HIM.
I'M A NOBEL PRIZE-WINNING SCIENTIST WITH SOME PERSONAL PROBLEMS, IS ALL.
I THOUGHT WE'D ALL EXCHANGE KNOWLEDGE TO SAVE THE WORLD.
ARE YOU TRYING TO TELL ME ALL MY PARALLEL EARTH COUNTERPARTS ARE--ARE ALL...
...CRIMINALS?
HEHE HEHE HEHEH HEHEHEHEH
MY TIME-TRAVEL TRICK KILLED MARVEL BEFORE HE COULD BE BORN ON MY WORLD.
I'VE BEEN SO BORED EVER SINCE.
I NEED NEW MARVELS TO TORTURE!

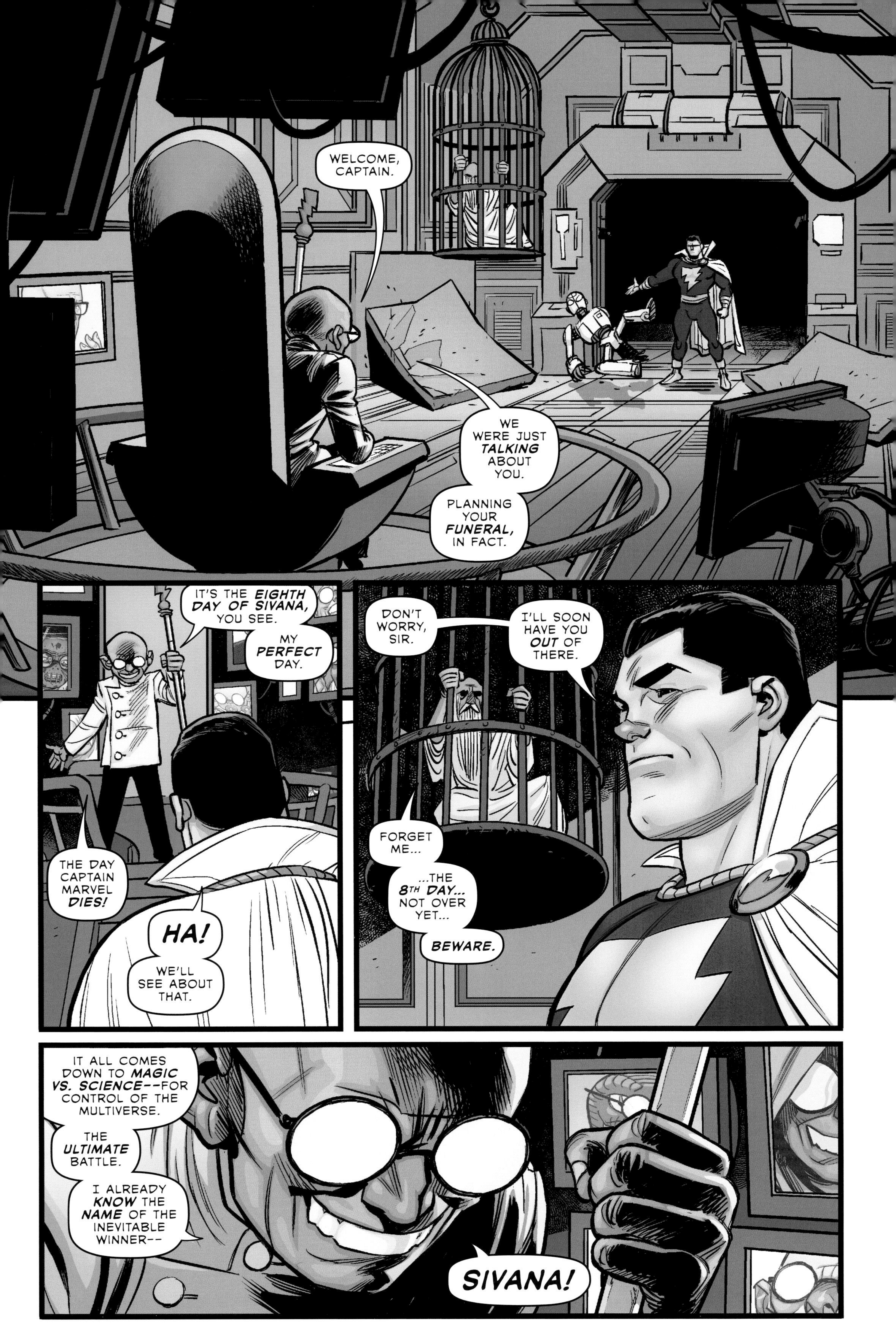

WELCOME, CAPTAIN.
WE WERE JUST TALKING ABOUT YOU.
PLANNING YOUR FUNERAL, IN FACT.
IT'S THE EIGHTH DAY OF SIVANA, YOU SEE.
MY PERFECT DAY.
THE DAY CAPTAIN MARVEL DIES!
HA!
WE'LL SEE ABOUT THAT.
DON'T WORRY, SIR.
I'LL SOON HAVE YOU OUT OF THERE.
FORGET ME...
...THE 8TH DAY... NOT OVER YET...
BEWARE.
IT ALL COMES DOWN TO MAGIC VS. SCIENCE--FOR CONTROL OF THE MULTIVERSE.
THE ULTIMATE BATTLE.
I ALREADY KNOW THE NAME OF THE INEVITABLE WINNER--
SIVANA!

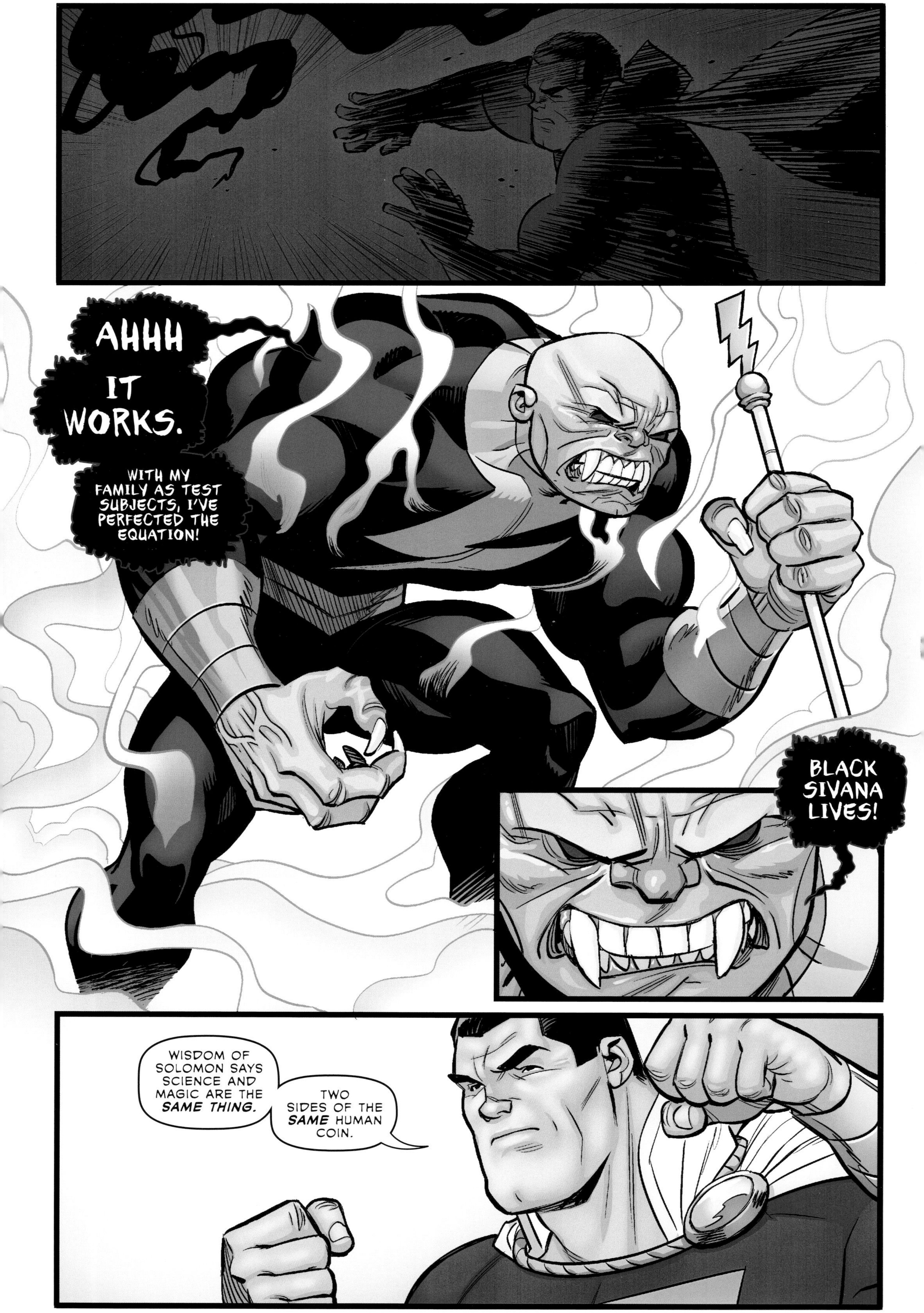
AHHH
IT WORKS.
WITH MY FAMILY AS TEST SUBJECTS, I'VE PERFECTED THE EQUATION!
BLACK SIVANA LIVES!
WISDOM OF SOLOMON SAYS SCIENCE AND MAGIC ARE THE *SAME THING.*
TWO SIDES OF THE *SAME* HUMAN COIN.

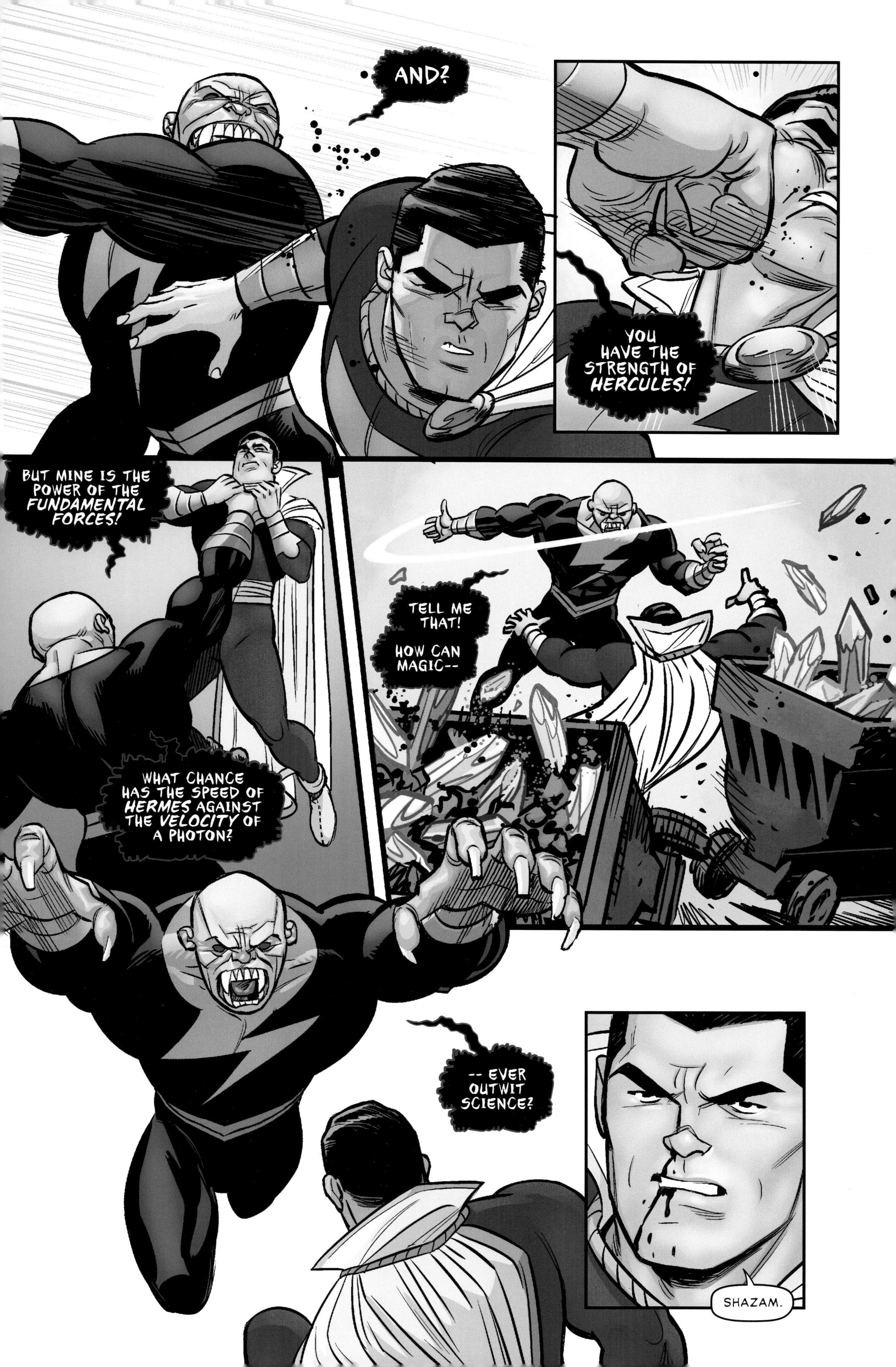
AND?
YOU HAVE THE STRENGTH OF HERCULES!
BUT MINE IS THE POWER OF THE FUNDAMENTAL FORCES!
TELL ME THAT!
HOW CAN MAGIC--
WHAT CHANCE HAS THE SPEED OF HERMES AGAINST THE VELOCITY OF A PHOTON?
-- EVER OUTWIT SCIENCE?
SHAZAM.

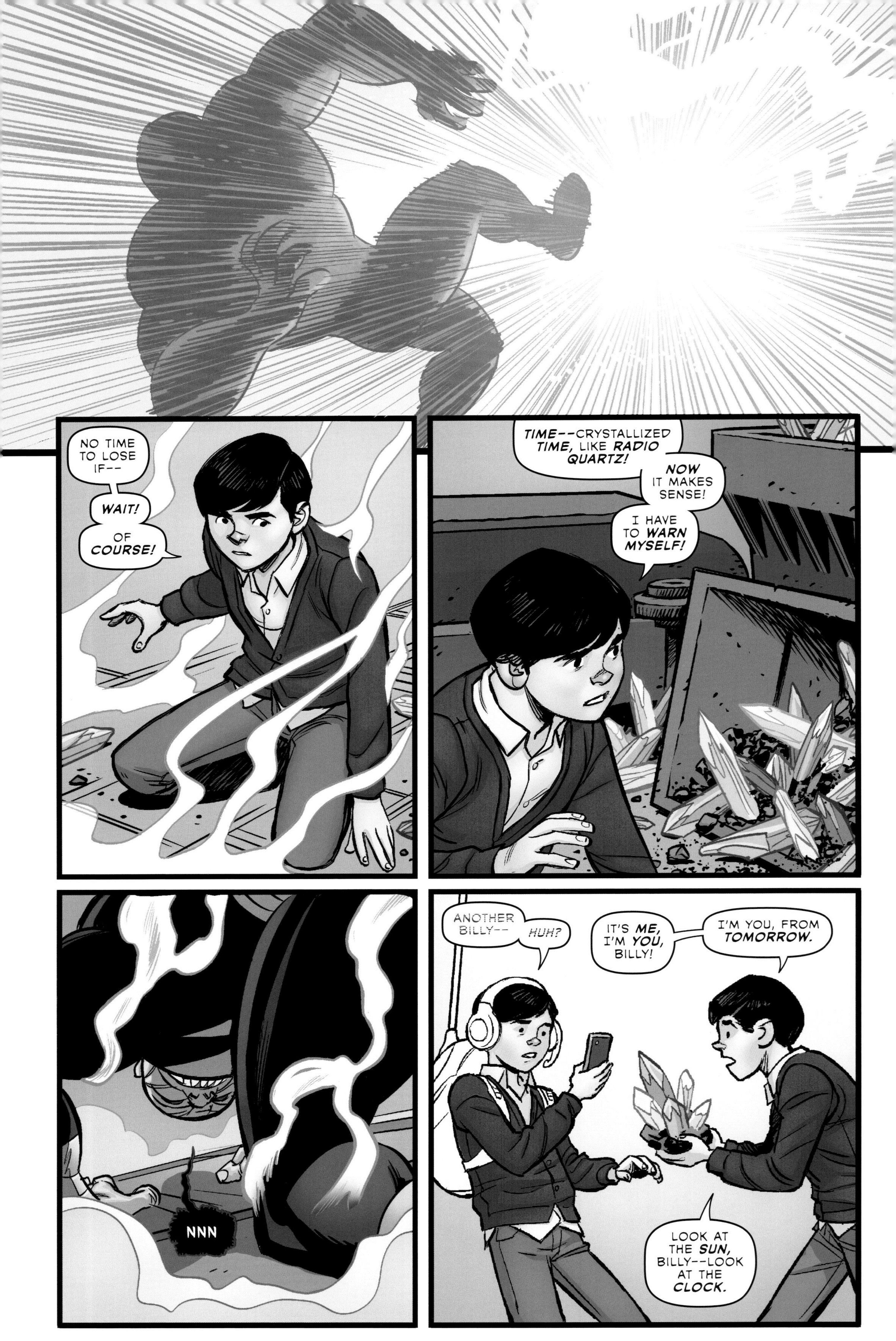
NO TIME TO LOSE IF--
WAIT!
OF COURSE!
TIME--CRYSTALLIZED TIME, LIKE RADIO QUARTZ!
NOW IT MAKES SENSE!
I HAVE TO WARN MYSELF!
NNN
ANOTHER BILLY--
HUH?
IT'S ME, I'M YOU, BILLY!
I'M YOU, FROM TOMORROW.
LOOK AT THE SUN, BILLY--LOOK AT THE CLOCK.

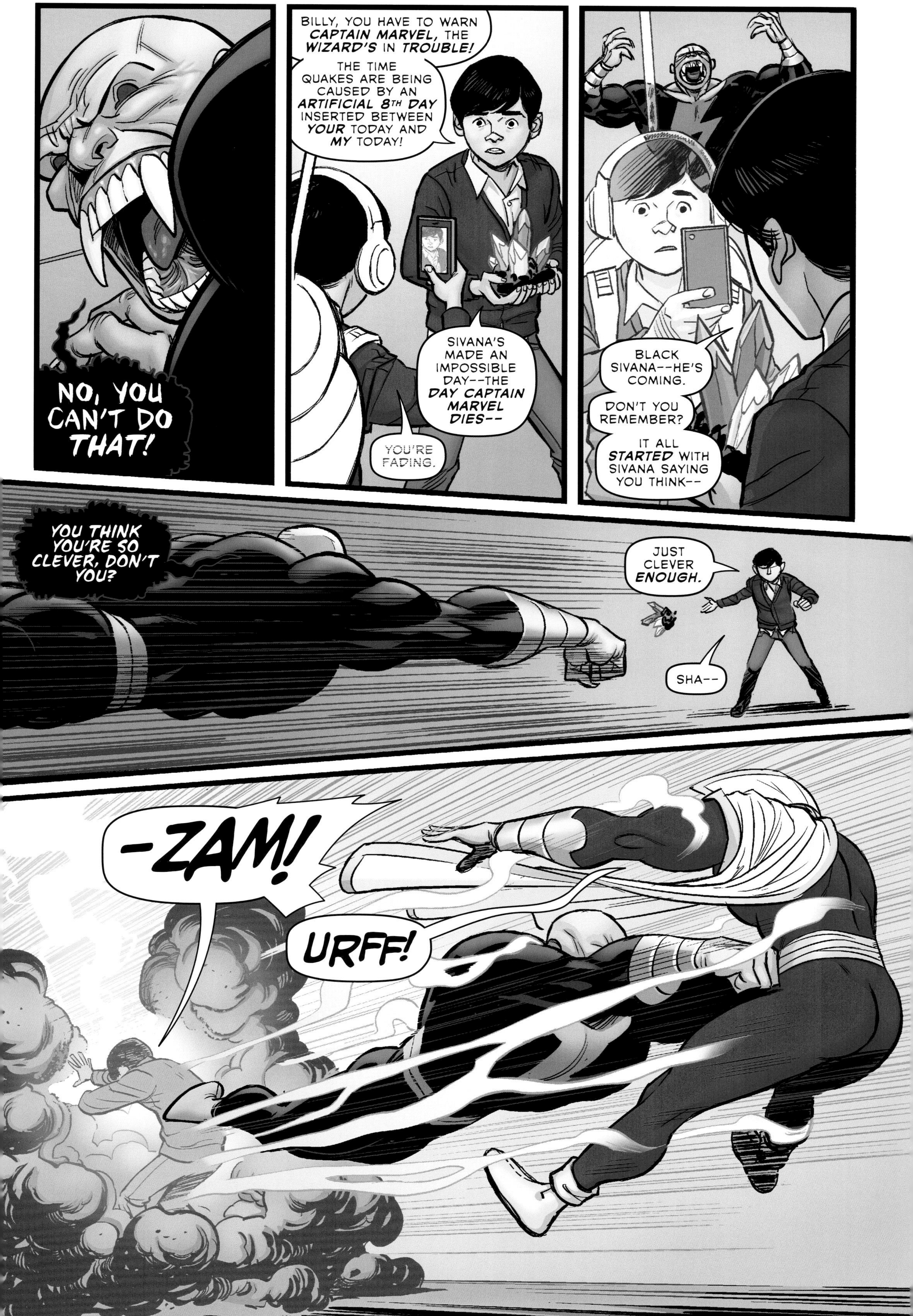
NO, YOU CAN'T DO THAT!
BILLY, YOU HAVE TO WARN CAPTAIN MARVEL, THE WIZARD'S IN TROUBLE!
THE TIME QUAKES ARE BEING CAUSED BY AN ARTIFICIAL 8TH DAY INSERTED BETWEEN YOUR TODAY AND MY TODAY!
SIVANA'S MADE AN IMPOSSIBLE DAY--THE DAY CAPTAIN MARVEL DIES--
YOU'RE FADING.
BLACK SIVANA--HE'S COMING.
DON'T YOU REMEMBER?
IT ALL STARTED WITH SIVANA SAYING YOU THINK--
YOU THINK YOU'RE SO CLEVER, DON'T YOU?
JUST CLEVER ENOUGH.
SHA--
-ZAM!
URFF!

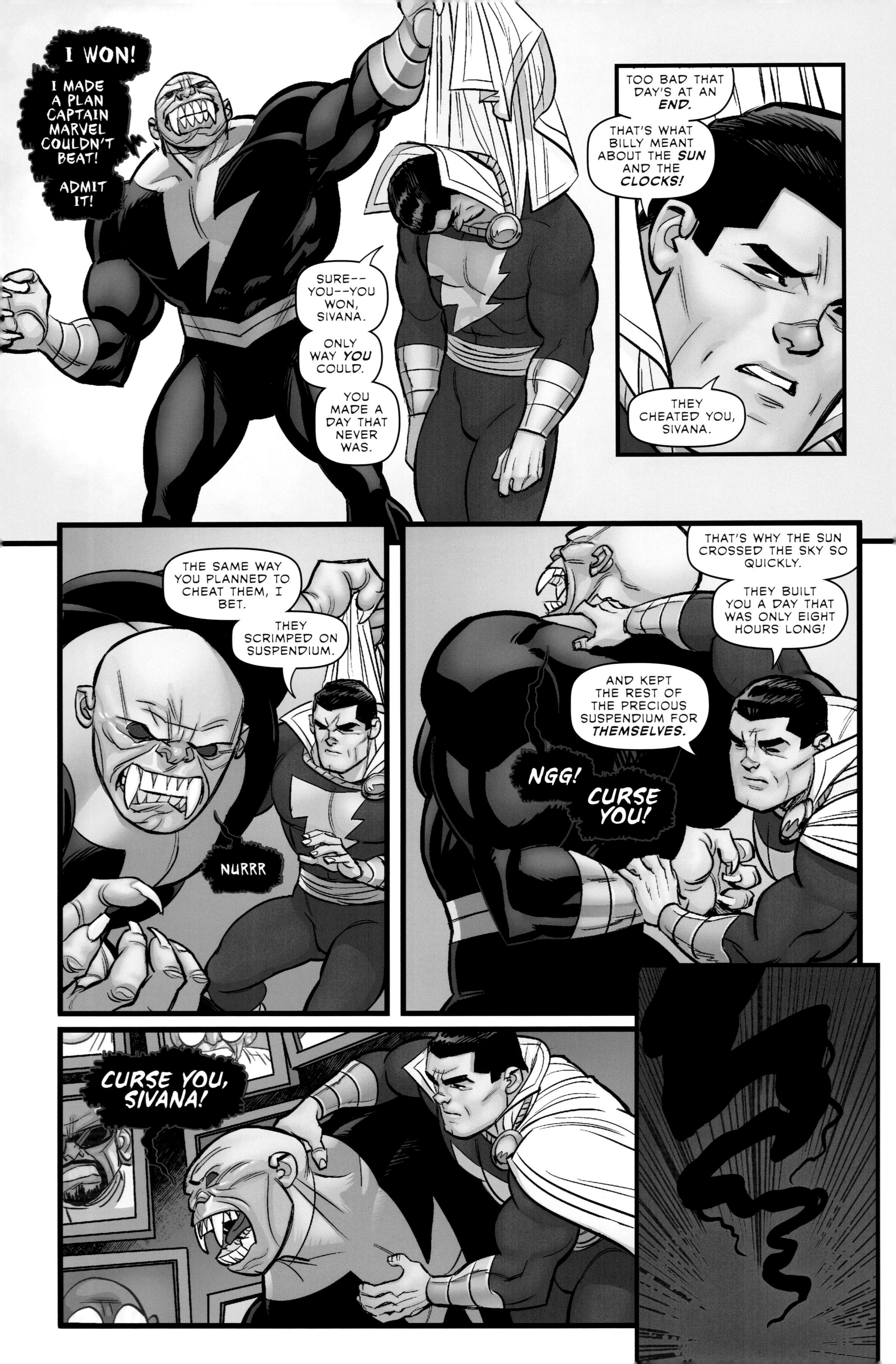
I WON!
I MADE A PLAN CAPTAIN MARVEL COULDN'T BEAT!
ADMIT IT!
SURE-- YOU--YOU WON, SIVANA.
ONLY WAY YOU COULD.
YOU MADE A DAY THAT NEVER WAS.
TOO BAD THAT DAY'S AT AN END.
THAT'S WHAT BILLY MEANT ABOUT THE SUN AND THE CLOCKS!
THEY CHEATED YOU, SIVANA.
THE SAME WAY YOU PLANNED TO CHEAT THEM, I BET.
THEY SCRIMPED ON SUSPENDIUM.
NURRR
THAT'S WHY THE SUN CROSSED THE SKY SO QUICKLY.
THEY BUILT YOU A DAY THAT WAS ONLY EIGHT HOURS LONG!
AND KEPT THE REST OF THE PRECIOUS SUSPENDIUM FOR THEMSELVES.
NGG!
CURSE YOU!
CURSE YOU, SIVANA!

SIVANA! SIVANA=$MEC2$! IT'S A **SCIENTIFIC PROOF!**

THAT WAS **YESTERDAY,** DOCTOR.

NEW DATA CAME TO LIGHT.

THERE WAS A SUDDEN **PARADIGM SHIFT.**

YOU **GOT** YOUR BIG CHANCE.

IN ALL TIME AND SPACE, THERE'S **ONE DAY** WHERE YOU WIN.

ON EVERY **OTHER** DAY, GENTLEMEN--

--YOU **LOSE** LIKE THE **LAST TIME!**

THIS ISN'T **OVER.**

NOW I'VE **SEEN** HER.

I WANT THAT **GIRL.**

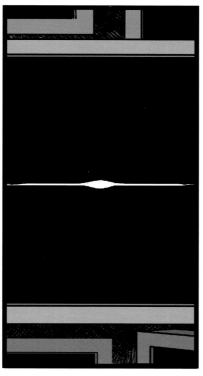

YOU NEVER **FAIL** ME, DO YOU, BOY?

I **CHOSE** MY CHAMPION WELL.

MEH!

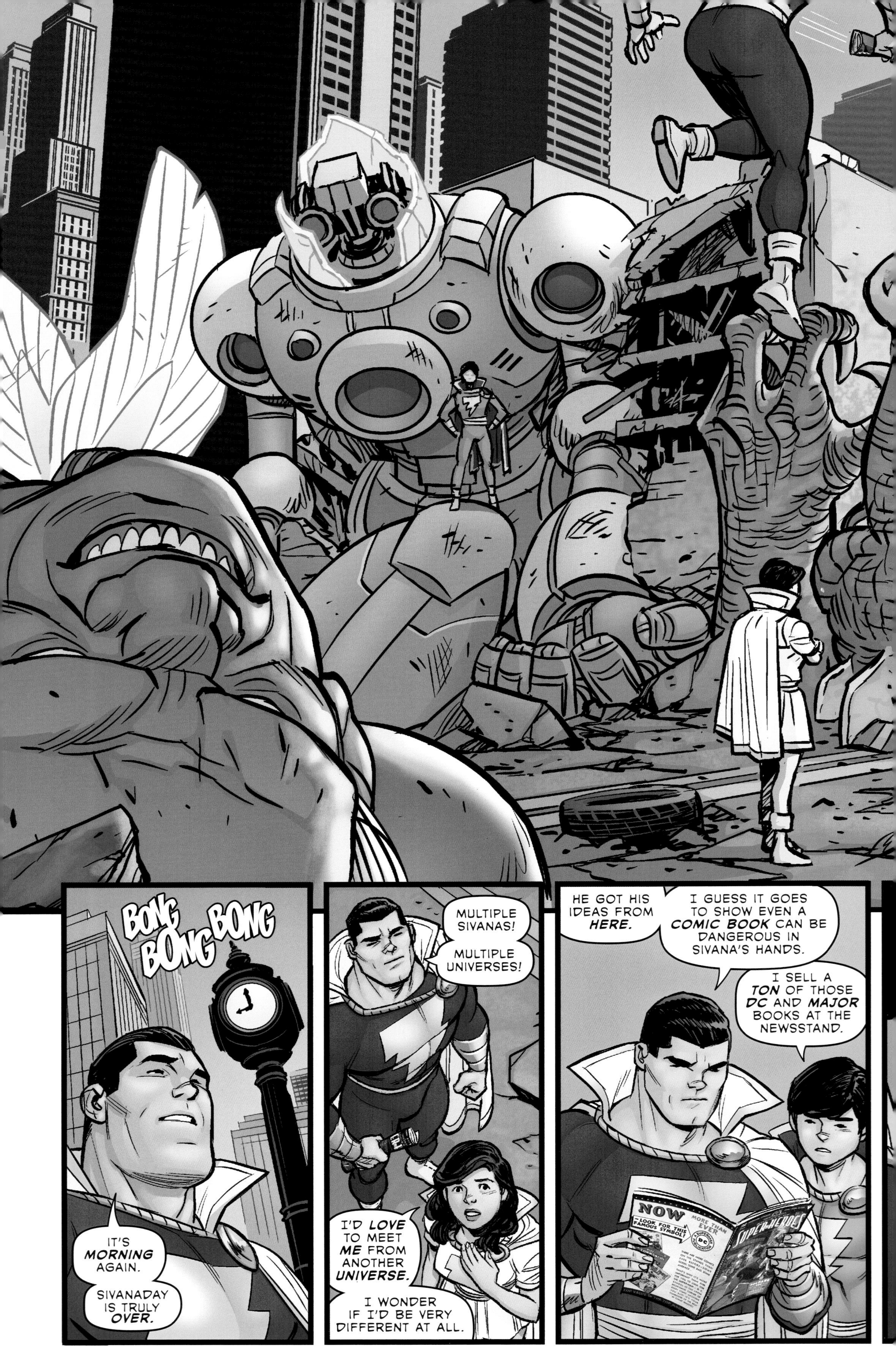
BONG BONG BONG
IT'S MORNING AGAIN.
SIVANADAY IS TRULY OVER.
MULTIPLE SIVANAS!
MULTIPLE UNIVERSES!
I'D LOVE TO MEET ME FROM ANOTHER UNIVERSE.
I WONDER IF I'D BE VERY DIFFERENT AT ALL.
HE GOT HIS IDEAS FROM HERE.
I GUESS IT GOES TO SHOW EVEN A COMIC BOOK CAN BE DANGEROUS IN SIVANA'S HANDS.
I SELL A TON OF THOSE DC AND MAJOR BOOKS AT THE NEWSSTAND.
NOW MORE THAN EVER
LOOK FOR THIS FAMOUS SYMBOL!
SUPER-HEROES

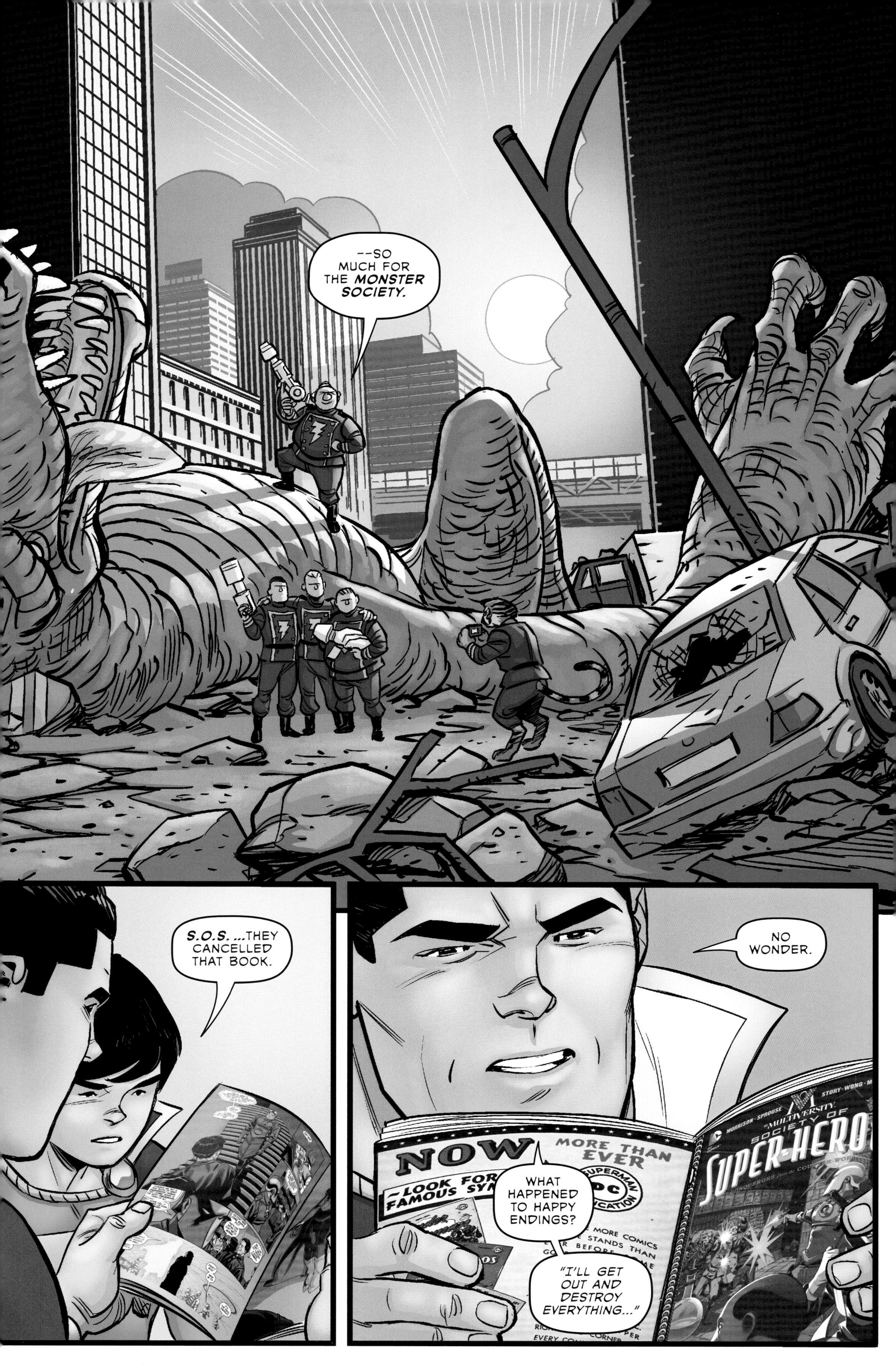
--SO MUCH FOR THE *MONSTER SOCIETY.*
S.O.S. ...THEY CANCELLED THAT BOOK.
NO WONDER.
WHAT HAPPENED TO HAPPY ENDINGS?
"I'LL GET OUT AND DESTROY EVERYTHING..."

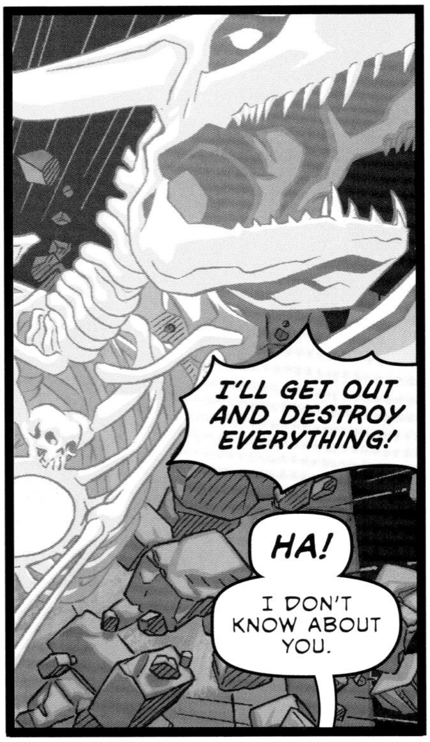
I'LL GET OUT AND DESTROY EVERYTHING!
HA!
I DON'T KNOW ABOUT YOU.

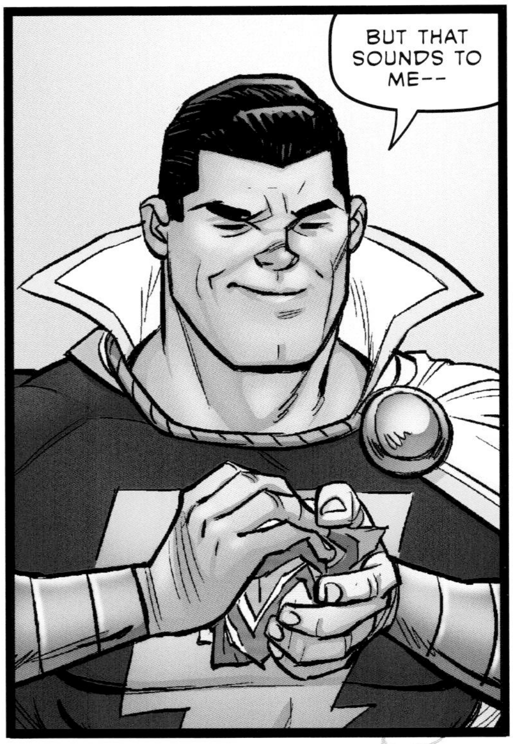
BUT THAT SOUNDS TO ME--

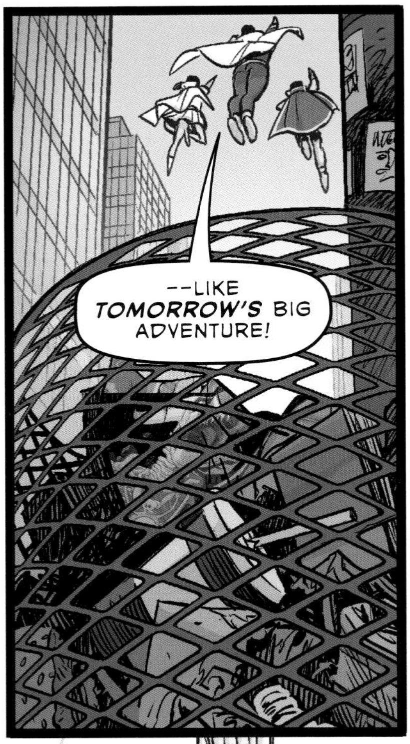
--LIKE *TOMORROW'S* BIG ADVENTURE!

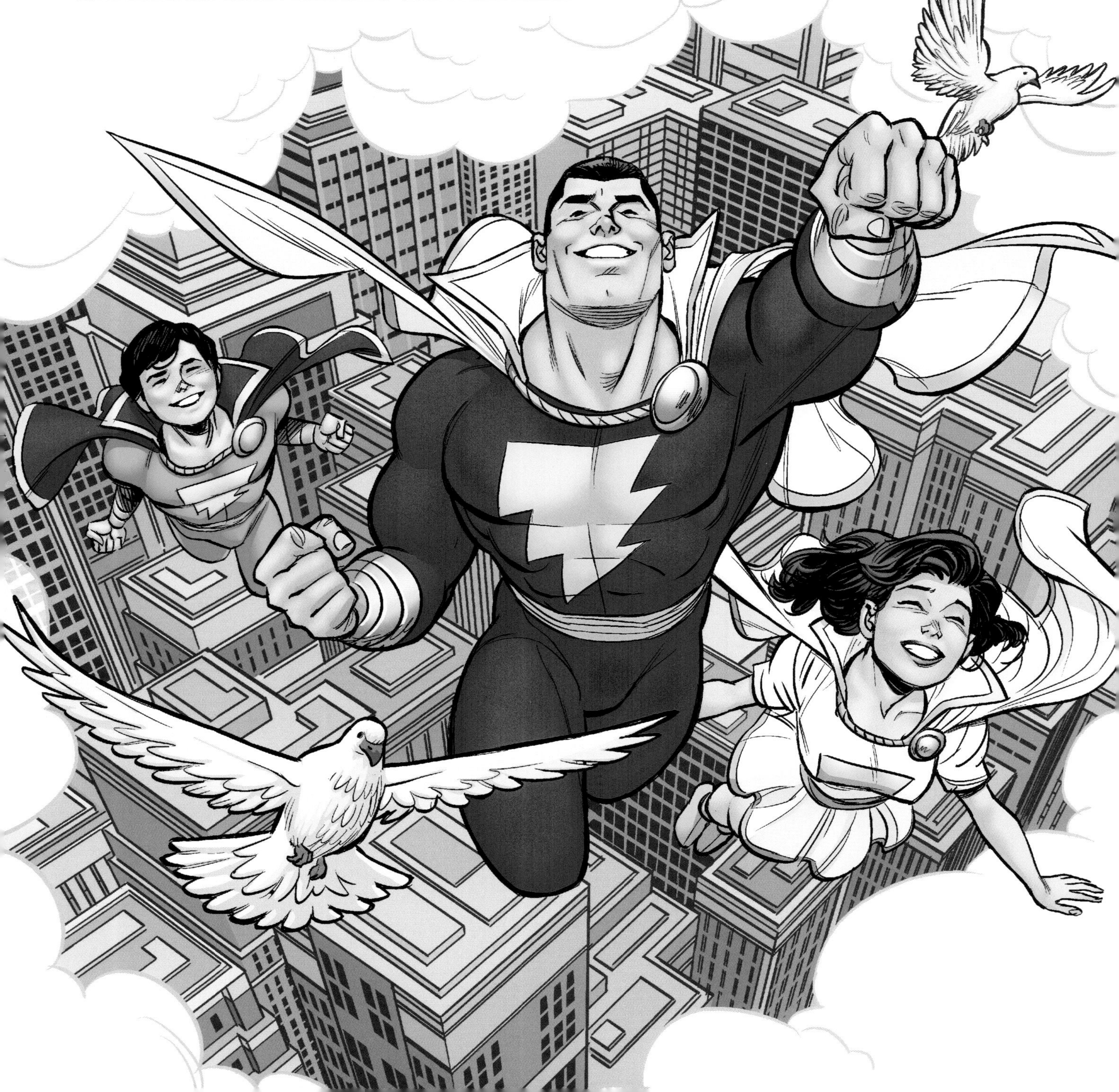

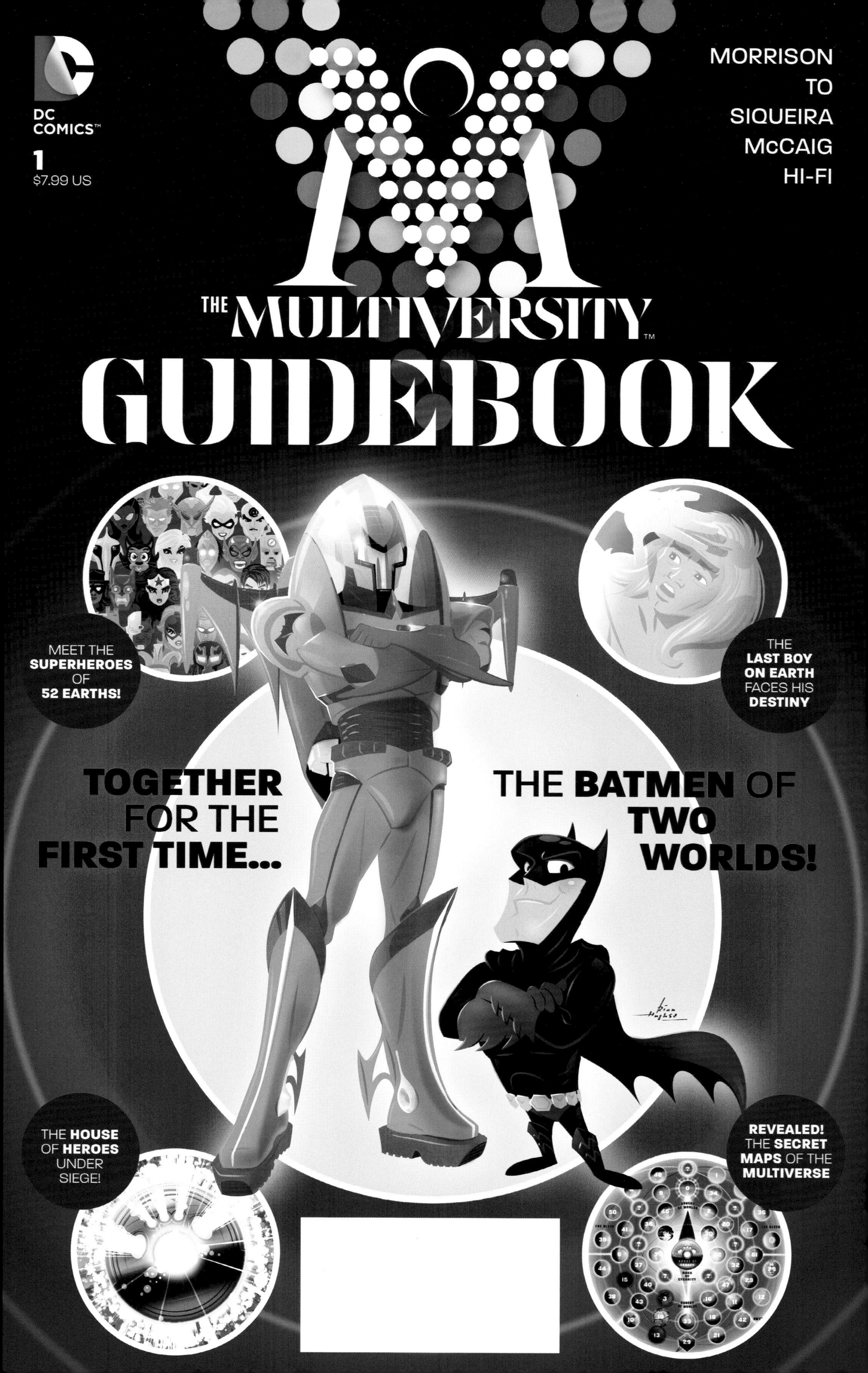
DC COMICS™
1
$7.99 US
MORRISON
TO
SIQUEIRA
McCAIG
HI-FI
THE MULTIVERSITY™
GUIDEBOOK
MEET THE SUPERHEROES OF 52 EARTHS!
THE LAST BOY ON EARTH FACES HIS DESTINY
TOGETHER FOR THE FIRST TIME...
THE BATMEN OF TWO WORLDS!
THE HOUSE OF HEROES UNDER SIEGE!
REVEALED! THE SECRET MAPS OF THE MULTIVERSE

CREDITS

Writer
GRANT MORRISON

BATMAN SECTION

Artist
MARCUS TO

Colorist
DAVE McCAIG

KAMANDI SECTION

Layouts
SCOTT McDANIEL

Finishes
PAULO SIQUEIRA

Colorist
HI-FI

Letters
TODD KLEIN

Cover
RIAN HUGHES

THE MULTIVERSE ARTISTS

- Earth-**0** Brett Booth and Norm Rapmund with Andrew Dalhouse
- Earth-**1** Gary Frank with Nathan Fairbairn
- Earth-**2** Nicola Scott and Trevor Scott with Pete Pantazis
- Earth-**3** David Finch with Sonia Oback
- Earth-**4** Juan Jose Ryp with Fairbairn
- Earth-**5** Cameron Stewart with Fairbairn
- Earth-**6** Marcus To with Tomeu Morey
- Earth-**7** Joe Prado with Marcelo Maiolo
- Earth-**8** Bryan Hitch with Alex Sinclair
- Earth-**9** Dan Jurgens and Rapmund with Pantazis
- Earth-**10** Mike Hawthorne with Fairbairn
- Earth-**11** Emanuela Lupacchino with Tomeu Morey
- Earth-**12** Jake Wyatt
- Earth-**13** Jae Lee with June Chung
- Earth-**14** ?
- Earth-**15** Prado with Gabe Eltaeb
- Earth-**16** Ben Oliver
- Earth-**17** Kalman Andrasofszky with Fairbairn
- Earth-**18** Andrew Robinson
- Earth-**19** Giuseppe Camuncoli and Richard Friend with Fairbairn
- Earth-**20** Chris Sprouse and Karl Story with Dave McCaig
- Earth-**21** Darwyn Cooke
- Earth-**22** Yildiray Cinar with Fairbairn
- Earth-**23** Gene Ha
- Earth-**24** ?
- Earth-**25** ?
- Earth-**26** Chris Burnham with Fairbairn
- Earth-**27** ?
- Earth-**28** ?
- Earth-**29** Declan Shalvey with Jordie Bellaire
- Earth-**30** Shalvey with Bellaire
- Earth-**31** Cinar with McCaig
- Earth-**32** Todd Nauck with Eltaeb
- Earth-**33** Hitch with Sinclair
- Earth-**34** Jeff Johnson with Fairbairn
- Earth-**35** Camuncoli and Friend with Fairbairn
- Earth-**36** Evan "Doc" Shaner with Fairbairn
- Earth-**37** Jed Dougherty with Eltaeb
- Earth-**38** Jon Bogdanove with McCaig
- Earth-**39** To with McCaig
- Earth-**40** Sprouse and Story with McCaig
- Earth-**41** Hawthorne with Fairbairn
- Earth-**42** To with McCaig
- Earth-**43** Kelley Jones with McCaig
- Earth-**44** Duncan Rouleau
- Earth-**45** Andy MacDonald with McCaig
- Earth-**46** ?
- Earth-**47** Scott Hepburn with Fairbairn
- Earth-**48** Camuncoli and Friend with Eltaeb
- Earth-**49** ?
- Earth-**50** Wyatt
- Earth-**51** Paulo Siqueira with Eltaeb

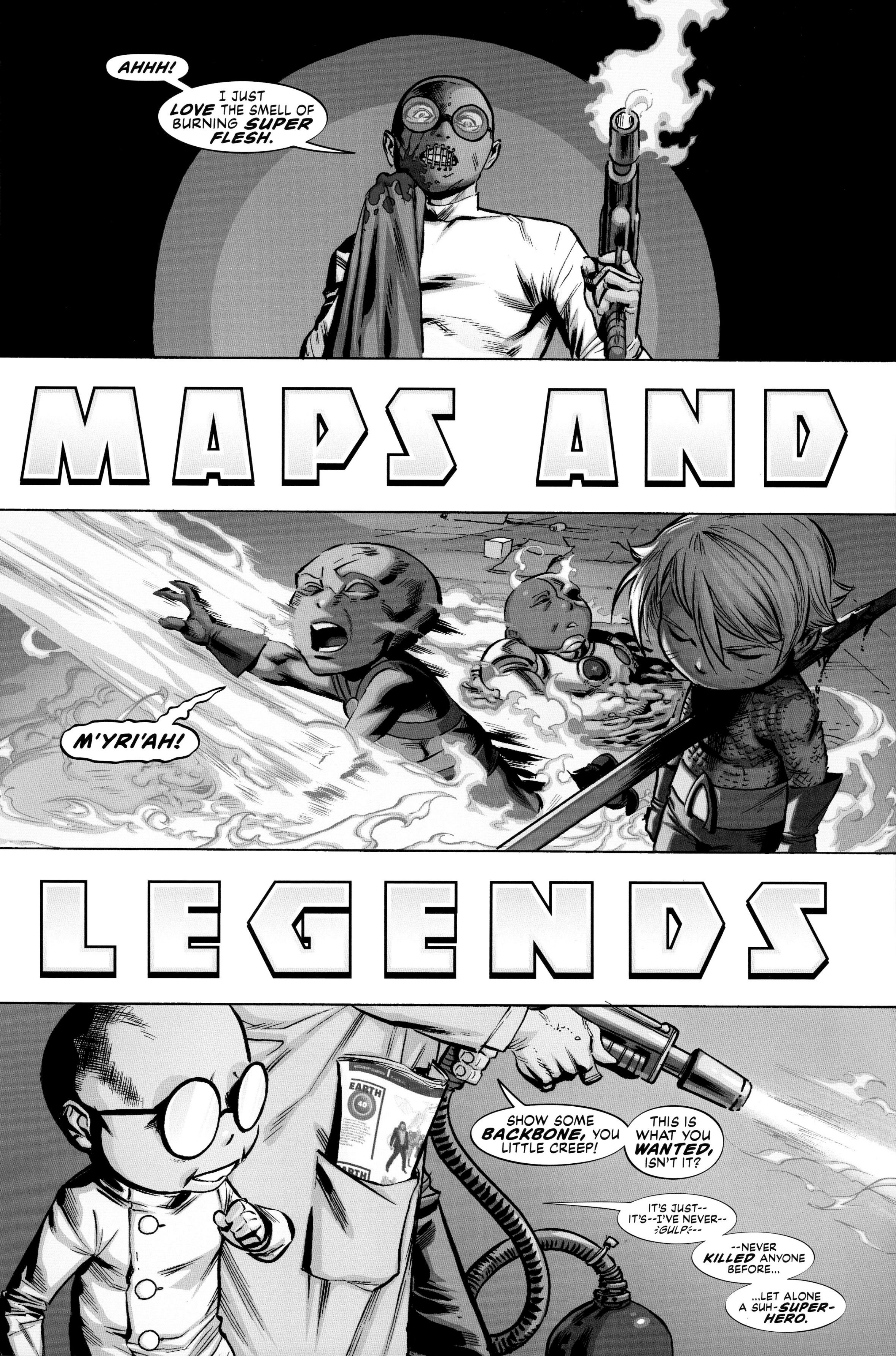
AHHH!
I JUST LOVE THE SMELL OF BURNING SUPER FLESH.
MAPS AND
M'YRI'AH!
LEGENDS
EARTH 40
SHOW SOME BACKBONE, YOU LITTLE CREEP!
THIS IS WHAT YOU WANTED, ISN'T IT?
IT'S JUST-- IT'S--I'VE NEVER-- <GULP>--
--NEVER KILLED ANYONE BEFORE...
...LET ALONE A SUH-SUPER-HERO.

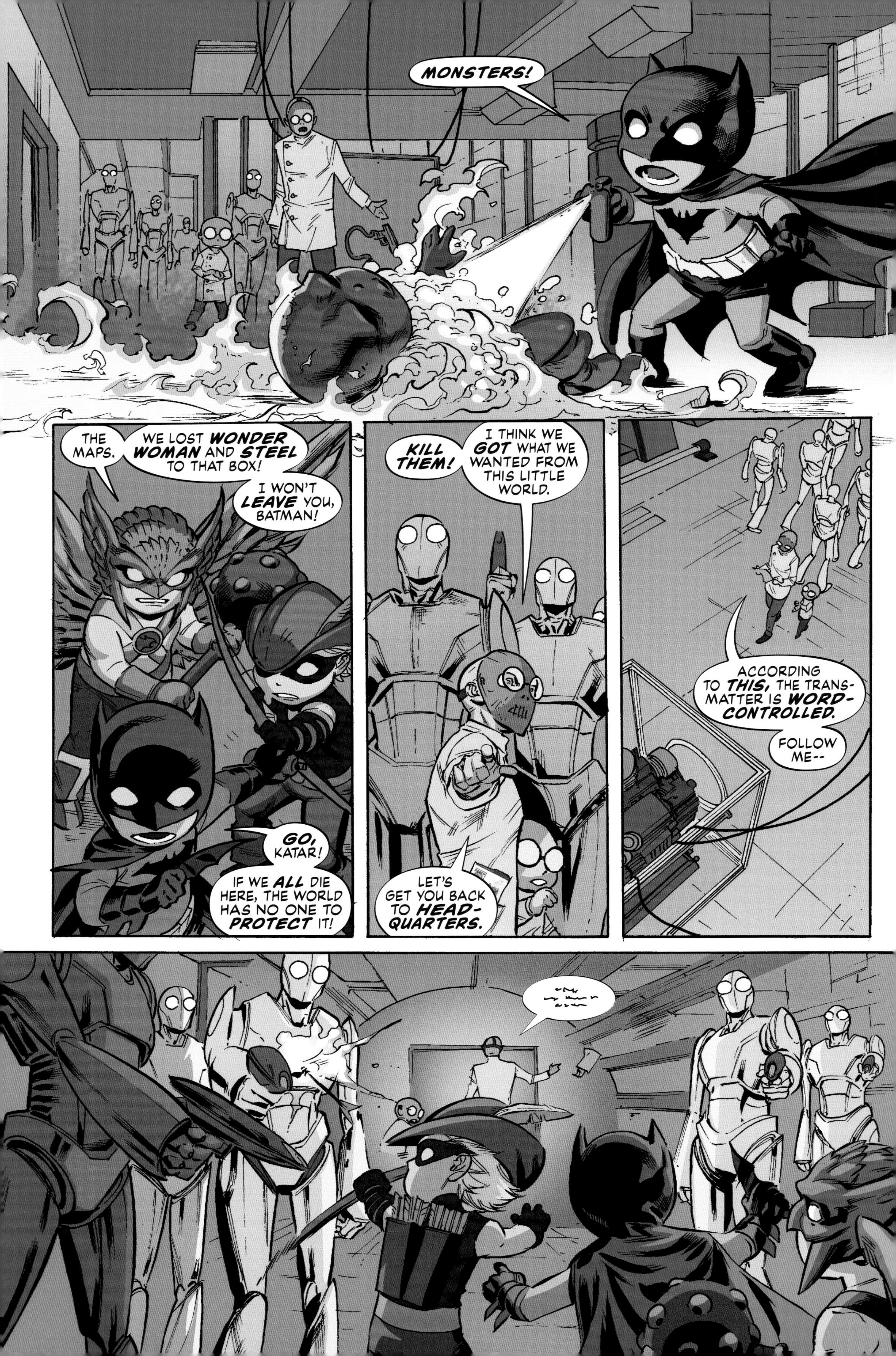
MONSTERS!
THE MAPS.
WE LOST WONDER WOMAN AND STEEL TO THAT BOX!
I WON'T LEAVE YOU, BATMAN!
GO, KATAR!
IF WE ALL DIE HERE, THE WORLD HAS NO ONE TO PROTECT IT!
KILL THEM!
I THINK WE GOT WHAT WE WANTED FROM THIS LITTLE WORLD.
LET'S GET YOU BACK TO HEAD-QUARTERS.
ACCORDING TO THIS, THE TRANS-MATTER IS WORD-CONTROLLED.
FOLLOW ME--

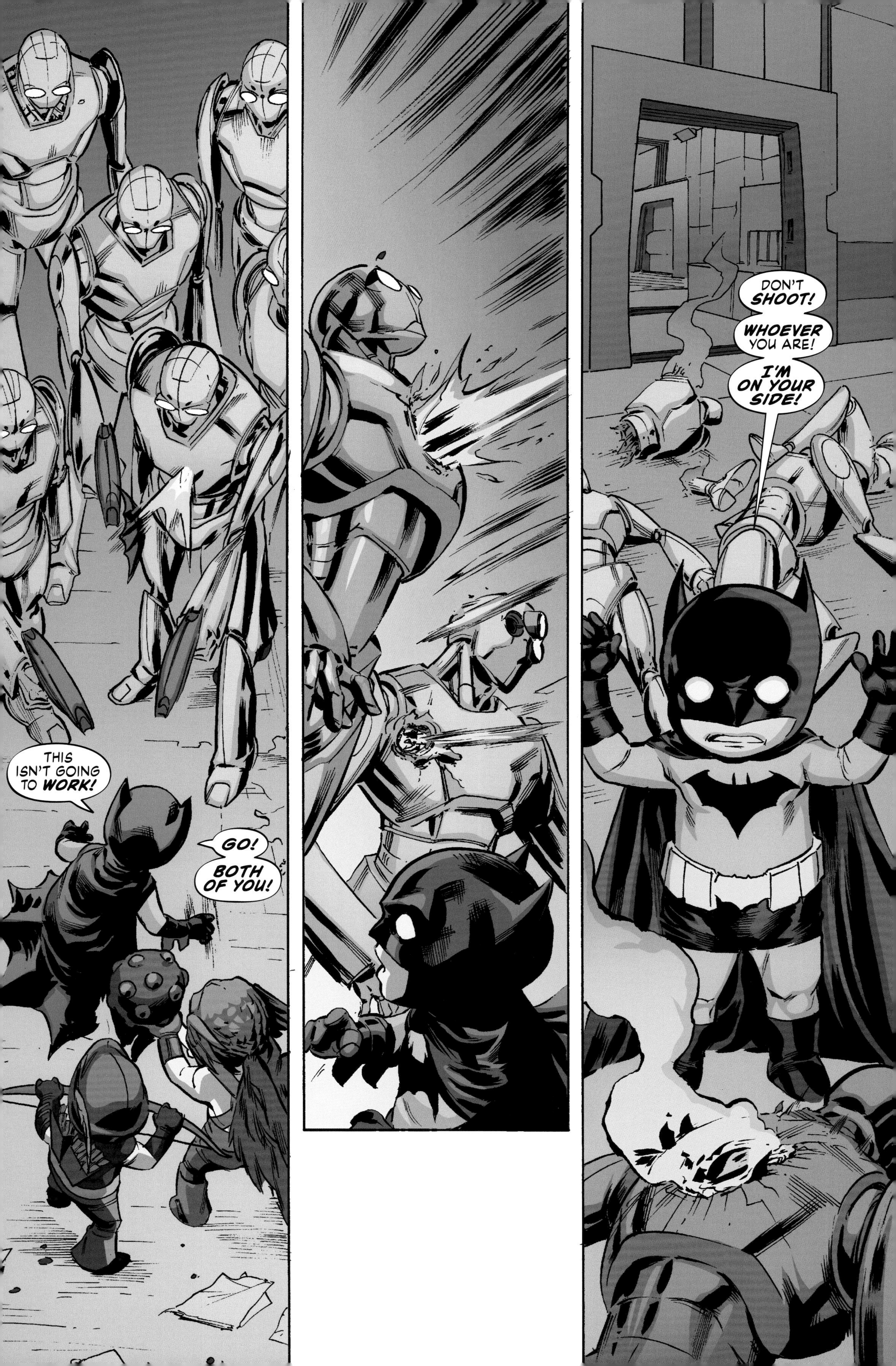
THIS ISN'T GOING TO WORK!
GO! BOTH OF YOU!
DON'T SHOOT!
WHOEVER YOU ARE!
I'M ON YOUR SIDE!

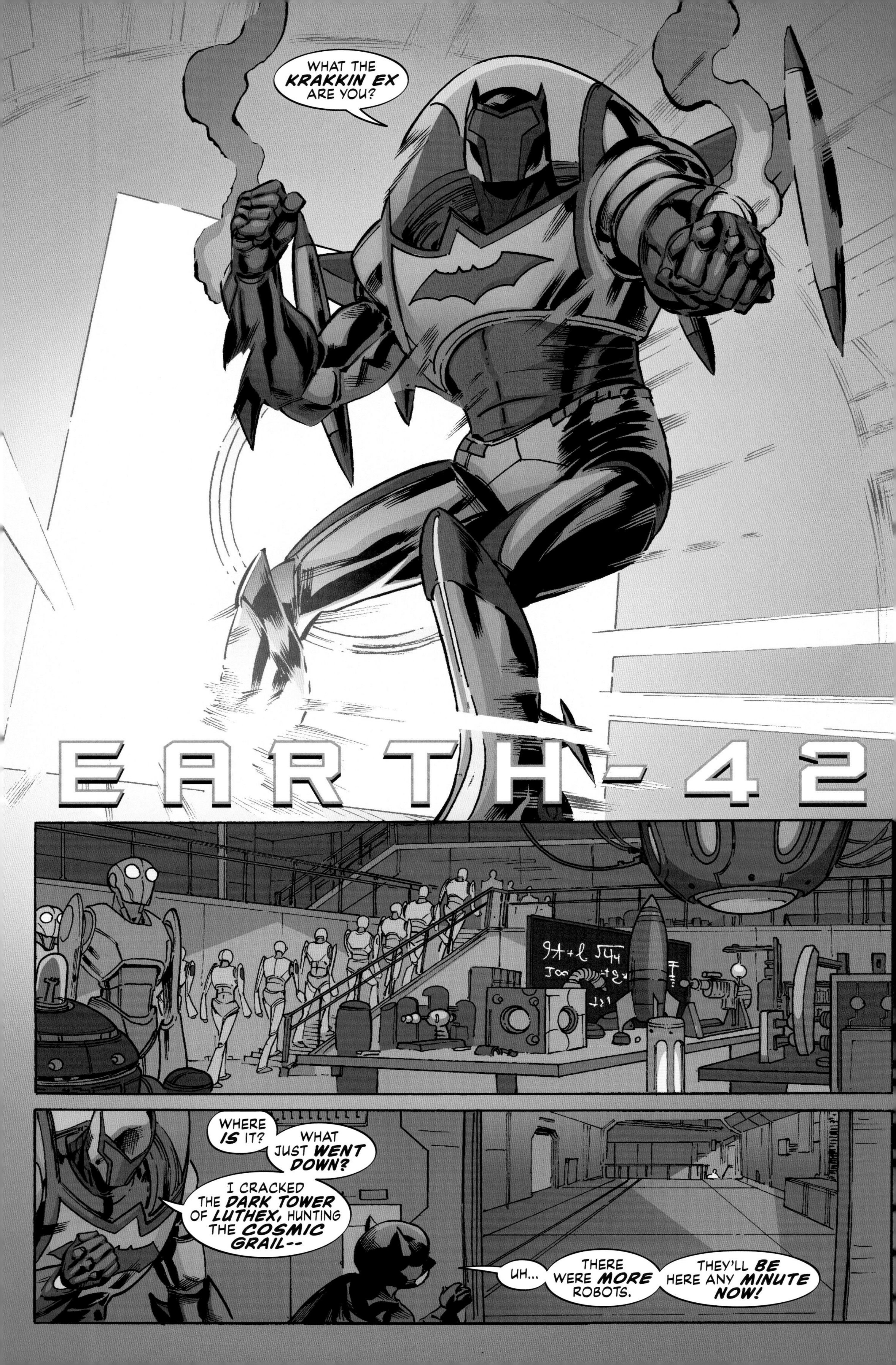
WHAT THE KRAKKIN EX ARE YOU?
EARTH-42
WHERE IS IT?
WHAT JUST WENT DOWN?
I CRACKED THE DARK TOWER OF LUTHEX, HUNTING THE COSMIC GRAIL--
UH...
THERE WERE MORE ROBOTS.
THEY'LL BE HERE ANY MINUTE NOW!

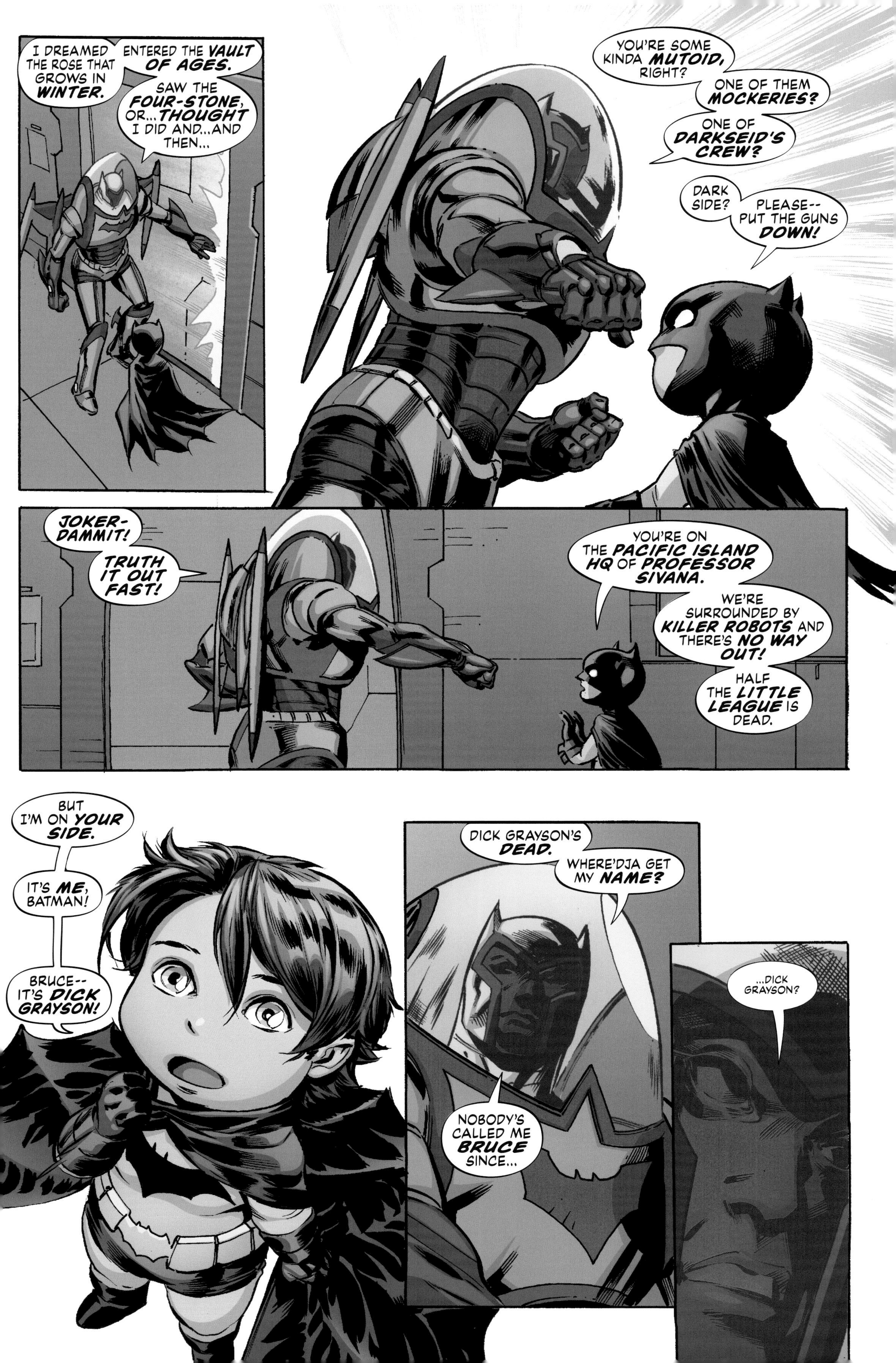
I DREAMED THE ROSE THAT GROWS IN WINTER.
ENTERED THE VAULT OF AGES.
SAW THE FOUR-STONE, OR...THOUGHT I DID AND...AND THEN...
YOU'RE SOME KINDA MUTOID, RIGHT?
ONE OF THEM MOCKERIES?
ONE OF DARKSEID'S CREW?
DARK SIDE?
PLEASE-- PUT THE GUNS DOWN!
JOKER-DAMMIT!
TRUTH IT OUT FAST!
YOU'RE ON THE PACIFIC ISLAND HQ OF PROFESSOR SIVANA.
WE'RE SURROUNDED BY KILLER ROBOTS AND THERE'S NO WAY OUT!
HALF THE LITTLE LEAGUE IS DEAD.
BUT I'M ON YOUR SIDE.
IT'S ME, BATMAN!
BRUCE-- IT'S DICK GRAYSON!
DICK GRAYSON'S DEAD.
WHERE'DJA GET MY NAME?
NOBODY'S CALLED ME BRUCE SINCE...
...DICK GRAYSON?

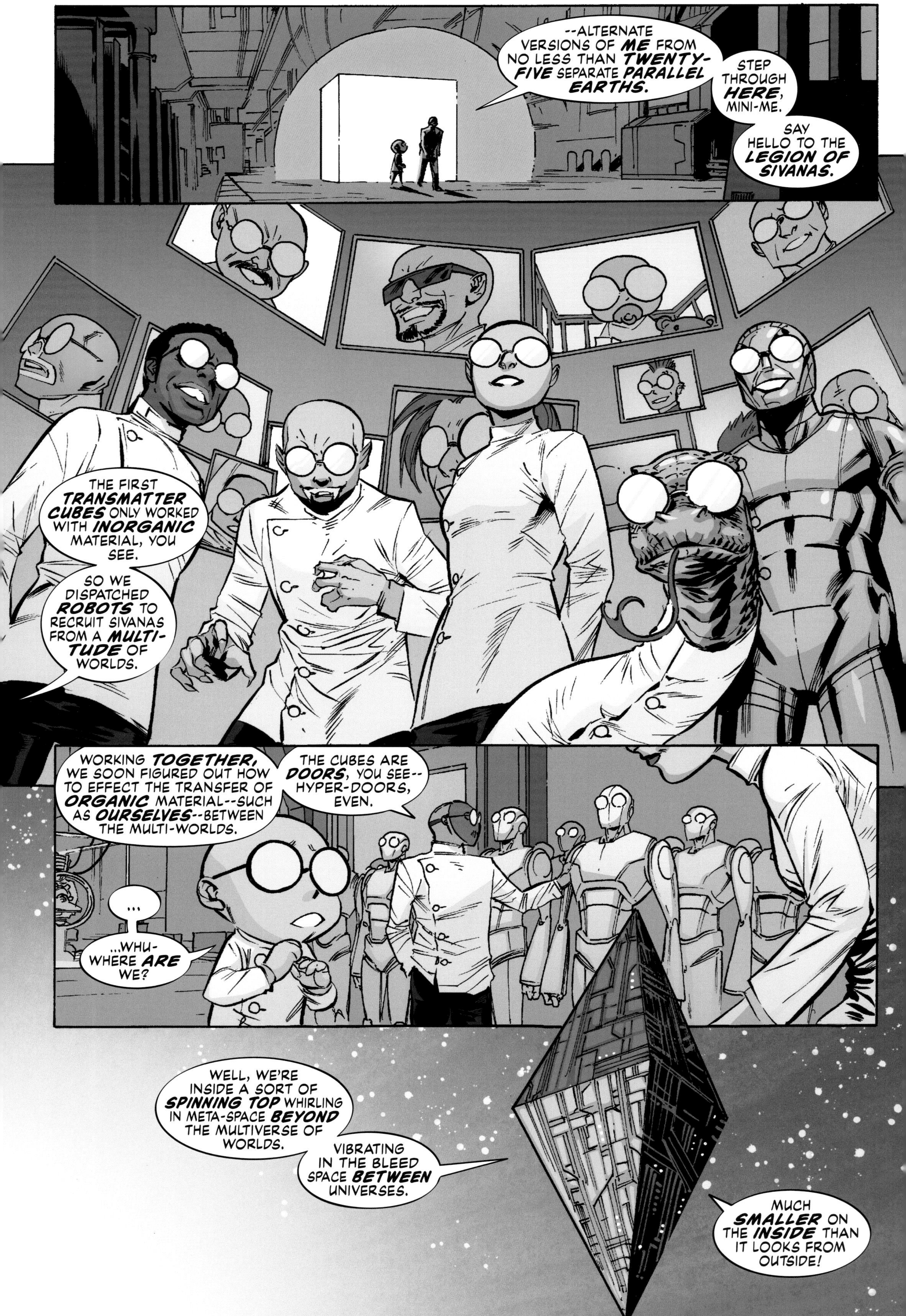
--ALTERNATE VERSIONS OF ME FROM NO LESS THAN TWENTY-FIVE SEPARATE PARALLEL EARTHS.
STEP THROUGH HERE, MINI-ME.
SAY HELLO TO THE LEGION OF SIVANAS.
THE FIRST TRANSMATTER CUBES ONLY WORKED WITH INORGANIC MATERIAL, YOU SEE.
SO WE DISPATCHED ROBOTS TO RECRUIT SIVANAS FROM A MULTI-TUDE OF WORLDS.
WORKING TOGETHER, WE SOON FIGURED OUT HOW TO EFFECT THE TRANSFER OF ORGANIC MATERIAL--SUCH AS OURSELVES--BETWEEN THE MULTI-WORLDS.
THE CUBES ARE DOORS, YOU SEE--HYPER-DOORS, EVEN.
...
...WHU-WHERE ARE WE?
WELL, WE'RE INSIDE A SORT OF SPINNING TOP WHIRLING IN META-SPACE BEYOND THE MULTIVERSE OF WORLDS.
VIBRATING IN THE BLEED SPACE BETWEEN UNIVERSES.
MUCH SMALLER ON THE INSIDE THAN IT LOOKS FROM OUTSIDE!

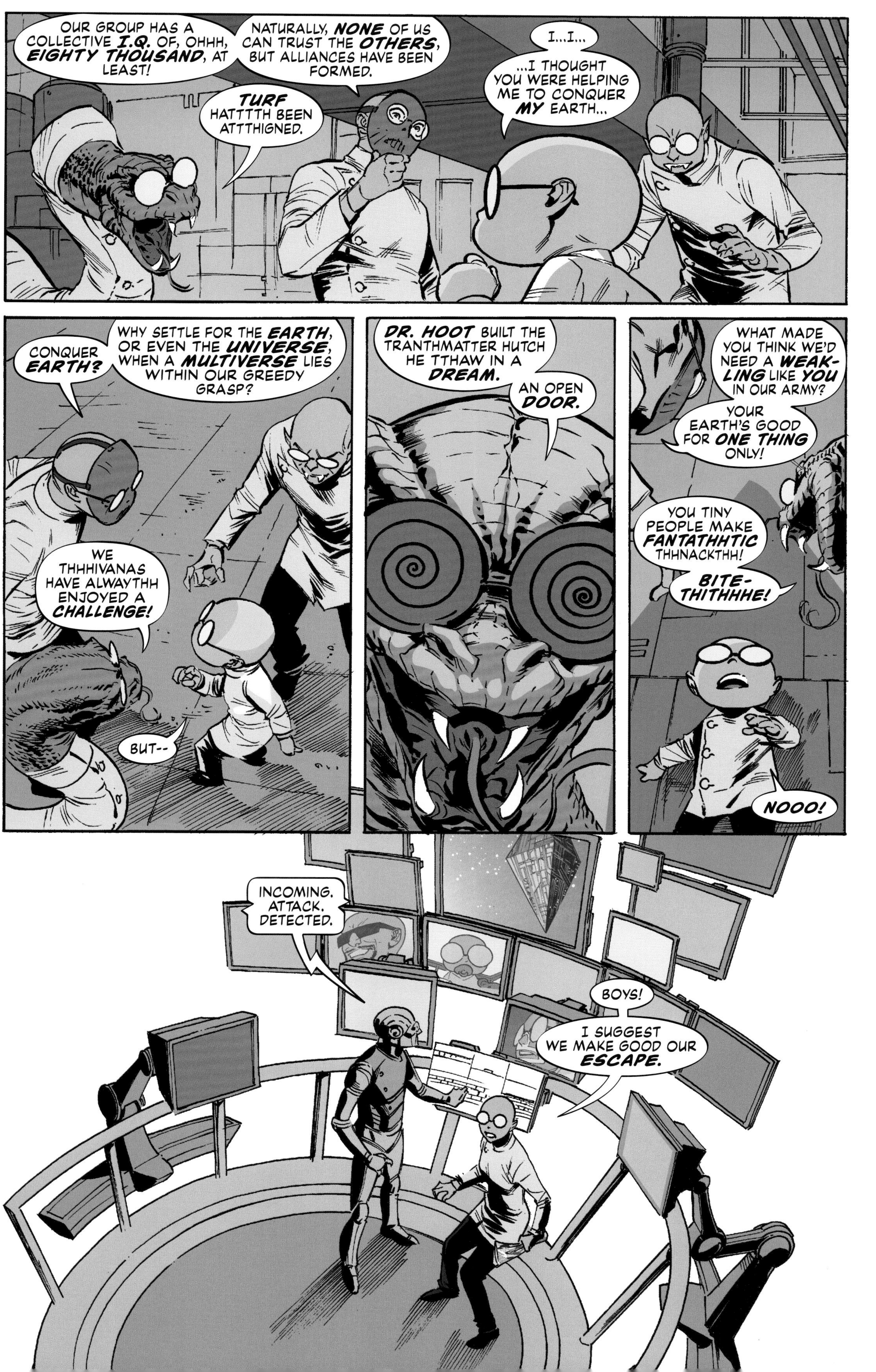
OUR GROUP HAS A COLLECTIVE I.Q. OF, OHHH, EIGHTY THOUSAND, AT LEAST!
NATURALLY, NONE OF US CAN TRUST THE OTHERS, BUT ALLIANCES HAVE BEEN FORMED.
TURF HATTTTH BEEN ATTTHIGNED.
I...I...
...I THOUGHT YOU WERE HELPING ME TO CONQUER MY EARTH...
CONQUER EARTH?
WHY SETTLE FOR THE EARTH, OR EVEN THE UNIVERSE, WHEN A MULTIVERSE LIES WITHIN OUR GREEDY GRASP?
WE THHHIVANAS HAVE ALWAYTHH ENJOYED A CHALLENGE!
BUT--
DR. HOOT BUILT THE TRANTHMATTER HUTCH HE TTHAW IN A DREAM.
AN OPEN DOOR.
WHAT MADE YOU THINK WE'D NEED A WEAK-LING LIKE YOU IN OUR ARMY?
YOUR EARTH'S GOOD FOR ONE THING ONLY!
YOU TINY PEOPLE MAKE FANTATHHTIC THHNACKTHH!
BITE-THITHHHE!
NOOO!
INCOMING. ATTACK. DETECTED.
BOYS!
I SUGGEST WE MAKE GOOD OUR ESCAPE.

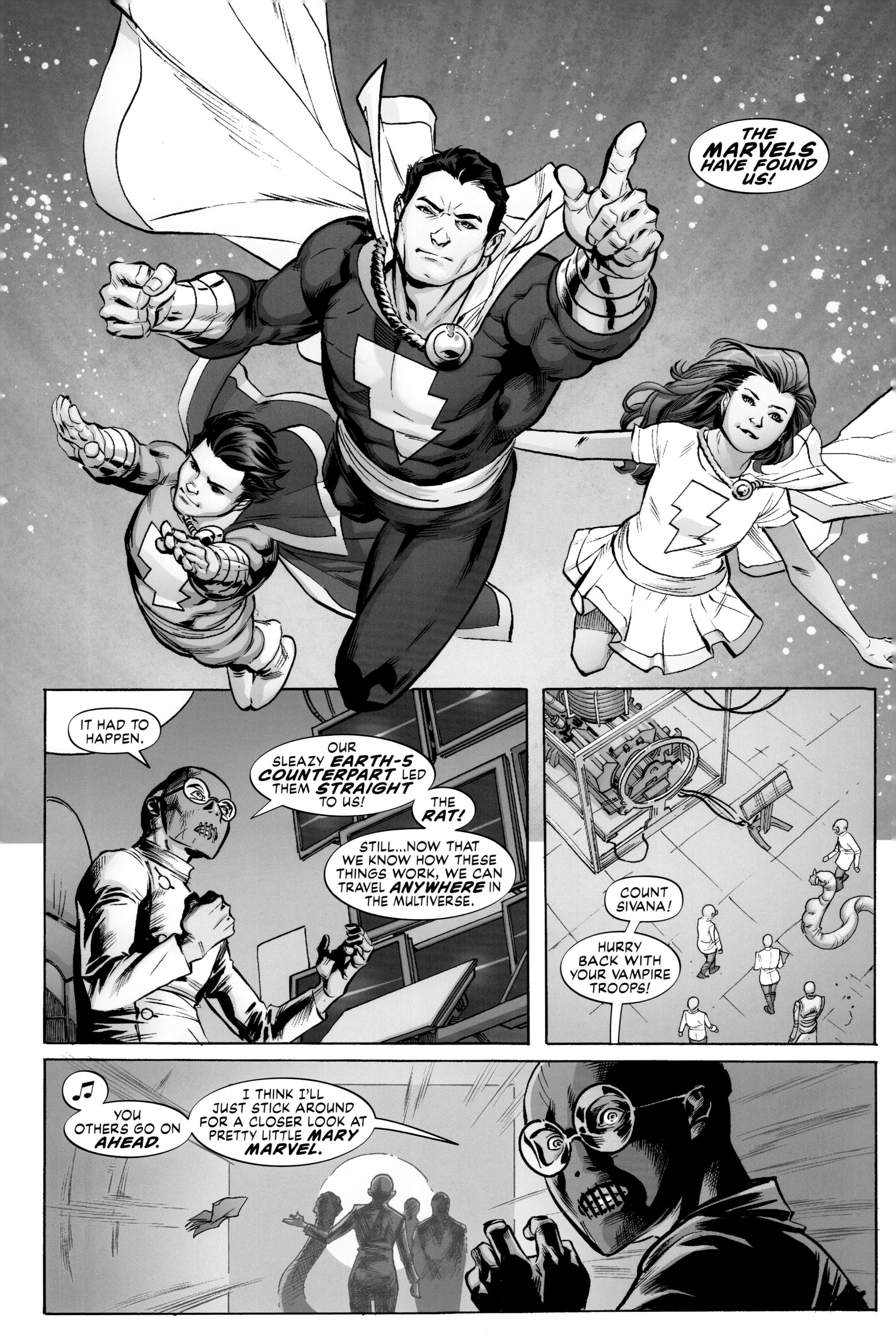
THE MARVELS HAVE FOUND US!
IT HAD TO HAPPEN.
OUR SLEAZY EARTH-S COUNTERPART LED THEM STRAIGHT TO US!
THE RAT!
STILL...NOW THAT WE KNOW HOW THESE THINGS WORK, WE CAN TRAVEL ANYWHERE IN THE MULTIVERSE.
COUNT SIVANA!
HURRY BACK WITH YOUR VAMPIRE TROOPS!
♫
YOU OTHERS GO ON AHEAD.
I THINK I'LL JUST STICK AROUND FOR A CLOSER LOOK AT PRETTY LITTLE MARY MARVEL.

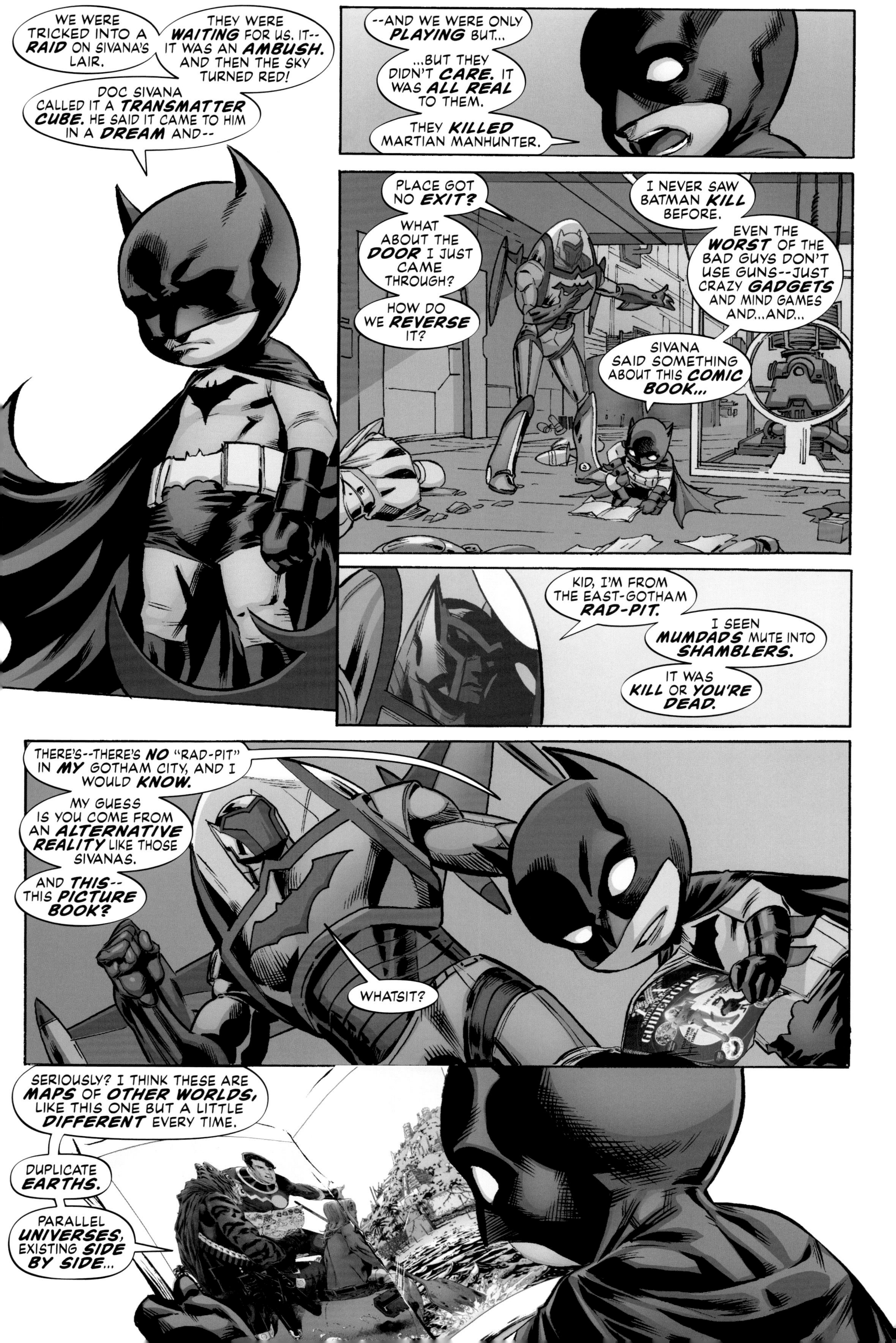
WE WERE TRICKED INTO A RAID ON SIVANA'S LAIR.
THEY WERE WAITING FOR US. IT-- IT WAS AN AMBUSH. AND THEN THE SKY TURNED RED!
DOC SIVANA CALLED IT A TRANSMATTER CUBE. HE SAID IT CAME TO HIM IN A DREAM AND--
--AND WE WERE ONLY PLAYING BUT...
...BUT THEY DIDN'T CARE. IT WAS ALL REAL TO THEM.
THEY KILLED MARTIAN MANHUNTER.
PLACE GOT NO EXIT?
WHAT ABOUT THE DOOR I JUST CAME THROUGH?
HOW DO WE REVERSE IT?
I NEVER SAW BATMAN KILL BEFORE.
EVEN THE WORST OF THE BAD GUYS DON'T USE GUNS--JUST CRAZY GADGETS AND MIND GAMES AND...AND...
SIVANA SAID SOMETHING ABOUT THIS COMIC BOOK...
KID, I'M FROM THE EAST-GOTHAM RAD-PIT.
I SEEN MUMDADS MUTE INTO SHAMBLERS.
IT WAS KILL OR YOU'RE DEAD.
THERE'S--THERE'S NO "RAD-PIT" IN MY GOTHAM CITY, AND I WOULD KNOW.
MY GUESS IS YOU COME FROM AN ALTERNATIVE REALITY LIKE THOSE SIVANAS.
AND THIS-- THIS PICTURE BOOK?
WHATSIT?
SERIOUSLY? I THINK THESE ARE MAPS OF OTHER WORLDS, LIKE THIS ONE BUT A LITTLE DIFFERENT EVERY TIME.
DUPLICATE EARTHS.
PARALLEL UNIVERSES, EXISTING SIDE BY SIDE...

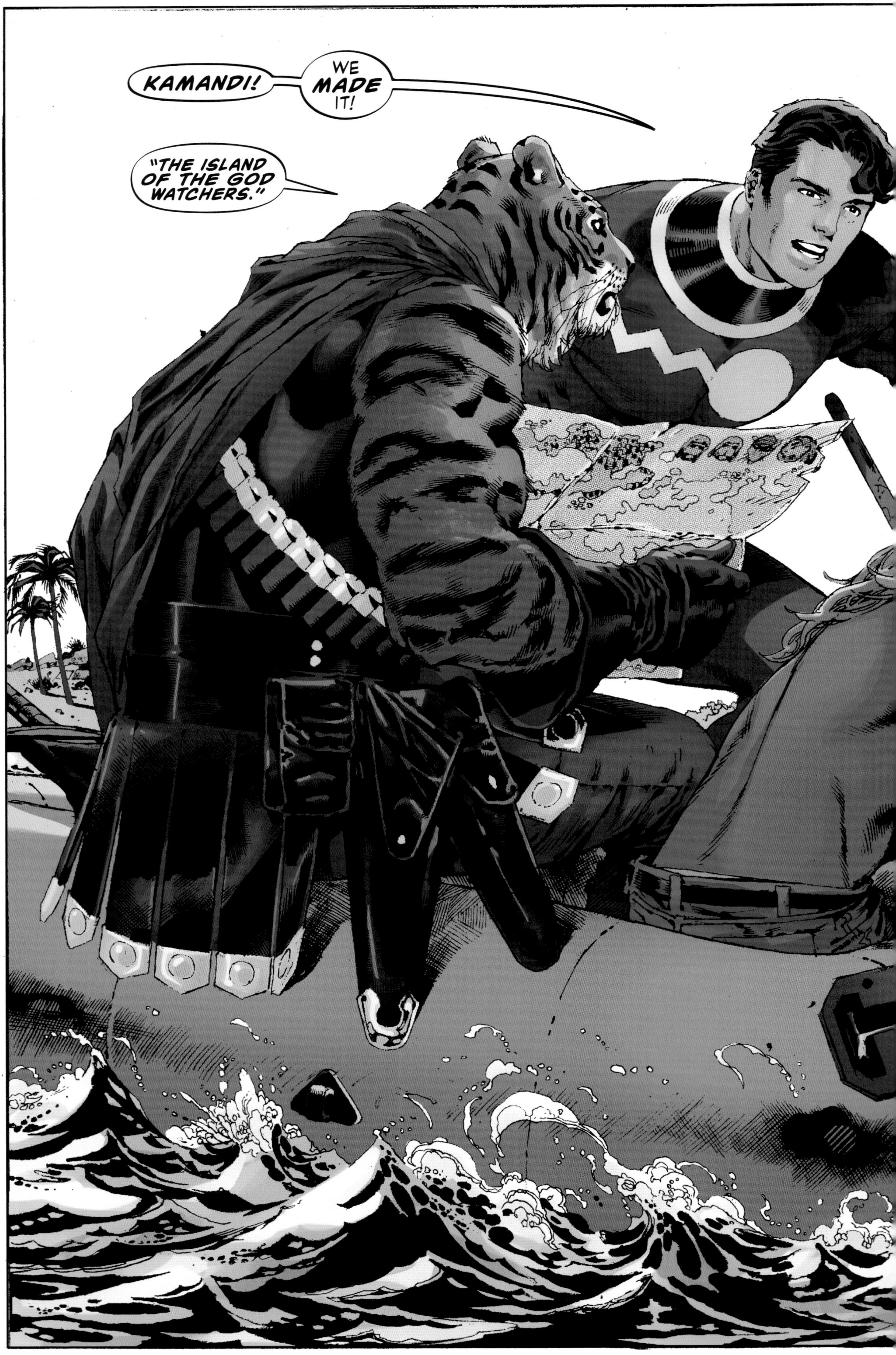
KAMANDI!
WE MADE IT!
"THE ISLAND OF THE GOD WATCHERS."

EARTH-51

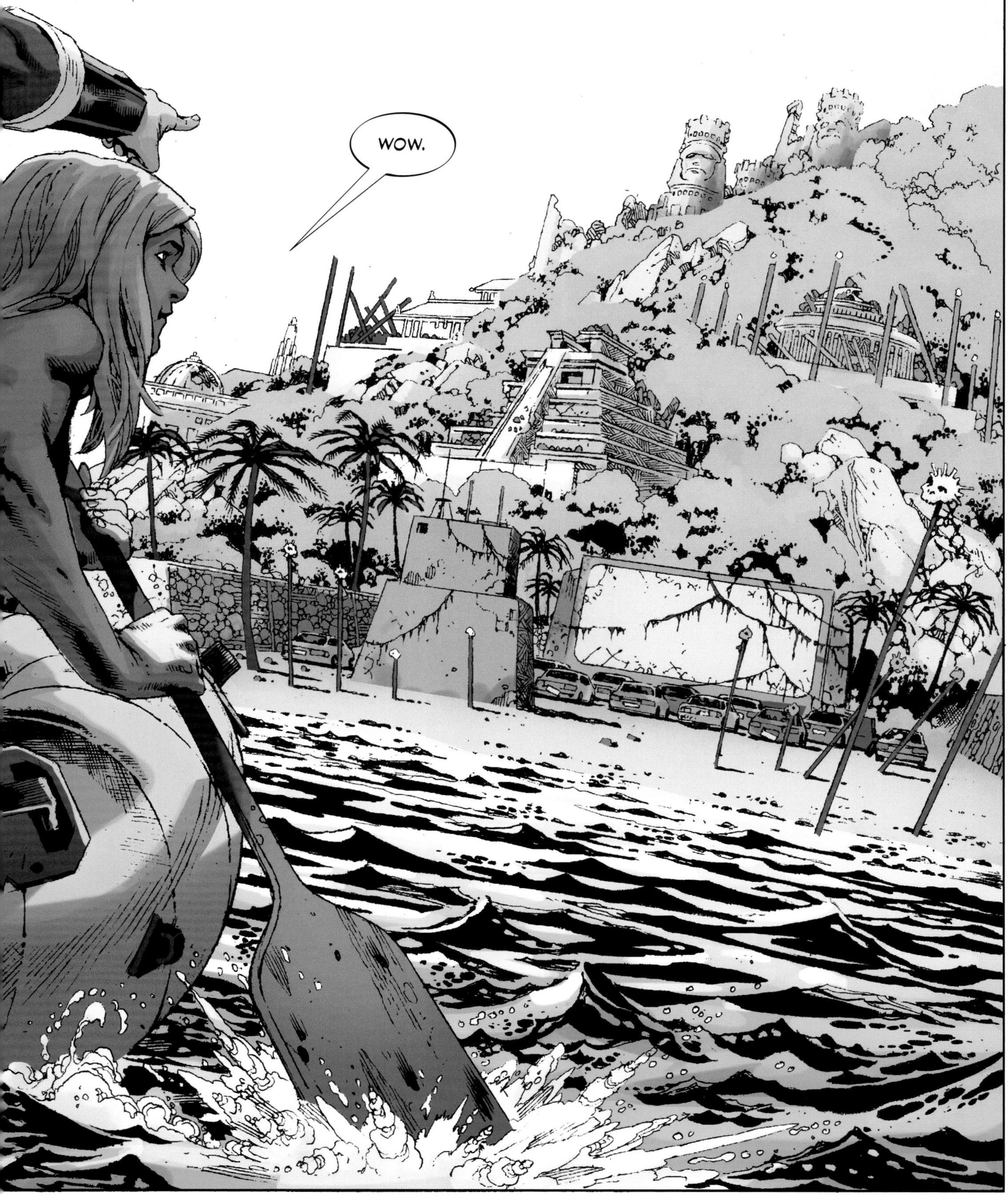

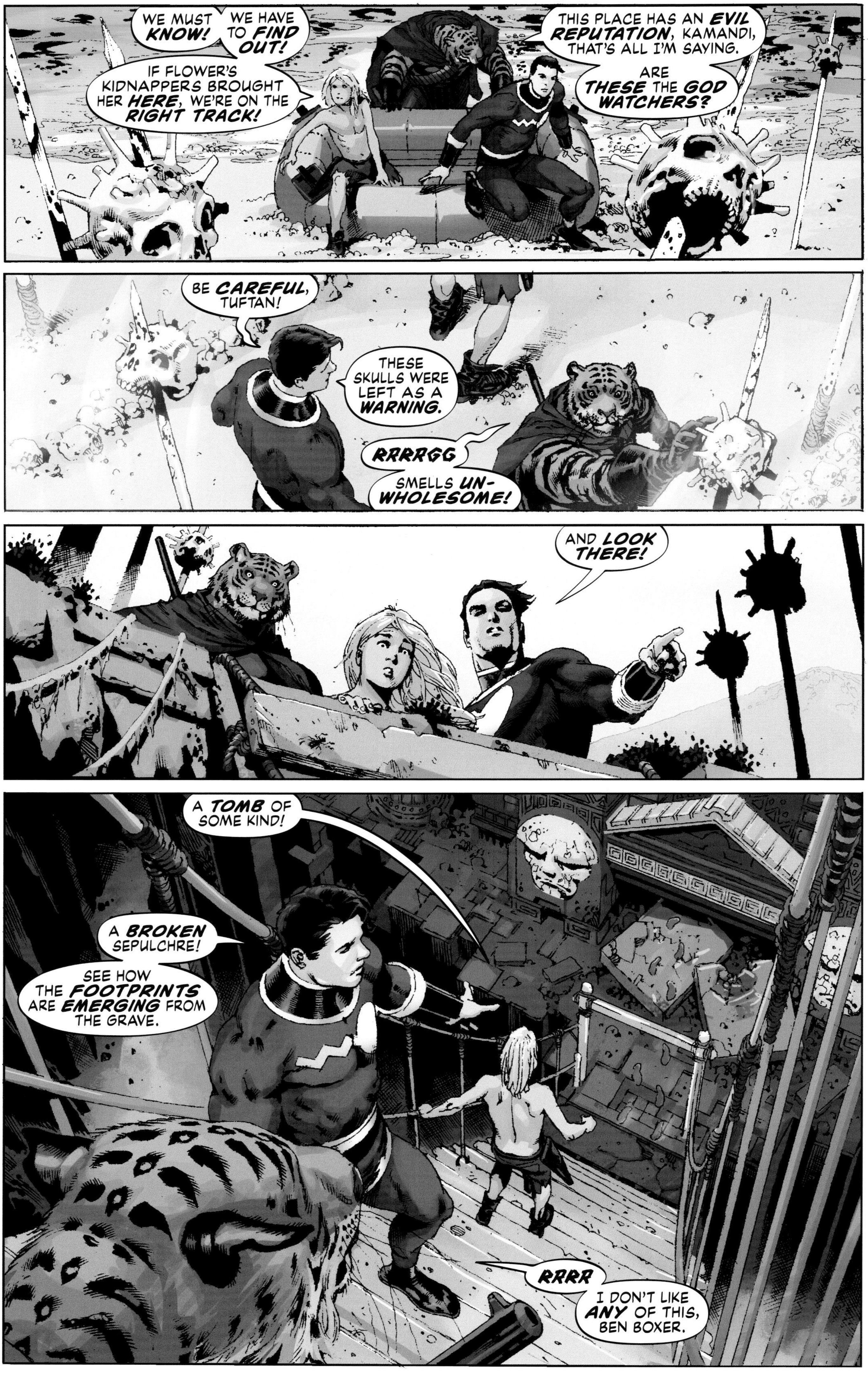
WE MUST KNOW!
WE HAVE TO FIND OUT!
IF FLOWER'S KIDNAPPERS BROUGHT HER HERE, WE'RE ON THE RIGHT TRACK!
THIS PLACE HAS AN EVIL REPUTATION, KAMANDI, THAT'S ALL I'M SAYING.
ARE THESE THE GOD WATCHERS?
BE CAREFUL, TUFTAN!
THESE SKULLS WERE LEFT AS A WARNING.
RRRRGG
SMELLS UN-WHOLESOME!
AND LOOK THERE!
A TOMB OF SOME KIND!
A BROKEN SEPULCHRE!
SEE HOW THE FOOTPRINTS ARE EMERGING FROM THE GRAVE.
RRRR
I DON'T LIKE ANY OF THIS, BEN BOXER.

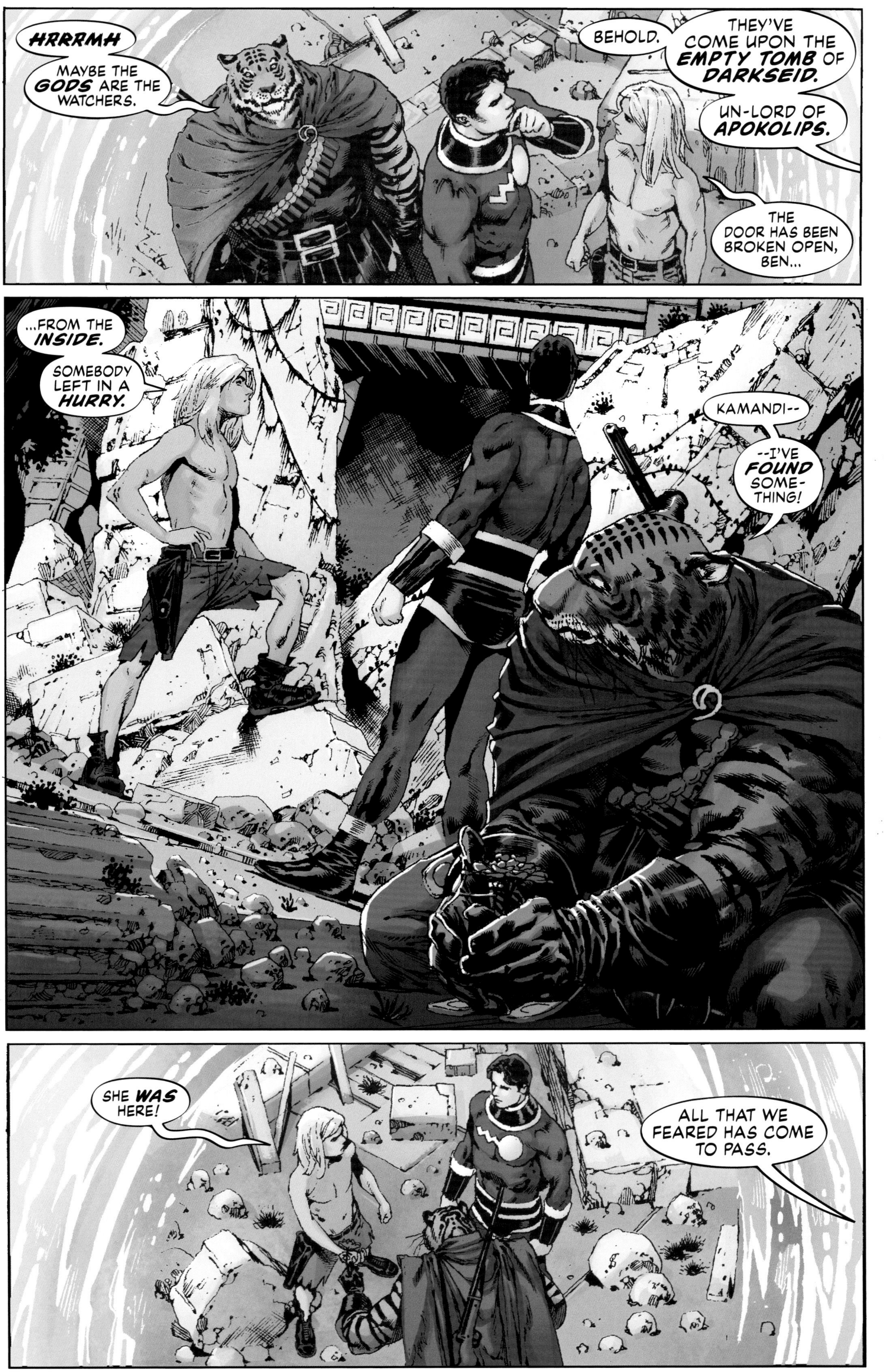
HRRRMH
MAYBE THE GODS ARE THE WATCHERS.
BEHOLD.
THEY'VE COME UPON THE EMPTY TOMB OF DARKSEID.
UN-LORD OF APOKOLIPS.
THE DOOR HAS BEEN BROKEN OPEN, BEN...
...FROM THE INSIDE.
SOMEBODY LEFT IN A HURRY.
KAMANDI--
--I'VE FOUND SOME-THING!
SHE WAS HERE!
ALL THAT WE FEARED HAS COME TO PASS.

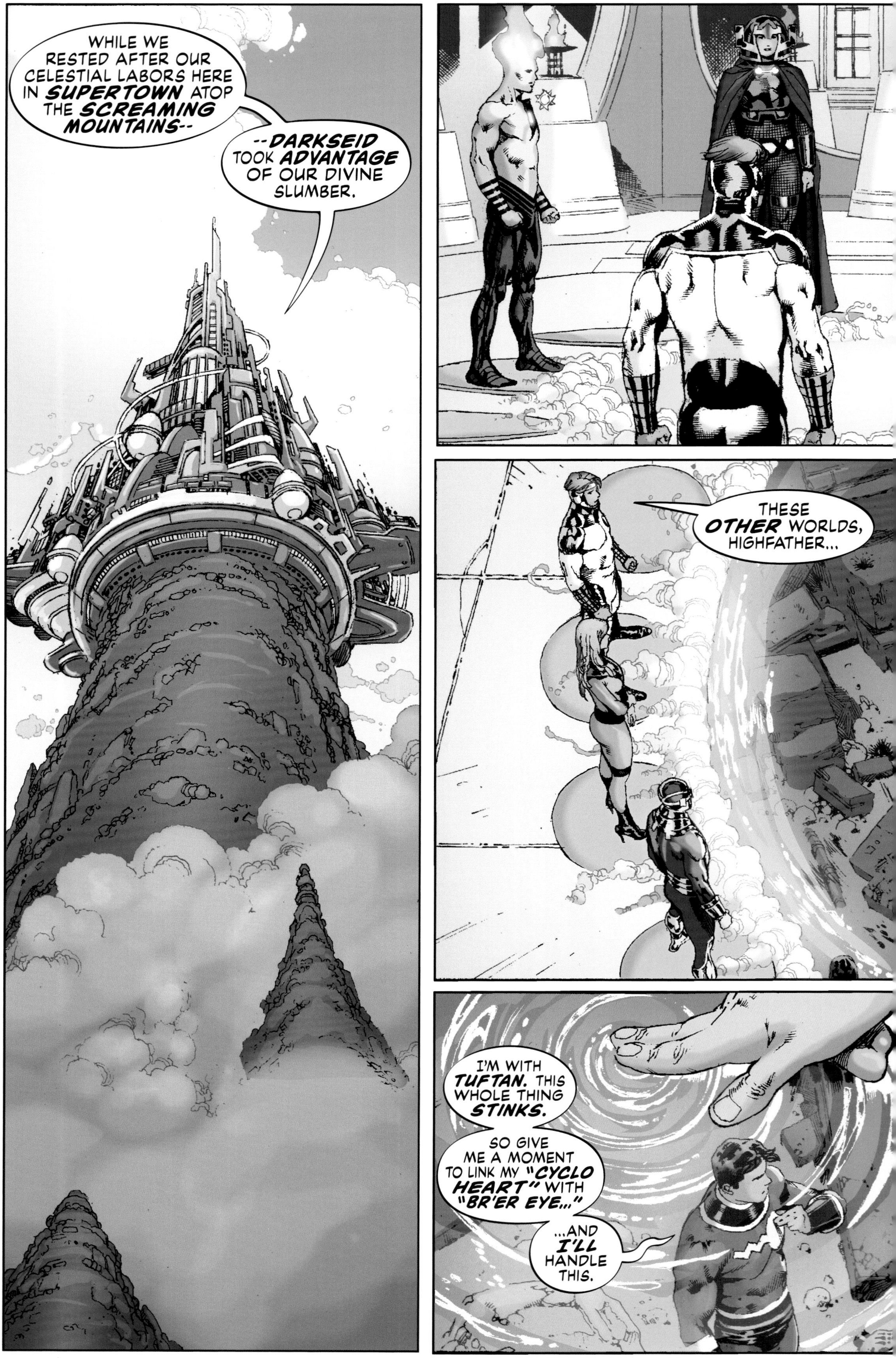

WHILE WE RESTED AFTER OUR CELESTIAL LABORS HERE IN SUPERTOWN ATOP THE SCREAMING MOUNTAINS--
--DARKSEID TOOK ADVANTAGE OF OUR DIVINE SLUMBER.
THESE OTHER WORLDS, HIGHFATHER...
I'M WITH TUFTAN. THIS WHOLE THING STINKS.
SO GIVE ME A MOMENT TO LINK MY "CYCLO HEART" WITH "BR'ER EYE..."
...AND I'LL HANDLE THIS.

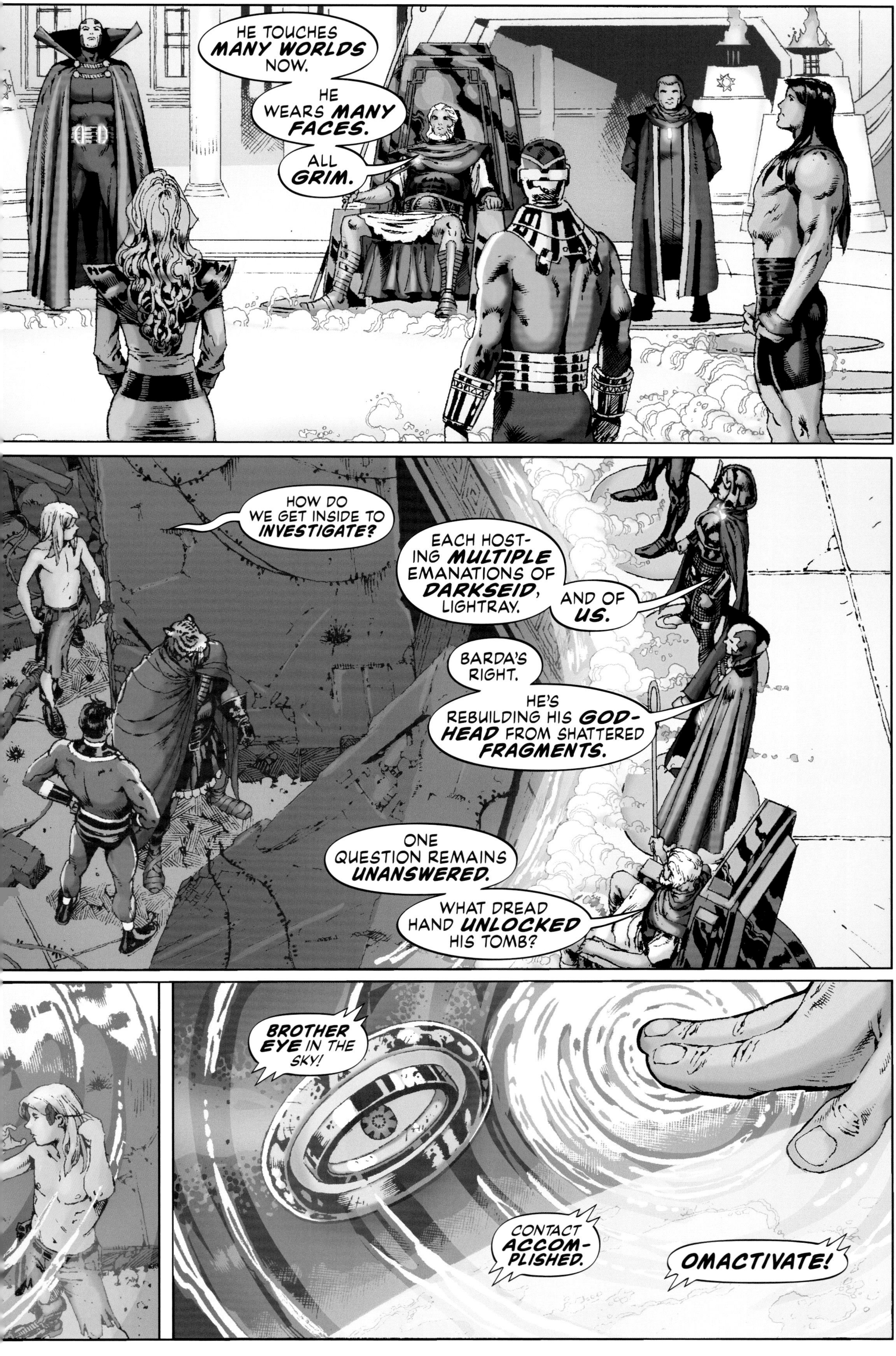
HE TOUCHES MANY WORLDS NOW.
HE WEARS MANY FACES.
ALL GRIM.
HOW DO WE GET INSIDE TO INVESTIGATE?
EACH HOSTING MULTIPLE EMANATIONS OF DARKSEID, LIGHTRAY.
AND OF US.
BARDA'S RIGHT.
HE'S REBUILDING HIS GODHEAD FROM SHATTERED FRAGMENTS.
ONE QUESTION REMAINS UNANSWERED.
WHAT DREAD HAND UNLOCKED HIS TOMB?
BROTHER EYE IN THE SKY!
CONTACT ACCOMPLISHED.
OMACTIVATE!

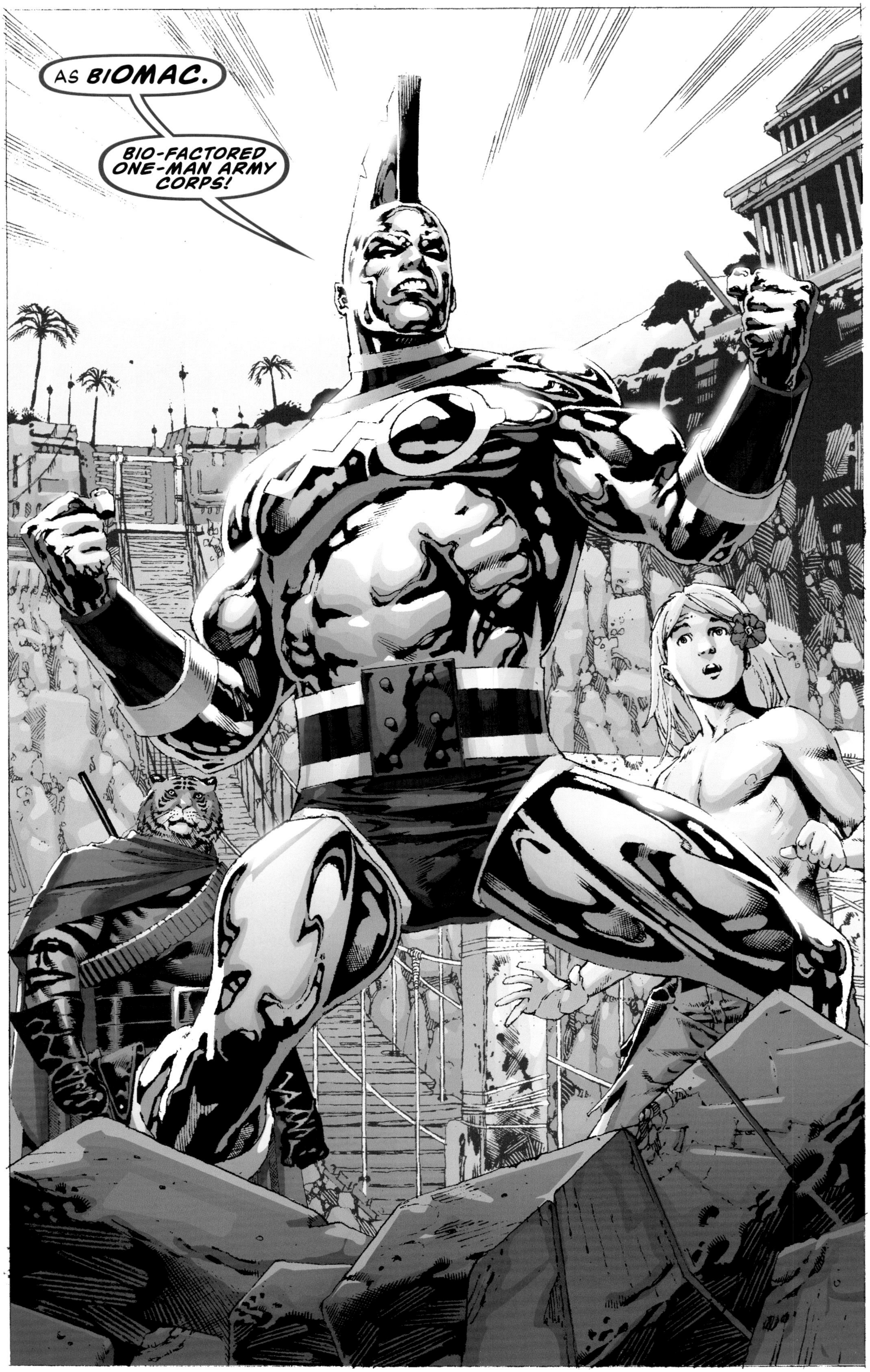
AS BIOMAC.
BIO-FACTORED ONE-MAN ARMY CORPS!

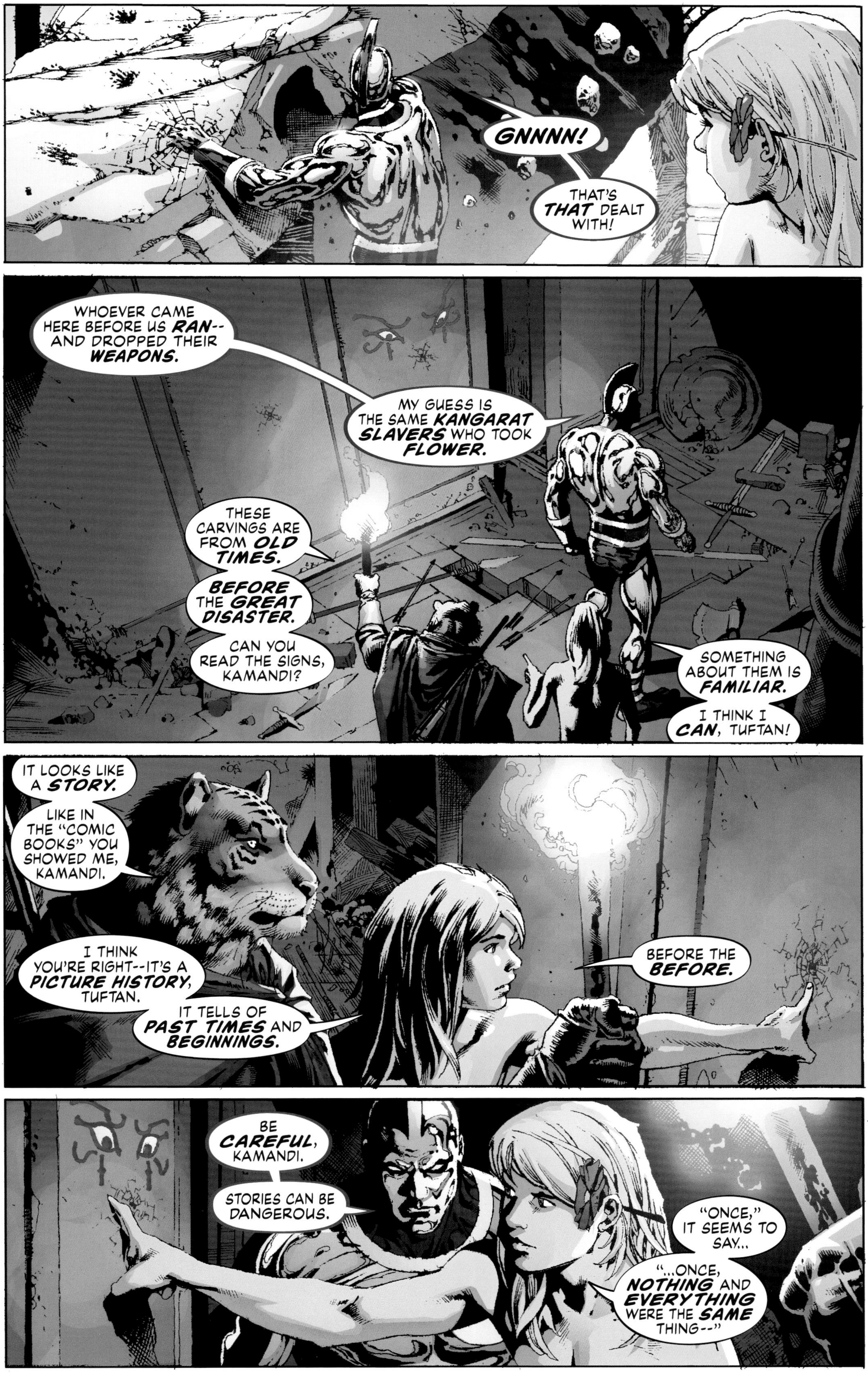
GNNNN!
THAT'S THAT DEALT WITH!
WHOEVER CAME HERE BEFORE US RAN-- AND DROPPED THEIR WEAPONS.
MY GUESS IS THE SAME KANGARAT SLAVERS WHO TOOK FLOWER.
THESE CARVINGS ARE FROM OLD TIMES.
BEFORE THE GREAT DISASTER.
CAN YOU READ THE SIGNS, KAMANDI?
SOMETHING ABOUT THEM IS FAMILIAR.
I THINK I CAN, TUFTAN!
IT LOOKS LIKE A STORY.
LIKE IN THE "COMIC BOOKS" YOU SHOWED ME, KAMANDI.
I THINK YOU'RE RIGHT--IT'S A PICTURE HISTORY, TUFTAN.
IT TELLS OF PAST TIMES AND BEGINNINGS.
BEFORE THE BEFORE.
BE CAREFUL, KAMANDI.
STORIES CAN BE DANGEROUS.
"ONCE," IT SEEMS TO SAY...
"...ONCE, NOTHING AND EVERYTHING WERE THE SAME THING--"

And Then!

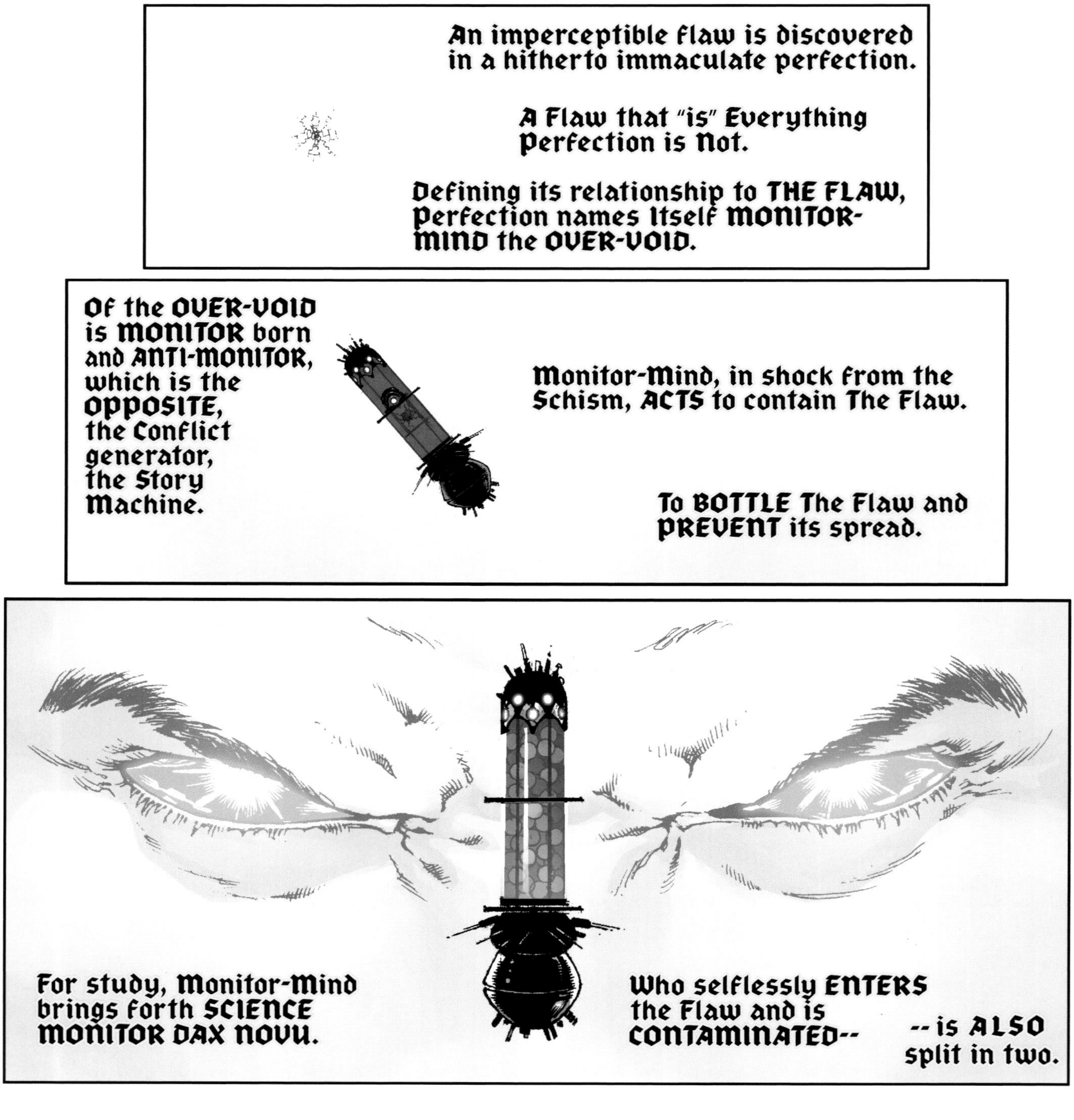

An imperceptible flaw is discovered in a hitherto immaculate perfection.
A Flaw that "is" Everything Perfection is Not.
Defining its relationship to THE FLAW, Perfection names Itself MONITOR-MIND the OVER-VOID.
Of the OVER-VOID is MONITOR born and ANTI-MONITOR, which is the OPPOSITE, the Conflict generator, the Story Machine.
Monitor-Mind, in shock from the Schism, ACTS to contain The Flaw.
To BOTTLE The Flaw and PREVENT its spread.
For study, Monitor-Mind brings forth SCIENCE MONITOR DAX NOVU.
Who selflessly ENTERS the Flaw and is CONTAMINATED--
--is ALSO split in two.

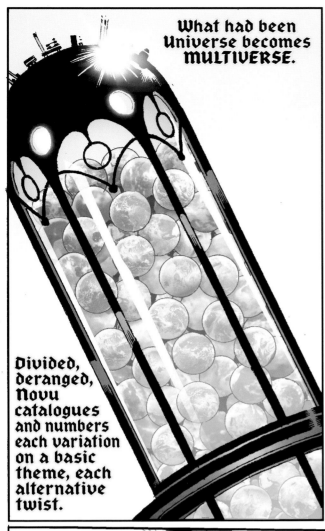

What had been Universe becomes MULTIVERSE.

Divided, deranged, Novu catalogues and numbers each variation on a basic theme, each alternative twist.

But Novu looks too close, too deep.

Infected by activity and process, by the endless play of matter and narrative--

--Novu is blinded, corrupted by the Flaw's lightning dazzle.

"AND SO BEGINS ALL THINGS...

"...WITH A *FLASH*..."

YOU MENTIONED OLD *COMIC BOOKS*.

NOW WHY WOULD *THESE* BE *HERE*?

COINCIDENCE, KAMANDI?

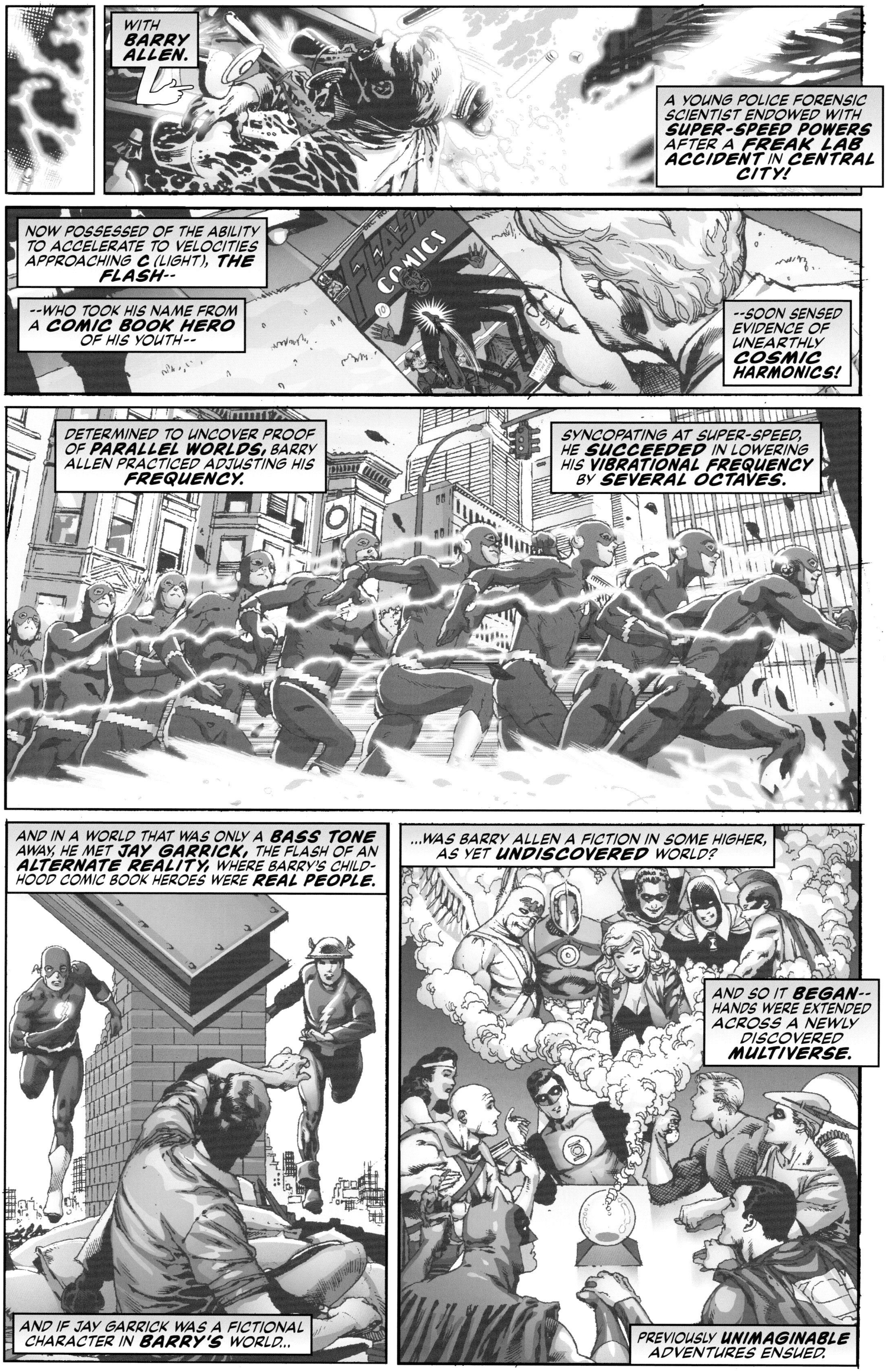
WITH BARRY ALLEN.
A YOUNG POLICE FORENSIC SCIENTIST ENDOWED WITH SUPER-SPEED POWERS AFTER A FREAK LAB ACCIDENT IN CENTRAL CITY!
NOW POSSESSED OF THE ABILITY TO ACCELERATE TO VELOCITIES APPROACHING C (LIGHT), THE FLASH--
--WHO TOOK HIS NAME FROM A COMIC BOOK HERO OF HIS YOUTH--
FLASH COMICS
--SOON SENSED EVIDENCE OF UNEARTHLY COSMIC HARMONICS!
DETERMINED TO UNCOVER PROOF OF PARALLEL WORLDS, BARRY ALLEN PRACTICED ADJUSTING HIS FREQUENCY.
SYNCOPATING AT SUPER-SPEED, HE SUCCEEDED IN LOWERING HIS VIBRATIONAL FREQUENCY BY SEVERAL OCTAVES.
AND IN A WORLD THAT WAS ONLY A BASS TONE AWAY, HE MET JAY GARRICK, THE FLASH OF AN ALTERNATE REALITY, WHERE BARRY'S CHILDHOOD COMIC BOOK HEROES WERE REAL PEOPLE.
AND IF JAY GARRICK WAS A FICTIONAL CHARACTER IN BARRY'S WORLD...
...WAS BARRY ALLEN A FICTION IN SOME HIGHER, AS YET UNDISCOVERED WORLD?
AND SO IT BEGAN--HANDS WERE EXTENDED ACROSS A NEWLY DISCOVERED MULTIVERSE.
PREVIOUSLY UNIMAGINABLE ADVENTURES ENSUED.

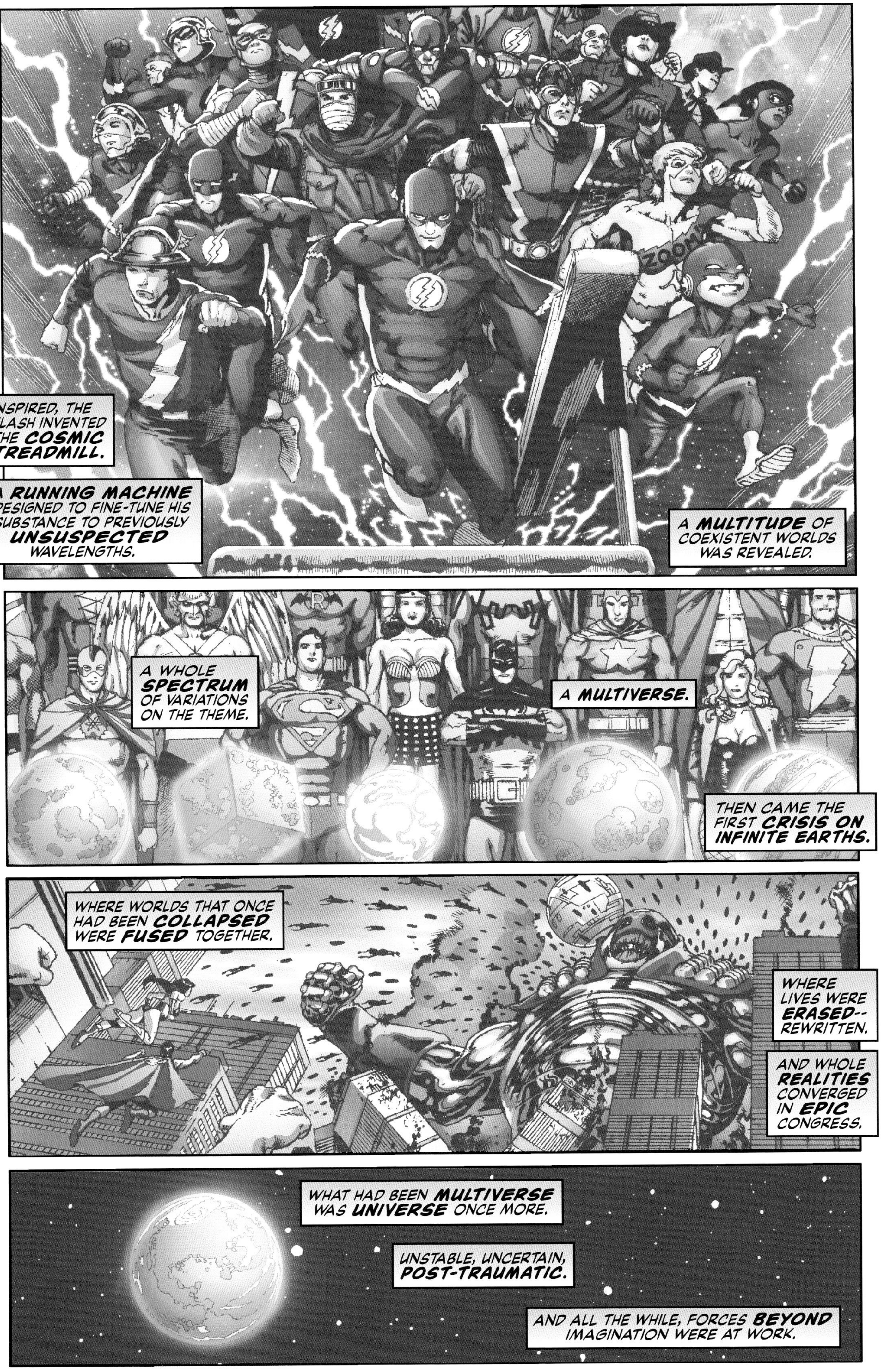
INSPIRED, THE FLASH INVENTED THE COSMIC TREADMILL.
A RUNNING MACHINE DESIGNED TO FINE-TUNE HIS SUBSTANCE TO PREVIOUSLY UNSUSPECTED WAVELENGTHS.
ZOOM
A MULTITUDE OF COEXISTENT WORLDS WAS REVEALED.
A WHOLE SPECTRUM OF VARIATIONS ON THE THEME.
A MULTIVERSE.
THEN CAME THE FIRST CRISIS ON INFINITE EARTHS.
WHERE WORLDS THAT ONCE HAD BEEN COLLAPSED WERE FUSED TOGETHER.
WHERE LIVES WERE ERASED--REWRITTEN.
AND WHOLE REALITIES CONVERGED IN EPIC CONGRESS.
WHAT HAD BEEN MULTIVERSE WAS UNIVERSE ONCE MORE.
UNSTABLE, UNCERTAIN, POST-TRAUMATIC.
AND ALL THE WHILE, FORCES BEYOND IMAGINATION WERE AT WORK.

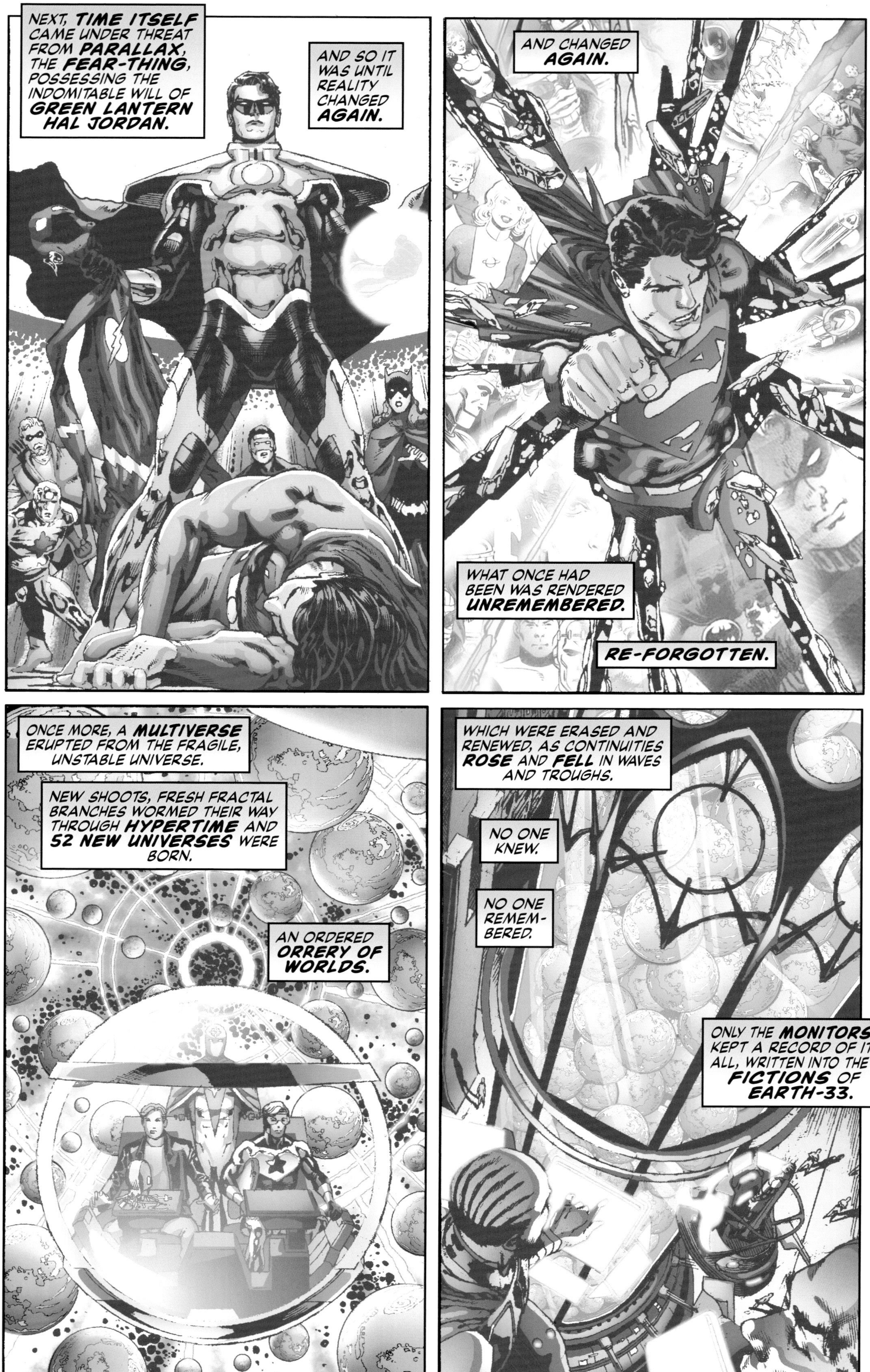
NEXT, TIME ITSELF CAME UNDER THREAT FROM PARALLAX, THE FEAR-THING, POSSESSING THE INDOMITABLE WILL OF GREEN LANTERN HAL JORDAN.
AND SO IT WAS UNTIL REALITY CHANGED AGAIN.
AND CHANGED AGAIN.
WHAT ONCE HAD BEEN WAS RENDERED UNREMEMBERED.
RE-FORGOTTEN.
ONCE MORE, A MULTIVERSE ERUPTED FROM THE FRAGILE, UNSTABLE UNIVERSE.
NEW SHOOTS, FRESH FRACTAL BRANCHES WORMED THEIR WAY THROUGH HYPERTIME AND 52 NEW UNIVERSES WERE BORN.
AN ORDERED ORRERY OF WORLDS.
WHICH WERE ERASED AND RENEWED, AS CONTINUITIES ROSE AND FELL IN WAVES AND TROUGHS.
NO ONE KNEW.
NO ONE REMEM- BERED.
ONLY THE MONITORS KEPT A RECORD OF IT ALL, WRITTEN INTO THE FICTIONS OF EARTH-33.

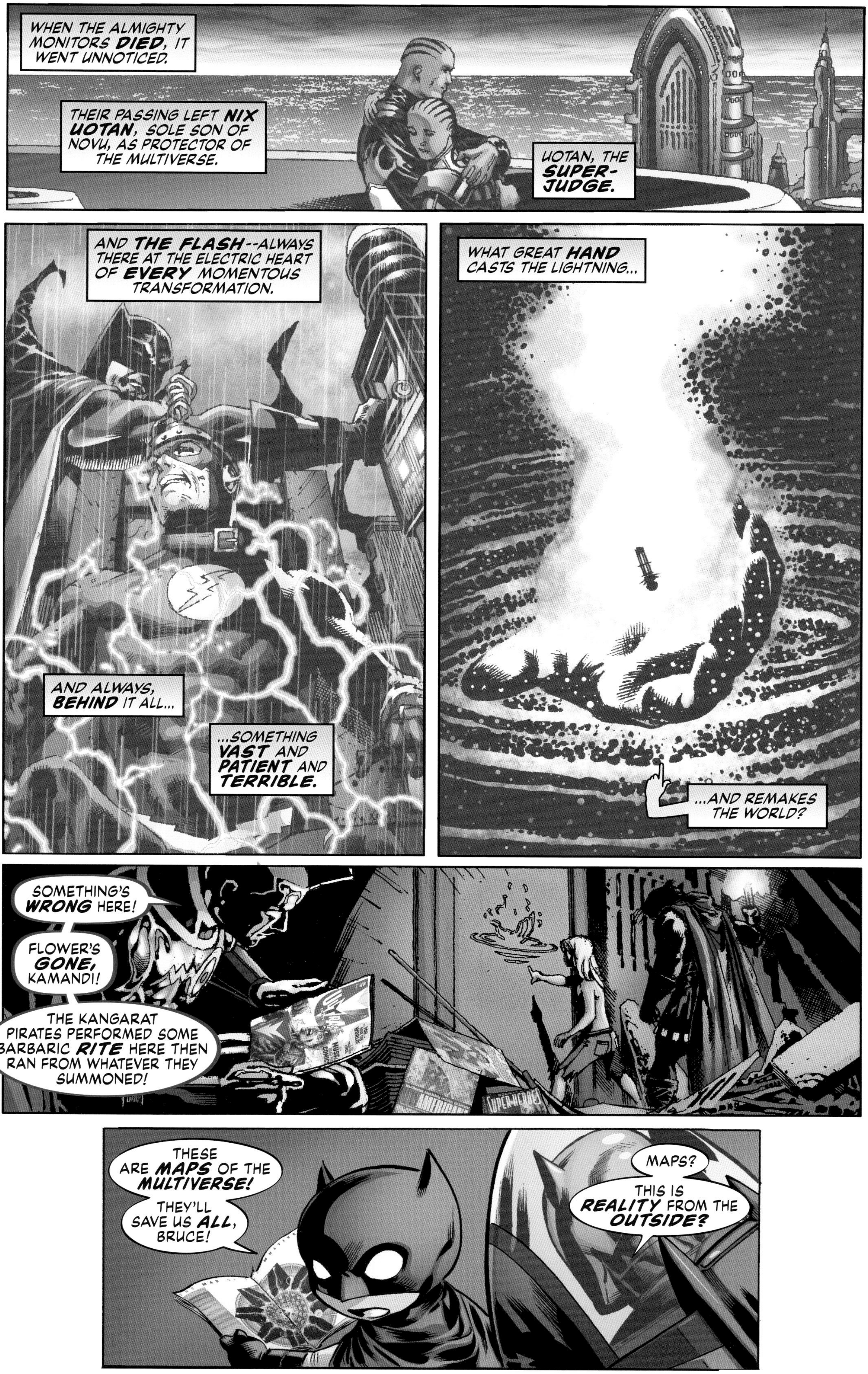

WHEN THE ALMIGHTY MONITORS DIED, IT WENT UNNOTICED.
THEIR PASSING LEFT NIX UOTAN, SOLE SON OF NOVU, AS PROTECTOR OF THE MULTIVERSE.
UOTAN, THE SUPER-JUDGE.
AND THE FLASH--ALWAYS THERE AT THE ELECTRIC HEART OF EVERY MOMENTOUS TRANSFORMATION.
AND ALWAYS, BEHIND IT ALL...
...SOMETHING VAST AND PATIENT AND TERRIBLE.
WHAT GREAT HAND CASTS THE LIGHTNING...
...AND REMAKES THE WORLD?
SOMETHING'S WRONG HERE!
FLOWER'S GONE, KAMANDI!
THE KANGARAT PIRATES PERFORMED SOME BARBARIC RITE HERE THEN RAN FROM WHATEVER THEY SUMMONED!
THESE ARE MAPS OF THE MULTIVERSE!
THEY'LL SAVE US ALL, BRUCE!
MAPS?
THIS IS REALITY FROM THE OUTSIDE?

THE MAP OF T

THE MULTIVERSAL VIBRATIONAL REALMS

SOURCE WALL

Here is the Limit even to Thought. Beyond lies only Monitor-mind, The Source and the Unknowable.

MONITOR SPHERE

Dwelling place of the mighty Monitor race — once countless in number, the 52 Monitors that remained after the CRISIS event were each tasked with the preservation and study of a separate universe.

LIMBO

Home of the Lost and Forgotten of the Orrery, Limbo is the furthest edge of the manifest DC universe. This is where matter and memory break down.

SPHERE OF THE GODS

From the heights of the Skyland Pantheons to the prison depths of the Underworld, this is the great realm of Archetypal Powers and Intelligences inhabited by Gods and New Gods, Demons, Angels and the Endless.

DREAM

On the borderlands is the magical realm of Morpheus the Dream-King, incorporating the Halls of The Endless, the Courts of Faerie and the Twelve Houses of Gemworld. Home to Oberon, Titania, Amethyst, Santa Claus and the Easter Bunny.

HEAVEN

The Silver City. The Word of the Voice. Home of the Spectre, Zauriel and the Guardian Angel Hosts of the Pax Dei — The Bull Host, The Eagle Host, The Lion Host and the Host of Adam.

NEW GENESIS

Sunlit lordly New Genesis is the proud home of the New Gods and the young Forever People. The floating city of Supertown is the dwelling place of Highfather, Orion, Lightray, Avia, Big Barda, Scott Free and others.

SKYLAND

Home of the Shining Ones, the Old Gods of Thunder and Lightning, Love and War and Death. Here is Asgard, Olympus, and the Throne of Zeus. The Pantheons of Celts, Mayans, the Divine Bureaucracies of China, and the Gods of Oceania, Mesopotamia and Egypt, the Loa and the Elohim are all gathered here, each with a peak of its own.

NIGHTMARE

The creepy-crawly Shadow Side of Morpheus's domain. Here is the Goblin Market where nothing is real. The Land of Nightshades. Home to the Bogeyman and the Corinthian, haunt of Witches, Yeth Hounds and Bad Dreams.

HELL

Known to some as Sheol, or Jigoku, the burning iron Place of Torment is home to Neron, Belial, Trigon, Azazel, Abnegazar, Rath, Ghast and the Demon Etrigan — high on a list of a legion of fiends. Here are the Djinns and the Fallen Angels, and the Haters of Humanity, waiting...

APOKOLIPS

The fiery planetasm ruled with the iron fist of the ultimate tyrant, Darkseid of the New Gods, and his cruel acolytes — Desaad the Torture God, Granny Goodness, Glorious Godfrey, Kalibak and many, many others.

UNDERWORLD

Here is Hades, Annwn, the realm of Pluto and the Throne of Erishkagal, the Land of No Return. Known also as The Phantom Zone, this gloomy prison of shades and formless shadows plays host to the criminals of the planet Krypton — General Zod, Ursa the She-Devil, Xadu the Phantom King and many others.

WONDERWORLD

Orbiting Creation itself at unimaginable velocities, Wonderworld is the "Worldquarters" of the long-lost Theocracy, a team of stupendous primal superheroes.

SPEED FORCE WALL

The Speed Force Wall is otherwise known to the denizens of the Orrery as the Speed of Light. It is only a limit to matter.

THE FREQUENCIES OF KWYZZ

Radio universe, home to KRAKKL the Defender.

ORRERY OF WORLDS

52 'brane universes vibrating in the same space, all at different frequencies, within the all-enclosing Bulk, otherwise known as Bleedspace. Four Bleed Siphons have been drilled in from the Monitor Sphere to the Orrery, to permit harvest of the miracle Ultramenstruum fluid.

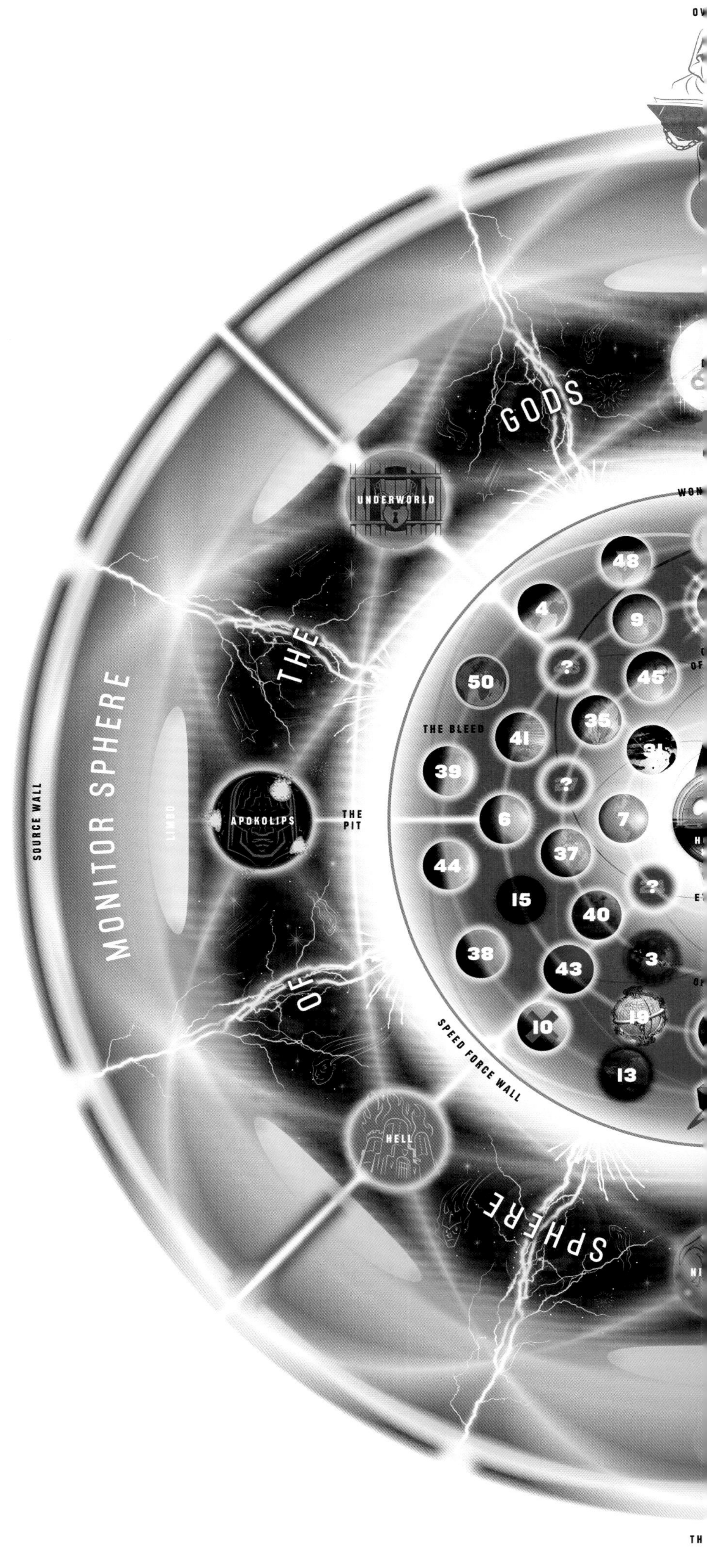

SOURCE WALL
MONITOR SPHERE
LIMBO
THE
GODS
UNDERWORLD
APOKOLIPS
THE PIT
OF
SPHERE
HELL
THE BLEED
SPEED FORCE WALL
48
4
9
45
50
35
41
39
6
7
37
44
15
40
38
43
3
10
13

E MULTIVERSE

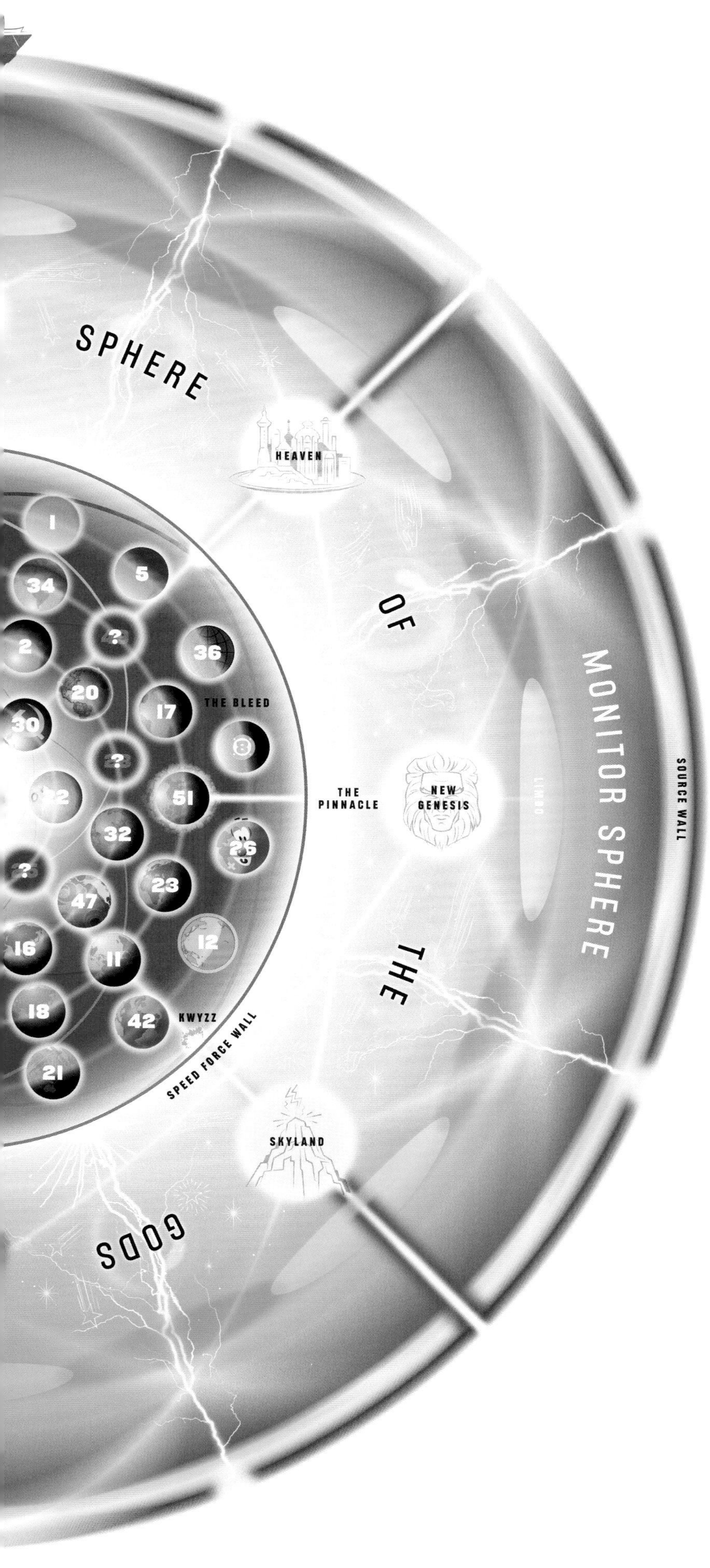

SPHERE OF THE GODS
HEAVEN
NEW GENESIS
SKYLAND
THE PINNACLE
MONITOR SPHERE
SOURCE WALL
LIMBO
THE BLEED
SPEED FORCE WALL
KWYZZ
1
5
34
?
2
36
20
17
30
?
8
22
51
32
26
?
23
47
12
16
11
18
42
21

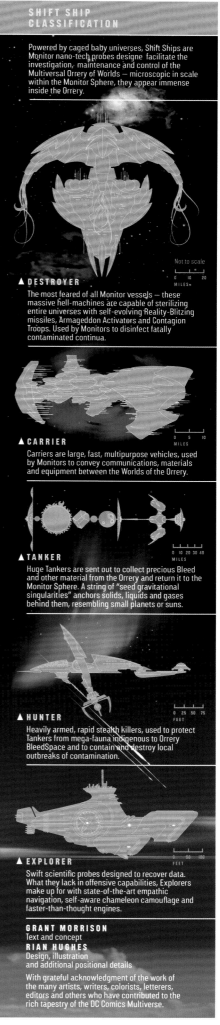

SHIFT SHIP CLASSIFICATION

Powered by caged baby universes, Shift Ships are Monitor nano-tech probes designe facilitate the investigation, maintenance and control of the Multiversal Orrery of Worlds — microscopic in scale within the Monitor Sphere, they appear immense inside the Orrery.

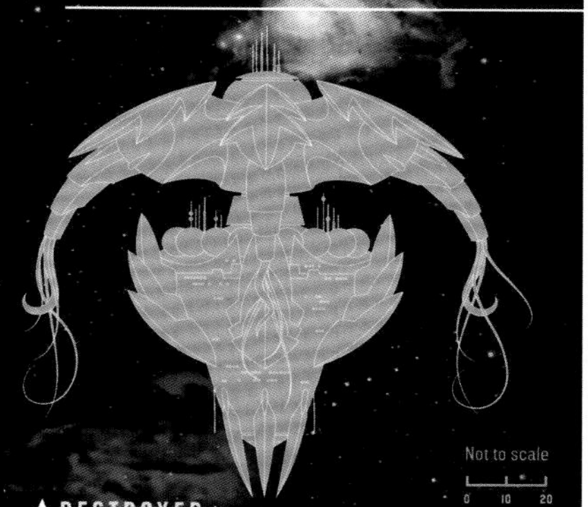

Not to scale
0 10 20
MILES

▲ DESTROYER

The most feared of all Monitor vessels — these massive hell-machines are capable of sterilizing entire universes with self-evolving Reality-Blitzing missiles, Armageddon Activators and Contagion Troops. Used by Monitors to disinfect fatally contaminated continua.

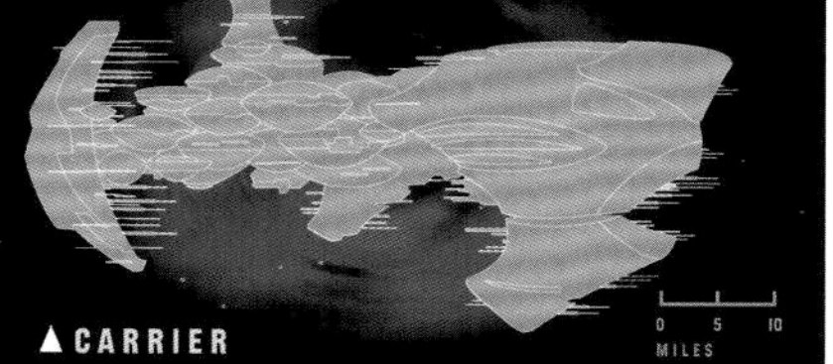

0 5 10
MILES

▲ CARRIER

Carriers are large, fast, multipurpose vehicles, used by Monitors to convey communications, materials and equipment between the Worlds of the Orrery.

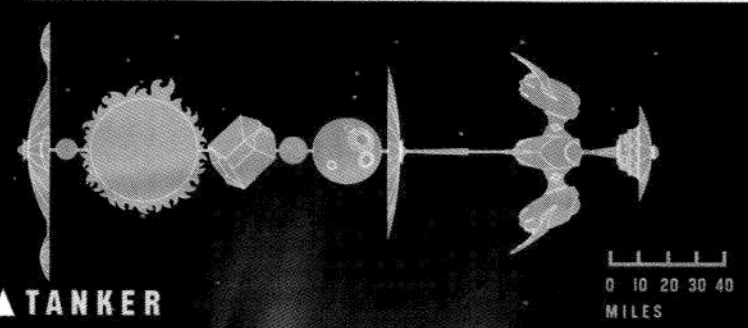

0 10 20 30 40
MILES

▲ TANKER

Huge Tankers are sent out to collect precious Bleed and other material from the Orrery and return it to the Monitor Sphere. A string of "seed gravitational singularities" anchors solids, liquids and gases behind them, resembling small planets or suns.

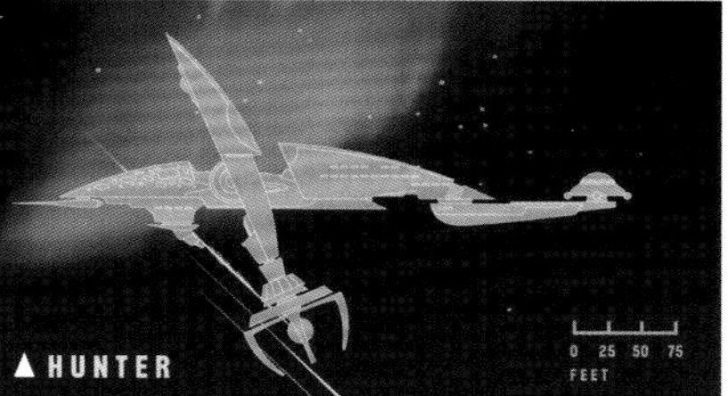

0 25 50 75
FEET

▲ HUNTER

Heavily armed, rapid stealth killers, used to protect Tankers from mega-fauna indigenous to Orrery BleedSpace and to contain and destroy local outbreaks of contamination.

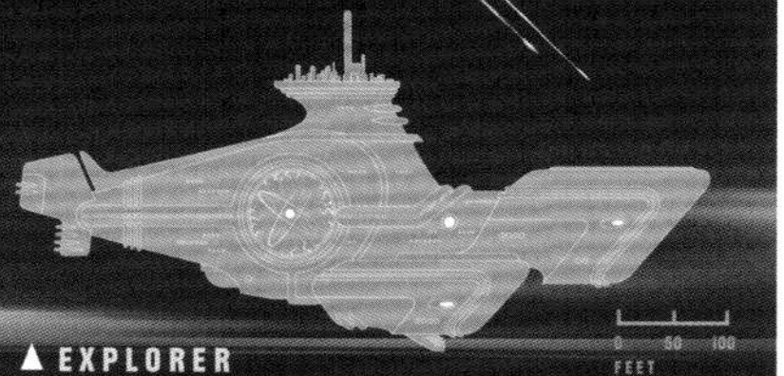

0 50 100
FEET

▲ EXPLORER

Swift scientific probes designed to recover data. What they lack in offensive capabilities, Explorers make up for with state-of-the-art empathic navigation, self-aware chameleon camouflage and faster-than-thought engines.

GRANT MORRISON
Text and concept
RIAN HUGHES
Design, illustration
and additional positional details

With grateful acknowledgment of the work of the many artists, writers, colorists, letterers, editors and others who have contributed to the rich tapestry of the DC Comics Multiverse.

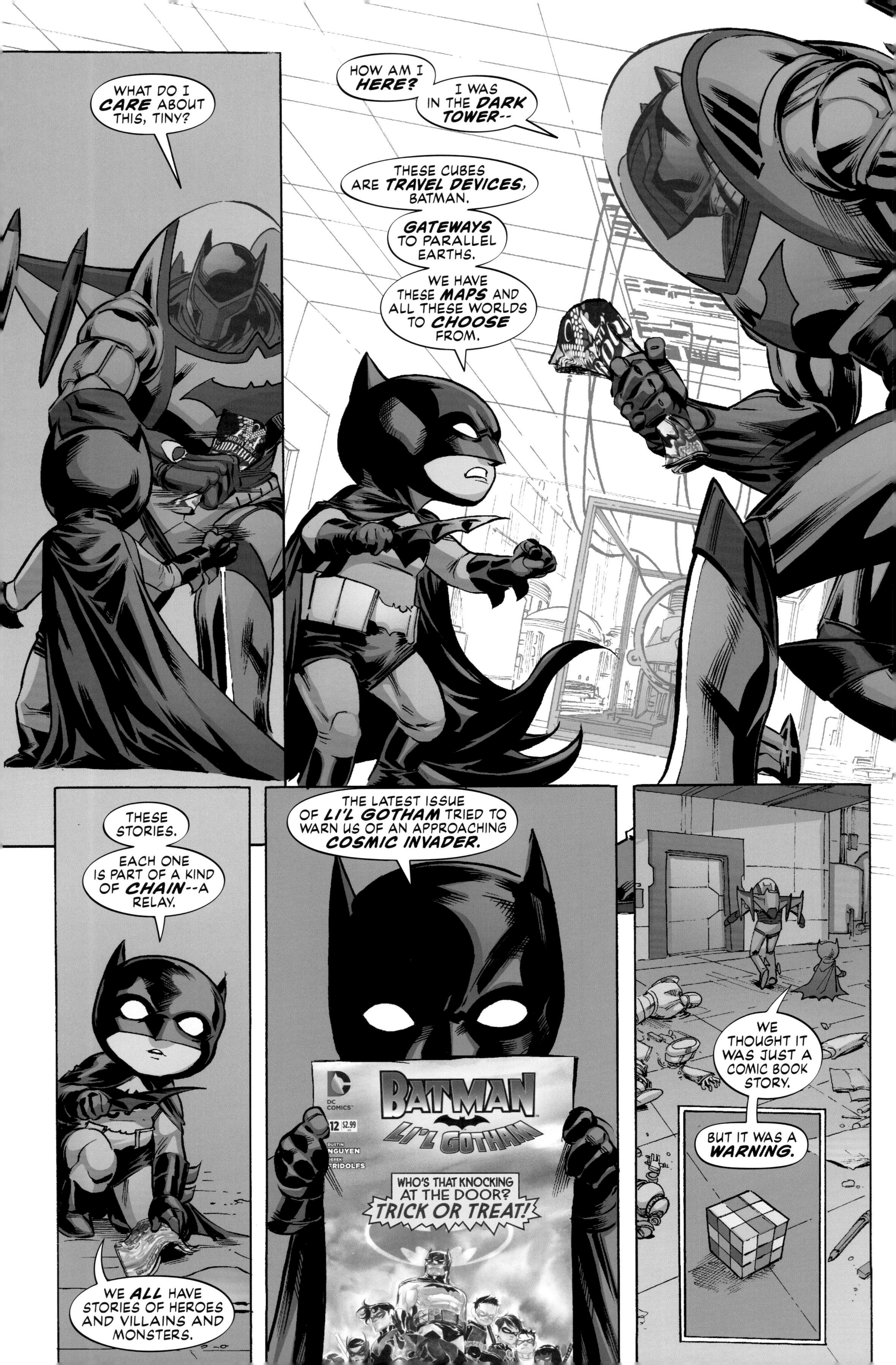
WHAT DO I CARE ABOUT THIS, TINY?
HOW AM I HERE?
I WAS IN THE DARK TOWER--
THESE CUBES ARE TRAVEL DEVICES, BATMAN.
GATEWAYS TO PARALLEL EARTHS.
WE HAVE THESE MAPS AND ALL THESE WORLDS TO CHOOSE FROM.
THESE STORIES.
EACH ONE IS PART OF A KIND OF CHAIN--A RELAY.
WE ALL HAVE STORIES OF HEROES AND VILLAINS AND MONSTERS.
THE LATEST ISSUE OF LI'L GOTHAM TRIED TO WARN US OF AN APPROACHING COSMIC INVADER.
DC COMICS
BATMAN
LI'L GOTHAM
12 $2.99
WHO'S THAT KNOCKING AT THE DOOR? TRICK OR TREAT!
WE THOUGHT IT WAS JUST A COMIC BOOK STORY.
BUT IT WAS A WARNING.

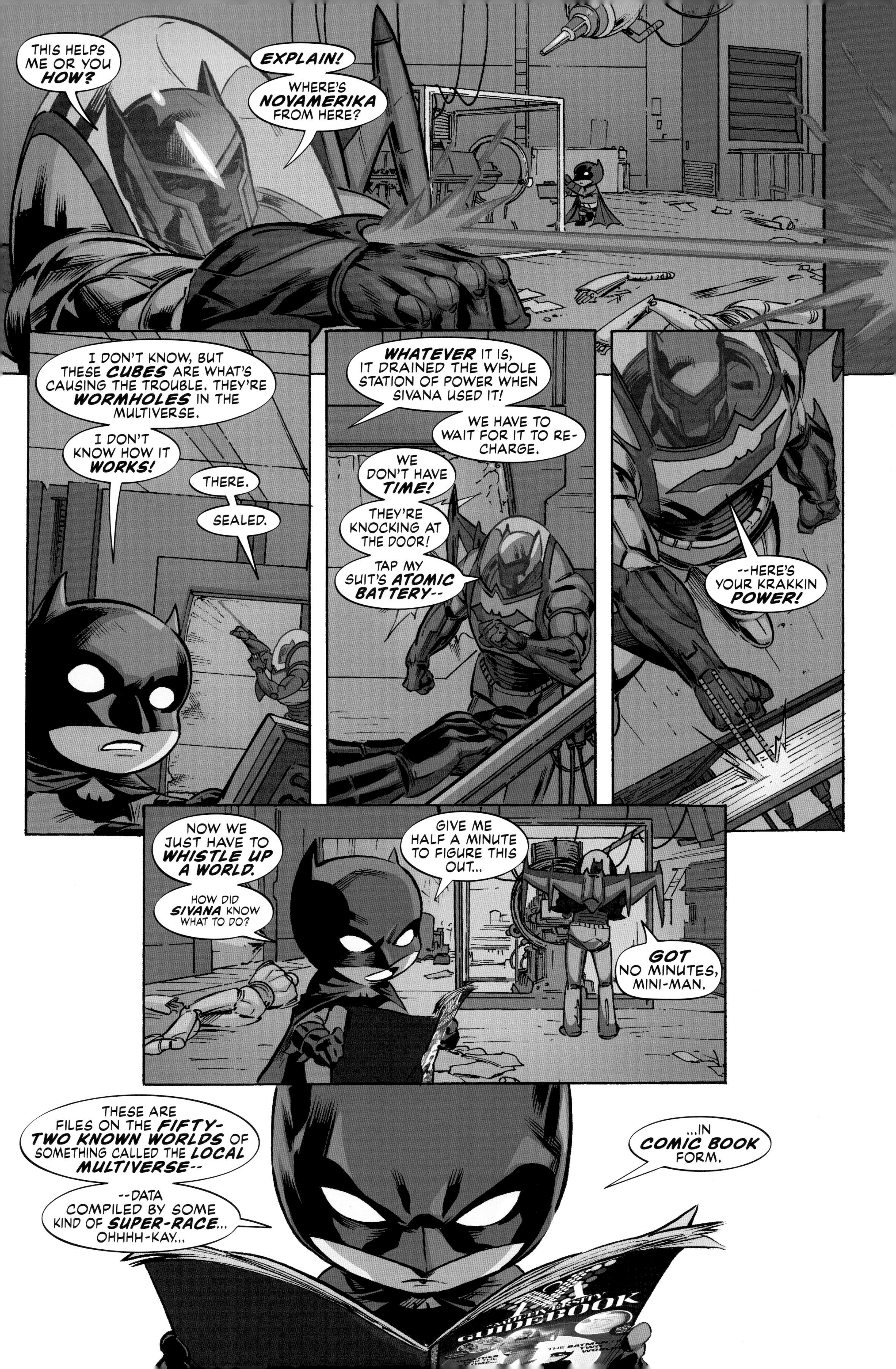

THIS HELPS ME OR YOU HOW?
EXPLAIN! WHERE'S NOVAMERIKA FROM HERE?
I DON'T KNOW, BUT THESE CUBES ARE WHAT'S CAUSING THE TROUBLE. THEY'RE WORMHOLES IN THE MULTIVERSE.
I DON'T KNOW HOW IT WORKS!
THERE.
SEALED.
WHATEVER IT IS, IT DRAINED THE WHOLE STATION OF POWER WHEN SIVANA USED IT!
WE HAVE TO WAIT FOR IT TO RE-CHARGE.
WE DON'T HAVE TIME!
THEY'RE KNOCKING AT THE DOOR!
TAP MY SUIT'S ATOMIC BATTERY--
--HERE'S YOUR KRAKKIN POWER!
NOW WE JUST HAVE TO WHISTLE UP A WORLD.
HOW DID SIVANA KNOW WHAT TO DO?
GIVE ME HALF A MINUTE TO FIGURE THIS OUT...
GOT NO MINUTES, MINI-MAN.
THESE ARE FILES ON THE FIFTY-TWO KNOWN WORLDS OF SOMETHING CALLED THE LOCAL MULTIVERSE--
--DATA COMPILED BY SOME KIND OF SUPER-RACE... OHHHH-KAY...
...IN COMIC BOOK FORM.
GUIDEBOOK

EARTH 0

Earth-0, also known as NEW EARTH, is the foundation stone of the Multiversal structure. It has survived several attacks, surgeries and reconstructions on the way to its current form. On Earth-0, the greatest young superheroes of the age are at the peak and pinnacle of their powers and achievements.

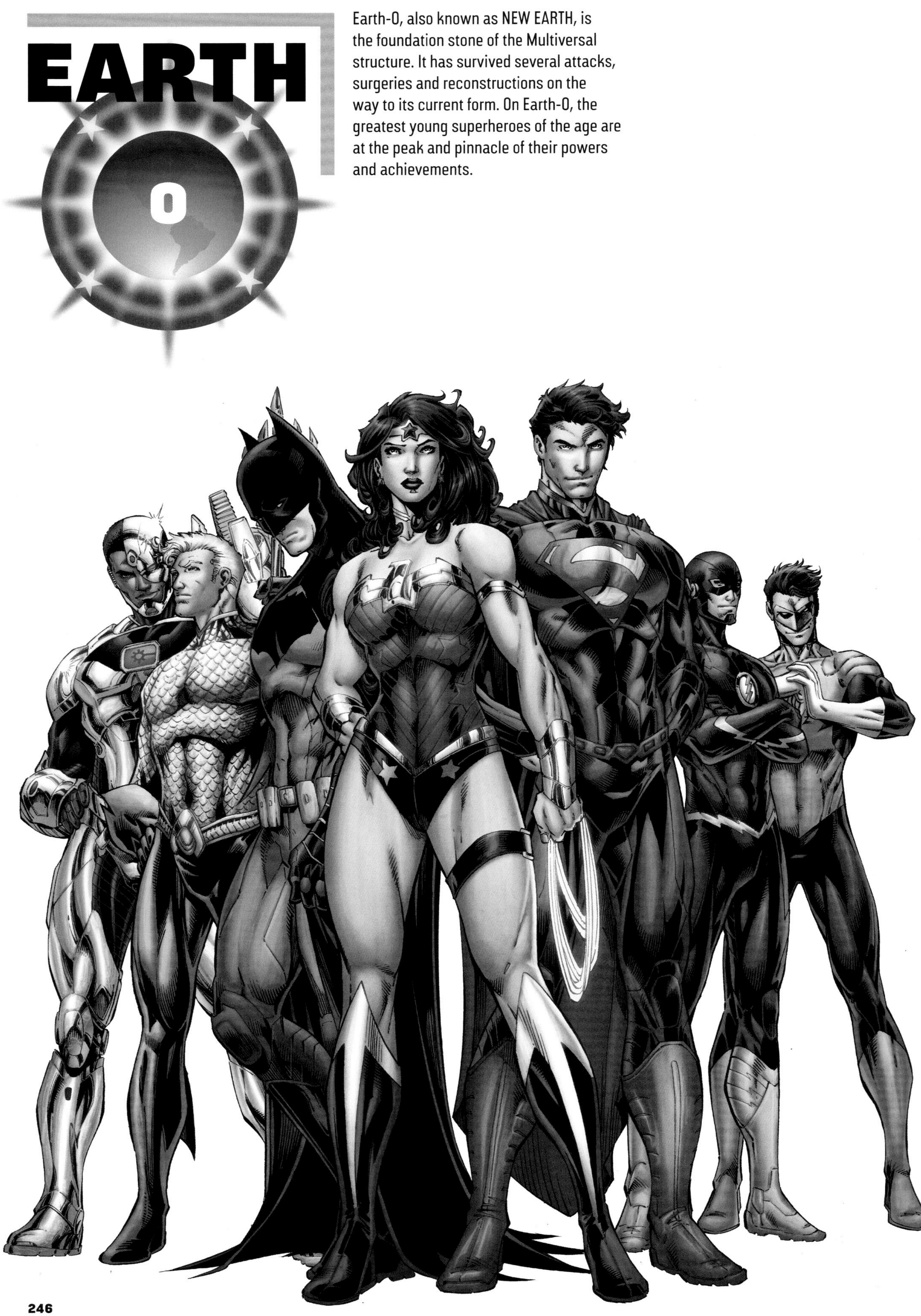

EARTH I

This freshly created Universe is still cooling and as yet unformed. Earth-I's known superbeings — SUPERMAN, BATMAN, WONDER WOMAN and the TEEN TITANS — are at the beginning of their careers. Time and space are still pliable, and nothing here is certain.

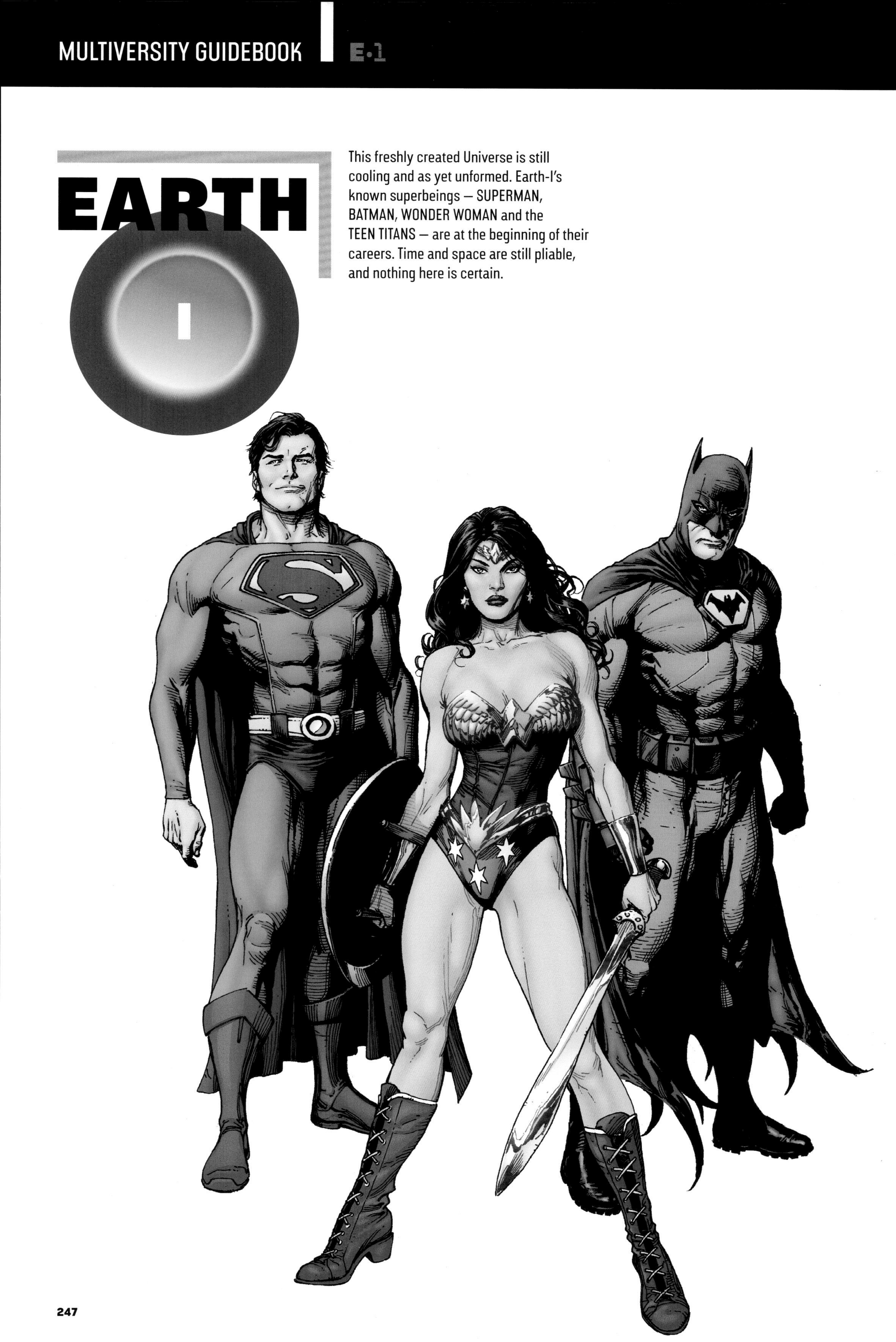

EARTH

2

Following the deaths of Superman, Batman and Wonder Woman in the War with the Great and Terrible Darkseid, a new generation of superheroes has emerged to continue the fight against immortal evil. This world includes a new BATMAN and SUPERMAN, RED TORNADO, DOCTOR FATE, FLASH, GREEN LANTERN, HAWKGIRL, HUNTRESS and POWER GIRL.

EARTH

3

This world is home to the villainous, despotic CRIME SYNDICATE OF AMERICA, including their leader, the tyrant ULTRAMAN, and his cohorts OWLMAN, SUPERWOMAN, JOHNNY QUICK, POWER RING, DEATHSTORM and ATOMICA — the world's greatest super-criminals in this universe, where Good and Evil are reversed.

EARTH 4

Earth-4's only superhuman being is CAPTAIN ALLEN ADAM, endowed with "quantum senses" following close-quarters interactions with an unstable neo-element known as U-235.

The PAX AMERICANA is a group of specialized, uniformed, peacekeeping operatives including PEACEMAKER, BLUE BEETLE and NIGHTSHADE. THE QUESTION of this world is a rogue crimebuster.

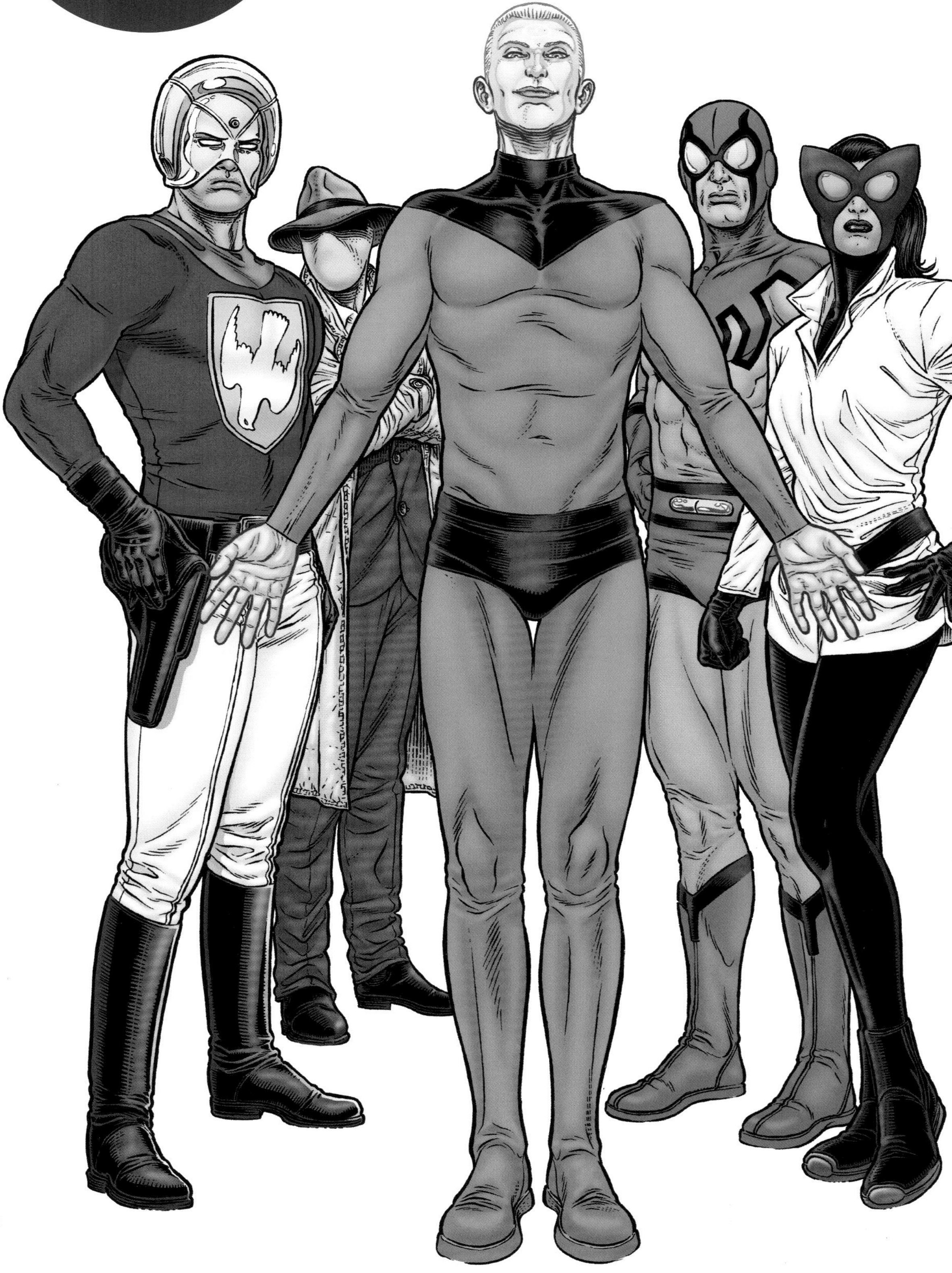

EARTH 5

Known throughout the Multiverse as "Thunderworld," this universe is the home of the Marvel Family paragons, their friends and their foes.

CAPTAIN MARVEL, CAPTAIN MARVEL JR., MARY MARVEL and the LIEUTENANT MARVELS fight an eternal battle to protect their world from monsters, aliens and the machinations of the power-mad genius DOCTOR SIVANA.

EARTH

The happening home of AQUAMAN, SANDMAN, BATMAN, GREEN LANTERN and other familiar names, given new and unfamiliar stories! On this world, SUPERMAN is a castaway cosmic cop from the planet Krypton. WONDER WOMAN wields the senses-sundering celestial staff of Manco Capac, the Inca Sun God, while the glistening GREEN LANTERN channels the peerless power of the wondrous World Tree Yggdrasil against the villainous REVEREND DARKK!

EARTH

On this world, the history of Earth-8 was recreated with subtle differences. In spite of its innovations and the protection of heroes like CRUSADER, GOLEM, "DOC" FUTURE, WALKÜRE, DEVILFIST and MICROBOT, Earth-7 was targeted and destroyed by the rapacious demons of the Gentry as part of their first incursion into the Multiverse. The sole survivor of Earth-7 is THUNDERER, an incarnate storm god.

EARTH

On this world, great power comes with great responsibility, and heroes often pay a high price for their dedication to justice. Earth-8 is home to the battlin' BUG, STUNTMASTER, bestial BIG BABY, HYPERIUS and MAJOR MAX.

Prominent hero teams include THE FUTURE FAMILY the 'Neo-human' G-('GENO-') MEN and THE RETALIATORS including DEADEYE, LADYBUG, KITE, WUNDAJIN, AMERICAN CRUSADER, RED DRAGON and MACHINEHEAD.

EARTH

Here, SUPERMAN is a human being of vast intellect and mental power, while the ATOM takes his place as Earth's foremost superhero. Here, the light-powered FLASH is the first baby born in space. Here, GREEN LANTERN can resurrect the dead. Here, JOKER is an anarchist prankster on the side of freedom, and BATMAN is a time-lost armored spirit seeking justice throughout eternity.

EARTH

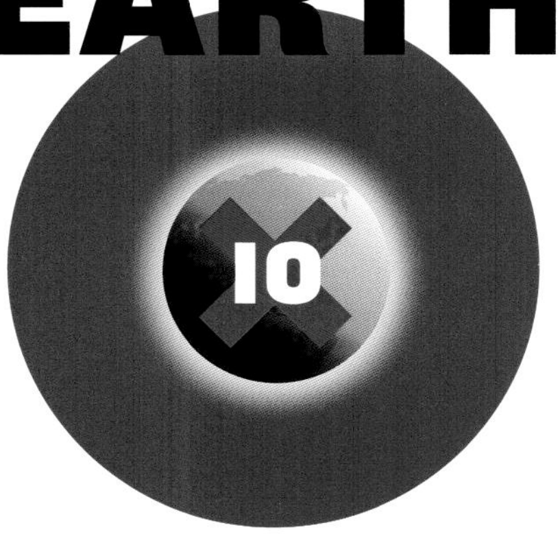
10

Also designated EARTH-X, history was altered here when the rocket carrying the infant super-being Kal-L of Krypton landed in Nazi-occupied Czechoslovakia in 1938. Eighty years after assuring a German victory in World War II, the troubled OVERMAN leads LEATHERWING, BRÜNHILDE, BLITZEN, and UNDERWATERMAN — as the NEW REICHSMEN — in their war against UNCLE SAM and his terrorist FREEDOM FIGHTERS — THE RAY, BLACK CONDOR, THE HUMAN BOMB, PHANTOM LADY, DOLL MAN and DOLL WOMAN.

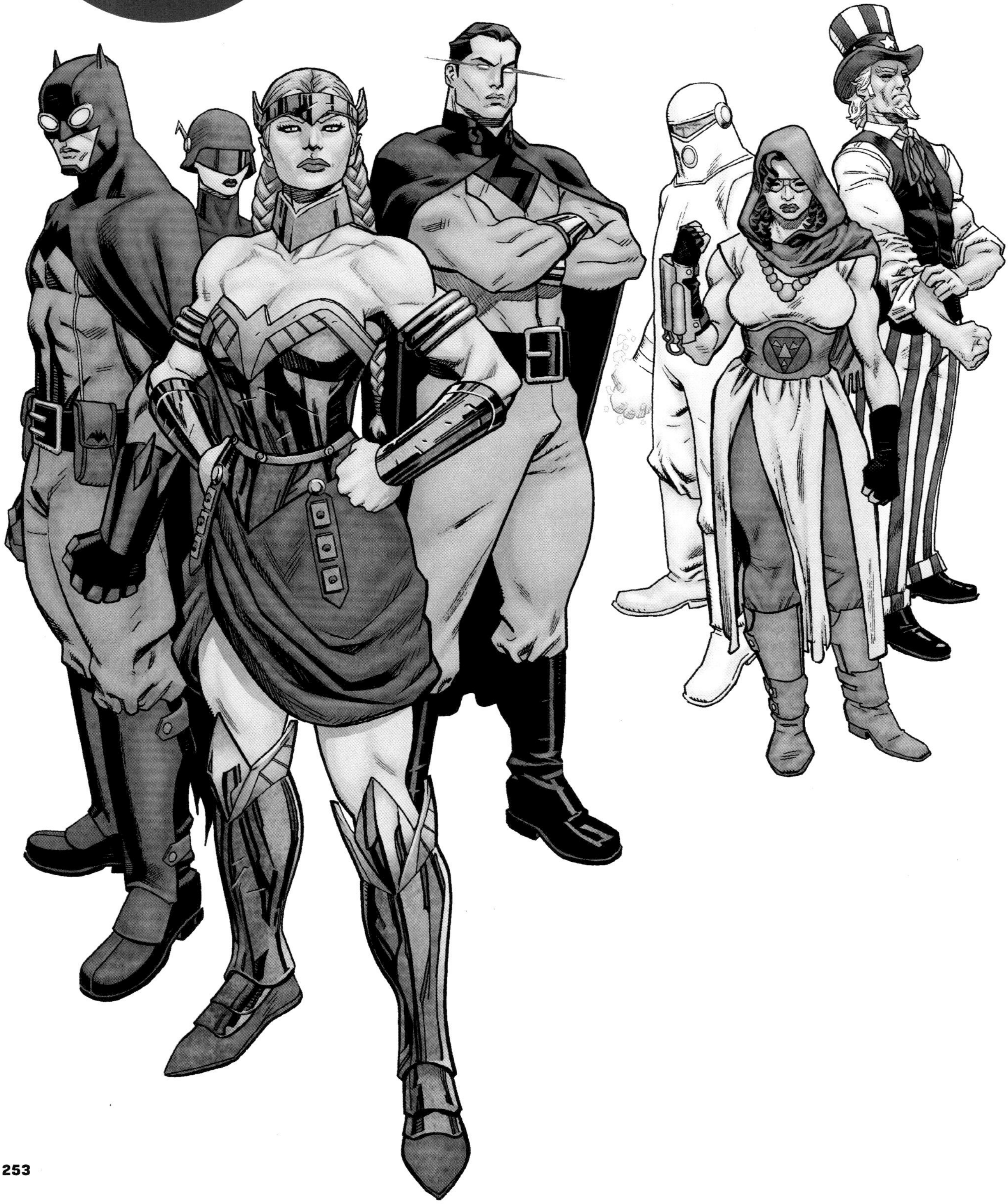

EARTH

On Earth-II, the Amazons of Themyscira imposed their law on the whole world and changed it forever, with new technology and philosophies, inspiring generations of women to take the lead in creating the future.

This world's JUSTICE GUILD comprises WONDEROUS MAN, AQUAWOMAN, BATWOMAN, SUPERWOMAN, JESSE QUICK, STAR SAPPHIRE, POWER MAN and ZATARA!

EARTH

With a timeline running slightly in advance of Earth-0, this is the near-future world of Batman's successor Terry McGinnis and his JUSTICE LEAGUE BEYOND allies, GREEN LANTERN, SUPERMAN, WARHAWK, AQUAGIRL, BIG BARDA, MICRON and others. Together they face the threats of an untamed future reality!

EARTH 13

On this world of permanent magical twilight, every day has 13 hours and each year has 13 months. Here, Etrigan the Demon, rocketed to Earth from the doomed planet Kamelot, fights evil in Merlin's name as SUPERDEMON!

Fellow members of the LEAGUE OF SHADOWS include HELLBLAZER, ANNATAZ, WITCHBOY, SWAMP-MAN, FATE, RAGMAN, DEADMAN and ENCHANTRESS.

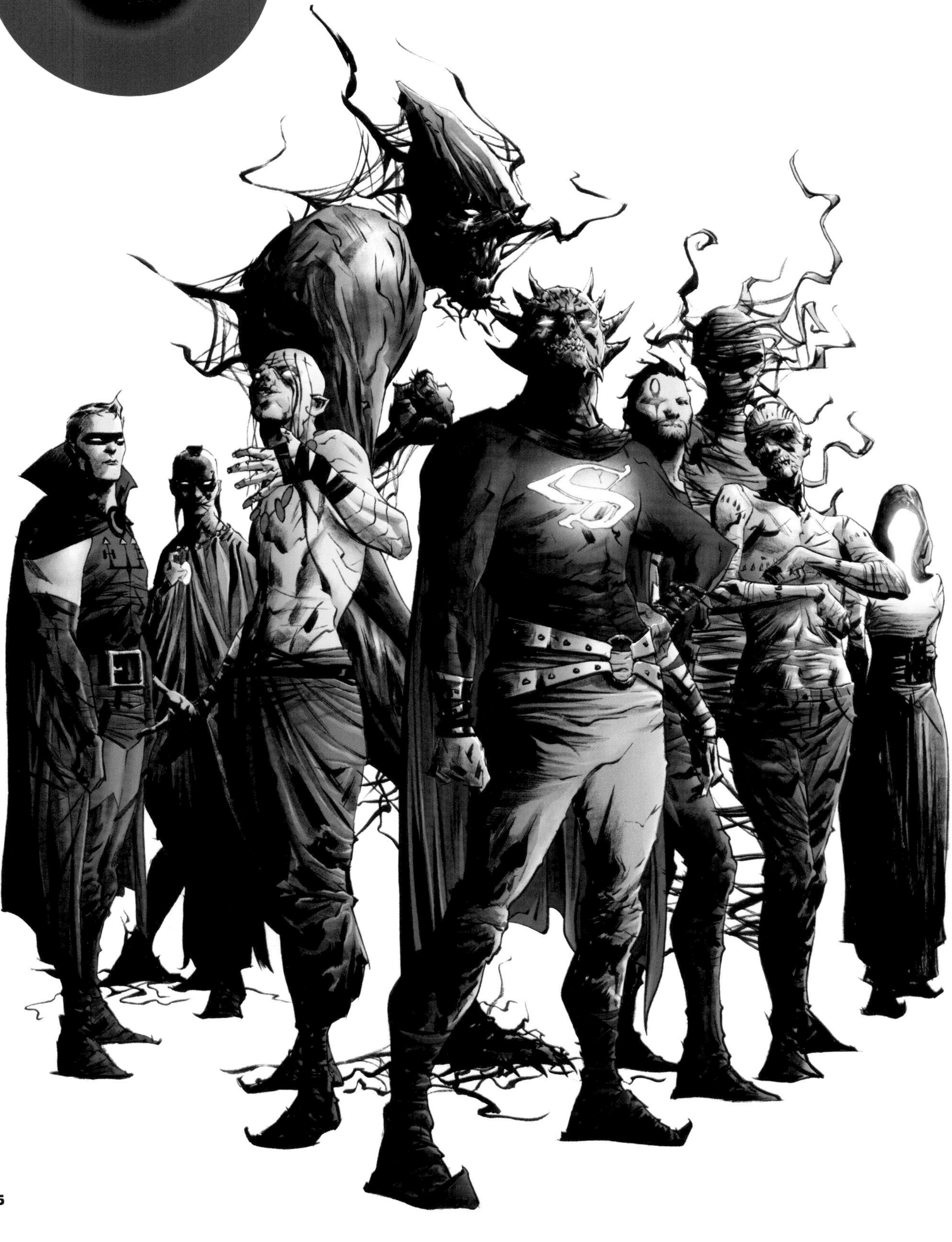

EARTH

Number I of 7 UNKNOWN WORLDS.

Created by an Inner Chamber of 7 Monitor Magi for a mysterious purpose yet to be revealed.

EARTH

The so-called Perfect Universe was destroyed during a rampage by the deranged and so-called SUPERBOY-PRIME of Earth-33, during which billions of fictional lives were lost and the delicate structure of spacetime itself was irreparably damaged.

A solitary, immensely powerful fragment of this universe — known as the COSMIC GRAIL — is said to remain, hidden somewhere among the many worlds of the Multiverse.

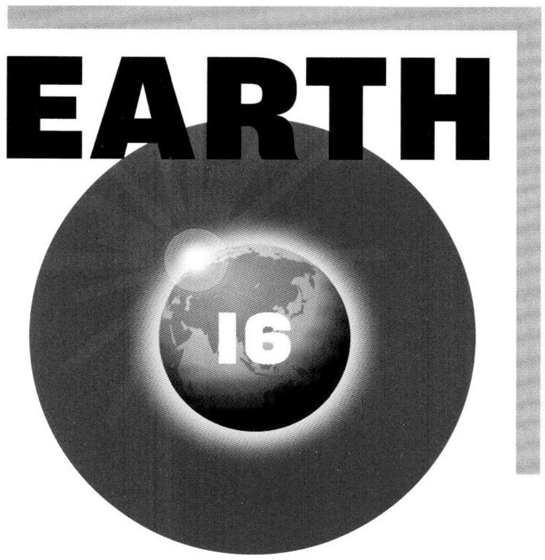
EARTH
16

Earth-Me — home of THE JUST — a world where peace, prosperity and boredom reign supreme. Here the Super-Sons of BATMAN and SUPERMAN are joined by others of a pampered second generation of superheroes, like SISTER MIRACLE, ARROWETTE, MEGAMORPHO and OFFSPRING.

While the older heroes of the JUSTICE LEAGUE indulge in nostalgic battle reenactments, the young live meaningless, self-absorbed lives.

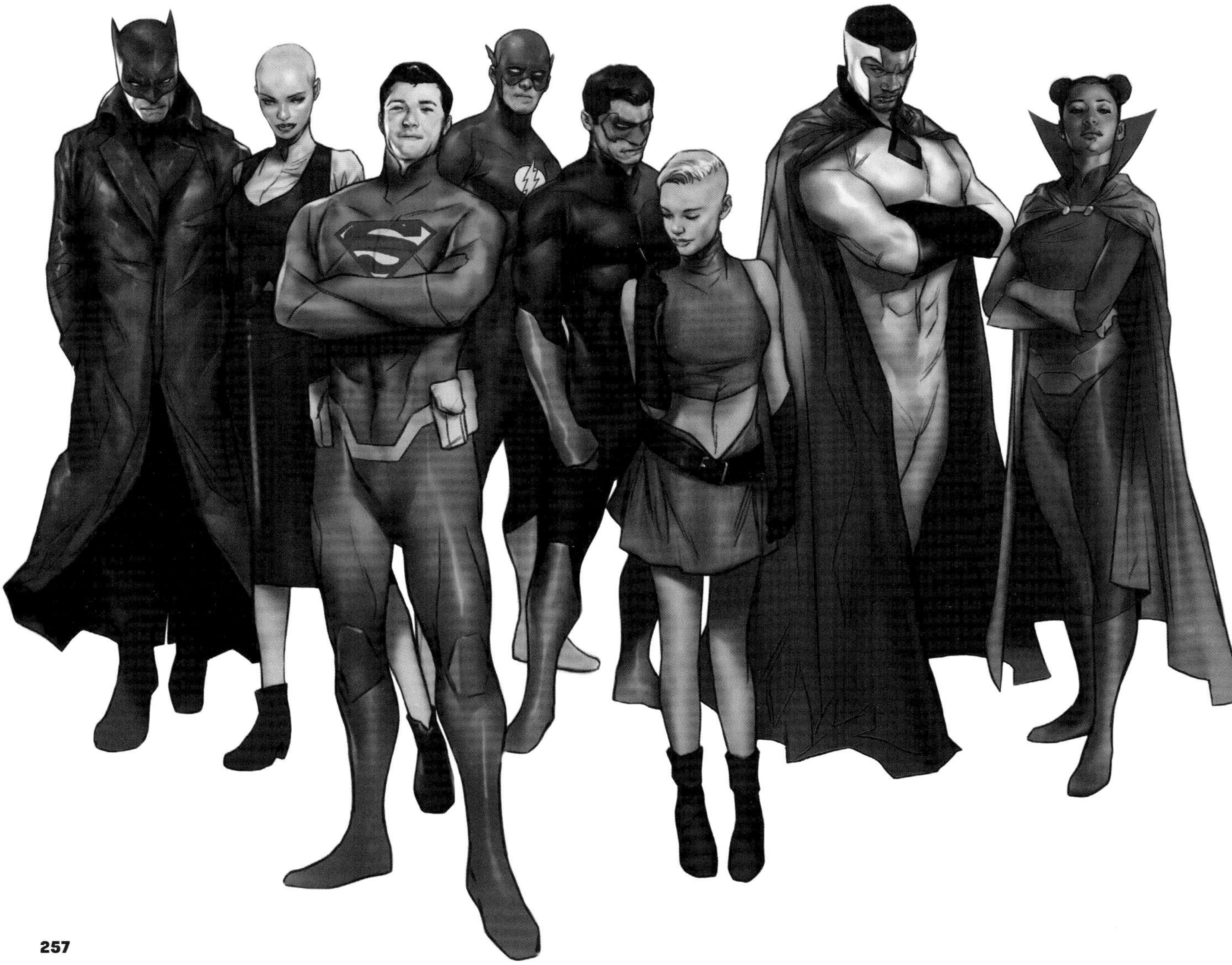

EARTH 17

CAPTAIN ADAM STRANGE leads his ATOMIC KNIGHTS OF JUSTICE on a desperate, last-chance quest to preserve the remnants of humanity 50 years after a nuclear war in 1963. Facing monstrous mutations, mad science and human heartbreak on the way to rebuilding the ruined world of 21st-century Novamerika, they seek the COSMIC GRAIL — the only weapon that will defend against the coming threat of DARKSEID the Destroyer.

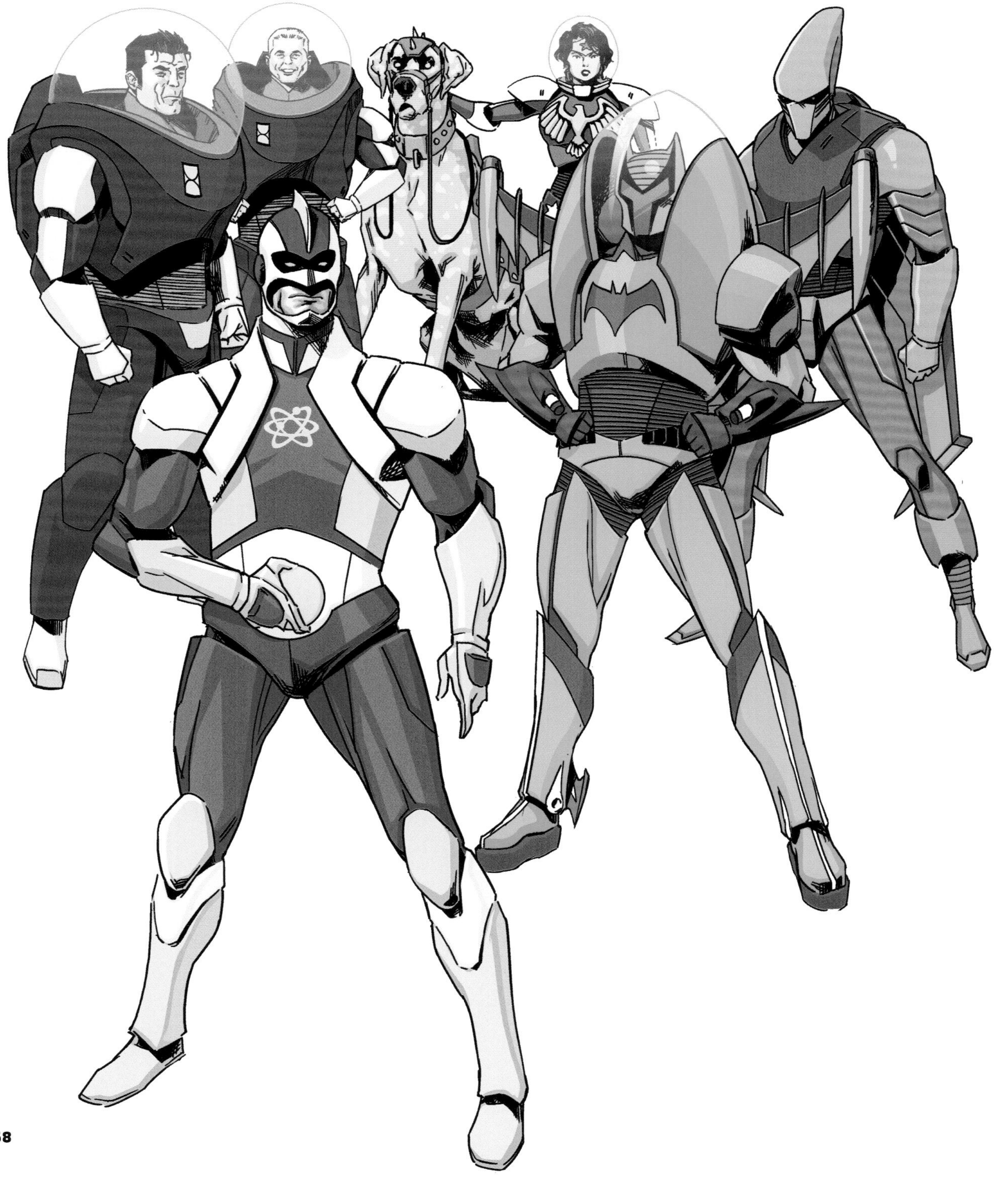

EARTH

Led by Saganowana, the SUPERCHIEF, the JUSTICE RIDERS are BAT-LASH, MADAME .44, STRONGBOW, EL DIABLO, CINNAMON, THE TRIGGER TWINS, FIREHAIR, TOMAHAWKMAN, JOHNNY THUNDER and POW-WOW SMITH.

They are sworn to protect a frontier world where the meddling Time Trapper froze technology and culture in the late 19th century. Here, human ingenuity has used the available resources of the 19th century to create everything humans take for granted in the 21st century, including a telegraph internet and air travel.

EARTH

Queen Victoria is dead. King Edward rules a 20th-century empire of new electric technology in a rapidly changing social landscape. Into this Modernist ferment, this world of new ideas and new futures, the super-humans have arrived! BAT MAN! ACCELERATED MAN! THE WONDER WOMAN! THE SHRINKING MAN and others face unexpected challenges as history takes a twisted turn!

EARTH 20

Home of the SOCIETY OF SUPER-HEROES, a team of adventurers and science champions assembled by DOC FATE to include GREEN LANTERN, THE MIGHTY ATOM, IMMORTAL MAN, LADY BLACKHAWK and the BLACKHAWKS.

Earth-20 occupies a binary universe, which tunes itself to occupy the same space as Earth-40 once every 100,000 years, with catastrophic consequences. See also EARTH-40.

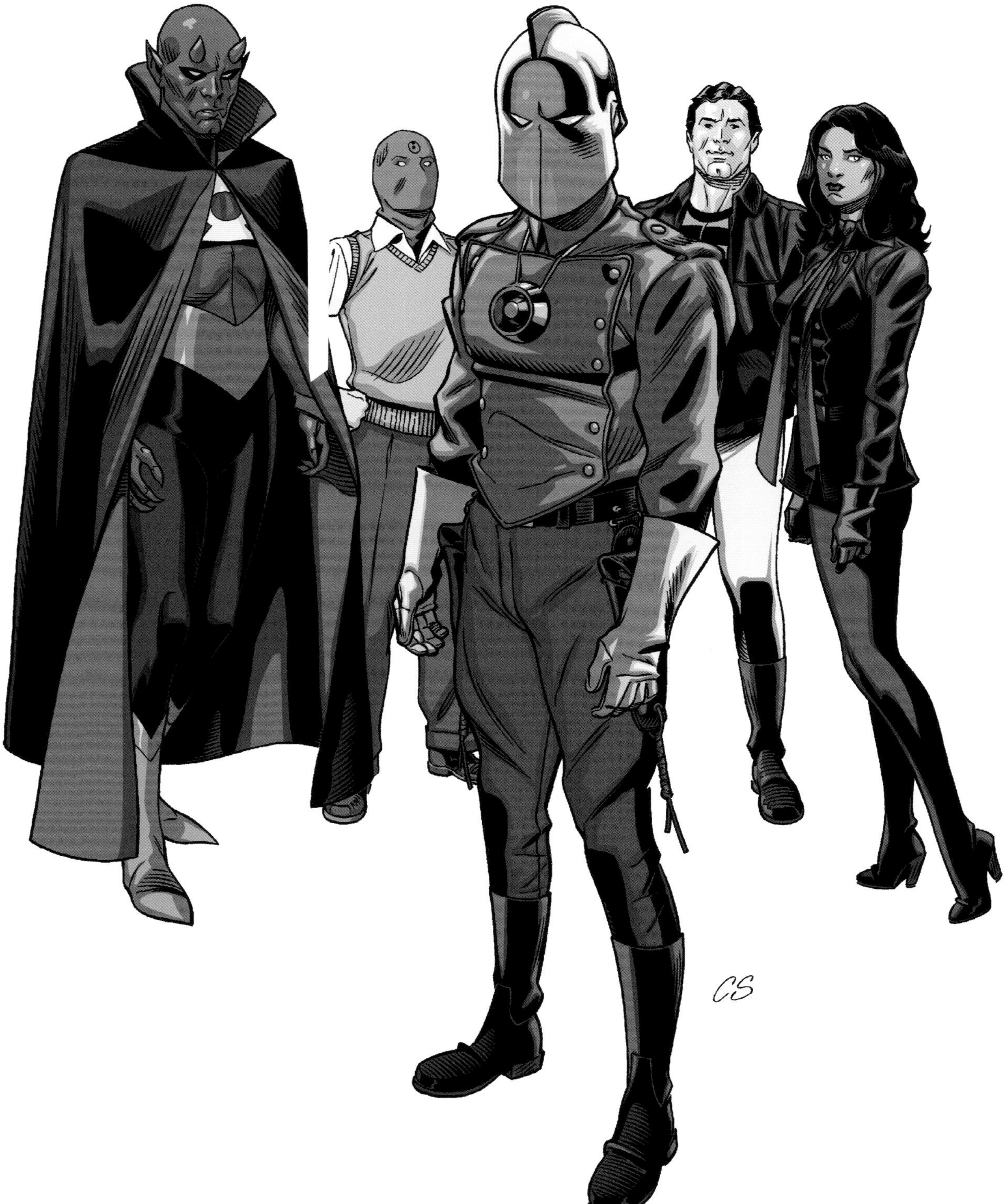

EARTH 21

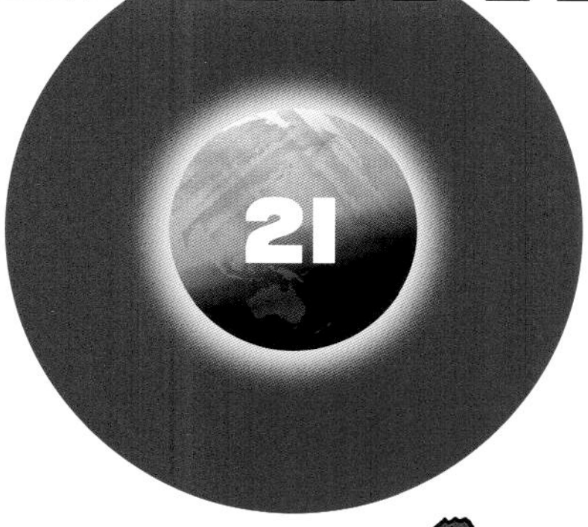

Here, a never-assassinated President John F. Kennedy stands forever poised to lead a newly superhuman, turned-on nation to the stars, while the indomitable young science heroes and pioneers of the JUSTICE LEAGUE OF AMERICA fight to protect their ideals against threats from this world — and others.

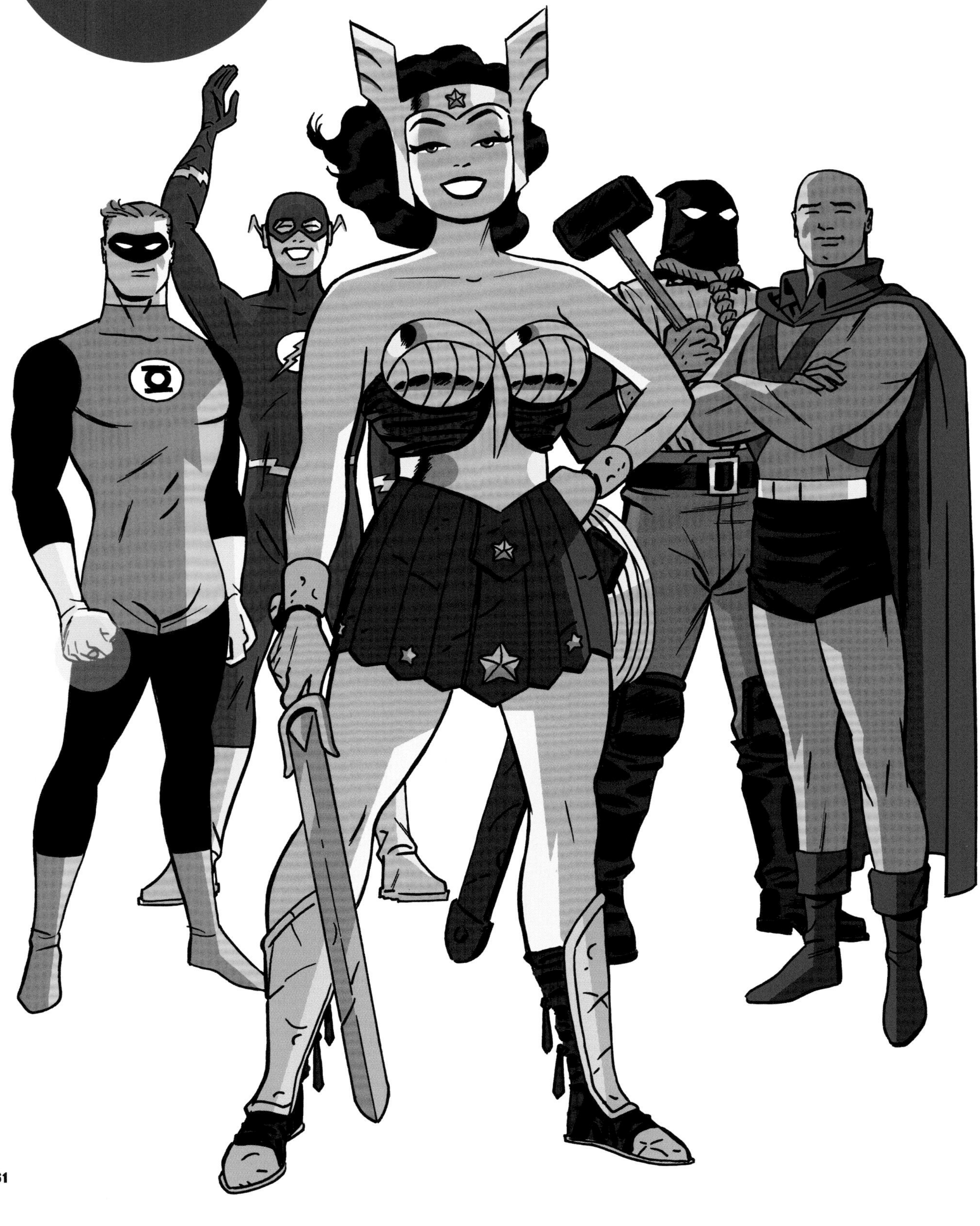

EARTH 22

Next door, by contrast, is an older world where the next generation of superhumans ran wild.

Here, Kansas was destroyed and civilization was brought to the brink of apocalypse before the timely return of a retired SUPERMAN.

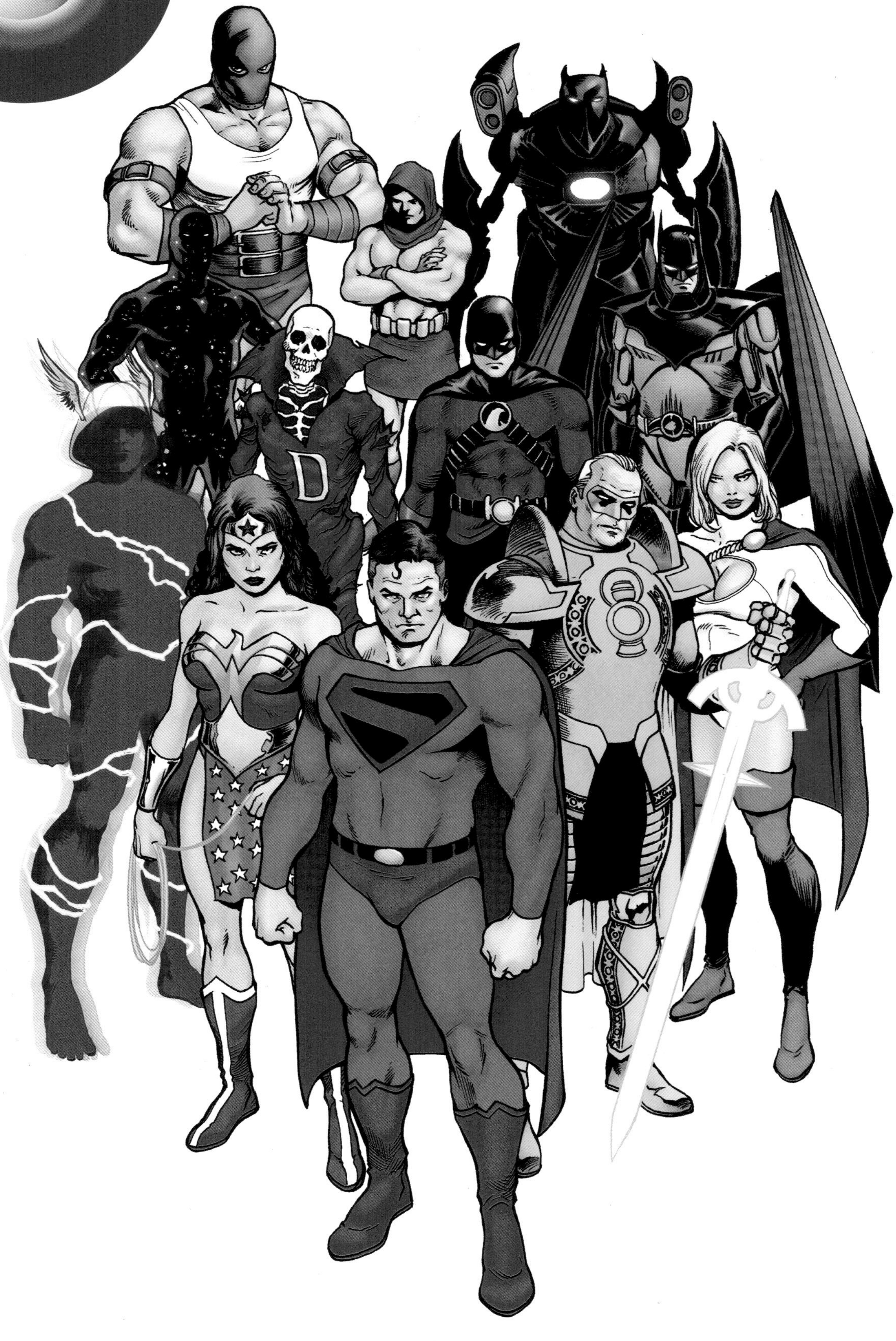

EARTH 23

The arrival on Earth of KAL-L of KRYPTON – this world's SUPERMAN – was the catalyst for a generation of superheroes including NUBIA the WONDER WOMAN, GREEN LANTERN, VIXEN, STEEL, MISTER MIRACLE, BLACK LIGHTNING and AMAZING MAN.

In his alter ego of Calvin Ellis, Superman is President of the United States of America.

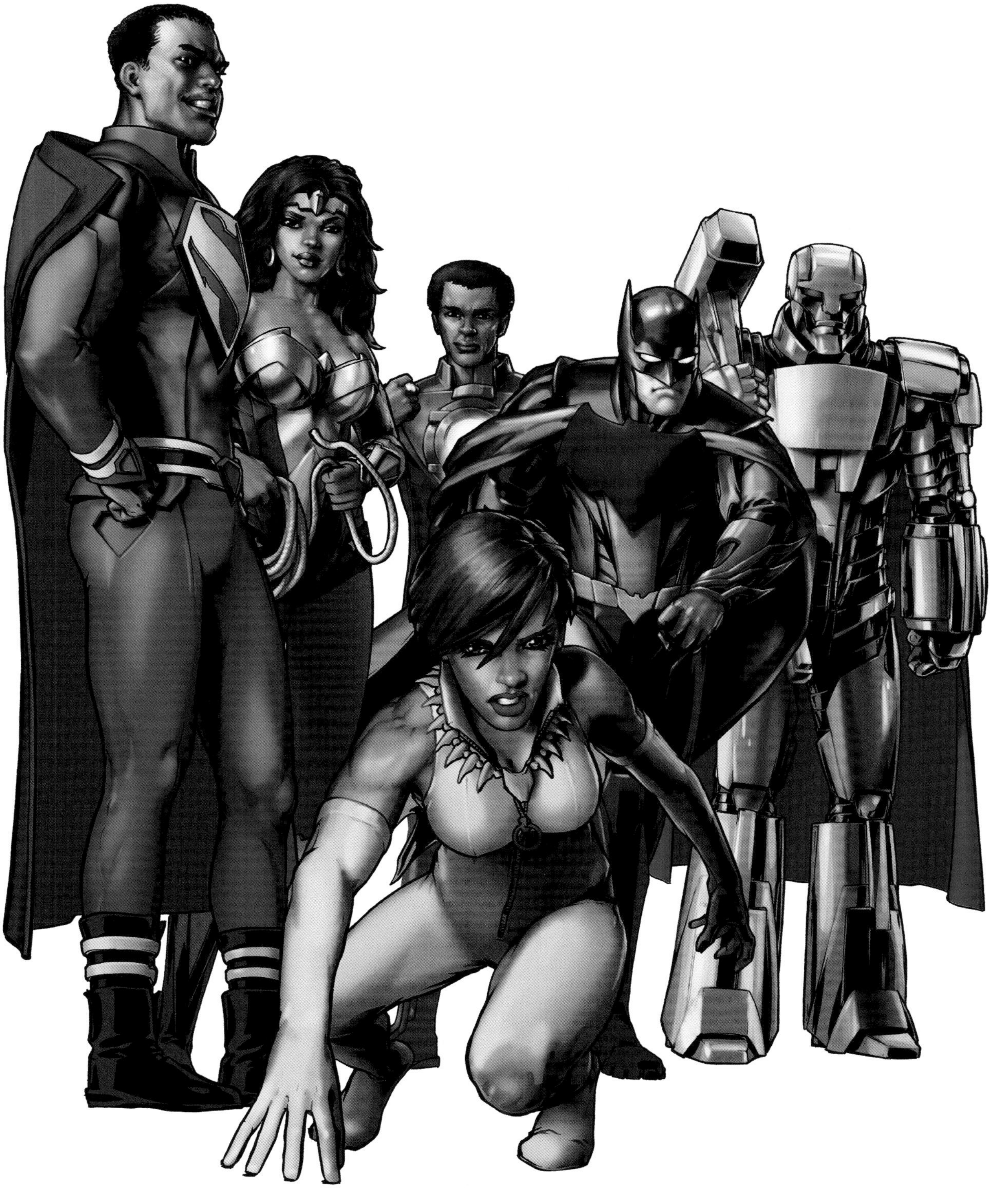

EARTH

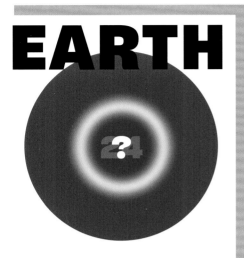

Number 2 of 7 UNKNOWN WORLDS. Created by an Inner Chamber of 7 Monitor Magi for a mysterious purpose.

EARTH

Number 3 of 7 UNKNOWN WORLDS. Created by an Inner Chamber of 7 Monitor Magi for a mysterious purpose.

EARTH

Earth-26 was briefly destroyed, but the so-called CARTOON PHYSICS governing this world permits the inhabitants of Earth-26 to survive almost any known physical assault. In his superheroic guise as CAPTAIN CARROT, comic book writer/artist Rodney Rabbit leads FASTBACK, AMERICAN EAGLE, RUBBERDUCK, YANKEE POODLE, PIG-IRON, ALLEY-KAT-ABRA and LITTLE CHEESE — a.k.a. the ZOO CREW.

EARTH

Number 4 of 7 UNKNOWN WORLDS. Created by an Inner Chamber of 7 Monitor Magi for a mysterious purpose.

EARTH

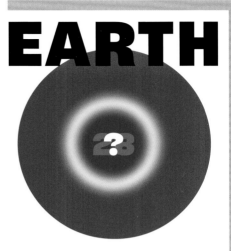

Number 5 of 7 UNKNOWN WORLDS. Created by an Inner Chamber of 7 Monitor Magi for a mysterious purpose.

EARTH

The square planet Htrae dominates Bizarroverse, a broken continuum with damaged laws of physics. BIZARRO-SUPERMAN leads his UNJUSTICE LEAGUE OF UNAMERICA on pointless, inexplicable and utterly futile adventures.

The Bizarroverse is crowded with nearby planets including Nnar, home of ADAM FAMILIAR; the overpopulated Sram, birthplace of the green SRAMIAN SNITCH; Raganaht, home planet of the flightless BIZARRO MANHAWK; Ao of the DISMISSERS OF THE UNIVERSE; etc, etc.

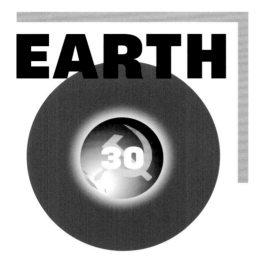

EARTH 30

World of the Soviet Superman, where Kal-L's rocket crash-landed on a Russian collective farm, resulting in a Communist Superman.

On Earth-30, BATMAN was a terrorist freedom fighter. GREEN LANTERN and BIZARRO were American super-weapons. Following the apparent death of Superman, this world prospered under the guidance of the LUTHOR FAMILY.

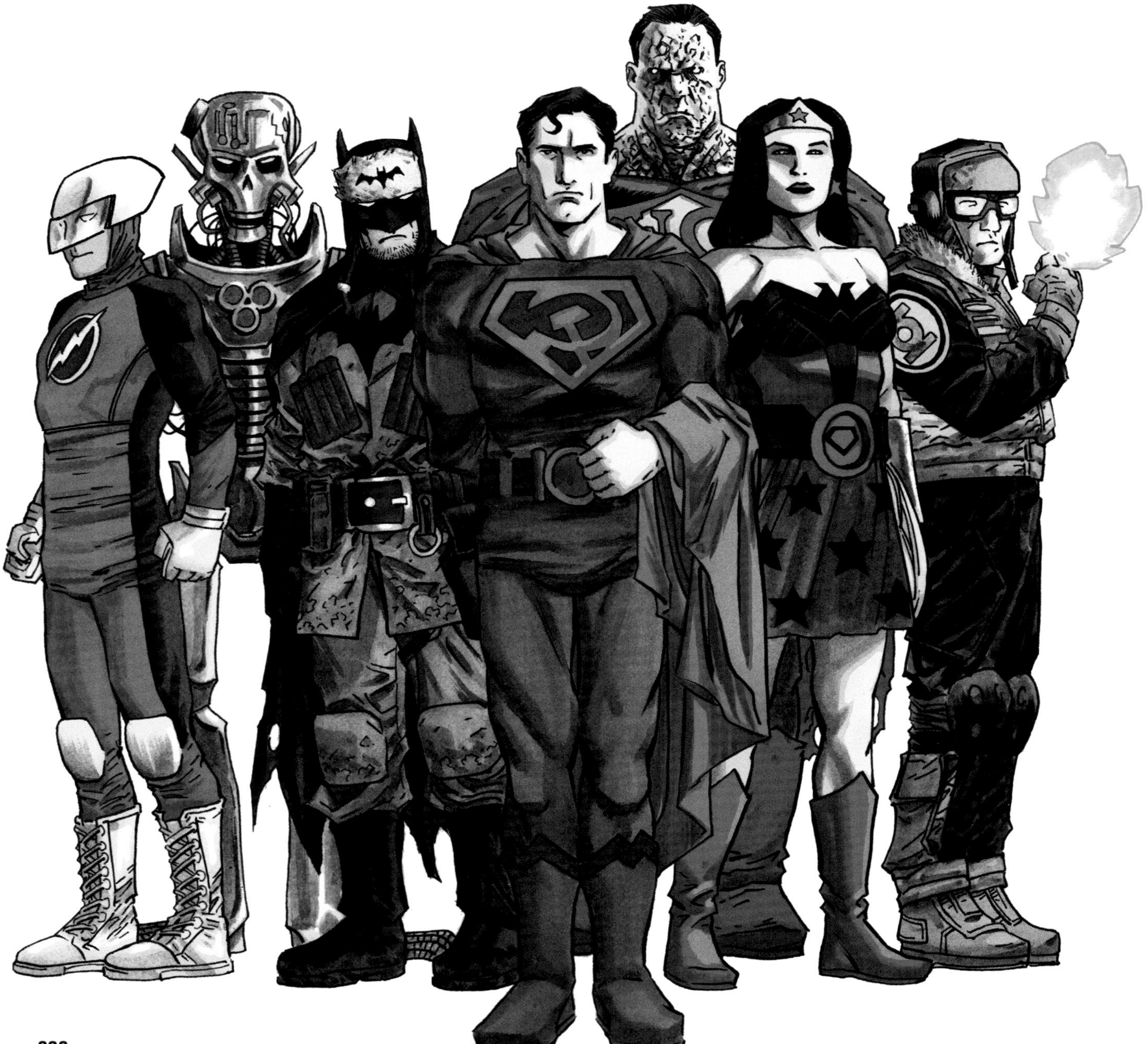

EARTH

Global warming, mega-tsunamis and tectonic shifts have created a post-apocalyptic drowned world.
CAPTAIN LEATHERWING and the crew of the Flying Fox — including ROBIN REDBLADE — fight to preserve the safety of the Seven Seas.

EARTH

Here, Bruce Wayne is Earth's Green Lantern and fights evil as BAT-LANTERN, alongside BLACK ARROW, WONDERHAWK, AQUAFLASH, SUPER-MARTIAN and other members of the JUSTICE TITANS.

EARTH
33

Known also as Earth-Prime, this mysterious world without superheroes exerts a powerful and unknown influence on the progress and development of the entire Multiverse.

Earth-Prime's only known superhuman inhabitant is known as ULTRA COMICS. That's him there...

EARTH

One of numerous superheroes based in the city of COSMOVILLE, SAVIOR was the last survivor of the ancient super-civilization of MU. Sent into the future to escape a doomed past, he inaugurated the LIGHT BRIGADE along with HERCULINA, RADMAN, GOODFELLOW, FORMULA-I, GHOSTMAN, MASTER MOTLEY, CUTIE, THE STINGRAY and many others.

EARTH

SUPREMO is the greatest hero of Earth-35, an awesome "pseudoverse" or artificial universe constructed by Monitor "ideominers" operating from harvesting stations in Earth-35 "concept space." Supremo is a proud member of the SUPER-AMERICANS, alongside heroes including STARCOP, MERCURY-MAN, MISS X, MORPHIN' MAN, MAJESTY — QUEEN OF VENUS, OLYMPIAN and THE OWL.

EARTH

The homeworld of JUSTICE 9, where the alien OPTIMAN fought bravely alongside such heroes as FLASHLIGHT, CYBERION, WAR-WOMAN, MER-MAN, BLACKBIRD, BOWBOY, IRON KNIGHT, RED RACER and more. Optiman was apparently killed by the Earth-45 monster SUPERDOOMSDAY.

EARTH

A world of lawless heroes and cynical champions. On Earth-37 technology accelerated through the '60s, '70s and '80s. The beat cellars of the '50s gave way to the underground Mars base colonies of the '80s and the Europa bases of the '90s and then to the interstellar world of TOMMY TOMORROW, MANHUNTER 2015 and the SPACE RANGERS.

EARTH

38

Here, Superman and Batman first appeared in the 1930s, aging normally as their children inherited a world of wonder and tragedy, where heroes and heroines alike carry the heroic baton into an unknown future.

EARTH

39

Home of the AGENTS OF W.O.N.D.E.R., an organization of United Nations super-spies — CYCLOTRON, DOCTOR NEMO, CORVUS, ACCELERATOR and PSI-MAN — each equipped with an item of miracle technology designed by visionary boy genius Happy DaVinci — the Cyclo-Harness, the Accelerator Circuit, the Ghost Chamber, the LightWing and the Cypher Suit. Repeated use of this technology might be addictive and ruinous.

EARTH

40

A "binary universe" resonating in "catastrophic harmony" with Earth-20, of which it is the evil reflex. Colliding every 100,000 years with its counterpart, Earth-40 is home to the SOCIETY OF SUPER-CRIMINALS including DOC FAUST, VANDAL SAVAGE, LADY SHIVA, BLOCKBUSTER and PARALLAX the FEAR-THING.
See also EARTH-20.

EARTH

41

A dark and violent world. Home of the "necro floral" avenger SPORE, gruff DINO-COP, NIMROD SQUAD, NIGHTCRACKER, THE SCORPION and SEPULCHRE.

EARTH

42

The tiny inhabitants of Earth-42 knew nothing of mortality, evil or violence until the death of their Superman at the hands of the Earth-45 thought-monster, SUPERDOOMSDAY — but their world hides a great and terrible secret.

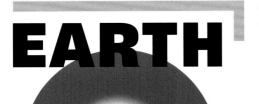

EARTH 43

A world of darkness and fear where super-vampires rule the night as the BLOOD LEAGUE.

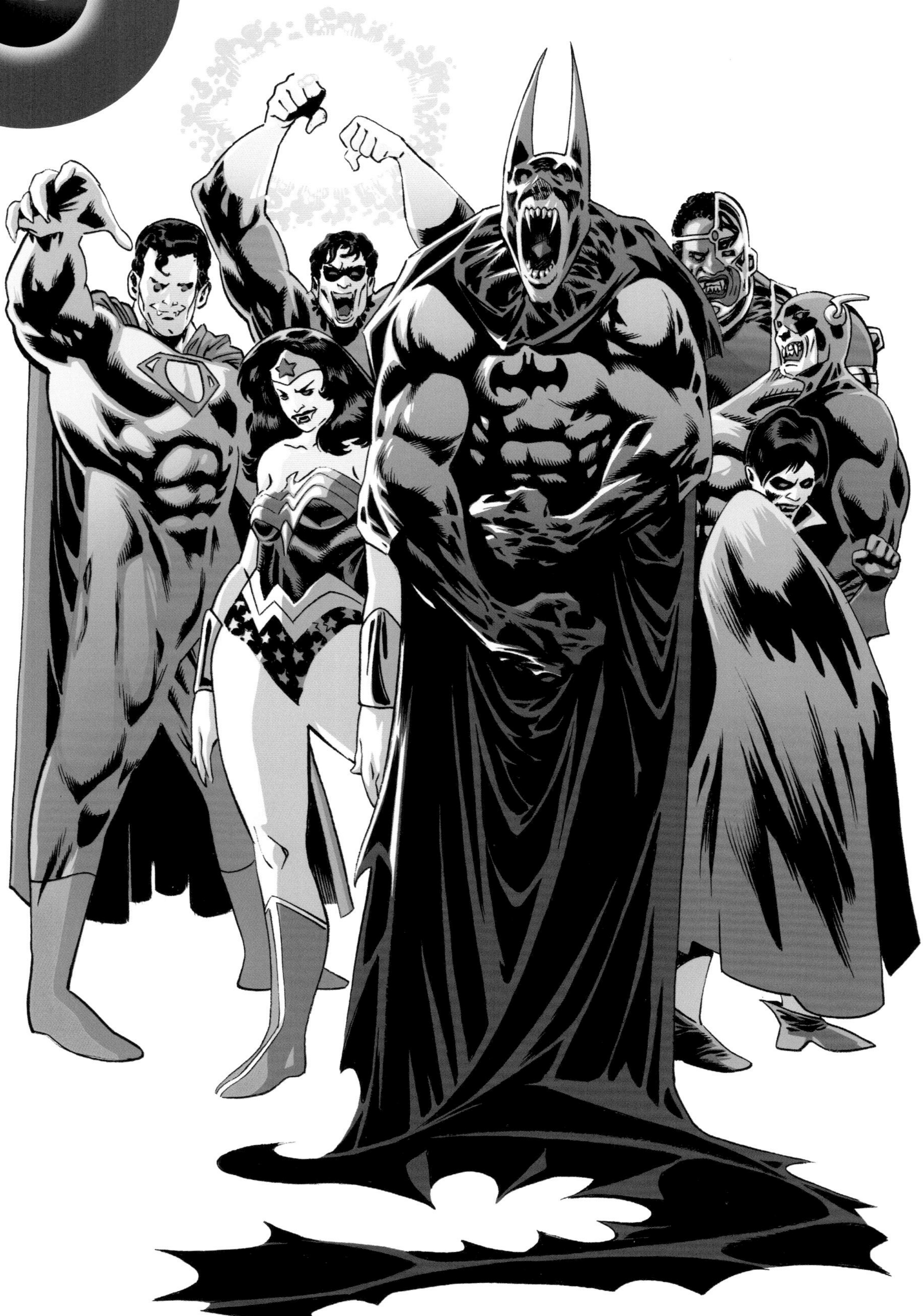

EARTH

44

The home of world-changing superhero A.I.s designed and built by the brilliant, bipolar Doctor Will Tornado. "There were no super-heroes — there was no one to save the world — so I built them," says DOC TORNADO of his creations.

THE METAL LEAGUE comprises GOLD SUPER-MAN, IRON BATMAN, PLATINUM WONDER WOMAN, MERCURY FLASH, Nth METAL HAWKMAN, TIN ELONGATED MAN, and LEAD GREEN ARROW.

EARTH

45™

On this world there were no superhuman beings until "SUPERMAN™" was created by CLARK KENT, LOIS LANE and JIMMY OLSEN using incredible new thought-powered technology. Co-opted by the business mavens of OVERCORP, Superman was redesigned as a monstrous, troubled anti-hero and came to be known as SUPERDOOMSDAY when his rampage through the worlds of the Multiverse resulted in the deaths of Superman of Earth-42 and Optiman of Earth-36 before his defeat at the hands of President Superman of Earth-23 and the Superman of Earth-0.

EARTH

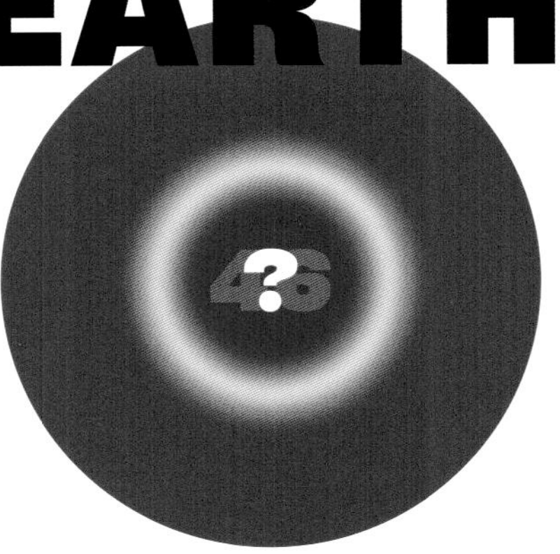
?

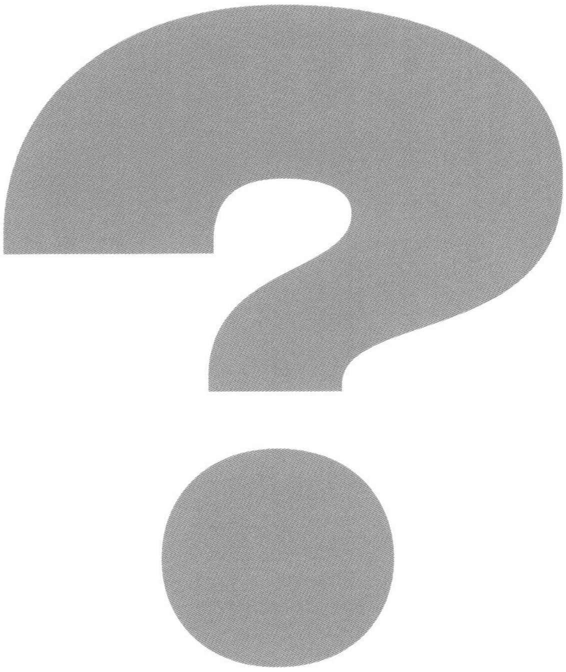

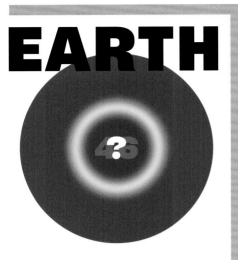

Number 6 of 7 UNKNOWN WORLDS. The second most mysterious of 7 UNKNOWN EARTHS.

EARTH

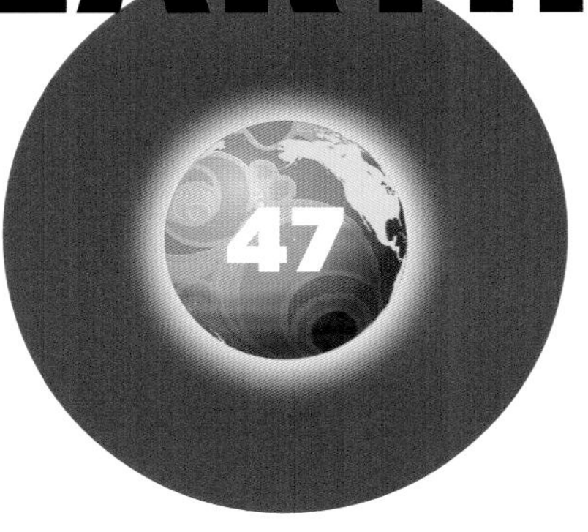
47

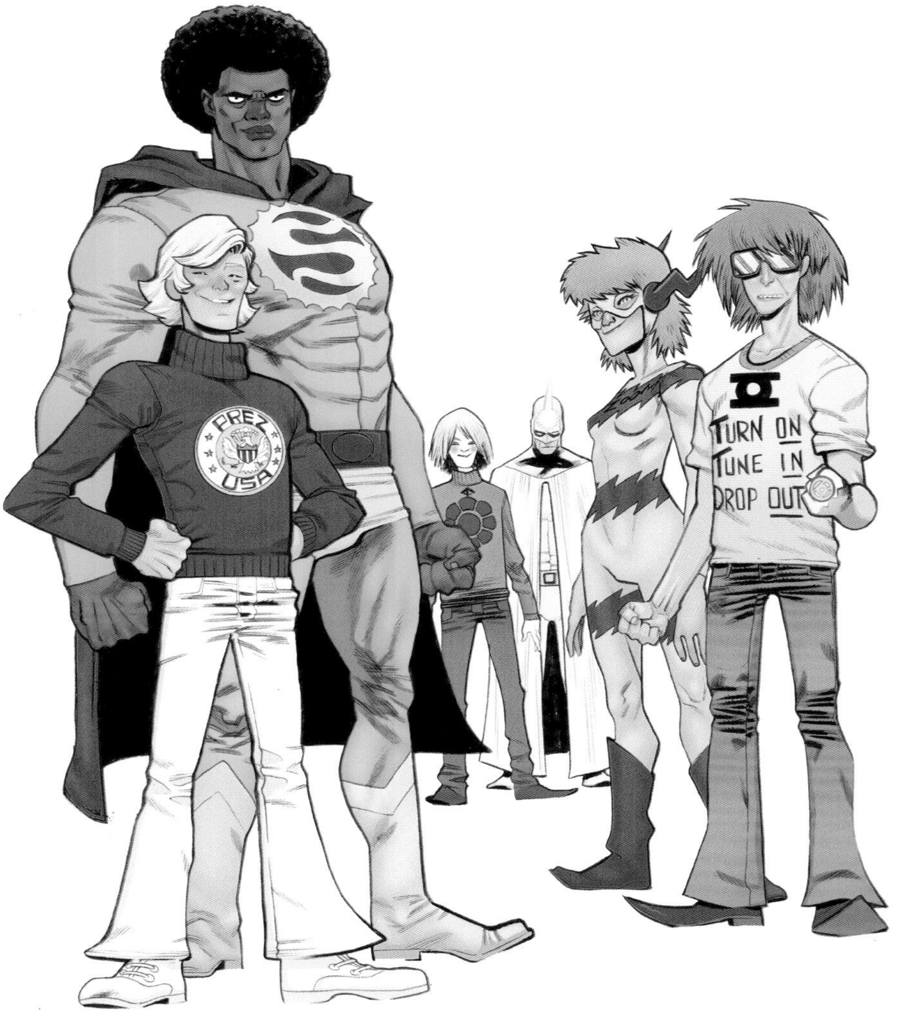
PREZ
USA
TURN ON
TUNE IN
DROP OUT

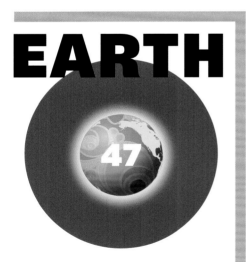

Home of the psychedelic champions of the LOVE SYNDICATE of DREAMWORLD led by SUNSHINE SUPERMAN, and including THE SHOOTING STAR, SPEED FREAK, MAGIC LANTERN and BROTHER POWER, THE GEEK.

The Love Syndicate is financed by the immortal teenaged President PREZ RICKARD. All is groovy.

EARTH 48

The Earth of the FORERUNNERS – a race of super beings bred to be harvested as ultimate protectors of the Multiverse itself. Rapid evolution has resulted in super-trees, super-dogs, mice and bacteria; super-weapons, super-food, super-TV shows. Every story is a crossover epic, every event an EVENT.

Sometimes known as Warworld, Earth-48 has been converted by benevolent aliens into a factory, designed to produce a race of Fifth World warriors to fight in the eternal war against Lord Darkseid. The Royal Family of Warworld includes LADY QUARK, LIANA, BROTHER EYES, ANTARCTIC MONKEY, DANGER DOG, LORD VOLT, KID VICIOUS and billions more.

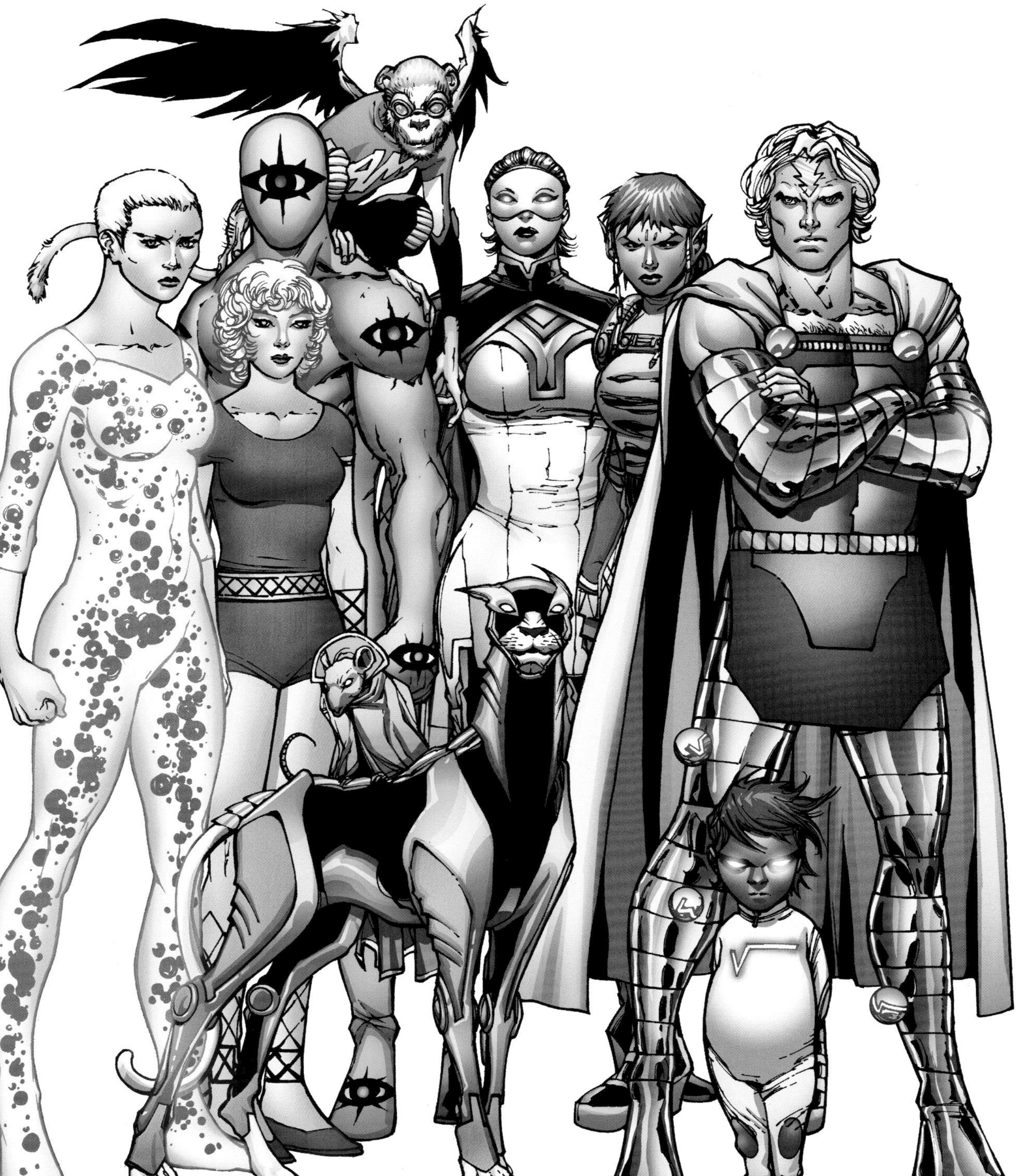

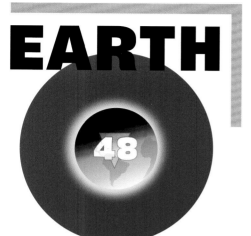

EARTH

Number 7 of 7 UNKNOWN WORLDS. The most mysterious of 7 UNKNOWN EARTHS.

EARTH

When PRESIDENT LEX LUTHOR murdered the FLASH, the SUPERMAN of this world took it upon himself to punish Luthor by death and instituted a global police state patrolled and maintained by the tyrannical, super-powered JUSTICE LORDS.

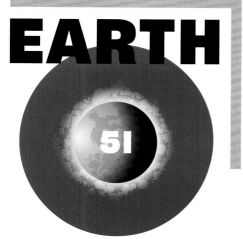

EARTH 51

On a fragile Earth ravaged by an unknown "Great Disaster," men act like beasts and beasts act like men!

Here, KAMANDI, the Last Boy on Earth, and his allies PRINCE TUFTAN of the Tiger-Men and BEN BOXER, a.k.a. biOMAC, have embarked on a mind-bending rescue mission to the ends of the earth, while vast, powerful and manipulative New Gods look on.

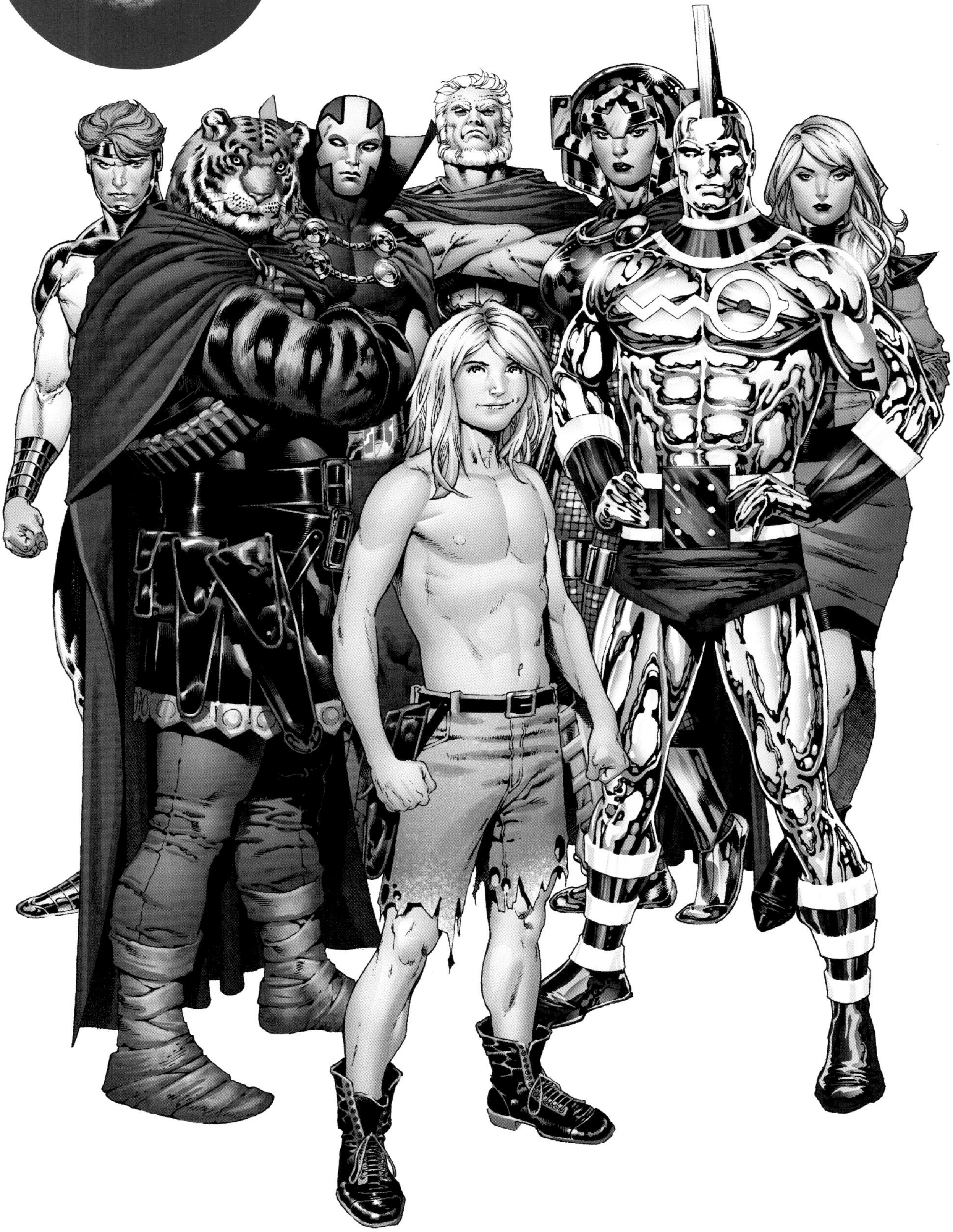

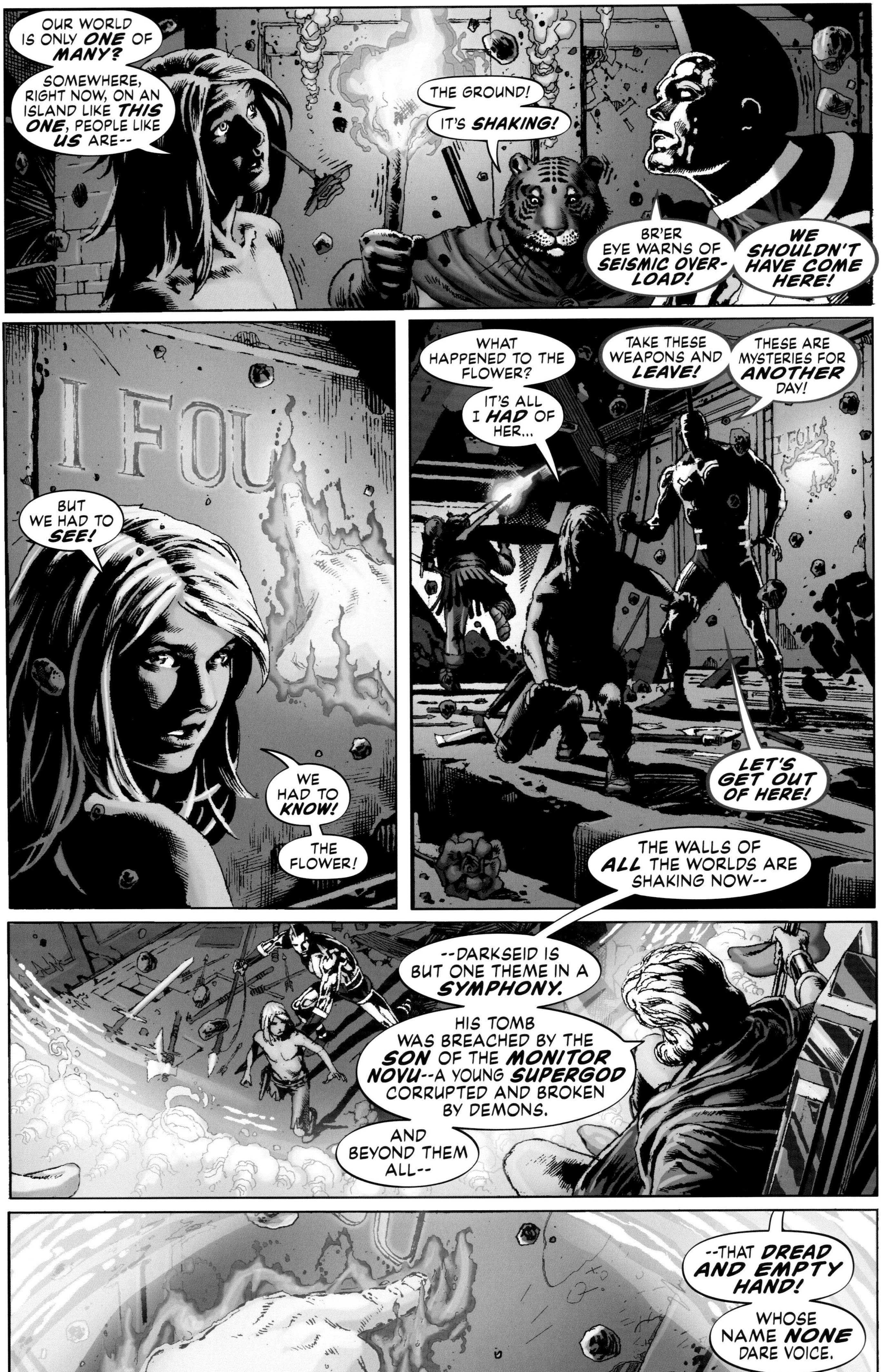

OUR WORLD IS ONLY ONE OF MANY?
SOMEWHERE, RIGHT NOW, ON AN ISLAND LIKE THIS ONE, PEOPLE LIKE US ARE--
THE GROUND!
IT'S SHAKING!
BR'ER EYE WARNS OF SEISMIC OVER-LOAD!
WE SHOULDN'T HAVE COME HERE!
I FOU
BUT WE HAD TO SEE!
WE HAD TO KNOW!
THE FLOWER!
WHAT HAPPENED TO THE FLOWER?
IT'S ALL I HAD OF HER...
TAKE THESE WEAPONS AND LEAVE!
THESE ARE MYSTERIES FOR ANOTHER DAY!
LET'S GET OUT OF HERE!
THE WALLS OF ALL THE WORLDS ARE SHAKING NOW--
--DARKSEID IS BUT ONE THEME IN A SYMPHONY.
HIS TOMB WAS BREACHED BY THE SON OF THE MONITOR NOVU--A YOUNG SUPERGOD CORRUPTED AND BROKEN BY DEMONS.
AND BEYOND THEM ALL--
--THAT DREAD AND EMPTY HAND!
WHOSE NAME NONE DARE VOICE.

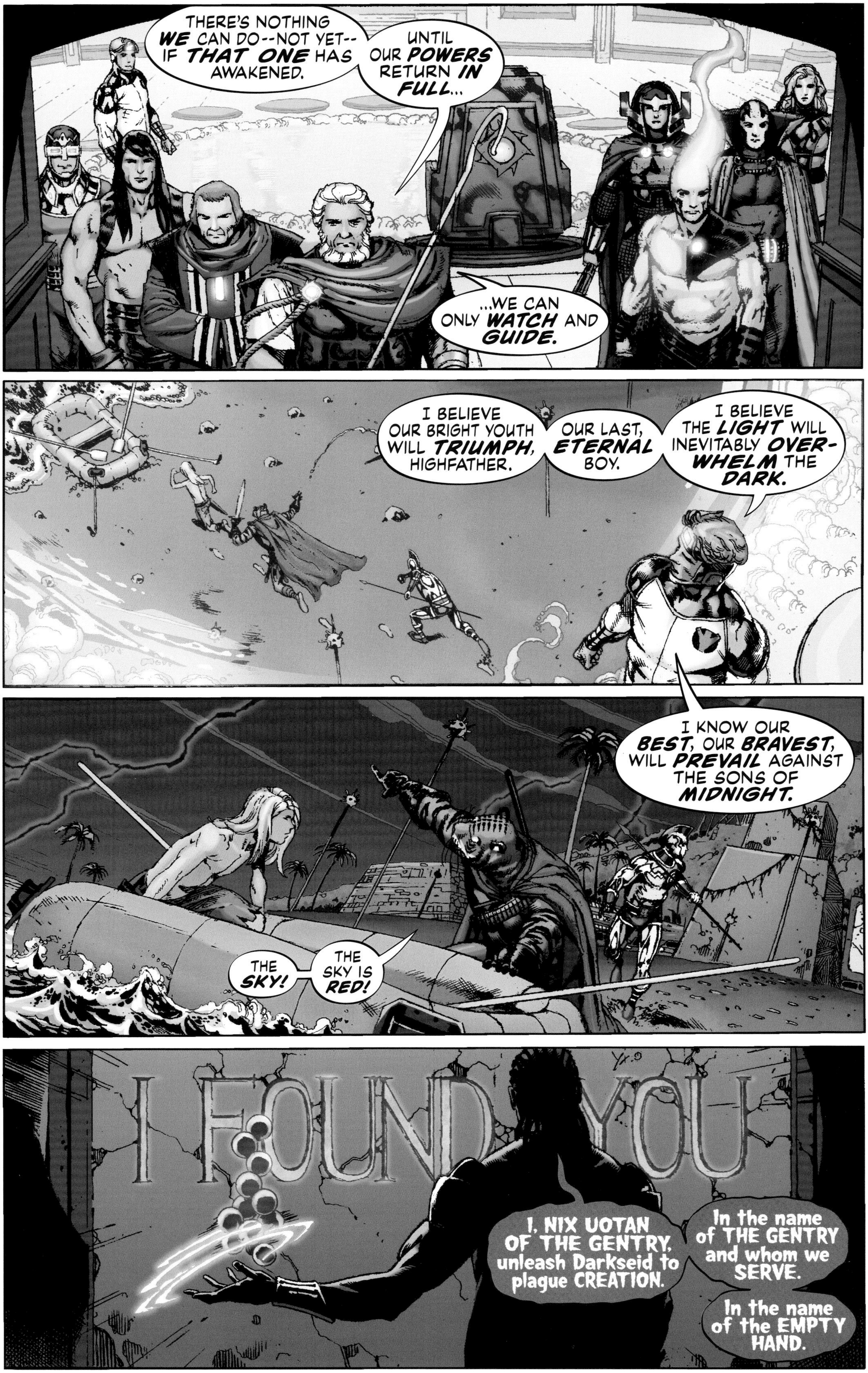
THERE'S NOTHING WE CAN DO--NOT YET-- IF THAT ONE HAS AWAKENED.
UNTIL OUR POWERS RETURN IN FULL...
...WE CAN ONLY WATCH AND GUIDE.
I BELIEVE OUR BRIGHT YOUTH WILL TRIUMPH, HIGHFATHER.
OUR LAST, ETERNAL BOY.
I BELIEVE THE LIGHT WILL INEVITABLY OVER-WHELM THE DARK.
I KNOW OUR BEST, OUR BRAVEST, WILL PREVAIL AGAINST THE SONS OF MIDNIGHT.
THE SKY!
THE SKY IS RED!
I FOUND YOU
I, NIX UOTAN OF THE GENTRY, unleash Darkseid to plague CREATION.
In the name of THE GENTRY and whom we SERVE.
In the name of the EMPTY HAND.

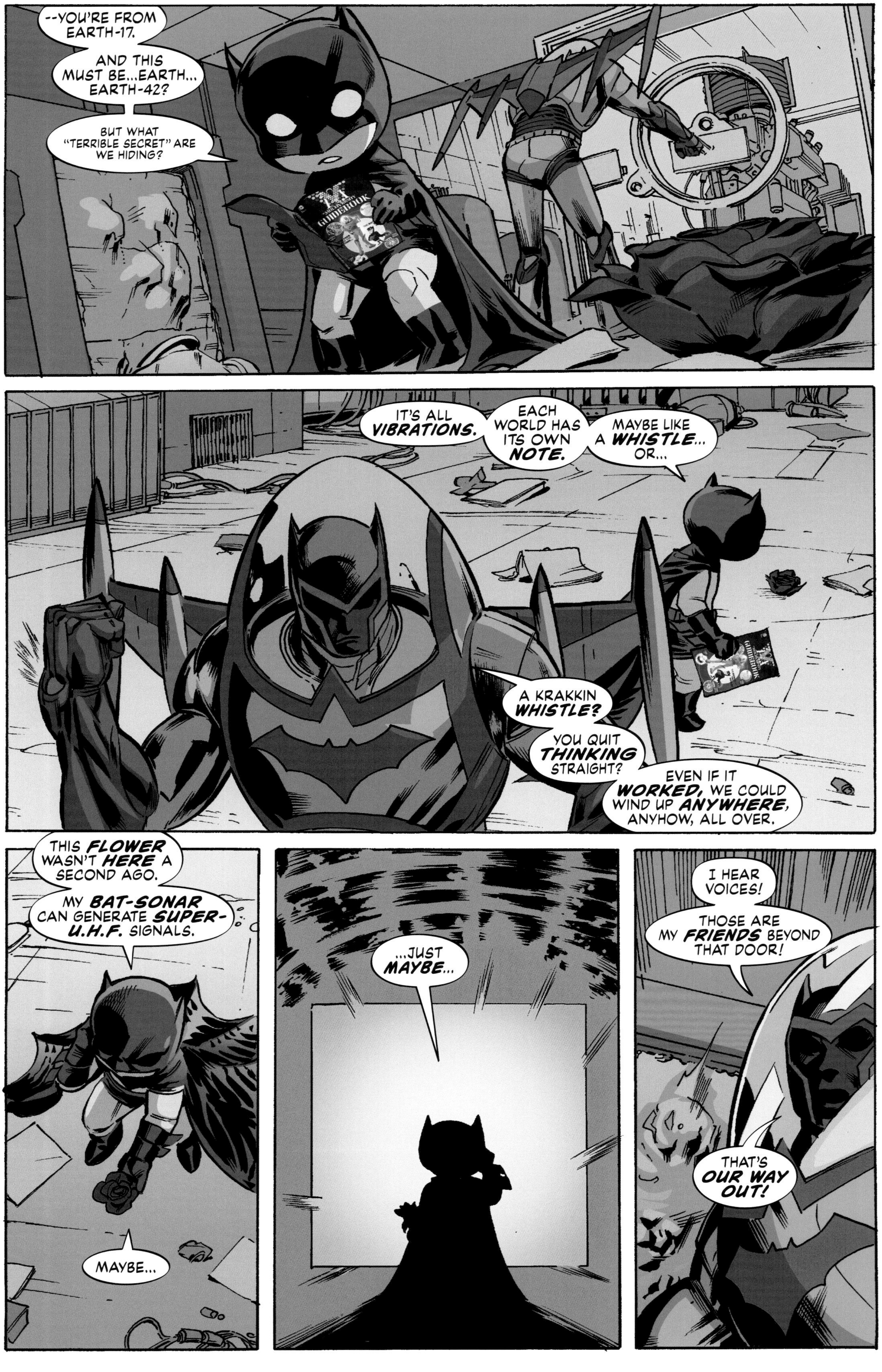
--YOU'RE FROM EARTH-17.
AND THIS MUST BE...EARTH... EARTH-42?
BUT WHAT "TERRIBLE SECRET" ARE WE HIDING?
GUIDEBOOK
IT'S ALL VIBRATIONS.
EACH WORLD HAS ITS OWN NOTE.
MAYBE LIKE A WHISTLE... OR...
A KRAKKIN WHISTLE?
YOU QUIT THINKING STRAIGHT?
EVEN IF IT WORKED, WE COULD WIND UP ANYWHERE, ANYHOW, ALL OVER.
THIS FLOWER WASN'T HERE A SECOND AGO.
MY BAT-SONAR CAN GENERATE SUPER-U.H.F. SIGNALS.
MAYBE...
...JUST MAYBE...
I HEAR VOICES!
THOSE ARE MY FRIENDS BEYOND THAT DOOR!
THAT'S OUR WAY OUT!

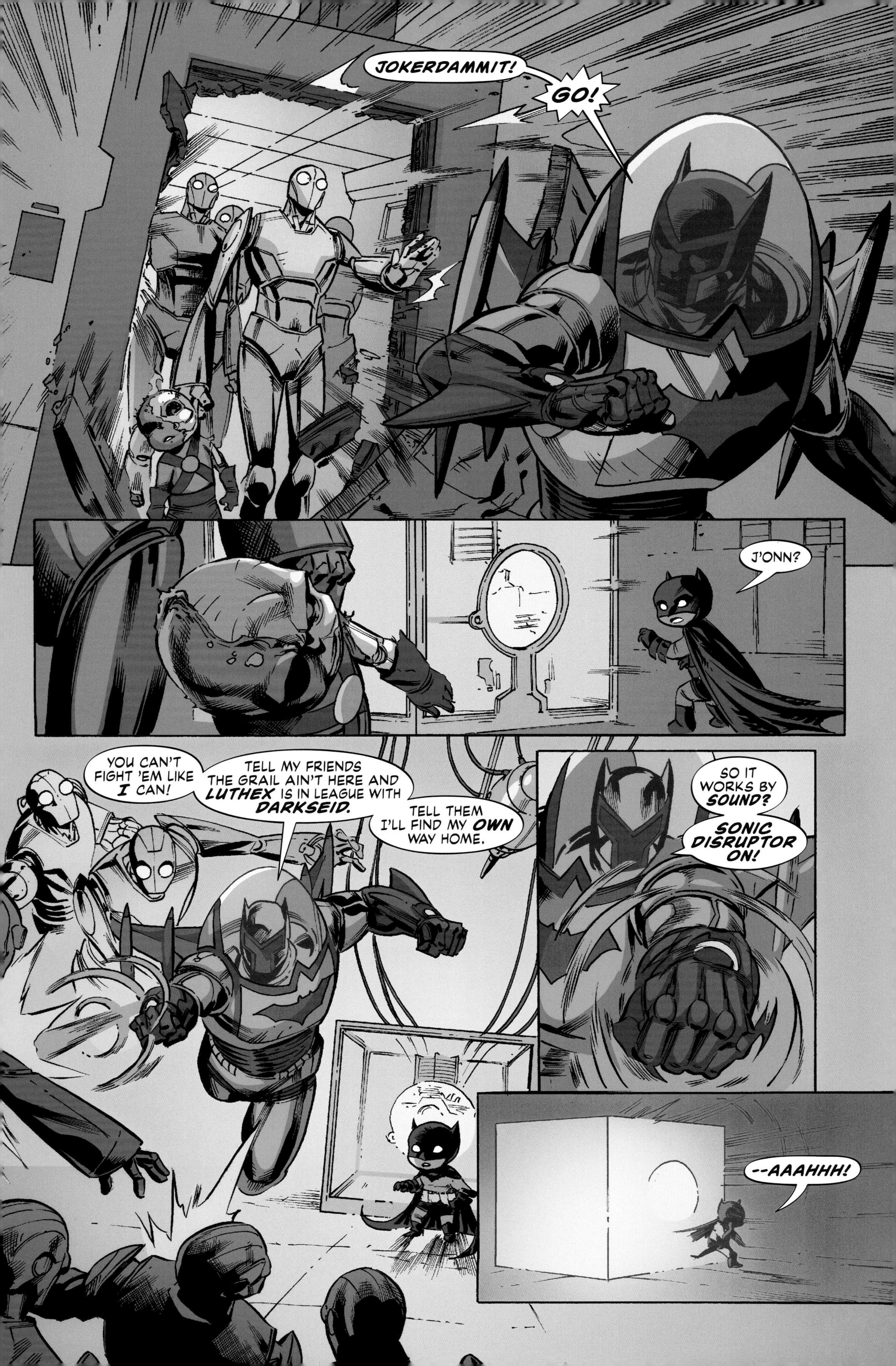
JOKERDAMMIT!
GO!
J'ONN?
YOU CAN'T FIGHT 'EM LIKE I CAN!
TELL MY FRIENDS THE GRAIL AIN'T HERE AND LUTHEX IS IN LEAGUE WITH DARKSEID.
TELL THEM I'LL FIND MY OWN WAY HOME.
SO IT WORKS BY SOUND?
SONIC DISRUPTOR ON!
--AAAHHH!

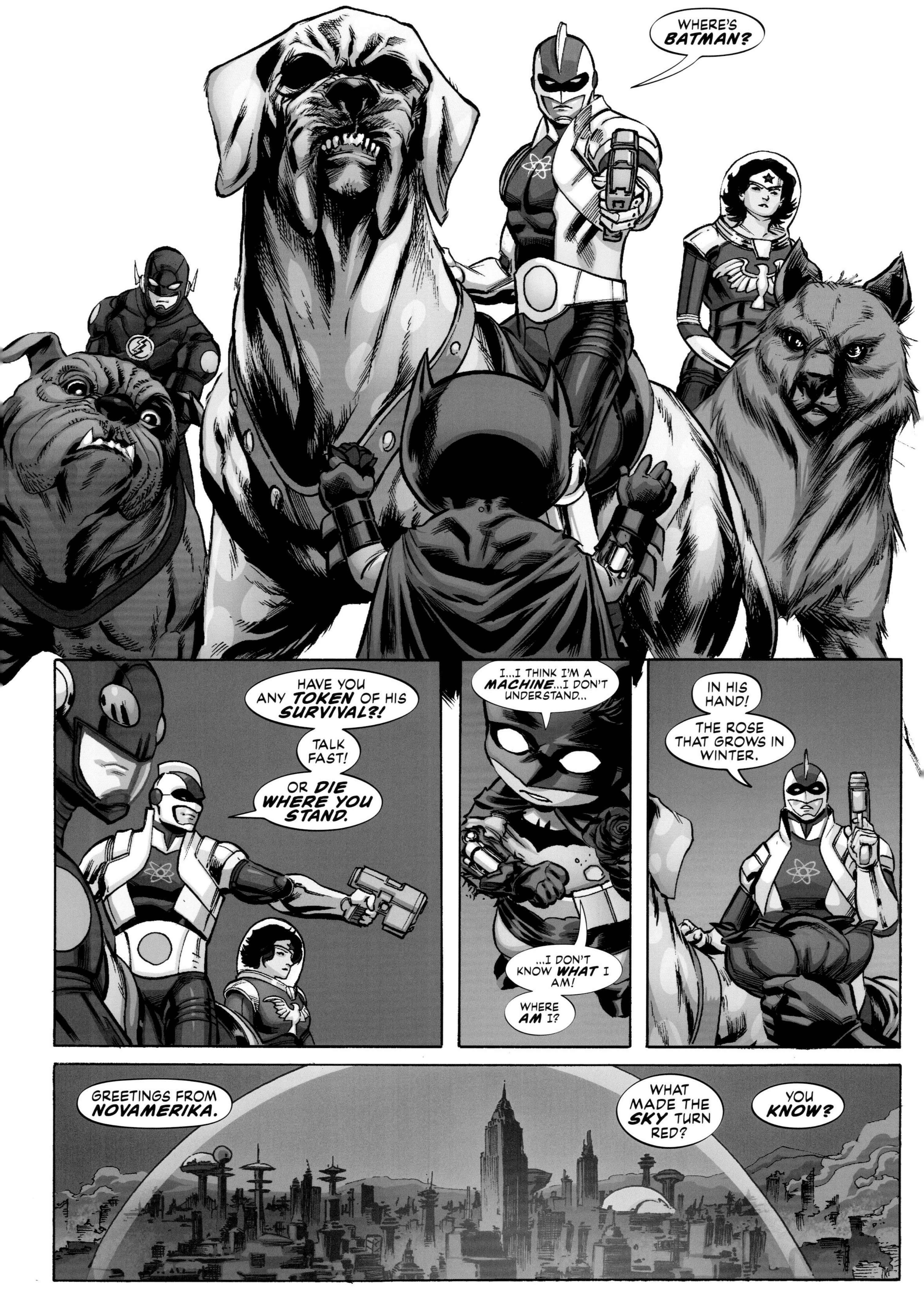
WHERE'S BATMAN?
HAVE YOU ANY TOKEN OF HIS SURVIVAL?!
TALK FAST!
OR DIE WHERE YOU STAND.
I...I THINK I'M A MACHINE...I DON'T UNDERSTAND...
...I DON'T KNOW WHAT I AM!
WHERE AM I?
IN HIS HAND!
THE ROSE THAT GROWS IN WINTER.
GREETINGS FROM NOVAMERIKA.
WHAT MADE THE SKY TURN RED?
YOU KNOW?

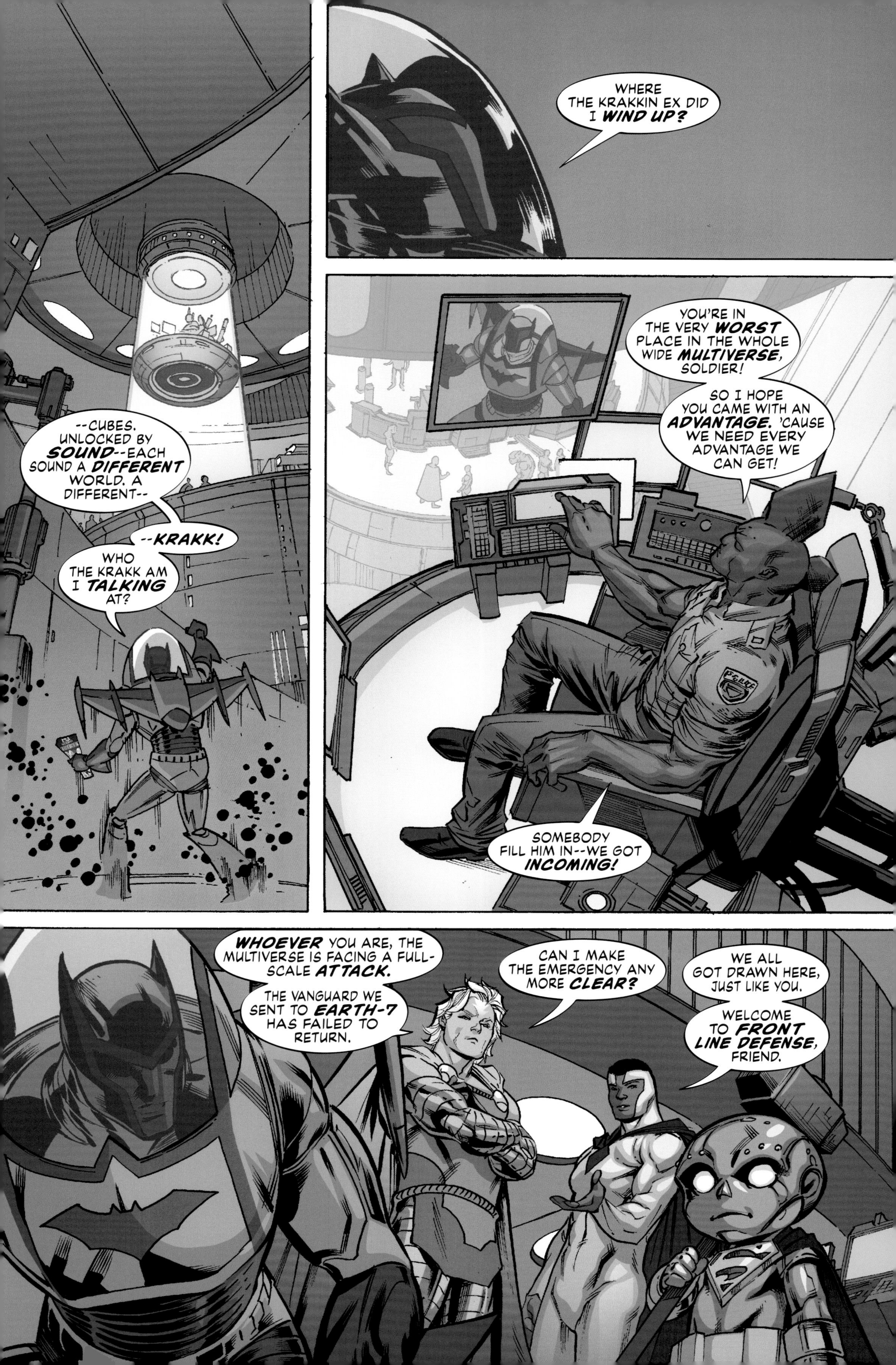
WHERE THE KRAKKIN EX DID I WIND UP?
--CUBES. UNLOCKED BY SOUND--EACH SOUND A DIFFERENT WORLD. A DIFFERENT--
--KRAKK!
WHO THE KRAKK AM I TALKING AT?
YOU'RE IN THE VERY WORST PLACE IN THE WHOLE WIDE MULTIVERSE, SOLDIER!
SO I HOPE YOU CAME WITH AN ADVANTAGE. 'CAUSE WE NEED EVERY ADVANTAGE WE CAN GET!
SOMEBODY FILL HIM IN--WE GOT INCOMING!
WHOEVER YOU ARE, THE MULTIVERSE IS FACING A FULL-SCALE ATTACK.
THE VANGUARD WE SENT TO EARTH-7 HAS FAILED TO RETURN.
CAN I MAKE THE EMERGENCY ANY MORE CLEAR?
WE ALL GOT DRAWN HERE, JUST LIKE YOU.
WELCOME TO FRONT LINE DEFENSE, FRIEND.

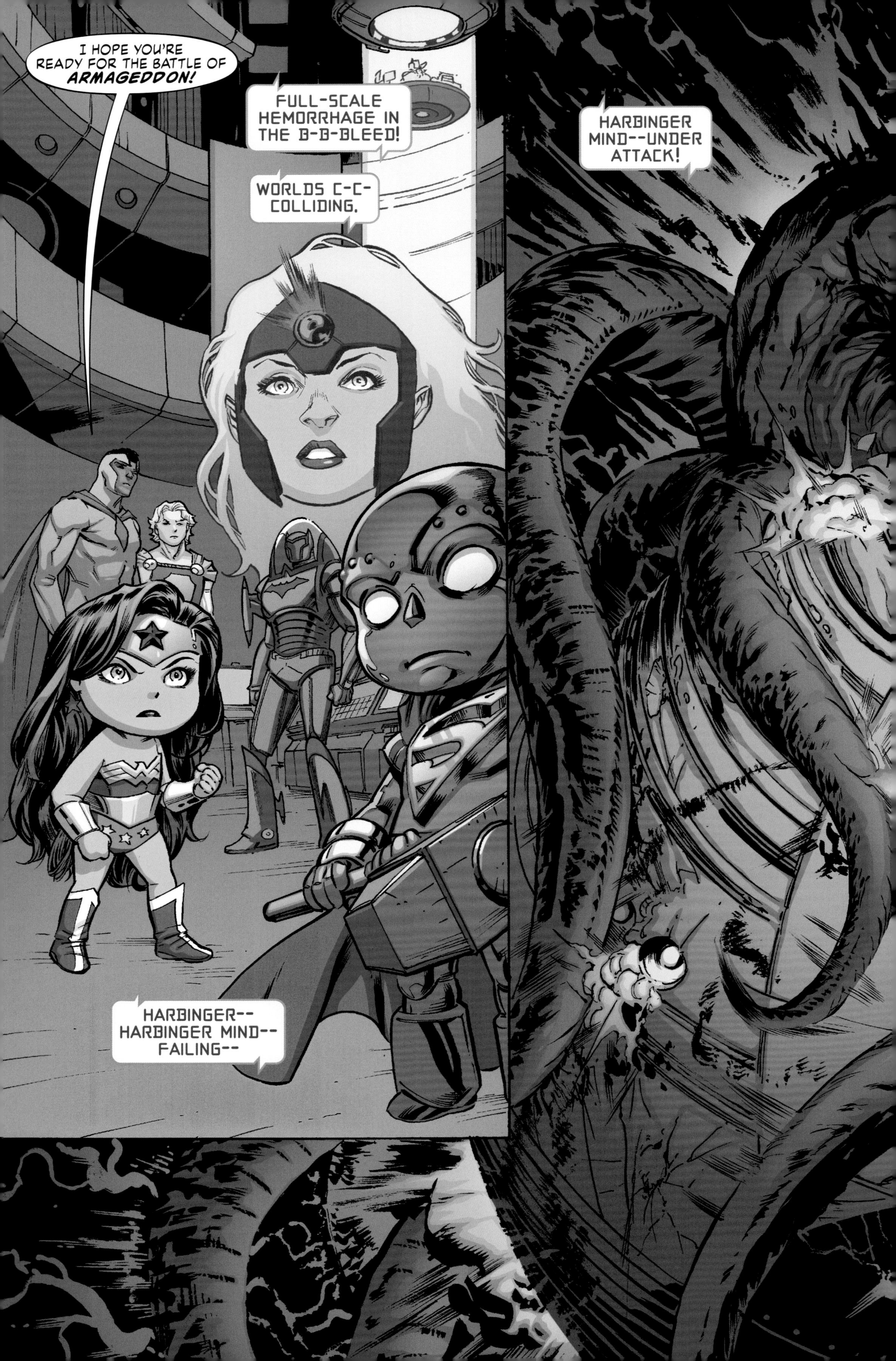
I HOPE YOU'RE READY FOR THE BATTLE OF *ARMAGEDDON!*
FULL-SCALE HEMORRHAGE IN THE B-B-BLEED!
WORLDS C-C-COLLIDING.
HARBINGER--HARBINGER MIND--FAILING--
HARBINGER MIND--UNDER ATTACK!

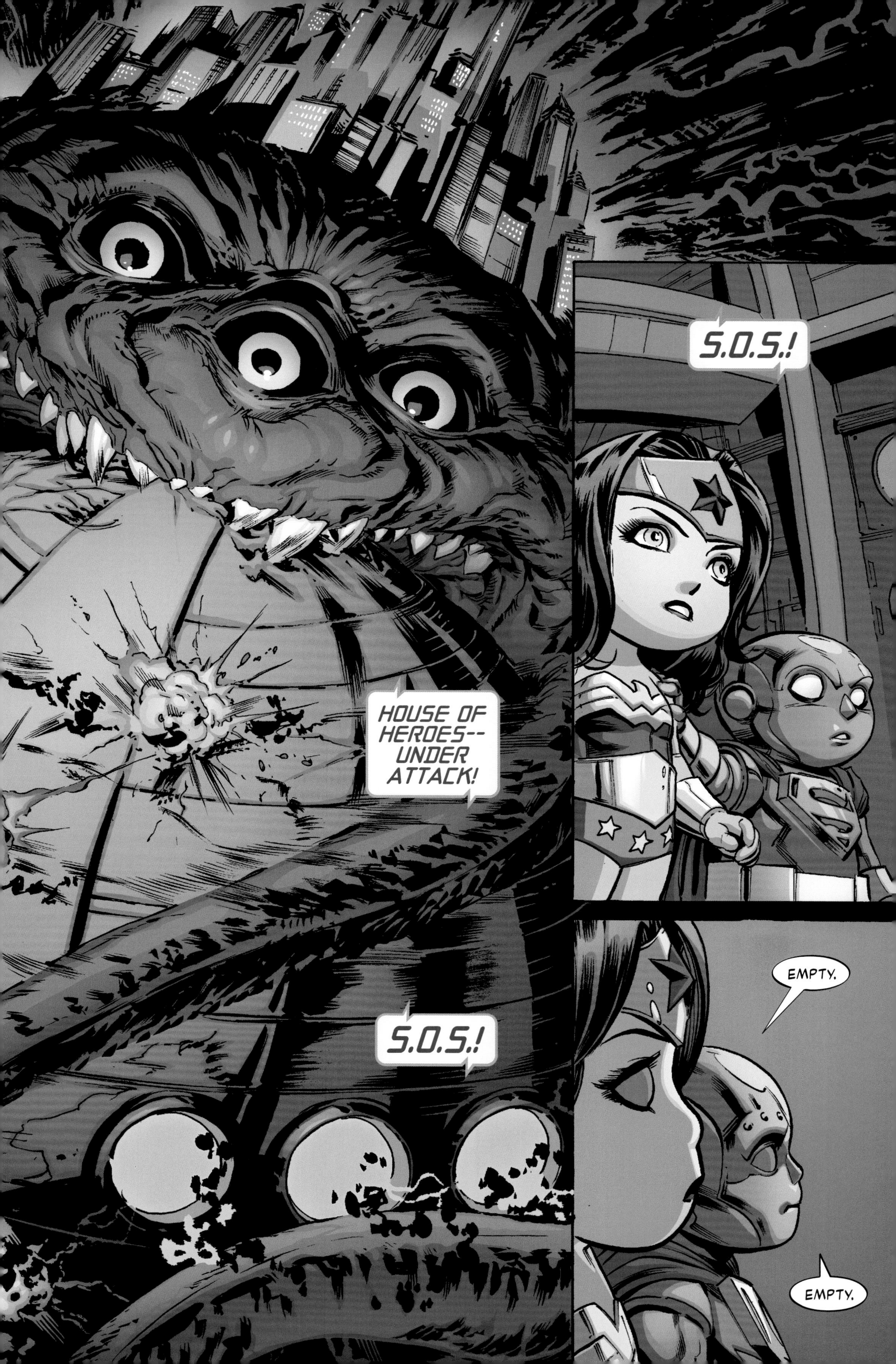
HOUSE OF HEROES-- UNDER ATTACK!
S.O.S.!
S.O.S.!
EMPTY.
EMPTY.

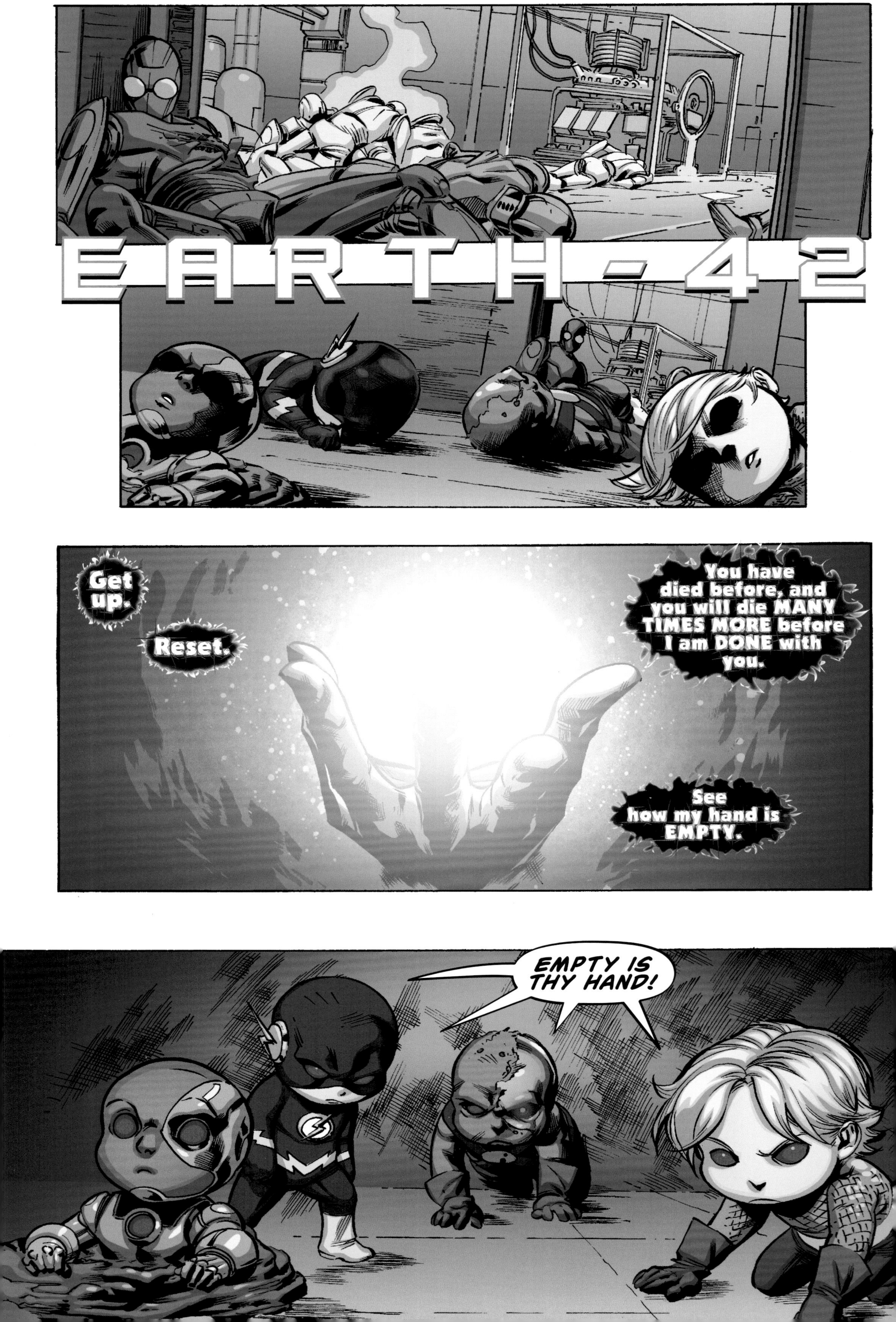
EARTH-42
Get up.
Reset.
You have died before, and you will die MANY TIMES MORE before I am DONE with you.
See how my hand is EMPTY.
EMPTY IS THY HAND!

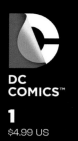

DC COMICS™

1

$4.99 US

THE MULTIVERSITY™

MORRISON
LEE
WILLIAMS
SINCLAIR

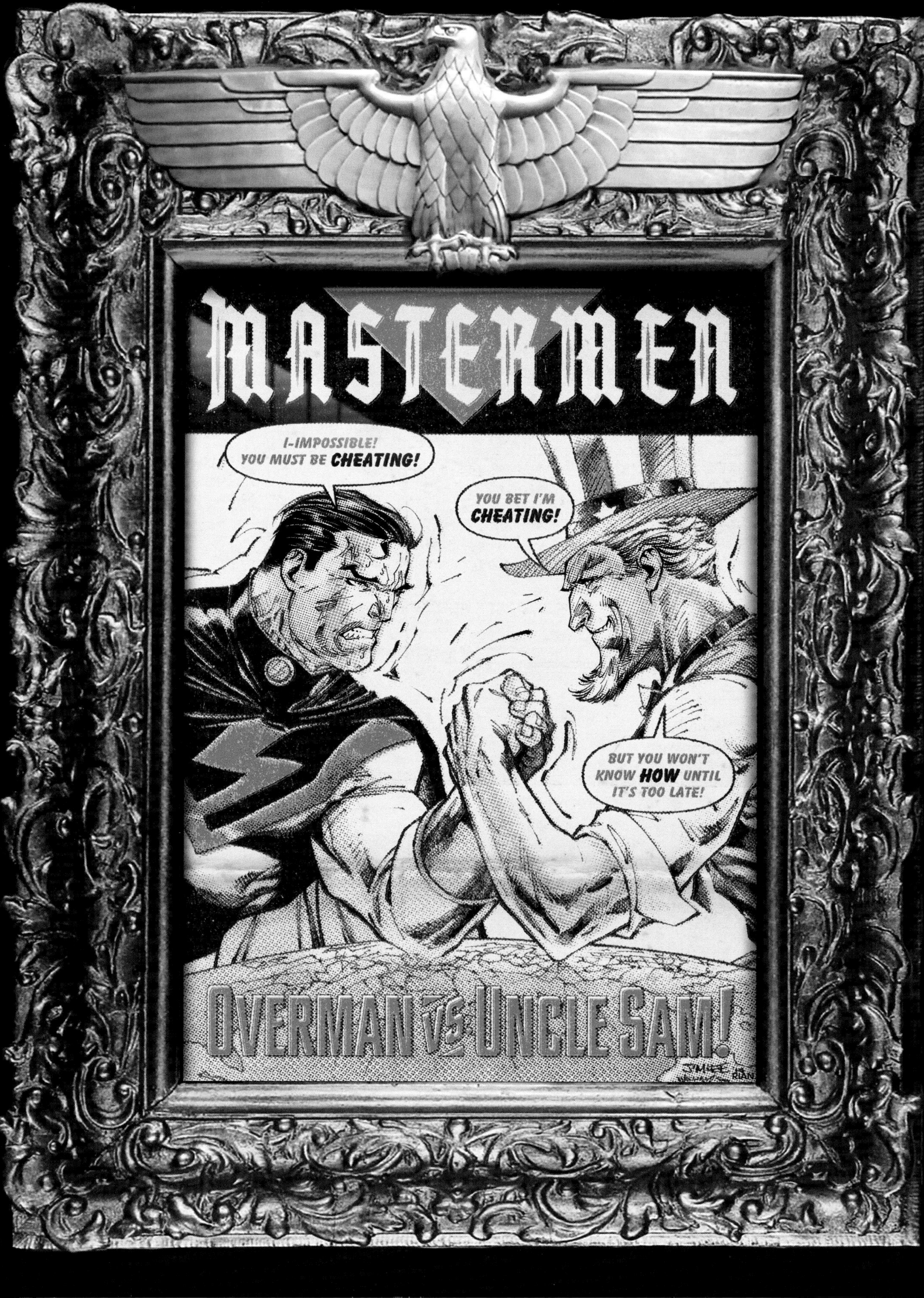
MASTERMEN
I-IMPOSSIBLE! YOU MUST BE CHEATING!
YOU BET I'M CHEATING!
BUT YOU WON'T KNOW HOW UNTIL IT'S TOO LATE!
OVERMAN vs UNCLE SAM!

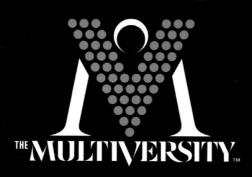

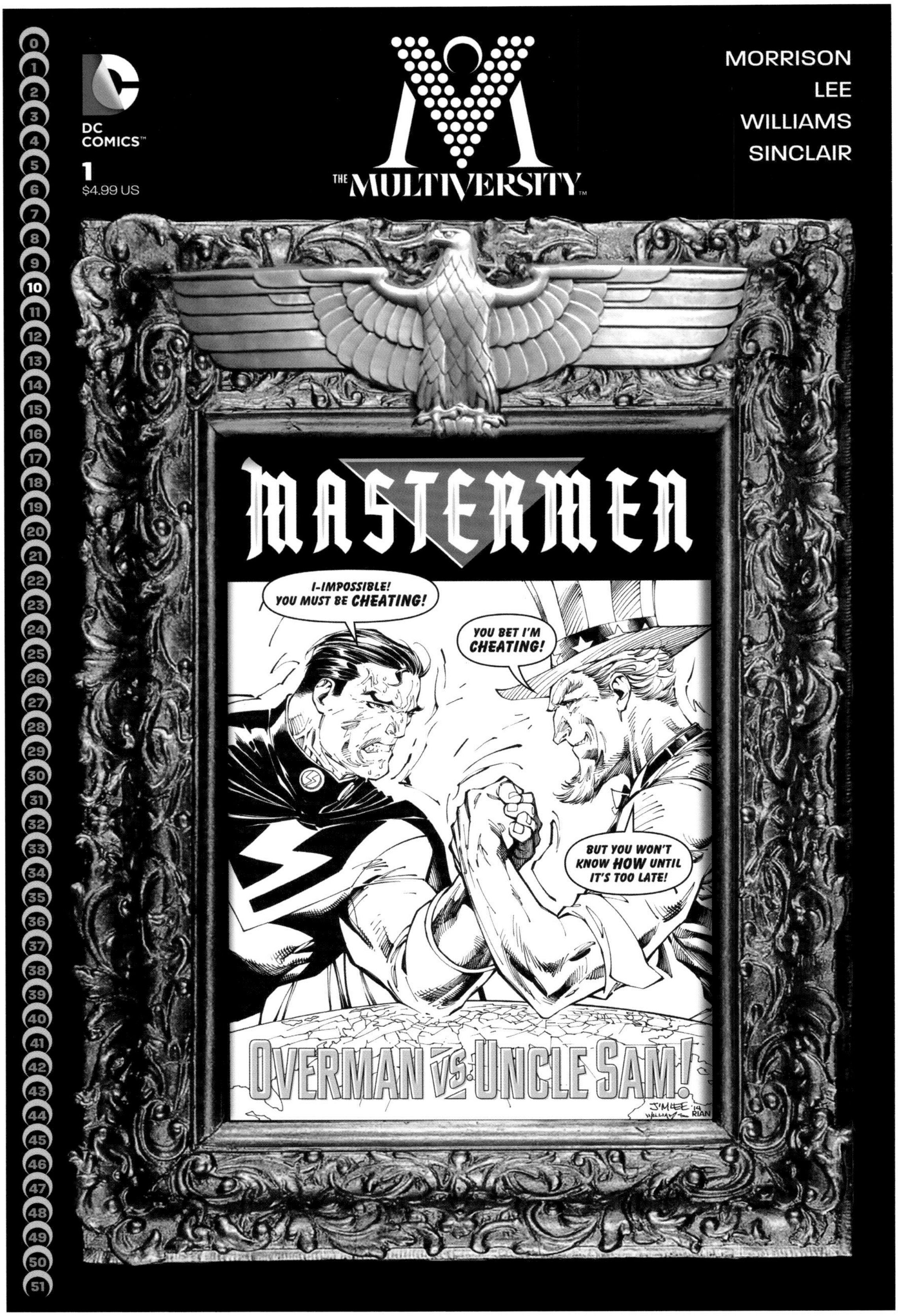

MORRISON
LEE
WILLIAMS
SINCLAIR
DC COMICS
1
$4.99 US
THE MULTIVERSITY
MASTERMEN
I-IMPOSSIBLE! YOU MUST BE CHEATING!
YOU BET I'M CHEATING!
BUT YOU WON'T KNOW HOW UNTIL IT'S TOO LATE!
OVERMAN VS. UNCLE SAM!

THE MULTIVERSITY: MASTERMEN
#1

Written by
GRANT MORRISON

Penciller
JIM LEE

Inkers
SCOTT WILLIAMS
SANDRA HOPE
MARK IRWIN
JONATHAN GLAPION

Colorists
ALEX SINCLAIR
JEROMY COX

Letterer
ROB LEIGH

Cover artists
JIM LEE with
RIAN HUGHES

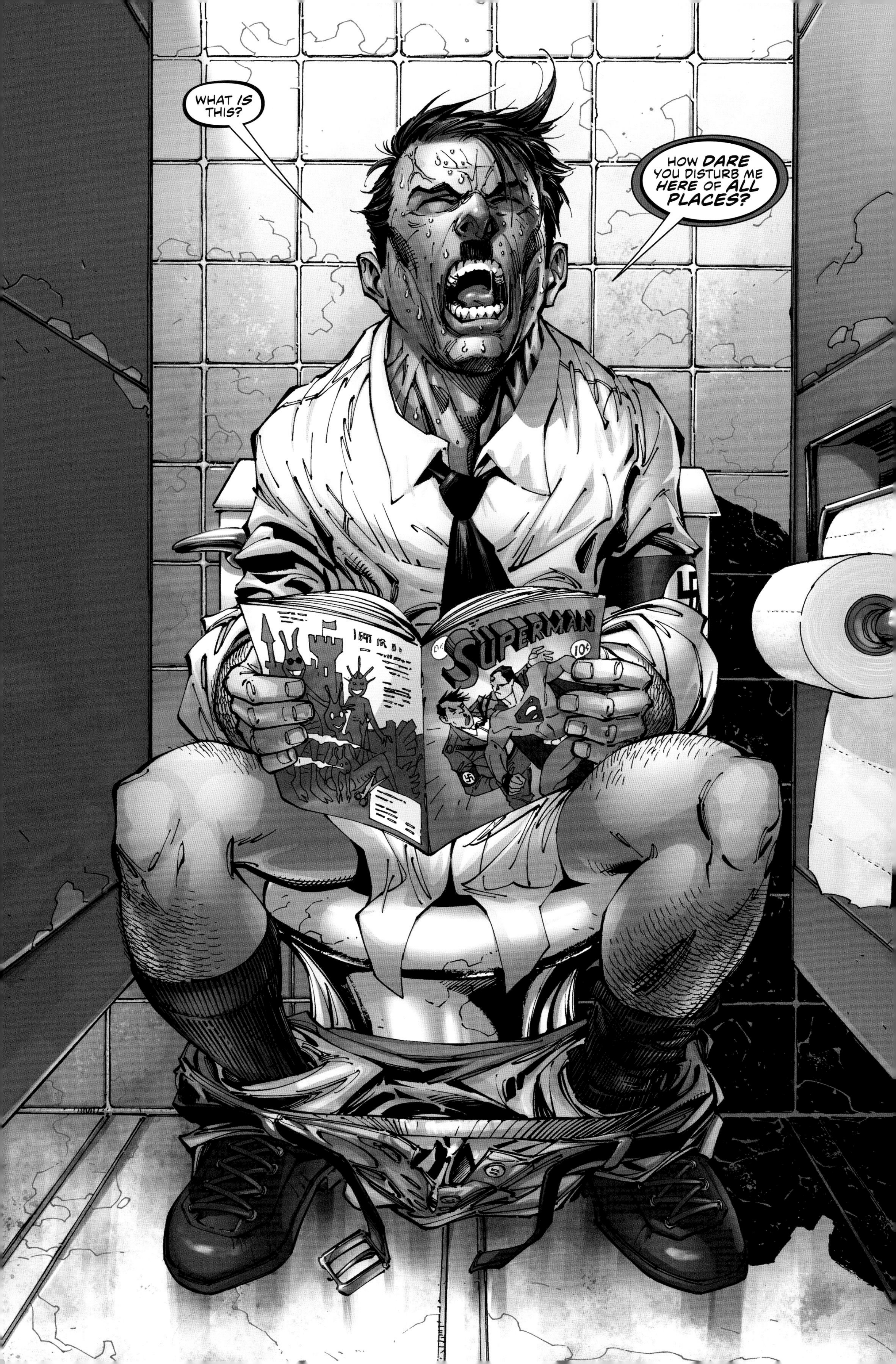
WHAT IS THIS?
HOW DARE YOU DISTURB ME HERE OF ALL PLACES?
SUPERMAN
10¢

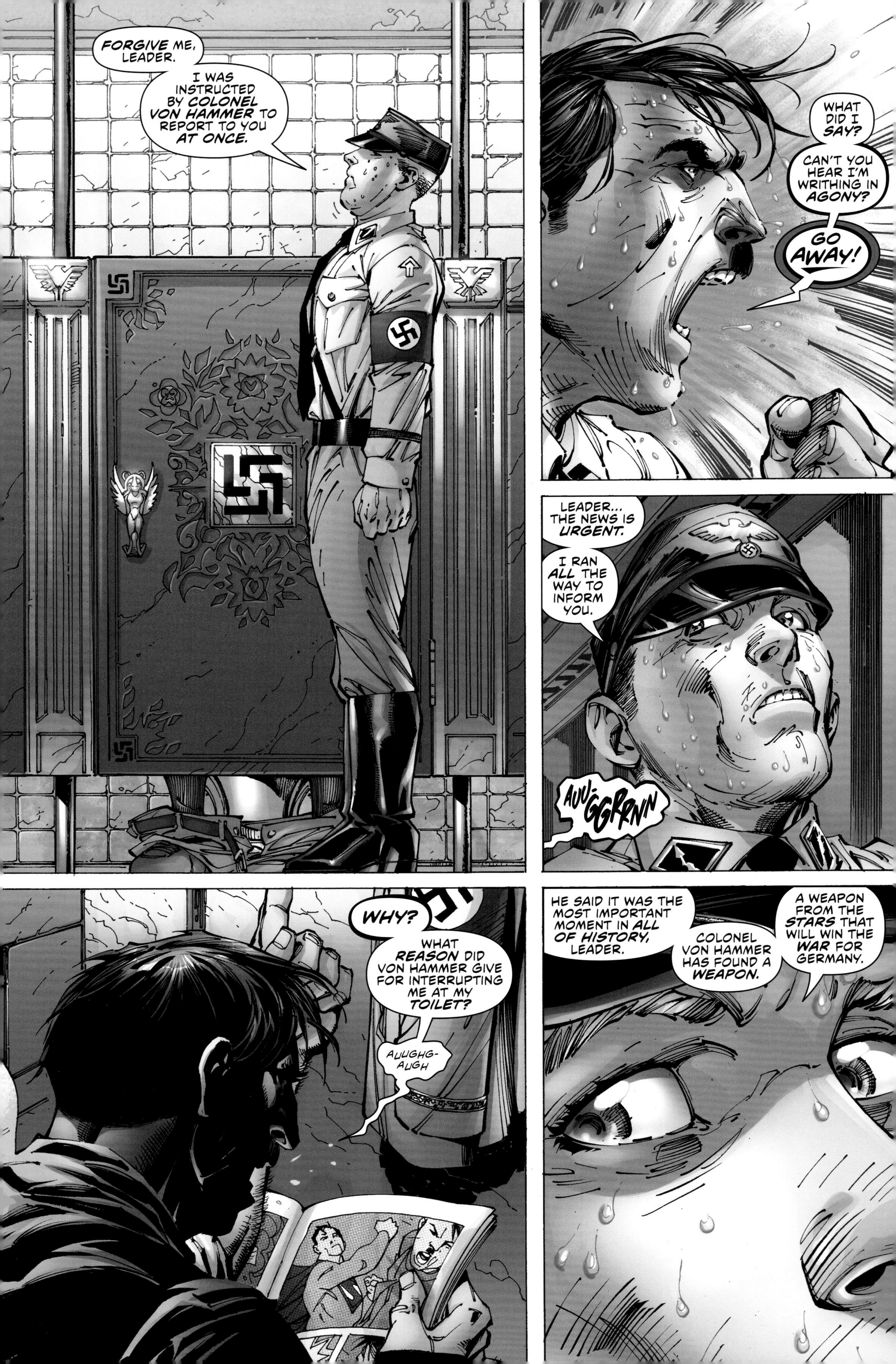
FORGIVE ME, LEADER.
I WAS INSTRUCTED BY COLONEL VON HAMMER TO REPORT TO YOU AT ONCE.
WHAT DID I SAY?
CAN'T YOU HEAR I'M WRITHING IN AGONY?
GO AWAY!
LEADER... THE NEWS IS URGENT.
I RAN ALL THE WAY TO INFORM YOU.
AUU-GGRRNN
WHY?
WHAT REASON DID VON HAMMER GIVE FOR INTERRUPTING ME AT MY TOILET?
AUUGHG-AUGH
HE SAID IT WAS THE MOST IMPORTANT MOMENT IN ALL OF HISTORY, LEADER.
COLONEL VON HAMMER HAS FOUND A WEAPON.
A WEAPON FROM THE STARS THAT WILL WIN THE WAR FOR GERMANY.

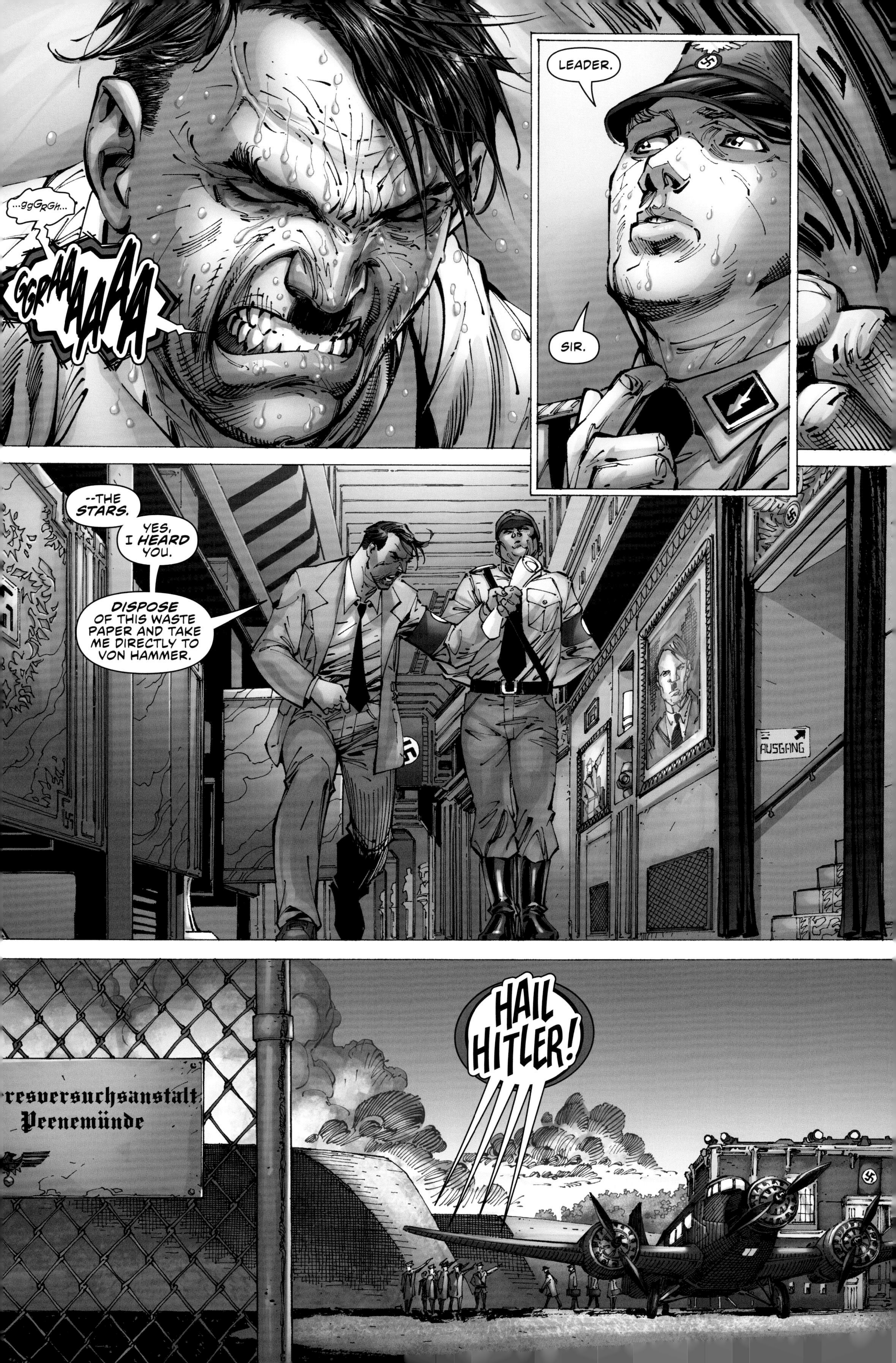
...ggGRGh...
GGRAAAAAAAA
LEADER.
SIR.
--THE STARS.
YES, I HEARD YOU.
DISPOSE OF THIS WASTE PAPER AND TAKE ME DIRECTLY TO VON HAMMER.
AUSGANG
resversuchsanstalt
Peenemünde
HAIL HITLER!

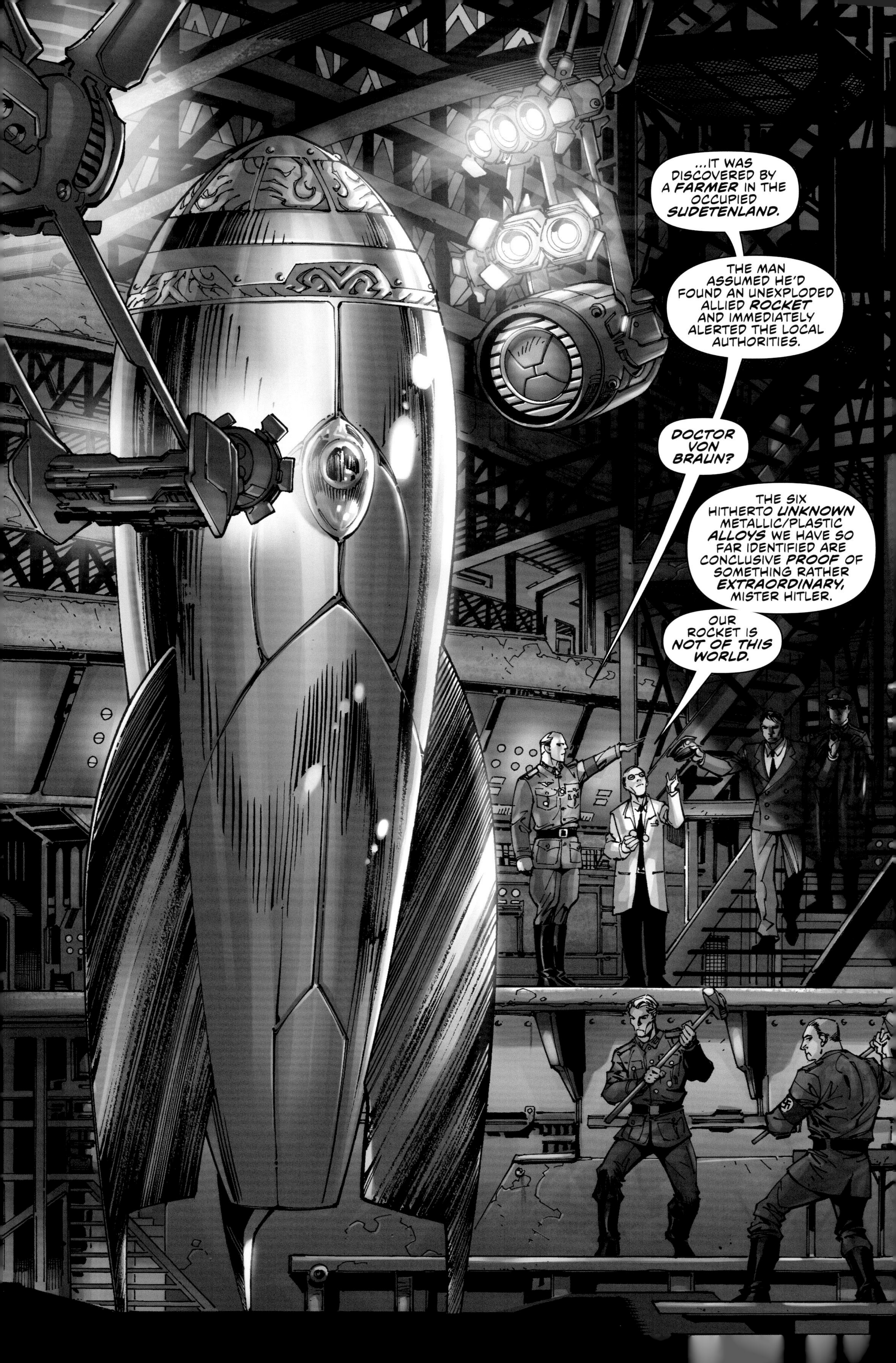
...IT WAS DISCOVERED BY A FARMER IN THE OCCUPIED SUDETENLAND.
THE MAN ASSUMED HE'D FOUND AN UNEXPLODED ALLIED ROCKET AND IMMEDIATELY ALERTED THE LOCAL AUTHORITIES.
DOCTOR VON BRAUN?
THE SIX HITHERTO UNKNOWN METALLIC/PLASTIC ALLOYS WE HAVE SO FAR IDENTIFIED ARE CONCLUSIVE PROOF OF SOMETHING RATHER EXTRAORDINARY, MISTER HITLER.
OUR ROCKET IS NOT OF THIS WORLD.

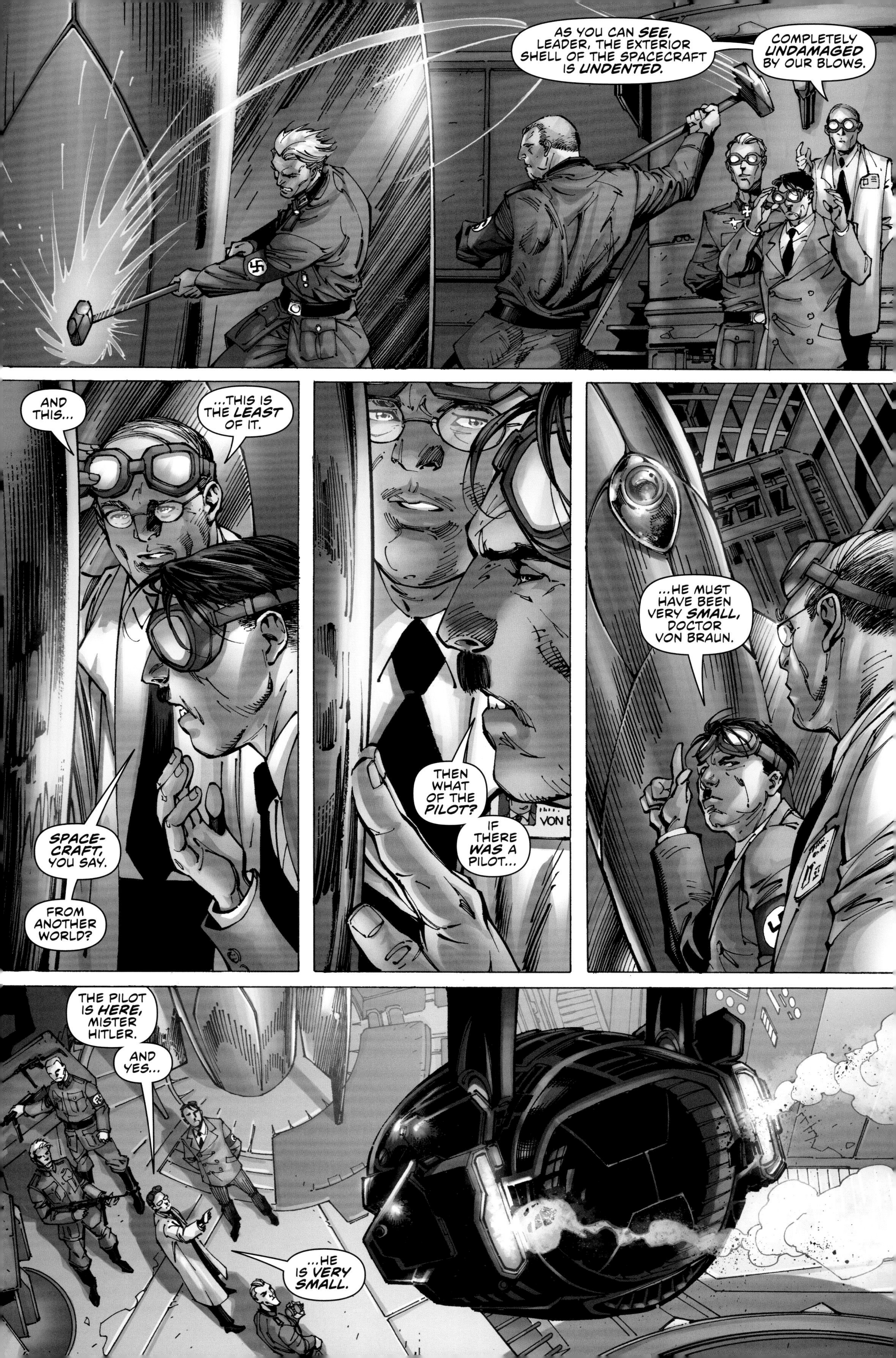
AS YOU CAN SEE, LEADER, THE EXTERIOR SHELL OF THE SPACECRAFT IS UNDENTED.
COMPLETELY UNDAMAGED BY OUR BLOWS.
AND THIS...
...THIS IS THE LEAST OF IT.
SPACE-CRAFT, YOU SAY.
FROM ANOTHER WORLD?
THEN WHAT OF THE PILOT?
IF THERE WAS A PILOT...
VON B
...HE MUST HAVE BEEN VERY SMALL, DOCTOR VON BRAUN.
THE PILOT IS HERE, MISTER HITLER.
AND YES...
...HE IS VERY SMALL.

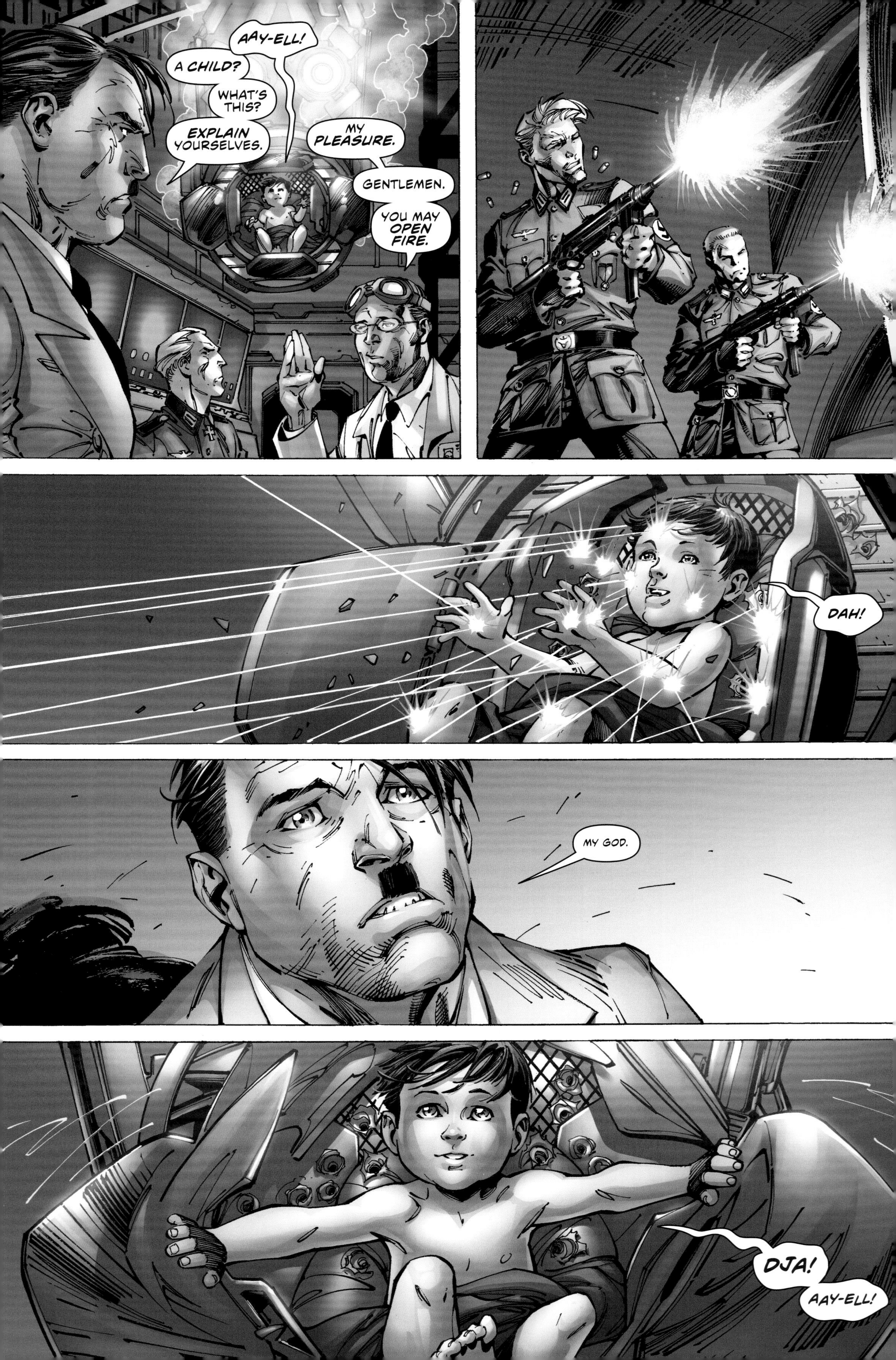
AAY-ELL!
A CHILD?
WHAT'S THIS?
EXPLAIN YOURSELVES.
MY PLEASURE.
GENTLEMEN.
YOU MAY OPEN FIRE.
DAH!
MY GOD.
DJA!
AAY-ELL!

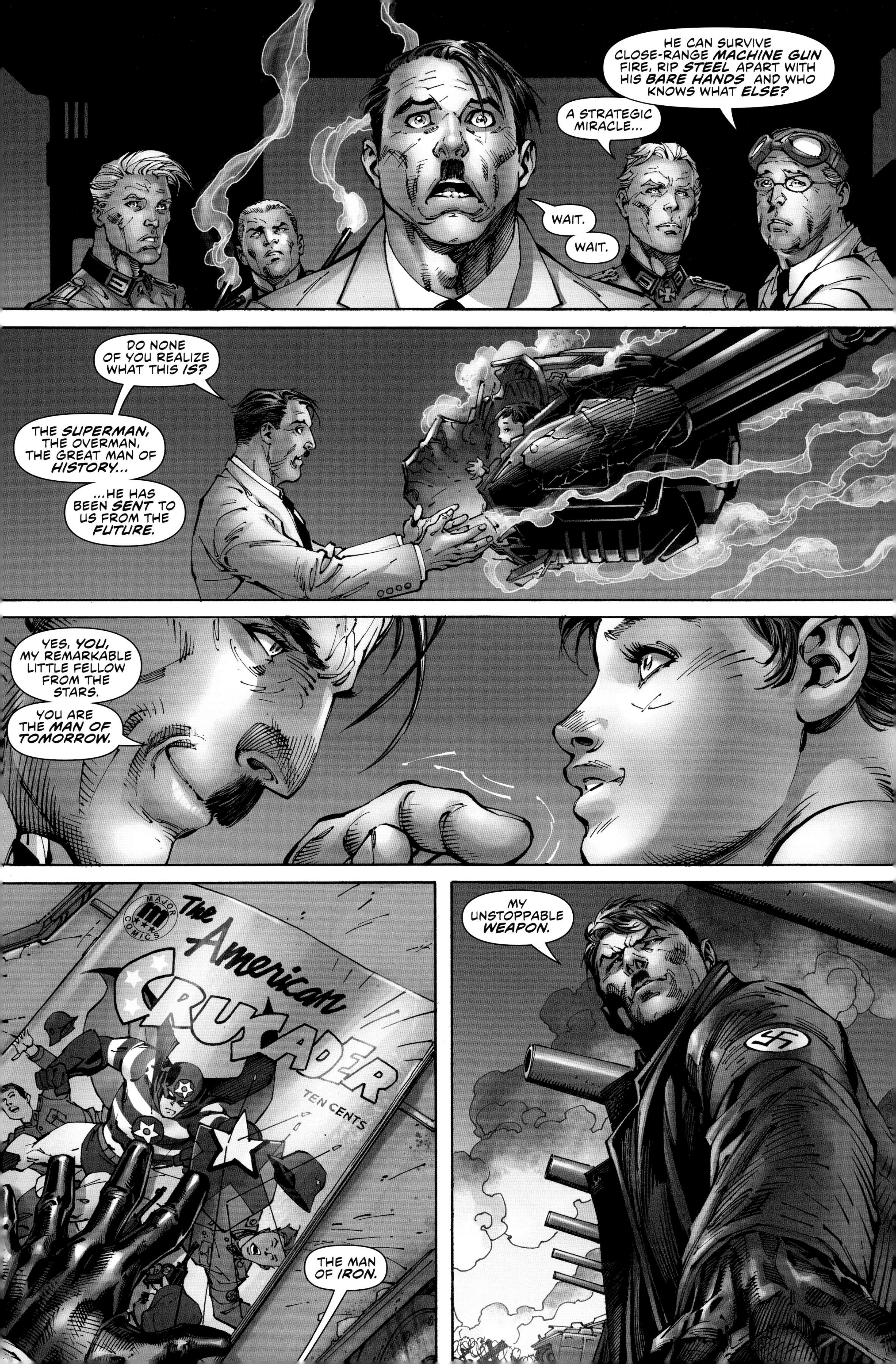

HE CAN SURVIVE CLOSE-RANGE MACHINE GUN FIRE, RIP STEEL APART WITH HIS BARE HANDS AND WHO KNOWS WHAT ELSE?
A STRATEGIC MIRACLE...
WAIT.
WAIT.
DO NONE OF YOU REALIZE WHAT THIS IS?
THE SUPERMAN, THE OVERMAN, THE GREAT MAN OF HISTORY...
...HE HAS BEEN SENT TO US FROM THE FUTURE.
YES, YOU, MY REMARKABLE LITTLE FELLOW FROM THE STARS.
YOU ARE THE MAN OF TOMORROW.
MAJOR COMICS
The American CRUSADER
TEN CENTS
THE MAN OF IRON.
MY UNSTOPPABLE WEAPON.

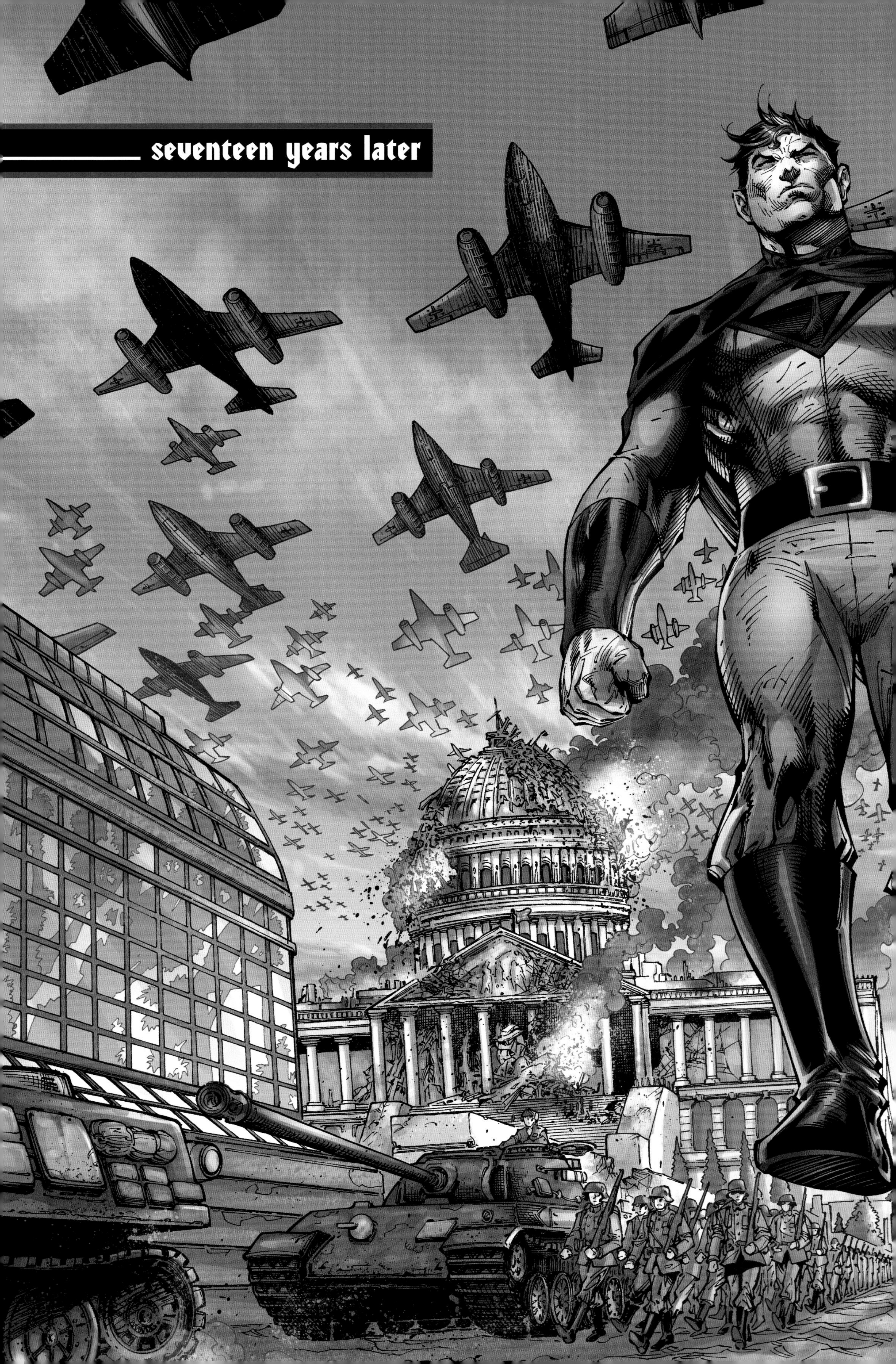
seventeen years later

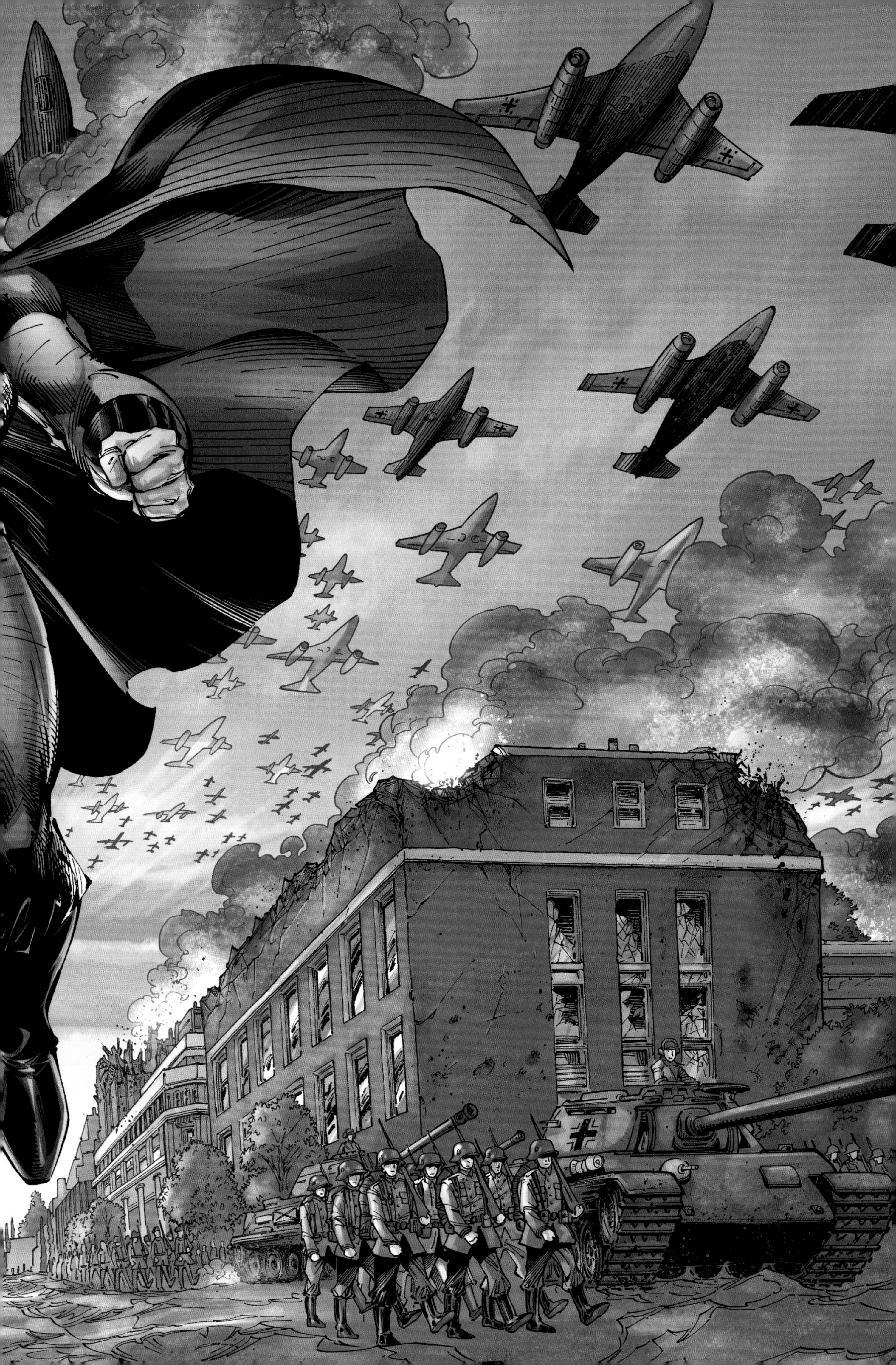

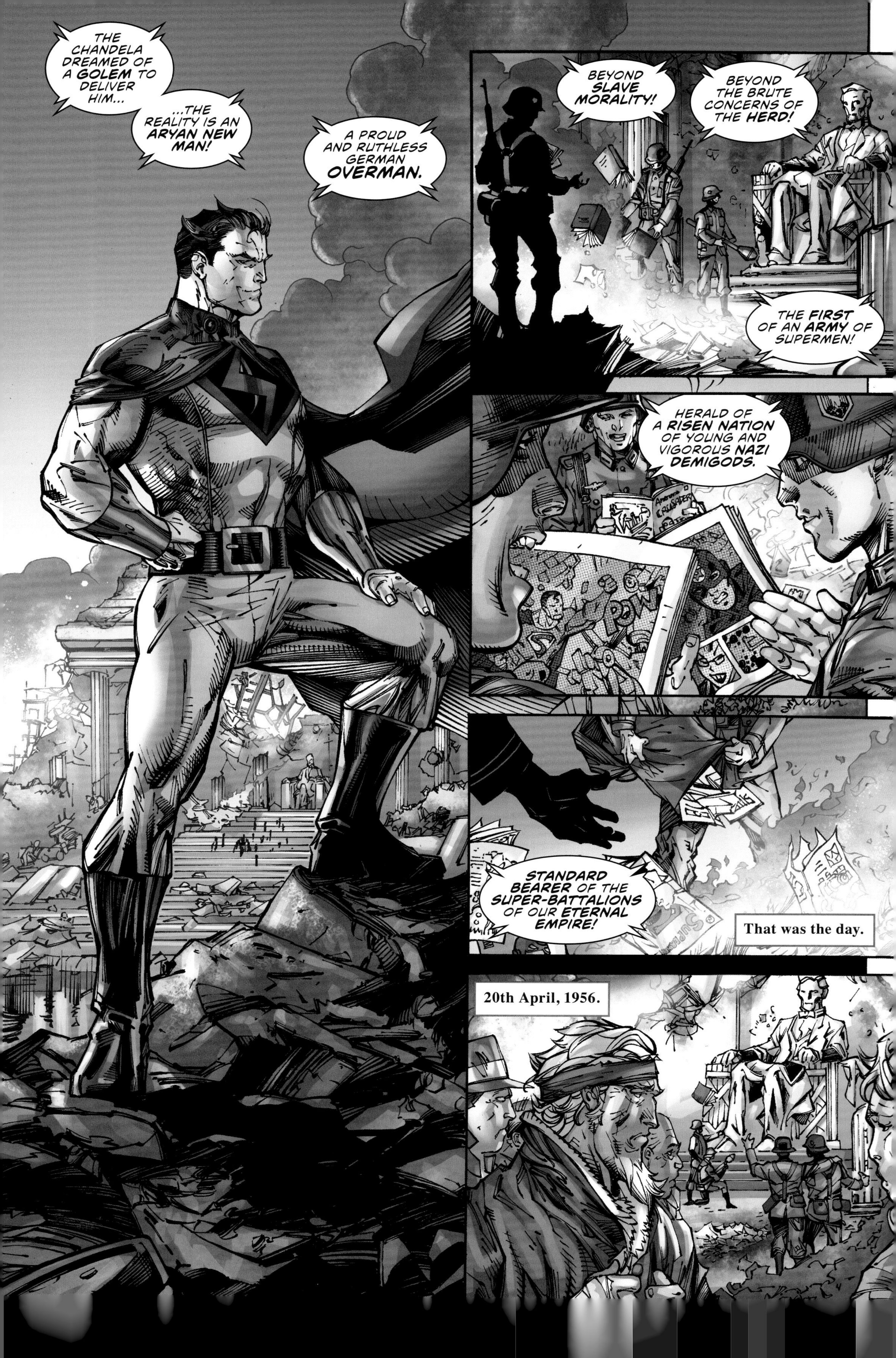

THE CHANDELA DREAMED OF A GOLEM TO DELIVER HIM...
...THE REALITY IS AN ARYAN NEW MAN!
A PROUD AND RUTHLESS GERMAN OVERMAN.
BEYOND SLAVE MORALITY!
BEYOND THE BRUTE CONCERNS OF THE HERD!
THE FIRST OF AN ARMY OF SUPERMEN!
HERALD OF A RISEN NATION OF YOUNG AND VIGOROUS NAZI DEMIGODS.
STANDARD BEARER OF THE SUPER-BATTALIONS OF OUR ETERNAL EMPIRE!
That was the day.
20th April, 1956.

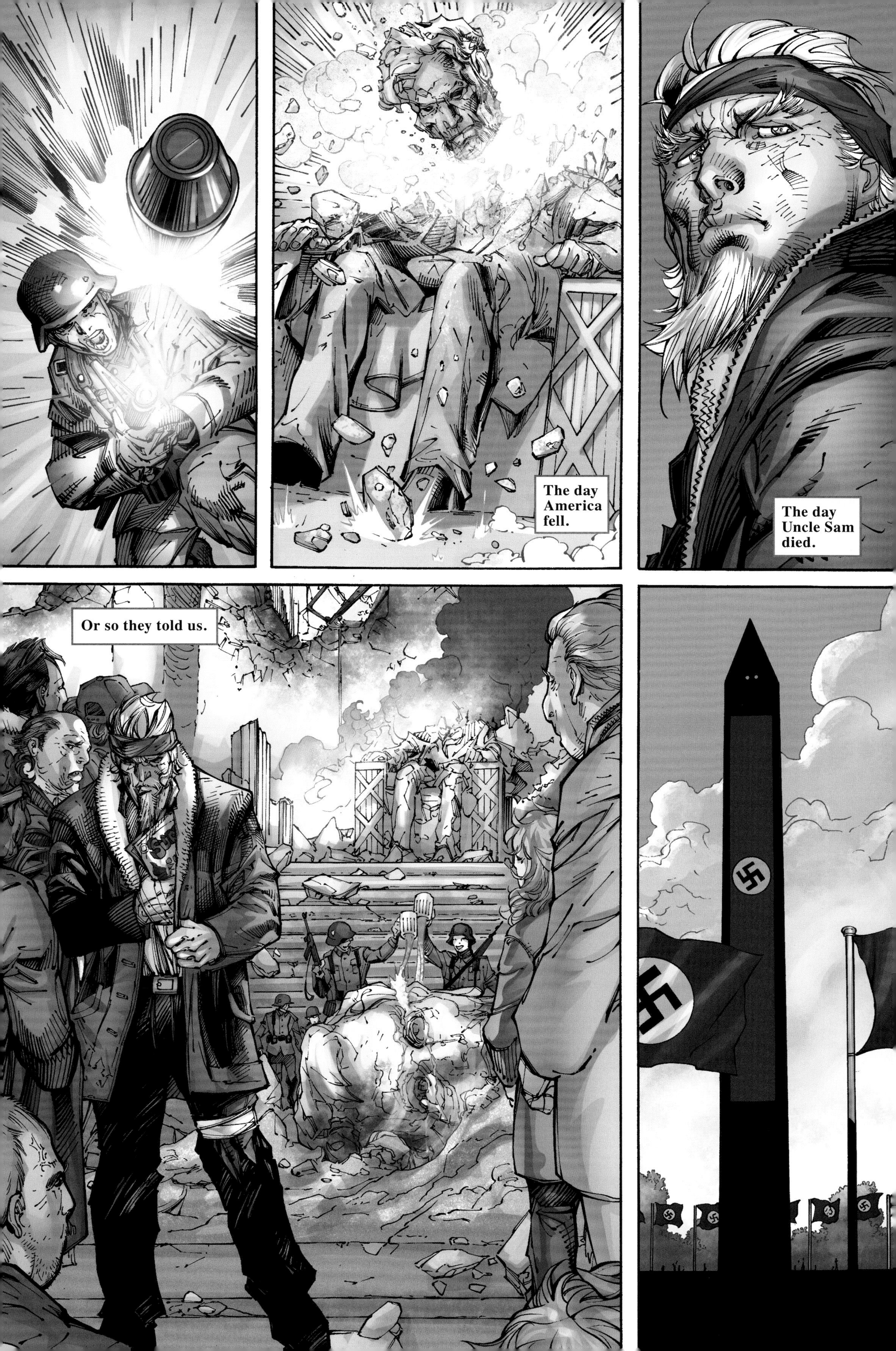
The day America fell.
The day Uncle Sam died.
Or so they told us.

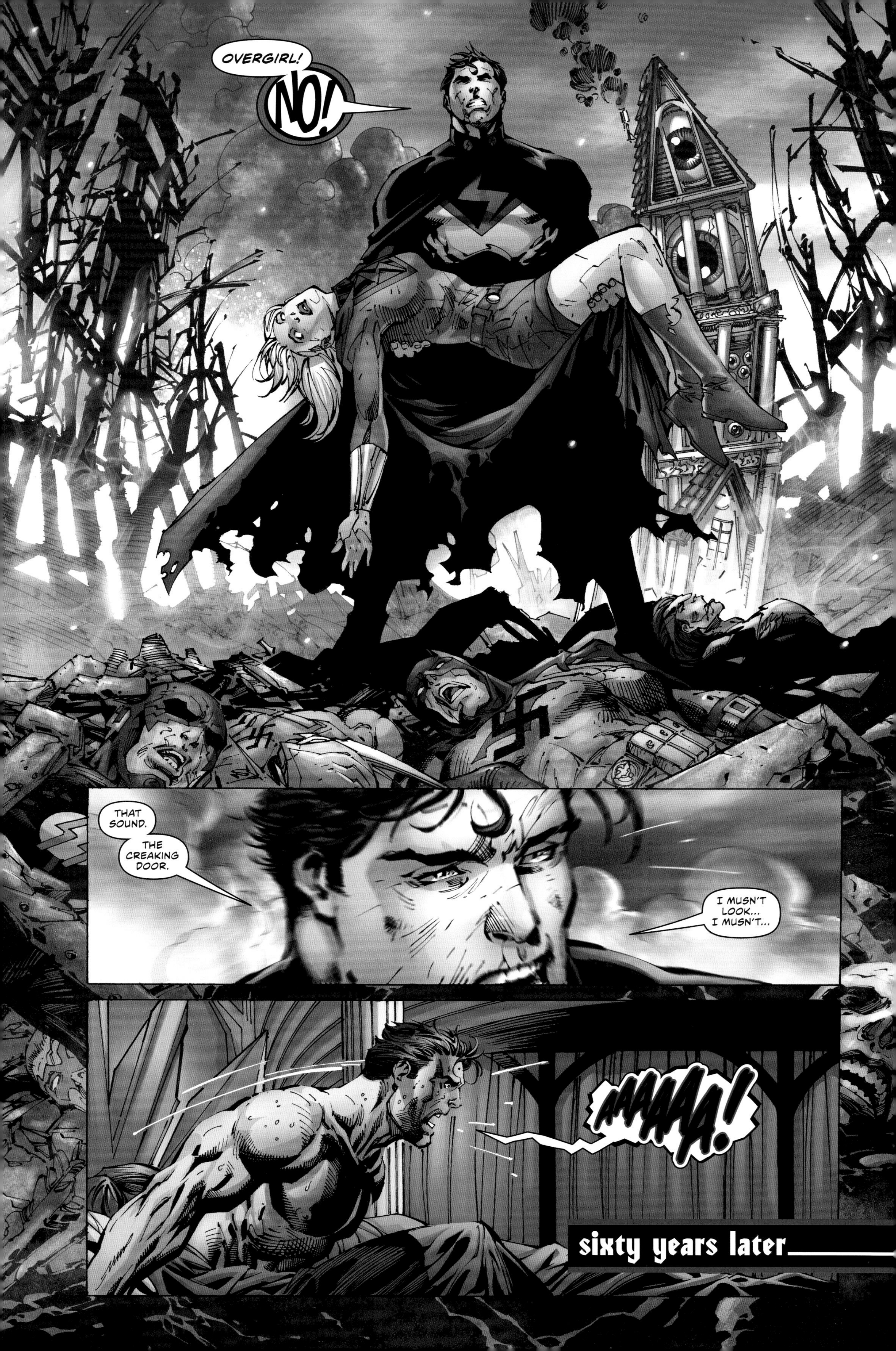

OVERGIRL!
NO!
THAT SOUND.
THE CREAKING DOOR.
I MUSN'T LOOK... I MUSN'T...
AAAAAAA!
sixty years later

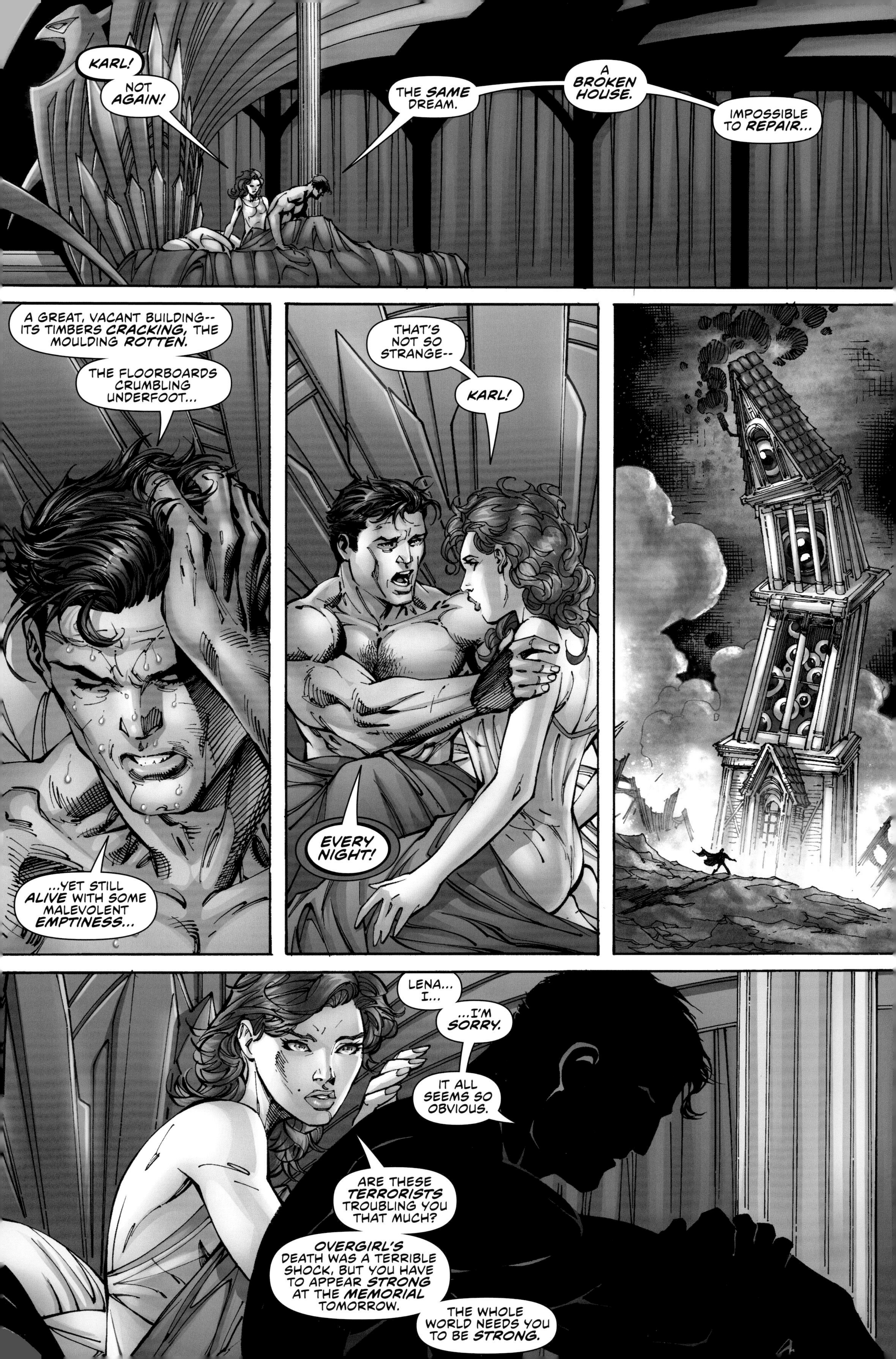
KARL!
NOT AGAIN!
THE SAME DREAM.
A BROKEN HOUSE.
IMPOSSIBLE TO REPAIR...
A GREAT, VACANT BUILDING-- ITS TIMBERS CRACKING, THE MOULDING ROTTEN.
THE FLOORBOARDS CRUMBLING UNDERFOOT...
...YET STILL ALIVE WITH SOME MALEVOLENT EMPTINESS...
THAT'S NOT SO STRANGE--
KARL!
EVERY NIGHT!
LENA... I...
...I'M SORRY.
IT ALL SEEMS SO OBVIOUS.
ARE THESE TERRORISTS TROUBLING YOU THAT MUCH?
OVERGIRL'S DEATH WAS A TERRIBLE SHOCK, BUT YOU HAVE TO APPEAR STRONG AT THE MEMORIAL TOMORROW.
THE WHOLE WORLD NEEDS YOU TO BE STRONG.

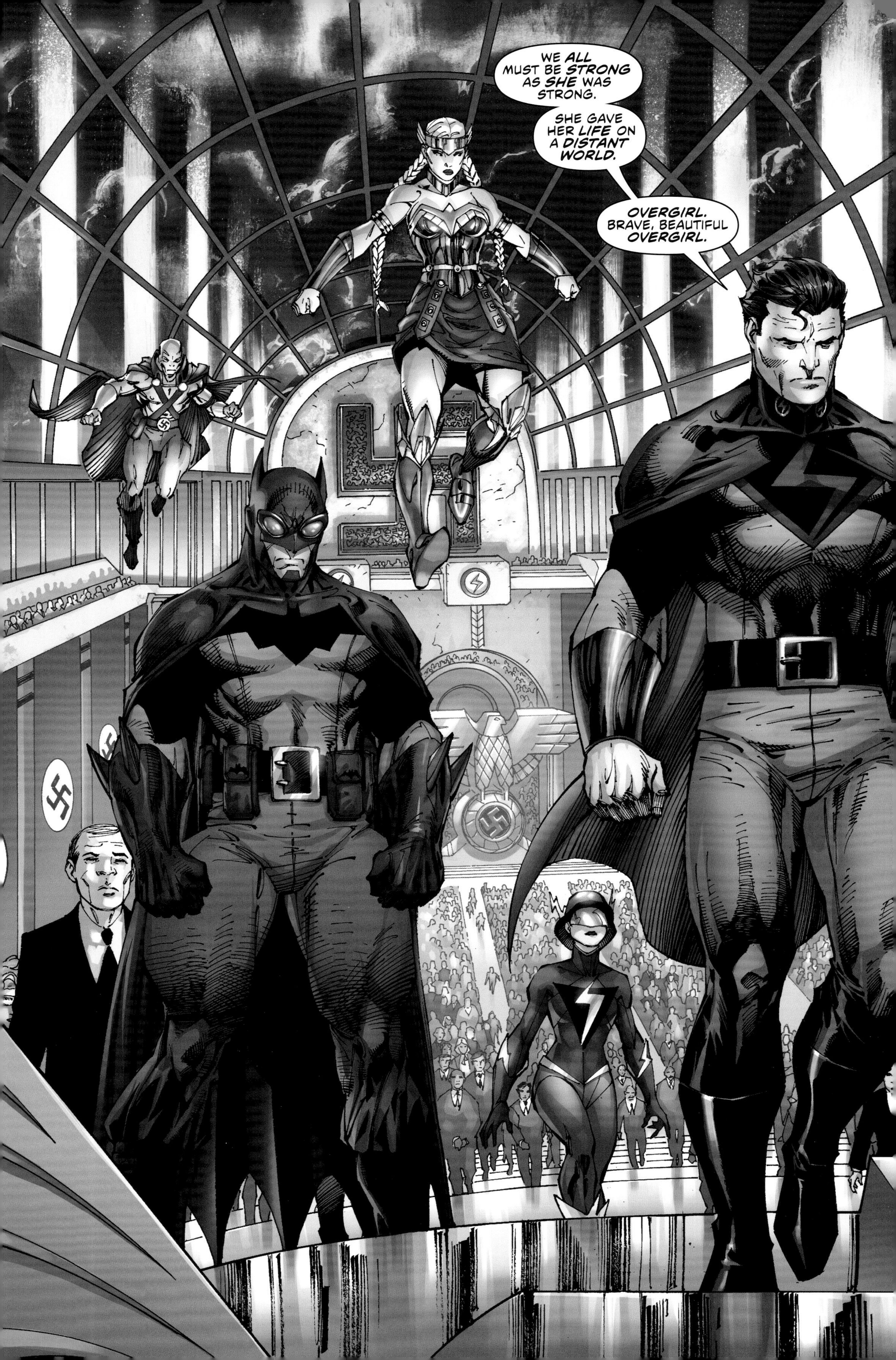
WE ALL MUST BE STRONG AS SHE WAS STRONG.
SHE GAVE HER LIFE ON A DISTANT WORLD.
OVERGIRL. BRAVE, BEAUTIFUL OVERGIRL.

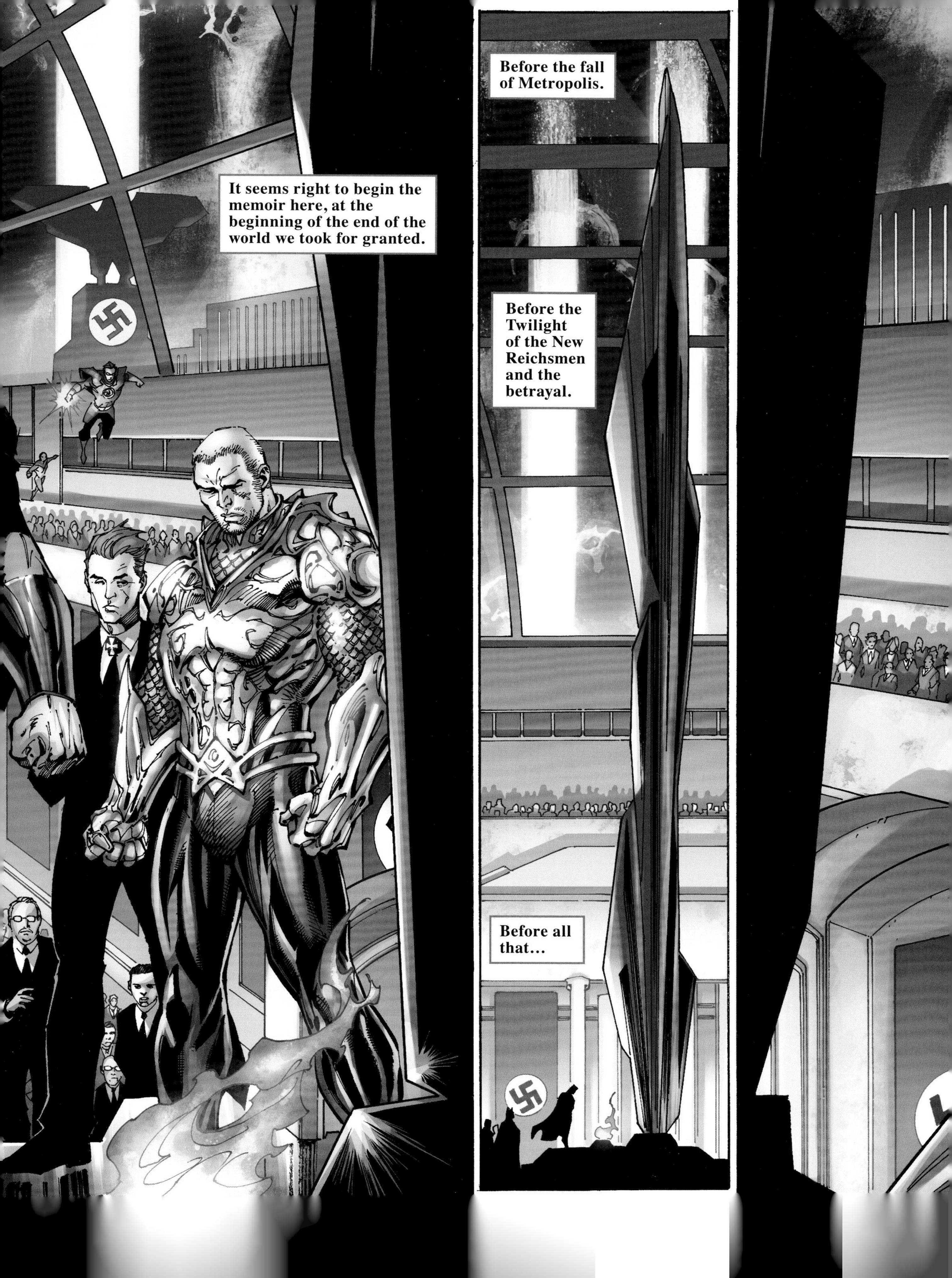

It seems right to begin the memoir here, at the beginning of the end of the world we took for granted.
Before the fall of Metropolis.
Before the Twilight of the New Reichsmen and the betrayal.
Before all that...

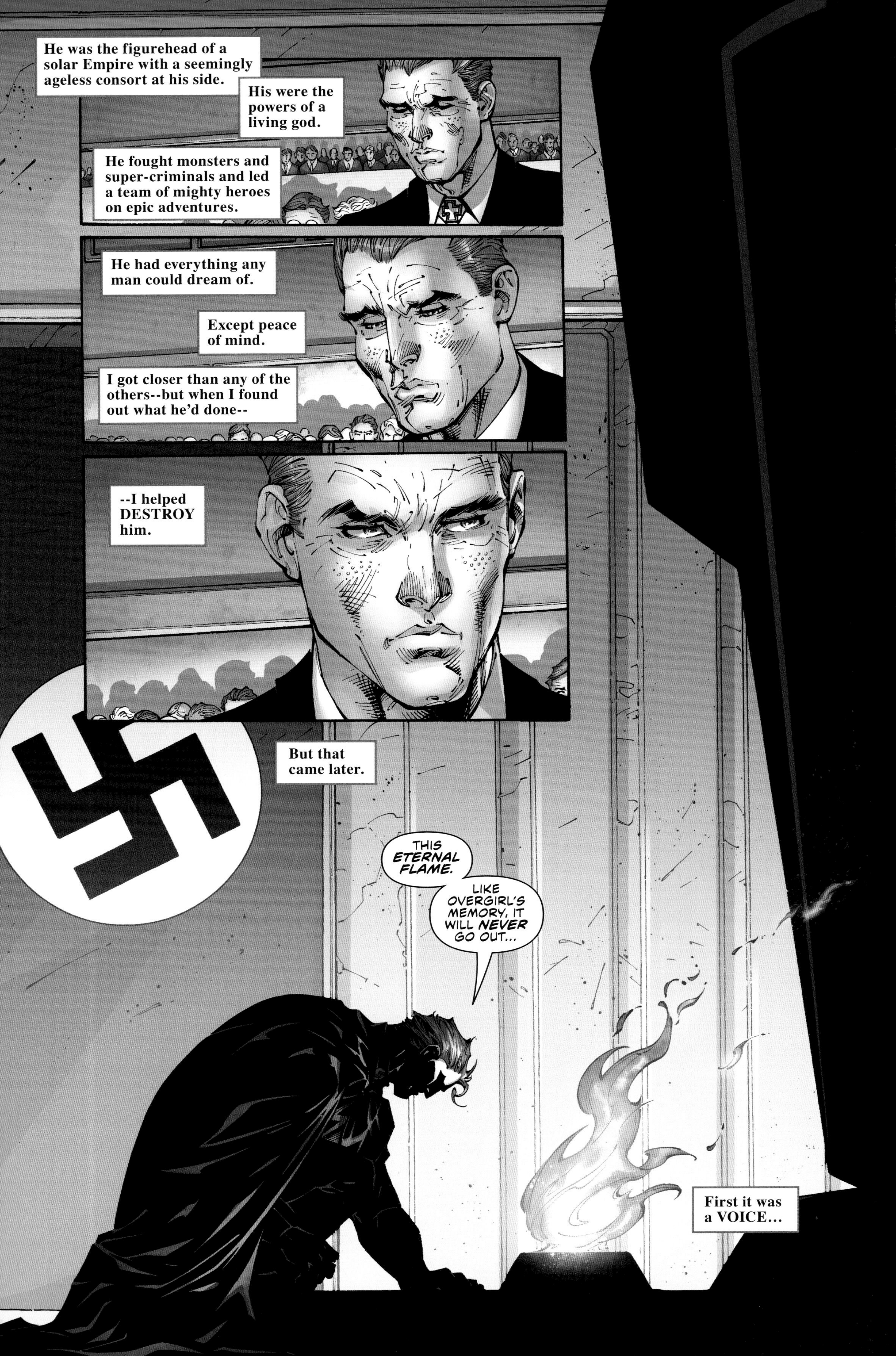
He was the figurehead of a solar Empire with a seemingly ageless consort at his side.
His were the powers of a living god.
He fought monsters and super-criminals and led a team of mighty heroes on epic adventures.
He had everything any man could dream of.
Except peace of mind.
I got closer than any of the others--but when I found out what he'd done--
--I helped DESTROY him.
But that came later.
THIS ETERNAL FLAME.
LIKE OVERGIRL'S MEMORY, IT WILL NEVER GO OUT...
First it was a VOICE...

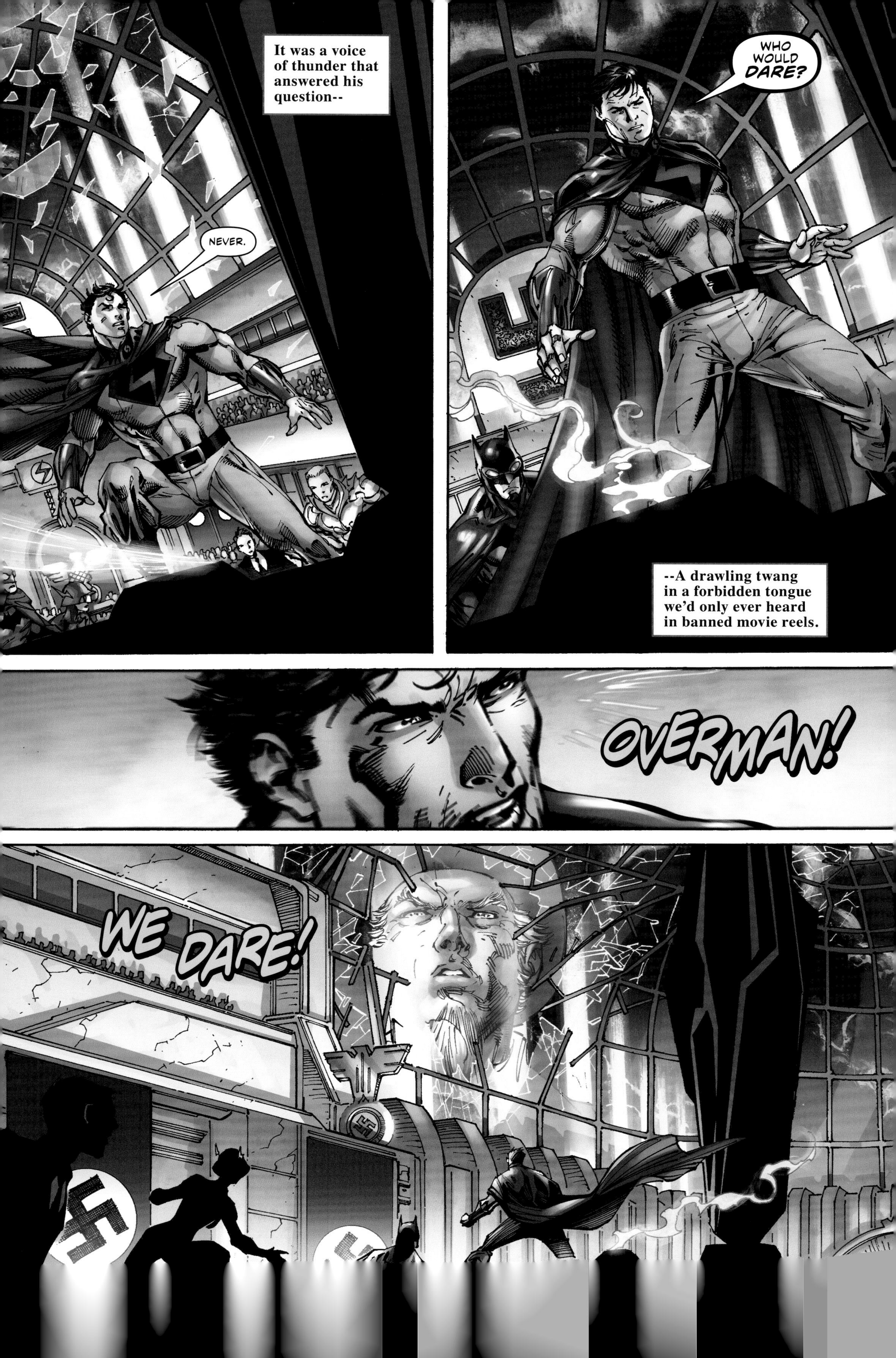
It was a voice of thunder that answered his question--
NEVER.
WHO WOULD DARE?
--A drawling twang in a forbidden tongue we'd only ever heard in banned movie reels.
OVERMAN!
WE DARE!

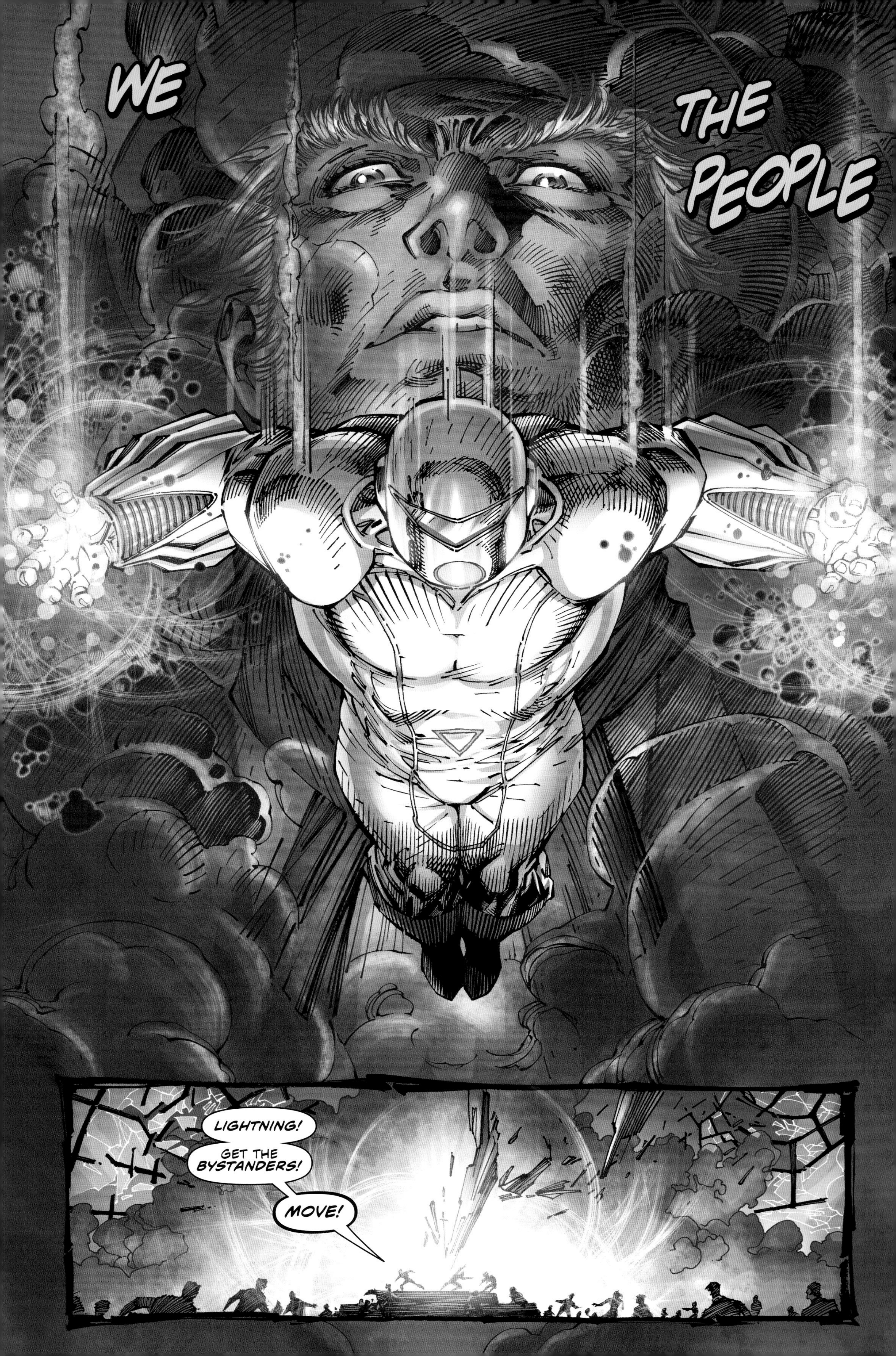
WE
THE
PEOPLE
LIGHTNING!
GET THE BYSTANDERS!
MOVE!

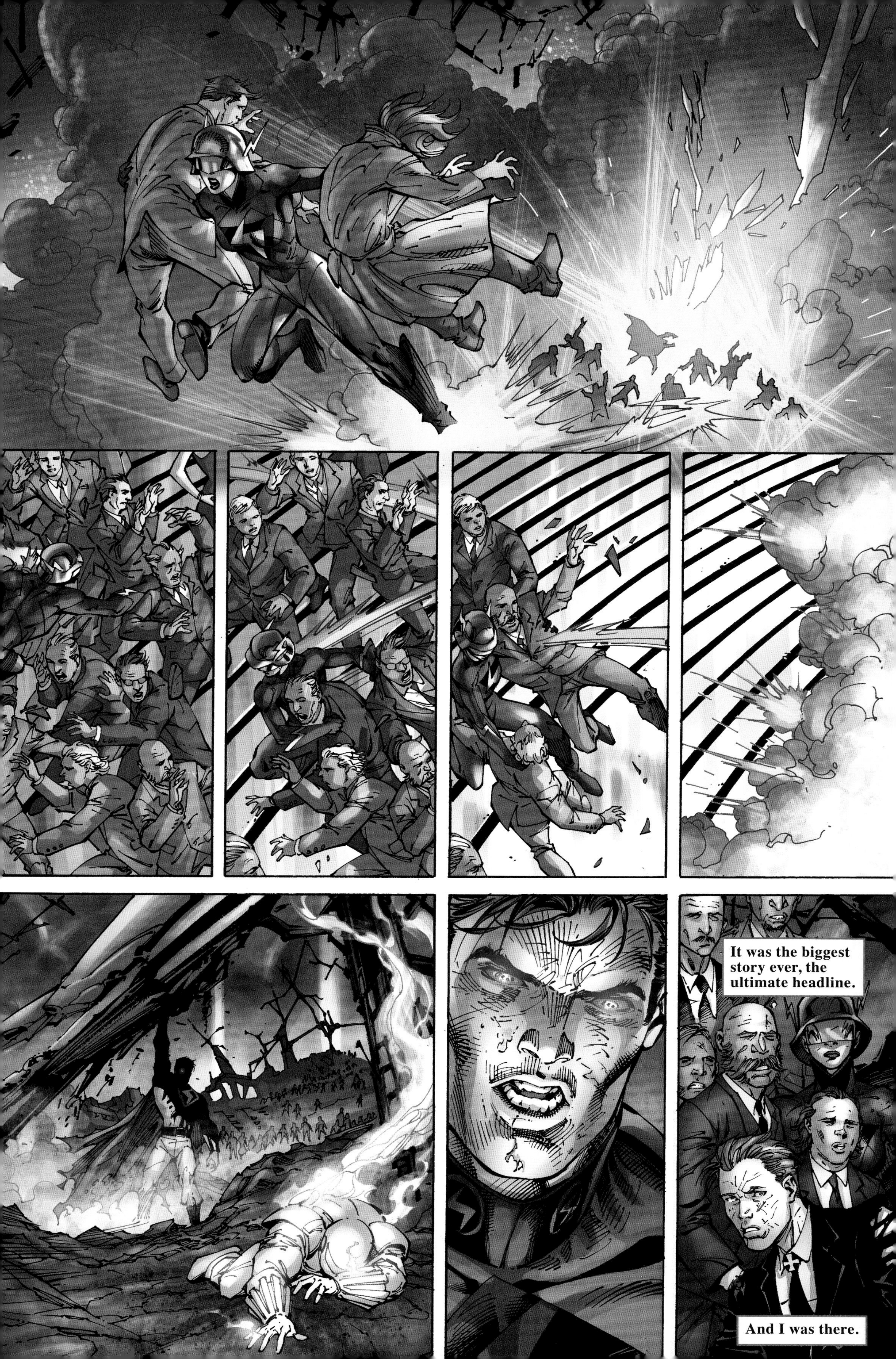
It was the biggest story ever, the ultimate headline.
And I was there.

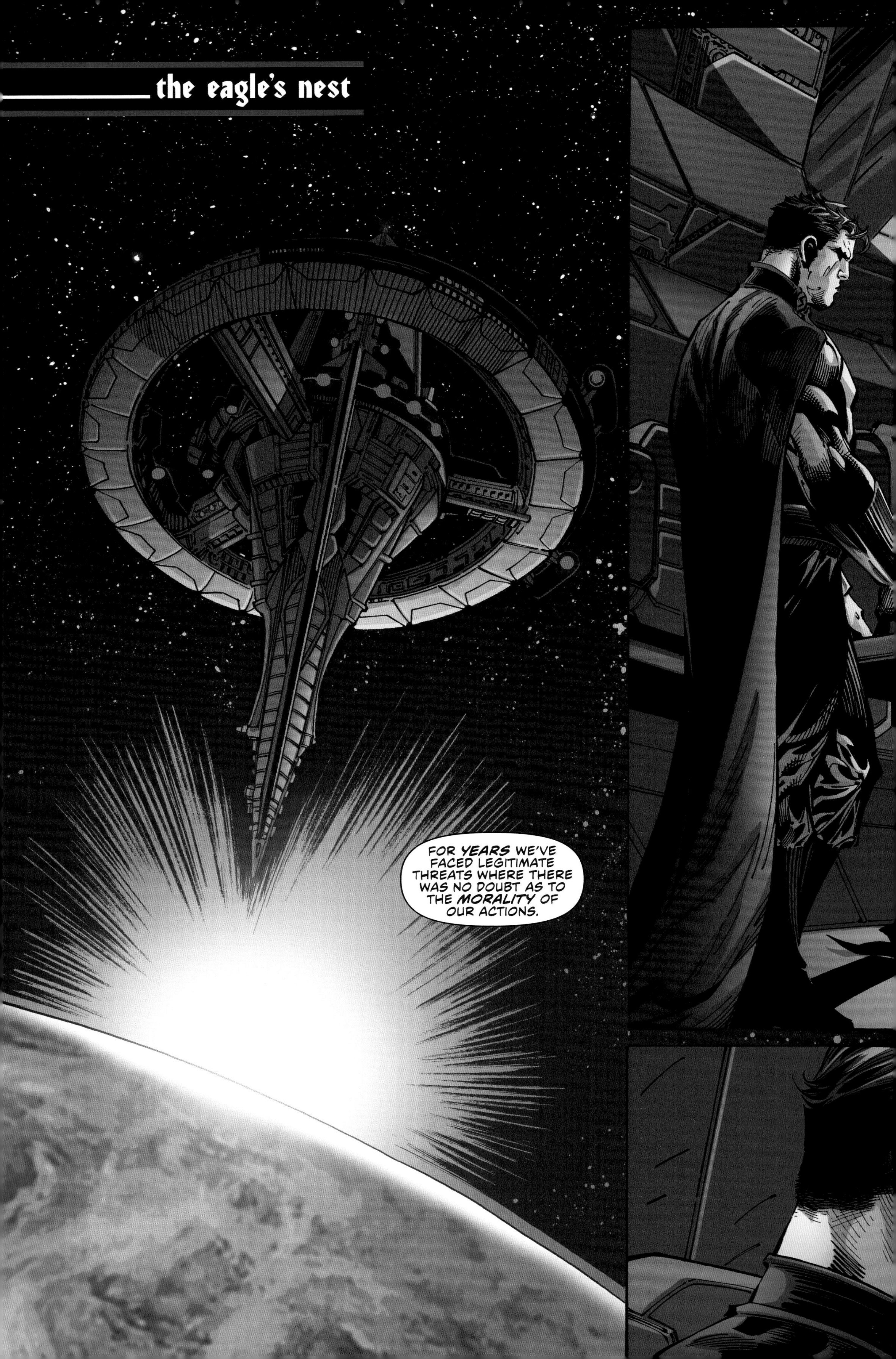
the eagle's nest
FOR YEARS WE'VE FACED LEGITIMATE THREATS WHERE THERE WAS NO DOUBT AS TO THE MORALITY OF OUR ACTIONS.

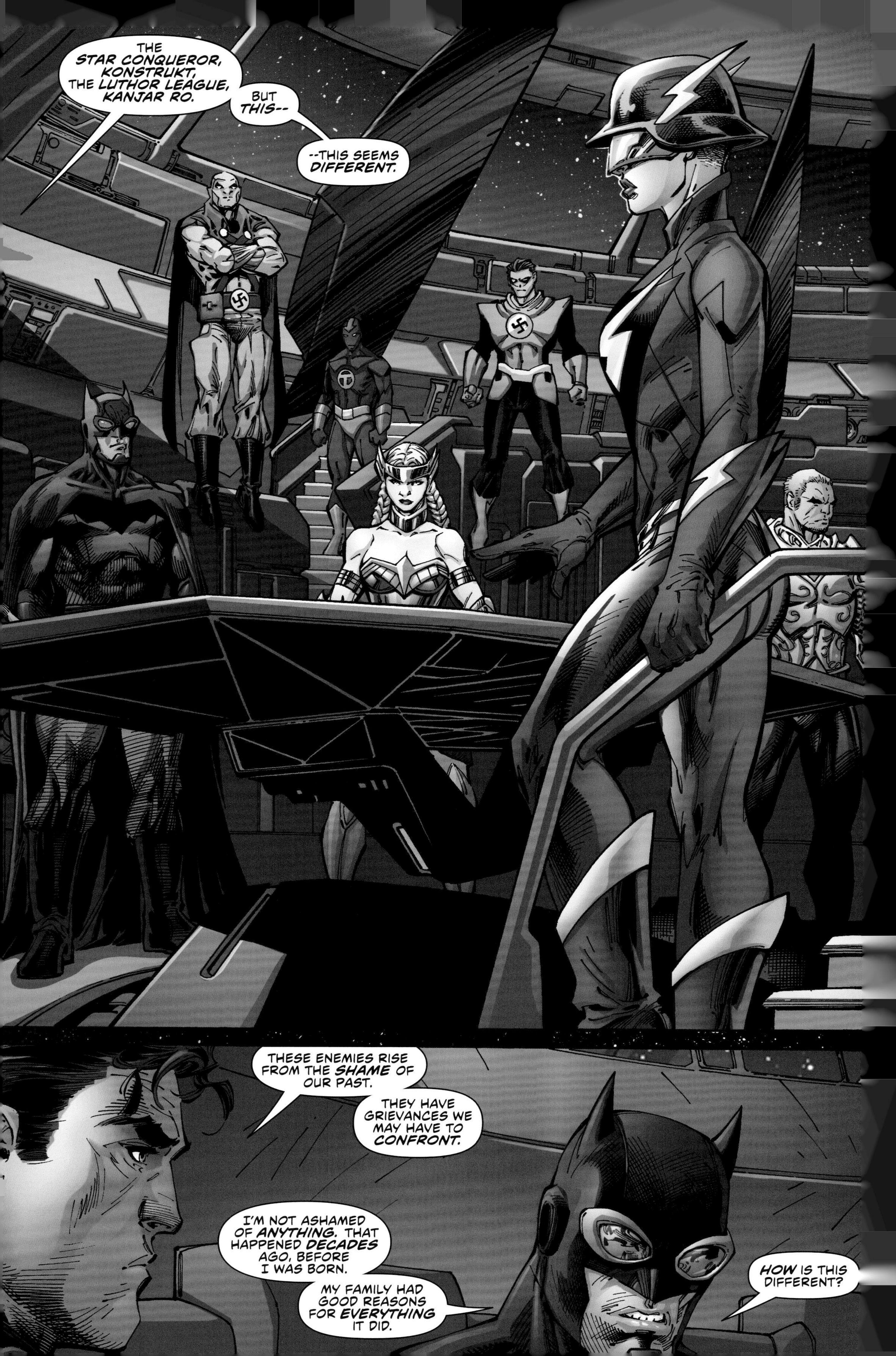

THE STAR CONQUEROR, KONSTRUKT, THE LUTHOR LEAGUE, KANJAR RO.
BUT THIS--
--THIS SEEMS DIFFERENT.
THESE ENEMIES RISE FROM THE SHAME OF OUR PAST.
THEY HAVE GRIEVANCES WE MAY HAVE TO CONFRONT.
I'M NOT ASHAMED OF ANYTHING. THAT HAPPENED DECADES AGO, BEFORE I WAS BORN.
MY FAMILY HAD GOOD REASONS FOR EVERYTHING IT DID.
HOW IS THIS DIFFERENT?

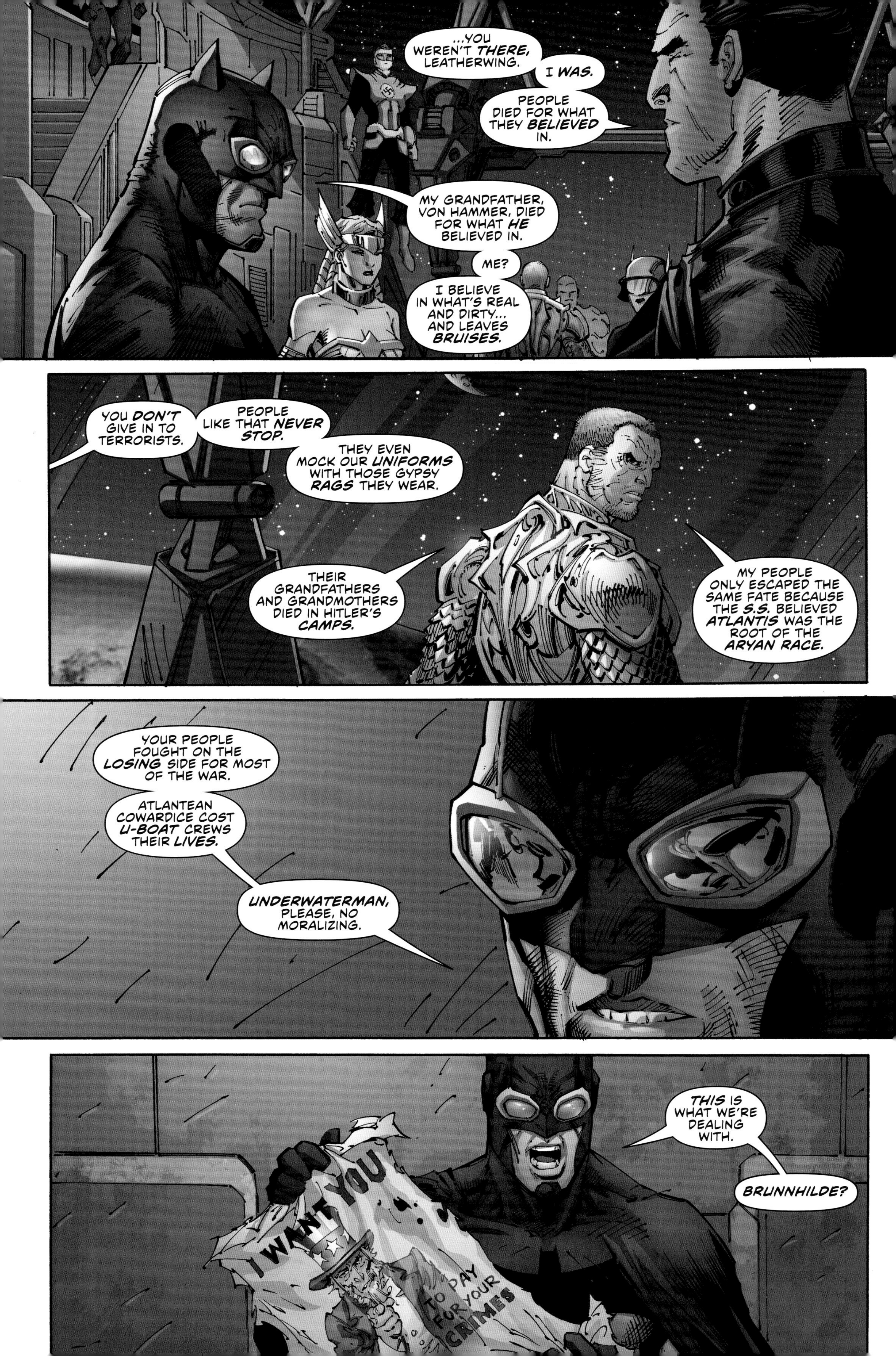
...YOU WEREN'T THERE, LEATHERWING.
I WAS.
PEOPLE DIED FOR WHAT THEY BELIEVED IN.
MY GRANDFATHER, VON HAMMER, DIED FOR WHAT HE BELIEVED IN.
ME?
I BELIEVE IN WHAT'S REAL AND DIRTY... AND LEAVES BRUISES.
YOU DON'T GIVE IN TO TERRORISTS.
PEOPLE LIKE THAT NEVER STOP.
THEY EVEN MOCK OUR UNIFORMS WITH THOSE GYPSY RAGS THEY WEAR.
THEIR GRANDFATHERS AND GRANDMOTHERS DIED IN HITLER'S CAMPS.
MY PEOPLE ONLY ESCAPED THE SAME FATE BECAUSE THE S.S. BELIEVED ATLANTIS WAS THE ROOT OF THE ARYAN RACE.
YOUR PEOPLE FOUGHT ON THE LOSING SIDE FOR MOST OF THE WAR.
ATLANTEAN COWARDICE COST U-BOAT CREWS THEIR LIVES.
UNDERWATERMAN, PLEASE, NO MORALIZING.
THIS IS WHAT WE'RE DEALING WITH.
BRUNNHILDE?
I WANT YOU
TO PAY FOR YOUR CRIMES

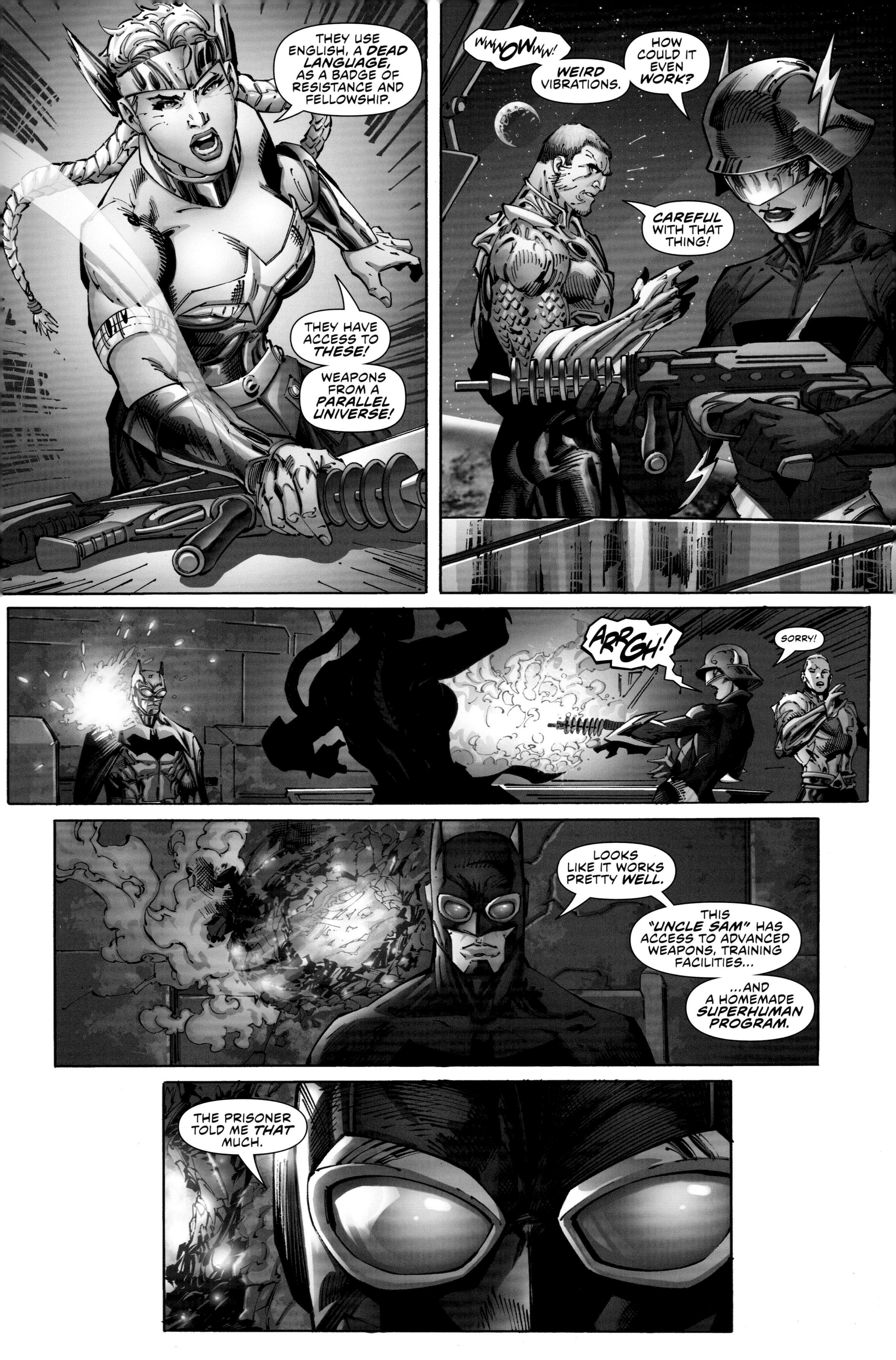
THEY USE ENGLISH, A DEAD LANGUAGE, AS A BADGE OF RESISTANCE AND FELLOWSHIP.
THEY HAVE ACCESS TO THESE!
WEAPONS FROM A PARALLEL UNIVERSE!
WWWOWWW!
WEIRD VIBRATIONS.
HOW COULD IT EVEN WORK?
CAREFUL WITH THAT THING!
ARRGH!
SORRY!
LOOKS LIKE IT WORKS PRETTY WELL.
THIS "UNCLE SAM" HAS ACCESS TO ADVANCED WEAPONS, TRAINING FACILITIES...
...AND A HOMEMADE SUPERHUMAN PROGRAM.
THE PRISONER TOLD ME THAT MUCH.

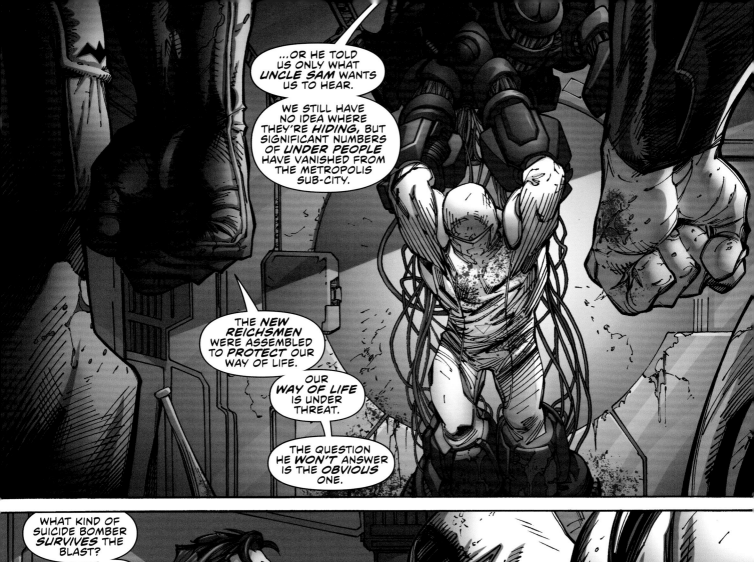

...OR HE TOLD US ONLY WHAT *UNCLE SAM* WANTS US TO HEAR.

WE STILL HAVE NO IDEA WHERE THEY'RE *HIDING*, BUT SIGNIFICANT NUMBERS OF *UNDER PEOPLE* HAVE VANISHED FROM THE METROPOLIS SUB-CITY.

THE *NEW REICHSMEN* WERE ASSEMBLED TO *PROTECT* OUR WAY OF LIFE.

OUR *WAY OF LIFE* IS UNDER THREAT.

THE QUESTION HE *WON'T* ANSWER IS THE *OBVIOUS* ONE.

WHAT KIND OF SUICIDE BOMBER *SURVIVES* THE BLAST?

Hmm.

AN *INVULNERABLE* ONE, PERHAPS.

LET'S KEEP HIM IN HIS *PROTECTIVE SUIT* UNTIL WE'VE COMPLETED OUR TESTS.

THERE'S SOMETHING *ODD* ABOUT HIS CELLULAR STRUCTURE...

...SOME KIND OF RAPID *HEALING* FACTOR.

GOOD.

THAT MEANS HE CAN TAKE THE SAME PAIN ALL OVER AGAIN.

YOU DON'T WANT LEATHERWING TO BEAT THE HELL OUT OF YOU A *SECOND TIME*, SURELY, MY FRIEND.

TALK TO *ME* INSTEAD.

TELL ME, WHAT IS IT YOU *WANT?*

WE WANT TO WATCH YOU *FALL* FROM THE SKY.

"MY FRIEND."

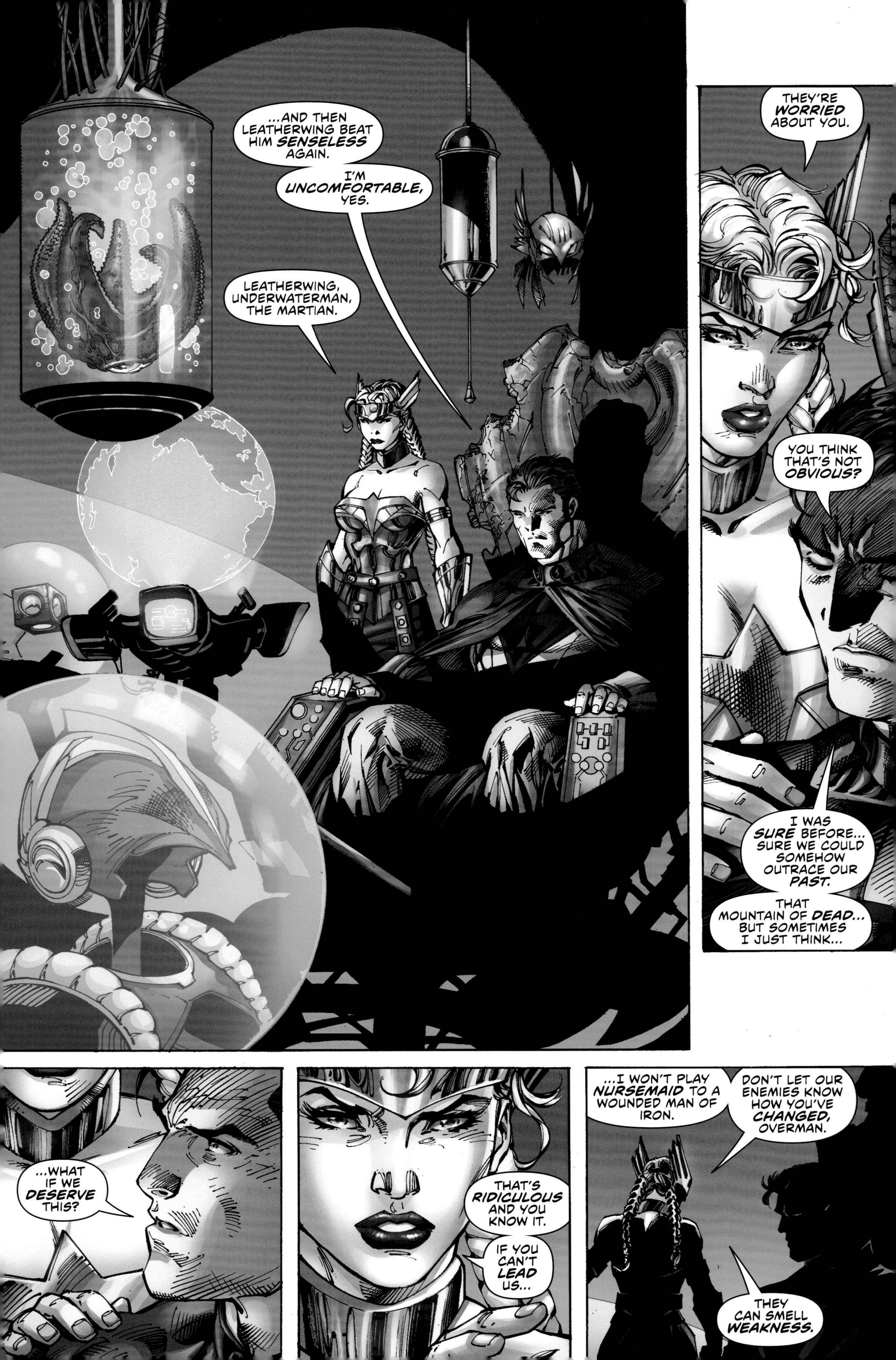

...AND THEN LEATHERWING BEAT HIM SENSELESS AGAIN.
I'M UNCOMFORTABLE, YES.
LEATHERWING, UNDERWATERMAN, THE MARTIAN.
THEY'RE WORRIED ABOUT YOU.
YOU THINK THAT'S NOT OBVIOUS?
I WAS SURE BEFORE... SURE WE COULD SOMEHOW OUTRACE OUR PAST.
THAT MOUNTAIN OF DEAD... BUT SOMETIMES I JUST THINK...
...WHAT IF WE DESERVE THIS?
THAT'S RIDICULOUS AND YOU KNOW IT.
IF YOU CAN'T LEAD US...
...I WON'T PLAY NURSEMAID TO A WOUNDED MAN OF IRON.
DON'T LET OUR ENEMIES KNOW HOW YOU'VE CHANGED, OVERMAN.
THEY CAN SMELL WEAKNESS.

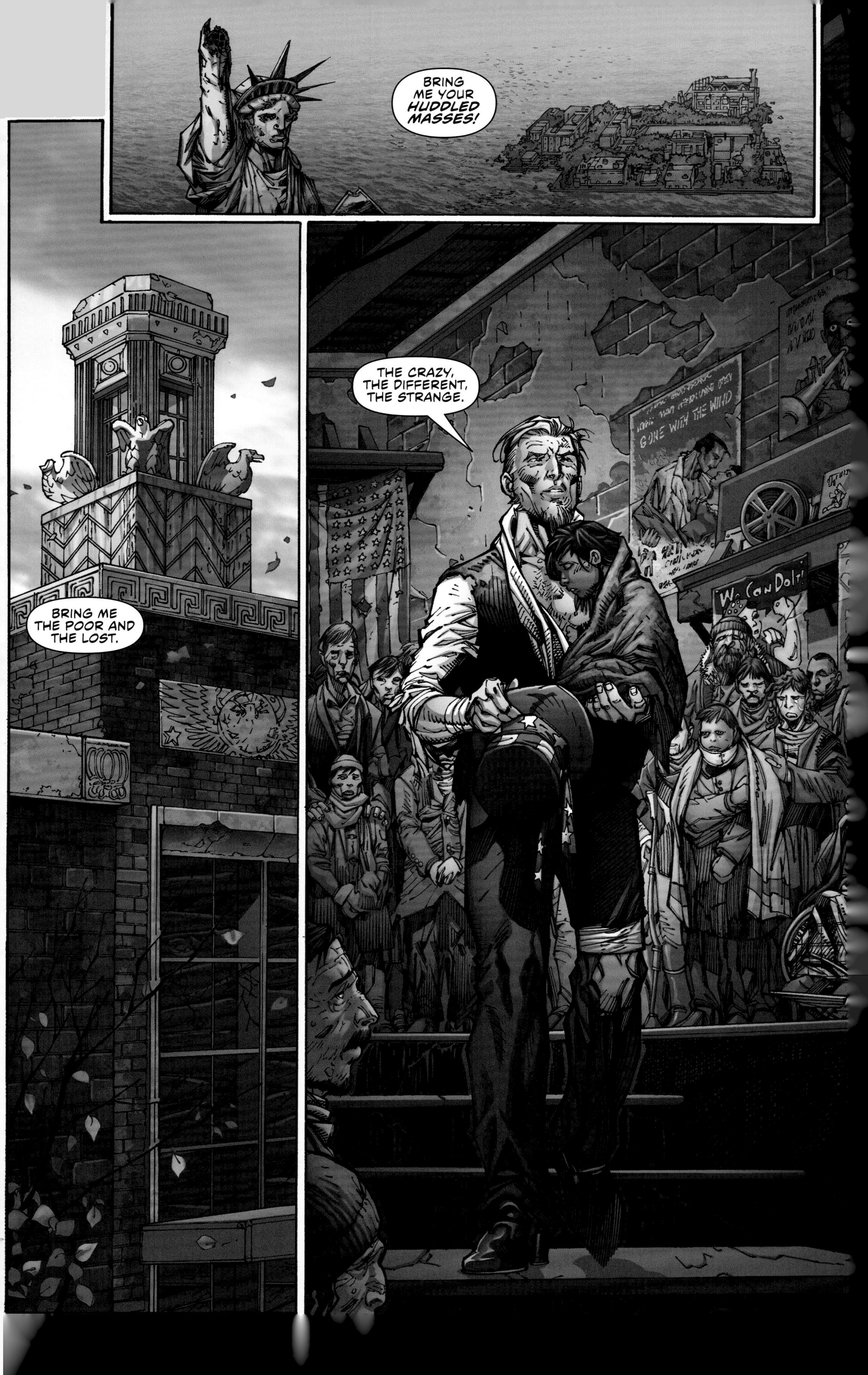
BRING ME YOUR HUDDLED MASSES!
BRING ME THE POOR AND THE LOST.
THE CRAZY, THE DIFFERENT, THE STRANGE.
GONE WITH THE WIND
We Can Do It!

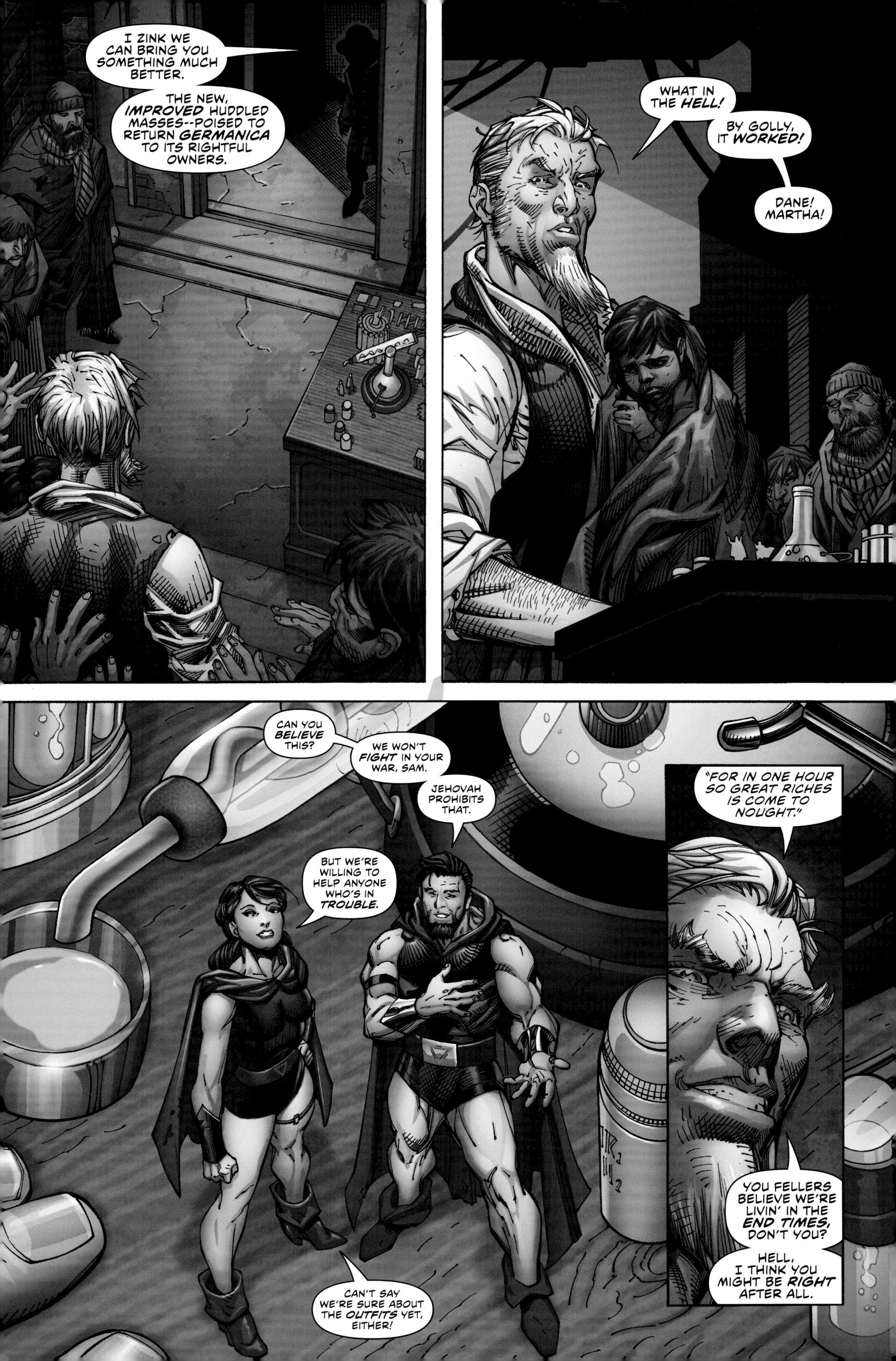
I ZINK WE CAN BRING YOU SOMETHING MUCH BETTER.
THE NEW, *IMPROVED* HUDDLED MASSES--POISED TO RETURN *GERMANICA* TO ITS RIGHTFUL OWNERS.
WHAT IN THE *HELL!*
BY GOLLY, IT *WORKED!*
DANE! MARTHA!
CAN YOU *BELIEVE* THIS?
WE WON'T *FIGHT* IN YOUR WAR, SAM.
JEHOVAH PROHIBITS THAT.
BUT WE'RE WILLING TO HELP ANYONE WHO'S IN *TROUBLE.*
CAN'T SAY WE'RE SURE ABOUT THE *OUTFITS* YET, EITHER!
"FOR IN ONE HOUR SO GREAT RICHES IS COME TO NOUGHT."
YOU FELLERS BELIEVE WE'RE LIVIN' IN THE *END TIMES,* DON'T YOU?
HELL, I THINK YOU MIGHT BE *RIGHT* AFTER ALL.

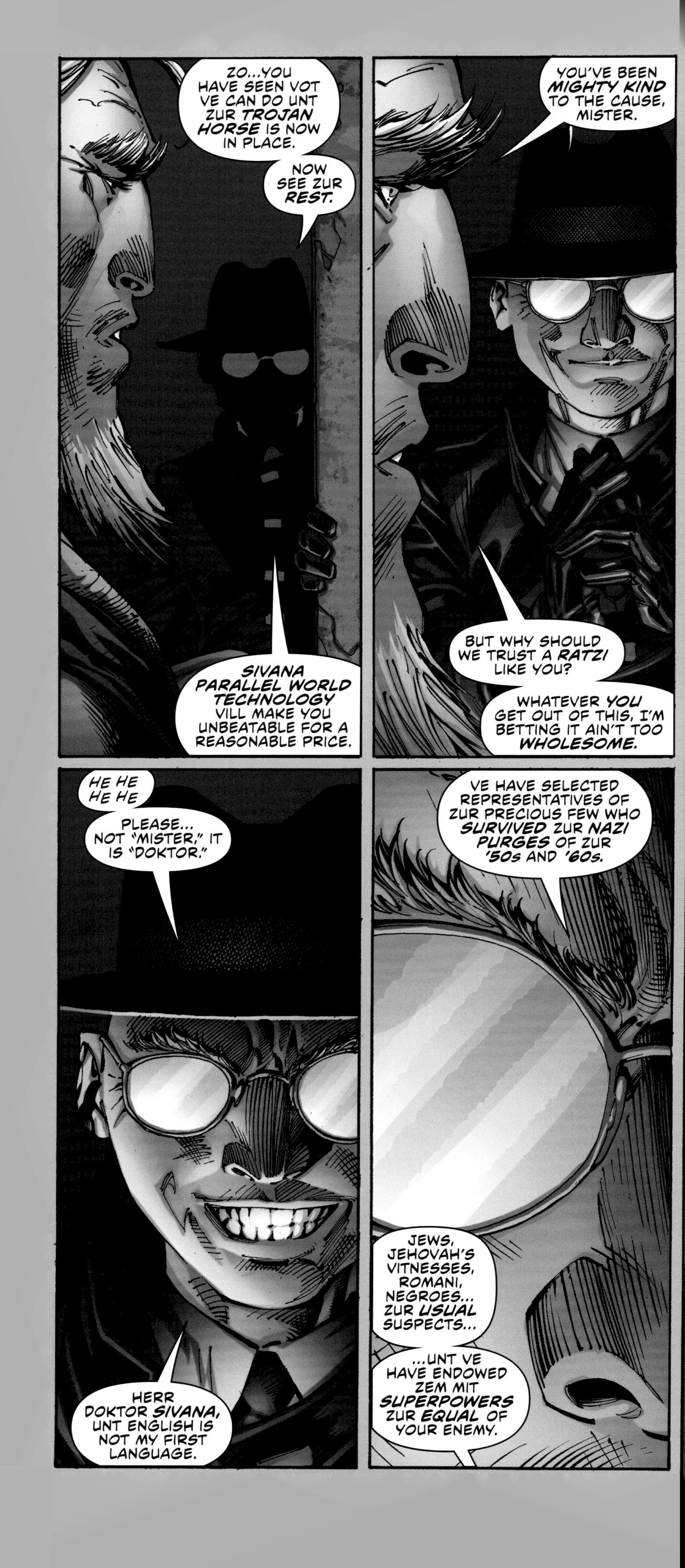
ZO...YOU HAVE SEEN VOT VE CAN DO UNT ZUR ***TROJAN HORSE*** IS NOW IN PLACE.
NOW SEE ZUR ***REST.***
SIVANA PARALLEL WORLD TECHNOLOGY VILL MAKE YOU UNBEATABLE FOR A REASONABLE PRICE.
YOU'VE BEEN ***MIGHTY KIND*** TO THE CAUSE, MISTER.
BUT WHY SHOULD WE TRUST A ***RATZI*** LIKE YOU?
WHATEVER ***YOU*** GET OUT OF THIS, I'M BETTING IT AIN'T TOO ***WHOLESOME.***
HE HE HE HE
PLEASE... NOT "MISTER," IT IS "DOKTOR."
HERR DOKTOR ***SIVANA,*** UNT ENGLISH IS NOT MY FIRST LANGUAGE.
VE HAVE SELECTED REPRESENTATIVES OF ZUR PRECIOUS FEW WHO ***SURVIVED*** ZUR ***NAZI PURGES*** OF ZUR ***'50s*** AND ***'60s.***
JEWS, JEHOVAH'S VITNESSES, ROMANI, NEGROES... ZUR ***USUAL*** SUSPECTS...
...UNT VE HAVE ENDOWED ZEM MIT ***SUPERPOWERS*** ZUR ***EQUAL*** OF YOUR ENEMY.

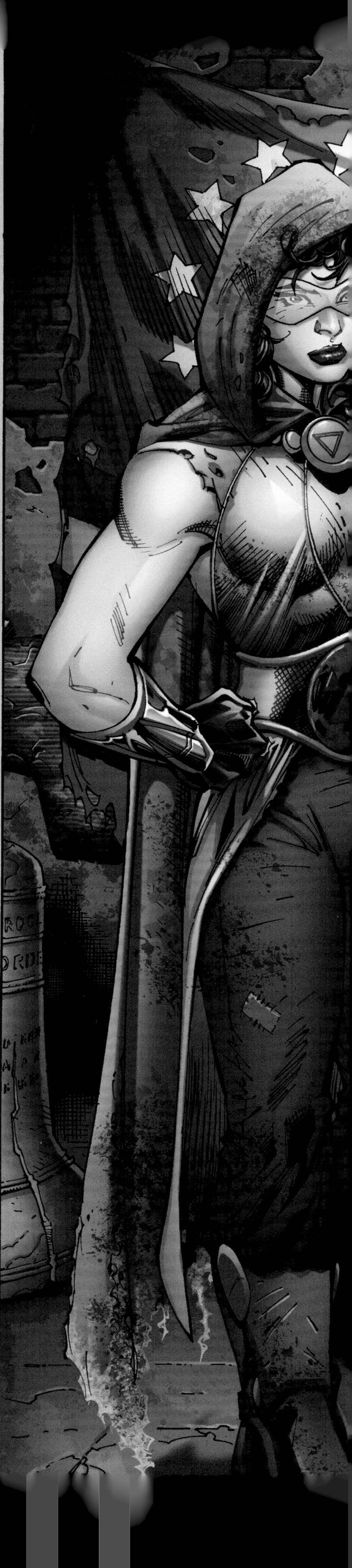

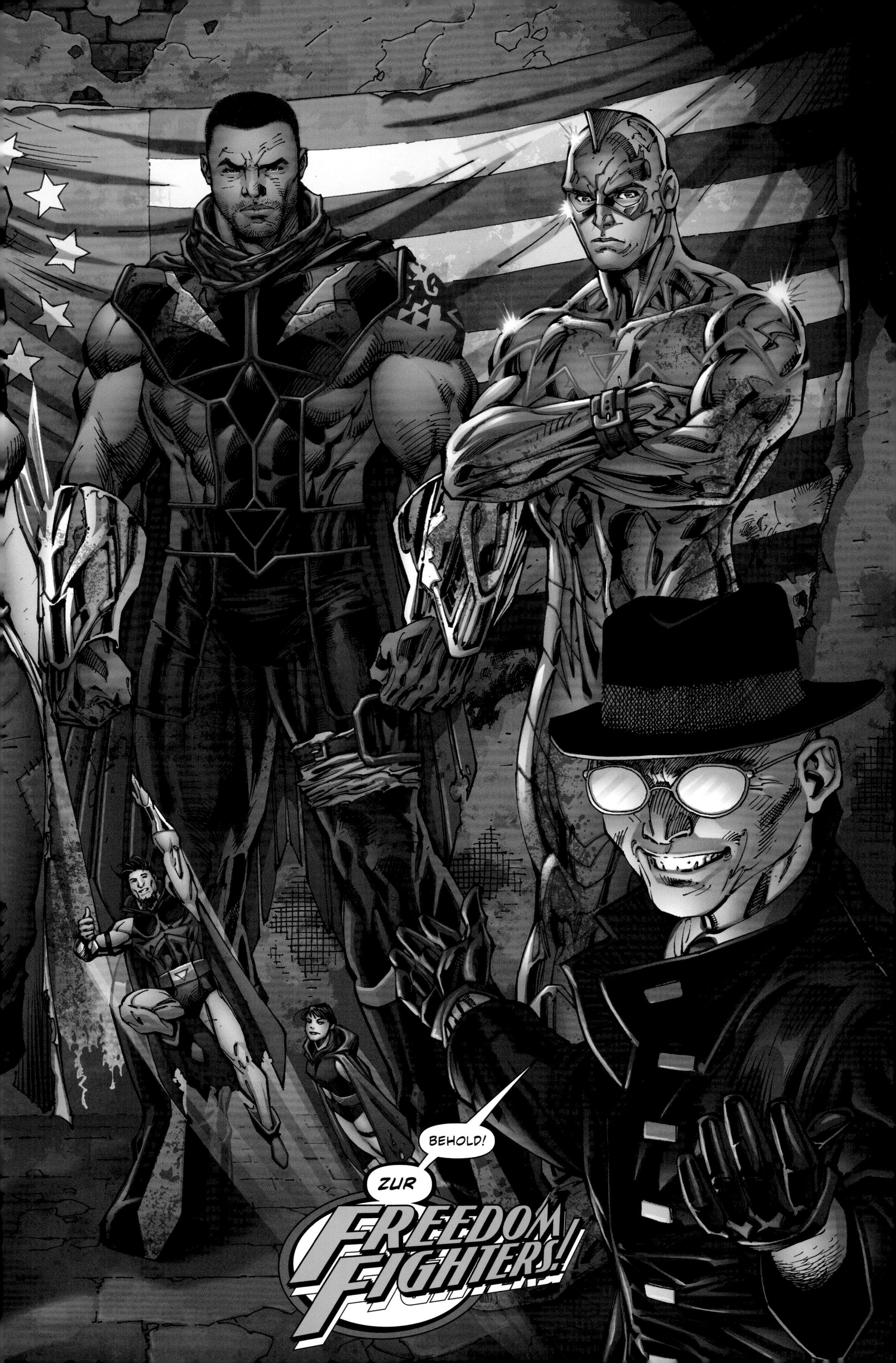
BEHOLD!
ZUR
FREEDOM FIGHTERS!

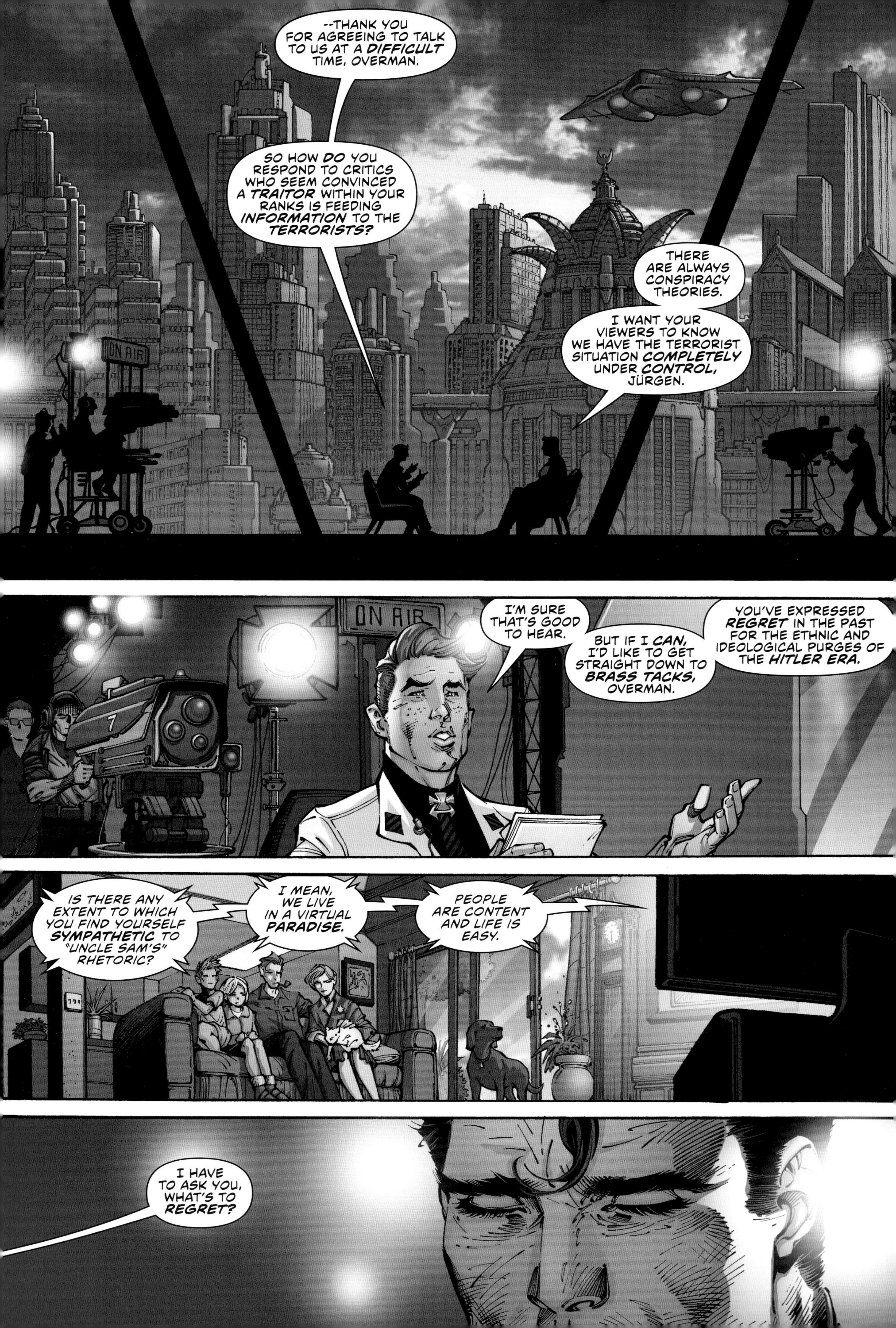

--THANK YOU FOR AGREEING TO TALK TO US AT A DIFFICULT TIME, OVERMAN.
SO HOW DO YOU RESPOND TO CRITICS WHO SEEM CONVINCED A TRAITOR WITHIN YOUR RANKS IS FEEDING INFORMATION TO THE TERRORISTS?
THERE ARE ALWAYS CONSPIRACY THEORIES.
I WANT YOUR VIEWERS TO KNOW WE HAVE THE TERRORIST SITUATION COMPLETELY UNDER CONTROL, JÜRGEN.
ON AIR
ON AIR
I'M SURE THAT'S GOOD TO HEAR.
BUT IF I CAN, I'D LIKE TO GET STRAIGHT DOWN TO BRASS TACKS, OVERMAN.
YOU'VE EXPRESSED REGRET IN THE PAST FOR THE ETHNIC AND IDEOLOGICAL PURGES OF THE HITLER ERA.
IS THERE ANY EXTENT TO WHICH YOU FIND YOURSELF SYMPATHETIC TO "UNCLE SAM'S" RHETORIC?
I MEAN, WE LIVE IN A VIRTUAL PARADISE.
PEOPLE ARE CONTENT AND LIFE IS EASY.
I HAVE TO ASK YOU, WHAT'S TO REGRET?

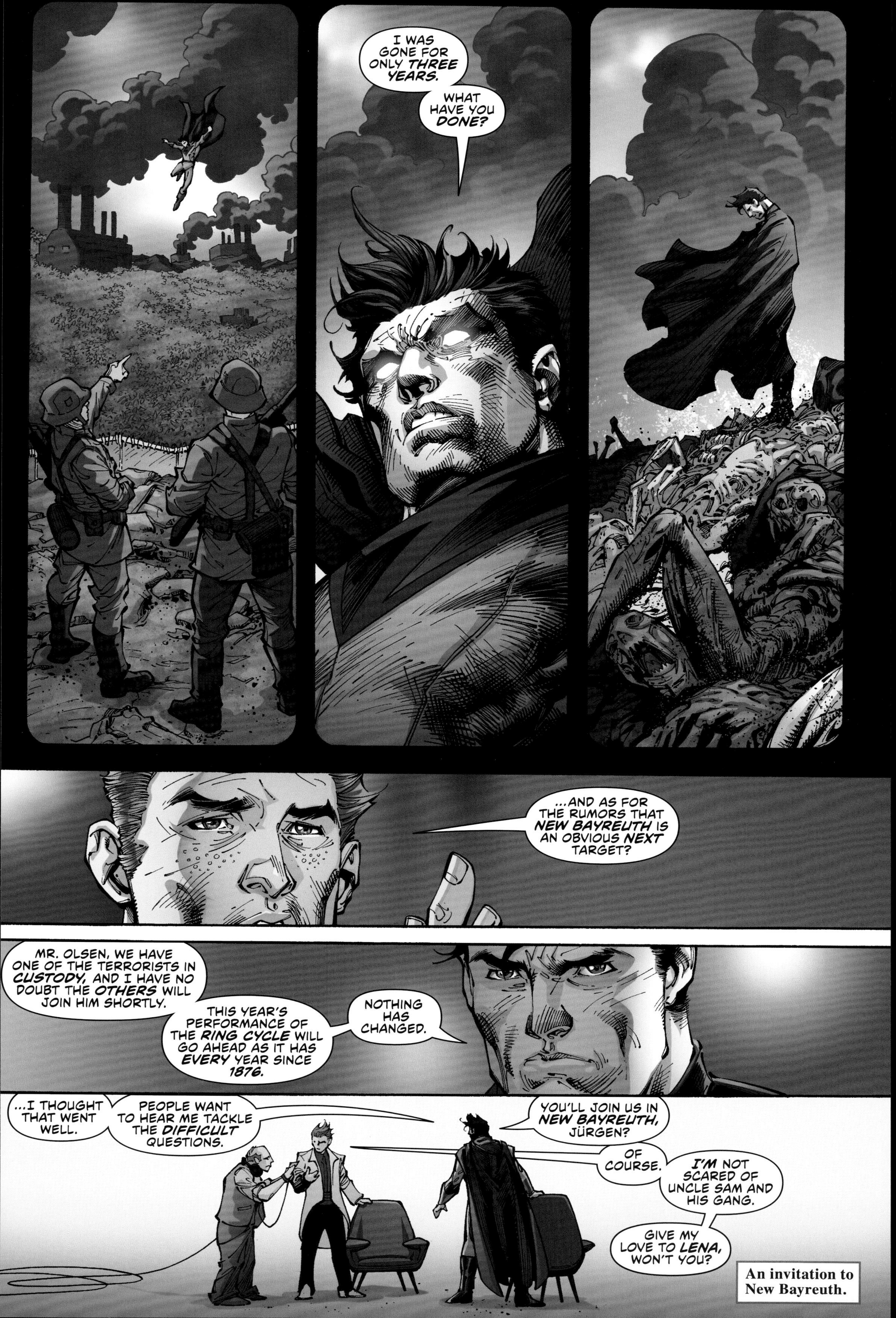

I WAS GONE FOR ONLY THREE YEARS.
WHAT HAVE YOU DONE?
...AND AS FOR THE RUMORS THAT NEW BAYREUTH IS AN OBVIOUS NEXT TARGET?
MR. OLSEN, WE HAVE ONE OF THE TERRORISTS IN CUSTODY, AND I HAVE NO DOUBT THE OTHERS WILL JOIN HIM SHORTLY.
THIS YEAR'S PERFORMANCE OF THE RING CYCLE WILL GO AHEAD AS IT HAS EVERY YEAR SINCE 1876.
NOTHING HAS CHANGED.
...I THOUGHT THAT WENT WELL.
PEOPLE WANT TO HEAR ME TACKLE THE DIFFICULT QUESTIONS.
YOU'LL JOIN US IN NEW BAYREUTH, JÜRGEN?
OF COURSE.
I'M NOT SCARED OF UNCLE SAM AND HIS GANG.
GIVE MY LOVE TO LENA, WON'T YOU?

An invitation to New Bayreuth.

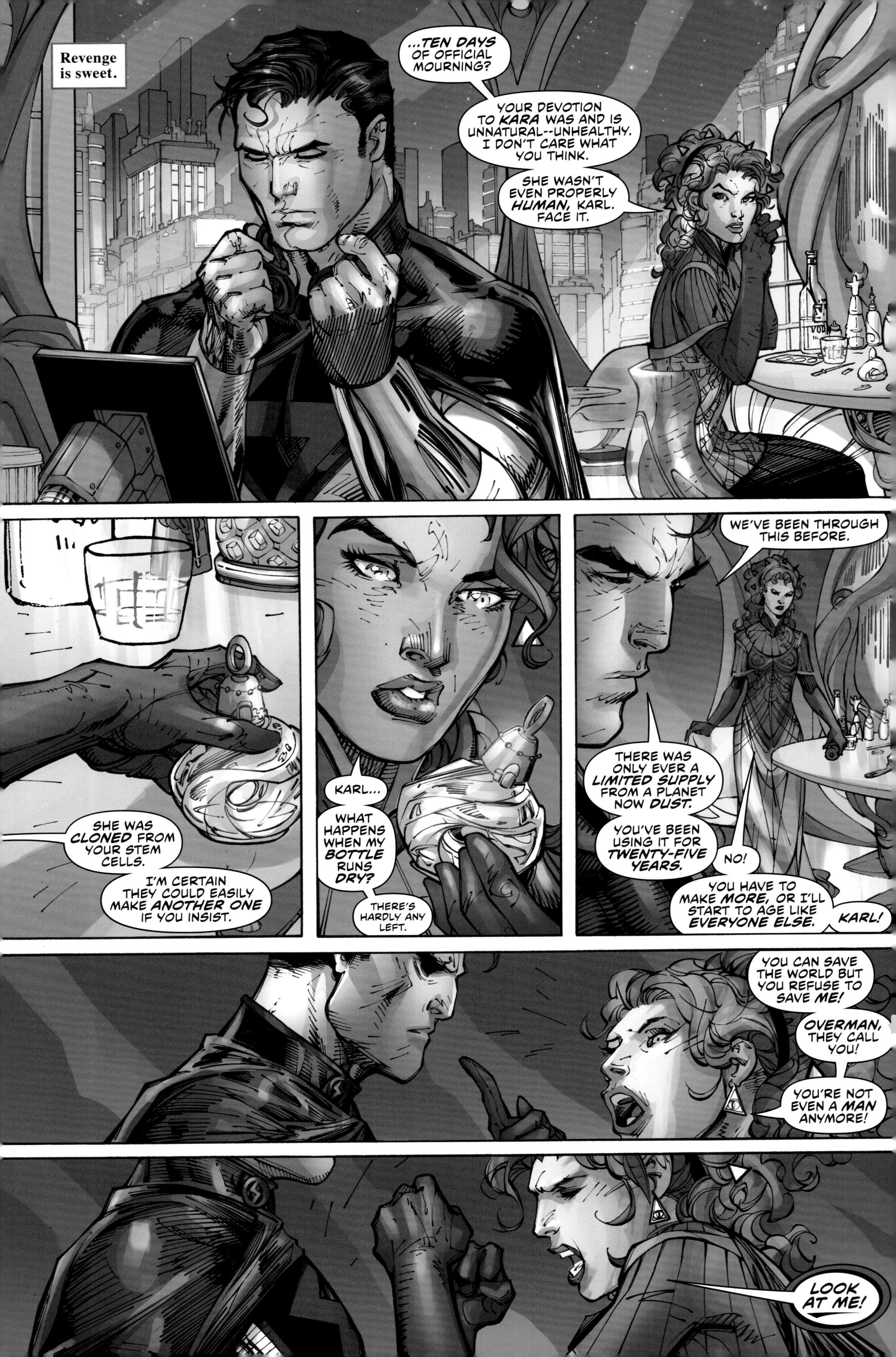

Revenge is sweet.
...TEN DAYS OF OFFICIAL MOURNING?
YOUR DEVOTION TO KARA WAS AND IS UNNATURAL--UNHEALTHY. I DON'T CARE WHAT YOU THINK.
SHE WASN'T EVEN PROPERLY HUMAN, KARL. FACE IT.
SHE WAS CLONED FROM YOUR STEM CELLS.
I'M CERTAIN THEY COULD EASILY MAKE ANOTHER ONE IF YOU INSIST.
KARL...
WHAT HAPPENS WHEN MY BOTTLE RUNS DRY?
THERE'S HARDLY ANY LEFT.
WE'VE BEEN THROUGH THIS BEFORE.
THERE WAS ONLY EVER A LIMITED SUPPLY FROM A PLANET NOW DUST.
YOU'VE BEEN USING IT FOR TWENTY-FIVE YEARS.
NO!
YOU HAVE TO MAKE MORE, OR I'LL START TO AGE LIKE EVERYONE ELSE.
KARL!
YOU CAN SAVE THE WORLD BUT YOU REFUSE TO SAVE ME!
OVERMAN, THEY CALL YOU!
YOU'RE NOT EVEN A MAN ANYMORE!
LOOK AT ME!

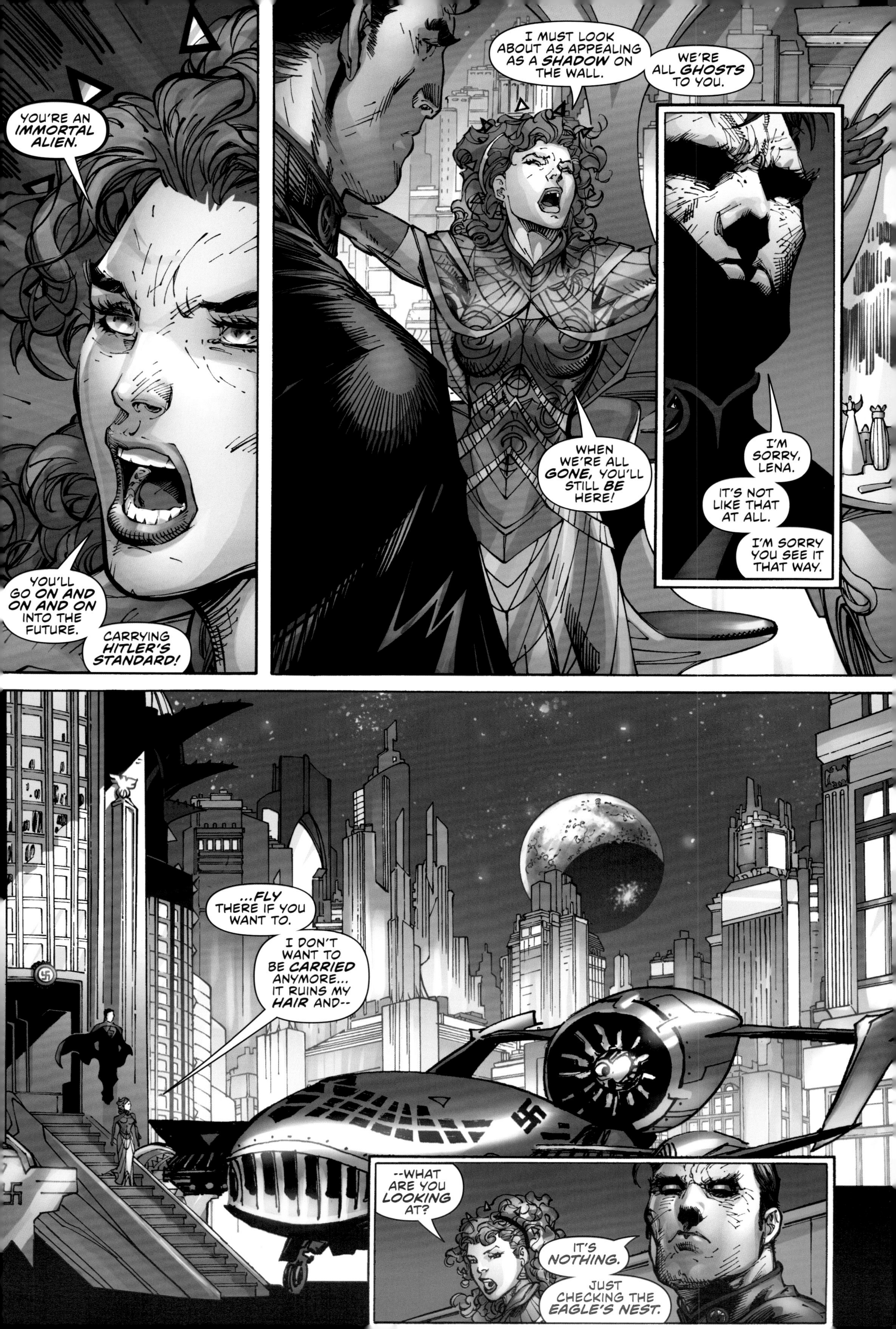

YOU'RE AN IMMORTAL ALIEN.
YOU'LL GO ON AND ON AND ON INTO THE FUTURE.
CARRYING HITLER'S STANDARD!
I MUST LOOK ABOUT AS APPEALING AS A SHADOW ON THE WALL.
WE'RE ALL GHOSTS TO YOU.
WHEN WE'RE ALL GONE, YOU'LL STILL BE HERE!
I'M SORRY, LENA.
IT'S NOT LIKE THAT AT ALL.
I'M SORRY YOU SEE IT THAT WAY.
...FLY THERE IF YOU WANT TO.
I DON'T WANT TO BE CARRIED ANYMORE... IT RUINS MY HAIR AND--
--WHAT ARE YOU LOOKING AT?
IT'S NOTHING.
JUST CHECKING THE EAGLE'S NEST.

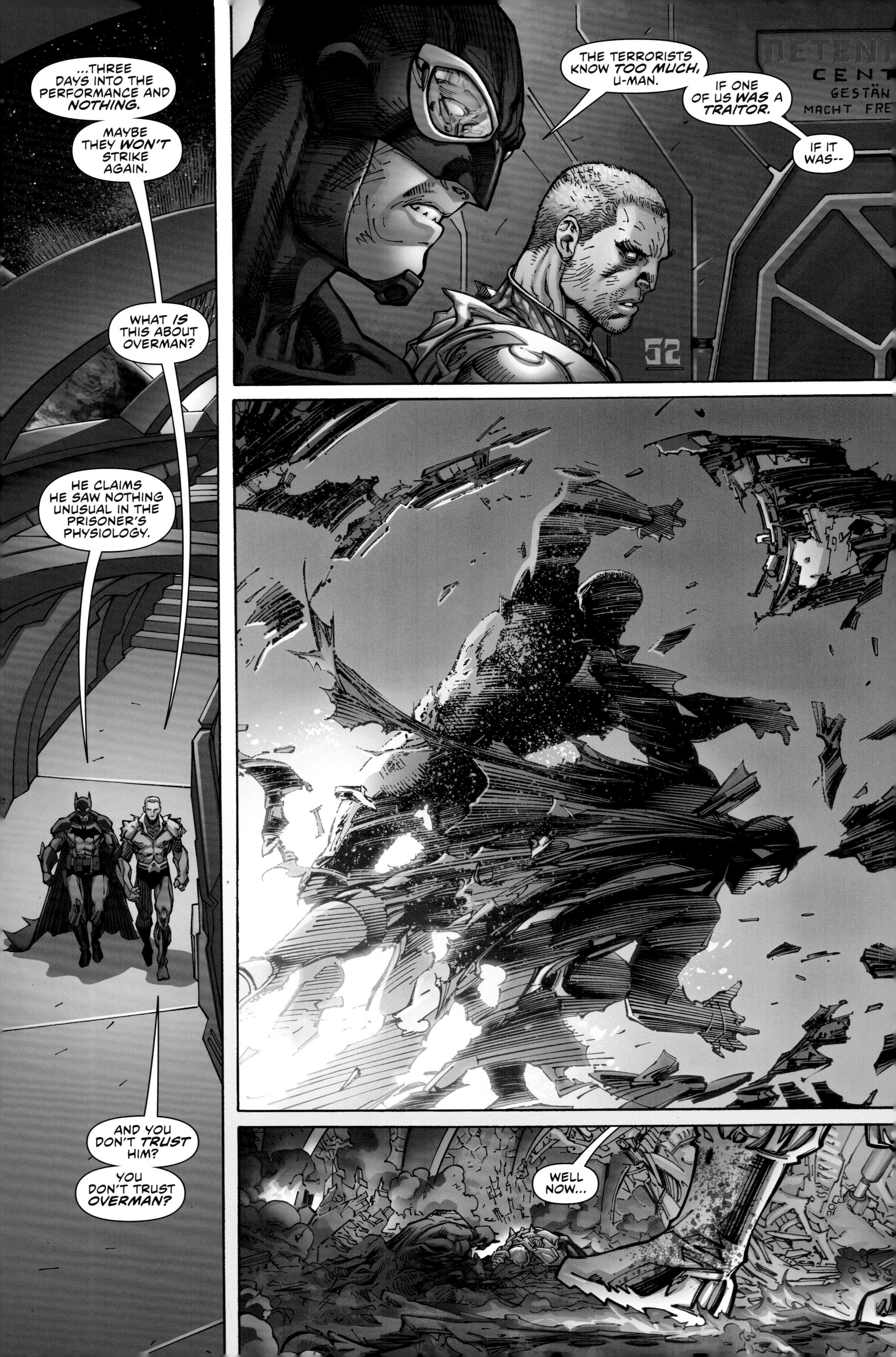
...THREE DAYS INTO THE PERFORMANCE AND NOTHING.
MAYBE THEY WON'T STRIKE AGAIN.
WHAT IS THIS ABOUT OVERMAN?
HE CLAIMS HE SAW NOTHING UNUSUAL IN THE PRISONER'S PHYSIOLOGY.
AND YOU DON'T TRUST HIM?
YOU DON'T TRUST OVERMAN?
THE TERRORISTS KNOW TOO MUCH, U-MAN.
IF ONE OF US WAS A TRAITOR.
IF IT WAS--
CENT
GESTÄN
MACHT FRE
52
WELL NOW...

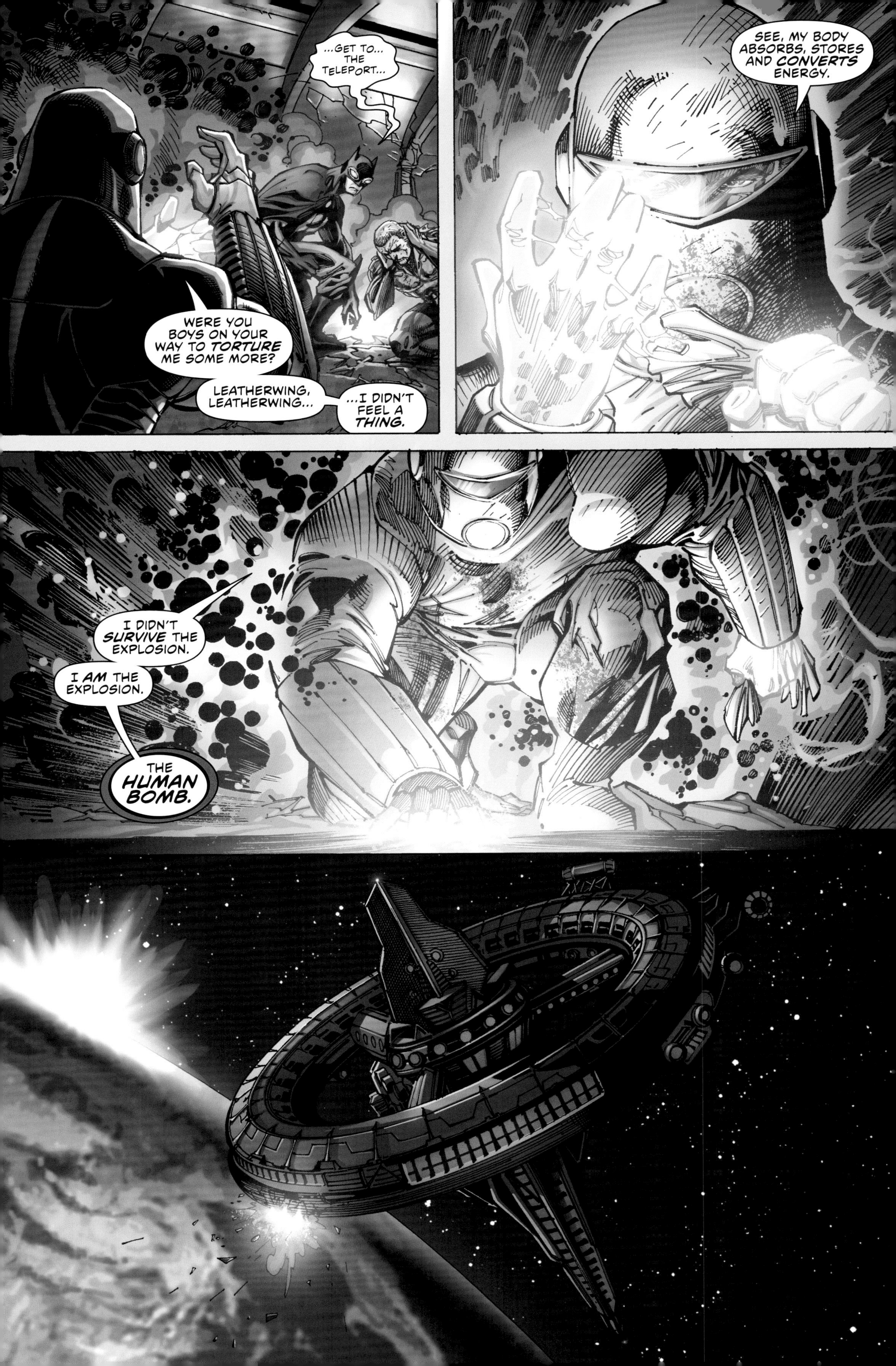
...GET TO... THE TELEPORT...
WERE YOU BOYS ON YOUR WAY TO TORTURE ME SOME MORE?
LEATHERWING, LEATHERWING...
...I DIDN'T FEEL A THING.
SEE, MY BODY ABSORBS, STORES AND CONVERTS ENERGY.
I DIDN'T SURVIVE THE EXPLOSION.
I AM THE EXPLOSION.
THE HUMAN BOMB.

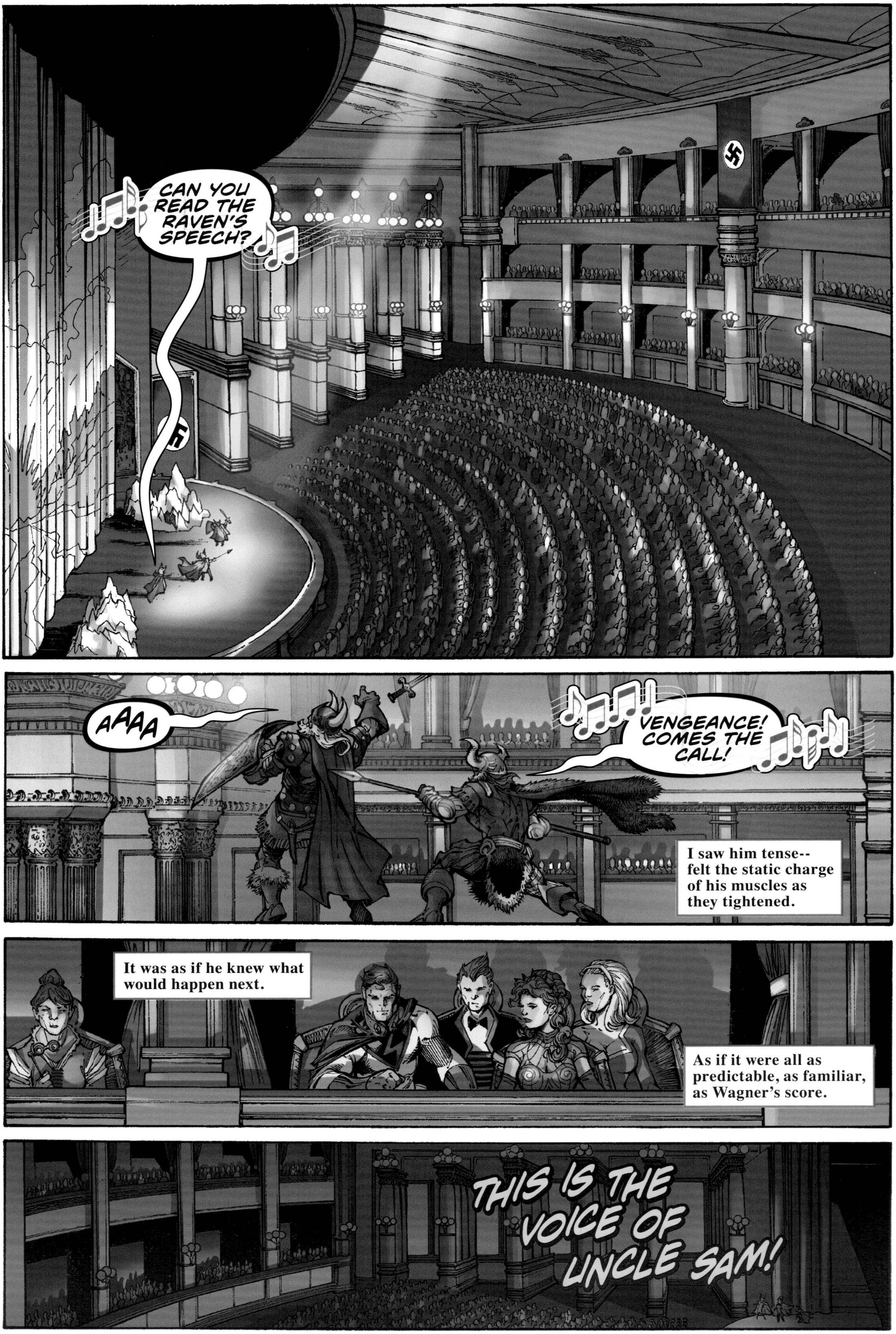
CAN YOU READ THE RAVEN'S SPEECH?
AAAA
VENGEANCE! COMES THE CALL!
I saw him tense--felt the static charge of his muscles as they tightened.
It was as if he knew what would happen next.
As if it were all as predictable, as familiar, as Wagner's score.
THIS IS THE VOICE OF UNCLE SAM!

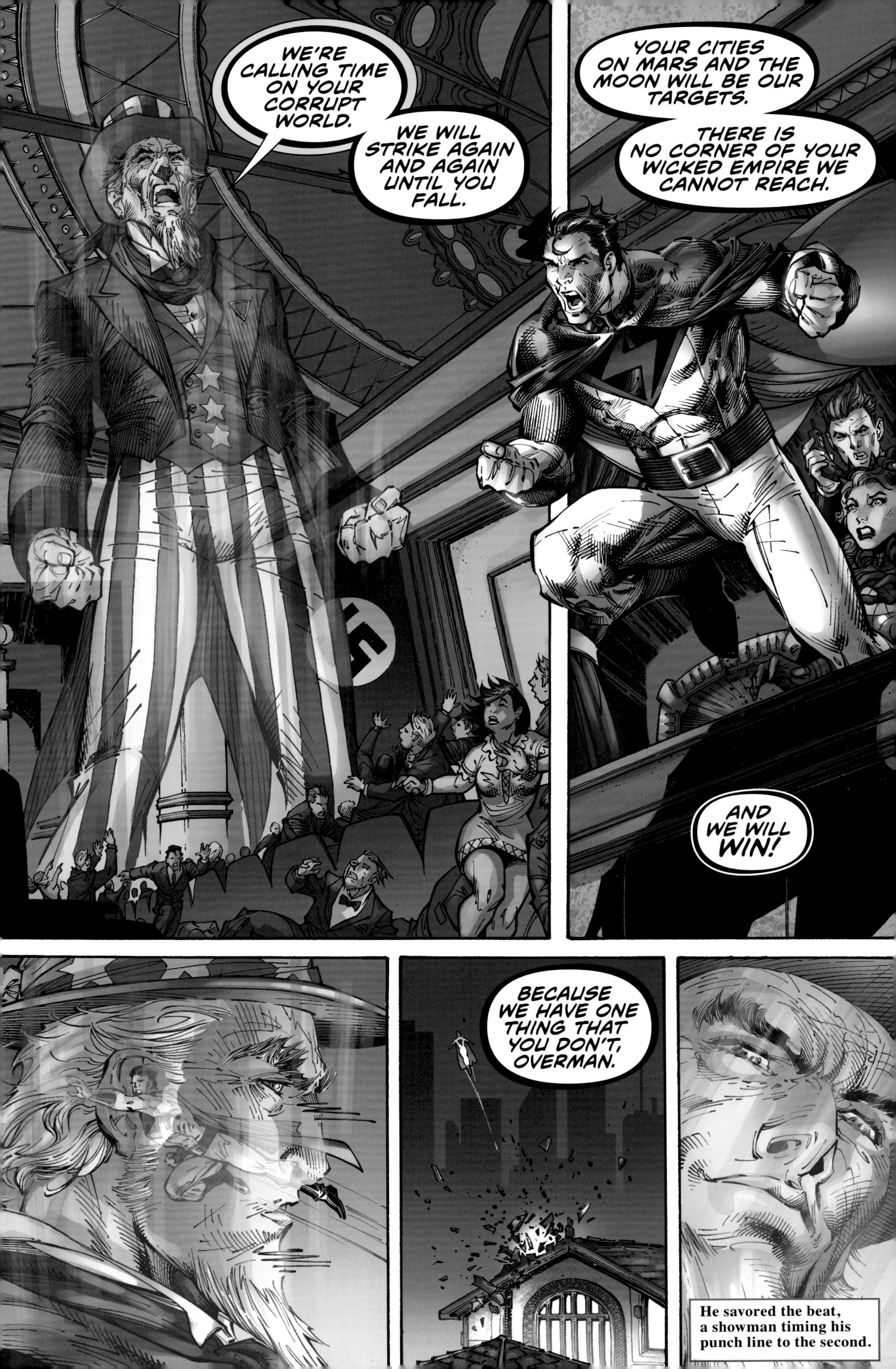
WE'RE CALLING TIME ON YOUR CORRUPT WORLD.
WE WILL STRIKE AGAIN AND AGAIN UNTIL YOU FALL.
YOUR CITIES ON MARS AND THE MOON WILL BE OUR TARGETS.
THERE IS NO CORNER OF YOUR WICKED EMPIRE WE CANNOT REACH.
AND WE WILL WIN!
BECAUSE WE HAVE ONE THING THAT YOU DON'T, OVERMAN.
He savored the beat, a showman timing his punch line to the second.

SOMETHING TO BELIEVE IN!

NINETY-EIGHT YEARS old, his strength failing under the massive weight of the Eagle's Nest as it hit the atmosphere.

His resolve failing.

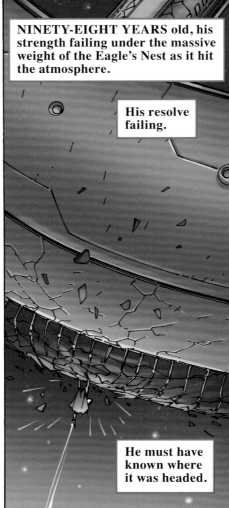

He must have known where it was headed.

WE WANT YOU!

TO PAY FOR YOUR CRIMES!

HEADS UP, RATZIS.

SAM SAYS YOU CAN RAM YOUR SIEGFRIED WHERE THE SUN DON'T SHINE.

He must have known where it would fall.

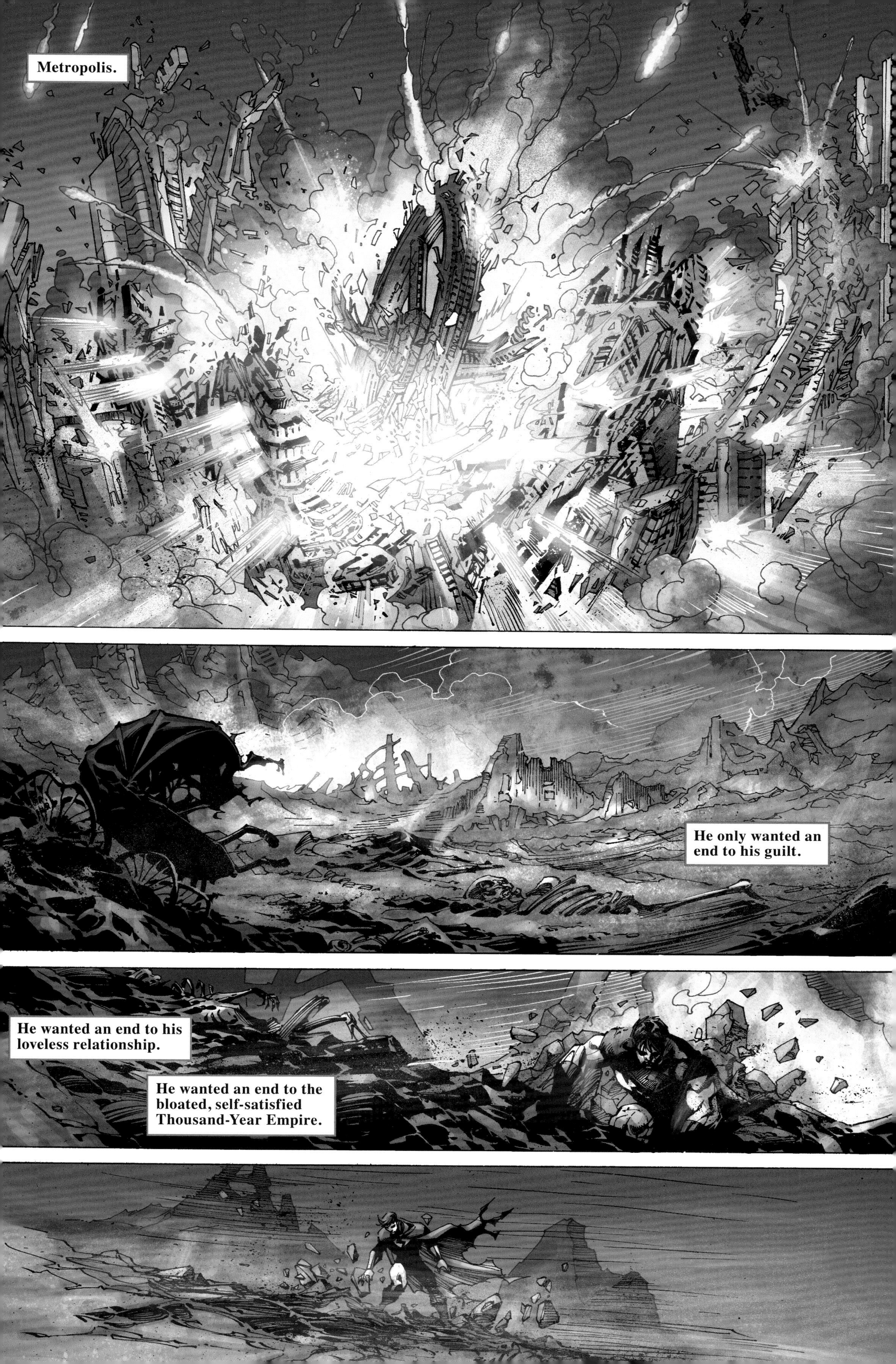
Metropolis.
He only wanted an end to his guilt.
He wanted an end to his loveless relationship.
He wanted an end to the bloated, self-satisfied Thousand-Year Empire.

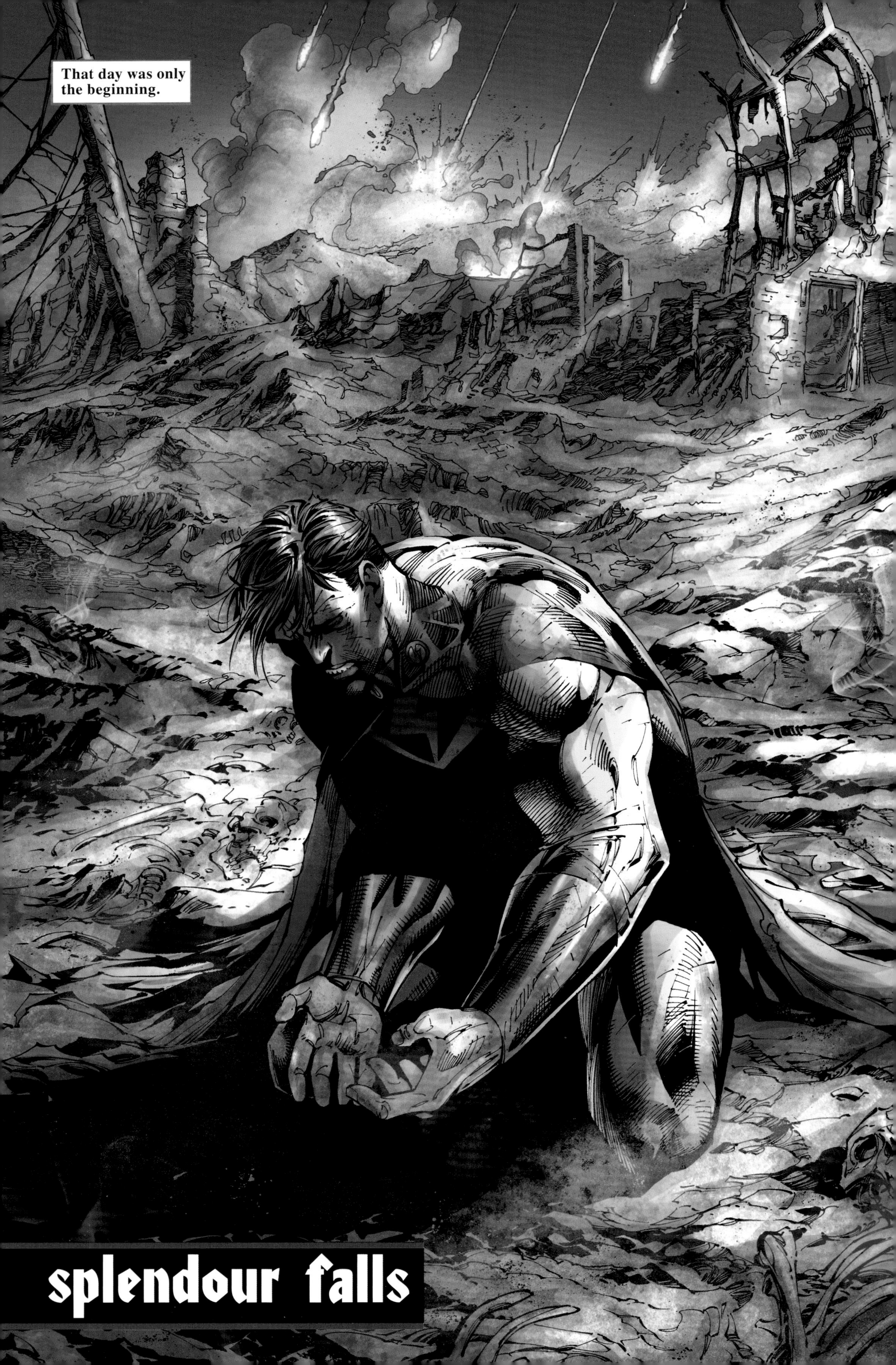
That day was only the beginning.
splendour falls

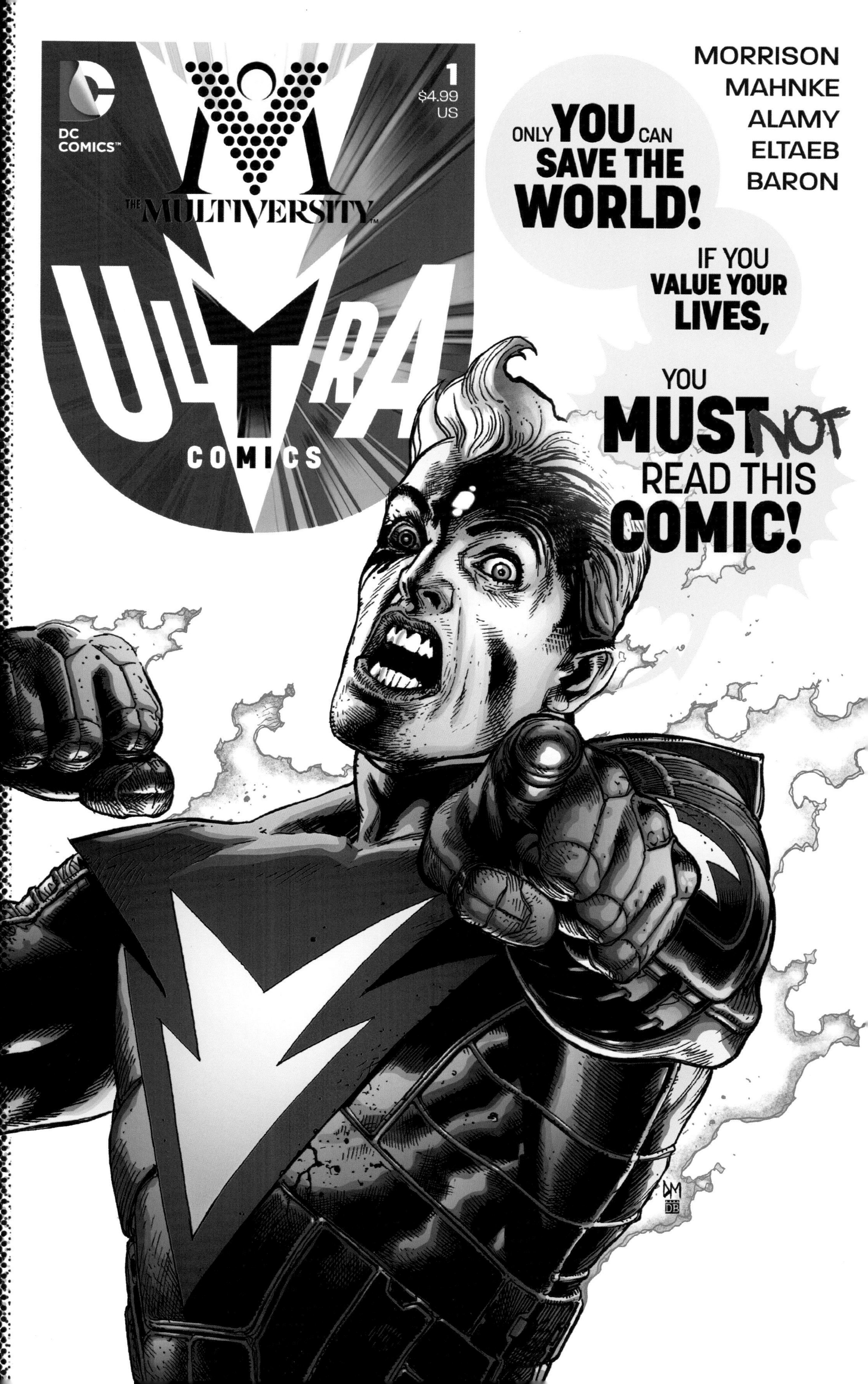
DC COMICS™
THE MULTIVERSITY™
1
$4.99
US
ULTRA
COMICS
MORRISON
MAHNKE
ALAMY
ELTAEB
BARON
ONLY YOU CAN SAVE THE WORLD!
IF YOU VALUE YOUR LIVES,
YOU MUST NOT READ THIS COMIC!

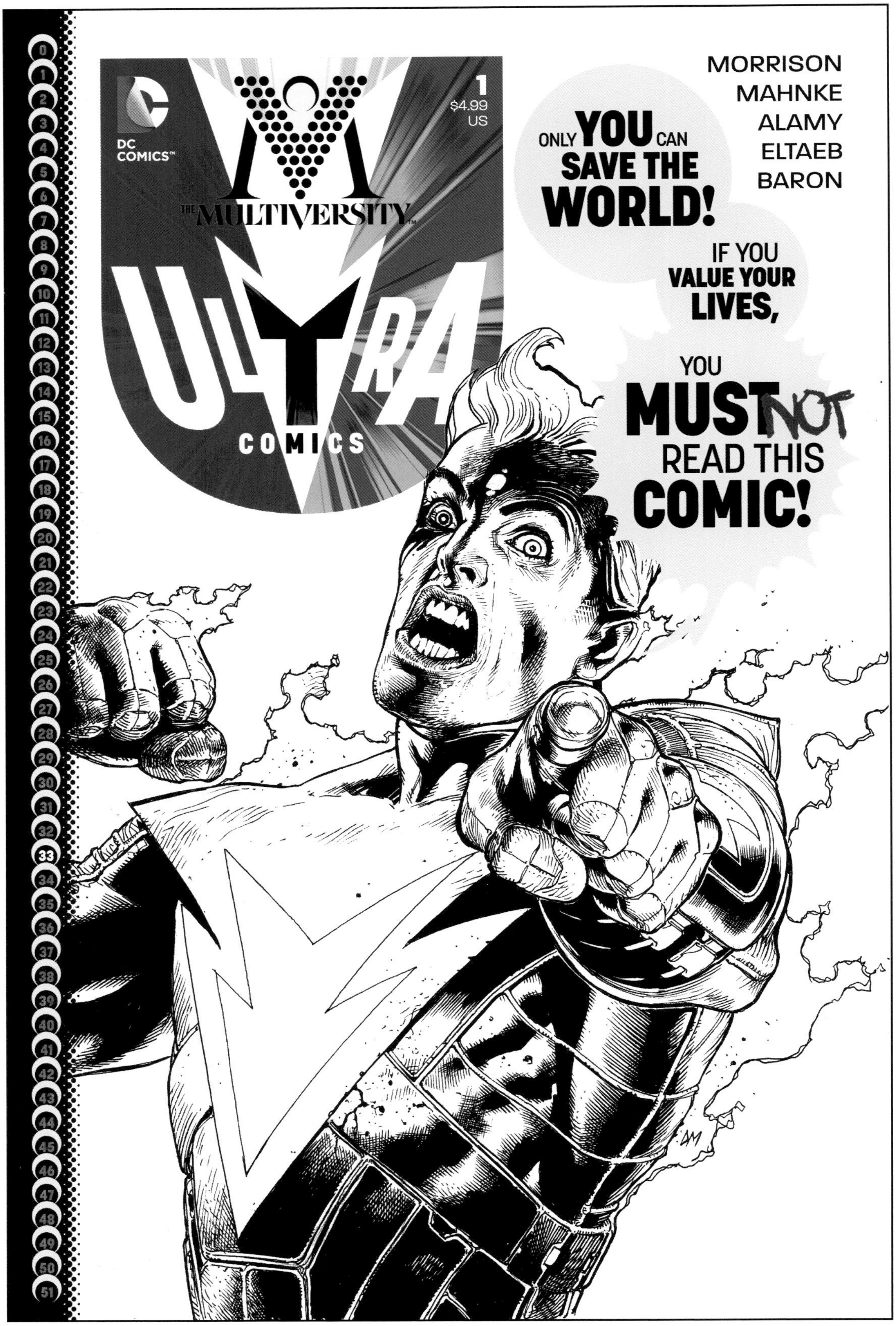
DC COMICS
1 $4.99 US
THE MULTIVERSITY
ULTRA COMICS
MORRISON
MAHNKE
ALAMY
ELTAEB
BARON
ONLY YOU CAN SAVE THE WORLD!
IF YOU VALUE YOUR LIVES,
YOU MUST NOT READ THIS COMIC!

THE MULTIVERSITY: ULTRA COMICS
#1

Written by
GRANT MORRISON

Penciller
DOUG MAHNKE

Inkers
CHRISTIAN ALAMY
MARK IRWIN
KEITH CHAMPAGNE
JAIME MENDOZA

Colorists
GABE ELTAEB
DAVID BARON

Letterer
STEVE WANDS

Cover artists
DOUG MAHNKE
with
DAVID BARON

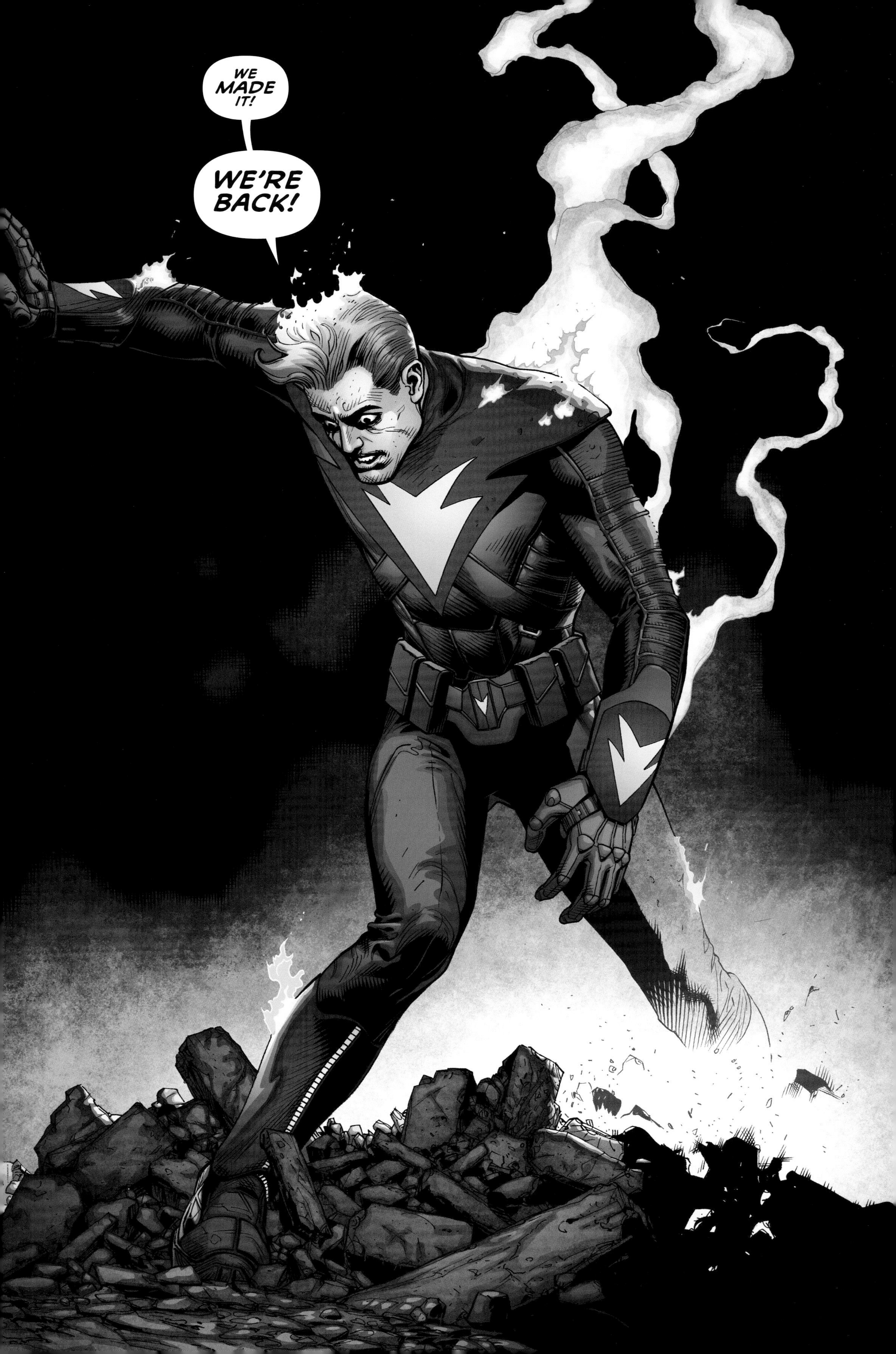
WE MADE IT!
WE'RE BACK!

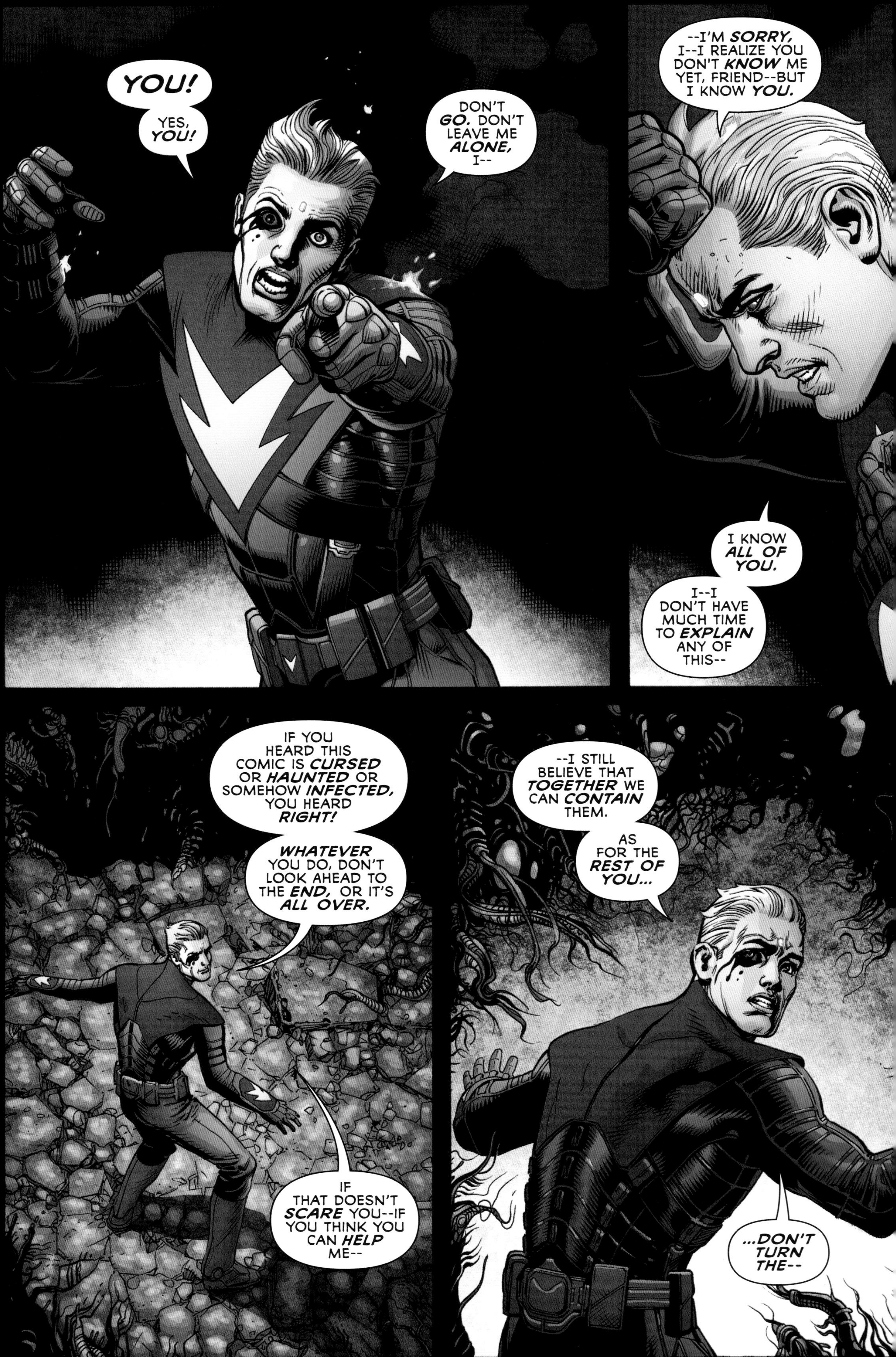
YOU!
YES, YOU!
DON'T GO. DON'T LEAVE ME ALONE, I--
--I'M SORRY, I--I REALIZE YOU DON'T KNOW ME YET, FRIEND--BUT I KNOW YOU.
I KNOW ALL OF YOU.
I--I DON'T HAVE MUCH TIME TO EXPLAIN ANY OF THIS--
IF YOU HEARD THIS COMIC IS CURSED OR HAUNTED OR SOMEHOW INFECTED, YOU HEARD RIGHT!
WHATEVER YOU DO, DON'T LOOK AHEAD TO THE END, OR IT'S ALL OVER.
IF THAT DOESN'T SCARE YOU--IF YOU THINK YOU CAN HELP ME--
--I STILL BELIEVE THAT TOGETHER WE CAN CONTAIN THEM.
AS FOR THE REST OF YOU...
...DON'T TURN THE--

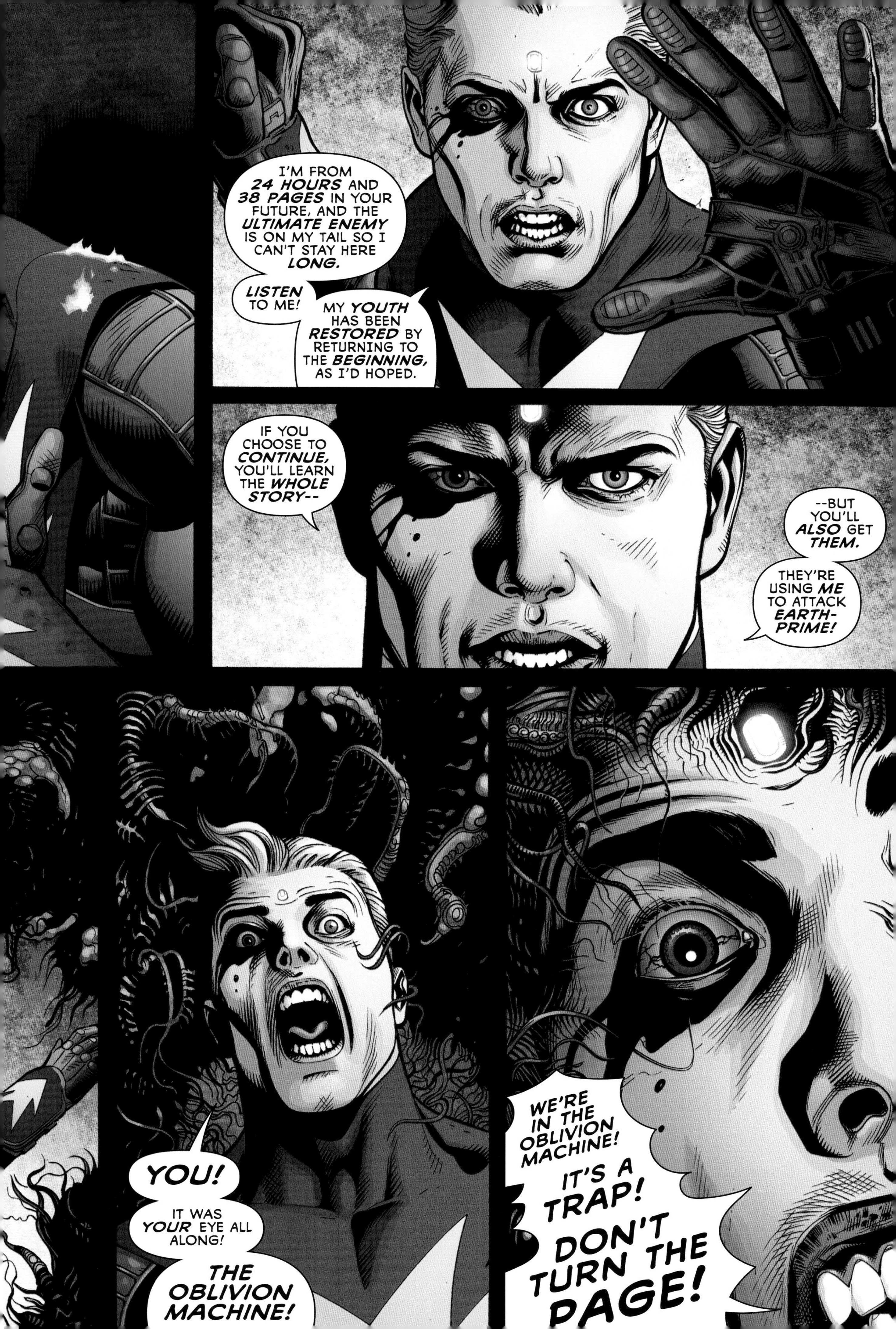
I'M FROM 24 HOURS AND 38 PAGES IN YOUR FUTURE, AND THE ULTIMATE ENEMY IS ON MY TAIL SO I CAN'T STAY HERE LONG.
LISTEN TO ME!
MY YOUTH HAS BEEN RESTORED BY RETURNING TO THE BEGINNING, AS I'D HOPED.
IF YOU CHOOSE TO CONTINUE, YOU'LL LEARN THE WHOLE STORY--
--BUT YOU'LL ALSO GET THEM.
THEY'RE USING ME TO ATTACK EARTH-PRIME!
YOU!
IT WAS YOUR EYE ALL ALONG!
THE OBLIVION MACHINE!
WE'RE IN THE OBLIVION MACHINE!
IT'S A TRAP!
DON'T TURN THE PAGE!

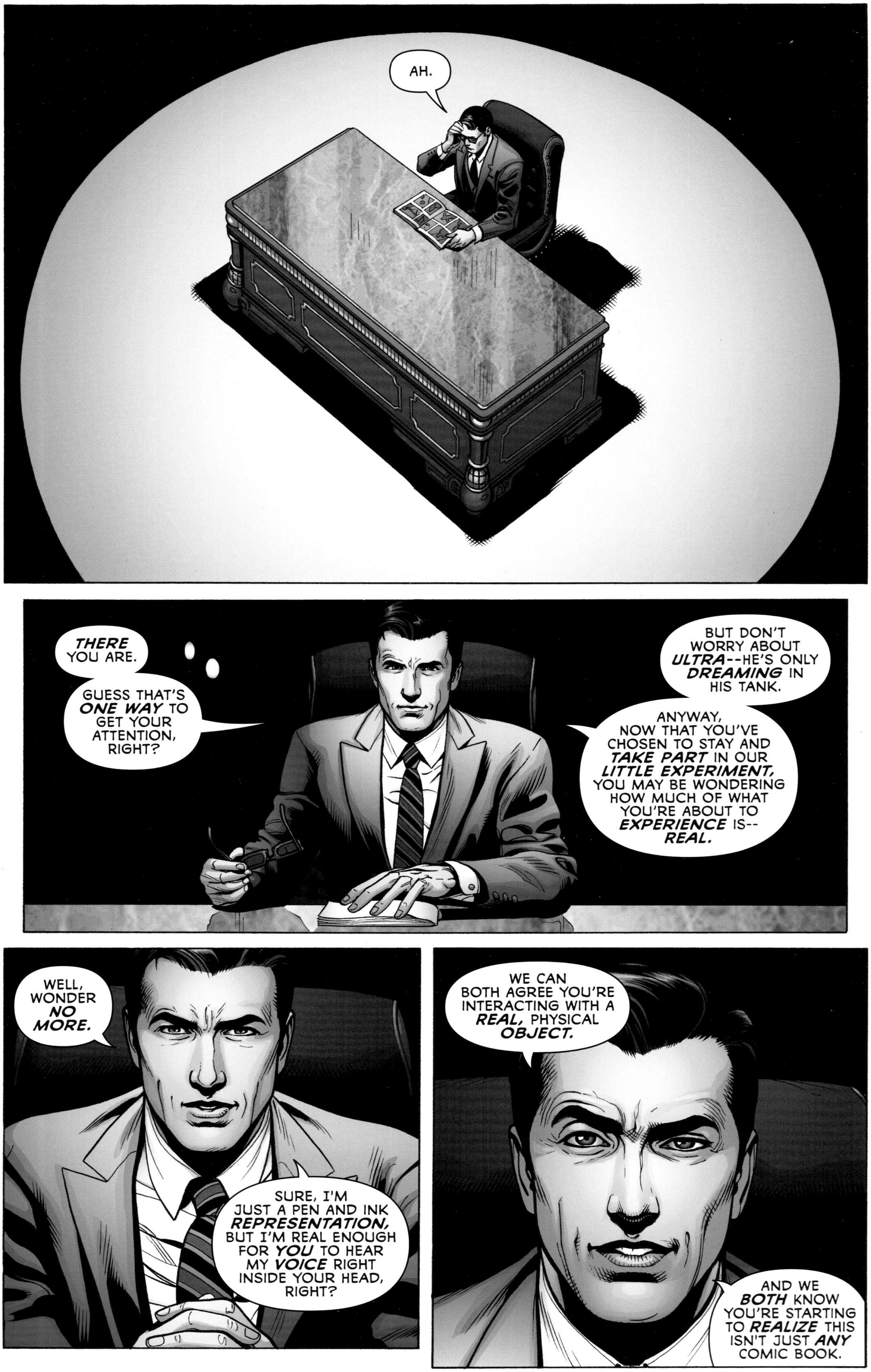
AH.
THERE YOU ARE.
GUESS THAT'S ONE WAY TO GET YOUR ATTENTION, RIGHT?
BUT DON'T WORRY ABOUT ULTRA--HE'S ONLY DREAMING IN HIS TANK.
ANYWAY, NOW THAT YOU'VE CHOSEN TO STAY AND TAKE PART IN OUR LITTLE EXPERIMENT, YOU MAY BE WONDERING HOW MUCH OF WHAT YOU'RE ABOUT TO EXPERIENCE IS-- REAL.
WELL, WONDER NO MORE.
SURE, I'M JUST A PEN AND INK REPRESENTATION, BUT I'M REAL ENOUGH FOR YOU TO HEAR MY VOICE RIGHT INSIDE YOUR HEAD, RIGHT?
WE CAN BOTH AGREE YOU'RE INTERACTING WITH A REAL, PHYSICAL OBJECT.
AND WE BOTH KNOW YOU'RE STARTING TO REALIZE THIS ISN'T JUST ANY COMIC BOOK.

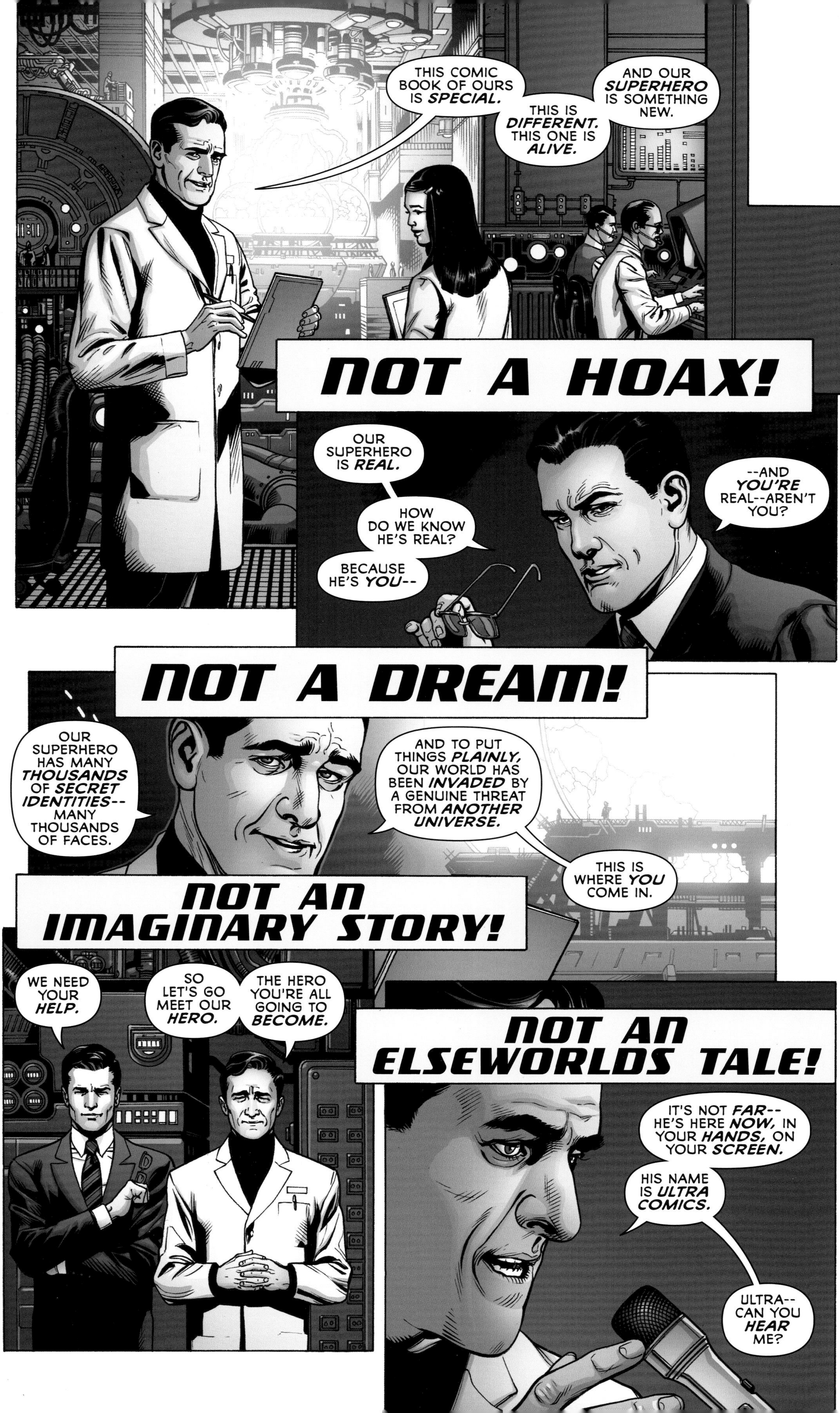

THIS COMIC BOOK OF OURS IS SPECIAL.
THIS IS DIFFERENT. THIS ONE IS ALIVE.
AND OUR SUPERHERO IS SOMETHING NEW.
NOT A HOAX!
OUR SUPERHERO IS REAL.
HOW DO WE KNOW HE'S REAL?
BECAUSE HE'S YOU--
--AND YOU'RE REAL--AREN'T YOU?
NOT A DREAM!
OUR SUPERHERO HAS MANY THOUSANDS OF SECRET IDENTITIES--MANY THOUSANDS OF FACES.
AND TO PUT THINGS PLAINLY, OUR WORLD HAS BEEN INVADED BY A GENUINE THREAT FROM ANOTHER UNIVERSE.
THIS IS WHERE YOU COME IN.
NOT AN IMAGINARY STORY!
WE NEED YOUR HELP.
SO LET'S GO MEET OUR HERO.
THE HERO YOU'RE ALL GOING TO BECOME.
NOT AN ELSEWORLDS TALE!
IT'S NOT FAR--HE'S HERE NOW, IN YOUR HANDS, ON YOUR SCREEN.
HIS NAME IS ULTRA COMICS.
ULTRA--CAN YOU HEAR ME?

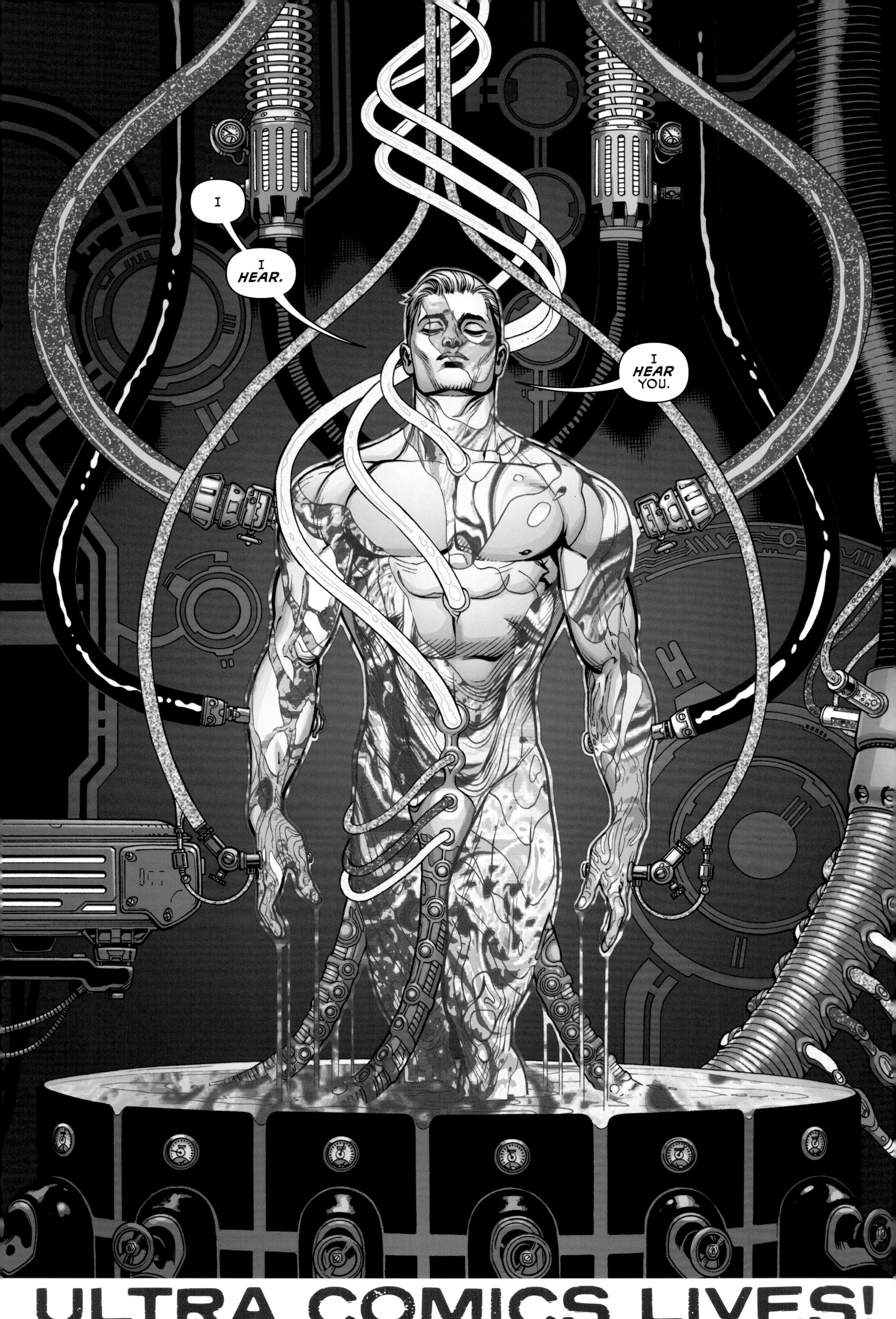
I
I HEAR.
I HEAR YOU.

ULTRA COMICS LIVES!

I HEAR YOU *LOUD AND CLEAR.*

INCREDIBLE!

MY BODY--MADE FROM *CELLULOSE PULP, SALT WATER, AND CARBON.*

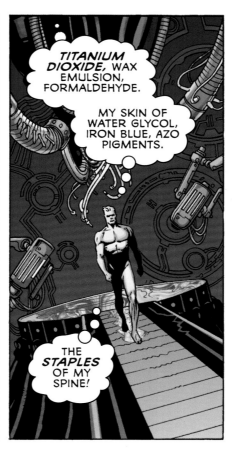

TITANIUM DIOXIDE, WAX EMULSION, FORMALDEHYDE.

MY SKIN OF WATER GLYCOL, IRON BLUE, AZO PIGMENTS.

THE *STAPLES* OF MY SPINE!

ULTRA COMICS.

MADE TO CONFRONT A THREAT NO *SINGLE ORDINARY BEING* COULD DEAL WITH!

DESIGNED AS THE ULTIMATE WARRIOR IN A BATTLE FOR YOUR *VERY SOULS!*

BUT *DON'T* BE ALARMED.

I'VE BEEN PRECISION-ENGINEERED TO HELP YOU *WIN* THAT WAR.

INSTALL *ULTRA COMICS™ PSYCHIC SHIELD TECHNOLOGY* SIMPLY BY CHOOSING TO READ THIS ISSUE COVER TO COVER!

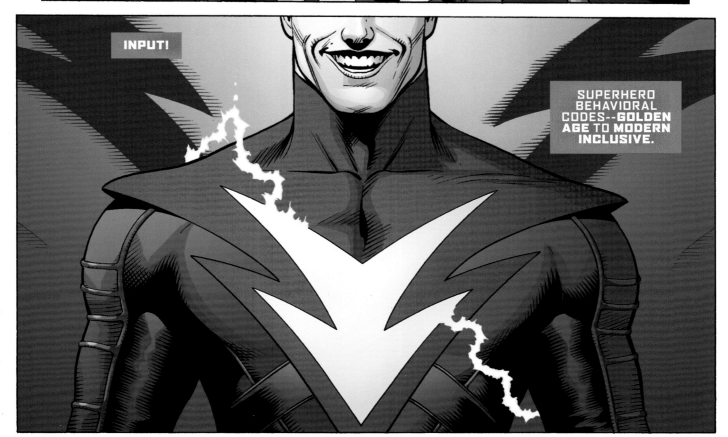

INPUT!

SUPERHERO BEHAVIORAL CODES--GOLDEN AGE TO MODERN INCLUSIVE.

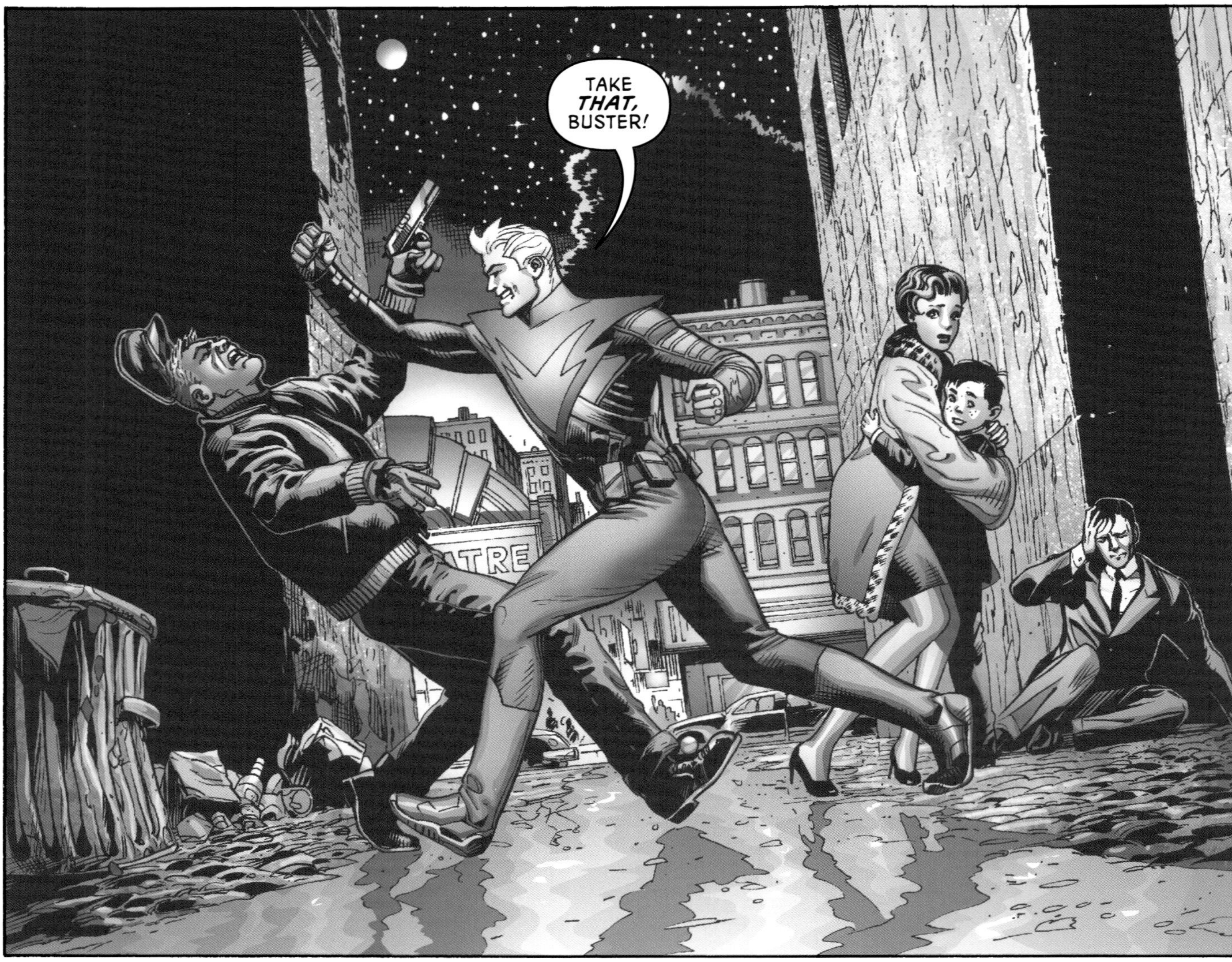
TAKE *THAT,* BUSTER!

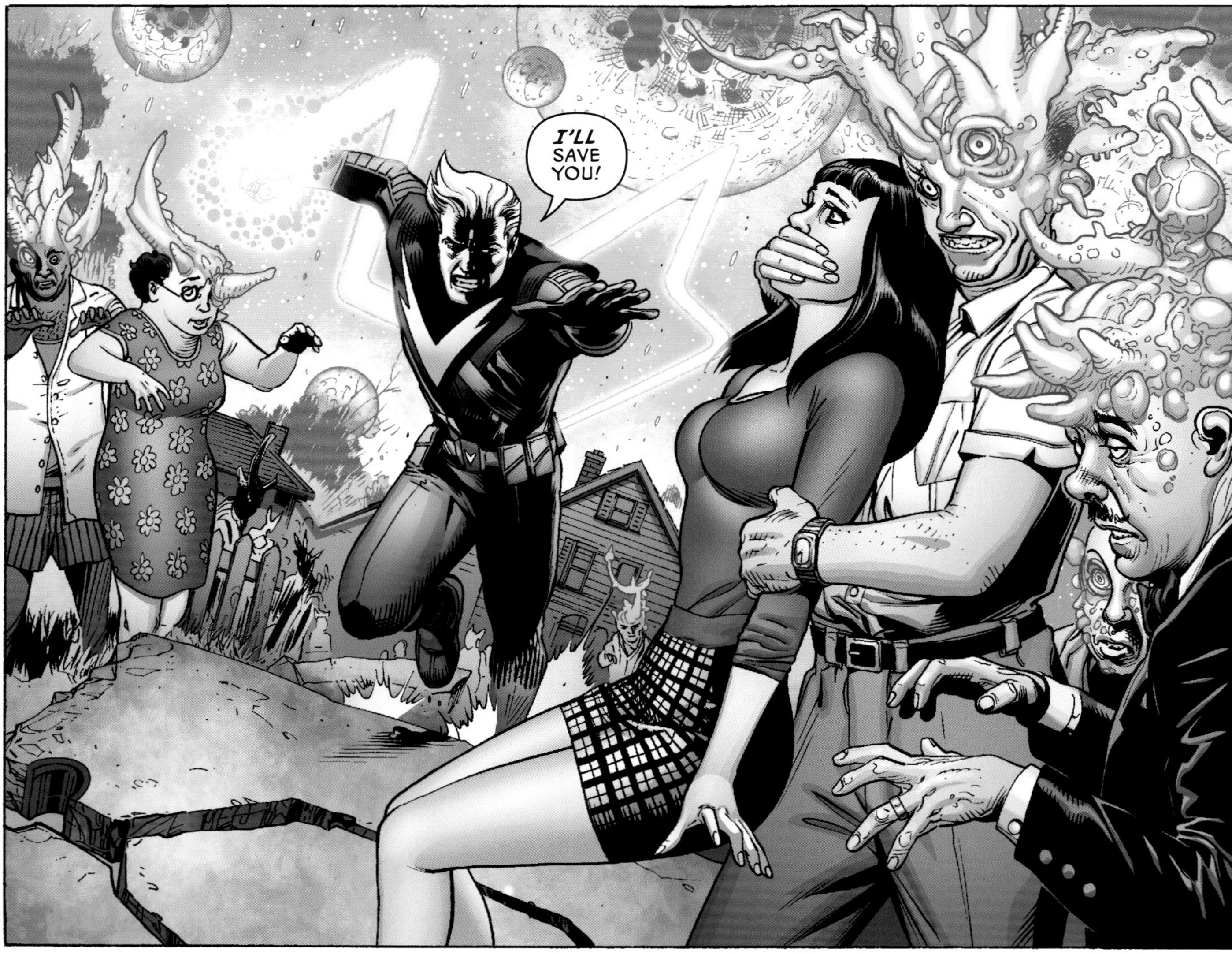
I'LL SAVE YOU!

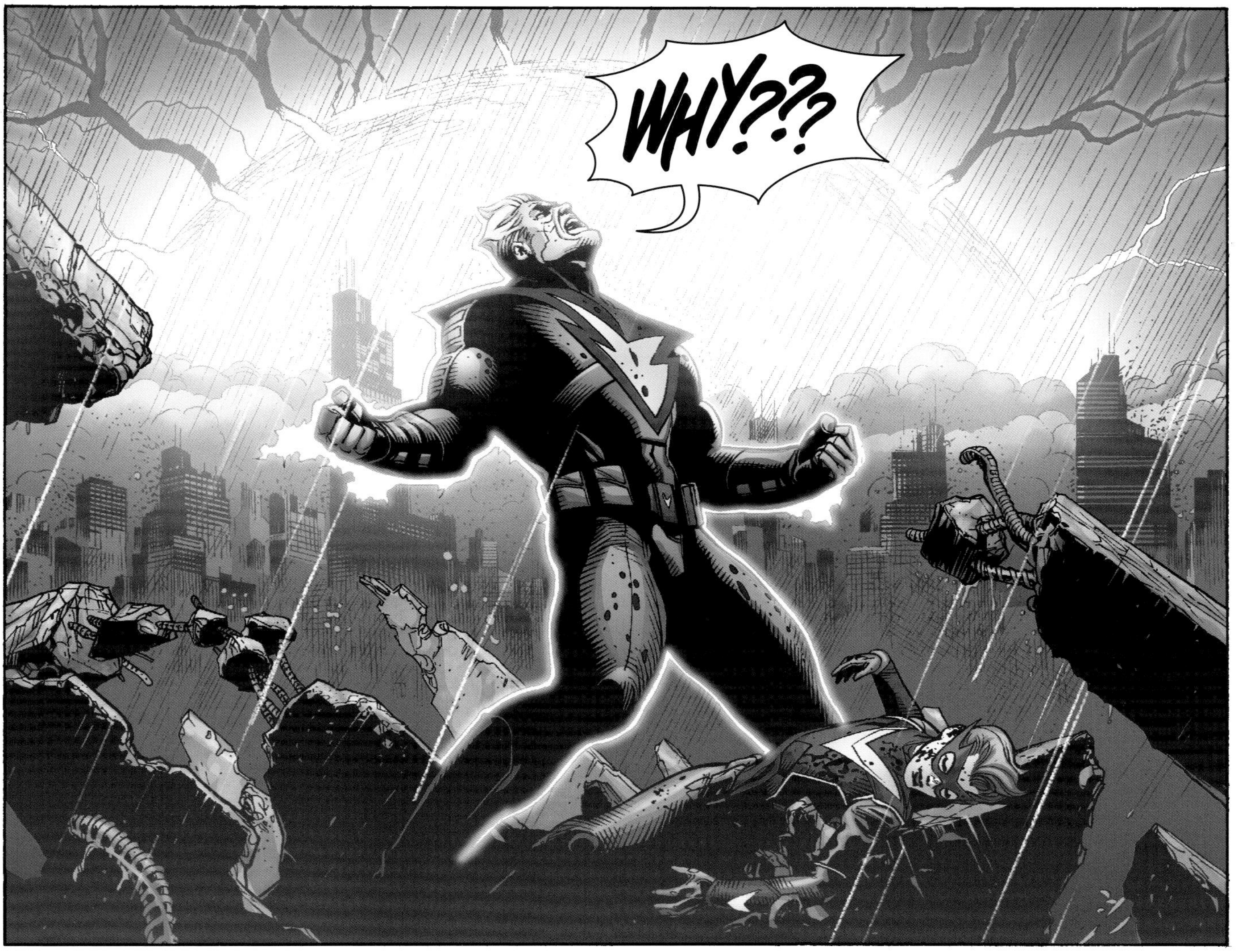
WHY???

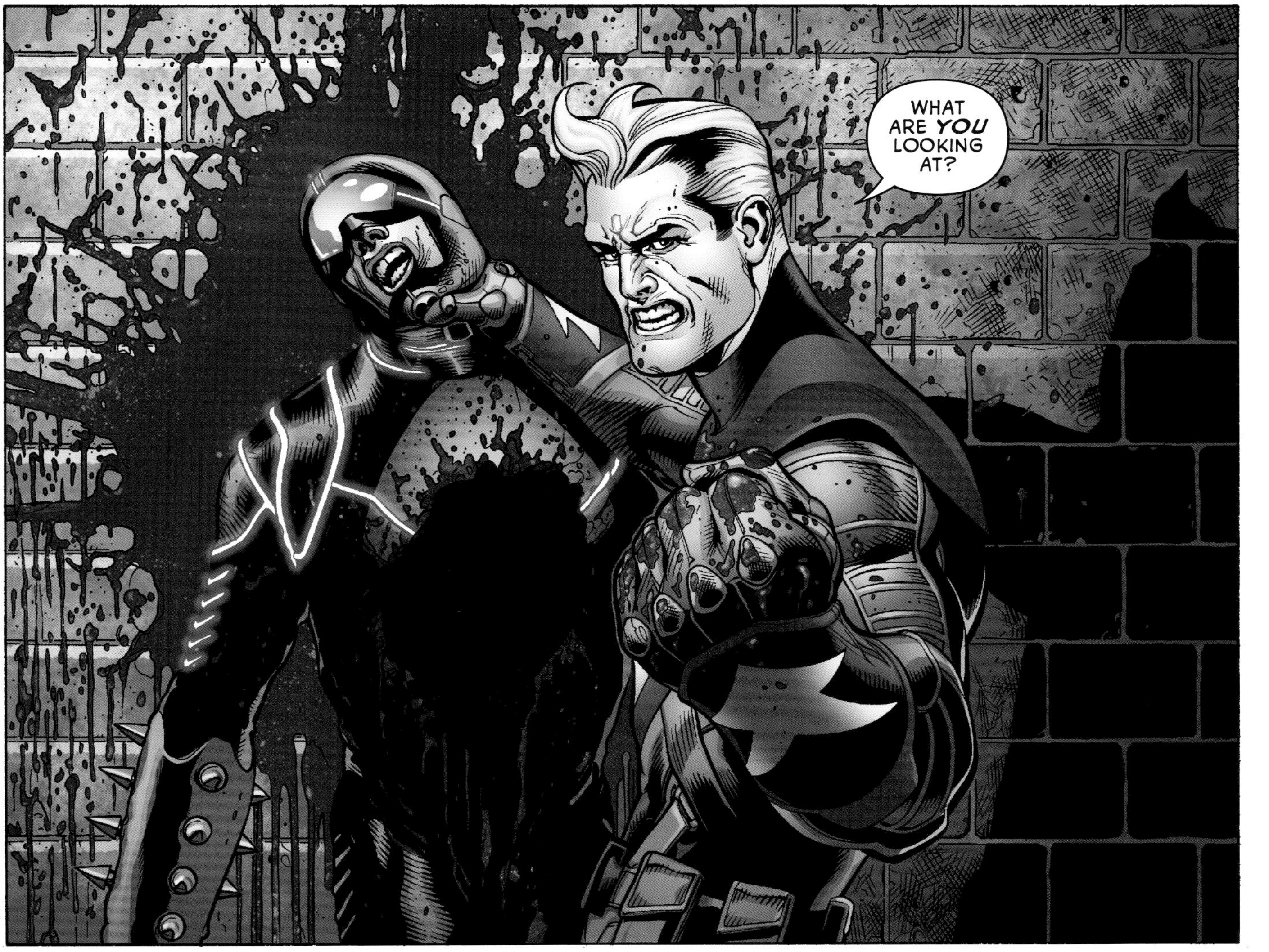
WHAT ARE *YOU* LOOKING AT?

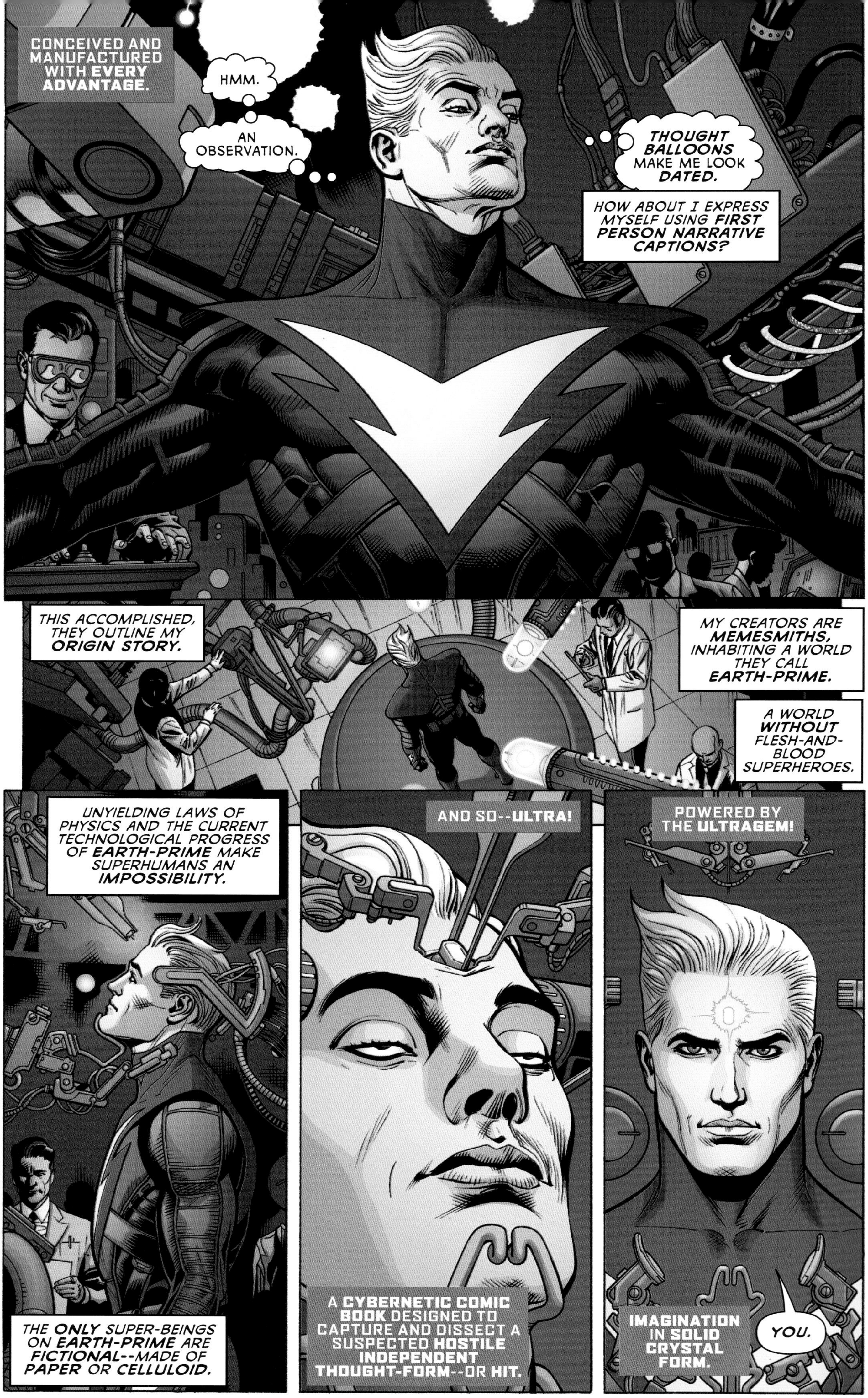
CONCEIVED AND MANUFACTURED WITH EVERY ADVANTAGE.
HMM.
AN OBSERVATION.
THOUGHT BALLOONS MAKE ME LOOK DATED.
HOW ABOUT I EXPRESS MYSELF USING FIRST PERSON NARRATIVE CAPTIONS?
THIS ACCOMPLISHED, THEY OUTLINE MY ORIGIN STORY.
MY CREATORS ARE MEMESMITHS, INHABITING A WORLD THEY CALL EARTH-PRIME.
A WORLD WITHOUT FLESH-AND-BLOOD SUPERHEROES.
UNYIELDING LAWS OF PHYSICS AND THE CURRENT TECHNOLOGICAL PROGRESS OF EARTH-PRIME MAKE SUPERHUMANS AN IMPOSSIBILITY.
THE ONLY SUPER-BEINGS ON EARTH-PRIME ARE FICTIONAL--MADE OF PAPER OR CELLULOID.
AND SO--ULTRA!
A CYBERNETIC COMIC BOOK DESIGNED TO CAPTURE AND DISSECT A SUSPECTED HOSTILE INDEPENDENT THOUGHT-FORM--OR HIT.
POWERED BY THE ULTRAGEM!
IMAGINATION IN SOLID CRYSTAL FORM.
YOU.

ALL OF YOU.

ONLY TOGETHER CAN WE BRING THE ULTRAGEM TO LIFE.

USING THE ULTRAGEM, THE ACCUMULATED POWER OF THOUSANDS OF MINDS--IN DIFFERENT TIMES AND PLACES--CAN BE HARNESSED!

UNITED!

FOCUSED HERE AT THE INTERFACE WHERE YOU AND ULTRA COMICS BECOME ONE LIVING ORGANISM!

NOT THAT I SHOULD NEED ANYONE'S HELP, BUT...

...FRIENDS?

AN UNFORESEEN ASSEMBLAGE OF NETWORKED MULTIPLE MINDS COMBINED IN ONE SINGLE SUPER-POWERED FORM!

MY BEST FRIENDS.

ARE WE-- CIRCUIT CLOSING--

--ARE I--

EARTH'S FIRST REAL SUPERHUMAN HERO!

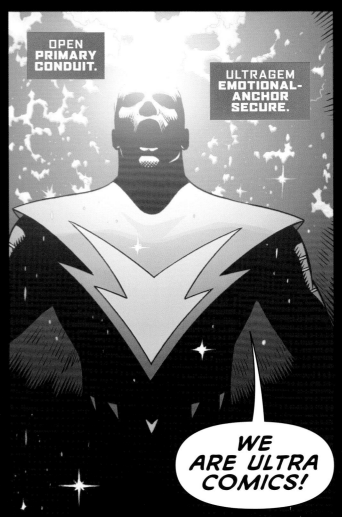

OPEN PRIMARY CONDUIT.

ULTRAGEM EMOTIONAL- ANCHOR SECURE.

WE ARE ULTRA COMICS!

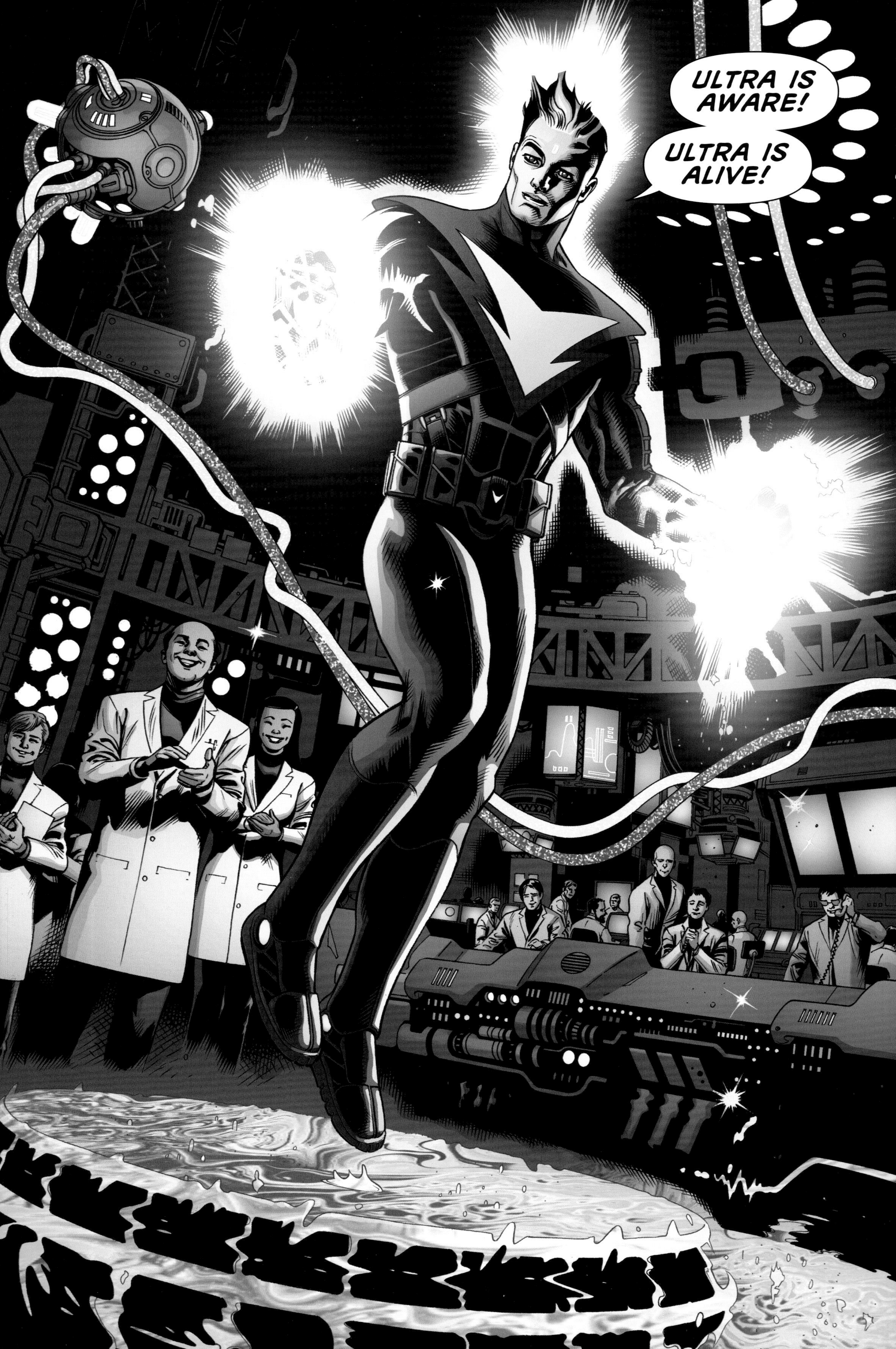
ULTRA IS AWARE!
ULTRA IS ALIVE!

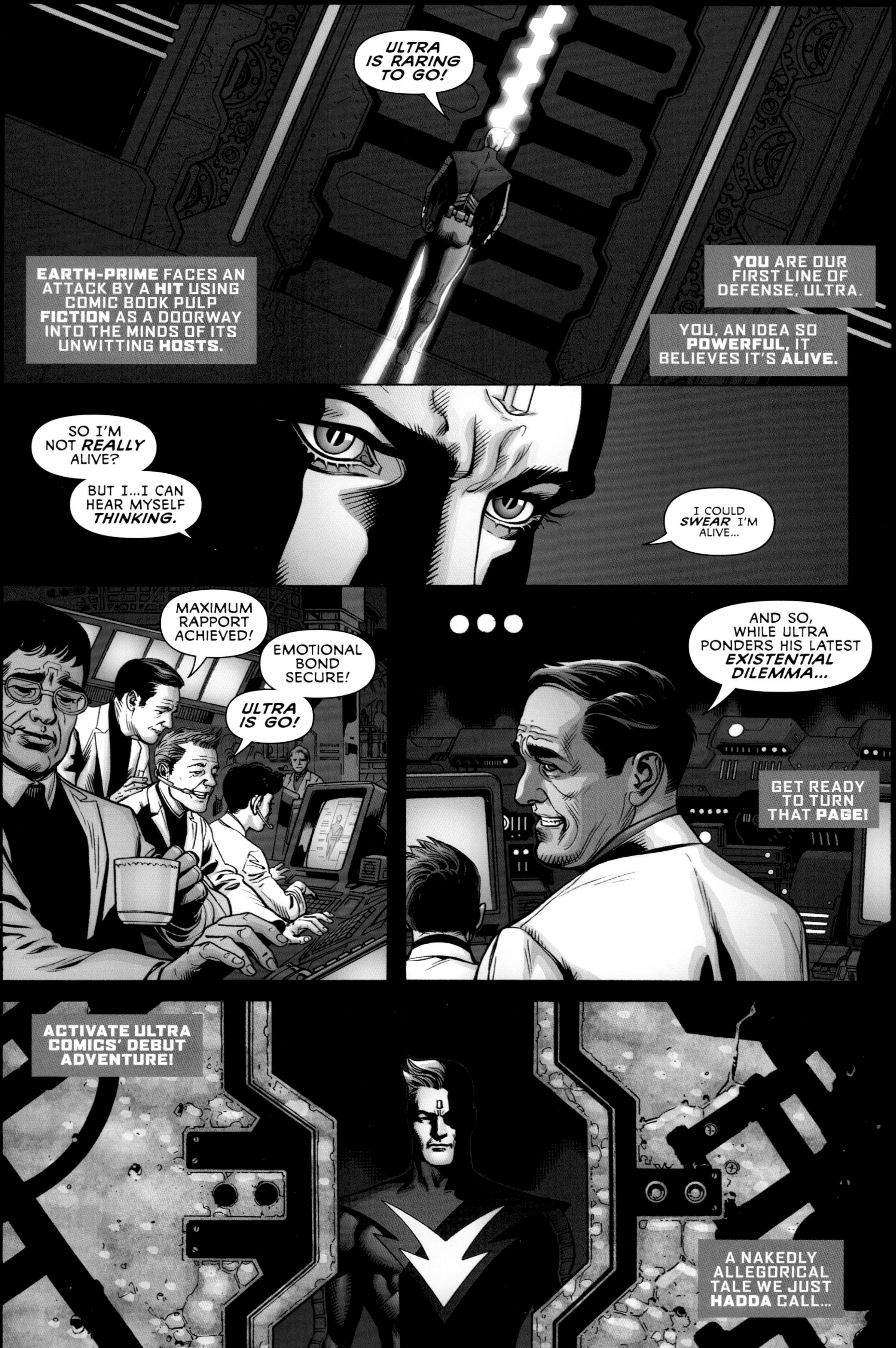
ULTRA IS RARING TO GO!
EARTH-PRIME FACES AN ATTACK BY A HIT USING COMIC BOOK PULP FICTION AS A DOORWAY INTO THE MINDS OF ITS UNWITTING HOSTS.
YOU ARE OUR FIRST LINE OF DEFENSE, ULTRA.
YOU, AN IDEA SO POWERFUL, IT BELIEVES IT'S ALIVE.
SO I'M NOT REALLY ALIVE?
BUT I...I CAN HEAR MYSELF THINKING.
I COULD SWEAR I'M ALIVE...
MAXIMUM RAPPORT ACHIEVED!
EMOTIONAL BOND SECURE!
ULTRA IS GO!
AND SO, WHILE ULTRA PONDERS HIS LATEST EXISTENTIAL DILEMMA...
GET READY TO TURN THAT PAGE!
ACTIVATE ULTRA COMICS' DEBUT ADVENTURE!
A NAKEDLY ALLEGORICAL TALE WE JUST HADDA CALL...

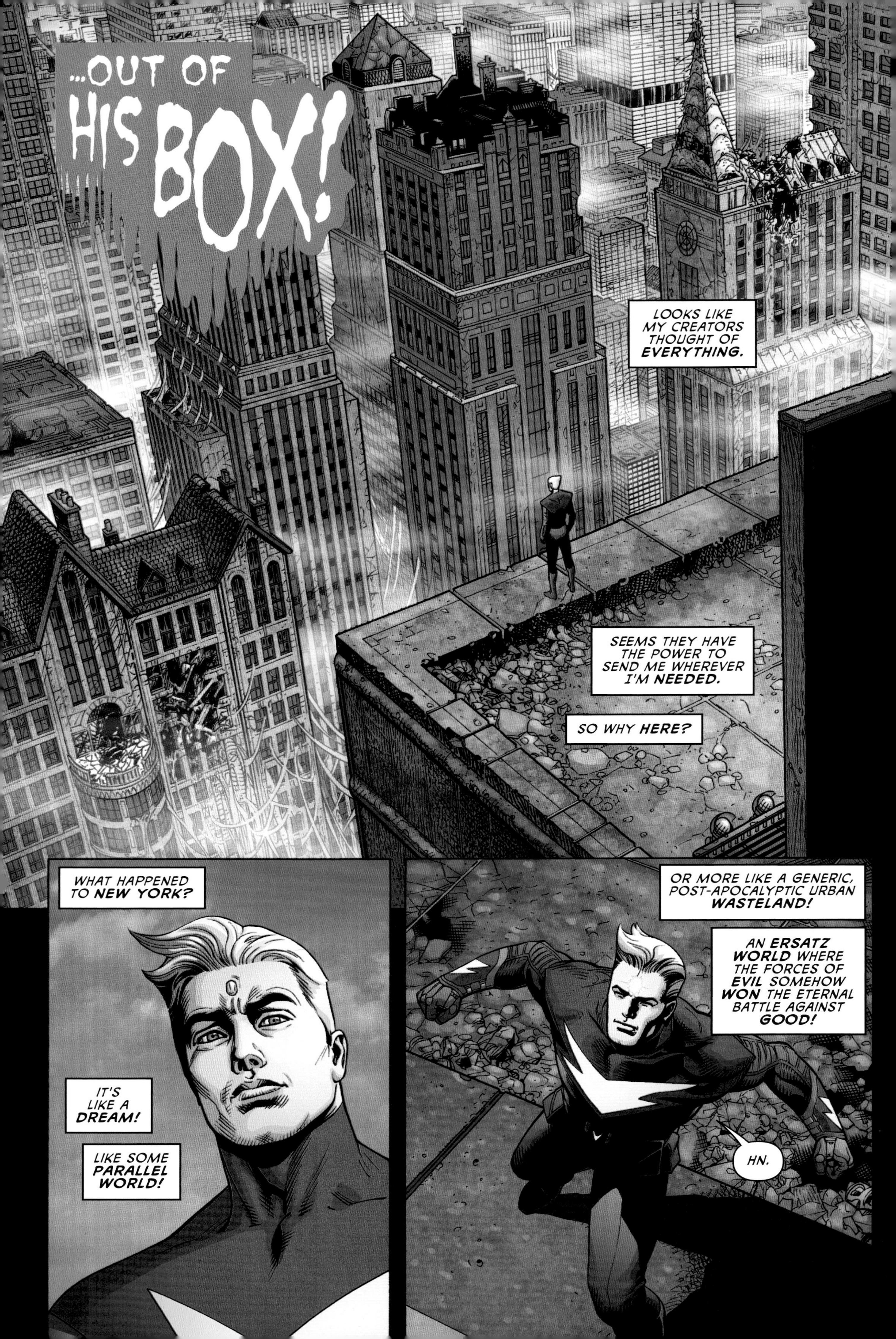
...OUT OF HIS BOX!
LOOKS LIKE MY CREATORS THOUGHT OF EVERYTHING.
SEEMS THEY HAVE THE POWER TO SEND ME WHEREVER I'M NEEDED.
SO WHY HERE?
WHAT HAPPENED TO NEW YORK?
IT'S LIKE A DREAM!
LIKE SOME PARALLEL WORLD!
OR MORE LIKE A GENERIC, POST-APOCALYPTIC URBAN WASTELAND!
AN ERSATZ WORLD WHERE THE FORCES OF EVIL SOMEHOW WON THE ETERNAL BATTLE AGAINST GOOD!
HN.

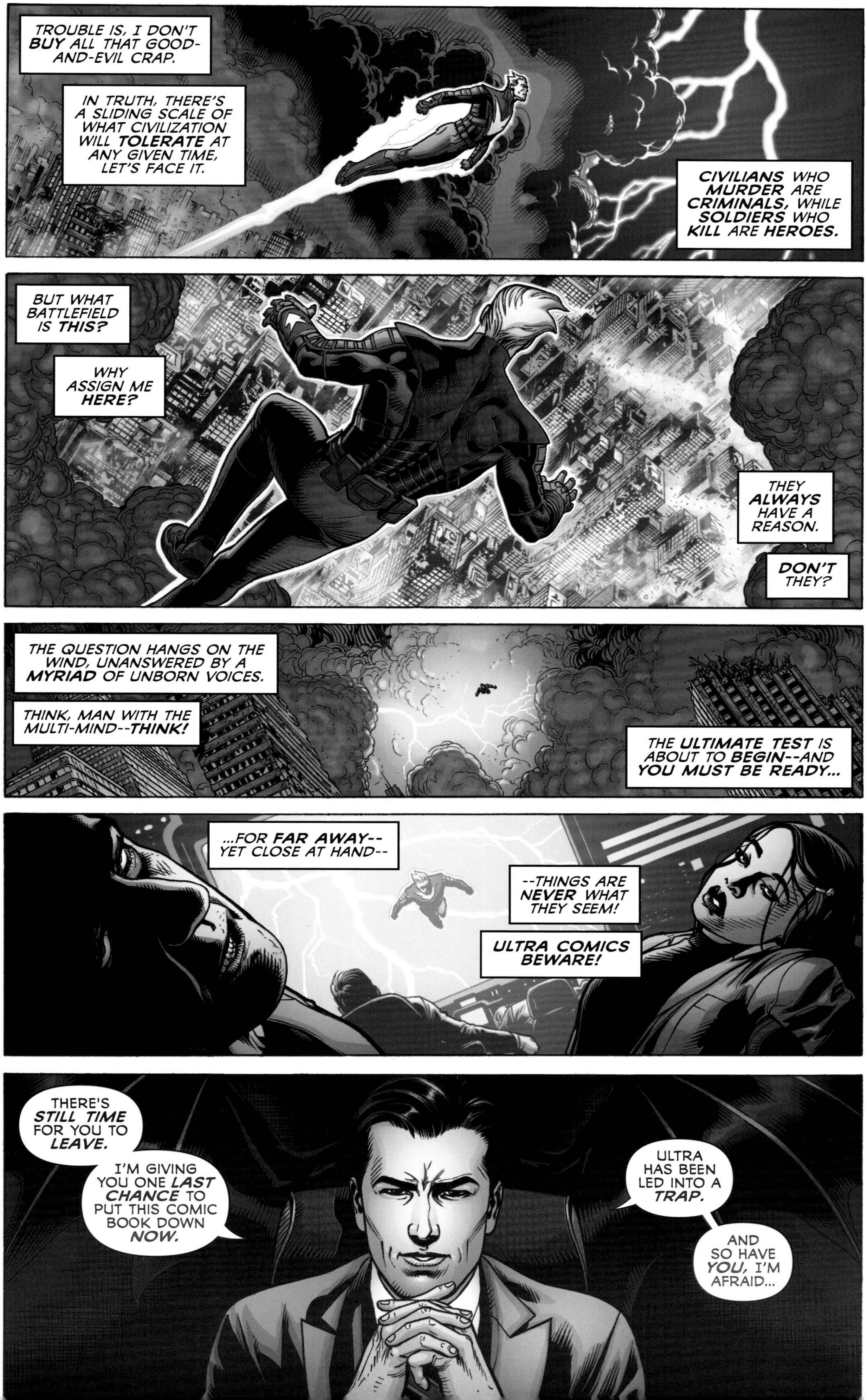
TROUBLE IS, I DON'T BUY ALL THAT GOOD-AND-EVIL CRAP.
IN TRUTH, THERE'S A SLIDING SCALE OF WHAT CIVILIZATION WILL TOLERATE AT ANY GIVEN TIME, LET'S FACE IT.
CIVILIANS WHO MURDER ARE CRIMINALS, WHILE SOLDIERS WHO KILL ARE HEROES.
BUT WHAT BATTLEFIELD IS THIS?
WHY ASSIGN ME HERE?
THEY ALWAYS HAVE A REASON.
DON'T THEY?
THE QUESTION HANGS ON THE WIND, UNANSWERED BY A MYRIAD OF UNBORN VOICES.
THINK, MAN WITH THE MULTI-MIND--THINK!
THE ULTIMATE TEST IS ABOUT TO BEGIN--AND YOU MUST BE READY...
...FOR FAR AWAY-- YET CLOSE AT HAND--
--THINGS ARE NEVER WHAT THEY SEEM!
ULTRA COMICS BEWARE!
THERE'S STILL TIME FOR YOU TO LEAVE.
I'M GIVING YOU ONE LAST CHANCE TO PUT THIS COMIC BOOK DOWN NOW.
ULTRA HAS BEEN LED INTO A TRAP.
AND SO HAVE YOU, I'M AFRAID...

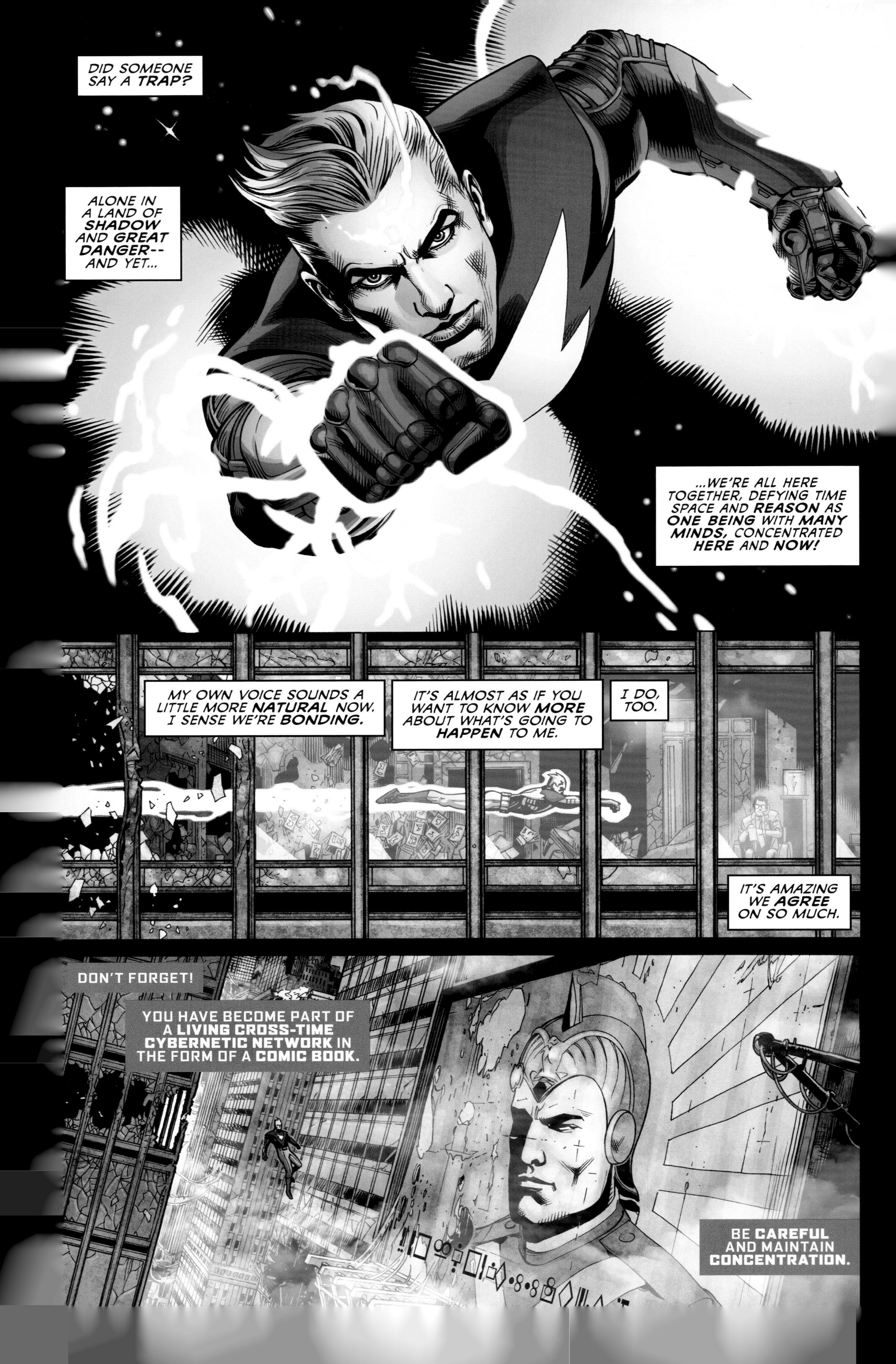
DID SOMEONE SAY A TRAP?
ALONE IN A LAND OF SHADOW AND GREAT DANGER-- AND YET...
...WE'RE ALL HERE TOGETHER, DEFYING TIME SPACE AND REASON AS ONE BEING WITH MANY MINDS, CONCENTRATED HERE AND NOW!
MY OWN VOICE SOUNDS A LITTLE MORE NATURAL NOW. I SENSE WE'RE BONDING.
IT'S ALMOST AS IF YOU WANT TO KNOW MORE ABOUT WHAT'S GOING TO HAPPEN TO ME.
I DO, TOO.
IT'S AMAZING WE AGREE ON SO MUCH.
DON'T FORGET!
YOU HAVE BECOME PART OF A LIVING CROSS-TIME CYBERNETIC NETWORK IN THE FORM OF A COMIC BOOK.
BE CAREFUL AND MAINTAIN CONCENTRATION.

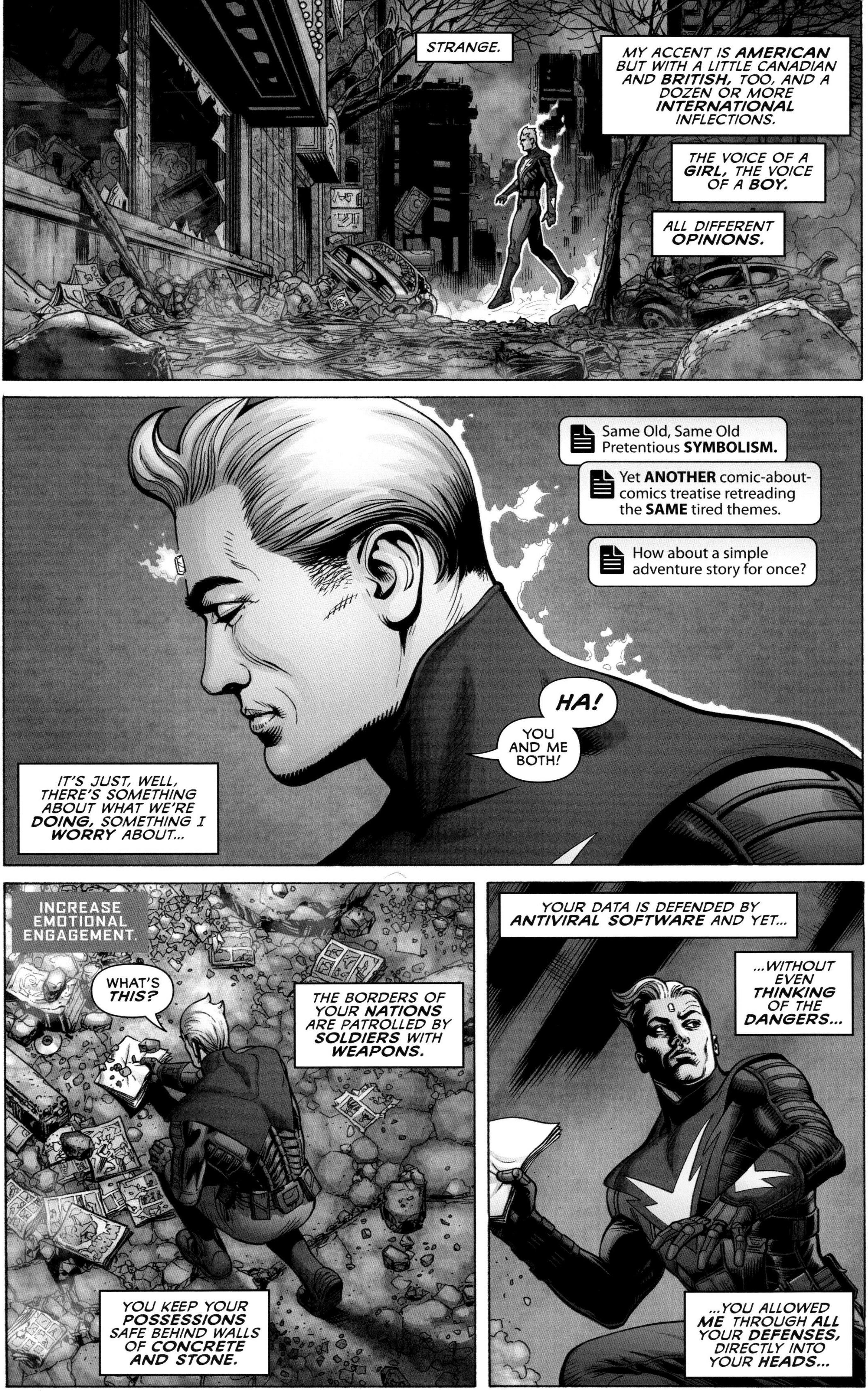
STRANGE.
MY ACCENT IS AMERICAN BUT WITH A LITTLE CANADIAN AND BRITISH, TOO, AND A DOZEN OR MORE INTERNATIONAL INFLECTIONS.
THE VOICE OF A GIRL, THE VOICE OF A BOY.
ALL DIFFERENT OPINIONS.
Same Old, Same Old Pretentious SYMBOLISM.
Yet ANOTHER comic-about-comics treatise retreading the SAME tired themes.
How about a simple adventure story for once?
HA!
YOU AND ME BOTH!
IT'S JUST, WELL, THERE'S SOMETHING ABOUT WHAT WE'RE DOING, SOMETHING I WORRY ABOUT...
INCREASE EMOTIONAL ENGAGEMENT.
WHAT'S THIS?
THE BORDERS OF YOUR NATIONS ARE PATROLLED BY SOLDIERS WITH WEAPONS.
YOU KEEP YOUR POSSESSIONS SAFE BEHIND WALLS OF CONCRETE AND STONE.
YOUR DATA IS DEFENDED BY ANTIVIRAL SOFTWARE AND YET...
...WITHOUT EVEN THINKING OF THE DANGERS...
...YOU ALLOWED ME THROUGH ALL YOUR DEFENSES, DIRECTLY INTO YOUR HEADS...

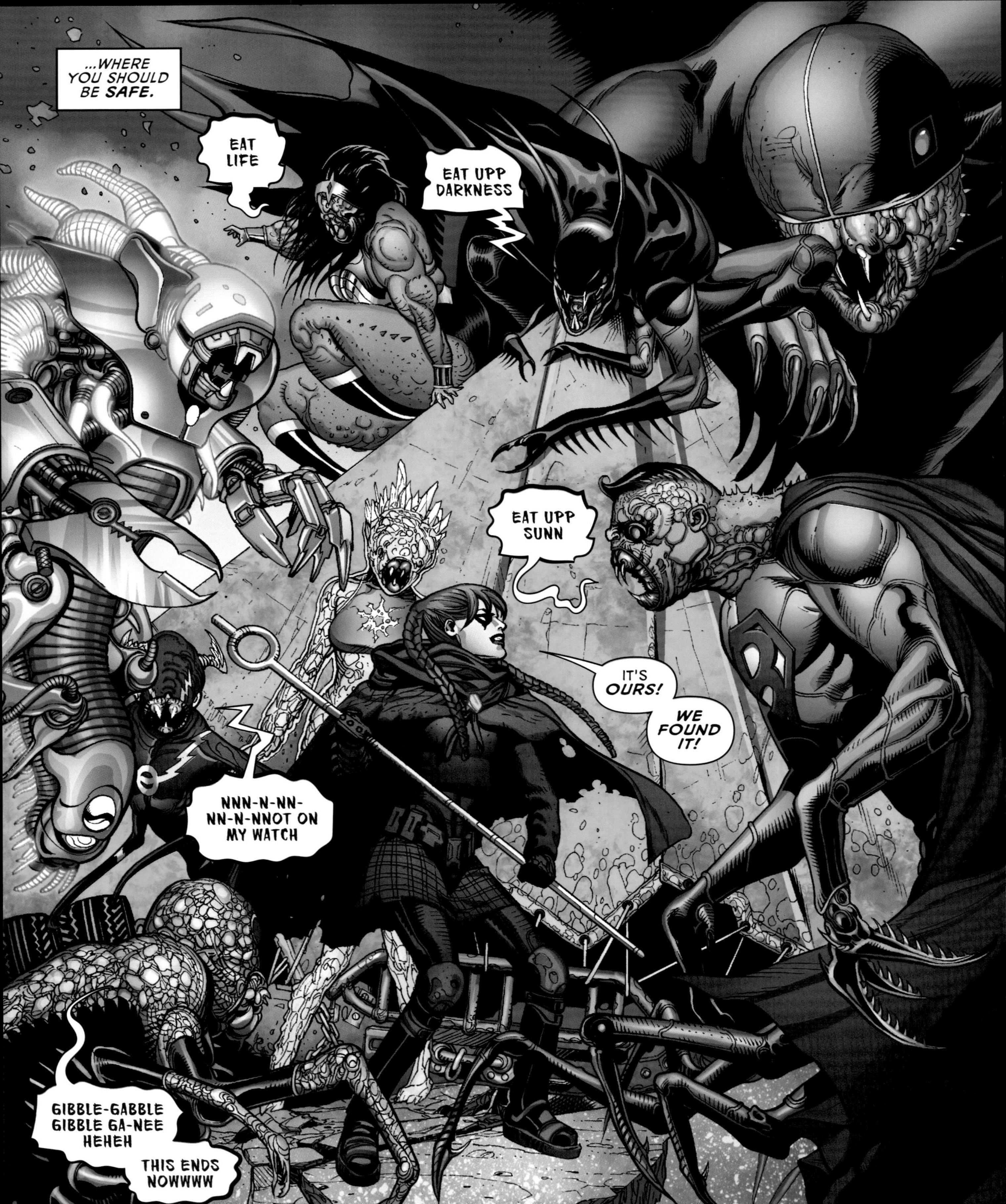
...WHERE YOU SHOULD BE SAFE.
EAT LIFE
EAT UPP DARKNESS
EAT UPP SUNN
IT'S OURS!
WE FOUND IT!
NNN-N-NN-NN-N-NNOT ON MY WATCH
GIBBLE-GABBLE GIBBLE GA-NEE HEHEH
THIS ENDS NOWWWW

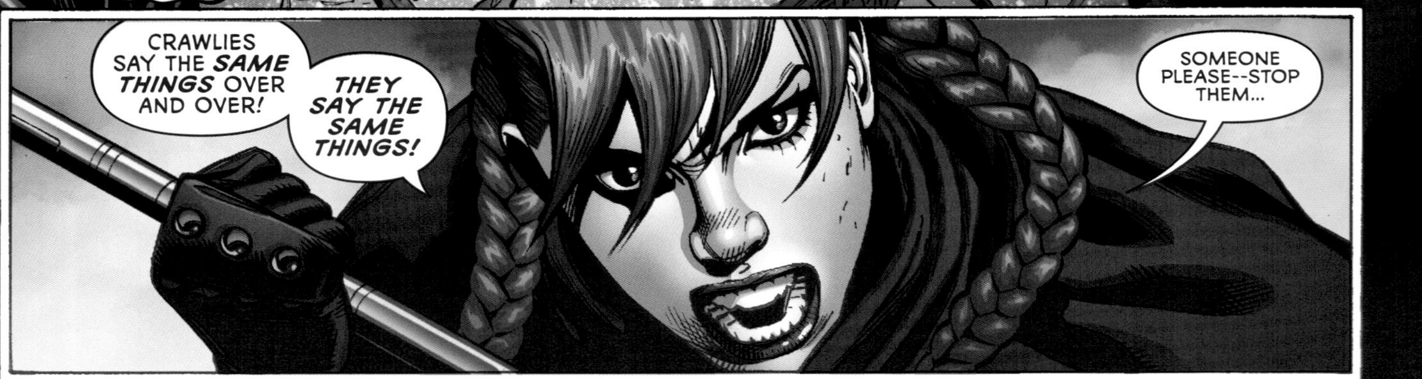
CRAWLIES SAY THE SAME THINGS OVER AND OVER!
THEY SAY THE SAME THINGS!
SOMEONE PLEASE--STOP THEM...

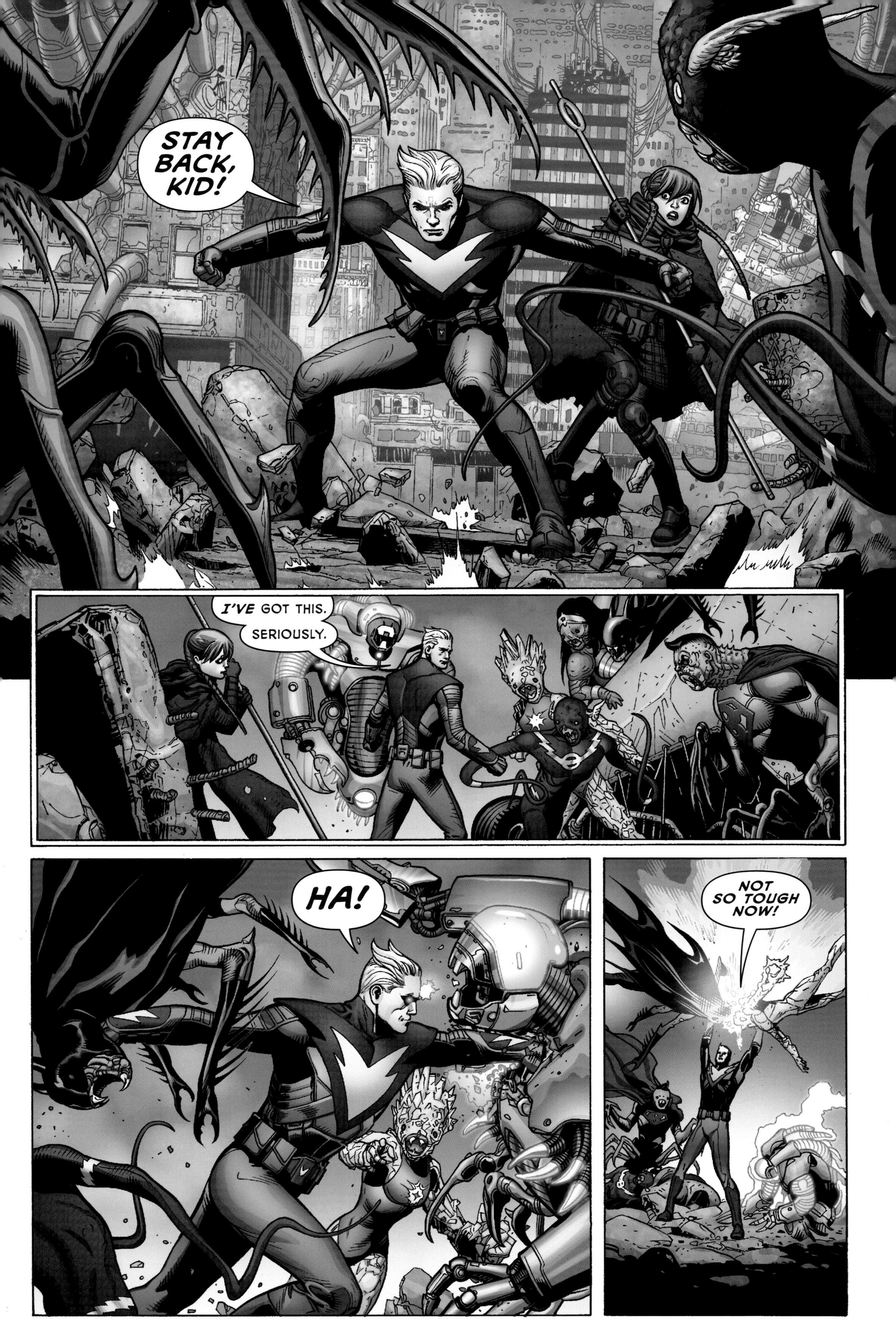
STAY BACK, KID!
I'VE GOT THIS.
SERIOUSLY.
HA!
NOT SO TOUGH NOW!

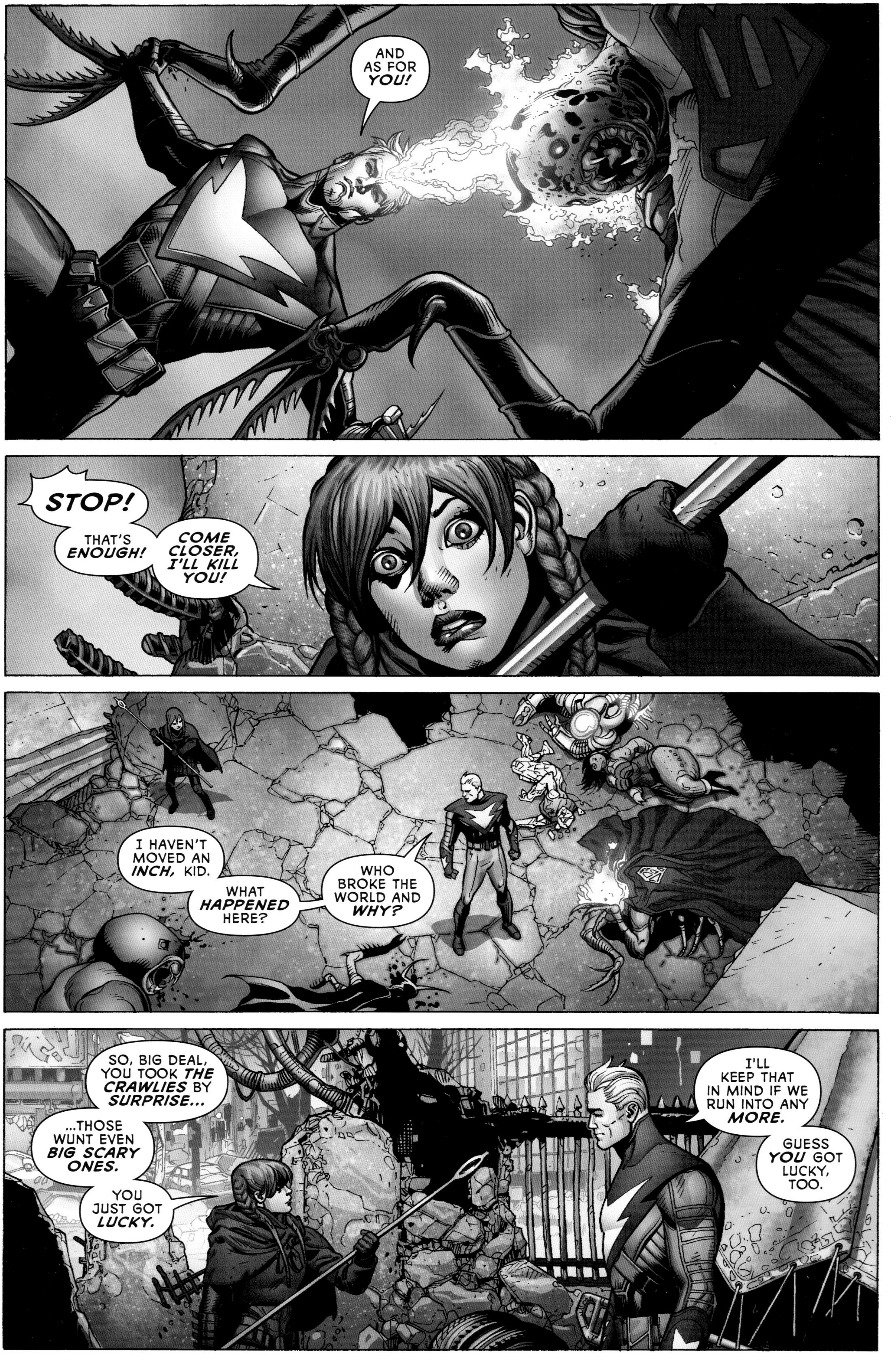
AND AS FOR YOU!
STOP!
THAT'S ENOUGH!
COME CLOSER, I'LL KILL YOU!
I HAVEN'T MOVED AN INCH, KID.
WHAT HAPPENED HERE?
WHO BROKE THE WORLD AND WHY?
SO, BIG DEAL, YOU TOOK THE CRAWLIES BY SURPRISE...
...THOSE WUNT EVEN BIG SCARY ONES.
YOU JUST GOT LUCKY.
I'LL KEEP THAT IN MIND IF WE RUN INTO ANY MORE.
GUESS YOU GOT LUCKY, TOO.

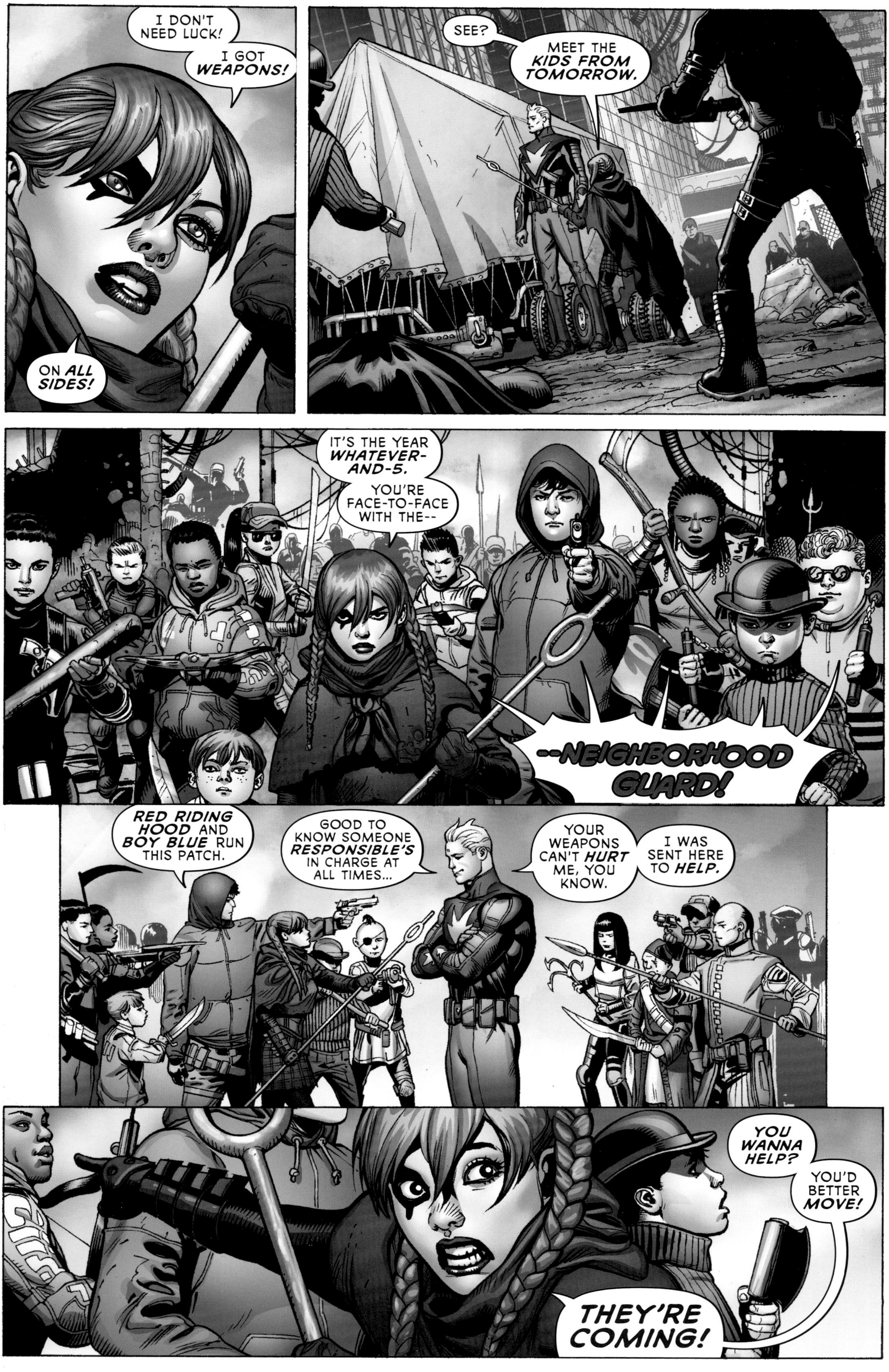

I DON'T NEED LUCK!
I GOT WEAPONS!
ON ALL SIDES!
SEE?
MEET THE KIDS FROM TOMORROW.
IT'S THE YEAR WHATEVER-AND-5.
YOU'RE FACE-TO-FACE WITH THE--
--NEIGHBORHOOD GUARD!
RED RIDING HOOD AND BOY BLUE RUN THIS PATCH.
GOOD TO KNOW SOMEONE RESPONSIBLE'S IN CHARGE AT ALL TIMES...
YOUR WEAPONS CAN'T HURT ME, YOU KNOW.
I WAS SENT HERE TO HELP.
YOU WANNA HELP?
YOU'D BETTER MOVE!
THEY'RE COMING!

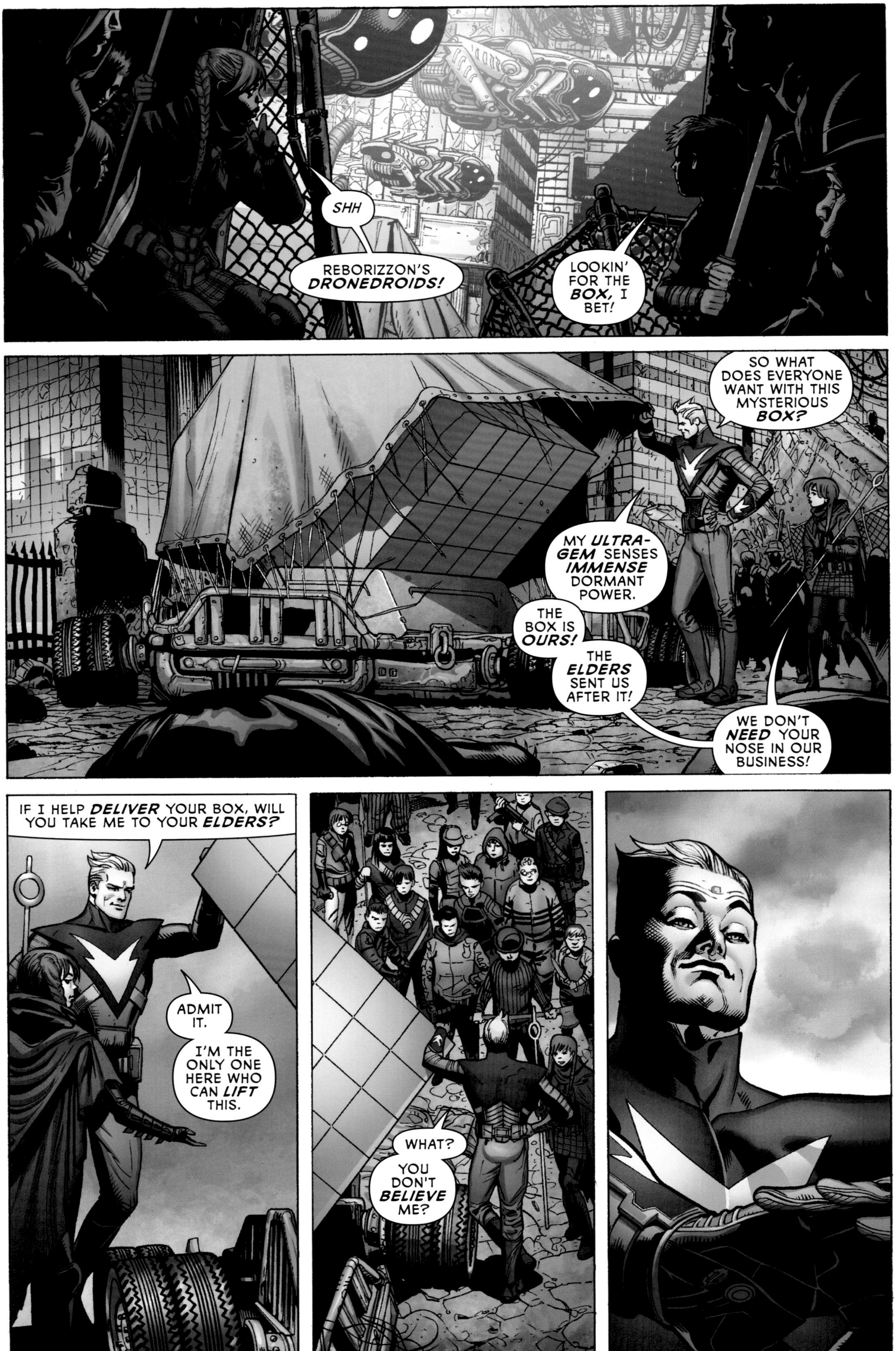
SHH
REBORIZZON'S DRONEDROIDS!
LOOKIN' FOR THE BOX, I BET!
SO WHAT DOES EVERYONE WANT WITH THIS MYSTERIOUS BOX?
MY ULTRA-GEM SENSES IMMENSE DORMANT POWER.
THE BOX IS OURS!
THE ELDERS SENT US AFTER IT!
WE DON'T NEED YOUR NOSE IN OUR BUSINESS!
IF I HELP DELIVER YOUR BOX, WILL YOU TAKE ME TO YOUR ELDERS?
ADMIT IT.
I'M THE ONLY ONE HERE WHO CAN LIFT THIS.
WHAT?
YOU DON'T BELIEVE ME?

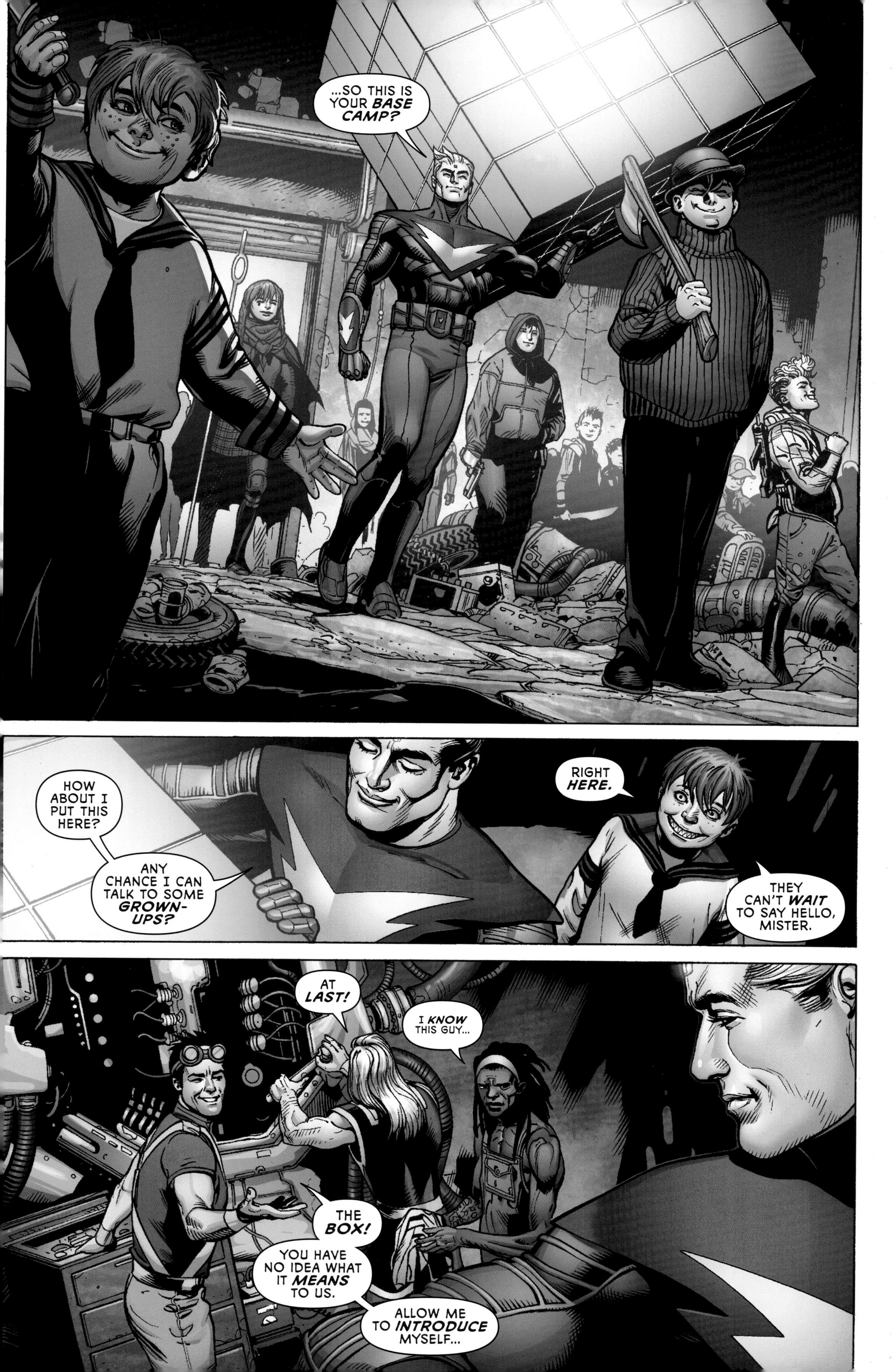
...SO THIS IS YOUR BASE CAMP?
HOW ABOUT I PUT THIS HERE?
ANY CHANCE I CAN TALK TO SOME GROWN-UPS?
RIGHT HERE.
THEY CAN'T WAIT TO SAY HELLO, MISTER.
AT LAST!
I KNOW THIS GUY...
THE BOX!
YOU HAVE NO IDEA WHAT IT MEANS TO US.
ALLOW ME TO INTRODUCE MYSELF...

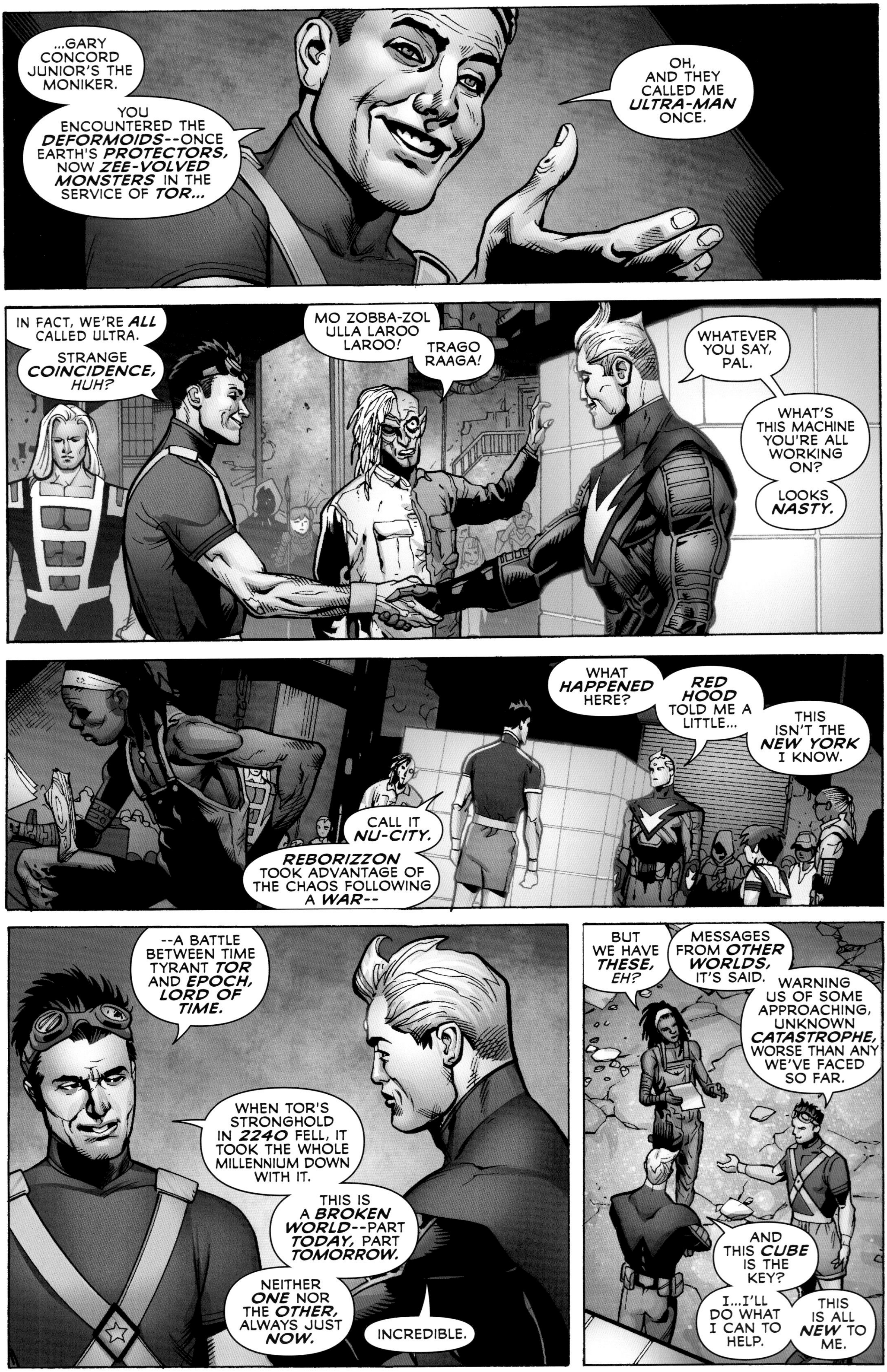

...GARY CONCORD JUNIOR'S THE MONIKER.
YOU ENCOUNTERED THE DEFORMOIDS--ONCE EARTH'S PROTECTORS, NOW ZEE-VOLVED MONSTERS IN THE SERVICE OF TOR...
OH, AND THEY CALLED ME ULTRA-MAN ONCE.
IN FACT, WE'RE ALL CALLED ULTRA.
STRANGE COINCIDENCE, HUH?
MO ZOBBA-ZOL ULLA LAROO LAROO!
TRAGO RAAGA!
WHATEVER YOU SAY, PAL.
WHAT'S THIS MACHINE YOU'RE ALL WORKING ON?
LOOKS NASTY.
WHAT HAPPENED HERE?
RED HOOD TOLD ME A LITTLE...
THIS ISN'T THE NEW YORK I KNOW.
CALL IT NU-CITY.
REBORIZZON TOOK ADVANTAGE OF THE CHAOS FOLLOWING A WAR--
--A BATTLE BETWEEN TIME TYRANT TOR AND EPOCH, LORD OF TIME.
WHEN TOR'S STRONGHOLD IN 2240 FELL, IT TOOK THE WHOLE MILLENNIUM DOWN WITH IT.
THIS IS A BROKEN WORLD--PART TODAY, PART TOMORROW.
NEITHER ONE NOR THE OTHER, ALWAYS JUST NOW.
INCREDIBLE.
BUT WE HAVE THESE, EH?
MESSAGES FROM OTHER WORLDS, IT'S SAID.
WARNING US OF SOME APPROACHING, UNKNOWN CATASTROPHE, WORSE THAN ANY WE'VE FACED SO FAR.
AND THIS CUBE IS THE KEY?
I...I'LL DO WHAT I CAN TO HELP.
THIS IS ALL NEW TO ME.

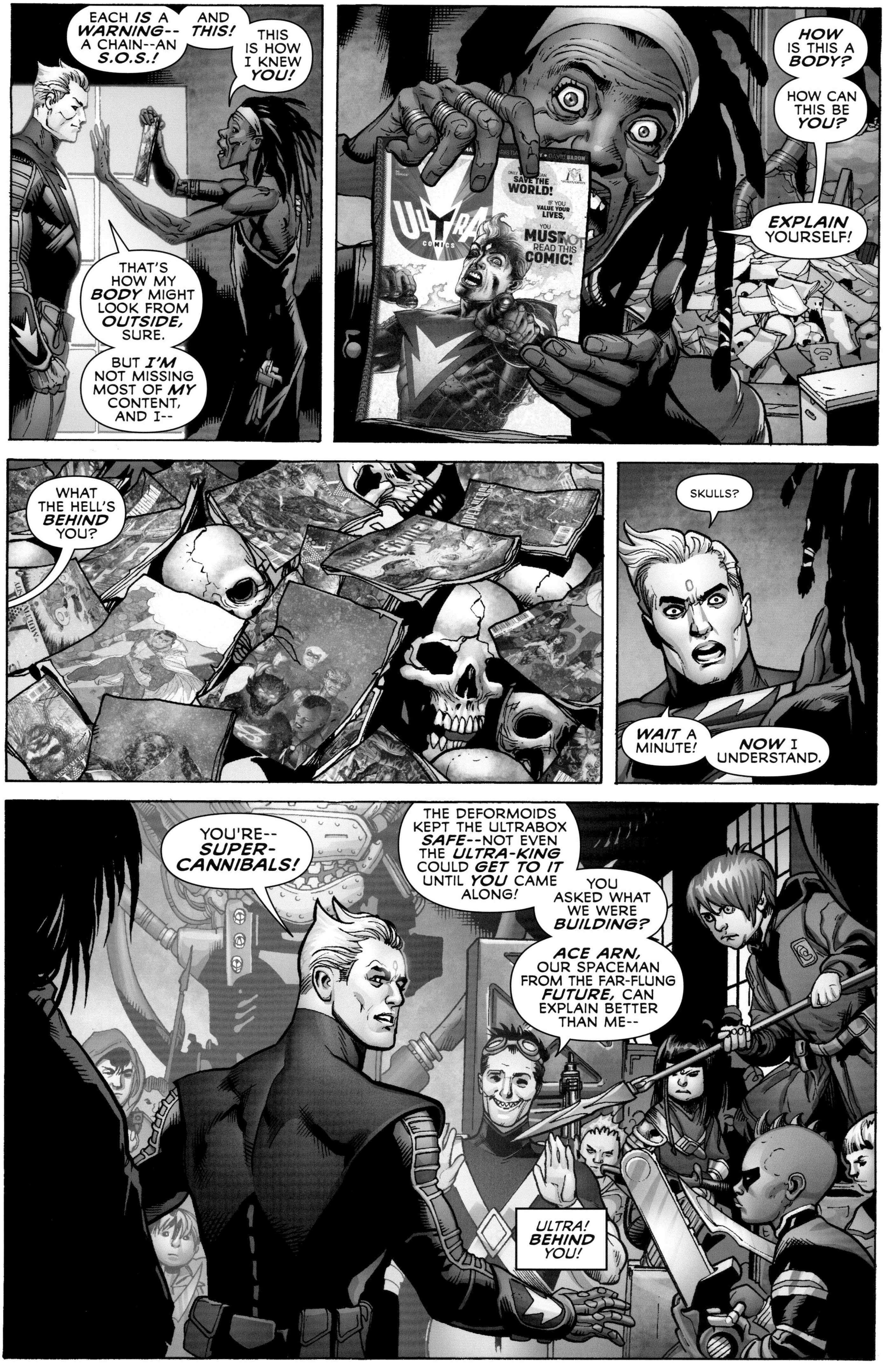

EACH *IS* A *WARNING*-- A CHAIN--AN *S.O.S.!*
AND *THIS!*
THIS IS HOW I KNEW *YOU!*
THAT'S HOW MY *BODY* MIGHT LOOK FROM *OUTSIDE,* SURE.
BUT *I'M* NOT MISSING MOST OF *MY* CONTENT, AND I--
HOW IS THIS A *BODY?*
HOW CAN THIS BE *YOU?*
EXPLAIN YOURSELF!
SAVE THE WORLD!
IF YOU VALUE YOUR LIVES,
YOU MUST
READ THIS COMIC!
ULTRA COMICS
WHAT THE HELL'S *BEHIND* YOU?
SKULLS?
WAIT A MINUTE!
NOW I UNDERSTAND.
YOU'RE-- *SUPER-CANNIBALS!*
THE DEFORMOIDS KEPT THE ULTRABOX *SAFE*--NOT EVEN THE *ULTRA-KING* COULD *GET TO IT* UNTIL *YOU* CAME ALONG!
YOU ASKED WHAT WE WERE *BUILDING?*
ACE ARN, OUR SPACEMAN FROM THE FAR-FLUNG *FUTURE,* CAN EXPLAIN BETTER THAN ME--
ULTRA! BEHIND YOU!

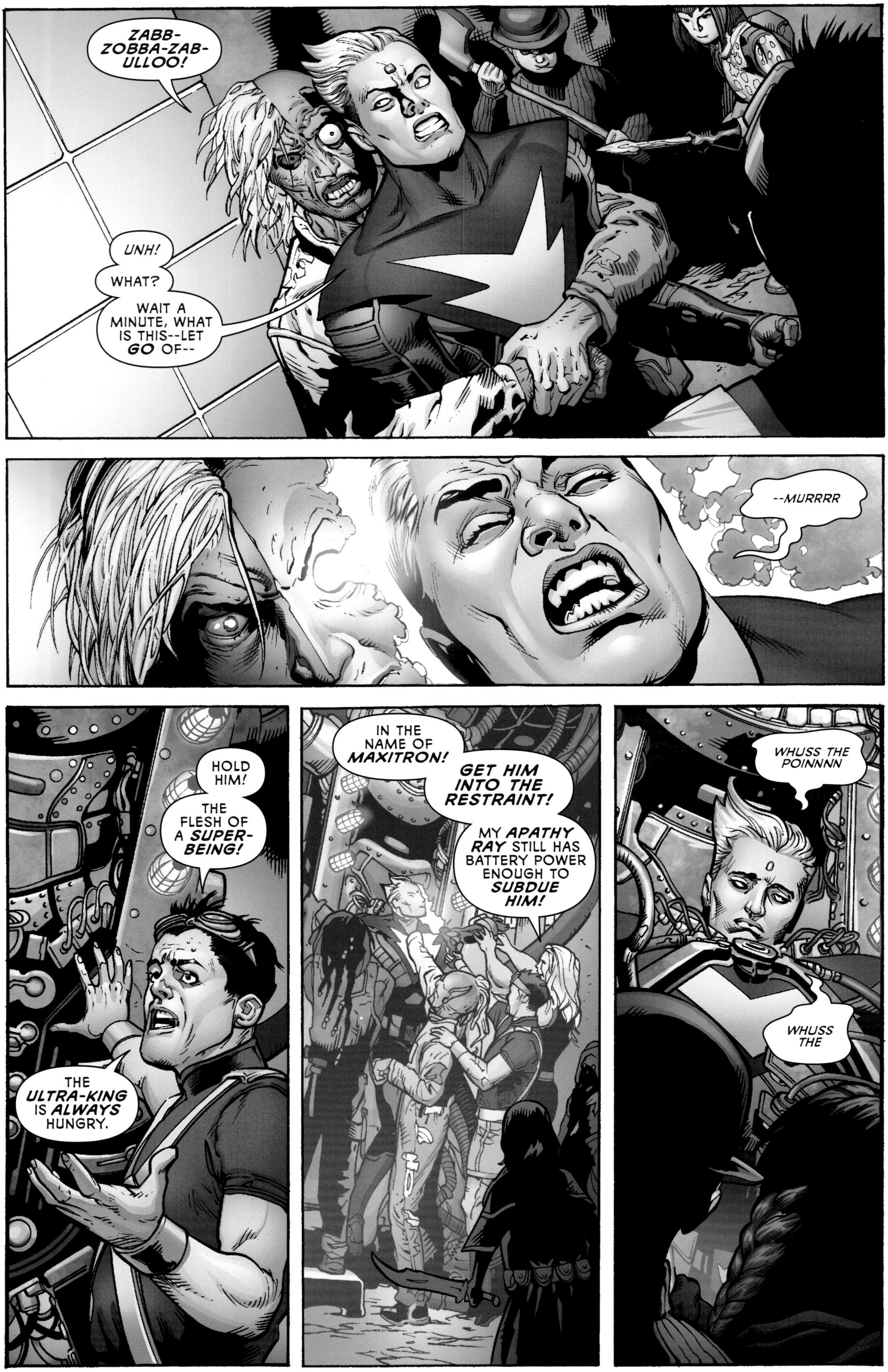
ZABB-ZOBBA-ZAB-ULLOO!
UNH!
WHAT?
WAIT A MINUTE, WHAT IS THIS--LET GO OF--
--MURRRR
HOLD HIM!
THE FLESH OF A SUPER-BEING!
THE ULTRA-KING IS ALWAYS HUNGRY.
IN THE NAME OF MAXITRON!
GET HIM INTO THE RESTRAINT!
MY APATHY RAY STILL HAS BATTERY POWER ENOUGH TO SUBDUE HIM!
WHUSS THE POINNNN
WHUSS THE

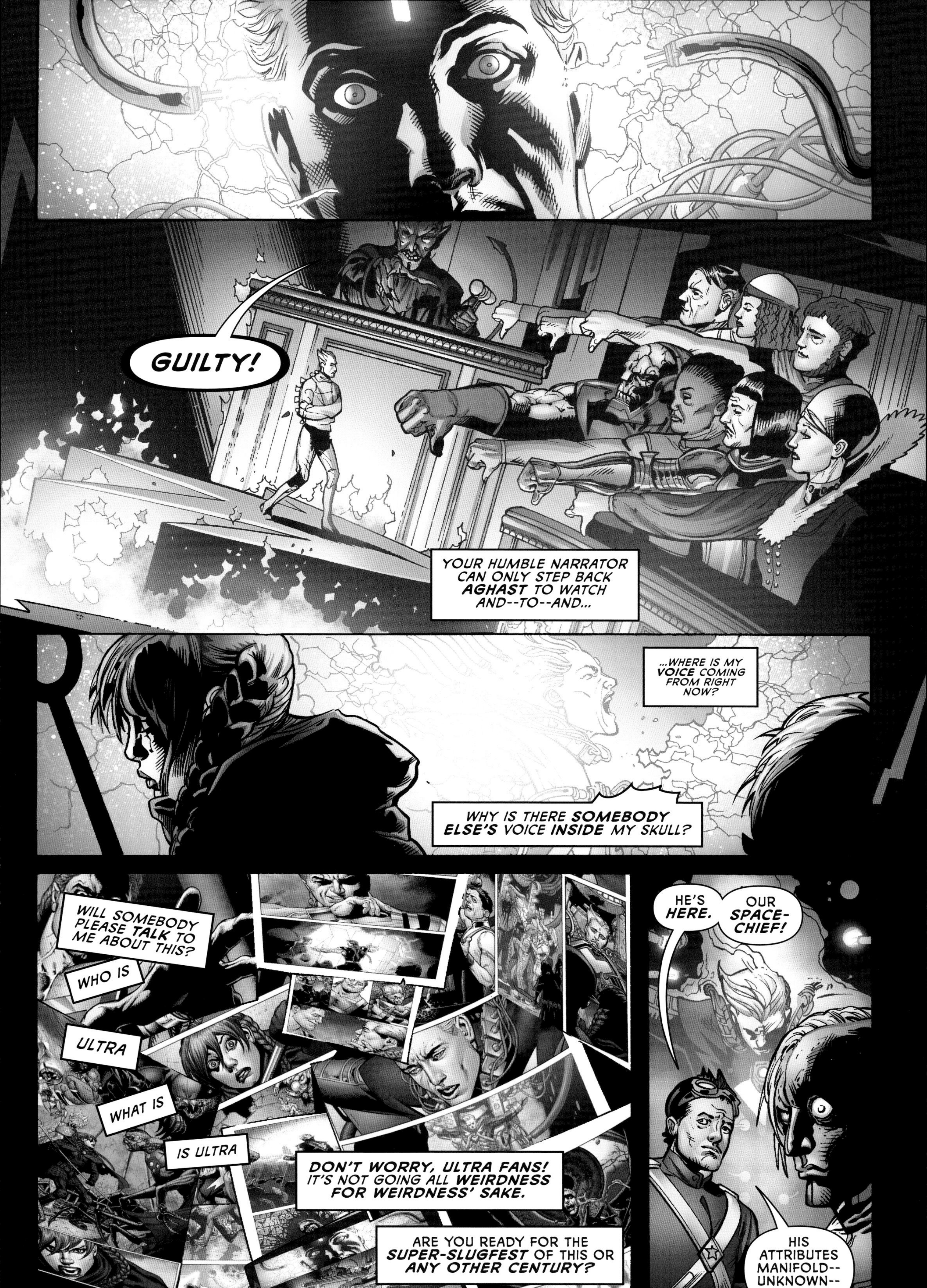
GUILTY!
YOUR HUMBLE NARRATOR CAN ONLY STEP BACK AGHAST TO WATCH AND--TO--AND...
...WHERE IS MY VOICE COMING FROM RIGHT NOW?
WHY IS THERE SOMEBODY ELSE'S VOICE INSIDE MY SKULL?
WILL SOMEBODY PLEASE TALK TO ME ABOUT THIS?
WHO IS
ULTRA
WHAT IS
IS ULTRA
DON'T WORRY, ULTRA FANS! IT'S NOT GOING ALL WEIRDNESS FOR WEIRDNESS' SAKE.
ARE YOU READY FOR THE SUPER-SLUGFEST OF THIS OR ANY OTHER CENTURY?
HE'S HERE.
OUR SPACE-CHIEF!
HIS ATTRIBUTES MANIFOLD-- UNKNOWN--

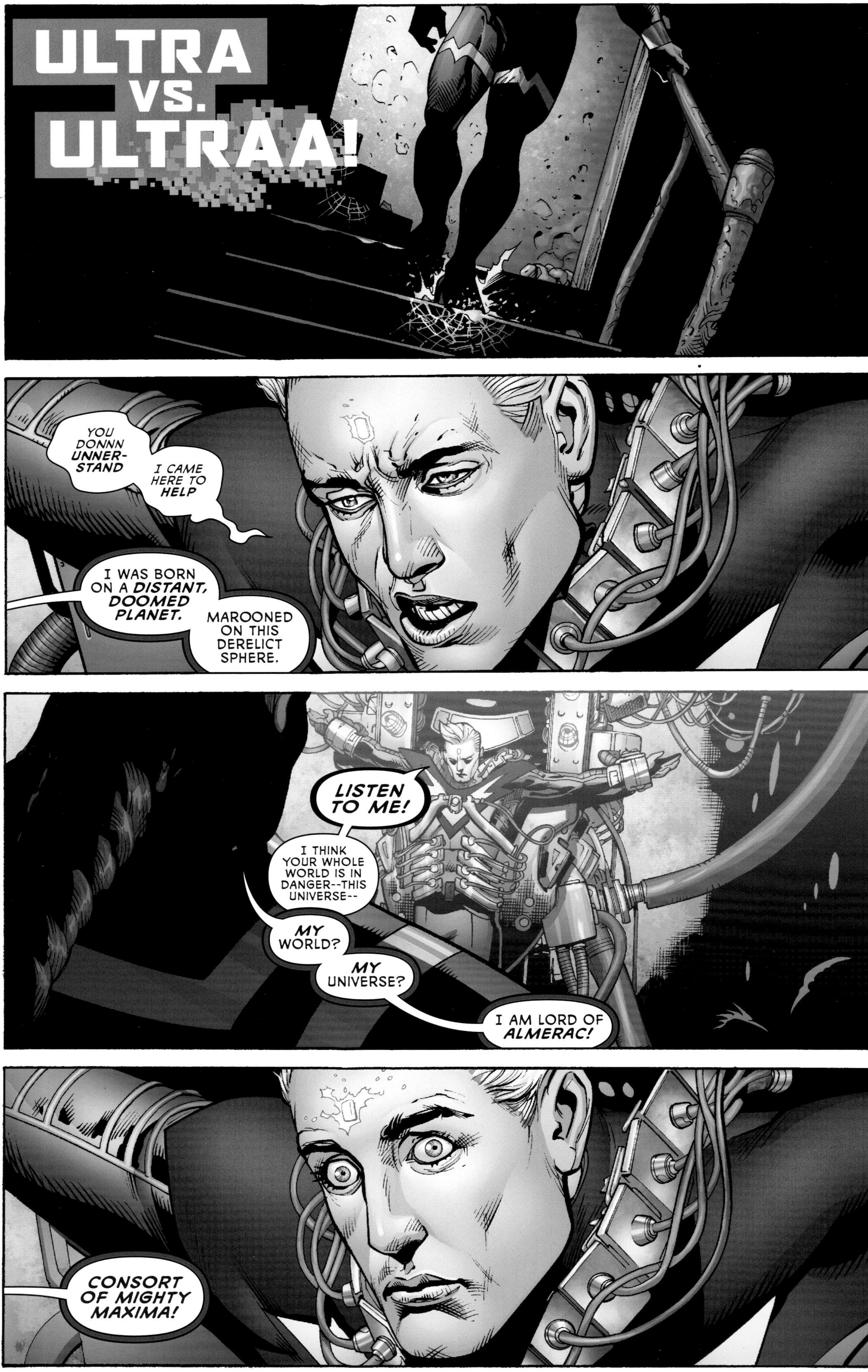
ULTRA VS. ULTRAA!
YOU DONNN UNNER-STAND
I CAME HERE TO HELP
I WAS BORN ON A DISTANT, DOOMED PLANET.
MAROONED ON THIS DERELICT SPHERE.
LISTEN TO ME!
I THINK YOUR WHOLE WORLD IS IN DANGER--THIS UNIVERSE--
MY WORLD?
MY UNIVERSE?
I AM LORD OF ALMERAC!
CONSORT OF MIGHTY MAXIMA!

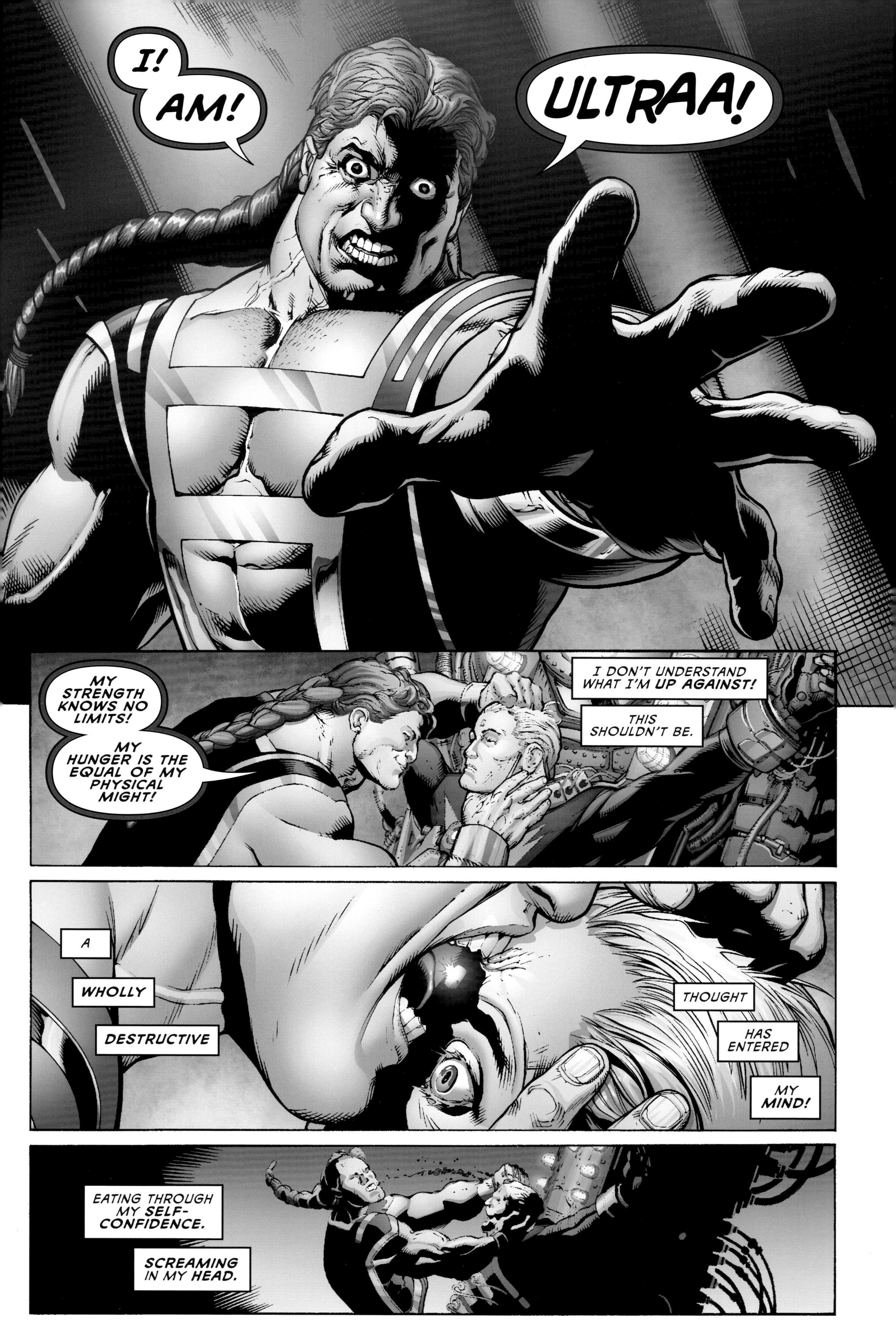
I! AM!
ULTRAA!
MY STRENGTH KNOWS NO LIMITS!
MY HUNGER IS THE EQUAL OF MY PHYSICAL MIGHT!
I DON'T UNDERSTAND WHAT I'M UP AGAINST!
THIS SHOULDN'T BE.
A
WHOLLY
DESTRUCTIVE
THOUGHT
HAS ENTERED
MY MIND!
EATING THROUGH MY SELF-CONFIDENCE.
SCREAMING IN MY HEAD.

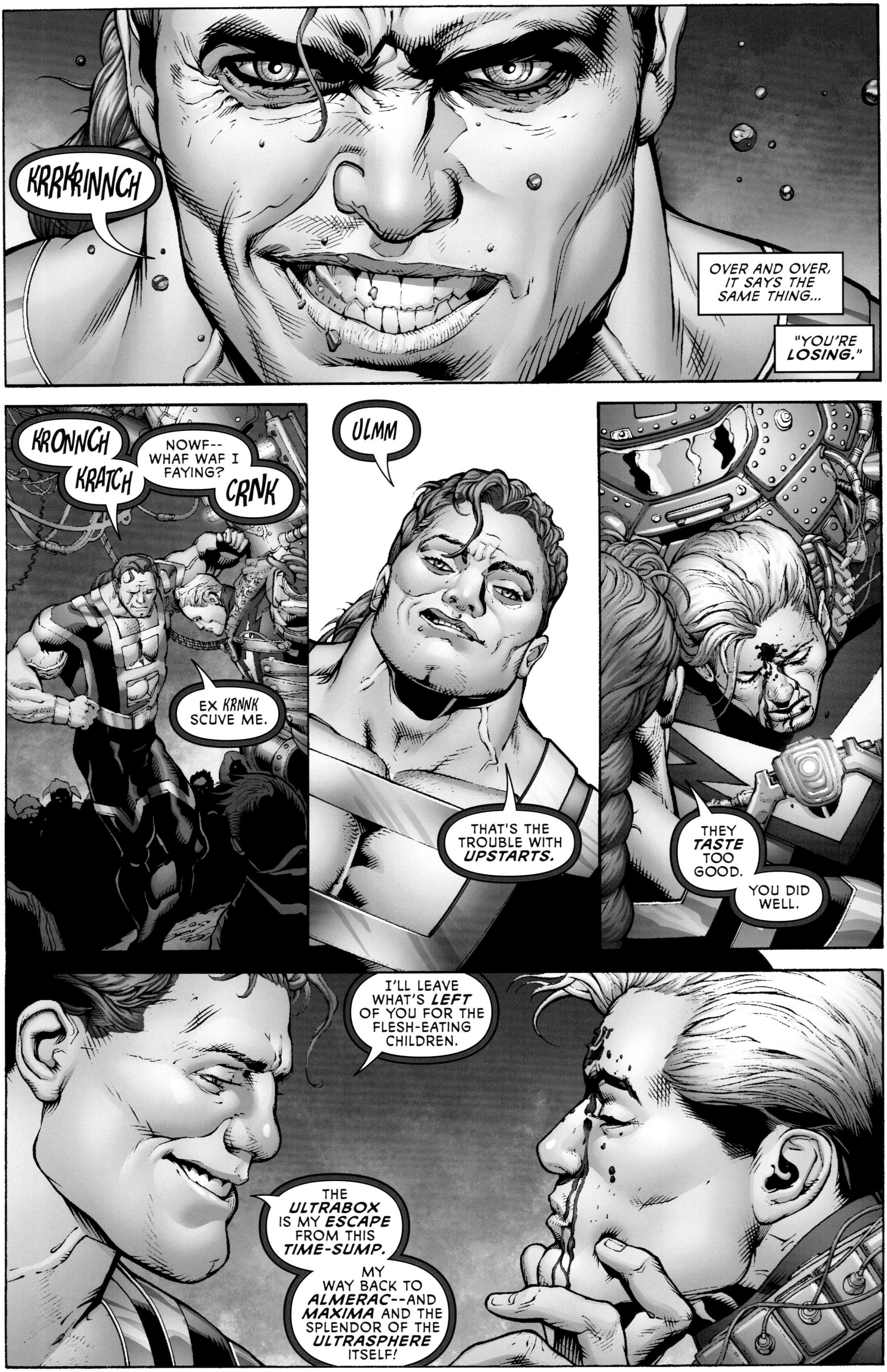
KRRKRINNCH
OVER AND OVER, IT SAYS THE SAME THING...
"YOU'RE LOSING."
KRONNCH
KRATCH
NOWF-- WHAF WAF I FAYING?
CRNK
EX KRNNK SCUVE ME.
ULMM
THAT'S THE TROUBLE WITH UPSTARTS.
THEY TASTE TOO GOOD.
YOU DID WELL.
I'LL LEAVE WHAT'S LEFT OF YOU FOR THE FLESH-EATING CHILDREN.
THE ULTRABOX IS MY ESCAPE FROM THIS TIME-SUMP.
MY WAY BACK TO ALMERAC--AND MAXIMA AND THE SPLENDOR OF THE ULTRASPHERE ITSELF!

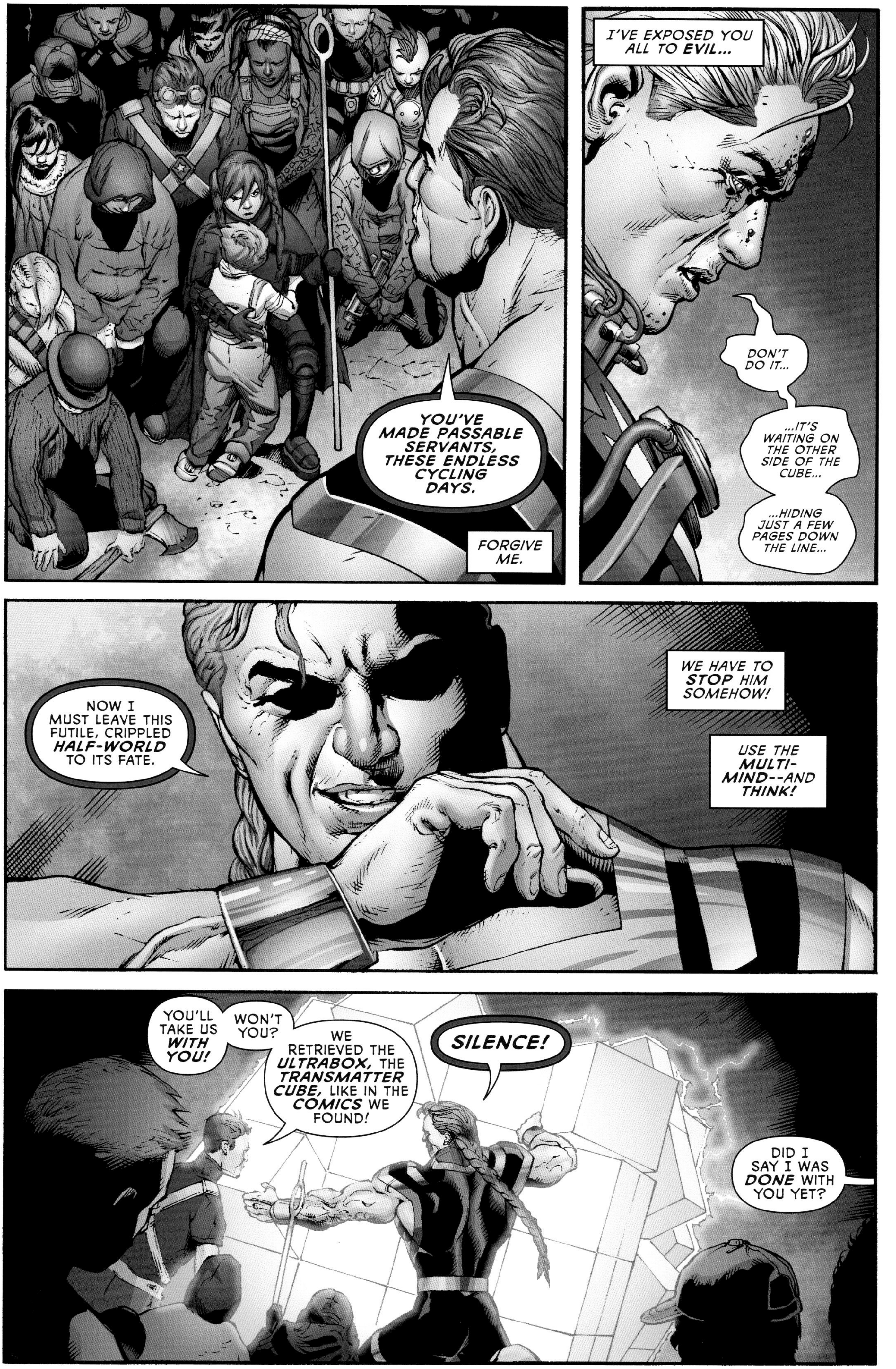
YOU'VE MADE PASSABLE SERVANTS, THESE ENDLESS CYCLING DAYS.
FORGIVE ME.
I'VE EXPOSED YOU ALL TO EVIL...
DON'T DO IT...
...IT'S WAITING ON THE OTHER SIDE OF THE CUBE...
...HIDING JUST A FEW PAGES DOWN THE LINE...
NOW I MUST LEAVE THIS FUTILE, CRIPPLED HALF-WORLD TO ITS FATE.
WE HAVE TO STOP HIM SOMEHOW!
USE THE MULTI-MIND--AND THINK!
YOU'LL TAKE US WITH YOU!
WON'T YOU?
WE RETRIEVED THE ULTRABOX, THE TRANSMATTER CUBE, LIKE IN THE COMICS WE FOUND!
SILENCE!
DID I SAY I WAS DONE WITH YOU YET?

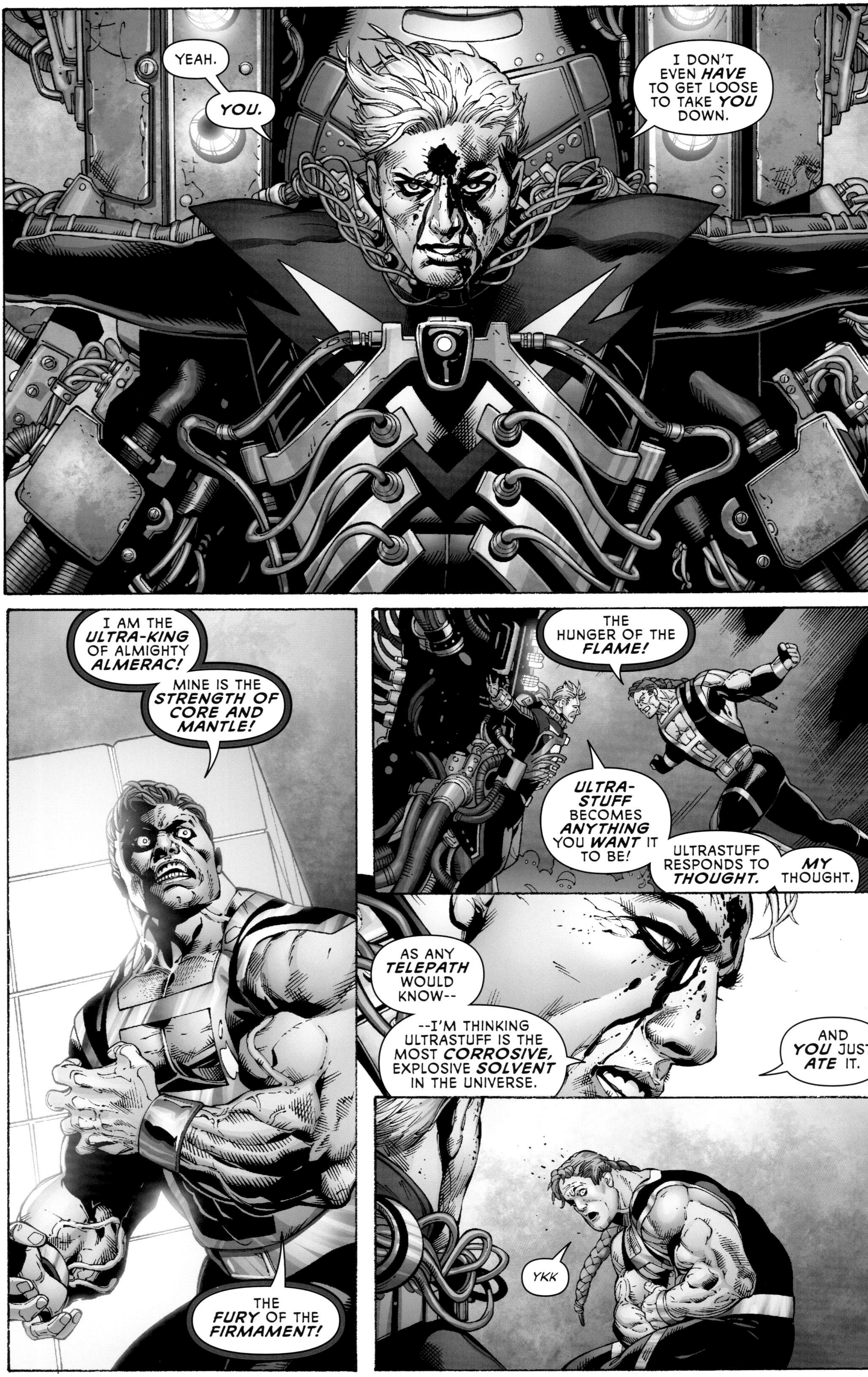
YEAH.
YOU.
I DON'T EVEN HAVE TO GET LOOSE TO TAKE YOU DOWN.
I AM THE ULTRA-KING OF ALMIGHTY ALMERAC!
MINE IS THE STRENGTH OF CORE AND MANTLE!
THE FURY OF THE FIRMAMENT!
THE HUNGER OF THE FLAME!
ULTRA-STUFF BECOMES ANYTHING YOU WANT IT TO BE!
ULTRASTUFF RESPONDS TO THOUGHT.
MY THOUGHT.
AS ANY TELEPATH WOULD KNOW--
--I'M THINKING ULTRASTUFF IS THE MOST CORROSIVE, EXPLOSIVE SOLVENT IN THE UNIVERSE.
AND YOU JUST ATE IT.
YKK

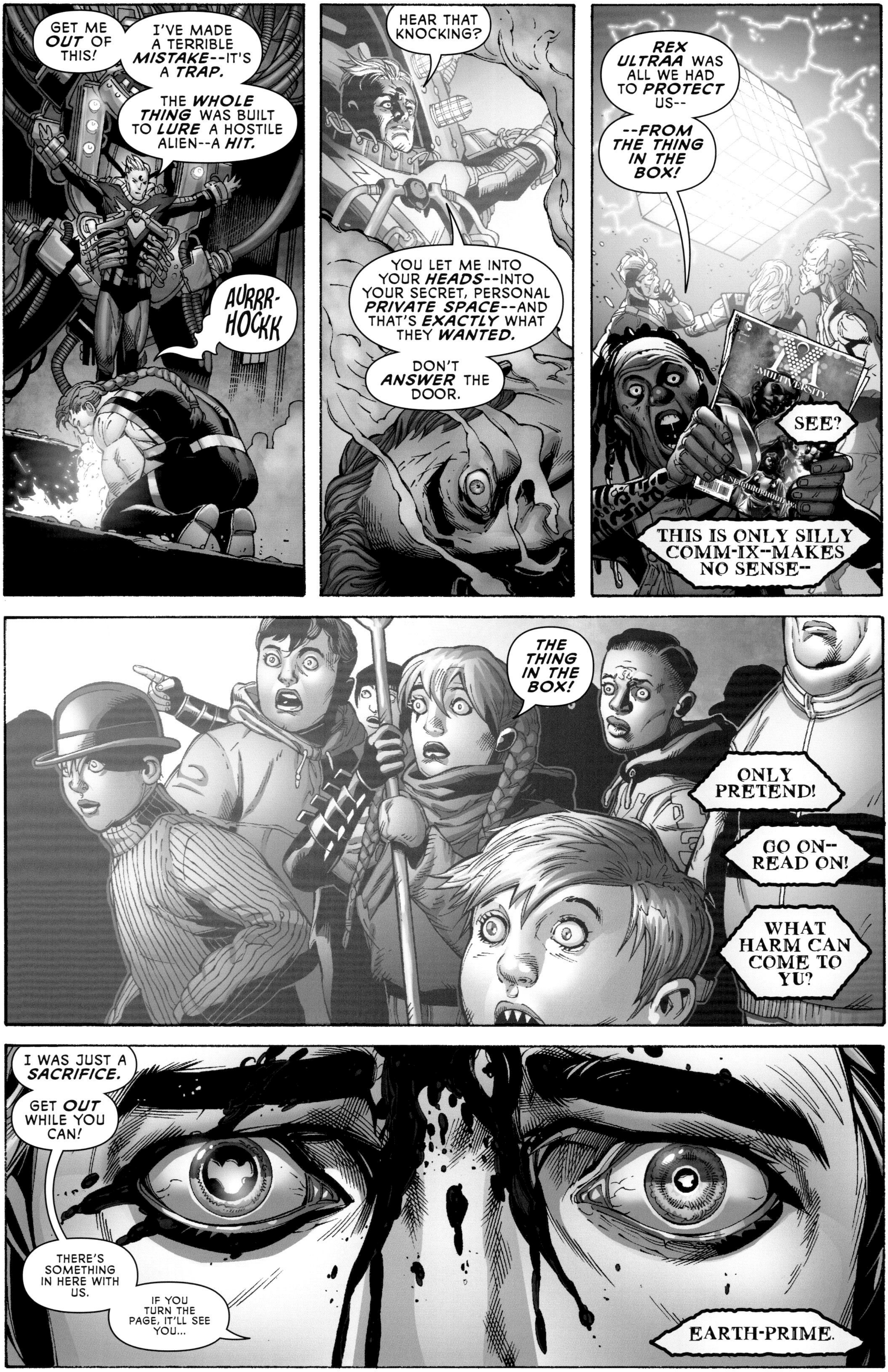
GET ME OUT OF THIS!
I'VE MADE A TERRIBLE MISTAKE--IT'S A TRAP.
THE WHOLE THING WAS BUILT TO LURE A HOSTILE ALIEN--A HIT.
AURRR-HOCKK
HEAR THAT KNOCKING?
YOU LET ME INTO YOUR HEADS--INTO YOUR SECRET, PERSONAL PRIVATE SPACE--AND THAT'S EXACTLY WHAT THEY WANTED.
DON'T ANSWER THE DOOR.
REX ULTRAA WAS ALL WE HAD TO PROTECT US--
--FROM THE THING IN THE BOX!
MULTIVERSITY
SEE?
THIS IS ONLY SILLY COMM-IX--MAKES NO SENSE--
THE THING IN THE BOX!
ONLY PRETEND!
GO ON--READ ON!
WHAT HARM CAN COME TO YU?
I WAS JUST A SACRIFICE.
GET OUT WHILE YOU CAN!
THERE'S SOMETHING IN HERE WITH US.
IF YOU TURN THE PAGE, IT'LL SEE YOU...
EARTH-PRIME.

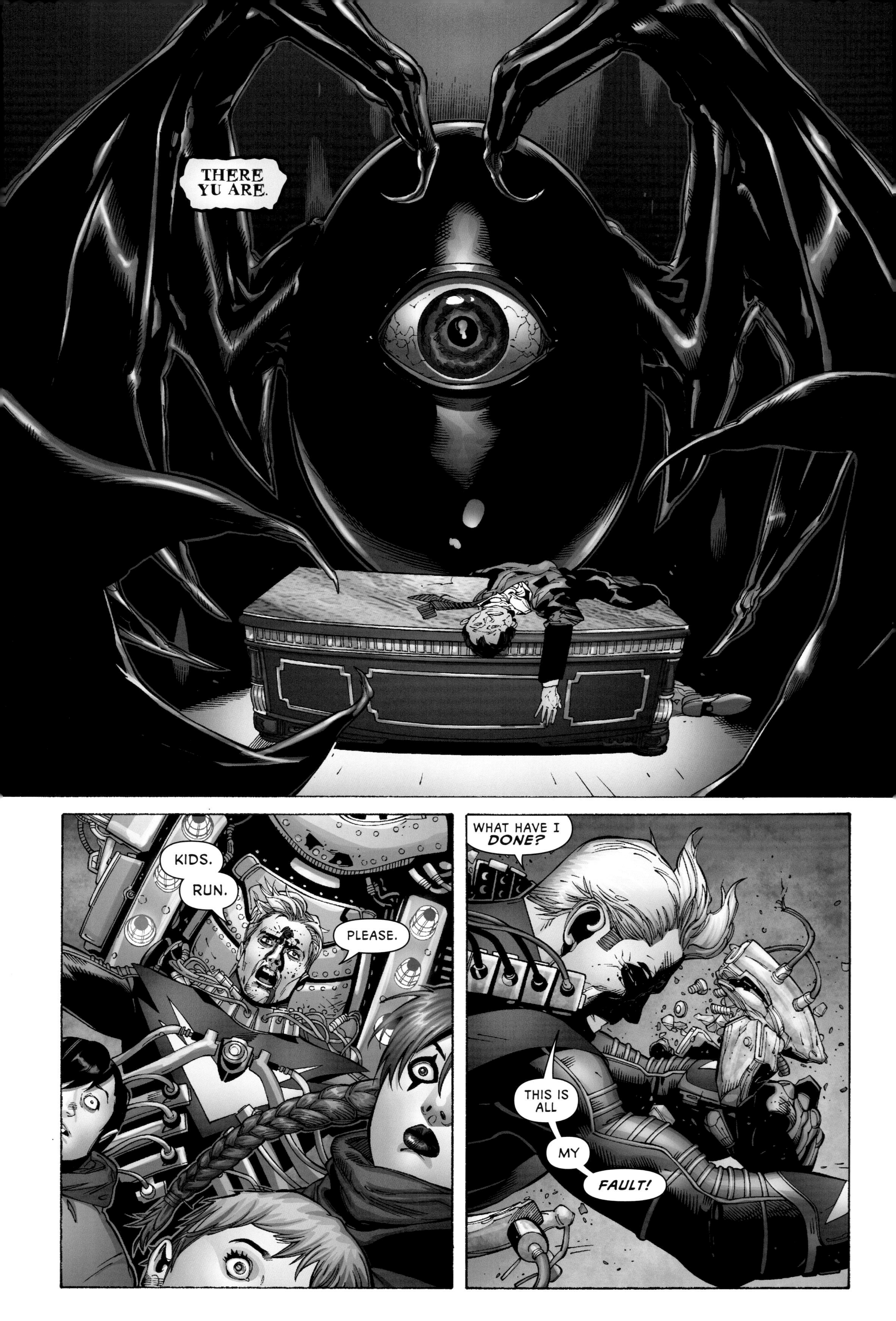
THERE YU ARE.
KIDS.
RUN.
PLEASE.
WHAT HAVE I DONE?
THIS IS ALL
MY
FAULT!

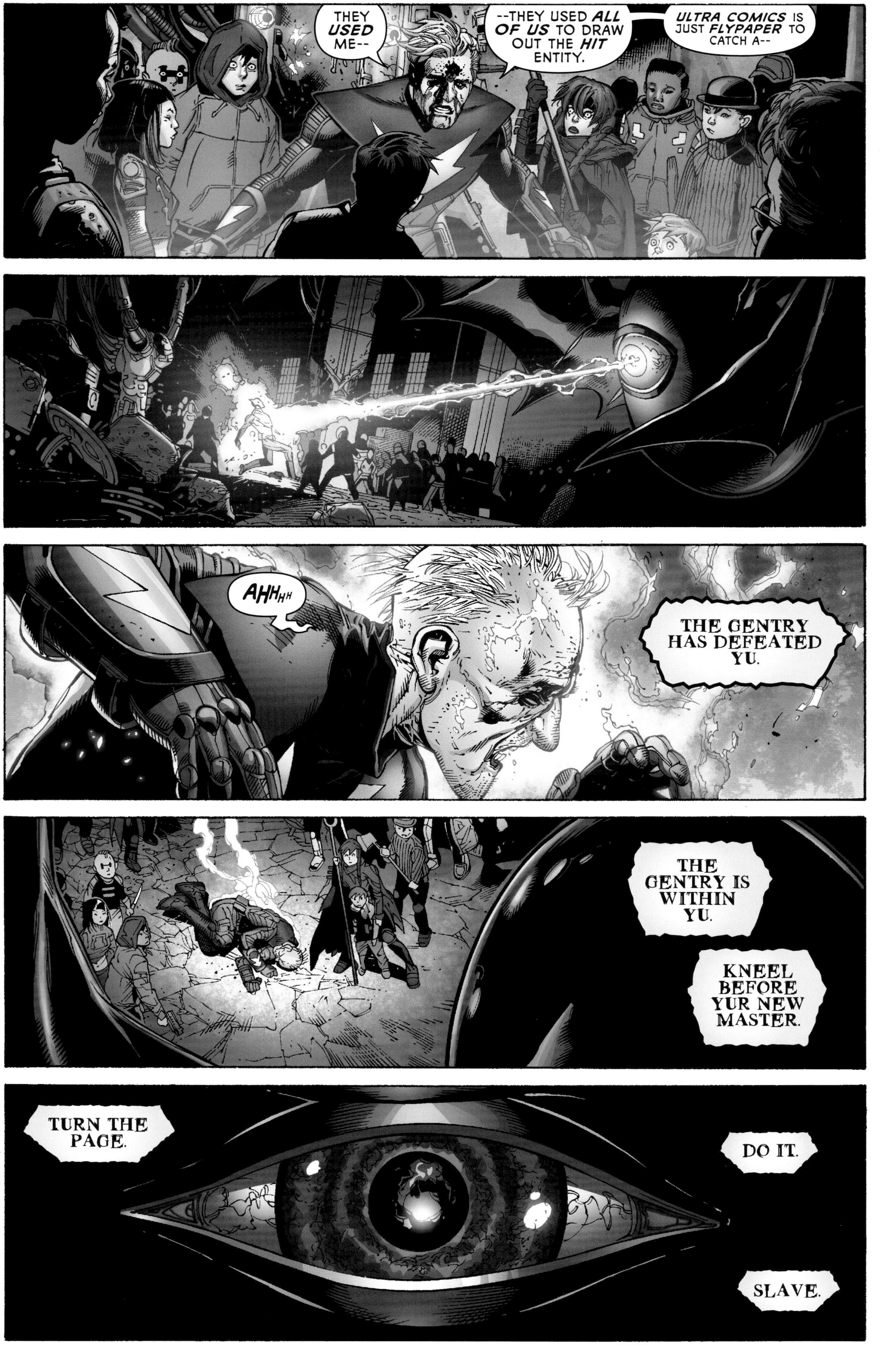

THEY USED ME--
--THEY USED ALL OF US TO DRAW OUT THE HIT ENTITY.
ULTRA COMICS IS JUST FLYPAPER TO CATCH A--
AHHHH
THE GENTRY HAS DEFEATED YU.
THE GENTRY IS WITHIN YU.
KNEEL BEFORE YUR NEW MASTER.
TURN THE PAGE.
DO IT.
SLAVE.

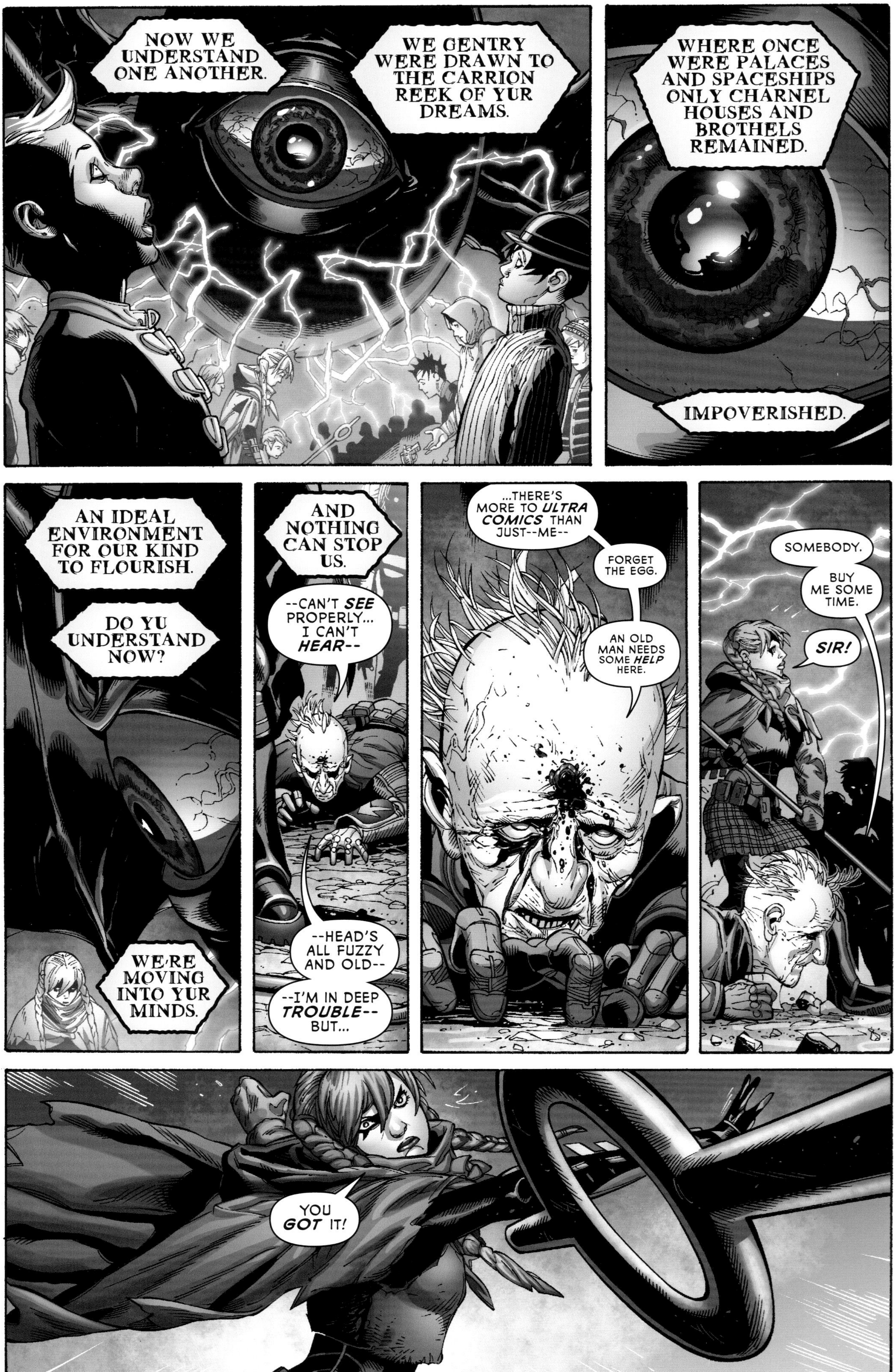
NOW WE UNDERSTAND ONE ANOTHER.
WE GENTRY WERE DRAWN TO THE CARRION REEK OF YUR DREAMS.
WHERE ONCE WERE PALACES AND SPACESHIPS ONLY CHARNEL HOUSES AND BROTHELS REMAINED.
IMPOVERISHED.
AN IDEAL ENVIRONMENT FOR OUR KIND TO FLOURISH.
DO YU UNDERSTAND NOW?
WE'RE MOVING INTO YUR MINDS.
AND NOTHING CAN STOP US.
--CAN'T SEE PROPERLY... I CAN'T HEAR--
--HEAD'S ALL FUZZY AND OLD--
--I'M IN DEEP TROUBLE-- BUT...
...THERE'S MORE TO ULTRA COMICS THAN JUST--ME--
FORGET THE EGG.
AN OLD MAN NEEDS SOME HELP HERE.
SOMEBODY.
BUY ME SOME TIME.
SIR!
YOU GOT IT!

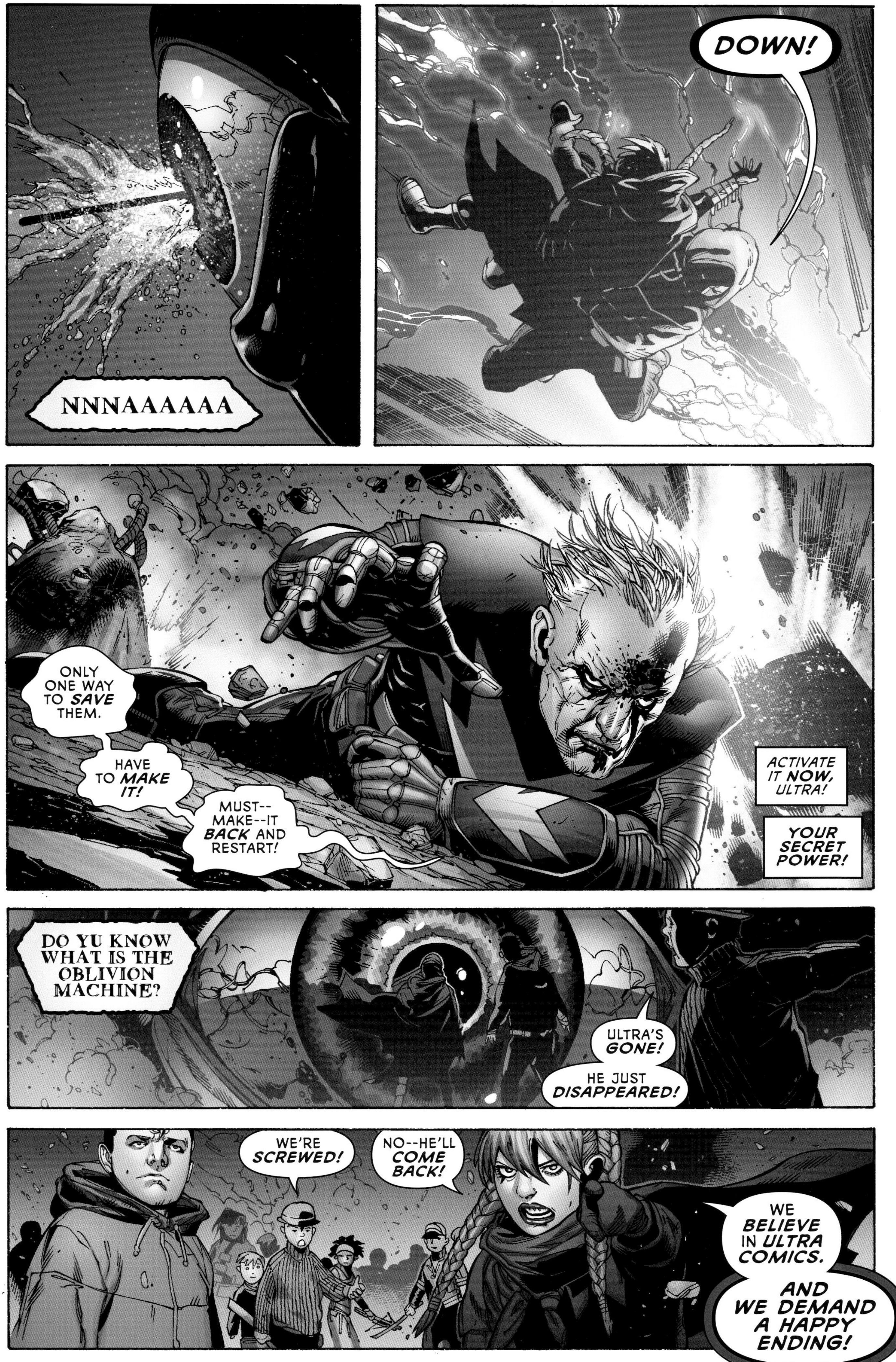
NNNAAAAAA
DOWN!
ONLY ONE WAY TO *SAVE* THEM.
HAVE TO *MAKE IT!*
MUST--MAKE--IT *BACK* AND RESTART!
ACTIVATE IT **NOW**, *ULTRA!*
YOUR SECRET POWER!
DO YU KNOW WHAT IS THE OBLIVION MACHINE?
ULTRA'S *GONE!*
HE JUST *DISAPPEARED!*
WE'RE *SCREWED!*
NO--HE'LL *COME BACK!*
WE *BELIEVE* IN *ULTRA COMICS.*
AND WE DEMAND A HAPPY ENDING!

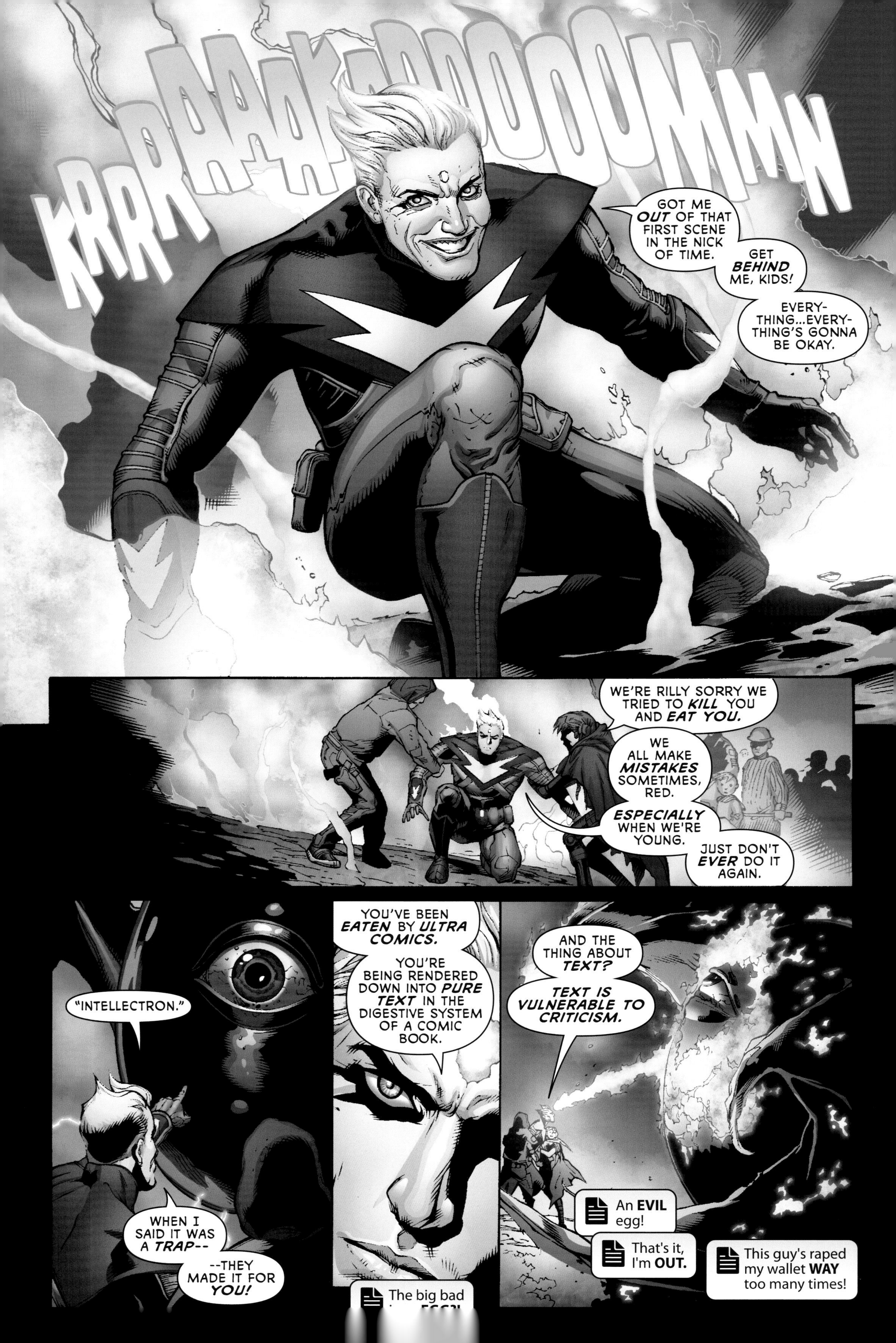
KRRRAAKADOOOOMMMN
GOT ME OUT OF THAT FIRST SCENE IN THE NICK OF TIME.
GET BEHIND ME, KIDS!
EVERY-THING...EVERY-THING'S GONNA BE OKAY.
WE'RE RILLY SORRY WE TRIED TO KILL YOU AND EAT YOU.
WE ALL MAKE MISTAKES SOMETIMES, RED.
ESPECIALLY WHEN WE'RE YOUNG.
JUST DON'T EVER DO IT AGAIN.
"INTELLECTRON."
WHEN I SAID IT WAS A TRAP--
--THEY MADE IT FOR YOU!
YOU'VE BEEN EATEN BY ULTRA COMICS.
YOU'RE BEING RENDERED DOWN INTO PURE TEXT IN THE DIGESTIVE SYSTEM OF A COMIC BOOK.
The big bad
AND THE THING ABOUT TEXT?
TEXT IS VULNERABLE TO CRITICISM.
An EVIL egg!
That's it, I'm OUT.
This guy's raped my wallet WAY too many times!

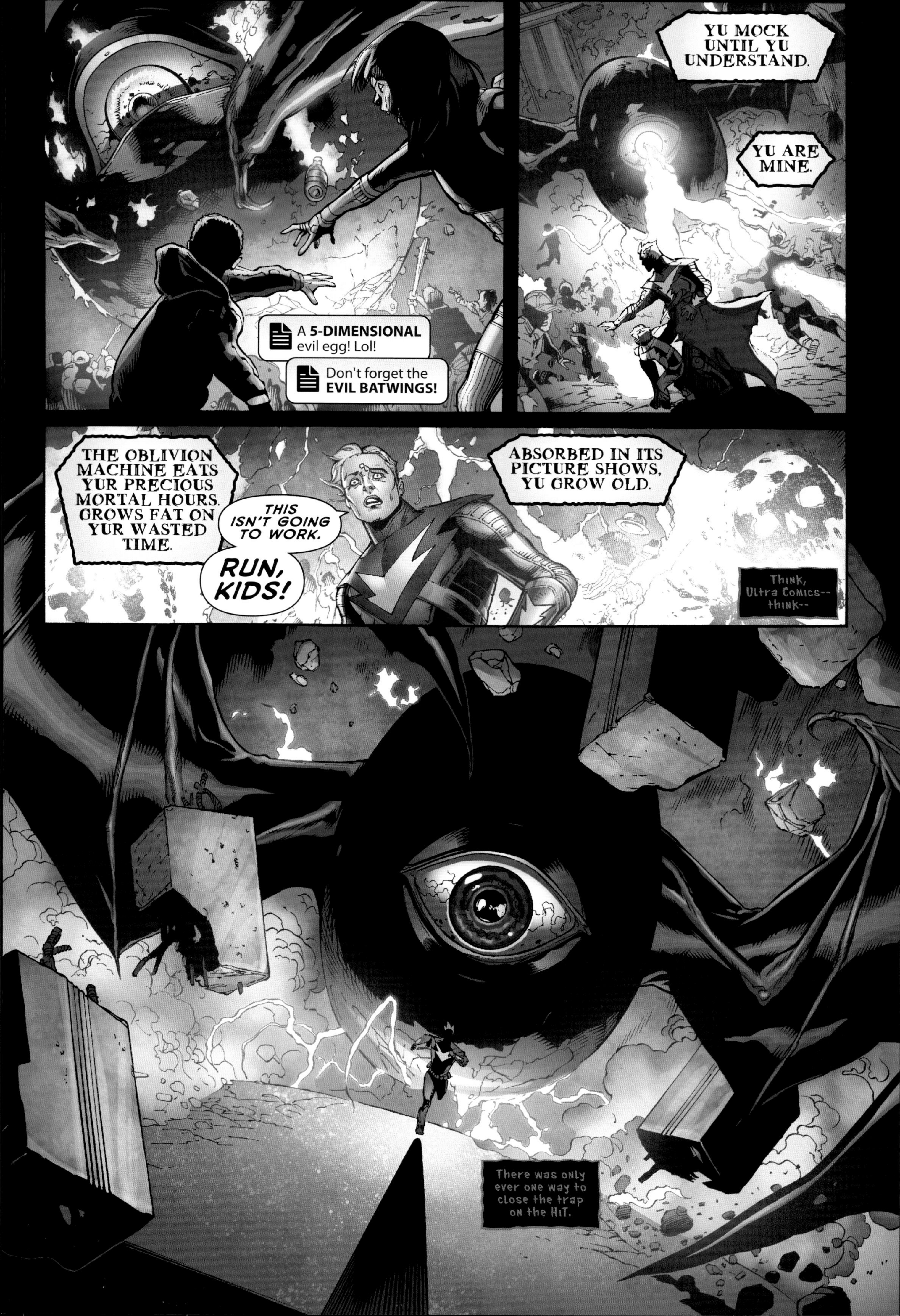
A 5-DIMENSIONAL evil egg! Lol!
Don't forget the EVIL BATWINGS!
YU MOCK UNTIL YU UNDERSTAND.
YU ARE MINE.
THE OBLIVION MACHINE EATS YUR PRECIOUS MORTAL HOURS. GROWS FAT ON YUR WASTED TIME.
THIS ISN'T GOING TO WORK.
RUN, KIDS!
ABSORBED IN ITS PICTURE SHOWS, YU GROW OLD.
Think, Ultra Comics-- think--
There was only ever one way to close the trap on the HiT.

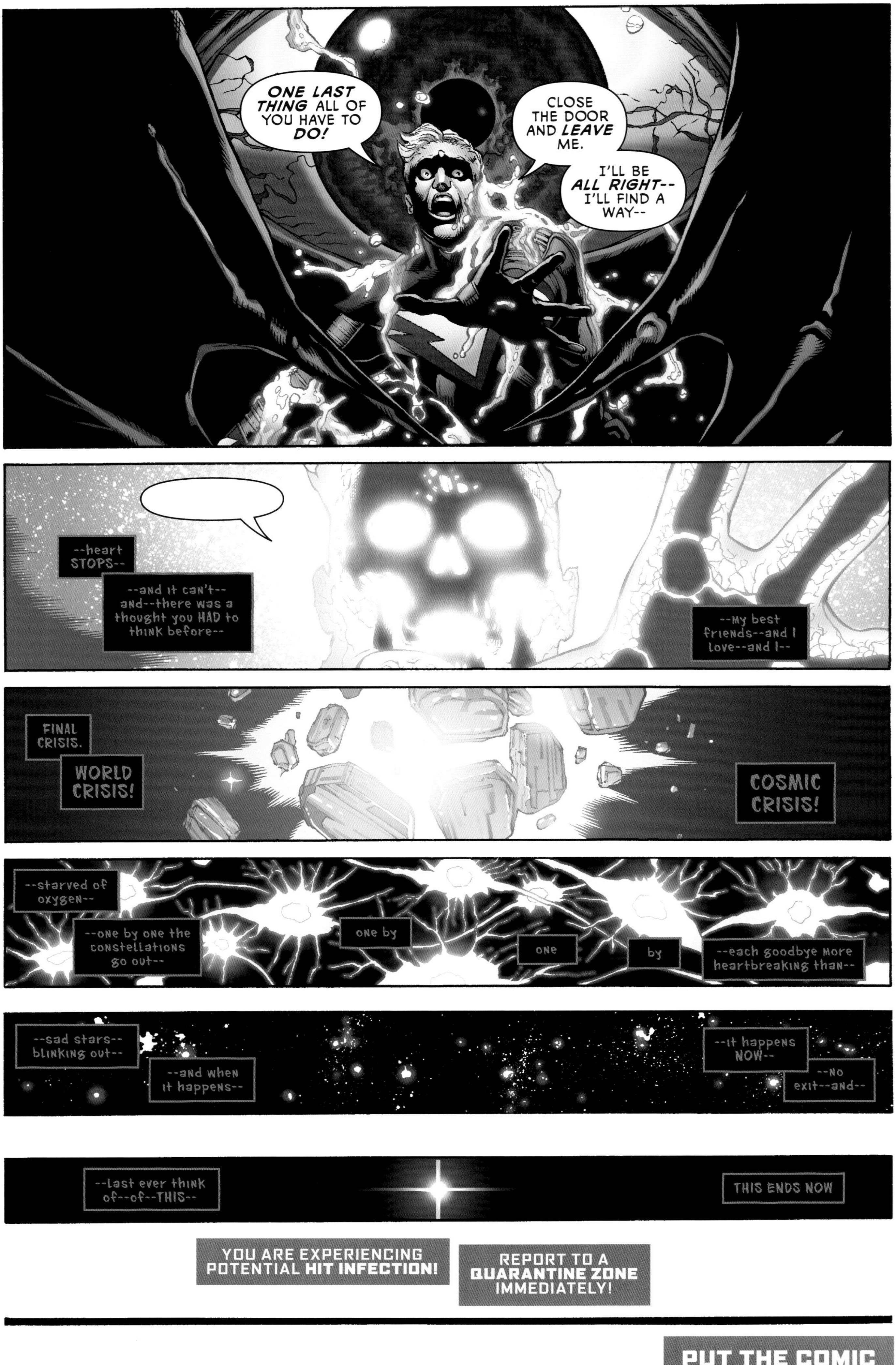
ONE LAST THING ALL OF YOU HAVE TO DO!
CLOSE THE DOOR AND LEAVE ME.
I'LL BE ALL RIGHT-- I'LL FIND A WAY--
--heart STOPS--
--and it can't-- and--there was a thought you HAD to think before--
--my best friends--and I love--and I--
FINAL CRISIS.
WORLD CRISIS!
COSMIC CRISIS!
--starved of oxygen--
--one by one the constellations go out--
one by
one
by
--each goodbye more heartbreaking than--
--sad stars-- blinking out--
--and when it happens--
--it happens NOW--
--no exit--and--
--last ever think of--of--THIS--
THIS ENDS NOW
YOU ARE EXPERIENCING POTENTIAL HIT INFECTION!
REPORT TO A QUARANTINE ZONE IMMEDIATELY!
PUT THE COMIC DOWN NOW!

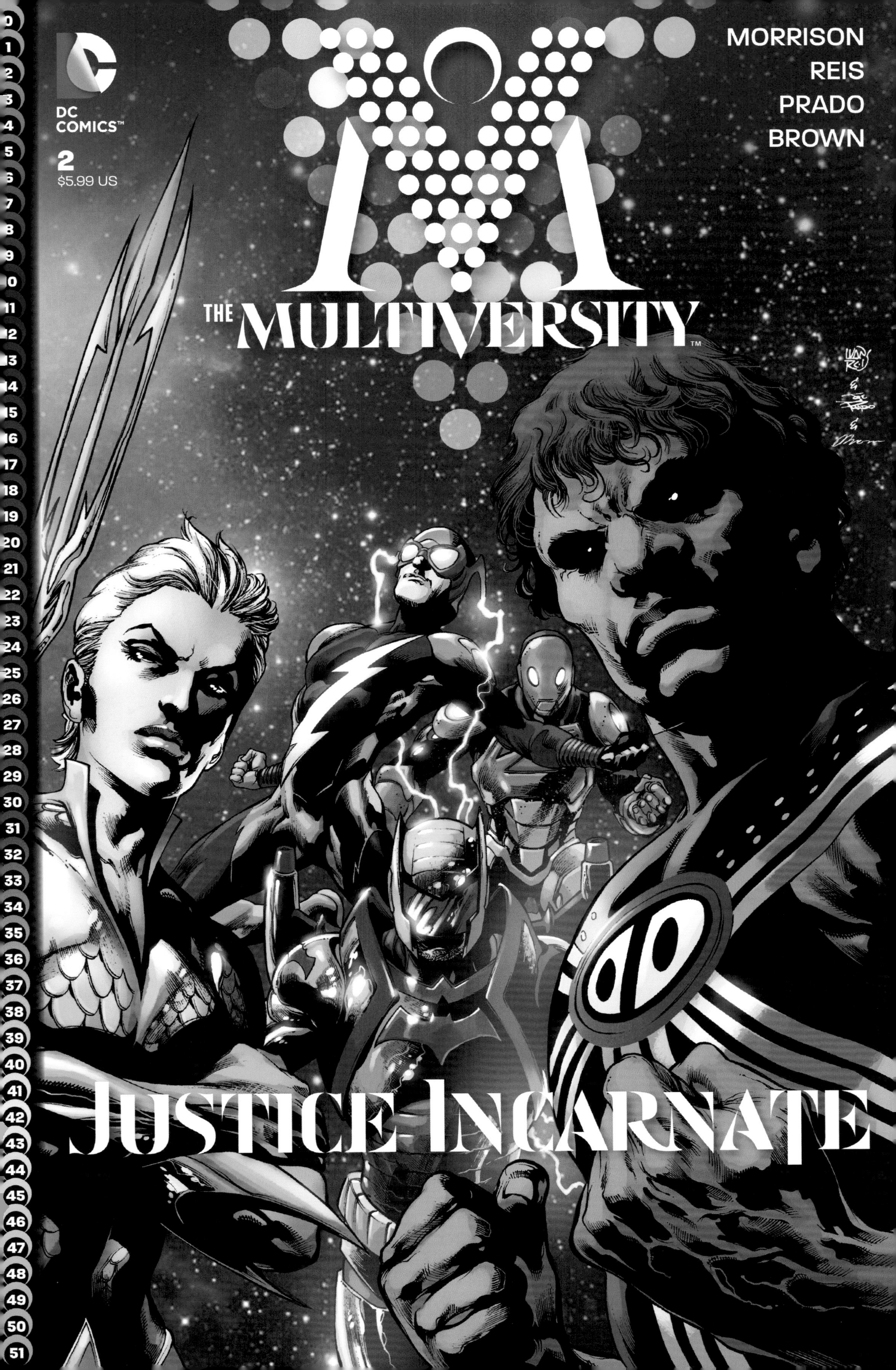
DC COMICS™
2
$5.99 US
MORRISON
REIS
PRADO
BROWN
THE MULTIVERSITY™
JUSTICE INCARNATE

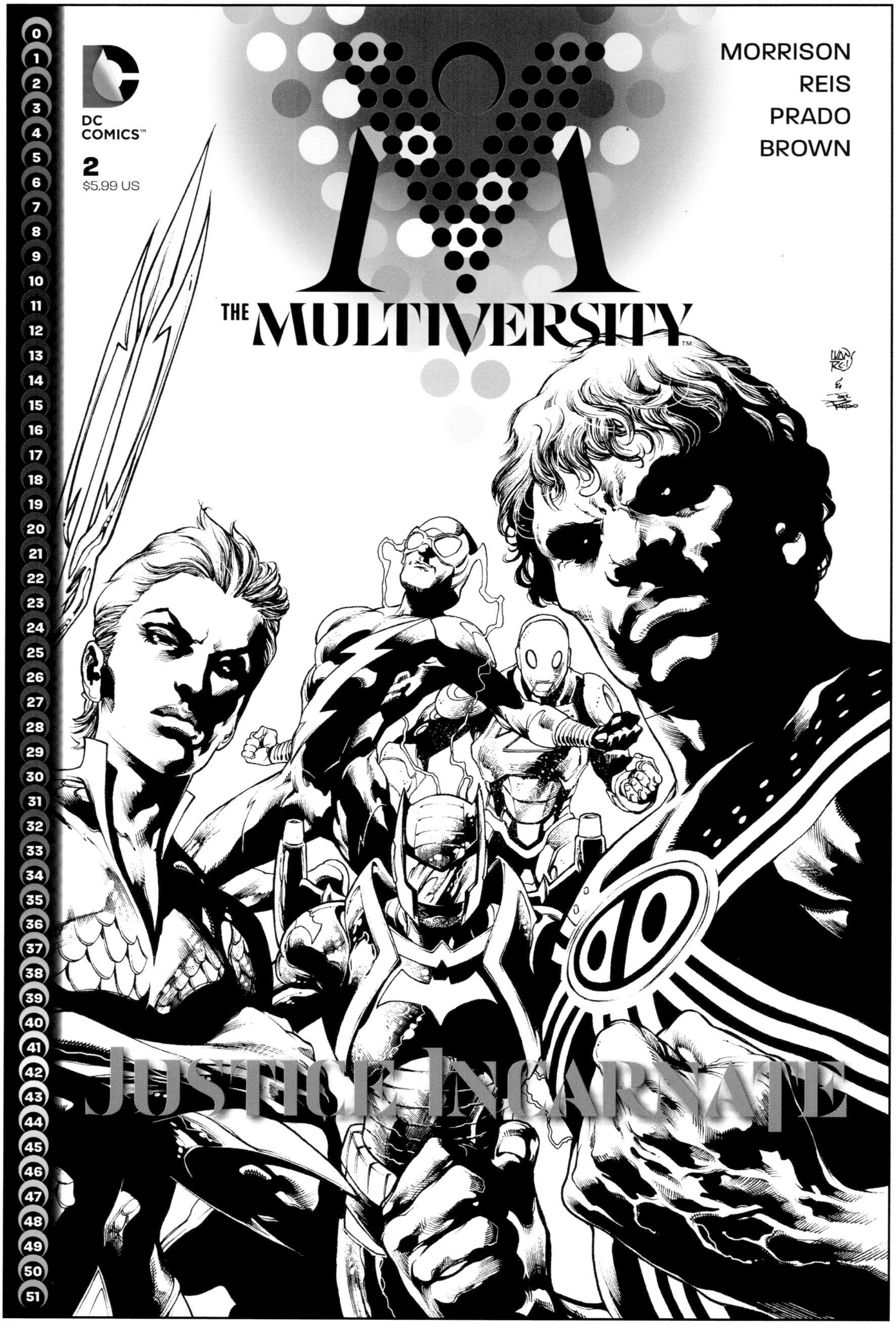
DC COMICS™
2
$5.99 US
MORRISON
REIS
PRADO
BROWN
THE MULTIVERSITY™
JUSTICE INCARNATE

THE MULTIVERSITY
#2

Written by
GRANT MORRISON

Penciller
IVAN REIS

Inkers
JOE PRADO
EBER FERREIRA
JAIME MENDOZA

Colorists
DAN BROWN
JASON WRIGHT
BLOND

Letterer
TODD KLEIN

Cover artists
IVAN REIS and
JOE PRADO with
DAN BROWN

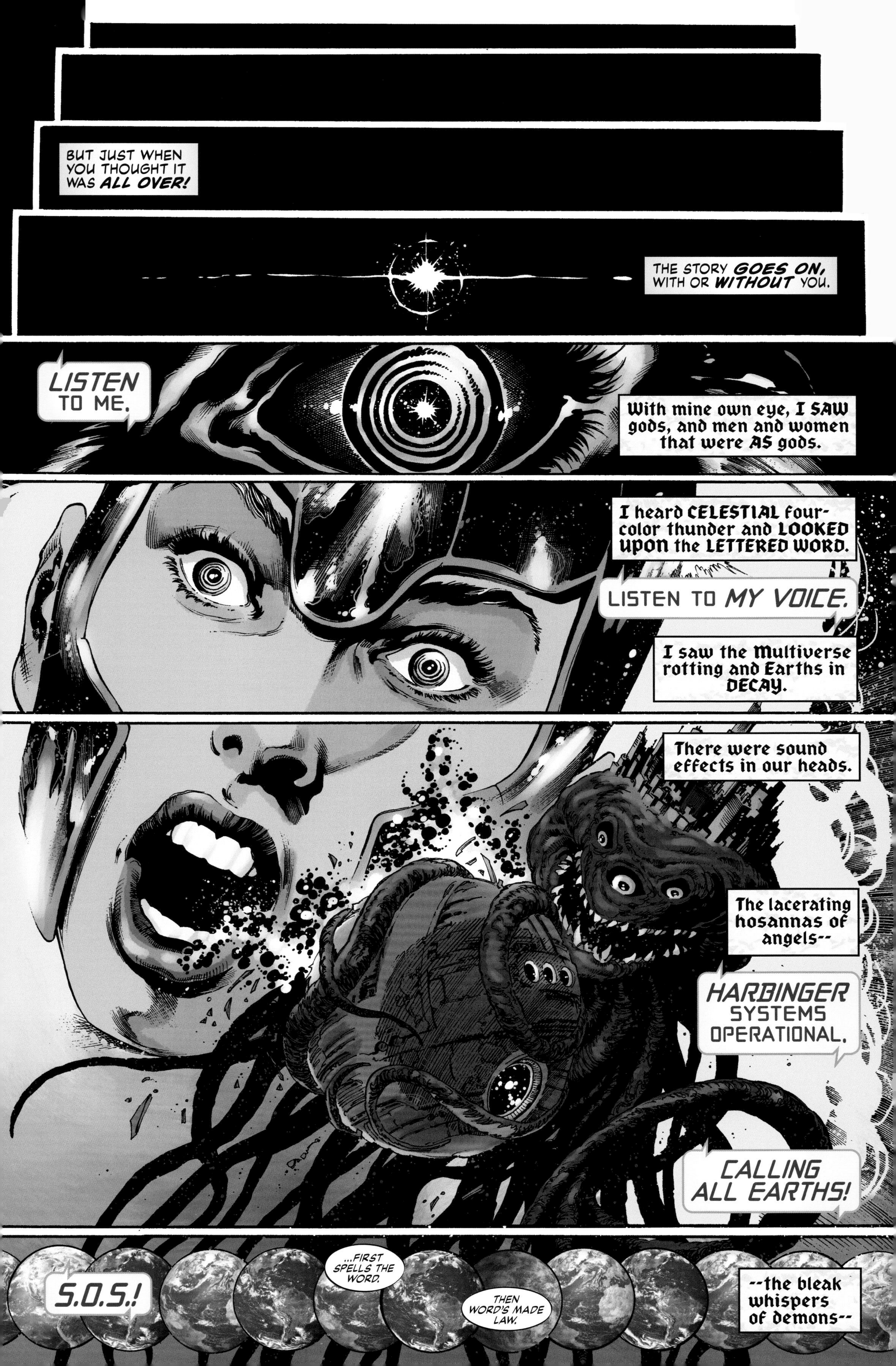
BUT JUST WHEN YOU THOUGHT IT WAS ALL OVER!
THE STORY GOES ON, WITH OR WITHOUT YOU.
LISTEN TO ME.
With mine own eye, I SAW gods, and men and women that were AS gods.
I heard CELESTIAL four-color thunder and LOOKED upon the LETTERED WORD.
LISTEN TO MY VOICE.
I saw the Multiverse rotting and Earths in DECAY.
There were sound effects in our heads.
The lacerating hosannas of angels--
HARBINGER SYSTEMS OPERATIONAL.
CALLING ALL EARTHS!
S.O.S.!
...FIRST SPELLS THE WORD.
THEN WORD'S MADE LAW.
--the bleak whispers of demons--

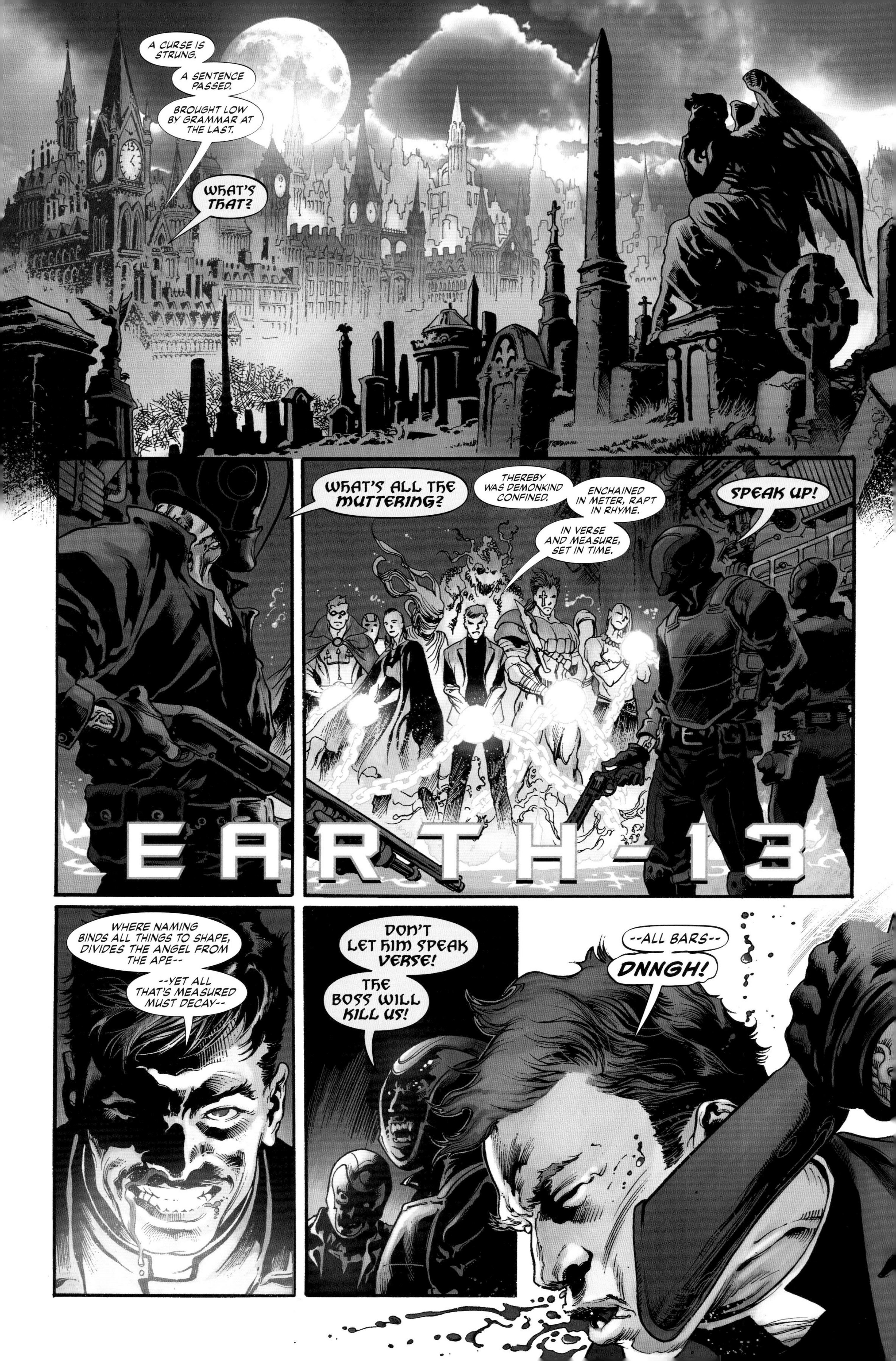
A CURSE IS STRUNG.
A SENTENCE PASSED.
BROUGHT LOW BY GRAMMAR AT THE LAST.
WHAT'S THAT?
WHAT'S ALL THE MUTTERING?
THEREBY WAS DEMONKIND CONFINED.
ENCHAINED IN METER, RAPT IN RHYME.
IN VERSE AND MEASURE, SET IN TIME.
SPEAK UP!
EARTH-13
WHERE NAMING BINDS ALL THINGS TO SHAPE, DIVIDES THE ANGEL FROM THE APE--
--YET ALL THAT'S MEASURED MUST DECAY--
DON'T LET HIM SPEAK VERSE!
THE BOSS WILL KILL US!
--ALL BARS--
DNNGH!

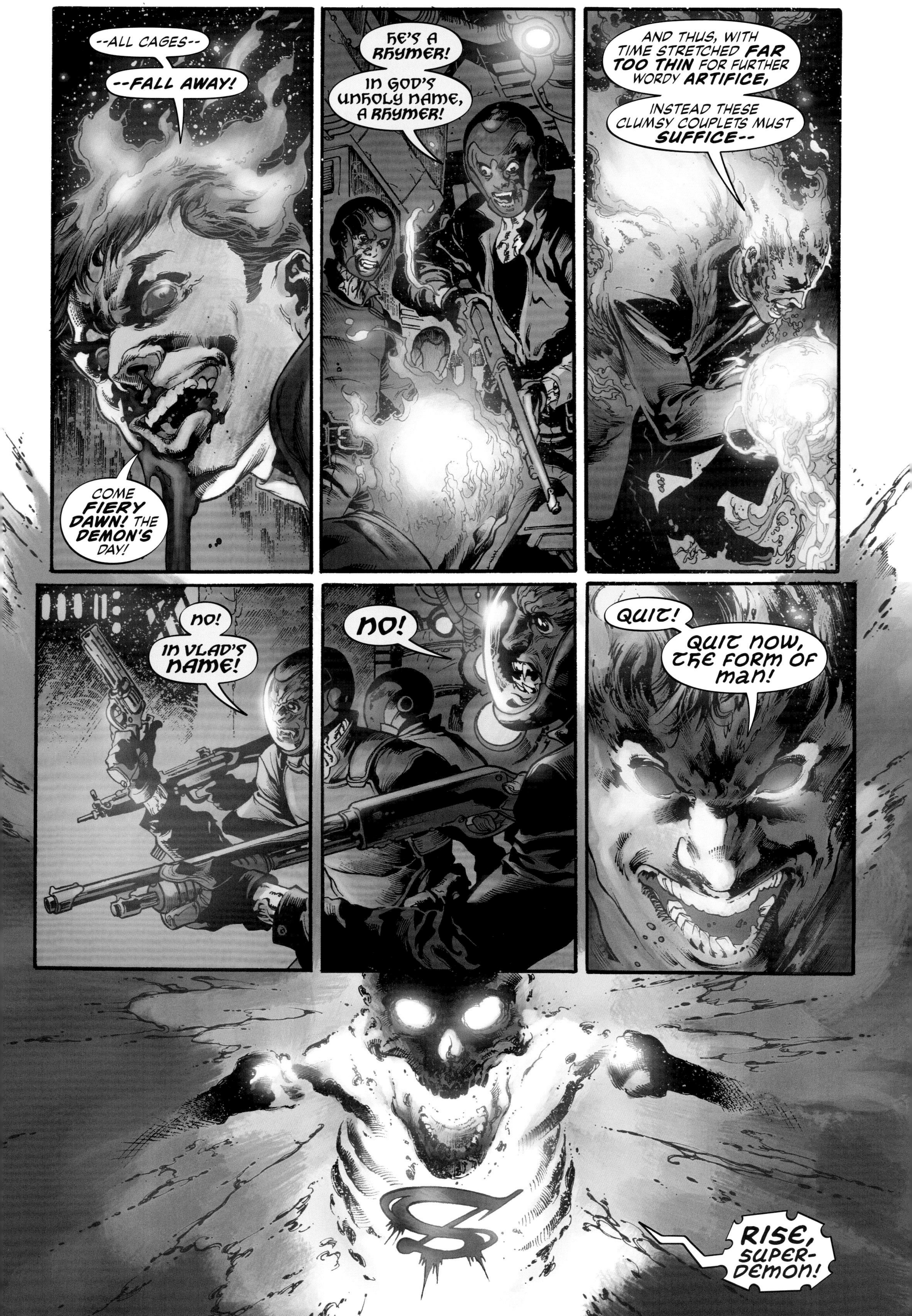
--ALL CAGES--
--FALL AWAY!
COME FIERY DAWN! THE DEMON'S DAY!
HE'S A RHYMER!
IN GOD'S UNHOLY NAME, A RHYMER!
AND THUS, WITH TIME STRETCHED FAR TOO THIN FOR FURTHER WORDY ARTIFICE,
INSTEAD THESE CLUMSY COUPLETS MUST SUFFICE--
NO!
IN VLAD'S NAME!
NO!
QUIT!
QUIT NOW, THE FORM OF MAN!
RISE, SUPER-DEMON!

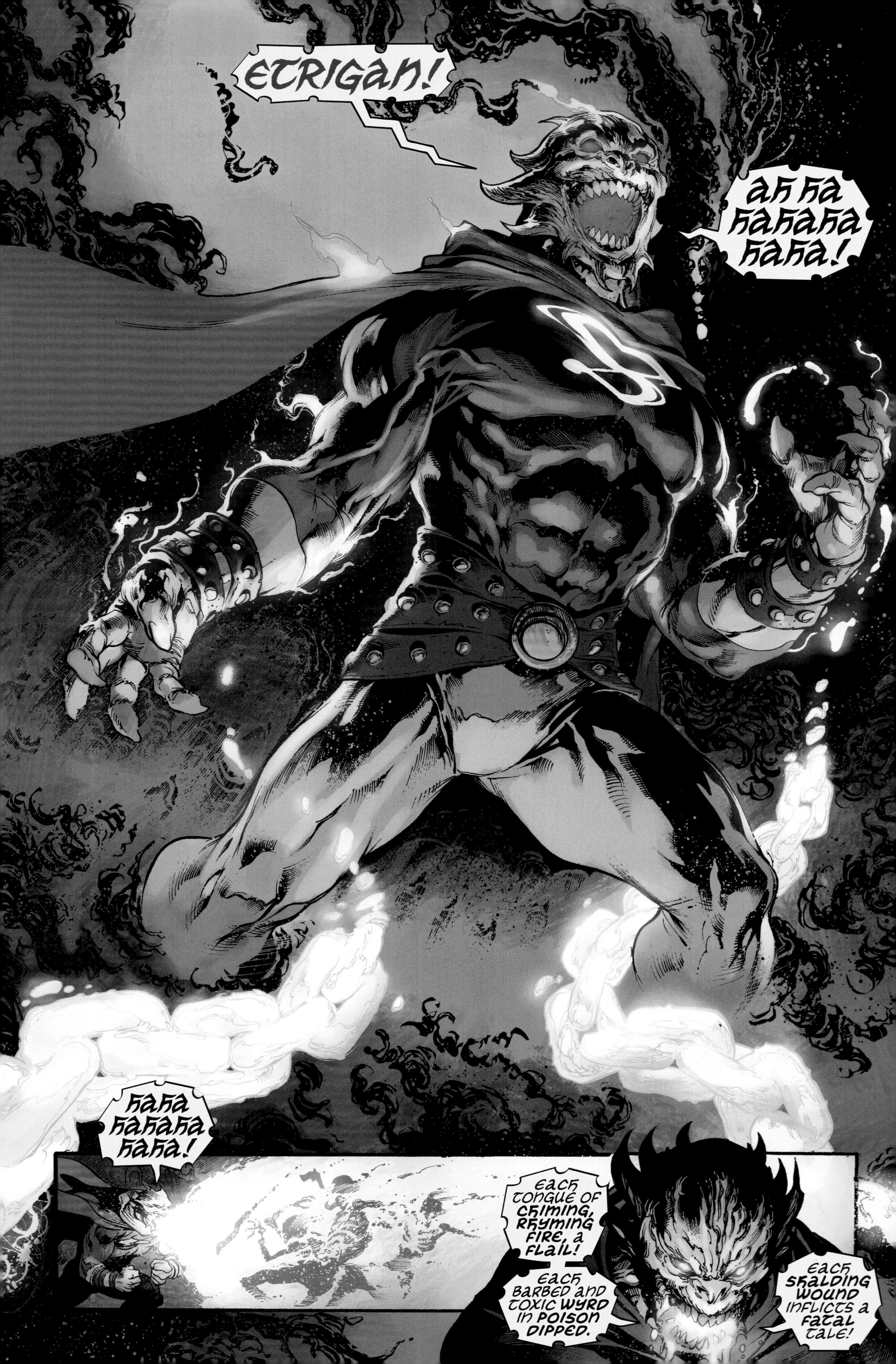
ETRIGAN!
AH HA HAHAHA HAHA!
HAHA HAHAHA HAHA!
EACH TONGUE OF CHIMING, RHYMING FIRE, A FLAIL!
EACH BARBED AND TOXIC WYRD IN POISON DIPPED.
EACH SKALDING WOUND INFLICTS A FATAL TALE!

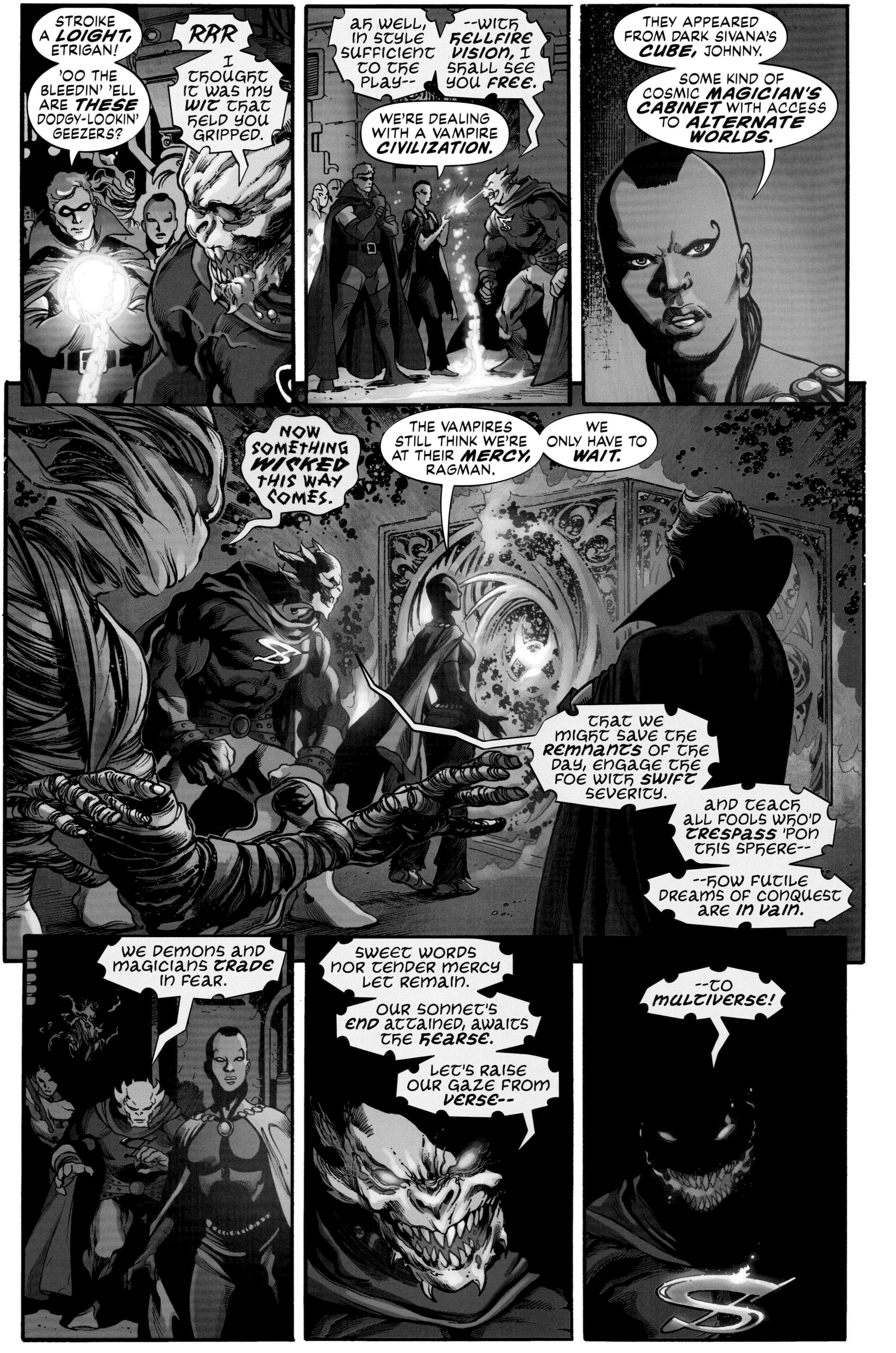
STROIKE A LOIGHT, ETRIGAN!
'OO THE BLEEDIN' 'ELL ARE THESE DODGY-LOOKIN' GEEZERS?
RRR
I THOUGHT IT WAS MY WIT THAT HELD YOU GRIPPED.
AH WELL, IN STYLE SUFFICIENT TO THE PLAY--
--WITH HELLFIRE VISION, I SHALL SEE YOU FREE.
WE'RE DEALING WITH A VAMPIRE CIVILIZATION.
THEY APPEARED FROM DARK SIVANA'S CUBE, JOHNNY.
SOME KIND OF COSMIC MAGICIAN'S CABINET WITH ACCESS TO ALTERNATE WORLDS.
NOW SOMETHING WICKED THIS WAY COMES.
THE VAMPIRES STILL THINK WE'RE AT THEIR MERCY, RAGMAN.
WE ONLY HAVE TO WAIT.
THAT WE MIGHT SAVE THE REMNANTS OF THE DAY, ENGAGE THE FOE WITH SWIFT SEVERITY.
AND TEACH ALL FOOLS WHO'D TRESPASS 'PON THIS SPHERE--
--HOW FUTILE DREAMS OF CONQUEST ARE IN VAIN.
WE DEMONS AND MAGICIANS TRADE IN FEAR.
SWEET WORDS NOR TENDER MERCY LET REMAIN.
OUR SONNET'S END ATTAINED, AWAITS THE HEARSE.
LET'S RAISE OUR GAZE FROM VERSE--
--TO MULTIVERSE!

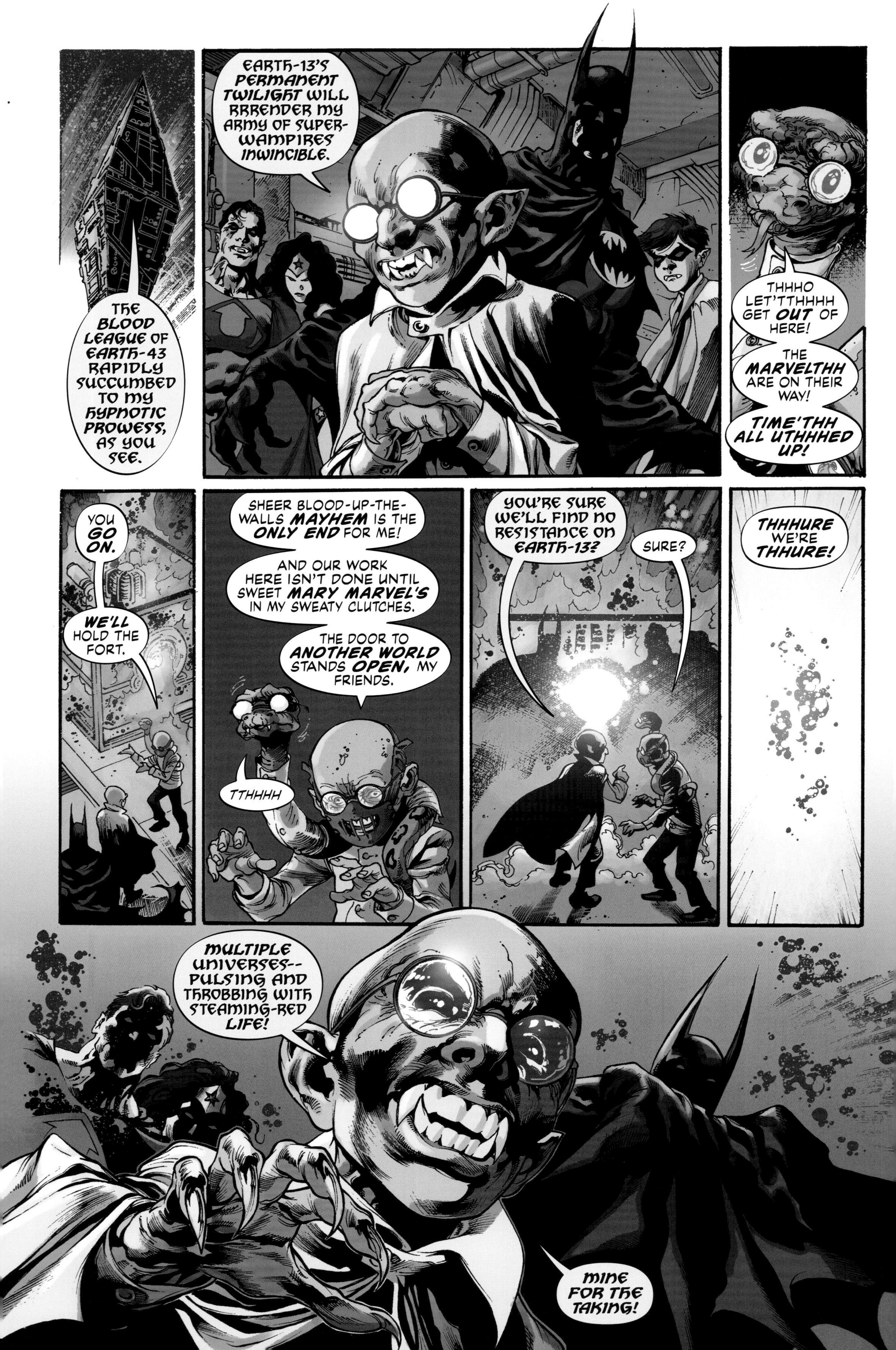
THE BLOOD LEAGUE OF EARTH-43 RAPIDLY SUCCUMBED TO MY HYPNOTIC PROWESS, AS YOU SEE.
EARTH-13'S PERMANENT TWILIGHT WILL RRRENDER MY ARMY OF SUPER-WAMPIRES INWINCIBLE.
THHHO LET'TTHHHH GET OUT OF HERE!
THE MARVELTHH ARE ON THEIR WAY!
TIME'THH ALL UTHHHED UP!
YOU GO ON.
WE'LL HOLD THE FORT.
SHEER BLOOD-UP-THE-WALLS MAYHEM IS THE ONLY END FOR ME!
AND OUR WORK HERE ISN'T DONE UNTIL SWEET MARY MARVEL'S IN MY SWEATY CLUTCHES.
THE DOOR TO ANOTHER WORLD STANDS OPEN, MY FRIENDS.
TTHHHH
YOU'RE SURE WE'LL FIND NO RESISTANCE ON EARTH-13?
SURE?
THHHURE WE'RE THHURE!
MULTIPLE UNIVERSES-- PULSING AND THROBBING WITH STEAMING-RED LIFE!
MINE FOR THE TAKING!

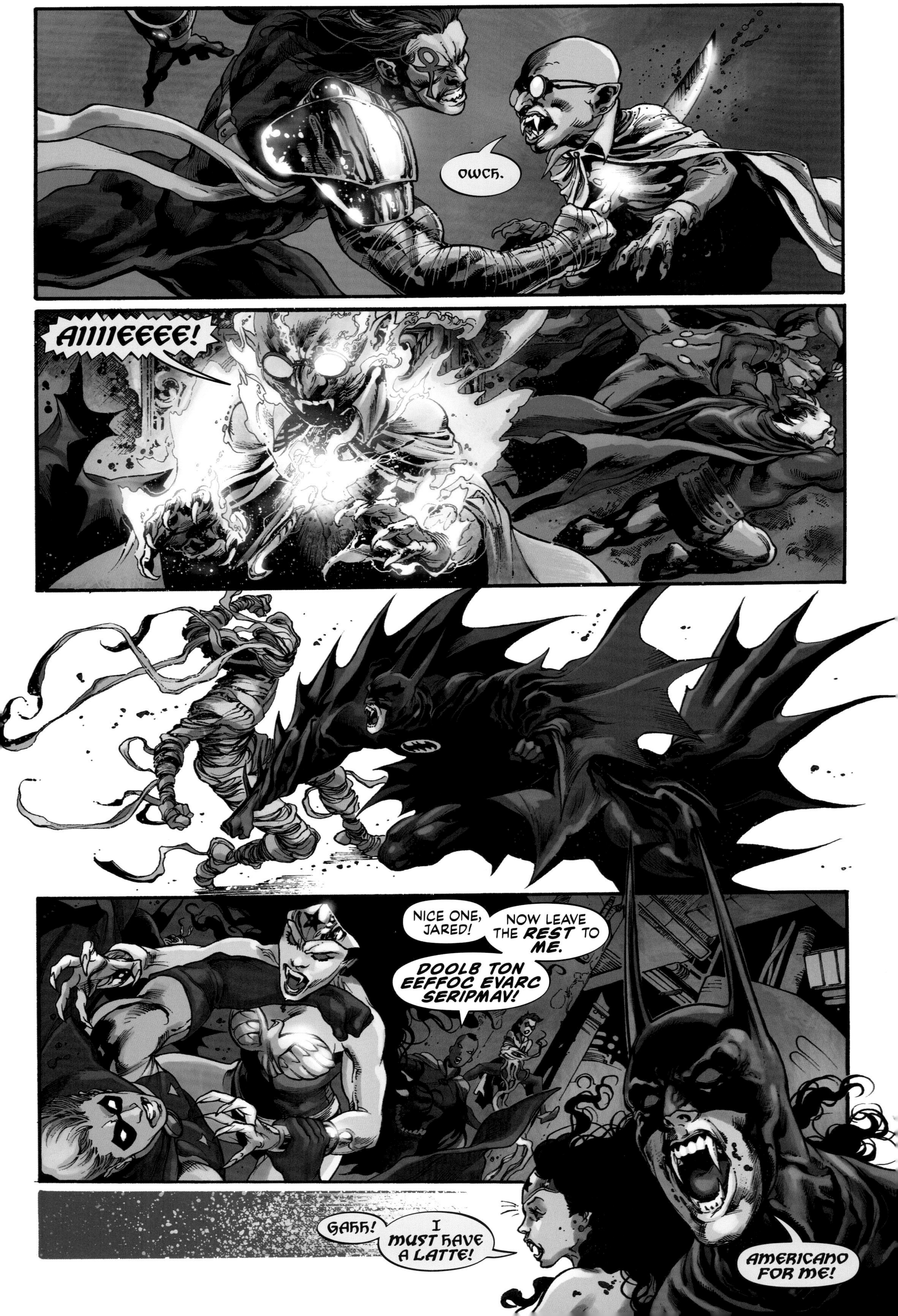
OWCH.
AIIIIEEEE!
NICE ONE, JARED!
NOW LEAVE THE REST TO ME.
DOOLB TON EEFFOC EVARC SERIPMAV!
GAHH!
I MUST HAVE A LATTE!
AMERICANO FOR ME!

:FF:

ONE LESS **IDIOT**.

NOW--

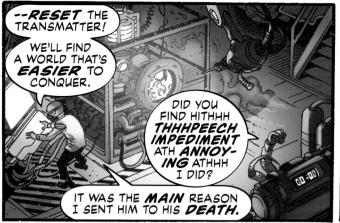

--**RESET** THE TRANSMATTER!

WE'LL FIND A WORLD THAT'S **EASIER** TO CONQUER.

DID YOU FIND HITHHH **THHHPEECH** IMPEDIMENT ATH **ANNOY-ING** ATHHH I DID?

IT WAS THE **MAIN** REASON I SENT HIM TO HIS **DEATH**.

WHAT THE **HELL'S** WRONG WITH YOUR **BREATH**?

THAT **SMELL**!

I--:URRP:

NOW IT'S **YOUR TURN**!

THE **CUBE'S** LOCATED A WORLD WHERE **YOU'LL** FIT RIGHT IN.

A HOT, DRY DESERT--

YOU THINK I'D TRUTHHHT A **THHHIVANA**?!

WE GO THHROUGH **TOGETHER**--

--OR **NOT** AT ALL.

HMMM.

AT **LEATHHHT** IT'THHHH NITHHHE AND **WARM**!

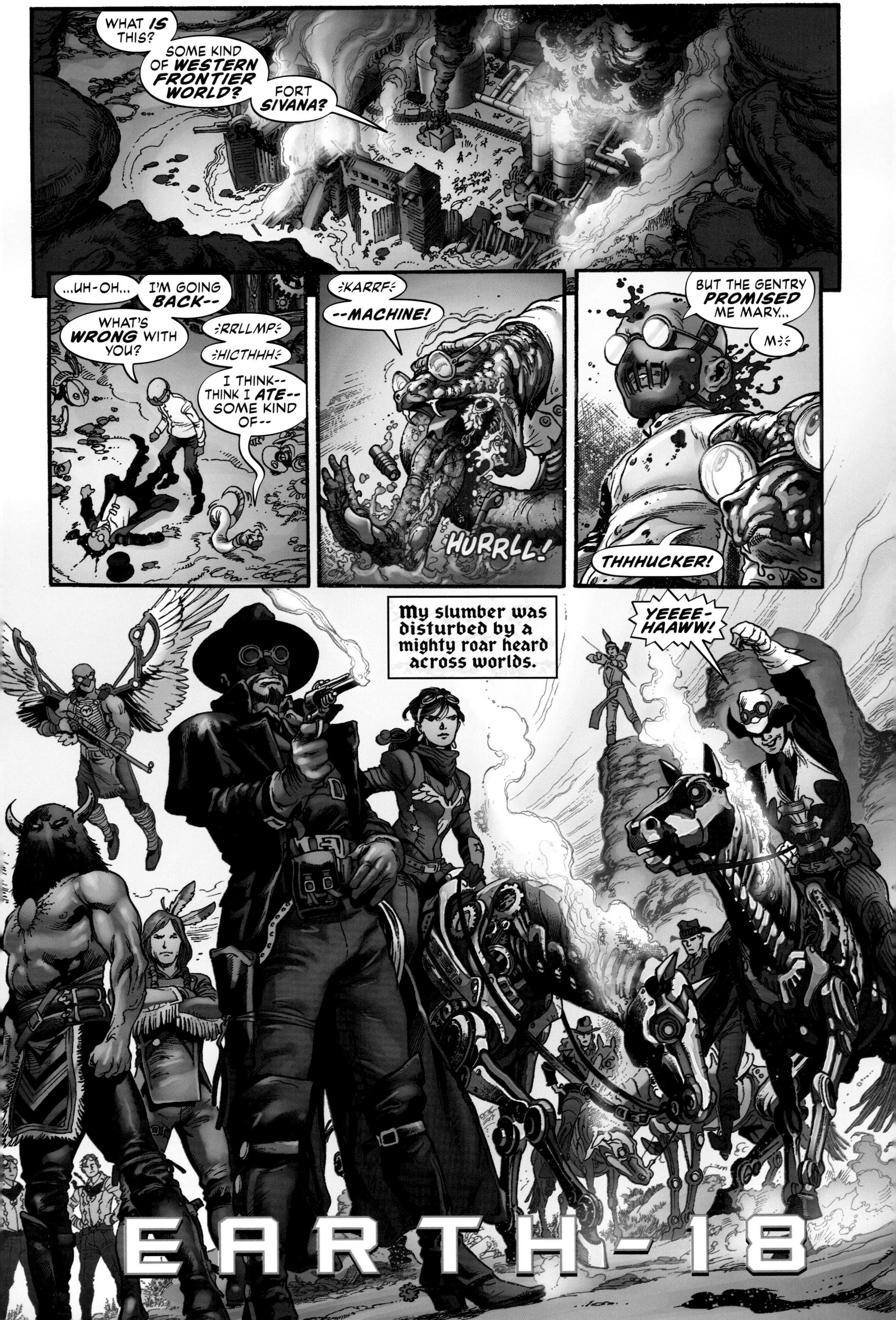
WHAT IS THIS?
SOME KIND OF WESTERN FRONTIER WORLD?
FORT SIVANA?
...UH-OH...
I'M GOING BACK--
WHAT'S WRONG WITH YOU?
RRLLMP
HICTHHH
I THINK-- THINK I ATE-- SOME KIND OF--
KARRF
--MACHINE!
HURRLL!
BUT THE GENTRY PROMISED ME MARY...
M
THHHUCKER!
My slumber was disturbed by a mighty roar heard across worlds.
YEEEE-HAAWW!
EARTH-18

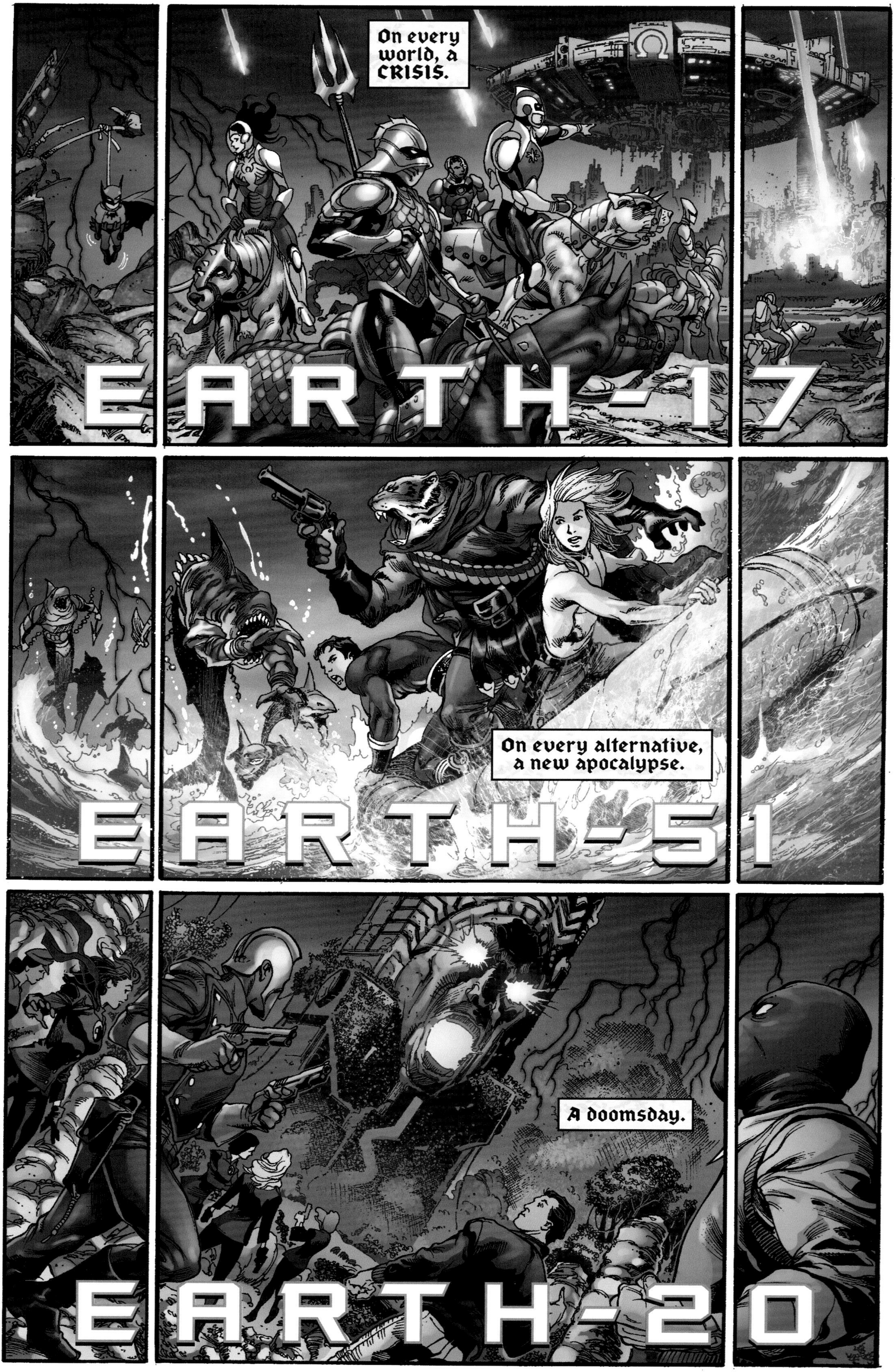
On every world, a CRISIS.
EARTH-17
On every alternative, a new apocalypse.
EARTH-51
A doomsday.
EARTH-20

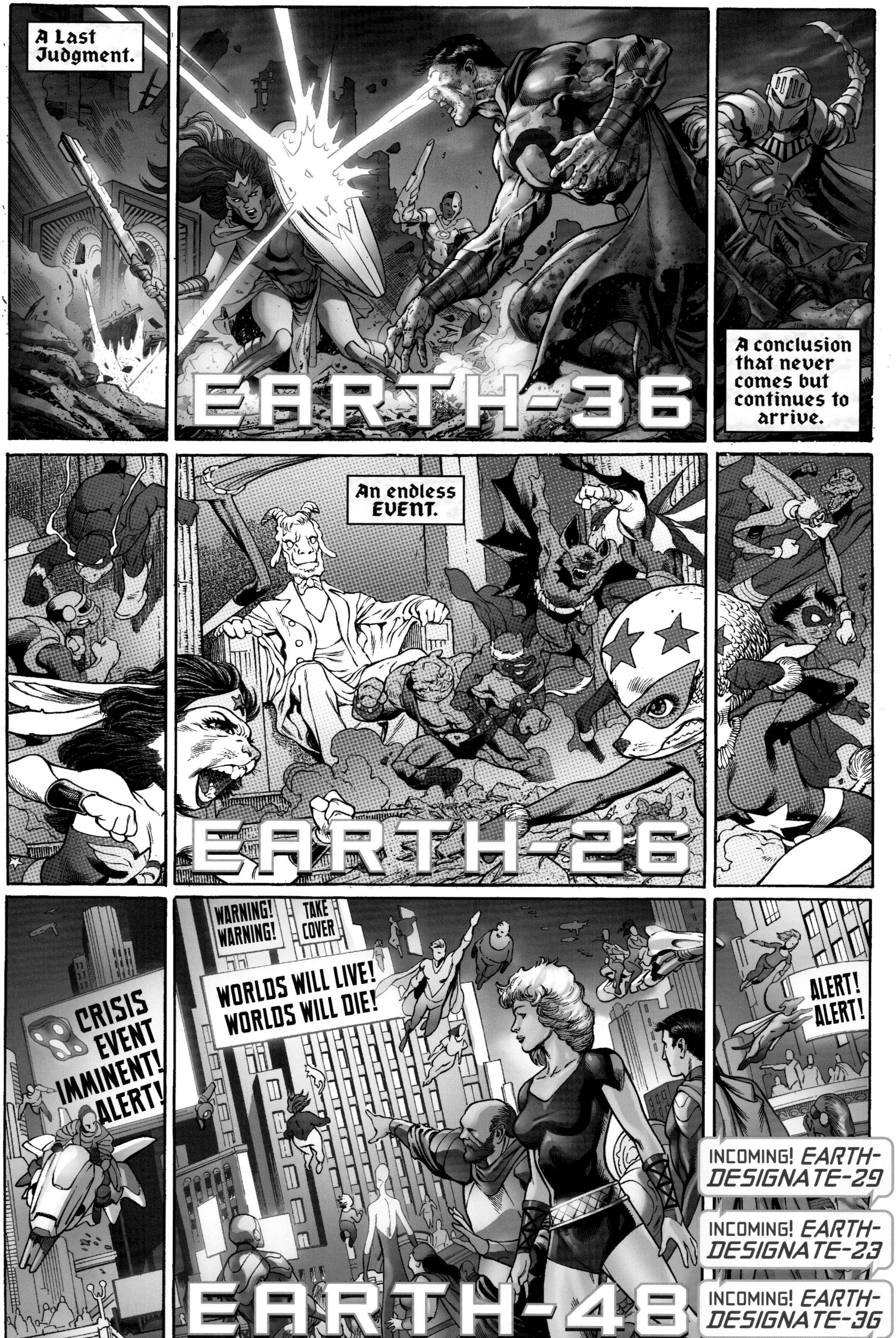
A Last Judgment.
EARTH-36
A conclusion that never comes but continues to arrive.
An endless EVENT.
EARTH-26
CRISIS EVENT IMMINENT! ALERT!
WARNING! WARNING!
TAKE COVER
WORLDS WILL LIVE! WORLDS WILL DIE!
ALERT! ALERT!
INCOMING! EARTH-DESIGNATE-29
INCOMING! EARTH-DESIGNATE-23
INCOMING! EARTH-DESIGNATE-36
EARTH-48

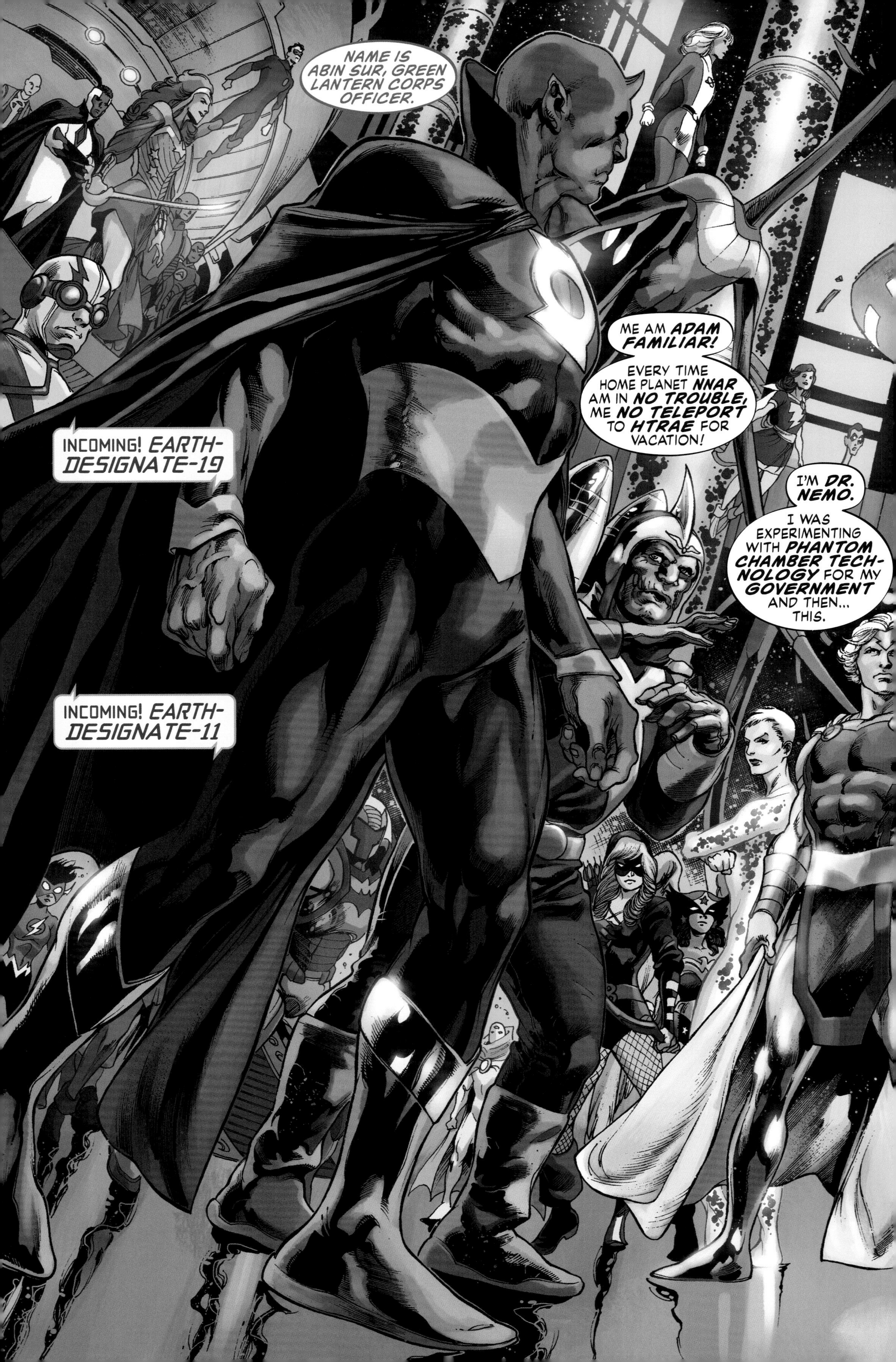
NAME IS ABIN SUR, GREEN LANTERN CORPS OFFICER.
ME AM ADAM FAMILIAR!
EVERY TIME HOME PLANET NNAR AM IN NO TROUBLE, ME NO TELEPORT TO HTRAE FOR VACATION!
INCOMING! EARTH-DESIGNATE-19
I'M DR. NEMO.
I WAS EXPERIMENTING WITH PHANTOM CHAMBER TECHNOLOGY FOR MY GOVERNMENT AND THEN... THIS.
INCOMING! EARTH-DESIGNATE-11

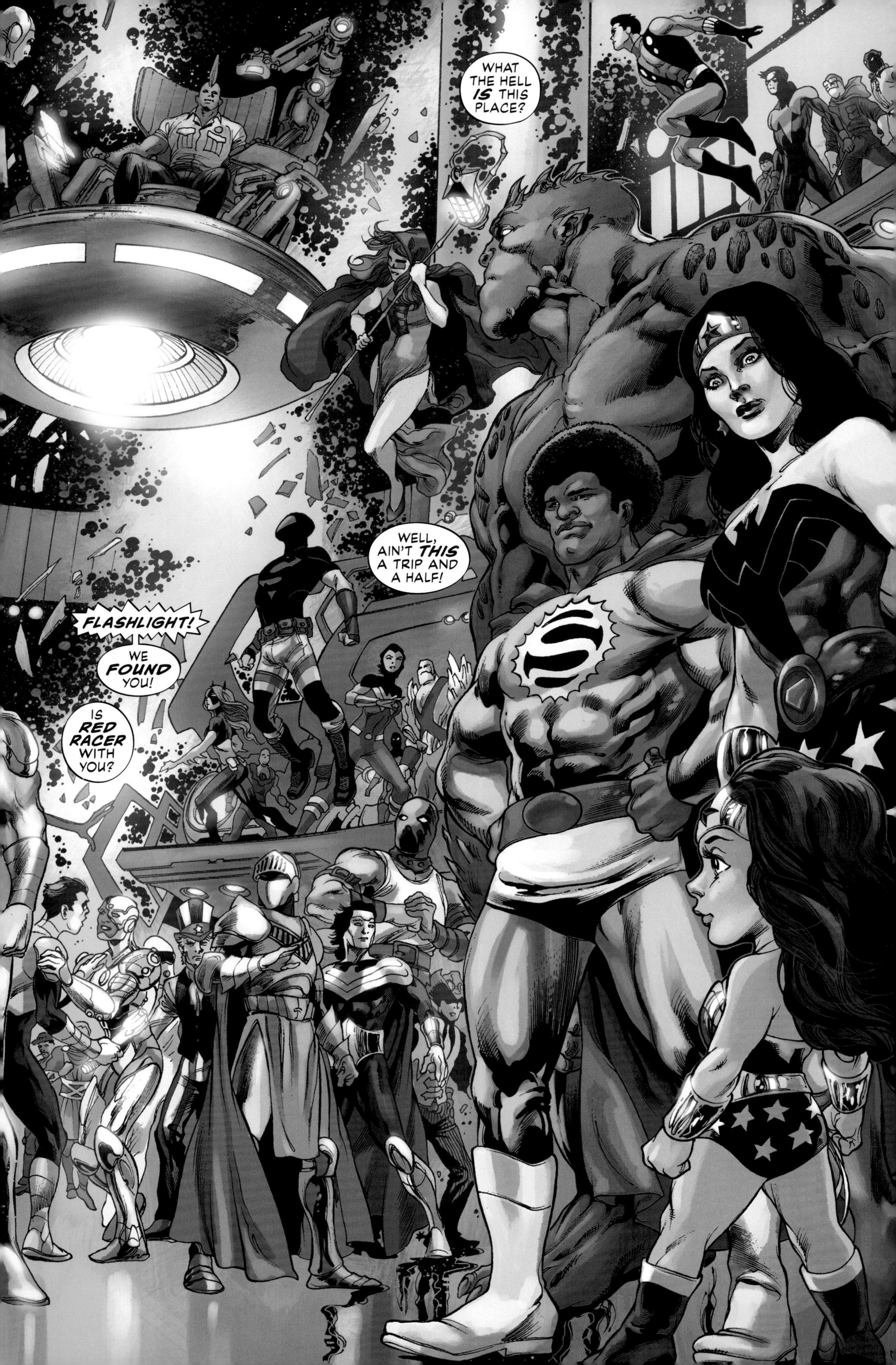
WHAT THE HELL *IS* THIS PLACE?
WELL, AIN'T *THIS* A TRIP AND A HALF!
FLASHLIGHT!
WE *FOUND* YOU!
IS *RED RACER* WITH YOU?

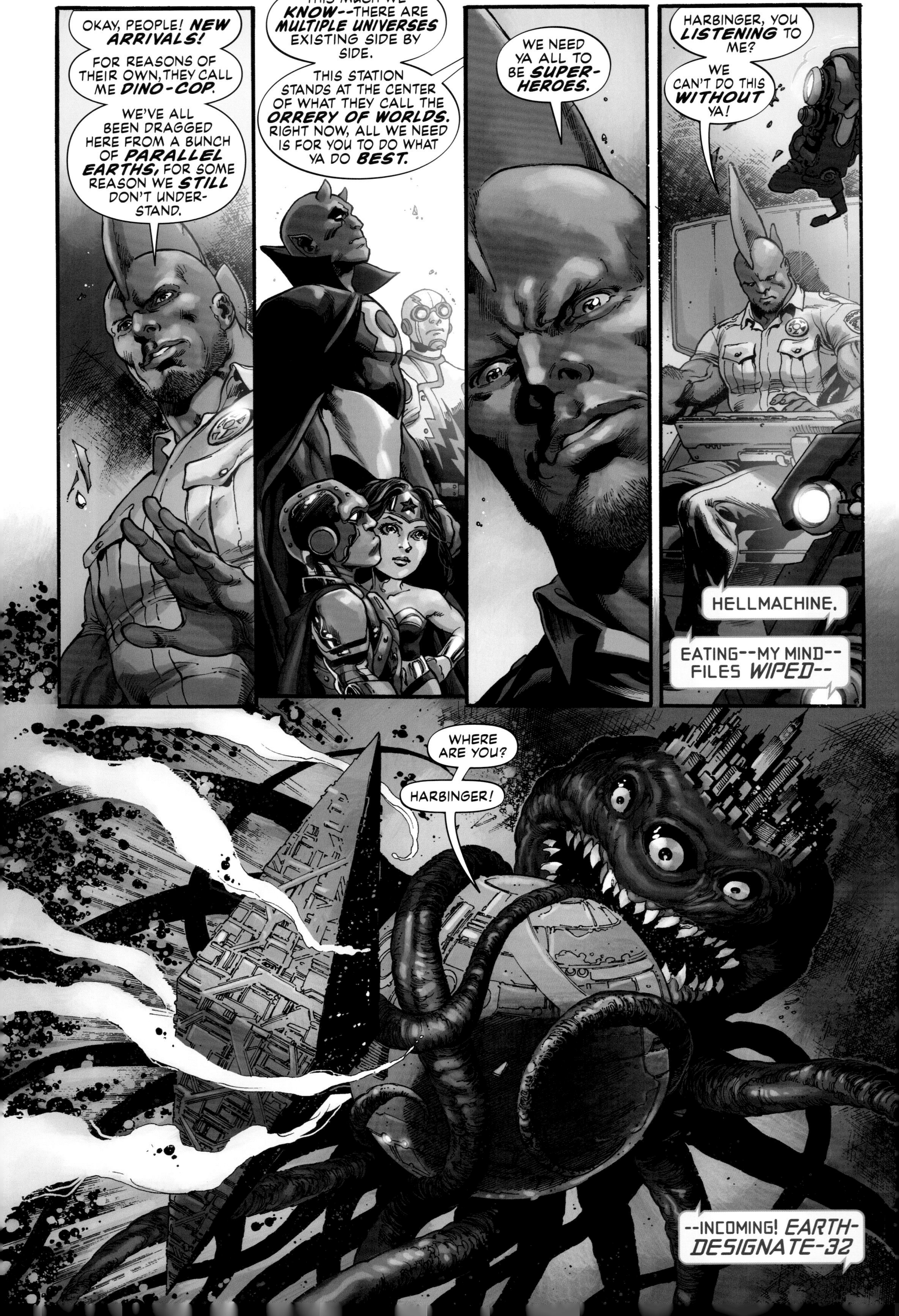
OKAY, PEOPLE! NEW ARRIVALS!
FOR REASONS OF THEIR OWN, THEY CALL ME DINO-COP.
WE'VE ALL BEEN DRAGGED HERE FROM A BUNCH OF PARALLEL EARTHS, FOR SOME REASON WE STILL DON'T UNDER-STAND.
THIS MUCH WE KNOW--THERE ARE MULTIPLE UNIVERSES EXISTING SIDE BY SIDE.
THIS STATION STANDS AT THE CENTER OF WHAT THEY CALL THE ORRERY OF WORLDS. RIGHT NOW, ALL WE NEED IS FOR YOU TO DO WHAT YA DO BEST.
WE NEED YA ALL TO BE SUPER-HEROES.
HARBINGER, YOU LISTENING TO ME?
WE CAN'T DO THIS WITHOUT YA!
HELLMACHINE.
EATING--MY MIND--FILES WIPED--
WHERE ARE YOU?
HARBINGER!
--INCOMING! EARTH-DESIGNATE-32

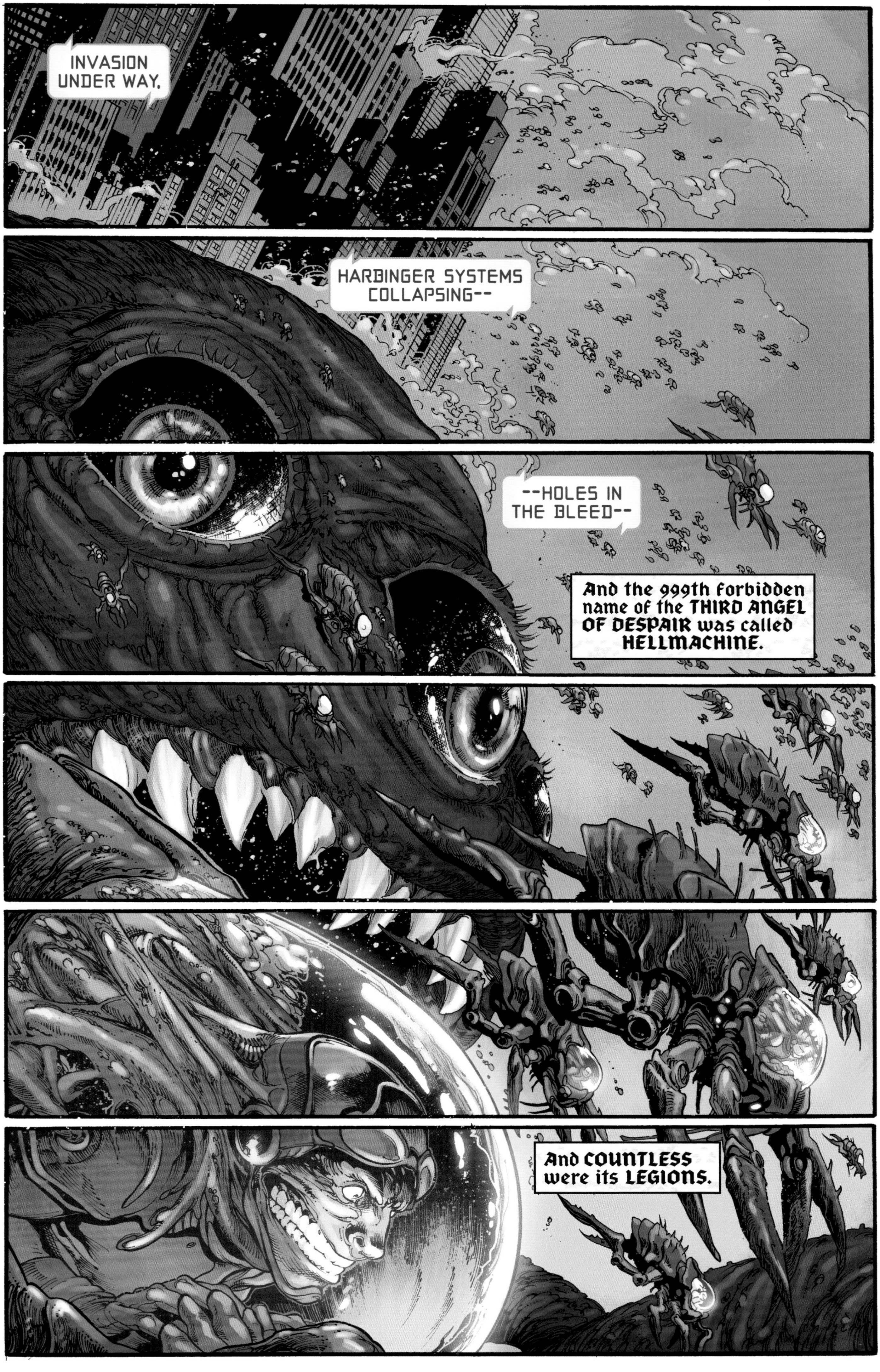
INVASION UNDER WAY.
HARBINGER SYSTEMS COLLAPSING--
--HOLES IN THE BLEED--
And the 999th forbidden name of the THIRD ANGEL OF DESPAIR was called HELLMACHINE.
And COUNTLESS were its LEGIONS.

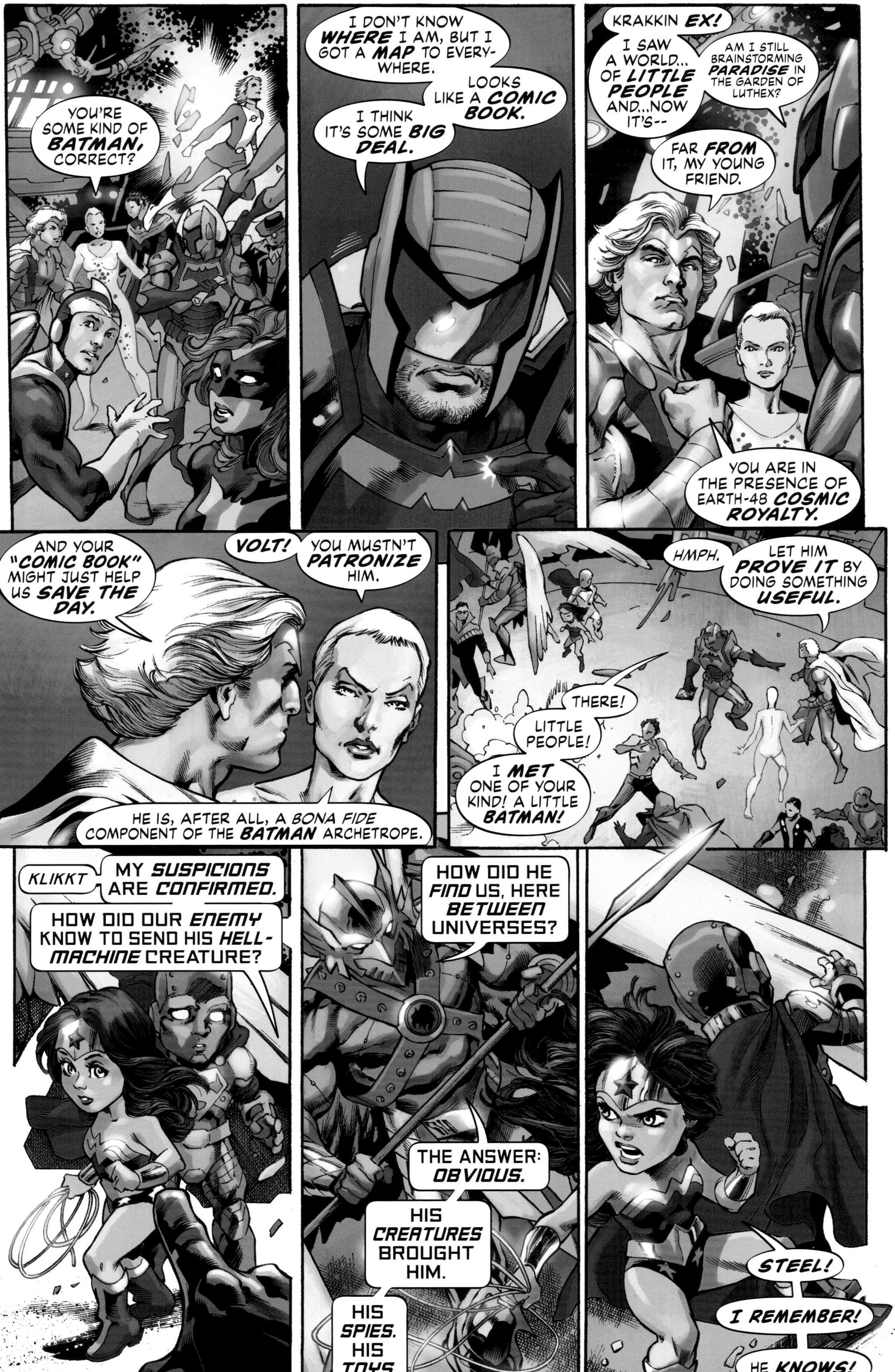
YOU'RE SOME KIND OF BATMAN, CORRECT?
I DON'T KNOW WHERE I AM, BUT I GOT A MAP TO EVERYWHERE.
LOOKS LIKE A COMIC BOOK.
I THINK IT'S SOME BIG DEAL.
KRAKKIN EX!
I SAW A WORLD... OF LITTLE PEOPLE AND...NOW IT'S--
AM I STILL BRAINSTORMING PARADISE IN THE GARDEN OF LUTHEX?
FAR FROM IT, MY YOUNG FRIEND.
YOU ARE IN THE PRESENCE OF EARTH-48 COSMIC ROYALTY.
AND YOUR "COMIC BOOK" MIGHT JUST HELP US SAVE THE DAY.
VOLT!
YOU MUSTN'T PATRONIZE HIM.
HE IS, AFTER ALL, A BONA FIDE COMPONENT OF THE BATMAN ARCHETROPE.
HMPH.
LET HIM PROVE IT BY DOING SOMETHING USEFUL.
THERE!
LITTLE PEOPLE!
I MET ONE OF YOUR KIND! A LITTLE BATMAN!
KLIKKT
MY SUSPICIONS ARE CONFIRMED.
HOW DID OUR ENEMY KNOW TO SEND HIS HELL-MACHINE CREATURE?
HOW DID HE FIND US, HERE BETWEEN UNIVERSES?
THE ANSWER: OBVIOUS.
HIS CREATURES BROUGHT HIM.
HIS SPIES. HIS TOYS.
STEEL!
I REMEMBER!
HE KNOWS!

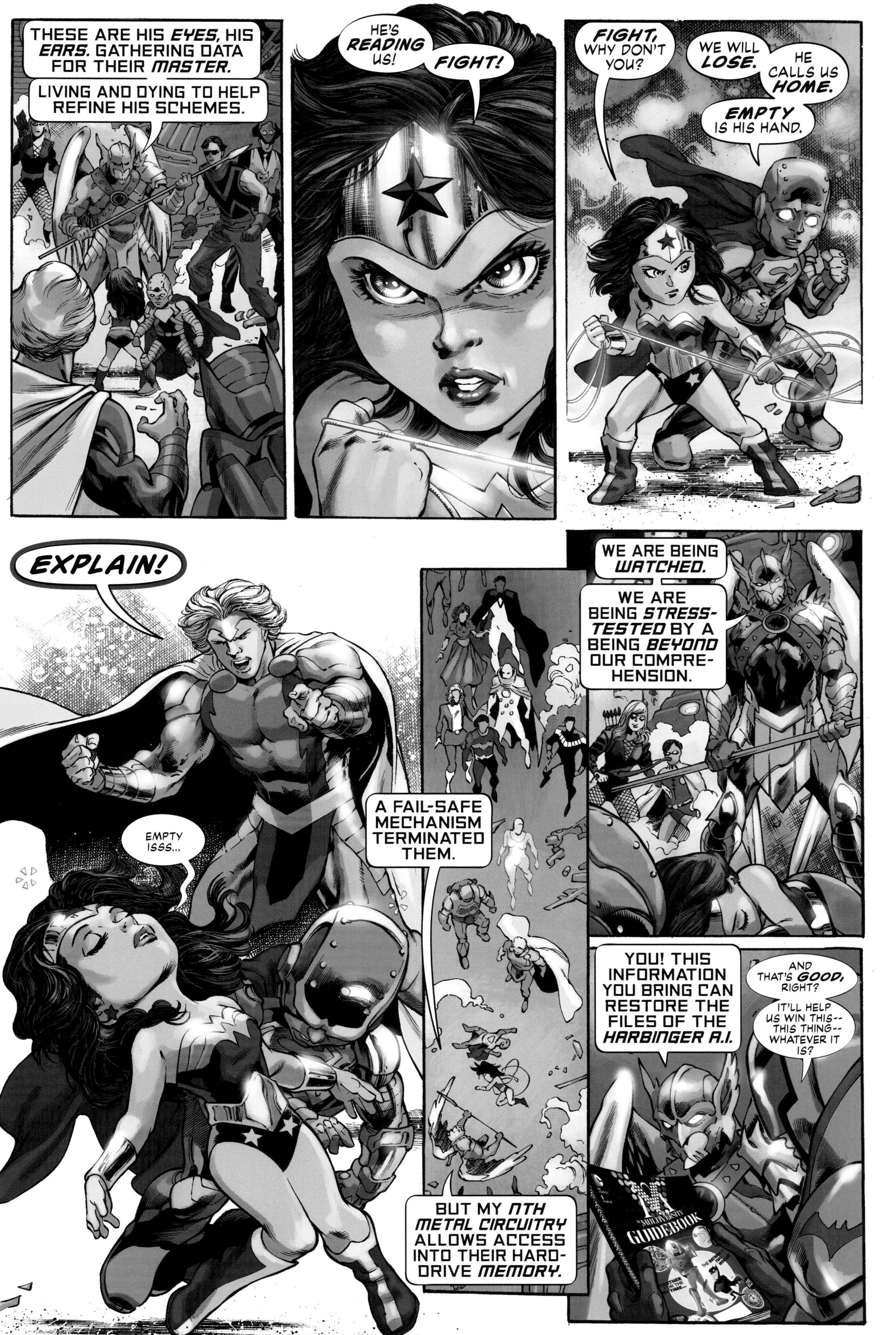
THESE ARE HIS *EYES*, HIS *EARS*. GATHERING DATA FOR THEIR *MASTER*.
LIVING AND DYING TO HELP REFINE HIS SCHEMES.
HE'S *READING* US!
FIGHT!
FIGHT, WHY DON'T YOU?
WE WILL *LOSE.*
HE CALLS US *HOME.*
EMPTY IS HIS HAND.
EXPLAIN!
EMPTY ISSS...
A FAIL-SAFE MECHANISM TERMINATED THEM.
BUT MY *NTH METAL CIRCUITRY* ALLOWS ACCESS INTO THEIR HARD-DRIVE *MEMORY*.
WE ARE BEING *WATCHED*.
WE ARE BEING *STRESS-TESTED* BY A BEING *BEYOND* OUR COMPRE-HENSION.
YOU! THIS INFORMATION YOU BRING CAN RESTORE THE FILES OF THE *HARBINGER A.I.*
AND THAT'S *GOOD*, RIGHT?
IT'LL HELP US WIN THIS-- THIS THING-- WHATEVER IT IS?
GUIDEBOOK

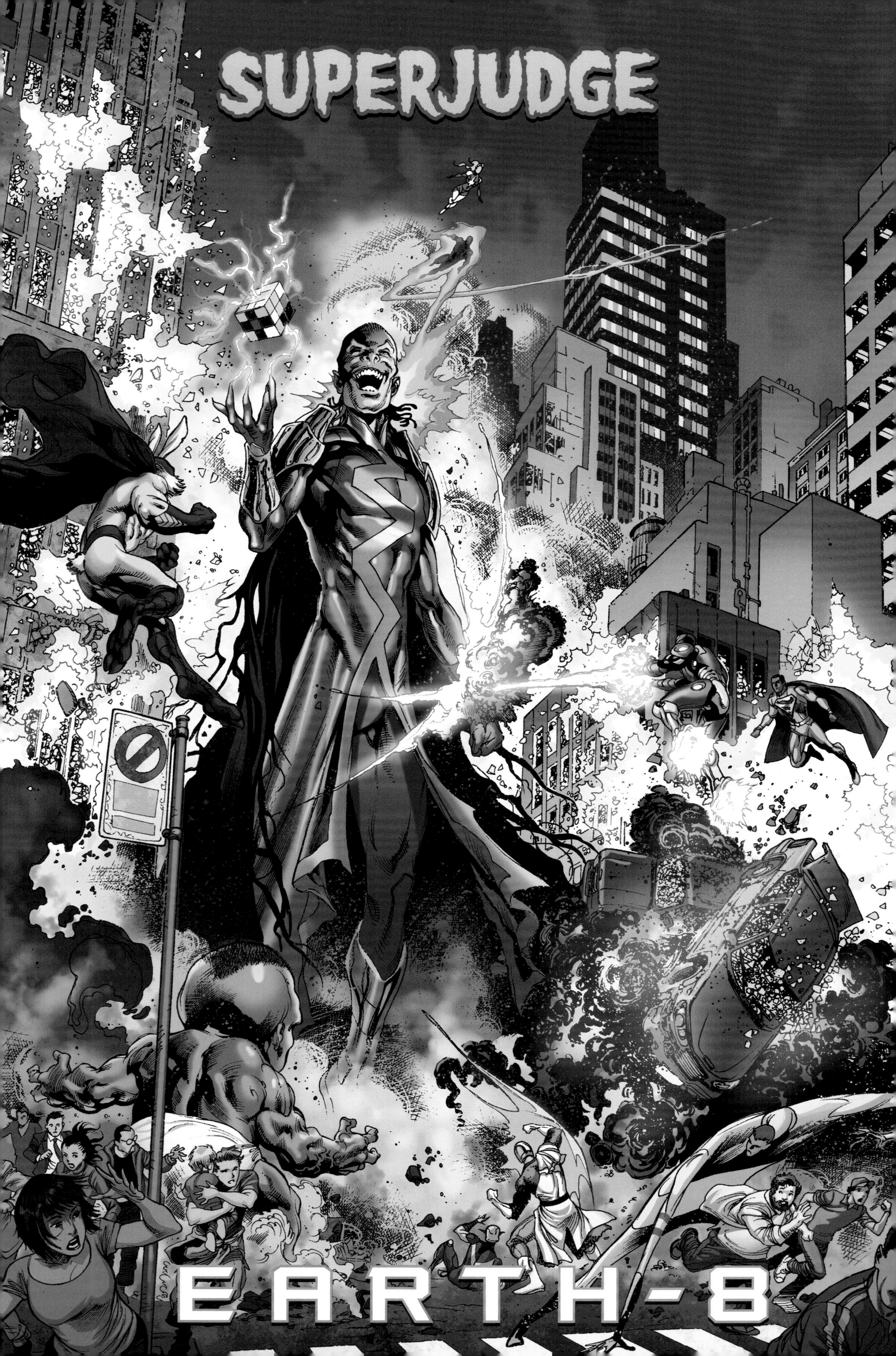
SUPERJUDGE
EARTH-8

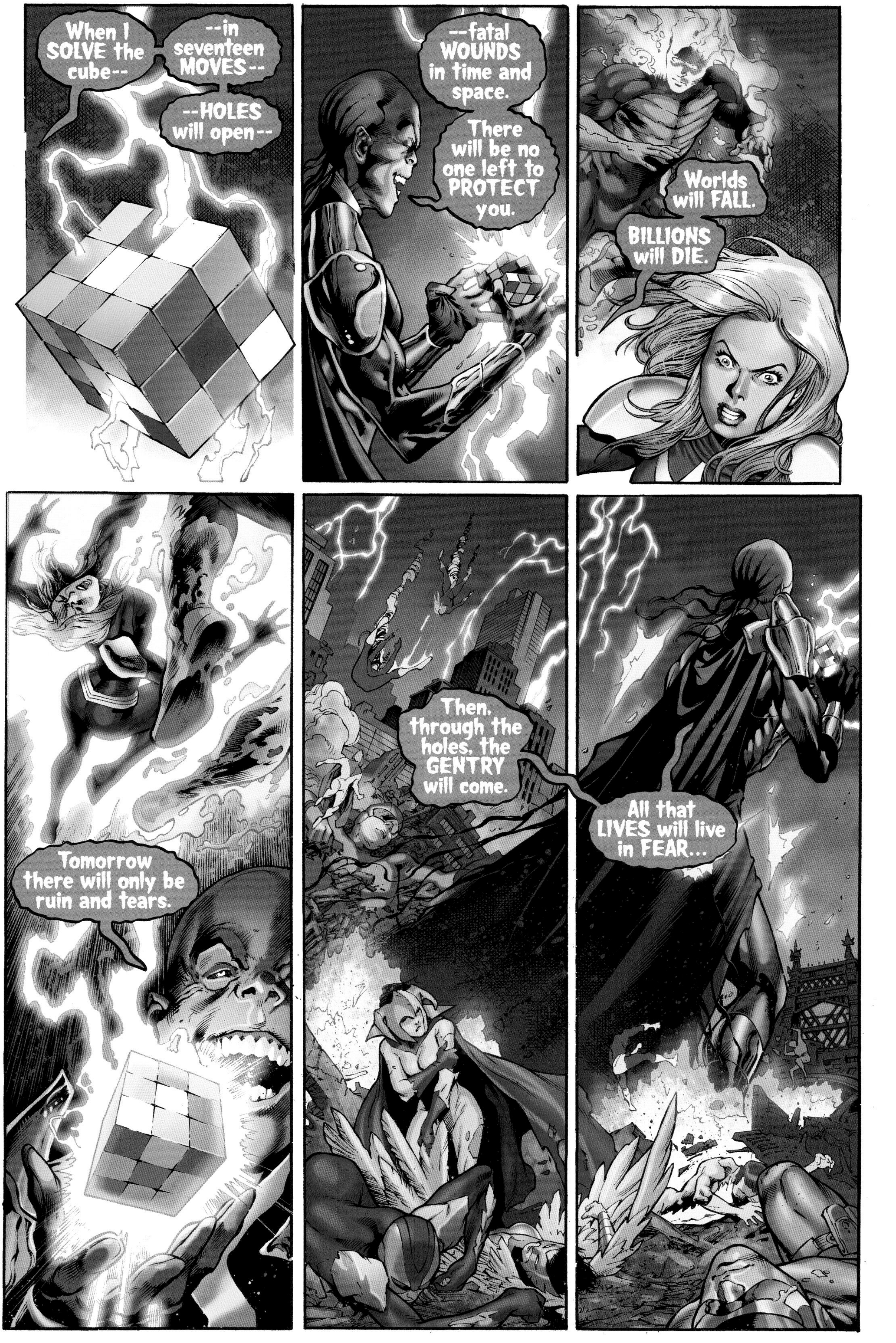
When I SOLVE the cube--
--in seventeen MOVES--
--HOLES will open--
--fatal WOUNDS in time and space.
There will be no one left to PROTECT you.
Worlds will FALL.
BILLIONS will DIE.
Tomorrow there will only be ruin and tears.
Then, through the holes, the GENTRY will come.
All that LIVES will live in FEAR...

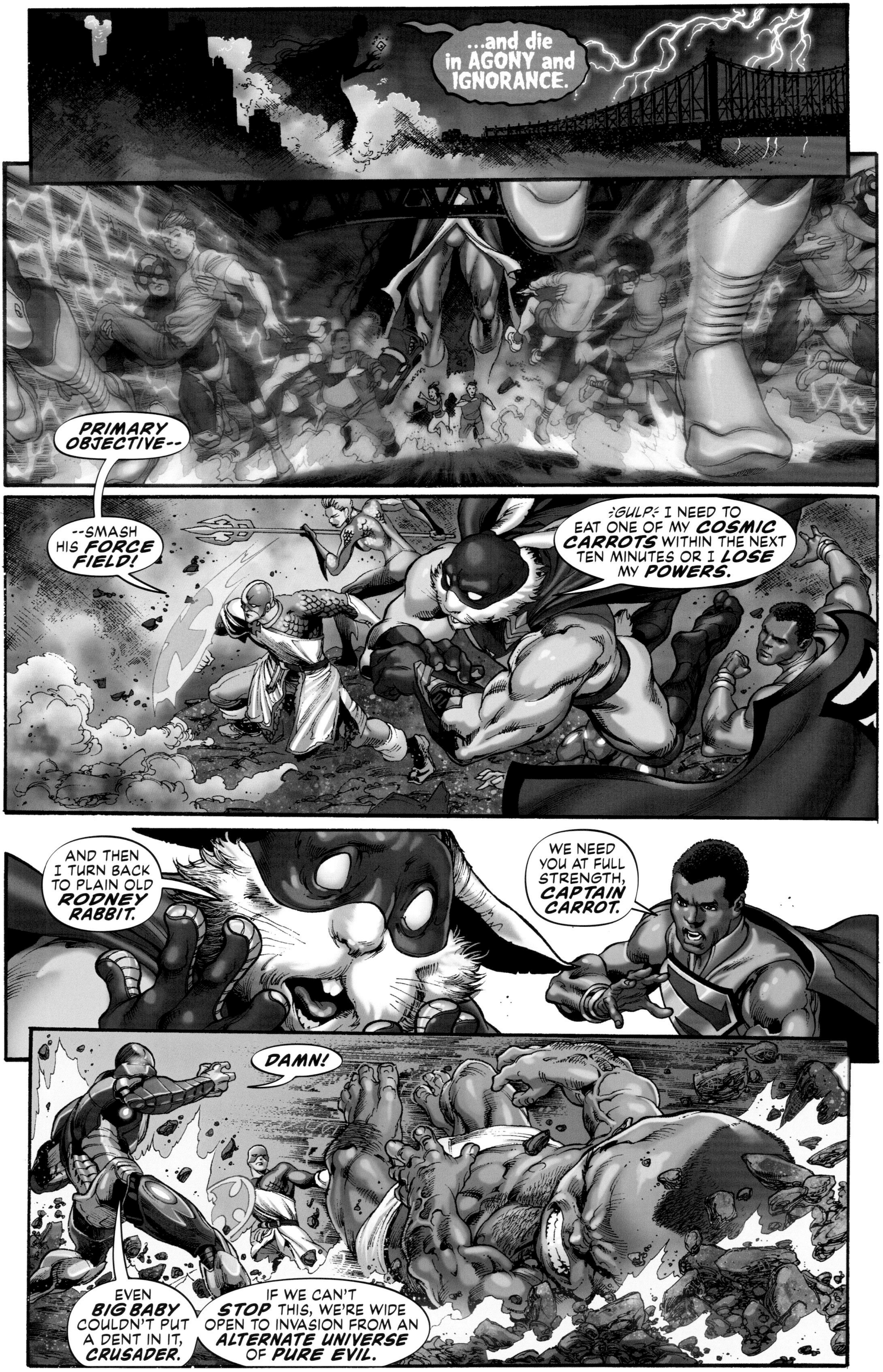

...and die in AGONY and IGNORANCE.
PRIMARY OBJECTIVE--
--SMASH HIS FORCE FIELD!
ᵹGULPᵹ I NEED TO EAT ONE OF MY COSMIC CARROTS WITHIN THE NEXT TEN MINUTES OR I LOSE MY POWERS.
AND THEN I TURN BACK TO PLAIN OLD RODNEY RABBIT.
WE NEED YOU AT FULL STRENGTH, CAPTAIN CARROT.
DAMN!
EVEN BIG BABY COULDN'T PUT A DENT IN IT, CRUSADER.
IF WE CAN'T STOP THIS, WE'RE WIDE OPEN TO INVASION FROM AN ALTERNATE UNIVERSE OF PURE EVIL.

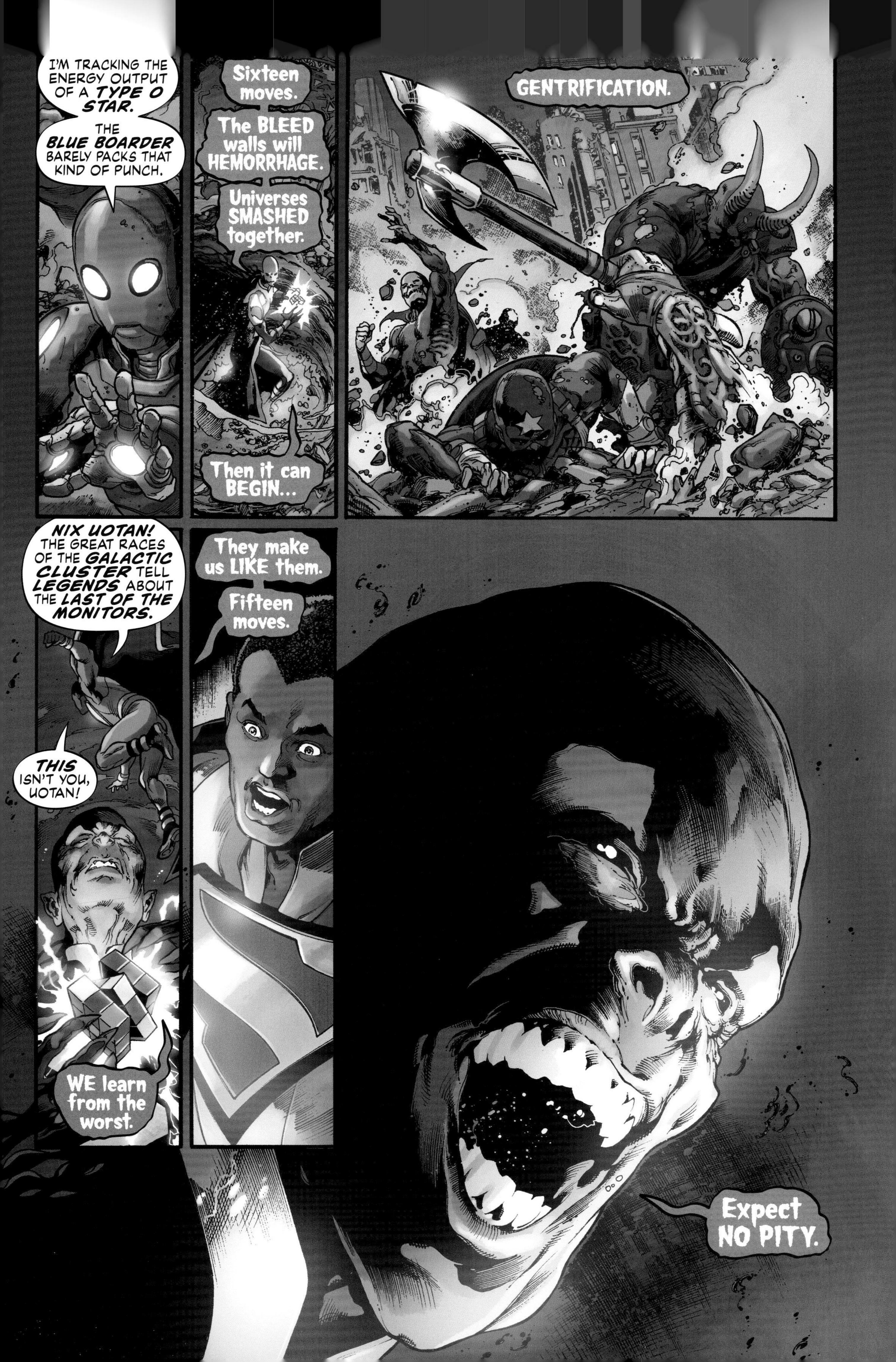
I'M TRACKING THE ENERGY OUTPUT OF A TYPE O STAR.
THE BLUE BOARDER BARELY PACKS THAT KIND OF PUNCH.
Sixteen moves.
The BLEED walls will HEMORRHAGE.
Universes SMASHED together.
Then it can BEGIN...
GENTRIFICATION.
NIX UOTAN! THE GREAT RACES OF THE GALACTIC CLUSTER TELL LEGENDS ABOUT THE LAST OF THE MONITORS.
THIS ISN'T YOU, UOTAN!
WE learn from the worst.
They make us LIKE them.
Fifteen moves.
Expect NO PITY.

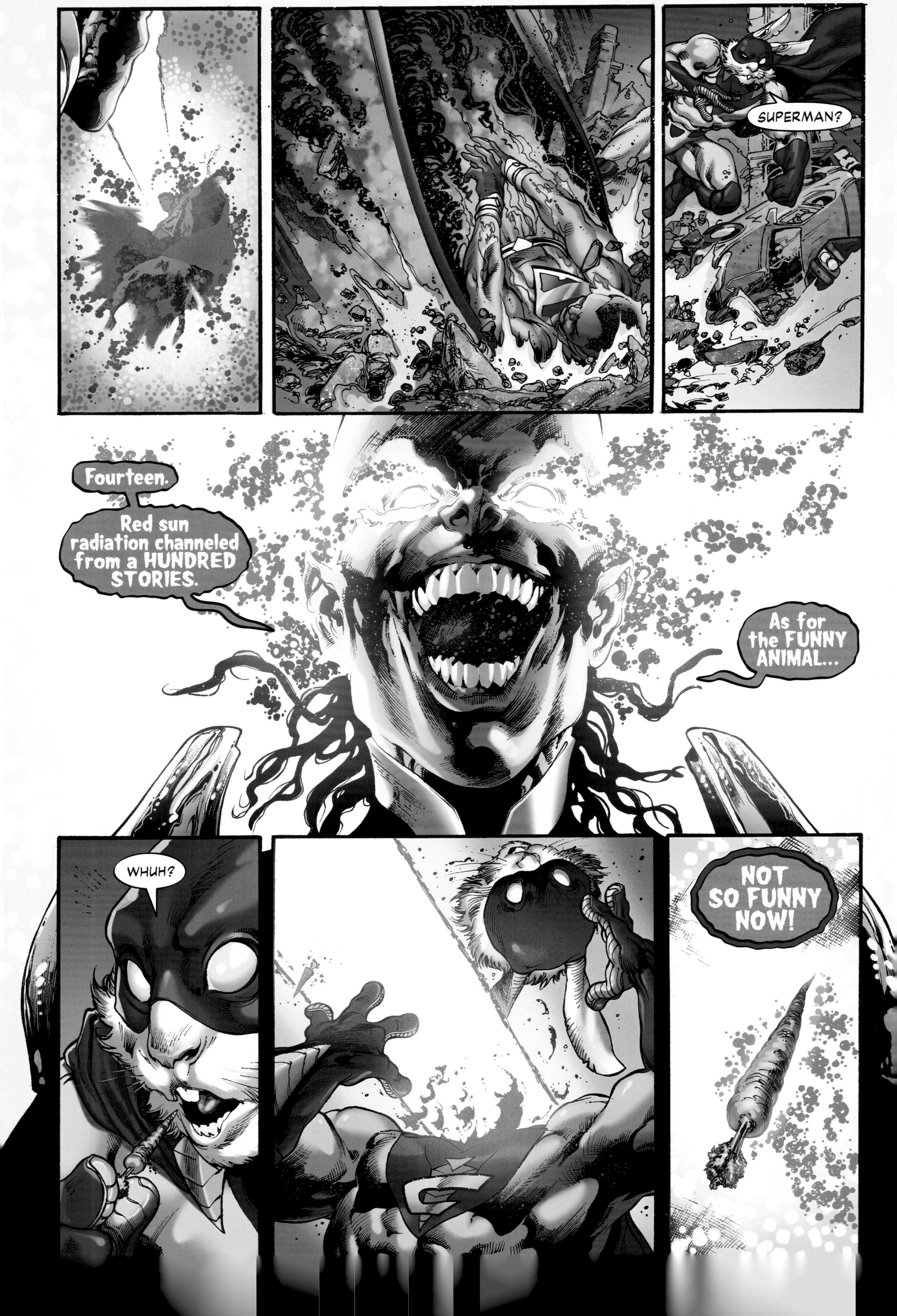
SUPERMAN?
Fourteen.
Red sun radiation channeled from a HUNDRED STORIES.
As for the FUNNY ANIMAL...
WHUH?
NOT SO FUNNY NOW!

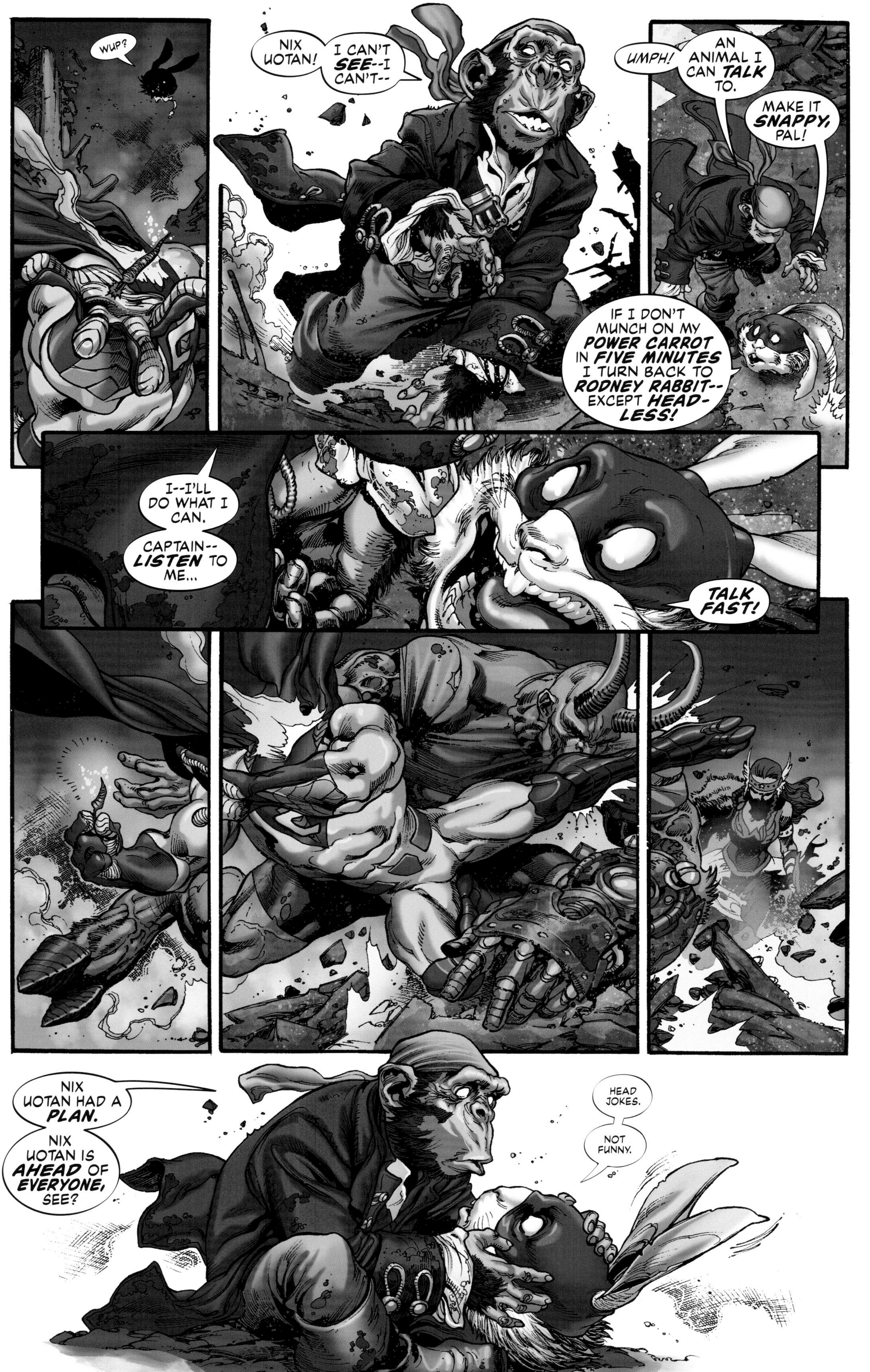
WUP?
NIX UOTAN!
I CAN'T SEE--I CAN'T--
UMPH!
AN ANIMAL I CAN TALK TO.
MAKE IT SNAPPY, PAL!
IF I DON'T MUNCH ON MY POWER CARROT IN FIVE MINUTES I TURN BACK TO RODNEY RABBIT--EXCEPT HEAD-LESS!
I--I'LL DO WHAT I CAN.
CAPTAIN--LISTEN TO ME...
TALK FAST!
NIX UOTAN HAD A PLAN.
NIX UOTAN IS AHEAD OF EVERYONE, SEE?
HEAD JOKES.
NOT FUNNY.

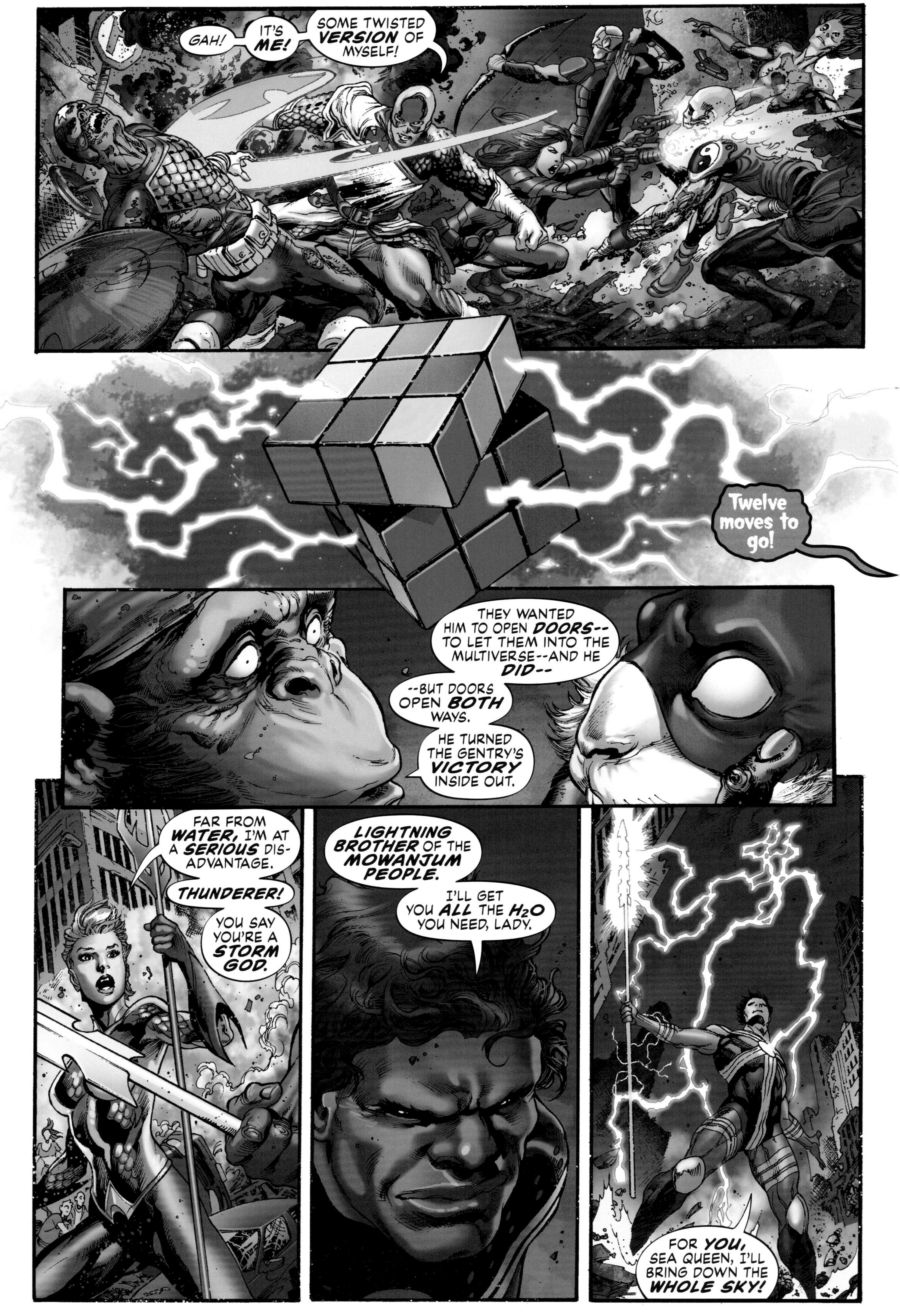

GAH!
IT'S ME!
SOME TWISTED VERSION OF MYSELF!
Twelve moves to go!
THEY WANTED HIM TO OPEN DOORS-- TO LET THEM INTO THE MULTIVERSE--AND HE DID--
--BUT DOORS OPEN BOTH WAYS.
HE TURNED THE GENTRY'S VICTORY INSIDE OUT.
FAR FROM WATER, I'M AT A SERIOUS DIS-ADVANTAGE.
THUNDERER!
YOU SAY YOU'RE A STORM GOD.
LIGHTNING BROTHER OF THE MOWANJUM PEOPLE.
I'LL GET YOU ALL THE H2O YOU NEED, LADY.
FOR YOU, SEA QUEEN, I'LL BRING DOWN THE WHOLE SKY!

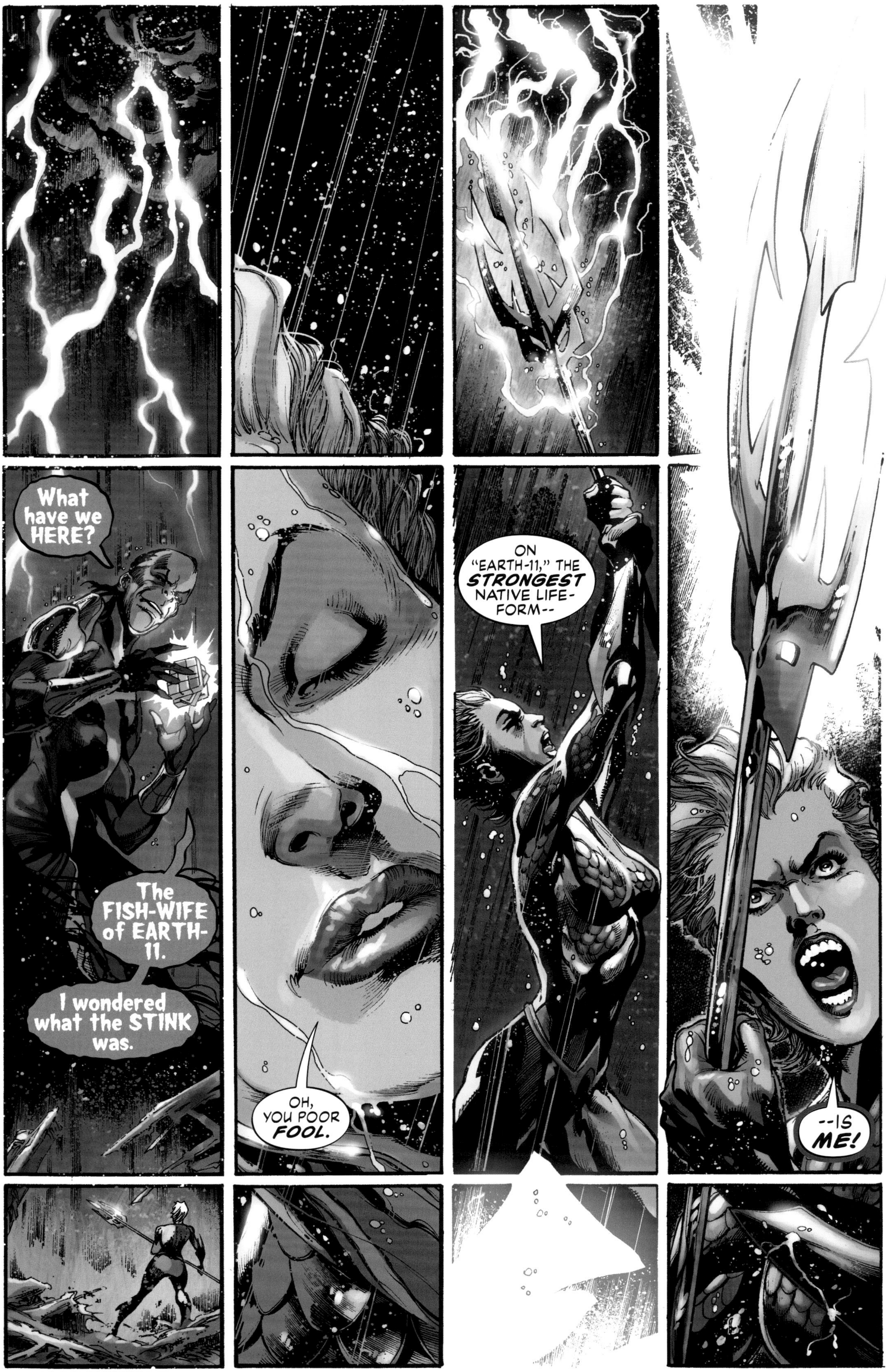
What have we HERE?
The FISH-WIFE of EARTH-11.
I wondered what the STINK was.
OH, YOU POOR FOOL.
ON "EARTH-11," THE STRONGEST NATIVE LIFE-FORM--
--IS ME!

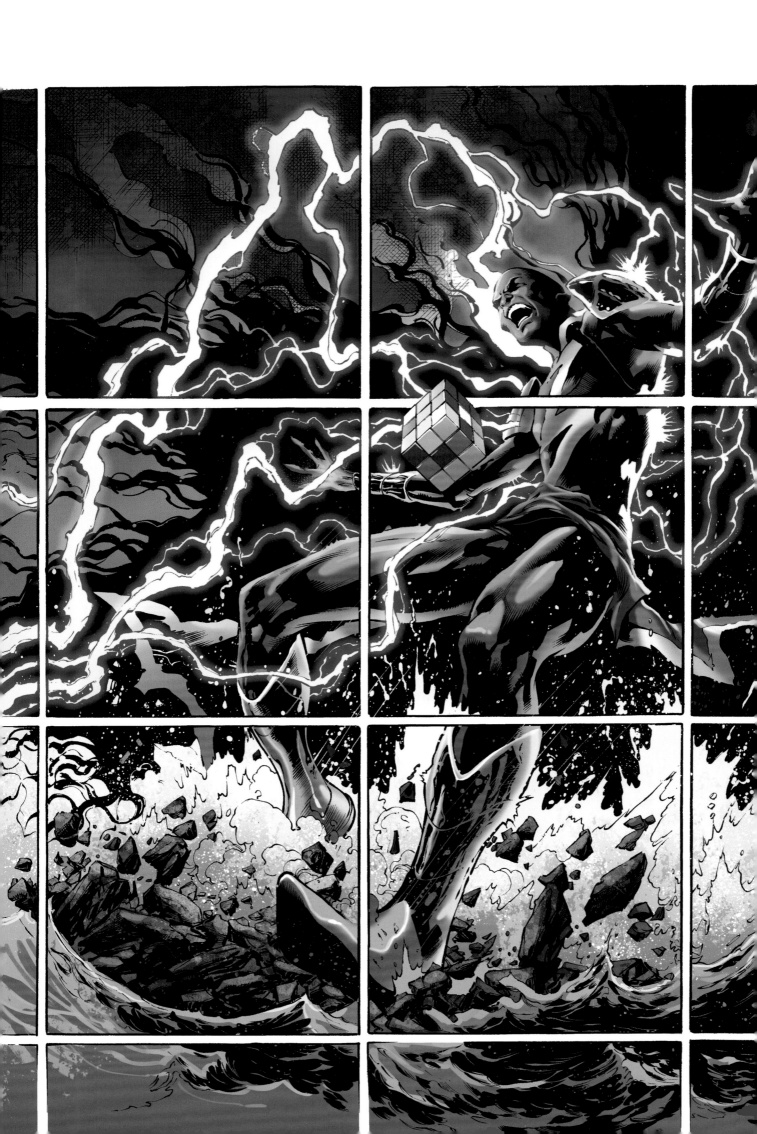

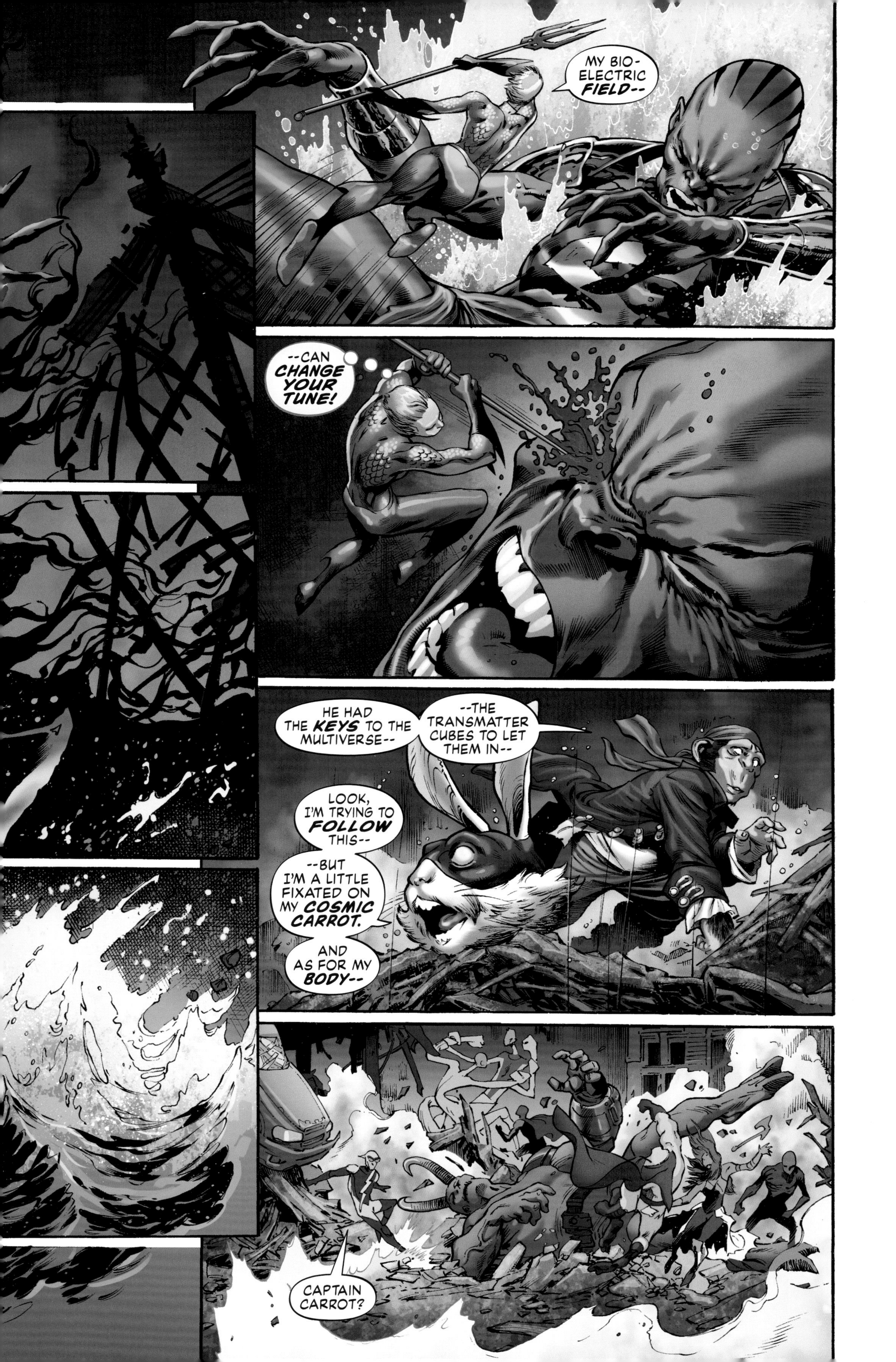
MY BIO-ELECTRIC FIELD--
--CAN CHANGE YOUR TUNE!
HE HAD THE KEYS TO THE MULTIVERSE--
--THE TRANSMATTER CUBES TO LET THEM IN--
LOOK, I'M TRYING TO FOLLOW THIS--
--BUT I'M A LITTLE FIXATED ON MY COSMIC CARROT.
AND AS FOR MY BODY--
CAPTAIN CARROT?

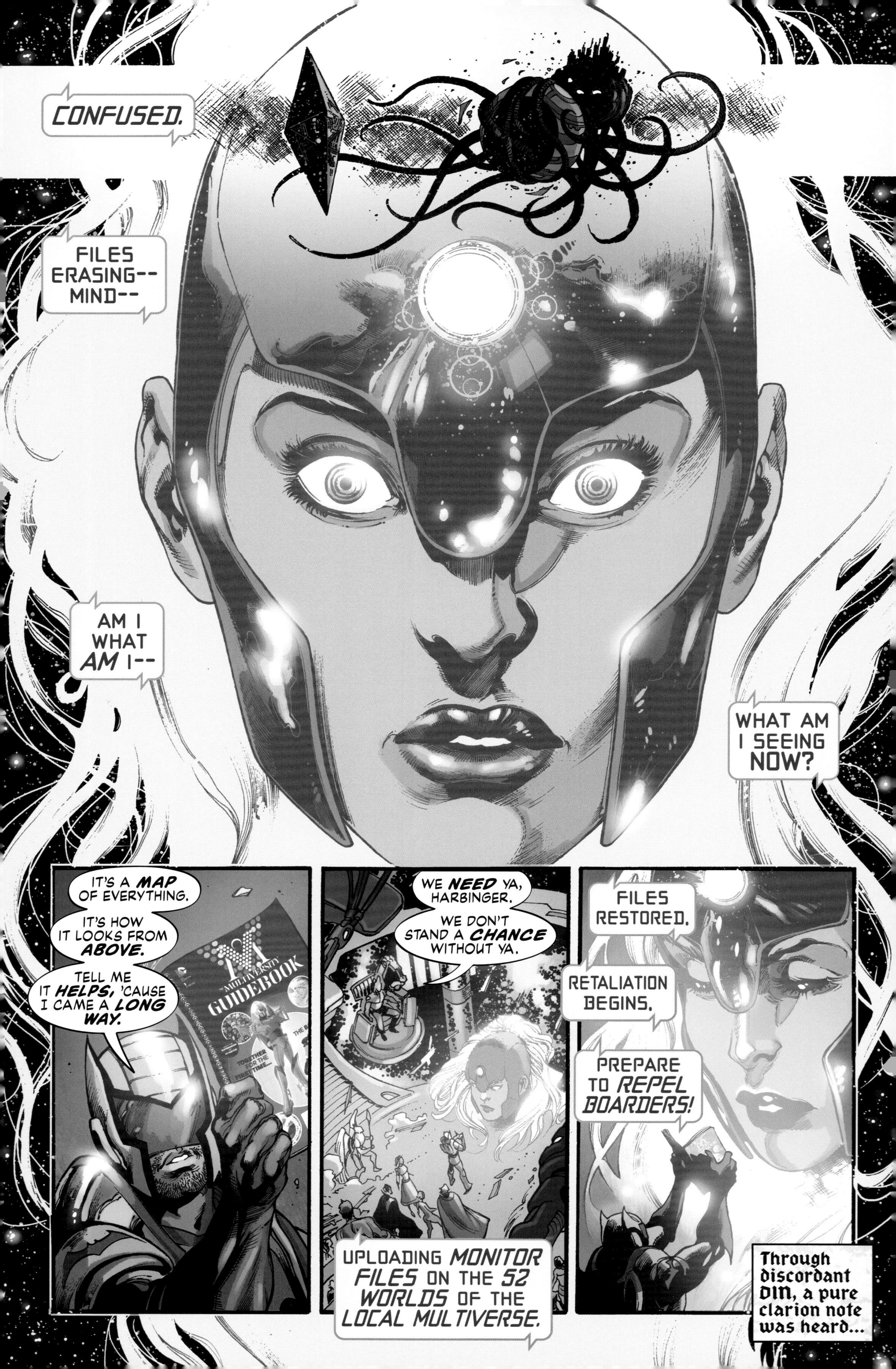
CONFUSED.
FILES ERASING-- MIND--
AM I WHAT AM I--
WHAT AM I SEEING NOW?
IT'S A MAP OF EVERYTHING.
IT'S HOW IT LOOKS FROM ABOVE.
TELL ME IT HELPS, 'CAUSE I CAME A LONG WAY.
MULTIVERSITY GUIDEBOOK
TOGETHER FOR THE FIRST TIME...
WE NEED YA, HARBINGER.
WE DON'T STAND A CHANCE WITHOUT YA.
UPLOADING MONITOR FILES ON THE 52 WORLDS OF THE LOCAL MULTIVERSE.
FILES RESTORED.
RETALIATION BEGINS.
PREPARE TO REPEL BOARDERS!
Through discordant DIN, a pure clarion note was heard...

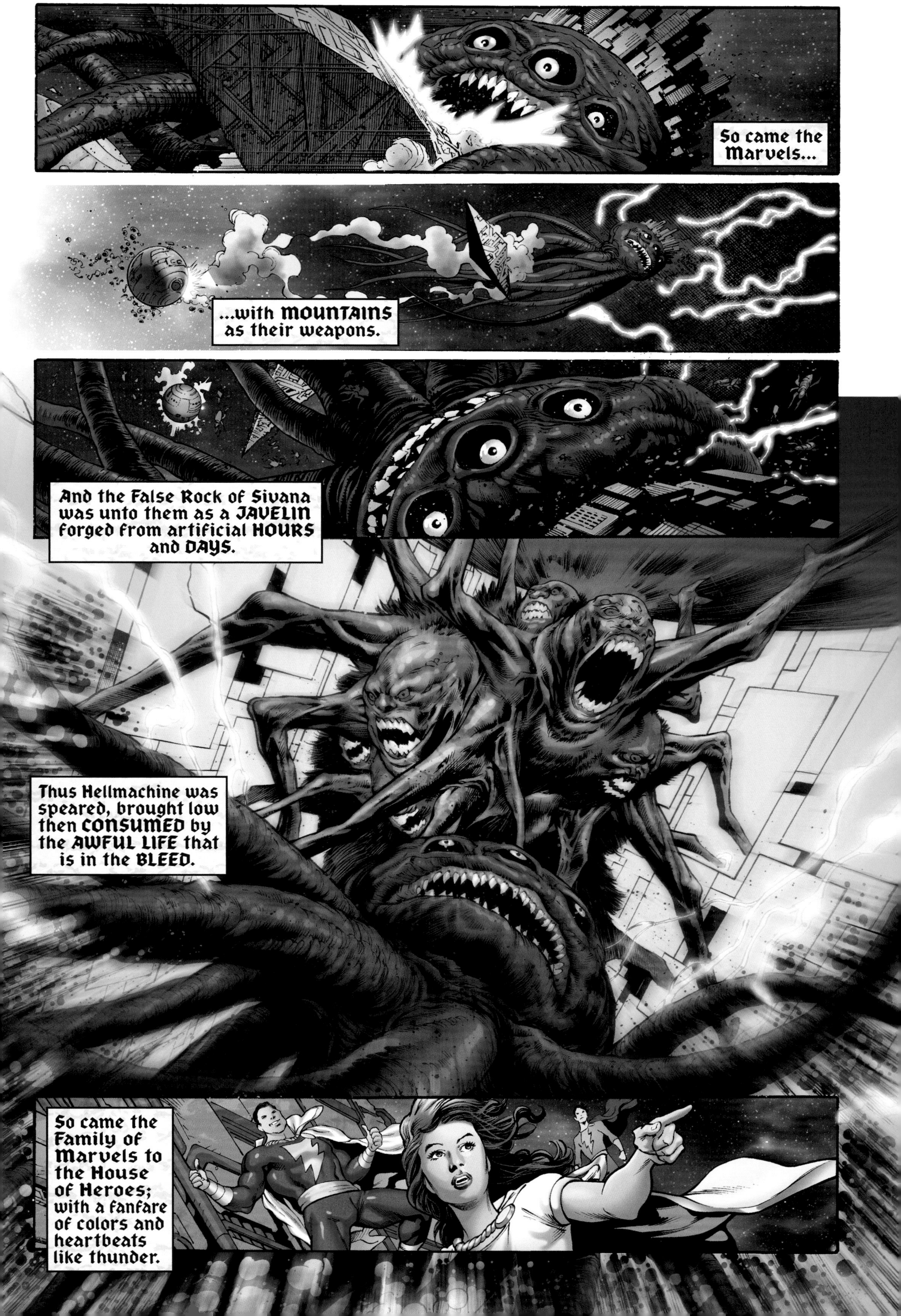
So came the Marvels...
...with MOUNTAINS as their weapons.
And the False Rock of Sivana was unto them as a JAVELIN forged from artificial HOURS and DAYS.
Thus Hellmachine was speared, brought low then CONSUMED by the AWFUL LIFE that is in the BLEED.
So came the Family of Marvels to the House of Heroes; with a fanfare of colors and heartbeats like thunder.

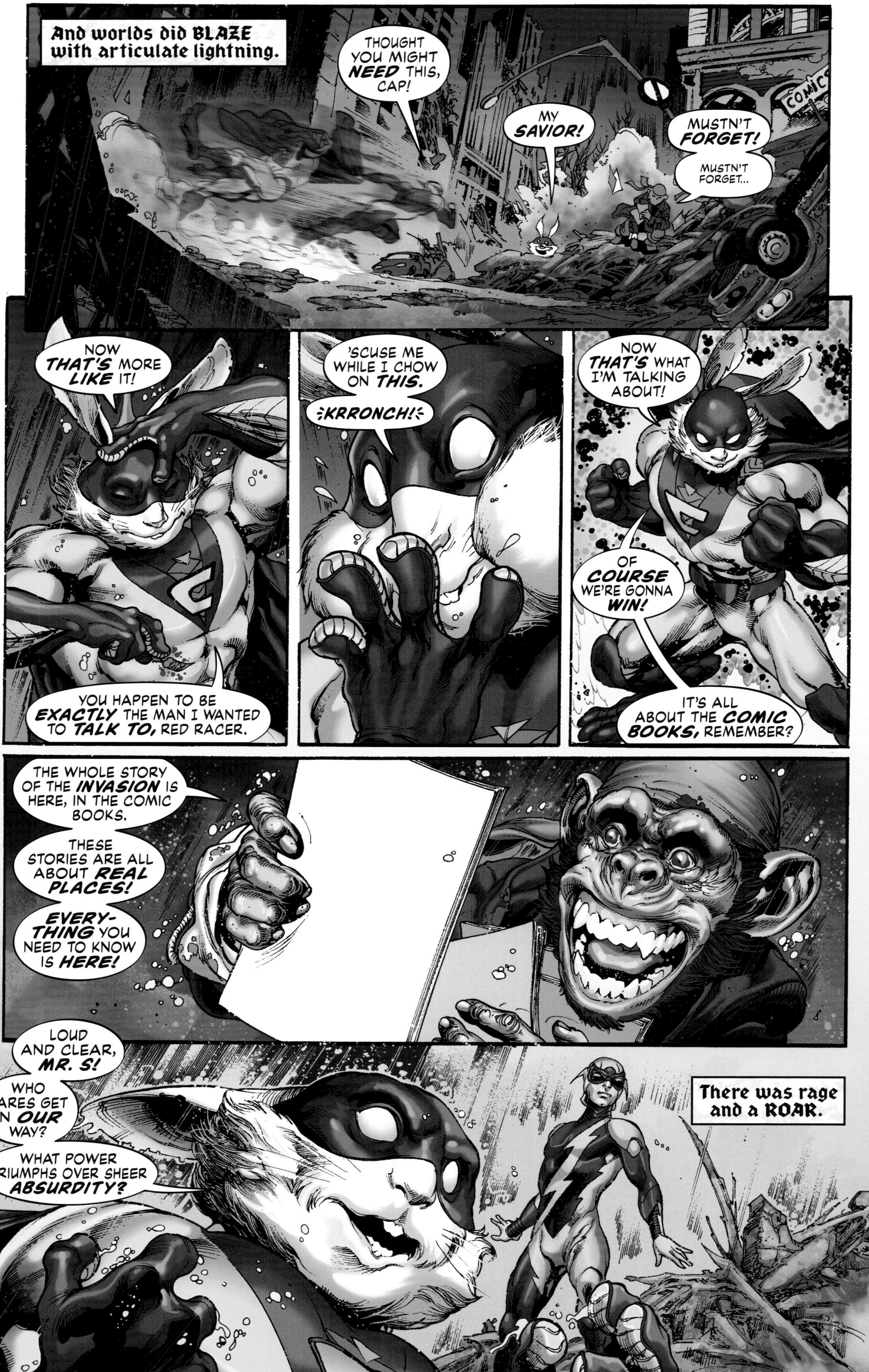
And worlds did BLAZE with articulate lightning.
THOUGHT YOU MIGHT NEED THIS, CAP!
MY SAVIOR!
MUSTN'T FORGET!
MUSTN'T FORGET...
COMICS
NOW THAT'S MORE LIKE IT!
YOU HAPPEN TO BE EXACTLY THE MAN I WANTED TO TALK TO, RED RACER.
'SCUSE ME WHILE I CHOW ON THIS.
KRRONCH!
NOW THAT'S WHAT I'M TALKING ABOUT!
OF COURSE WE'RE GONNA WIN!
IT'S ALL ABOUT THE COMIC BOOKS, REMEMBER?
THE WHOLE STORY OF THE INVASION IS HERE, IN THE COMIC BOOKS.
THESE STORIES ARE ALL ABOUT REAL PLACES!
EVERY-THING YOU NEED TO KNOW IS HERE!
LOUD AND CLEAR, MR. S!
WHO DARES GET IN OUR WAY?
WHAT POWER TRIUMPHS OVER SHEER ABSURDITY?
There was rage and a ROAR.

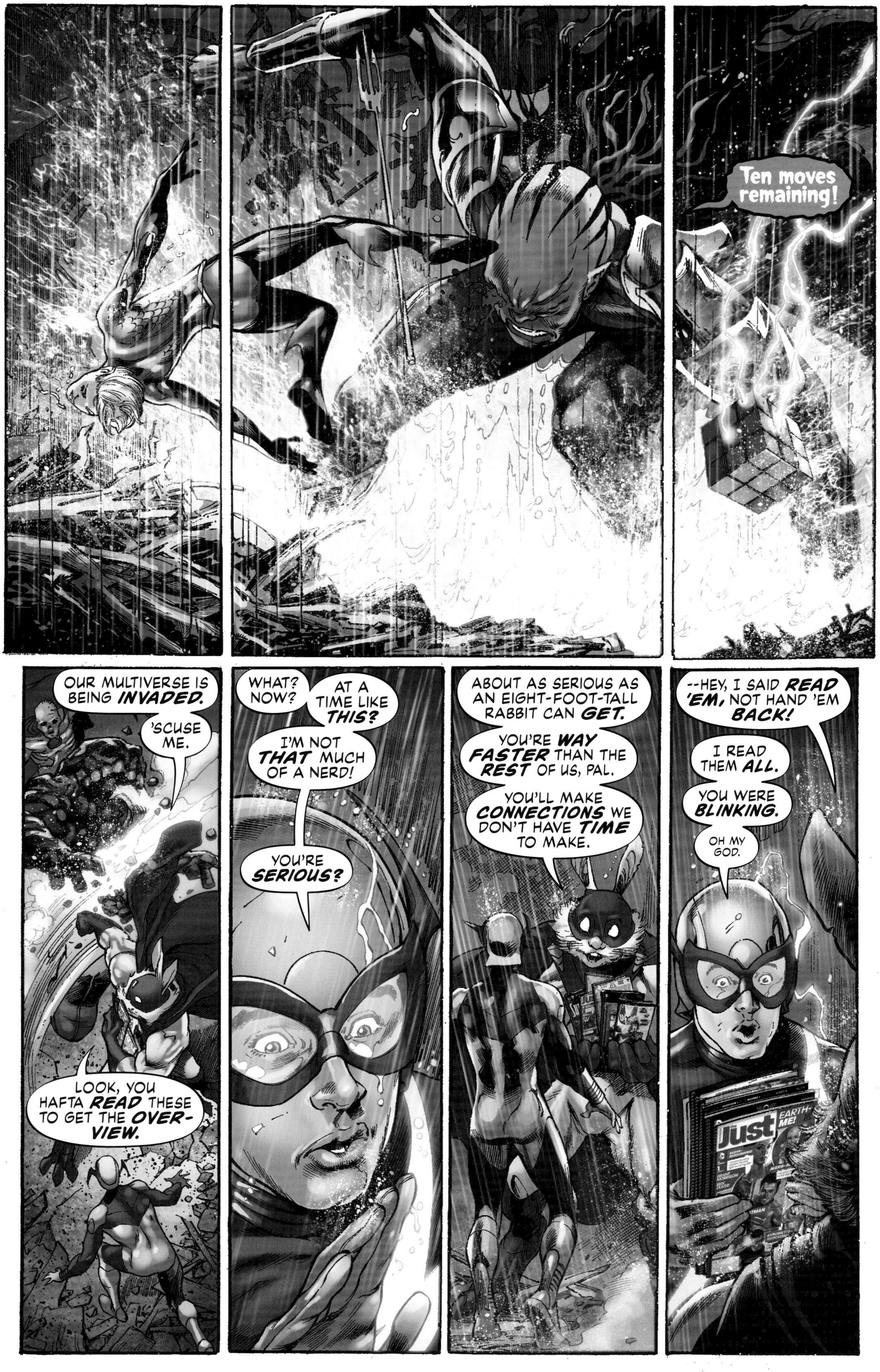
Ten moves remaining!
OUR MULTIVERSE IS BEING INVADED.
'SCUSE ME.
LOOK, YOU HAFTA READ THESE TO GET THE OVER-VIEW.
WHAT? NOW?
AT A TIME LIKE THIS?
I'M NOT THAT MUCH OF A NERD!
YOU'RE SERIOUS?
ABOUT AS SERIOUS AS AN EIGHT-FOOT-TALL RABBIT CAN GET.
YOU'RE WAY FASTER THAN THE REST OF US, PAL.
YOU'LL MAKE CONNECTIONS WE DON'T HAVE TIME TO MAKE.
--HEY, I SAID READ 'EM, NOT HAND 'EM BACK!
I READ THEM ALL.
YOU WERE BLINKING.
OH MY GOD.

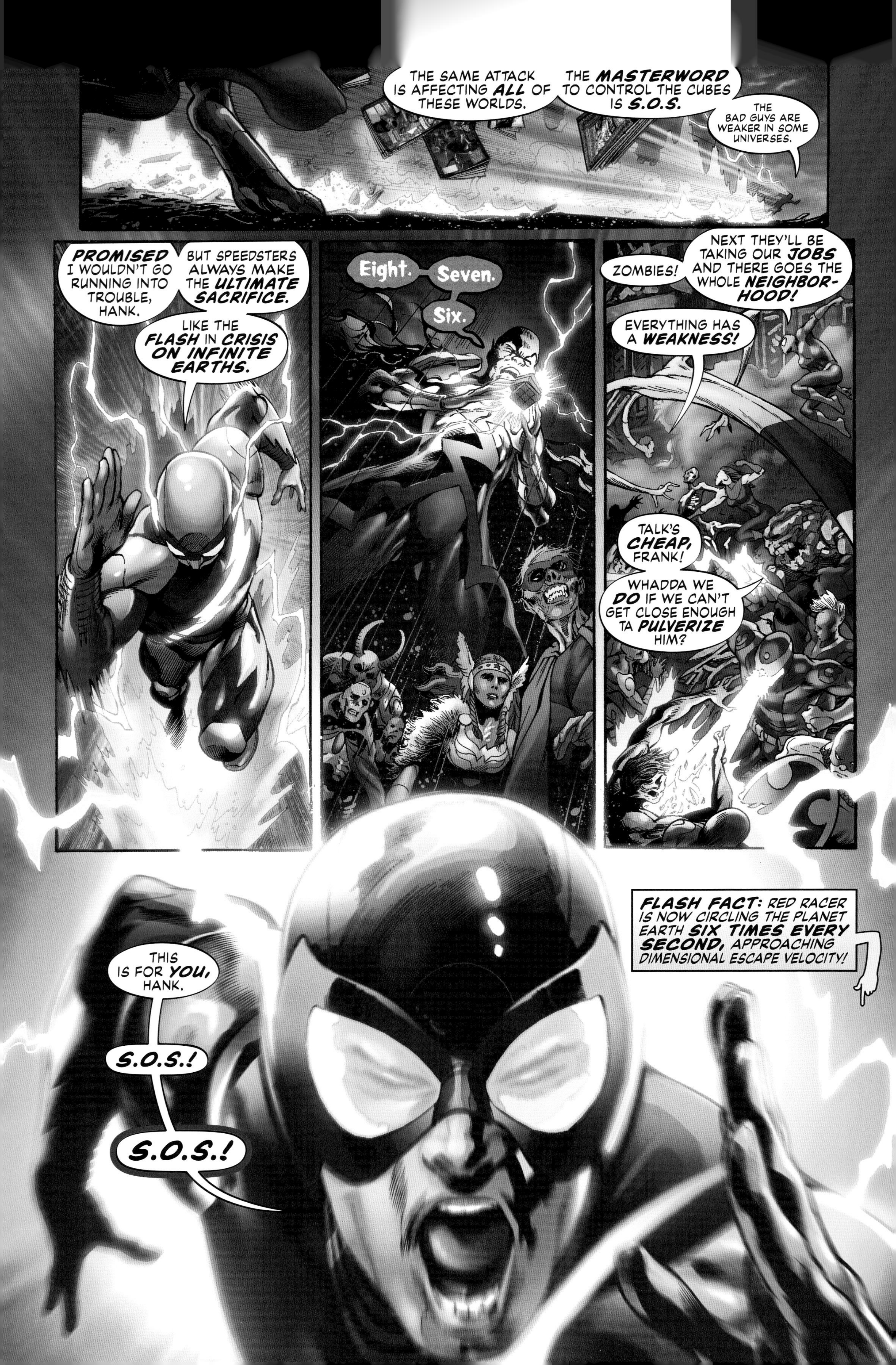

THE SAME ATTACK IS AFFECTING ALL OF THESE WORLDS.
THE MASTERWORD TO CONTROL THE CUBES IS S.O.S.
THE BAD GUYS ARE WEAKER IN SOME UNIVERSES.
PROMISED I WOULDN'T GO RUNNING INTO TROUBLE, HANK.
BUT SPEEDSTERS ALWAYS MAKE THE ULTIMATE SACRIFICE.
LIKE THE FLASH IN CRISIS ON INFINITE EARTHS.
Eight.
Seven.
Six.
ZOMBIES!
NEXT THEY'LL BE TAKING OUR JOBS AND THERE GOES THE WHOLE NEIGHBOR-HOOD!
EVERYTHING HAS A WEAKNESS!
TALK'S CHEAP, FRANK!
WHADDA WE DO IF WE CAN'T GET CLOSE ENOUGH TA PULVERIZE HIM?
FLASH FACT: RED RACER IS NOW CIRCLING THE PLANET EARTH SIX TIMES EVERY SECOND, APPROACHING DIMENSIONAL ESCAPE VELOCITY!
THIS IS FOR YOU, HANK.
S.O.S.!
S.O.S.!

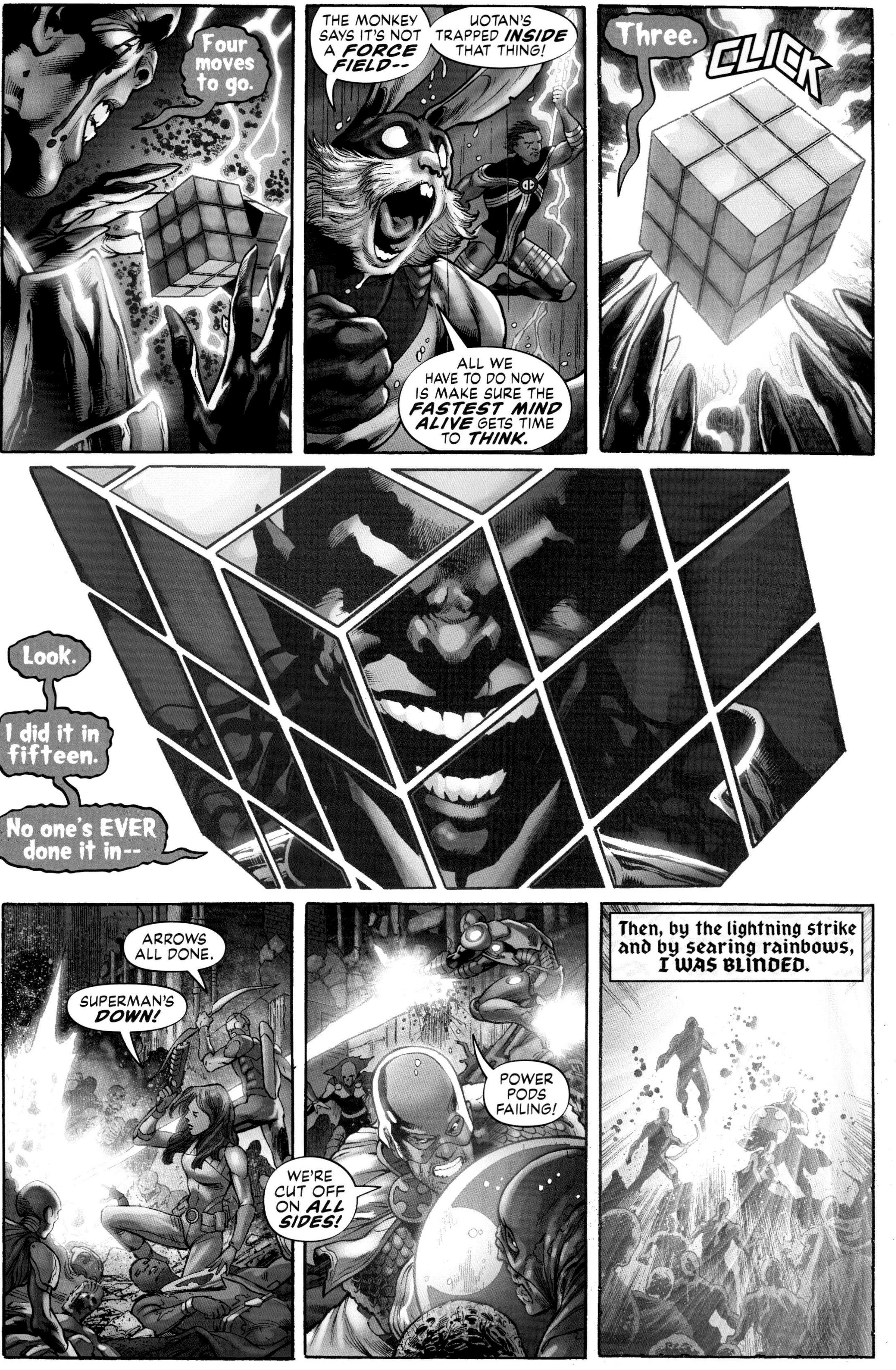
Four moves to go.
THE MONKEY SAYS IT'S NOT A FORCE FIELD--
UOTAN'S TRAPPED INSIDE THAT THING!
ALL WE HAVE TO DO NOW IS MAKE SURE THE FASTEST MIND ALIVE GETS TIME TO THINK.
Three.
CLICK
Look.
I did it in fifteen.
No one's EVER done it in--
ARROWS ALL DONE.
SUPERMAN'S DOWN!
POWER PODS FAILING!
WE'RE CUT OFF ON ALL SIDES!
Then, by the lightning strike and by searing rainbows, I WAS BLINDED.

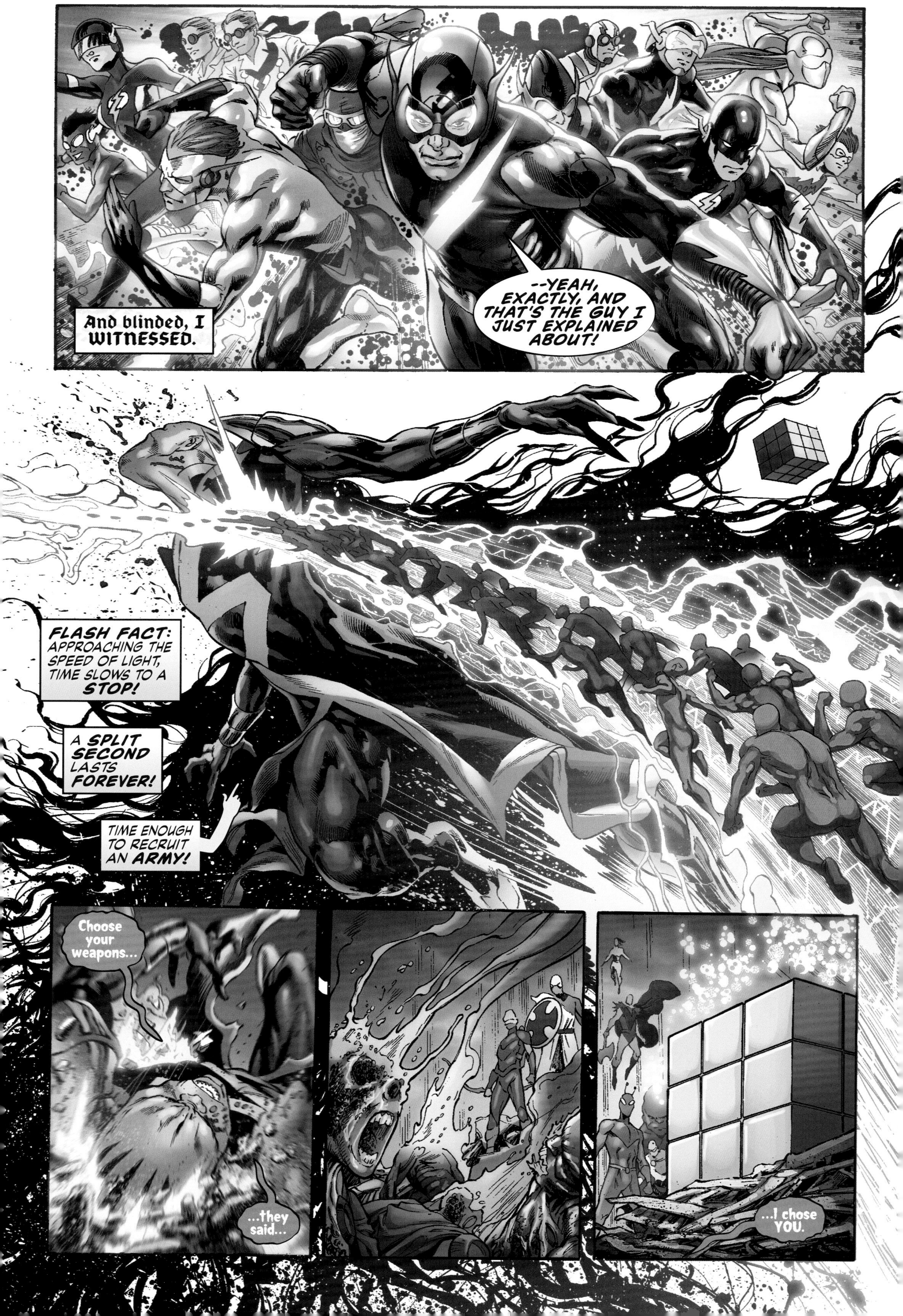
And blinded, I WITNESSED.
--YEAH, EXACTLY, AND THAT'S THE GUY I JUST EXPLAINED ABOUT!
FLASH FACT: APPROACHING THE SPEED OF LIGHT, TIME SLOWS TO A STOP!
A SPLIT SECOND LASTS FOREVER!
TIME ENOUGH TO RECRUIT AN ARMY!
Choose your weapons...
...they said...
...I chose YOU.

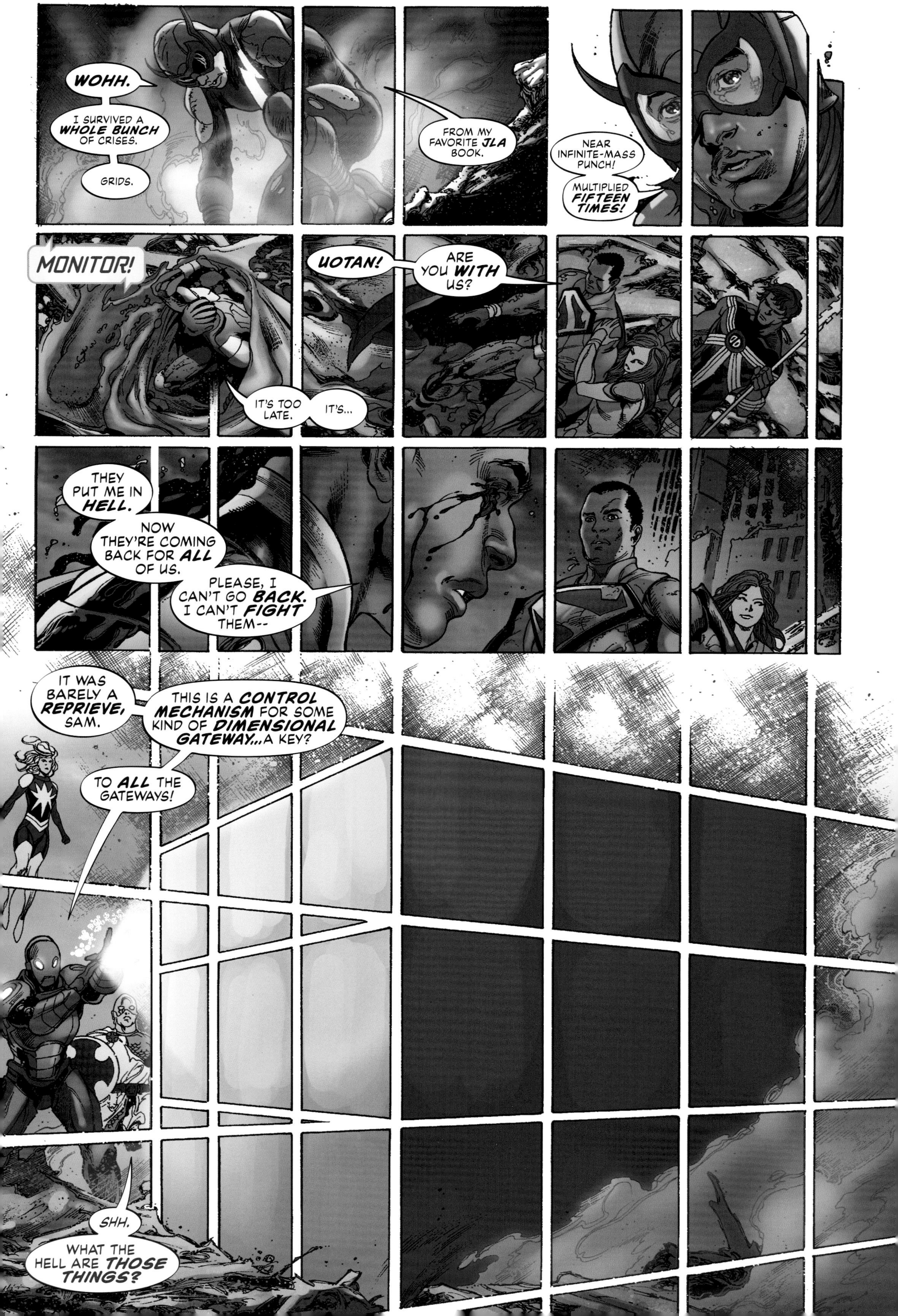
WOHH.
I SURVIVED A WHOLE BUNCH OF CRISES.
GRIDS.
FROM MY FAVORITE JLA BOOK.
NEAR INFINITE-MASS PUNCH!
MULTIPLIED FIFTEEN TIMES!
MONITOR!
UOTAN!
ARE YOU WITH US?
IT'S TOO LATE.
IT'S...
THEY PUT ME IN HELL.
NOW THEY'RE COMING BACK FOR ALL OF US.
PLEASE, I CAN'T GO BACK. I CAN'T FIGHT THEM--
IT WAS BARELY A REPRIEVE, SAM.
THIS IS A CONTROL MECHANISM FOR SOME KIND OF DIMENSIONAL GATEWAY...A KEY?
TO ALL THE GATEWAYS!
SHH.
WHAT THE HELL ARE THOSE THINGS?

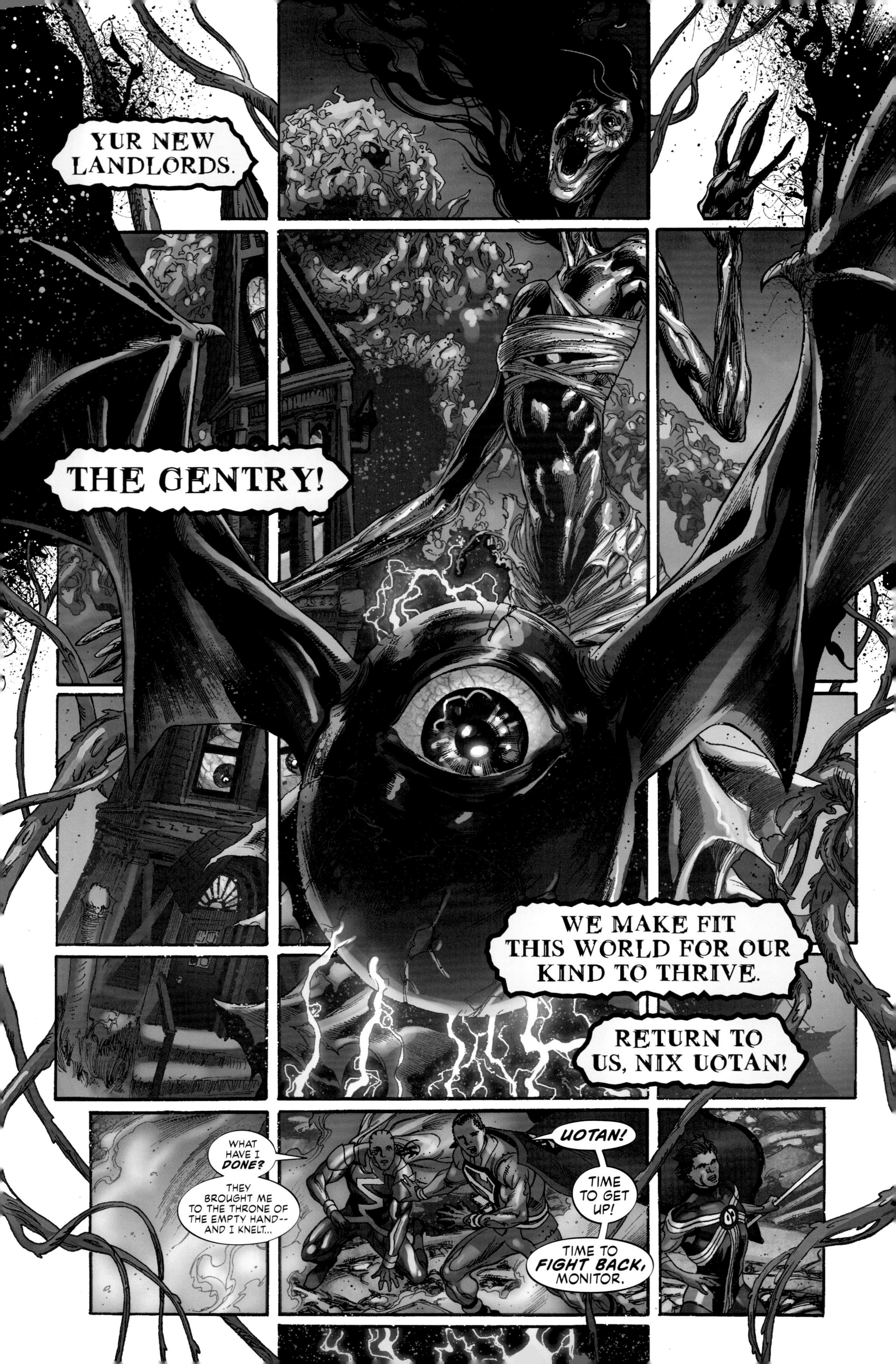
YUR NEW LANDLORDS.
THE GENTRY!
WE MAKE FIT THIS WORLD FOR OUR KIND TO THRIVE.
RETURN TO US, NIX UOTAN!
WHAT HAVE I DONE?
THEY BROUGHT ME TO THE THRONE OF THE EMPTY HAND-- AND I KNELT...
UOTAN!
TIME TO GET UP!
TIME TO FIGHT BACK, MONITOR.

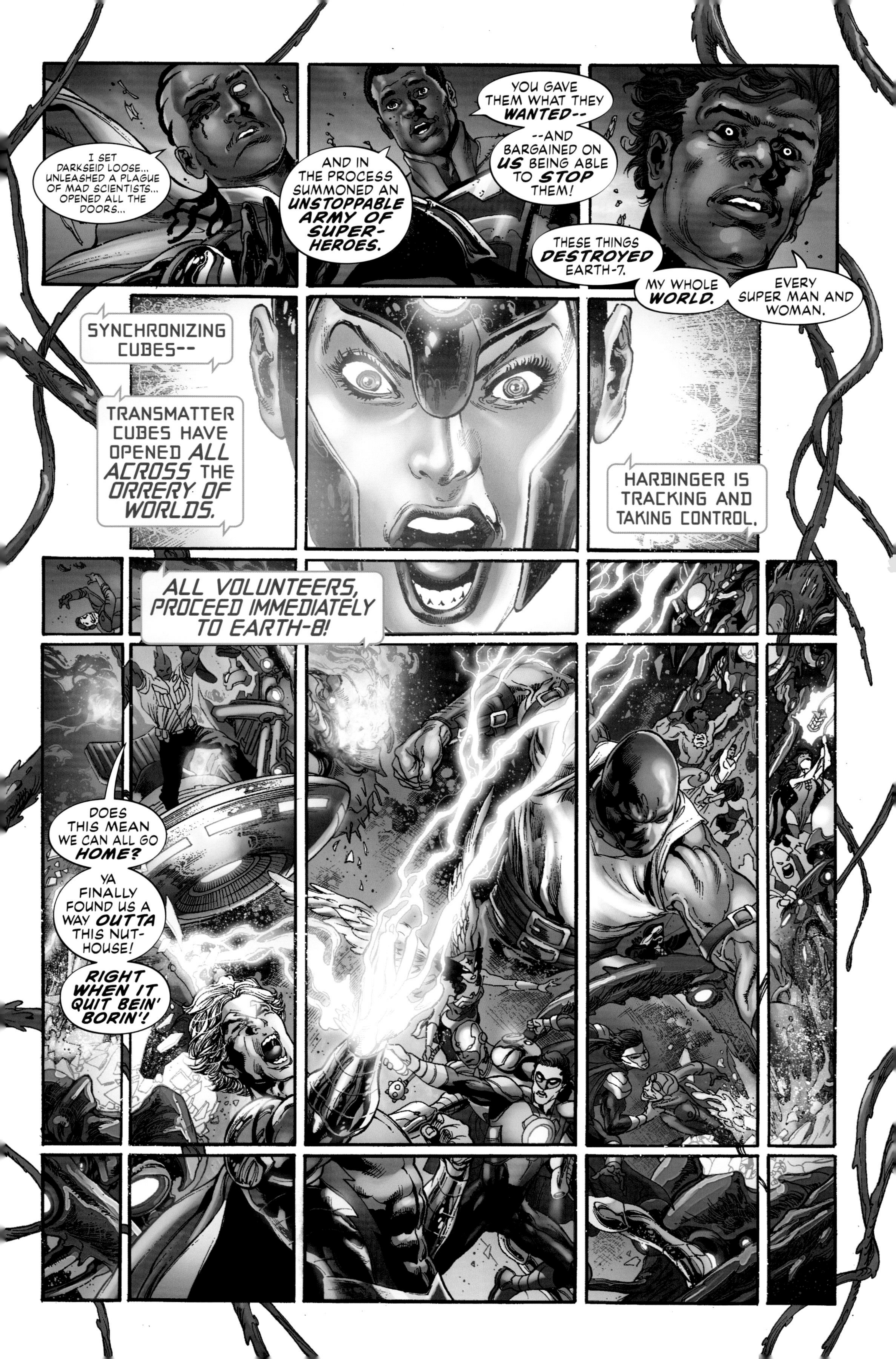

I SET DARKSEID LOOSE... UNLEASHED A PLAGUE OF MAD SCIENTISTS... OPENED ALL THE DOORS...
AND IN THE PROCESS SUMMONED AN UNSTOPPABLE ARMY OF SUPER-HEROES.
YOU GAVE THEM WHAT THEY WANTED--
--AND BARGAINED ON US BEING ABLE TO STOP THEM!
THESE THINGS DESTROYED EARTH-7.
MY WHOLE WORLD.
EVERY SUPER MAN AND WOMAN.
SYNCHRONIZING CUBES--
TRANSMATTER CUBES HAVE OPENED ALL ACROSS THE ORRERY OF WORLDS.
HARBINGER IS TRACKING AND TAKING CONTROL.
ALL VOLUNTEERS, PROCEED IMMEDIATELY TO EARTH-8!
DOES THIS MEAN WE CAN ALL GO HOME?
YA FINALLY FOUND US A WAY OUTTA THIS NUT-HOUSE!
RIGHT WHEN IT QUIT BEIN' BORIN'!

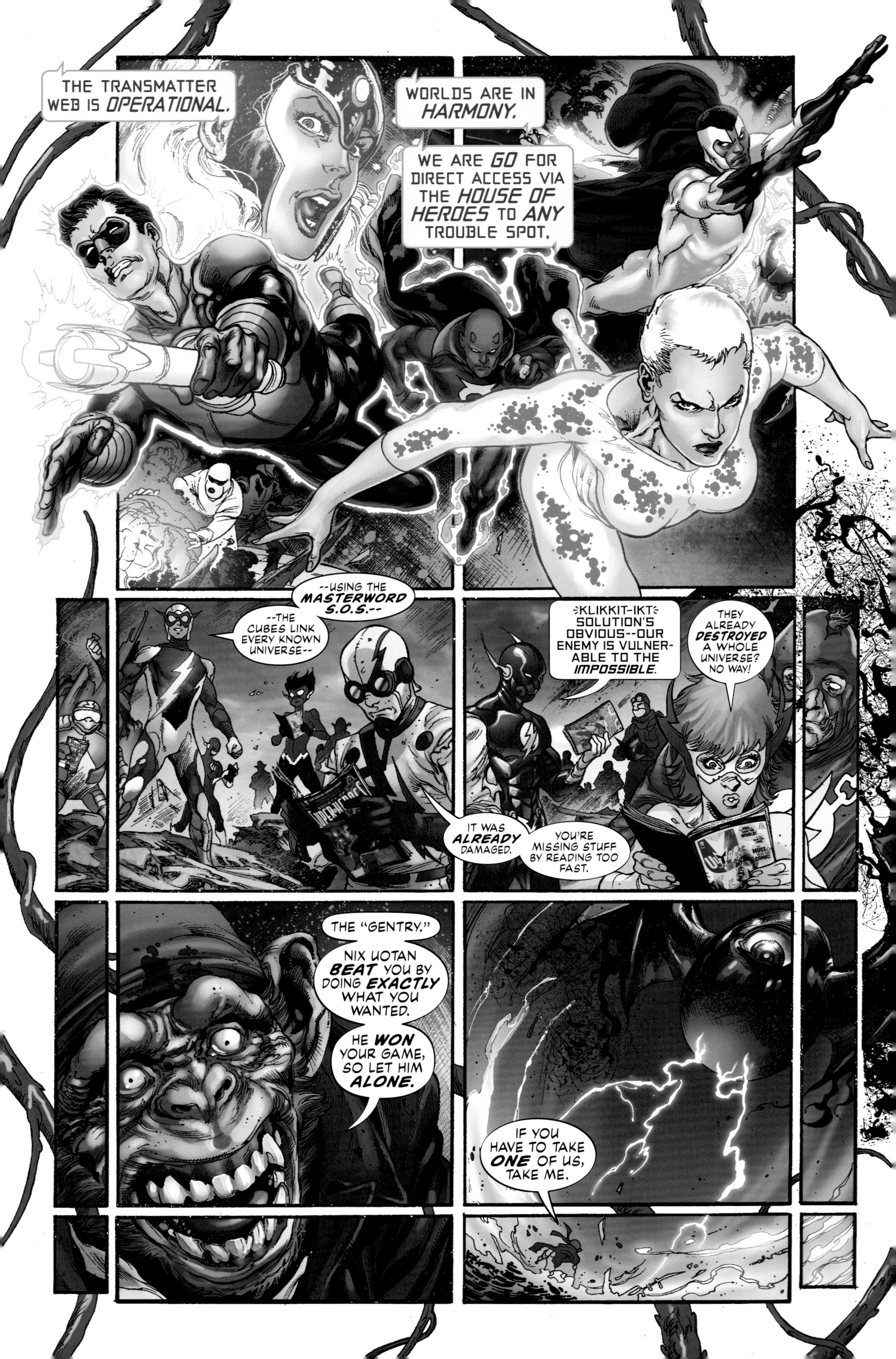
THE TRANSMATTER WEB IS OPERATIONAL.
WORLDS ARE IN HARMONY.
WE ARE GO FOR DIRECT ACCESS VIA THE HOUSE OF HEROES TO ANY TROUBLE SPOT.
--USING THE MASTERWORD S.O.S.--
--THE CUBES LINK EVERY KNOWN UNIVERSE--
IT WAS ALREADY DAMAGED.
YOU'RE MISSING STUFF BY READING TOO FAST.
KLIKKIT-IKT SOLUTION'S OBVIOUS--OUR ENEMY IS VULNERABLE TO THE IMPOSSIBLE.
THEY ALREADY DESTROYED A WHOLE UNIVERSE? NO WAY!
THE "GENTRY."
NIX UOTAN BEAT YOU BY DOING EXACTLY WHAT YOU WANTED.
HE WON YOUR GAME, SO LET HIM ALONE.
IF YOU HAVE TO TAKE ONE OF US, TAKE ME.

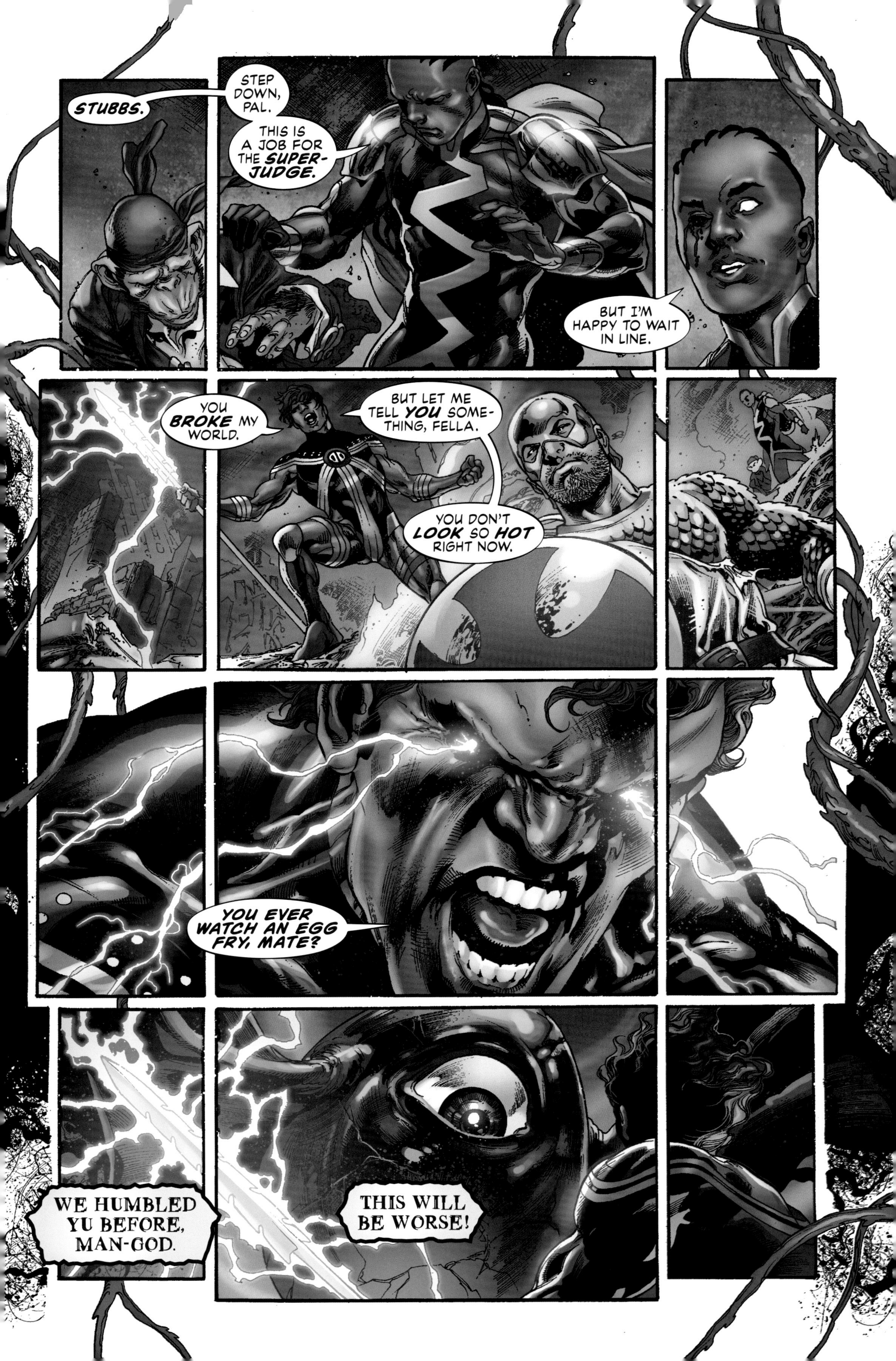
STUBBS.
STEP DOWN, PAL.
THIS IS A JOB FOR THE SUPER-JUDGE.
BUT I'M HAPPY TO WAIT IN LINE.
YOU BROKE MY WORLD.
BUT LET ME TELL YOU SOME-THING, FELLA.
YOU DON'T LOOK SO HOT RIGHT NOW.
YOU EVER WATCH AN EGG FRY, MATE?
WE HUMBLED YU BEFORE, MAN-GOD.
THIS WILL BE WORSE!

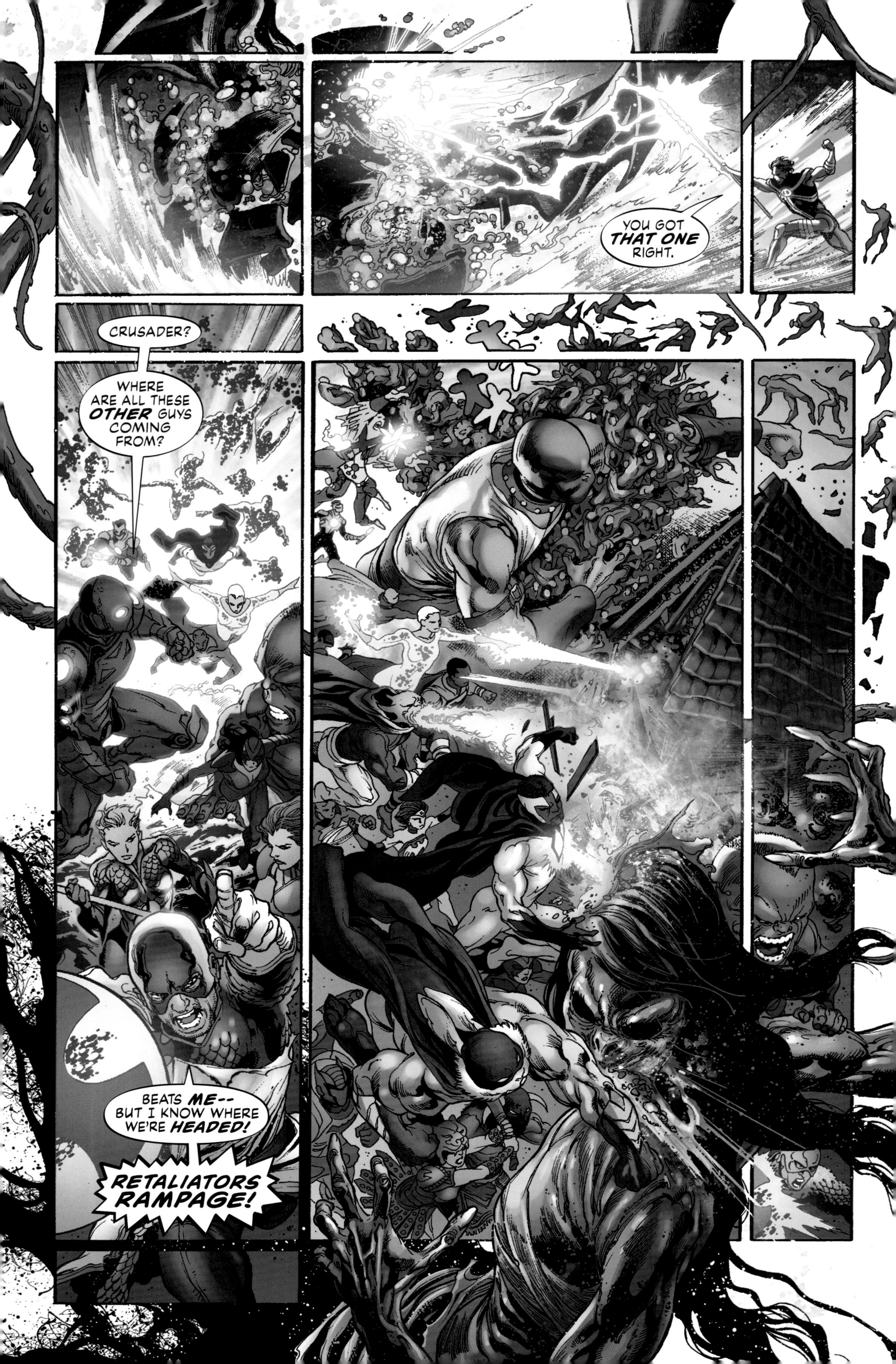
YOU GOT *THAT ONE* RIGHT.
CRUSADER?
WHERE ARE ALL THESE *OTHER* GUYS COMING FROM?
BEATS *ME*-- BUT I KNOW WHERE WE'RE *HEADED!*
RETALIATORS RAMPAGE!

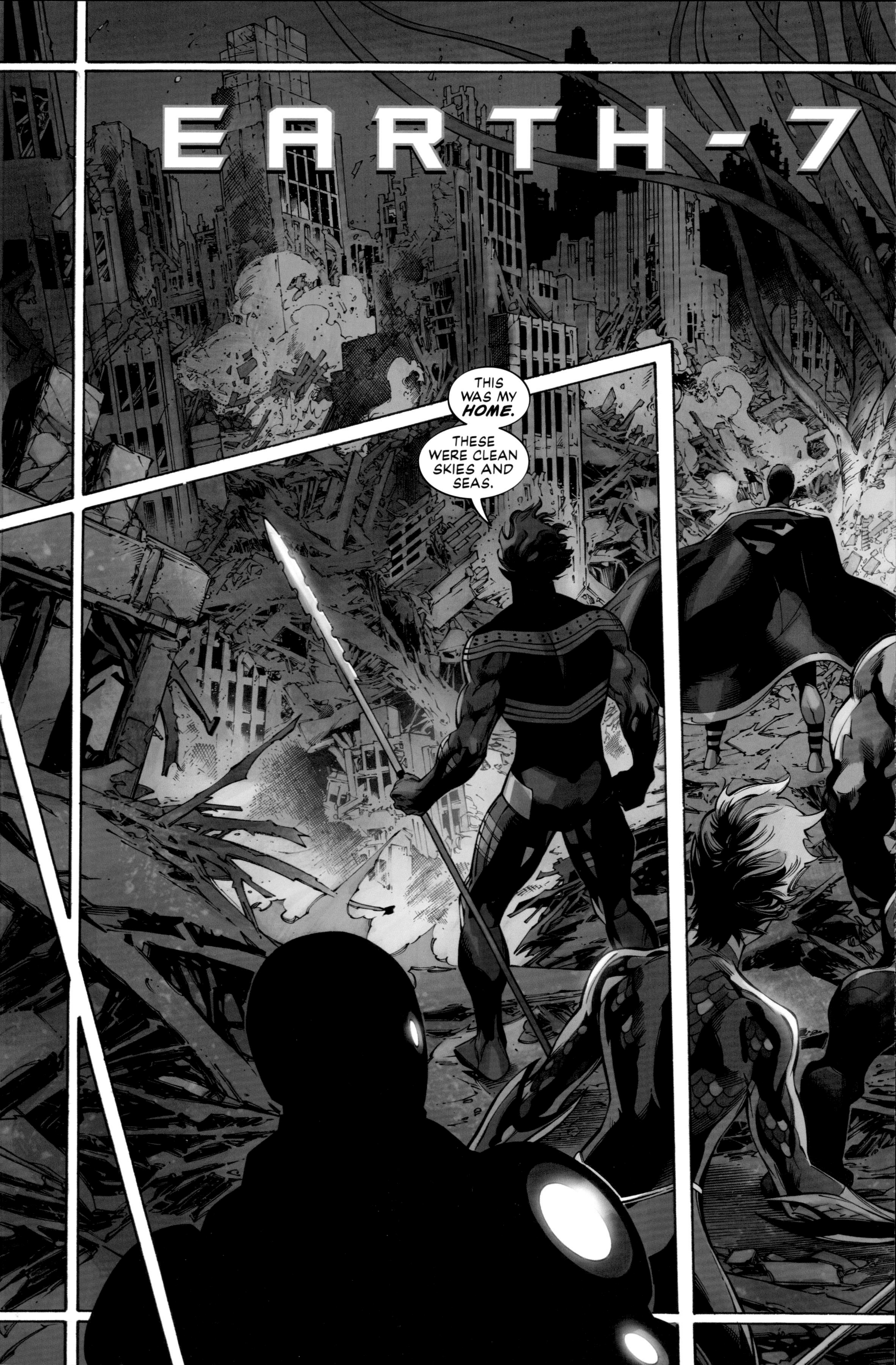
EARTH-7
THIS WAS MY HOME.
THESE WERE CLEAN SKIES AND SEAS.

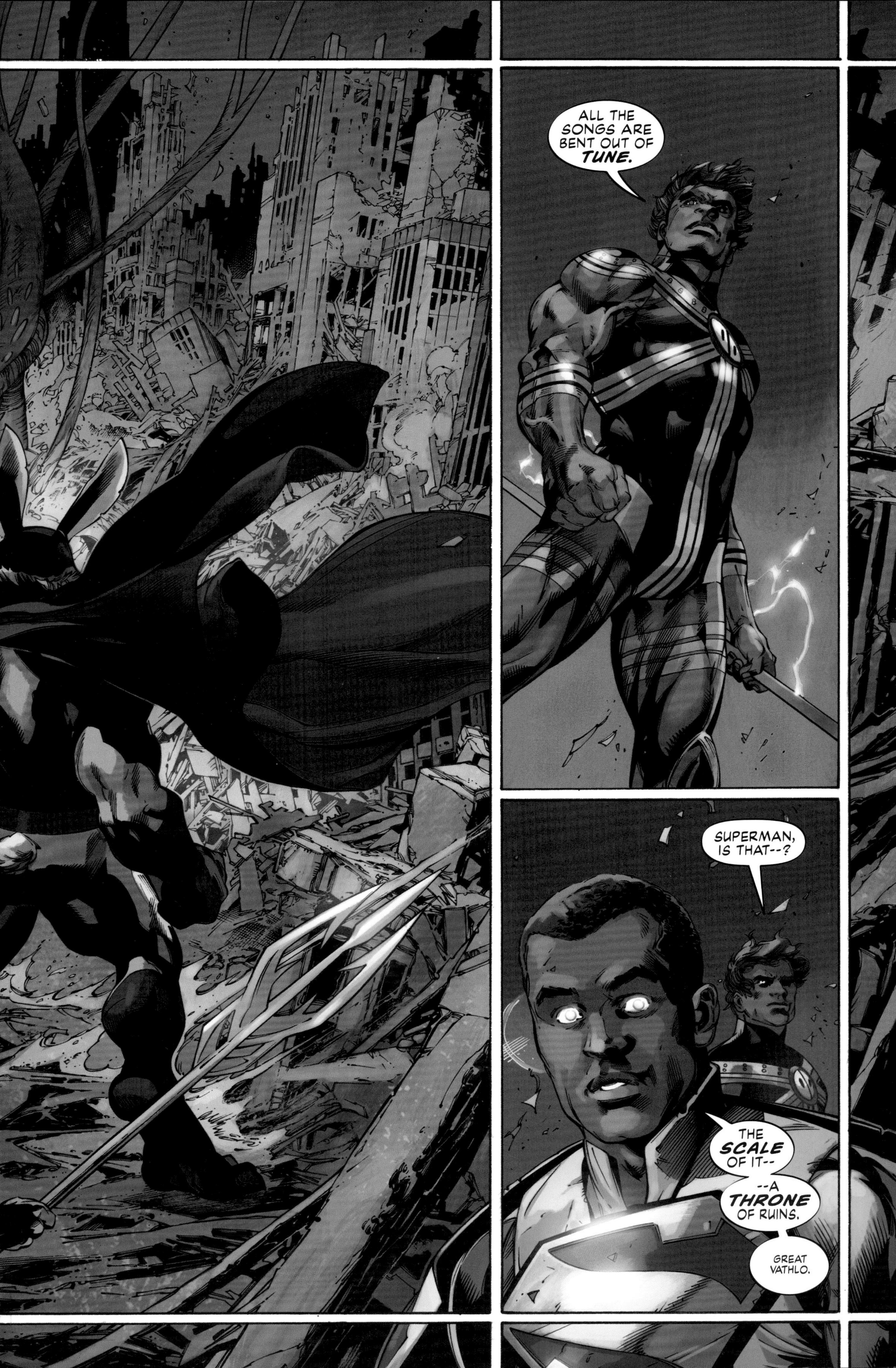
ALL THE SONGS ARE BENT OUT OF *TUNE.*
SUPERMAN, IS THAT--?
THE *SCALE* OF IT--
--A *THRONE* OF RUINS.
GREAT VATHLO.

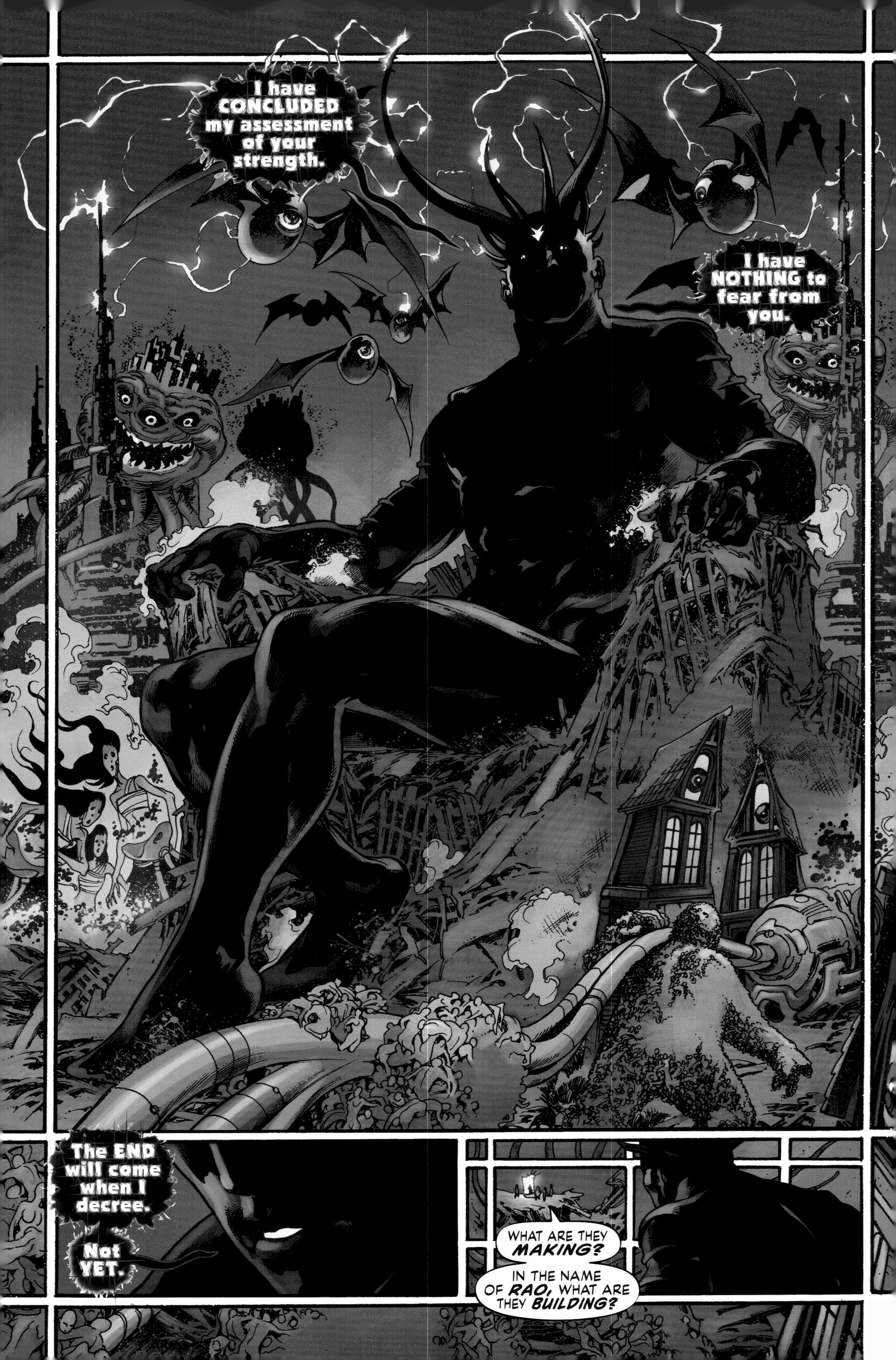
I have CONCLUDED my assessment of your strength.
I have NOTHING to fear from you.
The END will come when I decree.
Not YET.
WHAT ARE THEY MAKING?
IN THE NAME OF RAO, WHAT ARE THEY BUILDING?

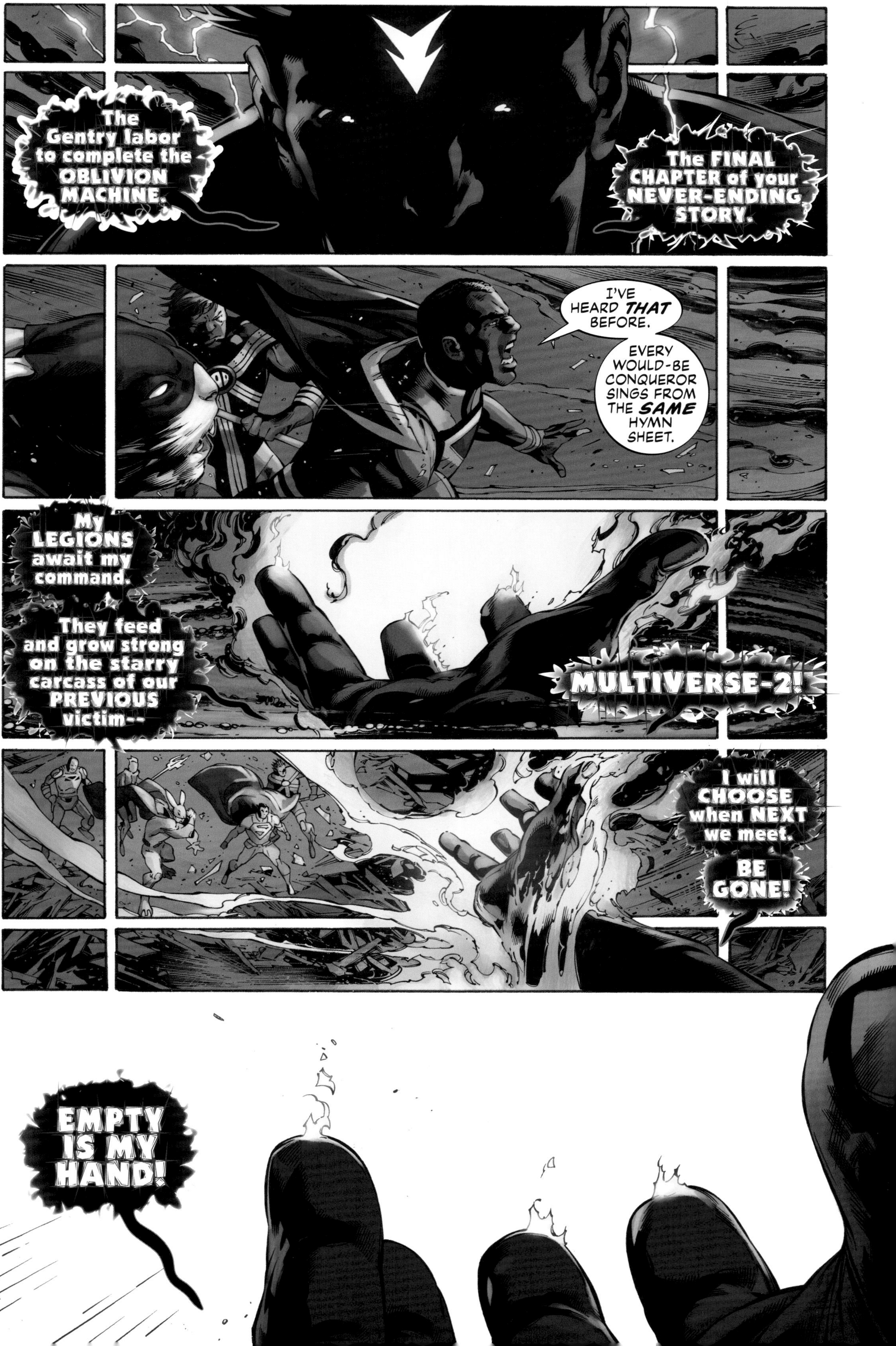
The Gentry labor to complete the OBLIVION MACHINE.
The FINAL CHAPTER of your NEVER-ENDING STORY.
I'VE HEARD THAT BEFORE.
EVERY WOULD-BE CONQUEROR SINGS FROM THE SAME HYMN SHEET.
My LEGIONS await my command.
They feed and grow strong on the starry carcass of our PREVIOUS victim--
MULTIVERSE-2!
I will CHOOSE when NEXT we meet.
BE GONE!
EMPTY IS MY HAND!

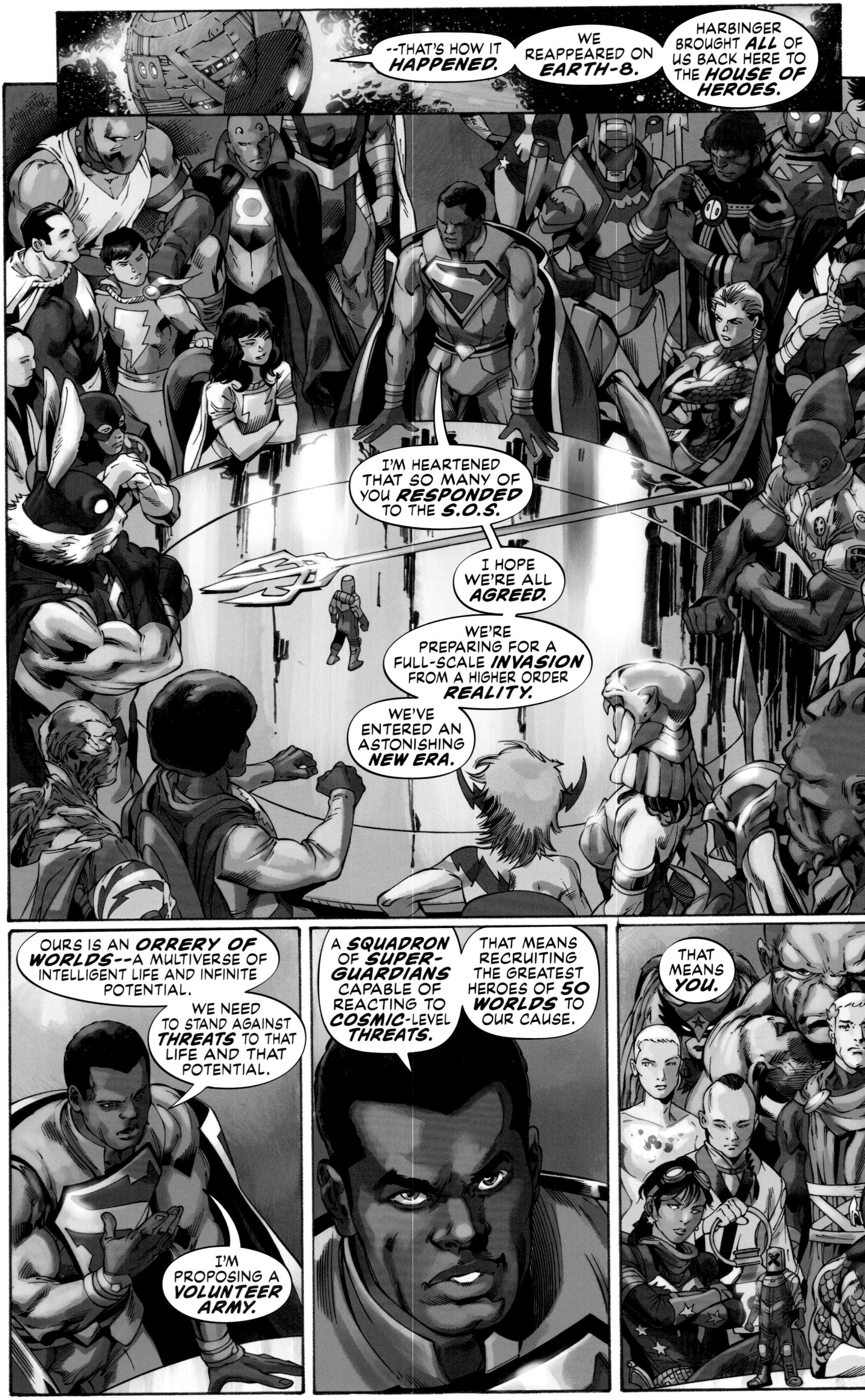
--THAT'S HOW IT HAPPENED.
WE REAPPEARED ON EARTH-8.
HARBINGER BROUGHT ALL OF US BACK HERE TO THE HOUSE OF HEROES.
I'M HEARTENED THAT SO MANY OF YOU RESPONDED TO THE S.O.S.
I HOPE WE'RE ALL AGREED.
WE'RE PREPARING FOR A FULL-SCALE INVASION FROM A HIGHER ORDER REALITY.
WE'VE ENTERED AN ASTONISHING NEW ERA.
OURS IS AN ORRERY OF WORLDS--A MULTIVERSE OF INTELLIGENT LIFE AND INFINITE POTENTIAL.
WE NEED TO STAND AGAINST THREATS TO THAT LIFE AND THAT POTENTIAL.
I'M PROPOSING A VOLUNTEER ARMY.
A SQUADRON OF SUPER-GUARDIANS CAPABLE OF REACTING TO COSMIC-LEVEL THREATS.
THAT MEANS RECRUITING THE GREATEST HEROES OF 50 WORLDS TO OUR CAUSE.
THAT MEANS YOU.

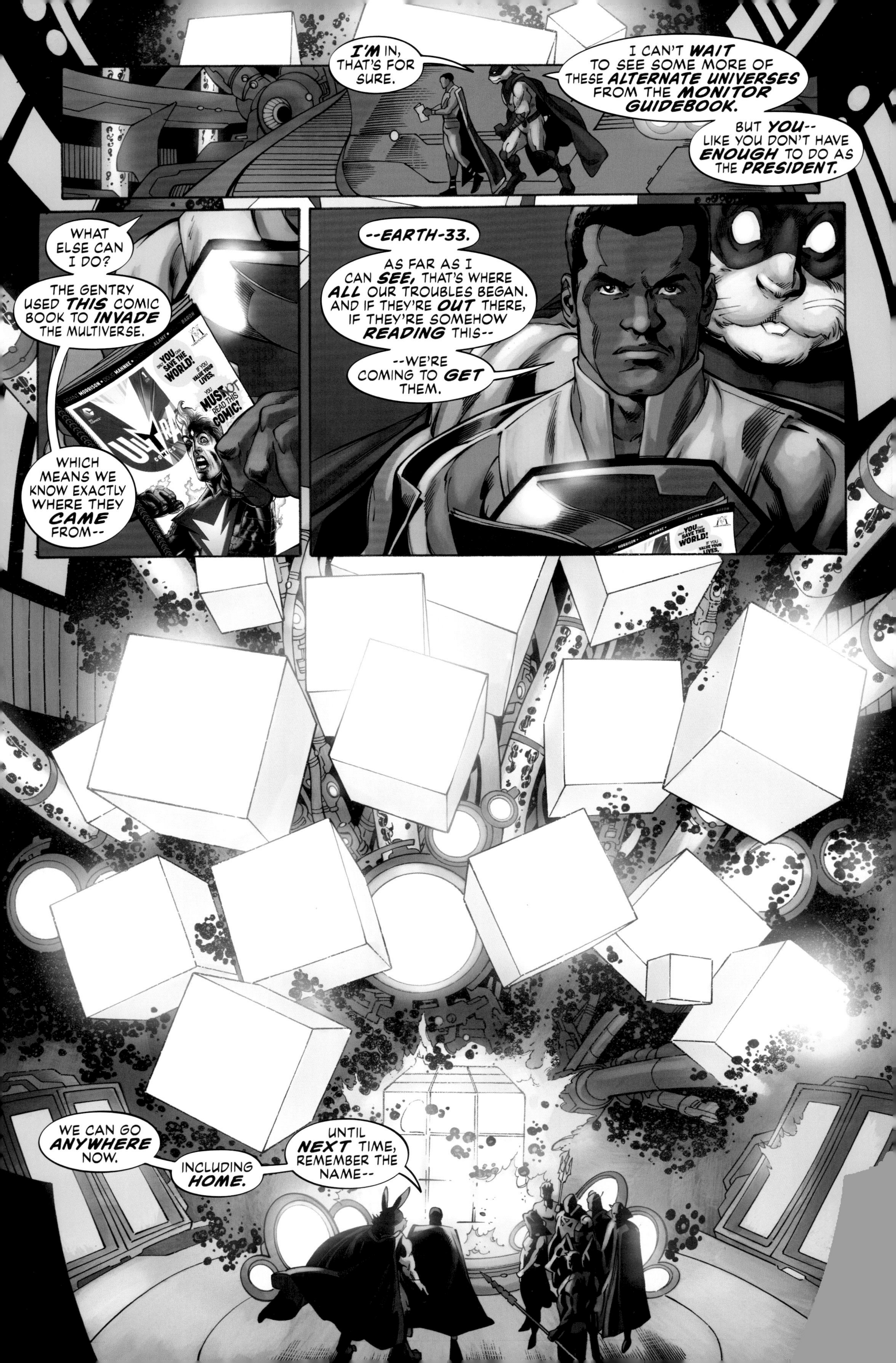
I'M IN, THAT'S FOR SURE.
I CAN'T WAIT TO SEE SOME MORE OF THESE ALTERNATE UNIVERSES FROM THE MONITOR GUIDEBOOK.
BUT YOU-- LIKE YOU DON'T HAVE ENOUGH TO DO AS THE PRESIDENT.
WHAT ELSE CAN I DO?
THE GENTRY USED THIS COMIC BOOK TO INVADE THE MULTIVERSE.
WHICH MEANS WE KNOW EXACTLY WHERE THEY CAME FROM--
--EARTH-33.
AS FAR AS I CAN SEE, THAT'S WHERE ALL OUR TROUBLES BEGAN. AND IF THEY'RE OUT THERE, IF THEY'RE SOMEHOW READING THIS--
--WE'RE COMING TO GET THEM.
WE CAN GO ANYWHERE NOW.
INCLUDING HOME.
UNTIL NEXT TIME, REMEMBER THE NAME--

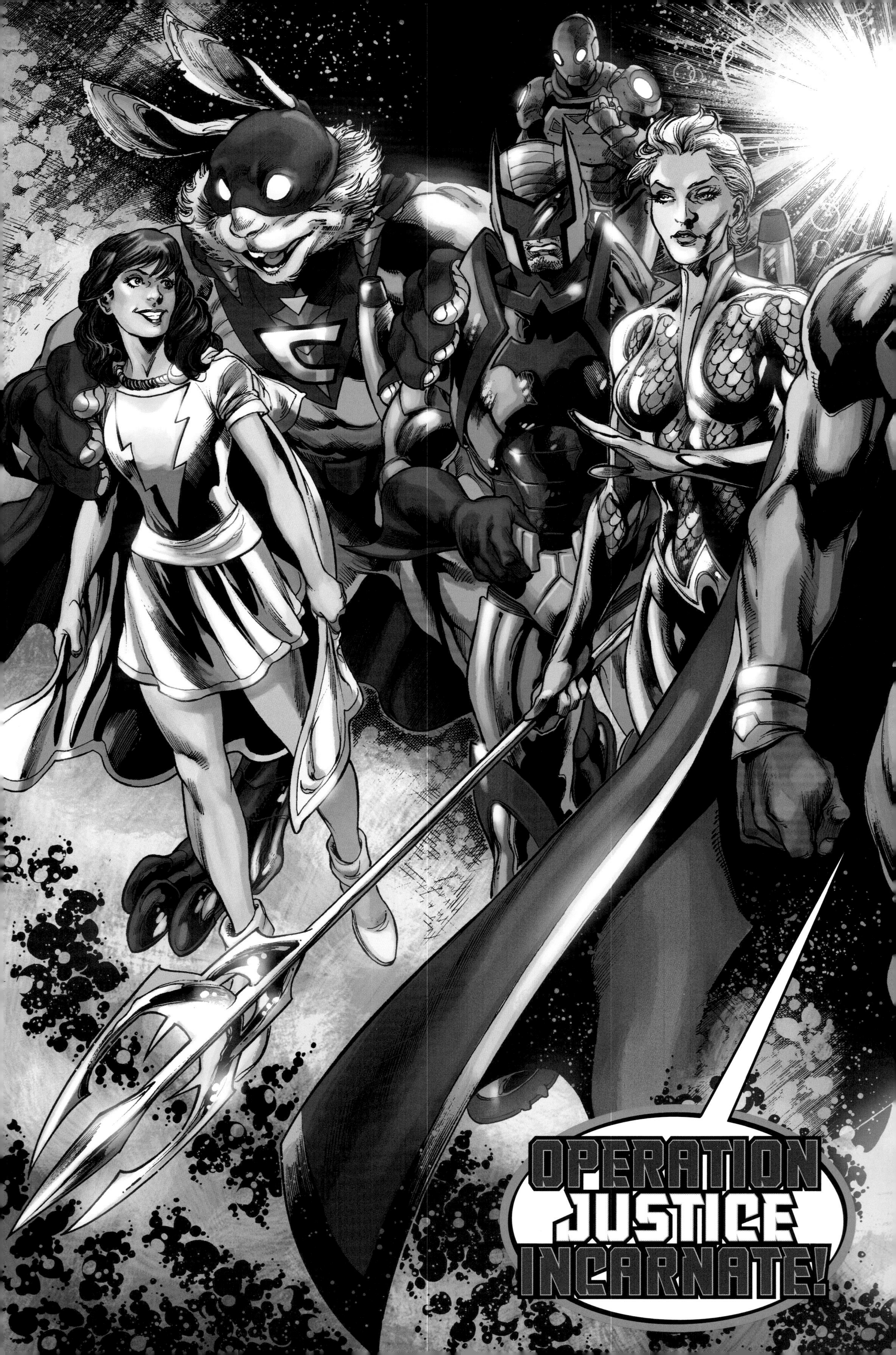
OPERATION JUSTICE INCARNATE!

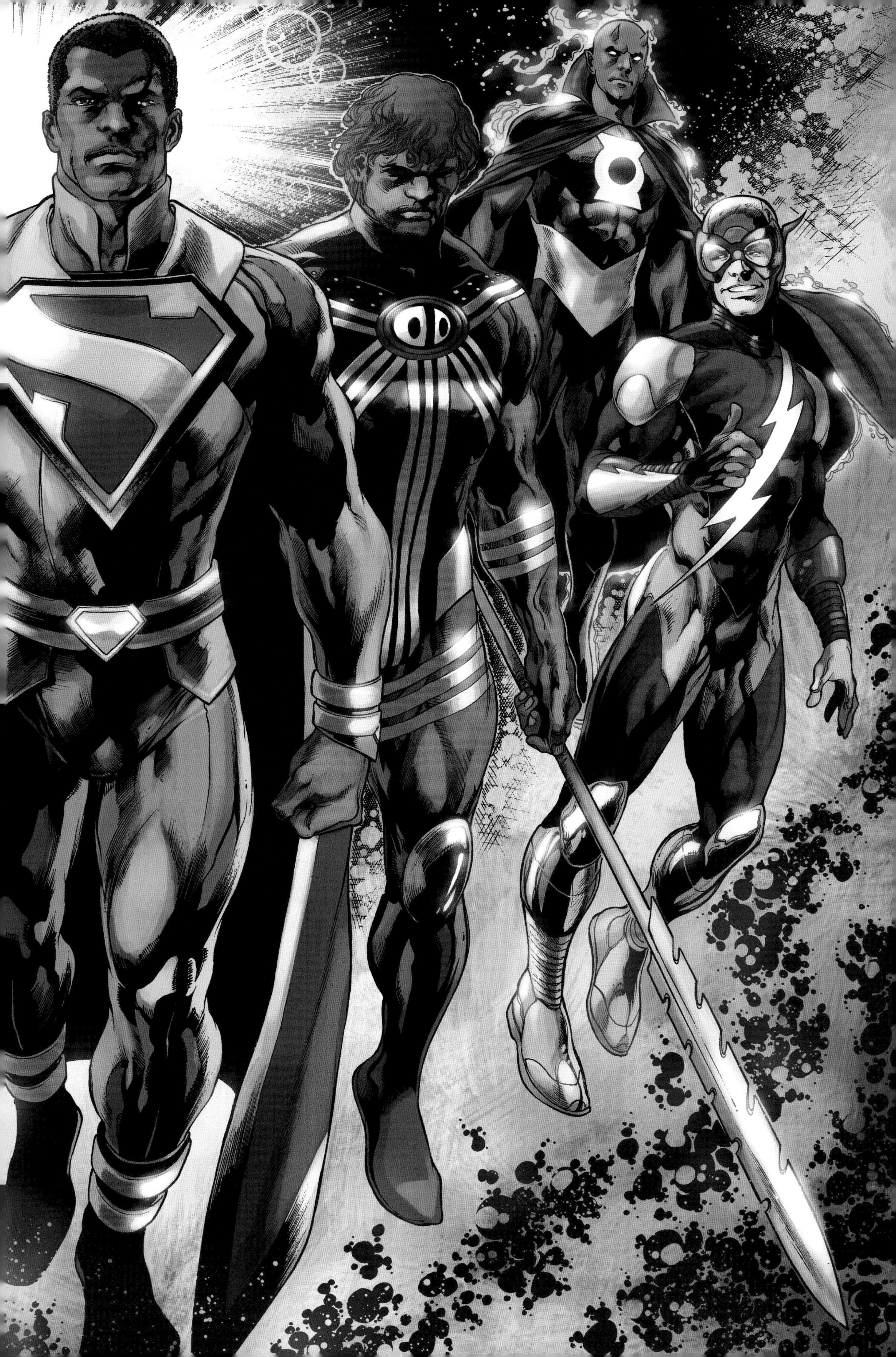

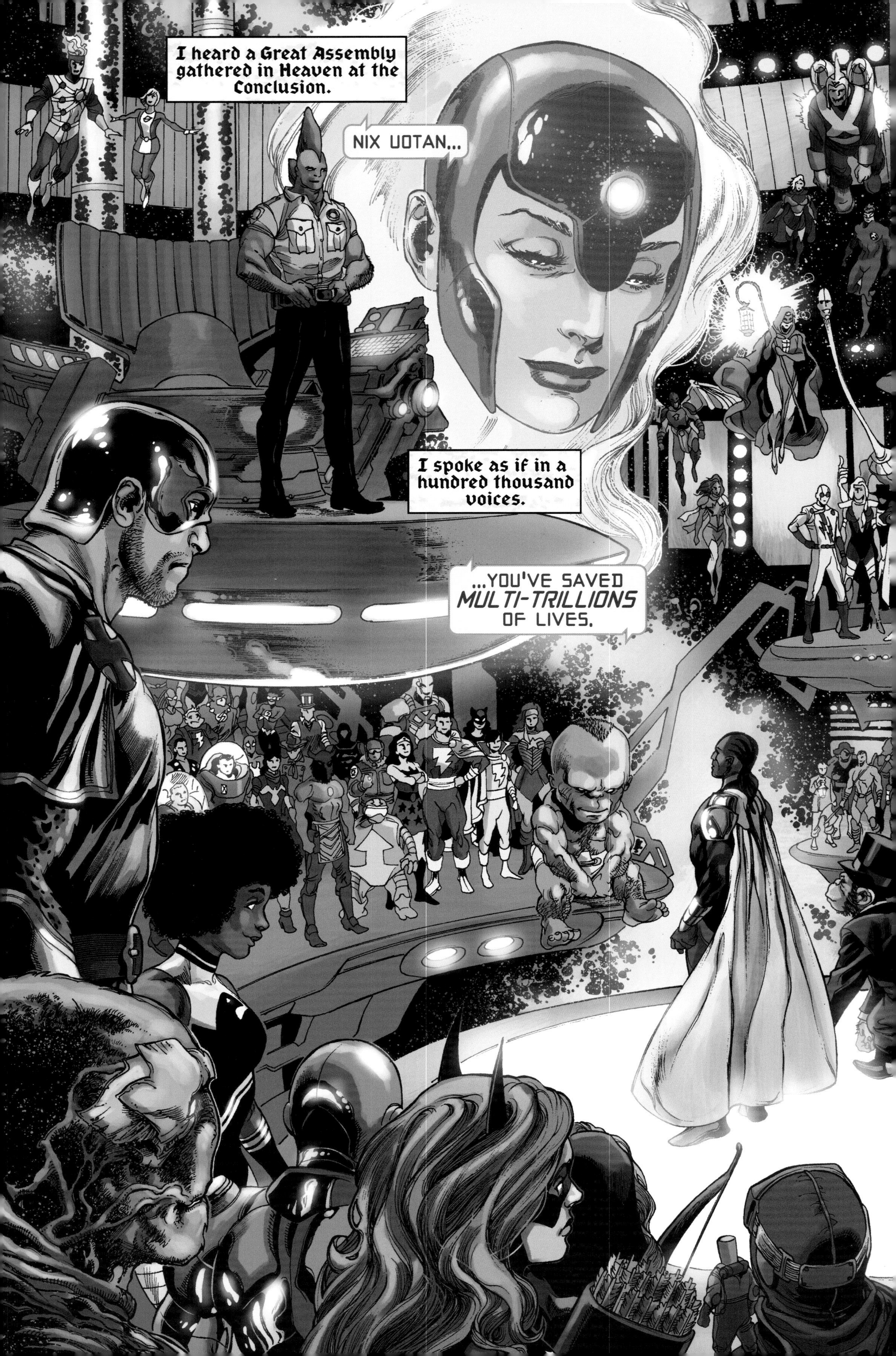
I heard a Great Assembly gathered in Heaven at the Conclusion.
NIX UOTAN...
I spoke as if in a hundred thousand voices.
...YOU'VE SAVED *MULTI-TRILLIONS* OF LIVES.

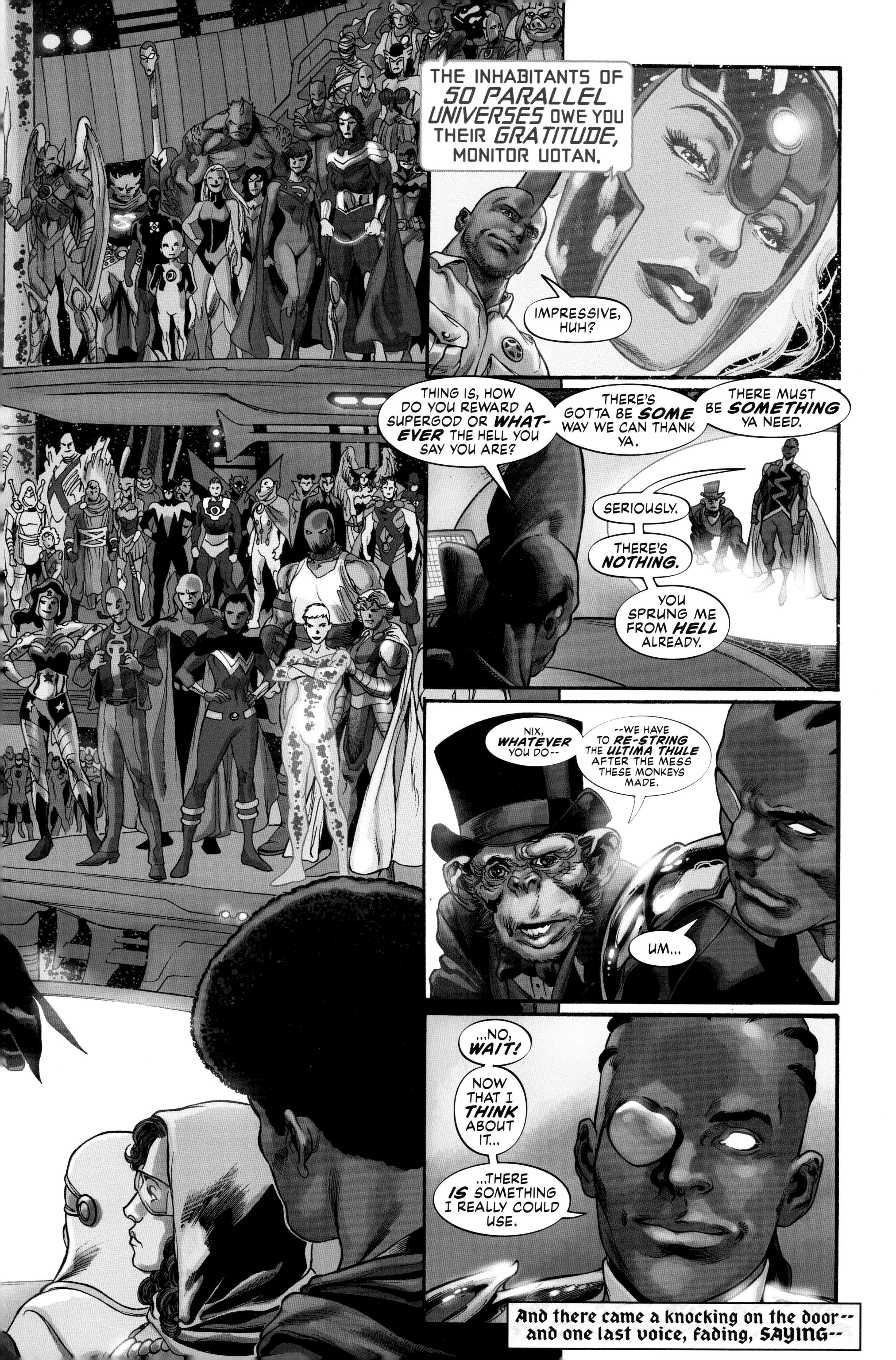
THE INHABITANTS OF 50 PARALLEL UNIVERSES OWE YOU THEIR GRATITUDE, MONITOR UOTAN.
IMPRESSIVE, HUH?
THING IS, HOW DO YOU REWARD A SUPERGOD OR WHAT-EVER THE HELL YOU SAY YOU ARE?
THERE'S GOTTA BE SOME WAY WE CAN THANK YA.
THERE MUST BE SOMETHING YA NEED.
SERIOUSLY.
THERE'S NOTHING.
YOU SPRUNG ME FROM HELL ALREADY.
NIX, WHATEVER YOU DO--
--WE HAVE TO RE-STRING THE ULTIMA THULE AFTER THE MESS THESE MONKEYS MADE.
UM...
...NO, WAIT!
NOW THAT I THINK ABOUT IT...
...THERE IS SOMETHING I REALLY COULD USE.
And there came a knocking on the door--
and one last voice, fading, SAYING--

WHEREVER LIFE CAN TAKE ROOT.

WHEREVER LIFE CAN FLOURISH.

LIFE WILL THRIVE AND LIFE WILL PROSPER.

GIVEN THE NEED.

GIVEN THE OPPORTUNITY.

BE CAREFUL WHAT YOU LET INTO YOUR *HEAD.*

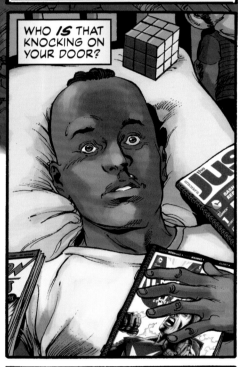

WHO *IS* THAT KNOCKING ON YOUR DOOR?

And then it was **CONTINUED** thereafter.

Unto all Eternity.

OW.

NO MORE *BYZANTINE* IMPLAUSIBLE EXCUSES.

YOU *OWE* ME--!

UH, SURE.

SURE, I OWE YOU.

AND *GUESS WHAT?*

COUNT 'EM.

EIGHT HUNDRED BUCKS.

EARTH-0

THE MULTIVERSITY:
THE DIRECTOR'S CUT
#1 and #2

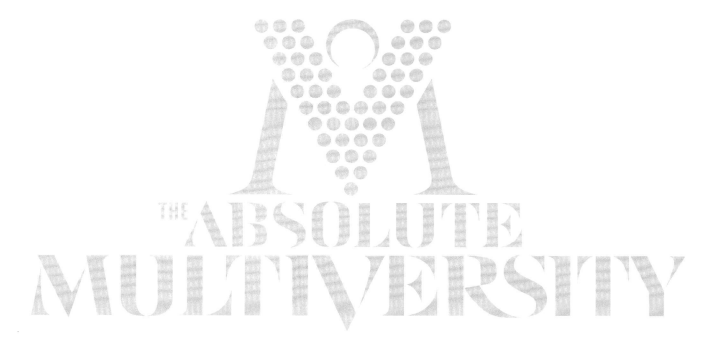

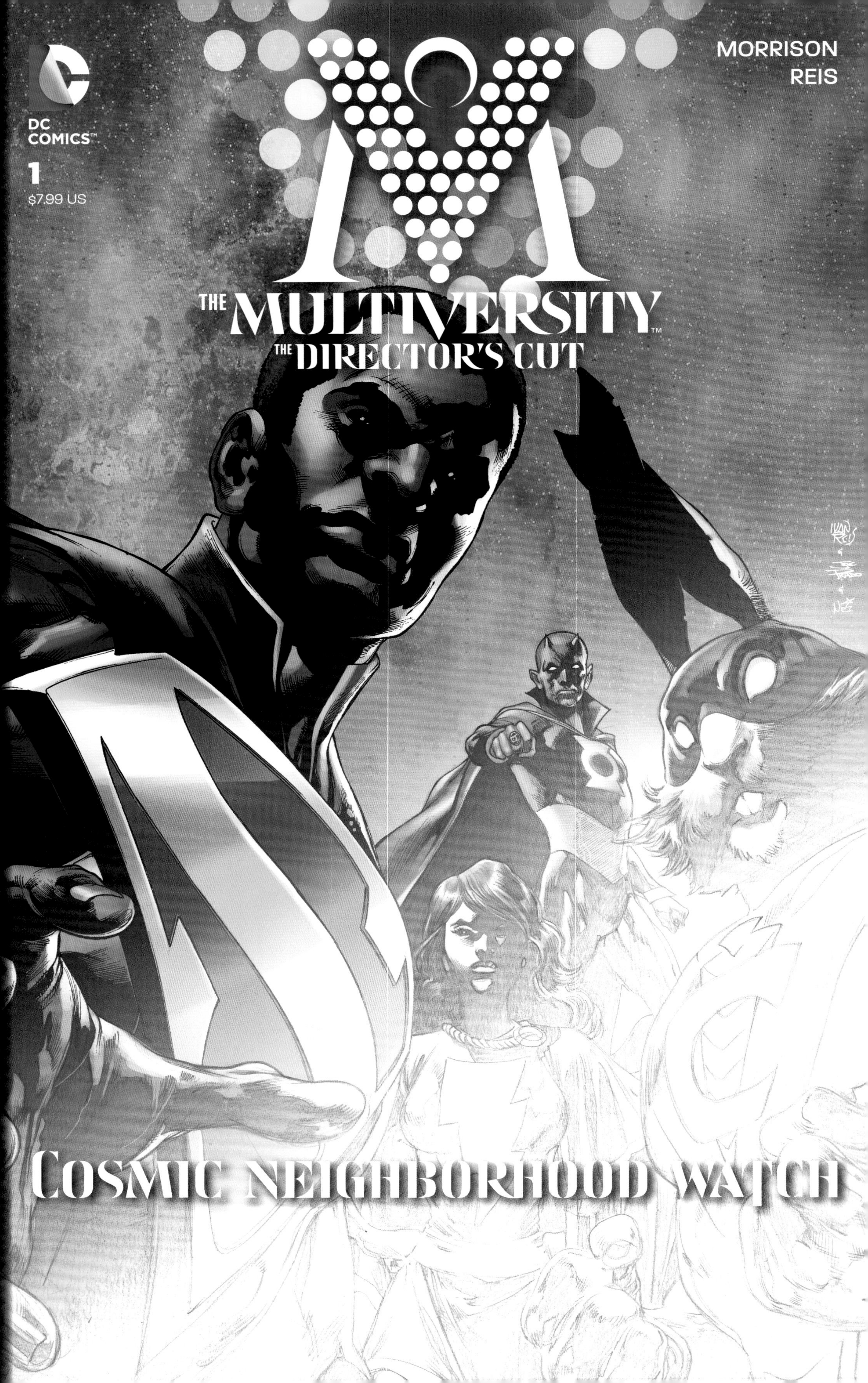
DC COMICS
1
$7.99 US
MORRISON
REIS
THE MULTIVERSITY
THE DIRECTOR'S CUT
COSMIC NEIGHBORHOOD WATCH

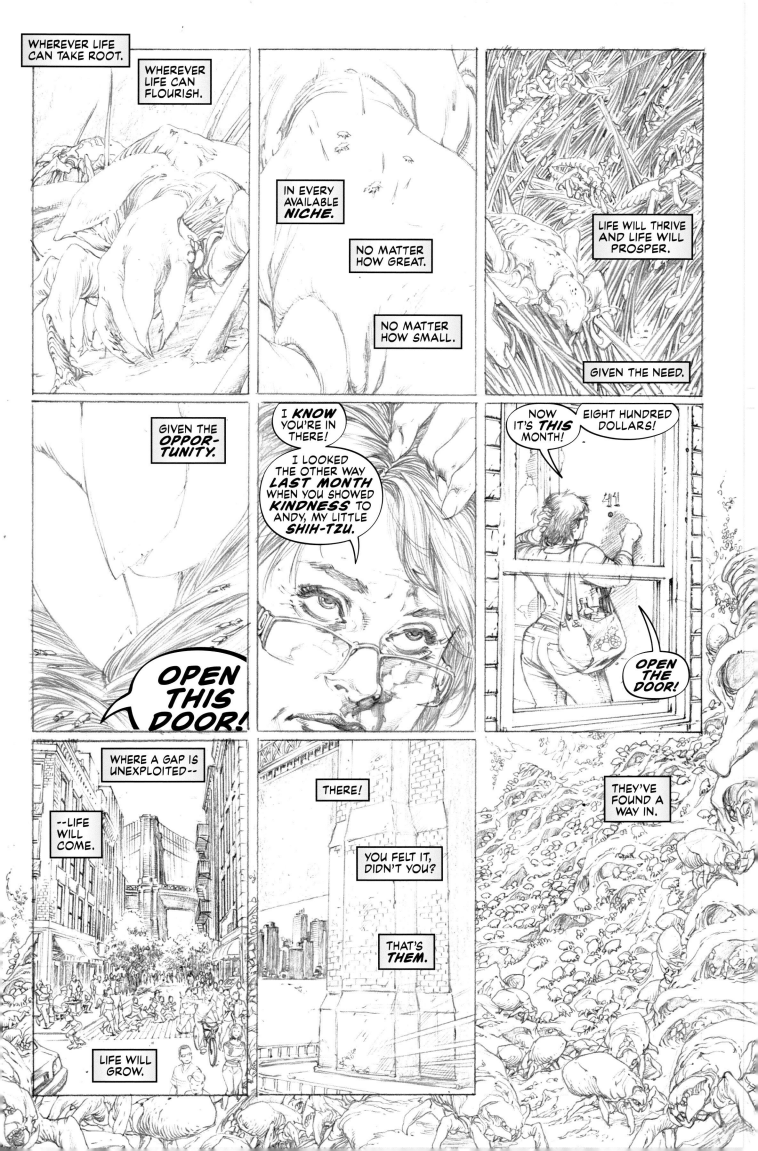

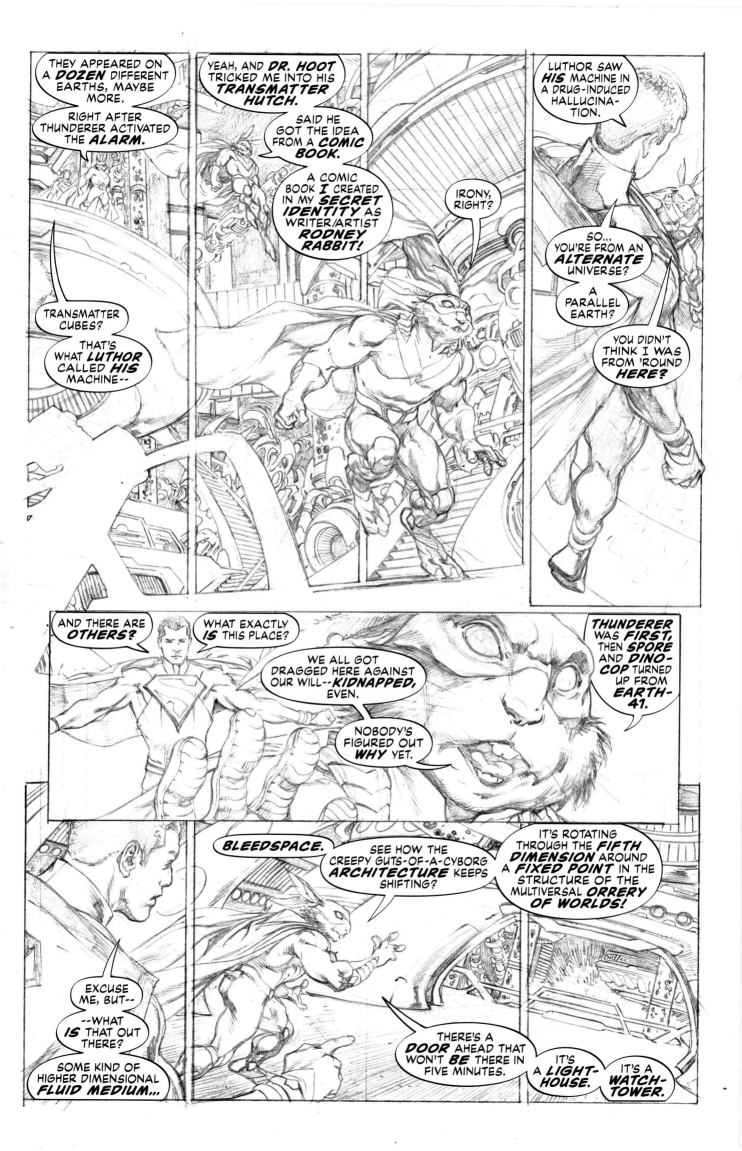

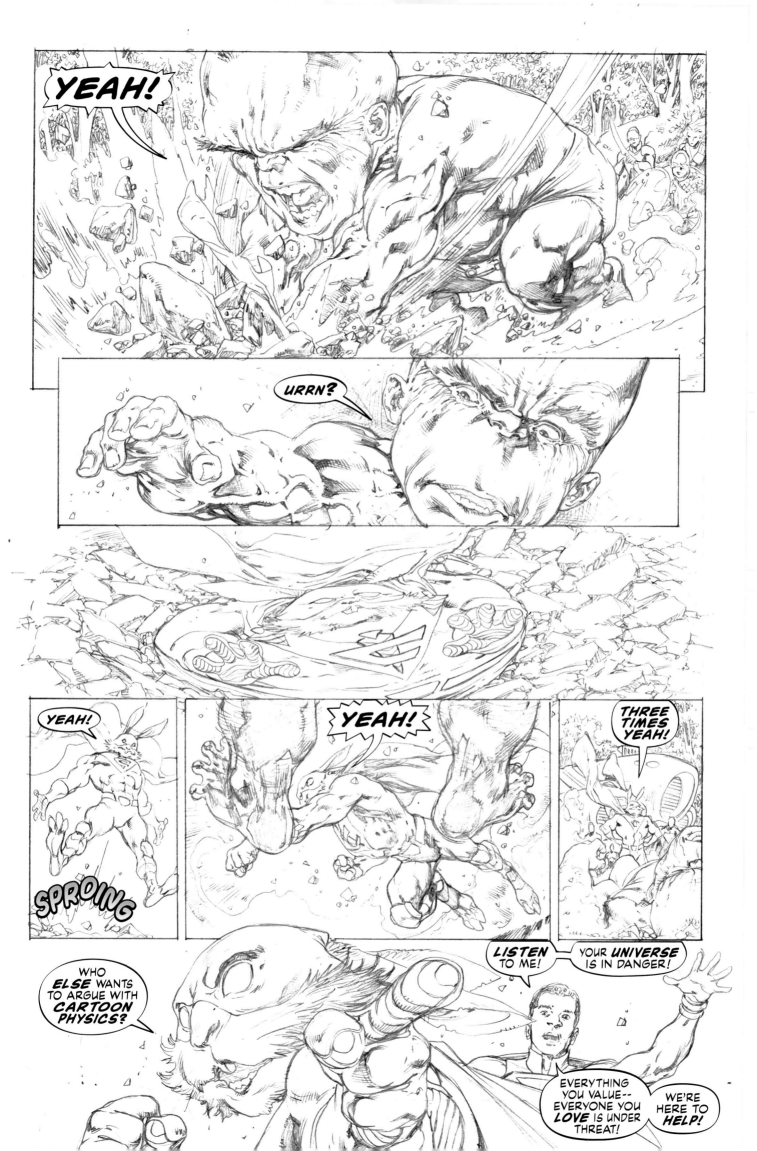

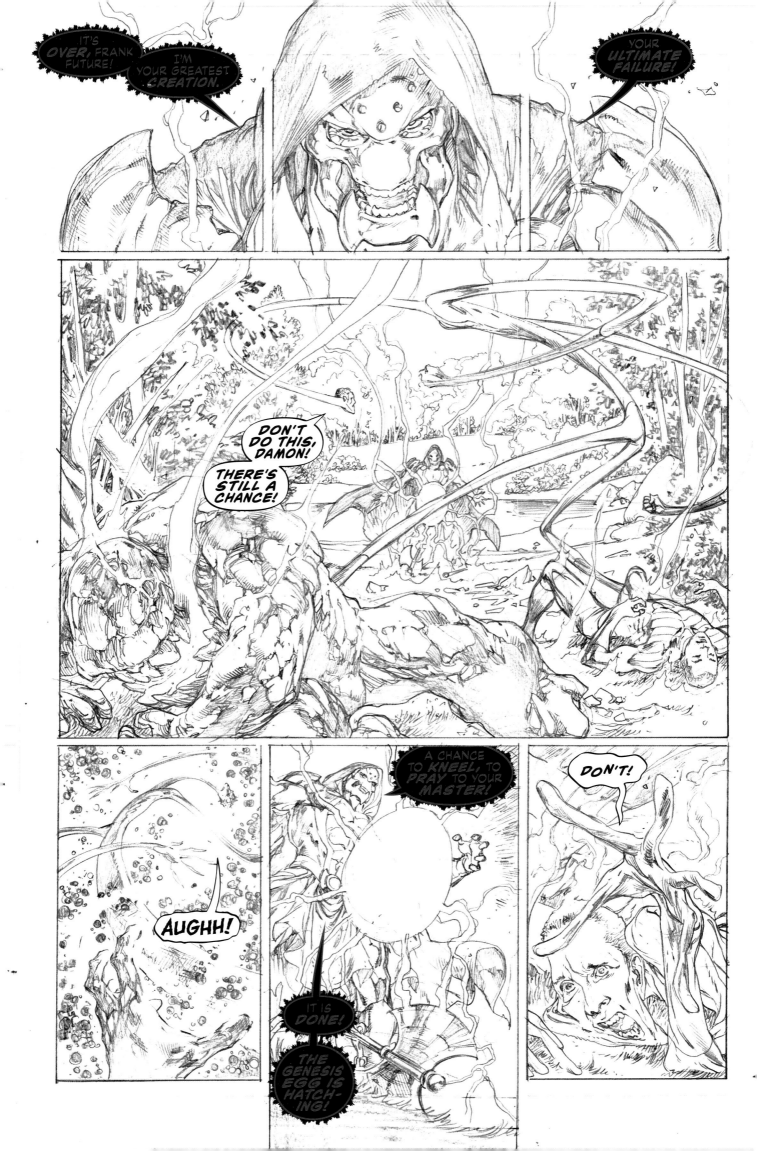

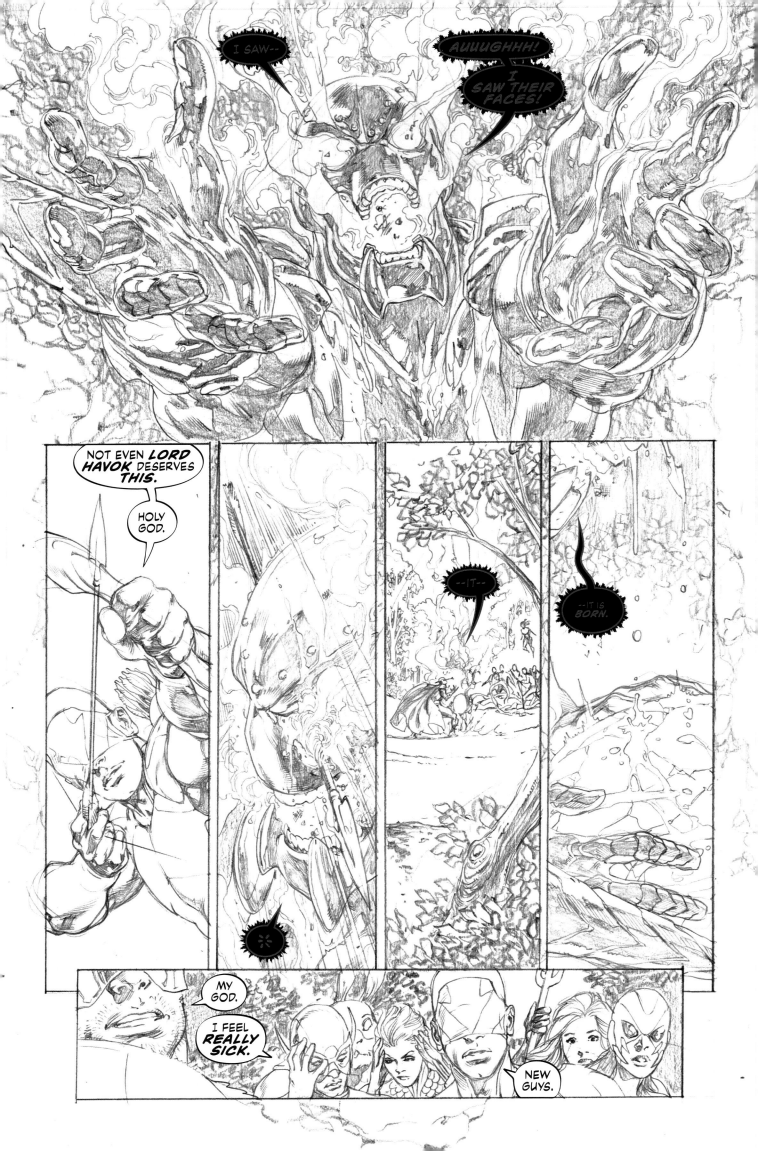

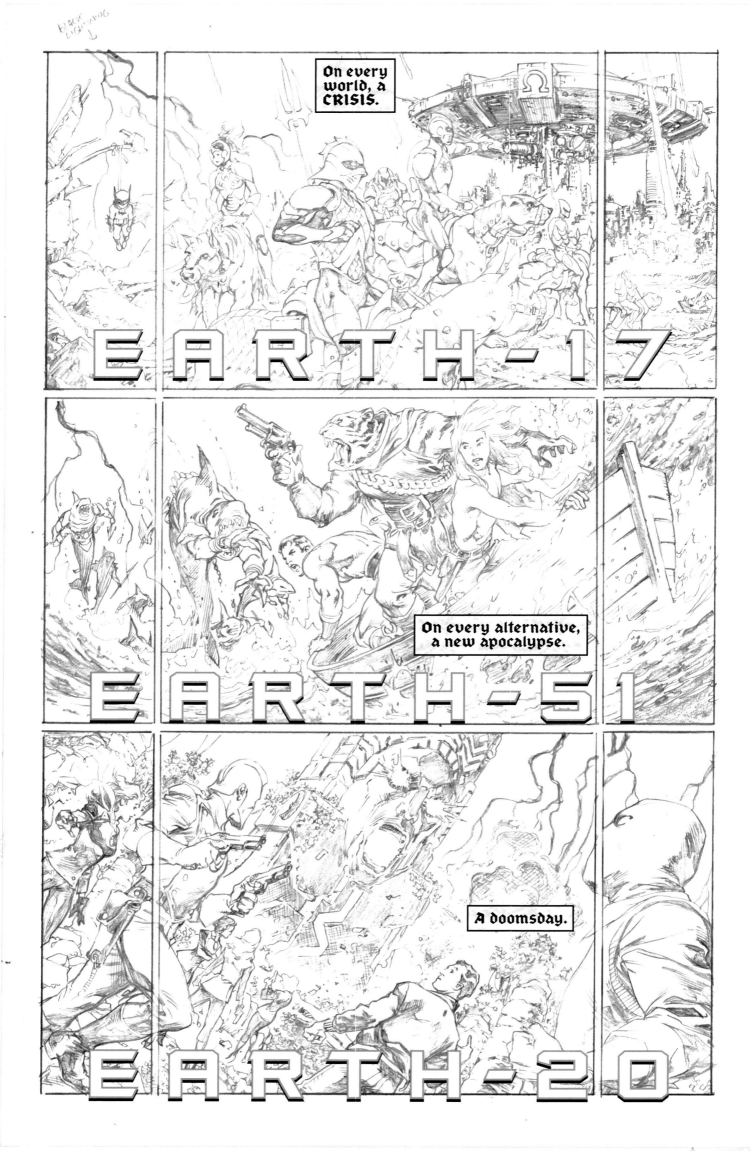

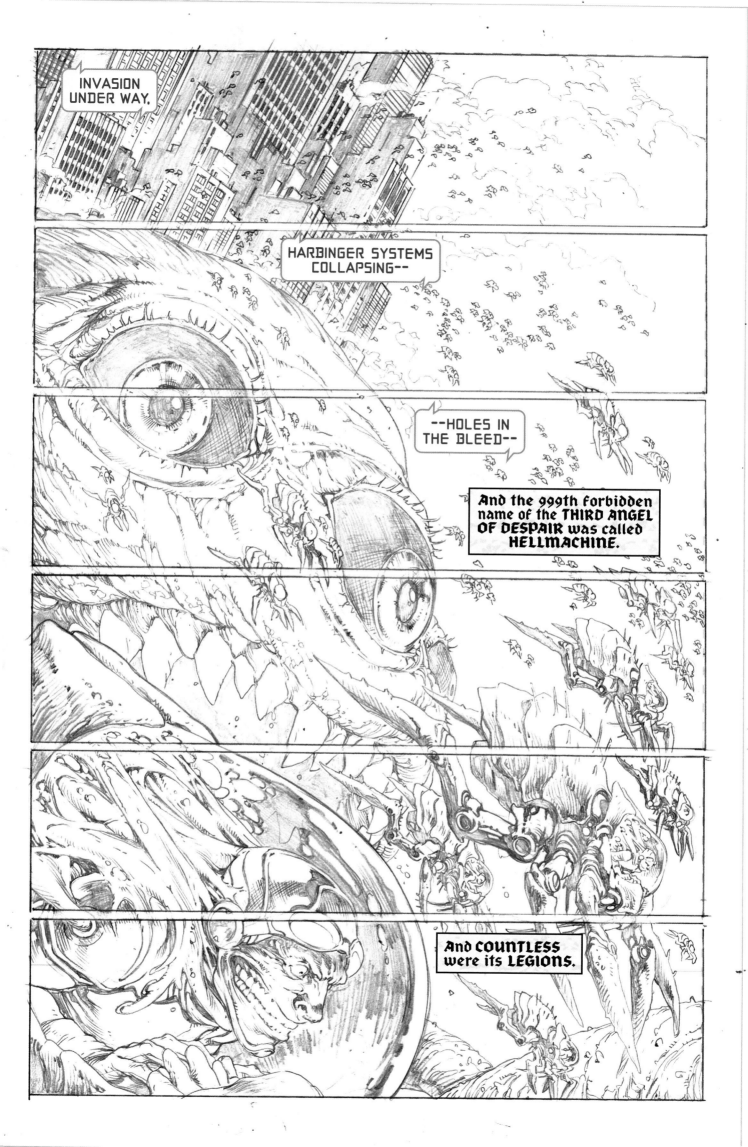

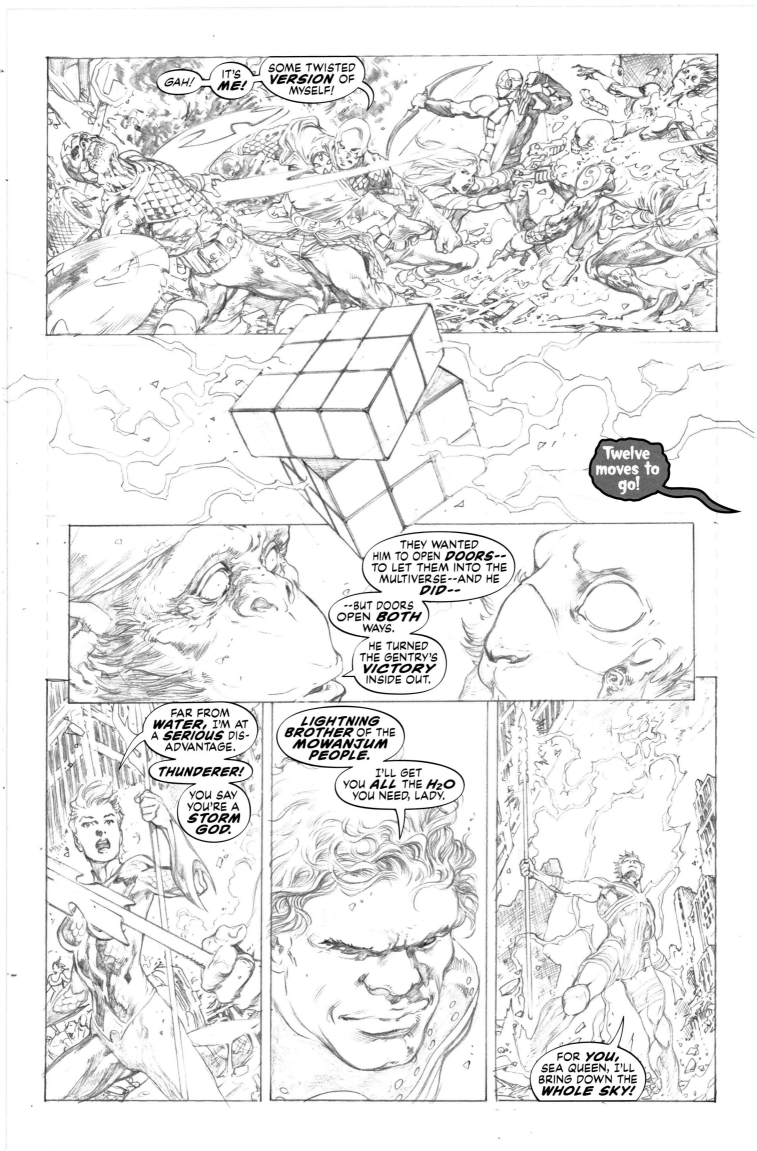

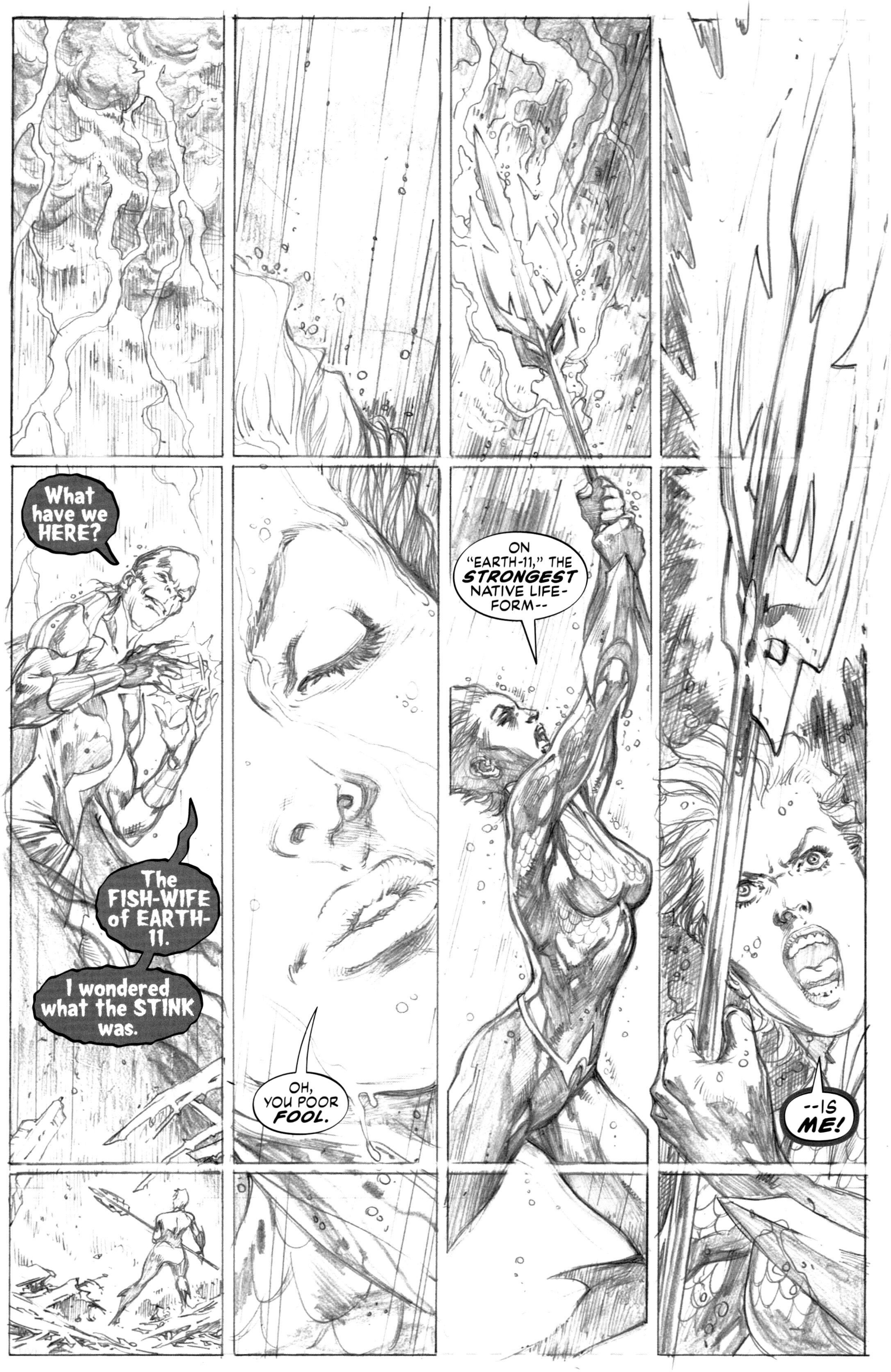
What have we HERE?
OH, YOU POOR FOOL.
ON "EARTH-11," THE STRONGEST NATIVE LIFE-FORM--
--IS ME!
The FISH-WIFE of EARTH-11.
I wondered what the STINK was.

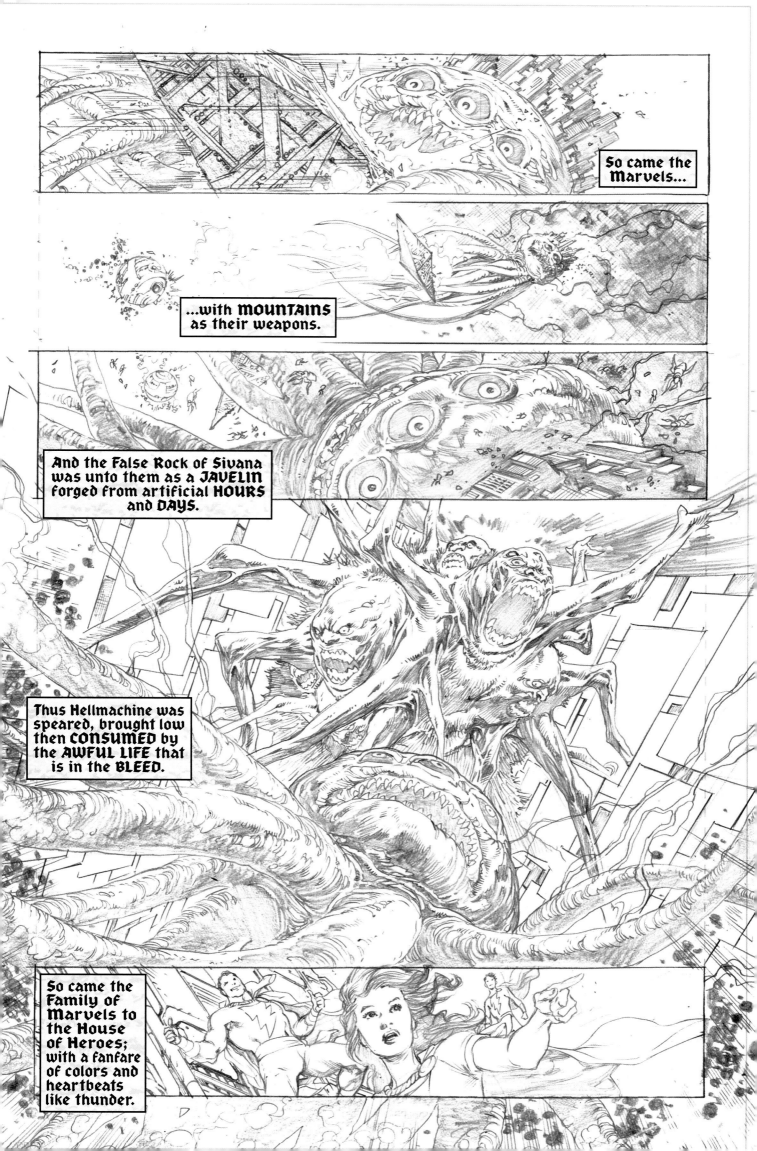

So came the Marvels...

...with **MOUNTAINS** as their weapons.

And the False Rock of Sivana was unto them as a **JAVELIN** forged from artificial **HOURS** and **DAYS**.

Thus Hellmachine was speared, brought low then **CONSUMED** by the **AWFUL LIFE** that is in the **BLEED**.

So came the Family of Marvels to the House of Heroes; with a fanfare of colors and heartbeats like thunder.

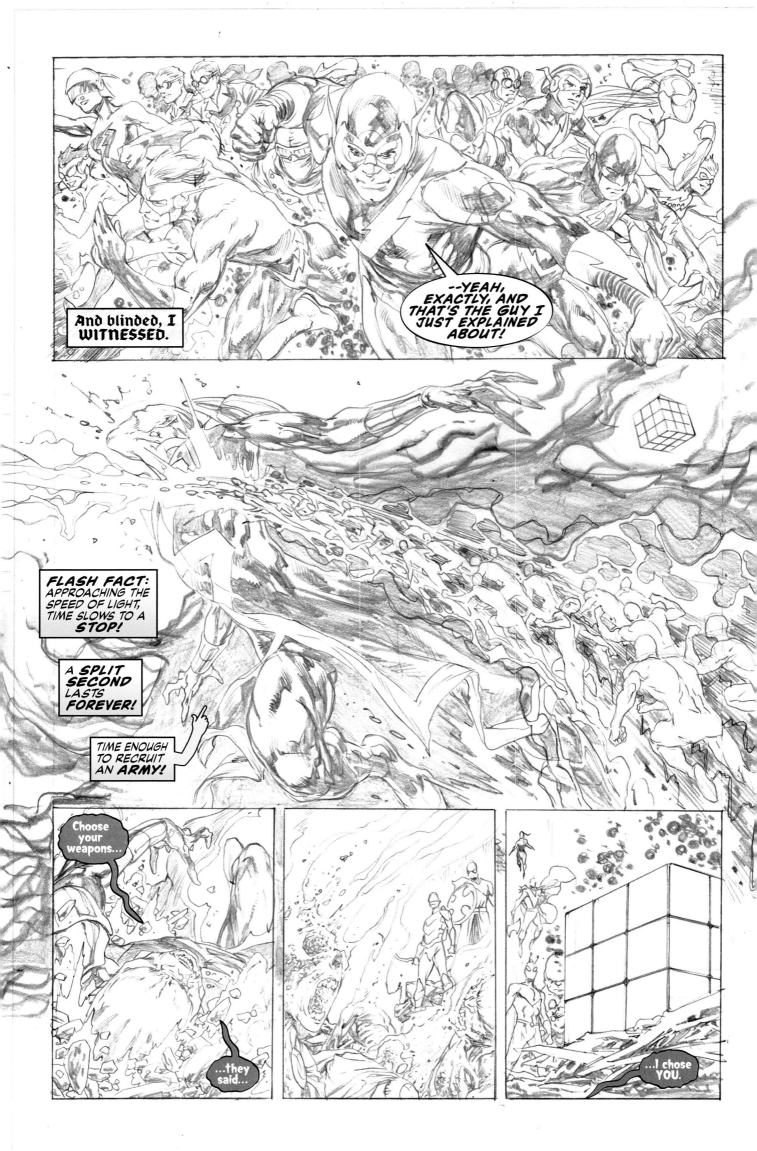

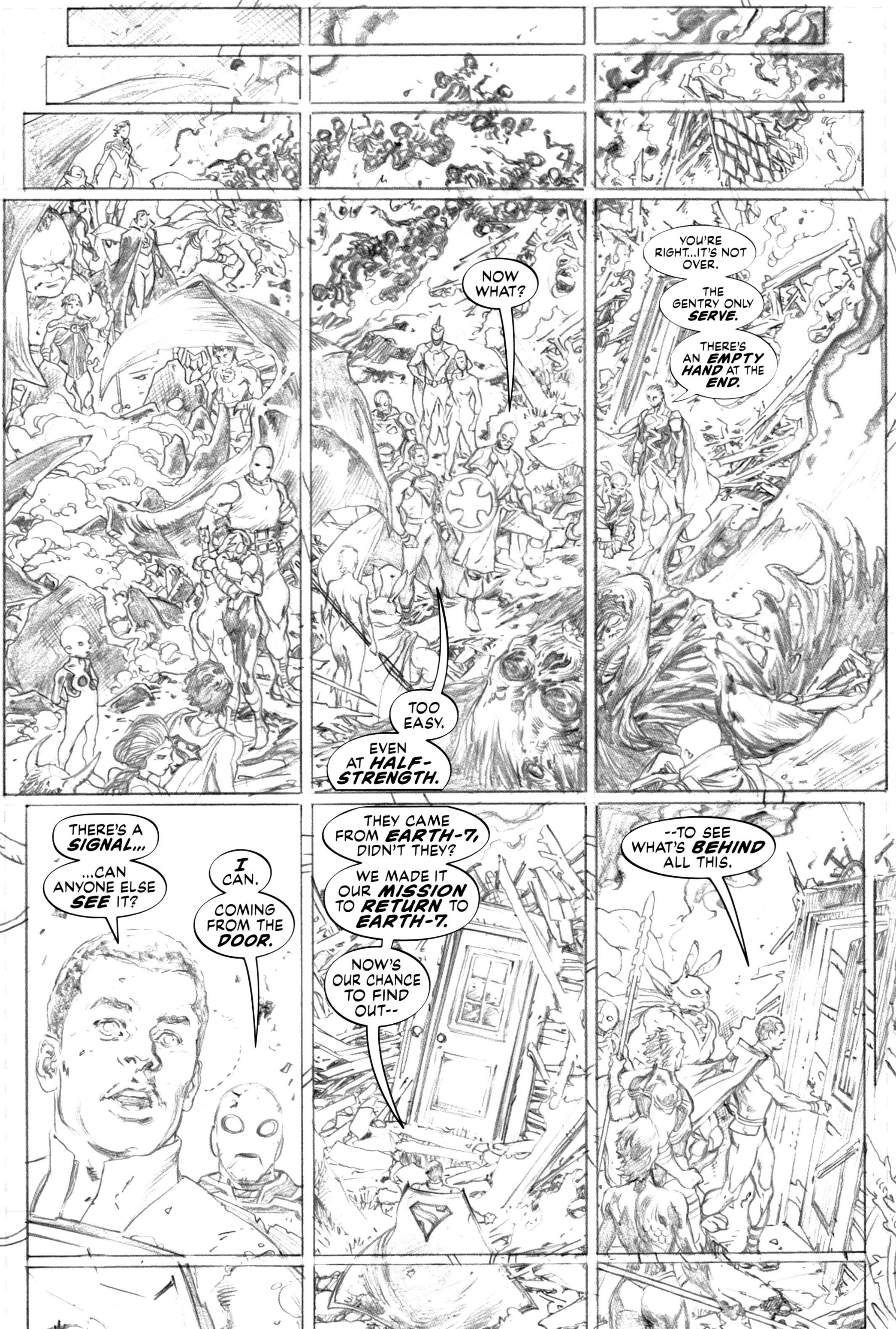
NOW WHAT?
TOO EASY.
EVEN AT HALF-STRENGTH.
YOU'RE RIGHT...IT'S NOT OVER.
THE GENTRY ONLY SERVE.
THERE'S AN EMPTY HAND AT THE END.
THERE'S A SIGNAL...
...CAN ANYONE ELSE SEE IT?
I CAN.
COMING FROM THE DOOR.
THEY CAME FROM EARTH-7, DIDN'T THEY?
WE MADE IT OUR MISSION TO RETURN TO EARTH-7.
NOW'S OUR CHANCE TO FIND OUT--
--TO SEE WHAT'S BEHIND ALL THIS.

PAX AMERICANA
THE DIRECTOR'S CUT
#1

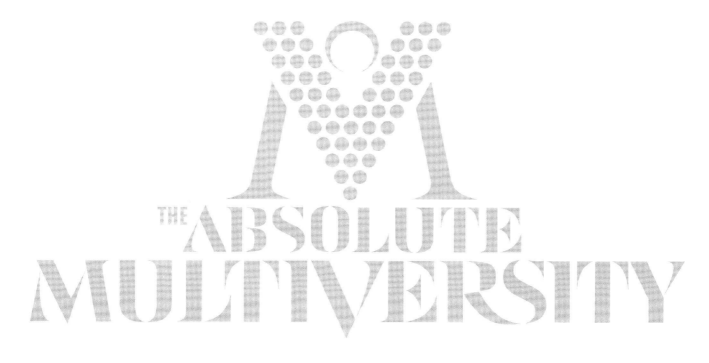

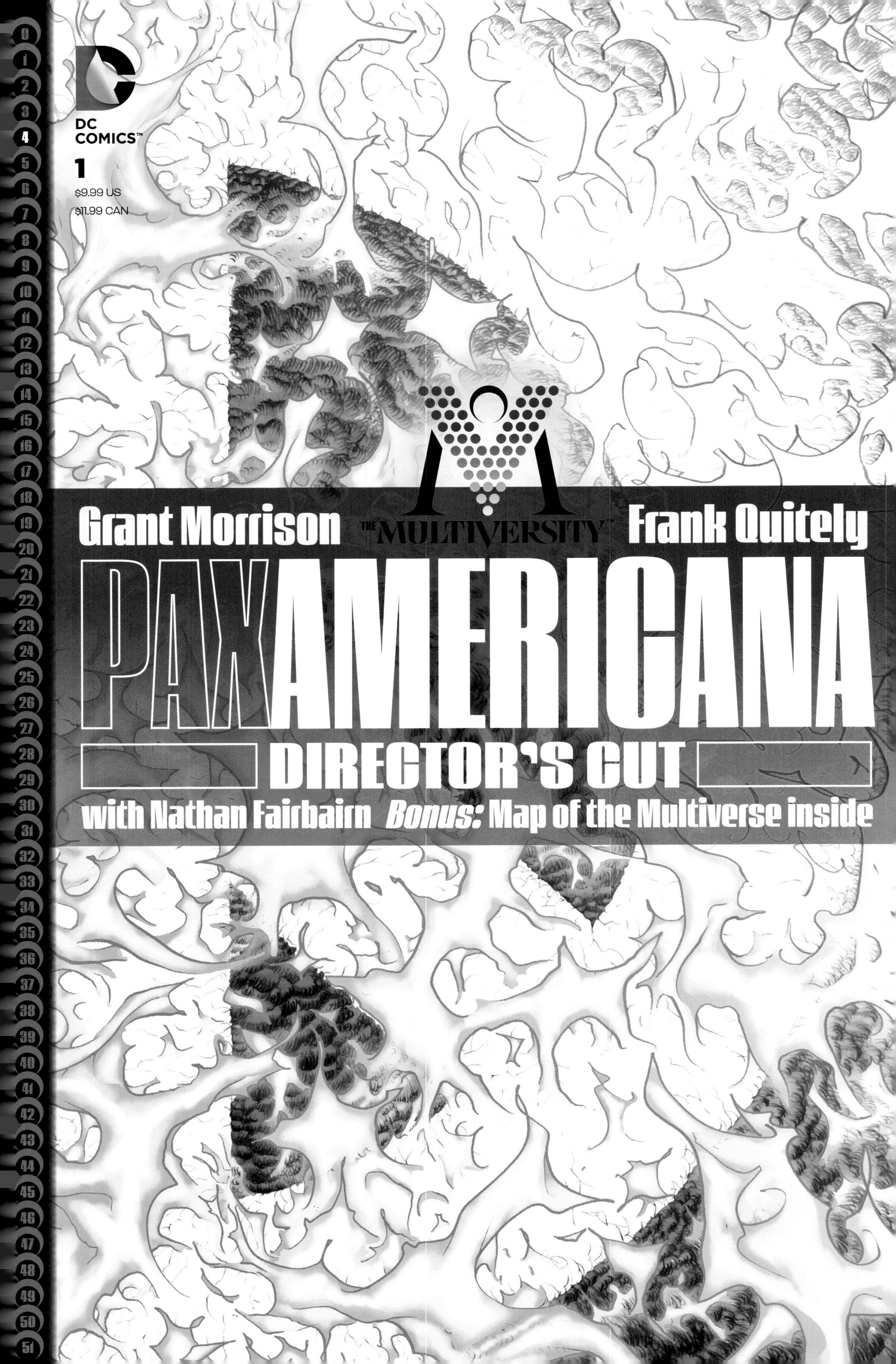
DC COMICS™
1
$9.99 US
$11.99 CAN
Grant Morrison
THE MULTIVERSITY™
Frank Quitely
PAX AMERICANA
DIRECTOR'S CUT
with Nathan Fairbairn
Bonus: Map of the Multiverse inside

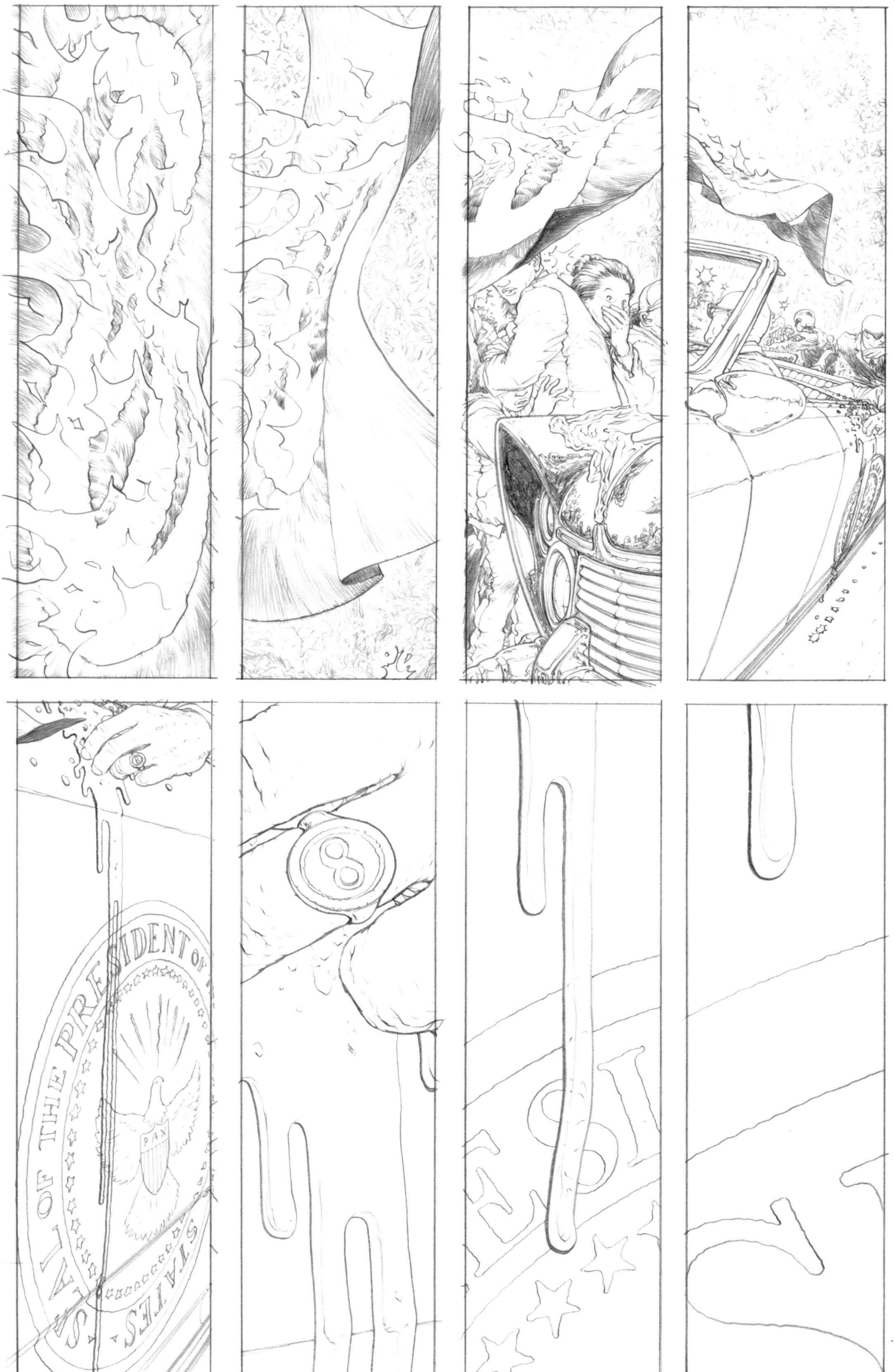
OF THE PRESIDENT
STATES
PAX

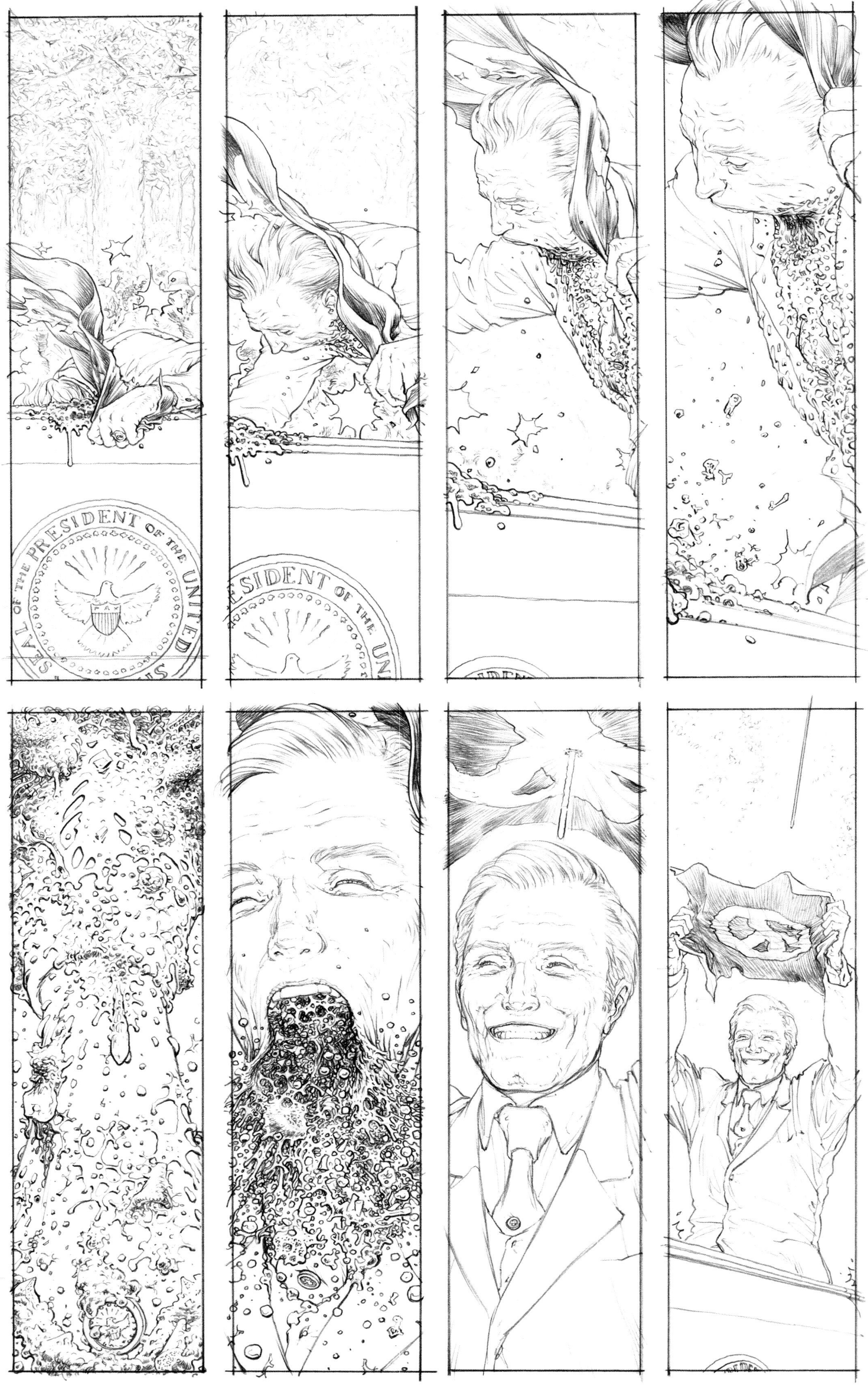
SEAL OF THE PRESIDENT OF THE UNITED

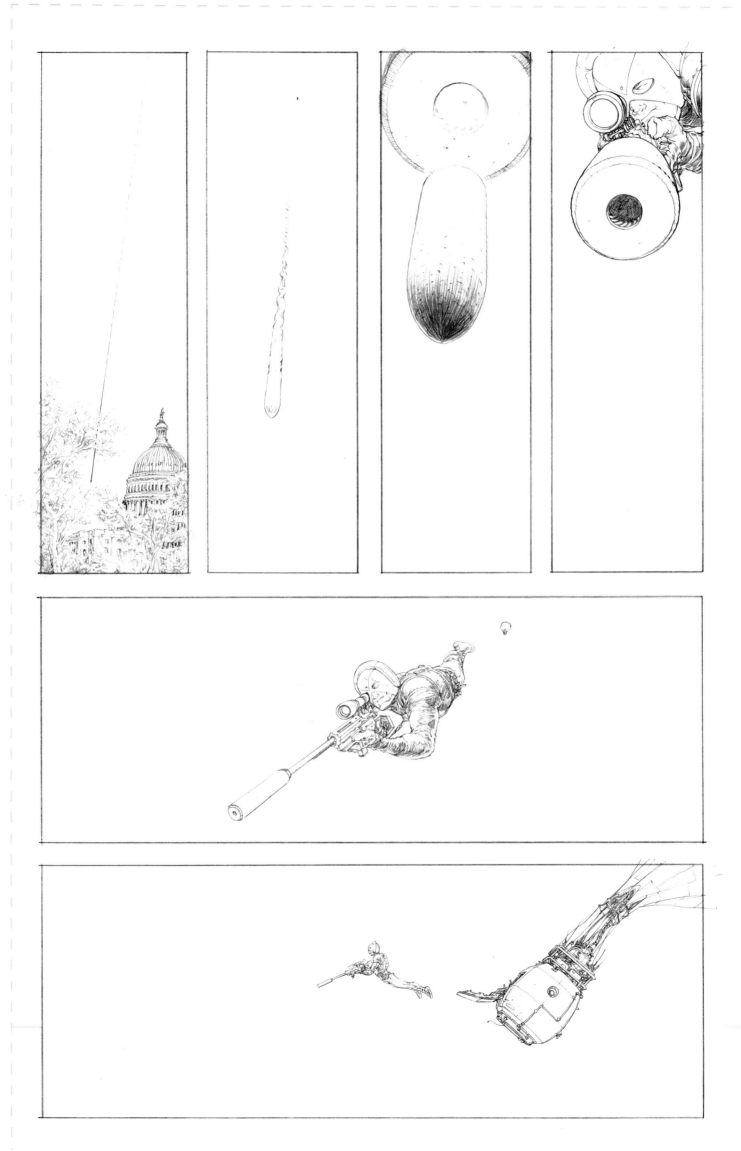

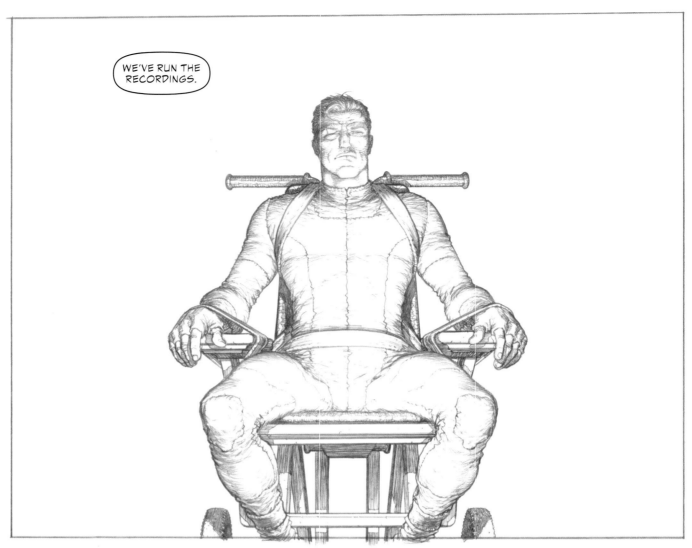

In Which We Burn

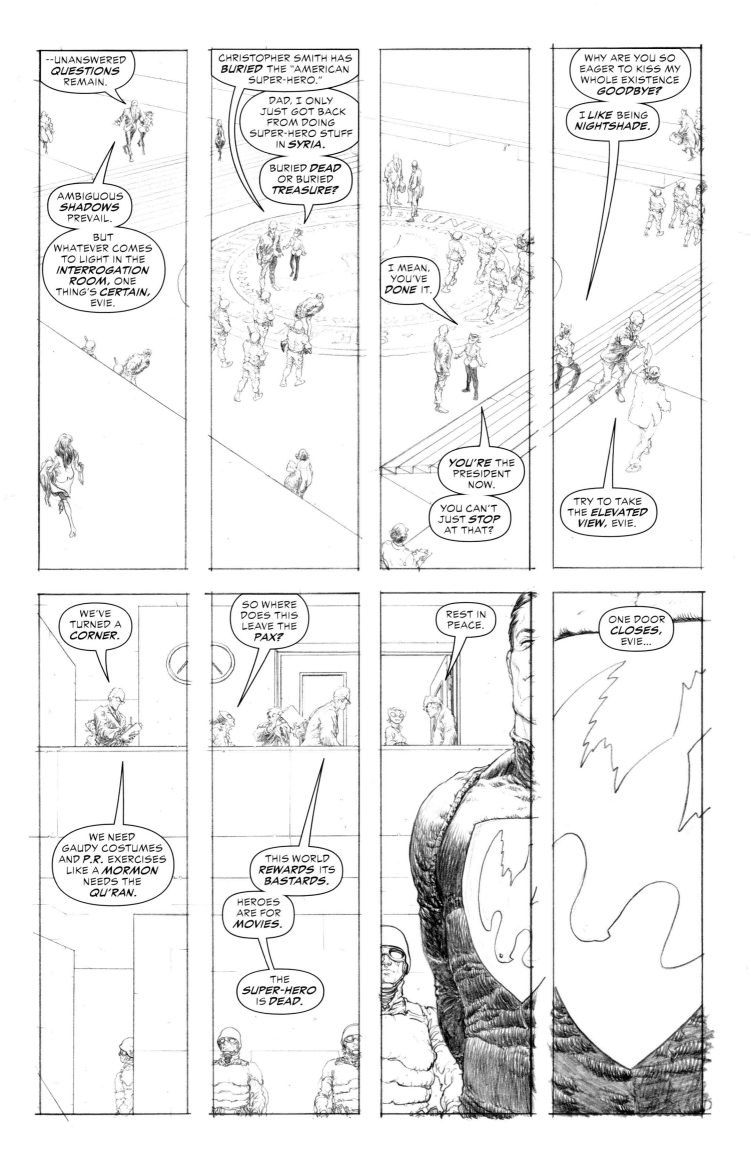

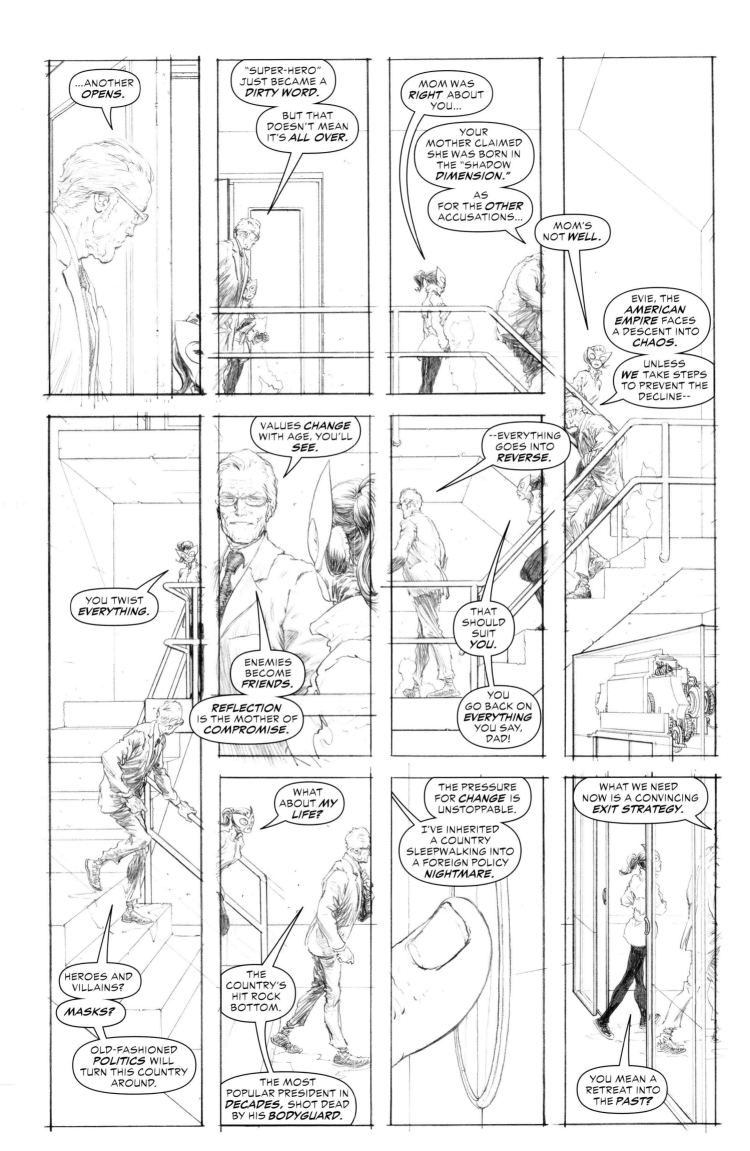

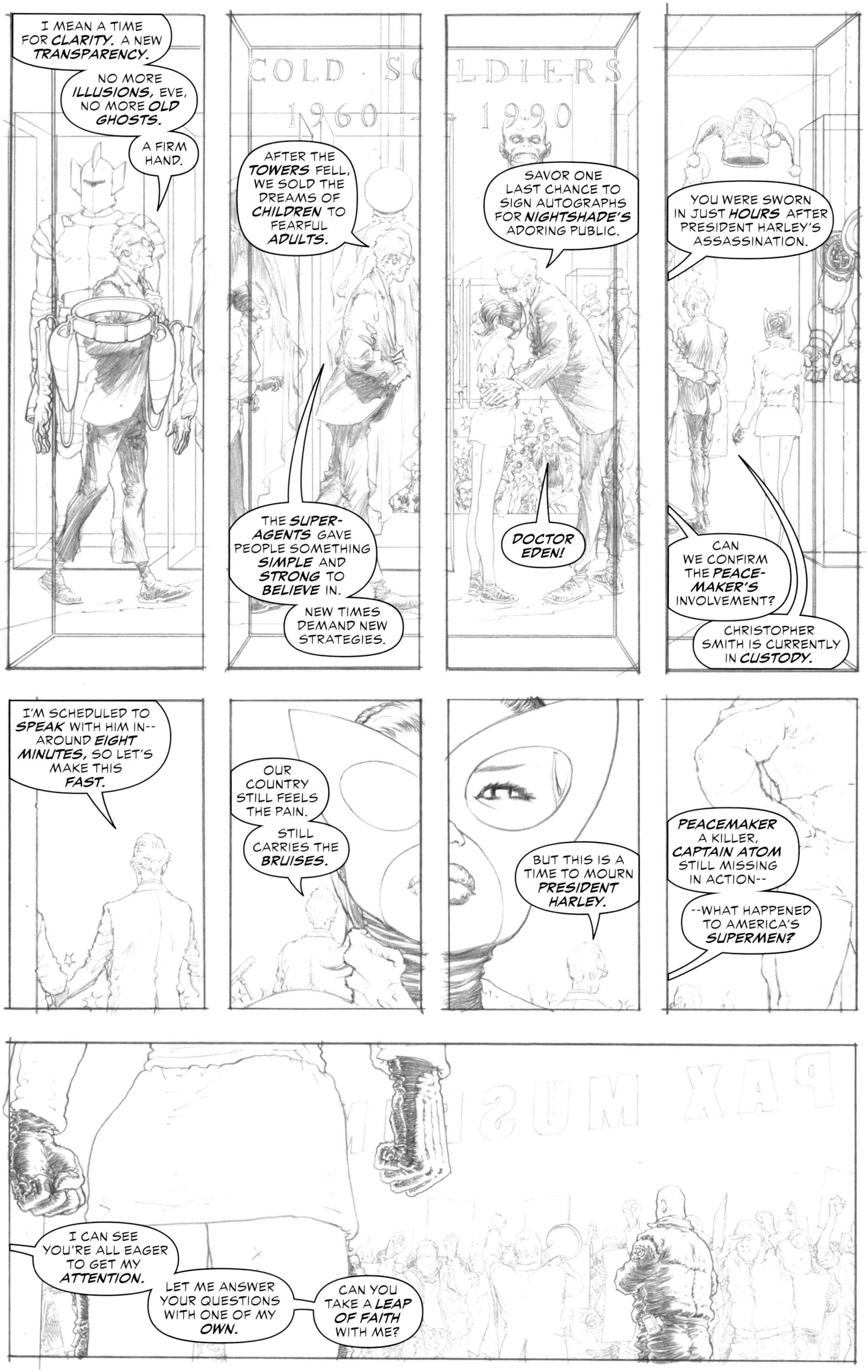
I MEAN A TIME FOR CLARITY. A NEW TRANSPARENCY.
NO MORE ILLUSIONS, EVE, NO MORE OLD GHOSTS.
A FIRM HAND.
COLD SOLDIERS 1960 - 1990
AFTER THE TOWERS FELL, WE SOLD THE DREAMS OF CHILDREN TO FEARFUL ADULTS.
THE SUPER-AGENTS GAVE PEOPLE SOMETHING SIMPLE AND STRONG TO BELIEVE IN.
NEW TIMES DEMAND NEW STRATEGIES.
SAVOR ONE LAST CHANCE TO SIGN AUTOGRAPHS FOR NIGHTSHADE'S ADORING PUBLIC.
DOCTOR EDEN!
YOU WERE SWORN IN JUST HOURS AFTER PRESIDENT HARLEY'S ASSASSINATION.
CAN WE CONFIRM THE PEACE-MAKER'S INVOLVEMENT?
CHRISTOPHER SMITH IS CURRENTLY IN CUSTODY.
I'M SCHEDULED TO SPEAK WITH HIM IN-- AROUND EIGHT MINUTES, SO LET'S MAKE THIS FAST.
OUR COUNTRY STILL FEELS THE PAIN.
STILL CARRIES THE BRUISES.
BUT THIS IS A TIME TO MOURN PRESIDENT HARLEY.
PEACEMAKER A KILLER, CAPTAIN ATOM STILL MISSING IN ACTION--
--WHAT HAPPENED TO AMERICA'S SUPERMEN?
I CAN SEE YOU'RE ALL EAGER TO GET MY ATTENTION.
LET ME ANSWER YOUR QUESTIONS WITH ONE OF MY OWN.
CAN YOU TAKE A LEAP OF FAITH WITH ME?

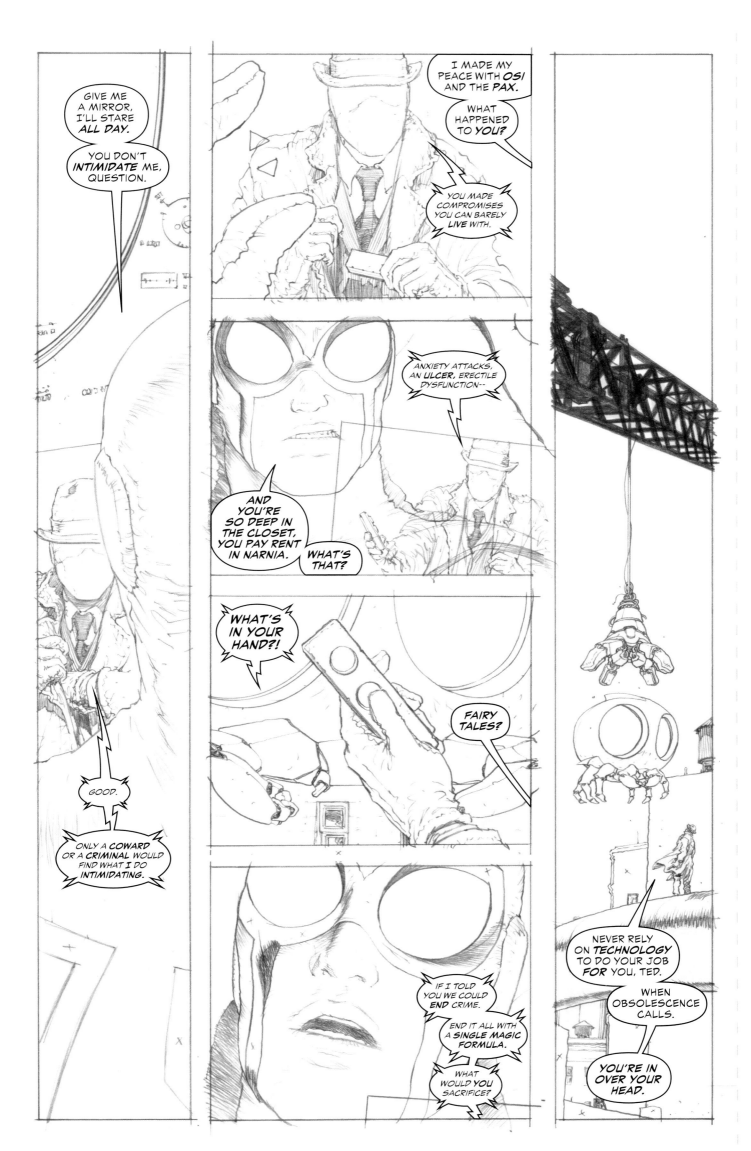

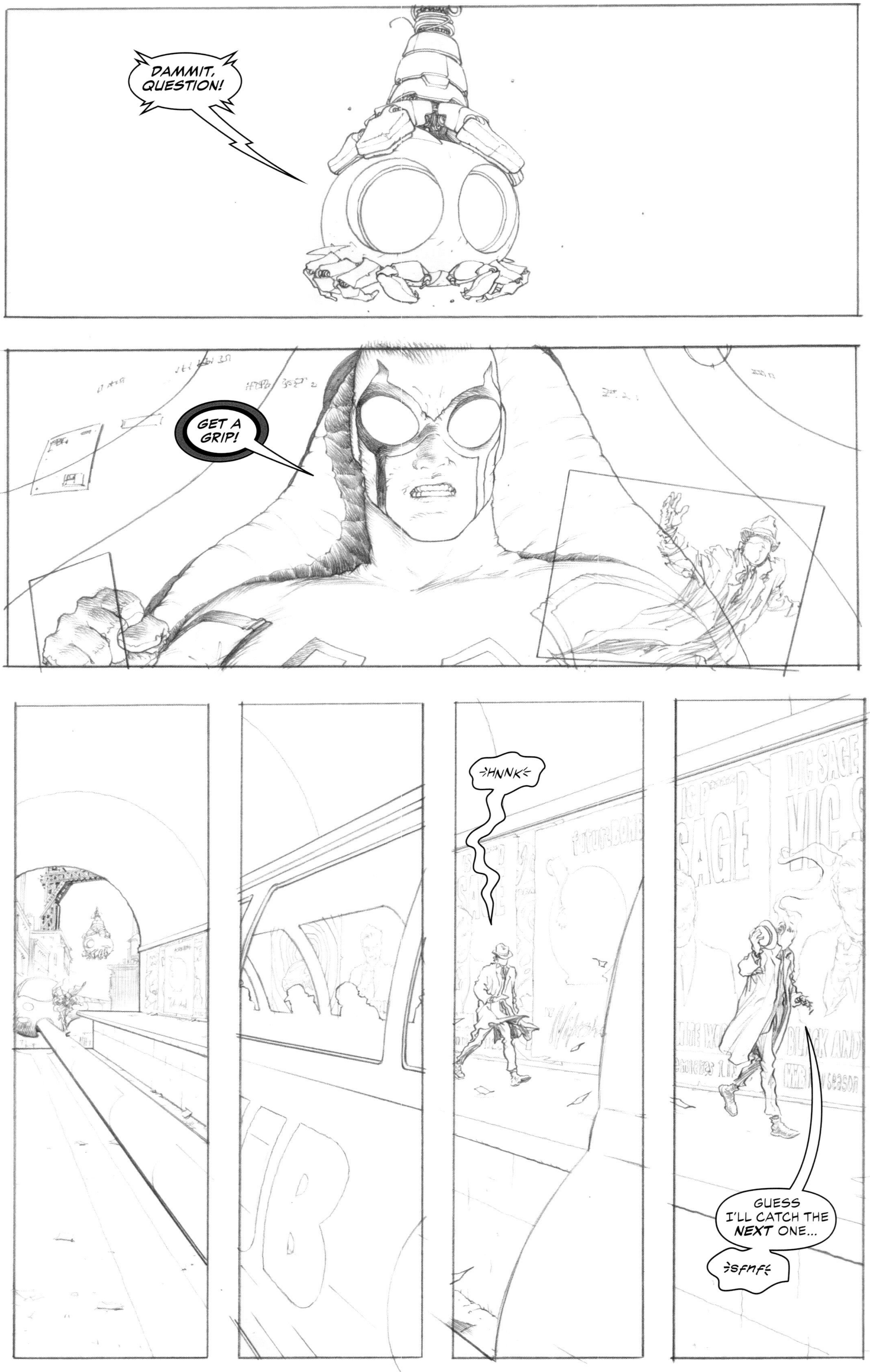
DAMMIT, QUESTION!
GET A GRIP!
HNNK
GUESS I'LL CATCH THE NEXT ONE...
SFNF

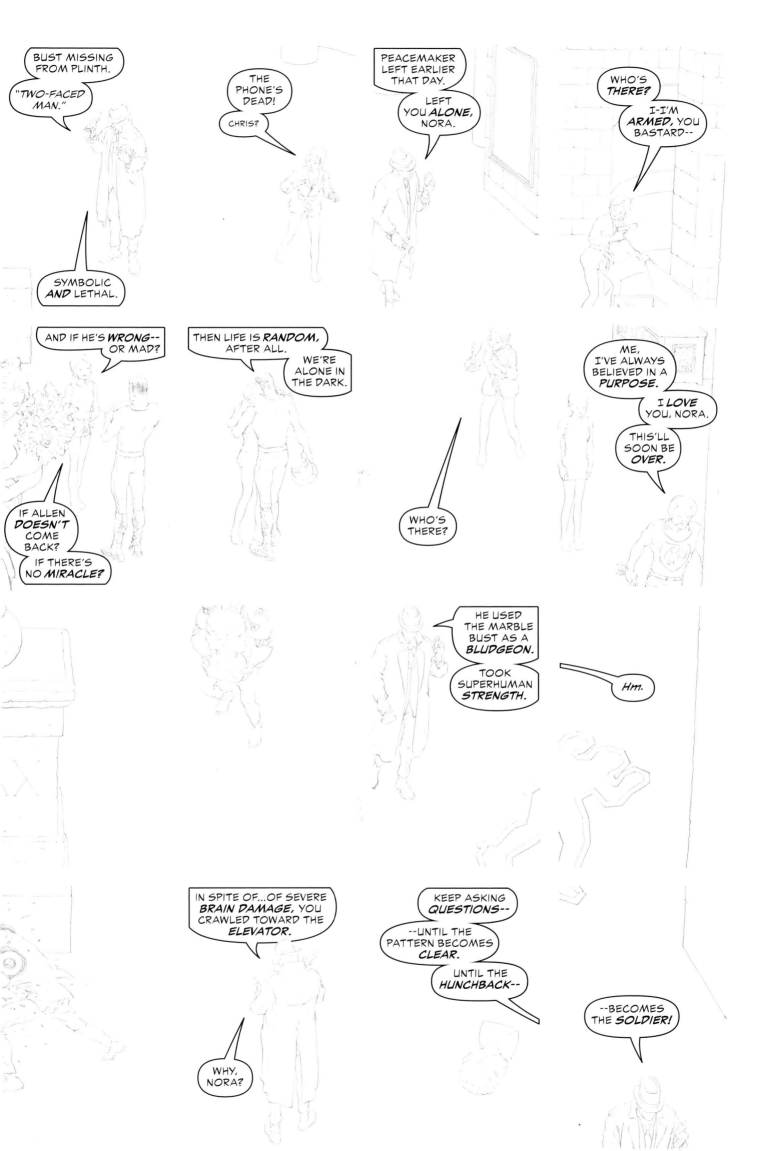

--ON PAGES *12 AND 13,* I CAUGHT SIGHT OF A MASSLESS TIME-SYMMETRICAL *BOSON.*

A *MÖBIUS LOOP* CURVING THROUGH *EIGHT* DIMENSIONS.

I HEARD SOMETHING KNOCKING ON THE *DOOR* TO *GET IN*--

Um, ah, CAPTAIN, THIS IS *DOCTOR McDOUGALL* IN THE *CONTROL ROOM.*

CAN WE PUT AWAY THE COMIC BOOK, PLEASE?

I'M THINKING HOW *OUR* UNIVERSE APPEARS FROM A *HIGHER DIMENSIONAL* PERSPECTIVE.

FLAT.

CAPTAIN--PLEASE *CONCENTRATE.*

THIS IS *PROFESSOR LYONS.*

COMMENCING *PARTICLE ACCELERATION,* ARE YOU READY?

COMPLETE YET ALWAYS BEGINNING AND ENDING.

ALWAYS *DIFFERENT.*

THE STORY'S *LINEAR,* BUT I CAN FLIP THROUGH THE PAGES IN *ANY* ORDER, ANY DIRECTION. *FORWARD* IN TIME TO THE *CONCLUSION.*

BACK TO THE *OPENING SCENE.*

THE CHARACTERS REMAIN *UNAWARE* OF MY SCRUTINY, BUT *THEIR* THOUGHTS ARE *TRANSPARENT,* WEIGHTLESS IN LITTLE CLOUDS.

THIS IS HOW A *2-DIMENSIONAL CONTINUUM* LOOKS TO *YOU.*

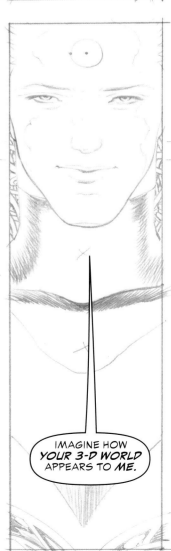

IMAGINE HOW *YOUR 3-D WORLD* APPEARS TO *ME.*

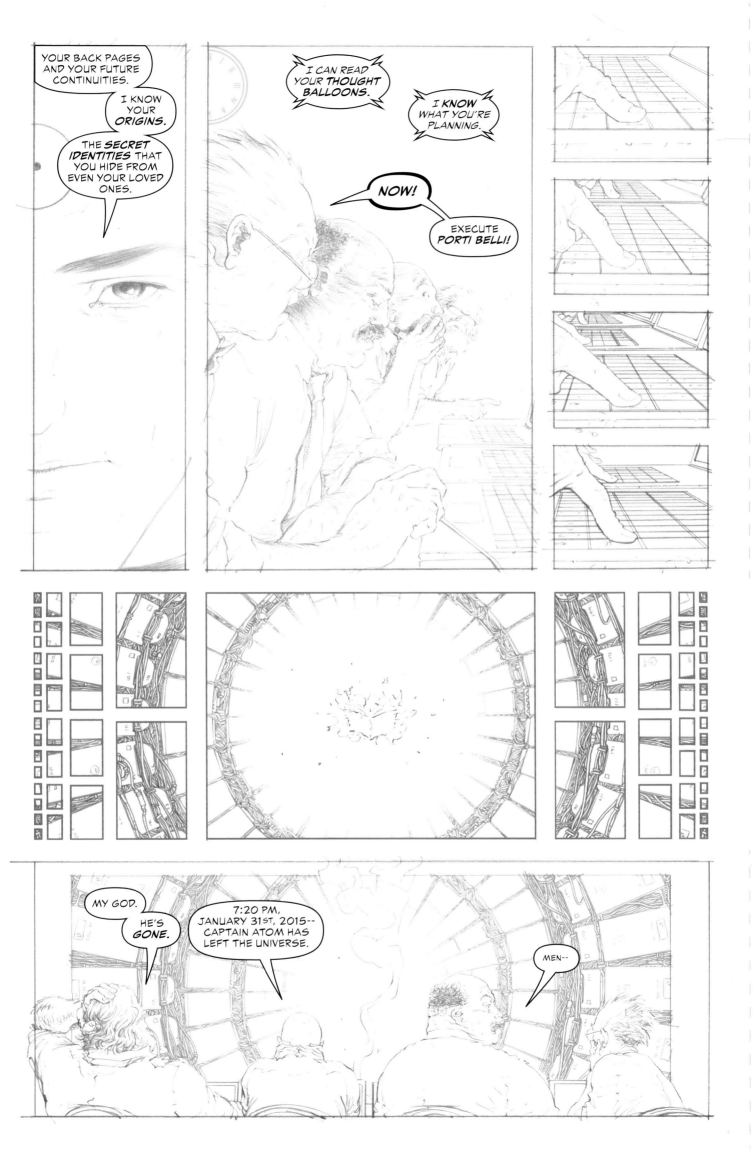

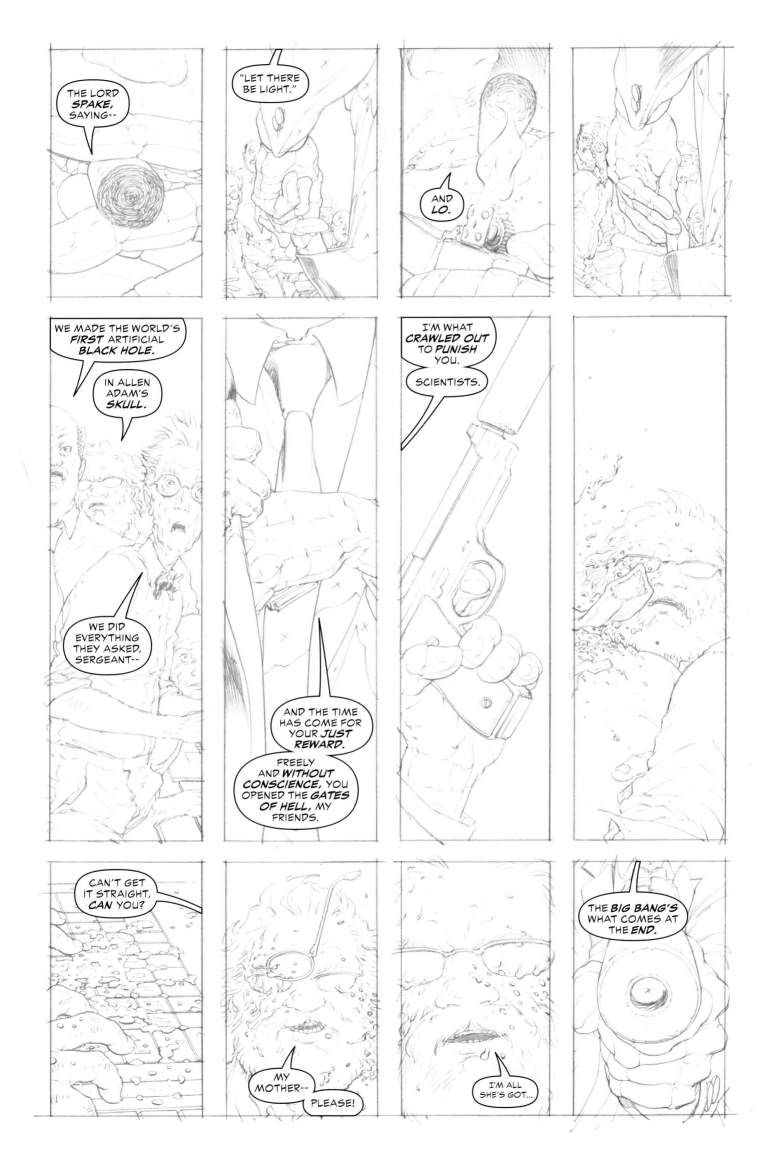

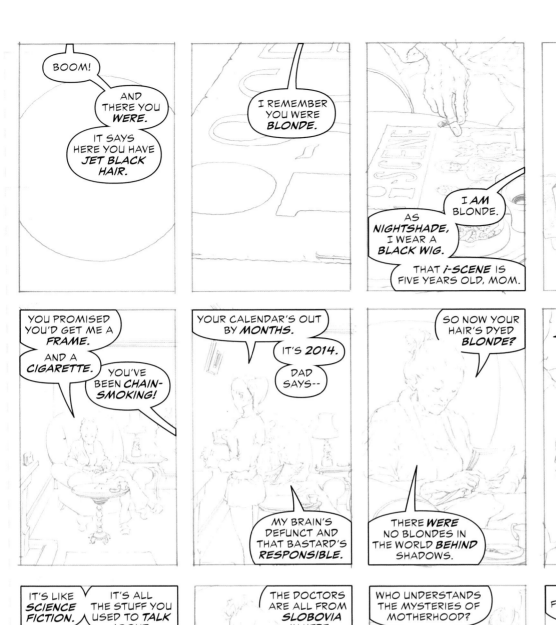

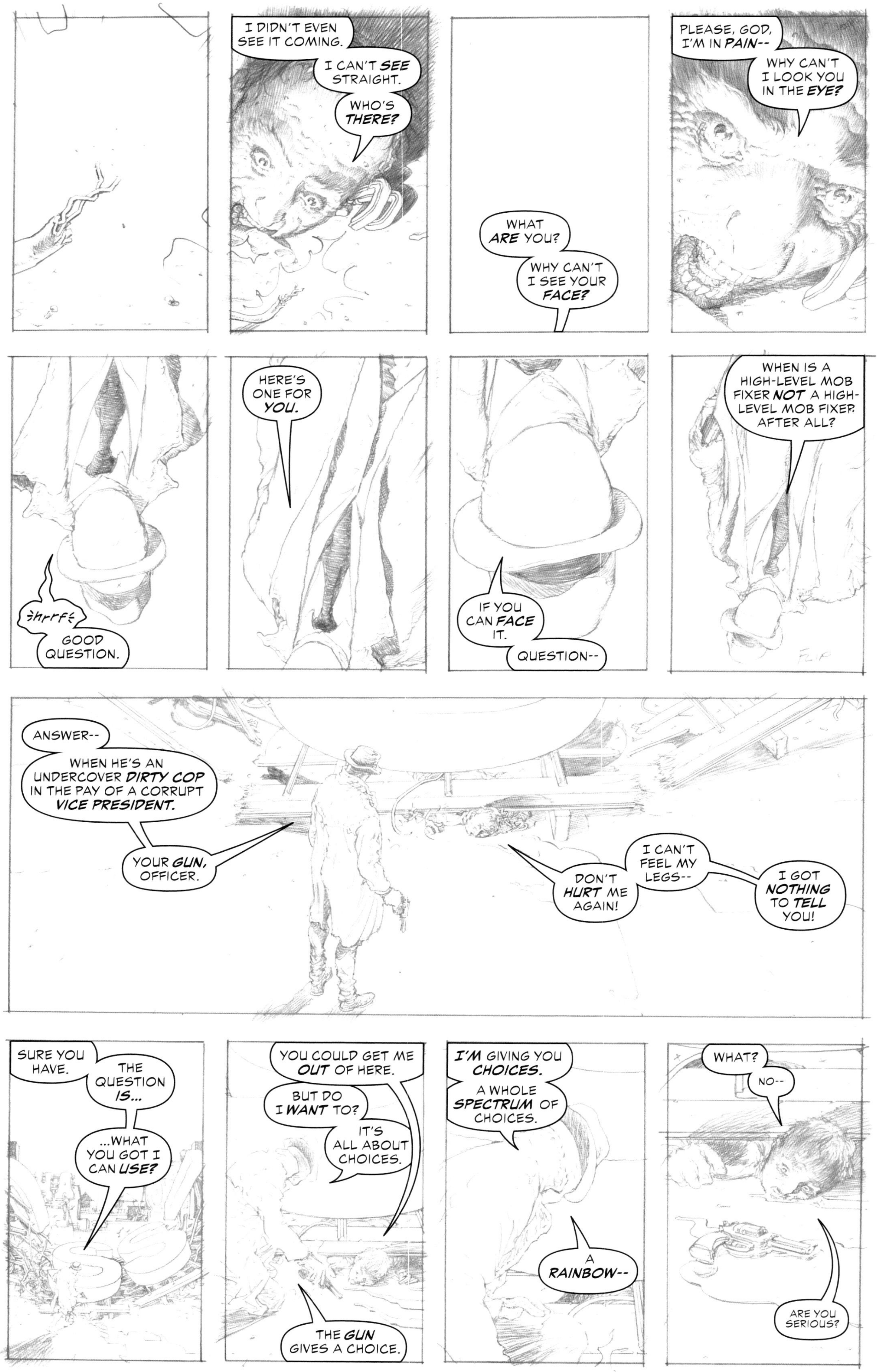
I DIDN'T EVEN SEE IT COMING.
I CAN'T SEE STRAIGHT.
WHO'S THERE?
WHAT ARE YOU?
WHY CAN'T I SEE YOUR FACE?
PLEASE, GOD, I'M IN PAIN--
WHY CAN'T I LOOK YOU IN THE EYE?
HRRF
GOOD QUESTION.
HERE'S ONE FOR YOU.
IF YOU CAN FACE IT.
QUESTION--
WHEN IS A HIGH-LEVEL MOB FIXER NOT A HIGH-LEVEL MOB FIXER, AFTER ALL?
ANSWER--
WHEN HE'S AN UNDERCOVER DIRTY COP IN THE PAY OF A CORRUPT VICE PRESIDENT.
YOUR GUN, OFFICER.
DON'T HURT ME AGAIN!
I CAN'T FEEL MY LEGS--
I GOT NOTHING TO TELL YOU!
SURE YOU HAVE.
THE QUESTION IS...
...WHAT YOU GOT I CAN USE?
YOU COULD GET ME OUT OF HERE.
BUT DO I WANT TO?
IT'S ALL ABOUT CHOICES.
THE GUN GIVES A CHOICE.
I'M GIVING YOU CHOICES.
A WHOLE SPECTRUM OF CHOICES.
A RAINBOW--
WHAT?
NO--
ARE YOU SERIOUS?

AS THEY *GROW,* SOCIETIES, LIKE INDIVIDUALS, PASS THROUGH IDENTICAL STAGES OF *DEVELOPMENT.* IT BREAKS DOWN INTO AN *EIGHT-STAGE COLOR-CODED* SYSTEM, WHERE THE FIRST LEVEL IS *BEIGE,* CORRESPONDING TO INFANCY.

THI... ...OF PRI... WHERE ...GICAL SUR... ...S ARE PA... ...INT.

THIS IS WHY THEY KICKED YOU OUTTA THE PAX!

NEXT COMES *PURPLE,* EQUIVALENT TO *MAGICAL THINKING* AND THE STAGE AT WHICH HUNTER/GATHERER SUBSISTENCE SOCIETIES EX...

RED IS ... *POWER* POLIT... ...T GANGS, WAR... ...IETIES-- THE ... ...WOS.

B'UE ... ...ENTALIST RE... ...NGE IS THE S... ...TIONAL ... ...ET THE ...EA.

WESTERN SOCIETY'S AT PLURALISTIC *GREEN* RIGHT NOW, BUT *YELLOW* COMES NEXT.

IF WE *MAKE* IT THAT FAR.

YELLOW INTEGRA... PLURAL...

A *TURQUOISE* SOCIETY WOULD RUN ON HOLISTIC, SYNERGISTIC ...PLES.

ME?

I TAKE A *FULL SPECTRUM* APPROACH TO PROBLEMS.

WITH *YOUR* KIND I EMPHASIZE THEMES OF PAIN, FEAR, *BASIC SURVIVAL.*

--PLEASE CALL AN *AMBULANCE--*

MY ORDERS COME FROM THE *SARGE...*

I CAN'T REACH--

THOSE ARE THE GUYS YOU WANT!

I'M *DEAD* WHEN THE SPARKS HIT THE WATER!

THAT'S A DIRTY, ROTTEN WAY TO GO!

I--I GOT *RUMORS* IS ALL--

--ABOUT KILLING *CAPTAIN ATOM.*

A SECRET *FORMULA...*

OH GOD, OH GOD.

WHAT KIND OF MAN WOULD *DO* THIS TO A HUMAN BEING?

I HAVE A *MOTHER--*

I'LL LET HER KNOW HER SON DIED *YELLOW.*

AS FOR *ME--*

--I'M A REGISTERED, CARD-CARRYING *SUPER-HERO.*

I DON'T SAVE *BAD GUYS.*

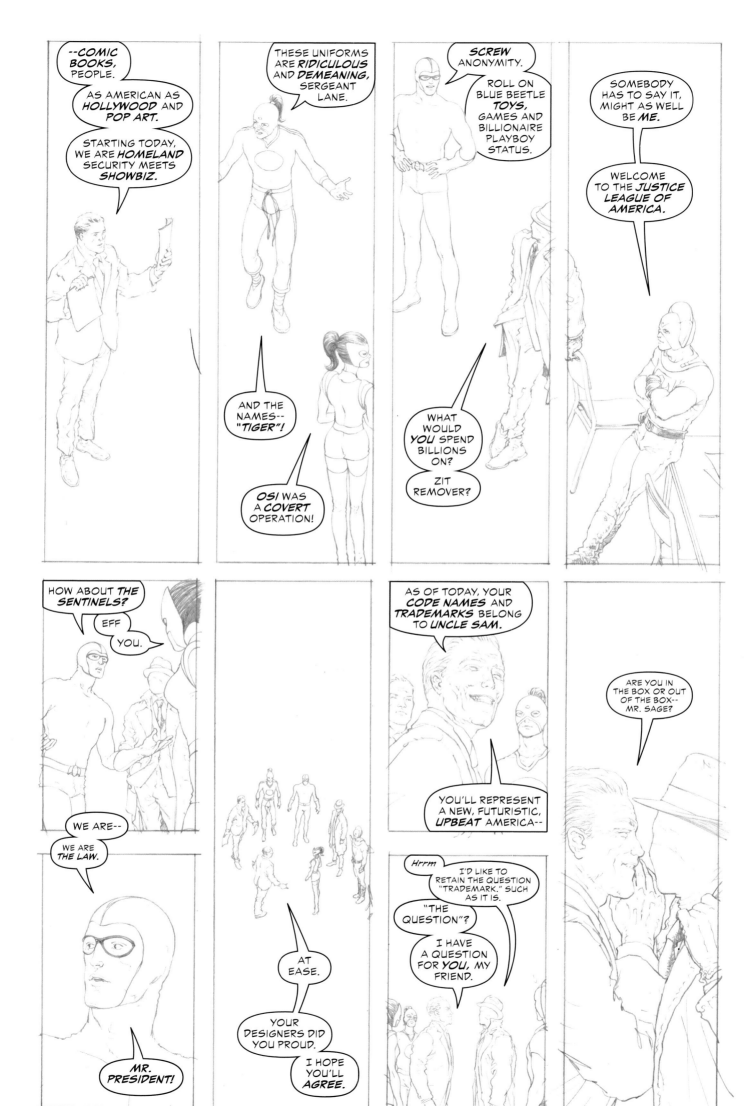

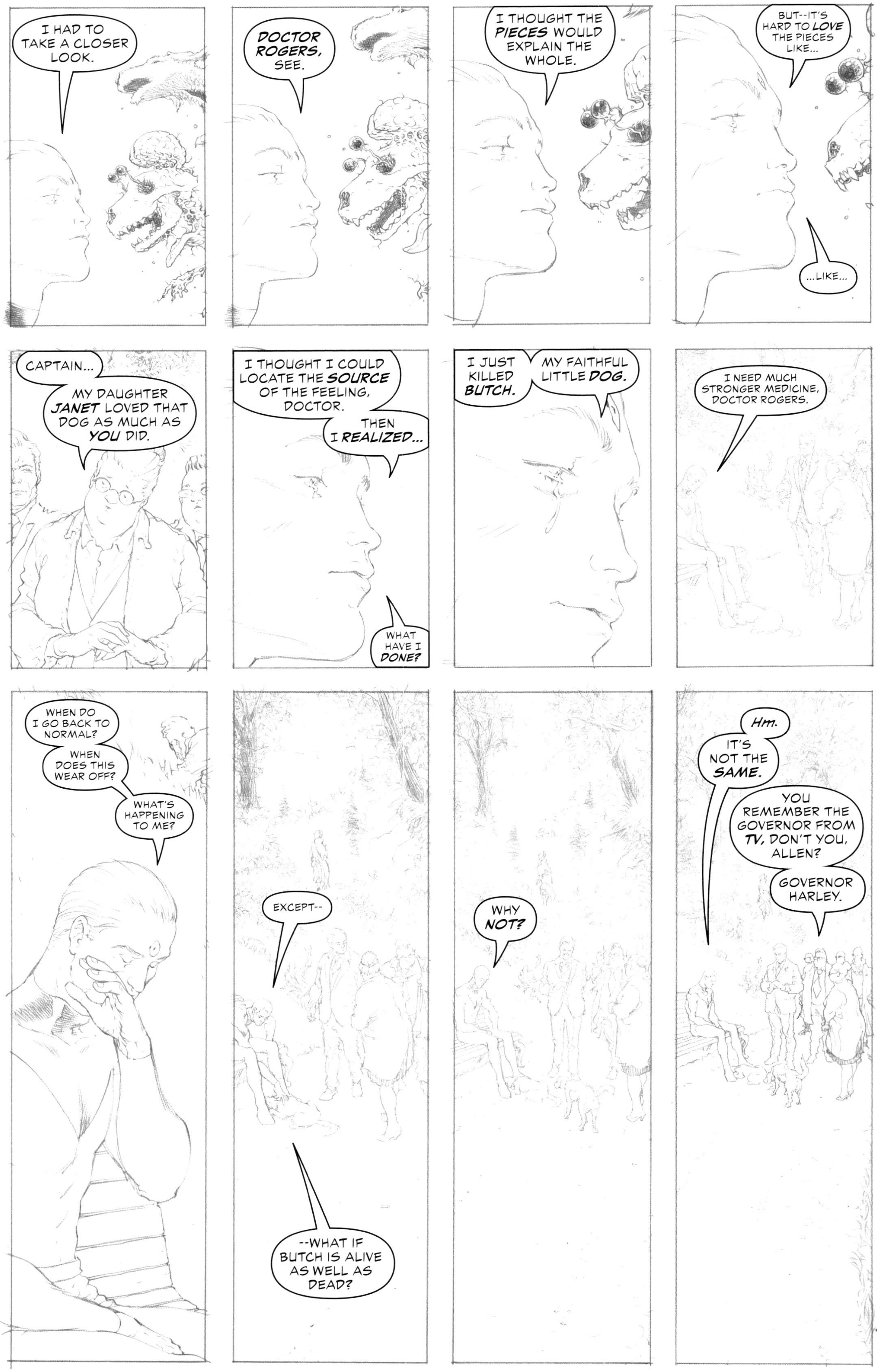
I HAD TO TAKE A CLOSER LOOK.
DOCTOR ROGERS, SEE.
I THOUGHT THE PIECES WOULD EXPLAIN THE WHOLE.
BUT--IT'S HARD TO LOVE THE PIECES LIKE...
...LIKE...
CAPTAIN...
MY DAUGHTER JANET LOVED THAT DOG AS MUCH AS YOU DID.
I THOUGHT I COULD LOCATE THE SOURCE OF THE FEELING, DOCTOR.
THEN I REALIZED...
WHAT HAVE I DONE?
I JUST KILLED BUTCH.
MY FAITHFUL LITTLE DOG.
I NEED MUCH STRONGER MEDICINE, DOCTOR ROGERS.
WHEN DO I GO BACK TO NORMAL?
WHEN DOES THIS WEAR OFF?
WHAT'S HAPPENING TO ME?
EXCEPT--
--WHAT IF BUTCH IS ALIVE AS WELL AS DEAD?
WHY NOT?
Hm.
IT'S NOT THE SAME.
YOU REMEMBER THE GOVERNOR FROM TV, DON'T YOU, ALLEN?
GOVERNOR HARLEY.

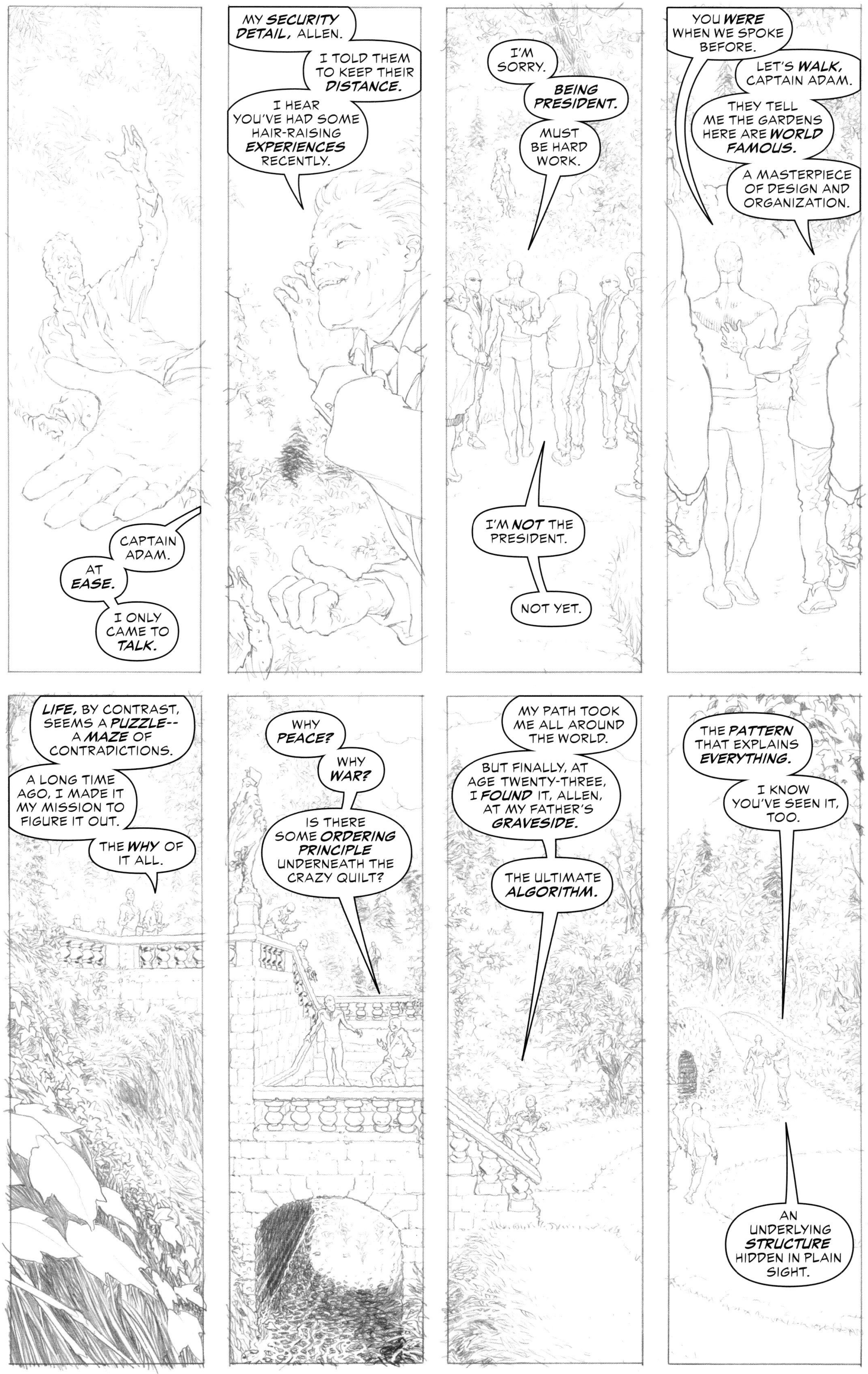
CAPTAIN ADAM.
AT EASE.
I ONLY CAME TO TALK.
MY SECURITY DETAIL, ALLEN.
I TOLD THEM TO KEEP THEIR DISTANCE.
I HEAR YOU'VE HAD SOME HAIR-RAISING EXPERIENCES RECENTLY.
I'M SORRY.
BEING PRESIDENT.
MUST BE HARD WORK.
I'M NOT THE PRESIDENT.
NOT YET.
YOU WERE WHEN WE SPOKE BEFORE.
LET'S WALK, CAPTAIN ADAM.
THEY TELL ME THE GARDENS HERE ARE WORLD FAMOUS.
A MASTERPIECE OF DESIGN AND ORGANIZATION.
LIFE, BY CONTRAST, SEEMS A PUZZLE-- A MAZE OF CONTRADICTIONS.
A LONG TIME AGO, I MADE IT MY MISSION TO FIGURE IT OUT.
THE WHY OF IT ALL.
WHY PEACE?
WHY WAR?
IS THERE SOME ORDERING PRINCIPLE UNDERNEATH THE CRAZY QUILT?
MY PATH TOOK ME ALL AROUND THE WORLD.
BUT FINALLY, AT AGE TWENTY-THREE, I FOUND IT, ALLEN, AT MY FATHER'S GRAVESIDE.
THE ULTIMATE ALGORITHM.
THE PATTERN THAT EXPLAINS EVERYTHING.
I KNOW YOU'VE SEEN IT, TOO.
AN UNDERLYING STRUCTURE HIDDEN IN PLAIN SIGHT.

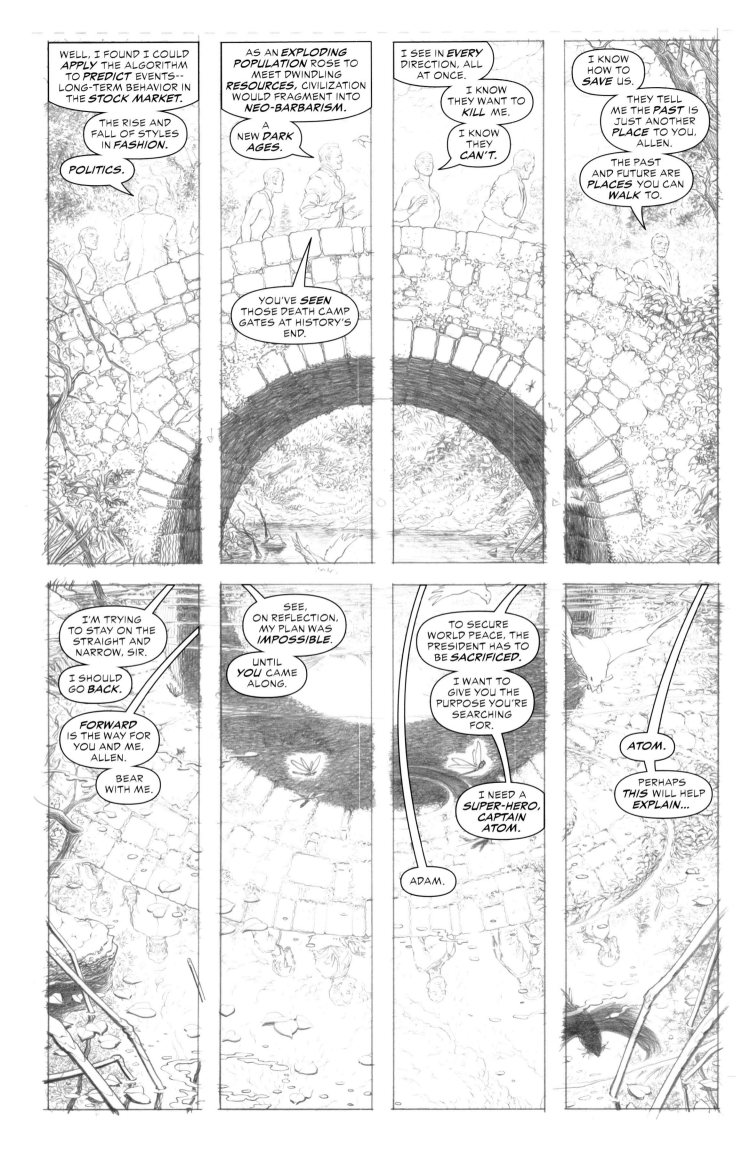

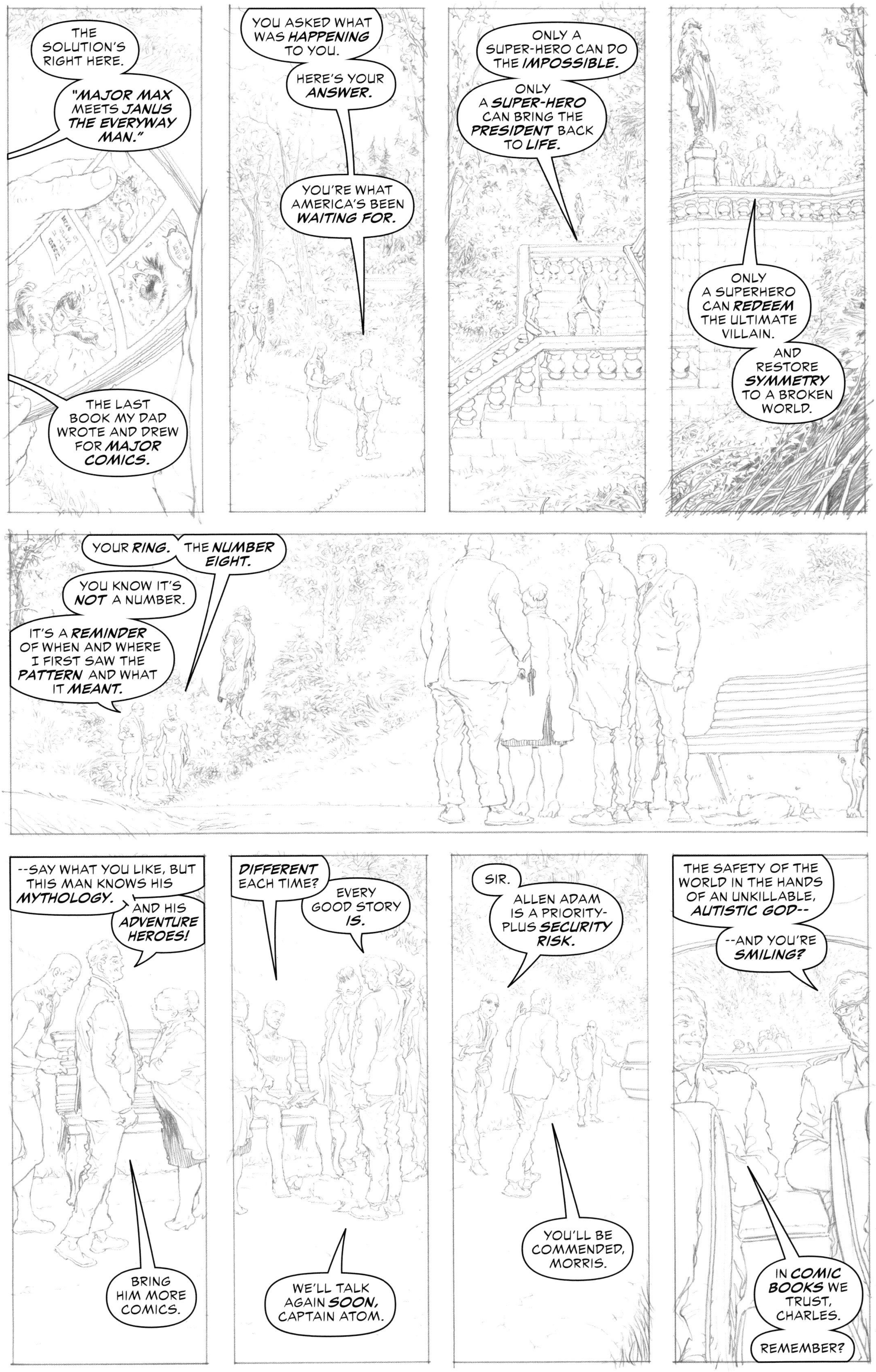
THE SOLUTION'S RIGHT HERE.
"MAJOR MAX MEETS JANUS THE EVERYWAY MAN."
THE LAST BOOK MY DAD WROTE AND DREW FOR MAJOR COMICS.
YOU ASKED WHAT WAS HAPPENING TO YOU.
HERE'S YOUR ANSWER.
YOU'RE WHAT AMERICA'S BEEN WAITING FOR.
ONLY A SUPER-HERO CAN DO THE IMPOSSIBLE.
ONLY A SUPER-HERO CAN BRING THE PRESIDENT BACK TO LIFE.
ONLY A SUPERHERO CAN REDEEM THE ULTIMATE VILLAIN.
AND RESTORE SYMMETRY TO A BROKEN WORLD.
YOUR RING.
THE NUMBER EIGHT.
YOU KNOW IT'S NOT A NUMBER.
IT'S A REMINDER OF WHEN AND WHERE I FIRST SAW THE PATTERN AND WHAT IT MEANT.
--SAY WHAT YOU LIKE, BUT THIS MAN KNOWS HIS MYTHOLOGY.
AND HIS ADVENTURE HEROES!
BRING HIM MORE COMICS.
DIFFERENT EACH TIME?
EVERY GOOD STORY IS.
WE'LL TALK AGAIN SOON, CAPTAIN ATOM.
SIR.
ALLEN ADAM IS A PRIORITY-PLUS SECURITY RISK.
YOU'LL BE COMMENDED, MORRIS.
THE SAFETY OF THE WORLD IN THE HANDS OF AN UNKILLABLE, AUTISTIC GOD--
--AND YOU'RE SMILING?
IN COMIC BOOKS WE TRUST, CHARLES.
REMEMBER?

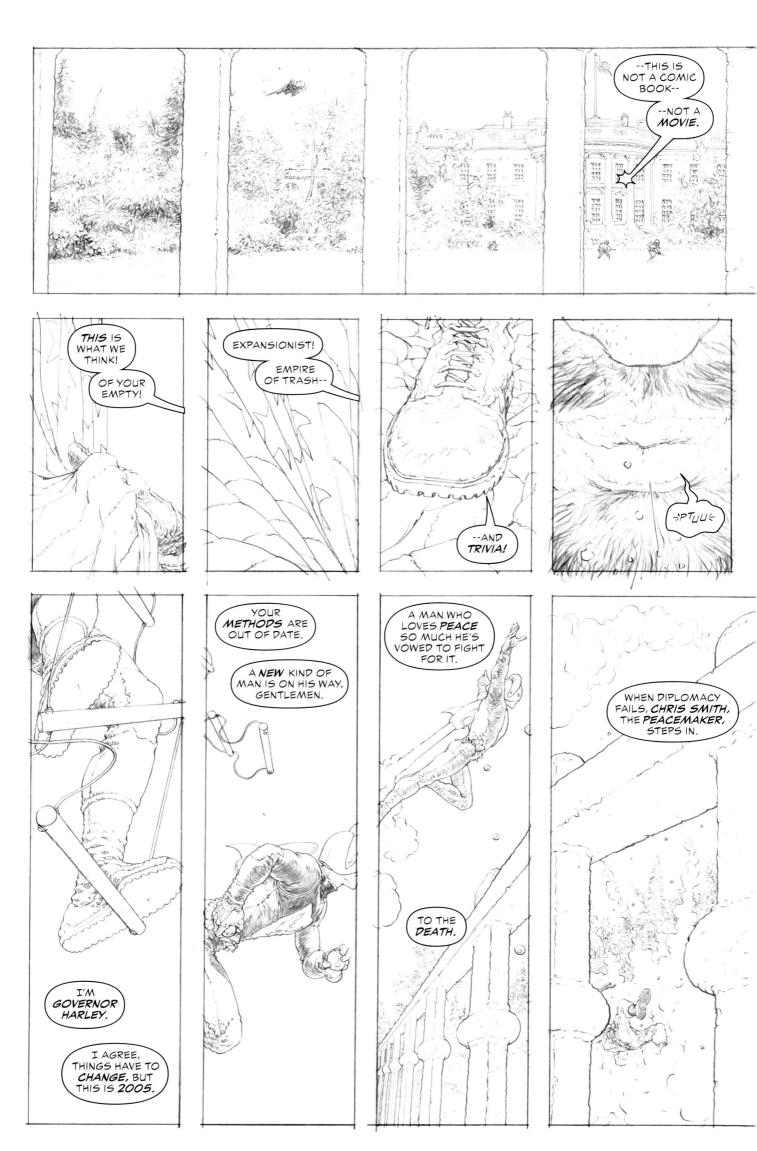

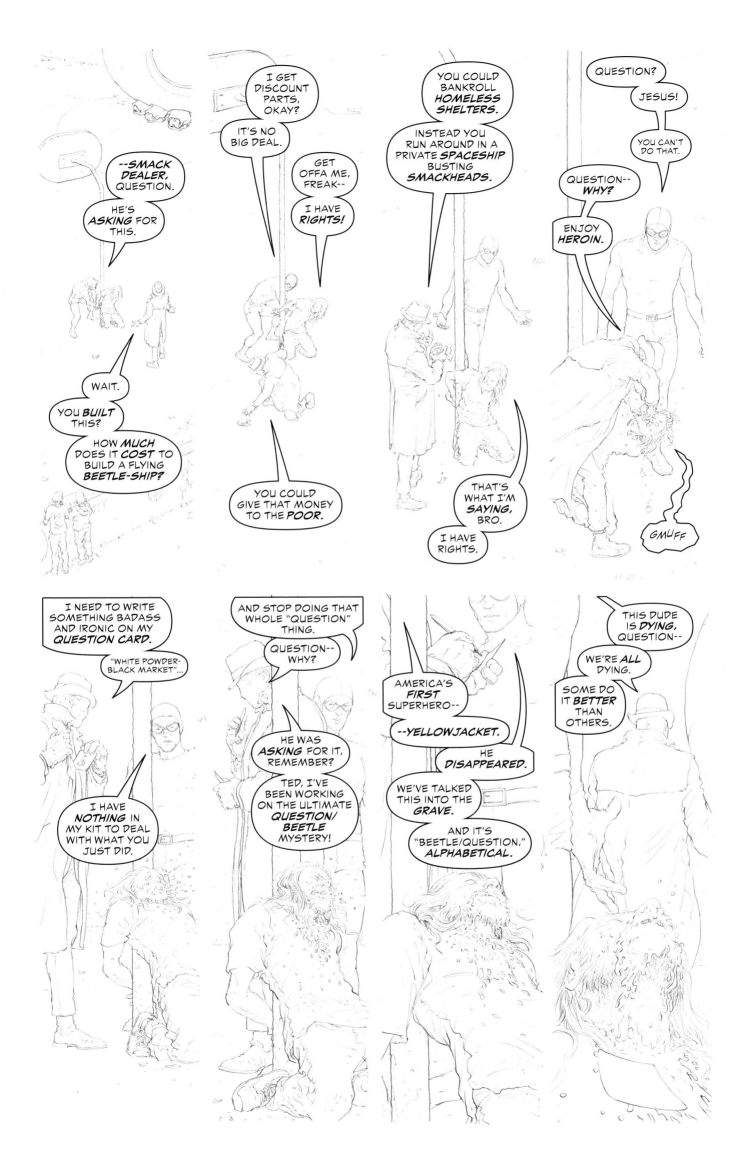

SYNCHRONIZING TRANSMATTER CUBES...

Access across Orrery of Worlds granted.
Variant covers, scripts, and other behind-the-scenes material from the making of *The Multiversity*.

THE ABSOLUTE MULTIVERSITY

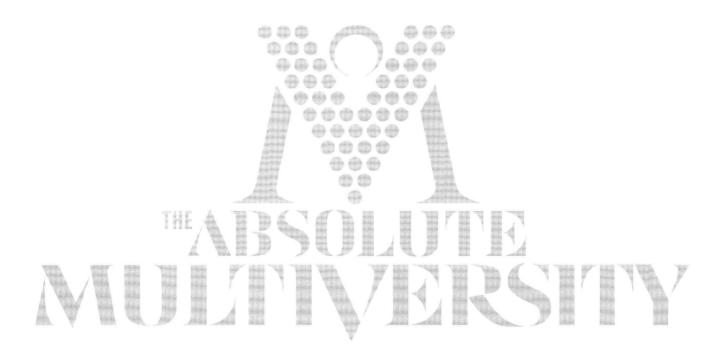

The Multiversity #1 variant cover by Chris Burnham with Nathan Fairbairn after Joe Shuster

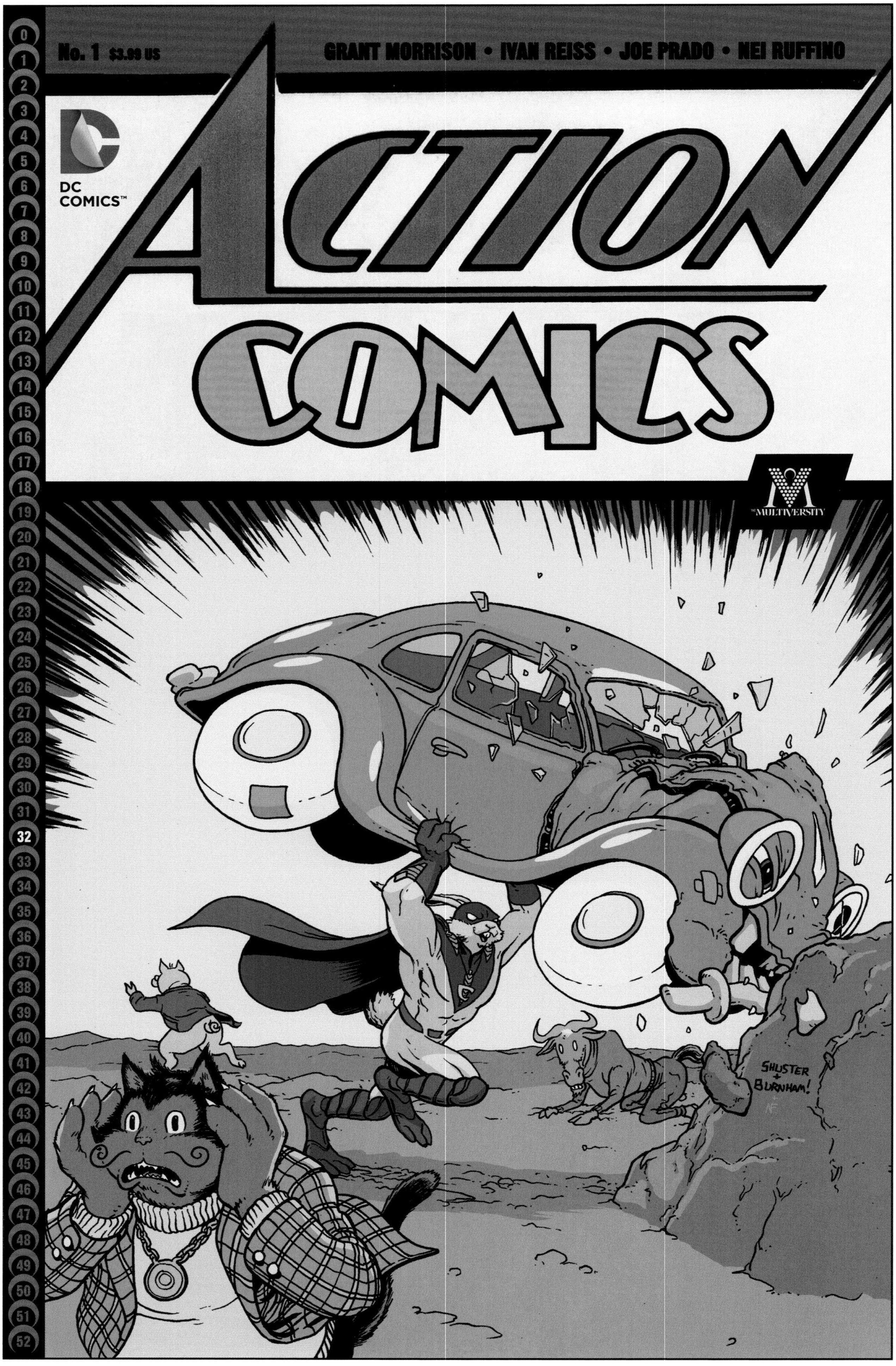

No. 1 $3.99 US
GRANT MORRISON • IVAN REISS • JOE PRADO • NEI RUFFINO
DC COMICS™
ACTION COMICS
THE MULTIVERSITY
SHUSTER + BURNHAM!
NF
0
1
2
3
4
5
6
7
8
9
10
11
12
13
14
15
16
17
18
19
20
21
22
23
24
25
26
27
28
29
30
31
32
33
34
35
36
37
38
39
40
41
42
43
44
45
46
47
48
49
50
51
52

The Multiversity *#1 variant cover by Bryan Hitch with Alex Sinclair*

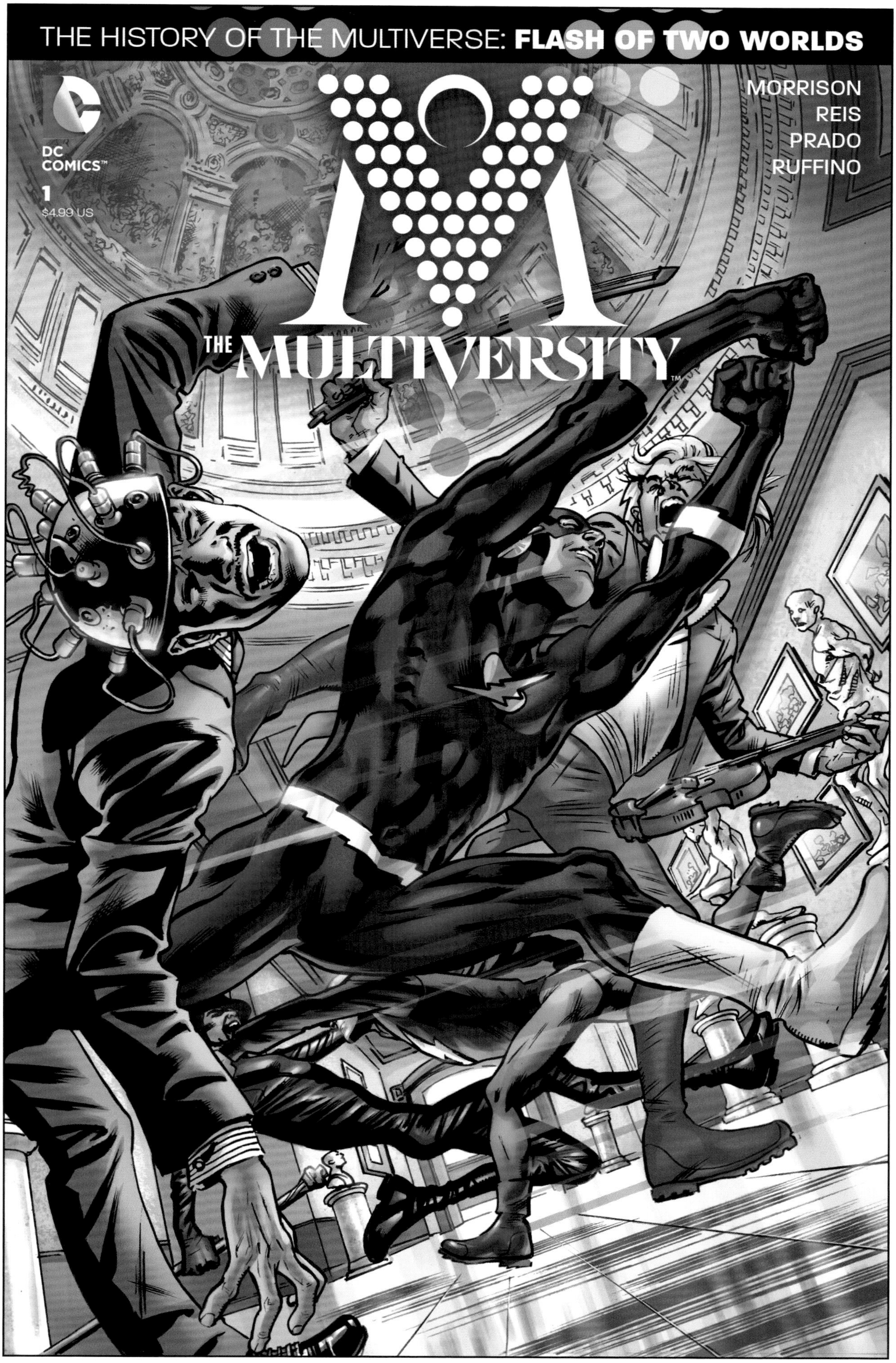
THE HISTORY OF THE MULTIVERSE: FLASH OF TWO WORLDS
DC COMICS
1
$4.99 US
THE MULTIVERSITY
MORRISON
REIS
PRADO
RUFFINO

The Multiversity #1 variant cover by Grant Morrison

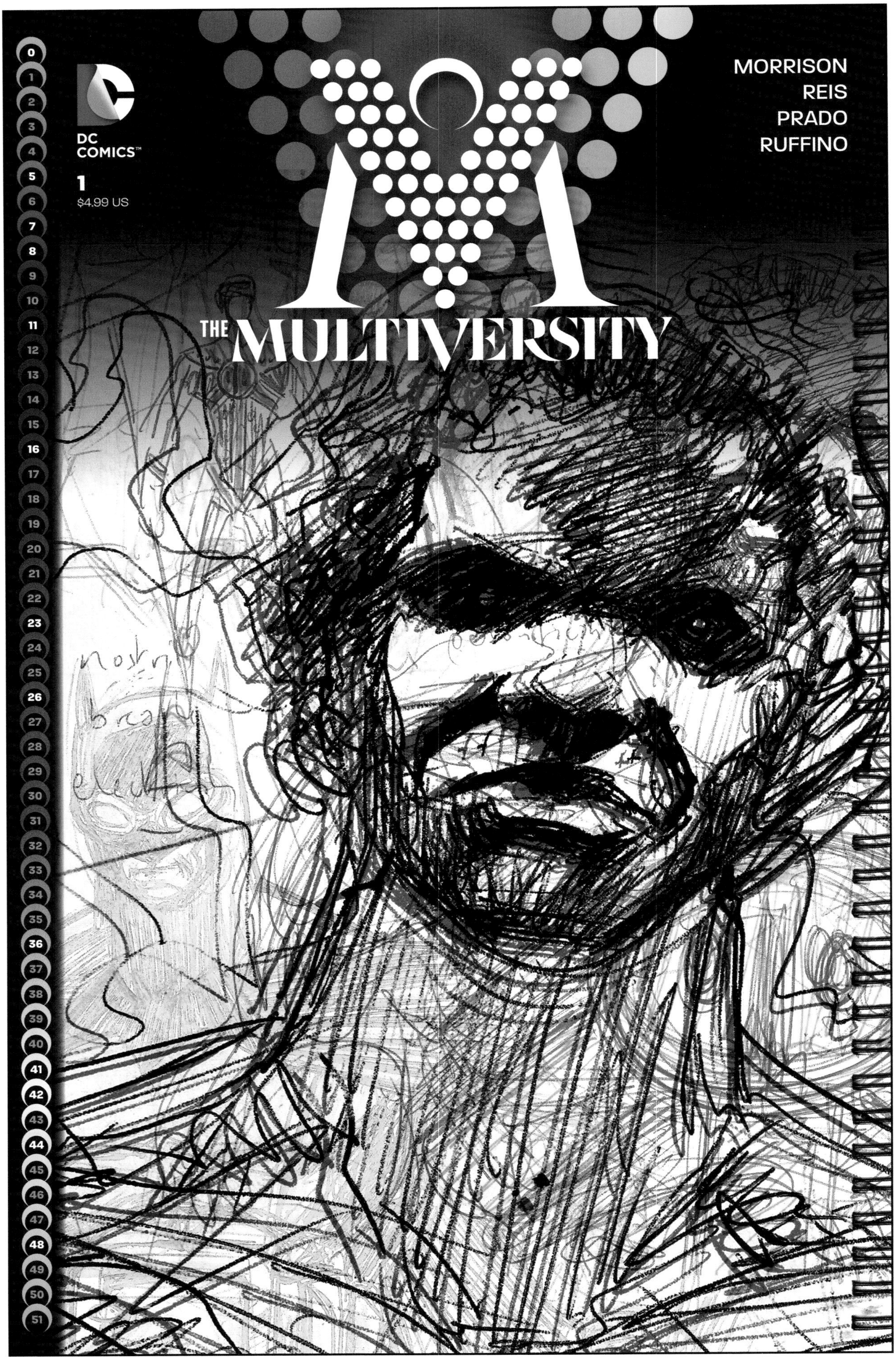
DC COMICS™
1
$4.99 US
MORRISON
REIS
PRADO
RUFFINO
THE MULTIVERSITY

Left: The Multiversity *#1 New York Comic Con variant cover by Ivan Reis and Joe Prado*
Right: The Multiversity *#1 Fan Expo Canada variant cover by Ivan Reis and Joe Prado*

DC COMICS
1
MORRISON
REIS
PRADO
RUFFINO
THE MULTIVERSITY
COSMIC NEIGHBORHOOD WATCH
NEW YORK COMIC CON OCTOBER 9-12, 2014
RATED T TEEN • DCCOMICS.COM

DC COMICS
1
MORRISON
REIS
PRADO
RUFFINO
THE MULTIVERSITY
COSMIC NEIGHBORHOOD WATCH
FAN EXPO CANADA
RATED T TEEN • DCCOMICS.COM

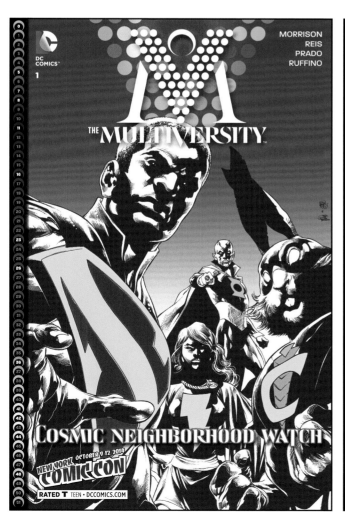

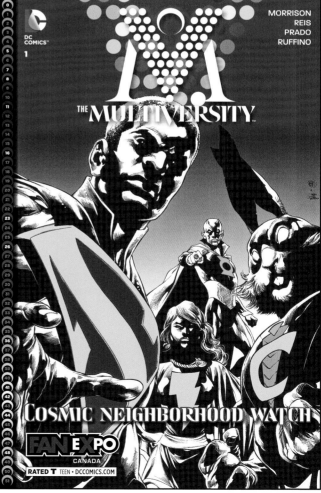

The Multiversity #2 variant cover by Michael Allred with Laura Allred after Mike Mignola

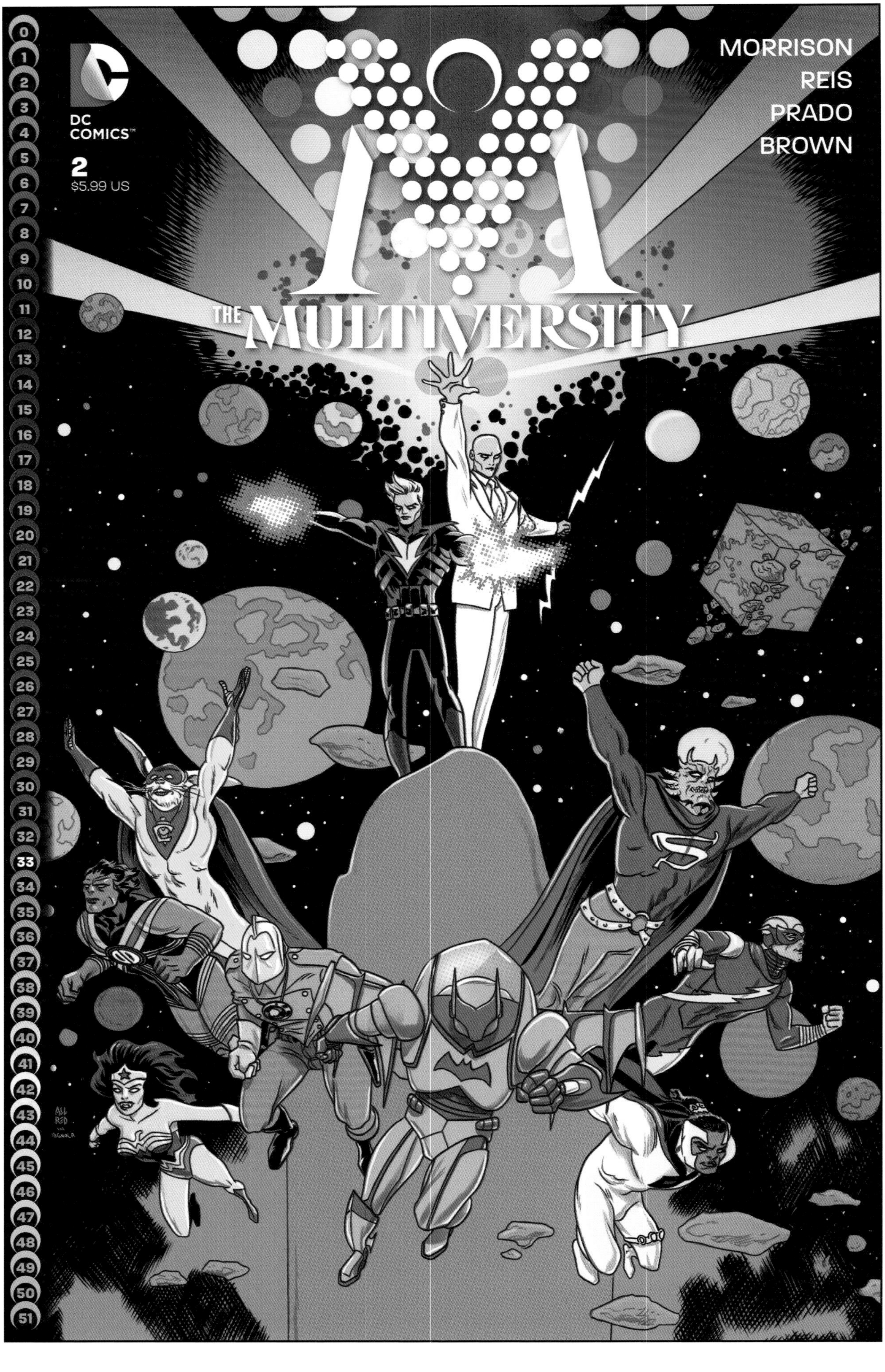
DC COMICS™
2
$5.99 US
MORRISON
REIS
PRADO
BROWN
THE MULTIVERSITY
0
1
2
3
4
5
6
7
8
9
10
11
12
13
14
15
16
17
18
19
20
21
22
23
24
25
26
27
28
29
30
31
32
33
34
35
36
37
38
39
40
41
42
43
44
45
46
47
48
49
50
51

The Multiversity #2 variant cover by Francis Manapul

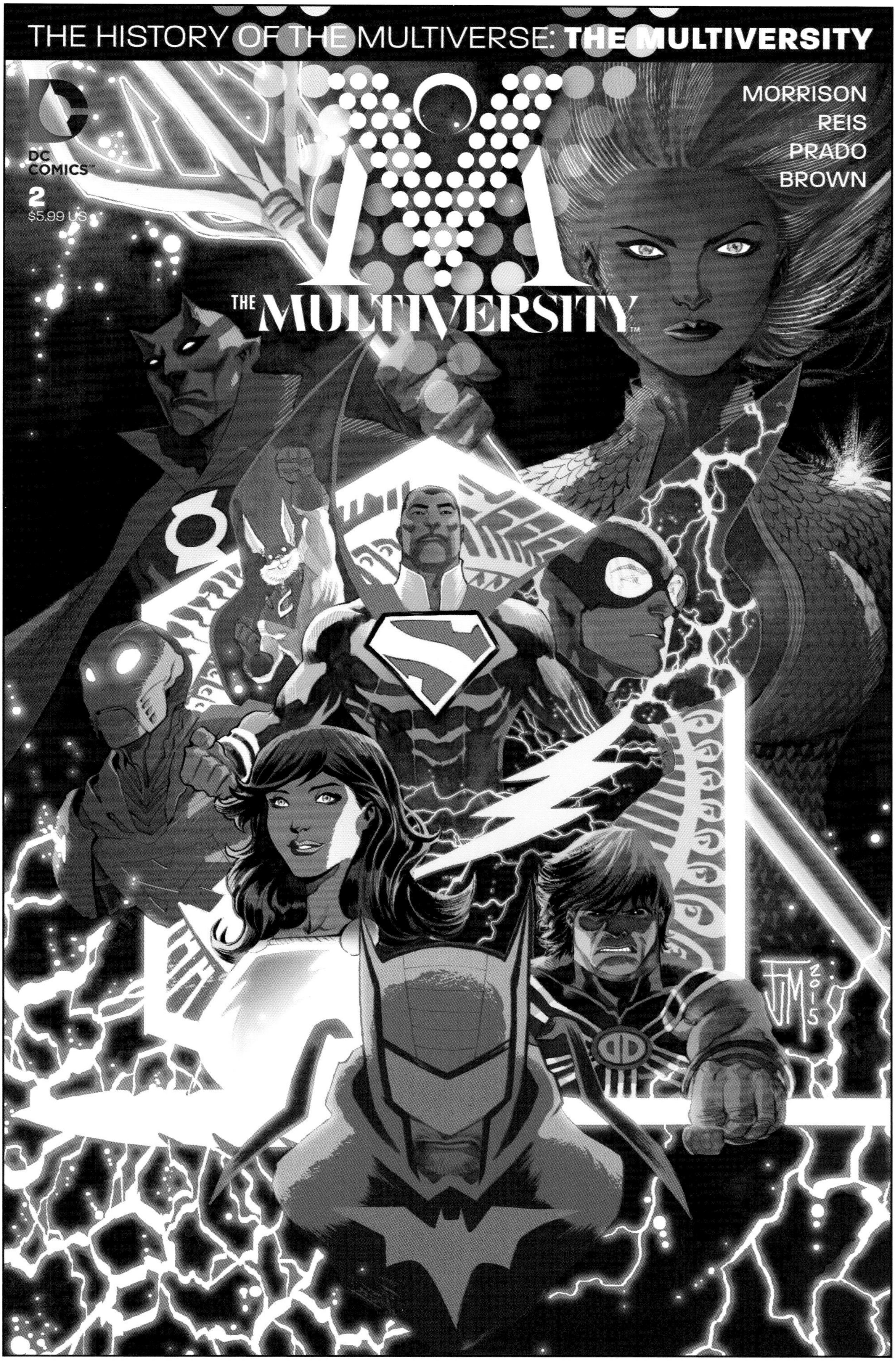
THE HISTORY OF THE MULTIVERSE: THE MULTIVERSITY
DC COMICS
2
$5.99 US
MORRISON
REIS
PRADO
BROWN
THE MULTIVERSITY
FJM 2015

The Multiversity *#2 variant cover by Grant Morrison*

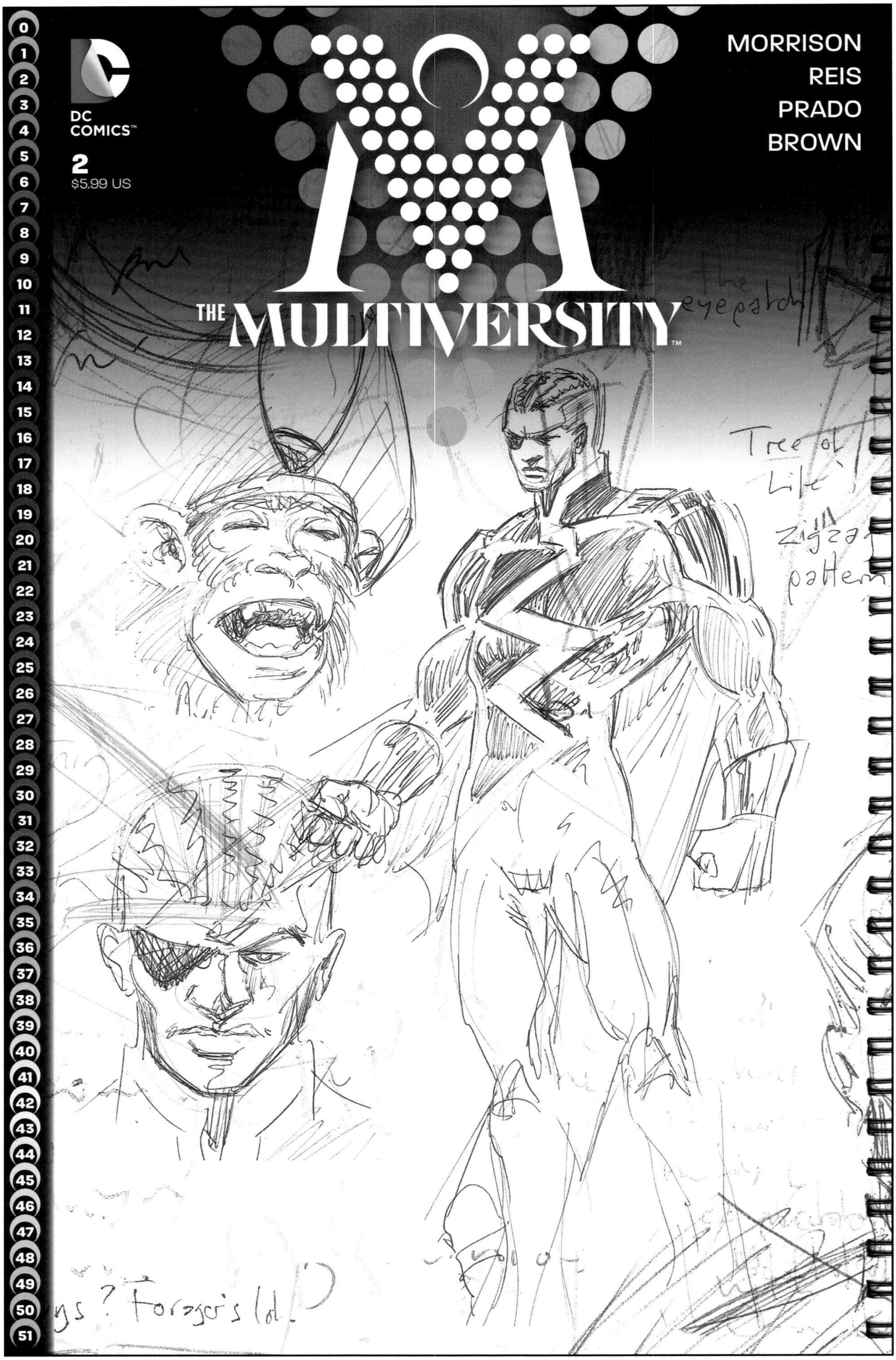
MORRISON
REIS
PRADO
BROWN
DC COMICS
2
$5.99 US
THE MULTIVERSITY
eyepatch
Tree of Life
Zigzag pattern

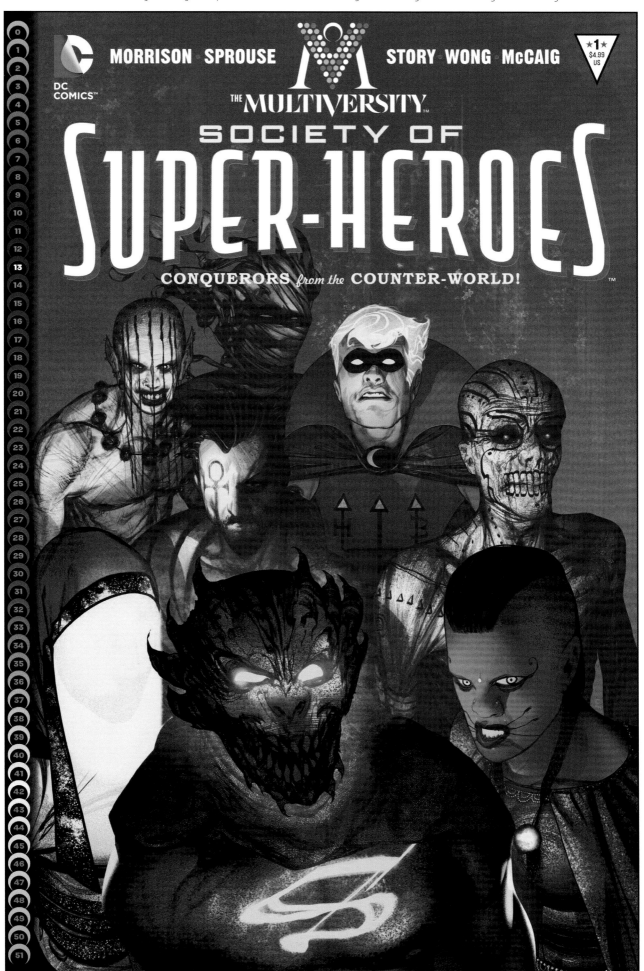

The Multiversity: Society of Super-Heroes *#1 variant cover by Grant Morrison*

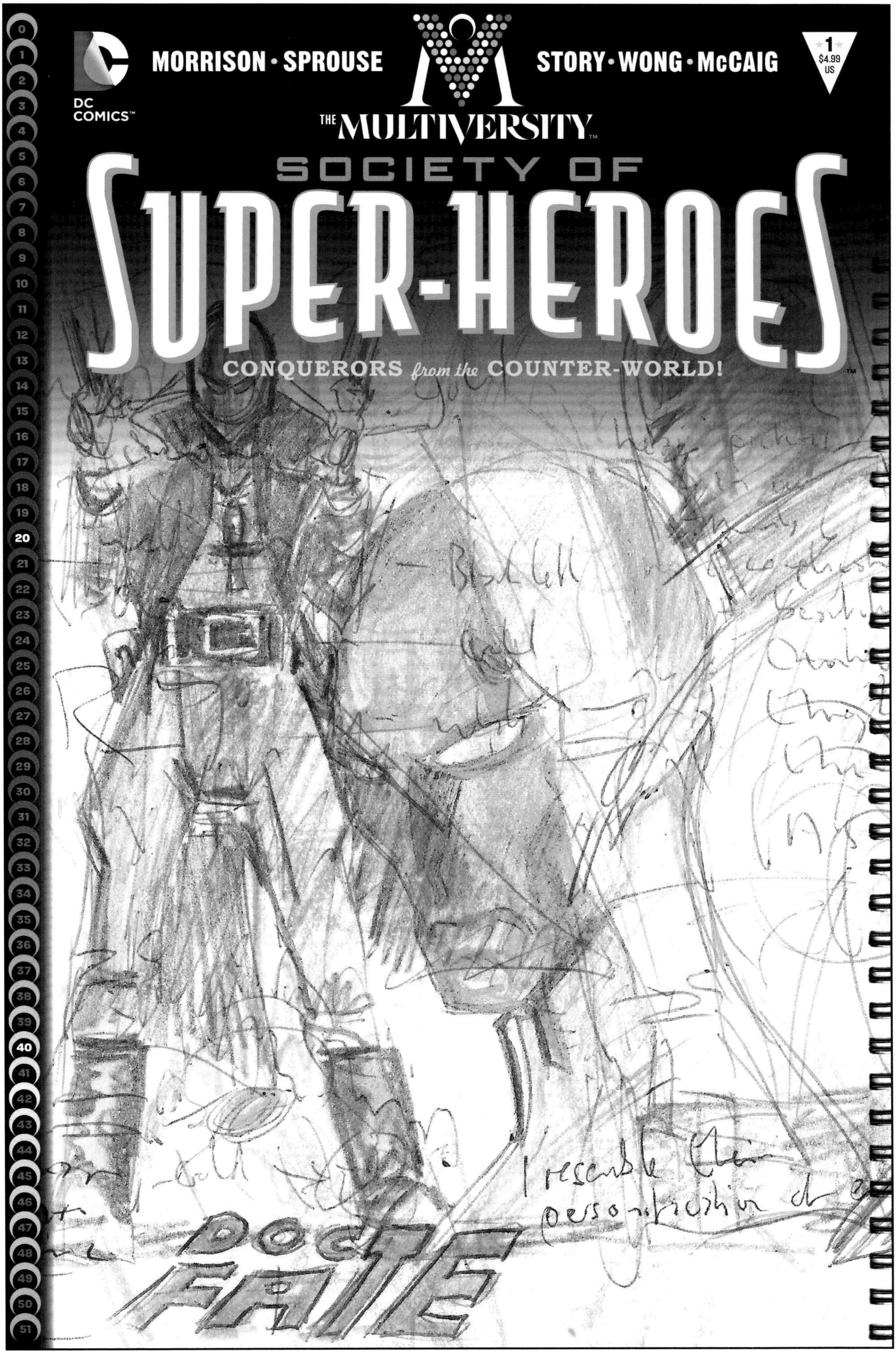
DC COMICS
MORRISON • SPROUSE
STORY • WONG • McCAIG
1
$4.99
US
THE MULTIVERSITY
SOCIETY OF
SUPER-HEROES
CONQUERORS from the COUNTER-WORLD!
FATE

The Multiversity: The Just *#1 variant cover by Dale Eaglesham with Gabe Eltaeb*

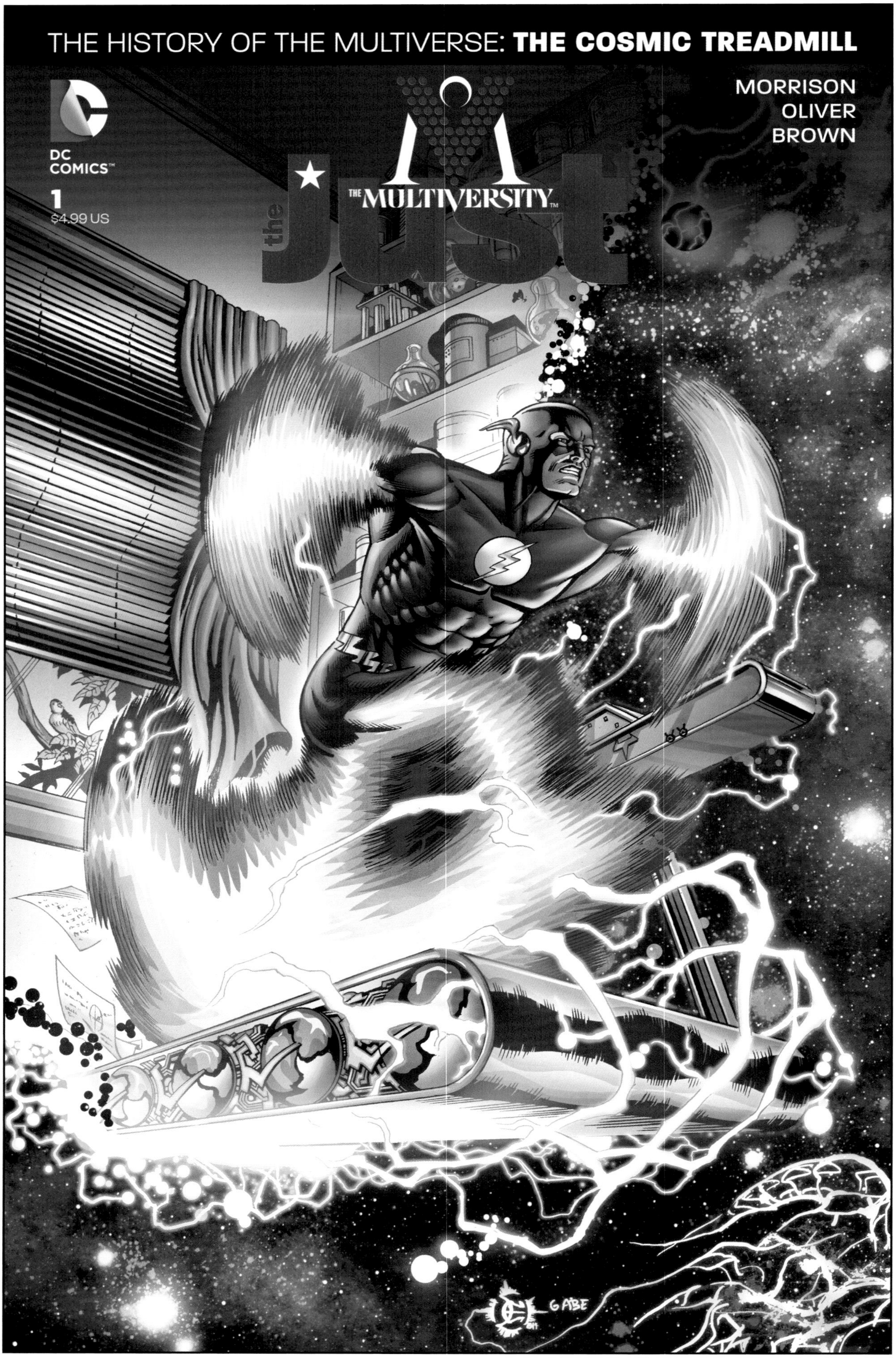
THE HISTORY OF THE MULTIVERSE: THE COSMIC TREADMILL
DC COMICS
1
$4.99 US
THE MULTIVERSITY
the Just
MORRISON
OLIVER
BROWN
GABE

The Multiversity: The Just *#1 variant cover by Eduardo Risso with Nathan Fairbairn after Mike Sekowsky, Murphy Anderson, and Jack Adler*

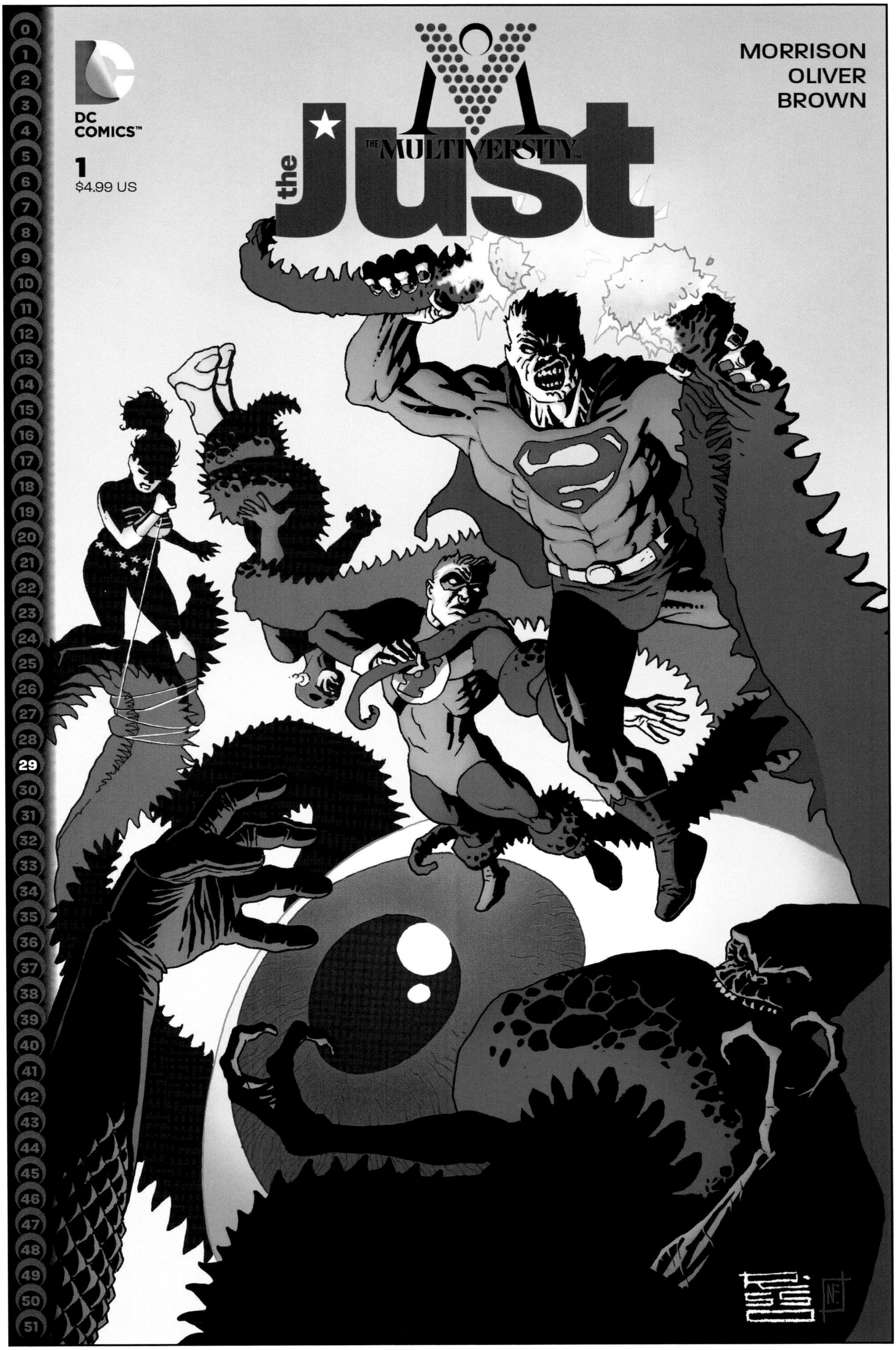

0
1
2
3
4
5
6
7
8
9
10
11
12
13
14
15
16
17
18
19
20
21
22
23
24
25
26
27
28
29
30
31
32
33
34
35
36
37
38
39
40
41
42
43
44
45
46
47
48
49
50
51
DC COMICS™
1
$4.99 US
THE MULTIVERSITY™
the Just
MORRISON
OLIVER
BROWN
NF

The Multiversity: The Just *#1 variant cover by Grant Morrison*

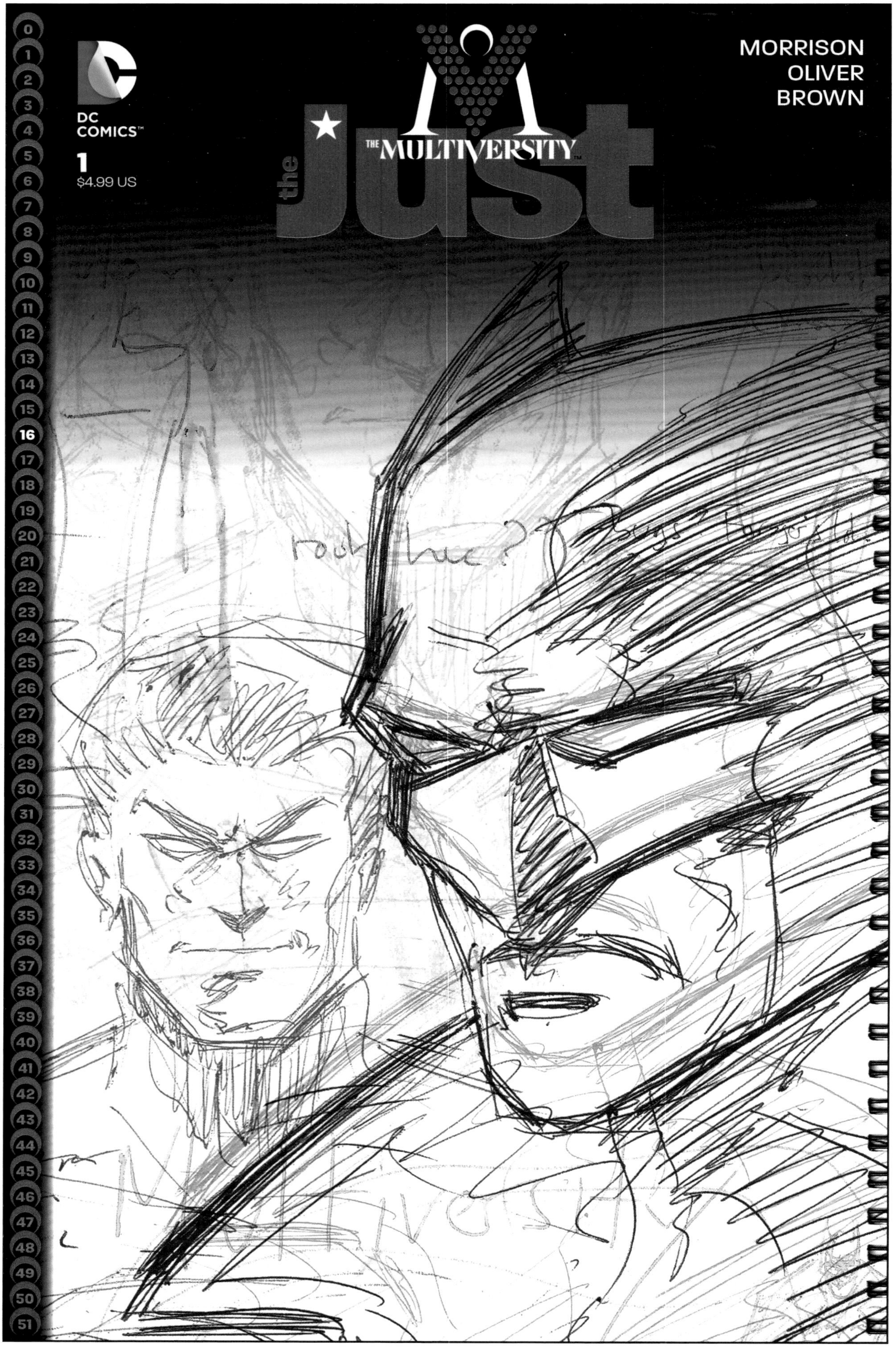
DC COMICS™
1
$4.99 US
THE MULTIVERSITY
the Just™
MORRISON
OLIVER
BROWN

The Multiversity: Pax Americana *#1 variant cover by Jae Lee with June Chung*

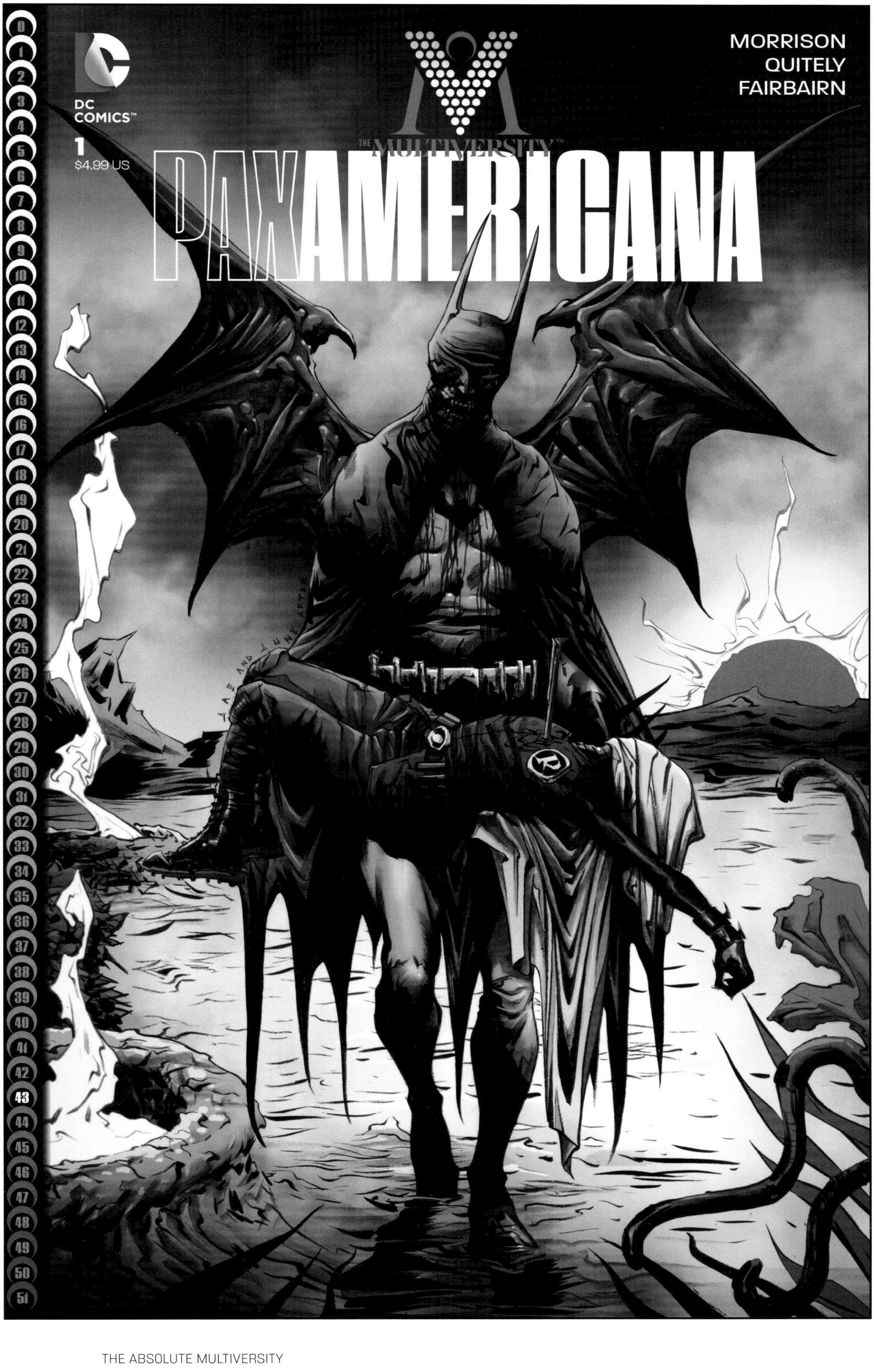
DC COMICS
1
$4.99 US
THE MULTIVERSITY
PAX AMERICANA
MORRISON
QUITELY
FAIRBAIRN

The Multiversity: Pax Americana *#1 variant cover by Patrick Gleason and Christian Alamy with Nathan Fairbairn*

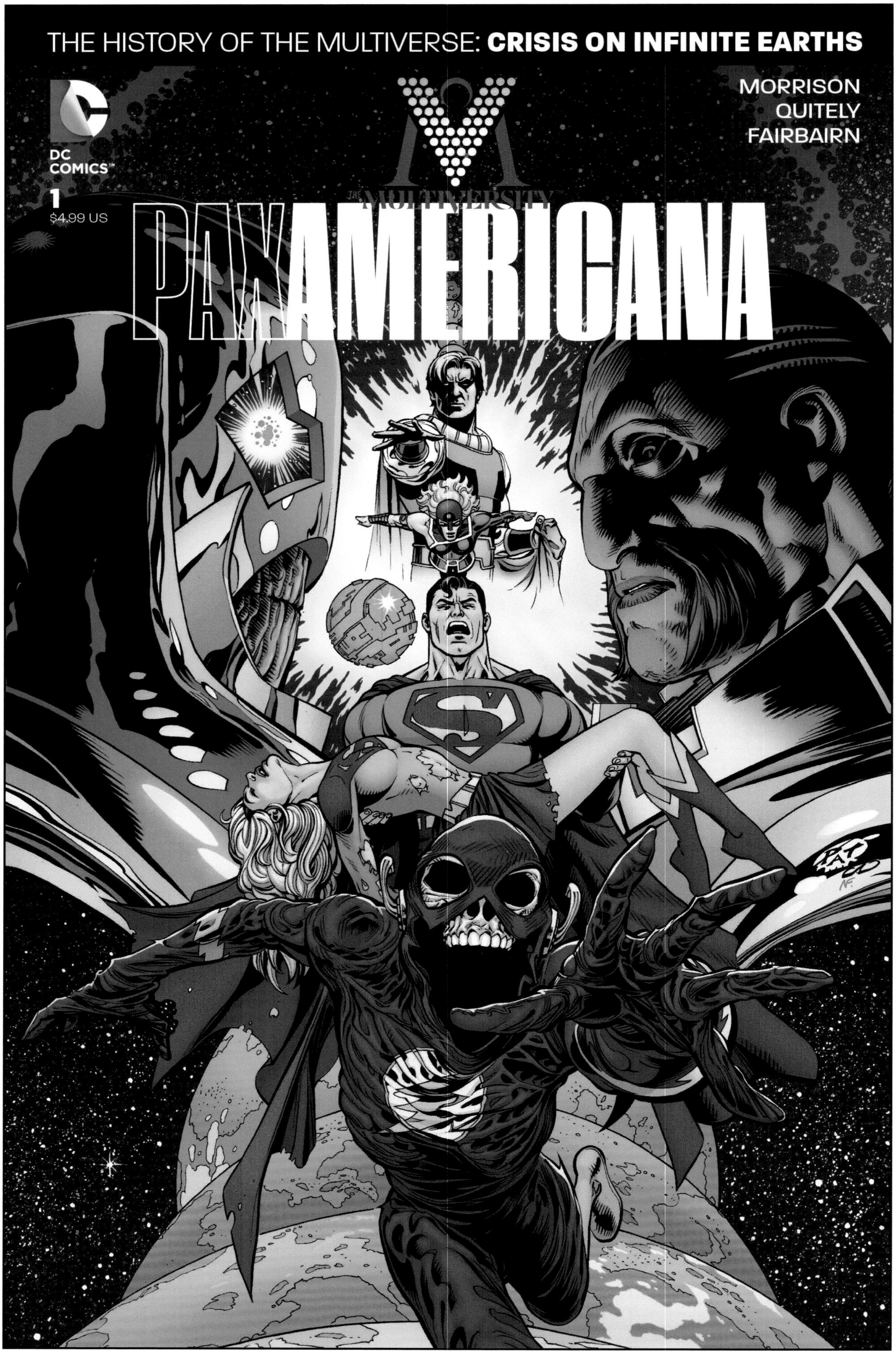
THE HISTORY OF THE MULTIVERSE: CRISIS ON INFINITE EARTHS
DC COMICS™
1
$4.99 US
MORRISON
QUITELY
FAIRBAIRN
THE MULTIVERSITY
PAX AMERICANA

The Multiversity: Pax Americana *#1 variant cover by Michael Cho*

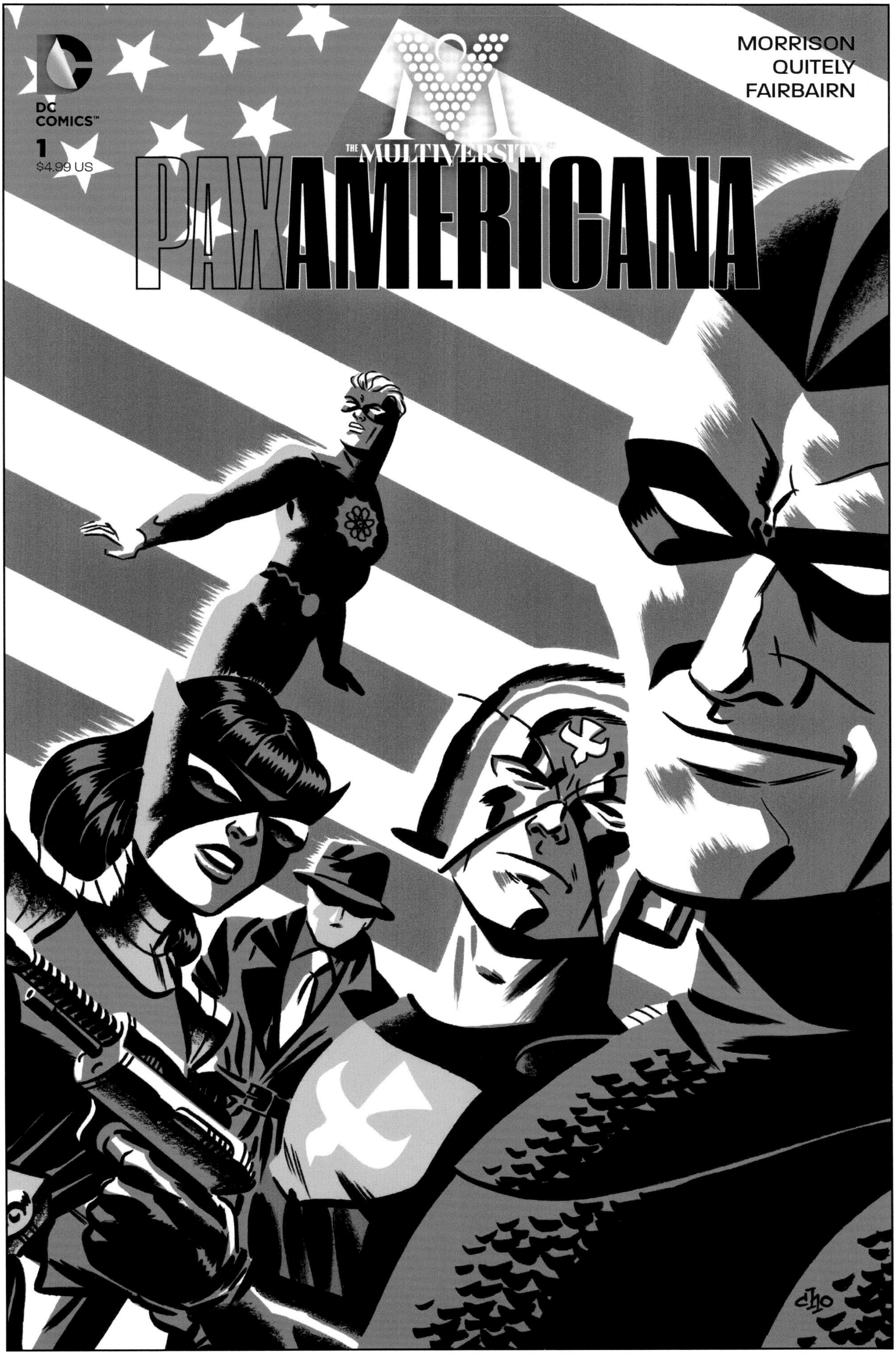
DC COMICS™
1
$4.99 US
THE MULTIVERSITY
PAX AMERICANA
MORRISON
QUITELY
FAIRBAIRN
cho

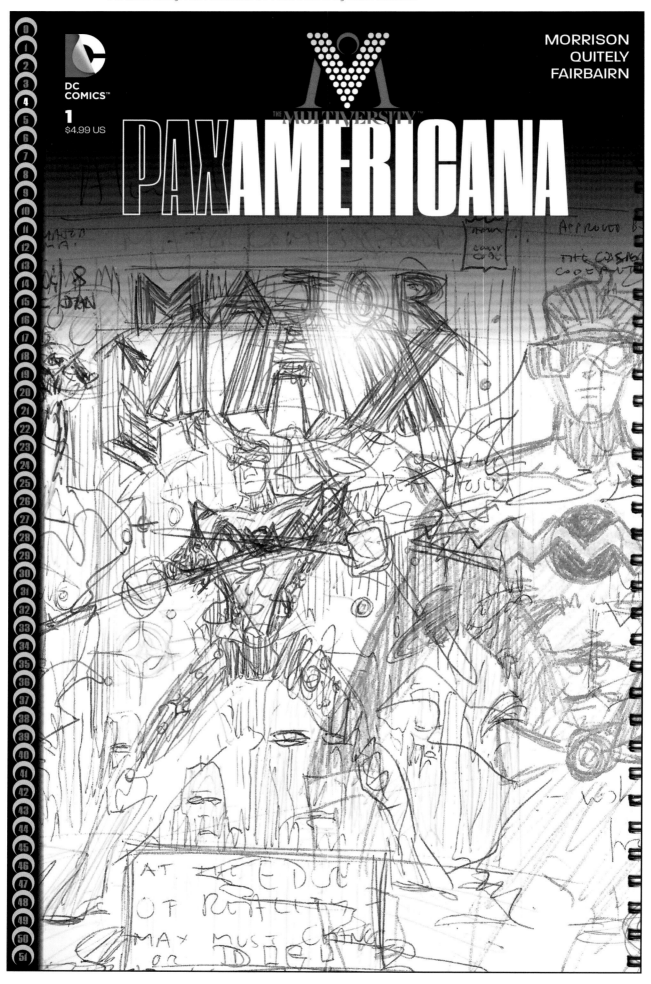

The Multiversity: Thunderworld Adventures *#1 variant cover by Cliff Chiang after Murphy Anderson*

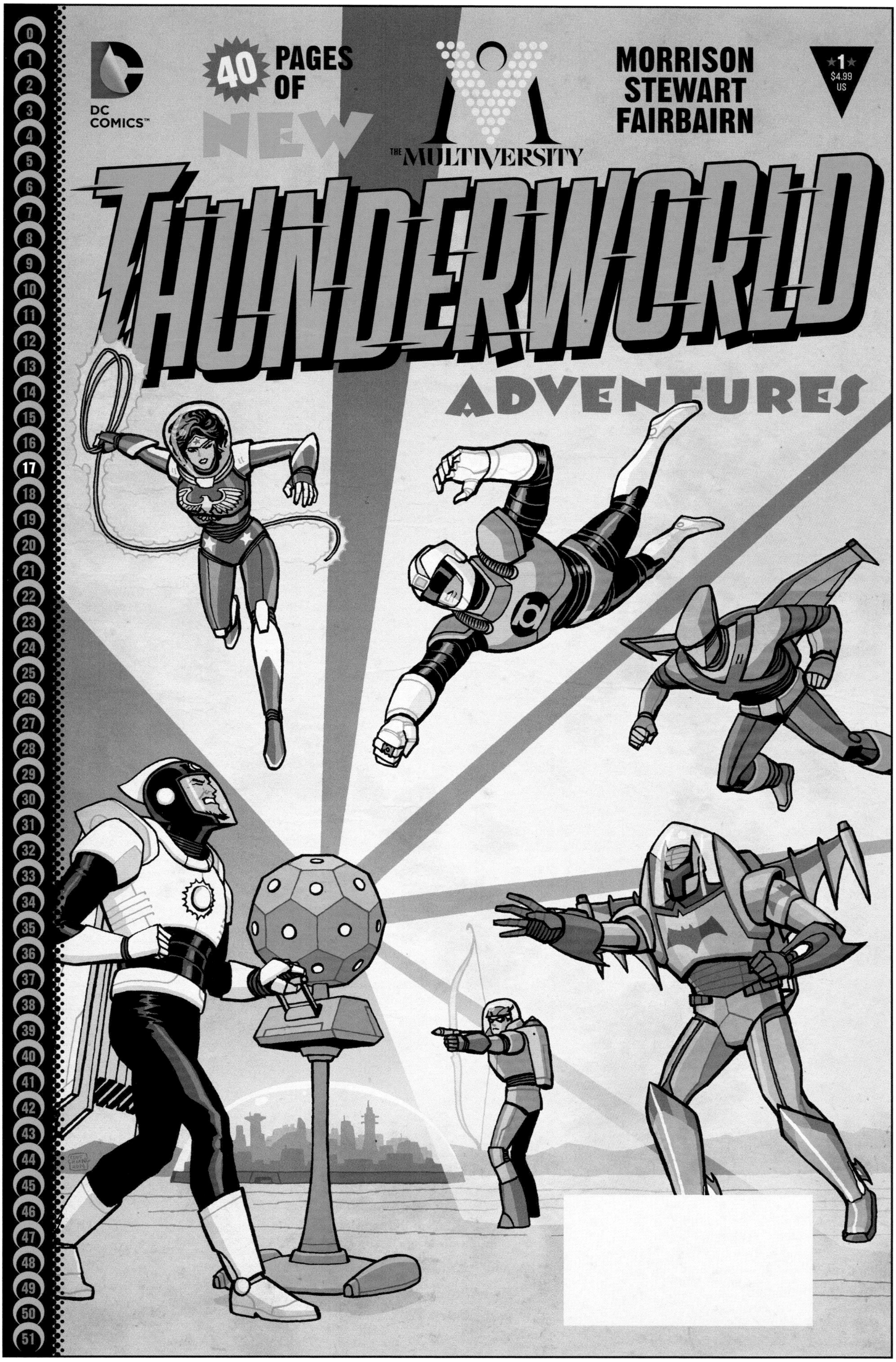
DC COMICS™
40 PAGES OF NEW
THE MULTIVERSITY
MORRISON
STEWART
FAIRBAIRN
1
$4.99 US
THUNDERWORLD
ADVENTURES

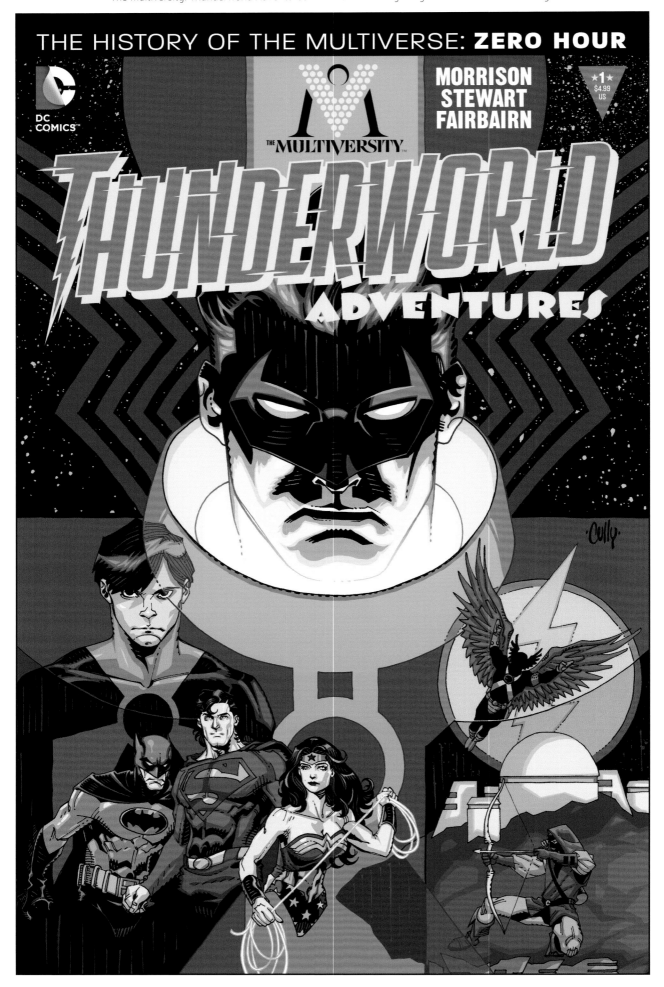

The Multiversity: Thunderworld Adventures #1 variant cover by Cully Hamner with Dave McCaig

The Multiversity Guidebook #1 variant cover by Phil Jimenez with Dave McCaig

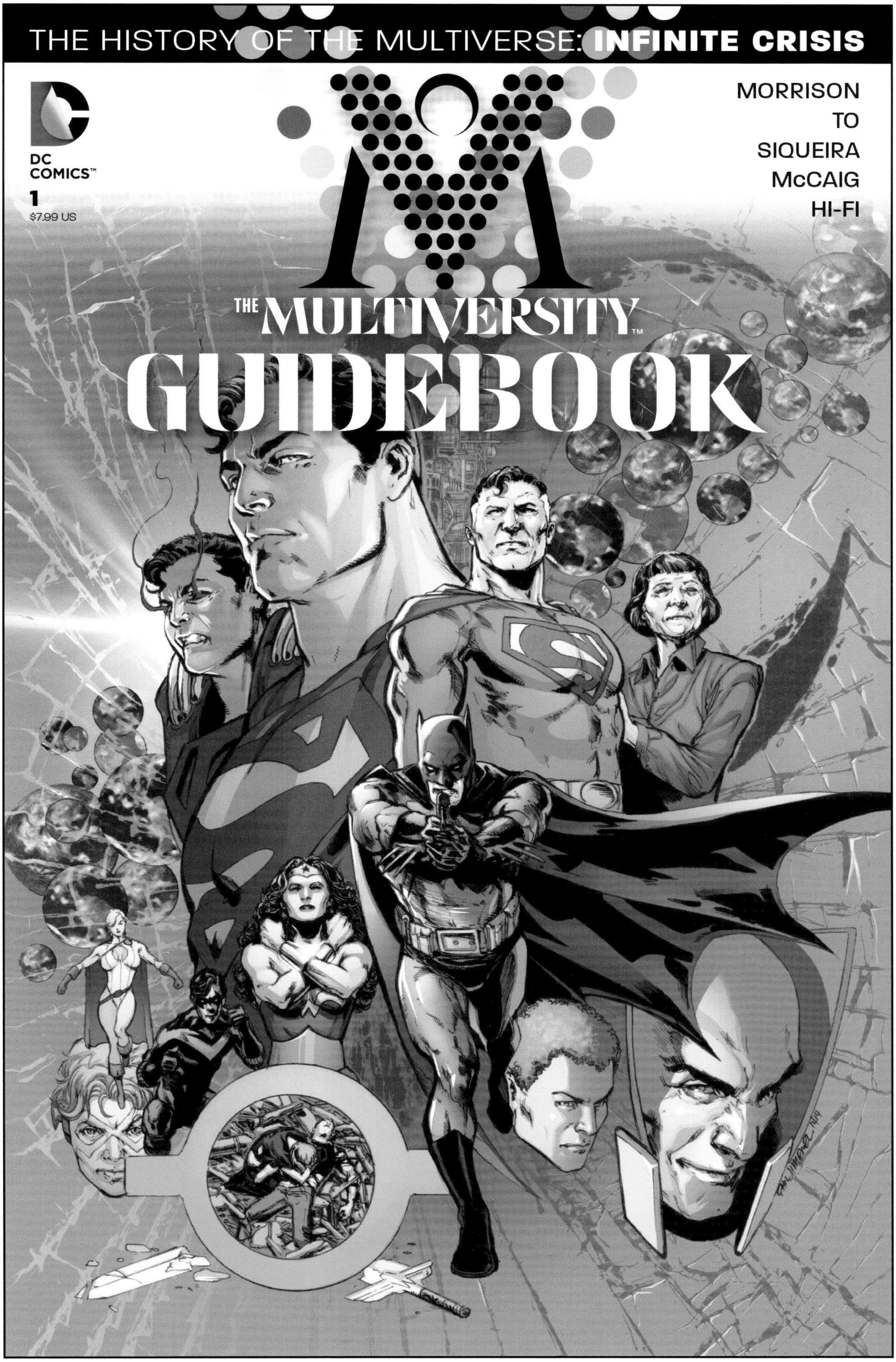
THE HISTORY OF THE MULTIVERSE: INFINITE CRISIS
DC COMICS™
1
$7.99 US
MORRISON
TO
SIQUEIRA
McCAIG
HI-FI
THE MULTIVERSITY™
GUIDEBOOK

The Multiversity Guidebook *#1 sketch variant cover by Rian Hughes*

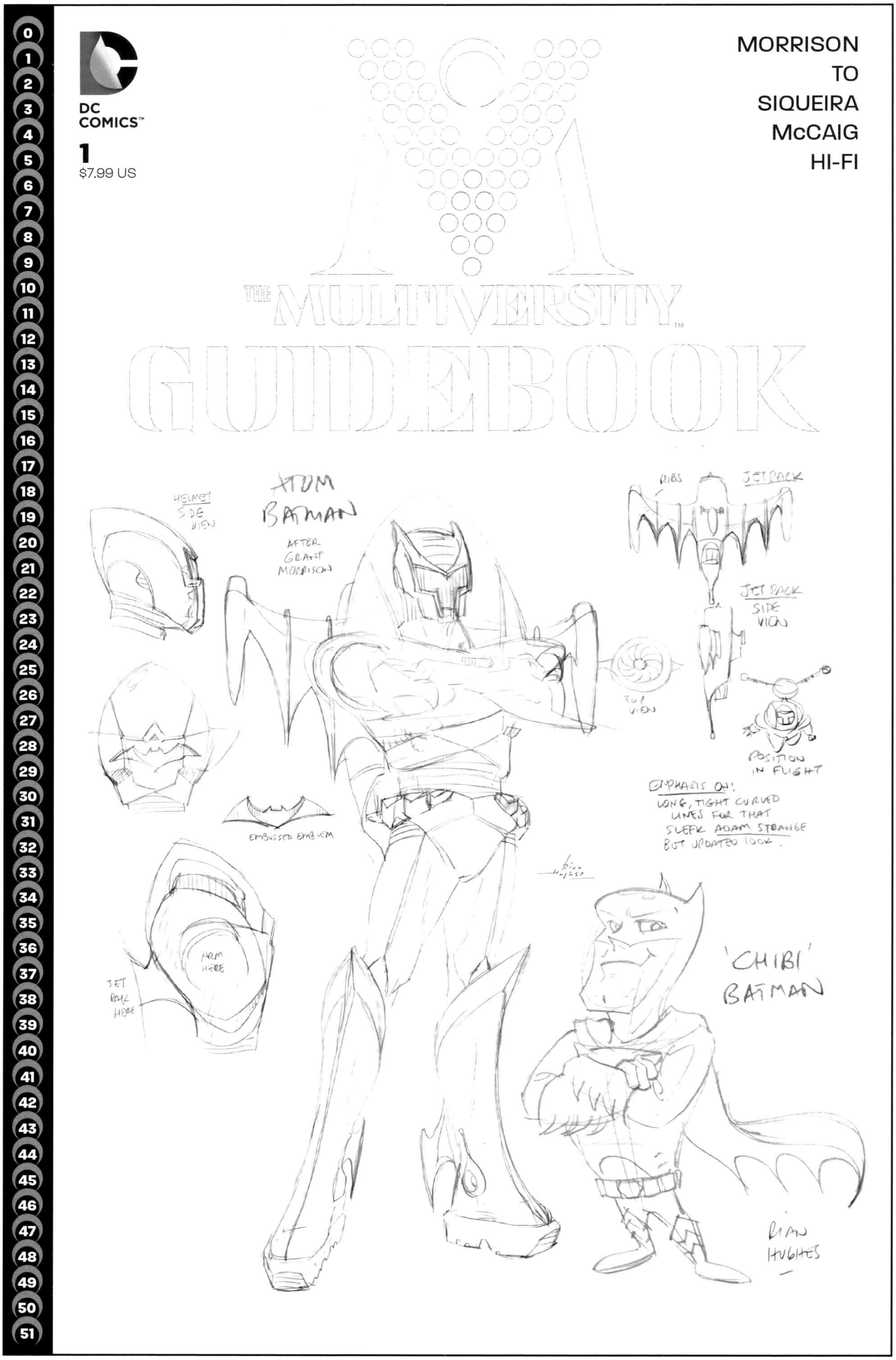
DC COMICS
1
$7.99 US
MORRISON
TO
SIQUEIRA
McCAIG
HI-FI
THE MULTIVERSITY
GUIDEBOOK
HELMET SIDE VIEW
ATOM BATMAN
AFTER GRANT MORRISON
RIBS
JET PACK
JET PACK SIDE VIEW
TOP VIEW
POSITION IN FLIGHT
EMPHASIS ON: LONG, TIGHT CURVED LINES FOR THAT SLEEK ADAM STRANGE BUT UPDATED LOOK.
EMBOSSED EMBLEM
ARM HERE
JET PACK HERE
'CHIBI' BATMAN
RIAN HUGHES

The Multiversity Guidebook *#1 variant cover by Grant Morrison*

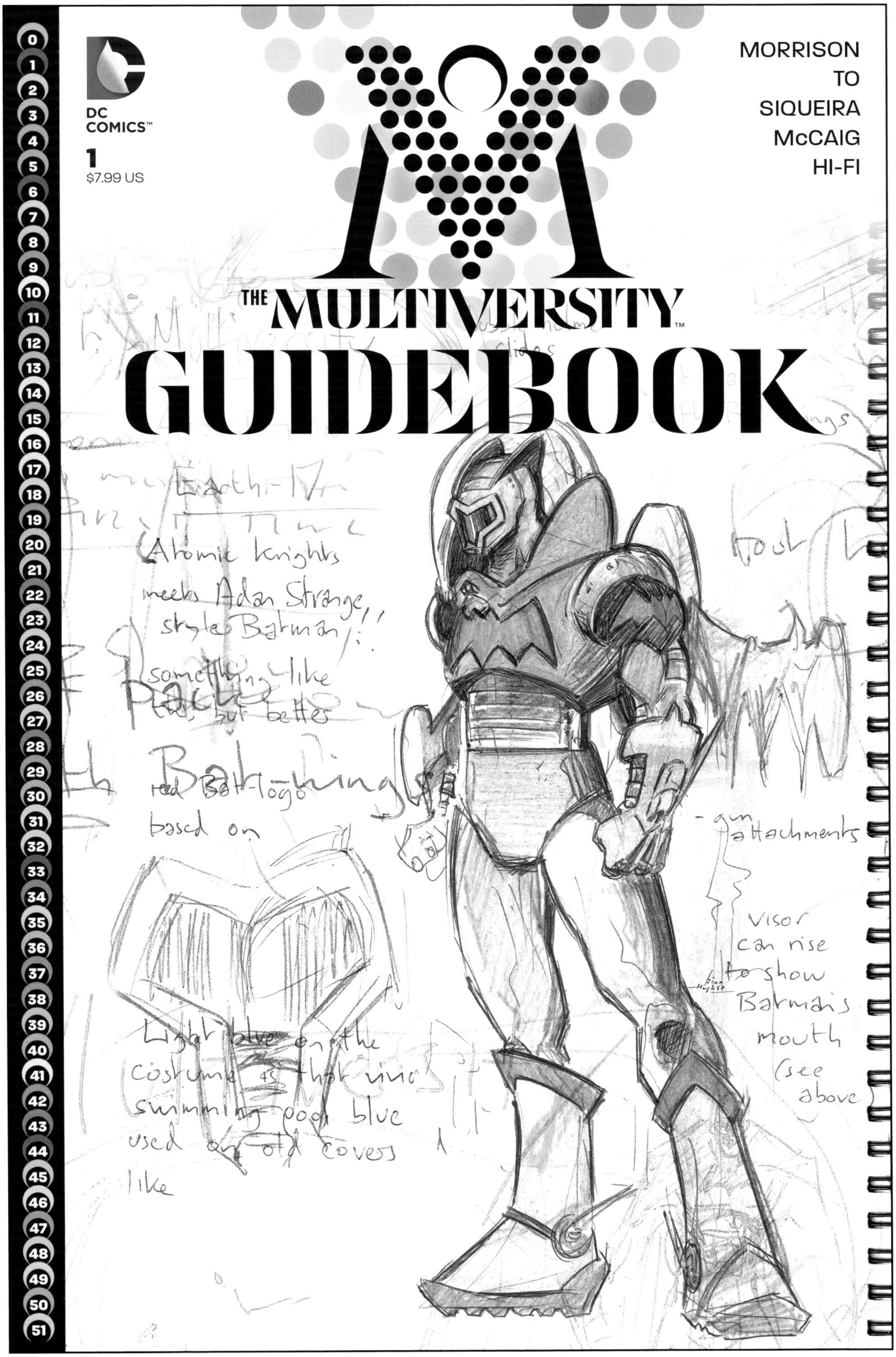
DC COMICS
1
$7.99 US
MORRISON
TO
SIQUEIRA
McCAIG
HI-FI
THE MULTIVERSITY
GUIDEBOOK
Earth-17
Atomic Knights
meets Adam Strange,
style Batman!!
something like
this, but better
red Bat-logo
based on
Light blue on the
costume is that vivid
swimming pool blue
used on old covers
like
- gun attachments
Visor
can rise
to show
Batman's
mouth
(see
above)

The Multiversity Guidebook *#1 second printing cover by Rian Hughes*

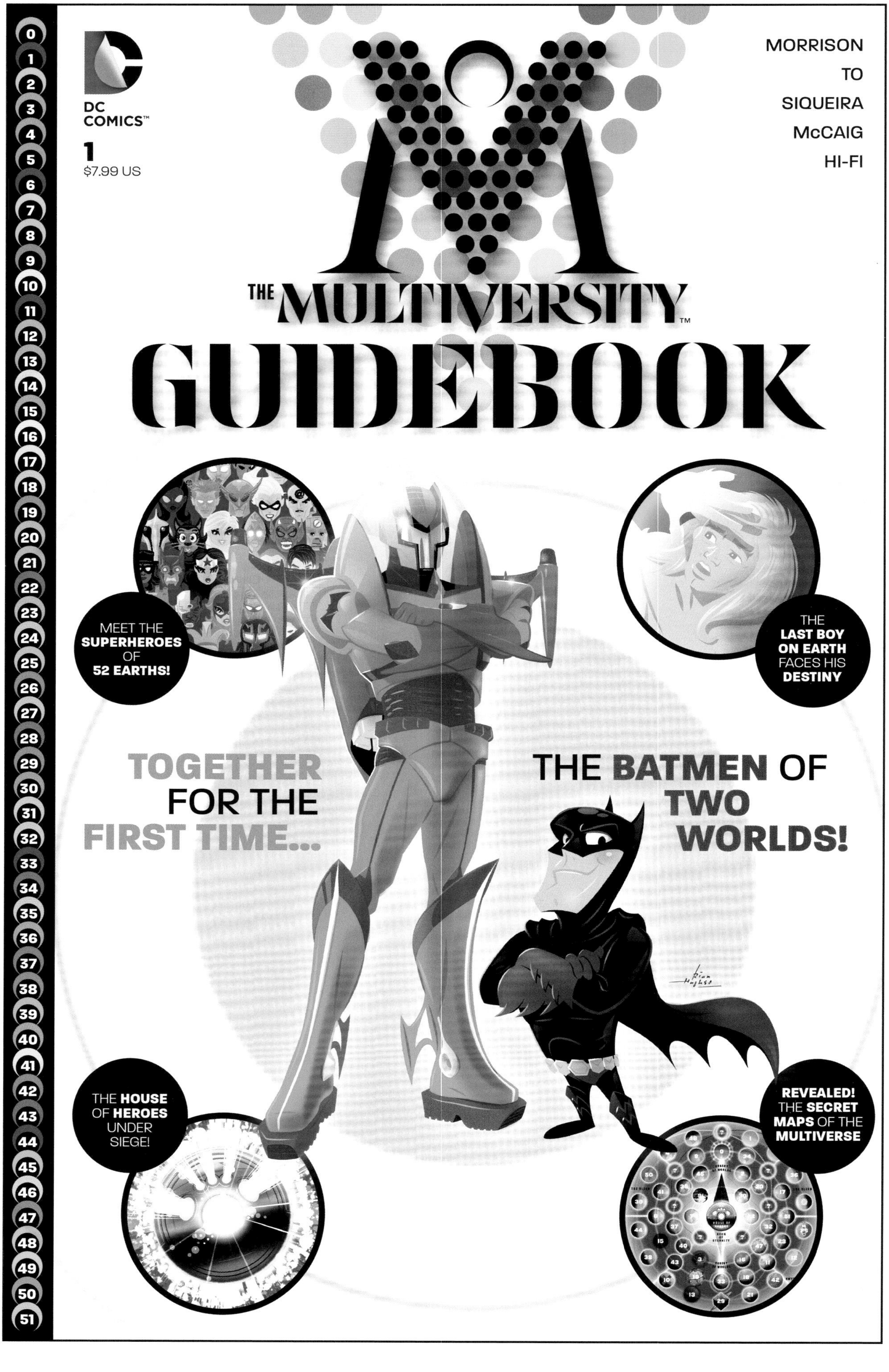
DC COMICS™
1
$7.99 US
MORRISON
TO
SIQUEIRA
McCAIG
HI-FI
THE MULTIVERSITY™
GUIDEBOOK
MEET THE SUPERHEROES OF 52 EARTHS!
THE LAST BOY ON EARTH FACES HIS DESTINY
TOGETHER FOR THE FIRST TIME...
THE BATMEN OF TWO WORLDS!
THE HOUSE OF HEROES UNDER SIEGE!
REVEALED! THE SECRET MAPS OF THE MULTIVERSE
0 1 2 3 4 5 6 7 8 9 10 11 12 13 14 15 16 17 18 19 20 21 22 23 24 25 26 27 28 29 30 31 32 33 34 35 36 37 38 39 40 41 42 43 44 45 46 47 48 49 50 51

The Multiversity: Mastermen *#1 variant cover by Aaron Kuder with Nathan Fairbairn after George Pérez and Dick Giordano*

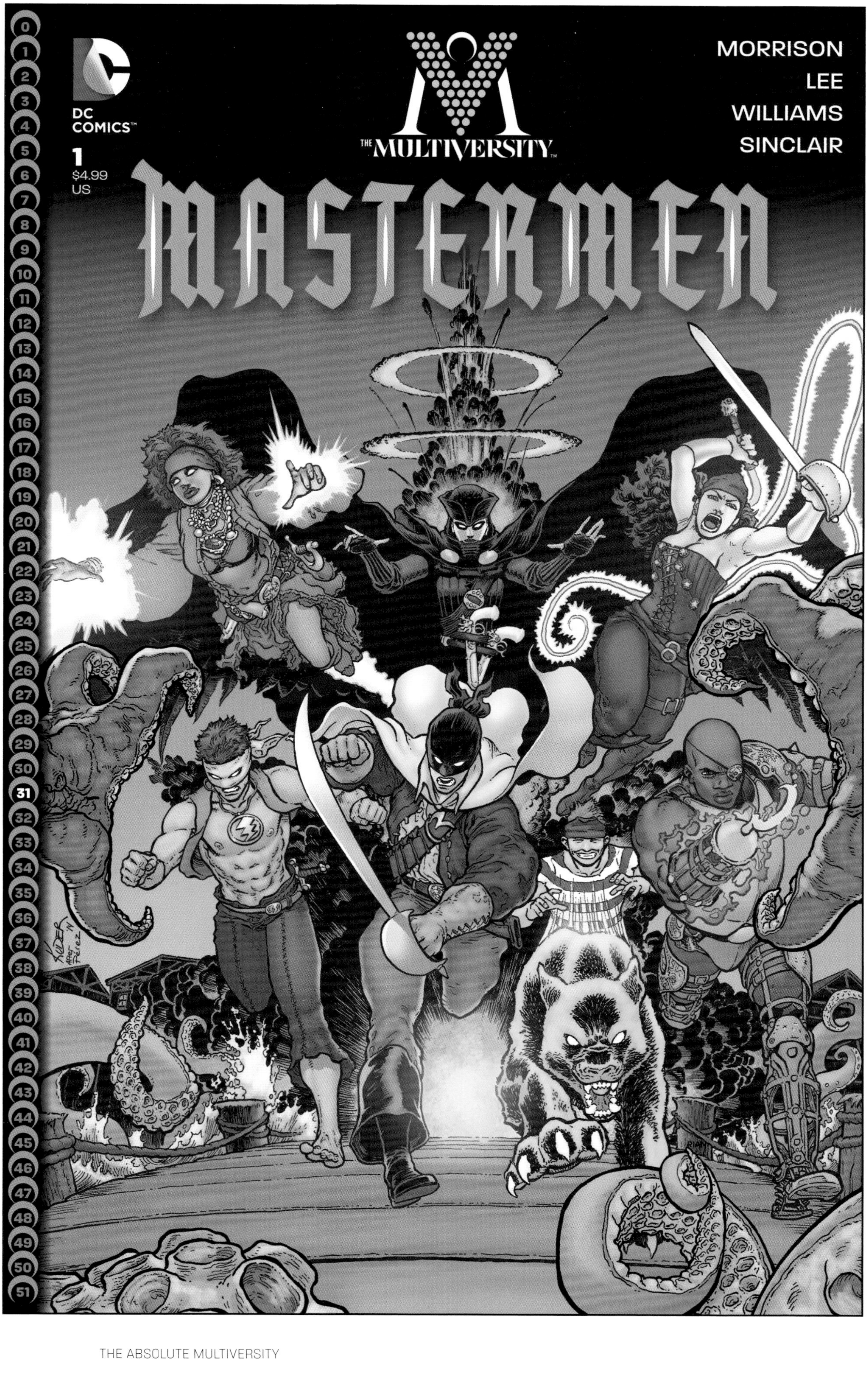
DC COMICS
1
$4.99 US
THE MULTIVERSITY
MASTERMEN
MORRISON
LEE
WILLIAMS
SINCLAIR

The Multiversity: Mastermen *#1 variant cover by Howard Porter with Tomeu Morey*

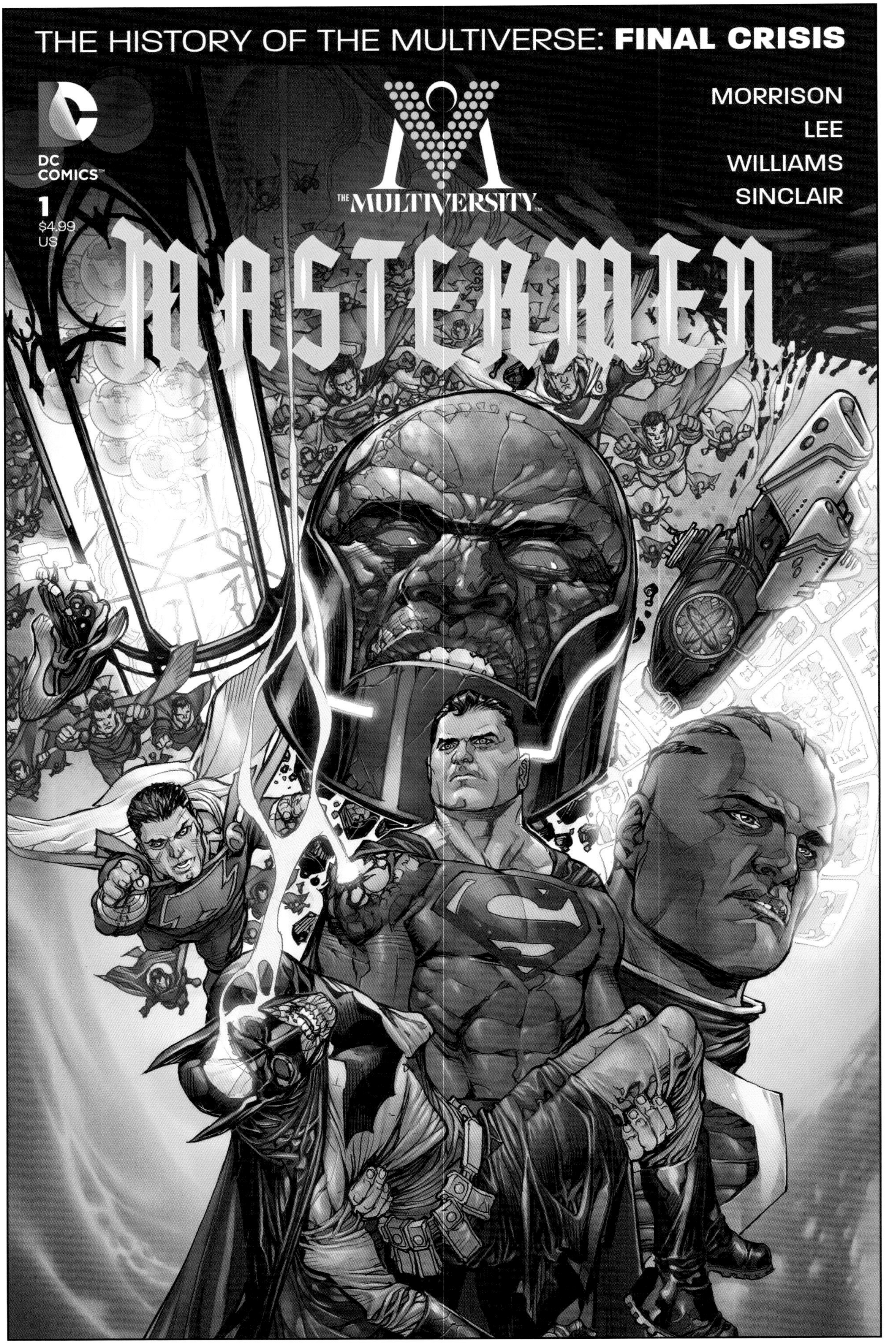
THE HISTORY OF THE MULTIVERSE: FINAL CRISIS
DC COMICS
1
$4.99 US
THE MULTIVERSITY
MASTERMEN
MORRISON
LEE
WILLIAMS
SINCLAIR

The Multiversity: Mastermen *#1 variant cover by Grant Morrison*

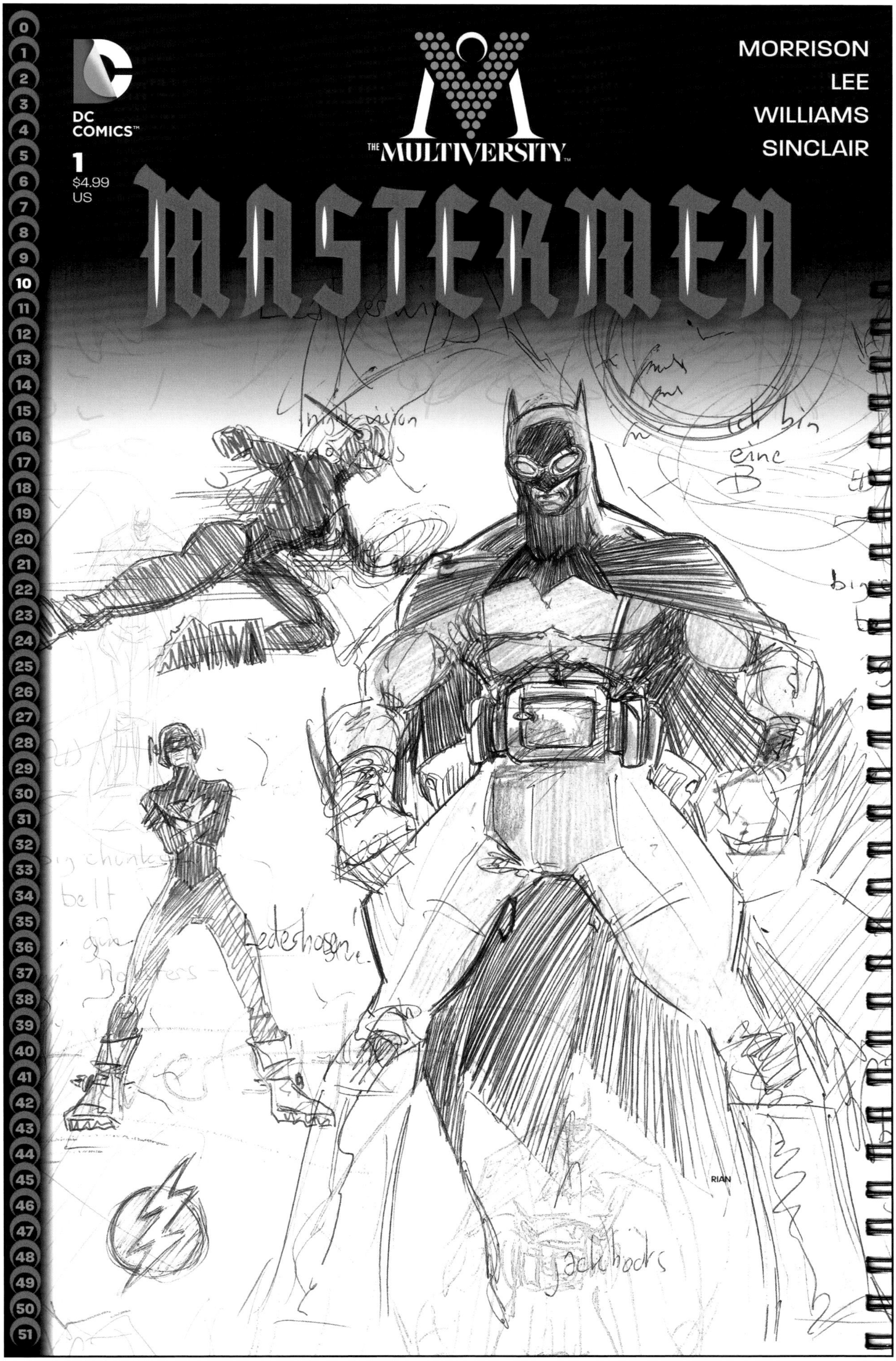
DC COMICS™
1
$4.99
US
THE MULTIVERSITY™
MASTERMEN
MORRISON
LEE
WILLIAMS
SINCLAIR
ich bin
eine
belt
jackboots
RIAN

The Multiversity: Ultra Comics *#1 variant cover by Duncan Rouleau after Mike Sekowsky and Murphy Anderson*

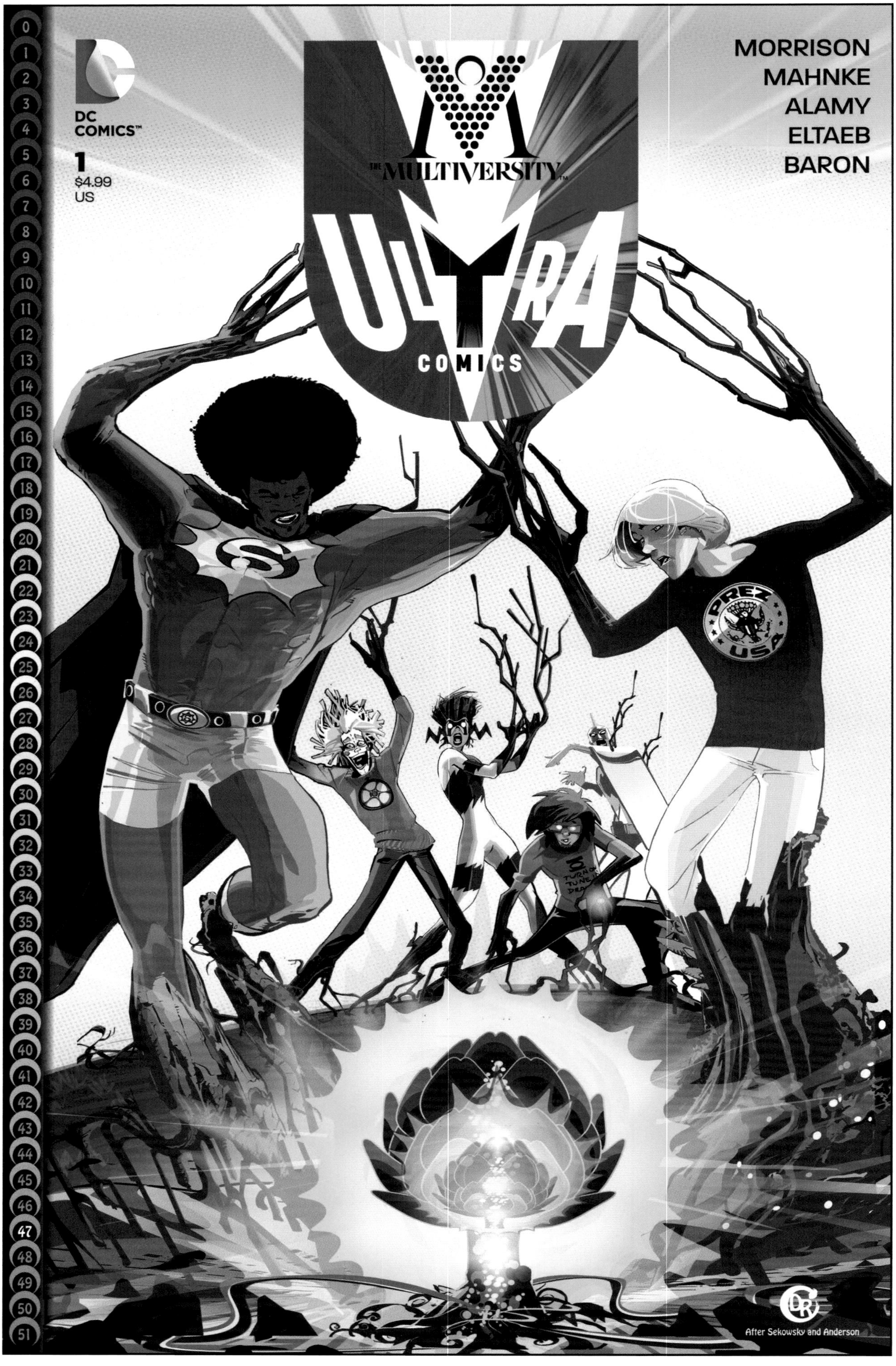

0 1 2 3 4 5 6 7 8 9 10 11 12 13 14 15 16 17 18 19 20 21 22 23 24 25 26 27 28 29 30 31 32 33 34 35 36 37 38 39 40 41 42 43 44 45 46 47 48 49 50 51
DC COMICS™
1
$4.99
US
THE MULTIVERSITY™
ULTRA
COMICS
MORRISON
MAHNKE
ALAMY
ELTAEB
BARON
PREZ
USA
After Sekowsky and Anderson

The Multiversity: Ultra Comics *#1 variant cover by Yanick Paquette with Nathan Fairbairn*

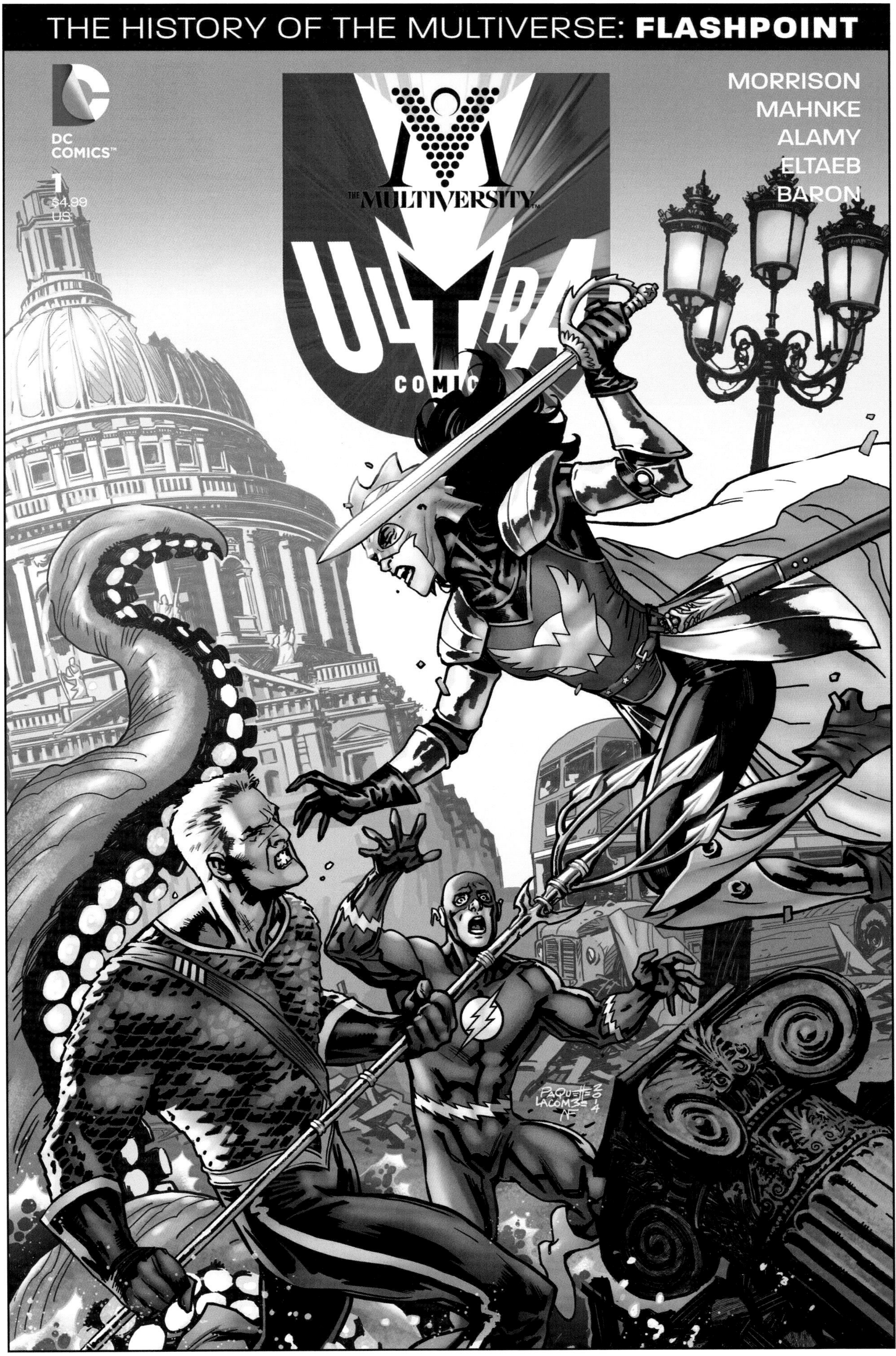

THE HISTORY OF THE MULTIVERSE: FLASHPOINT
DC COMICS
1
$4.99
US
MORRISON
MAHNKE
ALAMY
ELTAEB
BARON
THE MULTIVERSITY
ULTRA
COMIC
PAQUETTE 2014
LACOMBE
NF

The Multiversity: Ultra Comics *#1 variant cover by Grant Morrison*

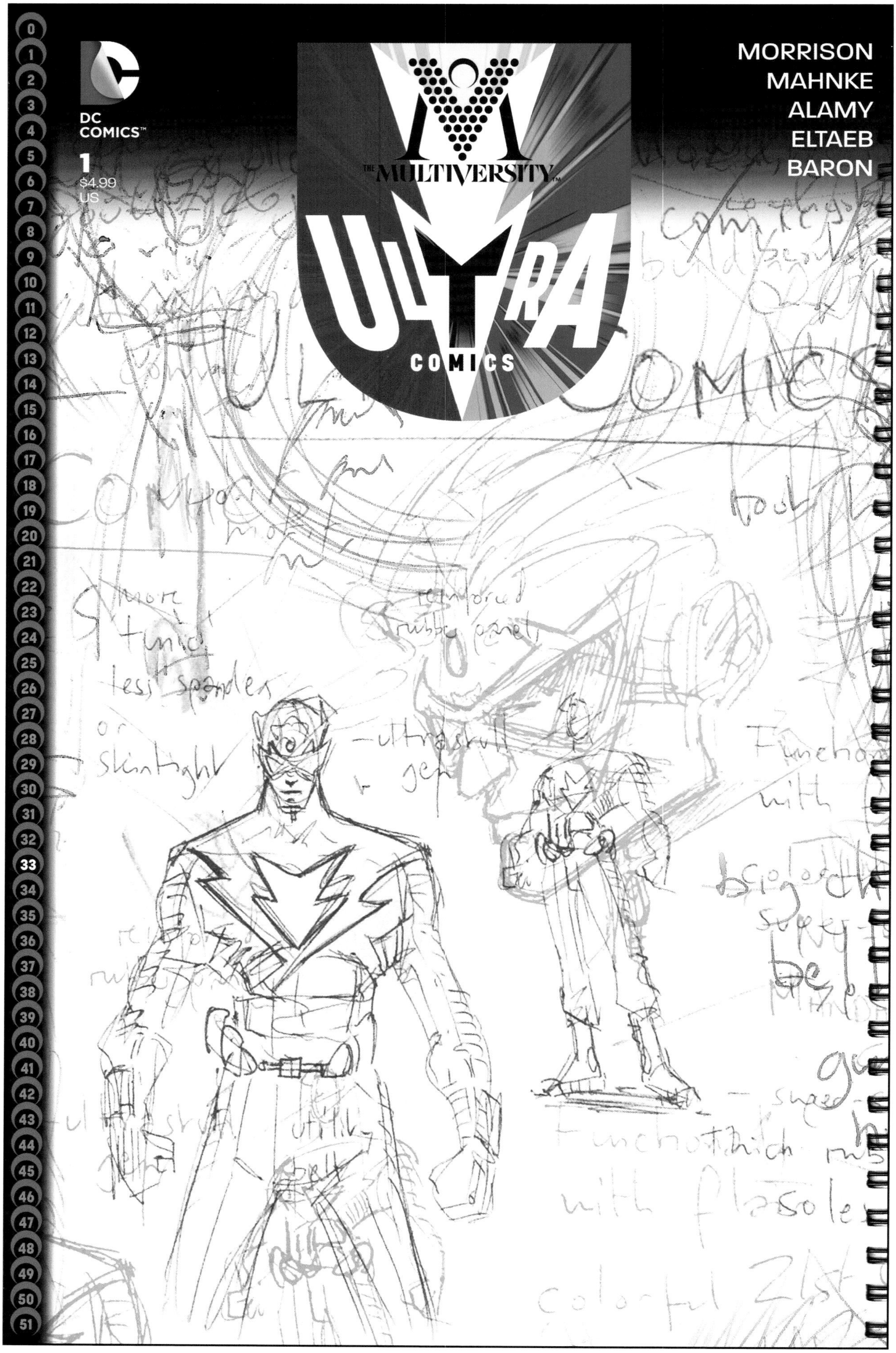
DC COMICS
1
$4.99
US
THE MULTIVERSITY
ULTRA
COMICS
MORRISON
MAHNKE
ALAMY
ELTAEB
BARON

THE MULTIVERSITY: PROPOSAL AND SCRIPT EXCERPTS

The original proposal for The Multiversity. *Text by Grant Morrison, October 2, 2009*

The Multiversity is an eight-issue series comprising six oneshots and a two-part concluding story.

Each issue takes place on a different parallel world from the DC Multiverse and functions as a number one issue and bible for potential series which could be spun off in a line of Multiverse books. Each issue is drawn by a different artist.

The books can be read independently but together they tell an epic tale of cosmic villainy and heroism.

The series redefines the Multiverse, separating it off from the DCU proper so that it can be developed as its own rich playground before we eventually do the big crossover event where our heroes meet their counterparts for the first time.

Taking a cue from the original "Flash of Two Worlds" story, we reveal that each world in the Multiverse publishes comic books about the heroes of the *other* worlds – once our characters realize this, they are able to use the books to strategise a response to the villains.

A major strand of our villain plot involves a comic book – *Ultraa the Unknown* – which is cursed or haunted in some way and causes the death of several heroes throughout the story.

Each book is 38 pages long.

THE SOCIETY OF SUPER-HEROES #1
Doom from the Counter-World

Set on Earth-20A, the Society ("Call S.O.S.!") are a group of DC adventure and mystic heroes done in a neo-pulp style.

Earth-20 is a world recovering from a devastating World War 2-style conflict. The Society is led by the masked occult adventurer known as Doctor Fate, and includes in its roster Immortal Man, The Mighty Atom, Lady Blackhawk, and Abin Sur the alien Green Lantern.

When they discover that their universe is part of a binary *pair* of universes, which are about to collide with terrifying consequences, the Society must face a menace they are barely equipped to deal with – from Earth-20B.

They are about to go to war with their own evil opposites, the Society of Super-Criminals – Doc Faust, Vandal Savage, Blockbuster, Lady Shiva, and Sinestro – on Earth-30.

They will uncover a terrifying plan that spans multiple realities and involves a monstrous cabal of godlike entities from the dark side of the Multiverse. Can they get a message to the rest of the Multiverse before it's too late?

MASTERMEN #1
Splendor Falls

Set on Earth-10 (inspired by the former Earth-X of the Freedom Fighters), a world where the Nazis won World War 2 thanks to a secret weapon – superbaby Kal-L. Rocketed to Earth from the doomed planet Krypton, he has been found in a field in the occupied Sudetenland.

Retro-engineering Kryptonian technology from Kal-L's escape rocket, Nazi scientists win the war for Hitler. Even the US falls in the early '50s and the world becomes a German-speaking Nazi "utopia."

70 years on and Hitler is long dead, along with all his enemies and victims – Nazism has been replaced by a more benign world order and the grown up Kal-L is now the troubled "hero" known as *Ubermensch*, or Overman. Leader of his world's Justice League – Leatherwing, Rhinemaiden, Underwaterman, Blitz – he presides over a calm, ordered, and prosperous Art Deco sci-fi civilization but is haunted by the guilt of the millions who died so this dream could prosper. Tortured by his conscience, he wonders if this world deserves to exist at all.

So when the vengeful ghosts of the past return in the form of Uncle Sam and his Freedom Fighters (each of them represents one of Sam's "huddled masses" – the last surviving members of the persecuted minorities wiped out by the Nazi purges decades before), will Overman fight to defend his world or stand back and watch it fall to chaos?

Mastermen sets up the Earth-10 universe for an ongoing book with a thoughtful modern Shakespearean drama type feel. These are powerful super-human beings dealing with big moral problems, compromises, gray areas, and contemporary ideas.

THE JUST #1
Earth Me

Set on Earth-7, On this world, the sons and daughters of the JLA – Chris Kent Superman, Damian Wayne Batman... Norman, Sister Miracle, Megamorpho, and others have grown up privileged in a perfect world with nothing much to do.

In this world, the legacy heroes of the '90s like Wally West, Kyle Rayner, and Connor Hawke have become the heavy hitters who look down on the new breed of wasters.

This is a tale of the superhero equivalent of showbiz brats, as they are forced into a confrontation with destiny and must learn the hard way about what really matters in life...

PAX AMERICANA #1
In Which We Burn

Set on Earth-4, this is the world of the Charlton heroes mixed with a little bit of the *Watchmen* characters that were based on the Charlton originals. It's an attempt to do a comic based on the *Watchmen* aesthetic, but updated and reimagined as something quite new and different.

This is the ultimate murder mystery set in an alternate world that's as convincing as we can make it, and features Captain Atom, the Question, Blue Beetle, and Nightshade.

Sporting a Delmore Schwartz quote – "Time is the fire in which we burn" – the cover depicts a burning peace sign, leading into a student riot that becomes a Presidential assassination.

When Chris Smith, the American super-agent known as the Peacemaker, is accused of the killing, an investigation begins which will change the lives of our heroes and the destiny of the world in which they live.

Told in an intricate sequence of backwards jumps in time, we learn the origins of the Pax team through the life of Chris Smith, the Peacemaker, and slowly learn how this idealistic young man has been manipulated by amoral super-intellects as a pawn in a plan that staggers the imagination...

THUNDERWORLD #1
Captain Marvel and the Day That Never Was!

Set on Earth-5, this is the SHAZAM! world that will attempt to be more faithful to the original spirit of the character while adding the kind of modern gloss and gravitas that readers of today need from their books. The idea is not to aim for some kind of nostalgic feel, but to capture the spirit of smart comics that are not just for kids or grown-ups but for everyone.

Think Pixar movies or how we did Superman in *All-Star* and think of that kind of fidelity to the core values of the feature, allied with a progressive, modern approach to storytelling and characterisation.

In this definitive adventure the Marvel Family must face their worst nightmare – a super-powered, costumed "Sivana Family" – as they fight an incredible battle on Earth and at the besieged Rock of Eternity.

Evil Professor Slvana has built his own artificial Rock of Eternity using Suspendium...he's made a New Day of villainy and it's this new day and what the cross-universe coalition of criminal masterminds do with it – that's brought the Multiverse to the attention of godlike predators.

ULTRAA THE UNKNOWN #1
Buy This Comic or Die!

Set on Earth-Prime, *Ultraa* is the cursed comic book at the heart of the plot. Created here, in our own world, *Ultraa* is a living comic book designed to trap a malign spirit.

The hero Ultraa is a "Pinnochio" style character – a fiction who longs to become real and who is given this one incredible chance to save all of reality. Locked into the pages of this book along with his ultimate enemy, Ultraa must fight to save us all.

THE MULTIVERSITY #1 and #2
House of Heroes

The greatest heroes of a dozen worlds team up to save all of reality in a two-part story that combines to form an "80-page giant" epic. The Multiversity is the ultimate cross-universe collection of superheroes working together to protect 52 universes and billions of worlds.

Nix Uotan, Hyperhero, from *Final Crisis* has uncovered a terrible plan to invade and destroy the Multiverse. Four terrifying and all-powerful god-like beings are playing a destructive *Clash of the Titans*-style game of gods, where human and superhuman lives are mere pawns in a scheme.

Assembled in the House of Heroes at the Rock of Eternity, and using as transport the shiftship *Ultima Thule* (from *Superman Beyond*), the Multiversity is a team of incredible superheroes led by the black Superman of Earth-25 (last seen in *Final Crisis*), and includes Mary Marvel, Captain Carrot, Wandjina (the Aboriginal "Thor" of Earth-8), and others.

Sivana's cross-universe coalition of bad guys has attracted the attention of the god-beings, and so begins an epic tale – a *Jason and the Argonauts*, an *Odyssey*, a *Mahabharata* – a sci-fi mythic adventure across multiple universes against a foe beyond all imagining. This is our chance to see a wider spread of worlds and check in with some of the more interesting of the 52 universes like the Marvel analogue Earth-8, the "reversed-gender" Earth-11 and others. We also get to meet some analogue characters for other comic companies like "Spore" for Spawn, "Dino-Cop" for Savage Dragon and many others.

And, of course, not everyone will make it back – and the Multiverse will never be the same again.

Right: Sketches by Frank Quitely for the opening sequence

ORIGINAL SCRIPT FOR THE MULTIVERSITY: PAX AMERICANA
Text by Grant Morrison

PAGE 1 *Frame 1*

Okay, the game we're playing with EARTH 4 – which is, of course, the parallel world home of the characters DC acquired from Charlton – is to create a world aesthetic which takes inspiration from both the original Charlton characters, and also from the most famous and celebrated iteration of those characters, *Watchmen*.

No-one's ever really taken up the challenge of *Watchmen*'s intricate, showy narrative tricks and structures, but that's what we're going to do here. Rather than copy *Watchmen*'s grids and transitions, we'll create our own updated version of that high-density semiotic overload approach to comic storytelling.

So we're using a basic eight-panel grid structure which allows us to employ a lot of new storytelling techniques here – the eight-grid breaks down into sixteen sometimes, as in *Dark Knight*. The eight-grid is here for a number of reasons, the most obvious of which appears in the final panel, explaining the recurring image of the 8-on-its-side Infinity symbol. The whole of the *Multiversity* series is based on the number 8, representing the musical octave – since its introduction in 1963 the DC Multiverse has been described as being made of overlapping "vibrations," like music, so the octave seems to me to represent the fundamental framework of the DCU. In this issue that number takes on a special significance. *Watchmen* is mostly set in November, the month of Alan Moore's birthday, so *Pax* is mostly set in January, which happens to be not only the month of my own birthday but ties into the central conceit of symmetrical time as personified by the two-faced Roman god Janus, who stands at the hinge of every year, looking to the past and the future simultaneously.

Where, for instance, Rorschach (*Watchmen*'s re-thinking of the Question character) had a black-and-white moral viewpoint inspired by the Objectivist Ayn Randian viewpoint of Steve Ditko, the Question's creator, *our* new version of the Question bases his bizarre M.O. on the developmental spectrum of philosopher Ken Wilber's Integral approach, which borrows its color coding from the Spiral Dynamics system. Instead of an Objectivist Ditko vigilante we have a post-Denny O'Neil Question who interprets the whole world through the lens of Spiral Dynamics. From the black-and-white morality of Ditko's worldview, we move to a spectrum of motivational colors (there are eight colors in the system of course!).

Time runs *backwards* through this issue, so that the last panel truly explains all the rest.

Our first panel shows a detail of the peace symbol, twisting now as it turns. The flames seem to be sucked into the drifting flag.

Over the next three pages we see the assassination of the U.S. president running backwards. The forward motion of the events is that we start with Chris Smith, the Peacemaker, diving from a high-altitude weather balloon, aiming his rifle from very, very high above the president and shooting.

The president's standing up in his limo with a peace flag held up over his head in both hands, so that's it's streaming behind him. A fiery bullet then smacks through the flag, igniting it before passing directly through the top of the President's head and exiting through his lower jaw. He then slumps forward over the side of the limo, letting go the burning flag which drifts toward the horrified spectators.

Frame 2
The burning flag ripples across the panel. It's less aflame again as time continues to run backward.

Frame 3
The flag's drifting toward the right side of the panel, losing flame. Behind it, we can see glimpses of people – a woman screaming with her hand at her mouth. A crowd lining the streets of a motorcade.

Frame 4
The flag burning a little less fiercely again is drifting off panel right. Behind are revealed bystanders, a fence keeping them from the road and the motorcade that's been passing. Cops pushing people back. Chaos.

Frame 5
Lower tier. We're looking at the side of a souped-up limousine – almost the Batmobile version of a Presidential convertible. Blood runs down the polished side of the car, over the seal of the USA. The flag appears in the lower left corner blowing away from the right hand hanging over the edge of the door.

Frame 6
Go in closer, running time backward, so the blood runs *up* the side of the car door, revealing more of the seal. A limp hand is wearing a ring with a distinctive number "8" on it. Although it's not really an 8 – it's an infinity sign. This hand is letting go of the flag.

Frame 7
Go in closer for an almost abstract *Watchmen*-ish shot of the blood trails running backward up the side of the door.

Frame 8
Closer on one drip running back up the polished metal.

PAGE 2 *Frame 1*
Top tier four show a dead man half hanging over the door of the wonder car. Blood runs up the side. This is *President Harley*. He's mid-50s and good-looking – or was until his head was blown away.

Frame 2
We pan across left to right. Blood runs backward up the

chassis. The dead man's slumped body seems to lift.

Frame 3
He rises with his head blown open, like a puppet jerking awake. The hand with the ring still clutches an edge of the flag as flame spreads from the impact hole in it.

Frame 4
The Prez's body lifts back up from its slumped position – the bullet hitting his flag trails flame – the Prez falls forward and his flag is now catching fire.

Frame 5
The bottom tier starts on a close up and the sequence then pulls back from the President's head. Close on bone fragments and blood in hyperforensic detail.

Frame 6
Pull back for a literal head shot – a flaming bullet has ploughed down through the president's head and is exiting through his lower jaw, taking the whole bottom half of his head with it, vaporising.

Frame 7
Pull back for a chest and shoulders shot. The President is smiling – he's smiling with the bullet inches from his head and *directly* above it as if it has been fired from directly overhead, which in fact it has.

Frame 8
Pull back to see him from the waist up – or further if you need space at the top for the bullet coming in. Move in on the burning bullet, now lifting up into the air away from the President's skull.

PAGE 3 *Frame 1*
Close on the intact bullet moving backwards through the air directly upward, with buildings in the background – specifically, parts of the skyline of Washington. The bullet's just catching fire here.

Frame 2
Pull back from the bullet and tilt our POV so we're looking *up* at the bullet as it zips away from us with clouds now in the background and open sky. Perhaps a hint of a tiny figure way up above but this might not be needed.

Left: Sketches by Frank Quitely for the opening sequence
Right: Layout by Frank Quitely for page 2

Frame 3
Follow the bullet back toward the silenced muzzle of a super hunting rifle with a puff of pressurized air that's being sucked back into the silencer.

Frame 4
And with the silencer in foreground, foreshortened immensely, we see the rifle behind and part of the face of a helmeted man who aims down the scope of the rifle.

Frame 5
The lower tier is halved horizontally to give us two long widescreen panels. In this one we see a full body shot of PAX agent Chris Smith, a.k.a. Peacemaker, wearing a HALO dive version of his suit – colored red and white and featuring his dove-in-a-shield logo. He's skydiving and taking aim directly downwards, eye to the gunsight. There's a reflective weather balloon high above. We can see the curve of the Earth he's so high up.

Frame 6
Second of the long panels. A kind of overhead establishing shot. We're looking down across the silvery curved surface of a weather balloon where we can see Peacemaker releasing himself from a harness and falling forward into his dive, holding his rifle across his chest, looking down, as he lets go and falls from a weather balloon...

Below: Thumbnails by Grant Morrison and layouts by Frank Quitely for pages 5-6

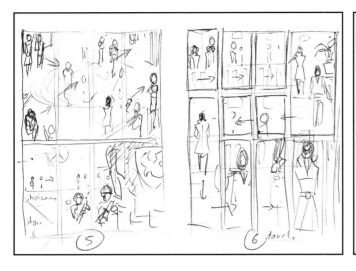

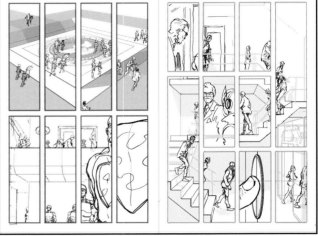

PAGE 10 *Frame 1*
The top tier shows a single image of the Bug snared by the magnet.

BEETLE: DAMMIT, QUESTION!

Frame 2
Second tier has a Bug interior shot. Controls sparking – Beetle raging.

BEETLE: GET A GRIP!

Frame 3
Bottom tier. Four panels showing the monorail station. The background stays the same, the Question and the train move across it.

Here the Question is a small figure walking into the monorail station tunnel, heading toward us.

This is where we begin to see the posters on the station wall – adding some *Watchmen*-style cultural texture, so apart from the main poster in the sequence – described in the next panel – there could be a Ford advert for the Ford Hydro – the back of a hydrogen-powered car, something between a Prius and a VW Beetle, almost insect-like. It's driving into an op art spiral effect. The ad's supposed to be jolly but has sinister undertones. In the center of the spiral is a hydrogen atom symbol. These new cars run on hydrogen, and top up at Air Garages.

YOUR GETAWAY CAR
2014 FORD HYDRO

Although not in this sequence, if we need other adverts we can have Beetle Brand protective clothes like super-cool silver padded winter parkas – maybe see some young dudes wearing these in street scenes. There's something sci-fi mod about his clothing lines – imagine a Beetle Brand store in every town, like Liam Gallagher's "Pretty Green" outlets. The clothes are all developed from innovations he's made to his Blue Beetle suit, his "peace keeping" armor, over the years. With the tagline *Costumes for Everyday Heroes*, it's like a kind of slightly rave/sci-fi take on American Apparel.

Blue Beetle – in his guise as wealthy, retired inventor who sold his company and several patents for billions of dollars to become a super-agent for the PAX after 9/11 – has lucrative

Below: Frank Quitely's art for the monorail station posters
Below right: Layout for pages 12-13 by Frank Quitely

VIC SAGE IS P*****D
VIC SAGE
BLACK & WHITE WORLD
New season premieres 1.12.13

your get-away car
2014 FORD HYDRO
HYDRO
FORD
HYDR

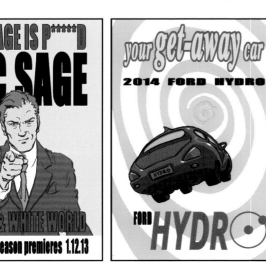

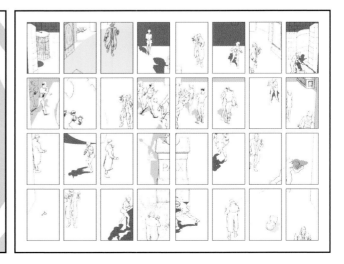

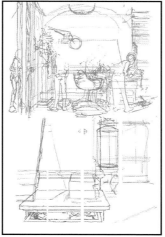
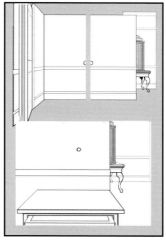
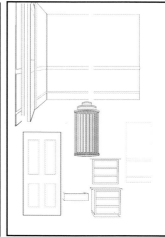

Above: A page's progress from initial thumbnails by Grant Morrison to final pencils by Frank Quitely

sidelines in games, fashion, publishing etc. His entrepreneurial spirit led him to seize on the brand-building possibilities of the "superhero" idea.

"Perfume by Nightshade" is *Futurebomb.*

People drink Atomade – a kind of super Red Bull that's rich in caffeine and marketed as a drink to give you the ability to multitask – a little "Red Bull gives you wings" cartoon of someone with multiple arms legs and head doing shit, like a Hindu god forced to work in an office.
ATOMADE = YOU2.

Popular computer games are *Pax Infantry 4: Lunar Jihad, Batman: Planet Arkham,* and *Hub City Racer.*

Right: Revised layout for page 11 by Frank Quitely

Frame 4
Continues Frame 2 – the monorail train passes across the panel and stops – doors open. It's early in the morning and there are very few people around.

Frame 5
The train moves on. The Question climbs onto the platform. There are posters on the station walls – one poster which is split in two by the panel borders shows the Question's alter ego, TV firebrand Vic Sage.

The poster shows Sage from the waist up, pointing with an accusing snarl (in his alter ego as Vic Sage, the Question also fights crime and corruption in a different way as the controversial host of his own TV show – a kind of Roger Cook/Despatches-style aggressive crusading and slightly over-the-top hysterical investigative reporter show where Vic Sage names names and sometimes gets involved in onscreen scuffles and punch-ups. Sage has orange hair and a confrontational stare.
VIC SAGE IS P****D!
BLACK AND WHITE WORLD
New season premieres 1.12.15
WWB

WWB is the TV network Sage worked for in the Charlton books. Give it a modern logo style, like NBC or FOX.
QUESTION: >HNNK<

Frame 6
Question comes towards us on the platform. He reaches up to take off his hat (have a look at the way Steve Ditko drew the "yellow mist" during the Question's transformation sequences – if you look online for the cover of Charlton's *Mysterious Suspense* issue #1 you'll see a particularly nice version of the sweeping "question mark" cloud – the process is only beginning here.
QUESTION: GUESS I'LL CATCH THE NEXT ONE.
QUESTION: >sfnf<

Top left, bottom: Cover sketches by Grant Morrison
Top right: Character sketches for the Gentry

KEYHOLE COMICS (GOLD KEY)
VICTORY COMICS (ATLAS 70s)
DOCTOR MANHATTAN
THE QUANTUM MAN
VICTORY COMICS
The STINGRAY
Harpoon guns
SPIRE COMICS (TOWER)
CYCLOTRON
CHAMP OF AMERICA
ANDY COMICS
Howard Chaykin style
Andy Comics
Goodguy the Great

MULTIVERSITY 1
THE GENTRY -
DEMONS OF THE GENTRY
INTELLECTRON - Earth-5
HELLMACHINE - Earth-4
DAME MERCILESS - Earth-16
DEMOGORGUN - Earth-20
LORD BROKEN - Earth-16
INTELLECTRON
HELLMACHINE
DAME MERCILESS
DEMOGORGUN
LORD BROKEN
Made of thousands of people with knives + forks

MULTIVERSITY
CREATION'S GREATEST HEROES
COSMIC
SOCIETY OF SUPER-HEROES
MULTIVERSITY 1
THE SOCIETY 1
PAX AMERICANA
THE JUST 1
PAX AMERICANA 1
quitely
black + white
consumed by fire.

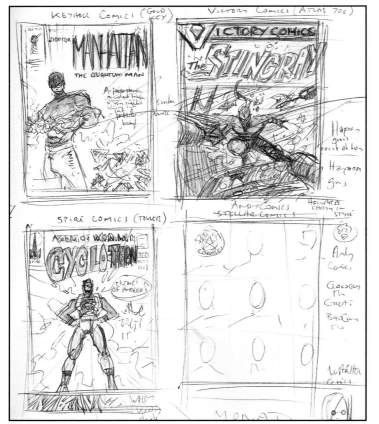

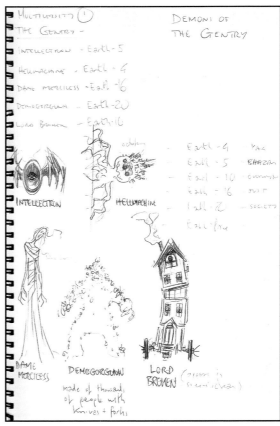

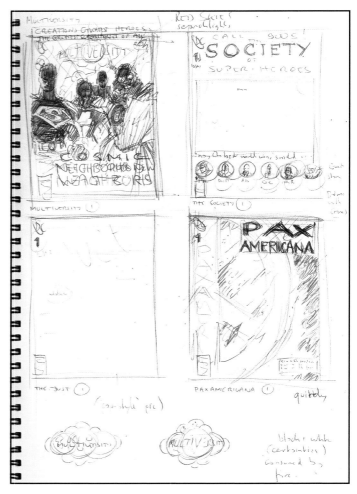

Top: Initial designs for Major Max by Grant Morrison
Bottom: Character designs for the Agents of W.O.N.D.E.R. by Grant Morrison

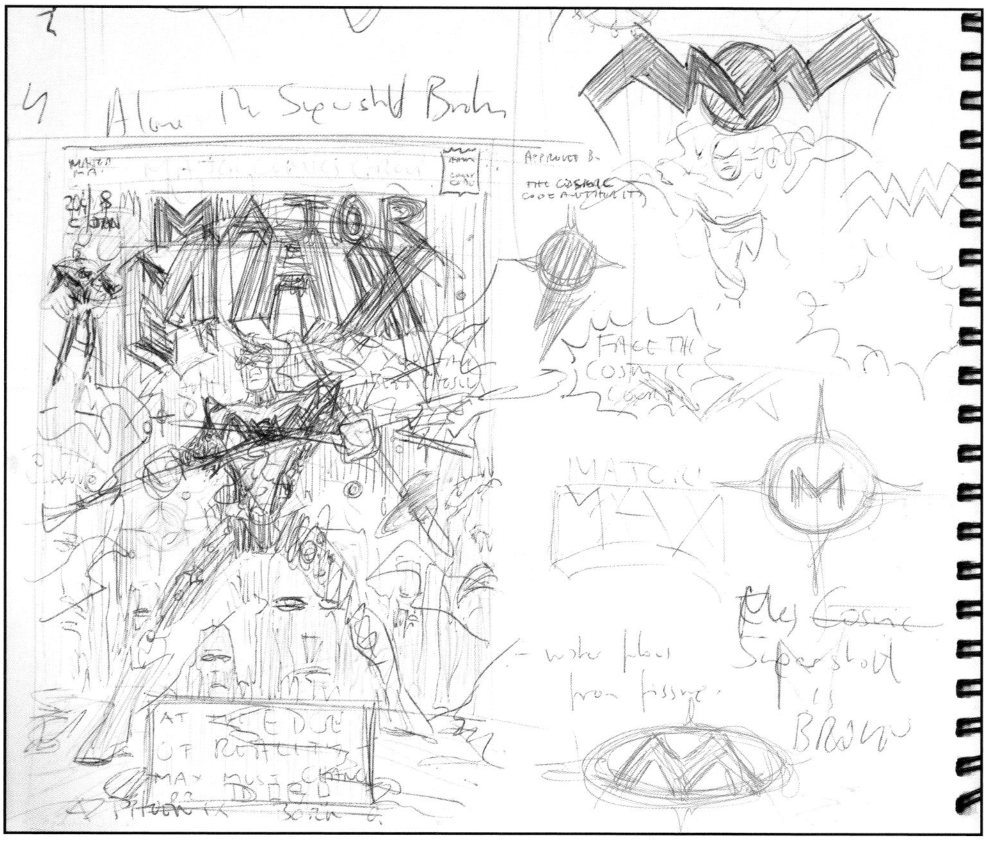
MAJOR MAX

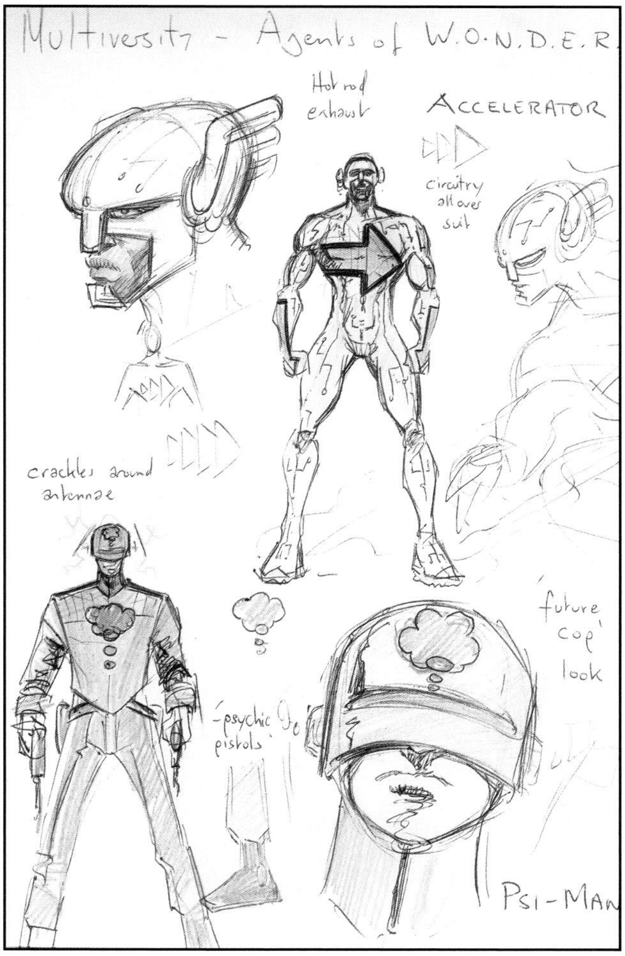
Multiversity - Agents of W.O.N.D.E.R.
Hot rod exhaust
ACCELERATOR
circuitry all over suit
crackles around antennae
future cop' look
psychic pistols
PSI-MAN

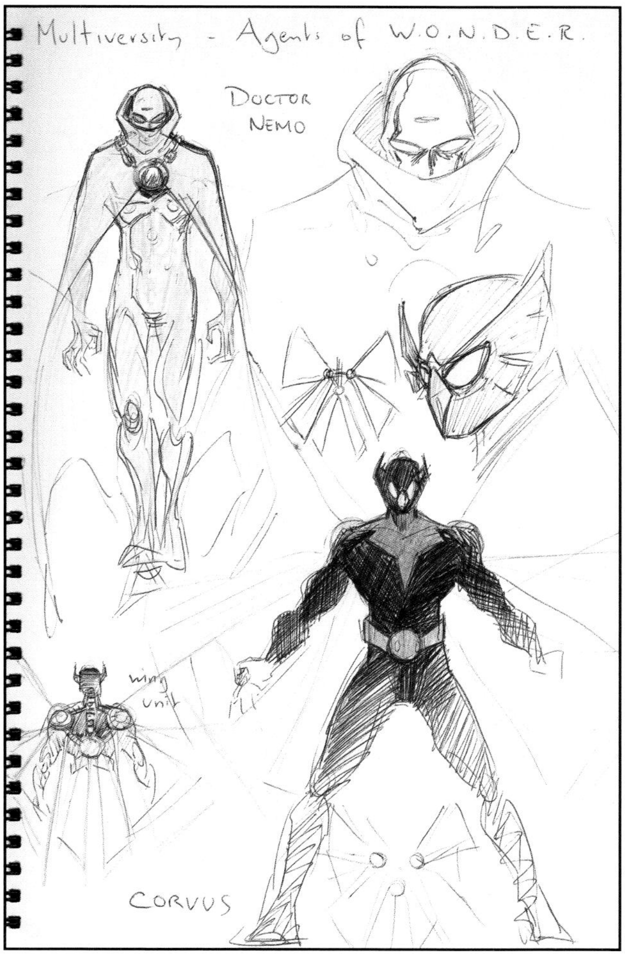
Multiversity - Agents of W.O.N.D.E.R.
DOCTOR NEMO
wing unit
CORVUS

The Multiversity: *final pencil art by Ivan Reis from issue #2*

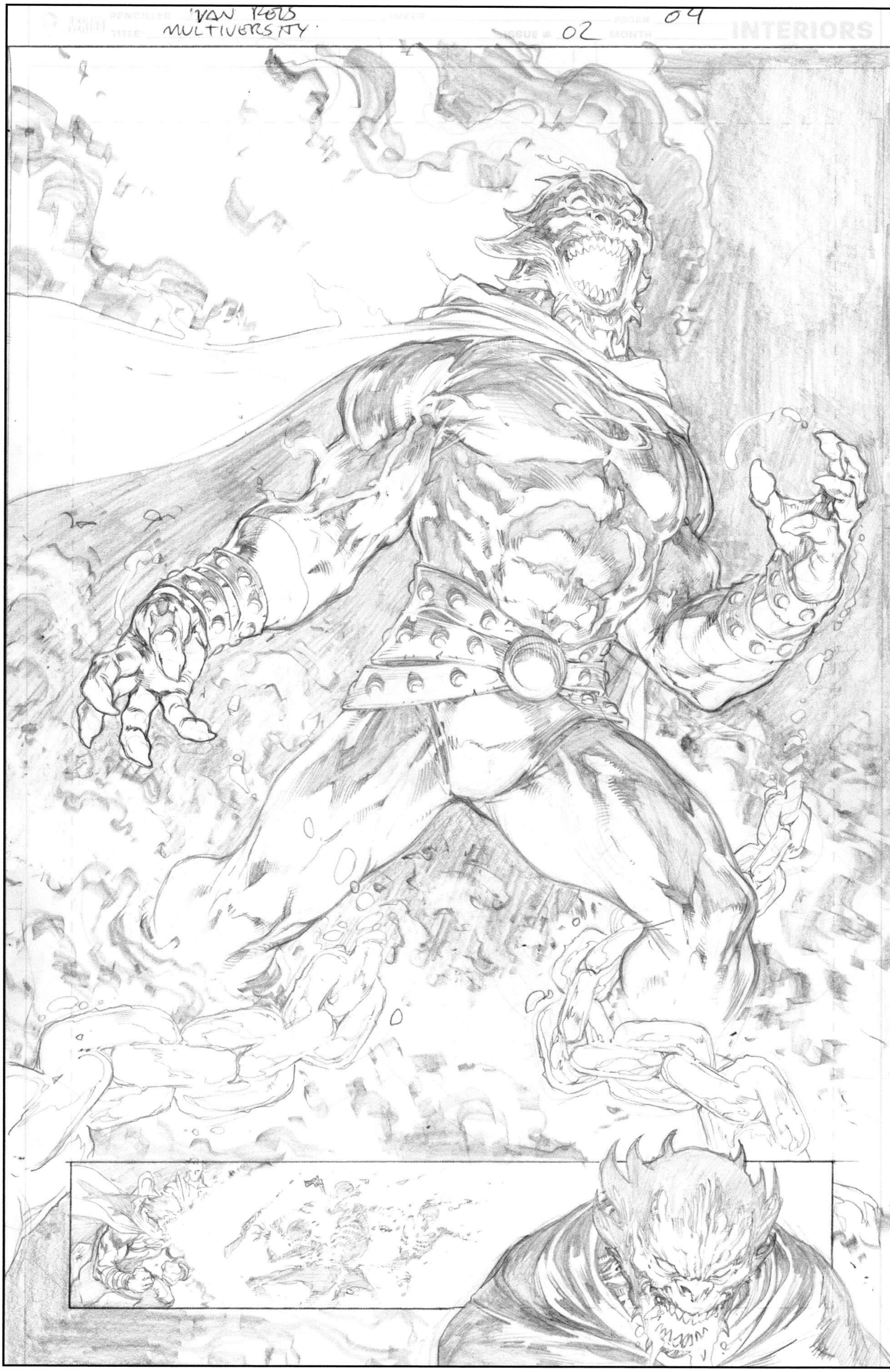
MULTIVERSITY
02
04
INTERIORS

Society of Super-Heroes *character sketches for Doc Fate and Abin Sur by Grant Morrison*

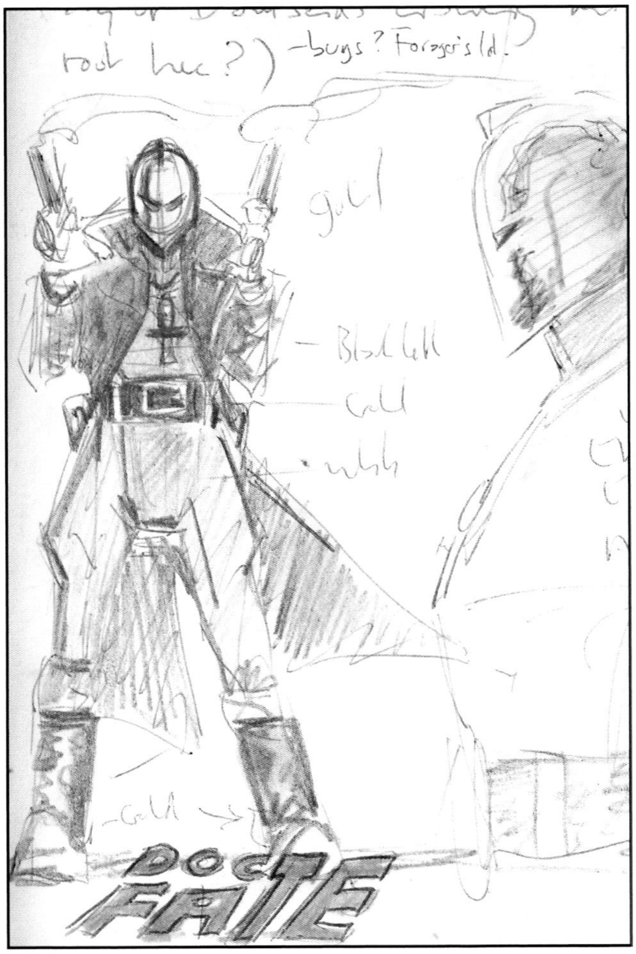
DOC FATE

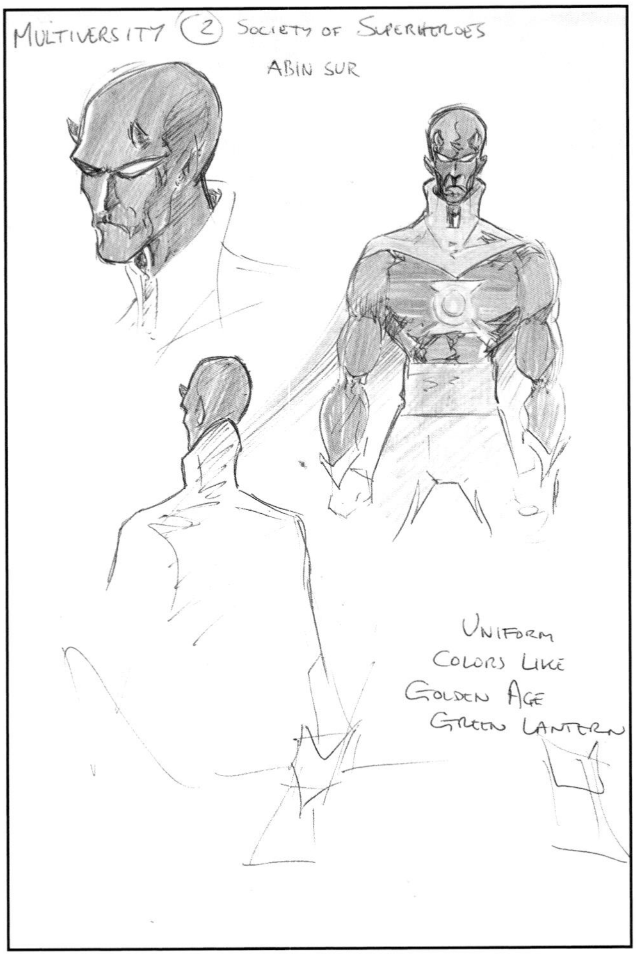
MULTIVERSITY (2) SOCIETY OF SUPERHEROES
ABIN SUR
UNIFORM
COLORS LIKE
GOLDEN AGE
GREEN LANTERN

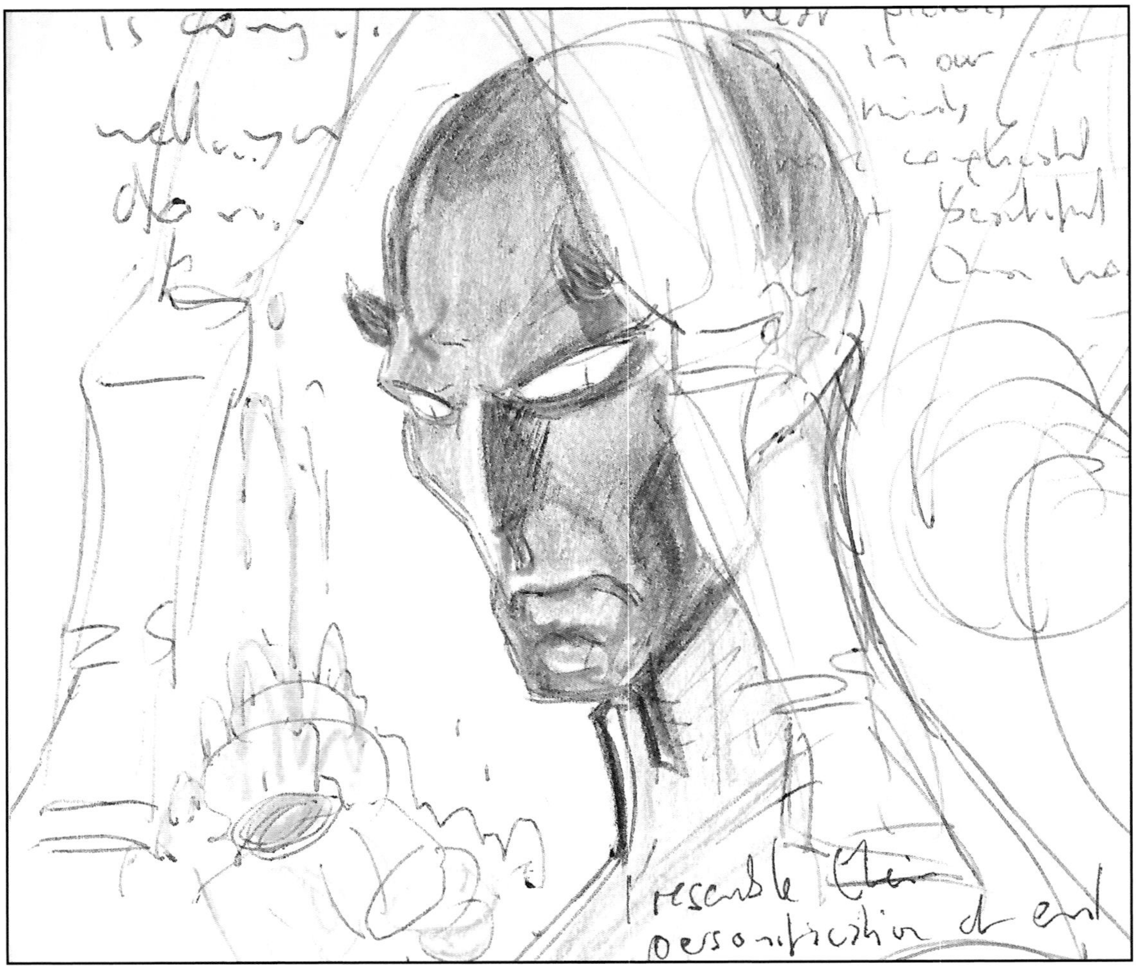

Final character designs by Chris Sprouse

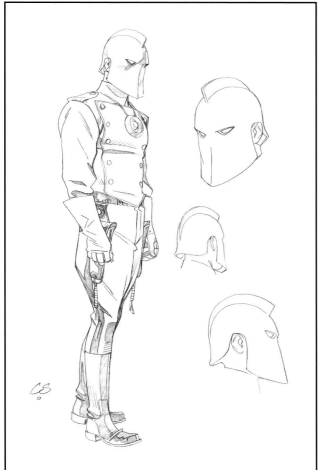

Top: The Just *initial sketches for the Atom by Grant Morrison* *Bottom: Thunderer sketch by Grant Morrison*

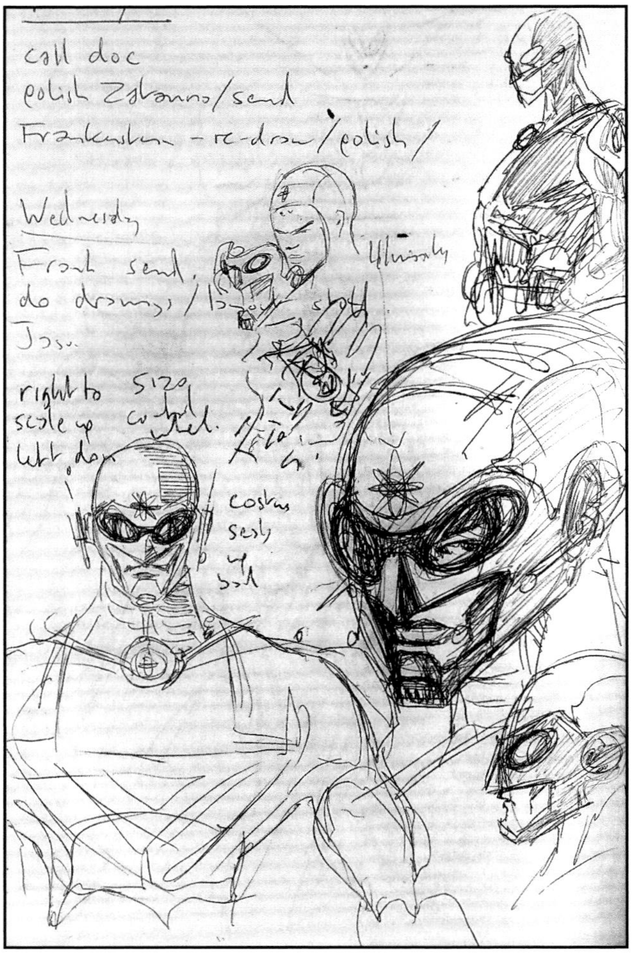
call doc
Wednesday

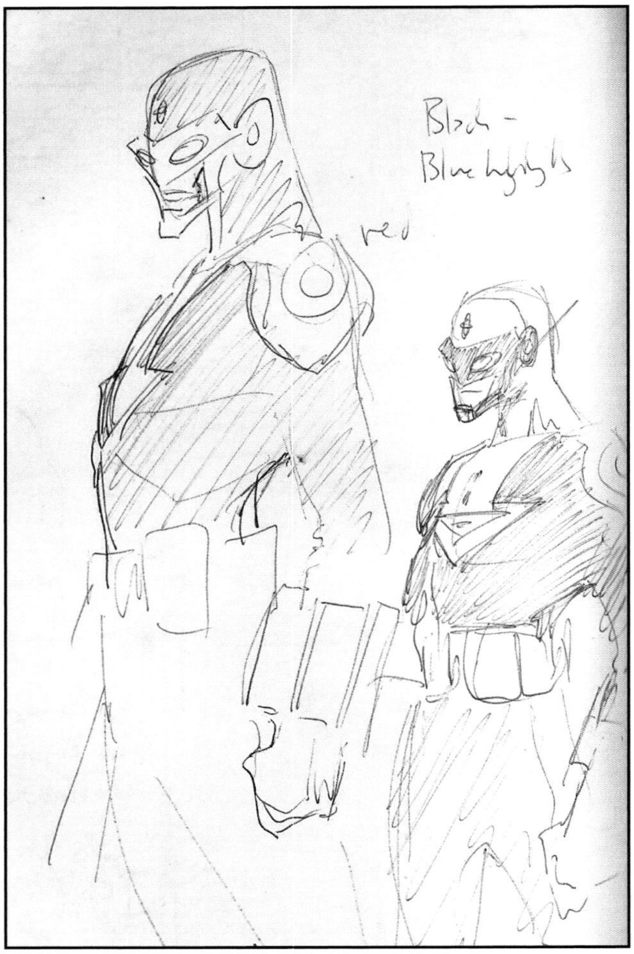

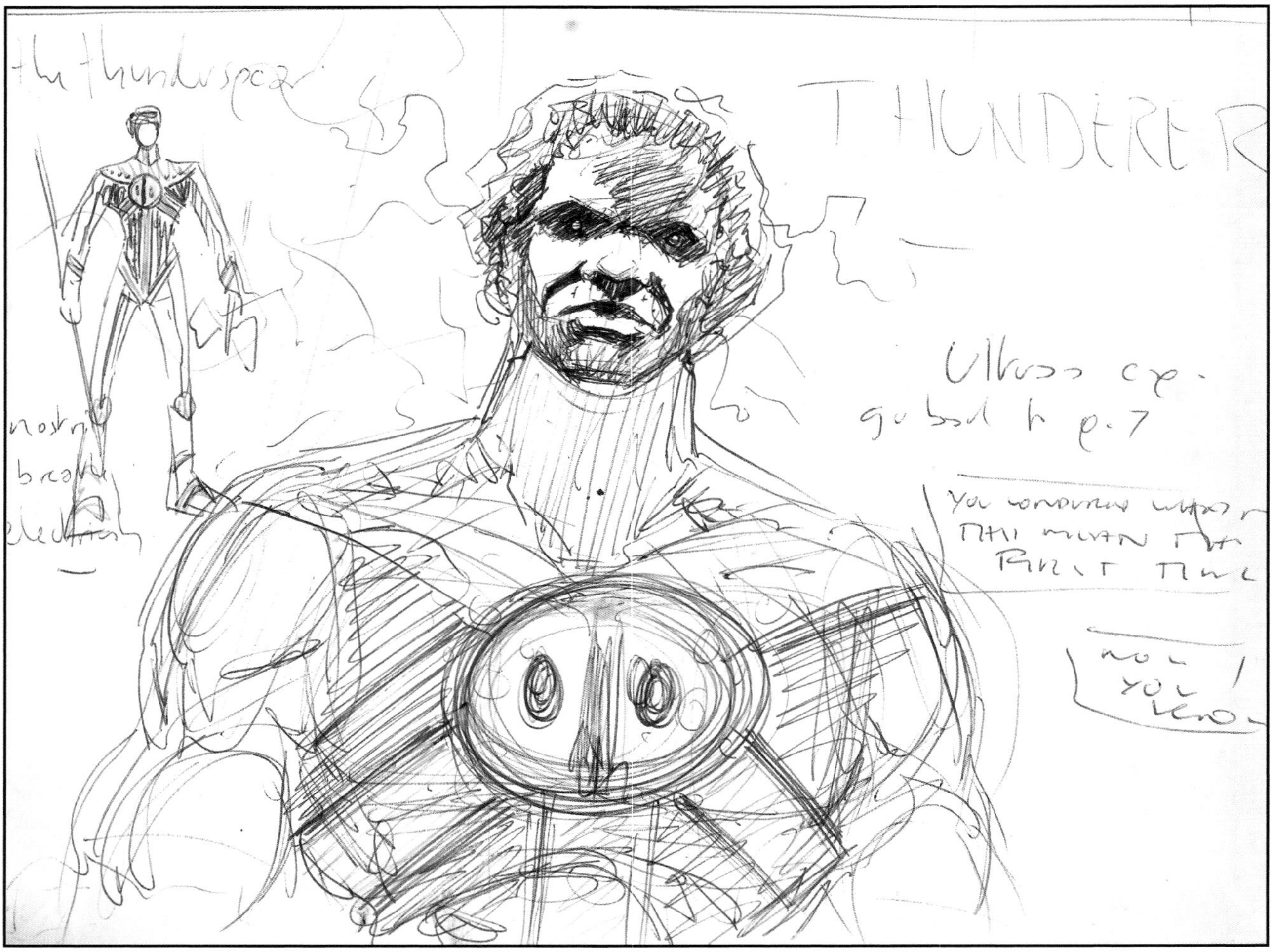
THUNDERER

Final The Just *character designs by Ben Oliver*

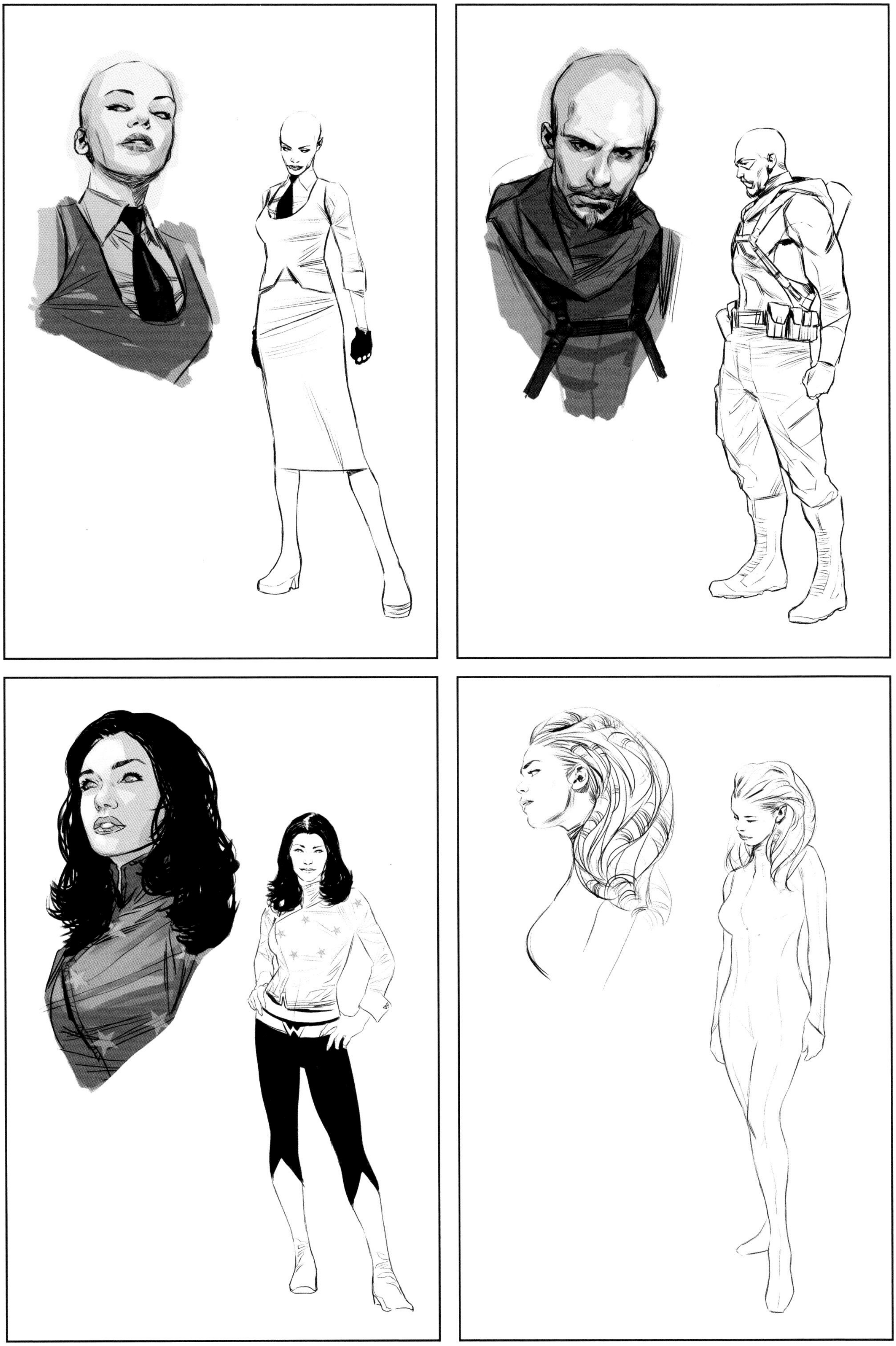

The Just: *final character designs by Ben Oliver*

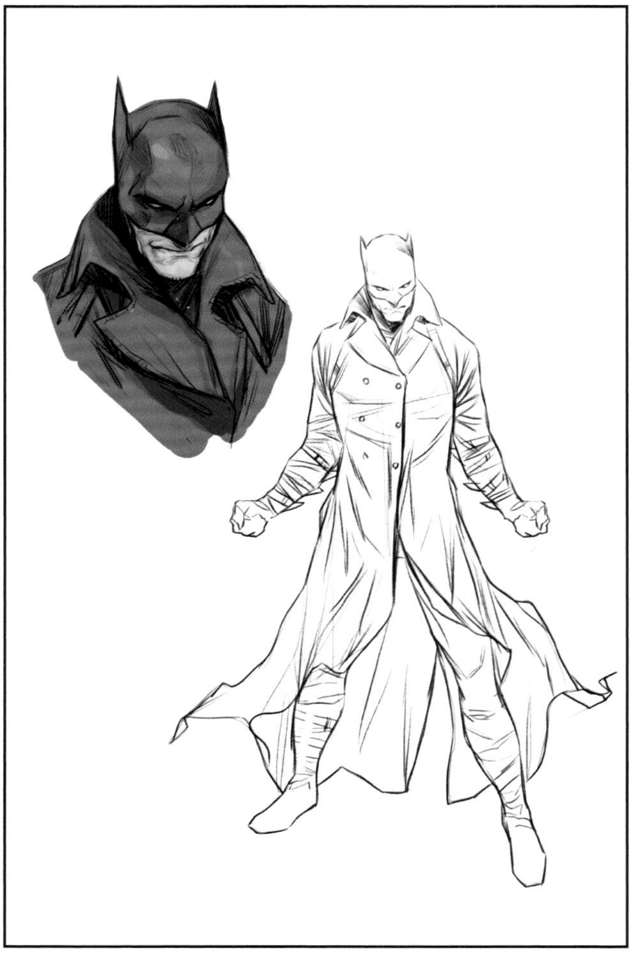

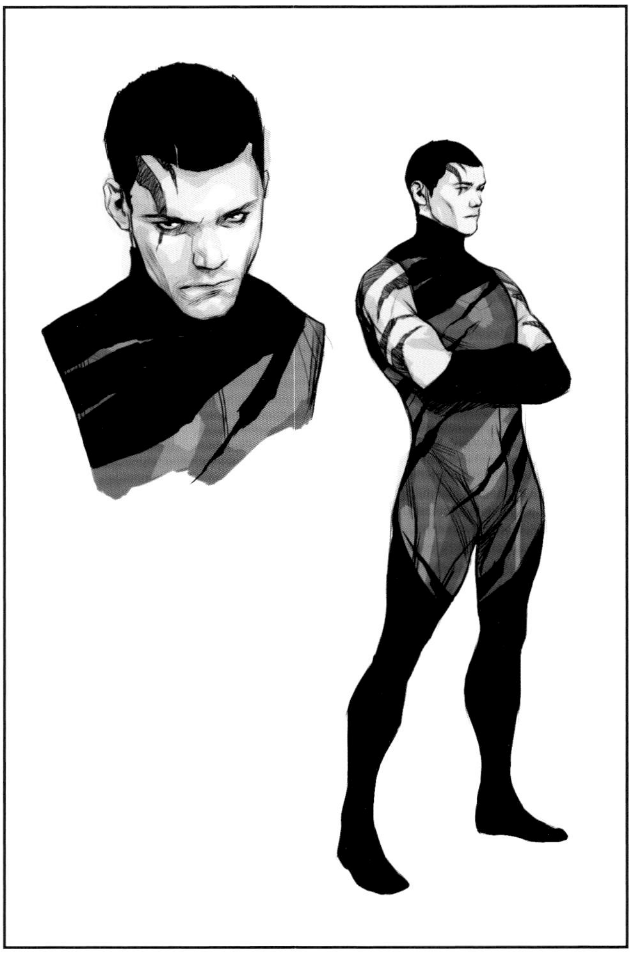

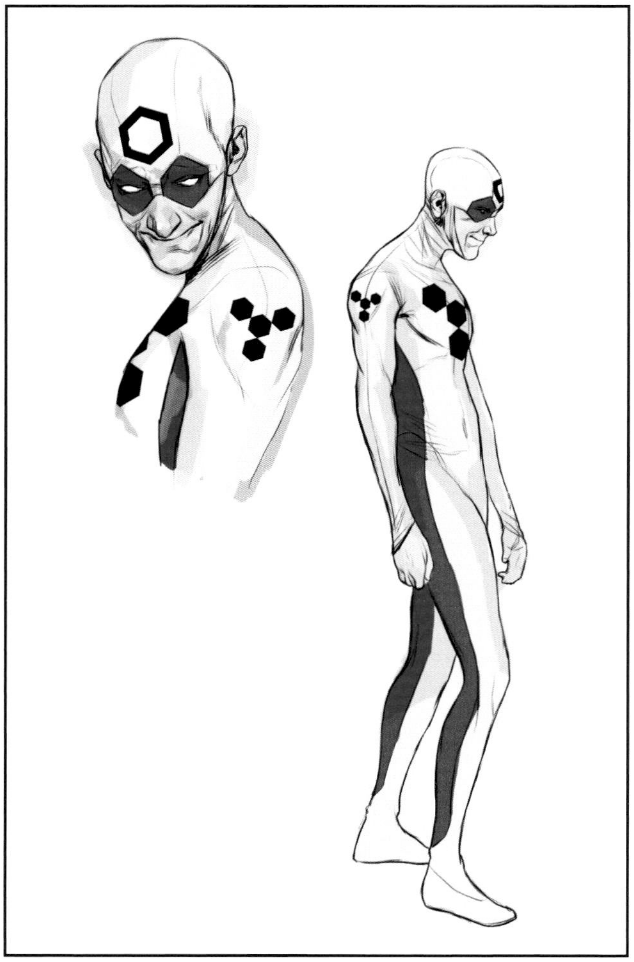

Pax Americana: *breakdown for page 28 by Grant Morrison*

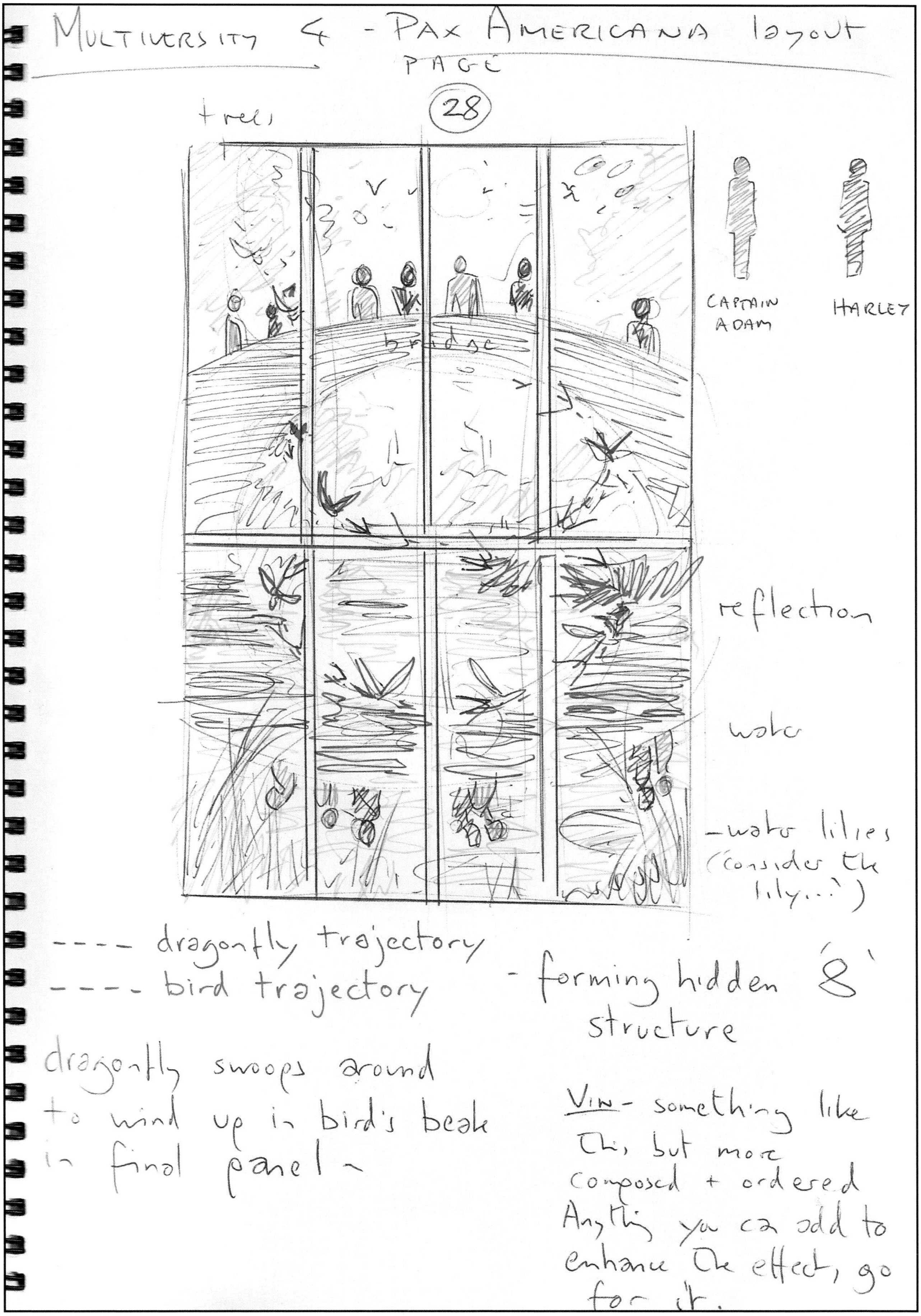

MULTIVERSITY 4 - PAX AMERICANA layout
PAGE
28
trees
bridge
CAPTAIN ADAM
HARLEY
reflection
water
- water lilies ('consider the lily...')
---- dragonfly trajectory
---- bird trajectory
- forming hidden '8' structure
dragonfly swoops around to wind up in bird's beak in final panel -
Vin - something like this, but more composed + ordered
Anything you can add to enhance the effect, go for it.

Pax Americana: *pencils for page 28 by Frank Quitely*

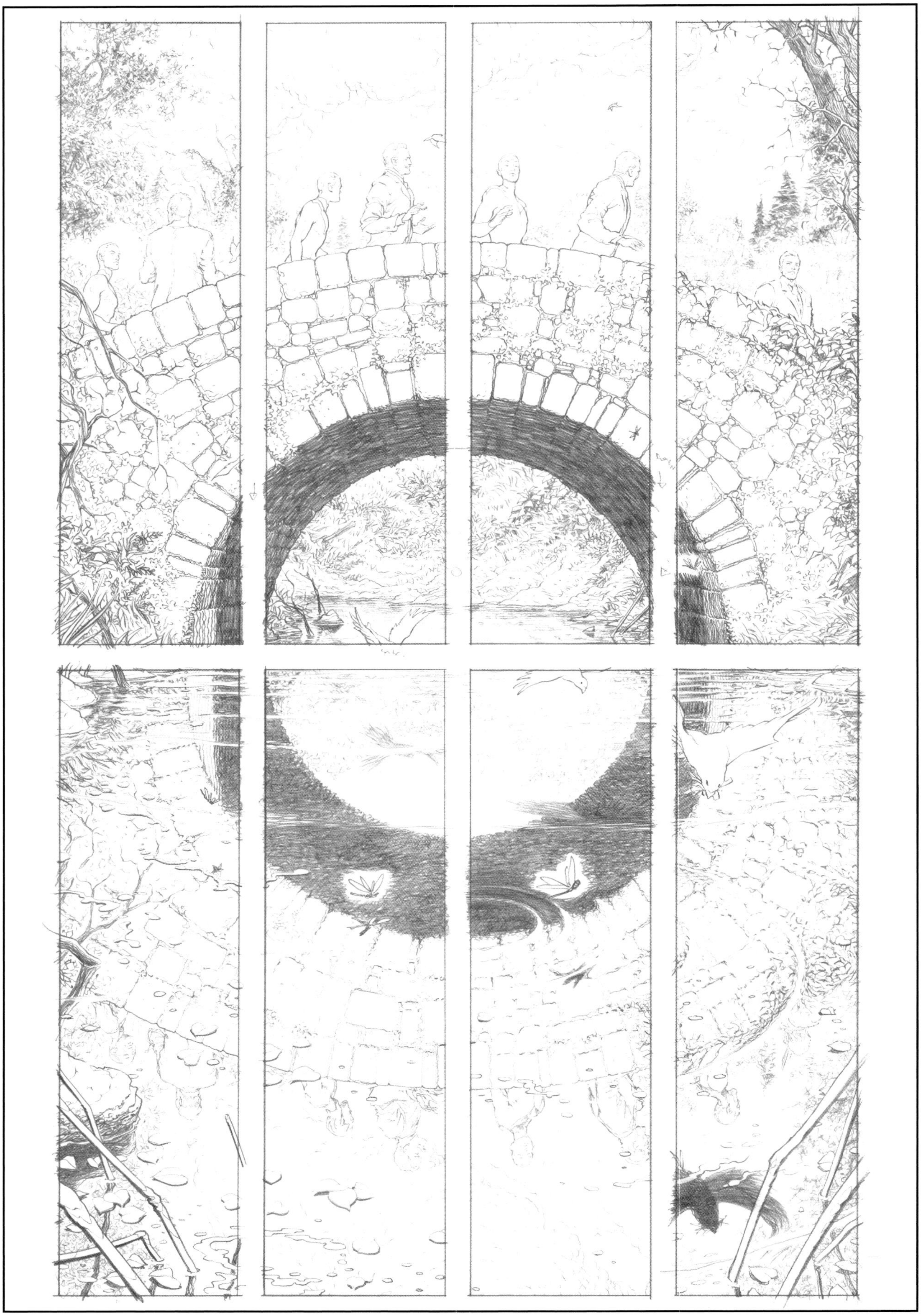

Final inks for page 28 by Frank Quitely

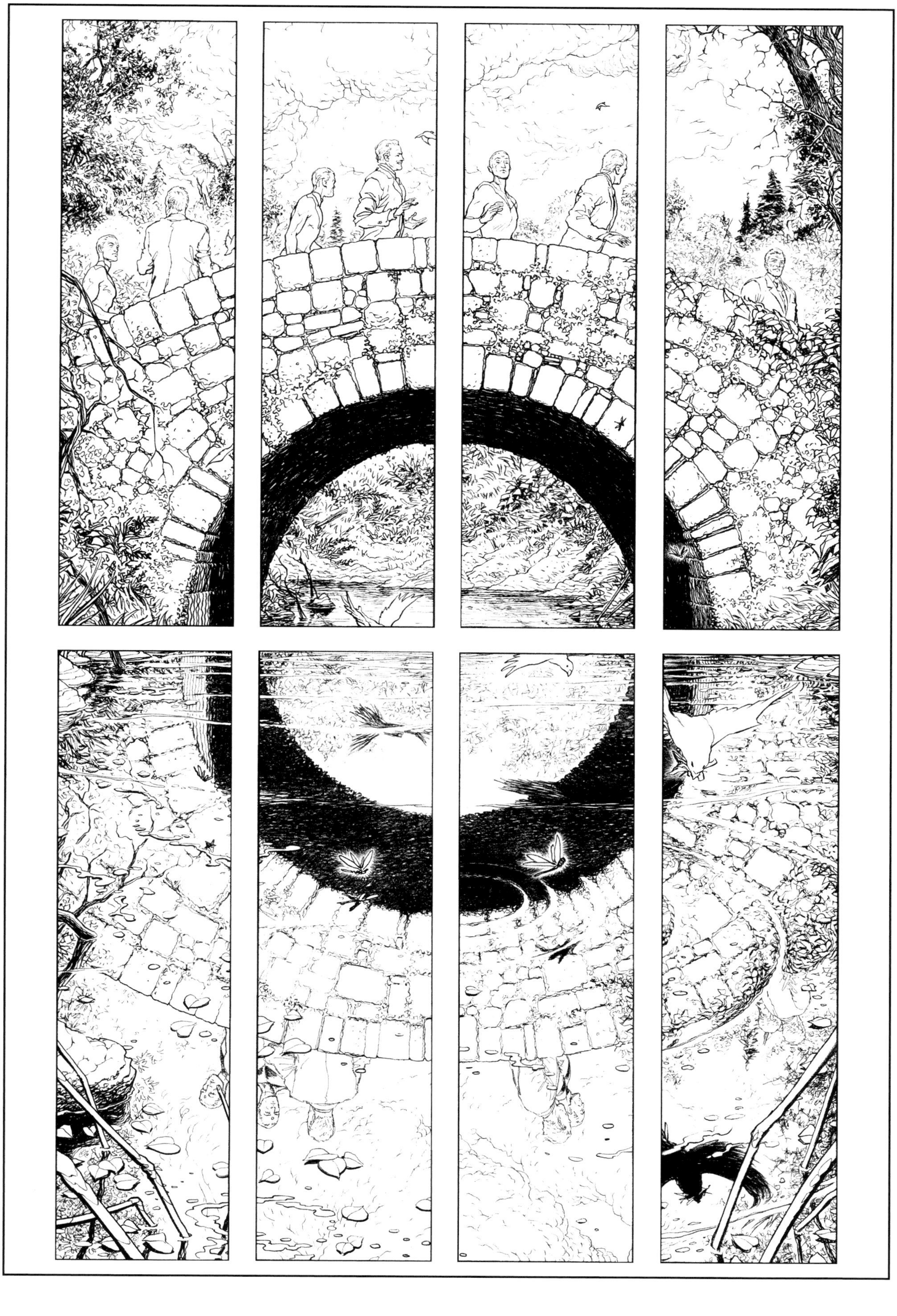

Thunderworld Adventures: *cover sketch by Grant Morrison*

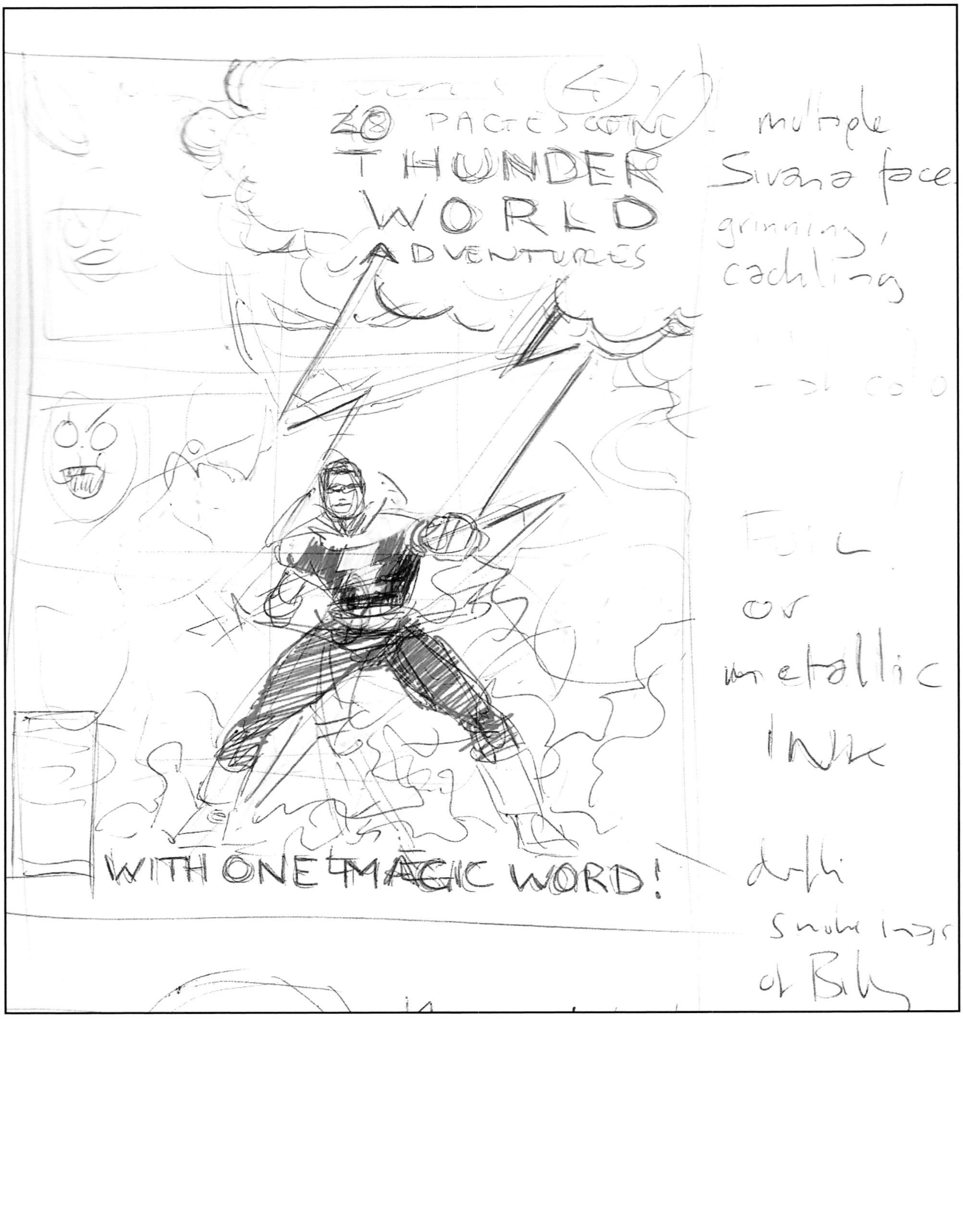
THUNDER WORLD ADVENTURES
multiple Sivana face grinning/cackling
Foil or metallic INK
WITH ONE MAGIC WORD!

Conceptual art and character designs by Cameron Stewart

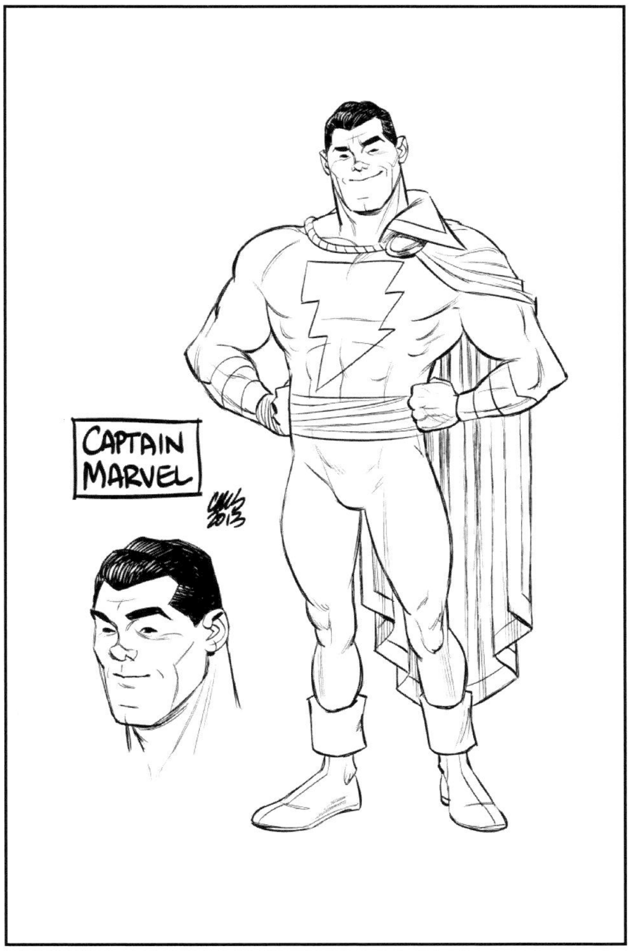
CAPTAIN MARVEL

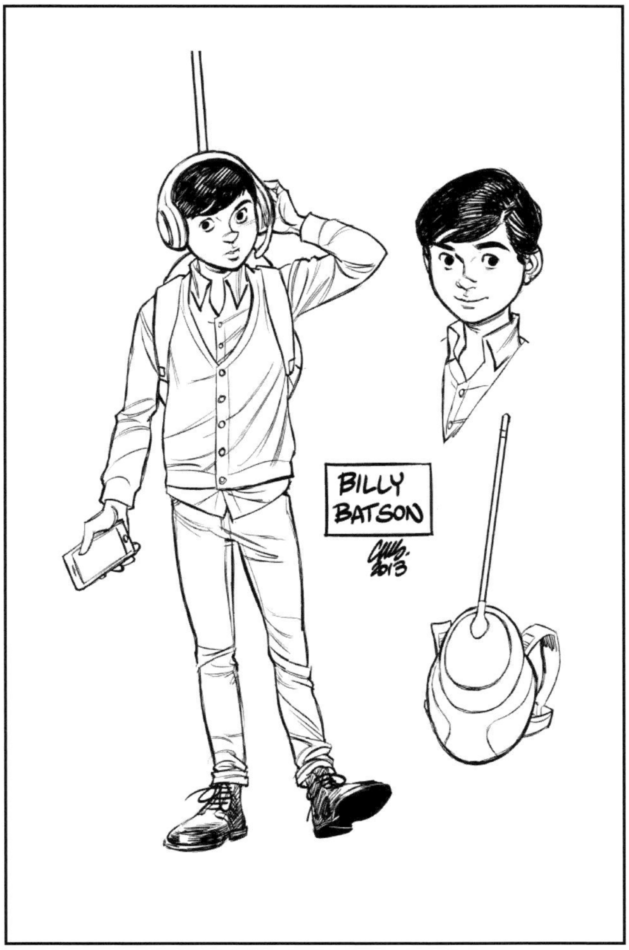
BILLY BATSON

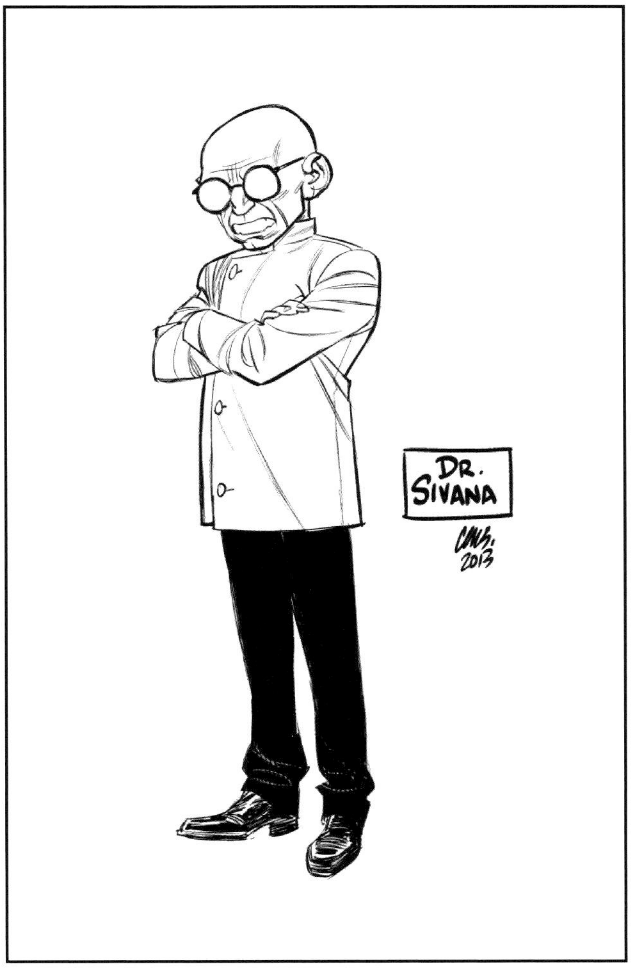
DR. SIVANA

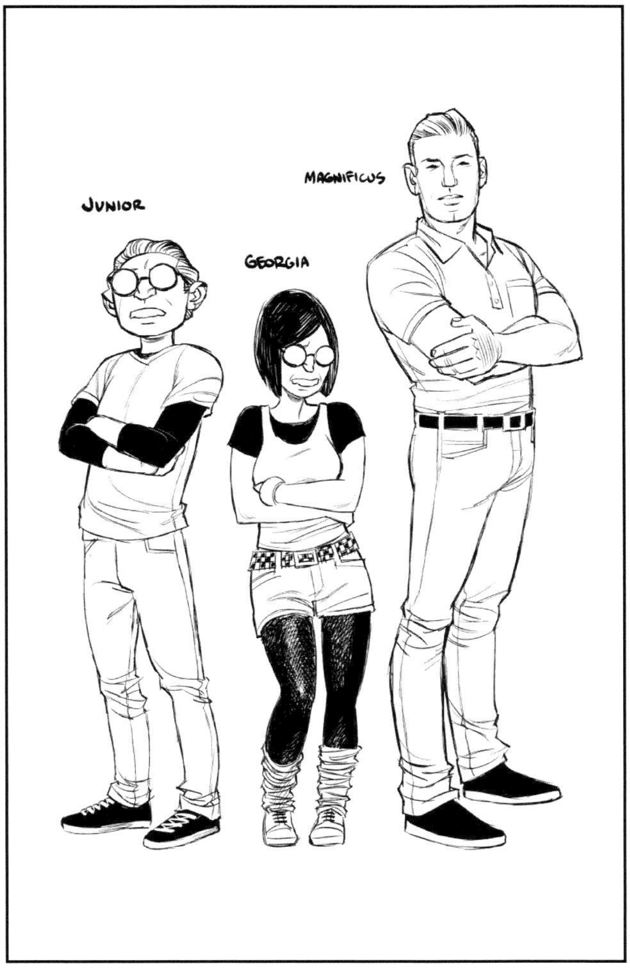
MAGNIFICUS
JUNIOR
GEORGIA

Thunderworld Adventures: layouts by Cameron Stewart for pages 2-5

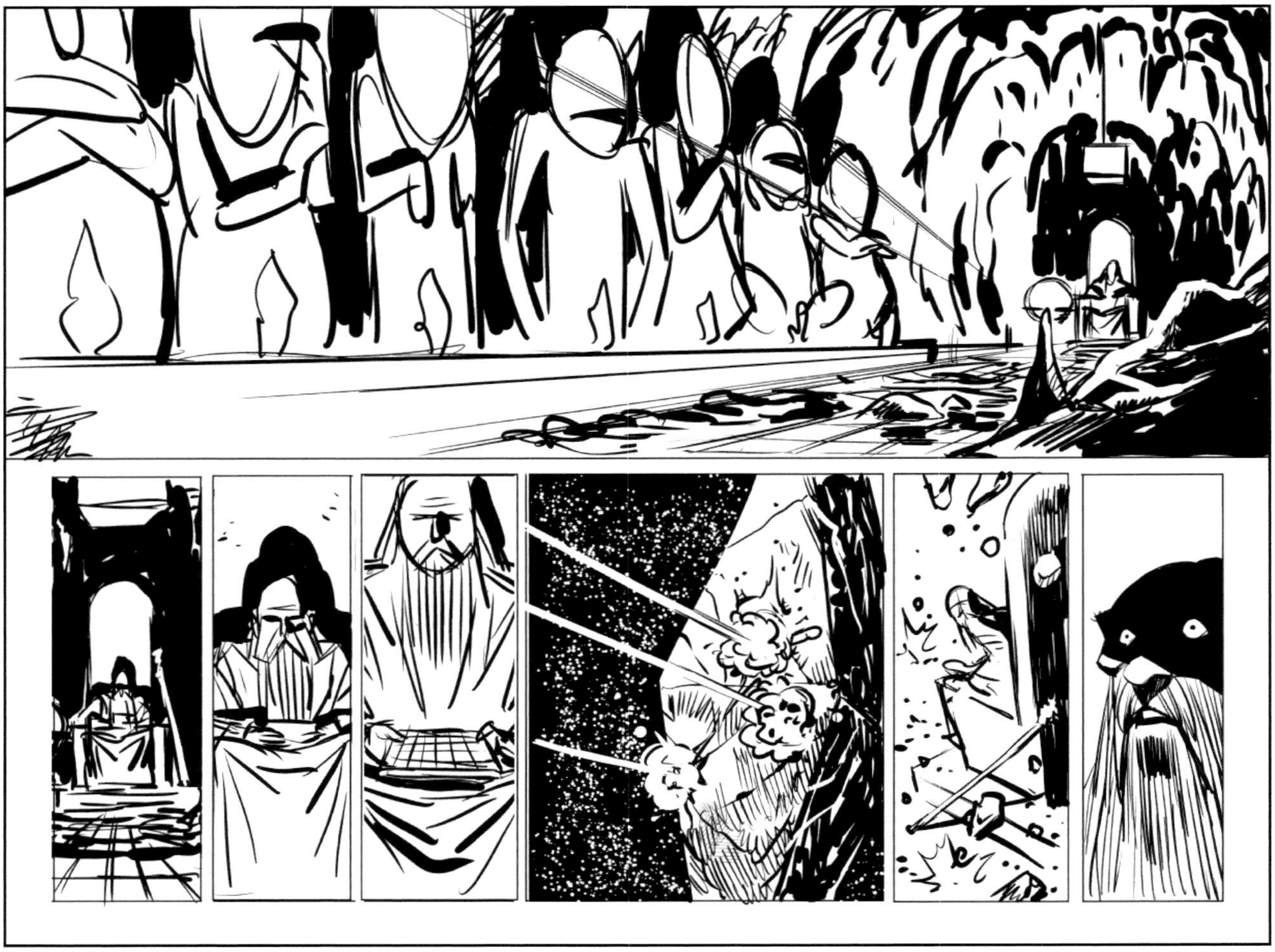

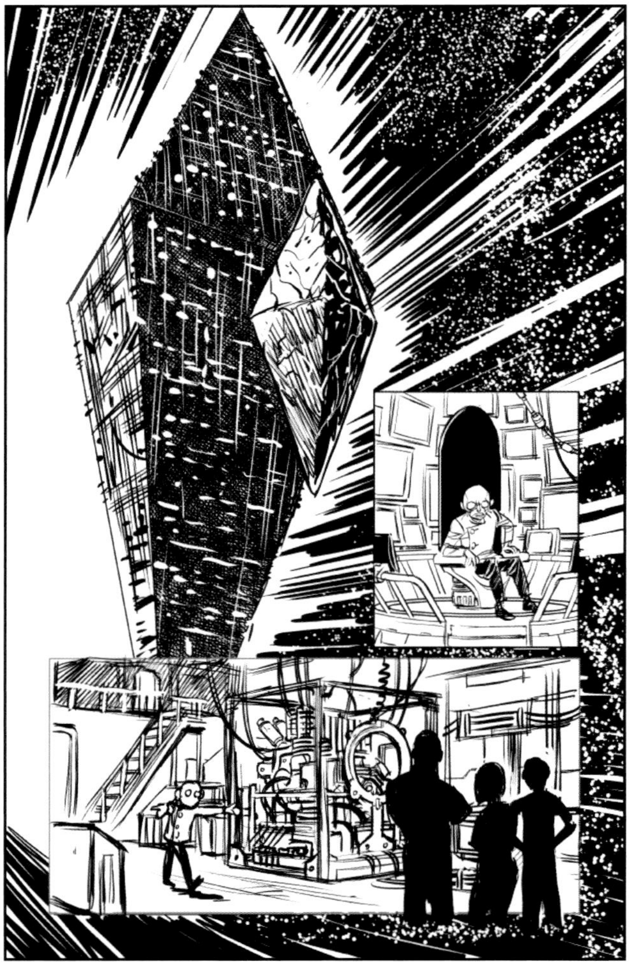

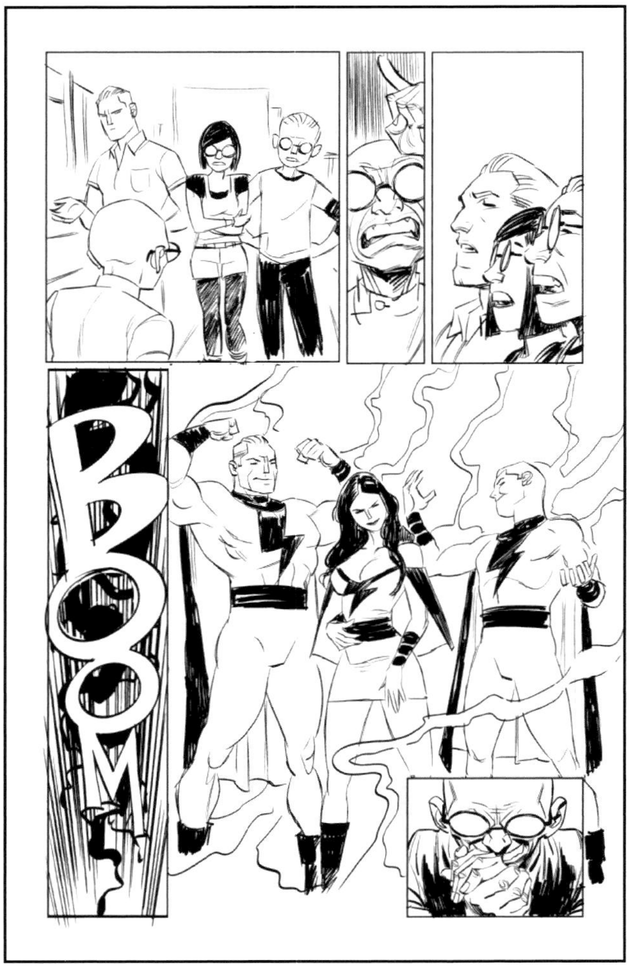
BOOM

The Multiversity Guidebook: *character design for the Atomic Batman by Grant Morrison*

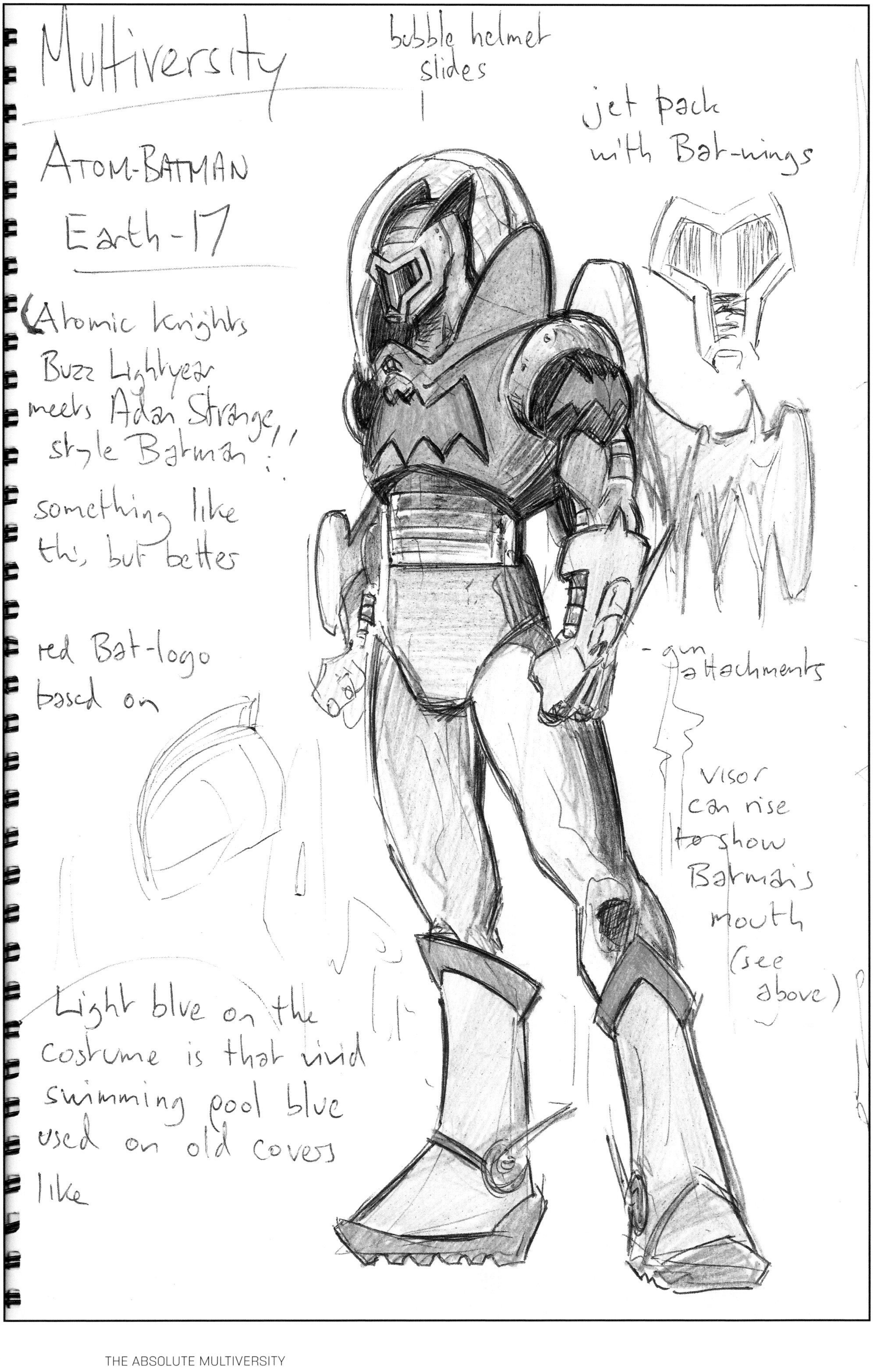

Multiversity
ATOM-BATMAN
Earth-17
Atomic Knights
Buzz Lightyear
meets Adam Strange,
style Batman!!
something like
this, but better
red Bat-logo
based on
Light blue on the
costume is that vivid
swimming pool blue
used on old covers
like
bubble helmet
slides
jet pack
with Bat-wings
- gun
attachments
visor
can rise
to show
Batman's
mouth
(see
above)

The Multiversity Guidebook: *breakdowns and layouts for pages 1-4 by Marcus To*

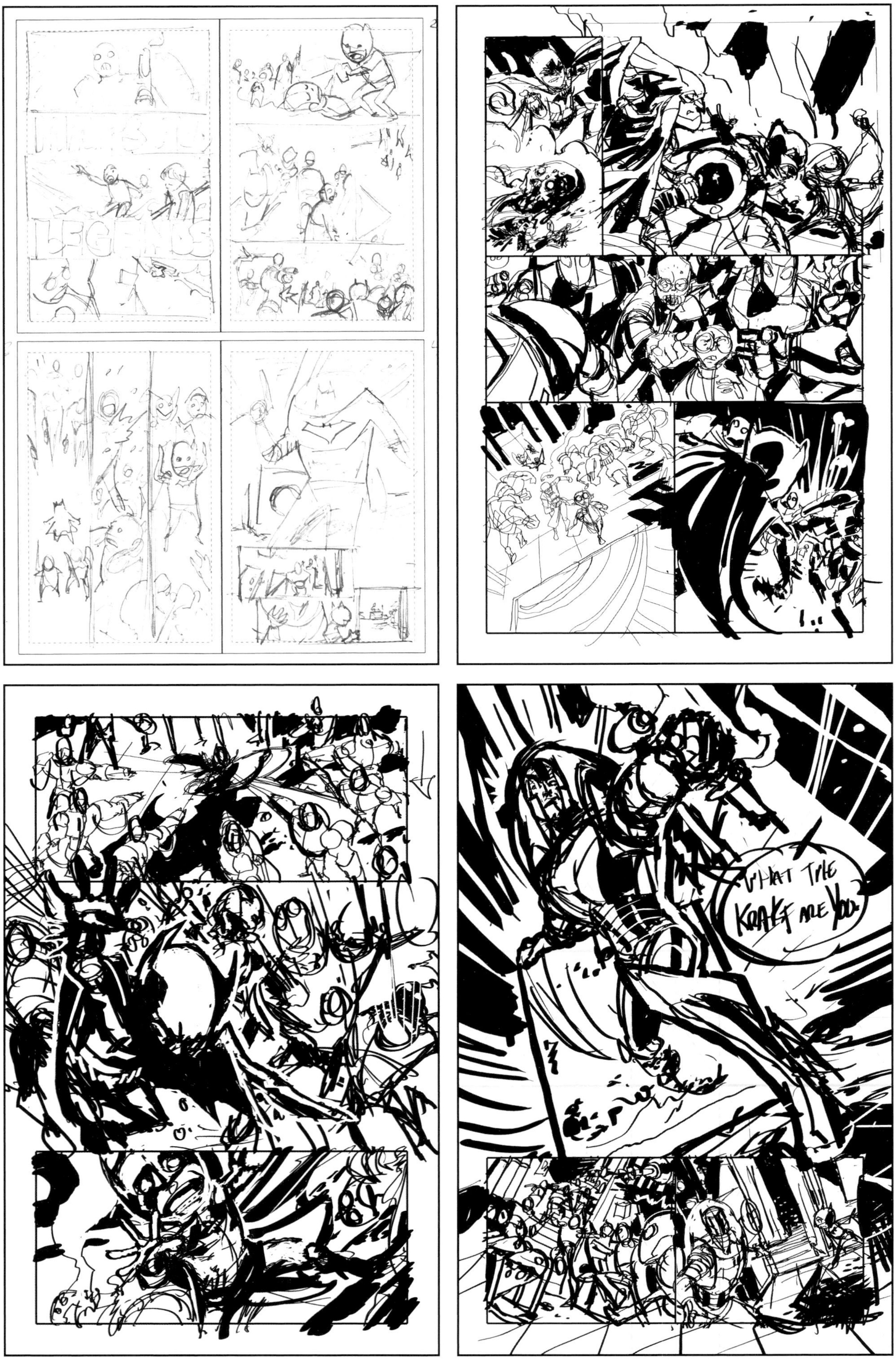
WHAT THE KRAKF ARE YOU?

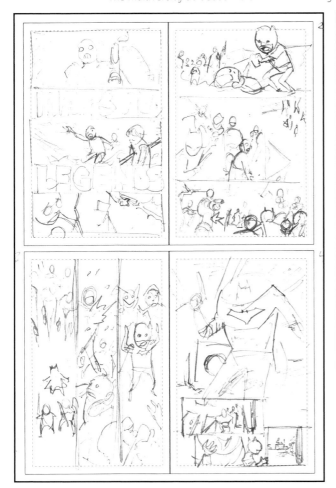

Layouts for pages 10-11 and 14-15 by Scott McDaniel

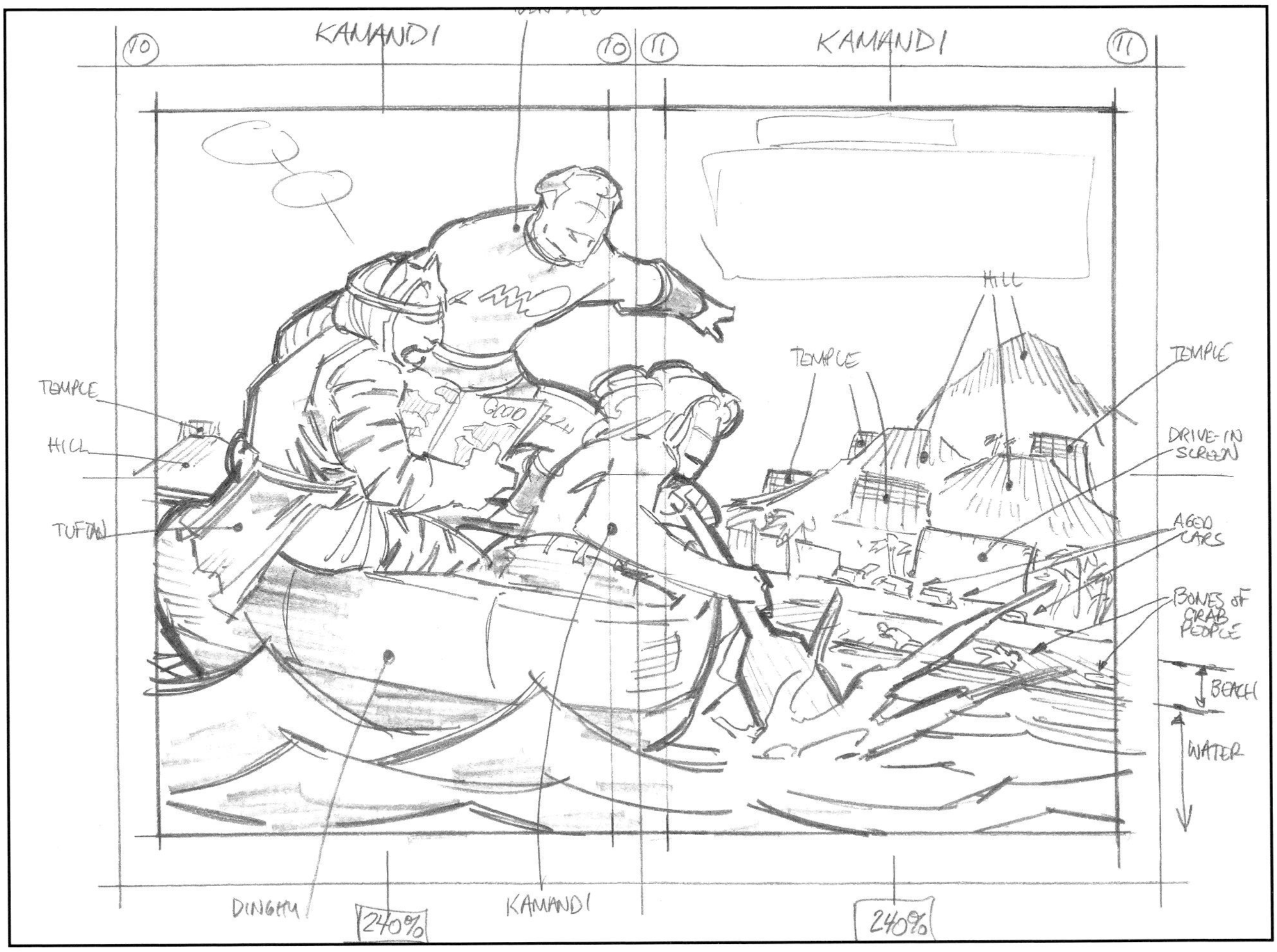
10
KAMANDI
10
11
KAMANDI
11
TEMPLE
HILL
TUFON
HILL
TEMPLE
TEMPLE
DRIVE-IN SCREEN
AGED CARS
BONES OF CRAB PEOPLE
BEACH
WATER
DINGHY
240%
KAMANDI
240%

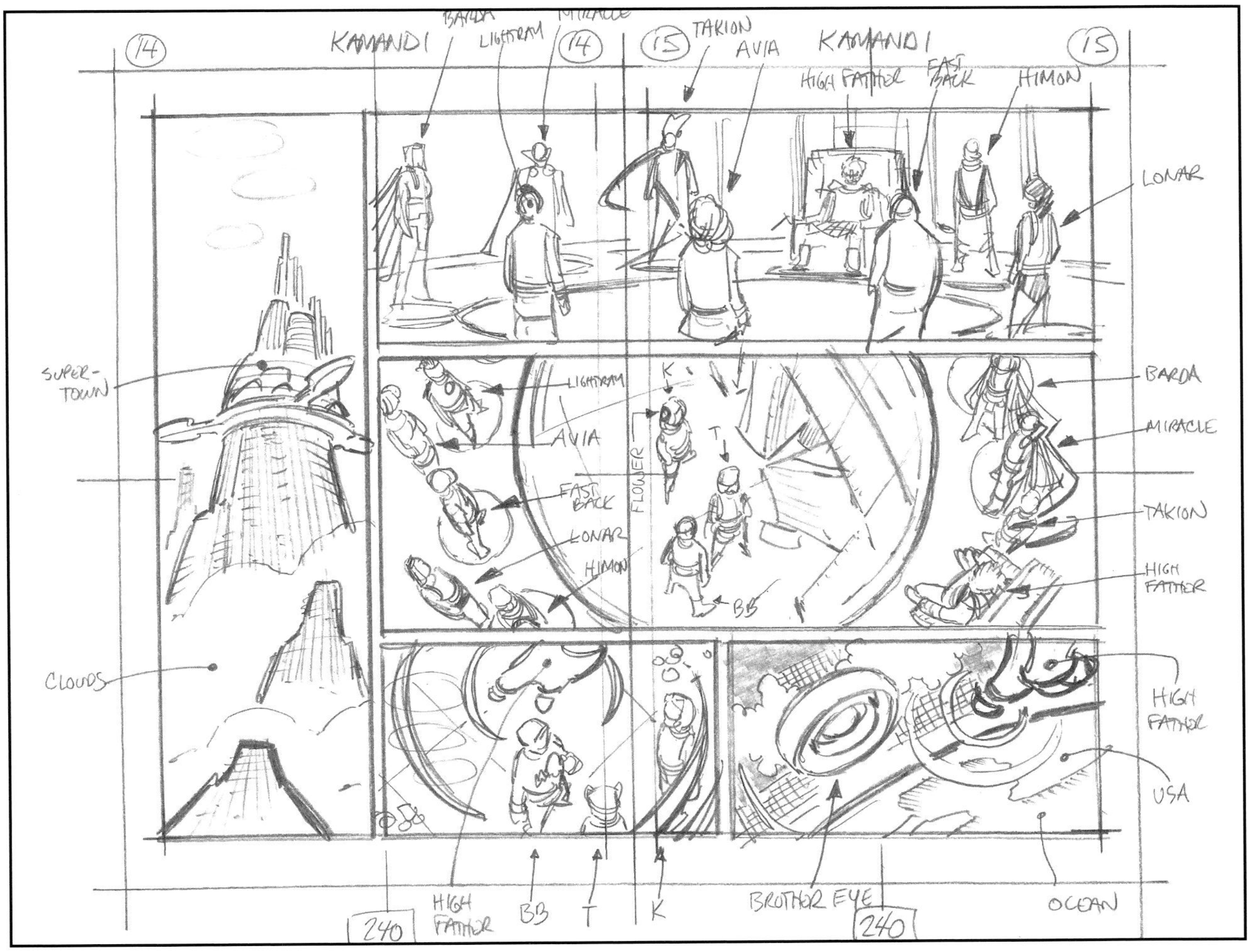
14
KAMANDI
BARDA
LIGHTRAY
MIRACLE
14
15
TAKION
AVIA
KAMANDI
HIGH FATHER
FAST BACK
HIMON
15
LONAR
SUPER-TOWN
LIGHTRAY
AVIA
FAST BACK
LONAR
HIMON
FLOWER
K
T
BB
BARDA
MIRACLE
TAKION
HIGH FATHER
CLOUDS
HIGH FATHER
USA
HIGH FATHER
BB
T
K
BROTHER EYE
OCEAN
240
240

Mastermen: *character design for Leatherwing by Grant Morrison*

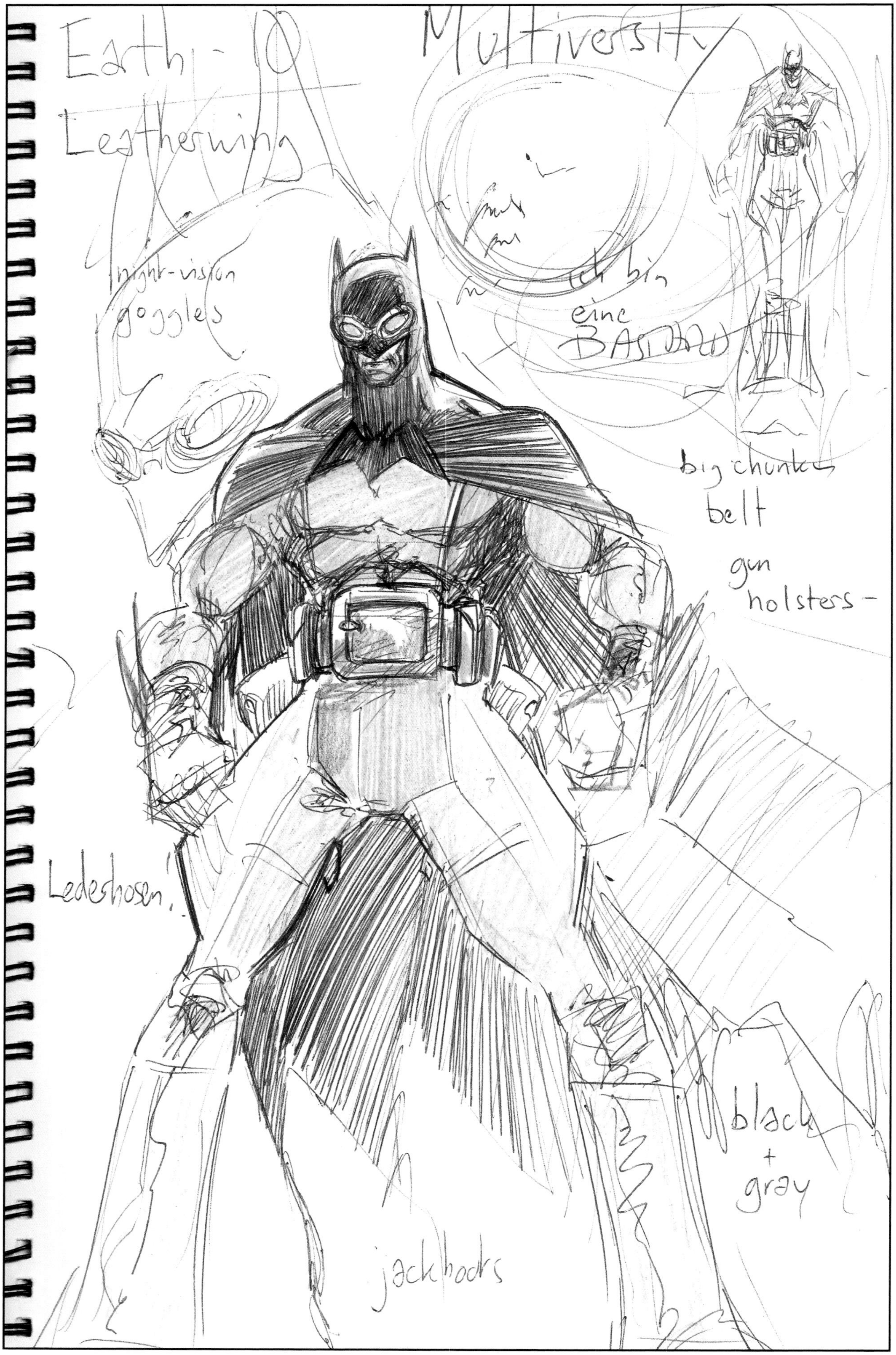
Earth-10
Multiversity
Leatherwing
night-vision goggles
ich bin eine
big chunky belt
gun holsters -
Ledershosen!
black + gray
jackboots

Character sketches for Blitzen by Grant Morrison

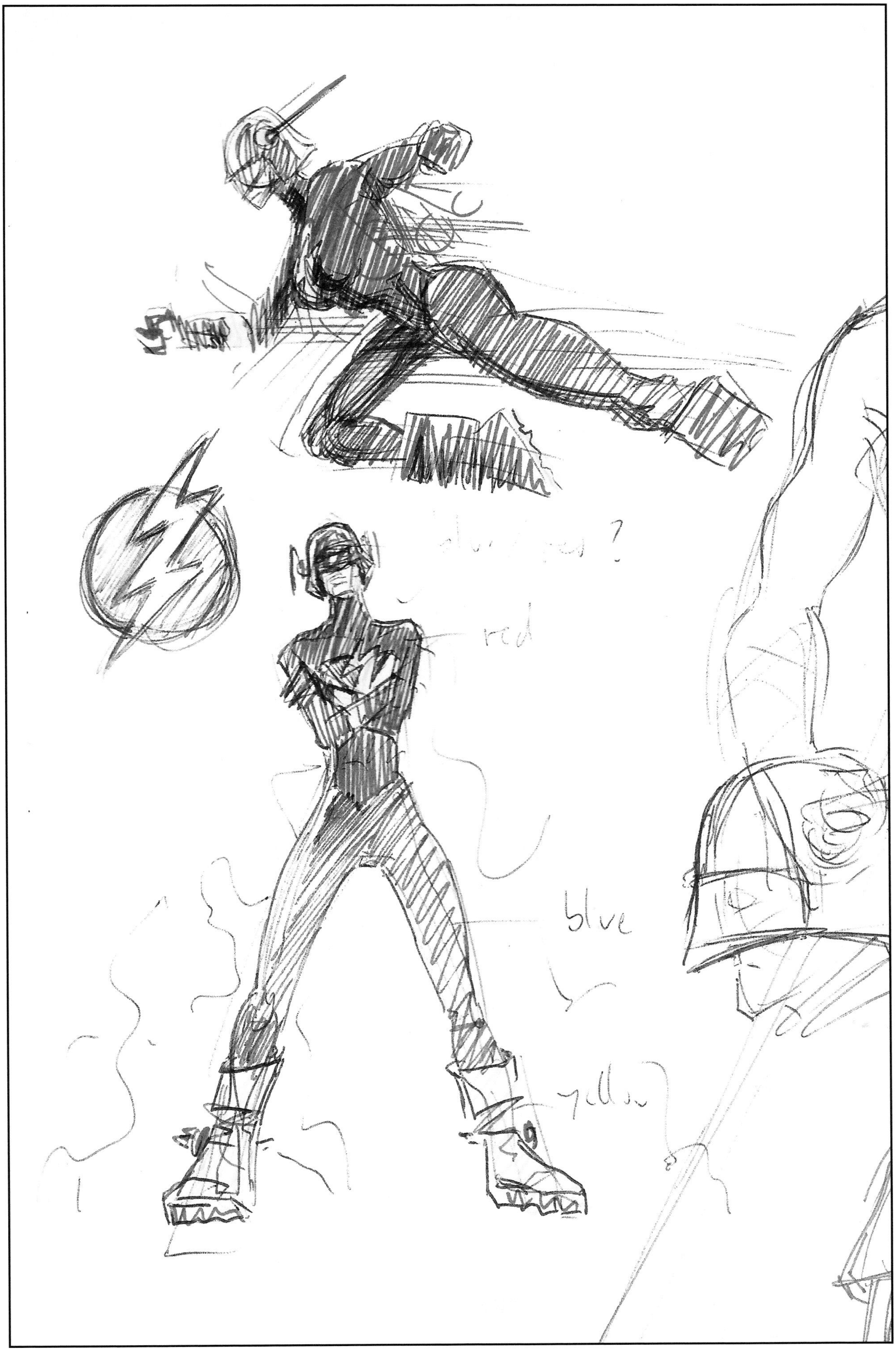
red
blue

Mastermen: *initial layout for pages 8-9 by Jim Lee*

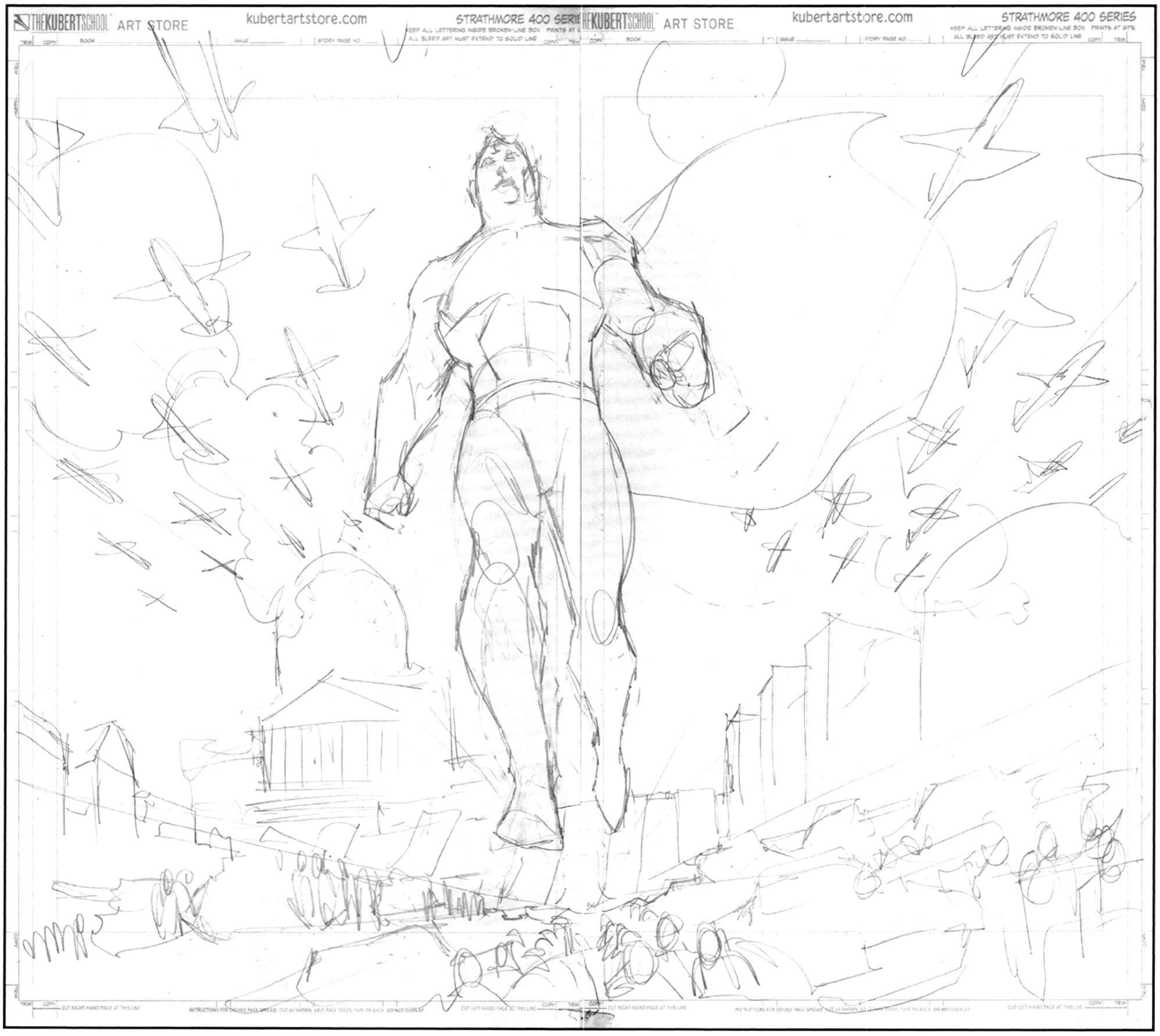
THEKUBERTSCHOOL ART STORE
kubertartstore.com
STRATHMORE 400 SERIES
KEEP ALL LETTERING INSIDE BROKEN-LINE BOX
ALL BLEED ART MUST EXTEND TO SOLID LINE

Final pencils for pages 8-9 by Jim Lee

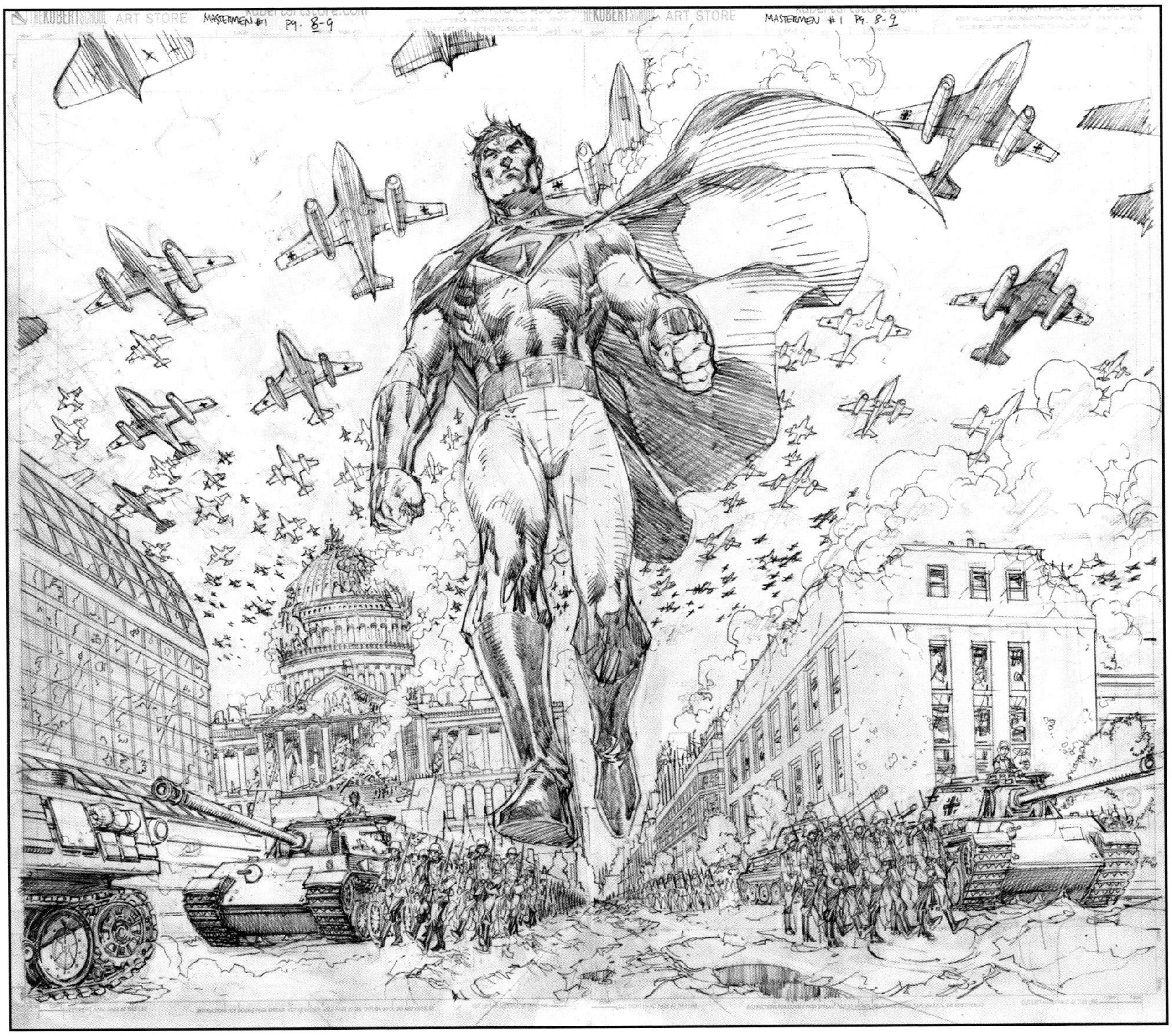
ART STORE
MASTERMEN #1 Pg. 8-9
ART STORE
MASTERMEN #1 Pg. 8-9

Ultra Comics: *character sketches for Ultra Comics by Grant Morrison*

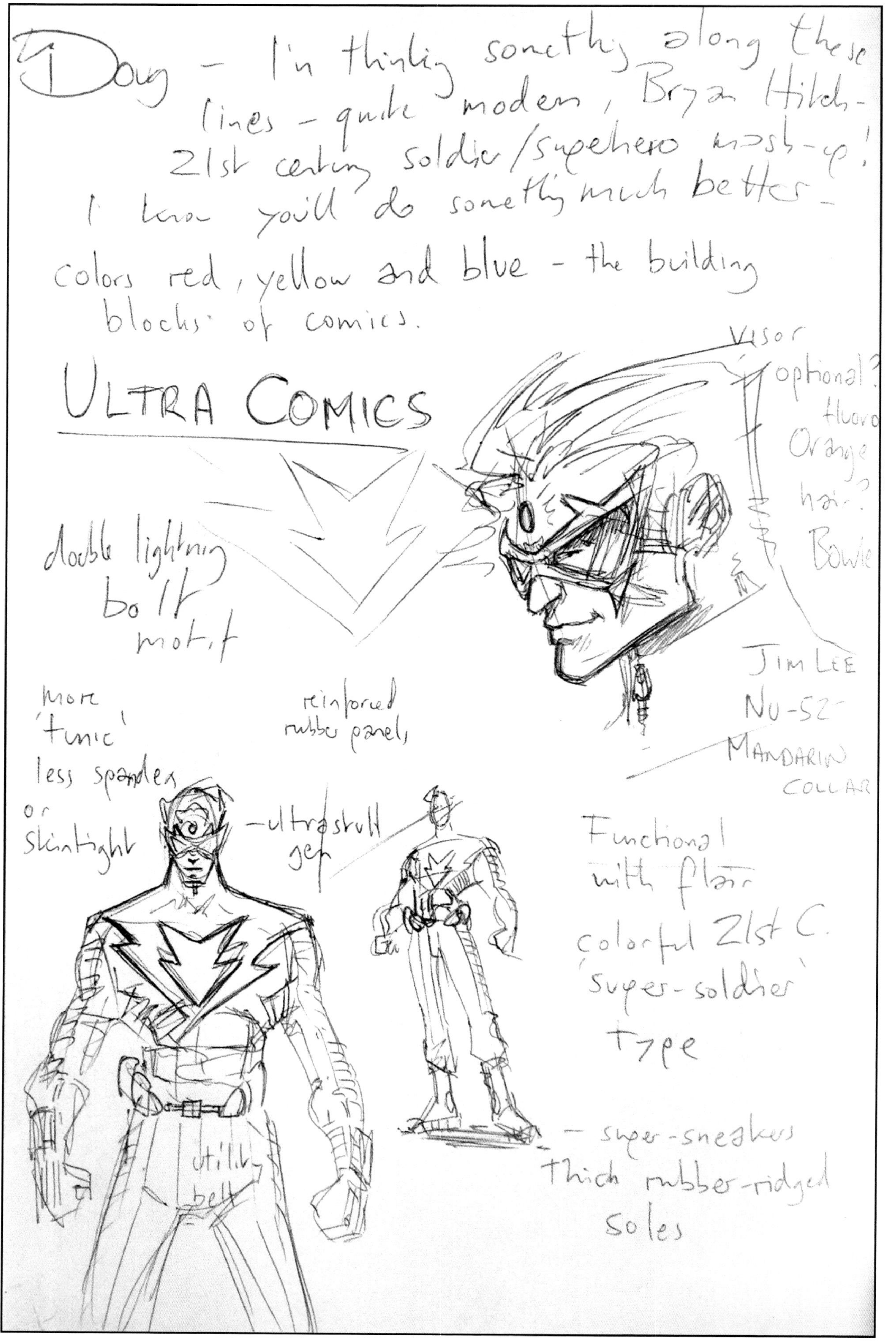

To Doug – I'm thinking something along these lines – quite modern, Bryan Hitch-
21st century soldier/superhero mash-up!
I know you'll do something much better –
colors red, yellow and blue – the building blocks of comics.
ULTRA COMICS
double lightning bolt motif
Visor optional?
fluoro Orange hair? Bowie
JIM LEE NU-52
MANDARIN COLLAR
more 'tunic' less spandex or skintight
reinforced rubber panels
–ultraskull gem
Functional with flair
colorful 21st C. 'super-soldier' type
utility belt
– super-sneakers thick rubber-ridged soles

Character design for Ultra Comics by Doug Mahnke

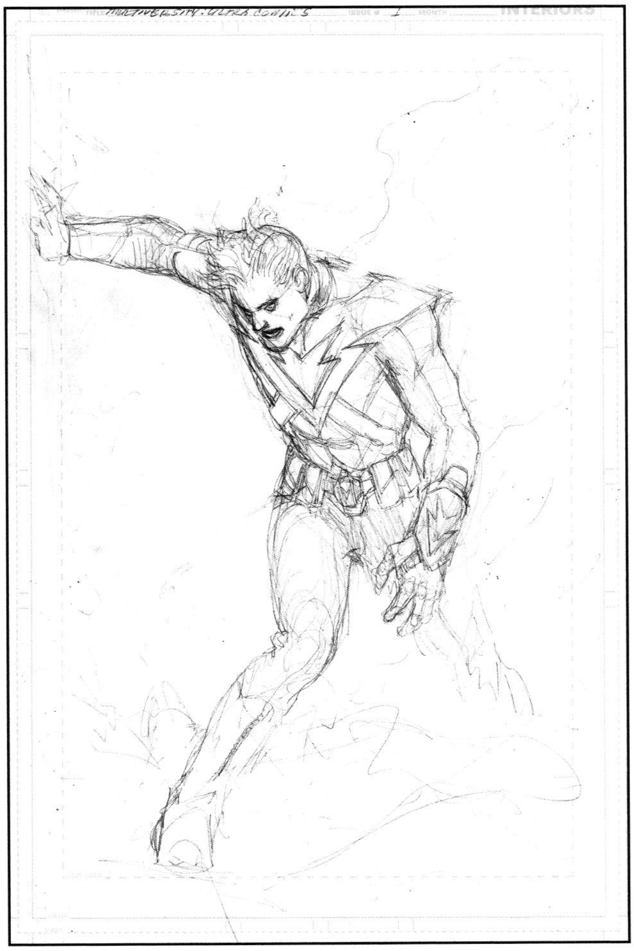
INTERIORS

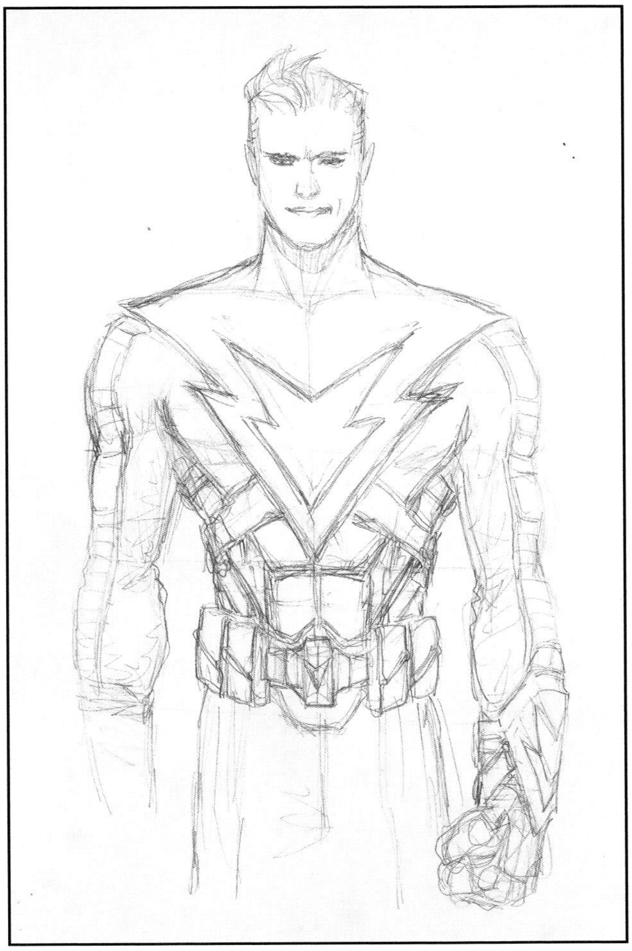

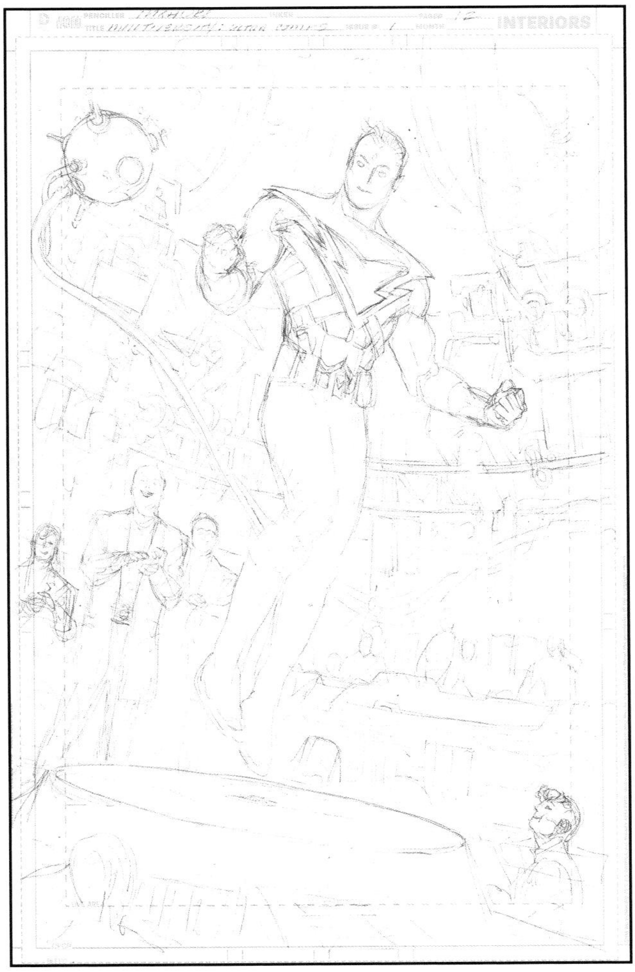
INTERIORS

MAPPING THE MULTIVERSE 1

Original script for the Multiverse Map by Grant Morrison, for The Multiversity *series designer Rian Hughes*

THE MULTIVERSITY GUIDEBOOK
The Multiverse Map (2 pages)
Writer: Grant Morrison

Artist: Rian Hughes

Hi Rian
Here to accompany my rough sketch *[opposite page]* are some notes to get you started. Absorb these, then let's get on the phone about this! Not all of this information will be useful but this is everything I'm thinking as I contemplate this goshdarned map!

All references can be looked up and consulted online.

Basically, the main influences on what I'm thinking here would be those kinds of Renaissance alchemical illustrations of the cosmos that show the hierarchy of the Earth and Heavens as a series of nested globes.

Here we're trying to systematize and depict how the Multiverse – or Orrery of Worlds – fits into the structure of DC's already established "higher" realms. In issue #1 of *Multiversity*, the aboriginal superhero Thunderer speaks of a "rainbow of worlds" and this is color-coded to represent that idea.

Think also of old sailing charts, Theosophical diagrams, Starfleet manuals, the sort of thing that would hang as a wall-chart in a primary school class of the future.

The biggest influence here is the art of Paul Laffoley (I have a Laffoley original on the wall and a number of limited edition prints which you may have seen when you were staying at my place. Check out Laffoley online – I'm a big fan of his work. He's an amazing character who had his foot amputated, and now wears a screw-on lion's paw in its place! He's a radical architect who designs Qabbalistic blueprints for imaginary soul-machines of the future...).

We're taking a cross-section through the structure so that it appears as a series of concentric circles or ripples of varying widths, each representing a different higher vibration of the DC Multiverse and surrounding God Realms, etc.

As we move through increasingly more rarefied and conceptual spheres, the colors move through the rainbow from red to violet. This rainbow effect is repeated in miniature, in reverse, around the outer ring where the entire manifest and conceptual universe surrenders to the Overvoid of the Monitor Sphere.

1. At the Bullseye position, we see a little graphic of the House of Heroes (see *Multiversity* #1). Just behind it, is the rhomboid shape of the Rock of Eternity (see *Thunderworld*, page 1). The central circle is lit so that the top half is black-shadowed. The Rock behind is lit so the bottom half is in black shadow. The effect of the circle on the rhomboid recalls a compass point spinning in the center of the chart.

2. The largest central circle is filled with 52 Alternate Earths, arranged in neat patterns around the compass of the House of Heroes/Rock of Eternity, labelled the Orrery of Worlds.

This central section is coloured in red tones to suggest the liquid Bleed substance in which all the worlds vibrate and are suspended.

The worlds could be numbered, but possibly not. It could look like a mess.

There are seven Unknown Worlds which could be colored differently or have a little "?" as their only identifying mark.

There is one cube-shaped Bizarro Earth where Bizarro reversal shows the familiar shapes of the continents as immense land-locked oceans, while the oceans are solid earth.

Four spokes connect the central circle to the outer Monitor Sphere – these are Bleed Siphons, like straws plugged into the Bleed so that Monitors can feast upon this Wonder Elixir. The Monitors are gone now but these Bleed drains still remain. Think of them as oil wells, sunk into the substance of reality itself to suck out the sweet nectar at the core of all things.

Around this central mandala of worlds are "ripples" of increasingly less dense energy – these are higher worlds of more rarefied concept and fundamental expression.

3. On the very edge of this ring where it touches the next, we have a little circle graphic labelled Wonderworld. Wonderworld appeared in *JLA* #13 (I think – I wrote the bloody thing) and was described as orbiting the boundaries of known reality.

4. A thin orange ring surrounds the central Multiverse. This ring represents the Speed Force Wall encountered by the Flash and is the limit of the known Multiverse. Eight crackling lightning-like paths link the outer wall of the Speed Force ring to the Source via the outer Monitor Sphere.

5. A wide yellow and black ring around the packed Earths depicts the Archetypal Circle or Platonic Realm, inhabited by personified cosmic principles, the living gods and pantheons of the DCU such as the Greek Gods of Olympus and any other pantheons we've verified are in the DCU.

This is the ring of Platonic or Archetypal forces, the Ring of Duality – Light vs. Dark, Good vs. Evil, Youth vs. Age, This vs. That, etc.

So, this big ring is a kind of Cosmic Clock – it is divided down the middle so that the left half is black and the right half is yellow. It has eight stations arranged symmetrically around the ring. Each of these little circles has a simple drawing to indicate location.

The left hand black half is labelled the Pit, the right hand yellow half is the Pinnacle.

The whole circle is labelled Sphere of the Gods.

In the 12 o'clock position, halfway between light and dark, is Faerie – home of Oberon and Titania, and the lighter Endless from *Sandman* – Dream, Destiny, Delirium.

In the 1:30 o'clock position, DC's version of Heaven is the Silver City. I'm not sure at this scale if it'll be possible to add little images suggestive of DC Heaven *[it wasn't]*, but if it is possible let's see the Spectre, Zauriel, and the 4 Angel Hosts of the Pax Dei – the Bull Host, the Eagle Host, the Lion Host, and the Host of Adam (the hosts have heads equivalent to their titles – Bulls have bull heads, Eagles have eagle heads, etc. The Host of Adam, the Order of Guardian Angels to which Zauriel belongs, have human faces of men and women).

In the 3 o'clock position – sunlit New Genesis, the beautiful blue green world of the New Gods of New Genesis. If we see any character heads or other illustrations let them be of Highfather, Orion, Lightray, Takion, and other New Gods.

In the 4:30 o'clock position is Olympus, which represents all of the DC "light" pantheons. This is where DC's Zeus, Hermes, and other Wonder Woman characters live. Other DC gods – Celtic gods, Norse, Hindu, or Mayan or whatever would also live in this sphere. Basically, Olympus stands for all pantheistic ideas about the Sky Home of the Gods, so it's also Asgard.

In the 6 o'clock position is Otherworld, containing all the weird, unclassifiable creatures of nightmare and fever, and the darker members of Sandman's Endless like Despair, Death, and Destruction.

In the 7:30 o'clock position is DC's version of Hell. Home of Etrigan, Trigon, Neron, Belial, Suge, and other DC major demons, alongside a New 52 version of the Demons 3 – Abnegazar, Rath, and Ghast.

In the 9 o'clock position is Apokolips, the fiery planet of Darkseid of the New Gods, with reeking firepit radiation spilling off into space. Evil Gods include Darkseid, Desaad, Kalibak, Granny Goodness, etc.

In the 10:30 o'clock position is Chaos – here exist all the opponents of the world's pantheons. In DC that means the realm of Hades, Hell, and Annwn.

Sixteen fine spokes or tracks lead from this circle to the Source Wall on the other Monitor Sphere circle.

Between the eight realms, in the yellow or black spaces, there are stars and human-faced comets or angel planets. This sphere most resembles some occult attempt to render the denizens of the human collective unconscious.

6. Next comes the Green Ring of Limbo. Limbo is the furthest edge of the manifest DC universe. This is where matter and memory break down. Limbo is represented as a kind of chain design – eight oval shapes linked by a single path, like a chain around everything.

7. Here is the blue-colored Monitor Sphere, as seen in *Final Crisis: Superman Beyond*.

8. The outer edge of Monitor Sphere is another thin rainbow, in reverse, from violet to red – and then red fades into the white of the page space, which is labelled Overvoid/the Source.

Down the left side of the diagram we're given a different view of the Multiversal Rainbow. Imagine an upright panel, graded from top to bottom, white to black to red to violet to black to white, depicting the increasingly tighter, faster wavelengths of the Multiverse and beyond.

Fat, spaced-out wavelengths down the red end at the bottom, begin to accelerate and squeeze together as we move to the blue end at the top and things get faster and faster. This is like a side section of the main image.

In a similar vertical panel on the right, or in a panel along the bottom depending on how you choose to arrange this information, we see little blueprint pictures of various classes of Monitor Shift-Ships – Carriers, Destroyers, Scouts. Below the images we have little explanatory caption boxes:

DESTROYER – things like these appeared in *Final Crisis: Superman Beyond*. A big ugly bacterial monster, that's capable of evolving and deploying its own reality-destroying weaponry.

CARRIER – as seen in *The Authority*.

TANKER – these vessels collect and return Bleed from the Orrery to the Monitor Sphere. Big, heavy-duty machines. You can make this design up, as we've never seen them before, although they're referenced in *Superman Beyond* #1.

EXPLORER – this class of scientific, data-recovering vehicles look like the *Ultima Thule*

A little label says Not to Scale – as we've seen, the *Ultima Thule* is about as big as a big pleasure cruiser, while the Authority's Carrier is fifty miles long. Destroyers are even bigger and bulkier. Perhaps there could be some kind of scale line under each ship to indicate its dimensions.

At the very top central position of the image, we see Destiny of the Endless with his open Book, as if reading this whole thing.

SOURCE
MONITOR SPHERE
HELL
THE SOURCE IS THE WHITE PAGE
THE MULTIVERSE and surrounding regions
CARRIER
YACHT
SHIFTSHIP
'COSMIC' CLOCK
panel on side shows classes of MONITOR PROBE SHIFTSHIPS

Grant Morrison's original rough sketch of the Mutiverse Map

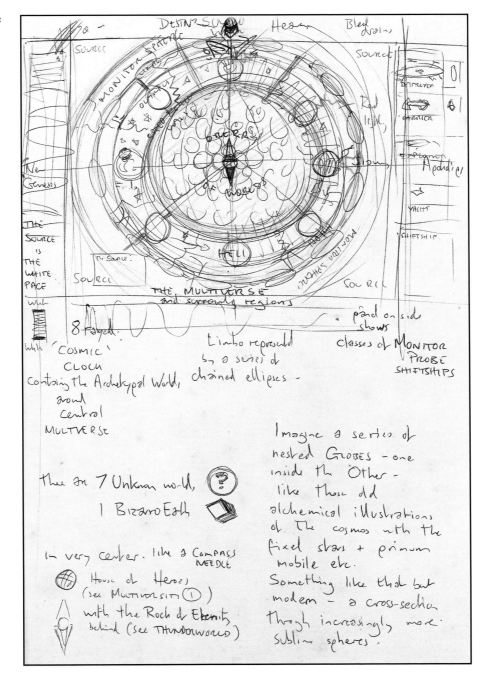

MAPPING THE MULTIVERSE 2

Design concepts and notes from The Multiversity *series designer Rian Hughes*

THE MULTIVERSE MAP: ORRERY OVERVIEW

The following is a summary of the internal workings and arrangement of the 52 worlds in the Orrery, building on Grant's outline and culled from our previous discussions, plus some new insights. Some of this may be suitable for public consumption, some may be best held back, either because it reveals too much about the mechanisms at work, it'll tie things down too firmly, or simply because it's good to maintain a little mystery.

THE ORRERY IS IN CONSTANT MOTION

It is continually evolving.

In this way we can explain all past and future iterations. We can neatly keep historical number designations canonical by simply saying that the position in the Orrery of a certain world has subsequently changed as the Orrery evolved. This is in addition to the simpler (but perhaps less satisfying) explanation that old mariner's maps may or may not accurately reflect the territory – that cartographers of new lands often just got it wrong.

If we want to get mystical, there are in fact certain theosophical theories that claim that the structure of the atom and the universe is evolving, changing slowly, and that new parts are being added to the "anu," the ultimate unit of matter in the scheme. (As these insights were arrived at by psychics over 100 years ago I'm not vouching for their authenticity, but as an imaginative and very thorough construct it is amazing.)

ORRERY ORBITALS

The Orrery has four "energy levels," from the inside to the outside. By analogy to atomic orbitals, let's call these 1 through 4, inside to outside. The inner orbital, 1, has a maximum of 6 worlds, 2 has 12, 3 has 16, 4 has 18. (By comparison, electron shells have 2, 6, 10, 14, and 18 electrons.)

The inner circles are more "real," at least in that comic book idea of real – more gritty, more morally ambivalent, more violent perhaps.

The outer worlds, being closer to the Platonic realms, are more idealized, simpler, more morally clear-cut, more cartoony.

NUMERICAL DESIGNATION

For the most part a matter of DC's historical precedence, and so somewhat arbitrary, though let's assume that 0 and 1 (and smaller numbers) have some kind of hierarchy over larger numbers.

Possibly the higher numbers indicate older, and the lower numbers younger, worlds. Could they have been created (via the method I discuss later) in numerical order?

If so, that would place the creation of some of the DCU "fictional" worlds before our own world! Who thought them up, if we weren't around to do so? Or did they somehow "self-create," without a Designer? Did creatures on one of them think up our own Earth-33, *us* – comic book artists, writers, and editors – and thus the Multiverse, of which they would be a part? There's an intriguing story idea right there...

ARCS

There are four major "arcs" that go from the Oculus (the "Eye") of the House of Heroes to the Speed Force Wall.

Passing through E-14, we have the Light and Dark Arcs. The Dark Arc takes a world off towards the darker realms on the left, the Light Arc to the right.

Passing through Bizarro World, we have the Green and Magenta Arcs. The Magenta Arc I've dubbed the Bizarro Arc, and worlds along this arc have something reversed or bizarre about them. The Green Arc's character is less defined, but seems to be of a dark and more sinister nature.

There are also four other lesser arcs which do not have specific colors or designations. These are sympathetic vibrations in the Bleed, and of unknown influence.

ORRERY QUADRANTS

A world's position relative to the Sphere of the Gods reveals the influences of those areas that lie outside the Orrery on the Orrery itself. Each world thus sits within a "concept space," governed by the eight Platonic ideals around it. So, when positioning a world, we have to consider: Left or right? Top or bottom? Inner circles or outer?

The top right quadrant represents the Idealized, the Good. Pure and noble worlds reside here.

The bottom right quadrant represents the Cartoon, the Reversed. The Flipped and Flippant.

The bottom left represents the Dark, the Supernatural, the Evil. I've called part of this area "the Gloaming."

The top left quadrant represents the Realistic, the Gritty – but also incorporates other company's worlds – Charlton, Tower, etc. Because of this, I suggested we rename Underworld "Otherworld," which didn't fly. (I realize that Underworld is opposite Skyland, and hence in an over/under pairing.) I suggest "The Otherworld Archipelago" could refer to the subsection of this quadrant that includes properties from other companies, as with the Gloaming.

We can, however, also postrationalise the Underworld imagery as suggestive of a vault, a locked basement. We even have a lock in the illustration. This is where characters and worlds that come from defunct companies have been residing, locked in old comics or in storage. All they need is a "key" (in the form of a company asset rights purchase) to release them into the light of the rest of the Orrery.

"TONALITY"

To summarize, each world has five possible "dimensions" that describe its position (it is thus 5D):

- Orbital (in/out)
- Top/bottom
- Left/right
- Arc (optional – not all worlds are on an arc)
- Numerical designation

With a little rejigging to get a neat acronym, this could be dubbed its TONALity (T.O.N.A.L.). A world's "tonality" completely describes its position and character in the Orrery.

Tonality also implies sound, music – Grant has previously mentioned that the Multiverse is based on eightfold octaves. So here "Multiversal Tonality" is our version of the Music of the Spheres.

It's interesting to try and figure out the properties of the mystery worlds using their positions as clues – much like Mendeleyev did with the periodic table, which gave clues to the nature of then-undiscovered elements.

THE SEVEN UNKNOWN WORLDS

Grant's seven unknown worlds I placed on two arcs, the Light and Dark Arcs.

These unknown worlds all have a "tonality," and as we hoped, people are already speculating on their character using their positions as a guide. Earth-14, the only world at the crossing point of these two arcs, has a second image, as if it is actually two worlds in superposition, a cell about to divide, perhaps. Or one world vibrating. Which brings us to...

THE BIRTH OF NEW WORLDS

As Grant suggests, we should incorporate a way for new worlds to enter the Orrery. Maybe Earth-14, overseen by the Theocracy, is where this happens: Earth-14 is in the early stages of birthing a new Earth. The exact process of this birthing is a mystery, but undoubtedly linked to the reproductive urges of the denizens of Earth-33, whose creativity knows no bounds.

Once given existence, where does this new Earth go? It has several options: it can move to the left or the right along the Dark or Light Arc, depending on its character, or even move out along the fourth orbital, as the cooling Earth-1 has done.

Interestingly, a new Earth is birthed close to Earth-0, the main venue of events in the current DCU mainstream, and so linked to what is happening there. As with Earth-0, it is opposite Earth-33, and thus creatively linked with it in a similar manner – both are powered by the creative energy channeled across the Rock of Eternity from the Real World.

BIZARRO WORLD

This new Earth is also in direct opposition to Bizarro World, which suggests that in its unformed state it also possesses dynamic opposites in balance, though still in potential and as yet unresolved.

Even more interestingly, this gives us an insight into the origins of the Bizarro World itself: an unresolved "sport" of the Orrery's birthing process, a world in which the shaping rational forces of world-building didn't fully separate and coalesce. Imagine a Universe that didn't fall into a single "matter or anti-matter" state like ours did, but somehow managed to mature while still containing contradictory superpositions of opposites – a paradoxical world in which a broken symmetry has produced unbalanced results.

THE DESTRUCTION/REMOVAL OF WORLDS

The arcs cross at the Speed Force Wall where the siphons enter the Orrery, and at these locations they either draw some kind of force through the Wall from that which lies outside, or power those outside forces.

Here, where siphons pierce the Force Wall, worlds may possibly exit the Orrery, becoming concepts in the Platonic Sphere of the Gods in a manner analogous to the spirit's ascent to the astral plane after death. Here, having already shed their physical forms, they then shed their etheric forms (the Astral Body), which whizzes around this sphere like elementals. These are the little sprites and faces that populate the Sphere of the Gods.

From here, a more rarified and pure "monad" can rise to the higher realms of Abstract Idea (if it's not caught up in Limbo first), and ultimately return to the Overmind, possibly to eventually become a Recycled Idea, or Rebooted Character.

There is even a direct shortcut along the length of the siphon that enables worlds considered to be ill-conceived, derivative, or otherwise detrimental to the cohesion of the Orrery to return directly to the Source. (Go straight to jail, do not pass go.)

If they're unlucky they might not exit the Orrery, and instead be annihilated and become one with the Speed Force Wall. The Speed Force Wall is very much like the event horizon surrounding a black hole – in fact, the Speed Force Wall may even consist entirely of earlier worlds from within the Orrery that have lost all cohesion and become smeared across the Vault of the Heavens to the point of paper-thin invisibility, just like the Cosmic Microwave Background (CMB) radiation is posited to be the afterglow of the Big Bang, and of all creation (here, destruction).

Whether information can be retrieved from these lost worlds, and whether the histories of the heroes and ordinary denizens that lived and died on them before the DCU was even conceived can be read, is open to debate.

If a world moves inward in the opposite direction, it'll end up in the center at the House of Heroes, and the vibrational rainbow mirror image of the Source Wall that is inside the central Oculus. This return to the Central Source could be envisaged as a return to a world in potential – all the stories that have happened on that world could be then contained within some kind of repository. Think of a collection of comics stored for all eternity in the great library of the House of Heroes (I'm winging it a bit here, as I don't know the details of the House of Heroes history – what it really is and how it came to be – so some of this may not be appropriate).

I do love the idea that at the very center of the DCU is a great library containing all the DC stories ever written – and possibly everything that has ever happened, whether written down or not – a kind of DC Akashic Library.

THE LIBRARY OF WORLDS

I imagine it'd look like the old British Library Reading Room in the British Museum, where Marx wrote *Das Kapital* and Bram Stoker and Conan Doyle were members. This was circular, with a round dome overhead and an oculus at the very top, which is perfect for our needs.

Here, just like the British Library, there is a spoked wheel arrangement of desks surrounded by rows and rows of books, the upper tiers reached by ladders; the dimly lit study desks have overstuffed armchairs upholstered in the leather hides of unknown animals, in which denizens from all around the Multiverse browse volumes, research their retconned pasts, look up lost loved ones, idly pass the time, save their worlds from imminent total destruction, or plot the subjugation of others; heroes and villains both, all respecting the hush any decent library insists on.

This is the quiet stillness at the very center of the Multiverse, the eye of the storm.

There would of course be a librarian, who would sit at a desk in the middle of the room where the spokes meet. This could be Destiny with his book (though he has just one, and this library has countless). Or it could be a new character – I imagine an officious and unhelpful pedant with a train-spotter's obsession with detail and an eidetic memory for the Library's arcane filing system that only he can understand. He wouldn't care if it was Darkseid himself come to check out a book – he'd still have to fill in the same forms as everyone else before he could get a reader's ticket. The archetypal faceless gray bureaucrat, lord of his own domain, for whom an orderly system unwaveringly governed by ironclad rules is of supreme importance.

The Librarian would also check visitors in and out, making sure they don't pilfer books, write in the margins, or sneak in unapproved noncanonical material. Being that for some worlds this is the only record that exists, altering any entry here would effectively rewrite the actual history of that world.

Of course, there would be missing volumes, misfiled volumes, strange items pressed between pages, books (these books obviously include comic books) that are not books at all but gateways to the worlds within; forbidden volumes; maps of the Multiverse itself (maps within maps!); historical maps of early drafts of the Multiverse before each shore had been explored...there'd also be a café selling inedible sandwiches and foul overpriced coffee, and an exhibition space showcasing weird relics from old and forgotten DCU stories that would serve the same purpose as Batman's Batcave, with its large Lincoln penny, old costumes, vehicles, gadgets, etc.

So we have several scenarios for removing an existing world from the Orrery: a complete physical destruction in situ; a return to the Source via a Siphon; an exit through the Force Wall via Earth-46 (which I imagine to be a department at DC selling off intellectual property like the family silver, or at the very least putting it in storage) to the Underworld; becoming a comic in the library of the House of Heroes; or a smearing into the CMB of the Force Wall.

REALIGNMENT

This process of birth and death can have consequences for the Orrery as a whole.

The arrangement of worlds must consequently adjust itself to regain harmonic balance, like an atom losing an electron and then rejigging its orbitals into a new energy-efficient base state. Worlds will thus move and realign in unpredictable ways – the Orrery will convulse and shuffle, then settle into a new configuration, which may be different locally or universally; new influences will then come to bear upon worlds due to their new positions. Though I here say "unpredictable," the worlds should only move along orbitals or arcs.

This would be called a "redesign" in Monitor terms, or a "crisis" to those resident within the Orrery. Not all "crises" need be major – worlds might imperceptibly move around their orbitals, or up or down an arc, while the rest of the Orrery remains relatively stable and unaffected.

Of course, there exist, buried somewhere in the Library's maps room, maps of all the older, pre-Crisis multiverses, and all the previous positions of the worlds within them. Think of those old mariner's charts crossed with Ptolemaic diagrams of the Heavens, written on parchment...There is a rumor that there may even be a map describing the very birth of the Multiverse itself, pieced together from information gleaned from the worlds lost to the Source Wall. An expedition deep into the labyrinthine and perhaps endless passages and rooms of the Library of Worlds is planned in search of it. They may be gone for years.

Crises, unlike sunspot cycles, don't seem to happen at regular intervals: *Crisis on Infinite Earths* (1985) > *Infinite Crisis* (2005-6) > *Final Crisis* (2008) > *Flashpoint* and New 52 (2011). So we can assume they're not natural events, but rather the work of some Intelligent (Re)Designers.

THE 52 WORLDS
These are my additions to Grant's original designations and descriptions, as seen in *The Multiversity Guidebook*:

Earth-0. The DCU. This sits directly opposite the Real World, Earth-33, and is joined to it by a link of creative energy that crosses the center of the "compass" and follows the channeling needle of the Rock of Eternity. It has four stars circling it (an homage to the old DC logos) which represent star quality, the four elements, the star attraction. This world is shining as the main jewel in the whole system.

Earth-1. Still cooling and unformed. Bright orange. Sits opposite the dark supernatural world of Earth-13.

Earth-2. Home of the JSA. Currently pocked with firepits after the war with Darkseid. This world sits opposite...

Earth-3. ...its shadow counterpart. Dark, shadowy, and ruined. Glowing hotspots reveal areas where damage is still cooling.

Earth-4. Pax Americana. The Charlton heroes, part of the Otherworld Archipelago (which is a poetic term taken from Grant's original suggestion, the Wildstorm Archipelago). This is the archipelago of worlds absorbed from other companies. Sits out on the edge, near the realm of Archetype and Platonic Symbol. Colored in a petrol-rainbow (which may be too subtle and I may have to bring it out more) to reflect one of the themes of the book.

Earth-5. Thunderworld. Bright and brash and morally straightforward. Opposite Earth-X/10.

Earth-6. Just Imagine Stan Lee. Dramatic Marvel-style speed/explosion lines emanate. On the horizontal Kirby Axis that runs from Apokolips to New Genesis through 6, 7, 22, and 51. *[Altered in final Guidebook.]*

Earth-7. The more realistic "Ultimates"-style DCU. Closer to the center, and thus more gritty and real. Realistically rendered continents. Destroyed by the Gentry.

Earth-8. The Marvel-style DCU. Grant: "In old continuity, this world was known as Angor and was introduced back in *Justice League of America* #87 in 1971. Angor was subsequently destroyed in a nuclear holocaust triggered by Lord Havok and the Extremists." Out near the imaginative realms of purer morals, next to Earth-51, the Kirbyverse. The 8 is a cross between the old DC bullet and reminiscent of the cyan and white number-in-a-circle Fantastic Four logo. Forms the Lee/Kirby Binary with Earth-51. Next to the simpler '60s-style comic heroes of Earth-36, in the Brightlands. Also looks like an eight ball, which suggests the Orrery is a pool table...

Earth-9. Tangent. This world has the swirly background of my *Sea Devils* design from back in '97.

Earth-10. Earth-X. Nazis. Down in the darker realms of the bottom left quadrant known as the Gloaming. Opposite the pure cheerful hopefulness of Thunderworld. Also opposite Red Son at 30, another murderous totalitarian ideology.

Earth-11. Gender-reversal. Lies on the Bizarro Reversal Arc, the spiral line that represents the opposite of the normal, and extends from the Force Wall, through Bizarro World, to the center, also passing through Earth-32 (Mash-up-verse)

and Red Son Earth-30. Has a direct connection through the Force Wall to Skyland. North is south, and south north.

Earth-12. The Animated Show world. "Aniverse?" Shaded with "cel" shading, and thick simple outlines. No graduated colors here! Forms part of the Outer Cartoon Rim along with 26, 42, and 20, which I'll get to soon...

Earth-13. Supernatural DCU. Shrouded in darkness, situated near Nightmare. Pinpricks of light show on its surface. Perpetual pea-souper gloom. In the Gloaming, which includes local worlds 10, 43, 15, and 40, and outlier Earth-37.

Earth-14. First of the Unknown Worlds. Grant: "Mentioned briefly in *Animal Man* #2. All we ever saw of it was a particular butterfly." I've positioned all these on two spiral arcs similar to the Bizarro Arc, like beads on a thread. Earth-14 lies at the top, and is obviously very important in the big scheme of things.

These arcs take us across all the realms of the Orrery, from the center out to the Rim, from the Pit to the Pinnacle. Earth-14 is the key to the infinite Multiverse Grant mentions. As previously suggested, it's interesting to figure out the properties of these mystery worlds using their positions as clues, much as Mendeleyev did with the periodic table.

Earth-15. Destroyed by Superboy-Prime in *Countdown* #30. A black cinder. It was a perfect world with perfect heroes, but residing in the Gloaming meant that couldn't last...

Earth-16. Grant: "The world of Bob Haney's Super-Sons continuity." The Just. Situated on the inner circle of Reality, but here it's Reality as in Reality TV shows. Close enough to our world for discomfort. I have added a paparazzi camera-flare "ping" bouncing off its artificially perfect sheen, and the magenta flouro color of a celebrity magazine (what that actually means on the ground I'm not sure...map and the territory again...).

Also home to the Justice League cartoon characters, which Grant is retrofitting here. We are at least in the quadrant where the cartoon worlds are, though closer in, and thus more "real."

Earth-17. Grant: "Previously described as a grim update on the Atomic Knights with dog-riding post-nuclear war paladins, but I thought it might be more fun to create a mash-up of DC's optimistic Atomic Age future with the nuked-out wastelands of EC sci-fi, set in a world that experienced a devastating nuclear exchange as a result of the Bay of Pigs crisis in 1963." Up near the optimistic '60s group. Cratered with atomic blasts.

Earth-18. Wild West DCU. Grant: "This one derives from an old Elseworlds book called *Justice Riders*."

Earth-19. Steampunk DCU, moving into early modernism, in an ornate sepia Victorian globe. Near the pea-soupers of Earth-13 and the vampires of Earth-43. In the Gloaming.

Earth-20. Pulp Hero world, home of the S.O.S., as seen in *Superman Beyond* #1. In the quadrant of idealized moral dilemmas. Opposite Earth-40. Uses an old illustration of the Earth by Frank R. Paul, famous pulp and comic book artist.

Earth-21. "Darwynverse." Out on the Outer Cartoon Arc. Bold, dynamic, clean-cut brushstrokes adorn this world.

Earth-22. Kingdom Come. In the central "realistic" sphere. Opposite the realistic "Ultimates"-style DCU. Craters filled with new oceans pockmark the surface.

Earth-23. World of Black Superman. Was opposite Milestone, Earth-41, which is now the world of Twilight.

Earth-24. Another unknown world.

Earth-25. Another unknown world.

Earth-26. "Carrotverse." Earth-C. The actual world has a face, the nose of which is caught in the number 26, breaking the fourth wall in typical cartoon fashion. On the Outer Cartoon Rim.

Earth-27. Another unknown world.

Earth-28. Another unknown world.

Earth-29. Bizarro World. On the Bizarro Arc. Opposite Earth-14, and just below Earth-33, which is interesting – again, this positioning has generated lots of discussion. The real world can be pretty dark and bizarre too...

Earth-30. "Red Son" world. With a hammer and sickle, but this is part of the number designation, just as the X is part of the number on Earth-10 – i.e., it's on the map, not something on the surface of the world (unlike Earth-48). That perennial distinction between the map and the territory...!

Earth-31. "Millerverse." Morally and actually black and white, gritty and covered with inky splatter. On the central gritty realistic circle and also in the realistic quadrant for a double dose of Real. [Became "Pirate" World.]

Earth-32. "Mash-up"-verse. On the Bizarro Arc. Note that this is actually the Moon, swapped with the Earth, and terraformed. The lunar "seas" are now bodies of water, and Tycho Crater a circular lake with a central island where the ruling elite have their capital.

Earth-33. Earth-Prime: *Us*. In balance with the DCU at Earth-0, which is kept alive by our powers of imagination, and with which we share a uniquely balanced two-way relationship. Earth-33 is the most realistically rendered world here, using an actual NASA photograph. There seems to be a ring around it which separates us from the Multiverse, and through which only memes can pass (via Ultra, and comics in general). Outside of fiction, we are currently aware of no aliens, no superheroes, no parallel worlds. We are utterly alone.

Earth-34. Grant: "First of a trio of faux-faux-DCUs." Earth-34 is home to *Astro City* analogues and others. Shares a dense mythology like the adjacent Earth-2.

Earth-35. Analogues of the Liefeld/Moore-verse. (Analogues of analogues.) Rendered with some trademark Liefeld crosshatching. Part of the Wildstorm Archipelago (renamed the Otherworld Archipelago).

Earth-36. Optimistic '60s world, looking like a Pan Am "the future's bright" logo.
    If possible, this seems the best place to put DC's romance titles, which no one has tried to fold into continuity but for which I have a soft spot. This is a world permanently stuck in an an idealized '50s/'60s romance story. *Happy Days* meets *The Stepford Wives*. Pinups. Fashion tips. Those paper dolls with outfits attached by tabs. The sexual revolution is just around the corner, but a girl or boy has still gotta look after their reputation.
    When I was curating the Image Duplicator show I became familiar with those old DC romance titles Roy Lichtenstein lifted from – there's some great but underappreciated art by Jim Mooney, Tony Abruzzo, etc. I imagine a world populated by misunderstood teens with complex love lives and boys in middle management jobs, street gangs or bands, something that looks like a Peter Blake painting or Richard Hamilton's "Just what is it that makes today's homes so different, so appealing?" montage of 1956. This world could somehow comment on the high art/low art debate, and the art world's appropriation of comics if we want to get really meta... [This idea was not included in the final description.]

Earth-37. "Chaykin *Thrillkiller*-verse." With trademark American Flagg-style Letratone coquille texture. Next door to Earth-40, part of the Pulp Antiheroes Binary.

Earth-38. Byrne's *Generations*-verse. Deep in the Gloaming, where heroes age and die...

Earth-39. The Spire Comics world of Cyclotron, Doctor Nemo, Corvus, and other Tower analogues. Features a Wally Wood (*T.H.U.N.D.E.R. Agents* artist) drawing of the Earth.

Earth-40. Anti-pulp heroes. Opposite Earth-20. Next door to Earth-37, part of the Pulp Antiheroes Binary. This uses a pulp image of the Earth from an old Alex Schomburg painting, which looks like a black-and-white grainy image from a matinee movie short.

Earth-41. The sci-fi universe of *Twilight* by Howard Chaykin and José Luis García-López. Bands of dark clouds, like pencil sketching, shroud the planet.

Earth-42. Superdeformed "Kawaii"-verse. The continents share the simplified, rounded appearance of their inhabitants. A cute plastic toy of a world, on the Outer Cartoon Rim. Smells like one of those Japanese erasers that look like fruit or ice cream. [Should I add a keychain?]
    Might Sugar and Spike reside here? Or Carrotworld?

Earth-43. Elseworld's *Red Rain* Vampireworld. Soaked in blood that rains down from red skies. Down in the Gloaming, with a direct connection through the Force Wall to Hell.

Earth-44. Metal Men. The Prof created new heroes because the world needed them, says Grant. So did Stan Lee, opposite. Not sure if both smoked pipes...

Earth-45. We have a mismatch here. This is now listed as the Image-style DCU.
    Previously this was: "On this world there were no superhuman beings until "Superman™" was created by Clark Kent, Lois Lane, and Jimmy Olsen using incredible thought-technology capable of bringing ideas to life as physical objects," hence the TM after the number and the crater.
    My postrationalization: the TM indicates the creator-rights self-publishing movement that Image grew out of originally, and is still championing, publishing only creator-owned books. [Reverted to original description.]

Earth-46. Another unknown world.

Earth-47. Grant: "A world that is a permanent psychedelic-fuelled Silver Age where every adventure is a John Broome Flash story." The super-psychedelic world of the Love Syndicate. The home of counterculture Underground comix analogues of DCU characters, drawn in a Crumb/Shelton *Wonder Warthog* style. Scooter of *Swing with Scooter*, Binky, and co. also chill out here.

Earth-48. The world of the Forerunners, where everything is Super. (But not in a Big Gay Al way.) Grant: "Just as human bone marrow creates immune defenses for the body, Earth-48 is the "marrow" of the Multiverse, churning out super-beings to protect the Multiversal megastructure." Here everything has a logo – and that includes the world, which is sporting a gigantic 48 written large across its continents. Upkeep of this massive feat of civil engineering is easy, due to the fact everyone is Super.

Earth-49. The most mysterious of the unknown worlds.

Earth-50. The world of the Justice Lords, which is the sinister, "dark" reflex of the Earth-12 *Batman Beyond* universe. Opposite the "light" animated world, and also drawn in the style of cel animation. Note the nongradated, cartoon atmosphere.

Earth-51. "Kirbyverse!" Enveloped in Kirby Krackle, on the Kirby Axis, which takes us from Apokolips to New Genesis, the Pit to the Pinnacle. Forms the Lee/Kirby Binary with Earth-8. Close to the Pinnacle and the New Gods in New Genesis. Opposite the Marvel-style DCUs of Earth-6 and Earth-7. The shape of the continents is taken from Kirby's Kamandi map.

KWYZZ

Up near the Speed Wall, where the siphon that passes through Skyland penetrates the Force Wall. It occurred to me that here you'd get creatures living from the energy as it comes into the Orrery, just like those unique creatures that live around black smokers, those deep-sea hot vents that spew nutrients up from the mantle.

I have also added unlabeled glows at the three other siphon vents too, for symmetry. These have yet to be described or explored. Kwyzz is the only one with blue electricity around it, however. Each is a different color.

ROCK OF ETERNITY

This channels the creative force between the Real World (where writers, artists, editors, and designers reside) and the DCU, Earth-33 to Earth-0, and back again, bringing comics from the DCU to the Real World. Tetrahedral in shape, it has six vertices and a central seventh, upon which sits the House of Heroes.

These two occupy the same space, but in different vibrational realms, so they intersect only in concept-space. They are in a quantum superposition that cannot be collapsed into unity because they occupy the central pivot of the Multiverse which is built on a fundamental duality: the interplay of imagination (internal, the creative process, the world of mind) and expression (external, the physical comic, expressed). Immaterial, "spirit" (though here I'm not using the word in a religious meaning, more to describe a motive force), and material. Black and white, up and down, in and out. Good and evil. Balanced opposing forces. The very epitome of the Heroic Struggle.

HOUSE OF HEROES

At the center there is another tiny reversed rainbow within the Oculus, a mirror of the outer Source Wall.

Within this, at the very center, is "white-hot calm" and "dense emptiness" – very much like the Overvoid or the Source. We have a yin/yang: Nothing is Everything in potential, unexpressed and undifferentiated; Everything is Nothing in potential, everything is expressed, differentiated.

See also the description of the Library of Worlds.

LIMBO

Note the siphons centrally penetrate the light green Limbo areas, the lightning the dark green.

MONITOR SPHERE

There is a faint bubble at the bottom, opposite the Monitor World. Added for symmetry, further details unknown...

I also added eight *very faint* bubbles between each of the illustrated worlds in the Sphere of the Gods. These I leave open to future interpretation.

There are four unnamed ellipses of force that connect the worlds in the Sphere of the Gods with each other and the Source Wall. These ellipses contain and describe the extent of the Speed Force Wall, and thence the Orrery itself. Two are blue, two are magenta.

SHIFT SHIP CLASSIFICATION

Other than the Carrier and the original *Ultima Thule*, these are new, and of my own design.

• *Destroyer* – Positions itself above a target world and shoots missiles or rays from the base downwards. The central part rotates to bring different mechanisms to bear. The prehensile tentacle arms slowly wave in the Bleed, and are used like the arms of a swimmer to keep the ship precisely in position.
• *Carrier* – As seen in *The Authority*. Designed by Hitch.
• *Tanker* – Rather than a big container with stuff inside (which seems silly in outer space) I envisaged a ship that trails a string of "seed gravitational singularities" (tame mini-black holes) behind it. These form the cores of spheres of various materials – gas, liquid, plasma – that are anchored like small planets or suns to them. These are towed behind a shield that protects the crew quarters and engines up front from radiation. Note that one substance has formed a crystal, the liquid sphere has ripples on its surface caused by micrometeorite strikes, the gas sphere is a hazy swirling ball in motion, and the plasma sphere is on fire, like a small sun.

• *Hunter* – A smaller, faster ship of my own devising. Armed with two caged universes (the same type that powers the Explorers) held in two rotating arms on each flank. These can shoot a ray of antimatter in any direction.
• *Explorer* – Based on the *Ultima Thule*, but with minor design adjustments. There are several types of Explorer ships, with different specifications.

APPENDIX

1. Limbo, Underworld, Otherworld, and the Phantom Zone: As Grant says somewhere – I forget where! – Limbo is the place where DC's and other companies' dormant properties languish, to be resurrected in the Otherworlds section of the Orrery. This suggests the connection between Limbo and the Orrery, passing through the top left siphon (let's call it the Underworld Siphon) into Earth-46, has a special role to play in this respect – a kind of exit/entrance to Limbo. I suggest that on Earth-46 a Council for Forgotten Worlds convenes, where these universes are considered for resurrection. There was a DC comic called *Forgotten Realms*, but as that was licensed from the D&D people I assume it's probably not available as a name?

The names of the other siphons are therefore the Heaven Siphon, the Skyland Siphon, and the Hell Siphon.

Here, on Earth-46, the characters from these worlds have to petition for release from Limbo – they prepare documents and present them to a Multiversal UN-style bureaucracy to get a hearing. I imagine a waiting room of obscure characters, passing time around the water cooler or reading 10-year-old copies of the Earth-46 version of *Reader's Digest*.

If Limbo and the Phantom Zone are one and the same, this means that all the currently unused characters, not just from DC but from every other comic company (or close analogues thereof), reside here. So it may even be possible to put together a team of (say) Moon Girl, Jet Dream and her Stunt-Girl Counterspies, Calvin and Hobbes, Patsy Walker, Angel Love, Mr. E, Dilbert, Bog Beast, Krazy Kat, Mod Wheels, Pogo, and the Freak Brothers (or, again, close analogues thereof) and pit them against General Zod and Lucy Van Pelt. Hobbes and Fat Freddy's Cat is a pairing I'd definitely pay to see...

2. The Fictive Membrane around Earth that only ideas can cross (via comics and other cultural artefacts) should obviously be called the Memebrane.

There is a symmetrically placed and similar-looking membrane around the New 52 Earth-0 Earth, though the exact properties of this are unknown.

3. The numbering of the worlds: as Earth-1 is still cooling, that supports the idea that the lower numbers are the younger worlds, the higher the older – which makes sense because Kamandi's post-apocalyptic future Earth is Earth-51, the New 52 is Earth-0.

So, just preceding the creation of our world, Earth-33, we have Earth-32, the Moon-with-oceans Mash-Up world. Just after is Earth-34, the Astro City world. Does our creation owe something to Earth-32, and Earth-34 owe something to us?

It could be that these worlds just coalesced earlier and later than our world, and it was millions of years before they supported superheroes, so we don't need to posit a direct creative link from world to world. But then, if there's a neat way to do so, why not?

4. The colors of the worlds in the Sphere of the Gods follow Josef Albers's Bauhaus color harmony theories. Hell is red, Skyland blue, Nightmare purple, New Genesis blue/green, Dream yellow. (I should note that Albers's scheme was just painterly, not symbolic.)

I did depart from this, though, as Underworld needed to be a dark subterranean gloomy gray, Heaven white. Apokolips is black (but with red firepits). So, we have a gray/white heaven/underworld pairing superimposed on the Albers scheme.

ANTI-MATTER MULTIVERSE

This is the opposite in all regards to the matter Multiverse. The worlds therein are designated with a minus when listed just by number (-33, -14) and written backwards or even backwards and upside down in full, for example: Ɛ̷Ɛ-ɥʇɹɐƎ.

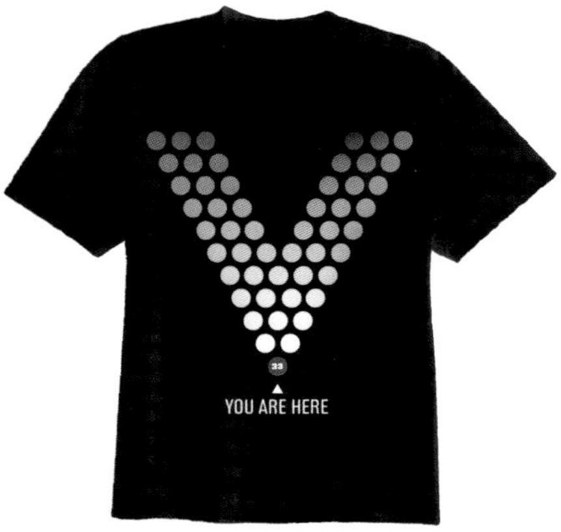
33
YOU ARE HERE
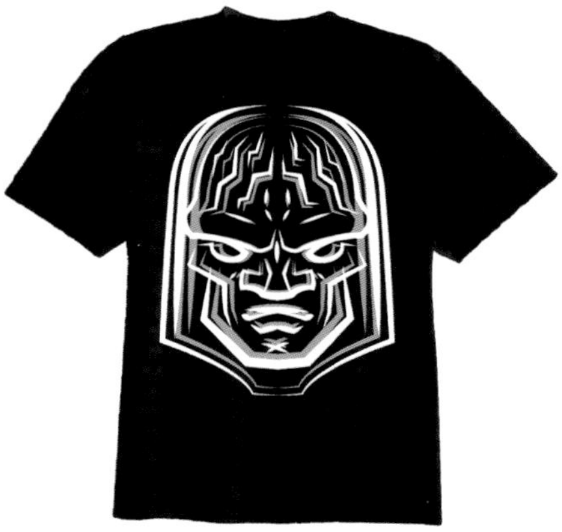
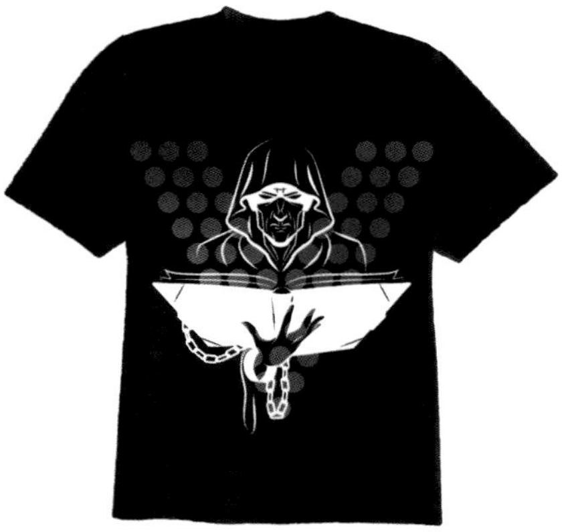

Above: Unused T-shirt design proposals
Below: The Map of the Anti-Matter Multiverse

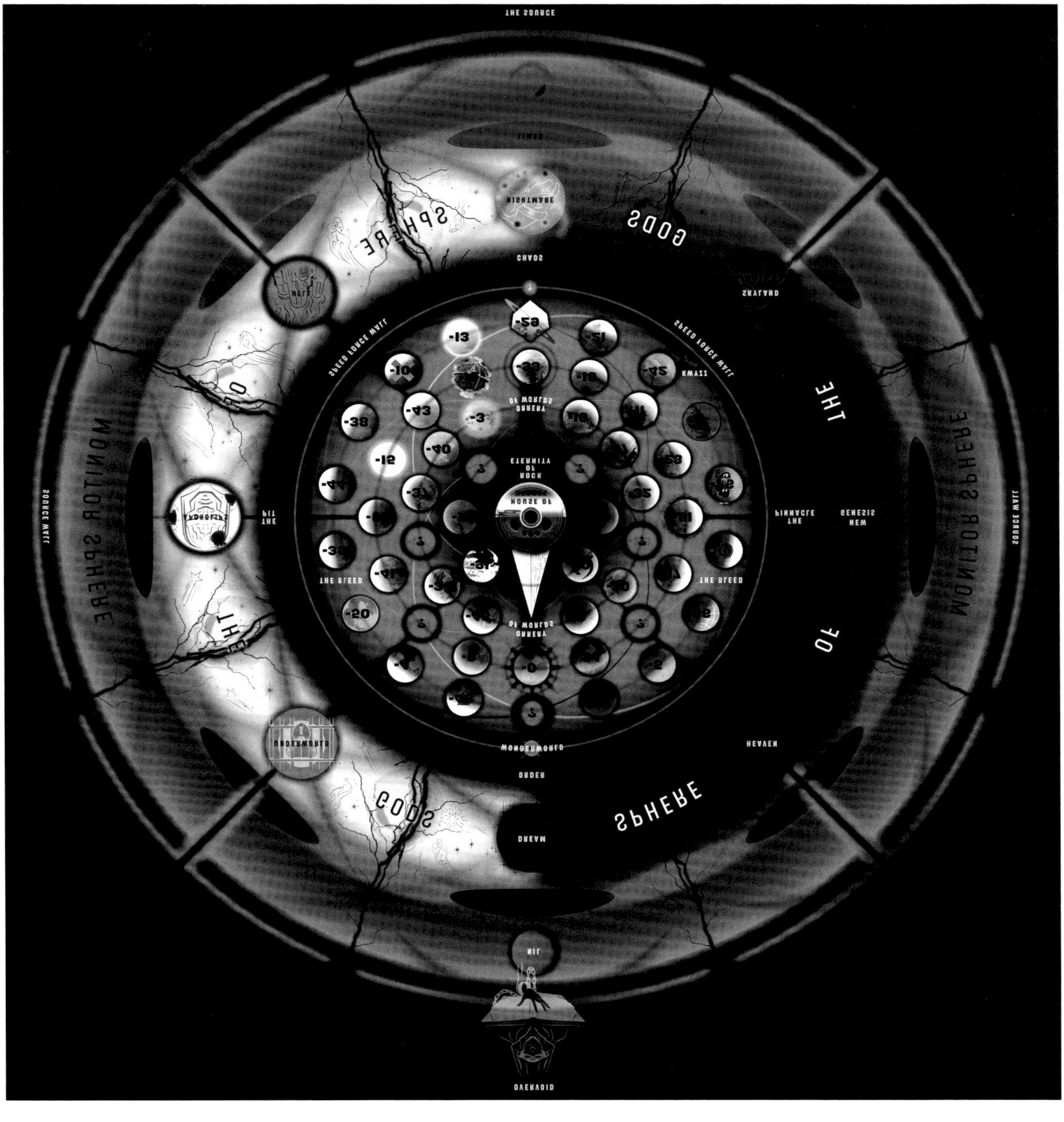

BIOGRAPHIES

GRANT MORRISON
Grant Morrison has been working with DC Comics for more than 20 years, beginning with his legendary runs on the revolutionary titles *Animal Man* and *Doom Patrol*. Since then he has written numerous bestsellers – including *JLA*, *Batman*, and *New X-Men* – as well as the critically acclaimed creator-owned series *The Invisibles*, *Seaguy*, *The Filth*, *WE3*, and *Joe the Barbarian*. In addition, Morrison has expanded the borders of the DC Universe in the award-winning pages of *Seven Soldiers*, *All-Star Superman*, *Final Crisis*, *Batman Incorporated*, *Action Comics*, *The Multiversity*, and *The Green Lantern*. He is also the co-creator of the 2017 hit Syfy television series *Happy!* based on his comic book of the same name, as well as a new TV adaptation of Aldous Huxley's *Brave New World* for NBCUniversal's Peacock streaming service.

In his secret identity, Morrison is a "counterculture" spokesperson, a musician, an award-winning playwright, and a chaos magician. He is also the author of the *New York Times* bestseller *Supergods*, a groundbreaking psycho-historic mapping of the superhero as a cultural organism. He divides his time between his homes in Los Angeles and Scotland.

IVAN REIS
Ivan Reis began his career in Brazil more than 25 years ago and has since worked for many American publishers, including Marvel and DC. For Marvel, he has drawn titles such as *Avengers*, *Iron Man*, and *Captain Marvel*; for DC, he has drawn *Batman*, *Superman*, *Green Lantern*, and *Aquaman*, as well as the major crossover events *Infinite Crisis*, *Blackest Night*, *Brightest Day*, *The Multiversity*, and *Rebirth*. Active in multiple media, Reis has also designed collectible consumer products and ad campaigns for DC Comics, including an exclusive poster for the movie *Batman v Superman: Dawn of Justice*, requested by director Zack Snyder. The winner of numerous accolades throughout his career and an exclusive DC Comics artist for many years, Reis's recent work includes *Man of Steel* and *Superman* with Brian Michael Bendis and *The Terrifics* with Jeff Lemire.

BEN OLIVER
Ben Oliver is a British comic book artist. His realistic style has made him a fan favorite on titles such as *Judge Dredd*, *The Authority*, *Ultimate X-Men*, and *Batwing*. He illustrated the third chapter of Grant Morrison's Multiversity saga, *The Multiversity: The Just*, and he spends his time mostly drawing. Mostly.

CHRIS SPROUSE
Chris Sprouse began working in comics in 1989, cutting his teeth on such series as *Legion of Super-Heroes*, *Legionnaires*, and *Hammerlocke*. In 1999 he co-created the world of *Tom Strong* with Alan Moore, and since then he has drawn countless adventures featuring Earth's Greatest Science Hero in the titles *Tom Strong*, *Tom Strong and the Planet of Peril*, and *Tom Strong and the Robots of Doom*. In addition to his work on *Ocean*, Sprouse has also contributed to *The Authority*; *Batman: The Return of Bruce Wayne*; and *The Multiversity: The Society of Super-Heroes*. He currently lives in Ohio.

FRANK QUITELY
Frank Quitely was born in Glasgow in 1968. Since 1988 he's drawn *The Greens* (self-published); *Blackheart*; *Missionary Man*; *Shimura*; *Inaba*; ten shorts for Paradox Press; six shorts for Vertigo; *Flex Mentallo*; *20/20 Visions*; *Batman: Scottish Connection*; *The Kingdom: Offspring*; *JLA: Earth 2*; *The Invisibles*; *Transmetropolitan*; *The Authority*; *Captain America*; *New X-Men*; *The Sandman: Endless Nights*; *WE3*; *All-Star Superman*; and *Batman and Robin*. He has also created covers for *Negative Burn*, *Judge Dredd Megazine*, *Classic 2000 AD*, *Jonah Hex*, *Books of Magick: Life During Wartime*, *Bite Club*, *American Virgin*, and *All-Star Batman*. He lives in Glasgow with his wife and three children. He used to design his own hats and clothing. Currently his favorite hobby is cooking.

PAULO SIQUEIRA
Paulo Siqueira is a Brazilian penciller and inker who has been active in the comic book industry since 2003. His art has been published by Avatar Press, DC Comics, Dynamite Entertainment, Marvel, and Zenescope Entertainment. Some of his most notable works include *Birds of Prey*, *Earth 2: World's End*, *Titans Hunt*, and *Wonder Woman: Rebirth* for DC, and *A-Force* and *Amazing Spider-Man* for Marvel. In addition to being a talented storyteller and interior artist, he is also an acclaimed cover artist.

CAMERON STEWART
Cameron Stewart's first major comics work was a celebrated run drawing DC's ongoing *Catwoman* series with writer Ed Brubaker from 2002 to 2003. He then joined forces with Grant Morrison to produce the miniseries *Seaguy*; *Seven Soldiers: The Manhattan Guardian*; and *Seaguy: Slaves of Mickey Eye*. In 2006 he was nominated for an Eisner Award for his work on the Jason Aaron-written graphic novel *The Other Side* from Vertigo, and in 2007 he launched his own webcomic, *Sin Titulo*, which won the 2009 Shuster Award for Outstanding Webcomic Creator and the 2010 Eisner Award for Best Digital Comic. Stewart lives and works in Montreal, Quebec.

MARCUS TO
Marcus To is a *New York Times* bestselling illustrator and storyteller who lives in Toronto, Canada. Throughout his career Marcus has drawn virtually every DC superhero, having worked on *Red Robin*, *Huntress*, *Batwing*, *Flash*, and *Wonder Woman*. His current work includes his creator-owned book *Joyride*. He is a proud member of the RAID Studio.

JIM LEE
Jim Lee is a renowned comic book artist and the publisher and chief creative officer of DC Entertainment. In addition to his executive positions, he is also the artist for many of DC Comics' bestselling comic books and graphic novels, including *All-Star Batman and Robin, the Boy Wonder*; *Superman: For Tomorrow*; *Justice League: Origin*; *Superman Unchained*; and *Suicide Squad*. He also served as the executive creative director for the *DC Universe Online* (DCUO), a massively multiplayer action game from Daybreak Game Company.

DOUG MAHNKE
Doug Mahnke embarked on a love affair with comics at the age of five, having received a pile of *Spider-Man* issues from a rugby-playing college student named Mike who lived in his basement. A consistent interest in the medium, coupled with some art skill, landed Mahnke a job drawing comics for Dark Horse at the age of 24. His first gig was illustrating a moody detective one-shot entitled *Homicide*, written by John Arcudi. The two went on to collaborate on Dark Horse's *The Mask* and their creator-owned series *Major Bummer*, originally published by DC. Since then Mahnke has worked almost exclusively for DC on a wide variety of titles, including *Superman: The Man of Steel*; *JLA*; *Justice League*; *Batman*; *Team Zero*; *Seven Soldiers: Frankenstein*; *Black Adam: The Dark Age*; *Stormwatch: P.H.D.*; *Final Crisis*; *Green Lantern*; *Superman/Wonder Woman*; *Superman*; and *Detective Comics*.

RIAN HUGHES
Rian Hughes is a graphic designer, illustrator, comic artist, writer, and typographer who has worked extensively for the British and American advertising, music, and comic book industries.

He has written and drawn comics featured in *2000 AD*, *Vertigo CMYK*, and *Batman: Black and White* and designed hundreds of logos for DC Comics, Marvel, and other companies, including Batman, the X-Men, Superman, James Bond, and the Avengers. He has also produced Hawaiian shirts, ranges for Swatch, and record sleeves for Ultravox and has designed typefaces that are available through his foundry, Device Fonts.

Rian has recently published his first novel, *XX*, which he describes as a "novel, graphic." Other publications include *Lifestyle Illustration of the '50s* and *Custom Lettering of the '20s and '30s*, while his comic strips have been collected in *Yesterday's Tomorrows* and *Tales from Beyond Science*, and his burlesque portraits in *Soho Dives, Soho Divas*. *Logo a Gogo* collects all his logo designs for the comic book world and beyond.

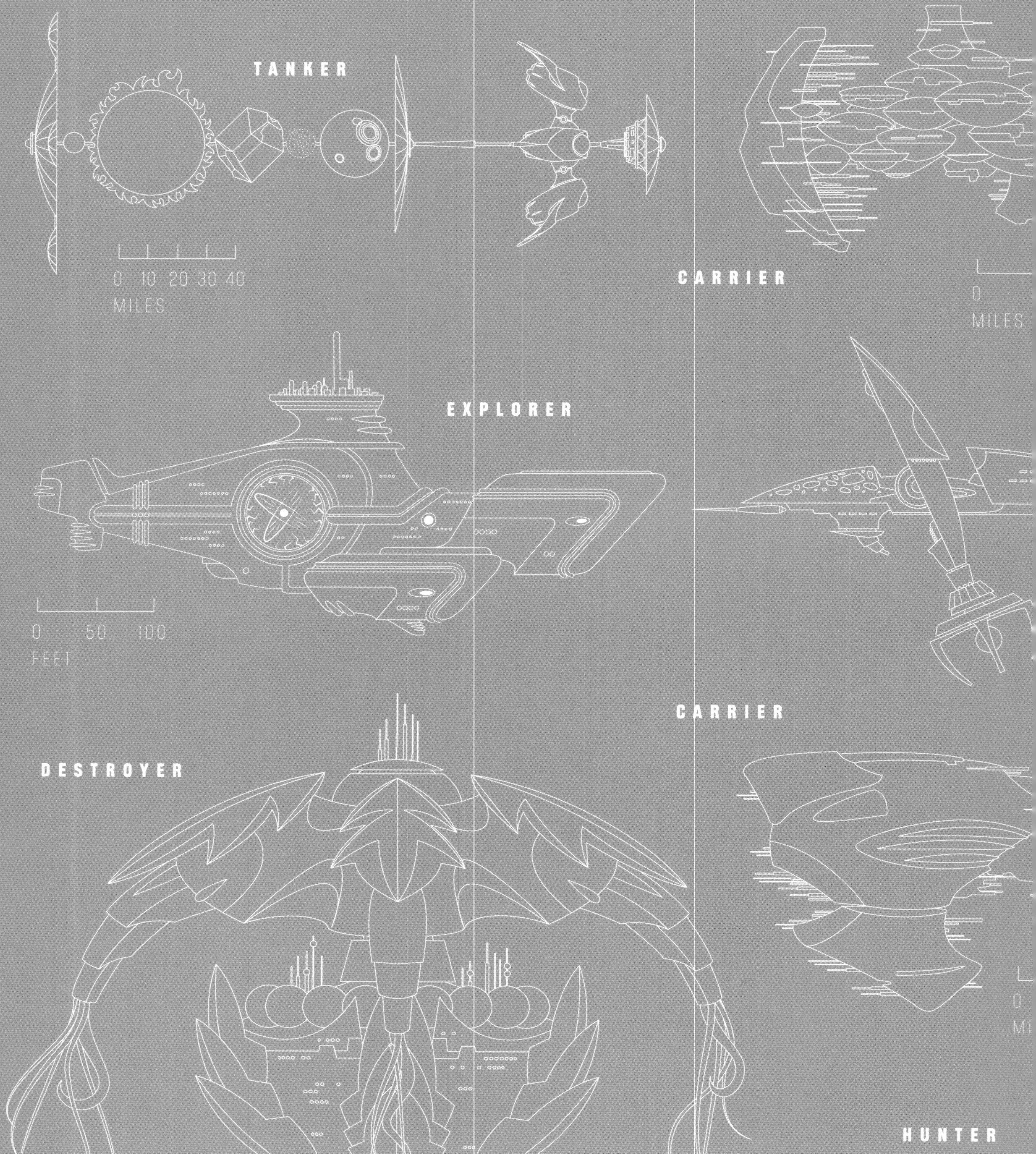
TANKER
0 10 20 30 40
MILES
CARRIER
0
MILES
EXPLORER
0 50 100
FEET
CARRIER
DESTROYER
0 10 20
MILES
HUNTER
0 25 50 75
FEET

SHIFT SHIP CLASSIFICATION | THE MULTIVERSI